KU-068-947

CONTENTS

INTRODUCTION

An executive once told me he doesn't travel anymore, he just goes from place to place. I wish I had his name so I could send him a copy of *The Wall Street Journal Guides to Business Travel*. Knowing your way around—knowing where to be at the right time, and where to get what you need *when you need it*—can save time and money. It could also save a deal. And it could put the joy back into travel.

For two years the world's #1 travel expert (Fodor's) and the world's #1 business authority (*The Wall Street Journal*) have been working to produce a series of guides that will give business travelers the savvy to succeed away from home. The result is the most comprehensive business travel guides ever published—the first that really qualify as an essential business tool.

It's useful pointing out the top hotels, although most of you already know where they are, at least in cities you visit regularly. What the *Journal* guides do, in addition, is rate each property for 29 different services of critical interest to business travelers—from fitness facilities to modem phone jacks, secretarial services, dry-cleaning and pressing, hairdryers, and in-room checkout.

We're also thorough—some would say fanatical—enough to tell you about the bed lighting. And the desk lighting. And the desks themselves. Not just whether they exist, but how good they are.

It's helpful to know the top restaurants, but only in the *Journal's* business travel guides will you find out whether tables are spaced far enough apart for confidential talks, or whether the ambience is best for hammering out a contract or for celebrating a deal. And only in the *Journal* guides will you learn about the current power-breakfast scene.

Not everyone is a CEO and not everyone (alas) is on a company expense account. And so, among reviews of hotels and restaurants are names of smaller, less obvious properties that keep standards up and prices down. We give stars to the best of the upscale restaurants and hotels, and we give stars to the best of the moderately priced ones, too.

We've tried to anticipate other needs as well. Such as where to find a late-night pharmacy, a gift basket, a tux. Or where to get slides made up an hour before a critical presentation. Or where to unwind—alone or with a client—after work.

And for a free afternoon, we suggest some fun ways to spend your time: Museum-hopping, yes, but also jogging, shopping, people-watching—ideas for speeding up the pace or slowing down.

The Wall Street Journal Guides to Business Travel are both for first-time travelers and frequent flyers; for traditionalists and trend-spotters; for long-term visitors and travelers on the run. Writers express their opinions with no holds barred, their goal being not so much to impose their tastes on you as to give you the information you need to make your own informed choices. Every property has been reviewed in person, virtually always by a long-time resident with an insider's way of looking at things. The result is an invaluable series of guides that satisfy the personal and professional needs of business travelers—those who never just go from here to there.

While every care has been taken to ensure the accuracy of the information in this guide, time brings change, and consequently the publisher cannot accept responsibility for errors that may occur. Prudent travelers will therefore want to call ahead to verify prices and other "perishable" information.

We encourage you to write and share your thoughts with us—positive or otherwise. We promise to take your comments seriously, to investigate all complaints, and to make changes when the facts warrant it. Write to Edie Jarolim, Editor, *The Wall Street Journal Guides to Business Travel*, Fodor's Travel Publications, 201 E. 50th Street, New York, NY 10022.

Michael Spring
Editorial Director
Fodor's Travel Publications

INTERNATIONAL DIALING CODES

Argentina 54
Buenos Aires 1
Australia 61
Melbourne 3
Sydney 2
Austria 43
Vienna 1
Belgium 32
Brussels 2
Bolivia 591
Santa Cruz 33
Brazil 55
Brasilia 61
Rio de Janeiro 21
Brunei* 673
Chile 56
Santiago 2
China, Rep. of 86
Beijing 1
Canton 20
Shanghai 21
Colombia 57
Bogota 1
**Czechoslavakia
42**
Prague 2
Denmark 45
Copenhagen 1
or 2
Ecuador 593
Quito 2
Egypt 20
Cairo 2
El Salvador* 503
Ethiopia 251
Addis Ababa 1
Finland 358
Helsinki 0
France 33
Lyon 7
Marseille 91
Paris 13, 14, or 16
**Germany,
Eastern† 37**
Berlin 9
**Germany,
Western† 49**
Berlin 30
Bonn 228
Cologne 221
Frankfurt 69
Munich 89
Greece 30

Athens 1
Hong Kong 852
Hong Kong 5
Kowloon 3
Hungary 36
Budapest 1
India 91
Bombay 22
New Delhi 11
Indonesia 62
Jakarta 21
Iran 98
Teheran 21
Iraq 964
Baghdad 1
Ireland 353
Dublin 1
Israel 972
Jerusalem 2
Tel Aviv 3
Italy 39
Florence 55
Milan 2
Rome 6
Japan 81
Nagoya 52
Osaka 6
Tokyo 3
Jordan 962
Amman 6
Kenya 254
Nairobi 2
Korea, Rep. of 82
Seoul 2
Kuwait* 965
Libya 218
Tripoli 21
Liechtenstein 41
All points 75
Luxembourg* 352
Malaysia 60
Kuala Lumpur 3
Mexico 52
Mexico City 5
Netherlands 31
Amsterdam 20
The Hague 70
Rotterdam 10
New Zealand 64
Auckland 9
Wellington 4
Nicaragua 505
Managua 2

Nigeria 234
Lagos 1
Norway 47
Oslo 2
Pakistan 92
Islamabad 51
Panama* 507
Peru 51
Lima 14
Phillippines 63
Manila 2
Poland 48
Warsaw 22
Portugal 351
Lisbon 1
Romania 40
Bucharest 0
**Saudia Arabia
966**
Riyadh 1
Singapore* 65
South Africa 27
Cape Town 21
Pretoria 12
Spain 34
Barcelona 3
Madrid 1
Sweden 46
Stockholm 8
Switzerland 41
Geneva 22
Zurich 1
Taiwan 886
Taipei 2
Thailand 66
Bangkok 2
Turkey 90
Istanbul 1
**United Arab
Emirates 971**
Abu Dhabi 2
Dubai 4
United Kingdom 44
Edinburgh 31
London 71 or 81
USSR 7
Leningrad 812
Moscow 95
Venezuela 58
Caracas 2
Yugoslavia 38
Belgrade 11

* *no city code required*
† *the former divisions of Germany are still reflected in separate telephone country codes and Berlin city codes*

WORLD TIME ZONES

Algiers, **54**
Anchorage, **16**
Athens, **61**
Atlanta, **32**
Auckland, **14**
Baghdad, **63**
Bangkok, **2**
Beijing, **6**
Berlin, **55**
Bogotá, **34**
Boston, **29**
Brussels, **48**
Budapest, **58**

Buenos Aires, **38**
Caracas, **35**
Chicago, **25**
Copenhagen, **46**
Dallas, **23**
Delhi, **67**
Denver, **21**
Dublin, **41**
Edmonton, **20**
Frankfurt, **49**
Geneva, **51**
Hong Kong, **8**
Honolulu, **15**
Istanbul, **60**

Jakarta, **5**
Jerusalem, **62**
Johannesburg, **66**
Lima, **36**
Lisbon, **43**
London (Greenwich), **42**
Los Angeles, **19**
Madrid, **44**
Manila, **9**
Mecca, **64**
Mexico City, **22**
Miami, **33**
Milan, **52**
Montréal, **28**

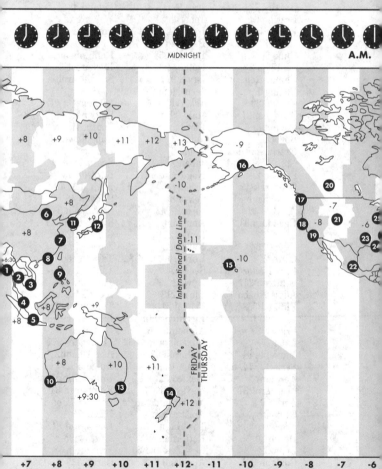

MIDNIGHT   A.M.

Numbers below vertical bands relate each zone to Greenwich Mean Time (0 hrs.).
Local times frequently differ from these general indications,
as indicated by light-face numbers on map.

FREQUENT FLYER AFFILIATIONS: HOTELS

AIRLINES	Adams Mark	Colony	Compri	Courtyard Inns	Canadian Pacific	Doubletree	Hilton	Holiday Inn	Hyatt	InterContinental	Lodge Inn	Marriott
Air Canada/ Aeroplan	✓			✓	✓							
Alaska Airlines/ Gold Coast												
Aloha Airlines/ Aloha Pass		✓										
American Airlines/ AAdvantage							✓		✓			✓
America West/ Flight Fund			✓			✓						✓
Canadian Airlines Int'l./ Canadian Plus				✓							✓	✓
Continental			✓			✓						✓
Delta/ Frequent Flyers							✓					✓
Hawaiian Airlines/ Gold Pass												
Midway/ Flyers First								✓				
Midwest Express/ Frequent Flyers												
Northwest/ World Perks									✓			✓
Pan Am/ World Pass										✓		
TWA/ Frequent Flyers	✓					✓						✓
United/ Mileage Plus							✓	✓				
USAir/ Frequent Traveler							✓	✓				✓

Ming Court	Omni	Radisson	Ramada	Red Lion	Sheraton	Stouffer	Westin	West Mark	Wyndham	Car Rentals	Alamo	Avis	Budget	Dollar	Hertz	National	Tilden	Thrifty
✓		✓			✓		✓					✓			✓			
				✓				✓			✓		✓		✓			
					✓								✓					
					✓				✓			✓			✓			
				✓									✓					✓
			✓										✓				✓	✓
		✓							✓							✓	✓	✓
											✓	✓			✓			
					✓							✓		✓				
	✓												✓					✓
																✓		
		✓					✓						✓		✓			
					✓						✓	✓	✓					
													✓					✓
								✓								✓	✓	
	✓	✓			✓	✓										✓	✓	✓

CONVERSION TABLES

Distance

To change kilometers to miles, multiply kilometers by .621. To change miles to kilometers, multiply miles by 1.61.

Km to Mi		Mi to Km	
1 = .62	10 = 6.2	1 = 1.6	10 = 16.1
2 = 1.2	11 = 6.8	2 = 3.2	11 = 17.7
3 = 1.9	12 = 7.5	3 = 4.8	12 = 19.3
4 = 2.5	13 = 8.1	4 = 6.4	13 = 20.9
5 = 3.1	14 = 8.7	5 = 8.1	14 = 22.5
6 = 3.7	15 = 9.3	6 = 9.7	15 = 24.2
7 = 4.3	16 = 9.9	7 = 11.3	16 = 25.8
8 = 5.0	17 = 10.6	8 = 12.9	17 = 27.4
9 = 5.6	18 = 11.2	9 = 14.5	18 = 29.0

To change meters to feet, multiply meters by 3.28. To change feet to meters, multiply feet by .305.

M to Ft		Ft to M	
1 = 3.3	10 = 32.8	1 = .31	10 = 3.1
2 = 6.6	11 = 36.1	2 = .61	11 = 3.4
3 = 9.8	12 = 39.4	3 = .92	12 = 3.7
4 = 13.1	13 = 42.6	4 = 1.2	13 = 4.0
5 = 16.4	14 = 45.9	5 = 1.5	14 = 4.3
6 = 19.7	15 = 49.2	6 = 1.8	15 = 4.6
7 = 23.0	16 = 52.5	7 = 2.1	16 = 4.9
8 = 26.2	17 = 55.8	8 = 2.4	17 = 5.2
9 = 29.5	18 = 59.0	9 = 2.7	18 = 5.5

Weight

To change kilograms to pounds, multipy pounds by 2.20. To change pounds to kilograms, multiply kilograms by .453.

Kg to Lb		Lb to Kg	
1 = 2.2	10 = 22.0	1 = .45	10 = 4.5
2 = 4.4	11 = 24.2	2 = .91	11 = 5.0
3 = 6.6	12 = 26.4	3 = 1.4	12 = 5.4
4 = 8.8	13 = 28.6	4 = 1.8	13 = 5.9
5 = 11.0	14 = 30.8	5 = 2.3	14 = 6.3
6 = 13.2	15 = 33.0	6 = 2.7	15 = 6.8
7 = 15.4	16 = 35.2	7 = 3.2	16 = 7.2
8 = 17.6	17 = 37.4	8 = 3.6	17 = 7.7
9 = 19.8	18 = 39.6	9 = 4.1	18 = 8.2

To change grams to ounces, multiply grams by .035. To change ounces to grams, multiply ounces by 28.4.

G to Oz		Oz to G	
1 = .04	10 = .35	1 = 28	10 = 284
2 = .07	11 = .39	2 = 57	11 = 312
3 = .11	12 = .42	3 = 85	12 = 341
4 = .14	13 = .46	4 = 114	13 = 369
5 = .18	14 = .49	5 = 142	14 = 398
6 = .21	15 = .53	6 = 170	15 = 426
7 = .25	16 = .56	7 = 199	16 = 454
8 = .28	17 = .60	8 = 227	17 = 483
9 = .32	18 = .63	9 = 256	18 = 511

Liquid Volume

To change liters to U.S. gallons, multiply liters by .264. To change U.S. gallons to liters, multiply gallons by 3.79.

L to U.S. Gal		U.S. Gal to L	
1 = .26	10 = 2.6	1 = 3.8	10 = 37.9
2 = .53	11 = 2.9	2 = 7.6	11 = 41.7
3 = .79	12 = 3.2	3 = 11.4	12 = 45.5
4 = 1.1	13 = 3.4	4 = 15.2	13 = 49.3
5 = 1.3	14 = 3.7	5 = 19.0	14 = 53.1
6 = 1.6	15 = 4.0	6 = 22.7	15 = 56.9
7 = 1.8	16 = 4.2	7 = 26.5	16 = 60.6
8 = 2.1	17 = 4.5	8 = 30.3	17 = 64.4
9 = 2.4	18 = 4.8	9 = 34.1	18 = 68.2

TOLL-FREE NUMBERS

Car Rentals

Ajax, 800/252–9756
Alamo, 800/327–9635
American, 800/527–0202
Ansa International, 800/527–0202
Atesa, 800/223–6114
Auto Europe, 800/223–5555
Autoglobe, 800/858–1515
Avis, 800/331–1212
Budget, 800/527–0700
Dollar, 800/421–6878
Enterprise, 800/325–8007
Europcar/National, 800/227–7368
General, 800/327–7607
Hertz, 800/654–3131
National, 800/328–4657
Sears, 800/527–0770
Thrifty, 800/367–2277

Airlines

Air Canada, 800/776–3000
Air France, 800/237–2747
Air New Zealand, 800/262–1234
Alitalia, 800/223–5730
American, 800/433–7300
British Airways, 800/247–9297
Canadian Airlines, 800/426–7000
Cathay Pacific, 800/233–2742
China Airlines, 800/227–5118
Continental, 800/525–0280
Delta, 800/221–1212
Finnair, 800/950–5000
Japan Airlines, 800/525–3663
KLM, 800/777–5553
Korean Air, 800/223–1155
Lufthansa, 800/645–3880
LOT, 800/223–0593
Malaysian Airline System, 800/421–8641
Midway, 800/621–5700
Northwest, 800/225–2525
Southwest, 800/531–5601
Pan Am, 800/221–1111
Philippine Airlines, 800/435–9725
Qantas, 800/227–4500
SAS, 800/221–2350
Singapore Airlines, 800/742–3333
Swissair, 800/221–4750
Thai Airways, 800/426–5204
Trump Shuttle, 800/247–8786
TWA, 800/221–2000
United, 800/241–6522
USAir, 800/428–4322

Hotels

Adams Mark, 800/231–5858
Ana, 800/858–4649
Best Western, 800/528–1234
Clarion, 800/252–7466
Colony, 800/367–6046
Comfort, 800/228–5750
Compri, 800/426–6774
Comfort, 800/228–5150
Days Inn, 800/547–7878
Doubletree, 800/528–0444
Federal Pacific, 800/225–9849
Four Seasons, 800/332–3442
Golden Tulip, 800/333–1212
Hilton, 800/445–8867
Holiday Inn, 800/465–4329
Hyatt Hotels & Resorts, 800/233–1234
InterContinental, 800/327–0200
InterEurope, 800/221–6509
Jolly, 800/221–2626
Jurys, 800/843–6664
Leading Hotels of the World, 800/223–6800
Mandarin Oriental, 800/526–6566
Marriott, 800/228–9290
Meridien, 800/543–4300
New Otani America, 800/421–8795
Nikko, 800/645–5687
Omni, 800/843–6664
Orient, 800/221–7982
Pan Pacific, 800/663–1515
Paradise Resorts, 800/367–2644
Preferred, 800/323–7500
Princess, 800/223–1818
Pullman, 800/223–9862
Quality Inns, 800/228–5151
Radisson/Movenpick, 800/333–3333
Ramada, 800/228–2828
Red Lion, 800/547–8010
Regent, 800/545–4000
Resinter, 800/221–4542
Ritz-Carlton, 800/241–3333
Royal, 800/534–9800
Shangri-La, 800/457–5050
Sheraton, 800/325–3535
Stouffer, 800/468–3571
Trusthouse Forte, 800/225–5877
Westin Hotels, & Resorts, 800/228–3000
Wyndham, 800/822–4200

THE WALL STREET JOURNAL AWARDS

Our dining and lodging critics were asked to list their favorite restaurants and hotels from three price categories: Very Expensive (*$$$$*), Expensive (*$$$*), and Moderate (*$$*).

Atlanta

Best Hotels
Ritz-Carlton, Buckhead, *$$$$*
Colony Square, *$$$*
Atlanta Airport Hilton, *$$*

Best Restaurants
Nikolai's Roof, *$$$$*
Savannah Fish Company, *$$$*

Bangkok

Best Hotels
Oriental, *$$$$*
Princess, *$$$*
Mermaid's Rest, *$$*

Best Restaurants
Le Banyan, *$$$$*
Thanying, *$$$*
Coca, *$$*

Boston

Best Hotels
Four Seasons, *$$$$*
Le Meridien, *$$$*
The 57 Park Plaza, *$$*

Best Restaurants
Le Marquis de Lafayette, *$$$$*
Biba, *$$$*
Legal Seafood, *$$*

Brussels

Best Hotels
SAS Royal, *$$$$*
Amigo, *$$$*

Best Restaurants
Comme Chez Soi, *$$$$*
La Maison du Boeuf, *$$$*
Ogenblik, *$$*

Chicago

Best Hotels
The Drake, *$$$$*
Richmont, *$$$*

Best Restaurants
The Everest Room, *$$$$*
Printer's Row, *$$$*
Berghoff, *$$*

Dallas/Fort Worth

Best Hotels
The Adolphus, *$$$$*
Hyatt Regency Dallas at Reunion, *$$$*
Embassy Suites Airport, *$$*

Best Restaurants
Routh Street Cafe, *$$$$*
Saint-Emilion, *$$$*
Joe T. Garcia's, *$$*

Frankfurt

Best Hotels
Steigenberger Frankfurter Hof, *$$$$*
Arabella Congress, *$$$*
Monopol, *$$*

Best Restaurants
Erno's Bistro, *$$$$*
Brückenkeller, *$$$*
Börsenkeller, *$$*

Geneva

Best Hotels
Les Bergues, *$$$$*
Hôtel du Rhône, *$$$*
Touring Balance, *$$*

Best Restaurants
Le Béarn, *$$$$*
Roberto, *$$$*
Brasserie Lipp, *$$*

Hong Kong

Best Hotels	*Best Restaurants*
Mandarin Oriental, *$$$$*	One Harbour Road, *$$$$*
Holiday Inn Harbour View, *$$$*	Guangzhou Garden, *$$$*
The Kowloon, *$$*	Casa Mexicana/Texas Rib House, *$$*

London

Best Hotels	*Best Restaurants*
Claridges, *$$$$*	Chez Nico, *$$$$*
The Gore, *$$*	Orso, *$$$*
	Wódka, *$$*

Los Angeles

Best Hotels	*Best Restaurants*
Hotel Bel-Air, *$$$$*	Patina, *$$$$*
New Otani Hotel and Gardens, *$$$*	Citrus, *$$$*
	Locanda Veneta, *$$*

Milan

Best Hotels	*Best Restaurants*
Hotel Palace, *$$$$*	Gaultiero Marchesi, *$$$$*
Hotel Brunelleschi, *$$$*	Boeucc, *$$$*

Montréal

Best Hotels	*Best Restaurants*
Four Seasons/Le Quatre Saison, *$$$$*	Café de Paris, *$$$$*
Delta, *$$$*	Le Mas des Oliviers, *$$$*
Le Nouvel Hotel, *$$*	

New York

Best Hotels	*Best Restaurants*
Carlyle, *$$$$*	Lutèce, *$$$$*
Sherry Netherland, *$$$*	Montrachet, *$$$*
Algonquin, *$$*	Union Square Cafe, *$$*

Paris

Best Hotels	*Best Restaurants*
Plaza Athénée, *$$$$*	Michel Rostang, *$$$$*
Novotel, *$$$*	Bellecour, *$$$*
L'Abbaye St.-Germain, *$$*	Lescure, *$$*

San Francisco

Best Hotels	*Best Restaurants*
Mandarin Oriental, *$$$$*	Masa's, *$$$$*
Prescott, *$$*	Stars, *$$$*
	Fog City Diner, *$$*

Seoul

Best Hotels	*Best Restaurants*
Westin Chosun, *$$$$*	Dae Won Gak, *$$$$*
Swiss Grand, *$$$*	Firenze, *$$$*
King Sejong, *$$*	Orchid Room, *$$*

Singapore

Best Hotels	*Best Restaurants*
Sheraton Towers, *$$$$*	The Pinnacle, *$$$$*
Omni Marco Polo, *$$$*	Li Bai, *$$$*
Carlton, *$$*	Choon Hoon Seng, *$$*

Sydney

Best Hotels	*Best Restaurants*
InterContinental, *$$$$*	Oasis Seros, *$$$$*
Old Sydney Parkroyal, *$$$*	Beppi's, *$$$*
Gazebo, *$$*	Paddington Inn Bistro, *$$*

Tokyo

Best Hotels	*Best Restaurants*
Seiyo Ginza, *$$$$*	La Belle Epoque, *$$$$*
Pacific Meridien, *$$$*	Sasashu, *$$$*
President, *$$*	

Toronto

Best Hotels	*Best Restaurants*
The Four Seasons Toronto, *$$$$*	Pronto, *$$$$*
Sheraton Centre, *$$$*	Bistro 990, *$$$*
Novotel Toronto Centre, *$$*	The Avocado Club, *$$*

Washington, DC

Best Hotels	*Best Restaurants*
The Willard, *$$$$*	Jockey Club, *$$$$*
The Jefferson, *$$$*	Dominique's, *$$$*
Hotel Washington, *$$*	

Zurich

Best Hotels	*Best Restaurants*
Savoy Baur en Ville, *$$$$*	Agnes Amberg, *$$$$*
Zum Storchen, *$$$*	Kronenhalle, *$$$*
	Bierhalle Kropf, *$$*

TWO-YEAR CALENDAR

1991

January
S	M	T	W	T	F	S
		1	2	3	4	5
6	7	8	9	10	11	12
13	14	15	16	17	18	19
20	21	22	23	24	25	26
27	28	29	30	31		

February
S	M	T	W	T	F	S
					1	2
3	4	5	6	7	8	9
10	11	12	13	14	15	16
17	18	19	20	21	22	23
24	25	26	27	28		

March
S	M	T	W	T	F	S
					1	2
3	4	5	6	7	8	9
10	11	12	13	14	15	16
17	18	19	20	21	22	23
$^{24}/_{31}$ 25	26	27	28	29	30	

April
S	M	T	W	T	F	S
	1	2	3	4	5	6
7	8	9	10	11	12	13
14	15	16	17	18	19	20
21	22	23	24	25	26	27
28	29	30				

May
S	M	T	W	T	F	S
			1	2	3	4
5	6	7	8	9	10	11
12	13	14	15	16	17	18
19	20	21	22	23	24	25
26	27	28	29	30	31	

June
S	M	T	W	T	F	S
						1
2	3	4	5	6	7	8
9	10	11	12	13	14	15
16	17	18	19	20	21	22
$^{23}/_{30}$ 24	25	26	27	28	29	

July
S	M	T	W	T	F	S
	1	2	3	4	5	6
7	8	9	10	11	12	13
14	15	16	17	18	19	20
21	22	23	24	25	26	27
28	29	30	31			

August
S	M	T	W	T	F	S
				1	2	3
4	5	6	7	8	9	10
11	12	13	14	15	16	17
18	19	20	21	22	23	24
25	26	27	28	29	30	31

September
S	M	T	W	T	F	S
1	2	3	4	5	6	7
8	9	10	11	12	13	14
15	16	17	18	19	20	21
22	23	24	25	26	27	28
29	30					

October
S	M	T	W	T	F	S
		1	2	3	4	5
6	7	8	9	10	11	12
13	14	15	16	17	18	19
20	21	22	23	24	25	26
27	28	29	30	31		

November
S	M	T	W	T	F	S
					1	2
3	4	5	6	7	8	9
10	11	12	13	14	15	16
17	18	19	20	21	22	23
24	25	26	27	28	29	30

December
S	M	T	W	T	F	S
1	2	3	4	5	6	7
8	9	10	11	12	13	14
15	16	17	18	19	20	21
22	23	24	25	26	27	28
29	30	31				

1992

January
S	M	T	W	T	F	S
			1	2	3	4
5	6	7	8	9	10	11
12	13	14	15	16	17	18
19	20	21	22	23	24	25
26	27	28	29	30	31	

February
S	M	T	W	T	F	S
						1
2	3	4	5	6	7	8
9	10	11	12	13	14	15
16	17	18	19	20	21	22
23	24	25	26	27	28	29

March
S	M	T	W	T	F	S
1	2	3	4	5	6	7
8	9	10	11	12	13	14
15	16	17	18	19	20	21
22	23	24	25	26	27	28
29	30	31				

April
S	M	T	W	T	F	S
			1	2	3	4
5	6	7	8	9	10	11
12	13	14	15	16	17	18
19	20	21	22	23	24	25
26	27	28	29	30		

May
S	M	T	W	T	F	S
					1	2
3	4	5	6	7	8	9
10	11	12	13	14	15	16
17	18	19	20	21	22	23
$^{24}/_{31}$ 25	26	27	28	29	30	

June
S	M	T	W	T	F	S
	1	2	3	4	5	6
7	8	9	10	11	12	13
14	15	16	17	18	19	20
21	22	23	24	25	26	27
28	29	30				

July
S	M	T	W	T	F	S
			1	2	3	4
5	6	7	8	9	10	11
12	13	14	15	16	17	18
19	20	21	22	23	24	25
26	27	28	29	30	31	

August
S	M	T	W	T	F	S
						1
2	3	4	5	6	7	8
9	10	11	12	13	14	15
16	17	18	19	20	21	22
$^{23}/_{30}$ $^{24}/_{31}$ 25	26	27	28	29		

September
S	M	T	W	T	F	S
		1	2	3	4	5
6	7	8	9	10	11	12
13	14	15	16	17	18	19
20	21	22	23	24	25	26
27	28	29	30			

October
S	M	T	W	T	F	S
				1	2	3
4	5	6	7	8	9	10
11	12	13	14	15	16	17
18	19	20	21	22	23	24
25	26	27	28	29	30	31

November
S	M	T	W	T	F	S
1	2	3	4	5	6	7
8	9	10	11	12	13	14
15	16	17	18	19	20	21
22	23	24	25	26	27	28
29	30					

December
S	M	T	W	T	F	S
		1	2	3	4	5
6	7	8	9	10	11	12
13	14	15	16	17	18	19
20	21	22	23	24	25	26
27	28	29	30	31		

Atlanta

by Robin Hohman

From the gold-covered dome of the state capitol to the trendiest nightspots in Buckhead, Atlanta is a combination of old Southern traditions and new moneyed power. It's southern, because it's in the South, but there are so many transplanted northerners that regional differences seem to matter less and less. Ask anybody working in Atlanta where they're from, and there's a good chance it's somewhere else.

Since the 1960s, business leaders have worked hard to combat northern perceptions of the South as a backward and racist region. Atlantans like to say it's a city too busy to hate, and, for the most part, that seems to be true. Atlanta businesspeople are primarily interested in getting ahead, in broadening the city's economic base, and in encouraging business travel and tourism.

Now a major airline hub, Atlanta had formerly been a railroad town. Soon after Hardy Ivy, the first settler, put down stakes here in 1833, it became known as Terminus, because the railroad line ended here. It became Marthasville a decade later and Atlanta soon after that, in 1845.

As a railroad and trade center, its importance to the Confederacy during the Civil War wasn't lost on the Union. Most of the city was burned by Gen. Sherman's forces before they began the famous march to the sea in 1864.

It was rebuilt rapidly after the war, and has been an important commercial center ever since. Coca-Cola and Georgia Pacific, among other commercial giants, call Atlanta home.

Atlanta scored a major coup when it earned the right to host the 1996 summer Olympics. In anticipation, the city began building the Georgia Dome, which will become home to the Atlanta Falcons football team in 1992 and a major site for some of the games. Organizers expect about 84,000 jobs to be created in preparation for the event.

Top Employers

Employer	Type of Enterprise	Parent*/ Headquarters
AT&T	Communications	Baskin Ridge, NJ

Atlanta Newspapers	Daily newspaper	Atlanta
The Coca-Cola Co.	Soft drink manufacturer	Atlanta
Delta Air Lines	Airline	Atlanta
General Motors	Automobile manufacturer	Dearborn, MI
Georgia Power	Utility	Atlanta
IBM	Computers	Armonk, NY
Lockheed Aeronautical Systems Co.	Airplane manufacturer	Burbank, CA
Rich's, Inc.	Department store	Campeau/Toronto
Southern Bell Telephone & Telegraph	Telecommuni-cations	BellSouth/Atlanta

if applicable

ESSENTIAL INFORMATION

Climate

Allergy sufferers alert: Atlanta's mostly mild temperatures, with two rainy seasons, one in winter and one in summer, are fodder for more than just good cotton. If pollen was a cash crop, Atlanta alone could pay off the national debt. If you suffer from allergies or asthma, bring your medication, and be prepared to use it.

What follows are average daily maximum and minimum temperatures for Atlanta.

Jan.	52F 11C 36 2	Feb.	54F 12C 38 3	Mar.	63F 17C 43 6
Apr.	72F 22C 52 11	May	79F 26C 61 16	June	86F 30C 67 19
July	88F 31C 70 21	Aug.	86F 30C 70 21	Sept.	83F 28C 65 18
Oct.	72F 22C 54 12	Nov.	61F 16C 43 6	Dec.	52F 11C 38 3

Airport

Hartsfield International Airport is located 10 miles south of downtown.

Airport Business Facilities

Mutual of Omaha Business Service Center (South Terminal next to the security checkpoint, tel. 404/761–0106) has fax machines, photocopying, notary public, ticket pickup, Western Union, and travel insurance.

Airlines

Delta Air Lines is based in Atlanta.

American, tel. 404/521–2655 or 800/433–7300.
Continental, tel. 404/436–3300 or 800/525–0280.
Delta, tel. 404/765–5000 or 800/221–1212.
Northwest, tel. 800/225–2525.
Pan Am, tel. 800/221–1111.
TWA, tel. 404/522–5738 or 800/221–2000.
United, tel. 404/394–2234 or 800/241–6522.
USAir, tel. 800/428–4322.

Between the Airport and Downtown

By Taxi
Taxis take 20 minutes if there's no traffic, 35–45 minutes in rush hour (6–9 AM, 3:30–6:30 PM). The cost between the airport and downtown hotels is set by the city; at press time it was $15 for one person, $16 for two people, and $18 for three.

By Train
This is the fastest, cheapest, most reliable way to go, especially during rush hours. MARTA trains take about 13 minutes to get downtown from a terminal near the Delta baggage claim carousels 8 and 9. Airport trains run on the north/south line; if you want to get to, or are coming from, an east/west stop, switch at the downtown Five Points Station. Trains leave for the airport every 12 minutes from Five Points. MARTA operates 5 AM–12:30 AM, Mon.–Sat., and 6 AM–midnight, Sun. Cost: 85¢. You need exact change or a token purchased from the machines. For MARTA schedule information call 404/848–4711.

By Shuttle Bus
The Atlanta Airport Shuttle (tel. 404/525–2177) takes about 20 minutes and stops at major downtown hotels. Cost: $7 one way, $12 round trip, higher to midtown and suburbs.

By Limousine
This is a more comfortable way to get to the airport than taxi, but you must reserve in advance and pay a 6% service tax. Prices run between $40 and $50, plus tax and tip. (*See* Important Addresses and Numbers below, for some company names.)

Car Rentals

The following companies have booths in the airport:

Ace Rent-A-Car, tel. 404/530–2210 or 800/533–6489.
Atlanta Rent-A-Car, tel. 404/297–0990.
Avis, tel. 404/530–2700 or 800/331–1212.
Budget, tel. 404/530–3000 or 800/527–0700.
Hertz, tel. 404/530–2900 or 800/654–3131.
National, tel. 404/530–2800 or 800/328–4657.
Snappy, tel. 404/968–0255.
Southern Rent-A-Car, tel. 404/436–2722.

Emergencies

Doctors
Piedmont Minor Emergency Clinic (3115 Piedmont Rd. NE, tel. 404/237–1755) is open 8 AM–8 PM Mon.–Sat.,

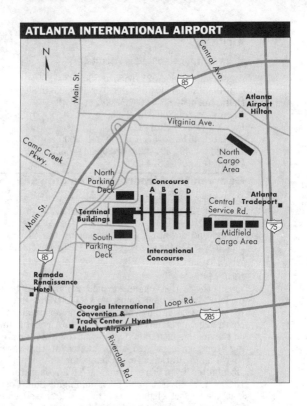

noon–8 Sun. **Medical Associations of Atlanta** (874 W. Peachtree St. NE, tel. 404/881–1714) is a physician referral service.

Dentists
Northern District Dental Society (tel. 404/270–1635) is a free dental referral service, with someone always on call.

Hospitals
Piedmont Hospital (1968 Peachtree Rd. N.W., tel. 404/350–2222).

Important Addresses and Numbers

Audiovisual rentals. Audio Visual Services (811 Marietta St. NW, tel. 404/875–7555), Image America (771 Miami Circle NE, tel. 404/266–3340).

Chamber of Commerce (234 International Blvd. NW, tel. 404/880–9000).

Computer rentals. Computer Business Solutions (2260–R Northwest Pkwy., Marietta, tel. 404/952–9930), PCR Personal Computer Rentals (1874 Piedmont Ave. NE, tel. 404/874–5394).

Convention and exhibition centers (233 Peachtree St. NE, tel. 404/521–6600).

Fax service. Action Fax (3620 DeKalb Technology Pkwy., Doraville, tel. 404/452–0502) will direct you to the closest facsimile station in the city.

Formal-wear rentals. Men's: Mitchell's Formal Wear (3976 Peachtree Rd., tel. 404/261–0761), Women's: Women's Overnight Sensations (4920 Roswell Rd. NW, tel. 404/250–0711).

Gift shops. Gift Baskets: Christie's Baskets (442 Sherwood Oaks Rd., tel. 404/469–6408), Flowers: Execu-Flower Service (5299 Roswell Rd. NE, tel. 404/252–5151).

Graphic design studios. Atlanta Graphics Center (6456 Warren Dr., Norcross, tel. 404/448–3920), Executive Arts (1916 Piedmont Rd. NE, tel. 404/325–0087).

Hairstylists. Unisex: Fugi's Hair Designers (in the Marriott Marquis at Peachtree Center, tel. 404/524–6622), Lenox Hair Studio (3355 Lenox Rd NE, tel. 404/261–8832).

Health and fitness clubs. *See* Fitness, below.

Information hot lines. Concert information (tel. 404/633–9623), movie listings (tel. 404/222–2070), sports scores (tel. 404/222–2030).

Limousine services. A-1 Limousine Services (tel. 404/299–2388 or 800/672–5466), Executive Limousine Service (tel. 404/763–1000 or 800/241–3943).

Liquor stores. Elite Liquor Store (1163 Peachtree St. NE, tel. 404/892–7892), Peachtree Road Package Store (1893 Peachtree Rd. NE, tel. 404/351–2994).

Mail delivery, overnight. DHL Worldwide Express (tel. 404/997–1635), Federal Express (tel. 404/321–7566), TNT Skypak (tel. 404/991–9191), United Parcel Service (tel. 404/432–9494), U.S. Postal Service Express Mail (404/765–7486).

Messenger services. Central Delivery Service of Atlanta (tel. 404/892–1350), Georgia Messenger Service Inc. (tel. 404/681–3278).

Office space rentals. Executive Office Center (3525 Piedmont Rd. N.E., tel. 404/233–0055), Secretariat Executive Center (3355 Lenox Rd. NE, Suite 750, tel. 404/262–2121).

Pharmacies, 24-hour. Treasury Drug (1061 Ponce de Leon Ave. NE, tel. 404/876–0381), Bells Ferry (1250 N. Cobb Dr., Marietta, tel. 404/427–7344).

Radio stations, all-news. WCNN 680 AM; WGST 640 AM.

Secretarial services. Convention Connection (1 CNN Center, Suite 553, tel. 404/872–1268), Manpower (260 Peachtree St. NW, Suite 900, tel. 404/659–3565).

Stationery supplies. Brown Office Supply Services (477 Peachtree St. NE, tel. 404/892–4770), Franklin's Printing Office Supplies and Copy Service will pick up and deliver (123 Peachtree St. NE, tel. 404/523–6931).

Taxis. Yellow Cabs (tel. 404/521–0200), Checker Cab (tel. 404/351–1111).

Train information. Amtrak (1688 Peachtree St. NW, tel. 404/881–3060), MARTA hot line (tel. 404/848–5072).

Travel agents. AAA Travel Agency (1100 Spring St. NW, tel. 404/843–4500), Maritz Travel (5605 Glen Ridge Dr., Suite 200, tel. 404/522–6515 or 800/334–6718).

Weather. Weather Line, WYNX (tel. 404/436–1550).

LODGING

Atlanta is a big convention town, which room availability and rates reflect. Prices change according to season and are usually higher in the late winter and spring when most conventions are held.

Buckhead is a trendy, expensive area, about four miles north of downtown, with numerous restaurants and the best stores. If you have business in midtown—between Buckhead and downtown—this is where you'll want to stay, though there's little nightlife or shopping here. Downtown can be very expensive, and gets very crowded during conventions and trade shows, but you can get around easily and won't need a car. The downtown and midtown hotel complexes are fairly safe, but it's best to be cautious walking around in these areas at night. An active street life keeps uptown Buckhead a safer bet.

Airport hotels cost 30–50% less than those downtown, but they're smaller and don't offer as many business services. Most provide a free shuttle bus to and from Hartsfield International, and downtown Atlanta is a 15-minute ride on a MARTA train, so a car is unnecessary if you stay in the airport area.

All of the hotels listed below offer corporate rates and weekend discounts; inquire when making reservations.

Highly recommended lodgings in each price category are indicated by a star ★.

Category	Cost*
$$$$ (Very Expensive)	over $150
$$$ (Expensive)	$105–$150
$$ (Moderate)	under $105

*All prices are for a standard double room, single occupancy, excluding 11% tax.

Numbers in the margin correspond to numbered hotel locations on the Atlanta Lodging and Dining maps.

Buckhead

❶ **Embassy Suites Hotel-Buckhead.** This quiet and comfort-
$$$ able all-suites hotel, in a pleasant if predictable atrium setting, offers many in-room extras geared specifically to the busy business traveler. Each double and king suite is equipped with a kitchen area, three sinks, a microwave oven, a small refrigerator, and a coffeemaker with coffee— good if you plan to do a lot of in-room business and don't want to have to call room service all the time. Living/dining areas have a sofa bed, an overstuffed chair, a dining table, and an extra phone. An all-you-can-eat breakfast and a cocktail hour are included in the suite price. For more space, ask for a room with a double bed, larger than those with kings. *3285 Peachtree Rd. NE, 30305, tel. 404/261–*

GREATER ATLANTA

Lodging

Atlanta Airport
Hilton, **7**

Atlanta Marriott
Gwinnett Place, **4**

Colony Square Hotel, **6**

Embassy Suites
Hotel-Buckhead, **1**

Hyatt Atlanta
Airport, **9**

Ramada Renaissance
Hotel/Atlanta-
Airport, **8**

Ritz-Carlton
Buckhead, **2**

Dining

The Dining Room, **2**

Harry Baron's, **3**

Houston's, **5**

DOWNTOWN ATLANTA

7733 or 800/362-2779, fax 404/261-7733, ext. 2198. Gen. manager, Ken Powers. 328 suites. AE, CB, D, DC, MC, V.

★ ❷ **Ritz-Carlton, Buckhead.** This is simply the most luxurious
$$$$ hotel in Atlanta, the place where the high-powered mon-eyed people meet. Some may find the white-gloved staff overattentive, but most appreciate the full service for both business and personal needs. Dark wood paneling, high-pile oriental rugs, and quality antique reproductions and paintings give the lobby the feel of an Old World hotel. Rooms are similarly elegant, with richly patterned drap-eries and spreads, and high four-poster beds with claw-and-ball feet. Twin rooms are small, but as gracefully dec-orated as the larger kings and suites. Views are not spec-tacular—rooms overlook the Phipps Plaza and Lenox Square shopping centers. But you can walk to these two malls, which are the best in Atlanta. The hotel's dining room is well worth trying (*see* Dining, below), the Lobby Lounge is a fine place to entertain a client, and the Café Bar offers jazz in the evenings (*see* After Hours, below, for both). *3434 Peachtree Rd. NE, 30326, tel. 404/237-2700 or 800/241-3333, fax 404/239-0078. Gen. manager, Ed Staros. 555 rooms, 14 suites. AE, CB, D, DC, MC, V.*

Downtown

❿ **Atlanta Hilton and Towers.** This fashionable hotel is aimed
$$$ at people who are willing to forgo some business services for a downtown location in an elegant setting. On the Tow-ers level, floors 26–28, you'll get extra-plush rooms, a bet-ter selection of bath toiletries, access to the Towers lounge, plus Continental breakfast, afternoon hors d'oeuvres, and self-serve cocktails from the wet bar in the lounge. The less expensive business-class section on the fifth floor has fewer VIP services than the Towers level, but offers complimentary Continental breakfast and pri-vate check-in and check-out. Nikolai's Roof (*see* Dining, below) is one of Atlanta's best restaurants and Trader Vic's (*see* After Hours, below) features its trademark ex-otic drinks. *255 Courtland St., 30303, tel. 404/659-2000 or 800/445-8667, fax 404/ 222-2868. Gen. manager, An-dre Schaeffer. 1,220 rooms, 60 suites. AE, CB, D, DC, MC, V.*

❽ **Atlanta Marriott Marquis.** Designed by Atlanta architect
$$$$ John Portman, the Marquis atrium is a towering maze of pink walls and black railings, punctuated by the trade-mark glass elevators constantly on the move. Rooms above the 10th floor have the best views; ask to face north to see the city, south to view the airport. The location, setting, and service here are first rate; the staff is large and friend-ly. However, the furnishings in some of the less expensive rooms seem tacky and out of date. In an ongoing renova-tion begun in 1990, richer, darker furniture was added to over half the rooms. The more expensive suites are well equipped. Concierge-level guests receive an ample Conti-nental breakfast and hors d'oeuvres in the concierge lounge. Champions (*see* Dining, below) is a fun place for a casual meal or drink. *265 Peachtree Center Ave., 30303, tel. 404/521-0000 or 800/228-9290, fax 404/586-6299. Gen. manager, Ted Renner. 1,674 rooms, 80 suites. AE, CB, D, DC, MC, V.*

❼ **Comfort Inn Hotel.** Despite the Comfort Inn's $2.5-million
$$ renovation when it changed hands in late 1989 (it used to

ATLANTA HOTEL CHART

HOTELS	Price Category	Banquet capacity	No. of meeting rooms	Secretarial services	Audiovisual equipment	Teletype news service	Computer rentals	In-room modem phone jack	All-news cable channel	Desk	Desk lighting	Bed lighting
Airport Hilton	$$	570	22	✓	✓	✓	✓	✓	✓	●	◐	◐
Colony Square	$$$	1500	14	✓	✓	-	✓	-	✓	◐	●	◐
Comfort Inn	$$	0	4	-	✓	-	-	-	✓	●	◐	◐
Embassy Suites Hotel-Buckhead	$$$	200	5	✓	✓	-	✓	✓	✓	●	●	●
Hilton and Towers	$$$	1700	49	✓	✓	-	✓	-	✓	◐	◐	●
Hyatt Atlanta Airport	$$	500	11	✓	✓	-	✓	-	✓	●	●	●
Hyatt Regency	$$$$	1400	37	✓	✓	✓	✓	✓	✓	◐	●	●
Marriott Gwinnett Place	$$	1000	13	✓	✓	-	✓	✓	✓	●	●	◐
Marriott Marquis	$$$$	2150	46	✓	✓	-	✓	✓	✓	●	●	●
Omni Hotel at CNN Center	$$	2000	99+	✓	✓	✓	✓	✓	✓	◐	●	◐
Ramada Renaissance	$$	620	23	-	✓	-	✓	-	✓	●	◐	◐
Ritz-Carlton Atlanta	$$$$	240	15	✓	✓	✓	✓	✓	✓	●	●	●
Ritz-Carlton Buckhead	$$$$	500	25	✓	✓	✓	✓	✓	✓	●	●	●
Westin Peachtree Plaza	$$$$	2800	41	✓	✓	✓	✓	✓	✓	●	●	●

$$$$ = over $150, $$$ = $105 -$150, $$ = under $105.
● good, ◐ fair, ○ poor.
All hotels listed here have photocopying and fax facilities.

| In-Room Amenities | | | | | | | | | | Hotel Amenities | | | | | | |
Nonsmoking rooms	In-room checkout	Minibar	Pay movies	VCR/Movie rentals	Hairdryer	Toiletries	Room service	Laundry/Dry cleaning	Pressing	Concierge	Barber/Hairdresser	Garage	Courtesy airport transport	Sauna	Pool	Exercise room
✓	✓	✓	✓	–	✓	◑	●	●	●	✓	✓	✓	✓	✓	●	●
✓	✓	–	✓	–	–	●	●	●	●	✓	✓	✓	–	–	●	●
✓	–	–	✓	–	–	○	◑	○	◑	–	–	✓	–	✓	◑	–
✓	✓	✓	✓	–	–	◑	●	◑	◑	–	–	✓	–	✓	●	◑
✓	✓	✓	✓	–	–	◑	◑	●	●	✓	✓	✓	–	✓	◑	◑
✓	–	–	✓	–	–	○	◑	●	●	✓	–	✓	✓	✓	○	○
✓	✓	✓	✓	–	✓	◑	●	●	◑	✓	✓	✓	–	✓	○	○
✓	✓	–	✓	–	–	○	◑	●	●	✓	–	✓	–	✓	●	◑
✓	✓	–	✓	–	–	◑	●	●	●	✓	✓	✓	–	✓	●	●
✓	✓	–	✓	–	–	○	◑	●	●	✓	✓	✓	✓	●	●	
✓	✓	–	✓	–	✓	○	◑	●	●	✓	–	✓	✓	✓	●	●
✓	✓	✓	–	✓	✓	○	●	●	●	✓	✓	✓	–	✓	–	–
✓	✓	✓	–	✓	✓	○	●	●	●	✓	✓	✓	–	✓	●	●
✓	✓	✓	✓	–	–	○	●	◑	◑	✓	–	✓	–	✓	●	●

Room service: ● 24-hour, ◑ 6AM-10PM, ○ other.
Laundry/Dry cleaning: ● same day, ◑ overnight, ○ other.
Pressing: ● immediate, ◑ same day, ○ other.

be the Hotel Ibis), its main attraction is still its price. During convention time, this hotel is booked. Yet it offers few business services and very basic rooms with limited storage space: only one desk drawer, no closets. A very narrow open-sided armoire is provided for clothing. Bathrooms, however, are extra large, and double rooms are fairly spacious. Although it's close to bustling Peachtree Street, the hotel is in a seedier part of town, across from the Greyhound bus station. Security people are visible, walking around with two-way radios. Women traveling alone may be uneasy in this neighborhood. *101 International Blvd., 30303, tel. 404/524–5555 or 800/535–0707. Gen. manager, Ian Saucer. 260 rooms. AE, CB, D, DC, MC, V.*

⑮   **Hyatt Regency Atlanta.** You pay for the name, location,
$$$$ and convention services here; luxurious rooms and elegant surroundings are not part of the package. The hotel's public areas are not in great condition, nor are the rooms; their Danish modern furnishings have seen better days, and the color scheme is dark and somewhat depressing, like the spiny greenery in the center atrium. There are no desk phones, some rooms have tables instead of desks, and there are few in-room extras. If working in your room is less important than a good location (right near the Apparel and Merchandise marts), and you'd rather mingle with the convention crowd at night than hole up in your room, the Hyatt will meet your needs. *265 Peachtree St., 30303, tel. 404/577–1234 or 800/228–9000, fax 404/588–4137. Gen. manager, Steve Mills. 1,279 rooms, 59 suites. AE, D, DC, MC, V.*

⑪   **Omni Hotel at CNN Center.** A downtown hotel in the com-
$$ plex that houses CNN, The Omni Coliseum, some foreign consulates, and the Associated Press, the Omni seems crowded only during Hawks games and the NCAA tournament. That's no reflection on the hotel's quality, because you get more for less here than you do at other downtown hotels, especially those on Peachtree Street. The Omni is an attractive establishment: the public spaces are huge and airy, and the staff is willing and attentive. Some of the suites are extremely large, at reasonable prices. Hallways are long and wide, adorned with crisp black-and-white movie stills from the MGM Library (now owned by the Turner Broadcasting System, which also owns the complex). Rooms are comfortable and spacious, if the furniture is a bit on the tacky side. There are balconies in some rooms, and all rooms have desks or tables with adequate lighting. The Bugatti Restaurant (*see* Dining, below) is highly recommended for its fine northern Italian fare. *100 CNN Center, 30305, tel. 404/659–0000 or 800/843–6664, fax through hotel switchboard. Gen. manager, William M. Thompson. 470 rooms, 29 suites. AE, CB, D, DC, MC, V.*

★ ⑯   **Ritz-Carlton, Atlanta.** For all its beauty and Old World
$$$$ charm, the downtown Ritz-Carlton is still not quite as lavish as its uptown cousin in Buckhead, but plenty of quality reproduction antiques, crystal chandeliers, Chinese lamps, plush rugs, and extensive in-room extras make this the second most luxurious hotel in town. Service, for business or pleasure, is impeccable. The deluxe accommodations are larger than the standard ones, with better views. Rooms on the Japanese floor come with tea service, slip-

pers, and Japanese porcelain dishes. There's no health club on premises (although one is planned), but guests can use facilities in the nearby Georgia Pacific building and the pool at the Westin Peachtree Plaza. The Café (*see* Business Breakfasts, *below*) offers an elegant setting for business meals. *181 Peachtree St. NE, 30303, tel. 404/659–0400 or 800/241–3333, fax 404/688–0400. Gen. manager, Darrell Sheaffer. 454 rooms, 22 suites. AE, CB, D, DC, MC, V.*

★ ⓮ **The Westin Peachtree Plaza.** This 73-floor glass cylinder in
$$$$ the heart of the business district is the tallest hotel in North America. Public areas are plush and luxurious, with gleaming marble, polished wood with brass accents, and handsome floral arrangements; the plaza's shops, restaurants, and lounges all display similar high-tech elegance. Guest rooms are angled around the center elevators; it can be a bit dizzying to walk in circles to find your room. Accommodations are smaller than in other luxury hotels, but floors above 46 offer spectacular city views (those facing north or south are the best). Floors 15 and 16 have the worst views, and tables instead of desks, but cost appreciably less. There are desks in most of the other rooms, and all are decorated with overstuffed chairs, modernistic furniture, and imported marble in the bathrooms. The staff is helpful and attentive. At the top of the building, the revolving Sun Dial restaurant is a good steakhouse with a great view, and The Savannah Fish Company serves up excellent seafood (*see* Dining, *below*, for both). *210 Peachtree at International Blvd. NE, 30303, tel. 404/659–1400 or 800/228–3000, fax 404/589–7424. Gen. manager, Herman Gammeter. 1,074 rooms, 48 suites. AE, CB, D, DC, MC, V.*

Midtown

★ ⓺ **Colony Square Hotel.** In the heart of the midtown business
$$$ district, across from the Woodruff Arts Center and near the High Museum of Art, the Colony Square is superfunctional. A full-service meeting site connected to a mini shopping mall, it offers just about everything you'll need except, possibly, excitement. The ambience here, like the hushed mauves and dusty blues throughout, is restrained. The towering main lobby and long, narrow corridors give the feel of an apartment building more than of a bustling hotel. Rooms are spacious and comfortable, if somewhat plain, and business amenities are good, especially on Colony Club floors, where suites have two telephones with three separate lines. Trellises (*see* Business Breakfasts, *below*) is a good spot for an early morning meeting. Overall, the value-to-price ratio here is much higher than on downtown Peachtree Street. *Peachtree at 14th St. NE, 30361, tel. 404/892–6000 or 800/422–7895, fax 800/876–3276. Gen. manager, Mark Hancock. 466 rooms, 34 suites. AE, CB, DC, MC, V.*

Gwinnett County

⓸ **Atlanta Marriott Gwinnett Place.** This is an attractive 17-
$$ story hotel about 25 miles northeast of downtown Atlanta, where you get more for less. A comfortable main lobby with cozy, overstuffed furniture lends a relaxed, easygoing atmosphere to this business-efficient hotel. Rooms are pleasant and, with two phones and a desk in each, well suited for the business traveler. Ten guest rooms are

equipped with computers, software, color monitors, and printers. Hallway lighting is inadequate, though, and women traveling alone may be uncomfortable here at night. New lighting and room renovations are in process. *1775 Pleasant Hill Rd., Duluth, 30136, tel. 404/923–1775 or 800/228–9290, fax 404/923–1775, ext. 7102 for hotel business, ext. 7103 for guests. Gen. manager, Kevin Regan. 295 rooms, 5 suites. AE, CB, D, DC, MC, V.*

Airport

★ **❼** **Atlanta Airport Hilton.** A full-service hotel practically
$$ touching the airport, the Hilton is high-tech yet comfortable. The exterior is contemporary stone-and-glass, but rooms are plush, well equipped, and exceedingly clean. Corner rooms, called Executive rooms, are very large; rooms –04 and –20 on each floor have extra-big tubs and stall showers. Better, more expensive accommodations are on the Towers level, with higher ceilings, bathroom TVs, access to the Towers lounge, and free Continental breakfast and afternoon hors d'oeuvres. *1031 Virginia Ave., Hapeville, 30354, tel. 404/767–9000 or 800/445–8667, fax 404/768–0185. Gen. manager, Jim Haughney. 501 rooms, 4 suites. AE, CB, D, DC, MC, V.*

❾ **Hyatt Atlanta Airport.** A cozy lobby with exotic flowers,
$$ reproduction antiques, a marble floor, and a decorative fountain give the Hyatt an ambience that's closer to downtown luxury than that at other airport hotels; it's not as well equipped for business travelers, however. Don't let the hospital-like basic brick exterior throw you; the hotel was formerly the Holiday Inn Crowne Plaza before it changed hands in mid-1989. A $5-million renovation blends the stark modern architecture with comfortable furnishings. Rooms, decorated in easy-to-take muted greens, are better than those at most mid-priced hotel chains. And more executive frills were laid on for the hotel's Regency Club level, opened in late 1990. The hotel's biggest draw for business travelers is that it's connected to the Georgia International Convention and Trade Center, with 17 meeting rooms and a 40,000-square-foot exhibit hall. *1900 Sullivan Rd., College Park, 30337, tel. 404/991–1234 or 800/228–9000, fax 404/991–5906. Gen. manager, Valerie Ferguson. 400 rooms, 9 suites. AE, CB, D, DC, MC, V.*

❽ **Ramada Renaissance Hotel/Atlanta-Airport.** If you're look-
$$ ing for a basic, moderately priced room close to I-85—and little else—this is the place to come. The layout is motel-modern, with small rectangular rooms radiating from the hall. Furnishings are too large for the rooms, so an extra chest of drawers is placed in the closet. There's some attempt at atmosphere in the main lobby, with a touch of Ramada burgundy to set off natural stone columns, but results are mixed. The staff can be less than friendly—unusual for Atlanta. *4736 Best Rd., College Park, 30337, tel. 404/762–7676 or 800/228–9898, fax 404/ 763–1913. Gen. manager, Chris Steinfals. 496 rooms, 57 suites. AE, CB, D, DC, MC, V.*

DINING

Atlanta has restaurants for almost every taste, and often at prices lower than those in other major metropolitan areas. Most hotel restaurants offer decent American fare, and there are good French and Italian restaurants throughout the city. Greek, Vietnamese, Korean, Indian, Thai, Spanish, and Mexican food are available, but not always authentic. Fresh seafood is hard to come by, except at a few downtown restaurants. Good Southern cooking is equally hard to find in this convention city, as is real downhome barbecue. The local celebrity crowd favors the trendy theme bistros and cafés in uptown Buckhead. Downtown and midtown fare is geared to traditional American palates.

Highly recommended restaurants in each price category are indicated by a star ★.

Category	Cost*
$$$$ (Very Expensive)	over $40
$$$ (Expensive)	$25–$40
$$ (Moderate)	under $25

per person, including appetizer, entrée, and dessert, and excluding drinks, service, and 6% sales tax.

Numbers in the margin correspond to numbered restaurant locations on the Atlanta Lodging and Dining maps.

Business Breakfasts

Atlanta offers a number of good hotel dining rooms for breakfast meetings. **The Café** in the Ritz-Carlton (tel. 404/659–0400) is cheerful and relaxed; menus run from griddle cakes and grits to Scottish smoked salmon; special fitness menus are also available. **Trellises,** in the Colony Square Hotel (tel. 404/892–6000), small and low-key, is one of the few full service restaurants in the midtown business district. Its tables and chairs are strategically placed for private conversation. The breakfast menu offers everything from bagels and lox to eggs Benedict. **The Atrium Café** (tel. 404/521–0000), on the garden level of the Atlanta Marriott Marquis, adjacent to Peachtree Center, offers a breakfast buffet with a variety of freshly baked breads, grits, and eggs prepared to order.

Cracker Barrel (2160 Delk Rd., SE, Marietta, tel. 404/951–2602), in an old country store setting, is not the place to impress people—unless they love homemade hotcakes dripping with real maple syrup, big slabs of bacon, eggs, and grits, and a huge hunk of watermelon for dessert. Nine separate restaurants ring the city, all about 20 minutes from downtown. They open at 6 AM; on Sunday, arrive before noon to avoid the after-church crowd. **The Waffle House** (2581 Piedmont Rd. NE, tel. 404/261–4475, various other locations) doesn't look like much, but it's open 24 hours a day, makes pecan waffles just right, and always has good, fresh coffee.

Buckhead

★ **②** **The Dining Room.** Soft linens and lavish flower arrange-
$$$$ ments set the tone for this elegant eatery that features
Chef Gunter Seeger's thoughtfully prepared nouvelle cuisine. The atmosphere is a bit stiff and the service somewhat cold, but if you want to make an impression, this is
the place to come. Menus are prix fixe, and change daily.
Popular appetizers include Olympia oysters in chive vinaigrette, and white Alaska salmon cake with citrus vinaigrette. Choice entrées include bass in red wine sauce, and
Jamison farm lamb with cabbage. Lime mousse with piña
colada sorbet and dark chocolate mousse with huckleber-
ry compote are among the excellent desserts. The wine
list is consistently strong. *Ritz-Carlton, Buckhead, 3434
Peachtree Rd., tel. 404/237–2700. Formal dress; jacket
and tie required. Reservations required. AE, CB, D, DC,
MC, V. Closed Sun. and holidays. Dinner only.*

③ **Harry Baron's.** Probably the only kosher-style deli in the
$$ country that serves grits, Harry Baron's is nevertheless
authentic in decor—that is, there isn't any, just the usual
salamis hanging over the glassed-in deli counter. You
don't come here to entertain but to satisfy a craving for
a Hebrew National hot dog with steaming sauerkraut, a
pastrami on rye, or a Dr. Brown's soda. There are plenty
of overstuffed sandwiches on the menu, some of them fea-
turing unusual combinations. Challah bread, borscht, ba-
gels, and lox are all available for takeout. *Phipps Plaza,
Buckhead, tel. 404/261–5288. Casual dress. No reserva-
tions. No credit cards; out-of-town checks accepted.
Closed Thanksgiving, Christmas, New Year's.*

⑤ **Houston's.** Part of a national, Texas-based chain, Hous-
$$ ton's serves up hearty portions of American standards
as well as some Southwest specialties. Deep burgundies,
dark woods, and brass accents give this place a clubby feel.
Parties of three or more should ask for the roomier round
tables in the middle of the restaurant. Try roasted chicken
with black bean sauce, or the Texas burger smothered in
chili, grated cheddar, onions, and jalapeño peppers. This
is not a place to discuss business—the noise level is fairly
high, with a constant din of soft rock in the background.
The wine menu is extremely limited, the beer selection is
better, and there's plenty of top-notch hard stuff. *2166
Peachtree St., tel. 404/351–2442. Casual dress, no cut-
offs. No reservations. AE, CB, DC, MC, V. Closed
Thanksgiving, Christmas.*

Downtown

⑪ **Bugatti Restaurant.** Oversized posters of the vintage cars
$$$ for which this restaurant was named line the walls of
Bugatti, which specializes in cuisine from northern Italy.
The large, high-back leather chairs and the well-spaced
tables make it a good choice for relaxing and private busi-
ness discussions. Zuppa di pesce, the house specialty, fea-
tures fish, shrimp, and mussels in a tomato base. Veal
lovers can find several different kinds of scaloppine, as well
as a good standard veal Parmesan. Another favorite is the
Italian Connection, which comes with medallions of veal,
beef, and jumbo shrimp. The wine selection is strong and
varied. *Omni Hotel, 100 CNN Center, tel. 404/659–0000.*

Casual dress. Reservations accepted. AE, CB, D, DC, MC, V. Closed Sun.

⑱ **Champion's.** More than 22 television sets, usually tuned to
$$ ESPN or the game of the day, make this a good place for
sports fans to relax with colleagues or dine alone. The
large, airy bar/restaurant is decorated with sports post-
ers and memorabilia. Food is basic bar fare, featuring
well-prepared nachos, salads, sandwiches, and burgers.
There's a very decent chili with red beans and a good se-
lection of beers and ales to chase it down. *Garden Level,
Marriott Marquis, 265 Peachtree Center Ave., tel. 404/
586–6359. Casual dress. Reservations suggested for lunch
weekdays. AE, D, DC, MC, V.*

⑰ **Dailey's.** This converted two-story warehouse has a good
$$$ bar and grill downstairs, and finer dining upstairs. The
basic bar menu is supplemented with some more imagina-
tive dishes, like baked salmon in parchment with garlic
butter and fresh dill, or avocado pasta. The larger upstairs
menu features veal, duck, and seafood entrées, and a dessert bar. The dining room is private but dark, especially at
night when candles are the main light source. Service is
not speedy: Be prepared to wait up to 90 minutes to be
seated for dinner, 20 for lunch. *17 International Blvd., tel.
404/681–3303. Casual but neat dress. No reservations.
AE, CB, DC, MC, V. Closed Christmas Eve, Christmas,
Thanksgiving.*

★ ⑲ **Nikolai's Roof.** This restaurant takes its cue from the opu-
$$$$ lent lifestyle of the last Czar of Russia, and the czar's pas-
sion for French food and wine. In an intimate setting, with
a fine view of the city, Chef Philippe Haddad serves up a
five-course, prix-fixe meal in classic French style, with a
liberal sprinkling of Russian specialties. The menu
changes monthly, and might offer an appetizer of pirozh-
kis followed by borscht, a house salad, roasted rack of
lamb served with white basil butter and garlic demi-glaze,
and a dessert soufflé. Russian vodkas are available, of
course, and there are nearly 200 wines, in all price ranges.
This is a restaurant for celebrating, entertaining, or im-
pressing, but reserve early; there's usually a three-week
wait for Saturday night, and during convention time you
could wait a month for a table. *255 Courtland St., atop the
Atlanta Hilton and Towers, tel. 404/659–3282. Jacket and
tie required. Reservations required. AE, CB, D, DC, MC,
V. Closed Christmas and New Year's Day. Dinner only,
two seatings nightly: at 6:30 and 9:30.*

⑬ **Pittypat's Porch.** This is *the* place for traditional, down-
$$$ home Southern cooking. The entrance to this Atlanta in-
stitution re-creates a pre-Civil War plantation porch, and
allows a rocking-chair view of the plain 18th-century-style
dining area below. The menu reflects the German, En-
glish, and French heritage of many Southern settlers.
Smoked pork loin and marinated venison and buffalo are
good choices among a variety of game and seafood dishes;
all entrées include a 39-item all-you-can-eat hors d'oeuvre
sideboard. The wine list is short, but why not try a mint
julep or an Ankle Breaker—rum, wild cherry brandy, or-
ange juice, and grenadine? This is a place to indulge; ta-
bles are tightly placed and the noise level makes it more
suitable for relaxing or entertaining than for discussing
serious business. *25 International Blvd., tel. 404/525–
8228. Casual dress. No reservations. AE, CB, DC, MC,*

V. Closed Thanksgiving, Christmas, New Year's Day. Dinner nightly, lunch only by appointment for 40 or more.

★ ⑭ **Savannah Fish Company.** The seafood served here is flown
$$$ in daily from the coast. Whether it's a bucket of Little Neck clams in white wine sauce or red snapper fried in just the right amount of butter, Chef Gerhardt Wind believes in excellence through simplicity. The daily menu reflects the day's catch, but there's always a full range of regional favorites, such as baby Boston scrod and lemon sole from the Northeast, or grouper and sea trout from the Southern coast. Be sure to try the famous Savannah Fish Stew, a bouillabaisse of yesterday's fish stock, brimming with julienne vegetables, and a touch of saffron and pernod. The decor is as fresh and appealing as the menu, with a 100-foot glassed-in waterfall, huge pots of yellow daisies, and a sumptuous white-tiled oyster bar. Always crowded during convention time, it's still a good place to discuss business or simply relax after work. *Westin Peachtree Plaza, Peachtree & International Blvd. NE, tel. 404/589–7456. Casual but neat. No reservations. AE, CB, D, DC, MC, V. Closed Christmas.*

⑭ **Sun Dial Restaurant.** As the name suggests, this restau-
$$$$ rant revolves, offering spectacular views of Atlanta from 73 floors above the city. Tables are crowded together in this popular eatery, but business talks are possible on a slow night, when you can ask to be seated apart from other diners. Among the excellent American specialties are smoked prime ribs, T-bone steaks, and lamb chops. The wine list is strong and varied, with selections from California, Italy, and France. Desserts range from simple cheesecake to the baroque Cloud Duster—marble pound cake filled with hazelnut-chocolate ice cream and topped with hot Southern Comfort sauce. Request a window seat and the staff will try to accommodate you—but there are no guarantees. *Westin Peachtree Plaza Hotel, Peachtree St. & International Blvd. NE, tel. 404/589–7506, ext. 7200. No jeans, no sneakers, men's shirts must have collars. Reservations advised. AE, CB, D, DC, MC, V.*

Midtown

★ ⑩ **The Abbey.** Waiters are dressed in monk's habits in this
$$$$ converted church built in 1915 with stained glass windows and vaulted ceilings. Tables are private enough for serious business discussions, but it's the sophisticated menu that brings most locals here. Among the recommended entrées are pheasant breast with sweetbreads in Madeira, and venison medallions in port sauce with sweet potato puree. For lighter fare, try the sautéed grouper with juniper berries in grapefruit sauce. The wine list is also commendable. *163 Ponce de Leon Ave. NE, tel. 404/876–8532. No jeans or tennis shoes; jacket optional. Reservations advised. AE, CB, D, DC, MC, V. Closed all legal holidays. Dinner only.*

FREE TIME

Fitness

Hotel Facilities

The **Atlanta Marriott Marquis** has a fully equipped health club, with an indoor/outdoor pool, sauna, and massages. The daily fee for nonguests is $5. The **Westin Peachtree – Plaza** is also fully equipped, with exercise bikes, Stairmaster, weight room, swimming pool, and sauna; massages are often available at an hour's notice. The cost (without massage) for nonguests is $7 per day or $20 per week.

Health Clubs

The **Atlanta Health and Racquet Club** (1775 Water Pl., tel. 404/952–3200) has the best facilities, including the regulation-size basketball court where the Atlanta Hawks practice when they're in town. Guest passes are $15 a day. Very close seconds are the **Sporting Club** (1515 Sheraton Rd., tel. 404/325–2700) and the newer **Sporting Club at Windy Hill** (300 Interstate North Parkway, tel. 404/953–1100). Rates for nonmembers are $20 a day ($11 if you are accompanied by a member), but the range of equipment and activities available is excellent.

Jogging

The best downtown jogging route is in **Piedmont Park,** about a 3½-mile run around ball fields, tennis courts, and Piedmont Lake. Call the **Atlanta Track Club** (3097 Shadowlawn Ave., tel. 404/231–9064) for alternatives.

Shopping

There are more than 22 malls in the greater Atlanta area, as well as an abundance of small shops. In Buckhead, **Lenox Square** (3393 Peachtree Rd. NE) boasts more than 200 shops, including high-fashion designer stores such as Louis Vuitton, Guy Laroche, and Brooks Brothers, as well as Macy's, Neiman Marcus, and Rich's. Adjacent, **Phipps Plaza** (3500 Peachtree at Lenox Rd.) counters with Sak's Fifth Avenue, Lord & Taylor, Tiffany & Co., Godiva Chocolates, Mark Cross, Abercrombie & Fitch, and more than 50 other high-priced specialty stores. Downtown, the **Peachtree Center Shopping Mall** (231 Peachtree St. NE) has more than 70 shops and restaurants, ranging from upscale designer stores to touristy gift boutiques.

More than $100 million was spent to redevelop **Underground Atlanta** (Peachtree St. and Central Ave. at Alabama St.), a megashopping complex with space for 130 shops, restaurants, and nightclubs—but it hasn't really caught on yet. Several shops closed down soon after opening, and the city is fighting to promote the concept. Expect to find plenty of "Southern" souvenirs that say "Hi, ya'll, from Atlanta." There's adequate parking, but streets are congested; consider taking a MARTA Peachtree Trolley bus from downtown.

Diversions

Atlanta Botanical Garden (Piedmont Rd. between 14th St. and Monroe Dr., tel. 404/876–5858) features both exotic and endangered plants, including a restored hardwood forest, vegetable rows, and Japanese gardens. In spring the blooming dogwoods are especially beautiful.

Chastain Park (216 W. Wieuca Rd., tel. 404/255–0723) and **Sugar Creek** (2706 Bouldercrest Rd., tel. 404/241–7671) are two of the best public golf courses, with carts and rental clubs available.

DeKalb Farmers Market (3000 E. Ponce de Leon Ave., Decatur, tel. 404/377–6400) has 106,000 square feet of fresh fruits, cheeses, and delicacies from around the world. Closed Mon.

High Museum of Art (1280 Peachtree St., tel. 404/892–3600), Atlanta's major museum, features permanent exhibits on the decorative arts and African folk arts, as well as changing special exhibits.

Martin Luther King, Jr., National Historic District (along Auburn Ave.) is a memorial to the life and death of the civil rights leader. It encompasses the **Center for Nonviolent Social Change** (449 Auburn Ave., tel. 404/524–1956), a community-oriented education center with a museum, library, and souvenir gift shop; tours of the district are offered here. Next to the Center is the **Ebenezer Baptist Church** (407 Auburn Ave.), where three generations of the King family preached. Adjacent to it is Dr. King's white marble tomb, with an eternal flame. A few doors up the street is Dr. King's birthplace (501 Auburn Ave., tel. 404/331–3919), which is managed by the National Park Service and open daily.

Museum of the Jimmy Carter Library (Carter Presidential Center, 1 Copenhill Ave. NE, tel. 404/331–3942) features photos, videotapes, and other memorabilia from the native Georgian's days at the White House.

Piedmont Park (Piedmont Ave. between 10th and 14th Sts.) is closed to automobile traffic, and is a popular spot to picnic, jog, or bicycle.

Professional Sports

The **Braves,** Atlanta's baseball team (tel. 404/577–9100), and the **Falcons,** the city's football team (tel. 404/261–5400), play at the Atlanta/Fulton County Stadium. Atlanta's basketball players, the **Hawks** (tel. 404/681–3605), appear at the Omni Coliseum.

The Arts

Atlanta offers high-quality symphony, ballet, and regional theater. The city's young, moneyed population also helps attract top rock groups in the largest arena in town, the **Omni Coliseum** (100 Techwood Dr. NW, tel. 404/681–2100). Traditionalists can hear the Atlanta Symphony Orchestra and the Atlanta Opera Association at **Symphony Hall** in the **Woodruff Arts Center** (1280 Peachtree St. NE, tel. 404/892–2414); there are also free classical concerts in the summer at **Chastain and Piedmont parks.** The **Alliance Theater,** also at the Woodruff Arts Center, presents a mix of classic Broadway musicals, comedies, and drama.

The **Fox Theatre** (660 Peachtree St., tel. 404/881–2000), built in the 1920s and now a national landmark, is still a grand showcase for current films, Broadway hits, and popular music. The Atlanta Ballet, which has a repertoire ranging from classical to modern, used to perform at the Fox, but now may be seen at the **Atlantic Civic Center** (395 Piedmont Ave. NE, tel. 404/523–1879).

For listings, check *Atlanta* magazine, Friday's *Atlanta Journal-Constitution*, or *Creative Loafing*, a free tabloid distributed throughout the city.

Ticket agencies include **Ticket Master** (1 Georgia Center, 600 W. Peachtree St., Suite 2550, tel. 404/249–6400) and **Turtle's Records & Tapes** (2385 Peachtree Rd. NE, tel. 404/261–8130; ask about other outlets throughout the city).

After Hours

Bars and Lounges
The lounges at the **Ritz Carlton Atlanta** (tel. 404/659–0400) and **Buckhead** (tel. 404/237–2700) are both elegant and perfect for a quiet drink with a client. If you want to have a late-night sandwich or relax over a fresh draft, head for **Manuel's Tavern** (602 N. Highland Ave., tel. 404/525–3447). **Trader Vic's Mai Tai Bar** at the Atlanta Hilton and Towers (Courtland & Harris Sts. NE, tel. 404/659–2000) is mostly visited by the convention crowd, who come here to taste the best tropical drinks in town, including the bar's famous namesake.

Blues Clubs
The most popular club for New Orleans–style blues is **Blind Willie's** (818 N. Highland Ave., tel. 404/456–4433). **Blues Harbor** (3179 Peachtree Rd., tel. 404/261–6717) wails nightly with Chicago-style blues.

Country Music Clubs
Miss Kitty's Saloon & Dance Hall (Underground Atlanta, tel. 404/524–4614) combines traditional country and western with today's Southern rock.

Jazz Clubs
Upscale, laid-back jazz aficionados will appreciate the combo at **The Café Bar** at the Ritz-Carlton Buckhead (tel. 404/237–2700). Somewhat gimmicky, **Dante's Down the Hatch** (3380 Peachtree Rd., tel. 404/266–1600) features The Paul Mitchell Trio, fondue, and wine in the "hold" of a replica of a sailing ship. **Walter Mitty's Jazz Café** (816 N. Highland Ave., tel. 404/876–7115) offers high style for a well-to-do crowd.

Rock Clubs
The Cotton Club (1021 Peachtree St., tel. 404/874–2523) is a loud, contemporary rock club. **The Metroplex** (388 Marietta St., tel. 404/523–1468) screams nightly with heavy metal, punk, reggae, and new wave music.

For Singles
Atkins Park Bar & Grill (794 N. Highland Ave., tel. 404/876–7249) is an old-time neighborhood bar, where a casually dressed, mostly young (20s and 30s) clientele come to drink, eat, and listen to rock. **Confetti** (3909 Roswell Rd., tel. 404/237–4238) is a good place to drink, dance, and meet upscale singles.

Bangkok

by Collin Piprell

Bangkok, with an official population of 5.8 million, and an actual one of perhaps twice that, is the only significant city in Thailand, and as such staggers along as the political, administrative, financial, commercial, and cultural capital of the country. Real-estate values have sky-rocketed in recent years, evidence of boom times. Thailand's GNP growth-rate figures have recently been revised upward to 13.2% for 1988 and 12% for 1989. Optimism is the order of the day, with business and tourism thriving.

The downside to all this is that Bangkok has become a simmering concrete jungle of largely unplanned and uncontrolled construction, of rush hours that frequently seem to extend from 7 AM to 8 PM, of traffic jams that go on for years. The heat and the pollution are often oppressive.

But charming traditional areas of tree-shaded streets and canals, vibrant open markets, ubiquitous street vendors, and people very hospitable to visitors all help lower one's blood pressure. There's also shopping in modern comfort, with many new arcades and department stores. Leisure hours can be filled as well by visiting the many temples and other ancient sites in the city, or by taking one of the many fascinating half-day or full-day canal or river tours. For the business traveler, there is an abundance of fine hotels at good value, and some of the best dining, both Thai and international, in Asia.

Bustling street markets here are found side-by-side with mushrooming department stores and high-rise office and apartment complexes. The minimum daily wage has recently gone from B78 to B90 ($3.12 to $3.60), yet Mercedes-Benzes and BMWs carrying an official import duty of 600% queue up at the traffic lights. A bottle of beer in a five-star hotel costs more than most construction workers earn in a day. Pleasant faces everywhere attest to Thailand's reputation as the Land of Smiles, yet this country has one of the highest murder rates in the world (not to worry—the killings are mainly linked to family disputes and local "business conflicts"; the streets of Bangkok are safer than those of most world capitals). Blaring nightclubs often close their doors not long before the orange-robed Buddhist monks set out on their serene early-morning alms rounds.

Top Employers

Employer	Type of Enterprise	Parent*/ Headquarters
Bangchak Petroleum	Petroleum refining	Bangkok
Bangkok Bank	Finance	Bangkok
Cal Tech Oil	Petroleum refining	Chevron/ Dallas, TX
Esso Standard Thailand	Petroleum refining	Exxon/ Dallas, TX
Seagate Technology	Computerwares	Scottsdale, AZ
Shell Co. of Thailand	Petroleum refining	Shell Oil/ London
Siam Cement	Cement	Bangkok
Thai Airways International	Airline	Bangkok
Thai Farmers Bank	Financial services	Bangkok
Thai Oil	Petroleum refining	Bangkok

*if applicable

ESSENTIAL INFORMATION

We include the Bangkok telephone area code (02) with all numbers listed below. If you are calling from outside Thailand, omit the 0 from the code. If you are calling from within Bangkok, omit the area code altogether.

The currency of Thailand is the baht, abbreviated throughout the chapter as B.

Government Tourist Offices

Tourist Authority of Thailand. In North America: 5 World Trade Center, Suite 2449, New York, NY 10048, tel. 212/432–0433; 3440 Wilshire Blvd., Los Angeles, CA 90010, tel. 213/382–2353.
In the United Kingdom: 49 Albemarle St., London W1X 3FE, tel. 071/499–7679.
In Thailand: Ratchadamnoen Rd., tel. 02/282–1143. You can pick up maps and tourist information from the TAT desk at the airport as well.

Foreign Trade Information

In the United States: Thai Trade Center, 5 World Trade Center, Suite 2447, New York, NY 10048, tel. 212/466–1777; 3440 Wilshire Blvd., Suite 1101, Los Angeles, CA 90010, tel. 213/380–5943.
In Canada: Office of the Commercial Counsellor, Royal Thai Embassy, 396 Cooper St., Suite 310, Ottawa K2P 2H7, Ontario, tel. 613/238–4002; Thai Trade Center, 105 736 Cranveille St., Vancouver V6Z 1C3, tel. 604/687–6400.

In the United Kingdom: Thai Trade Center, St. Peter's Sq., Elisabeth House, 3rd Floor, Manchester M2 3DF, tel. 061/236–0445.

Entry Requirements

U.S., Canadian, and U.K. Citizens
Passport and ongoing ticket required. A visa is required for stays of more than 15 days. A 15-day transit visa can be obtained upon arrival at the airport by presenting your passport and an ongoing ticket. Apply through Thai embassies or consulates for visas allowing longer stays.

Note: After 90 days in Thailand within any one calendar year, you are subject to tax, and must provide tax-clearance documents before you are permitted to leave the country.

Climate

There are only three seasons in Bangkok: winter (November–February), summer (March–June), and the rainy season (July–September). A glance at the table of average monthly temperatures might suggest that there's little difference between the winter season and the summer, or "hot," season, but this is very misleading. The hot season is sweltering—sunny and humid. Tourists generally prefer the winter months, which are sunny and dry. The rainy season is actually easy to accommodate to because the rain is usually a single half-hour to one-hour deluge at 3 or 4 PM. At other times of the day, the weather can be quite pleasant. What follows are the average daily maximum and minimum temperatures for Bangkok.

Jan.	89F	32C	Feb.	91F	33C	Mar.	93F	34C
	68	20		72	22		75	24
Apr.	95F	35C	May	93F	34C	June	91F	33C
	77	25		77	25		75	24
July	89F	32C	Aug.	89F	32C	Sept.	89F	32C
	75	24		75	24		75	24
Oct.	88F	31C	Nov.	88F	31C	Dec.	88F	31C
	75	24		72	22		68	20

Airport

Bangkok Airport, otherwise known as **Don Muang Airport,** consists of a modern, well-designed international terminal and a domestic terminal one-quarter mile away. The airport is 25 kilometers (16 miles) north of the main business/commercial areas of the city.

Airlines

Thai Airways International, the national carrier, has the most domestic flights in and out of Don Muang Airport, and offers international service from London, Seattle, and Toronto. British Airways offers direct service from London. Delta flies directly from Portland, Oregon; Northwest flies from New York, Seattle, San Francisco, and Los Angeles; and United Airlines has direct service from San Francisco. All flights from U.S. cities have rests at Tokyo and Taipei.

British Airways, tel. 02/236–2000; 800/243–6822.
Delta, tel. 02/237–6838; 800/241–4141.
Northwest, tel. 02/253–4822; 800/447–4747.
Thai Airways International, tel. 02/233–8810; 800/426–5204.
United, tel. 02/253–0558; 800/538–2929.

Between the Airport and Downtown

Taxis, airport limousines, and hotel buses provide transportation into town and back. Travel time depends on the traffic, which in turn depends on a variety of factors such as weather and time of day (rush hours 7–9 AM, 4–7 PM). It should take about 45 minutes to travel by taxi between Don Muang Airport and the city center under the most favorable conditions. In rush hour during the rainy season, 1–2½ hours is a better safety margin.

By Taxi
Be wary of independent operators at the airport; they may overcharge you for the trip into town. Instead, obtain a taxi reservation at the counter as you leave the customs area; a driver will lead you to the taxi. Always verify the price before you get in the cab. The fare for any Bangkok destination should be B300.

By Bus
Thai Airways has minibus service between the airport and Bangkok's major hotels. Buses depart when full and take approximately 90 minutes to reach town. The cost is B100. You can also make the trip by air-conditioned local bus for only B15; Bus No. 4 and Bus No. 10 both stop at the Rama Garden Hotel and a few of the other hotels in the Silom business district.

By Train
Trains into Bangkok's central railway station run every hour from 5:30 AM to 9 PM. The fare is B5 for a local train, B13 for an express. The trip from the airport to the main downtown train station (Hua Lumpong) takes about 40 minutes.

Car Rentals

There are no car-rental counters at the airport; however, if you contact one of the agencies listed below, confirming your flight number, they will deliver a car to the airport for you.

Autorent Interleasing, tel. 02/255–7700 or 02/255–4280.
Avis, tel. 02/233–5256; 800/331–1212.
Hertz, tel. 02/251–7575 or 02/253–6251; 800/654–3131.
Toyota Rental and Leasing, tel. 02/233–0169 or 02/234–5021.

Emergencies

For a list of approved physicians and clinics in Bangkok that belong to the International Association for Medical Assistance to Travelers, contact IAMAT, 417 Center St., Lewiston, NY 14092, tel. 716/754–4883.

Hospitals and Clinics
Bangkok Christian Hospital (124 Silom Rd., tel. 02/233–6981/9), **The Bangkok Nursing Home** (9 Convent Rd., tel. 02/233–2610/9), **Phyathai 2 Hospital** (943 Phaholyothin

Rd., tel. 02/279–9580/90), **Bangkok Adventist Hospital** (430 Pitsanuloke Rd., tel. 02/281–1422).

Dentists
Dental Clinic (7 South Sathorn Rd., tel. 02/287–1036), **Dental Poly Clinic** (2111–2113 New Petchburi Rd., tel. 02/314–5070).

Police
Tel. 191 or 123 for emergency assistance. **Tourist Police** (509 Vorachak Rd., tel. 195 or 221–6206) have been trained to assist foreigners with problems or complaints, and have at least a rudimentary command of English.

Ambulance
Tel. 246–0199.

Important Addresses and Numbers

Note: Multiple phone numbers are given where possible, because exchanges are often oversubscribed and lines often out of order.

American Express (333 Silom Rd., Bangkok Bank Bldg., tel. 02/236–0276).

Audiovisual rental. Advance Vision (36/1 Soi Attakarnprasit, Sathorn Tai Rd., tel. 02/286–8377).

Bookstores (English-language). Asia Books (221 Sukhumvit Rd., tel. 02/252–7277; Landmark Plaza, 138 Sukhumvit Rd., tel. 02/252–5839), D.K. Books (244 Soi 2, Siam Sq., tel. 02/251–6335; CCT Bldg., 109 Suriwong Rd., tel. 02/236–2899), Elite Books (second-hand) (593/5 Sukhumvit Rd., tel. 02/258–0221).

British Embassy (1031 Wireless Rd., tel. 02/252–0191).

Canadian Embassy (Boonmitr Bldg. 11F, 138 Silom Rd., tel. 02/234–1561/8).

Chamber of Commerce (150 Rajabophit Rd., tel. 02/225–0086 or 02/225–4900/12).

Computer rentals. Computerist Co. (Tada Bldg., 55 Rajaprarop Rd., tel. 02/247–1282/3), Cybernetics Co. (62/17–8 Thaniya Rd., tel. 02/234–4551/2), Microway LP (727 Sukhumvit Rd., tel. 02/258–8922), Summit Computer (197/1 Silom Rd., tel. 02/234–3931/4).

Convention and exhibition centers. Thai-Japanese Culture Center Hall (Ratchadapisek Rd., tel. 02/247–3201); the new National Convention Center on Ratchadapisek Road debuts in October 1991. Of the major hotels, the Central Plaza (tel. 02/541–1234), the Ambassador (tel. 02/254–0444), the Shangri-La (tel. 02/236–7777), and the Siam InterContinental (tel. 02/253–0355) have the most extensive convention facilities.

Fax services. Bureau Bangkok (503 Panawong Bldg., 104 Suriwong Rd., tel. 02/235–0200/9, ext. 68), Bangkok Business Services (Ploy Mitr Bldg. 3F, 81 Soi 2, Sukhumvit Rd., tel. 02/251–0649 or 02/251–9534).

Formal-wear rentals. Women: Sangiem Gown (1/8 Wat Mahathat La., Maharaj, tel. 02/221–1817), Ussanee Shop (30–1 Maharaj, tel. 02/221–4440). Formal rentals for men aren't common in Bangkok. Your hotel will be able to tell you which tailor shops in the vicinity offer rentals.

Gift shops. Chocolates: Central Chidlom Department Store (1027 Ploenchit Rd., tel. 02/252–6811), Central Lad Phrao Department Store (1691 Phaholyothin Rd., tel. 02/541–1309/10), Tokyo Department Store (Mah Boonrong Center, Rama 1 Rd., tel. 02/217–9100); Flowers: Central Flower Shop (144/25 Silom Rd., tel. 02/235–1844, 191 Silom Rd., tel. 02/235–9680), Daffodil Florists (169 Silom Rd., tel. 02/235–1559), White Rose (390 Sukhumvit Rd., tel. 02/258–1929/30).

Graphic design studios. Blake and Associates (59 Soi Lang Suan, Ploenchit Rd., tel. 02/254–3555).

Hairstylists. Men: The Barber Shop (Dusit Thani Hotel, tel. 02/236–0450/9), Fantasy (Central Plaza Hotel, tel. 02/541–1234), The Health Club (Regent Hotel, tel. 02/251–6127); Women: Anna Beauty Shop (Regent Hotel, tel. 02/251–6127), Elizabeth Arden (Dusit Thani Hotel, tel. 02/236–0450/9), Primrose (Central Plaza Hotel, tel. 02/541–1234); Unisex: Scala (186/11 Soi Siam Sq. 1, Rama 1 Rd., tel. 02/251–3502).

Health and fitness clubs. *See* Fitness, below.

Limousine service. Thai Airways International, at the airport (tel. 02/523–1253).

Liquor stores. Foodland Supermarket (Patpong II Chai Store, 1413–7 Sukhumvit Rd., tel. 02/392–3068), Kim Nguan Lee (334/18 Rama IV, tel. 02/236–1793), Villa Supermarket (591/1 Soi Daegudom, Sukhumvit Rd., tel. 02/258–5072). Most modern department stores carry a good selection of spirits; however, the wines sometimes show signs of having been improperly handled and stored.

Mail delivery, overnight. DHL International (tel. 02/260–7600), Federal Express (tel. 02/249–9850), TNT Skypak (02/381–2050), UPS (02/511–2190).

Messenger service. Orient Super Express Corp. (tel. 02/237–6284/6).

News Programs (English-language). Local news reporting on TV and radio is largely business oriented and wholly dictated by the government Public Relations Department. Foreign news coverage on the radio tends to consist of readings from the *Bangkok Post*. Television: local and international news at 7:30 PM on channels 3, 7, and 11 with simultaneous English soundtrack on radio FM 105.5, 103.5, and 88, respectively; news at 8 PM on channel 9 with simultaneous radio English broadcast of soundtrack on FM 107; CNN international news and local news in English at 9 PM on channel 5. Some of the bigger hotels carry the CNN satellite network. Radio: 107 FM at 7 AM and 7 PM; 97 FM at 7 AM, 8 AM, 11 AM, noon, and 7 PM—see newspaper for program listings.

Office space rental. Executive Business Center (92 North Sathorn Rd., 18F Sathorn Thani II, tel. 02/236–6120/1), Instant Service Offices (Silom Center Bldg. 16F, tel. 02/233–0985/9), The Privilege Business Center (888/206–7, Mahatun Plaza Bldg. 3F, Ploenchit Rd., tel. 02/254–

9325/9); Suriwong Business Center (Panjaphat Bldg. 6F, Suriwong Rd., tel. 02/237–6831).

Pharmacies, late-night. Foodland Supermarket Pharmacy (No. 9 Patpong II Rd., tel. 02/233–2101). Some nonprescription medications and sundries may be found at the 7-Eleven stores, which are currently springing up all over the city.

Secretarial services. Bangkok Business and Secretarial Office (5/6 Soi Saladaeng, Silom Rd., tel. 02/233–4768 or 02/235–7321), Bangkok Business Services (Ploy Mitr Bldg. 3F, 81 Soi 2, Sukhumvit Rd., tel. 02/251–0649 or 02/251–9534).

Stationery supplies. P&C Stationery (114/20 Silom Rd., tel. 02/233–7556; 11/1 Soi Ruenruedee, Sukhumvit Rd., tel. 02/251–8910), Siam Marketing (262/7–264 Soi 3, Siam Sq., tel. 02/252–2857).

Taxis. *See* Getting Around, below.

Theater Tickets. *See* The Arts, below.

Thomas Cook (191 South Sathron Rd., tel. 02/213–2663/5).

Trade Ministry. Ministry of Commerce (Dept. of Foreign Trade, Sanamchai Rd., tel. 02/225–1315/39 or 02/223–1481/5).

Train information. Bangkok Railway Station (Hua Lampong) (Rama IV Rd., tel. 02/223–0341/8).

Translation services. Bangkok Business and Secretarial Office (5/6 Soi Saladaeng, Silom Rd., tel. 02/233–4768 or 02/235–7321), The Translators (SSC Bldg. 3F, Rajaprasong Corner, 133/19 Gaysorn Rd., tel. 02/252–1303/4 or 02/255–1085/6).

U.S. Embassy (95 Wireless Rd., just down from the Hilton Hotel, tel. 02/252–5040).

Telephones

To use a public phone, simply pick up the receiver, deposit a coin, and dial. Some phones take only the old B1 coin, others take only the new B1 coin, which is smaller; neither type of phone will take the oldest and largest version of the B1 coin, which is also still in circulation. Hotel pay phones sometimes require the insertion of three B1 coins to make a call. Still others require a B5 coin (there are three varieties in circulation, at least one of which should fit the phone-box slot). It's wise to carry a selection of coins. Currency complications notwithstanding, it's usually easy to complete a local call. One other thing to watch for, however—although most phones let you talk as long as you like, some cut you off with little warning after a few minutes. In Bangkok, dial 13 for an English-speaking operator.

Tipping

A bellhop who carries your bags to the room should get B10–B50, depending on the category of hotel and your own inclinations. Tip room-service waiters who have given good service B10–B50. In a five-star hotel, it is appropriate to tip the concierge B50–B100. In restaurants where there is a 10% service charge calculated into your bill, there's no need to tip unless the service has been exceptional. Thais will often leave only B10–B20, even when the bill is sizable. Loose change is generally sufficient (although a B1 tip is considered an insult). Don't tip taxi drivers, except under truly extraordinary circumstances; chances are they've already included a nice tip in the fare they've negotiated.

DOING BUSINESS

Hours

Businesses: weekdays 8:30–5. **Banks:** weekdays 8:30–3:30. **Shops:** most open daily from 9 or 10 to 8 or later. **Department stores:** 9–6 or later, with some open till 9.

National Holidays

New Year's Day; Makhabucha Day, Feb./Mar.*; Apr. 6, Chakkri Day; Apr. 13, Songkran Day; May 1, Labor Day; Ploughing Ceremony, May*; Visakhabucha Day, May/June*; Asalahabucha Day, July/Aug.*; Rains Retreat, July/Aug.*; Aug. 12, Queen's Birthday; Oct. 23, Chulalongkorn Day; Dec. 5, King's Birthday; Dec. 10, Constitution Day; New Year's Eve.

*These holidays are lunar based and change yearly.

Getting Around

Addresses in Bangkok often include a *soi* number as well as a road name. For example, "Sukhumvit, Soi 12," "Soi 12 Sukhumvit," and "Soi 12, Sukhumvit Road," all refer to Soi 12, which is a secondary street running off a main road, in this case Sukhumvit. Just to make things more confusing, the soi usually has a name as well as a number; Sukhumvit Soi 21, for example, is also known as Soi Asoke. In locating a building on the main road itself, locals more often use its proximity to a soi than they do its street number. For example, "Sukhumvit Soi 17" would describe the address of Asia Books more often than would "221 Sukhumvit Road." Throughout the chapter we include the soi number/name and the road name of each address as often as possible.

By Car
Unless you are familiar with Bangkok traffic and the sometimes rather informal rules of the road, it might be best to rent both a car and driver, as the difference in cost is minimal. Otherwise, be prepared to deal with the frustration of navigating your way around this city. Bangkok traffic has long been notorious, but it has become outrageous. Rush hour often extends right through the day, from 7 AM to 8 PM. Adjust your estimated travel time accordingly.

By Taxi
Radio taxis are nonexistent in Bangkok, so you must either have someone at your hotel arrange to have a taxi pick you up, or flag one down on the street; fortunately, they are never in short supply. No one taxi fleet is more reliable than another, but it is not wise to accept offers of cabs that don't have posted signs or licenses.

Taxis are not metered, and bargaining is essential before climbing into the cab. Many taxi drivers do not speak English, but all understand the finger count (i.e., showing one finger means B10, two means B20, and so on). Ask at your hotel what the appropriate fare from one point to another will be. Otherwise, accept 65%–75% of the cabbie's quote. Taxis that operate from the major hotels are expensive, by local standards, but the drivers tend to speak more English and have a better idea where to find things. In heavy traffic, and for short trips, the ubiquitous *tuk-tuk*, or three-wheel covered motorcycle, is faster and cheaper than a taxi. However, tuk-tuk drivers rarely speak English or really know where it is you want to go. Overall, you'll do better by sticking with cabs.

By Public Transportation
If you don't mind crowds, the bus service is surprisingly efficient, and on some routes at some times of day, a bus may be almost as fast as a taxi. Air-conditioned buses are especially comfortable. Fares are B5–B13. Exact change is not needed. Look before you get on, though—there may be standing room only. Buses run 6 AM–10 PM. English maps with bus routes are readily available.

Protocol

Appearances are important anywhere, but this is especially true in a society such as this one. Keep your cool; be unfailingly polite, deferring to those you consider senior to yourself; carry business cards; dress appropriately; show generosity whenever possible.

Appointments
Western businesspeople should be punctual, but they should not get upset if Thais are not as careful to be on time. The traffic provides a universal excuse for lateness and missed appointments. Also, try to avoid scheduling meetings after 3:30 because the locals appreciate the opportunity to get an early start on the evening rush-hour trip home.

Places to meet for business include offices, hotel lobbies, and restaurants (for lunch or dinner). Men may be invited to "member clubs" (similar to old-style Playboy clubs). Thais are a sociable people who enjoy combining business and pleasure. Before Thais ask whether your business trip was successful, they are likely to ask if it was *sanuk*, whether it was fun. In Thailand, the person who makes the invitation pays for the meal or the drinks; it is not customary to split the bill, a practice the Thais call "American share." If it isn't clear who extended the invitation, then it's often the senior-most person at the table who has the honor of paying. If you are the only foreigner present, it might be diplomatic to make the offer.

Customs
Khun (pronounced coon) stands in place of "Mr." or "Ms." and can be used alone or with the person's first name. Family names are not often used, so you should have no inhibition about addressing even someone very senior by his or her first name, so long as it is prefaced by "Khun." However, never introduce yourself as "Khun George" or "Khun Mary."

When you first meet a Thai, it is a good idea to wait a moment to see whether he or she intends to shake hands. Thai businesspeople are coming to adopt this alien convention, but the *wai* is still the more customary greeting. This involves bowing forward and bringing the hands up together in a prayerful attitude to somewhere between the chest and the forehead, depending on the degree of respect being communicated. If your Thai counterpart wais instead of offering a hand, then you can take your choice: A slight bow of respect is probably adequate, supposing the other assumes you are unfamiliar with local custom; otherwise, wai in return, though you needn't worry about degrees of formality—knowledge of relative status and deference owed takes a wealth of cultural experience.

Have business cards available. It is customary in Thailand to exchange these upon first meeting, and your status might be suspect if you can't produce one. Some of the department stores (*see* Shopping, below) can produce business cards on the spot.

Although Thailand is often referred to as the "Land of Smiles," these smiles may signify all sorts of things, depending on the circumstances. One thing is certain, however—a smile will get you everywhere in this culture. If you can remember that, even when hot and frustrated, your business and social dealings will be more rewarding. A premium is placed on maintaining a *jai yen*, or "cool heart." Public displays of anger can result in a costly loss of face. Rule no. 1 is never lose your temper; and if you do, smile anyway. Try repeating to yourself one of the Thais' favorite expressions: *Mai pen rai* ("Never mind; it doesn't matter").

Direct criticism is taboo in Thailand, especially in public. This should moderate your own expectations of critical feedback. It is also unwise to criticize Thai politics or society when speaking to Thais, at least until you know your way around the culture. Never criticize the monarchy. It is in fact against the law, and that law is taken very seriously.

Dress
In general, both men and women should dress for business in Thailand as they would at home (e.g., for men, the classic business suit and tie are conventional; the jacket is often removed in the heat of the summer when short sleeves are the norm; for women, suits or simple, stylish dresses are acceptable). If you go to a big hotel restaurant, or to a dinner theater at the Landmark or the Shangri-La Hotel, you may feel most comfortable in a jacket and tie, though they aren't required. Certainly, shorts and T-shirts are not welcome in the better-class restaurants (though Thais are very tolerant, and probably no one would object). But in general people dress for comfort. When visiting temples, conservative dress is advised, especially for women, who should not have bare shoulders or knees.

Gifts
It is politic, when invited to a Thai home or when showing appreciation for some favor received, to offer a small gift (it really is the thought that counts). Best is a small souve-

nir of your country; liquor or sweets are also acceptable. Flowers, however, are deemed more appropriate to funerals.

Toasts and Greetings

Using a few Thai phrases will generate a disproportionate amount of goodwill. Phrases are slightly different for men and women.

Hello, how are you? *Sah-WAS-dee KOP* (when addressing women), *sah-WAS-dee KAH* (when addressing men).
Well, thank you. *Sah-BAI-dee*.
Thank you. *KAWP khun KOP* (women), *KAWP khun KAH* (men).
You're welcome. *Mai-pen-RAI*.
Excuse me. *Koh-TAWT KOP* (women), *koh-TAWT KAH* (men).
Nice to have met you. *Sah-WAS-dee KOP* (women), *sah-WAS-dee KAH* (men).
Goodbye. *Sah-WAS-dee KOP* (women), *sah-WAS-dee KAH* (men).
Cheers! *CHO-keh-dee KOP* (women), *CHO-keh-dee KAH* (men).

LODGING

Bangkok is booming. In 1960, a mere 15 international-class hotels served the needs of its business and holiday visitors. Today, there are at least 50 hotels of that standard in Bangkok, several of them international prize-winners. Still, book well in advance, especially in the tourist high season (November–March). Bangkok is full of new, upscale accommodations. If you're looking for quaint old places with their own pleasingly eccentric personalities, you're largely out of luck—assuming you also want comfort and convenience as a business traveler.

Given the heat and frustration of negotiating traffic, travelers usually find that a good hotel near their area of business is a necessary asylum.

Excellent service, of a caliber higher than you'll experience in Europe or North America, is more the rule than the exception in Thailand. First-class business hotels in this city also offer good business facilities, dining, and ambience. The main criterion in making a choice, thus, is proximity to your place of business. You might consider a moderately priced hotel—many of them are ideally located and, if they lack certain business services or fitness centers, they are normally within easy range of places that offer these facilities. Truly cheap hotels in Bangkok can be a false economy.

There are primarily four areas of interest to the business traveler. Bangkok really has no single definable "downtown." The closest candidate is the financial/commercial/entertainment area centered on Silom Road. Adjoining this district is the Sukhumvit Road/Rama I/Ploenchit area, which is mainly a commercial and tourism district, with many good hotels that also afford easy access to Silom Road. In the new and fast-growing Vipawadee-Rangsit Road/Ratchadapisek Road business and commercial district are, among other headquarters, the Board of Investment, the Petroleum Authority of Thailand, the Export Promotion Board, and Thai Airways. Finally, the United Nations/Royal Palace area on Rattanakosin Island is close to the various international agencies (e.g., UNICEF, FAO, ESCAP, ILO, etc.) and many Thai government ministries.

Highly recommended lodgings in each price category are indicated by a star ★ .

Category	Cost*
$$$$ (Very Expensive)	over B3,000
$$$ (Expensive)	B1,500–B3,000
$$ (Moderate)	under B1,500

All prices are for a standard double room, single occupancy, excluding 11% tax and 10% service charge.

Numbers in the margin correspond to numbered hotel locations on the Bangkok Lodging and Dining map.

Silom Road District

★ ❷⑤
$$$$
Dusit Thani. After the Oriental, the Dusit is the oldest five-star hotel in Bangkok. Its distinctive architecture, with the crowning Prussian helmet spire, has become part of the popular image of the city. Decorated throughout with Thai antiques, both public areas and guest rooms are masterpieces of tasteful design. In celebration of its 20th anniversary, in 1990, the hotel underwent a $10-million renovation, which diminished none of its charm. In the main lobby a sunken lounge with live chamber music opens onto a lush atrium garden. The many regular customers often develop affections for particular Landmark Deluxe rooms and suites, which are worth the extra cost to those who value butler service and individual character in room decor. Even standard rooms are plush, though, and everything from the desk to the bathroom is generously proportioned and supplied with amenities. Business services include a multilingual simultaneous translation system, reference library, news service, and a Rolls-Royce fleet; fitness facilities (*see* Fitness, below) include squash courts and massage. The hotel has several fine restaurants, including the Mayflower (*see* Dining, below), and after-hours spots like Bubble's (a lively disco) and the Tiara Room (*see* After Hours, below), which attracts local socialites for dinner and dancing. *Rama IV Rd., tel. 02/ 236–0450/9 or 800/448–8355, fax 02/236–6400/7238. Gen. manager, Daniel P. McCafferty. 487 double/singles, 33 suites. AE, DC, MC, V.*

⑮
$$$$
Holiday Inn Crowne Plaza. This recent addition (1989) to Bangkok's luxury hotels is a definite cut above the garden-variety Holiday Inn. The high ceilings and vast spaces of the public areas are given human scale by cozy islands of seating nooks and bars in *sala*-style (wood paneled, tile-roofed rooms-within-rooms). Light color schemes, plenty of lamps, lots of draperies, and plush chairs lend a cheerful and homey atmosphere to large guest rooms that are well insulated against Silom Road traffic noise. The Executive Tower, which opened December 1990, features even

BANGKOK

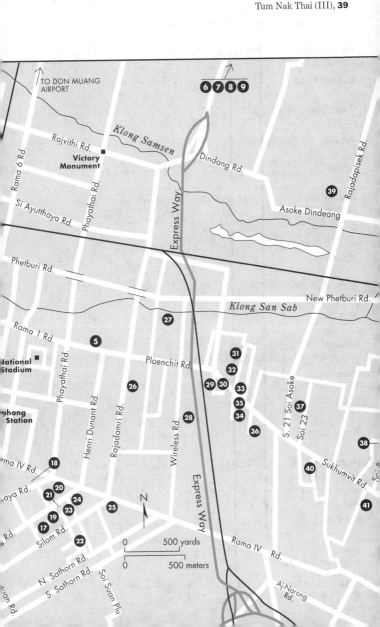

BANGKOK HOTEL CHART

HOTELS	Price Category	Banquet capacity	No. of meeting rooms	Fax	Telex	Photocopying	Secretarial services	Audiovisual equipment	Translation services	International direct dial	Computer rentals	In-room modem phone jack
Airport Hotel	$$$	300	4	✓	✓	✓	✓	✓	-	-	-	-
Ambassador/Convention	$$$$	2000	10	✓	✓	✓	✓	✓	✓	✓	✓	✓
Central Plaza	$$$$	3800	25	✓	✓	✓	✓	✓	✓	✓	✓	-
Dusit Thani	$$$$	2000	7	✓	✓	✓	✓	✓	✓	✓	-	-
Federal	$$	0	0	-	-	-	-	-	-	-	-	-
Hilton	$$$$	1900	7	✓	✓	✓	✓	✓	✓	✓	✓	-
Holiday Inn Crowne Plaza	$$$$	250	5	✓	✓	✓	✓	✓	✓	✓	✓	✓
Landmark	$$$$	600	8	✓	✓	✓	✓	✓	✓	✓	✓	-
Mandarin	$$$	2200	10	✓	✓	✓	✓	✓	✓	-	-	-
Mermaid's Rest (New Wing)	$$	0	0	✓	✓	✓	✓	-	✓	-	-	✓
Montien	$$$	750	5	✓	✓	✓	✓	✓	✓	✓	-	-
Oriental	$$$$	200	7	✓	✓	✓	✓	✓	✓	✓	✓	-
Princess	$$$	120	1	✓	✓	✓	✓	✓	✓	✓	-	-
Ra-Jah	$$	750	1	✓	✓	-	-	-	-	-	-	-
Rama Garden	$$$	1000	3	✓	✓	✓	✓	✓	✓	-	✓	-
Regent of Bangkok	$$$$	1200	6	✓	✓	✓	✓	✓	✓	✓	✓	-
Royal Orchid Sheraton	$$$$	3000	10	✓	✓	✓	✓	✓	✓	✓	✓	-
Shangri-La	$$$$	200	9	✓	✓	✓	✓	✓	✓	✓	✓	-
Siam InterContinental	$$$$	1000	5	✓	✓	✓	✓	✓	✓	✓	✓	-

$$$$ = over B3,000, $$$ = B1,500 - B3,000, $$ = under B1,500.
● good, ◑ fair, ○ poor.

All-news cable channel	Desk	Desk lighting	Bed lighting	**In-Room Amenities** Nonsmoking rooms	In-room checkout	Minibar	Toiletries	Room service	Laundry/Dry cleaning	Pressing	**Hotel Amenities** Barber/Hairdresser	Garage	Courtesy airport transport	Sauna	Pool	Exercise room
✓	●	◐	●	✓	–	●	●	●	●	●	✓	–	✓	✓	◐	◐
–	◐	●	●	–	–	●	●	●	◐	●	✓	✓	–	✓	●	●
✓	●	●	●	✓	–	●	◐	●	●	●	✓	✓	✓	✓	●	◐
✓	●	●	●	–	–	●	●	●	●	●	✓	✓	✓	✓	◐	●
–	◐	○	○	–	–	–	–	●	○	●	✓	–	–	–	○	–
–	●	●	◐	✓	✓	✓	●	●	●	●	✓	✓	–	●	●	●
✓	●	●	●	✓	–	●	●	●	●	●	✓	✓	✓	–	●	●
✓	●	●	●	–	✓	●	●	●	●	●	✓	✓	✓	✓	●	●
–	●	●	●	–	✓	✓	◐	●	●	●	✓	✓	✓	–	◐	–
✓	○	◐	◐	–	✓	○	◐	◐	◐	◐	–	–	–	–	◐	–
✓	◐	◐	◐	–	–	✓	◐	●	●	●	✓	✓	–	–	◐	–
✓	●	●	●	–	–	●	●	●	●	●	✓	✓	✓	✓	●	●
✓	●	●	●	–	◐	✓	●	●	●	◐	–	–	–	–	●	◐
–	◐	◐	◐	–	–	–	–	●	●	●	✓	✓	–	✓	●	–
–	◐	◐	●	–	–	✓	○	●	●	●	✓	✓	–	✓	●	●
✓	●	●	●	✓	–	✓	●	●	●	●	✓	✓	–	✓	●	●
✓	●	●	●	✓	✓	✓	●	●	●	●	✓	✓	✓	✓	●	●
✓	●	●	●	–	✓	✓	●	●	●	●	✓	–	✓	✓	●	●
✓	●	●	●	–	–	✓	●	●	●	●	✓	–	–	–	●	●

Room service: ● 24-hour, ◐ 6AM-10PM, ○ other.
Laundry/Dry cleaning: ● same day, ◐ overnight, ○ other.
Pressing: ● immediate, ◐ same day, ○ other.

BANGKOK HOTEL CHART

HOTELS	Price Category	Business Services Banquet capacity	No. of meeting rooms	Fax	Telex	Photocopying	Secretarial services	Audiovisual equipment	Translation services	International direct dial	Computer rentals	In-room modem phone jack
Swan	$$	0	0	-	-	-	-	-	-	-	-	-
Tarntawan Place	$$$	0	1	✓	✓	✓	✓	✓	-	✓	-	-
Viengtai	$$	400	5	✓	✓	✓	-	✓	-	-	-	-
Wall Street Inn	$$	0	0	✓	✓	✓	✓	✓	✓	✓	-	-

$$$$ = over B3,000, $$$ = B1,500 - B3,000, $$ = under B1,500.
● good, ◐ fair, ○ poor.

All-news cable channel	Desk	Desk lighting	Bed lighting	**In-Room Amenities** Nonsmoking rooms	In-room checkout	Minibar	Toiletries	Room service	Laundry/Dry cleaning	Pressing	**Hotel Amenities** Barber/Hairdresser	Garage	Courtesy airport transport	Sauna	Pool	Exercise room
-	◑	◑	◑	-	-	-	-	●	◑	◑	✓	-	-	-	○	-
-	◑	◑	●	-	-	✓	○	●	●	●	-	✓	-	-	-	-
-	○	◑	●	-	-	-	-	◑	●	●	-	-	-	-	◑	-
-	●	◑	○	-	-	✓	○	●	●	●	-	-	-	-	-	-

Room service: ● 24-hour, ◑ 6AM-10PM, ○ other.
Laundry/Dry cleaning: ● same day, ◑ overnight, ○ other.
Pressing: ● immediate, ◑ same day, ○ other.

larger rooms and suites, special breakfast and meeting lounges, and a large fitness center. *981 Silom Rd., tel. 02/238–4300 or 800/465–4329, fax 02/238–5289. Gen. manager, Mr. Uno Jaritz. 207 twins, 171 doubles, 7 suites (324 rooms, 21 suites in Executive Tower). AE, DC, MC, V.*

⓲ **Mandarin Hotel.** Very centrally located, this comfortable
$$$ hotel costs less than some of its neighbors. Perhaps one is prejudiced by the less-than-grand entrance off Rama IV Road, but the public areas of this more-than-adequate hotel strike one on first glance as being a touch seedy. The rooms themselves just miss being elegant: The deeply carved and painted Chinese wooden furniture contend to set the tone with the cold white of the minibar fridge staring out from under the TV and the somewhat worn carpets. Service is friendly and competent. *Rama IV Rd., tel. 02/234–1390/9 or 800/448–8355, fax 02/237–1620. Acting Gen. manager, Chet Assawapimonpron. 332 doubles, 60 singles, 8 suites. AE, DC, MC, V.*

⓴ **Montien Hotel.** Though a stone's throw from the notorious
$$$ Patpong red-light district, this hotel is anything but dubious. It is also as close to the business and financial center as any hotel in the city. The lobby provides a gracious, beautifully lighted retreat from the bustle just outside. For the business guest, the two Executive Floors in particular are recommended. They include special business-class guest rooms, meeting rooms, and a private lounge where complimentary breakfast is served and free coffee is available all day. Rooms on the south side overlook the bright lights and bustle of Patpong Road, while others have a poolside view. The hotel's Jade Garden restaurant (*see* Dining, below) is well known for an outstanding dim-sum brunch. There is no fitness center, but Lumphini Park jogging is nearby. *54 Suriwong Rd., tel. 02/233–7060 or 800/448–8355, fax 02/236–5219. Gen. manager, Peter Daetwiler. 470 doubles, 30 suites (89 business-class rooms). AE, DC, MC, V.*

★ ⓫ **Oriental Hotel.** After claiming "Best Hotel in the World"
$$$$ and other top awards in polls by *Business Traveler Magazine, Executive Traveler*, and numerous other respected business publications, this famous hotel hardly needs an introduction. It has a well-deserved reputation for providing the best service in a country where good service is the rule (the staff–guest ratio is 2.2:1). The Oriental has a large and loyal number of regular guests—a roster of royalty, film stars, and business executives that has included everyone from Prince Philip to Billy Idol. The hotel enjoys a superb riverside location, but is also close to the business hub of the city. The public areas range from the bright and airy elegance of the lobby of the River Wing, to the Authors' Lounge, which evokes the more leisurely Asia of Somerset Maugham. Standard rooms are decorated in cool green-and-cream tones, utilizing lots of Thai cottons and silks with teak accents. The Terrace (*see* Dining, below) is a good spot for a business breakfast, and there are also several popular nightspots on the premises, notably the Bamboo Bar, Sala Rim Nam, and Diana's (*see* After Hours, below). Other amenities include squash courts, a golf driving range, a jogging track, and a Thai cooking school. *48 Oriental Ave., tel. 02/236–0400 or 800/448–*

8355, fax 02/236–1939. Gen. manager, Kurt Wachtveitl. 360 doubles, 34 suites. AE, DC, MC, V.

⓾ **Royal Orchid Sheraton.** Like its sister hotels on the river, $$$$ the Royal Orchid offers a wonderfully scenic location. The design of the lobby fails to take full advantage of its privileged setting, however—you almost have to go looking for the river. Standard rooms are not notably large, but are superbly designed, with an accent on simplicity and quality of craftsmanship. Light-teak paneling sets off the tans and coffee-creams of the walls, bedspread, and curtains. All guest rooms enjoy a view of the Chao Phya, called the "River of Kings," through enormous picture windows. The Rim Nam Coffeeshop (*see* Business Breakfasts, below) is a good place for a morning meeting with a river view, while the Benkay (*see* Dining, below) is one of the city's finest Japanese restaurants. Commuting from the Royal Orchid to the business/commercial area is rather slow because of the one-way street system. *2 Captain Bush La., Siphya Rd., tel. 02/234–5599 or 800/325–3535, fax 02/236–8320. Gen. manager, Peter B. Hollaus. 573 double/single rooms, 203 deluxe rooms and suites. AE, DC, MC, V.*

★ ⓬ **Shangri-La.** A much-larger neighbor of the Oriental, simi- $$$$ larly perched on the colorful Chao Phraya River, this hotel has also won honors in worldwide hotel rankings since opening in 1986. This monumental work of modern architecture manages to offer an impressively grand lobby as well as pleasingly intimate little terraces and corner patios. The architects were also careful to provide river views from every room and suite. Furnished with deep, upholstered chairs and sofas, cabinets and tables in teak, and decorated in subdued pastels, the rooms are maintained in immaculate condition. The Shangri-La is situated within easy reach of the Silom area, and offers first-class business services. The Horizon Floor (21), with special suites and services for businesspeople, has a private lounge for breakfast meetings. The Shang Palace Restaurant is another good venue for early-morning meetings (*see* Business Breakfasts, below). The hotel sometimes offers English-language dinner theater (*see* After Hours, below). Fitness facilities include squash courts, a golf driving range, and river cruises. The hotel also has its own 24-hour medical clinic. Business services will improve with the completion of a new convention hall plus an annex of business suites, each with its own computer, fax, and other office facilities. *89 Soi Wat Suan Plu, tel. 02/236–7777 or 800/448–8355, fax 02/236–8579. Gen. manager, Franz Wyder. 33 standard rooms, 420 doubles, 222 singles, 52 suites. Two rooms for disabled guests. AE, DC, MC, V.*

⓮ **Swan Hotel.** Shabby but clean, this moderately priced es- $$ tablishment puts you in the vicinity of places such as the Oriental and its sisters on the river. A tendency toward cracked vinyl seat covers in the small-but-friendly lobby echoes the basic-yet-adequate furnishings of the guest rooms. Noise from the tuk-tuks in the laneway bordering the hotel filters into rooms in the front, so ask for a room overlooking the pool or one in back. There are showers but no bathtubs. There are no business services, but fax, telex, and photocopying services are available at the general post office nearby. Short on luxury, the Swan offers a price that is right for tight budgets. *31 Custom House La., New Rd., tel. 02/234–8594 or 02/233–8444, no fax. Gen. manager, Nopporn Thorkaew. 40 doubles, 16 singles. No credit cards.*

㉑ **Tarntawan Place.** In the heart of the business and enter-
$$$ tainment district, down a little cul-de-sac off Suriwong Road, this relatively new (1989) inn strives to offer accommodations and services for the business traveler at better rates than the deluxe hotels in the neighborhood. So far, its guests are evenly divided between Westerners and Japanese. The Tarntawan's smallish lobby is of the character-less fast-food-chain variety. The well-maintained rooms are new, with predominately light colors lending a cheerful atmosphere. Chairs and beds are comfortably average, neither too hard nor too soft. VIP suites come with large, marble whirlpool baths. Because they are shielded from the traffic on Suriwong, rooms on the south side are quiet-er. The quality of the service is good, with everyone eager to please, though the staff doesn't always speak English very well. *A Maeping Hotel Group hotel. 119/5–10 Suriwong Rd., tel. 02/238–2620/39, fax 02/238–3228. Gen. manager, Vanjai Supanyaprubt. 70 rooms, 7 suites. AE, DC, MC, V.*

㉔ **Wall Street Inn.** Its moderate rates and location in the
$$ business district make the Wall Street Inn, completed in 1989, hard to beat. Japanese travelers make up the great-est percentage of guests, perhaps due to the many Japa-nese offices and nightclubs in the immediate area. Standard rooms are small and windowless, but functional; furnishings in natural-grain wood are still reasonably at-tractive; walls are bare of ornament. Bathtubs in the plain bathrooms are cramped. Deluxe rooms have full-size tubs and windows, though the quality of the view may make you wonder if windows are a good thing. The staff is most obliging and competent. There is no pool or fitness center, but the hotel has a traditional Thai massage parlor, and Lumphini Park is nearby for jogging. Overall, this is an acceptable budget alternative. *37/20–24 Soi Suriwong Plaza, Suriwong Rd., tel. 02/235–6068, fax 02/236–3619. Gen. manager, Suchin Kitisomprayoonkul. 75 rooms. AE, DC, MC, V.*

Sukhumvit/Ploenchit Area

㉝ **Ambassador Hotel and Convention Center.** This is the big-
$$$$ gest of Bangkok's hotels, with three wings ranging in cost from expensive to very expensive. With two large aviaries (one of them full of talking parrots), extensive business and convention facilities, and 100 shops on the premises, this establishment calls itself "Ambassador City" with some cause. The lobbies also tend to give the impression of colossal scale. The Tower Wing offers five-star luxury, but even the lower-priced Sukhumvit Wing, which is exposed to some noise from busy Sukhumvit Road, is quite plush. Nicely upholstered, comfortable chairs and couches are found in rooms in each of the wings, while brightly pat-terned bedspreads and curtains add an upbeat note. Se-lect a room above the sixth floor to avoid the noise coming from the hotel's popular clubs, notably Flamingo, the Rolls Royce Members Club, and the Leo Members Club (*see* After Hours, below). The hotel's fitness center (*see* Fitness, below) is one of the largest in the city. A pleasant

and efficient business center caters to business travelers, who make up about half of the hotel's guest list. *171 Sukhumvit Rd., tel. 02/254–0444 or 02/255–0444, fax 02/ 253–4123. Gen. manager, Mr. Kacuo Micutani. Tower Wing: 396 rooms, 24 suites; Main Wing: 400 rooms; Sukhumvit Wing: 190 rooms. AE, DC, MC, V.*

★ ㉛ **Federal Hotel.** Built in the late 1960s, this was an R&R ho-
$$ tel for U.S. troops during the Vietnam conflict. Today, it remains a bargain—functional and basic, but clean and good value for money, with little hint of the seediness of most similarly priced hotels in Bangkok. The lobby is a shade gloomy and somewhat cramped, and the rooms are utilitarian. The cushioned bamboo and wicker furniture is comfortable enough, but bedsprings and carpets show slight signs of wear. Aside from fax and telex, look for your business services outside the hotel. This is the best budget choice in the Sukhumvit/Ploenchit commercial district. *27 Soi 11, Sukhumvit, tel. 02/252–5143 or 02/253– 4768–9, fax 02/253–5332. Gen. manager, Mr. Tiam-chandr Chayangkura. 90 rooms. No credit cards.*

★ ㉗ **Hilton Hotel.** Since it opened in 1983, the Hilton has been
$$$$ popular with both business and diplomatic travelers for its location, ambience, and outstanding business services. Even in a city where marvelous hotel architecture is the rule, the five-story Hilton is outstanding. The open, airy design of its three atrium wings, together with abundant indoor greenery and skylighting, take full advantage of the hotel's setting in Nai Lert Park, 8.5 acres of lush tropical gardens with jogging track, pool, and lotus ponds. Deluxe rooms face the garden, Superior rooms front the city. Furnishings are simple and modern, with a white-and-cream color scheme accented by patches of cheery yellow on tables and desktops. All rooms are spacious and well appointed, but those overlooking the garden are especially pretty, with colorful bougainvillea spilling off each balcony. Ma Maison (*see* Dining, below), the hotel's premier French restaurant, is an elegant location for entertaining clients for lunch or dinner, while Suan Saronrom (*see* Business Breakfasts, below) is better suited for morning meetings. This hotel is just a 15-minute walk from the U.S. Embassy. It also features one of the best pools in the city (try the poolside barbecue) and a well-equipped and well-supervised fitness center, including both squash and tennis courts. *2 Wireless Rd., tel. 02/253–0123 or 800/445– 8667, fax 02/253–6509. Gen. manager, Bernard E. Brack. 295 singles/doubles, 37 suites, 43 "parlors." AE, DC, MC, V.*

㉚ **Landmark Hotel.** Completed in 1988, the Landmark Hotel
$$$$ is another newcomer catering primarily to business travelers. The public rooms, with their solid teak paneling and polished brass fittings, create a feeling of tasteful quality and luxury. The Rolls-Royces out front, part of the hotel's limousine fleet, add to the effect. Guest rooms begin on the eighth floor, well removed from traffic noise on busy Sukhumvit Road. All are spacious and luxuriously appointed with a number of convenient features, including safes, well-stocked minibars, and videotext computer terminals that allow guests to send faxes and call up stock-market updates, airline schedules, and weather forecasts. The hotel also offers 20 temporary offices for rent, complete with their own business center. English-language

dinner theater (*see* After Hours, below) is sometimes performed at the Landmark. Sui Sian (*see* Dining, below) is the hotel's fine Cantonese restaurant. There are also squash courts, private saunas, and a fitness center with carpeting and wood paneling. *138 Sukhumvit Rd., tel. 02/254-0404, fax 02/253-4259. Gen. manager, David Wiig. 360 singles/doubles, 55 suites. AE, CB, DC, MC, V.*

★ ㉟ **Mermaid's Rest.** The unaffectedly warm service suits the
$$ homey atmosphere of this quaint inn, where business services and ambience are better than in many of the more expensive hotels. With no desk or bath, rooms in the Old Wing are too basic for business travelers; however, rooms in the New Wing are quiet, bright, and comfortable, with highly polished parquet floors and handsome wooden furniture designed to maximize the use of the available space. Standard rooms have a shared bath and are cooled by fans; best bets are the deluxe rooms, which have air conditioning, private baths, television sets, and balconies. Guests are primarily European, many of whom are business travelers. This is good value for those on a tight budget. *39 Soi 8, Sukhumvit Rd., tel. 02/253-3410, fax 02/253-2401. Gen. manager, Mr. Ib Ottesen. 48 rooms. AE, DC, V; 5% service charge added for credit-card transactions.*

㉙ **Ra-Jah Hotel.** Centrally located and convenient to both
$$ the Sukhumvit/Ploenchit and Silom areas, the 14-story Ra-Jah Hotel is best described as modest verging on shabby. Some of the decor of the lounge and restaurant areas is peculiar but interesting—images of what might have happened had the Aztecs conquered southeast Asia. The room decor is a bit cold, with stark-white walls trimmed in pastels and worn-but-still-aggressively blue or green carpeting. Nevertheless, the simple furnishings are functional and comfortable. The hotel doesn't offer much in the way of business services, but rooms are clean and reasonably spacious, and the service is fine. Chinese, French, Arabs, and Americans are among the guests who frequent this hotel. *18 Soi 4, Sukhumvit Rd. tel. 02/255-0040, fax 02/255-7163. Gen. manager, Mr. Surat Kointrakul. 450 doubles/singles/suites. AE, DC, MC, V.*

★ ㉖ **Regent of Bangkok Hotel.** Believed by many to be the best
$$$$ business hotel in Bangkok, the Regent is ideally located equidistant from the Sukhumvit/Ploenchit and Silom business areas. Great square pillars in the lobby soar to a vast, softly glowing ceiling representation of the mythological Thai cosmos in a dozen shades of silk. Guest rooms are especially large and luxurious, decorated in the best tropical woods, with elegant bedspreads of pure silk, large writing desks, and substantial seating areas with chairs and sofa. All the elements combine to create feelings of grandeur and intimacy at the same time. The hotel's Spice Market (*see* Dining, below) serves some of the best Thai cuisine in town; The Lobby (*see* Business Breakfasts, below) is an excellent spot for morning meetings and is part of the reason that, architecturally, this is one of Bangkok's most interesting hotels. Management sees to it that the whole establishment functions as a single unit aimed at meeting the needs of business travelers, with convention and business services of an appropriate caliber. *155 Rajadamri Rd., tel. 02/251-6127 or 800/545-4000, fax 02/253-9195.*

Gen. manager, William D. Black. 405 rooms. AE, DC, MC, V.

❺ Siam InterContinental Hotel. One of two central garden
$$$$ hotels (the other is the Hilton), the Siam InterContinental
offers ready access to both the Sukhumvit/Ploenchit and
Silom business/shopping/entertainment areas. Its 26
acres of parkland, together with its botanical gardens and
the traditional-style "Thai Village" surrounding the main
pond, provide an asylum from the hectic pace and congestion of modern Bangkok. The artful use of large indoor
plants and lots of glass blurs the boundaries between lush
grounds and air-conditioned interior. In the guest rooms,
large writing desks, posh sofas, and deep winged-back
chairs provide all the working space and comfort one could
need. In the more-expensive garden rooms on the ground
floor, brightly patterned carpets add contrast to cool,
quiet color schemes, while sliding glass doors open onto
the lush greenery. Business facilities include 24-hour
news service. Landscaped jogging trails and a putting
green and driving range make up the unique outdoor fitness center. Dinner theater (*see* After Hours, below) is often performed at the hotel's restaurant. Only a few
minutes away on foot are several major shopping areas
with English-language cinemas and lots of good restaurants. *967 Srapatum Palace Property, Rama I Rd., tel.
02/253-0355/7 or 800/332-4246, fax 02/253-2275. Gen.
manager, Henri Blin. 400 rooms. AE, DC, MC, V.*

United Nations/Royal Palace Area

★ ❹ Princess Hotel. This small but elegant hotel is the best
$$$ business traveler's base in the Royal Palace/United Na-
tions end of town. The Dusit Thani Group took over in
1987, bringing with it its flair for management and fine
service. The small lobby offers views of gardens on two
sides, while recessed crystal chandeliers and potted
plants complete a mood of quiet intimacy. The rooms are
at once restful and stylish; subdued color combinations of
blues or tans and beiges set off the Oriental furnishings in
dark-stained woods. Spacious, well-lighted desks provide
adequate work space; however, bathrooms and tubs are
very small. Special executive rooms are located on the
Princess Floor, which has its own private lobby and
breakfast room. The hotel is not only close to the UN agen-
cies and several government ministries, but also to some
major tourist attractions as well as a number of fine river-
side restaurants. *269 Larn Luang Rd., tel. 02/281-3088
or 800/448-8355, fax 02/280-1314. Gen. manager, Vora-
pong Vanakong. 55 superior, 50 deluxe, 5 suites, and 50
executive. AE, DC, MC, V.*

❸ Viengtai Hotel. Its proximity to the United Nations and its
$$ tried-and-true accommodations make this modest property the favorite moderately priced hotel in this part of
town. Guests are 70% Thais, with Sri Lankans and Indians with business at UN agencies making up much of the
remainder. The U.S. Peace Corps has been the main
American contingent, having had a contract with this hotel for years. Regular guests prefer the quiet rooms on the
5th–8th floors at the back of the building, away from the
street. Rooms are more than adequate for the price,
though carpets and bedspreads are worn, and there is that
slight mustiness that pervades older budget hostelries

the world over. Beds are comfortable, and there is a small television set that receives plenty of Thai programming. The pool is fairly large and well maintained, but situated in a dreary setting. *42 Tanee, tel. 02/282–8119/23, fax 02/ 280–3527. Gen. manager, Mr. Surin Maneedul. 200 rooms. AE, DC, MC, V.*

Airport and Vipawadi-Rangsit/ Ratchadapisek

8 **Airport Hotel.** Connected to the airport by a covered walk-
$$$ way, this hotel is extremely convenient for those with late-night or early-morning flights. The hotel's "ministay" plan permits travelers with a short stopover in Bangkok to take a room for three hours at just B350. The steel-and-glass lobby is surprisingly small and purely functional. Rooms, in contrast, are large and pleasant, with tasteful if somewhat minimal furnishings in warm rust-and-cream tones. The quietest of the soundproofed rooms overlook the pool and garden in the central court. Service is cordial and efficient. Current expansion plans will soon add a business center, expanded banquet facilities, and a floor of specially equipped business-class rooms. *A Siam Lodge Group Hotel. 333 Chert Wudthakas Rd., tel. 02/566– 1020–1 or 800/448–8355, fax 02/566–1941. Gen. manager, Leo Muehlebach. 100 doubles, 180 singles, 20 suites. AE, DC, MC, V.*

★ **7** **Central Plaza Hotel.** The Central Plaza Hotel is situated
$$$$ midway between the airport and Silom Road, in the middle of one of the city's fastest-growing business districts. The west side of the hotel affords a view of the Railway Golf Course; the remaining sides lend a lofty perspective on the city's hellbent horizontal and vertical growth. The refreshingly cool, green lobby is a welcome hideaway, the atmosphere enhanced by the soothing white noise of the cascading waterfall. Rooms are quietly graceful, with pearly grays, soft creams, and tans in understated floral designs; Thai prints, bronze mythological figures, and temple-dog lampstands remind guests that they are in Thailand. The two floors of the Dynasty Club offer even better accommodations, with large, handsomely furnished sitting areas, stereo units, bars, kitchen facilities, and dining areas plus butler/valet service, a common lounge for business guests, and special security (guests get an elevator passkey to their own floor). Among the hotel's numerous restaurants and bars is Dynasty (*see* Dining, below), a popular spot for Chinese cuisine. Business facilities include a multilingual simultaneous translation system. Current traffic conditions can make getting to the Silom Road business/commercial center of the city a bit trying—the hotel's only real disadvantage. *1695 Phaholyothin Rd., tel. 02/541–1234 or 800/448–8355, fax 02/541–1087. Acting Gen. manager, Suthikiati Chirathivat. 348 standard rooms, 73 connecting rooms, 103 suites. AE, DC, MC, V.*

6 **Rama Garden Hotel.** This place is neither here nor there—
$$$ it's close to the airport, but not as close as the Airport Hotel; it's also close to the Vipawadi-Rangsit/Ratchadapisek business district, but not as close as the Central Plaza. Still, it's a good second choice in either case. Separated from the highway by a spacious park, this hotel has a quiet atmosphere. However, furnishings appear a bit spartan

and worn for an expensive hotel; and standard rooms are somewhat rundown and nondescript, with cushioned bamboo furniture and minibars that can only be unlocked by room-service staff. Rooms on the west side of the hotel overlook the pools and garden. Fitness facilities include two squash courts, three tennis courts, and a jogging trail. It's a long commute to the Silom and Sukhumvit areas, but free shuttle-bus service is available. *9/9 Vipawadi-Rangsit Rd., tel. 02/579–5400 or 800/448–8355, fax 02/561–1025. Gen. manager, Aswin Ingkakul. 228 doubles, 128 singles, 12 suites. AE, DC, MC, V.*

DINING

Bangkok is one of the best cities in the world for food—perhaps *the* best, if you take into account prices as well as quality and service—with an enormous variety of dining experiences. You can sample street food from the swarms of midday and evening vendors, or you can dine on gourmet fare served with impeccable skill in surroundings of splendid elegance. There are riverside restaurants, garden restaurants, and dinner cruises on the river. Aside from the wonderful Thai cuisine, which is of consistently high quality both in terms of ingredients and art, you can find almost any cuisine imaginable in Bangkok.

When eating Thai food, take a lesson from the Thai proverb: "A real Thai does as he likes." Don't worry too much about which eating implement to use, or which drink or dish should accompany others. As a rule of thumb, spicy food is usually accompanied by sweet, sour, and salty dishes; if you orchestrate these while you eat, the notoriously hot Thai cuisine should become quite manageable. In any case, copious doses of rice or lime juice are effective antidotes. If you would prefer to avoid overly spicy chilis, specify that you want your food *mai pet*, or not hot.

Note: In Thailand, although it is considered a little unusual for people to eat by themselves in public, there is no problem with it. You should feel comfortable dining alone in any of the restaurants listed here unless otherwise noted.

Highly recommended restaurants in each price category are indicated by a star ★.

Category	Cost*
$$$$ (Very Expensive)	over B400
$$$ (Expensive)	B200–B400
$$ (Moderate)	under B200

*per person, including appetizer, entrée, and dessert, but excluding drinks, service, and 11% sales tax.

Numbers in the margin correspond to numbered restaurant locations on the Bangkok Lodging and Dining map.

Wine and Beer

Restaurants offer one "red table wine" and one "white table wine," but local wines are not recommended because they tend to taste like cooking sherry. The excellent

Singha is the most popular local beer; Klosters is brewed under license and costs more. A third variety, Amarit, is available on draft in some places. All three are stronger than American beers and are often served with ice cubes. Imported brands, where available, are expensive.

Traditional Thai restaurants allow customers to bring wine or liquor with them, and provide ice, mixes, and service. Most don't even charge corkage. Thais often drink whiskey or brandy with soda or cola before, during, and after the meal. It is considered bad form to let someone's glass run empty, and the attentive and dangerously unobtrusive restaurant staff will see to it that yours doesn't, either; it may require some effort to keep track of just how much you've had to drink. Never pour your own drink unless you've first poured for your companions. Finishing your glass entirely is a signal that you're ready to leave.

Business Breakfasts

Business breakfasts are not particularly popular among Thais, but should you nevertheless need a place to meet over breakfast, the following are exceptional for their ambience, food, and service: **The Lobby** (Regent Hotel, tel. 02/251–6127), the **Suan Saronrom** (Hilton Hotel, tel. 02/253–0123), and **The Terrace** (Oriental Hotel, tel. 02/236–0400). The **Rim Nam Coffeeshop** (Royal Orchid Sheraton, tel. 02/234–5599) is a good place for a business breakfast with a river view. Alternatively, you could try the dim sum for brunch at the **Shang Palace** (Shangri-La Hotel, tel. 02/236–7777), the **Jade Garden** (Montien Hotel, tel. 02/233–7060), or **Maria Restaurant** (50–52 Bldg. 4, Rajadamnern Rd., tel. 02/224–1793).

Silom Road Area

★ ⑩ **Benkay.** One of Bangkok's best Japanese restaurants, this
$$$$ elegant little place overlooking the Chao Phraya River is favored by Japanese and Westerners alike for business lunches and dinners. The three small private rooms, decorated with the opulent minimalism at which the Japanese excel, are recommended when business takes precedence over a view. Otherwise, ask for a table by the river, especially at night. Waitresses are attentive and friendly. The main dining area includes teppanyaki and sushi counters where diners will feel entirely comfortable eating alone. The menu offers inventions of the chef such as sushi with shrimp eggs, a treat for the eyes as much as for the palate. The *gyuniku-yudofu* (a hot pot of sliced beef, bean curd, and vegetables) and *dobin mushi* (steamed seafood custard served in earthen teapots) are two other favorites. There are also special monthly features, as well as menus designed to coincide with festive occasions in Japan. Green-tea ice cream makes a refreshing dessert. *Royal Orchid Sheraton, 2 Captain Bush La., Siphya Rd., tel. 02/234–5599. Casual but neat dress. Reservations required for the private rooms. AE, DC, MC, V.*

㉒ ㉕ **Bussaracum.** This place is very popular with foreigners
$$$ who want to enjoy Royal Thai cuisine, a range of dishes traditionally favored at the Thai court; the Thais tend to stay away because of the prices. The visitor unaccustomed to the heat and blare of downtown Bangkok will welcome

the cool contrast to the street offered by this restaurant's subdued colors and lighting. The building itself is a modest house on a formerly quiet sidestreet. Bussaracum is a good spot for business lunches; the VIP rooms are nicely furnished, and each has its own bar. Popular dishes include steamed sea bass with chili paste, and sweet-and-sour shrimp. What many find most memorable are the painstakingly prepared appetizers—little birds fashioned of taro and nestled alongside shrimp in beds of shredded salad; mushrooms stuffed with seasoned shrimp fashioned to resemble tiny turtles; plates and platters decorated with geometrical shapes of carved watermelons, rose apples, and pineapples; delicate tomato roses resting in leaves of papaya and guava. A branch in the Dusit Thani Hotel offers the same food and service. *35 Soi Pipat, tel. 02/235–8915. Jacket and tie advised. Reservations advised, especially for the private rooms. AE, DC, MC, V.*

★ ⑲ **Coca.** A perennial favorite with locals, this is a good spot
$$ for an informal business lunch or dinner. Coca's specialty is Thai-style sukiyaki, which incorporates a piquant sauce. Each table comes equipped with a central gas cooker so you can prepare your own meal selected from an array of fresh ingredients on the menu. Or you can leave the work to the waitress. Noodle dishes are another favorite. Also recommended are the varieties of shark's fin soups or the stuffed king prawns the size of small lobsters. The Soi Tantawan branch is especially well decorated, with three large floors: the ground floor in Chinese decor with large, round tables and a convivial atmosphere; the first floor with Thai murals and carved screens and chairs, in VIP rooms suitable for more formal meetings; and the second floor with mirrored ceiling, big chandeliers, and high-backed chairs of vaguely Western Art Deco provenance. The same menu is available at Coca in Siam Square. *2 locations: 8 Soi Tantawan, Suriwong Rd., tel. 02/236–9323; 416/3–8 Henri Dunant Rd., tel. 02/251–6337. Casual but neat dress. Reservations advised; one week's notice requested for VIP rooms. AE, DC, V.*

⑬ **Himali Cha Cha.** This is a good alternative to the Moghul
$$ Room (*see* below) if you're at the Chao Phraya end of Silom Road and have a yen for Northern Indian food. Behind the tiled facade you'll discover a cozy little warren with lots of Western customers. The exposed-wood beams have all been hand carved in intricate Indian motifs, while the walls are decorated in a collage of chipped glass and Kashimi cotton. The warmth of the surroundings is enhanced by the presence of Himali Cha Cha himself, chief cook, part owner, and solicitous inquirer after the well-being of his guests. Given the somewhat close quarters and the ambient chatter and clatter of fellow diners, this restaurant is better suited for a relaxed meal than for serious business discussions. All the northern-style specialties are here, with the chicken tandoori and mutton masala being two perennial favorites. Chicken Kashmiri, with a creamy sauce incorporating fruits and nuts, is another specialty. *1229/11 New Rd., tel. 02/235–1569. Casual but neat dress. Reservations advised. AE, DC, V.*

⑳ **Jade Garden.** Fine Cantonese cuisine and good value make
$$$ this restaurant well worth visiting for dim-sum brunch or dinner. The Jade Garden boasts that it manages its superb dishes without the aid of MSG, a rarity in this part of the

world. The decor is similarly assured in its effects, with a remarkable wood-beam ceiling and softly lighted Chinese print screens. This fine restaurant is suitable for business or pleasure. Private dining rooms are available with advance notice; otherwise ask for the corner table in the main dining room—it's partly partitioned off and affords extra privacy. Two favorite dinner specials are fried Hong Kong noodles, and pressed duck with tea leaves. Look for the monthly "special promotion," a dish featuring some seasonally available ingredient. *Montien Hotel, 54 Suriwong Rd., tel. 02/233-7060. Casual but neat dress. Reservations advised; 24-hour advance notice required for private rooms. AE, DC, MC, V.*

★ ㉕ **Mayflower.** Captains of industry, royalty, and heads of
$$$$ state are counted among the regular customers who frequent the five stylishly opulent private rooms and the main dining area of the Mayflower. Carved wooden screens and quality porcelain vases set a tone of simple-but-luxurious refinement. Furnishings are decidedly modern, yet somehow contribute to a traditional Chinese ambience that perfectly complements the outstanding Cantonese food. In order to provide the best service possible, a computerized record is kept of the guests—of their food preferences, the size of their families, important anniversaries, etc. Tables are set with chopsticks and spoons, but knives and forks are available. Two of the best items on the menu are the piquant abalone-and-jellyfish salad, and the Drunken Chinese Chicken—steamed, skinned, and boned chicken doused with Chinese liquor and served with two sauces, one sweet and one spicy. The shark's-fin soup and the dim sum are also worth sampling. An excellent wine list assumes price is no object. Waitresses wear slinky silk dresses slit to the hip. *Dusit Thani Hotel., Rama IV Rd., tel. 02/236-0450. Jacket and tie advised. Reservations required; 2–3 day advance notice required for private rooms. AE, DC, V.*

⑰ **Once Upon a Time.** Here is an inexpensive place to relax
$$ and enjoy Thai food in an unusual setting that manages to be at once very central and off the beaten path. It's popular with Thais, but foreigners, mostly residents, have just started to discover it. There are weathered wooden shingles and shutters everywhere, small, sparkling lights in the trees outside at night, and a maze of half-partitioned rooms inside—both downstairs and upstairs. Walls are decorated with period photos of the Thai royal family, movie stars, and beauty queens. The music is traditional Thai, both taped and live. From the garden tables and the downstairs dining area, the quaint atmosphere of days gone by is only slightly marred by the sound of traffic from the other side of the wall. The menu is good, and authentic all the way. Experiment, by all means, but ask for advice on spiciness—ask for *mai pet* (not hot) if in doubt. Western customers often order the chopped pork with chili sauce or the beef fillet with pickled garlic. *Miang kham* (a traditional snack of dried shrimp, dried coconut, peanuts, pineapple, lime, chili pepper, and sweet tamarind sauce mixed to taste and rolled together in a green leaf) makes an excellent appetizer. Although the service is very friendly and willing, English is not a strong suit here. *67 Soi Anuman Rajathon Decho, Suriwong, tel. 02/233-8493. Casual but neat dress. Reservations advised. AE, V.*

㉖ **Spice Market.** This restaurant offers an unusual and pleas-
$$$ ing decor, one reminiscent of an old East India Company
trading outpost, with spices on display everywhere, add-
ing to the warmth of the service and atmosphere. Specia-
lizing in home-style Thai cooking, Spice Market is fine for
casual business meals or dining alone; the staff is adept at
making customers feel at home. Check their "chili guide,"
which rates items according to their degree of spiciness.
This may be a good place to begin with Thai food; the expe-
rience will help you survive subsequent gustatory explo-
rations. Popular dishes with Thai and foreign customers
alike are *tom yam kung* (hot-and-sour prawn soup), and
gaeng keeow waan (sweet green curries). *Regent of Bang-
kok Hotel, 155 Rajadamri Rd., tel. 02/251–6127. Casual
but neat dress. Reservations advised. AE, DC, MC, V.*

★ **⓰** **Thanying.** This stylish restaurant is decorated in the tra-
$$$ ditional Thai manner, though it is full of fascinating an-
tiques from all over Asia. Sitting in a walled compound,
the building looks more like a private home than a restaurant. Inside, the impression is maintained in the relaxed
and cozy atmosphere, with classical Thai musicians performing quietly in the background (Wednesday and Sunday) in one of the three main rooms. The owner is a movie
star who has specialized in portraying royalty. Appropriately enough, the menu is genuine Royal Thai cuisine, all
of it beautifully presented with carved fruits, vegetables,
flowers, and the best of service. This attracts many Thai
customers as well as foreign visitors. For something unusual in the hot season, try the *khao chae* (fragrant iced
rice), traditionally a favorite at the Thai court. This seemingly simple but amazingly refreshing dish actually incorporates a lot of ingredients and takes considerable time to
prepare; only the best chefs, such as the one here, can prepare it correctly. The fragrance comes partly from the jasmine buds that are floated in the rice. Grilled and boneless
whole sea bass with chili sauce is a favorite main dish.
Thanying is appropriate for business lunches. *10 Pra-
muan Rd., tel. 02/236–4361. Casual but neat dress. Reservations advised. AE, DC, MC, V.*

Sukhumvit/Ploenchit Area

★ **㉞** **Le Banyan.** Come to this old Thai house—warm, intimate,
$$$$ and vaguely colonial in style—for first-rate French cooking. This restaurant is roughly equivalent to Ma Maison
(*see* below) in terms of quality of food, service, ambience,
and prices (although the wines are somewhat less costly).
The service is considered by some to be even better. Tending towards nouvelle cuisine, the chef also experiments
with Asian influences, occasionally adding a Thai accent of
lemon grass, ginger, or Thai basil. Pressed duck à la
Rouennaise, incorporating a sauce prepared with the
juices of the bird and red wine, is one of the duck specialties; a large silver-plated duck press normally takes center stage in the dining room. The King Lobster makes a
delicious alternative. Lots of Thais come here to be seen,
and indeed it is one of the most impressive spots in town to
entertain. Recent expansion added a private dining room
suitable for business lunches and dinners; great care was
taken to preserve the period charm of the building. *59 Soi
8, Sukhumvit Rd., tel. 02/253–5556. Jacket advised. Res-*

ervations required. AE, DC, MC, V. Closed Mon. Dinner only.

28 **Le Bistrot.** While not quite in the same league as Le Ban-
$$$ yan—one is not so likely to go around tripping over maître
d's and the like—Le Bistrot nevertheless offers excellent
service, atmosphere, and classic French cuisine, all at a
lower price. The chic modern decor doesn't detract from
the intimacy. Sit at one of the tables at the back to conduct
business discussions undistracted by the comings and go-
ings of staff and customers. The food is classic French,
with plenty of caloric cream sauces. Among the favorite
dishes is chateaubriand with béarnaise sauce. Grilled king
prawns with peppercorns in a cognac-and-fresh-cream
sauce is also a nice way to blow a diet. Custard-apple
sherbert is a specialty. *20/17–9 Soi Ruam Rudee,
Ploenchit Rd., tel. 02/251–2523. Casual but neat dress.
Reservations advised. AE, DC, MC, V.*

36 **Cabbages and Condoms.** Though the name is peculiar, the
$$ Thai home cooking served here is delicious and moderately priced. This somewhat ramshackle old house behind a
fence on a sidestreet belongs to a nonprofit organization of
the Population and Community Development Association,
and proceeds go to family-planning education. Service is
slow, but otherwise much like the decor—simple and homey. Customers are mostly resident Westerners, with a
sprinkling of Thais. There are a couple of semiprivate dining rooms in addition to the small main room. The International Business Associates meet in the private Hilltribe
Room on Friday evenings; join them for insiders' tips on
Thailand. *8 Soi 12, Sukhumvit Rd., tel. 02/251–0402/3.
Casual dress. Reservations advised. AE, DC, MC, V.*

★ **37** **Le Dalat.** This relative newcomer became so popular so
$$$ fast it has already moved into larger and more lavish
premises. Its open, airy design takes in two floors with
rooms and little nooks for those who want privacy for an
informal business meeting. Le Dalat offers a delicious va-
riety of Vietnamese specialties, using the freshest ingre-
dients prepared with consistent flair. (Vietnamese food is
currently enjoying something of a fad in Bangkok, and
there are several very good competitors.) Try the fondue
with beef or shrimp, served with either international or
Vietnamese sauces. For those who can't get enough of raw
fish but are tired of sashimi, there's the *goi ca* (literally,
"fish dish"; raw fish prepared with spices and mint)—deli-
cious. *47/1 Soi 23, Sukhumvit Rd., tel. 02/258–4192. Casu-
al but neat dress. Reservations advised. AE, DC, MC, V.*

41 **Lemongrass.** One of the few upscale places where you can
$$$ find regional Thai specialties, Lemongrass is very popular
with Thais, resident Westerners, and visitors alike,
though it is somewhat overrated. Portions are stingy (the
main menu is sometimes described as Thai nouvelle cuisine), and the cluttered decor is reminiscent of a Victorian
drawing room. The rooms do lend an atmosphere of casual
intimacy and warmth, however—this is a good place to relax. The lemon chicken and duck curry are house specialties worth trying, as is a glass of *nam takrai*—a cold,
sweet drink brewed from lemongrass. *5/1 Soi 24,
Sukhumvit Rd., tel. 02/258–8637. Casual but neat dress.
AE, DC, MC, V.*

38 **L'Opera.** A slice of Italy, this quaint family bistro specia-
$$$ lizes in a variety of homemade pastas and other authentic

Italian fare. The staff takes pride in working here; many members have remained over the years, despite cutthroat competition. A recent expansion and a move from one side of the street to the other led to initial growing pains, but these have been ironed out. The bay-window table is nice but, given its proximity to the air conditioner, you might want to wear a parka. This is a fine spot to eat when you have a craving for *tortelli*, large ravioli stuffed with spinach and cheese, or *spadarrata*, a pleasing combination of seafood with garlic-and-white-wine sauce. *53 Soi 39, Sukhumvit Rd., tel. 02/258–5606. Casual but neat dress. Reservations advised. AE, DC, MC, V.*

㉗ **Ma Maison.** This is the most frequently recommended
$$$$ place for first-class Continental food, with French dishes in the nouvelle tradition. The designers took great care in recreating a traditional Thai house, while at the same time providing views of the pool and garden outside. Popular favorites here include prime rib beef, and red grouper cooked at tableside in a luscious cream sauce. Ma Maison is upscale enough for entertaining and comfortable enough for serious discussions over lunch or dinner. *Hilton Hotel, 2 Wireless Rd., tel. 02/253–0123. Jacket and tie advised. Reservations required. AE, DC, MC, V.*

㉜ **Moghul Room.** Many of Bangkok's Indian residents attest
$$$ that this restaurant serves the best northern Indian food in the city. The traditional tandoori meats and breads are excellent. The chefs can also prepare a sumptuous *ghozi* (actually an Arabian specialty)—a whole sheep stuffed with chickens stuffed with eggs and rice—if you give them a day's notice. There is a vegetarian menu as well. The decor is pleasant, with lots of tapestries and carpets. Reserve a table, particularly if you would like to sit on the mezzanine. The Moghul Room is conveniently located, opposite the Ambassador Hotel and almost as close to several other recommended hotels, and is best for dining alone or for a casual meal with associates. *1/16 Soi 11, Sukhumvit Rd., tel. 02/253–6989. Casual but neat dress. Reservations advised. AE, DC, MC, V.*

㉚ **Sui Sian.** The Sui Sian serves great, if a tiny bit inconsis-
$$$$ tent, Cantonese cuisine. Certainly the decor, the service, and the design of both the main dining area and the private rooms make this an appropriate spot for lunch or dinner meetings in this area of town. The main dining rooms, with their inward facing, bamboo-tiled eaves, give the feel of a courtyard, an impression reinforced by the splendid jade trees on display. The Peking duck is particularly good here. Or if you're in an extravagant mood, and need a tonic, try the pricey Ancient Master Jumps the Wall—a soup incorporating everything from black chicken, deer tendons, abalone, shark fin, dried scallops, fish maw, turtle, sea cucumber, mushrooms, and a selection of secret Chinese herbs. *Landmark Hotel, 138 Sukhumvit Rd., tel. 02/254–0404. Jacket and tie advised. AE, DC, MC, V.*

Vipawodi-Rangsit/Ratchadapisek Road Area

❾ **㊵** **D'Jit Pochana.** This branch of the D'Jit Pochana restau-
$$ rant chain is within relatively easy reach of the airport and is a convenient destination for home-cooked Thai meals for travelers staying at the Airport Hotel. The restaurant is made up of numerous rooms—including several large pri-

vate rooms suitable for business dinners—on different levels; guests must climb stairs from the street level to reach the entrance, and then go up or down more stairs to the various dining rooms. Request a room with a view of the fountain and pond in the garden; other rooms look out over the road. Among the many specialties are *gai haw bai toey* (chicken cooked in plantain leaves and served with a delicate sauce) and *tom kaa gai* (a fortifying soup made with coconut milk, chicken, Siamese ginger, lemongrass, lime juice, coriander leaves, and just enough chili to lend interest). The Sukhumvit Soi 20 branch, oldest of the D'Jit Pochna restaurants, has long been a favorite recommendation for newcomers to the city, and is still a comfortable, if modest, place to meet for lunch or dinner in this area of town. *26/368–80 Gp 6 Phaholyothin Rd., tel. 02/531–1644; 62 Soi 20, Sukhumvit Rd., tel. 02/258–1597. Casual but neat dress. No reservations. AE, DC, MC, V.*

★ **7** **Dynasty Restaurant.** The prime minister, the army chief of
$$$$ staff—virtually every senior member of the government, the military, and the local business establishment—come here to feast on outstanding Cantonese cuisine. In addition to the main dining area, 11 quiet rooms provide unsurpassed locations for business lunches or dinners (nine of them accommodate 10 people each, the other two hold up to 50). The deep red carpeting, heavy traditional Chinese furniture, masterfully carved screens, and porcelain objets d'art contribute to the hushed ambience and quietly elegant atmosphere. The Peking duck and shark's-fin dishes prepared by two first-rate Hong Kong chefs are among the draws. Seasonal specialties include everything from "hairy crab" (October–November) to "Taiwanese eels" (March), with only fresh ingredients used. The service—efficient and friendly without being obtrusive—couldn't be improved. There is such a demand for dinner seating here that expansion plans are under way. *Central Plaza Hotel, 1695 Phaholyothin Rd., tel. 541–1234. Jacket and tie advised. Reservations required; book at least one day ahead. AE, DC, MC, V.*

★ **39** **Tum Nak Thai (III).** Sprawling over 10 acres, with seating
$$ for 3,000, a staff of hundreds, a computer center, and spotters with walkie-talkies to keep it all happening, this outdoor restaurant is often recommended largely on the basis of its size. It is credited with being the largest in the world by the Guinness Book of Records. Some of the waitresses use roller skates, the better to convey your food to you before it gets cold. Despite all this, the food is remarkably good (but inconsistent, which isn't surprising when you consider that more than 150 cooks are employed here), and the surroundings are pleasant, with trees and waterfalls and terraced dining levels. There is traditional Thai music and dance for entertainment. With all the distractions, Tum Nak Thai is inappropriate for any but the most informal of business meetings. For a nice light meal or part of a larger feast, try the *gai yang* (grilled chicken with sweet-and-peppery sauce) and *somtam* (green papaya salad); this combination is a Northeastern Thai favorite that has become equally popular in Bangkok. Order "sticky rice" to go with it—it's traditional, and for very good reason, since it takes the edge off the hot salad. *131 Ratchadapisek Rd., tel. 02/276–1810. Casual dress. Weekend reservations advised. AE, DC, MC, V.*

United Nations/Royal Palace Area

❶ **Kaloang Seafood.** This local favorite is a little off the beat-
$$ en track, but it's worth the effort if you want the genuine
flavor of riverside Bangkok and good seafood as well. Be-
ginning at the National Library, the soi leading down to
the place is charmingly ethnic, and the restaurant itself is
open, built on a ramshackle pier. Although there is no air-
conditioned area, fans and the breeze off the river keep
things comfortably cool most evenings. The more observ-
ant customer will notice right away that almost all the
waiters/waitresses are transvestites. (Transvestism is
tolerated with good humor in Thai culture.) Service is
nonetheless friendly and competent, if initially somewhat
disconcerting. The grilled seafood platter is both gener-
ous and cheap, while the grilled giant river prawns are
also a bargain. Try the *yam pla duk foo* (puffed and deep-
fried catfish with peanuts, green mango, lime, and chilis).
It is rather spicy, be warned, but it complements cold beer
as few things in this world do. While Kaloang is a fun local
place to unwind, it is not appropriate for business meals.
Solo businesswomen might feel a little uncomfortable,
both with the area and with dining alone. *2 Sri Ayutthaya
Rd., tel. 02/281–9228 or 02/282–7581. Casual dress. BYOB
for wine. No reservations. AE, DC, MC, V.*

❷ **Krua Wang Nar.** This riverside restaurant serves magnifi-
$$ cent Thai food, including some of the best seafood in town.
It is also very near the National Museum, the National
Theater, the Royal Palace, and other cultural attractions.
Krua Wang Nar is noisy in the evenings, the decor is fairly
appalling (with pillars and plaster mermaids and several
TVs blaring away at once), and there seems to be a tendency for Westerners to be given smarmy and intrusive
service. However, a prime location on the river, a comfortable, air-conditioned dining section, and high-quality food
are among the factors that make this restaurant very popular with Thais and with growing numbers of foreigners.
Everything listed on the extensive menu is good, particularly *pla somlee pow* (baked cottonfish with ginger and
garlic) and *pae sa pla chon* (steamed serpenthead fish with
vegetables). This is not the place for business lunches or
dinners with serious intent. *17/1 Chao Fa Rd., tel. 02/224–
8552–3. Casual dress. BYOB for wine. Reservations advised, especially for a table by the water. DC, V.*

㉓ **Patpong Area Snacks**

Patpong roads I and II together are a jungle of bars and
restaurants. What follows is only a selection of the best
and cheapest places to get a quick snack. There are lots of
Western fast-food outlets in the area—Kentucky Fried
Chicken, Chicken Divine, McDonald's, A&W, etc. But
why not try something different?

Breakfast
Tip Top (46–48 Patpong I, tel. 02/02–2355) is an unpretentious—indeed, humble—institution that opens at 7
AM, and offers a tasty Thai-style breakfast for only B25. The
jok (savory rice porridge) includes shrimp or chicken with
spring onions, fresh ginger, garlic, and a raw egg (if de-
sired). The *pad thai* (Thai-style noodles) is also good.

Lunch
Derby King (74 Patpong I, tel. 02/234–8354) offers an old-fashioned, homey decor and great burgers, hoagies, heroes, deli-style sandwiches, and more at B50–B80.

Lunch, Dinner, and Late-Night Snacks
Mizu's Kitchen (32 Patpong I, tel. 02/233–6447), established in 1954, serves lunch for B80 and dinner for around B120; try the Sarika steak or the sizzling Saba fish steak, broiled with soy sauce and lime. **New Red Door** (40 Patpong I, tel. 02/234–9355) is favored by local revelers for midnight snacks (served till 12:30 AM); the fried Shanghai noodles are great. Most items on the menu cost B50–B100. **Bale** (1 Patpong Bldg. 2F, Patpong I or II, tel. 02/234–0290) serves something new from Vietnam—crisp toasted French baguettes with a tasty filling of various meats, pâté, crunchy pickled vegetables, mayonnaise, coriander, and chiles—for only B45.

FREE TIME

Fitness

Hotel Facilities
All of the following facilities are open to the general public. The **Ambassador Hotel** (tel. 02/254–0444) has one of the biggest and best-equipped fitness centers in the city, including pool, sauna, and Jacuzzi. Cost: B200 per day. The **Dusit Thani** (tel. 02/236–0450–9) also has an excellent club, including tennis and squash courts, and its rates for one day are B150 for the gym, B200 with sauna. The **Landmark Hotel** (tel. 02/254–0404) has a small but well-equipped and well-supervised gym together with lavish massage, steam bath, Jacuzzi, and sauna facilities, including private saunas; the daily rate is B200, excluding squash and pool.

Health and Fitness Clubs
The **Fitness Clinic Health Club** (16/15 Soi Somkhit Ploenchit, tel. 02/251–0392) accepts both male and female day members at B150 per day (gym), B100 (sauna), and B100 (Jacuzzi). The gym has free weights and Nautilus machines; supervised aerobics may be followed by sauna and Jacuzzi.

Jogging
There are miles of jogging trails in **Lumphini Park,** nestled right in the business hub of the city, within an easy walk of the Regent, the Dusit Thani, the Montien, and the Wall Street Inn. The **Hilton Hotel** has a nice trail in its park; the **Siam InterContinental** up on Rama I Road has some good routes, too. **Sanam Luang,** a big, tree-lined circuit in front of the Royal Palace, is popular with local Thais as a place to jog, though traffic exhaust gets more than a little thick at times.

Shopping

Popular gifts and souvenirs of Thailand include silk and cotton material and fashions, leather goods, lacquerware, gems and jewelry, antiques (both genuine and, overtly or covertly, reproductions), prints of traditional-style paintings, pewter, wood carvings, and ceramics (especially *celadon* with its characteristic green crackled glaze).

The **Silom/Suriwong** area has hundreds of shops and street vendors selling everything, from rubbish to excellent quality goods, at prices both reasonable and unreasonable. The **Rajadamri/Ploenchit/Pratunam** commercial district caters to foreigners and Thais alike, with gigantic department stores and arcades overshadowing clusters of little shops; leather goods and clothing are two of the bargains available here. The **Siam Square/Mah Boonkrong** area is a bit pricey, but offers a wealth of variety and interest, with movie theaters and lots of good restaurants to provide sanctuary from the maddening crowds of shoppers. The **Sampeng/Klong Tom** area of **Chinatown** is fun to visit if you have the time and patience to look for something of quality and to bargain for it once found. In the **Vipawadi-Rangsit/Ratchadapisek Road** area, go to Chatuchak Park on the weekends to explore the **Weekend Market,** said to be the largest market in Asia. There is more to see here than you'll ever manage in one morning or afternoon (mornings are cooler). You can buy anything from Siamese fighting fish to antiques to big rocks for your garden. The aquarium fish and pet section is in itself worth the trip.

Amarin Plaza (500 Ploenchit Rd., tel. 02/256–9111) houses a number of upscale shops, including the fancy **Sogo** Japanese department store. Locals favor the reasonable prices and good selection of merchandise at the **Central Department Store** (1027 Ploenchit Rd., tel. 02/251–9201; 306 Silom Rd., tel. 02/233–6930; 1691 Phaholyothin Rd., tel. 02/541–1020–9). **Robinson Department Store** (No. 2 Silom Rd., tel. 02/235–0471; 139 Ratchadapisek Rd., tel. 02/245–4811) is popular as well.

For a good selection of loose gems and jewelry, try **Wilai's Gems** (89/19 Wireless Rd., tel. 02/250–0532–3 or 02/250–1885) or **Beng Hwa Jewelers** (1233 New Rd., tel. 02/233–9359). **Jim Thompson Thai Silk** (9 Suriwong Rd., tel. 02/234–4900–4) is perhaps the most respected name in locally produced silk. **Khanitha** (362 Siam Center, Rama I Rd., tel. 02/251–2933; 113/3–5 Suriwong Rd., tel. 02/233–1004) has some of the most sought-after silk fashions. **Naraiphan** (127 Rajaprarob Rd., tel. 02/252–4670–9) offers a huge selection of Thai handicrafts at reasonable prices. The **River City Complex** (23 Rongnamkhaeng Rd., tel. 02/237–0077) has dozens of shops selling gems, silk fashions, handicrafts, antiques, and reproductions. Of particular note is the **Golden Triangle** (No. 301, third floor, River City, tel. 02/237–0078), which carries an interesting selection of hill-tribe clothes, silver jewelry, and antique textiles.

Diversions

The Ancient City (Kilometer 33, Sukhumvit Highway, tel. 02/222–8145) is billed as The World's Largest Outdoor Museum. It consists of dozens of famous monuments and buildings of historical and cultural interest, all reproduced in loving detail, some of them full-scale, some of them reduced. If you haven't time to travel all over Thailand to see the originals, this makes a good substitute. The exhibits are spaced out over a large area of lush parkland, and, if the weather isn't too hot, strolling from one site to the next is very pleasant. You can stop for drinks or lunch at the replica of a traditional Thai village, with houses and shops built out over a large pond, teak bridges and walkways linking them.

If you have a full day to sightsee, consider one of the cruises to **Ayutthaya,** the old capital of Thailand. Here, the partially restored ruins of magnificent architecture and fabulous statuary help visitors envision the glory of Thailand's past. Normally, the trip entails a cruise up and a bus back or vice versa, with a buffet lunch on the boat and stops at the Summer Palace (Bang Pa In) and the Thai Handicrafts Center. To arrange cruises, contact *Oriental Queen I and II* (tel. 02/236–0400–9, ext. 3133) or *River Sun Cruise* (tel. 02/237–0077, ext. 16).

Canal and river tours are among the best ways to get to know Bangkok. You can negotiate for a private longtail boat taxi at a number of riverside piers; the fare will depend on your bargaining skills. A standard tour will take you up a *klong* (canal) or two on the Thonburi side of the river, where you can see some of the charming traditional teak architecture of the houses and shops on stilts along the waterways. You can also travel up and down the Chao Phraya River past waterside temples and old Thai-style houses by scheduled express boat (Chao Phraya Express, tel. 02/411–4992).

Golf is all the rage currently, and golf courses are springing up faster than Thais can grow turf for the greens—at last count more than 30 courses in and around Bangkok were competing for members. The **Navathanee Golf Club** (22 Mu 1, Sukhaphiban 2 Rd., Bangkapi, tel. 02/374–6127) and the **Rose Garden Golf Course** (4/8 Soi 3 Sukhumvit, tel. 02/253–02197) are the best courses in Bangkok. Weekdays are still generally quiet—a good time to plan a game. On the weekends, courses are very crowded, due in part to those players who hire three caddies (one to carry the clubs, one to spot balls, and one for the parasol to help beat the heat). Thai caddies are usually female.

Massages are a common indulgence here. Of the varieties available, the traditional Thai "physical massage," is entirely legitimate and quite therapeutic if the masseuse is competent. Most of the better hotels have facilities on the premises. You can also experience a relaxing, hour-long massage at the Temple of the Reclining Buddha (Wat Po), long a learning center of the healing arts, including massage.

If you have just a couple of days to relax in Bangkok during your business travels, or if you want a memorable setting for informal business discussions, then a **river cruise** on the Chao Phraya River—traveling by luxurious converted rice barge—couldn't be improved upon. The *Mekhala I, II,* and *III* bear little resemblance to working barges, aside from the design of their hulls and their pace. Leaving at 3 PM from a landing directly across from the Shangri-La Hotel, you cruise at a leisurely rate, enjoying the colorful life along this River of Kings. The set dinner is a pleasing combination of Thai dishes tailored to suit Western palates. Overnight, the boat anchors by a charmingly rustic Buddhist temple. The cabins are masterpieces of design, and include private hot-and-cold showers; a mobile telephone is provided, too. Breakfast on deck the next day is followed by more cruising and a couple of interesting side tours by longtail boat. A bus takes you from Ayutthaya, the site of the old capital, back to Bangkok by late afternoon. The attentive and multitalented crew is good at making special arrangements, if the standard schedule doesn't suit you. This is probably the nicest single thing you could do for yourself if you have only limited sightseeing time in Bangkok. Contact Asia Voyages/Ted Cook Tours (In the U.S.: P.O. Box 1398, Newport Beach, CA 92663, tel. 714/654–8300 or 800/828–6877; In Bangkok: Ground Floor, Charn Issara Tower, 942/38 Rama IV Rd., tel. 02/235–4100–4).

A free morning is all the time you'll need to take a **temple walking tour.** Begin with the **Temple of the Emerald Buddha** (Wat Phra Keo, tel. 02/222–8181) next to the Royal Palace. This complex of buildings is one of the most recognizable symbols of Thai culture and shouldn't be missed. From the hallucinogenic extravagance of this architecture, you can get to the more mundane attractions of the **Temple of the Reclining Buddha** (Wat Po, tel. 02/222–0933) behind the Grand Palace in 10 minutes on foot. This enormous temple is the oldest center of learning in Thailand, and still a much-used center of community life. The souvenir stands, snake-keepers, and the school tour groups seem as much a part of the scene as do the monks and the traditional massage center. When you leave Wat Po, catch a ferry across the road and visit the **Temple of Dawn** (Wat Arun, tel. 02/282–1143) on the west bank of the Chao Phraya River. Climb up on this spectacular example of Khmer architecture for a fine view of the city and the river.

The Arts

Bangkok is getting more and more world-class performers now that the new **Thailand Cultural Center** is open (Ratchadapisek Rd., tel. 02/245–7711–9 for information on programs). The **National Theater** (Chao Fah Rd., tel. 02/221–5861) also puts on interesting shows, including the visually exciting *khon*, or classical dance drama. Check the **Goethe Institute** (18/1 Soi Ngarmduplee Rama IV, tel. 02/287–1991) and the **Alliance Française** (29 South Sathorn Rd., tel. 02/213–2122) for their current programs of music and films.

The better hotels can probably arrange for tickets. If not, you can purchase tickets at Central Department stores (*see* Shopping, above), D.K. Books in Siam Square (tel. 02/251–6335), Asia Books (221 Sukhumvit Rd., tel. 02/252–7277), or theater box offices.

After Hours

Patpong I and Patpong II roads are lined with a variety of establishments that are considered a must by many visitors, despite the hype, noise, and hustle. Everything from quiet restaurant bars to raunchy live sex shows is available. For quiet conversation over drinks with associates, stick to the more subdued bars and lounges in the major hotels.

Bars and Lounges

An upscale scene is found in the **Bamboo Bar** (Oriental Hotel, tel. 02/236–0400) where the smart set listens to live singers and drinks expensive drinks. The **Tiara Room** (Dusit Thani Hotel, tel. 02/236–0450–9) is a trendy and very pricey supper club showcasing live entertainment. The **New Madrid Cocktail Lounge** (80 Patpong II, second level, tel. 02/234–6905) is a good spot as well, though it is rather exclusively male in tone. **Bourbon Street** (Soi 22, Sukhumvit Rd., tel. 02/259–0328/9) is a favorite among resident Americans for its warm and friendly bar and spicy Cajun/Creole food.

Discos

There are popular discos in some of the larger hotels; notable examples are **Diana's** (Oriental Hotel, tel. 02/236–0400), **Bubbles** (Dusit Thani Hotel, tel. 02/236–0450), and the **Flamingo** (Ambassador Hotel, tel. 02/254–0444).

Dinner Theater

Professional English-language dinner theater can sometimes be found at the **Landmark** (tel. 02/254–0404), **Siam InterContinental** (tel. 02/253–0355), and **Shangri-La Hotel** (tel. 02/236–7777). Various restaurants, such as the **Baan Thai** (7 Soi 22, Sukhumvit Rd., tel. 02/258–5403), **Dusit Rim Tarn** (889 Charoennakorn Rd., tel. 02/437–9671), **Sala Rim Nam** (Oriental Hotel, tel. 02/236–0400), and **Silom Village** (286 Silom Rd., tel. 02/253–0355), offer a classical Thai dance show with dinner.

Dinner Cruises

Dinner cruises are a magnificent way to while away three hours of an evening. Try either **Kanab Nam Restaurant** (765/20 Ratchanithee Rd. near Krung Thon Bridge, tel. 02/433–6611; departures at 7 and 8 PM) or **Yok Yor Restaurant** (No. 3 Visuthikaset Rd., tel. 02/281–1829; departs at 8 PM). Guests are expected to arrive an hour before departure.

Jazz/Music Clubs

Bobby's Arms (Patpong II Carpark Bldg. 2F, 114/1–2 Soi Charuwan, tel. 02/233–6828), a British-style pub, has live Dixieland on Sundays from 8 PM. Sarasin Road, at the north end of Lumphini Park, offers a more lively scene for those in the 20–40 range. **Brown Sugar** (231/20 Soi Sarasin, tel. 02/250–0103) is a friendly pub that's predominantly jazz oriented; **Round Midnight** (106/2 Soi Lang Suan, tel. 02/251–0652) features rock and pop; and the **Old West Saloon** (231/17 Soi Sarasin, tel. 02/252–9510) is for country-and-western fans. Arrive early on weekend nights if you want a table. Live fusion, jazz, and rock can be enjoyed with food and drink in the pubby atmosphere of **Saxophone** (3/8 Victory Monument, Phaya Thai Rd., tel. 02/246–5472) or **Blue Moon** (145 Gaysorn Rd., tel. 02/253–7553).

For Singles

Men who appreciate a gentleman's club–type lounge will enjoy **Crown Royal** (9/7 Patapong II, tel. 02/234–3741), where regulars include everyone from foreign-service personnel to former Air America pilots. The **Rolls Royce Members Club** (Ambassador Hotel, tel. 02/254–0444) is another alternative for single men. In the interests of sexual equality, women might check out the **Leo Members Club**

(Ambassador Hotel, tel. 02/254–4444), where young Thai men serve as escorts and dancers for an exclusively female clientele. Singles of either sex will feel comfortable and find it easy to meet people at any of the hotel bars and lounges and live music clubs listed above.

Boston

by Mary Frakes

Boston is a paradox. Often called one of the most European of U.S. cities, it is nevertheless best known as the birthplace of the American Revolution. Tradition is knit into its bones, in the red-brick Victorian bow-front townhouses of Beacon Hill and the Back Bay, yet its economy has been closely linked to the most modern of industries, high-tech. Known for its conservative tastes in art and fashion—remnants of the days when being "banned in Boston" could boost book or ticket sales elsewhere—the city has universities that still produce some of the most challenging new minds of each generation. The slick and the staid exist side by side in a city on a human scale, which has assimilated—sometimes uneasily—different cultures without losing its unique character.

The "Massachusetts miracle"—the economic recovery of the 1980s—has ended, and Boston's major industries are struggling to cope with hard times, mergers, and downsizing.

A classic example is high technology, which fueled much of Boston's growth in the previous decade as the area's universities turned out computer whizzes. Employment in the computer industry was lower in 1989 than it was at the decade's beginning, reflecting increased domestic and foreign competition. Several of the largest companies along Route 128, the high-tech beltway outside the city limits, have been the victims of mergers or takeovers.

Defense companies, which profited from the Reagan administration's largesse in defense spending, are nervous about an extended downturn, though their emphasis on research and development makes them less vulnerable than hardware manufacturers. Financial services and construction have been hard-hit by a sluggish real estate market, though construction jobs are expected to pick up in several years once major public works, such as the third harbor tunnel and reconstruction of the Central Artery, begin.

The service sector has expanded steadily, though the state's poor economic health has slowed even that growth. However, the more optimistic economists say a depressed economy should help hold down costs and thus make it easier for businesses to find labor and space.

Boston's primary growth product remains brains: The city's more than 50 colleges and universities have traditionally supplied the rest of the nation with thinkers and leaders in every field. That emphasis on intellectual achievement, coupled with a strong sense of history and an increasingly diverse ethnic population, has created a city where world-class musical groups and art museums coexist with such big-city problems as racism and poverty.

Top Employers

Employer	Type of Enterprise	Parent*/ Headquarters
Amoskeag Co.	Real estate development	Boston
Digital Equipment Corp.	Computers	Maynard, MA
EG & G Inc.	Electronics	Wellesley, MA
General Cinema Corp.	Movie theaters	Newton, MA
Gillette Co.	Personal products	Boston
New England Telephone and Telegraph	Telecommunications	Boston
Raytheon Corp.	Defense contractor	Lexington, MA
Sheraton Corp.	Hotels	Boston
Stop and Shop	Grocery chain	Braintree, MA
Wang Laboratories, Inc.	Computers	Lowell, MA

*if applicable

ESSENTIAL INFORMATION

Climate

What follows are the average daily maximum and minimum temperatures for Boston.

Jan.	36F	2C	**Feb.**	38F	3C	**Mar.**	43F	6C
	20	−7		22	−6		29	−2
Apr.	54F	12C	**May**	67F	19C	**June**	76F	24C
	38	3		49	9		58	14
July	81F	27C	**Aug.**	79F	26C	**Sept.**	72F	22C
	63	17		63	17		56	13
Oct.	63F	17C	**Nov.**	49F	9C	**Dec.**	40F	4C
	47	8		36	2		25	−4

Airport

Logan International Airport is 3 miles southwest of downtown Boston.

Airport Business Facilities

Mutual of Omaha Business Service Center (Terminal C, tel. 617/569–4635) has fax machines, photocopying, notary public, secretarial service, ticket pickup, Western Union, travel insurance, cash advance, phone suites, and two conference rooms.

Airlines

Other than the Trump and Pan Am shuttles to New York, which operate hourly, the most frequent service by national carriers flying into Logan is offered by Delta and USAir. The following airlines serve Logan Airport:

American, tel. 617/338–6755 or 800/334–7400.
Continental, tel. 617/569–8400 or 800/231–0856.
Delta, tel. 617/567–4100 or 800/221–1212.
Midway, tel. 800/621–5700.
Northwest, tel.617/267–4885 or 800/225–2525.
Pan Am, tel. 800/221–1111.
Trump Shuttle, tel. 800/247–8786.
TWA, tel. 617/367–2800 (domestic), 617/367–2808 (international), or 800/221–2000.
United, tel. 800/241–6522.
USAir, tel. 617/482–3160 or 800/428–4322.

Between the Airport and Downtown

Although Logan airport is only 3 miles from downtown, it includes a stretch under Boston Harbor in a two-lane tunnel. There can be massive traffic jams, not only during rush hour (8–10AM and 4–6 PM) but at peak weekend travel times (Sunday evenings). Depending on city traffic and tunnel conditions, it can take anywhere from five minutes to an hour to get downtown.

If you don't have a lot of luggage and it's rush hour, the fastest way to get downtown is either via the water shuttle or the MBTA subway system, called "the T." For direct service to your hotel, an airport shuttle bus serves many area hotels. For information about ground transportation to and from Logan International, call 617/561–1769 or 800/235–6426.

By Taxi
There are cab stands outside each terminal. Barring major traffic delays, the trip should take 5–15 minutes to downtown. Cost: about $15, though a flat rate is available if a cab is shared.

By Helicopter
Hub Express (tel. 800/962–4744) links Logan's Terminal B with Boston City Heliport, near the World Trade Center, and four suburban sites: the New England Executive Park in Burlington (Rte. 128, north of the city); Waltham's Vista International Hotel; Norwood Municipal Airport; and the Sheraton Boxborough (Rte. 495). Each site has hourly service Mon.–Fri., 6 AM–8:30 PM. Cost: $59 basic fare; Trump Shuttle passengers fly free to downtown Boston, pay $10 to Rte. 128, and $20 to Boxborough; passengers on some routes of American, United, TWA, USAir, Delta, Midway, and Midwest Express pay $20 with advance reservations.

By Subway
The **MBTA's Blue Line,** which operates 5:30 AM–1 AM, links the airport with commuter rail service, downtown bus terminals, and interstate train service. The T runs about every 10 minutes and takes about 5 minutes to downtown. Free shuttle buses connect the subway terminal with all airline terminals. Cost: 75¢.

By Bus
Airways Transportation (tel. 617/267–2981) has regularly scheduled daily service to most major Boston hotels. Cost: $6.50.

By Water Shuttle
A small (50-passenger) ferry between Logan Airport and Rowes Wharf in downtown Boston operates every 15 minutes Mon.–Fri., 6 AM–8 PM and every half-hour weekends, noon–8, except July 4, Thanksgiving, and Christmas. Travel time is about 7 minutes. Cost: $7.

Car Rentals

The following companies have booths at the airport:

American, tel. 617/569–3550 or 800/527–0202.
Avis, tel. 617/424–0800 or 800/331–1212.
Budget, tel. 617/561–2300 or 800/527–0700.
Dollar, tel. 617/569–5300 or 800/421–6878.
Hertz, tel. 617/569–7272 or 800/654–3131.
Thrifty, tel. 617/569–6500 or 800/367–2277.

Emergencies

Doctors
Beth Israel Hospital has a physician referral service (330 Brookline Ave., tel. 617/735–5356), as does **New England Baptist Hospital** (125 Parker Hill Ave., tel. 800/447–5558).

Dentists
The Dental Cooperative of Massachusetts (tel. 617/262–9734) offers a dental referral service. The **New England Medical Center** (750 Washington St., tel. 617/956–5472), affiliated with Tufts University, has a dental clinic, as does **Massachusetts General Hospital** (55 Fruit St., tel. 617/726–5508).

Hospitals
Massachusetts General (55 Fruit St., tel. 617/726–2000), **Beth Israel Hospital** (330 Brookline Ave., tel. 617/735–3337), **Brigham and Women's Hospital** (75 Francis St., tel. 617/732–5500), **New England Medical Center** (750 Washington St., tel. 617/956–5000).

Important Addresses and Numbers

Audiovisual rentals. A.D. Handy (44 Bromfield St., tel. 617/542–3954), Mass Audio Visual Equipment (1167 Massachusetts Ave., Arlington, tel. 617/646–5410), Projection Video Services (39 Dalton St., tel. 617/262–3664).

Chamber of Commerce (600 Atlantic Ave., tel. 617/227–4500).

Computer rentals. Rentex Office Equipment (337 Summer St., tel. 617/423–5567), City Office Equipment (66 L St., South Boston, tel. 617/542–8378), PCR Personal Computer Rentals (10 Cedar St., Suite 19, Woburn, tel. 617/933–5993).

Convention and exhibition centers. Bayside Exposition Center (200 Mt. Vernon St., Dorchester, tel. 617/825–5151), John B. Hynes Veterans Memorial Convention Center (Prudential Tower, Suite 225, tel. 617/954–2300), World Trade Center Boston (Commonwealth Pier, tel. 617/439–5000).

Fax service. Copy Cop (2 locations: 260 Washington St., tel. 617/367–3370, 815 Boylston St., tel. 617/267–9267).

Formal-wear rentals. Formalwear Ltd. (15 Elm St., Waltham, tel. 617/899–5727), Read and White (54 Chauncy St., tel. 617/542–7444).

Gift shops. Gift Baskets: Beaubasket (1250 Washington St., Norwood, tel. 617/769–7755), Candy: The Chocolate Truffle (100 Tower Office Park, Suite I, Woburn, tel. 617/933–4616), Flowers: Winston Flowers, 131 Newbury St., tel. 617/536–6861).

Graphic design studios. Bezdek Design (24 Mt. Auburn St., Cambridge, tel. 617/547–6609), Independent Design Studios (451 D St., tel. 617/439–4944), Woodard/Black (419 Western Ave., tel. 617/782–3050).

Hairstylists. Unisex: Cramer's Hair Studio (Copley Place Shopping Center, tel. 617/267–4146), MJN at Harringtons (883 Boylston St., tel. 617/262–5587).

Health and fitness clubs. *See* Fitness, below.

Information hot lines. Boston Tourism and Convention Center (tel. 617/536–4100), Boston Globe Sports Scoreboard (tel. 617/265–6600), Ticketmaster Concert Line (tel. 617/332–9000), Boston Jazz Line (tel. 617/262–1300).

Limousine services. Ambassador Services (tel. 617/227–7844), Fifth Avenue Limousine Service of Boston (tel. 617/286–1590 or 800/343–2071).

Liquor stores. Merchants Wine and Spirits (6 Water St., tel. 617/523–7425), Marty's (193 Harvard Ave., Brighton, tel. 617/782–3250), Simmons Package Store (210 Cambridge St., tel. 617/227–2223).

Mail delivery, overnight. DHL Worlwide Express (tel. 617/846–8901), Federal Express (tel. 617/542–6142), TNT Skypak (617/884–9780), UPS (tel. 617/561–8483), U.S. Postal Service Express Mail (tel. 617/654–5676).

Messenger services. Boston Bicycle Couriers (tel. 617/426–7575) delivers within Boston, Statewide Delivery (tel. 617/242–9005) delivers outside Boston.

Office space rental. Headquarters (2 locations: 50 Milk St., tel. 617/451–6868, World Trade Center, tel. 617/439–5300).

Pharmacies, late-night. Back Bay Pharmacy (1130 Boylston St., tel. 617/267–5331), Phillips Drug (155 Charles St., tel. 617/523–1028 or 523–4372).

Radio stations, all-news. WEEI, 590 AM; WHDH, 850 AM.

Secretarial services. Drake International (80 Boylston St., Suite 333, tel. 617/542–7812), Office Support Management (715 Boylston St., 5th floor, tel. 617/262–5464), Staff Builders Convention Services (18 Tremont St., tel. 617/ 523–1880).

Stationery supplies. Back Bay Stationers (2 locations: 711 Boylston St., tel. 617/267–0445, 85 Arch St., tel. 617/542– 0001).

Taxis. Boston Cab Association (tel. 617/536–5010), Boston City Taxicab Co. (tel. 617/859–0855), Checker Cab (tel. 617/536–7000), Independent Taxi Operators Association (tel. 617/426–8700), Red & White Cab (tel. 617/742–9090), Town Taxi (tel. 617/536–5000).

Theater Tickets. *See* The Arts, below.

Train information. Amtrak (tel. 617/482–3660 or 800/392– 6099), Commuter Rail (tel. 617/227–5070 or 800/392– 6099). Trains for destinations north leave from North Station (150 Causeway St.); those heading south go from South Station (Atlantic Ave. and Summer St.).

Travel agents. Crimson Travel (3 locations: 53 State St., tel. 617/742–7060; 245 Summer St., tel. 617/720–2300; 2 Government Center Plaza, tel. 617/742–8500), Garber Travel (4 locations: 1047 Commonwealth Ave., tel. 617/ 787–0600; 44 School St., tel. 617/723–4400; 265 Franklin St., tel. 617/439–6773; Prudential Center Plaza, tel. 617/ 437–7200),

Weather (tel. 617/923–1234).

LODGING

Business travelers generally stay either downtown or near the Hynes Convention Center at Copley Square. Downtown is closer to Logan Airport and rail transportation, and most convenient for the financial district. The area around the convention center in the more residential Back Bay neighborhood is handy for conventioneers and those doing business with the major insurance companies. A few of the hotels listed are in the theater district, just about halfway between downtown and Back Bay. Hotel rates in Boston rival those of bigger cities, and most rates do not include parking, which can cost $10–$20 a night. The busiest times of the year are June, when students from the city's many colleges graduate, and fall, when students return and tourists come to see the foliage. Most of Boston's older hotels, like the Parker House, are situated in the financial district. Boston's newer mega hotels are for the most part centered around the Prudential Center in the Back Bay.

All the hotels listed below offer corporate rates and weekend discounts; inquire when making reservations.

Highly recommended lodgings in each price category are indicated by a star ★.

Category	Cost*
$$$$ (Very Expensive)	over $180
$$$ (Expensive)	$110–$180
$$ (Moderate)	under $110

All prices are for a standard double room, single occupancy, excluding 9.7% tax.

Numbers in the margin correspond to numbered hotel locations on the Boston Lodging and Dining map.

Downtown/Center City

★ ❷❾ **Boston Harbor Hotel.** If a room with a view is your top priority, it's hard to beat having a choice of either Boston
$$$$ Harbor or the heart of downtown. But the real advantage here is the ease of access to Logan Airport; this is the downtown terminus for the seven-minute water shuttle across the harbor. This newest of Boston's luxury hotels (1987) is also within walking distance of the financial district. The lobby features an antique map collection, oil portraits, and salmon and gray marble. The decor of the public areas and rooms is upscale Anglophile. Guest rooms, decorated with mahogany reproductions, are on floors 8–16; the Rotunda suites have a view of both harbor and city, though the room configuration can be awkward. Oversize club chairs and floor lamps are good for lounging and reading. In summer, there's a small outdoor terrace café, and the Rowes Wharf Bar has an outstanding selection of single-malt Scotches. *Small Luxury Hotels. 70 Rowes Wharf, 02110, tel. 617/439–7000 or 800/752–7077, fax 617/330–9450. Gen. manager, Francois Nivaud. 206 rooms, 24 suites. AE, CB, D, DC, MC, V.*

❷❺ **Bostonian.** Only minutes from Logan Airport, this small,
$$$$ European-style luxury hotel occupies three historic buildings across from Faneuil Hall. Converted to hotel use over the last decade, the somewhat undersized rooms were renovated in 1989. All have balconies and original watercolors. Weekend traffic in tourist season can be noisy, so try to avoid rooms closest to the Central Artery. Rooms in the oldest of the buildings (the Harkness) have working fireplaces and beamed ceilings; those in the other buildings mix contemporary metal with Chippendale reproductions. Some suites have whirlpool baths. Seasons, the hotel restaurant (*see* Dining, below), is excellent. *Fisher Hotel Group. Faneuil Hall Marketplace, 02109, tel. 617/523–3600 or 800/343–0922, fax 617/523–2454. Gen. manager, Timothy Kirwan. 153 doubles, 10 suites. AE, DC, MC, V.*

❷❷ **Lafayette Hotel.** This luxury hotel, built in 1985, does its
$$$ best to ignore the fact that it's located on the edge of the so-called Combat Zone—a downtown area within walking distance of Quincy Market, South Station, and the financial district. Though the Zone is being gentrified, walking at night is still not recommended. The lobby is on the second floor, away from the street level, and the atmosphere is sedate, with impressive flower arrangements, mahogany furniture, and soft music. Chippendale reproduction furniture, marble-topped nightstands, and botanical prints give the rooms a traditional feel, and upholstered armchairs are comfortable for lounging. The corner suites on

each floor are the most spacious, and odd-numbered rooms up to 37 have a view of the statehouse. The three butler-staffed concierge floors have juicers, hair-dryers, and robes in each room plus access to the central lounge, which features a complimentary Continental breakfast and afternoon tea, a billiard table, and a small sundeck. The formal dining room, Le Marquis de Lafayette, is one of the best restaurants in the city (*see* Dining, below). *Swissotel. 1 Ave. de Lafayette, tel. 617/451–2600 or 800/992–0124, fax 617/451–0054. Gen. manager, Liam Madden. 320 doubles, 44 suites, 117 business class. AE, CB, D, DC, MC, V.*

★ ② **Le Meridien.** When Air France converted the former Federal Reserve Bank into a hotel in 1981, it managed to blend ornate Renaissance revival granite-and-limestone architecture with traditional French elegance. The low-ceilinged, contemporary marble lobby is a striking counterpoint to the ornate marble carving over the door frames and gilded ceilings elsewhere in the building. In the heart of the financial district, Le Meridien is convenient to the airport, South Station, the north-south expressway (the Central Artery), and the Massachusetts Turnpike. Rooms on the top three of the nine floors have sloping glass windows with panoramic city views. Suites have recently been renovated, but you must specify if you want a desk in the room. Rooms on the third floor are smaller than the others, and those near the health club can be noisy; there are some bi-level loft suites on the second floor. The Julien lounge, a piano bar with N.C. Wyeth murals of American political figures, and the Julien restaurant (*see* Dining, below) are both favorites of the city's business leaders. Café Fleuri (*see* Business Breakfasts, below) draws them in in the morning. *250 Franklin St., 02110, tel. 617/451–1900 or 543-4300, fax 617/423–3844. Gen. manager, Hugues Jaquier. 304 doubles, 22 suites, AE, CB, D, DC, MC, V.*

② **Parker House.** The lobby, with its ornately embossed brass elevator doors and elaborately carved ceiling friezes, looks as grand as the original hotel, built in 1854, where Charles Dickens stayed and Parker House rolls were created in the kitchen. The present hotel, built in 1927, has long been associated with politics; John F. Kennedy announced his presidential candidacy here, and proximity to the statehouse means a clientele rife with government officials. It's also close to Boston Common and around the corner from the Downtown Crossing shopping area; you might have to contend with congested traffic if you have a rush hour appointment, but not much noise filters up to the rooms at night (the quietest rooms face School Street). As with many older hotels, room size can vary greatly. Desks are marble-topped and decor is traditional. Parker's dining room, with its crystal chandeliers, mahogany paneling, and wing chairs, is a mecca for political wheeling and dealing at lunch. *Omni Hotels. 60 School St., 02108, tel. 617/227–8600 or 800/843–6664, fax 617/ 742–4729. Gen. manager, Laurence Jeffrey. 476 doubles, 70 suites. AE, CB, D, DC, MC, V.*

Back Bay

❸ **Back Bay Hilton.** This triangular, concrete 26-story hotel, built in 1982, is just around the corner from the Hynes Convention Center; as a result, its primary market is conventioneers and business travelers. One of the virtues of

BOSTON

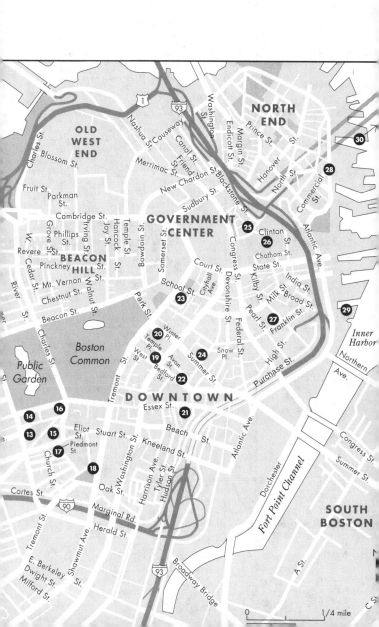

BOSTON HOTEL CHART

HOTELS	Price Category	Business Services Banquet capacity	No. of meeting rooms	Secretarial services	Audiovisual equipment	Teletype news service	Computer rentals	In-room modem phonejack	All-news cable channel	Desk	Desk lighting	Bed lighting
Back Bay Hilton	*$$$*	250	14	-	✓	-	✓	-	-	-	-	◗
Boston Harbor	*$$$$*	120	7	✓	✓	-	-	✓	✓	●	◗	●
Bostonian	*$$$$*	75	2	✓	✓	-	-	✓	✓	○	○	◗
Boston Park Plaza	*$$*	1500	35	-	✓	-	-	-	✓	○	-	●
Colonnade	*$$$*	350	7	✓	✓	-	-	✓	✓	●	●	◗
Copley Plaza	*$$$*	1000	9	✓	✓	-	✓	✓	-	◗	◗	●
Copley Square	*$$*	40	1	-	-	-	-	-	-	-	-	●
The 57 Park Plaza/ Howard Johnson	*$$*	600	11	✓	✓	-	-	-	✓	◗	●	◗
Four Seasons	*$$$$*	300	6	✓	✓	-	-	✓	✓	●	●	●
Guest Quarters Suite Hotel	*$$$*	160	8	-	✓	-	-	✓	✓	◗	●	◗
Lafayette	*$$$*	300	16	✓	✓	-	-	✓	✓	●	●	◗
Logan Airport Hilton	*$$$*	250	21	-	✓	-	-	✓	✓	◗	◗	◗
Marriott Copley Place	*$$$$*	2200	37	✓	✓	-	-	-	✓	◗	●	◗
Le Meridien	*$$$*	250	8	✓	✓	✓	✓	✓	✓	◗	●	●
Parker House	*$$$*	300	14	-	✓	-	-	-	✓	●	●	◗
Ritz-Carlton	*$$$$*	275	12	✓	✓	-	✓	-	✓	○	◗	◗
Sheraton Boston Hotel and Towers	*$$$*	1160	41	✓	✓	-	✓	✓	✓	-	-	●
Tremont House	*$$*	350	7	✓	✓	-	✓	-	✓	◗	◗	◗
Westin	*$$$$*	1400	24	-	✓	-	-	✓	✓	◗	◗	◗

$$$$ = over $180, **$$$** = $110-$180, **$$** = under $110.
● good, ◗ fair, ○ poor.
All hotels listed here have photocopying and fax facilities.

| In-Room Amenities | | | | | | | | | | Hotel Amenities | | | | | | |
Nonsmoking rooms	In-room checkout	Minibar	Pay movies	VCR/Movie rentals	Hairdryer	Toiletries	Room service	Laundry/Dry cleaning	Pressing	Concierge	Barber/Hairdresser	Garage	Courtesy airport transport	Sauna	Pool	Exercise room
✓	–	–	✓	–	✓	◐	◐	●	●	✓	–	✓	–	–	●	●
✓	–	✓	✓	✓	✓	●	●	●	◐	✓	✓	✓	–	✓	●	●
✓	–	✓	✓	✓	✓	●	●	●	◐	✓	–	–	✓	–	–	–
✓	✓	–	✓	–	–	○	●	●	◐	✓	✓	–	–	–	–	–
✓	–	✓	✓	–	✓	●	●	●	◐	✓	✓	–	–	–	○	●
✓	✓	✓	✓	✓	✓	◐	◐	●	◐	✓	✓	–	–	–	–	–
✓	–	–	✓	–	✓	◐	–	●	◐	✓	–	✓	–	–	–	–
✓	✓	✓	–	–	–	○	◐	●	●	–	✓	✓	–	✓	◐	–
✓	–	✓	–	–	✓	●	●	●	●	✓	–	✓	–	✓	●	●
✓	✓	✓	✓	✓	–	◐	◐	●	◐	✓	–	✓	–	✓	○	–
✓	✓	–	✓	–	–	◐	●	●	◐	✓	–	✓	–	✓	◐	○
✓	✓	–	–	–	–	○	○	●	●	✓	–	✓	–	–	○	–
✓	✓	–	✓	–	–	◐	●	●	◐	✓	–	✓	–	✓	●	●
✓	✓	✓	✓	–	–	●	●	◐	◐	✓	–	✓	–	✓	●	●
✓	✓	–	✓	✓	–	◐	◐	◐	○	✓	✓	–	–	–	–	–
✓	–	✓	–	✓	✓	●	●	●	●	✓	✓	–	–	✓	–	●
✓	✓	–	✓	✓	–	◐	●	●	◐	✓	✓	–	–	–	●	●
✓	–	✓	–	–	–	○	◐	●	◐	–	–	–	–	–	–	–
✓	✓	✓	✓	–	–	◐	●	●	◐	✓	–	–	–	–	◐	◐

Room service: ● 24-hour, ◐ 6AM-10PM, ○ other.
Laundry/Dry cleaning: ● same day, ◐ overnight, ○ other.
Pressing: ● immediate, ◐ same day, ○ other.

large chains is consistency, and you'll find few surprises at this Hilton. New management has promised to redo the rooms' uninspiring decor, including the ubiquitous round-table with overhead light and two side chairs. Rooms are soundproofed, the elevator is enclosed by glass partitions, and there are only 16 rooms per floor, so it's one of the quietest hotels around. The rooms on the north side of the uppermost floors have a view of the Charles River; corner rooms are largest and have balconies. The health club is one of the best of the hotel fitness facilities; hotel guests pay a minimal charge. *40 Dalton St., 02115, tel. 617/236–1100 or 800/874–0663, fax 617/236–1506. Gen. manager, Alan Lewis. 337 doubles, 3 suites. AE, CB, D, DC, MC, V.*

❺ **Colonnade.** Built in 1972 and renovated in 1989–90, this is
$$$ where Gerald Ford stayed to open the city's Bicentennial celebration. The exterior has all the charm of a concrete bunker, but the interior is that of a small luxury hotel. Rooms feature either contemporary oak furniture with black accents and coppery autumn colors, or mahogany furniture with a rose and black color scheme; executive suites have a dining table and sitting area. Bathrooms are on the small side; the newer ones with an Art Deco look seem larger. Rooms on the north side overlook the Christian Science Monitor building's reflecting pool and the Prudential Center; rooms facing south get less street noise. The Hynes Convention Center, Symphony Hall, and Copley Place shopping are nearby. Zachary's, the hotel's sleek gray and black dining room, is well regarded. Don't expect to use the rooftop pool except in summer; it's not enclosed. *Preferred Hotels. 120 Huntington Ave., 02116, tel. 617/424–7000 or 800/962–3030, fax 617/424–1717. Gen. manager, Sayed Saleh. 277 doubles, 11 suites. AE, CB, DC, MC, V.*

❾ **Copley Plaza.** A major renovation program in 1989 gave
$$$ new sparkle to this aging turn-of-the-century dowager. The gray-stone building, adorned with a bow-front, was designed by Henry Hardenbergh, architect of New York City's Plaza Hotel. The public areas now shine with bright lighting, gleaming gold leaf, pink marble, and ornately carved ceilings; the Grand Ballroom is straight out of 18th-century Vienna. The refurbished rooms, spread over seven floors, have a bland, uniformly beige decor and don't live up to the grandeur downstairs—though they are spacious, particularly the suites. Quietest rooms are in the central corridor, but they have the worst views; best views are in front, overlooking Copley Square and Trinity Church. The Plaza Dining Room (*see* Dining, below) and the Plaza Bar (*see* After Hours, below) with their leaded-glass doors and clublike atmosphere, are institutions. *138 St. James Ave., 02116, tel. 617/267–5300 or 800/826–7539, fax 617/267–7668. Gen. manager, Jan Chovanec. 287 doubles, 109 singles, 44 suites. AE, CB, DC, MC, V.*

❼ **Copley Square.** You won't impress anyone by staying here,
$$ except maybe your accountant. However, in a city where hotel rates tend to be high, this has always been a mecca for those seeking a reputable hotel bargain. Built in 1891 and renovated most recently in 1985, it appeals to many European travelers who like its intimate scale and often opt for the less expensive, shared bathrooms. The hotel bears the scars of age—chipped molding; relatively small, 1940s-era bathrooms; dark, mismatched furniture; indi-

vidual window-unit air conditioners; and an old steam-heat radiator system. However, it's clean and it's convenient to the Hynes Convention Center and Back Bay. Single rooms can be odd-shaped and small; best bets are the corner rooms, which are the largest, and rooms ending in 10 and 11, which have newer bathrooms. Courtyard rooms on upper floors are quietest. In the basement is Café Budapest, an appealing Hungarian restaurant with a romantic atmosphere. *Saunders Hotels. 47 Huntington Ave., 02116, tel. 617/536–9000 or 800/225–7062, fax 617/267–3547. Gen. manager, Jose Estrompa. 46 singles, 54 doubles, 11 suites. Coffeemakers in rooms. AE, CB, D, DC, MC, V.*

❻ **Marriott Copley Place.** This and the Westin (*see* below) are
$$$$ the two behemoths of Copley Place. One of the city's largest hotels, this 38-story modern structure was built in 1984, along with the rest of the posh Copley Place shopping complex. Most of the hotel's clientele is drawn from the big conventions at the nearby Hynes Center. The cavernous lobby is sleek pink-and-gray marble. Rooms feature Queen Anne-style furniture and pastel colors. The concierge floor has a complimentary Continental breakfast, hors d'oeuvres, and dessert, as well as concierge service. A Charles River view is available on the 30th floor and above. It's big, it's efficient, and it's not far from the Prudential Center. *110 Huntington Ave., 02116, tel. 617/236–5800 or 800/228–9290, fax 617/424–9378. Gen. manager, Jurgen Giesbert. 1001 doubles, 77 suites, 69 business class. AE, CB, D, DC, MC,V.*

⓬ **Ritz-Carlton.** Visiting royalty and heads of state stay here
$$$$ (the Aga Khan, Prince Charles, and the Kennedys, for example). Until the nearby Four Seasons opened, this was *the* place to stay in Boston. It was built in 1927, expanded in 1981 to add condominiums and additional rooms, and renovated in 1985. Service is the top priority here; the staff-to-guest ratio is high, and it's the only place in town that still has white-gloved elevator operators (who double as security guards). Some of the white-and-gold French Provincial furnishings are a touch old-fashioned, such as the vanity tables that serve as desks in some rooms. Newer rooms have bigger baths and floor-to-ceiling windows; however, many people still choose the older section, which has a pantry on all floors, buttons for calling the butler, and some working fireplaces. Interior courtyard rooms have no view, and you can't be guaranteed one of the coveted rooms facing the Public Garden even if you request it. The Ritz Café (*see* Business Breakfasts, below) hosts many movers and shakers in the morning, the hotel Dining Room attracts the same affluent crowd for lunch and dinner (*see* Dining, below), and the hotel bar (*see* After Hours, below) brings them in later in the evening. *15 Arlington St., 02117, tel. 617/536–5700 or 800/241–3333, fax 617/536–1335. Gen. manager, Sigi Brauer. 168 doubles, 68 singles, 42 suites. AE, CB, D, DC, MC, V.*

★ ❹ **Sheraton Boston Hotel and Towers.** If you're staying at the
$$$ Sheraton and attending a convention at the Hynes, you could stay indoors for your entire trip. The 29-story hotel has a direct link with not only the convention center but also the Prudential Center complex. It gets a lot of business from conventioneers, the city's consular corps, soloists at nearby Symphony Hall, and visiting sports teams. Rooms are large, modern, and comfortable, especially on

the four Towers floors, which have their own separate staff, a private lounge, complimentary Continental breakfast and hors d'oeuvres, and small conference rooms. Lanai suites open onto the skylit pool, which has a roof that opens in summer. Rooms above the 15th floor in the north tower overlook the Charles River; corner suites may have a four-poster bed, a wet bar, and a pantry. The business center, complete with desktop publishing facilities, is convenient to the convention center entrance. *39 Dalton St., Prudential Center, 02199, tel. 617/236–2000 or 800/325–3535, fax 617/236–1702. Gen. manager, Stephen Foster. 1,085 doubles, 45 suites, 120 business class. Voicemail messages in rooms, in-house graphics service. AE, CB, D, DC, MC, V.*

8 **Westin.** This 36-story hotel in the Copley Place office/
$$$$ shopping complex has all the conveniences—and impersonality—of a big-city chain facility. Built in 1983, it rivals the Marriott in height; rooms above the 16th floor have a good view of the Charles River (corner rooms have the best panorama as well as sitting areas). Even-numbered floors have bleached oak furniture, the odd floors mahogany; both include Colonial armoires for the TV and either a burgundy or gray color scheme. The bottled water in the bathrooms is a nice touch, as are operative windows and voice-mail messages. Floors 24–29 are the corporate floors, which have added perks such as complimentary breakfast. The hotel restaurant, Turner Fisheries (*see* Dining, below), is a fine setting for a business talk. *10 Huntington Ave., 02116, tel. 617/262–9600 or 800/228–3000, fax 617/424–7483. Gen. manager, David C. King. AE, CB, D, DC, MC, V.*

Brighton

1 **Guest Quarters Suite Hotel.** This 1985 post modern hotel is
$$$ five miles west of downtown, a trip that can take up to a half hour when traffic is heavy. However, it's the only Boston hotel that concentrates so heavily on suites; all but 22 rooms have a separate sitting room and kitchenette, and the executive suites have a small conference table. As a result, the hotel is popular with recruiters, government officials, and business travelers who must hold small seminars or stay for extended periods. All rooms have a view of the Charles River and either Harvard or Boston; the river's proximity is underlined by the rowing scull that hangs in the skylit atrium lobby. The bi-level loft rooms on the upper floors are the most expensive. A courtesy van from the water shuttle and complimentary Continental breakfast are pluses, and there's a cabaret nightly at Scullers (*see* After Hours, below), the hotel's restaurant. *400 Soldiers Field Rd., Brighton, 02134, tel. 617/783–0090 or 800/424–2900, fax 617/673–0987. Gen. manager, Mark Fallon. 22 doubles, 320 suites. AE, CB, D, DC, MC, V.*

Theater District

13 **Boston Park Plaza.** The lobby here speaks of the days
$$ when the Boston Park Plaza was the flagship for the Statler hotels: all cream and gilt molding, with ornate wrought iron and mahogany railings on the mezzanine balconies. Built in 1927, the hotel is showing a bit of age these days, but the location is still a good one: adjacent to the theater district and a block from the Public Garden. Some

smaller rooms have been merged into one and are spacious; others are still small. Be sure to ask for an outside room, which looks out over the city. The upgraded Plaza Towers rooms have extra amenities, complimentary Continental breakfast, and access to a lounge and meeting room. Furnishings are ersatz Oriental bamboo or light Colonial-style pine with abstract pastels; bathrooms are somewhat cramped. The Terrace Room hosts the Forbidden Broadway comedy revue (*see* After Hours, below). *Saunders Hotels. 64 Arlington St., 02117, tel. 617/426–2000 or 800/225–2008, fax 617/426–5545. Gen. manager, Joseph N. Malone. 873 doubles, 25 suites, 82 business class. Voicemail service in rooms. AE, CB, D, DC, MC, V.*

★ ⓱ **The 57 Park Plaza Hotel/Howard Johnson.** Even though
$$ the rooftop sign says Howard Johnson's, don't look for an orange roof or fried clams; this is an independently owned hotel. The lobby proclaims the difference with streamlined black lacquer Deco furniture, mirrors, frosted glass torchères, and soft rose and blue upholstery. Close to New England Medical Center, Chinatown, and the theater district, it caters to business travelers and families looking for a downtown bargain. All rooms in this big, 1970s-style concrete box are the same size and have balconies; the decor is contemporary, with soft pink and gray pastels and black lacquer trim on mahogany or light oak furnishings. Suites have small bathtubs. Executive rooms include a snack box, complimentary newspapers, and hair-dryers in the bathroom. If you don't want to pay for luxuries but need a comfortable, modern facility, this is a good choice. *200 Stuart St., 02116, tel. 617/482–1800 or 800/654–2000, fax 617/451–2750. Gen. manager, Donald Walsh. 276 doubles, 26 suites, 24 business class. Free parking. AE, CB, D, DC, MC, V.*

★ ⓰ **Four Seasons Hotel.** Rivaling the traditional Ritz as
$$$$ Boston's finest hotel, the Four Seasons has a superb location, across from the Public Garden, only a few blocks from the theater district, and equidistant from the Hynes Center and the financial district. The hotel occupies eight of this 1985 building's 15 stories; the other floors feature luxury condominiums. Oil portraits of proper Bostonians decorate the rather impersonal but antique-filled lobby. In the guest rooms, contemporary blond wood furnishings, brass touches, and spacious baths are the norm. Rooms in the front, including all of the suites, have a garden view. Fresh flowers and shaving/makeup mirrors in the bathrooms, free disposable bathing suits in the health clubs, and shaving kits on request are typical of the hotel's thoughtfulness. Shoeshines, newspapers, and limos to downtown are complimentary. The staff is not only efficient but friendly. The hotel dining room, Aujourd'hui (*see* Dining, below) is excellent. This is as glamorous as Boston gets, which is not very. *200 Boylston St., 02116, tel. 617/338–4400 or 800/332–3442, fax 617/423–0154. Gen. manager, Robin Brown. 272 doubles, 13 suites, 3 business class. AE, CB, DC, MC, V.*

⓲ **Tremont House.** In its 66 years, this theater district hotel
$$ with grandiose meeting spaces has been the national headquarters for the Elks. A down-at-the-heels has-been until a 1984 renovation, the Tremont now is a good choice for travelers on a budget. Rooms have dark Colonial furnishings and vary greatly in size (some are tiny), but the

ones on the upper floors of the west side overlook Back Bay. If you're concerned about noise, avoid the sixth floor, which is over the banquet area. The hotel also includes the Stage Deli, a sandwich place that stays open late; a 1950s-style rock 'n' roll bar; and the Roxy nightclub (*see* After Hours, below). The area is being revitalized, but it's best to be judicious late at night. *Quality Inns. 275 Tremont St., tel. 617/426–1400 or 800/228–5151, fax 617/482–6730. Gen. manager, Gregory Hargrave. 234 doubles, 34 suites. Bus tour office. AE, CB, D, DC, MC, V.*

Airport

③⓪
$$$
Logan Airport Hilton. The only airport hotel in Boston, this four-building complex immediately adjacent to the airport was renovated in 1989. The newest building is a 14-story tower; the oldest section, a two-story structure, houses the pool. *Logan International Airport, East Boston, 02128, tel. 617/569–9300 or 800/445–8667, fax 617/569–3981. Gen. manager, Richard Eaton, 542 doubles, 5 suites, 24-hour shuttle to airport. AE, CB, DC, MC, V.*

DINING

The quality of Boston dining has come a long way from the days of bland, overcooked seafood and heavy cream sauces. Interest in fine dining began about a decade ago in hotel dining rooms, many of which continue to be notable for their ambience and high quality. However, some of the best new entries are bistros that appeal to the Bostonian common-sense ethos of good quality at a good price. Though many of these bistros—Biba's, Hammersley's, Cornucopia—are expensive, the menus are flexible enough to allow for moderately priced dining as well. Chef/owners, many of whom started in the large hotel rooms and have since opened places of their own, are bringing creativity and flair to menus that emphasize good-sized portions, seasonal local foods, and inventive techniques and ingredients.

Highly recommended restaurants in each price category are indicated by a star ★.

Category	Cost*
$$$$ (Very Expensive)	over $45
$$$ (Expensive)	$30–$45
$$ (Moderate)	under $30

per person, including appetizer, entrée, and dessert, but excluding drinks, service, and 5% sales tax.

Numbers in the margin correspond to numbered restaurant locations on the Boston Lodging and Dining map.

Business Breakfasts

Café Fleuri (tel. 617/451–1900) has the best Sunday brunch in town, and the regular breakfast isn't shabby, either. The location, in the Meridien Hotel in the financial district, makes it perfect for a working breakfast in a cheerful, skylit atrium setting. The menu includes more than just the eggs-and-bacon standards. **Ritz Café** (tel.

617/536–5700) in the Ritz-Carlton is where power breakfasts are the norm for politicians, financiers, and executives of all stripes—not to mention people getting fueled
up for a day of shopping on Newbury Street. The Scotch
salmon is always popular, as are the eggs Benedict and
steak with eggs. Window seats are popular and difficult to
get.

For more casual morning dining the bustling **Café Tremont**
(60 School St., tel. 617/ 227–8600) is convenient to the
statehouse and downtown; it also has a self-serve takeout
pastry counter. **Rebecca's** (21 Charles St., tel. 617/742–
9747) specializes in baked goods and people-watching on
Beacon Hill. **Charlie's Sandwich Shoppe** (429 Columbus
Ave., tel. 617/536–7669) opens at 6 AM weekdays and is
usually packed with people ordering the enormous portions
of down-home food, especially the pancakes. **Au Bon Pain,**
which specializes in croissants, muffins, and pastries, has
a number of outlets, both takeout and eat-in, all over the
city.

Downtown

⑲ **Cornucopia.** It took a pioneering spirit to open an upscale
$$$ restaurant on a side street off Downtown Crossing near
the slowly gentrifying Combat Zone, but the gamble
has paid off. This two-level Art Deco room is warm and ap-
pealing, with geometric-patterned stained-glass chan-
deliers over oak tables. The imaginative New American
menu changes monthly, but often reflects a balance of
East and West, such as sesame-crusted catfish with fried
Chinese noodles in a spicy Thai sauce; or dishes that star
New England ingredients, such as grilled pork chop with
apples, sausage, and sage stuffing. The restaurant places
great importance on wine and even suggests ones to ac-
company specific dishes. There is a good selection of wines
by the glass. Women alone should be careful at night in
this neighborhood. The downstairs can be a bit noisy; if
you want serious conversation, go upstairs. *15 West St.,
tel. 617/338–4600. Dress: casual but neat. No reserva-
tions. AE, DC, MC, V. Closed Sun. and for dinner Mon.*

㉔ **Dakota's.** Located in the Downtown Crossing shopping
$$$ area, this Texas-influenced grill aims squarely at a
straightforward business clientele. The room is quietly
comfortable, with black wainscoting, salmon and cream
marble floor, and brass sconces—the food may be southwestern, but the look is sedate Boston. The menu includes
standards such as roast chicken, grilled rainbow trout,
swordfish, and haddock; Southwest accents include venison sausage quesadillas, tortilla soup, and crab cakes
made with minced serrano peppers. On the lobby level of
the 101 Arch Street building, Dakota's is a bit difficult to
find, and service can be haphazard. *34 Summer St., tel.
617/737–1777. Jacket and tie suggested. AE, MC, V.
Closed Mon.*

㉖ **Durgin-Park.** Diners who come to this Quincy Market res-
$$ taurant have to be hungry enough to cope with enormous
portions and have the time to stand in line for them.
Durgin-Park has been serving hearty New England fare
since the 1830s, when the building was a working produce
and meat market instead of a tourist attraction; it requires
only a little imagination to picture burly working men sit-

ting around communal tables and chowing down. The communal tables are still here, as are homey old New England dishes such as Indian pudding and huge haunches of prime rib. Lunch is a little calmer than dinner, though both are crowded during peak tourist seasons; poor ventilation in summer can leave you sweaty after all that vigorous eating. It would be difficult to do business here, especially when you're elbow-to-elbow with strangers, but the atmosphere is uniquely old Boston. *340 Faneuil Hall Marketplace, North Market Building, tel. 617/227–2038. Casual dress. No reservations. No credit cards.*

㉗ **Julien.** When the former Federal Reserve Bank became
$$$$ the Hotel Meridien, the owners turned part of it into a formal dining room, and some say it's still where the money is; the clientele draws heavily on the financial district. High ceilings, a limestone balcony, crystal chandelier, and heavy silver befit the elegant room, and wing chairs afford plenty of privacy for important discussions. Owned by Air France, the restaurant is a culinary collaboration between a young American chef and a four-star consulting chef from France; the result is a French-oriented menu that makes extensive use of local ingredients and cooking techniques that give lighter results than the traditional cream-laden Escoffier-style fare. Dishes change seasonally, but might include duck glazed with a Caribbean-spiced caramel sauce, pomegranate seeds, and watercress; or roasted lobster with artichoke hearts and lemon verbena juice. The wine list is largely French and well selected. *250 Franklin St., tel. 617/451–1900. Jacket and tie required. Reservations required. Dinner only on weekends and July–Aug. AE, CB, D, DC, MC, V.*

★ ㉒ **Le Marquis de Lafayette.** Although it's located on the edge
$$$$ of the Combat Zone, the Lafayette Hotel's dining room has an upscale image and a clientele of top-echelon businesspeople. French consulting chef Louis Outhier created the menu, and the atmosphere is that of an English club, with hunting prints and oil portraits on the walls, and crested china and a long-stemmed rose in a crystal vase on each table. Formally attired waiters provide deft, unobtrusive service. The seasonal menu might include a breast of pheasant with potato and pheasant hash, poached foie gras in lentils, or grouper steak with fried lotus root. The banquettes in the rear of the small room, shielded from the entrance, afford the most privacy. *1 Ave. de Lafayette, tel. 617/451–2600. Jacket and tie required. Reservations advised. AE, CB, DC, MC, V.*

㉑ **Mei Lei Wa.** If you've been negotiating into the late night,
$$ the Cantonese food here just might be able to break up the stalemate. There are not a lot of late-night choices in Boston, and Mei Lei Wa, by contrast, is open till 4 AM and takes credit cards—a rare combination in Chinatown. The decor is standard Chinese restaurant—unadorned. Especially good are the roast duck, which has crispy skin flavored with cinnamon, cloves, and anise; and clams in black-bean sauce. *21 Edinboro St., tel. 617/482–6840. Casual dress. AE, DC, MC, V.*

★ ㉘ **Restaurant Jasper.** Owner Jasper White, who trained a
$$$$ number of the city's best chefs when he was at Seasons (*see* below), has won a national reputation with his updated New England specialties since he opened this restaurant on the waterfront. A loyal business clientele

dominates this subdued Art Deco room, decorated in chic black and white, with exposed brick walls that hark back to the time when this space was occupied by a molasses factory. Dishes change almost nightly, but lean heavily on local game and seasonal produce. Typical fare might be as nouvelle as a salad of grilled duck with cranberries and spiced nuts, or as traditional as a New England boiled dinner cooked to perfection. Desserts such as a superb crème brulée or chocolate bread pudding may be New England inspired, but are anything but Puritan. *240 Commercial St., tel. 617/523–1126. Reservations required. Jacket and tie required. AE, CB, DC, MC, V. Dinner only.*

㉙ **Rowe's Wharf.** If you want a waterfront view of Boston
$$$ Harbor without the noise and mediocre food of tourist-ridden megarestaurants, this is the place. Though it was built in 1987, this large dining room of the Boston Harbor Hotel is replete with traditional touches such as upholstered armchairs, gathered swag curtains, mahogany paneling, and shaded wall sconces. It's a comfortable, low-key setting for thoughtful discussions, as well as a good choice for a working breakfast or lunch. Though the room itself is large, pillars and banquettes break the space into a gallery of smaller areas, and one section is set aside for more casually dressed diners. The food is subdued New American, with entrées such as fricassee of lobster and sea scallops on fresh herb pasta, and duck breast with a leek confit and honey-ginger glaze. Some of the items are designated as being heart healthy. *70 Rowe's Wharf, tel. 617/439–7000. Jacket suggested. Reservations suggested. AE, CB, DC, MC, V.*

㉕ **Seasons.** This highly respected restaurant has been the
$$$$ training ground for some of Boston's best-known chefs. Located in the Bostonian Hotel, it is close to both the financial district and City Hall; it's also only minutes from Logan airport, making it perfect for a business breakfast on the way out of town. Chef William Poirier has upheld the restaurant's tradition of excellence with a menu of New American cuisine with well-executed exotic touches. The menu changes seasonally; the duckling with ginger and scallions has been a perennial favorite, but a winter menu might also include caraway venison with wood mushrooms and cheese pierogi, or swordfish with chickpeas, eggplant, and taramosalata. The wine list is exclusively—and comprehensively—American, and the waiters, many of whom have been on the staff for years, are knowledgeable enough to make excellent recommendations. Large windows overlook the Faneuil Hall bustle, and the overhead ceiling draperies are drawn back at night for a view of the sky. *North and Blackstone Sts., tel. 617/523–3600. Jacket required. Reservations suggested. AE, DC, MC, V.*

Back Bay

⓫ **Grill 23.** The gray suits of insurance, the law, and banking
$$$$ are prominent at this dining room in the renovated Salada Tea building. This is a classic steak house, from the mahogany paneling, gigantic marble columns, and white-jacketed waiters, right down to the brass plaques on the bar that identify the favorite seats of its regular customers. Best tables are around the lower-level dining room. The house salad, a melange of vegetables, is rightly

praised, and the menu concentrates on doing one thing
well: grilling meat and seafood. Typical dishes include a
mixed grill and beef Wellington. If you want a burger for
lunch, you'll have to come early; inexplicably for a steak
house, they can run out. *161 Berkeley St., tel. 617/542–
2255. Jacket and tie advised. Reservations suggested. AE,
CB, D, DC, MC, V. Closed Sun. dinner only Fri. and Sat.*

❷ L'Espalier. When Moncef Meddeb announced he was sell-
$$$$ ing this temple of Boston haute cuisine, Boston feared the
new owner wouldn't keep up Meddeb's high standards.
However, Frank McClelland, Meddeb's second in command, has upheld the tradition of fine cuisine in this elegant spot that occupies two floors of a renovated Back Bay
townhouse. Marble fireplaces grace each of the three
rooms; the mahogany-paneled dining room upstairs is
clubby, while the other two dining rooms have a lighter
feel. A three-course prix fixe menu might include such
New American dishes as roast rack of lamb with a maple
mustard crust served with an apple-and-goat-cheese tart
and a shallot rosemary sauce, or grilled tuna and swordfish with shrimp risotto and olive basil butter. The atmosphere is quiet, and the intimate feel appropriate for
important business dinners. A tasting menu is available
on request. There's a well-selected wine list, and service is
punctilious. *30 Gloucester St., tel. 617/262–3023. Jacket
and tie required. Reservations required. AE, MC, V.
Closed Sun.*

❾ Plaza Dining Room. The Edwardian dining room at the
$$$$ Copley Plaza Hotel has always been elegant, but it has
taken on additional luster after a recent refurbishing by
new owners and the importation of two top chefs from Le
Marquis de Lafayette. High-backed, tapestry-covered
chairs, crystal chandeliers, a lavishly molded ceiling, and
mahogany Palladian-arched mirrors create a formal atmosphere suitable for the most serious business dinners,
while a baby grand plays discreetly in the background.
The extensive menu lists seasonal dishes that are classically French with some innovative touches. For example,
fillet of salmon is served with cepes mushrooms and leeks
flavored with walnut oil; warm oysters are topped with
caviar; and roasted rack of lamb is accented with salt-
cured lemon peels and sweet garlic. The wine list is designed to impress, and the library at the entrance is perfect for an after-dinner brandy. Service is meticulous. *138
St. James Ave., tel. 617/267–5300. Jacket and tie required. Reservations advised. AE, CB, DC, MC, V.*

⓬ Ritz Dining Room. This is where generations of Bostoni-
$$$$ ans have come to celebrate special occasions. After more
than a half century, the dining room of the Ritz-Carlton
has perfected its regal ways; the service is efficient, the
white and gold decor properly refined. The view of the
Public Garden is exquisite, the Sunday brunch is lavish,
conversations and the dinner music from the white grand
piano are discreetly subdued, and the array of silverware
offers the perfect opportunity to demonstrate one's social
aplomb. The kitchen focuses on such classic Continental
fare as steak Diane and Dover sole in a lemon-butter
sauce, and long-time local favorites like lobster in bourbon
sauce. This is not the place to impress someone with cutting-edge tastes. *15 Arlington St., tel. 617/536–3700.*

Jacket and tie required. Reservations required. AE, CB, D, DC, MC, V.

❽ Turner Fisheries. Businesspeople come to Turner Fisher-
$$ ies, in the Westin at Copley Place, for fresh, well-prepared seafood served in a comfortable, spacious room. Booths are paneled with gray wainscoting, and the room is adorned with mahogany sideboards and green-shaded lamps. Subdued contemporary jazz fills in the background. Locals usually begin with the chowder, which packs a rich punch. Seafood items can be ordered broiled, grilled, fried, baked, or blackened; other specialties include several kinds of smoked fish and steamed mussels served with a choice of sauces. There's plenty of privacy, especially in the booths, and the atmosphere is conducive to quiet talk. *10 Huntington Ave., tel. 617/424–7425. Dress: casual but neat. AE, CB, D, DC, MC, V.*

South End

★ ❿ Hamersley's Bistro. This small storefront in the up-and-
$$$ coming South End is known for its innovative yet unpretentious fare. Chef/owner Gordon Hamersley creates his hearty stews and braised dishes in an open kitchen at the back of the intimate restaurant. The black-and-white decor is simple but enlivened with posters. Specialties on the seasonal menu include a delectable lemon-garlic roasted chicken and a grilled mushroom and garlic sandwich; Sunday nights are prix fixe with slightly lower prices. The wine list has reasonably priced entries from Portugal, Spain, and Australia, as well as from France and the U.S. The noisy, informal atmosphere and small size make Hamersley's unsuitable for heavy-duty business negotiations. For women alone, the surrounding neighborhood can still be dicey after dark; it's best to take a cab directly to and from the restaurant. *578 Tremont St., tel. 617/267–6068. Dress: casual but neat. Reservations advised, especially on weekends. AE, MC, V.*

Theater District

❶❻ Aujourd'hui. This temple of understated elegance, the for-
$$$$ mal dining room of the Four Seasons Hotel, has been around for less than a decade, but it has become one of the power rooms in town. Tables overlooking the Public Garden are especially sought after. All tables are discreetly separated for important discussions, the carpet is thick, the staff is reverent. The food is anything but cold roast Boston; chef Mark Baker has earned a reputation for an inventive hand with regional ingredients and New American recipes. Though entrées such as braised lobster ragout with grilled corn and sauvignon blanc, or rack of lamb with kalamata olives and goat cheese ravioli can sometimes be extremely rich, the menu, which changes seasonally, also contains low-calorie, low-cholesterol spa cuisine. Aujourd'hui is also recommended for breakfast meetings. *200 Boylston St., tel. 617/338–4400. Jacket and tie advised. Reservations advised. AE, DC, MC, V.*

★ ❶❹ Biba. Chef Lydia Shire's culinary innovations were so re-
$$$ nowned that her casual restaurant, opened in 1989, quickly became a Boston favorite. She serves up earthy dishes that borrow inspiration from all five continents and can be as simple as spaghetti with breadcrumbs or as arty as wood-roasted swordfish with zucchini flowers and shrimp

risotto. The eclectic decor combines Turkish-pattern upholstery on the banquettes, a spectacular redrailed staircase, and a cryptic mural of well-fed diners. The informal atmosphere encourages spontaneous conversations with people at the next table; this is not a place for private discussions. Menu items are grouped not as appetizers, salads, vegetables, entrées, and desserts, but as "meats" or "legumina" or the challenging "offal"; the format encourages grazing—combining small, inexpensive portions. The extensive wine list emphasizes adventurous selections from lesser-known areas rather than renowned older vintages. The downstairs bar, where street-level windows offer interesting people-watching, is good for late-night snacks or single diners. *272 Boylston St., tel. 617/426–7878. Dress: casual but neat. Reservations advised. AE, MC, V.*

★ ⓯ **Legal Seafood.** "If it isn't fresh, it isn't Legal" is this Bos-
$$ ton institution's slogan. And that freshness is what keeps drawing crowds to this restaurant located in the theater district, despite waits for a table so long you could go out and dig your own clams. Legal restaurants (there are branches in Cambridge and several other suburbs) get the top of the catch. This wood-paneled restaurant is open and airy, with large windows that let in lots of light. Most entrées are of the standard fried-boiled-broiled-grilled variety with few elaborate sauces. The renowned clam chowder comes in a calorie-reduced version, and the fried calamari taste like seafood instead of rubber bands. Don't bring a client if you're in a hurry or are uncomfortable being served before he or she is; dishes come out whenever they're ready. *27 Columbus Ave., tel. 617/426–4444. Casual dress. No reservations. AE, CB, D, DC, M, V.*

⓴ **Locke-Ober Café.** After more than 100 years, this is still
$$$ the place where old-line Brahmins can find food that conforms with Boston tradition. The decor is solid and comfortable as well, featuring mahogany paneling, lace curtains, and brass trim. Tables are well spaced so conversations can be confidential. The location is conveniently near downtown, just off the Common. The specialty is lobster Savannah, a generous portion of shellfish in a rich cream sauce, but grilled chops, Dover sole, and finnan haddie are also menu staples. The Men's Bar downstairs is now open to women, though the female nude portrait that gets draped in black when Harvard loses to Yale is still there. *4 Winter Place, tel. 617/542–1340. Jacket and tie required. Reservations required. AE, CB, DC, MC, V.*

FREE TIME

Fitness

Hotel Facilities
The Westin (tel. 617/262–9600) offers a $7 day-pass for nonguests, which includes the use of the pool and equipment room. The excellent facilities at the **Back Bay Hilton** (tel. 617/262–2050) are run by FitCorp (*see* below), and are available to nonguests for $12 per day.

Health Clubs
In addition to the fitness center at the Back Bay Hilton, noted above, **FitCorp** has a downtown facility (133 Federal St., tel. 617/542–1010), also charging a $12 per-visit rate.

The **Spa at the Heritage** (75 Park Plaza, tel. 617/426–6999) has a $25 per-visit rate, plus discounts on aerobics classes and complimentary day passes for guests of the Ritz-Carlton, Copley Plaza, and Park Plaza hotels. **Boston Athletic Club** (653 Summer St., tel. 617/269–4300) allows travelers staying at a Boston hotel access to Nautilus equipment and tennis, racquetball, and basketball courts on a $20 per-visit rate. The **Greater Boston YMCA's** facilities (316 Huntington Ave., tel. 617/536–7800), are available to members of other Ys free with a photo ID.

Jogging
The **Esplanade,** which runs from Charles Street the length of the city along the Charles River, is the city's best route; at rush hour, though, you'll have to contend with exhaust fumes from Storrow Drive. **Boston Common** and the **Public Garden** also are popular, but to be avoided after dark.

Shopping

Some of the best souvenirs to take home from Boston are edible—maple syrup and live lobsters packed to travel have long been favorites. Most of the city's tourist attractions carry replicas of documents or artifacts of the Revolutionary War era.

The most popular shopping areas for visitors are the **Quincy Market/Faneuil Hall** "festival marketplace" developments, just off Atlantic Avenue, along the waterfront near City Hall. The most expensive shopping is along **Newbury Street,** which has fashion boutiques, furriers, art galleries, home design stores, and small cafés; **Boylston Street,** where designer names such as Hermes, Saint Laurent, and Escada have appeared in recent years; and **Copley Place,** an indoor mall that houses Gucci, Louis Vuitton, Tiffany, and Neiman Marcus. The Downtown Crossing area has the city's two major department stores: **Jordan Marsh** (450 Washington St., tel. 617/357–3000) and **Filene's** (426 Washington St., tel. 617/357–2100), which is above but no longer affiliated with **Filene's Basement,** whose automatic markdowns have created some legendary shopping frenzies.

Other highly regarded stores include **Louis Boston** (234 Berkeley St., tel. 617/965–6100) and **Brooks Brothers** (46 Newbury St., tel. 617/267–2600) for menswear; **Suzanne** (35 Newbury St., tel. 617/266–4146) and **Charles Sumner** (16 Newbury St., tel. 617/536–6225) for designer women's clothing; **Shreve, Crump and Low** (350 Boylston St., tel. 617/267–9100) for jewelry, silver, china, and antiques; and **FAO Schwarz** (338 Boylston St., tel. 617/266–5101) for toys.

Diversions

The red-brick bowfront townhouses and cobblestone streets of **Beacon Hill,** which date back to the early 1800s, are good territory for exploring on foot and absorbing the proper Bostonian atmosphere. Louisburg Square, at one end of Mount Vernon Street, has been home to William Dean Howells and the Bronson Alcotts; the enclosed patch of green is open only to the adjacent residents.

The 50-acre **Boston Common,** where colonials grazed cattle, and the adjacent **Public Garden** provide green space in the city's heart. The Public Garden, with its carefully tended formal plantings and summer swan-boat rides on a small pond, is the oldest botanical garden in the United States. Neither the Common nor the Garden, however, is recommended after dark.

Old Granary Burying Ground and nearby Park Street Church, at Boylston and Tremont streets, mark the beginning of the city's **Freedom Trail,** a walking tour that follows a line of red bricks to the city's most historic sites; a map is available at the Visitors' Information Booth just across the street on the corner of Boston Common. The church was the place where William Lloyd Garrison campaigned against slavery; the burying ground holds the remains of Samuel Adams, John Hancock, Paul Revere, and the victims of the Boston Massacre.

Across the river from Boston is busy **Harvard Square** and **Harvard Yard,** though there's little room to "pahk your cah." Take a break at one of the many bookstores or cafés there.

The **Museum of Fine Arts** (465 Huntington Ave., tel. 617/ 267–9300) is one of the country's outstanding museums, with extensive collections of Asian and Egyptian artifacts, American fine and decorative arts, and Impressionist paintings. On the Fenway Park side is the Tenshin Garden, a Japanese meditation area.

The **New England Aquarium** (Central Wharf, tel. 617/973– 5200) has some of the most engaging performers in the city. A four-story, 187,000-gallon observation tank houses sharks and other inhabitants of the deep. Dolphin and sea lion shows take place aboard the floating pavilion *Discovery*.

At the **Old North Church** (193 Salem St., tel. 617/523– 6676), lanterns that signaled "one if by land and two if by sea" prompted Paul Revere's famous ride. The church is in the North End, an Italian enclave that is rapidly being gentrified.

The **Old Statehouse** (206 Washington St., tel. 617/720– 3290) served as the seat of Colonial government until the Revolution and as the capitol of the commonwealth until a new state house was built on Boston Common. It now holds a collection of marine memorabilia and Revolutionary War artifacts. In front is a circle of cobblestones that mark the site of the Boston Massacre, when a group of British soldiers fired into a crowd of jeering colonials.

The original **Paul Revere House** (19 North Sq., tel. 617/ 523–1676) is hidden beneath restoration clapboard and practically none of the furnishings belonged to the famous patriot and silversmith, but it is the site of the oldest house in Boston. Tours are self guided.

The **Quincy Market** area, prior to the 1970s renovation, was filled with produce and meat vendors rather than boutiques and trendy cafés. Some of the original vendors are still here, though. **Faneuil Hall** (pronounced "Fan'l"), at one end of Quincy Market, distinguished by a grasshopper weathervane, has since Colonial days been the scene of political debates; it houses a number of historic paintings, including a Gilbert Stuart portrait of George Washington. The street level is packed with shops geared to tourists.

The *USS Constitution*'s (Charlestown Navy Yard, tel. 617/426–1812) voyages now are limited to July 4, when the ship is taken into Boston Harbor. Undefeated during its service against pirates and in the War of 1812, it now is a floating history lesson. Guided tours.

Professional Sports

Basketball. Boston Celtics (Boston Garden, tel. 617/523–3030); **Baseball.** Boston Red Sox (Fenway Park, tel. 617/267–8661); **Hockey.** Boston Bruins (Boston Garden, tel. 617/227–3223); **Football.** New England Patriots (Sullivan Stadium, Foxboro, tel. 617/543–1776).

The Arts

No matter what art forms a visitor prefers, Boston is a cultural mecca. Its musical resources are particularly rich. It is home to the world-renowned **Boston Symphony Orchestra,** which appears at Symphony Hall. The **New England Conservatory of Music** is affiliated with Jordan Hall. For opera, head for the **Opera Company** of Boston's home at the Opera House. Contemporary **jazz** can be heard at the Berklee Performance Center. Boston's reputation as a tryout ground for Broadway productions has faded in recent years, but **touring companies** still get booked into the large downtown theaters, such as the Colonial, Shubert, Wilbur theaters, and the Wang Center for the Performing Arts. The number of art film houses has dwindled substantially, but various universities and organizations sponsor a number of film series.

Bostix (Faneuil Hall Marketplace, tel. 617/723–5181) sells half-price tickets for same-day theater productions. No sales are made by phone. Most ticket brokers charge a service fee and take major credit cards. Among them are: **Ticketmaster** (tel. 617/931–2000); **Ticketmaster of New England** (tel. 617/787–8000); **Concert Charge, Sport-Charge, TheatreCharge** (tel. 617/497–1118); **Concertix,** (tel. 617/876–7777); **Charg-Tix** (617/542–8511); **Teletron** (617/720–3434 or 800/382–8080).

Berklee Performance Center, 136 Massachusetts Ave., tel. 617/266–1400.
Colonial Theatre, 106 Boylston St., tel. 617/426–9366.
Jordan Hall, 33 Gainsborough St., tel. 617/536–2412.
Opera House, 539 Washington St., tel. 617/426–5300.
Shubert Theatre, 265 Tremont St., tel. 617/426–4520.
Symphony Hall, 301 Massachusetts Ave., tel. 617/266–1492.
Wang Center for the Performing Arts, 268 Tremont St., tel. 617/482–2595.
Wilbur Theatre, 246 Tremont St., tel. 617/426–1988.

After Hours

Boston's Puritan founders bequeathed a tradition of ending evenings early, but that has begun to change a bit. Because of the large student population, the rock scene is lively, and in recent years, clubs catering to an older audience have opened, particularly some excellent jazz clubs.

And Boston is one of the great breeding grounds for standup comedy; Jay Leno got his start here, for one. The *Boston Globe*'s Thursday Calendar section provides extensive listings of current and coming events, as does the weekly *Boston Phoenix*.

Bars and Lounges

The **Bay Tower Room** (60 State St., tel. 617/723–1666) has a subdued yet glamorous atmosphere and a stunning view of downtown Boston. The **Bull and Finch Pub** (84 Beacon St., tel. 617/227–9605), the model for the TV series *Cheers*, is good for a beer and a sandwich. The bar upstairs in the **Hampshire House** (84 Beacon St., tel. 617/227–9600) has a fireplace where you can relax with a glass of port. The clubby **Ritz Bar** at the Ritz-Carlton (tel. 617/536–5700) has long been a favorite of the city's powerful; try for a window table. **St. Cloud** (Tremont and Clarendon Sts., tel. 617/353–0202) draws an upscale crowd, as does **Rocco's** (5 S. Charles St., tel. 617/723–6800), which is close to the theater district.

Cabarets

Forbidden Broadway in the Terrace Room of the Boston Park Plaza Hotel (tel. 617/426–2000) has been skewering theatrical icons for years and is updated annually to spoof the latest hits. One of the best bargains in town is the **Theatre Lobby and Cabaret** (216 Hanover St., tel. 617/227–9872), which has a café, a lively revue, and a lounge with live entertainment on the weekends. The **Plaza Bar** at the Copley Plaza (tel. 617/267–5300) has a cabaret format with lush Indo-Anglo decor; seating is a bit crowded. **Sculler's** at the Guest Quarters Suite Hotel (tel. 617/783–0090) features both local and national performers. **Club Cabaret at the Club Café** (209 Columbus Ave., tel. 617/536–0972) is the most theatrical of the city's cabarets and books everything from folk singers to female impersonators.

Comedy Clubs

Comedy Connection (76 Warrenton St., tel. 617/426–6339) has long been one of Boston's premier comedy clubs, booking top national comedians. Its neighbor, **Nick's Comedy Stop** (100 Warrenton St., tel. 617/482–0930), concentrates more on local comics. **Dick Doherty's Comedy Vault** (124 Boylston St., tel. 617/267–6626) includes improvisational comedy as well as magic acts.

Jazz Clubs

Some of the best clubs are across the river in Cambridge. The Charles Hotel's sleek **Regattabar** (1 Bennett St., tel. 617/876–7777) books top-flight national acts. **Nightstage** (823 Main St., tel. 617/497–8200) boasts excellent acoustics and sight lines for an interesting mix of jazz, blues, world music, and rock. There are the two-hour **Jazzboat** cruises on Boston Harbor on Fridays from June–Sept., departing from Central Wharf (tel. 617/876–8742). **Diamond Jim's Piano Bar** hosts a singalong Wed.–Sat. (710 Boylston St., tel. 617/566–8651).

For Singles

Zanzibar (1 Boylston Place, tel. 617/451–1955), open Wed.–Sat., an upscale mix of faux marble, rattan furniture, and palm trees, leans toward financial-district late-baby-boomer types who still like to shake a tailfeather. **Citi** (15

Lansdowne St., tel. 617/262-2424), open Thurs.-Sun., is all neon disco, light show, and elbow-to-elbow dancing. The **Roxy** (279 Tremont St., tel. 617/227-7699), open Thurs.-Sat., is a palatial setting with two tiers of supper-club-style banquettes and tables with a surprising mix of contemporary pop interspersed with an occasional big-band set.

Brussels

by Eric Sjogren

In 1967, when the European Commission—the executive branch of the European Economic Community—made the city its home, Brussels became the "capital of Europe." The geography was right, for Brussels is just about equidistant from London, Paris, and Bonn, and the politics were right, for no one could suspect Belgium of wanting to dominate the EEC. Perhaps most important, Brussels had the capacity to house some 10,000 European civil servants and their families. Some years later, and for much the same reasons, NATO dug in.

Around the 1960s, American multinational companies, including Goodyear, Procter & Gamble, 3M, Honeywell, and Monsanto, also began setting up European headquarters in Brussels. They were attracted, in part, by tax incentives and a highly productive work force. Also, many expatriate executives from small U.S. cities found it easier to adjust to Brussels (population: 1 million) than to such overpowering metropolises as Paris and London. Today, the American Chamber of Commerce has more than 800 members in Brussels, and the U.S. corporate presence is strong: Nearly all leading American advertising, public relations, auditing/management consulting, and executive search firms have offices here. Not surprisingly, the city's second largest industry is meetings and conventions, and it ranks third worldwide as a convention spot.

Belgium has two cultures that coexist in a somewhat uneasy linguistic truce: In the northern half, Flanders, the people speak Flemish, similar to Dutch; in the southern half, Wallonia, they speak French. Brussels is officially bilingual, but the long-running dispute between the two groups has led to much unnecessary duplication in the administrative and political life of the nation, and having to negotiate occasionally in two foreign languages can be frustrating for business travelers.

Top Employers

Employer	Type of Enterprise	Parent*/ Headquarters
BASF Belgium	Chemicals	BASF AG/Ludwigshafen, Germany
Delhaize	Retailing	Brussels

Esso	Oil	Exxon Inc./ Dallas, Texas
GB-Inno-BM	Retailing	Brussels
Intercom	Electricity	Brussels
Petrofina	Oil	Brussels
Philips Belgium	Appliances	Philips NV/ Eindhoven, The Netherlands
RTT	Telephone	Brussels
Solvay	Chemicals	Brussels
Wagons-Lits	Transportation	Brussels

*if applicable

ESSENTIAL INFORMATION

We include the Brussels telephone area code (02) with all numbers listed below. If you are calling from outside Belgium, omit the zero from the code. If you are calling within the city, drop the code altogether.

The currency in Belgium is the franc, abbreviated throughout the chapter as BF.

Government Tourist Offices

Belgian National Tourist Office. In North America: 745 Fifth Ave., Suite 714, New York, NY 10151, tel. 212/758–8130.
In the United Kingdom: Premier House, 2 Gayton Rd., Harrow, Middlesex HA1 2XU, tel. 081/861–3300.
In Brussels: Hôtel de Ville, Grand'Place, tel. 02/513–89–40.

Foreign Trade Information

Consulate General of Belgium. In the United States: 50 Rockefeller Plaza, New York, NY 10020, tel. 212/586–5110; 333 N. Michigan Ave., Rm. 2000, Chicago, IL 60601, tel. 312/263–6624; 61000 Wilshire Blvd., Suite 1200, Los Angeles, CA 90048, tel. 213/857–1244.
In Canada: 1001 De Maisonneuve Ouest, Suite 1250, Montréal H3A 3C8, Quebec, tel. 514/849–7394; 8 Kings St. East, Suite 1901, Toronto M5C 1B5, Ontario, tel. 416/364–5283.
The Belgian Embassy in the United Kingdom: 103 Eaton Sq., London SW1W 9AB, tel. 071/235–5422.

Entry Requirements

U.S. and Canadian Citizens
Passport only required. Visa required for stays longer than 90 days.

U.K. Citizens
Passport only.

Climate

What follows are the average daily maximum and minimum temperatures for Brussels.

Jan.	40F	4C	Feb.	45F	7C	Mar.	50F	10C
	31	−1		32	0		36	2
Apr.	58F	14C	May	65F	18C	June	72F	22C
	41	5		47	8		52	11
July	74F	23C	Aug.	72F	22C	Sept.	70F	21C
	54	12		54	12		52	11
Oct.	59F	15C	Nov.	49F	9C	Dec.	43F	6C
	45	7		38	3		32	0

Airport

Brussels' National Airport, generally known as Zaventem, is 7½ miles northeast of the city. It is reasonably functional, though you may encounter long lines at passport control (check that you're in the right line—most are for European Community nationals) and long waits for baggage. Smoking is not allowed.

Airlines

The Belgian airline, Sabena, departs from New York, Chicago, and Boston. There is no domestic air service within Belgium, but buses run from the airport to Antwerp, Ghent, and Liege.

American, tel. 02/508–7700; 800/433–7300.
Pan Am, tel. 02/751–8195; 800/221–1111.
Sabena, tel. 02/511–9030; 800/873–3900.
TWA, tel. 02/513–7916; 800/421–8480.

Between the Airport and Downtown

By Taxi
Autolux Mercedes airport taxis (tel. 02/425–6020) are plentiful, and if you purchase a round-trip, you get a 25% discount. Figure on 30 minutes during rush hours (8–9 AM and 4–5 PM) and 20 minutes otherwise for a trip downtown. The most direct (but not necessarily the fastest) route is via the Chaussée de Louvain. Cost: about BF 1,000 one way; BF 1,500 round-trip. AE, DC, MC, V accepted. No tips.

By Train
Trains run every 20 minutes from 5:24 AM to 11:46 PM to Gare du Nord (15 minutes) in the north end of town, and to Gare Centrale (19 minutes) in center city; once an hour they extend to Gare du Midi (27 minutes) in the south end. Get information and tickets in the arrivals hall. Cost: first class, BF 105; second class, BF 70 (add BF 30 if you buy your ticket on the train).

By Bus
Free courtesy buses serve the airport hotels.

Car Rentals

The following companies have booths in the airport arrivals hall:

AT, tel. 02/722–3106.
Avis, tel. 02/537–1280; 800/331–2112.

Budget, tel. 02/538–8075; 800/527–0700.
Europcar/InterRent, tel. 02/721–0592; 800/227–7368.
Hertz, tel. 02/513–2886; 800/654–3001.

Emergencies

For a list of approved physicians and clinics in Brussels that belong to the International Association for Medical Assistance to Travelers, contact IAMAT, 417 Center St., Lewiston, NY 14092, tel. 716/754–4883.

For round-the-clock crisis information in English, call Help Line, tel. 02/648–4014.

Doctors
Referral service, tel. 02/648–8000 or 02/479–1818.

Dentists
Referral service, tel. 02/426–1026 or 02/428–5888.

Hospitals
Clinique Parc Leopold (38 Rue Froissart, tel. 02/230–4980), **Hôpital de Braine l'Alleud** (35 Rue Wayez, Braine l'Alleud, tel. 02/384–6060), **Hôpital Universitaire St. Pierre** (322 Rue Haute, tel. 02/538–0000), **Institut Edith Cavell** (32 Rue Edith Cavell, tel. 02/348–4001).

Ambulance
Tel. 100.

Police
Tel. 101.

Important Addresses and Numbers

American Express (2 Place Louise, tel. 02/512–7040 travel services), (100 Boulevard Souverain, tel. 02/660–4989 card services).

Audiovisual rentals. AVP Audio Visual Partners (205 Ave. Kersbeek, tel. 02/376–0045), Diavision (18 Ave. Emile Duray, tel. 02/649–9485).

Bookstores (English-language). House of Paperbacks (813 Chaussée de Waterloo, tel. 02/343–1122), Librairie de Rome (50 Ave. Louise, tel. 02/511–7937), W.H. Smith (71–75 Blvd. Adolphe Max, tel. 02/219–5034).

British Embassy (28 Rue Joseph II, tel. 02/217–9000).

Canadian Embassy (2 Ave. de Tervuren, tel. 02/735–6040).

Convention and exhibition centers. Auditorium Hamoir (12 Ave. Hamoir, tel. 02/374–1981), Brussels Congress Center (Palais des Congres, 3 Coudenberg, tel. 02/513–4130), Centre International de Conferences de Bruxelles (Parc des Expositions, tel. 02/478–4860), Expo Rogier Center (32A Rue du Progres, tel. 02/218–5091).

Fax service. *See* Office space rental, below.

Formal-wear rentals. Francy Tailor (56 Rue des Colonies, tel. 02/217–8494), John Kennis (12 Ave. Marnix, tel. 02/513–2303).

Gift shops. Chocolates: Neuhaus (25 Galerie de la Reine, tel. 02/512–6359); Flowers: Kuipers (93 Rue du Marché-aux-Herbes, tel. 02/513–0291); Gift baskets: Rob (7–9 Chaussée d'Ixelles, tel. 02/513–3910).

Graphic design studios. Design Board (50 Ave. G. Lecointe, tel. 02/375–3962), Fox Studios (255 Chaussée de Waterloo, tel. 02/537–8505).

Hairstylists. Unisex: Jacques Dessange (245 Galerie Louise, tel. 02/512–9472), Men: Philippe (39 Rue des Eperonniers, tel. 02/513–3773), Women: Roger (88 Ave. Louise, tel. 02/512–2581).

Health and fitness clubs. *See* Fitness, below.

Limousine service. Avis (tel. 02/513–1051), Brussels Limousine Service (tel. 02/216–1901).

Liquor stores. Amis du Vin (47 Rue du Marais, tel. 02/218–2840), Millesime (968 Chaussée de Waterloo, tel. 02/374–5983). Wine and spirits can also be purchased in all grocery stores and supermarkets.

Mail delivery, overnight. DHL Worldwide Express (tel. 02/720–9500), Federal Express (tel. 02/722–7777), TNT Skypak (tel. 02/720–7190), UPS (tel. 02/751–7777).

Messenger services. Free Lance Express (tel. 02/725–0050), Taxipost (tel. 02/217–1204), or by regular taxi (*see* below).

News programs (English-language). Radio: BBC World Service (MW 648 kh, 463m, every hour on the hour), Radio 4 (LW 198 kh, 1515m, 7:30–9:30 AM and 7 PM); TV: BBC 1 (7:30–10 AM, 2, 7, and 10 PM), BBC 2 (11:30 PM).

Office space rentals. Burotel (4 Rue de la Presse, tel. 02/217–8360, and at the Airport Sheraton, tel. 02/725–3039), Contact Business Center (9–21 Rue Capouillet, tel. 02/536–8686), HQ Services (149 Ave. Louise, tel. 02/534–1000) all offer telex, fax, word processing, and secretarial services as well.

Pharmacies, late-night. One pharmacy in each district stays open 24 hours; the roster is posted in all pharmacy windows. In an emergency, tel. 02/479–1818.

Secretarial services. Randstad Interim (8–10 Rue des Princes, tel. 02/217–2320), Wings Interim (51 Rue de Joncker, tel. 02/537–7240); also *see* Office space rental, above.

Stationery supplies. Nias (59 Rue Neuve, tel. 02/217–6310), Papéterie Brugmann (230–232 Ave. Brugmann, tel. 02/343–7844).

Taxis. Taxis ATR (tel. 02/242–2222), Taxis Oranges (tel. 02/513–6200), Taxis Verts (tel. 02/347–4747 or 02/511–2244, the largest).

Theater tickets. *See* The Arts, below.

Thomas Cook (4 Grand'Place, tel. 02/513–2843, financial services), Wagons-Lits Tours (144 Ave. E. Plasky, tel. 02/736–6007, travel services).

Trade Ministry. Office Belge du Commerce Exterieur (162 Blvd. E. Jacqmain, tel. 02/219–4450).

Train information. SNCB (85 Rue de France, tel. 02/219–2640).

Translation services. Berlitz Translation Center (36 Ave. des Arts, tel. 02/513–9274), Lexitech (119 Chaussée Saint-Pierre, tel. 02/640–0385), Mendez (8 Ave. Franklin Roosevelt, tel. 02/647–2700).

U.S. Embassy (27 Blvd. du Regent, tel. 02/513–3830).

Telephones

To use a coin-operated telephone, lift the receiver and insert two BF-5 coins for local calls or two BF-20 coins for long distance; wait for the dial tone; dial the number; insert additional coins when signal indicates. International calls can be made from phone booths that bear a strip depicting European Community flags. Many pay phones are operated by Telecards, which you can buy at any post office on weekdays from 9 to 5 in denominations of BF 200 and BF 1000.

Tipping

Tip doormen carrying bags BF 100; porters carrying bags to your room should also receive BF 100. Tip concierges BF 100 for any services apart from giving information. Service is included in room-service bills, but an additional BF 50–100 (either added to the check or given directly to the staff member) is appreciated. A 16% service charge is added to all restaurant bills, so no tip is necessary or expected, even in the most expensive establishments. Tips are also included in taxi fares. Tip bathroom attendants BF 10, movie ushers BF 20.

DOING BUSINESS

Hours

Businesses: weekdays 9–5. **Banks:** weekdays 9–4; some are open Sat., 9–noon. **Shops:** generally Mon.–Sat., 10–7; some close for lunch.

National Holidays

New Year's Day; Easter Sun. and Mon.; May 1, Labor Day; Ascension Day (Thurs. 40 days after Easter); Whit Mon. (Mon. following Whitsun. or Pentecost, which is 50 days after Easter); July 21, Belgian Independence Day; Aug. 15, Assumption; Nov. 1, All Saints Day; Nov. 11, Armistice Day; Christmas.

When a national holiday falls on a Saturday or Sunday, employees are entitled to take another day off, usually the following Monday. Also, Belgians often take their four weeks vacation in July and August; many restaurants and some shops close at that time.

Getting Around

By Car
Driving in Brussels is easy once you've accepted the fact that Belgian drivers will risk collision rather than give up their right of way. Aside from rush hours (8–9 AM and 4–5 PM), traffic jams are rare in Brussels. You will need a valid U.S. driver's license, your passport, and a credit card in order to rent a car. Insurance usually costs extra.

By Taxi

It is next to impossible to hail a cab. If you are not near a taxi stand, phone for one (*see* Important Addresses and Numbers, above)—there's usually only a five- to 10-minute wait.

By Public Transportation

The Métro is easy to use. There are two main lines: No. 1 runs east to west and No. 2 runs northwest around the city center to the Gare du Midi. The two lines intersect at Arts-Loi. The Métro runs from 5:30 AM to midnight, and is supplemented by tram and bus service. For BF 40, you can buy a ticket good for 1 hour on all 3 modes of transportation; 10-trip cards cost BF 250 and can be purchased at newspaper kiosks.

Protocol

Appointments

Punctuality is the rule, for both business and social engagements. The lobbies and bars of major hotels are suitable places to meet.

Customs

Belgian businesspeople are getting used to the American habit of using first names, but it's still advisable to use surnames until you get to know someone. Shake hands with everybody, both on arrival and departure. Business cards are generally exchanged at the end of a meeting.

Dress

Although there is a trend toward more casual wear, suits (for women as well as men) are still the norm in offices, especially at the executive level.

Gifts

When invited for dinner at a private home, flowers, a box of chocolates, or a bottle of wine are appropriate. To make a real impression, bring a small gift typical of your home state or region.

Toasts and Greetings

French and Flemish are the official languages in Brussels, so it's good to know a little of both. (In Flemish, "kh" sounds the same as the first sound in the Spanish name *Jose.*):

Good morning, *Bonjour* (bohn ZHOOR); *Goede dag* (khoo-duh DAHK).
How are you? *Comment allez-vous?* (com-ahnt ahl-ay VOO); *Hoe gaat het met U?* (hoo khat het MEH-too).
Have a nice day, *Bonne journée* (bohn zhoor-NAY); *Prettige dag* (preh-tik-uh dakh).
Thank you, *Merci beaucoup* (mer-see boh-COU); *Dank U wel* (dahn-kuh vell).
Good-bye, *Au revoir* (oh ruh-VWAHR); *Tot ziens* (toht zeens).
Nice to have met you, *Ravi d'avoir fait votre connaissance* (rah-VEE da-VOUAR fay VO-truh con-nay-SAHNS); *Aangenaam kennis gemaakt te hebben met U* (ahn-kheh-NAHM ken-nis KHEH-mahkt tuh heb-en MEH-too).
To your health, *A votre santé* (ah VOH-truh sahn-TAY); *Gezondheid* (keh-ZOND-hide).

LODGING

Business travelers outnumber tourists in Brussels by 4 to 1, and their ranks are steadily growing. In response, many new hotels especially designed for businesspeople have sprung up, and many more are preparing to open.

Most of the new properties fall into the deluxe category, so finding accommodations that combine comfort with low or moderate prices can be difficult. For stays of a week or more, you might want to consider renting an apartment with a kitchenette (BF 15,000–BF 40,000 per week). For listings, contact T.I.B. (Hotel de Ville de Bruxelles, Grand'Place, 1000 Brussels, tel. 02/513–8940, fax 02/514–0129).

Because of Brussels' modest size, the location of your hotel is not as important as it might be in a city that's more spread out. An airport property makes sense if you're in town exclusively to meet with one of the many U.S. companies headquartered in that vicinity, or if you plan to travel extensively. The main attraction of a downtown site is the ambience of the Old City and proximity to the Brussels Congress Center. An uptown hotel makes it marginally easier to get to appointments with Belgian businesses, ministries, professional bodies, and with the European Commission.

Most of the properties listed below offer corporate rates and/or weekend discounts; inquire when making reservations.

Highly recommended lodgings in each price category are indicated by a star ★.

Category	Cost*
$$$$ (Very Expensive)	over BF 8,500
$$$ (Expensive)	BF 5,500–BF 8,500
$$ (Moderate)	BF 2,500–BF 5,500
$ (Inexpensive)	under BF 2,500

all prices are for a standard double room, single occupancy, including 6% value added tax, 9% city tax, and 16% service charge.

Numbers in the margin correspond to numbered hotel locations on the Brussels Lodging and Dining maps.

Downtown

★ ⑮
$$$

Amigo. Built in 1958, this six-story, privately owned hotel stands on the site of the old city jail, a block from the Grand'Place. Reminiscent of a manor house done in Spanish Renaissance style, with touches of Louis XV, Amigo attracts an 80% business clientele, mainly bankers and diplomats. Rooms vary in size and are priced in three categories; the best buy is a junior suite. If you value quiet rather than a view, ask for an inside room, and if air conditioning is a priority, be sure to request a room with it. The hotel's airport limo service costs less than a taxi. *1–3 Rue d'Amigo, 1000, tel. 02/511–5910, fax 02/513–5277. Gen.*

manager, Pierre Bouchard. 183 rooms, 11 suites. AE, DC, MC, V.

㉕ Royal Windsor. Refurbishment of this 1972-vintage hotel
$$$$ was completed in 1990, and the rooms are now tastefully decorated with blond oak paneling and marble bathrooms. Unfortunately, the business center fell by the wayside during the renovation, the low ceiling in the lobby makes the place feel cramped, and the rooms are small. Located near Grand'Place, this is a good choice if you have business at the Brussels Congress Center or downtown. Corporate guests include Exxon and GM executives; the majority of the guests are American, followed by British and Scandinavian business travelers. The dining room, Les Quatre Saison, is one of the best hotel restaurants in Brussels; the Clubby Waterloo Bar is a good place for drinks with a colleague, and the Crocodile Club disco attracts an international crowd (*see* After Hours, below, for both). Service throughout the hotel is friendly and efficient. *A Warwick International hotel. 5 Rue Duquesnoy, 1000, tel. 02/511–4215, fax 02/511–6004. Gen. manager, Guy Welter. 290 doubles. AE, DC, MC, V.*

★ ⑲ SAS Royal Hotel. This seven-story deluxe hotel, opened in
$$$$ 1990, was the first in Brussels especially designed for business travelers. There's a business center and an Office-for-a-Day rental service. The split-level, greenery-filled atrium incorporates a section of the original city wall that dates back to 1134 AD. Rooms range in style from oriental, with wicker furniture and Asiatic art; to Scandinavian, with light-wood furnishings and parquet floors; to Italian, with angular fixtures and colorful bedspreads. All rooms come with trouser presses, security locks, and spyholes; Royal Club extras include electronic safes, private lounge, and free use of the fitness center, which has an exercise room computerized for individual workout programs (*see* Fitness, below). The Sea Grill restaurant acquired a Michelin star in record time. The hotel's Old City site is great for ambience, but not extremely convenient for business appointments. *47 Rue du Fossé-aux-Loups, 1000, tel. 02/219–2828, in U.S., 800/221–2350, fax 02/219–6262. Gen. manager, Werner Knechtli. 263 rooms, 6 executive rooms, 12 junior suites. AE, DC, MC, V.*

Uptown

⑬ Albert Premier. This no-frills, modern hotel offers the bas-
$ ics at a very good price. First opened in the 1920s, it was totally refurbished in 1988 in a low-key, Art Deco style. The blue and gun-metal-gray guest rooms are a bit somber, but those facing the courtyard are very quiet; none are air-conditioned. The guests tend to be European businesspeople and tour groups from Italy and Spain. The staff's English is just passable, and the restaurant is open for breakfast and special functions only. The hotel is in a rather run-down part of town; women traveling alone are not advised to stay here. *20 Place Rogier, 1210, tel. 02/217–2125, fax 02/217–9331. Owner/manager, Salomon Levy. 285 rooms. AE, DC, MC, V.*

③ Forum. An extensive face-lift of this 1980 hotel was com-
$$ pleted in 1990, giving it a cool, attractive Art Deco look, but the Forum still retains its sensible prices. If you're on a tight budget and want to avoid the impersonality of the big chains, this is a good choice. The rooms are basic but

GREATER BRUSSELS

Lodging
Airport Sheraton, **2**
Forum, **3**
Mayfair, **7**
Trois Tilleuls, **11**

Dining
Bruneau, **1**
Le Camboge, **5**
La Charlotte aux Pommes, **4**
L'Elephant Bleu, **9**
Rick's Café Americain, **6**
Truffe Noire, **8**
Villa Lorraine, **10**

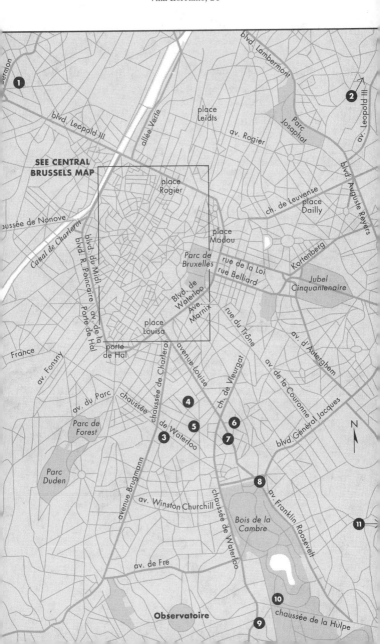

CENTRAL BRUSSELS

Lodging
Albert Premier, **13**
Amigo, **15**
Hilton International Brussels, **22**
Royal Windsor, **20**
SAS Royal Hotel, **19**
Sheraton Hotel & Towers, **12**
Sofitel, **23**

Dining
Aux Armes de Bruxelles, **17**
Comme Chez Soi, **14**
La Grande Porte, **21**
La Maison du Boeuf, **22**
La Maison du Cygne, **16**
Ogenblik, **18**

comfortable, though bathrooms are small, and there are no desks or air-conditioning; the quietest rooms are in the back overlooking the garden; and one on each of the seven floors comes equipped with a kitchenette. There is an attractive ground-floor breakfast room. New owners are making a determined effort to improve service. Tram and bus stops are nearby. *2 Ave. du Haut-Pont, 1060, tel. 02/343-0100, fax 02/347-0054. Gen. manager, Frederic Faucher. 75 rooms, 3 suites. AE, DC, MC, V.*

㉒ **Hilton International Brussels.** One of the first high rises to
$$$$ be built in Brussels in the 1960s, this hotel is still a distinctive landmark. American executives find the same bland Hilton here that they know and love at home. Only the most recently renovated rooms on the third and fourth floors have desks. Five more expensive Executive floors (16–20) offer better views and a private lounge. Advantages include the 24-hour room service and the excellent location near Port Louise (where the smartest shops are). The local business crowd heads for the second-floor Maison du Boeuf (*see* Dining, below), the Hilton Bar (*see* After Hours, below), or the garden terrace coffee shop (*see* Business Breakfasts, below). There's no extra charge for children sharing your room. *38 Blvd. de Waterloo, 1000, tel. 02/504-1111, fax 02/504-2111. Gen. manager, Robert Maslin. 365 rooms. AE, DC, MC, V.*

❼ **Mayfair.** If personalized service and an attractive location
$$$$ are priorities, this is the place to stay. On Avenue Louise, one of the city's most elegant streets, and near the Bois de la Cambre, a lovely place to jog, the Mayfair caters to American, British, and Japanese business travelers. The spacious and elegant lobby opens out onto a garden filled with statues. The 10-story property is 20 years old, but has been renovated in several stages: "studio" rooms, equipped with good-sized desks, were refurbished in 1989; suites were refitted three years earlier. All rooms have blond wood furnishings and a neutral, modern style; two are equipped with Jacuzzis, and four have been redone with large makeup mirrors and extra toiletries. *A Chisan hotel. 381-383 Ave. Louise, 1050, tel. 02/649-9800, fax 02/640-1764. Gen. manager, Edmo Muccioli. 95 rooms, 4 suites. AE, DC, MC, V.*

⓬ **Sheraton Hotel & Towers.** When Sheraton set out to chal-
$$$$ lenge the Brussels Hilton in the early 1970s, it built a hotel a few stories higher, with rooms a bit more spacious, in a style a little more opulent. What it couldn't rival was the Hilton's location. The neighborhood around the Sheraton is improving, but, though it is close to the World Trade Center, it remains an area not recommended for women alone after dark. All rooms feature good-sized desks, but bathrooms are on the small side. Guests on Tower floors (20–28) can check in while sitting in a special lounge, where complimentary breakfast and cocktail snacks are served. The club-like Rendezvous Bar (*see* After Hours, below) is quite spacious and well suited for business conversations, as is Le Pavillon (*see* Business Breakfasts, below). The top floor boasts the only hotel pool in town, with sauna, exercise room, and poolside bar (*see* Fitness, below). *3 Place Rogier, 1210, tel. 02/219-3400, fax 02/218-6618. Gen. manager, Andre Pendaries. 483 rooms, 43 suites. AE, DC, MC, V.*

BRUSSELS HOTEL CHART

HOTELS	Price Category	Business Services										
		Banquet capacity	No. of meeting rooms	Fax	Telex	Photocopying	Secretarial services	Audiovisual equipment	Translation services	International direct dial	Computer rentals	In-room modem phone jack
Airport Sheraton	$$$	500	9	✓	✓	✓	✓	✓	✓	✓	-	-
Albert Premier	$	65	9	✓	✓	✓	-	✓	-	✓	-	-
Amigo	$$$	200	6	✓	✓	✓	-	✓	-	✓	-	-
Forum	$$	80	1	✓	✓	✓	-	-	-	✓	-	-
Hilton International	$$$$	400	11	✓	✓	✓	✓	✓	✓	✓	-	-
Mayfair	$$$$	40	4	✓	✓	✓	-	✓	-	✓	-	-
Royal Windsor	$$$$	350	4	✓	✓	✓	✓	-	✓	✓	-	✓
SAS Royal	$$$$	300	14	✓	✓	✓	✓	✓	-	✓	-	✓
Sheraton Hotel and Towers	$$$$	680	11	✓	✓	✓	✓	✓	-	✓	✓	-
Sofitel	$$$	80	6	✓	✓	✓	-	✓	-	✓	-	-
Trois Tilleuls	$$	50	0	✓	-	-	-	-	-	✓	-	-

$$$$** = over BF 7,000, **$$$** = BF 5,000-7,000, **$$ = under BF 5,000.
● good, ◖ fair, ○ poor.

All-news cable channel	Desk	Desk lighting	Bed lighting	In-Room Amenities / Nonsmoking rooms	In-room checkout	Minibar	Toiletries	Room service	Laundry/Dry cleaning	Pressing	Hotel Amenities / Barber/Hairdresser	Garage	Courtesy airport transport	Sauna	Pool	Exercise room
-	●	●	◐	✓	-	✓	○	●	●	◐	-	✓	-	-	-	-
-	◐	○	◐	-	-	✓	-	-	●	●	-	-	-	-	-	-
-	●	●	●	-	-	✓	◐	●	●	●	-	✓	-	-	-	-
-	◐	◐	●	-	-	✓	○	◐	●	●	-	✓	-	-	-	-
-	●	●	◐	✓	-	✓	●	●	●	◐	-	✓	-	✓	-	-
✓	●	●	●	✓	-	✓	●	●	●	◐	-	✓	-	-	-	-
-	●	◐	◐	✓	-	✓	●	●	●	◐	-	✓	-	-	-	-
✓	●	●	●	✓	✓	✓	●	●	●	●	-	✓	-	✓	-	●
✓	●	●	●	✓	-	✓	●	●	●	●	-	✓	-	✓	●	●
-	●	●	●	✓	-	✓	●	●	●	●	-	✓	-	-	-	●
-	-	-	●	-	-	-	○	◐	●	◐	-	-	-	-	-	-

Room service: ● 24-hour, ◐ 6AM-10PM, ○ other.
Laundry/Dry cleaning: ● same day, ◐ overnight, ○ other.
Pressing: ● immediate, ◐ same day, ○ other.

㉓ **Sofitel.** This six-story hotel, built in 1989, has a great up-
$$$ town location, across the street from the Hilton, attract-
ing mainly French and U.S. business travelers. It boasts
an ultra-chic shopping arcade and a spacious second-floor
lobby with picture windows. Public rooms and bedrooms
are decorated in the warm brown and beige tones charac-
teristic of this French hotel chain. Executive rooms are re-
ally junior suites with sitting areas; bathroom telephones
and bathrobes are standard in all rooms. The Sofitel may
offer fewer services than its neighbor across the way, but
its rooms cost a good deal less, and there is no extra charge
for double occupancy. *40 Ave. de la Toison d'Or, 1000, tel.
02/514–2200 (in U.S., 800/221–4542), fax 02/514–5744.
Gen. manager, Bert Hummel. 160 rooms, 11 executive
rooms. AE, DC, MC, V.*

⑪ **Trois Tilleuls.** Business lunchers from nearby U.S. firms
$$ enjoyed the first-rate restaurant in this residential area,
Boisfort, so much that they suggested to the owner that he
branch out into the hotel business. The result: four well-
equipped, individually decorated rooms upstairs from the
dining room, renting at very reasonable rates, in an unprepossessing, semidetached villa. Nearby is an annex
with an additional room and two apartment-like suites,
also available for a very reasonable price. Most guests are
repeat customers. Expect comfort and excellent cooking,
but not the range of amenities associated with major hotels. A firm offering secretarial services and office space is
in the vicinity. *8 Berensheide, 1170, tel. 02/672–3014, fax
02/673–6552. Gen. managers, Guy and Adrienne Vander
Perre. 5 rooms, 2 suites. AE, DC, MC, V.*

Airport

② **Airport Sheraton.** Long on efficiency and short on charm,
$$$ this five-story property, opened in 1989, is the ultimate
airport hotel; you can push your baggage trolley from the
terminal to its front door. A vast, glass-walled atrium
punctuated with works by Belgian sculptors encloses the
lobby, restaurant, and bar. The rooms are identical to one
another, all humdrum modern hotel style, but the triple-
glazed windows afford an interesting—and silent—view
of airport activity. Many U.S.-based, high-tech compa-
nies are nearby, hence the high proportion of American
business travelers here. Sabena Airlines has an office in
the hotel lobby, and there's free shuttle service to down-
town. *Brussels National Airport, 1930 Zaventem, tel. 02/
725–1000 (in U.S. and Canada, 800/325–3535), fax 02/
725–1155. Gen. manager, Fred Welke. 296 rooms, 8
suites. AE, DC, MC, V.*

DINING

When history writers eventually come to decide why
Brussels was chosen as the home of the European Com-
mission and NATO, they may very well determine it was
because of the food. Twenty-five Brussels restau-
rants—out of 1,500—have one or more of the coveted
rosettes awarded by the Guide Michelin. (That's more
than twice as many as in all of London.) In days gone by,
Belgian cooking was as copious as it was robust and
rich. Since nouvelle cuisine emerged, however, young

chefs have gained the courage to create lighter, prettier dishes.

In Belgium, it is still rare for a woman to dine out alone or host a dinner. This can cause embarrassment in business situations; for example, in deluxe restaurants, only the host gets the menu with prices. Usually, the wife of the owner/chef is responsible for the dining room, so it's a good strategy to make her your ally.

Lunch is the meal associated with business discussions. Dinner is more a time to celebrate a deal, to butter up a client, or to say thank you. If the cost of the meal is to be reimbursed by a local business, be sure to get a *fiche TVA*, an official receipt giving the Value Added Tax details.

Note: The restaurants cited below are located in disparate areas of the city; except for in the vicinity of Grand'Place, where a great many eateries are concentrated, there are no large or distinct restaurant districts in Brussels.

Highly recommended restaurants in each price category are indicated by a star ★.

Category	Cost*
$$$$ (Very Expensive)	over BF 3,000
$$$ (Expensive)	BF 2,001–BF 3,000
$$ (Moderate)	BF 1,000–BF 2,000
$ (Inexpensive)	under BF 1,000

per person, including appetizer, entrée, dessert, 6% value added tax and 16% service charge, but excluding drinks.

Numbers in the margin correspond to numbered restaurant locations on the Brussels Lodging and Dining maps.

Wine

Most Belgians drink wine—preferably French—with their meals. There are no local vineyards. In many restaurants you can order wine by the glass or *pichet*, a small carafe holding about two glasses.

Beer and Ale

Beer is consumed in large quantities at almost all hours here. Belgium produces some 400 different brews. The most popular are the light lagers, such as Stella Artois and Jupiter; Duvel is a refermented and considerably stronger beer. Order *une blanche* and you'll get a bittersweet wheat beer. Trappist beer, strong and smooth, with a creamy head of froth, is brewed in several monasteries. Gueze and Kriek, which have a raspberry flavor, are spontaneous fermentation beers—the traditional brews consumed with such gusto in scenes painted by Breughel.

Business Breakfasts

Belgians who do business with or work for American companies have reluctantly come to terms with the power breakfast, but most others are astonished by the idea. The most suitable venues for such meetings are discreet hotel coffee shop/restaurants, especially the **Café d'Egmont** (tel. 02/513–8877) at the Hilton and **Le Pavillon** (tel. 02/219–3400) at the Sheraton.

Downtown

⑰ **Aux Armes de Bruxelles.** Hidden among the tourist traps
$ in the Ilot Sacre, the Armes de Bruxelles attracts a largely local clientele with its well-prepared Belgian classics: turbot *waterzooi* (a creamy stew of potatoes, vegetables, and fish), a variety of steaks, and french fries (which Belgians, with some justification, believe they prepare better than anyone else). A favorite here is mussels, steamed, Provençale, or in white wine, served in huge portions. There's no decor to speak of, and paper cloths cover the tightly packed tables, but the place is cheerful and light, and service is friendly (if frequently overstretched). This is a good choice for a relaxed, inexpensive evening. *13 Rue des Bouchers, tel. 02/511–2118. Casual dress. Reservations advised. AE, DC, MC, V. Closed Mon. and June.*

★ ⑭ **Comme Chez Soi.** The name means "Just Like Home," but
$$$$ unless mom was a gourmet chef, the cooking here is far from most domestic fare. Pierre Wynants, the third generation owner/chef of this once-modest establishment near Gare du Midi, draws on the best of yesteryear in his menu, while cutting down drastically on cream and butter. He's famous for his silky mousses of Ardennes ham, eel, and game. Also popular are his oxtail salad with leeks and fresh coriander, saddle of young rabbit with lemon and basil, and escalopes of duck's liver with port and ginger. The Art Nouveau dining room, once a bistro, squeezes in 40, so there's not much privacy. The kitchen is bigger, and the fabulous wine cellar bigger still. The secret of Comme Chez Soi is that you really do feel at home in this temple of gastronomy. Save this for a rare treat or big celebration; fax your reservation weeks ahead. *23 Place Rouppe, tel. 02/512–2921, fax 02/511–8052. Jacket and tie required. Reservations required. AE, DC. Closed Sun., Mon., July, Christmas week.*

㉑ **La Grande Porte.** Let your hair down in this old-time place—
$ in the bar with the player piano or in any of several smaller rooms decorated with pictures, posters, and marionettes. The short menu includes a number of quintessentially Belgian dishes, such as *carbonade à la flamande* (beef and onions stewed in beer) or *ballekes à la marollienne* (spicy meat balls). The spaghetti and risottos are fine, too, and portions are copious. Bruxellois from all walks of life come here to enjoy the ambience. Service is casual but friendly. *9 Rue Notre Seigneur, tel. 02/512–8998. Casual dress. AE, DC, MC, V. Closed Sat. and Sun. lunch.*

⑯ **La Maison du Cygne.** Dining at Le Cygne is a sensuous ex-
$$$$ perience. The setting, in one of the old guild houses on the Grand'Place, is incomparable. The paneled dining room upstairs is hung with oil paintings; the ground floor room is somewhat less formal. Tailcoated waiters glide rather than rush to attend your every wish. The cuisine is classic French: saddle of lamb, braised turbot, duckling with onions, and game in season. The wine list is extensive and excellent. The phrase *"luxe, calme, et volupte"* could have been invented for this establishment, which is most suitable for grand and special occasions. *2 Rue Charles Buls (Grand'Place), tel. 02/511–8244. Jacket and tie required.*

*Reservations advised. AE, DC, MC, V. Closed Sat.
lunch, Sun., Aug., Christmas week.*

★ ⓲ **Ogenblik.** This small, split-level restaurant off the Galerie
$$ Royales has all the appurtenances of an old-time bistro:
green-shaded lamps over marble-topped tables, sawdust
on the floor, and waiters in T-shirts. However, there is
nothing casual about the cuisine: boned chicken with
sweetbreads and goose liver, millefeuille of lobster and
salmon, saddle of lamb with fresh young vegetables. The
selection of Beaujolais is particularly good. Portions are
more than ample. Unpretentious and open until midnight,
Ogenblik is a fun place to relax with your peers in the
Grand'Place area. *1 Galerie des Princes, tel. 02/511–6151.
Casual dress. No reservations after 8 PM. AE, DC, MC, V.
Closed Sun.*

Uptown

★ ❶ **Bruneau.** Chef Jean-Pierre Bruneau remains relatively
$$$$ unknown outside Belgium, in spite of having earned a rare
three-star rating from Michelin. His elegant domain is
near the huge church of the Basilique, a 10–15 minute cab
ride north from downtown, where Flemish begins to be
the favored language. The paneled, Louis XVI-style main
dining room is filled with round tables, perfect for private
conversations; the upstairs has facilities for private par-
ties. New creations are marked by an asterisk on the
menu; you'll find specialties such as scallops served warm
with coriander and lobster sauce, or soufflé-of-prawn lasa-
gna. Desserts are fabulous, and the wine list is superb.
Choosing the seasonal, fixed-price menu cuts your bill al-
most in half. If you want to impress local VIPS (especially
if they are Flemish) with your knowledge of the Brussels
culinary scene, this is the place to come. *73 Ave. Broustin,
tel. 02/427–6978. Jacket and tie required. Reservations re-
quired. AE, DC, MC, V. Closed Tues. dinner, Wed., mid-
June to mid-July, Christmas week.*

❺ **Le Camboge.** This Cambodian restaurant, tastefully deco-
$$ rated with Kampuchean statuary, is on a corner a few
blocks from the advertising agencies of Avenue Louise.
It's packed for lunch and dinner seven days a week with a
youngish crowd, mostly professional, good-natured, and
nearly 100% Belgian. Try the *banh-xeo* (rice pancakes
with pork and shrimp), *a moc* (chicken en papillote with
Cambodian seasoning), or prawns with cashew nuts.
There's a perfectly acceptable white house wine, or you
can opt for beer or jasmine tea. Good for a pleasant lunch
or for nonostentatious entertaining. *77 Rue Washington,
tel. 02/537–7098. Casual dress. Reservations advised.
AE, DC, MC, V.*

★ ❹ **La Charlotte aux Pommes.** The best of a number of good
$$ restaurants on the lively Place du Châtelain and in the im-
mediate vicinity, La Charlotte aux Pommes is poised half-
way between its bistro past and a beckoning future as
"grand maison." The lunchtime crowd is heavy on busi-
ness types in earnest conversation about positioning
and strategies. Many choose the fixed-price *Dejeuner
d'Affaire*, a great value at BF 690, as is the four-course
Menu Plaisir (served both at lunch and dinner) at BF 990.
The talented young chef, Axel Vijt, serves up a cuisine
that is both nouvelle and substantial; entrées include
lightly grilled scallops, raviolis stuffed with escargot or

salmon, and great lamb chops. Desserts are imaginative too. Service is brisk and very friendly. If you intend to talk business, ask for a round table. *40 Place du Châte-lain, tel. 02/640–5388. Jacket and tie required. Reservations advised. AE, D, MC, V. Closed Sat., Sun., Carnival week, mid-Aug.–mid-Sept.*

❾ L'Elephant Bleu. The brainchild of Karl Steppe, a Belgian
$$ antiques dealer turned restaurateur, this Thai establishment is in the vanguard of the Oriental food renaissance in Brussels. A wealth of Thai statuettes and objets d'art fill the garden-like dining room, and the Thai staff members wear beautiful silk costumes. The young, well-to-do clientele come here for refined exotic flavors, at once sweet and spicy. Try the citronella-flavored shrimp soup, stuffed chicken wings, or *kaotang natang* (a fresh seafood salad with small rice cakes). Located in the southern part of town, towards Waterloo, (a 15-minute cab ride from the center), this is a good place to entertain junior managerial staff. *1120 Chaussée de Waterloo, tel. 02/374–4962. Casual dress. Reservations advised. AE, DC, MC, V. Closed Sat. lunch.*

★ ㉒ La Maison du Boeuf. It's been a long time since this Hilton
$$$ restaurant served only prime cuts from Texas. The spacious, attractive dining room overlooking Parc d'Egmont attracts officials from the Ministry of Foreign Affairs (across the park), as well as businesspeople from nearby offices. Turbot in champagne sauce, fillet of sole with crayfish sabayon, and young pigeon stuffed with black mushrooms are among the specialties—as is, still, sirloin steak. This restaurant's service is fast and attentive, and the wine list is excellent, making it eminently suitable for business luncheons and dinners. The Library, a private dining room, may be reserved. *Hotel Hilton, 38 Blvd. de Waterloo, tel. 02/513–8877. Jacket and tie required. Reservations advised. AE, DC, MC, V.*

❻ Rick's Café Americain. As you might expect, this Avenue
$$ Louise tavern, now into its second decade, is decorated with old movie posters and publicity photos. Unlike Humphrey Bogart's place in Casablanca, however, the fare here is pure American: hamburgers, chili, and pizza, followed by Grandma's apple pie. The quality is high, and the rushed-but-friendly staff always has time to refill your coffee cup. Otherwise, beverages run to beer and booze, and customers are three deep at the bar at peak hours. On Sundays, American families show up in droves for the huge brunch. *344 Ave. Louise, tel. 02/647–7530. Jacket and tie at lunch; informal evenings and weekends. Reservations advised. AE, DC, MC, V.*

★ ❽ La Truffe Noire. So far, few foreign visitors have discov-
$$$$ ered this upscale restaurant off Avenue Louise, although it began to attract a loyal following of local business leaders, diplomats, and European Commission panjandrums soon after it opened in 1988. The cuisine draws on classic Italian and modern French cooking. A favorite appetizer is carpaccio, prepared at the table by owner/maître d'Luigi Ciciriello and served with long strips of truffle and Parmesan cheese. Entrées include ravioli filled with minced truffles and wild mushrooms, and hake sautéed with herbs with a prawn bisque. A consummate maître d', Luigi makes all guests feel important and cared for, as does his well-groomed and attentive young staff. Tables

are well spaced for privacy. Guests taken to the Truffe
Noire will be impressed by your sophisticated choice, but
beware—they may also get the idea that money is no object. *12 Blvd. de la Cambre, tel. 02/640-4422. Jacket and
tie required. Reservations required. AE, DC, MC, V.
Closed Sat. lunch, Sun., last two weeks of Aug., Christmas week.*

⑩ **Villa Lorraine.** Generations of American business travel-
$$$$ ers have been introduced to the three-hour Belgian lunch
at the opulent Villa on the edge of the Bois de la Cambre.
The green terrace room, light and airy, always attracts
more diners than the stuffier inside rooms. The French
cuisine may be more classic than at other great Brussels
restaurants, but you still dine supremely on such standbys
as red mullet in artichoke vinaigrette, crayfish cooked in
chicken stock with white wine and a dash of Armagnac, or
Bresse duckling with peaches and green pepper. For dessert, the headwaiter might propose tiny slices of half a
dozen dreamy cakes. There is a comfortable bar with
leather armchairs for pre- and post-prandial drinks. A
half-price set luncheon menu is a good value. *Villa Lorraine, 75 Ave. du Vivier-d'Oie, tel. 02/374-3163. Jacket
and tie required. Reservations advised. AE, DC, MC, V.
Closed Sun., July.*

FREE TIME

Fitness

Hotel Facilities
The most complete hotel fitness centers are those at the
SAS Royal Hotel (tel. 02/511-8888), the **Brussels Sheraton**
(tel. 02/219-3400), and the **Holiday Inn** (Brussels National
Airport, 1920 Diergem, tel. 02/720-5865). You don't have
to be a guest to use the facilities: A session at the SAS
Royal costs BF 750; at the Sheraton, BF 800; and at the
Holiday Inn, BF 500.

Health Clubs
A full range of facilities can be found at the **California Club**
(280-300 Chaussée d'Ixelles, tel. 02/640-9344), which
costs BF 250, and the **European Athletic City** (25A Ave.
Winston Churchill, tel. 02/345-3077), which costs BF 300.

Jogging
For in-town jogging, use the **Parc de Bruxelles;** for more
extensive workouts, head for the **Bois de la Cambre.**

Shopping

The classic Belgian souvenir is lace. Authentic handmade
lace is available at **F. Rubbrecht** (23 Grand'Place, tel.
02/512-0218); a large selection of both old and modern lace
can be found at the **Manufacture Belge de Dentelles** (6-8
Galerie de la Reine, tel. 02/511-4477). Fine hand-dipped
chocolates, another popular gift selection, are made and
sold at **Wittamer** (6 Grand Sablon, tel. 02/512-3742),
Nihoul (298-302 Ave. Louise, tel. 02/648-3796), and **Mary**
(180 Rue Royale, tel. 02/217-4500). If your tastes run to
tableware, you'll find a substantial range of Val Saint-
Lambert crystal pieces at **Art et Selection** (83 Rue Marché-
aux-Herbes, tel. 02/511-8448).

The 150-year-old **Galeries Royales,** just off the Grand'-Place, was Europe's first shopping arcade. The area is lined with old, staid, and expensive shops. In contrast, the **Rue Neuve** and **City 2,** on Place Rogier, are fun and inexpensive (though women alone should avoid these areas after dark). **Grand Sablon** is an elegant square surrounded by picture galleries and antiques shops; it is also host to a lively antiques market every Saturday and Sunday morning. The most fashionable boutiques and shops are along **Avenue de la Toison d'Or** and its arcades, and **Avenue Louise.** The latter is a prime area for window shopping and has plenty of cafés for the weary.

The best department stores in town are **Inno,** at three locations (111 Rue Neuve, tel. 02/211–2111; 41 Chaussée d'Ixelles, tel. 02/512–7800; and 699 Chaussée de Waterloo, tel. 02/345–3890), and **Sarmalux** (15 Rue Neuve, tel. 02/212–8714 and 12 Ave. Louise, tel. 02/513–8494).

Virtually all of the top French and Italian name designers have boutiques in Brussels. **Olivier Strelli** (72 Ave. Louise, tel. 02/511–2134) is the best-known Belgian fashion designer; **Bouvy** (52 Ave. de la Toison d'Or, tel. 02/513–0748) carries a selection of upscale ready-to-wear for both women and men. **Dujardin** (8–10 Ave. Louise, tel. 02/513–6070) is an outstanding shop specializing in pricey clothing for children; **Delvaux** (31 Galerie de la Reine, tel. 02/512–7198 and 24 Ave. de la Toision d'Or, tel. 02/513–0502) carries handbags and other leather goods of their own design, beautifully executed, and quite expensive.

Diversions

Art Nouveau was Belgium's contribution to the architecture and decorative art of *la belle époque* in the early years of this century. The architect Victor Horta was its leading exponent, and his house is now the **Horta Museum** (25 Rue Americaine, tel. 02/537–1692). Other houses by Horta and his friends dot the city. Architectural tours are arranged by Arau (tel. 02/513–4761).

Bois de la Cambre, a 300-acre wooded park, begins at the end of Avenue Louise; thousands of Bruxellois use it for walking, jogging, riding, playing with kids and dogs, or just plain lazing about. The park merges into the Forêt de Soignes, a 10,000-acre beech forest.

Bruges, a perfectly preserved medieval city, is one of Europe's outstanding travel attractions. Only an hour from Brussels by rail or road, it's a good choice for a weekend getaway. It has a charming array of small canal-side hotels, including De Orangerie (10 Kartuizerinnenstraat, tel. 050/34–16–49) and Die Swaene (1 Steenhouwersdijk, tel. 050/34–27–98), as well as several wonderful restaurants.

The **Grand'Place,** with its 15th-century Town Hall and 17th-century guild houses in Flemish Baroque, is the glory of Brussels. This is where the locals go to enjoy parades, concerts, festivals, and fine restaurants. The tourist office in the Town Hall can supply private guides (BF 2,200 for three hours) and booklets on the area. On a street corner three blocks south you'll find the saucy statuette of Manneken Pis, originally used as a public drinking fountain.

The **Musée Royale d'Art Ancien** (Place Royale 1, tel. 02/513–9630) contains a huge collection of old masters, including some spectacular Breughel, Memling, Petrus Christus, and Hieronymus Bosch. The adjoining new Musée d'Art Moderne is architecturally exciting; it houses mostly modern Belgian art including Permeke, Ensor, Magritte, and Delvaux.

Waterloo, 12 miles south of Brussels, has become a favored residential area for American expatriates. The 1815 battlefield, to the south, is dominated by the Lion Monument. Wellington's and Napoleon's headquarters are both museums. The new Visitors Center features audiovisuals and scale models of the battle. For information on guided tours, call the Guides 1815 (tel. 02/385–0625).

The Arts

Opera and ballet have enjoyed a spectacular renaissance in recent years, and the restored opera house, **Théâtre Royal de la Monnaie** (Place de la Monnaie, tel. 02/218–1211), is a gem. Operas and other spectacles are also often staged at the **Cirque Royal** (81 Rue de l'Enseignement, tel. 02/218–2015). International classical concert artists and groups perform at the **Palais des Beaux Arts** (23 Rue Ravenstein, tel. 02/ 512–5045); pop and rock groups appear at **Forest National** (36 Ave. de la Globe, tel. 02/345–9050). Among French-speaking theaters, the avant-garde are the most interesting, especially **Théâtre 140** (140 Ave. Eugene Plasky, tel. 02/733–9708) and **Théâtre Varia** (78 Rue du Sceptre, tel. 02/640–8258).

Most Brussels movie theaters are modern, featuring comfortable chairs and Dolby sound, not to mention lobby bars. At any given time, there will be 25–30 English-language movies showing. The best theater uptown is **Acropole** (Galerie de la Toison d'Or, tel. 02/511–4328). The new **Kinepolis** (Heysel Bruparck, near the northern ring road, tel. 02/479–5252) boasts 26 theaters under one roof. Look for listings in *The Bulletin*.

Brussels' English-language news weekly, *The Bulletin*, contains complete listings of all events. For theater tickets, try **TIB Tourist and Information Office** (Brussels City Hall, Grand'Place, tel. 02/513–8940).

After Hours

Cafés in Brussels serve both coffee and alcohol. There is at least one on almost every street corner, and many of them stay open until the last customers have left. The favorite tipple is beer, which Belgium produces in staggering varieties. Brussels is short on nightlife other than at the cafés. At heart, this remains a large, provincial town.

Bars and Lounges
The **Hilton Bar** (tel. 02/513–8877) is a central meeting point, almost always packed with people for drinks before dinner; the Sheraton's **Rendezvous Bar** (tel. 02/219–3400) offers more privacy; and the Royal Windsor's **Waterloo Bar** (tel. 02/511–4215) exudes a British ambience. **Falstaff** (25 Rue Henri Maus, tel. 02/511–9877) is a famous and

crowded old tavern in Art Nouveau style. **La Fleur en Papier Doré** (53 Rue des Alexiens, tel. 02/511–1659) draws a crowd that is attracted by its surrealistic decor. **De Ultime Hallicunatie** (316 Rue Royale, tel. 02/217–0614) is a handsome Art Nouveau bar with a youngish and mostly Flemish clientele; it's a good place for dinner and dancing on Fridays and Saturdays. **Le Nemrod** (61 Blvd. de Waterloo, tel. 02/511–1127) has a fireplace, and hunting trophies line the walls; its location is handy both as a meeting place and for a drink after a show.

Jazz Clubs

The Brussels Jazz Club (13 Grand'Place, tel. 02/512–4093) is open nightly except Wed. and Sun. Most other venues are cheap and cheerful cafés with local jazz bands blowing up a storm on the weekends. Check out the **Bierodrome** (21 Place Fernand Cocq, tel. 02/512–0456), **Travers** (11 Rue Traversière, tel. 02/218–1509), and **Preservation Hall** (3 Rue de Londres, tel. 02/511–0304). *The Bulletin* has the details.

Discos

Discos come and go in Brussels. Here are a few where the clientele is not too embarrassingly young: **Le Mirano** (38 Chaussée de Louvain, tel. 02/218–5772) draws a self-styled jet set (Sat. only); **Le Cocoon Club** (Le Vaudeville, 14 Rue de la Montagne, tel. 02/512–4997) is another trendy spot; and **Crocodile Club** (Hotel Royal Windsor, tel. 02/ 511–4215) attracts an international clientale.

Nightclubs

Among a not terribly distinguished lot, **Show Point** (14 Place Stephanie, tel. 02/511–5364) puts on the flashiest striptease. Other clubs are located in nearby Rue Capitaine Crespel, cheek by jowl with the English-language Anglican Holy Trinity church.

Chicago

by Elizabeth Gardner

For many, the name "Chicago" still conjures up images of gangsters and tommy guns, stockyards and packing-houses; in the popular imagination it's a grimy industrial town whose climate is severe and whose denizens are rough-and-ready workmen. Few non-Chicagoans know that the city's motto is *Urbs in Horto,* "City in a Garden," and first-time visitors are often astonished to see Grant Park's acres of blooms, sailboats gliding on Lake Michigan, and lush green parkland along the lakefront; to find elegant and sophisticated shops along Michigan Avenue's Magnificent Mile; and to view handsome and impressive buildings, old and new, designed by world-class architects.

Like many American cities, Chicago prospered in the 1980s as middle-class urban pioneers migrated from the safety of the suburbs back to the city. In the 1960s, Lincoln Park, along the lakefront north of downtown, was plagued by crime and blight; now it's inhabited by bankers, physicians, lawyers, and other professionals who restored the 1890s-vintage two-family houses and are snapping up new $300,000 town houses. Upscale buyers are spilling into adjacent neighborhoods to the north and west as well, even invading a former industrial corridor along the Kennedy Expressway. The city's many ethnic neighborhoods on the northwest, west, and south sides—black, Mexican, Polish, Irish, Italian, Ukrainian, and Indian, to name a few—remain relatively stable, and gentrification has not yet disenfranchised the poor.

Chicago's almost even split between black and white residents (about 40% of each, with the remaining 20% divided among Hispanic and "other") doesn't diminish political acrimony and violence, though visitors are unlikely to encounter overt racism in the downtown and Near North Side neighborhoods that contain the city's major hotels and businesses.

Chicago enjoys a diverse economy. Although packinghouses, factories, and steel mills are gone, many corporate greats, including Quaker Oats, Helene Curtis, and Johnson Publishing, remain. The city is a hub for retailing, banking and insurance, commodities trading, drug and hospital supply companies, advertising, printing, and educational publishing. The suburbs to the north and west are home to many corporate headquarters. Chicago also has a large concentration of high-tech medical centers, including Rush-Presbyterian-St. Lukes, Northwestern Memorial Medical Center, Loyola University Medical Center, and the University of Chicago Hospitals.

The community was shaken when Sears Roebuck, the city's largest employer, threatened to leave Illinois for more hospitable economic climes. A package of tax breaks and incentives persuaded the company to stay in the Chicago area.

The center of Chicago business is the Loop, so-called because of the elevated train tracks that loop around its borders (Lake St., Wabash Ave., Van Buren St., and Wells St.). The Loop is home to the financial district, several major retailers, City Hall, and state and federal offices. (Helmut Jahn's futuristic State of Illinois Building at Randolph and Clark streets, also called Spaceship Chicago, is part of the redevelopment of the north Loop.) Most of the city's historic skyscrapers are in this area. The Loop deteriorated in the 1960s and 1970s as major retailers fled and downtown movie theaters were taken over by porno and kung-fu flicks, but it's slowly being reclaimed by new development and renovation.

Rampant office and hotel development is reshaping Chicago's other main business district, North Michigan Avenue. Travelers are likely to see scaffolding and torn-up streets for several years to come.

Top Employers

Employer	Type of Enterprise	Parent*/ Headquarters
Abbott Laboratories	Health care supply	Abbott Park, IL
Baxter International	Health care supply	Deerfield, IL
Commonwealth Edison	Utility	Chicago
Dominick's Finer Foods	Grocery	Chicago
Illinois Bell	Telephone	Ameritech/ Chicago
Jewel Food Stores	Grocery	American Stores Co./Salt Lake City, UT
Marshall Field	Retail	Dayton-Hudson Corp./Minneapolis
Sears Roebuck and Co.	Retail	Chicago
United Airlines	Transportation	UAL Corp./Elk Grove Village, IL

*if applicable

ESSENTIAL INFORMATION

Climate

Strong winds off Lake Michigan can be pleasantly cool in the summer or bone-chilling in the winter. (Chicago's nickname, The Windy City, was inspired not by the weather but by the hot air emitted by its politicians.) The height of summer usually brings temperatures in the 80s and 90s and humidity up to 100%. Winter temperatures range from the mid-30s to well below zero and can change from one to the other overnight. Snow has been scarce for the past few years, but the occasional blizzard and other sudden storms often cause travel delays.

What follows are the average daily maximum and minimum temperatures for Chicago.

Jan.	32F	0C	Feb.	34F	1C	Mar.	43F	6C
	18	−8		20	−7		29	−2
Apr.	55F	13C	May	65F	18C	June	75F	24C
	40	4		50	10		60	16
July	81F	27C	Aug.	79F	26C	Sept.	73F	23C
	66	19		65	18		58	14
Oct.	61F	16C	Nov.	47F	8C	Dec.	36F	2C
	47	8		34	1		23	−5

Airports

Chicago is served by two major airports. **O'Hare International Airport,** about 20 miles northwest of downtown, is one of the world's busiest. All major airlines, both national and international, serve O'Hare. It's big and sprawling; expect a walk of up to 20 minutes if you have to change carriers. Free shuttle buses on the lower (arrival) level take passengers from terminal to terminal and to remote parking lots. **Midway Airport,** about seven miles southwest of downtown, is more pleasant—much smaller and less congested. It's a hub for Midway Airlines, but other carriers use it as well. Some commuter planes and private aircraft fly out of tiny **Meigs Field,** on the lakefront just south of downtown.

Airport Business Facilities

O'Hare International Airport. The **O'Hare Hilton Hotel** (across the street from Terminal 2, tel. 312/686–8000) has a business center on the lower level with fax machines, photocopying, notary public, secretarial service, cash advance, and conference rooms with catering service. It also has day rates for rooms and a health club. **Skyberg** (in the Rotunda between Terminals 2 and 3, tel. 312/686–6101) has five conference rooms with catering service, and fax machines, photocopier, and secretarial services.

Midway Airport. There are no business facilities at this airport.

Airlines

All major domestic airlines serve Chicago, and it is a hub city for United, Midway, and American.

Air Canada, tel. 800/422–6232.
American, tel. 800/433–7300.
British Airways, tel. 800/247–9297.
Continental, tel. 312/686–6500 or 800/525–0280.
Delta, tel. 312/346–5300 or 800/221–1212.
Midway, tel. 312/767–3400 or 800/621–5700.
Northwest, tel. 312/349–4900 or 800/225–2525.
Pan Am, tel. 800/221–1111.
TWA, tel. 312/938–3000 or 800/221–2000.
United, tel. 312/569–3000 or 800/241–6522.

Between the Airport and Downtown

By Taxi
Metered taxis connect both airports to Near North Side and downtown Chicago. Each O'Hare terminal has a taxi stand; there is one taxi stand at Midway. Cost from O'Hare: $20–$30, plus tip; from Midway: about $12, plus tip. The Kennedy Expressway is the only route from O'Hare to the city; the trip takes 20–30 minutes at best, but can stretch to more than an hour during rush hours (7–9 AM and 3:30–7:30 PM) or bad weather. From Midway, the best route is north on Cicero Avenue to the Stevenson Expressway, then east to Lake Shore Drive and north to downtown and the Near North Side. The trip takes 20–30 minutes.

By Bus
Continental Air Transport minivans (tel. 312/454–7799) connect most major hotels with both Midway and O'Hare. The fare from O'Hare is $10.75; from Midway, $8. The O'Hare trip can take more than an hour because buses make several stops en route; the Midway run takes about 30 minutes. Vans operate from O'Hare from 6 AM to 11:30 PM, from Midway from 8 AM to 8:30 PM. Check with the company for exact travel times.

By Public Transportation
The Chicago Transit Authority's rapid transit station at O'Hare is in the underground concourse near terminal 3; you can reach it from any terminal without going outside.

If you're heading to the Near North Side or downtown and don't have much luggage, this is an inexpensive way to go, and, at rush hour, probably the fastest. Cost: $1.25. The first stop downtown is at Washington and Dearborn streets; the trip takes 40–50 minutes. From here you can take a taxi to your hotel or change to other rapid transit lines. Note, however, that the CTA train is best avoided late at night. There is no convenient public transportation from Midway Airport.

Car Rentals

All major national companies have booths at O'Hare and Midway.

Avis, tel. 312/694–5600 or 800/331–1212.
Budget, tel. 312/686–6800 or 800/527–0700.
Hertz, tel. 312/686–7272 or 800/654–3131.
National, tel. 312/694–4640 or 800/227–7368.
Sears, tel. 312/686–6780 or 800/527–0770.
Thrifty, tel. 708/298–3383 or 800/367–2277.

CHICAGO O'HARE INTERNATIONAL AIRPORT

Emergencies

Doctors
Northwestern Memorial Hospital's **HealthPlus** (Two Illinois Center Concourse, 233 N. Michigan Ave., tel. 312/649–2390) is open 8–6.

Dentists
The **Chicago Dental Society Emergency Service** (tel. 312/726–4321) makes 24-hour referrals.

Hospitals
In the Near North Side, **Northwestern Memorial Hospital** (Superior St. at Fairbanks Ct., tel. 312/908–2000); near the Loop, **Rush-Presbyterian-St. Lukes Medical Center** (1753 W. Congress Pkwy., tel. 312/942–5000).

Important Addresses and Numbers

Audiovisual rentals. Mills Recording Systems (316 N. Michigan Ave., tel. 312/332–4116), Video Replay, (118 W. Grand Ave., tel. 312/822–0221).

Chamber of Commerce (200 N. LaSalle St., tel. 312/580–6900).

Computer rentals. Computerland (153 E. Ohio St., tel. 312/661–0160), Computer Rental Centers (130 E. Randolph St., tel. 312/938–0087).

Convention and exhibition center (McCormick Pl., 2300 S. Lake Shore Dr., tel. 312/791–7000).

Fax services. Instant Printing Centers (200 S. Clark St., the Loop, tel. 312/726–6275; 180 N. LaSalle St., the Loop, tel. 312/263–6212; at the Merchandise Mart, tel. 312/670–2330).

Formal-wear rentals. Gingiss Formal Wear (185 N. Wabash Ave., tel. 312/263–7071), Seno Formal Wear (6 E. Randolph St., tel. 312/782–1115).

Gift shops. Chocolates: Godiva (10 S. LaSalle St., tel. 312/855–1588; Water Tower Place, 845 N. Michigan Ave., tel.

312/280–1133), Neuchatel (Avenue Atrium, 900 N. Michigan Ave., tel. 312/787–1301); Florists: Alice's Garden (Avenue Atrium, 900 N. Michigan Ave., tel. 312/649–2100), Amlings (151 E. Wacker Dr., tel. 312/265–4647; 2 N. Riverside Plaza, tel. 312/265–4647).

Graphic design studio. Artisan (575 W. Madison St., tel. 312/902–2969).

Hairstylists. Unisex: The Beauty Salon at Marshall Field (835 N. Michigan Ave., Water Tower Place, tel. 312/951–9054; 111 N. State St., the Loop, tel. 312/781–3651), Palmer House Hair Salon (17 E. Monroe St., tel. 312/201–0202), Jonathan's (875 N. Michigan Ave., tel. 312/664–9119).

Health and fitness clubs. *See* Fitness, below.

Information hot lines. Time (tel. 312/976–1616), financial markets (tel. 312/976–8100), stock market (tel. 312/976–3434), traffic (tel. 312/976–8646), sports (tel. 312/976–8383), toll-free entertainment information (tel. 312/FINEART).

Limousine services. Chicago Limousine Service (tel. 312/726–1035), Gold Coast Regency (tel. 312/227–1000).

Liquor stores. Chalet Wine and Cheese Shop (40 E. Delaware Pl., tel. 312/787–8555), Sam's Wines and Liquors (1000 W. North Ave., tel. 312/664–4394), Zimmerman's (213 W. Grand Ave., tel. 312/332–0012). Both Sam's and Zimmerman's deliver large orders.

Mail delivery, overnight. DHL Worldwide Express (tel. 708/456–3200), Federal Express (tel. 312/559–9000), TNT Skypak (312/992–2090), UPS (tel. 708/990–2900), U.S. Post Office Express Mail (tel. 312/765–3525).

Messenger services. Arrow (tel. 312/489–6688), Cannonball (tel. 312/829–1234).

Office space rental. U.S. Office (333 W. Wacker Dr., tel. 312/444–2000).

Pharmacies, late-night. Walgreen's (757 N. Michigan Ave., tel. 312/664–8686, open 24 hours; 25 S. Wabash Ave., tel. 312/641–1856).

Radio stations, all-news. WBBM 780 AM; WMAQ 670 AM.

Secretarial services. A-EC Secretarial Services (39 S. LaSalle St., tel. 312/236–6847), Executive Word Processing (612 N. Michigan Ave., tel. 312/337–7535), The Paper Works (105 W. Madison St., tel. 312/726–3442).

Stationery supplies. Order from Horder (111 W. Washington Blvd., tel. 312/648–7216; 211 E. Ontario St., tel. 312/648–7223; and Merchandise Mart Plaza, tel. 312/648–7205).

Taxis. Flash Cabs (tel. 312/561–1444), Yellow and Checker cabs (tel. 312/829–4222).

Theater tickets. *See* The Arts, below.

Train information. Amtrak (Jackson and Canal Sts., tel. 800/872–7245), Metropolitan Rail, suburban commuter trains (tel. 312/836–7000).

Travel agents. AAA Travel Agency (111 E. Wacker Dr., tel. 312/861–0771), Ask Mr. Foster (645 N. Michigan Ave., tel. 312/828–9230; 203 N. LaSalle St., tel. 312/726–4799).

Weather (tel. 312/976–1212).

LODGING

Chicago hotels are clustered in three main areas: the Loop, or downtown; Michigan Avenue and the Near North Side (that is, near the Loop); and around O'Hare Airport.

In general, the glossiest and most expensive hotels are in the Near North Side, where there has been a surge of hotel construction in the last decade. Many trade associations, advertising agencies, publishers, and television studios have their offices here. Michigan Avenue, the main drag of the Near North Side, is also Chicago's shopping mecca. Just to the west of the Near North Side is the River North neighborhood, Chicago's SoHo, bounded by Clark Street on the east and the Chicago River on the west. Art galleries abound here, along with boutiques and photography and design studios.

The Loop, or downtown, is home to city, state, and federal government offices, the financial district, and many law firms. Most Loop hotels are older and often less expensive than those in the Near North Side. Major cultural attractions—Orchestra Hall, the Art Institute, the Field Museum of Natural History, the Auditorium Theater, and the Lyric Opera—are all in the Loop, as are many of Chicago's renowned architectural masterpieces.

The Merchandise Mart, a magnet for wholesale buyers, is at the Chicago River between Wells and Orleans streets, about equidistant between downtown and the Near North Side. The nearest hotels are the Nikko and the Holiday Inn Mart Plaza.

McCormick Place, south of the Loop on the lakefront, is the largest convention center in the nation. Only one hotel, the McCormick Center, is within walking distance of McCormick Place, but all major trade shows provide free shuttle service to Loop and Near North hotels. McCormick Place is 10–15 minutes by taxi from most hotels. The McCormick Place Annex is right across Lake Shore Drive from the main building.

Women traveling alone may prefer to stay in the Near North Side; despite City Hall's efforts at rejuvenation, the Loop tends to be deserted and a little spooky at night.

A number of the hotels listed below offer corporate rates and weekend discounts; inquire when making reservations.

Highly recommended lodgings in each price category are indicated by a star ★.

Category	Cost*
$$$$ (Very Expensive)	over $150
$$$ (Expensive)	$100–$150
$$ (Moderate)	under $100

All prices are for a standard double room, single occupancy, excluding 12.4% tax.

Numbers in the margin correspond to numbered hotel locations on the Chicago Dining and Lodging maps.

Near North Side/Michigan Avenue

★ ❷
$$$
Claridge. If you're paying your own expenses and looking for something simple but comfortable, this small, recently renovated 1930s hotel is a good value. Public areas are tastefully decorated in dark wood and green marble; the attractive contemporary-style guest rooms tend toward mauves, grays, and other neutral colors. Corner rooms are the most spacious. In-room amenities aren't lavish, but almost any toilet article is available from the concierge. Most business needs can be accommodated, too. The Gold Coast location is quiet, but offers easy access to the Rush Street singles scene and North Michigan Avenue. The house restaurant, J.P.'s, serves outstanding, moderately priced seafood. *A Golden Tulip hotel. 1244 N. Dearborn Pkwy., 60610, tel. 312/787–4980 or 800/245–1258, fax 312/266–0978. Gen. manager, Michael Depoy. 173 rooms, 3 suites. AE, CB, D, DC, MC, V.*

★ ❻
$$$$
Drake. The grandest of Chicago's landmark hotels, the Drake is popular with upscale business travelers and visiting heads of state. Built on the lakefront in the style of an Italian Renaissance palace, the hotel opened in 1920 and has been listed in the National Register of Historic Places since 1981. The location across from Oak Street Beach offers easy access to the lakefront jogging path. Public areas are lavishly decorated, with oak accents and crystal chandeliers; the lobby boasts a spectacular marble fountain. Rooms are generally spacious and decorated in traditional style, with floral prints and comfortable, upholstered furniture; lakefront views cost more, but non-lakefront rooms tend to be bigger. Bathrooms include robes, hairdryers, and scales. The staff is friendly and helpful; elevators are a little slow despite the presence of elevator operators. The Cape Cod Room and the Oak Terrace (*see* Business Breakfasts, below) serve reliable fare; there's tea in the Palm Court in the late afternoon. *A Hilton International hotel. 140 E. Walton Pl., 60611, tel. 312/787–2200 or 800/445–8667, fax 312/787–1431. 535 rooms, 65 suites. Gen. manager, Victor Burt. AE, CB, D, DC, MC, V.*

❼
$$$$
Four Seasons. A hotel-within-a-skyscraper, this lavish $300-million hostelry has a seventh-floor lobby with the ambience and attention to detail of an 18th-century English manor house, complete with a wood-burning fireplace. Handcrafted woodwork, luxurious, Oriental-style floral carpets, and botanical prints are featured throughout public areas and rooms. There's even a touch of humor—life-size Seward Johnson sculptures of travelers and workmen. Standard rooms are small, though bathrooms are large and well appointed. Most rooms have ter-

rific views of the city or the lake; there's no extra charge for a lake view. The Four Seasons has one of the more luxurious health clubs in town, and an excellent restaurant, The Seasons (*see* Business Breakfasts, below), that features creative American cuisine. The Avenue Atrium, the more upscale of Michigan Avenue's two vertical malls, is in the same building. *A Four Seasons hotel. 120 E. Delaware Pl., tel. 312/280–8800 or 800/332–3442, fax 312/280–9184. Gen. manager, Hans Williman. 344 rooms, 121 suites, 16 apartments. AE, CB, D, DC, MC, V.*

❺ Mayfair Regent. A small hotel in the European tradition, $$$$ the Mayfair Regent is popular with visiting concert artists. It's on the lakefront, and many of its well-appointed rooms have spectacular views to the north and east, though a number of south-facing rooms look onto the backs of other buildings. A recent management change has brought a less formal ambience and less stringent standards of service, but the multilingual staff remains highly attentive to travelers' needs. Rooms have phones at bedside, on desks, and in the bathrooms, which are also equipped with makeup and shaving mirrors and scales. Of the Regent's two restaurants, the Ciel Bleu (*see* Business Breakfasts, below), on the top floor, offers expensive, adequate French food in a beautiful setting. *181 E. Lake Shore Dr., 60611, tel. 312/787–8500 or 800/545–4000, fax 312/664–6194. Gen. manager, Michael Burchett. 200 rooms, 30 suites. AE, CB, D, DC, MC, V.*

❸ Le Meridien. High-tech is the hallmark of this sleek gray $$$$ midrise building, completed in 1988. Services are what you'd expect from a hotel in this price category: Each guest room has a CD player, videocassette recorder, and several two-line phones, with a hot line to the video-rental store next door. Walls are extra thick, and the music systems have preset volume controls so that your neighbors won't blast you out. Every room lamp is on a rheostat for perfect lighting conditions. Phones are equipped for conference calling. Separate bathtubs and showers are standard in all bathrooms. The hotel's equally glossy meeting rooms have state-of-the-art audiovisual equipment operated through space-age control panels. Public areas feature gray marble, original photographs by Robert Mapplethorpe, and piped-in classic jazz. *21 E. Bellevue Pl., 60611, tel. 312/266–2100 or 800/266–2101, fax 312/266–2141. Gen. manager, Ken Withrow. 247 rooms, 41 suites. AE, CB, DC, MC, V.*

❶ Omni Ambassador East. The renowned Pump Room, the $$$$ restaurant where celebrities have their pictures taken in Booth One, put the Ambassador East on the map; elegance, charm, and gracious service keep it there. Located in the residential Gold Coast neighborhood, it's slightly off the beaten business track (about a 10–15 cab ride from the Loop); it's popular with movie stars and other celebrities, as well as with business travelers who want to get away from the bustle of the Loop and Michigan Avenue. The lobby has an Old World elegance, with crystal chandeliers, marble floors, and curving banisters. Rooms have reproductions of 19th-century American furnishings. They vary in size and shape, consistent with the building's 1920s vintage, but all are comfortable. Many members of the staff have been here a long time. *1301 N. State Pkwy.,*

NEAR NORTH SIDE CHICAGO

W. Schiller St.

N Dearborn St.

N. State Parkway

1

2

E Division St.

N. Clark St.

U.S. 41

Lake Shore Dr.

Lake Michigan

0   440 yards

0   400 meters

N

3

Michigan Ave.

Oak

4

6

5

V. Oak St.

W. Walton St.

E. Walton St.

N. Rush St.

**Washington
Square**

7

E. Delaware St.

8

9

E. Chestnut St.

10

11

Pearson St.

N. Dearborn St.

12

*Lake Sh
Park*

13

E. Superior St.

N. State St.

N. Wabash Ave.

N. Rush St.

E. Huron St.

14

E. Erie St.

17

18 **19**

E. Ontario St.

E. Ohio St.

22

E. Grand St.

E. Illinois St.

St.

Kinzie St.

N

Chicago River

DOWNTOWN CHICAGO

Lodging

Chicago Hilton and Towers, **38**
Fairmont, **30**
Holiday Inn Mart Plaza, **23**
Hotel Nikko, **25**
Hyatt Regency Chicago, **28**

McCormick Center Hotel, **39**
Midland, **34**
Palmer House, **33**
Swiss Grand Hotel, **29**

Dining

Berghoff, **36**
Billy Goat Tavern, **27**
The Everest Room, **35**

Harry Caray's, **24**
Nick's Fishmarket, **32**
Printer's Row, **37**
Shaw's Crab House and Blue Crab Lounge, **26**
Walnut Room, **31**

CHICAGO HOTEL CHART

HOTELS	Price Category	Business Services									Desk	Desk lighting	Bed lighting
		Banquet capacity	No. of meeting rooms	Secretarial services	Audiovisual equipment	Teletype news service	Computer rentals	In-room modem phone jack	All-news cable channel			
Chicago Hilton and Towers	$$$$	2100	55	✓	✓	-	✓	✓	✓	◐	●	●
Claridge	$$$	60	4	✓	✓	-	✓	✓	-	◐	●	●
Drake	$$$$	535	29	✓	✓	✓	✓	✓	✓	◐	●	●
Fairmont	$$$$	1600	14	✓	✓	-	✓	✓	✓	◐	●	●
Four Seasons	$$$$	500	18	✓	✓	-	✓	✓	✓	●	●	●
Holiday Inn Mart Plaza	$$$	700	14	-	✓	-	-	✓	✓	◐	◐	●
Hotel Nikko	$$$$	700	11	✓	✓	-	✓	✓	✓	●	●	●
Hyatt Regency Chicago	$$$$	2600	72	✓	✓	-	✓	✓	✓	○	◐	●
Hyatt Regency O'Hare	$$$$	1500	45	✓	✓	-	✓	✓	✓	●	●	●
Le Meridien	$$$$	130	6	✓	✓	-	✓	✓	✓	●	●	●
Mayfair Regent	$$$$	50	3	✓	✓	-	✓	-	✓	◐	●	●
McCormick Center	$$$	1000	20	-	✓	-	-	✓	✓	◐	●	◐
Midland	$$$	450	12	✓	✓	-	✓	✓	✓	○	○	●
O'Hare Hilton	$$$	275	56	✓	✓	-	✓	✓	✓	◐	◐	◐
Omni Ambassador East	$$$$	120	11	✓	✓	-	✓	-	✓	●	●	●
Palmer House	$$$	1600	68	✓	✓	-	✓	✓	✓	○	◐	●
Park Hyatt	$$$$	150	6	✓	✓	✓	✓	✓	✓	●	●	●
Radisson Suite Hotel O'Hare Airport	$$$	725	8	-	✓	-	-	✓	✓	●	●	●

$$$$ = over $150, **$$$** = $100-$150, **$$** = under $100.
● good, ◐ fair, ○ poor.
All hotels listed here have photocopying and fax facilities.

In-Room Amenities	Nonsmoking rooms	In-room checkout	Minibar	Pay movies	VCR/Movie rentals	Hairdryer	Toiletries	Room service	Laundry/Dry cleaning	Pressing	Hotel Amenities	Concierge	Barber/Hairdresser	Garage	Courtesy airport transport	Sauna	Pool	Exercise room
	✓	✓	✓	✓	✓	-	●	●	●	●		✓	✓	✓	-	✓	●	●
	✓	-	✓	✓	✓	✓	◐	●	●	●		✓	-	-	-	-	-	-
	✓	✓	✓	✓	-	-	●	●	●	◐		✓	✓	-	-	-	-	-
	✓	-	✓	-	-	✓	●	●	●	●		✓	-	✓	-	-	-	-
	✓	✓	✓	-	✓	✓	●	●	●	●		✓	✓	-	✓	-	●	●
	✓	-	-	✓	-	-	○	◐	●	●		-	✓	✓	-	-	◐	◐
	✓	✓	✓	✓	-	✓	●	●	●	●		✓	-	-	-	✓	-	●
	✓	✓	✓	✓	-	✓	●	●	●	●		✓	✓	●	-	-	-	-
	✓	✓	-	✓	✓	-	◐	●	●	●		✓	✓	✓	✓	✓	◐	●
	✓	✓	✓	-	✓	✓	●	●	●	●		✓	-	✓	-	-	-	-
	✓	-	✓	-	-	-	◐	◐	●	●		✓	-	-	-	✓	●	●
	✓	-	✓	-	✓	-	○	◐	●	-		✓	-	-	-	-	-	◐
	✓	✓	-	✓	-	-	◐	●	●	◐		-	-	✓	-	-	-	◐
	✓	✓	-	✓	-	✓	◐	●	●	●		✓	-	✓	-	-	-	-
	✓	✓	✓	✓	-	-	○	◐	●	●		✓	✓	✓	-	✓	●	●
	✓	-	✓	✓	-	✓	●	●	●	●		✓	-	✓	-	-	-	-
	✓	-	✓	✓	-	-	◐	○	●	◐		-	-	✓	✓	✓	●	●

Room service: ● 24-hour, ◐ 6AM-10PM, ○ other.
Laundry/Dry cleaning: ● same day, ◐ overnight, ○ other.
Pressing: ● immediate, ◐ same day, ○ other.

CHICAGO HOTEL CHART

HOTELS	Price Category	Business Services Banquet capacity	No. of meeting rooms	Secretarial services	Audiovisual equipment	Teletype news service	Computer rentals	In-room modem phone jack	All-news cable channel	Desk	Desk lighting	Bed lighting
Richmont	*$$$*	30	1	-	-	-	-	-	✓	◖	●	●
Ritz-Carlton	*$$$$*	640	6	✓	✓	-	✓	✓	✓	◖	●	●
Hotel Sofitel Chicago at O'Hare	*$$$$*	700	11	✓	✓	✓	✓	✓	✓	●	●	●
Swiss Grand	*$$$$*	450	31	✓	✓	✓	✓	-	✓	●	●	●

$$$$ = over $150, **$$$** = $100–$150, **$$** = under $100.
● good, ◖ fair, ○ poor.
All hotels listed here have photocopying and fax facilities.

| In-Room Amenities | | | | | | | | | | Hotel Amenities | | | | | | |
Nonsmoking rooms	In-room checkout	Minibar	Pay movies	VCR/Movie rentals	Hairdryer	Toiletries	Room service	Laundry/Dry cleaning	Pressing	Concierge	Barber/Hairdresser	Garage	Courtesy airport transport	Sauna	Pool	Exercise room
✓	✓	✓	✓	-	-	◐	◐	●	●	-	-	-	-	-	-	-
✓	✓	✓	✓	✓	✓	●	●	●	●	✓	-	✓	-	-	●	●
✓	✓	✓	✓	-	-	●	◐	●	●	✓	-	✓	✓	✓	●	●
✓	✓	✓	-	-	✓	●	●	●	●	✓	-	✓	-	✓	●	●

Room service: ● 24-hour, ◐ 6AM-10PM, ○ other.
Laundry/Dry cleaning: ● same day, ◐ overnight, ○ other.
Pressing: ● immediate, ◐ same day, ○ other.

60610, *tel. 312/787–7200 or 800/842–6664, fax 312/787–4760. Gen. manager, David Colella. 275 rooms, 52 suites. AE, CB, DC, MC, V.*

⑫ **Park Hyatt.** Behind the unprepossessing façade of this
$$$$ high rise are extremely luxurious (and costly) rooms, a plush, comfortable lobby filled with overstuffed armchairs, and one of the best French restaurants in the city. La Tour (*see* Business Breakfasts, below) looks out on the historic Water Tower, and is a popular spot for all types of power meals, particularly breakfast and lunch. All guest rooms were refurbished in 1989, and are done in subtle tones of peach, beige, and green. Fruit baskets, cookies, and thrice-daily maid service are standard. Bathrooms have high quality fixtures and toiletries, as well as telephones and televisions. There's no health club, but guests can request exercise bikes and rowing machines in their rooms. The Park Hyatt is a favorite with upscale corporate travelers, politicians, and movie stars. You get the kind of luxury you'd expect for the steep price tag. *800 N. Michigan Ave., 60611, tel. 312/280–2222 or 800/228–9000, fax 312/280–1963. Gen. manager, Marc Ellin. 255 rooms, 43 suites. AE, CB, DC, MC, V.*

★ ⑲ **Richmont.** This is an intimate establishment in recently
$$$ renovated quarters convenient to North Michigan Avenue. Charming rather than luxurious, comfortably rather than elegantly appointed, the Richmont offers an excellent value. It's not well equipped for meetings or other business needs, but is a good choice for someone who doesn't need these services. Continental breakfast and hors d'oeuvres at cocktail time are included in the basic room rate. The hotel restaurant is the delightful Rue St. Clair, an "American bistro." *162 E. Ontario St., 60611, tel. 312/787–3580 or 800/621–8055, fax 312/787–1299. Gen. manager, Frances Moore. 193 rooms, 26 suites. AE, CB, D, DC, MC, V.*

⑪ **Ritz-Carlton.** Like its sister hotel, the Four Seasons, the
$$$$ Ritz occupies space in a skyscraper that also houses a vertical shopping mall, Water Tower Place. Built in the 1970s, the hotel has a 12th-floor lobby with a skylighted fountain surrounded by bronze sculptures, modern chandeliers, and lots of plants. Rooms are spacious; most have been recently redecorated. Twin sinks are standard in each bathroom. The excellent health club includes a 52-foot lap pool; it's also used by residents of the condominiums that occupy the upper floors of the building. The Bar (*see* After Hours, below) is highly regarded among the club-going crowd for its live music and dancing; the Dining Room is one of Chicago's finer restaurants; and The Café (*see* Business Breakfasts, below) is a good place for an early meeting. *A Four Seasons hotel. 160 E. Pearson St., 60611, tel. 312/266–1000 or 800/332–3442, fax 312/266–9498. Gen. manager, Nicholas Mutton. 431 rooms, 81 suites. AE, CB, DC, MC, V.*

Downtown/The Loop

㊳ **Chicago Hilton and Towers.** This massive, opulent conven-
$$$$ tion hotel was built in 1927 and had a $200-million renovation in 1985. Its facilities, amenities, and South Michigan Avenue location make it a good choice for business travelers, though you may want to steer clear if the hotel is holding more than one large meeting; restaurants and other

facilities can become congested. The 1,543 rooms include 626 double-doubles, which have two double beds and two bathrooms. Most popular rooms are those with one king-size bed and a view of Lake Michigan. Business travelers prefer the more expensive Towers rooms, which have a service desk on each floor, complimentary Continental breakfast, a lounge with honor bar, and extensive business services. Bathtubs in all the rooms tend to be small. A state-of-the-art health club, featuring Universal weight machines, saunas, and a 60-foot lap pool, makes this hotel worth the stay. The Grand Ballroom, a tribute to the French Empire, is worth a look even if you're not staying here. Kitty O'Shea's (*see* After Hours, below) is a fun place to relax at the end of the day. *720 S. Michigan Ave., 60605. tel. 312/922–4400 or 800/445–8667, fax 312/922–5240. Gen. manager, Gerhardt Seibert. AE, CB, D, DC, MC, V.*

30 **Fairmont.** This 45-story, neoclassic, pink granite struc-
$$$$ ture is one of Chicago's most attractive new hotels (late 1980s), and offers wonderful lake or city views in all accommodations. The unusually spacious rooms are comfortably furnished in a variety of period styles; antiques and original artwork grace the public areas. All bathrooms include TV set, telephone, scale, an oversize tub, and separate shower. Windows can be opened slightly to get the fresh lake breezes—an unusual feature in a high-rise hotel; another plus is extra-long beds. Clever design places every room no more than four doors from an elevator. An Art Deco lounge offers evening cabaret entertainment. *200 N. Columbus Dr., 60601, tel. 312/565–8000 or 800/527–4727, fax 312/856–1032. Gen. manager, Wolf Lehmkuhl. 694 rooms, 66 suites. AE, CB, DC, MC, V.*

23 **Holiday Inn Mart Plaza.** Situated atop the Apparel Center
$$$ and next door to the Merchandise Mart, this 1970s hotel principally serves business travelers. Rooms are standard-issue Holiday Inn, comfortable but not lavish; bathrooms are spacious. There's no health club, but there is a heated indoor swimming pool. If you have business at the Mart, the location may make up for the relative lack of amenities and business services. *350 N. Orleans St., 60654, tel. 312/836–5000 or 800/465–4329, fax 312/836–0223. Gen. manager, William J. Horine. 525 rooms, 14 suites. AE, CB, D, DC, MC, V.*

★ 25 **Hotel Nikko.** One of Chicago's newest and most beautiful
$$$$ hotels, the Nikko is on the Chicago River, about four blocks west of the main hotel district, and convenient to the Merchandise Mart. Exquisite pieces of Oriental art decorate the public areas; the south side of the lobby is glassed in, giving views of a traditional Japanese garden and a riverfront park. Dark grays and black predominate in the design scheme. The standard, contemporary-style rooms have marble baths, separate dressing areas, and full-length mirrors; visitors can also request rooms with traditional Japanese decor and tatami sleeping mats. The three top floors have their own check-in and check-out, a special concierge, and complimentary breakfast and hors d'oeuvres. Business services include a library and executive lounge. One of the Nikko's two restaurants, Benkay, is esteemed locally for its fine Japanese food. *Owned by Japan Air Lines. 320 N. Dearborn St., 60610, tel. 312/744–1900 or 800/645–5687, fax 312/527–2650. Gen. manager,*

Pete Dangerfield. 425 rooms, 26 suites. AE, CB, D, DC, MC, V.

28 **Hyatt Regency Chicago.** It's alarmingly easy to get lost in
$$$$ this huge convention hotel, which is divided into East and
West Towers. The Hyatt is one of three hotels in the Illinois Center complex (the others are the Fairmont and the
Swiss Grand). You'll be comfortably housed if you stay
here to attend a meeting, but if your business is elsewhere, you may prefer one of the smaller, less crowded hotels. Accommodations are adequate but not luxurious,
though amenities include hair dryers and access to a
brand-new health club in Illinois Center. A club floor offers free Continental breakfast, concierge, and a lounge.
Catch a Rising Star Comedy Club (*see* After Hours, below)
is on the premises. *151 E. Wacker Dr., 60601, tel. 312/565–
1234 or 800/233–1234, fax 312/565–2966. Gen. manager,
Rod Young. 2,033 rooms, 175 suites. AE, CB, D, DC, MC,
V.*

34 **Midland.** This small hotel in the heart of the financial dis-
$$$ trict was built as a men's club in the 1920s. The Beaux
Arts lobby has vaulted arches and a gold-leaf ceiling.
Rooms are small but comfortable and were recently redec-
orated with black lacquer furniture and tones of mauve
and gray; amenities aren't lavish. The clientele is predom-
inantly business travelers. There's a free English-style
taxi to downtown locations and a complimentary breakfast
buffet. The taxi also transports joggers to the lakefront
jogging path weekday mornings at 6:30, and provides
them with Walkmans and orange juice. The exercise room
is limited to a few weight machines, but guests have free
access to the Randolph Combined Fitness Center a few
blocks away. The 12 meeting rooms have been decorated
in the styles of various Chicago architects, including
Frank Lloyd Wright and Louis Sullivan. Staff is friendly
and helpful. *A Grand Tradition hotel. 172 W. Adams St.,
60603, tel. 312/332–1200 or 800/621–2360 (outside Illi-
nois), fax 312/332–5909. Gen. manager, Myron Levy. 257
rooms, 4 full suites, 50 executive junior suites. AE, CB,
D, DC, MC, V.*

33 **Palmer House.** Built more than 100 years ago by Chicago
$$$ merchant Potter Palmer, this landmark hotel in the heart
of the Loop has some of the most ornate and elegant public
areas in the city. The gilded Victorian lobby, up a flight of
stairs from the street-level concourse, is worth a visit even
if you're staying elsewhere. The clientele is a mix of tourists and business travelers; the atmosphere can be hectic
and the service a little brusque during peak times. Recently renovated rooms are comfortable though not luxurious; if you're not staying in the Towers executive floors,
you're likely to have to do your work on the bed. Smallish
bathrooms include full-length mirrors. The hotel has sev-
en restaurants, among them the French Quarter, a good
place for a business breakfast. *A Hilton property. 17 E.
Monroe St., 60603, tel. 312/726–7500 or 800/445–8667, fax
312/947–1707. Gen. manager, James Claus. 1,600 rooms,
88 suites, 500 corporate class. AE, CB, D, DC, MC, V.*

29 **Swiss Grand Hotel.** Despite its size, this sleek, triangular,
$$$$ 45-story hotel, designed by Chicago architect Harry
Weese and opened in 1988, offers a quiet European ambience, as well as spacious rooms, and services designed
specifically for the business traveler. The business center

includes a library of current business and trade magazines, as well as up-to-the-minute stock exchange reports. Each guest room has two-line phones, an oversize writing desk, and a separate seating area. Among the state-of-the-art meeting rooms is a theater with banked seats. You can buy fresh bread and pastries at the in-house bakery, which also supplies them to the hotel's restaurants. *A Swissotel property. 323 E. Wacker Dr., 60601, tel. 312/565-0565 or 800/654-7263, fax 312/565-0540. Gen. manager, Costas Vafoupoulos. 625 rooms, 34 suites. AE, CB, D, DC, MC, V.*

McCormick Place

39 **McCormick Center Hotel.** This isolated high rise is the
$$$ only place to stay if you have to shuttle back and forth more than a few times a day between your hotel and a trade show at the McCormick Place convention center, right across the street. Rooms are attractively furnished, following a recent renovation. Several restaurants and a health club can take care of basic needs, but for culture, nightlife, really good food, and easy access to the major business areas, you're better off staying in the Loop or Near North Side, where you can get equally nice accommodations at similar prices. That said, it should be noted that the hotel does provide complimentary limousine service to the business districts. *451 E. 23rd St., 60616, tel. 312/791-1900 or 800/621-6909, fax 312/791-0634. Gen. manager, Joseph Duellman. 650 rooms, 40 suites. AE, CB, D, DC, MC, V.*

O'Hare Airport

$$$$ **Hotel Sofitel Chicago at O'Hare Airport.** This luxury hotel, opened in 1987, has public areas richly appointed with marble, wood, glass, and Oriental rugs. Rooms are furnished in country French–style, with light-wood furniture and floral prints. There's a 24-hour concierge, and turndown service includes a red rose and a chocolate truffle. An in-house French bakery is a good place to pick up last-minute gifts. Business services are exceptionally good for the airport area. *5550 N. River Rd., Rosemont, 60018, tel. 708/678-4488 or 800/233-5959, fax 708/678-4244. Gen. manager, Pierce Johnson. 305 rooms, 16 suites. AE, CB, D, DC, MC, V.*

$$$$ **Hyatt Regency O'Hare.** You can't miss the quartet of shiny copper-color towers that mark this institution among O'Hare-area hotels. In typical Hyatt style, a central atrium soars eight stories to the glass roof, and elevators are glass-enclosed. Both the lobby and guest rooms have been recently outfitted with new carpeting and furniture; two club floors offer concierge service and a private lounge with honor bar. A new ballroom was just added. A good health club has a dome-enclosed swimming pool, exercise machines, Jacuzzi, and sauna. There are three restaurants, including a revolving dining room on the top of the hotel. *9300 W. Bryn Mawr Ave., Rosemont, 60018, tel. 708/696-1234 or 800/223-1234, fax 708/696-1418. Gen. manager, Paul Tang. 1,100 rooms, 60 suites, 400 business class. AE, CB, D, DC, MC, V.*

$$$ **O'Hare Hilton.** The only hotel within walking distance of the airport (connected to the terminals by an underground walkway), this cement pile tends to fill up without

even trying, especially when bad weather delays flights overnight. As a result, it doesn't try terribly hard. You can get a perfectly comfortable basic room, but amenities are scarce for the price. If you need more than a place to sleep and have time to shop around, look farther afield. *Box 66414, O'Hare International Airport, 60666, tel. 312/686–8000 or 800/445–8667, fax 312/686–0073. Gen. manager, Bruce Ulrich. 885 rooms. AE, CB, DC, MC, V.*

$$$ **Radisson Suite Hotel O'Hare Airport.** This low rise has two-room suites furnished in a comfortable, homelike style, with casual light-wood furnishings. Each living room has a kitchen area with a wet bar, refrigerator, microwave, sofabed, and dining table with four chairs. Each suite has two television sets and two phones. Room service hours are limited. Room rates include an American-style breakfast and complimentary evening cocktails. *5500 N. River Rd., Rosemont, 60018, tel. 708/678–4000 or 800/333–3333, fax 708/671–3059. Gen. manager, Mark Marotta. 296 suites. AE, CB, D, DC, MC, V.*

DINING

The list below concentrates on restaurants in the Loop, Near North Side, and River North neighborhoods, where business travelers are likely to be staying. Proximity dictates the stamping grounds for locals—financiers dine in the Loop near the banking district; politicians eat near City Hall; advertising and public relations people gather at eateries on North Michigan Avenue. Brownbagging is also popular among the city's professionals; Chicago is a get-down-to-business city where lunch hour is likely to last no more than 60 minutes.

Virtually every type of dining experience is available in this former steak-and-potatoes city. Some of Chicago's notable restaurants are in its hotels, such as La Tour in the Park Hyatt. But for a real taste of Chicago dining, it's best to leave your hotel room and explore.

Highly recommended restaurants are indicated by a star ★.

Category	Cost*
$$$$ (Very Expensive)	over $40
$$$ (Expensive)	$26–$40
$$ (Moderate)	$13–$25
$ (Inexpensive)	under $13

per person, including appetizer, entrée, and dessert, but excluding drinks, service, and 8.5% sales tax.

Numbers in the margin correspond to numbered restaurant locations on the Chicago Lodging and Dining maps.

Business Breakfasts

For breakfast meetings, local businesspeople generally prefer hotel restaurants. Of these, the Mayfair Regent's **Ciel Bleu** (tel. 312/787–8500) has good food and a superb view. Other spots with plush, pleasant surroundings, good food, and an atmosphere conducive to talk include

The Seasons at the Four Seasons (tel. 312/280–8800), **The Café** at the Ritz-Carlton (tel. 312/266–1000), and **Oak Terrace,** at the Drake (tel. 312/787–2200).

La Tour, at the Park Hyatt (tel. 312/280–2230), is the most popular spot in town for power breakfasts, partly because of the "see and be seen" floor-to-ceiling windows that look out on North Michigan Avenue's Water Tower Park. The menu features standard breakfast fare (eggs, fresh fruit, and pastries), but everything is well prepared and beautifully presented.

Lou Mitchell's (565 W. Jackson Blvd., tel. 312/939–3111), one of the city's great breakfast spots, features fresh double-yolked eggs in 14 kinds of omelets, as well as pancakes, French toast, and Belgian waffles. Be prepared to stand in line, and to be seated at a long communal table. It's not ideal for meetings, but fun if you have extra time and don't mind a side trip to the west Loop.

The Loop

★ ❸❻ **Berghoff.** This bustling Loop institution serves German
$$ food in a huge wood-panel dining room where historic photographs of the area hang. A menu of classics (Wiener schnitzel, sauerbraten) are augmented by American favorites. Berghoff Beer (light and dark) is on tap, as is root-beer. Because it's a popular lunch spot with the business crowd, expect a wait of about 15 minutes at midday; the noise level does not permit serious discussions. The food varies from competent to excellent. The brisk efficiency of the service, delivered by formally dressed and very correct waiters, does not encourage lingering over coffee. *17 W. Adams St., tel. 312/427–3170. Casual dress. Reservations accepted for parties of 6 or more. AE, MC, V.*

★ ❸❺ **The Everest Room.** On the 40th floor of a high rise in the
$$$$ heart of the financial district, the Everest Room is arguably the best French restaurant in town. Meals are graciously served in an elegant setting with a spectacular view. Chef Jean Joho combines classic French techniques with those of his native Alsace. Entrées change frequently; among recent offerings were fish fillet wrapped and roasted in potato with thyme; yellowfin tuna tournedos sautéed medium rare with shallots; and breast of squab with truffle coulis and Napa cabbage. A fine wine list, including many Alsatian vintages, complements the menu. Service is polished and efficient; prices are high. This is a place to come to celebrate a deal; one would not want to be distracted from the food by a business discussion. *440 S. LaSalle St., tel. 312/663–8920. Jacket and tie required. Reservations required. AE, DC, MC, V. Closed Sun., holidays.*

❸❷ **Nick's Fishmarket.** This dark room has the feel of a tradi-
$$$ tional club, furnished in leather and wood and adorned with sports paintings. Phones can be requested and plugged into jacks at each booth. The large seafood menu often includes catfish, frog legs, Hawaiian opakapaka, and abalone. Although ingredients are fresh, they can be overcooked; share your concern with the efficient wait staff. A few pasta and beef dishes are also available. *1 First National Plaza, tel. 312/621–0200. Jacket and tie recommended. Reservations advised. AE, DC, MC, V. Closed Sun., holidays.*

★ ❸⁷ **Printer's Row.** Located in and named after the recently
$$$ chic loft neighborhood in the South Loop, this warm and
attractive restaurant offers some of the most interesting
and satisfying American cuisine in Chicago. Polished,
dark wood and neutral colors provide a quiet backdrop for
owner and chef Michael Foley's constantly changing fare.
New ideas and approaches bring forth such creative
dishes as grilled mallard duck with radicchio and endive in
port wine sauce, and ragout of sweetbreads with aromatic
vegetables and pasta. Daily specials augment the menu
and include at least one dish low in fat and sodium. An ex-
cellent wine list features a large selection of fine ports, co-
gnacs, and armagnacs. Tables are well spaced and the
noise level is low; this is a good place for business discus-
sions. *550 S. Dearborn St., tel. 312/461–0780. Jacket re-
quired. Reservations recommended, required on week-
ends. AE, CB, D, DC, MC, V. No lunch Sat., closed Sun.*

❸¹ **Walnut Room.** Marshall Field's dining room, with its wood
$$ archways and beams and Oriental screens and carpets, is
reminiscent of a Victorian-era English tearoom. Long a
haven for businesspeople seeking a relaxed, unhurried
lunch spot, the Walnut Room serves standard, comforting
fare: beef tenderloin tips Stroganoff, Field's own chicken
pot pie, roast free-range chicken, and a fresh fish of the
day, as well as a large selection of salads and sandwiches.
A traditional English tea, complete with scones and
Devonshire cream, is served at 3 PM. Bar service is available, too. Avoid the Walnut Room during Christmas season unless you want to battle the crowds who come to have
lunch under Field's two-story Christmas tree. *111 N.
State St., tel. 312/781–1000. Casual dress. No reservations. AE, MC, V. No dinner. Closed Sun., holidays.*

Near North Side

★ ❶⁴ **Avanzare.** This chic Italian restaurant has two handsome
$$$ rooms dominated by traditional brass accents, leather
banquettes, and marble floors; a full-length mirrored bar
separates the dining rooms. The main room tends to be
noisy; for serious discussions, try to get a table on the
mezzanine. A dozen carefully prepared pastas appear on
the regular menu, but the best offerings are usually on a
list of daily specials. Entrées might include ravioli stuffed
with mushrooms in shallot butter sauce, or succulent
braised baby pheasant with fennel. The tuna carpaccio ap-
petizer, paper-thin slices of raw tuna in soy sauce with av-
ocado and sweet onion, is a good starter. The freshness
and quality of the ingredients is outstanding. Reason-
ably priced Italian wines are available by the glass or
the bottle. *161 E. Huron St., tel. 312/337–8036. Casual
dress. Reservations recommended. AE, CB, DC, MC, V.*

❷⁷ **Billy Goat Tavern.** A favorite hangout for reporters from
$ the *Chicago Tribune*, just across the street, this self-serv-
ice bar-and-grill features the "chizboorgers" made famous
by John Belushi on "Saturday Night Live" in the 1970s.
Come for the atmosphere, a quick bite, and a cold brew
that won't set you back a day's pay. *430 N. Michigan Ave.
(lower level), tel. 312/222–1525. Casual dress. No reser-
vations. No credit cards.*

❶⁰ **Chestnut Street Grill.** Modeled after the famous Tadich
$$$ Grill in San Francisco, this Water Tower Place establish-
ment serves some of the best fresh seafood you'll find in

the Chicago area. Offerings vary from day to day; the catch is flown in from the coasts and prepared in a variety of ways, including charcoal-grilled. An excellent sourdough bread starts each meal; a few nonfish dishes, salads, and a selection of low-calorie, low-sodium dishes round out the menu. The restaurant is attractive, with tile floors, dark wood, and reproductions of details from buildings by notable Chicago architects—for example, the ornamental ironwork of Louis Sullivan. The brisk and efficient service also makes it a popular setting for business lunches; tables in the back tend to be quietest. *845 N. Michigan Ave., tel. 312/280–2720. Casual dress. Reservations accepted for lunch, and at dinner for 6 or more. AE, CB, D, DC, MC, V.*

❽ Crickets. The ladies who lunch tend to lunch at this Chica-
$$$$ go institution, something you wouldn't guess from the atmosphere—a dark, crowded room with toy airplanes, tanks, cars, and industrial signs hanging from the ceiling. Tables in this trendy spot (trendy, that is, for a middle-aged corporate crowd) are close together; sharing conversations with those nearby is inevitable and considered part of the fun. The eclectic menu features traditional French dishes: appetizers usually include pâté maison, baked oysters, and ragout of snails. Popular entrées include veal medallions with wild mushroom sauce, tournedos of beef with Zinfandel shallot sauce, and sweetbread medallions with tarragon-truffle sauce. For dessert, try Crickets's original cheesecake. Some wines are available by the glass; the wine list is extensive. *100 E. Chestnut St., tel. 312/280–2100. Jacket required. Reservations required. AE, CB, DC, MC, V. Closed for dinner, Sun., some holidays.*

❶⑥ The Eccentric. Restaurateur Richard Melman has teamed
$$ up with talk-show host Oprah Winfrey to open this aptly named adventure in dining. The pair built a combination of French café, Italian coffeehouse, and English pub into a space formerly occupied by a car dealership; the restaurant can seat about 400. Works by local artists adorn the walls. The food is surprisingly good, given the novelty value of the enterprise. Steaks and chops stand out, as do Oprah's mashed potatoes with horseradish (the only dish on the menu attributed directly to her). For dessert, try the butterscotch or bittersweet chocolate pot de crème. There is a selection of wines by the glass, as well as a variety of designer beers. And keep an eye out for Oprah. *159 West Erie St., tel. 312/787–8390. Casual dress. No reservations. Closed Sun. AE, CB, DC, M, V.*

❶⑤ Ed Debevic's. This imitation 1950s diner serves a swell
$ meatloaf, along with other diner fare, in a high-camp atmosphere that features gum-chewing, wisecracking waitresses, Jell-o salads, and "Ed Debevic's Beer, Aged in Its Own Bottle." Try the exemplary tuna sandwich and the homemade cream pies. A cult spot, Ed's tends to be packed evenings and weekends, but may be a good bet for a quick lunch during the week. Rock 'n' roll in the main room can make it difficult to talk; conversation is easier in the back room, where the noisiest things are the televisions tuned to the soaps and vintage sitcoms. Ed's is in the heart of the River North gallery neighborhood, just west of the Near North Side. Your meal here is likely to make an amusing anecdote for your co-workers back home. *640*

N. Wells St., tel. 312/664–1707. Casual dress. No reservations; the wait may be substantial. No credit cards. Closed
some holidays.

★ ⑬ **Eli's The Place for Steak.** The lounge and dining room of
$$$ this Chicago institution have the ambience of a private
club, with soft lights, thick carpets, and lots of leather and
warm woods—a good setting for quiet conversation. Eli's
developed its outstanding reputation through an unflag-
ging commitment to top-quality ingredients, prepared
precisely to the customer's taste in generous portions.
Prime aged steaks are the specialty of the house; you'll
also find superb, thickly cut veal chops and splendid
calves' liver. For dessert, order Eli's cheesecake, now sold
nationally in countless varieties. 215 E. Chicago Ave., tel.
312/642–1393. Jacket required. Reservations required.
AE, DC, MC, V. Closed holidays.

★ ㉑ **Gordon.** A favorite spot for Chicago's power-lunch crowd—
$$$$ it is quiet and well located in the River North loft dis-
trict—Gordon consistently offers some of the city's most
innovative contemporary American fare. Rococo furnish-
ings include Oriental rugs and swag curtains along the
walls; tables have fresh flowers. The menu changes often;
popular entrées include seared tuna with red-tomato-and-
chive vinaigrette, grilled beef tenderloin with cabernet-
braised mushrooms and marjoram, and roasted sweet-
breads with chanterelle mushrooms, prosciutto, and
chardonnay. There's a respectable wine list, with a good
selection available by the glass. Service is friendly and ef-
ficient. On weekends, there's piano music and dancing. 500
N. Clark St., tel. 312/467–9780. Jacket required. Reserva-
tions required. AE, CB, DC, MC, V. Closed hol-
idays.

㉔ **Harry Caray's.** Holy cow! It's a celebrity restaurant
$$$ where the food is decent and the owner, the veteran Chica-
go Cubs announcer, really stops by now and then. The
menu is Italian-American; steaks and chops share the bill
with pastas, veal dishes, salads, and cold platters. Baseball memorabilia decorate the walls. This is a good after-
work spot for sports fans who don't take the dining experience too seriously. 33 W. Kinzie St., tel. 312/465–9269.
Casual dress. AE, CB, D, DC, MC, V. Closed some holidays.

★ ⑱ **Hatsuhana.** Many sushi and sashimi lovers regard this
$$$ restaurant as the best of its kind in Chicago; its broad se-
lection of fish is infallibly fresh and carefully prepared.
The decor is characteristically Japanese—tasteful and
streamlined; diners sit at a long, angled sushi bar or
at wooden tables. Appetizers include broiled spinach in
sesame-soy sauce, and steamed egg custard with shrimp,
fish, and vegetables. Daily specials might include steamed
baby clams in sake, and king mackerel with soybean
paste. Service can be unpredictable. 160 E. Ontario St.,
tel. 312/280–8287. Casual dress. Reservations recom-
mended. AE, DC, MC, V. Closed Sun., holidays, and Sat.
lunch.

⑳ **Honda.** Owned and operated by a Tokyo restaurateur,
$$$ Honda offers one of the most varied Japanese menus in the
city. Its sushi and sashimi are among Chicago's best; it
also lays claim to one of the country's first kushi bars,
where vegetables and morsels of meat and seafood are
grilled or deep-fried. Customers sit at the kushi bar or

sushi bar, or in one of several dining rooms. Call a day in advance to reserve a tatami room, where diners remove their shoes and sit on the floor (a well under the table lets you stretch your legs). Visiting Japanese will find a large array of familiar dishes, including *chawan mushi* (steamed vegetables and fish in an egg custard) and *chasoba* (noodles in cold green tea). Sukiyaki is prepared for you at your table. Service can be uncoordinated, especially when large parties order a variety of entrées. *540 N. Wells St., tel. 312/923–1010. Casual dress. Reservations accepted. Closed Sun., Sat. lunch. AE, CB, DC, MC, V.*

❾ **The 95th.** Splendidly situated at the top of Chicago's third-
$$$$ tallest building, The 95th will impress clients with its spectacular view and elegant atmosphere, created by subdued lighting, lavish place settings, and contemporary-style chandeliers. The food's good, too. The entrées emphasize seafood and poultry, with dishes like Gulf shrimp with spinach linguine in tomato-basil butter, and roasted quail with ratatouille and rosemary butter. The wine list is large and reasonably priced, and there's a good choice by the glass. Spacious and quiet, The 95th is a good spot to talk business, as long as you can keep from looking out the window. An adjoining bar and lounge (*see* After Hours, below) is often crowded, but never frantic, and offers equally spectacular views. *John Hancock Building, 875 N. Michigan Ave., tel. 312/987–9596. Jacket required at dinner. Reservations recommended; weekend reservations required. AE, CB, DC, MC, V.*

❼ ㉒ **Pizzeria Uno/Due.** Chicago deep-dish pizza originated in
$ these two informal restaurants. Still run by the original owner, Ike Sewell, Uno has been remodeled to resemble its franchised cousins in other cities, but its pizzas retain their light crust and distinctive tang. Those not accustomed to pizza on a Chicago scale may want to skip the salad. Beer and soft drinks can be ordered by the pitcher. The wait is usually shorter at Pizzeria Due, which is a block away and has the same menu, more traditional decor, and longer hours. Some say Uno's pizza is better, but both establishments offer about the best in town. *Uno, 29 E. Ohio St., tel. 312/321–1000; Due, 619 N. Wabash Ave., tel. 312/943–2400. Casual dress. No reservations; phone-ahead orders accepted weekdays only. AE, DC, MC, V.*

㉖ **Shaw's Crab House and Blue Crab Lounge.** This New En-
$$$ gland–style crab house has a large room with exposed brick and wood, and an adjoining lounge with an oyster bar. Both are very popular, and tend to be packed at peak hours; come for after-work relaxation rather than quiet conversation. Appetizers include fried calimari, steamed blue mussels, and Maryland crab cakes. In addition to the standard shellfish dishes—simply and honestly prepared—are such daily fresh fish specials as grilled Hawaiian tuna with purslane and tomato relish, and grilled Pacific king salmon with herb marinade. A few chicken and beef items are also available. *21 E. Hubbard St., tel. 312/527–2722. Casual dress. Reservations accepted for lunch only; the wait at dinner can be substantial. AE, DC, MC, V. Lounge closed Sun.*

★ ❹ **Spiaggia.** This softly lighted, rose-color dining room at the
$$$$ north end of the chic Magnificent Mile vies with trendy New York or Los Angeles eateries for sophistication, qual-

ity of food—and price. The ambience is quietly elegant, service is gracious and knowledgeable, and business-people come here to make an impression. Variations on Northern Italian cuisine include crisp pizza with a paper-thin crust and topped with duck and goat cheese; ravioli filled with lobster meat in a delicate sauce; and paper-white grilled veal chop with rosemary. The large, all-Italian wine list is excellent, but yields few bargains. Café Spiaggia, next door, offers many of the same dishes at lower prices. *1 Magnificent Mile (Oak St. at Michigan Ave.), tel. 312/280–2750. Jacket required; no denim. Reservations recommended. AE, CB, D, DC, MC, V. No lunch Sun.*

FREE TIME

Fitness

Hotel Facilities
Good hotel fitness clubs are at the **Hilton** (tel. 312/922–4400), which has the best pool, and the **Nikko** (tel. 312/744–1900), which has an excellent selection of aerobic and weight machines, but no pool. However, neither is available to nonguests. Hotels without facilities often have agreements with local clubs.

Health Clubs
Many of the health clubs listed have arrangements with hotels for use of their facilities; inquire at your hotel. **Downtown Sports Club** (441 N. Wabash Ave., tel. 312/644–4880), with a day rate of $12, has agreements with several hotels. The top Chicago sports clubs do not accept nonmembers, but the following, all convenient and well equipped, take visitors on a per-diem basis: **Onterie Fitness Center** (466 E. Ontario St., tel. 312/642–0031), cost $10; **Charlie Club** (112 S. Michigan Ave., tel. 312/726–0510), cost $15; **Chicago Health and Racquet Clubs** (25 E. Washington Blvd., tel. 312/327–7755), cost $10; **Grand Ohio Athletic Club** (211 E. Ohio St., tel. 312/661–0036), cost $10; **Combined Fitness Center** (1235 N. LaSalle St., tel. 312/787–8400), cost $10.

Jogging
There's a 19-mile running and bicycle path, with mileage markers, along the lakefront through Lincoln and Grant parks. Enter at Oak Street Beach (across from the Drake Hotel) or at Grand Avenue (underneath Lake Shore Drive), or by going through Grant Park on Monroe Street or on Jackson Boulevard. It's well used in the early morning and late afternoon, especially north from the Loop, but be wary after dark and in the sparsely populated section south of McCormick Place.

Shopping

The two main shopping areas are **North Michigan Avenue** (also called the Magnificent Mile), between the Chicago River and Oak Street, and **the Loop.**

The city's two largest department stores, **Marshall Field** and **Carson Pirie Scott,** anchor the Loop's State Street–Wabash Avenue area (which has declined since the years when it was known as "State Street, that great street"). Marshall Field (111 N. State St., at the corner of Randolph

St., tel. 312/781–1000) is in the midst of a $110-million renovation; the bargain basement has been replaced with "Down Under," a series of small boutiques that sell clothing, luggage, picture frames, Chicago memorabilia, and Field's famous Frango mints, which many consider to be Chicago's greatest edible souvenirs. Second only to Marshall Field for many years, Carson Pirie Scott (1 S. State St., tel. 312/641–7000), the work of architect Louis Sullivan, is protected by landmark status, and well worth visiting for its ornate iron scrollwork.

The Magnificent Mile, Chicago's most glamorous shopping district, stretches along Michigan Avenue from the Chicago River to Oak Street. It's lined on both sides with some of the most sophisticated names in retailing: **Tiffany** (715 N. Michigan Ave., tel. 312/944–7500), **Gucci** (900 N. Michigan Ave., tel. 312/664–5504), **Chanel** (990 N. Michigan Ave., tel. 312/787–5500), **I. Magnin** (830 N. Michigan Ave., tel. 312/751–0500), and **Bonwit Teller** (875 N. Michigan Ave., tel. 312/751–1800), to name just a few.

Aside from dozens of designer shops, Michigan Avenue also features two "vertical malls." **Water Tower Place** (835 N. Michigan Ave., tel. 312/440–3165) contains branches of Lord & Taylor and Marshall Field, as well as seven floors of specialty stores. The **Avenue Atrium** (900 N. Michigan Ave., tel. 312/915–3916) houses the new Chicago branch of Bloomingdale's, along with dozens of smaller boutiques. Generally, the merchandise found here is more sophisticated, and more expensive, than that in Water Tower Place.

Diversions

The ArchiCenter (330 S. Dearborn St., tel. 312/782–1776) is the starting point for guided tours of the city's buildings and historic homes, led by the Chicago Architecture Foundation; also available here are maps of Chicago landmarks so that you can take your own architectural tour of the Loop.

The Art Institute (Michigan Ave. at Adams St., tel. 312/443–3600) has a world-renowned collection of French Impressionist art, as well as outstanding medieval and Renaissance works, Asian art, and photography.

Even if your business doesn't take you there, the Art Moderne–style **Chicago Board of Trade** (141 W. Jackson St.) is worth a visit for its stunning 1930s lobby.

The **Field Museum of Natural History** (Lake Shore Dr. at Roosevelt Rd., tel. 312/922–9410), the **Shedd Aquarium** (1200 S. Lake Shore Dr., tel. 312/939–2426), and the **Adler Planetarium** (1300 S. Lake Shore Dr., tel. 312/322–0304) occupy the same peninsula just south of the Loop, jutting out into Lake Michigan. If a visit to this neighborhood gives you museum overload, the adjoining park is a good place to walk and take in a great view of the skyline.

The Museum of Contemporary Art (237 E. Ontario St., tel. 312/280–2660) concentrates on works created after 1940.

Navy Pier, at the far eastern end of Grand Avenue, juts out almost a mile into Lake Michigan, and is used exclusively by walkers, joggers, and cyclists. It's a good place to get away from it all on a sunny day and enjoy the lake breezes, the cry of the gulls, and spectacular views of downtown and Near North skylines. If you're at McCormick Place, the serene promenade between the convention center and the lakefront is another good "time-out" spot.

The small **Terra Museum** (664 N. Michigan Ave., tel. 312/664-3939) contains an excellent collection of American art, including pieces by Whistler, Sargeant, Hopper, Avery, Stella, and Wyeth.

Professional Sports

Chicago's hockey team, the **Black Hawks,** (tel. 312/733-5300) and basketball team, the **Bulls** (tel. 312/943-5800) play at the Chicago Stadium. The city's football club, the **Bears** (tel. 312/663-5100) plays at Soldier Field. For baseball, see the **Cubs** (tel. 312/878-2827) at Wrigley Field, and the **White Sox** (tel. 312/924-1000) at Comiskey Park.

The Arts

The Chicago Symphony is internationally renowned, and the city's Lyric Opera is one of the best opera companies in the United States today. In addition, the Auditorium Theater holds a variety of first-rate subscription concerts and recital series throughout the year. Although road-show productions of Broadway hits come to Chicago, the true vigor of the city's theater springs from the multitude of small ensembles that have made a home here, ranging from the critically acclaimed Steppenwolf Company to the often satirical Body Politic.

Tickets for concerts and plays are available through **Theater Tix** (tel. 312/902-1919), **Ticketmaster** (tel. 312/559-1212), and **Ticketron** (tel. 312/902-1919). For a full listing of current attractions, call **Curtain Call** (tel. 312/977-1755). For half-price tickets on the day of the performance, check the **Hot Tix booth** (24 S. State St., no telephone).

Auditorium Theater, 70 E. Congress Pkwy., tel. 312/922-2110.
Body Politic Theater, 2261 N. Lincoln Ave., tel. 312/871-3000.
Chicago Symphony, Orchestra Hall, 220 S. Michigan, tel. 312/435-8122.
Lyric Opera, 20 N. Wacker Dr., tel. 312/332-2244.
Steppenwolf Theater Company, 2851 N. Halsted St., tel. 312/472-4141.

After Hours

Hotel bars are popular among businesspeople looking for a quiet drink and a place to talk; the atmosphere at the Park Hyatt (tel. 312/280-2222), the Four Seasons (tel. 312/280-8800), and the Drake (tel. 312/787-2200) is particularly pleasant. Nightlife options listed below are within an easy walk or short cab ride of the downtown and Near North Side hotels. The Near North is very lively on weekends, as are two lakefront neighborhoods—Lincoln Park and Lakeview. Women on their own will feel more at ease on North Michigan Avenue than in the Loop, which tends to be deserted after dark.

Bars and Lounges

The Bar at the Ritz-Carlton (tel. 312/266–1000) is popular with sophisticated clubbers; **Kitty O'Shea's** at the Hilton (tel. 312/922–4400) re-creates the atmosphere of an Irish pub. For a great view, try the bar at **The 95th,** in the John Hancock Building (tel. 312/987–9596).

Blues Clubs

Blue Chicago (937 N. State St., tel. 312/642–6261) is the best blues club in the Near North Side; in the Loop, check out **Buddy Guy's Legends** (754 S. Wabash Ave., tel. 312/427–1190), run by one of Chicago's own blues legends.

Cabarets

Milt Trenier's Lounge (610 Fairbanks Ct., tel. 312/266–6226) is lounge cabaret with a jazz quintet on the weekends.

Comedy Clubs

Second City (1608 N. Wells St., tel. 312/642–8189), the granddaddy of them all (and some say past its prime), is a short cab ride from the Near North Side; there are usually two different revues playing at the same time. Also try **Chicago Improv** (504 N. Wells St., tel. 312/782–6387), or **Catch a Rising Star** (Hyatt Regency, tel. 312/565–4242).

Jazz Clubs

The **Jazz Showcase,** in the Blackstone Hotel (tel. 312/427–4300), books name acts for serious listeners; don't come here if you want background music. For boisterous after-work and noon jazz, try **Andy's** (11 E. Hubbard St., tel. 312/642–6805). For something more intimate, go to the **Gold Star Sardine Bar** (680 N. Lake Shore Dr., tel. 312/664–4215).

For Singles

Chicago's famous Rush Street singles scene, popular with professionals in their 20s, is actually on Division Street between Clark Street and State Street. Its legendary singles bars include **Mother's** (26 W. Division St., tel. 312/642–7251) and **Butch McGuire's** (20 W. Division St., tel. 312/337–9080). **Eddie Rocket's** (9 W. Division St., tel. 312/787–4881) has dancing. For a more "amusement park" atmosphere that gives you something to do besides cruise, try the **North Pier** development, on the river at 455 East Illinois Street, which combines bars, museums, shops, restaurants, and miniature golf.

Dallas/Fort Worth

by Jeff Siegel

Dallas is neither the cowtown depicted in numerous Western movies, nor the cutthroat oil town of the "Dallas" TV series.

Founded as an Indian trading post in 1841, it was settled in 1855 by a group of French, Belgians, and Swiss, who came with dreams of a Utopian colony that never quite worked out. But the culture they brought helped transform the frontier town into the modern metropolis it is today.

Fort Worth, by contrast, was a major cattle-drive point in the last century, and it retains a good deal of the down-home friendliness of a Western frontier town. During the westward expansion, a garrison was based here to protect settlers; although it was never a fortress, it was later named Fort Worth for Gen. William Worth, a hero of the Mexican War.

As the Southwestern economy collapsed in the second half of the 1980s, the Metroplex (the local term for Dallas, Fort Worth, and the area between them) seemed to be riding out the storm. But instead of learning from the mistakes made in Houston and New Orleans, the area's bankers continued to lend money to the area's real estate developers, who continued to build. The result? Major, locally owned banks and savings and loans were wiped out, and the construction industry floundered.

The key to recovery, local leaders say, lies in how carefully the government manages all of its foreclosed properties. How the volatile situation in the Gulf will impact on Texas's economy is also for the future to determine. In the meantime, several major national companies have moved to the area in the past few years—Exxon to Las Colinas, J.C. Penney to Richardson, and GTE to Irving—and that has helped the economy.

Top Employers

Employer	Type of Enterprise	Parent*/ Headquarters
AMR Corp.	Airlines	Fort Worth
Burlington Northern	Transportation	Dallas

Dresser Industries	Oil field services	Dallas
Electronic Data Systems	Computers	Dallas
Halliburton Industries	Oil	Dallas
J.C. Penney	Retailer	Dallas
LTV	Holding company	Dallas
Kimberly-Clark	Consumer goods	Irving, TX
Texas Instruments	Computers	Dallas
Texas Utilities	Utilities	Dallas

*if applicable

ESSENTIAL INFORMATION

Climate

What follows are the average daily maximum and minimum temperatures for Dallas and Fort Worth.

Jan.	56F	13C	**Feb.**	61F	16C	**Mar.**	67F	19C
	36	2		40	4		47	8
Apr.	76F	24C	**May**	83F	28C	**June**	90F	32C
	56	13		63	17		72	22
July	94F	34C	**Aug.**	94F	34C	**Sept.**	88F	31C
	76	24		74	23		68	20
Oct.	79F	26C	**Nov.**	67F	19C	**Dec.**	58F	14C
	58	14		47	8		38	3

Airports

Dallas-Fort Worth International (DFW), with its Airtrans intraterminal subway system, is the main airport for both cities. DFW is 13 miles northwest of downtown Dallas and 17 miles northeast of downtown Fort Worth. Try to avoid changing planes at DFW if it means transferring between any of the five terminals. The Airtrans trains are inconvenient at best, and the walk is always too long, particularly with luggage.

Dallas' **Love Field,** six miles from downtown, is smaller and more convenient for Dallas passengers, but it is serviced only by Southwest. (Continental has received federal permission, but hasn't started service as of press time.) **Suburban Addison Airport,** 14 miles north of downtown Dallas, is a major commuter and general aviation facility.

Airport Business Facilities

The **Hyatt** (near the American Airlines terminal, tel. 214/453–1234) has fax machines, photocopying, a fitness center, and day rates for rooms with bed, desk, and telephone.

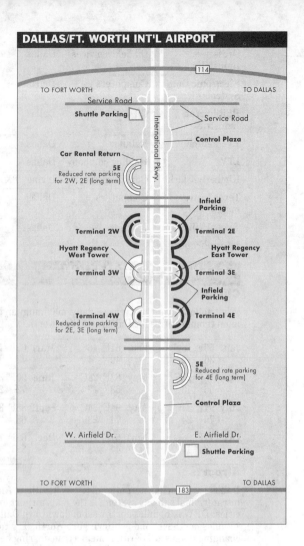

Airlines

Dallas-Fort Worth International is a major hub for American Airlines (the airline's headquarters are a mile and a half away); Love Field is home to Southwest.

American, tel. 214/267–1151 or 800/433–7300.
Continental, tel. 214/263–0523 or 800/525–0280.
Delta, tel. 214/630–3200 or 800/221–1212.
Southwest, tel. 214/640–1221 or 800/531–5601.

Between the Airports and Downtown

The trip from Dallas-Fort Worth International and downtown Dallas and Fort Worth takes 20–40 minutes, depending on rush-hour (6:30 AM–8:30 AM and 4 PM–6:30 PM) conditions.

By Taxi
It's a $25 cab ride (on the meter) to downtown Dallas and $22 (flat fee) to downtown Fort Worth. Expect to pay about $15 to the North Dallas business corridor (10–20 minutes along the LBJ Fwy.) and about $10 to the Las Colinas office sprawl (10–20 minutes along Hwy. 114).

By Bus
The blue-and-yellow **SuperShuttle** minivans (tel. 817/329–2000) offer scheduled service between DFW and Love Field and most of Dallas and Fort Worth, including both downtown areas, North Dallas, and Las Colinas. They operate 24 hours a day and have courtesy phones at the baggage areas. The fare structure is complicated: $10 to a downtown Dallas hotel, $12 to a downtown Dallas business, $11 to a downtown Fort Worth hotel, $18 to a downtown Fort Worth business, $12 to a North Dallas hotel, and $15 to a North Dallas business. The length of the trip depends not only on traffic, but on the number of passengers in the van and how many stops the driver has to make.

Fort Worth's public transportation system, The T, offers a $7 shuttle between the airport and downtown from 5 AM to 10 PM. The trip takes about an hour.

By Limousine
Limaxi (tel. 214/748–6294) offers service to Dallas and Fort Worth in stretch Hondas that seat six. The fare to downtown Dallas is $35 (flat fee for the car) plus $2 toll and 20% gratuity. The fare to downtown Fort Worth and North Dallas is $35 for the first 15 minutes and $10 for each additional 15 minutes, plus toll and tip. Corporate rates are available.

Car Rentals

These companies have locations at both airports.

Avis, tel. 214/574–4130 (DFW), 214/357–0301 (Love Field), or 800/331–1212.
Budget, tel. 214/871–9500 or 800/527–0700.
Hertz, tel. 214/453–0370 (DFW), 214/350–7071 (Love Field), or 800/654–3131.
National, tel. 214/574–3400 (DFW), 214/357–0478 (Love Field), or 800/227–7368.

These companies have locations near both airports, and operate shuttle services between the terminals and their sites.

Enterprise, tel. 214/986–1890 (DFW), 214/358–8831 (Love Field), or 800/325–8007.
Snappy, tel. 817/577–2655 (DFW), 214/357–8167 (Love Field), or 800/321–7159.
Thrifty, tel. 214/929–1320 (DFW) or 214/357–2821 (Love Field).

Emergencies

Prologue (tel. 214/256–2283 or 800/362–8677) is a free referral service for doctors and dentists.

Doctors
PrimaCare (tel. 214/263–0190) has 16 clinics, open 8 AM–10 PM daily.

Dentists

Horizon Dental Centers has several locations in Dallas County (downtown Dallas, tel. 214/720–7770) and six in Tarrant County (east Fort Worth, tel. 817/451–8825). **The Dallas County Dental Society** (tel. 214/654–7367) provides emergency service after 5 PM and on weekends. **The Fort Worth District Dental Society** (tel. 817/924–7111) offers 24-hour emergency service.

Hospitals

Baylor University Medical Center (3500 Gaston Ave., Dallas, tel. 214/820–0111) is five minutes from downtown. **Humana Hospital Medical City Dallas** (7777 Forest La., Dallas, tel. 214/661–7000) is in the heart of the North Dallas corridor. **All Saints Episcopal Hospital** (1400 8th Ave., Fort Worth, tel. 817/926–2544) is five minutes from downtown.

Important Addresses and Numbers

Audiovisual rentals. AVW Audio Visual (2233 Irving Blvd., Dallas, tel. 214/638–0024), J&S Audio Visual Communications (4407 Beltwood Pkwy. N., No. 112, Dallas, tel. 214/239–9133), Texas Audio Visuals (1822 N. Sylvania Ave., Fort Worth, tel. 817/831–3116).

Chambers of Commerce. Dallas Chamber of Commerce (1201 Elm St., Suite 2000, Dallas, tel. 214/746–6600), North Dallas Chamber of Commerce (10707 Preston Rd., Dallas, tel. 214/368–6486), Fort Worth Chamber of Commerce (777 Taylor St., Fort Worth, tel. 817/336–2491).

Computer rentals. First National Computer (4843 Keller Springs Rd., Dallas, tel. 214/380–8700), InfoRent (5001 Infomart, Dallas, tel. 214/746–5030), Computer Store (2700-B W. Berry St., Fort Worth, tel. 817/924–7772).

Convention and exhibition centers. Dallas Convention Center (650 S. Griffin St., Dallas, tel. 214/658–7000), Dallas Market Center (2100 Stemmons Fwy., Dallas, tel. 214/655–6100), Infomart (1950 Stemmons Fwy., Dallas, tel. 214/746–3500), Reunion Arena (777 Sport St., Dallas, tel. 214/658–7070), Tarrant County Convention Center (1111 Houston St., Fort Worth, tel. 817/332–9222), Will Rogers Memorial Center (330 W. Lancaster St., Fort Worth, tel. 817/870–8150).

Fax services. ActionFax (6390 LBJ Fwy., Dallas, tel. 214/661–2913), Alphagraphics (Renaissance Tower, Dallas, tel. 214/698–0556; 777 Main St., Fort Worth, tel. 817/870–2660).

Formal-wear rentals. Culwell & Son (13020 Preston Rd., Dallas, tel. 214/661–8282), Al's Formal Wear (315 Throckmorton St., Fort Worth, tel. 817/335–9493).

Gift shops. Chocolates: Godiva Chocolatier (73 Highland Park Ave., Dallas, tel. 214/559–0397; 13350 Dallas Pkwy., Dallas, tel. 214/458–1821), Russel Stover (800 Houston St., Fort Worth, tel. 817/332–3434); Florists: Liland's (2101 Abrahms Rd., Dallas, tel. 214/823–9505), John A. Winters (1021 N. Sylvania Ave., Fort Worth, tel. 817/831–1281).

Graphic design studios. The Artwerks Group (6116 N. Central Exp., Dallas, tel. 214/361–7750), Laser Publications (5005 Birch Hollow La., Fort Worth, tel. 817/294–7107).

Hairstylists. Unisex: Toni & Guy (443 North Park Center, Dallas, tel. 214/750–0067), Skiles (Tandy Center, Fort Worth, tel. 817/870–2588).

Health and fitness clubs. *See* Fitness, below.

Limousine services. Dallas-Fort Worth Limousines (tel. 817/467–5355), Limaxi (tel. 214/748–6294).

Liquor stores. Marty's (3316 Oak Lawn Ave., Dallas, tel. 214/526–7796), Sigel's (5757 Greenville Ave., Dallas, tel. 214/739–4012), Majestic (4520 Camp Bowie Blvd., Fort Worth, tel. 817/731–0634).

Mail delivery, overnight. DHL (tel. 214/471–1999, Dallas) Federal Express (tel. 214/358–5271, Dallas; tel. 817/332–6293, Fort Worth; or 800/238–5355), Purolator (tel. 800/645–3333), TNT Skypack (tel. 214/929–8720, Dallas), U.S. Postal Service Express Mail (tel. 214/760–4640, Dallas; tel. 817/625–3616, Fort Worth).

Messenger service. Dial-A-Messenger (tel. 214/630–2921, Dallas; tel. 214/263–1316, Fort Worth).

Office space rentals. Executive Suites of Dallas (1440 W. Mockingbird La., Suite 205, Dallas, tel. 214/634–4428), Fort Worth Executive Center (Fort Worth Club Tower, Fort Worth, tel. 817/336–0800).

Pharmacies, late-night. Eckerd Drugs (7028 Greenville Ave., Dallas, tel. 214/369–3706; 2414 Jacksboro Hwy., Fort Worth, tel. 817/626–8255).

Radio stations, all news. KRLD 1080AM; KDBN 1480AM, business news.

Secretarial services. Parkway Professional Suites (5050 Quorum Dr., Suite 700, Dallas, tel. 214/980–4126), Professional Suites (1700 Pacific Ave., Dallas, tel. 214/922–9888), Summit Secretarial Services (307 W. 7th St., Suite 1800, Fort Worth, tel. 817/332–7096).

Stationery supplies. Bizmart (2998 Stemmons Fwy., Dallas, tel. 214/637–6110; 6732 Camp Bowie, Fort Worth, tel. 817/732–1503).

Taxis. Executive Taxi (tel. 214/554–1212, Dallas and Mid-Cities), Terminal Taxi (tel. 214/350–4445, Dallas), American Taxi Cab (tel. 817/429–8829, Fort Worth).

Theater tickets. *See* The Arts, below.

Train information. Amtrak, Dallas (Union Station, 400 S. Houston Ave., tel. 214/653–1101 or 800/872–7245), Amtrak, Fort Worth (Union Station, 1601 Jones St., tel. 817/334–0268 or 800/872–7245).

Travel agents. Maritz Travel (11353 Emerald St., Dallas, tel. 214/484–1010), Travel Service Everywhere (306 Main St., Fort Worth, tel. 817/332–7434 or 800/433–5703).

Weather (tel. 214/787–1111).

LODGING

The Dallas-Fort Worth area has not one central business district but four: downtown Fort Worth, downtown Dallas, North Dallas, and Las Colinas. Real estate business might bring you to any of these locales. Downtown Dallas also has banking and oil service–related firms, while North Dallas, which runs east–west along LBJ Freeway, about 10 miles north of downtown, has a concentration of the city's high-tech industry. Fort Worth is home to a number of investment concerns. A good many banks are sited in the planned Las Colinas development, located midway between Dallas and the Dallas Fort Worth International Airport; this area has more office space than any Texas city except Dallas and Houston.

With the exception of the Mansion on Turtle Creek, all the hotels listed below offer corporate rates and weekend discounts; inquire when making reservations.

Highly recommended lodgings in each price category are indicated by a star ★ .

Category	Cost*
$$$$ (Very Expensive)	over $175
$$$ (Expensive)	$111–$175
$$ (Moderate)	under $111

All prices are for a standard double room, single occupancy, excluding 13% tax.

Numbers in the margin correspond to numbered hotel locations on the Dallas and Fort Worth Lodging and Dining maps.

Downtown and Near Downtown Dallas

★ ㉗
$$$$
Adolphus Hotel. This old-fashioned hotel has been a fixture in the heart of downtown for more than 75 years, and remains the place of choice for visitors who care about charm and class. A complete renovation a few years ago restored much of its turn-of-the-century comfort, luxury, and service. Guests range from celebrities like rocker Tom Petty to visiting oil executives. The most elegant rooms include four-poster beds and original art. Most rooms have a refrigerator and a second phone in the bathroom. The hotel offers a variety of advantages: a central location minutes from anything of importance downtown; complimentary limousine service anywhere downtown; and complete in-house audiovisual services. There's also one of Dallas's most highly rated (and expensive) restaurants, The French Room. Suites cost more than $1,000 a night. *1321 Commerce St., 75202, tel. 214/742–8200; 800/221–9083; in Texas, 800/441–0574; fax 214/747–3532. Gen. manager, Jeff Trigger. 413 rooms, 21 suites. AE, CB, MC, V.*

㉕
$$$$
Fairmont Hotel. The Dallas outpost of the ritzy national chain attracts everyone from society matrons, who like being next door to the Dallas Museum of Art, to visiting stockbrokers, who like the Fairmont's four-star touches. The two-tower building (one tower is 24 stories high, the other 19), which occupies a city block on the northwest edge of downtown, underwent a multimillion dollar reno-

GREATER DALLAS

Lodging

Dallas Parkway Hilton, **11**

D-FW Hilton Executive Conference Center, **1**

Doubletree at Lincoln Center, **13**

Embassy Suites DFW Airport, **3**

Four Seasons Hotel and Resort, **5**

Grand Kempinski Dallas, **8**

Hyatt Regency DFW, **2**

Marriott Mandalay at Los Colinas, **6**

Marriott Quorum, **9**

Westin Galleria, **12**

Dining

Blue Mesa Grill, **10**

Cacheral, **4**

Celebration, **15**

Gershwin's, **14**

May Dragon, **7**

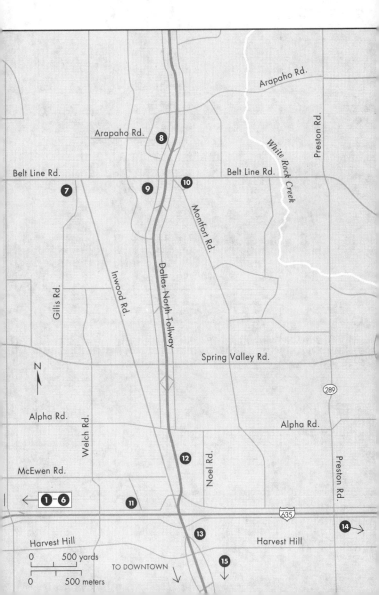

DOWNTOWN DALLAS

vation in the past few years, and every room was refurbished and modernized in earth tones. The ornate lobby features plush carpeting and bright wall hangings. The Fairmont is now considered to be on par with the Adolphus. The Pyramid Room is noted for its Continental cuisine. The Venetian Room, a supper club, features live music. *1717 N. Akard St., 75201. tel. 214/720–2020 or 800/527–4727, fax 214/720–5269. Gen. manager, Rolf Schraegle. 500 rooms, 50 suites. AE, CB, DC, MC, V.*

★ ㉙ **Hyatt Regency Dallas at Reunion.** This 50-story glass-and-
$$$ steel tower with the tennis ball on top is one of the tallest buildings in the city, and has become a recognizable part of Dallas's skyline. On a clear day, the view from the revolving lounge at the top of the ball extends past Fort Worth. Rooms, furnished in earth tones, are a step up from those in most Hyatts, and each one has a view of the waterfalls in the atrium. The on-site shops, arranged in bazaarlike fashion throughout the entire building, are as good as any in Dallas. The hotel is adjacent to Reunion Arena, home of the NBA's Dallas Mavericks and host to conventions and special events (which means guests can range from rowdy conventioneers to conservative church groups). On the negative side, the Hyatt is tucked on the southwestern edge of downtown, six blocks from the city center, and the neighborhood is not a good place to wander after dark. *300 Reunion Blvd., 75207, tel. 214/651–1234 or 800/228–9000, fax 214/742–8126. Gen. manager, Todd Martin. 943 rooms. AE, MC, V.*

⑰ **Loews Anatole.** This plush, modern hotel is one of the best
$$$$ examples of what Dallas was like in the 1980s, when insolvent was never used in the same sentence with savings and loan. Both Ronald Reagan (during the 1984 Republican convention) and Bruce Springsteen (during his "Born in the USA" tour) stayed here. The Anatole's lobby/atrium is all glass, chrome, and tile. The hotel gets tonier—some would say more ostentatious—from there. Rooms on the concierge floor feature Continental breakfast, free use of the hotel's health clubs, and complimentary cocktails. Rooms have separate sitting areas with desks; many have two phones. The location on the city's trade-show corridor, minutes from convention locations and a 10-minute cab ride from downtown, is a plus. The neighborhood on the west side of the hotel is not the best. *2201 Stemmons Fwy., 75207, tel. 214/748–1200 or 800/223–0888, fax 214/761–7242. Gen. manager, John Thacker. 1,475 rooms, 145 suites. AE, CB, DC, MC, V.*

⑲ **The Mansion on Turtle Creek.** The Mansion, built as a pala-
$$$$ tial private home, serves as a lobby and restaurant to an adjoining, nine-story tower in a quiet residential neighborhood about 10 minutes from downtown. The staff's reputation for service is legendary, and tales abound of the extraordinary lengths to which employees go for the cadre of regular guests. If you're not a regular, though, the service can be abrupt. All rooms, decorated in Southwestern colors, open onto balconies or private patios; bathrooms are fitted with Italian marble. The lobby boasts antique furnishings, paintings, and sculpture. This is where the rich and powerful stay, from cotton and oil barons to world celebrities. The hotel's restaurant serves innovative Southwestern cuisine, and is also a good place for business breakfasts (*see* Dining, below). *A Rosewood ho-*

FORT WORTH

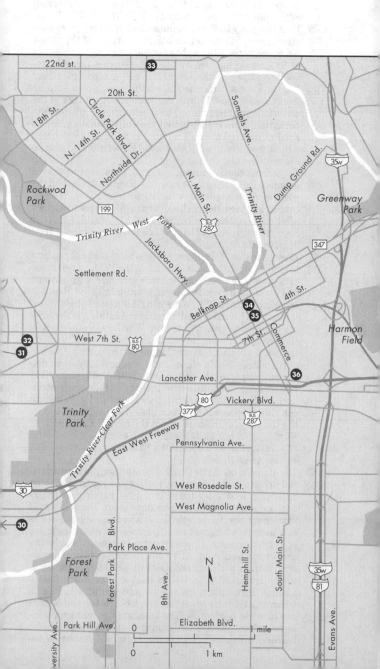

tel. 2821 Turtle Creek Blvd., 75219, tel. 214/559–2100 or 800/223–6800, fax 214/528–4187. Gen. manager, Philip Wood. 128 rooms, 14 suites. AE, CB, DC, MC, V.

㉓ **Stoneleigh Hotel.** In the mid-1980s, this former luxury
$$$ apartment hotel underwent its first renovation in almost 30 years. The lobby's original brass chandeliers, parquet floor, and marble columns were restored, and rooms were comfortably refurnished in tasteful tones of green and brown. Today, the Stoneleigh looks much like many of the small, well-appointed hotels that dot New York's best neighborhoods. It's in the Turtle Creek section, a 10-minute cab ride from downtown or the Market Center corridor, and just blocks away from the McKinney Avenue shopping and restaurant district. What the Stoneleigh lacks in business services it makes up for in comfort. The rooms are bigger than those in most chain hotels, and many have living rooms and kitchens. *2927 Maple Ave., 75201, tel. 214/871–7111; 800/255–9299; in Texas; 800/336–4242; fax 214/871–7111, ext. 1213. Gen. manager, Gary Bruton. 140 rooms, 10 suites. AE, MC, V.*

North Dallas

⓫ **Dallas Parkway Hilton.** This 15-story stucco building is
$$ tucked away behind some service roads, next to an auto dealership. The building is a startling shade of pink, but it's one of the few places in North Dallas where you can get a reasonably priced room. Lobby and rooms are standard Hilton. Colors are assembly-line hues of pink, tan, and beige, and furniture seems flimsy. The hotel business center (open weekdays 8 AM–5 PM) handles most secretarial services. Amenities on the Hilton Club Floor include free local phone calls. Guests can purchase temporary membership to the International Athletic Club, a few blocks north, for $7. *4801 LBJ Fwy., 75244, tel. 214/661–3600 or 800/445–8667, fax 214/385–3156. Gen. manager, Mike Meehan. 296 rooms, 13 suites. AE, CB, DC, MC, V.*

⓭ **Doubletree at Lincoln Centre.** The former Lincoln Hotel,
$$$ on the south side of the LBJ Freeway and east of the Dallas North Tollway, is a convenient base for shopping and doing business. The tinted glass-and-steel building is attached to the three-tower Lincoln Centre office complex by skyways. It's fancier now than when it was the Lincoln, and room rates have risen accordingly. The spacious, high-ceiling lobby overlooks a lake. Rooms are on the small side, though, and the furniture is standard hotel issue—thinly padded arms on the chairs and inexpensively constructed desks and tables. Guests can purchase a temporary membership for the health club facilities in the Lincoln City Club in the adjacent complex. The hotel restaurant, Crockett's, handles Southwestern cuisine respectably. *5410 LBJ Fwy., 75240, tel. 214/934–8400 or 800/528–0444, fax 214/701–5244. Gen. manager, Joe Palmieri. 509 rooms, 21 suites. AE, MC, V.*

★ ❽ **Grand Kempinski Dallas.** This 15-story establishment (the
$$$$ former Registry Hotel) might be the best business hotel in North Dallas; it's certainly the most impressive. Owned by Lufthansa's hotel division, this luxury hostelry is maintained with Teutonic efficiency. It's a blend of the European grand hotel tradition and Southwestern high tech, with a large marble-tile lobby, a business center, and a health club with better equipment than that of many pri-

HOTELS	Price Category	Business Services — Banquet capacity	No. of meeting rooms	Secretarial services	Audiovisual equipment	Teletype news service	Computer rentals	In-room modem phonejack	All-news cable channel	Desk	Desk lighting	Bed lighting
Adolphus	$$$$	750	17	✓	✓	-	✓	✓	✓	◐	●	●
Dallas Parkway Hilton	$$	450	23	✓	✓	-	✓	✓	✓	●	◐	◐
DFW Hilton Executive Conference Center	$$$	900	30	✓	✓	-	-	✓	✓	●	◐	◐
Doubletree at Lincoln Centre	$$$	1200	21	✓	✓	-	-	✓	✓	●	●	◐
Embassy Suites DFW Airport	$$	400	10	✓	✓	-	-	-	✓	●	●	◐
Fairmont	$$$$	180	24	✓	✓	-	✓	✓	✓	◐	◐	◐
Four Seasons Hotel and Resort	$$$	300	26	✓	✓	-	✓	✓	✓	●	●	◐
Grand Kempinski	$$$$	3000	22	✓	✓	-	-	✓	✓	●	●	●
Green Oaks Inn	$$	450	16	-	✓	-	-	-	✓	●	◐	◐
Hilton Fort Worth	$$	600	15	✓	✓	-	-	✓	✓	●	◐	◐
Hyatt Regency Dallas at Reunion	$$$	3000	12	✓	✓	✓	-	✓	✓	●	●	◐
Hyatt Regency DFW	$$$	1800	80	✓	✓	-	-	✓	✓	●	●	●
Loews Anatole	$$$$	3600	80	✓	✓	✓	✓	✓	✓	●	●	●
The Mansion on Turtle Creek	$$$$	145	5	✓	✓	-	✓	✓	✓	●	●	●
Marriott Mandalay at Las Colinas	$$$$	450	14	-	✓	-	-	✓	✓	●	◐	◐
Marriott Quorum	$$$	700	10	✓	✓	-	✓	✓	✓	●	◐	◐
Stoneleigh	$$$	230	3	✓	✓	-	-	✓	✓	●	●	◐
Westin Galleria	$$$	1690	20	-	✓	-	-	✓	✓	●	●	◐
The Worthington	$$$	950	17	-	✓	-	-	-	✓	◐	◐	◐

$$$$ = over $175, $$$ = $111 -$175, $$ = under $111.
● good, ◐ fair, ○ poor.
All hotels listed here have photocopying and fax facilities.

In-Room Amenities										Hotel Amenities						
Nonsmoking rooms	In-room checkout	Minibar	Pay movies	VCR/Movie rentals	Hairdryer	Toiletries	Room service	Laundry/Dry cleaning	Pressing	Concierge	Barber/Hairdresser	Garage	Courtesy airport transport	Sauna	Pool	Exercise room
✓	✓	-	-	-	✓	●	●	●	●	✓	✓	✓	-	-	-	-
✓	-	-	-	-	✓	●	●	◐	◐	-	-	-	-	✓	◐	-
✓	✓	-	✓	-	-	●	◐	◐	◐	✓	-	-	✓	✓	●	●
✓	✓	-	✓	✓	-	◐	◐	◐	◐	✓	-	-	✓	✓	◐	-
✓	-	✓	-	-	-	●	◐	◐	◐	-	-	-	✓	✓	◐	-
✓	✓	-	-	-	-	●	●	●	●	✓	-	-	-	-	-	-
✓	✓	✓	-	-	✓	●	◐	◐	◐	✓	✓	-	-	✓	●	●
✓	✓	-	✓	✓	-	●	◐	◐	◐	✓	-	-	-	✓	●	●
✓	-	-	-	-	✓	●	●	◐	◐	-	-	-	-	✓	●	●
✓	✓	-	-	-	-	●	●	◐	◐	-	-	✓	-	✓	◐	-
✓	-	✓	-	-	-	●	●	◐	◐	✓	-	✓	✓	-	●	●
✓	✓	✓	✓	-	-	◐	◐	●	●	✓	✓	✓	✓	✓	◐	●
✓	-	✓	✓	-	-	●	●	◐	◐	✓	✓	-	✓	✓	●	●
✓	-	-	-	✓	-	●	●	●	●	✓	-	-	-	✓	●	-
✓	✓	-	✓	-	-	●	◐	-	-	✓	-	✓	-	✓	◐	●
✓	✓	-	✓	✓	✓	◐	◐	●	●	✓	-	✓	-	✓	◐	●
-	✓	✓	✓	-	-	◐	◐	◐	◐	✓	✓	✓	✓	-	○	-
✓	✓	✓	✓	✓	-	◐	●	◐	◐	✓	✓	✓	✓	✓	◐	●
✓	-	-	✓	-	-	●	●	◐	●	✓	-	✓	-	✓	●	●

Room service: ● 24-hour, ◐ 6AM–10PM, ○ other.
Laundry/Dry cleaning: ● same day, ◐ overnight, ○ other.
Pressing: ● immediate, ◐ same day, ○ other.

vate facilities. In addition to the usual secretarial services, the business center includes extensive audiovisual services. On the concierge floors (14 and 15) each room has three phones and fresh flowers. *15201 Dallas Pkwy., 75248, tel. 214/386–6000; 800/527–1690; in Texas, 800/442–2039; fax 214/991–6937. Gen. manager, Michael Spencer. 492 rooms, 37 suites. AE, DC, MC, V.*

❾ **Marriott Quorum.** This seven-year-old Marriott property
$$$ fits in nicely with the other glass-and-steel buildings along the Dallas North Parkway. The 12-story hotel finished a room renovation program in 1989. The lobby, a mix of off-white marble and natural wood, isn't as big as many others in North Dallas. Rooms are standard issue, outfitted in shades of green and mauve; king corner accommodations are most spacious. The hotel is just south of Belt Line Road, convenient to both Prestonwood Town Center and The Galleria, and right around the corner from the bars and restaurants that line Belt Line Road in Dallas and Addison. The hotel's nightclub is popular with the younger, professional crowd that stays at the Quorum, and many of the guests are lawyers and real estate developers who do business in the silver towers along the Parkway. *14901 Dallas Pkwy., Addison, 75240, tel. 214/661–2800 or 800/228–9290, fax 214/934–1731. Gen. manager, Stephen Benkowitz. 537 rooms, 10 suites. AE, MC, V.*

⓬ **Westin Galleria.** The 21-story Westin helped pioneer a tru-
$$$ ly Dallas concept—the hotel/shopping mall. It's one of the anchors at The Galleria, where Macy's is the most downscale department store. There's a mall entrance on the second floor of the hotel, near the meeting rooms. It's not the swankiest spot in North Dallas, and it's starting to fray at the far edges. The lobby, for instance, is surprisingly small, and checking out can take time on busy days. Rooms are small, too, but the location, right in the middle of the North Dallas business center, couldn't be better. *13340 Dallas Pkwy., Addison, 75240, tel. 214/934–9494 or 800/228–3000, fax 214/851–2869. Gen. manager, Steve Shalit. 417 rooms, 14 suites. AE, DC, MC, V.*

DFW International Airport/Las Colinas

❶ **D-FW Hilton Executive Conference Center.** This is the
$$$ loneliest hotel in the Dallas-Fort Worth area, isolated in a prairie 2½ miles north of DFW International Airport. Rooms are standard Hilton, but the business and recreational facilities are outstanding—an amphitheater, a 14,000-square-foot exhibit hall, teleconferencing and satellite capabilities, 24-hour access to audiovisual services, a two-level fitness center with tennis and racquetball courts, and even an affiliation with the neighboring Austin Ranch for Texas-style entertainment and parties. Hilton has made an effort to deal with the hotel's remote location; there is a free shuttle service to the airport, and rental cars can be picked up and dropped off at a site at the hotel. Still, don't get any cravings for pizza late at night. *Box 759, Grapevine, 76051, tel. 817/481–8444 or 800/645–1019, fax 817/481–3160. Gen. manager, Juan Aquinde. 411 rooms. AE, CB, DC, MC, V.*

★ ❸ **Embassy Suites DFW Airport.** This goofy-looking hotel—
$$ it has a cupola, and extended eaves—is one of the best business values in the Dallas-Fort Worth area. Functional rather than fancy, it features a prime location at the south

entrance to DFW International, minutes from the terminals and halfway between Dallas and Fort Worth. Standard Embassy Suites have separate bedrooms and sitting rooms. There's free breakfast, an audiovisual service center, and a courtesy bus to the nearby Centerpoint Athletic Club, which hotel guests can use on a per-diem basis. *4650 W. Airport Fwy., Irving, 75062, tel. 214/790–0093 or 800/ 362–2779, fax 214/790–4768. Gen. manager, Josef Puhringer. 308 rooms. AE, MC, V.*

❺ **Four Seasons Hotel and Resort.** This hotel looks like a
$$$ Frank Lloyd Wright–designed country club, with low ceilings, earth-hugging shapes, and earth colors. It takes up a large portion of the Las Colinas office center—some 300 rooms and suites, a couple of golf courses, a separate building for the health club, an amphitheater, and a media center providing design, print, and graphic services. Each room has a balcony that overlooks the TPC course (site of the Professional Golfers' Association's GTE Byron Nelson Classic) and oversized bathrooms, some with separate showers and bathtubs. There are two sets of rates: the standard European plan and the conference plan, which includes meals, use of the health and conference facilities, gratuities, and airport transportation. *4150 N. MacArthur Blvd., Irving, 75038, tel. 214/717–0700 or 800/ 332–3442, fax 214/717–2550. Gen. manager, Jim Fitzgibbon. 312 rooms, 3 suites. AE, CB, DC, MC, V.*

❷ **Hyatt Regency DFW.** An air of hustle and bustle pervades
$$$ this Hyatt, the largest airport hotel in the world. The hotel has two towers, 14 stories on the east side, 13 stories on the west. Guests can register at either (unless they are part of a group). Rooms are relatively spacious and somewhat above standard issue. The Hyatt also has its own Airtrans courtesy van station and provides shuttle service to the terminals. The Business Communications Center features a 24-hour dictation service. Guests can also use the Hyatt Bear Creek Golf and Racquet Club, five minutes away at the southern edge of the airport; resort/hotel packages are available. *Box 619014, DFW Airport, 75261, tel. 214/453–8400 or 800/228–9000, fax 214/453–0638. Gen. manager, Abdul Suleman. 1,320 rooms, 49 suites. AE, MC, V.*

❻ **Marriott Mandalay at Las Colinas.** Marriott bought the
$$$$ Mandalay several years ago, and since then has toned down the Oriental motif (although bronze Siamese elephants still greet guests at the door) and upgraded the business services. The Mandalay is well located, in the middle of Las Colinas near shopping, the monorail, and the canal (with its water taxis). The regal-looking lobby is decorated in beige and gold and boasts a fountain. Many rooms have an Oriental motif and are comfortably furnished with sitting areas. King single rooms are exceptionally spacious. The Mandalay is well known for its weekend specials, one of which includes golf at nearby Fossil Creek. Weekend discounts can be as much as half the weeknight rate. The hotel's French restaurant, Enjolie, is among the trendiest in the Dallas area. *221 E. Las Colinas Blvd., Irving, 75039, tel. 214/556–0800 or 800/228–9290, fax, 214/869–9053. Gen. manager, Jim Kauffman. 322 rooms, 98 suites. AE, MC, V.*

Fort Worth

③⓪ **Green Oaks Inn.** From the outside, it looks like a motel
$$ from a 1950s travelogue, but the interior is clean, the staff
is efficient, and most business travelers consider this the
leading business hotel in west Fort Worth. The lobby is
low-ceilinged, with brick walls and a fireplace. Rooms are
nondescript but quiet and decently furnished. The ball-
room holds 1,000. It's a five-minute drive to Carswell Air
Force Base and General Dynamics's Fort Worth division,
and 10 minutes to downtown Fort Worth along the West
Freeway. Ridgemar Mall is across the street. An on-site
American Airlines AAirlink office lets passengers check in
for their flights at the hotel. *A Kahler hotel. 6901 West
Fwy., 76116, tel. 817/738–7311; 800/433–2174; in Texas,
800/772–2341; fax 817/377–1308. Gen. manager, Her-
mann Jung. 273 rooms, 9 suites. AE, MC, V.*

③⑥ **Hilton Fort Worth.** An extensive renovation began in 1990
$$ for this 12-story property on the south edge of downtown,
near I–30, and across from the Fort Worth Water Gar-
dens. Ask for an updated room. The hotel isn't as centrally
located as several others downtown, and it's a healthy
walk to Sundance Square. However, the Tarrant County
Convention Center is only three blocks from here. The
lobby, decorated in Southwestern pinks, is narrow and
can get crowded at check-out time. The Hilton's business-
floor service includes free local calls and the chain's
corporate amenities. *1701 Commerce St., 76102, tel. 817/
335–7000 or 800/445–8667, fax 817/335–7850. Gen. manager, Nelson Barnes. 424 rooms, 10 suites. AE, MC, V.*

★ ③④ **The Worthington Hotel.** Built in 1981, this white lump of a
$$$ building is one of the newest in a downtown that prides it-
self on its 19th-century roots. It is, nonetheless, Fort
Worth's preeminent luxury hotel, with two waterfalls in
the lobby, high tea every afternoon from 3 to 5, and rooms
with separate sitting areas. The lobby's contemporary
look is carried through to the room, which are decorated in
pastels, with comfortable furnishings. Closets are extra
large. The Worthington is part of Sundance Square, the
center of the city's efforts to invigorate its downtown with
upscale shops and restaurants. It's also across the street
from the Tandy Center Shopping mall and six blocks from
the Tarrant County Convention Center. The health club
includes an indoor pool and workout classes for guests.
The Reflections restaurant, serving nouvelle cuisine in an
Art Deco room, is the leading Fort Worth power lunch
spot. *200 Main St., 76102, tel. 817/870–1000; 800/433–
5677; in Texas, 800/772–5977; fax, 817/332–5679. Gen.
manager. Robert Jameson. 438 rooms, 69 suites. AE,
MC, V.*

DINING

Eating out is a social event in the Dallas-Fort Worth area.
People go to restaurants to be seen and to impress others,
and they very often dress up to do it. The food is often inci-
dental (which explains why this area is one of the last bas-
tions of nouvelle cuisine).

The Dallas-Fort Worth area is best known for two kinds of
cuisine: Southwestern—a "nouvelle Mexican" style, often

involving mesquite grilling as well as unusual combinations and the use of native American ingredients such as blue corn—pioneered by such Dallas chefs as Stephen Pyles at Routh Street Café and Dean Fearing at The Mansion on Turtle Creek; and Tex-Mex, a heavier North Texas derivative of traditional Mexican cooking that features enchiladas and fajitas. The chicken and sour cream enchilada, for instance, was invented in this area, and the ultimate Tex-Mex restaurant is Fort Worth's Joe T. Garcia's.

Thanks to Texas's Baptist heritage, all of Dallas (except for downtown and near north areas) and almost every suburban city between Dallas and Fort Worth is dry (Fort Worth itself is wet). There is no BYOB, either. Some restaurants get around the law by asking patrons to pay an additional fee to join the restaurant's private club.

Remember two names—the Dixie House and Black-Eyed Pea—if you want to eat but don't want to make a production out of it. These popular chain restaurants, located throughout the Dallas-Fort Worth area, feature homestyle cooking (the chicken-fried steak is as good as anything in a diner in West Texas) at reasonable prices.

Highly recommended restaurants in each price category are indicated by a ★.

Category	Cost*
$$$$ (Very Expensive)	over $50
$$$ (Expensive)	$25–$50
$$ (Moderate)	under $25

per person, including appetizer, entrée, and dessert, but excluding drinks, service, and 8% sales tax.

Numbers in the margin correspond to numbered restaurant locations on the Dallas-Fort Worth Lodging and Dining maps.

Business Breakfasts

Power breakfasts are not very popular in this rather traditional area, where people prefer to do their wheeling and dealing a bit later in the day. The main exception to this rule is **The Mansion on Turtle Creek** (214/526–2121); important matters are discussed over everything from fruit platters and bagels and lox to huevos rancheros and raspberry buttermilk pancakes in the mansion's sunny, tile-floor Promenade Room. Reservations (preferably a day in advance) are required; breakfast is served weekdays from 7–10:30, weekends until 11:30.

Downtown Dallas

26
$$$
Dakota's. An elevator on Akard Street takes guests down to this wood-paneled dining room, a popular lunch spot for local businesspeople; the modern but clublike room never gets too crowded or noisy for serious talk. The menu features New American food, combining the best elements of Southwestern and nouvelle cuisines. (In other words, Dakota's serves vegetables like jicama, but doesn't make a meal out of them.) The best entrées are mesquite grilled: try the smoked pork tenderloin or the swordfish. The wine

list, though expensive, offers some interesting California choices. The restaurant has valet parking, and is extremely popular with couples on the weekend. *600 N. Akard St., tel. 214/740–4001. Jacket and tie suggested. Reservations required. AE, MC, V.*

㉒ **Lawry's, The Prime Rib.** The menu is extremely limited
$$$ and the waitresses dress in kitschy 19th-century costumes, but Dallas adores this entry from the national chain. It's almost always busy at lunch and dinner, particularly with older businessmen dining together or with their families; you're likely to be taken here if your Dallas business contact is fairly traditional. Sandwiches are served at lunch, but roast beef is the only entrée offered at dinner. The prime rib lives up to Lawry's reputation, and the Victorian library atmosphere works well. But the side dishes, served à la carte, are undistinguished. *3008 Maple Ave., tel. 214/521–7777. Jacket and tie required. Reservations required. AE, MC, V.*

⑲ **The Mansion on Turtle Creek.** This opulent restaurant
$$$$ helped pioneer Southwestern cuisine, and it is a mecca for the beautiful, celebrated, and powerful in the Dallas-Fort Worth area. Located some 15 minutes from downtown, in a hotel of the same name, the Mansion is one of the city's premier power lunch spots, and the only place for a power breakfast. But don't expect to be treated well (or even civilly) unless you are known to the staff—which is a shame, as the cooking is as good as any in the city. A different menu is featured daily. Chef Dean Fearing's vision of Southwestern cuisine features such specialties as tortilla soup, warm lobster tacos, and halibut with cashews in a basil sauce, all stunningly presented. *2821 Turtle Creek Blvd., tel. 214/526–2121. Jacket and tie required. Reservations required. AE, DC, MC, V.*

⑱ **Mucky Duck.** This is a surprisingly near-authentic En-
$$ glish pub (even though it's in the back of a shopping center), complete with dart boards, an Irish bartender who can talk about "The Troubles," legitimate pub grub, and Fuller Extra Special Bitter on tap. Mucky Duck is a neighborhood hangout for young professionals in the affluent Turtle Creek area, 15 minutes north of downtown Dallas, and never gets too raucous (although there is live folk-rock music Thursday through Sunday nights). It's popular, too, with students from Southern Methodist University. Come for lunch (try the shepherd's pie) or to unwind after work; it's even possible to talk business over a pint. Women seem to feel especially comfortable here. *3102 Welborn St., Suite 100, tel. 214/522–7200. Casual dress. No reservations. AE, MC, V.*

㉔ **Newport's.** The Dallas-Fort Worth area, some 300 miles
$$ from the nearest ocean, is not famous for seafood, but Newport's, a fashionable and upscale spot on lower McKinney Avenue, just minutes from downtown Dallas, is among the best of the lot. The fish is flown in fresh daily, and the menu and prices change depending on the day's catch. The restaurant was part of an old brewery and has lots of exposed brick and wood and an open kitchen. It is popular among calorie-conscious executives at lunch; somewhat off the beaten path, Newport's never gets too noisy to preclude business discussion. Menu specialties include grilled fresh grouper and swordfish. *703 McKinney*

Ave., tel. 214/954-0220. Jacket suggested. Reservations suggested. AE, MC, V.

㉘ The Palm. The Dallas outpost of this steak-and-lobster
$$$$ chain is the place in Big D for a power lunch. It's almost impossible to walk into the downtown location at lunchtime and not recognize a face from the papers or television; Southwest Airlines chairman Herb Kelleher likes The Palm so much that the restaurant has reserved a Southwest Airlines room. The service and decor are much the same as at the Palms in New York, Washington, and Los Angeles—caricatures of customers on the dark wall and waiters who graduated from the Don Rickles School of Charm and go out of their way to ignore women dining without men. The lunch menu is unexceptional; the dinner menu features all of the things The Palm is famous for, including 12-pound lobsters and steaks the size of placemats. *701 Ross Ave., tel. 214/698-0470. Jacket suggested. Reservations suggested. AE, DC, MC, V.*

★ ㉑ Routh Street Café. Chef Stephen Pyles's restaurant is as
$$$$ good as everyone says it is. Opened in 1985, Routh Street Café now ranks with top-class restaurants all over the world. The staff is pleasant, too. It's an ideal place to entertain clients, talk business, or just enjoy an outstanding meal. The five-course, fixed-priced menu offers several choices for each course; options change daily. The cuisine is Southwestern: Try the tamale tart for a starter and the barbecued rib-eye steak as an entrée. Weekend reservations must be made at least one week in advance. Pyles has opened a more casual restaurant, Baby Routh, a few blocks down the street, to handle the overflow. *3005 Routh St., tel. 214/871-7161. Jacket and tie required. Reservations required. Dinner only. Closed Sun. and Mon. AE, MC, V.*

North Dallas

⑩ Blue Mesa Grill. This is the quintessential Dallas restau-
$$ rant, where fashion-conscious people come more for the atmosphere than for the food. Customers come to sit in one of the cowhide-covered booths; to relax at a table in front of the Texas-sized fireplace; or to drink a blue margarita (this is one of the few wet areas in dry North Dallas). The cuisine is modeled on Mark Miller's Coyote Café in Santa Fe, but fortunately it is not as trendy. There are fajitas to go along with the corn pasta, cheese chili rellenos, fried yam chips, and duck-filled *taquitos* (similar to tacos). Blue Mesa is a popular lunch spot for many executives who work in North Dallas along the crowded tollway/parkway corridor; the atmosphere is more laid back at dinner. *5100 Belt Line Rd., Village on the Parkway, Addison, tel. 214/934-0165. Casual but neat. No reservations. AE, MC, V.*

⑦ May Dragon. One of the most popular business lunch spots
$$ in North Dallas, this moderately priced Chinese restaurant is always crowded with men in three-piece suits talking to other men in three-piece suits. It isn't noisy, it isn't trendy, and it's not a place to impress clients with elegant decor or fine cuisine. But the service is impeccable, the atmosphere is comfortable, and it's possible to make deals here. The menu mixes Hunan and Szechuan, which means it offers such dishes as lobster in ginger root-and-scallion sauce, and beef stir-fried with vermicelli. *4848 Belt Line*

Rd., Addison, tel. 214/392–9998. Casual but neat. Reservations suggested. AE, MC, V.

Near North Dallas

⑭ **Gershwin's.** This major yuppie watering hole is the fron-
$$$ tier between wet and dry Dallas. On Friday and Saturday
nights, the crowd at the bar stretches from the front door
to the kitchen; don't even think about trying to have a seri-
ous discussion here. The restaurant has a New Orleans fla-
vor, both in its menu—with plenty of fresh grilled fish
including the obligatory blackened redfish—and in its de-
cor—neo-French Quarter, with brick walls, plenty of
glass, and a piano player. There's also a creditable bread
pudding. The tables in back, adjacent to the kitchen, are
the most private. The wine list is adequate, but over-
priced. *8442 Walnut Hill La., tel. 214/373–7171. Casual
but neat. AE, MC, V.*

East Dallas

⑯ **Bohemia.** The Dallas-Fort Worth area (with its Scottish-
$$ Irish heritage) doesn't have many great ethnic restaurants. This intimate, candlelit dining room, serving East
European–style cuisine, is one of the exceptions. The Bo-
hemia, which has about a dozen tables, takes up the front
room of a two-story house between the boutique-filled
shops of the pricey Upper McKinney Avenue neighborhood and a decidedly more blue-collar section of East Dallas. It is not part of the city's trendy dining scene; the
crowd is older and quieter than at other, similarly priced
restaurants. Highlights of the Czech-influenced menu include marvelously light dumplings that come with every
meal, beef Prague (a type of stew), and very traditional
Wiener schnitzel and chicken paprika. The short, inexpensive wine list features East European labels. *2810 N.
Henderson Ave., tel. 214/826–6290. Casual but neat. Dinner only. Reservations required. Closed Mon., Tues.,
and the week between Christmas and New Year's. AE,
MC, V.*

⑳ **Lakewood Plaza Grill.** There's nothing spectacular about
$$$ this two-level neighborhood spot in the Lakewood section,
a 15-minute cab ride from downtown Dallas—just a good
meal in comfortable surroundings. The decor is glass with
black-and-white tile, the service is usually efficient, and
it's possible to have dinner and to talk without being both-
ered by overzealous waiters. Try to get a table upstairs,
where it's quieter and more secluded. The menu is eclec-
tic, with choices as simple as hamburgers and salads shar-
ing space with items like venison sausage. Any of the
grilled chicken specialties is worth sampling. The wine
list, with Texas and California selections, is good. *6334
LaVista Dr., tel. 214/826–5226. Casual but neat. No res-
ervations. AE, DC, MC, V.*

West Dallas

★ ⑮ **Celebration.** This is one of the few places in the Dallas area
$$ to get an honest meal at a moderate price, which explains
why customers wait for up to an hour almost every night;
come before 6:30 or after 9 if you want to avoid the crowds.
The restaurant, in a renovated house in a residential
neighborhood near Love Field, is a good choice for a leisurely, casual meal after a day of serious meetings. Ask

for a booth; they're farther from the large tables with yelling children. The menu features traditional Texas/Southern cooking—chicken-fried steak, meat loaf, fried catfish, and pot roast—combined with daily specials, bowls of vegetables, and a wine list with several Texas selections. The food is served family style, and most entrées are all-you-can-eat. There is also a newer location in Fort Worth, in the old Crystal Ice House near the Cultural District. *4503 W. Lovers La., tel. 214/351–5681. Casual dress. Reservations required for parties of 6 or more. AE, MC, V.*

Fort Worth

★ ③ **Joe T. Garcia's.** This is the ultimate Tex-Mex restaurant,
$$ where cowboy-boot-clad customers drink Mexican beer and the bartenders mix potent margaritas. Don't plan on doing any business here; rather, celebrate after it's done. Joe T's, as it is fondly known, doesn't take credit cards, doesn't accept reservations, and doesn't serve anything other than beef and chicken fajitas and cheese enchiladas. There's usually a wait for tables, and on Saturday nights the wait can stretch to an hour. Don't be deterred by the location: a ramshackle old house in north Fort Worth a few blocks south of the Stockyards. In spring or fall it's pleasant to eat outside on the patio. *2201 N. Commerce St., tel. 817/624–0266. Casual dress. No reservations. No credit cards.*

★ ③ **Saint-Emilion.** It doesn't look like much from the outside,
$$$ but this tiny, buff-color brick building nestled between doctors' offices in west Fort Worth is one of the two or three best restaurants in Tarrant County. Saint-Emilion serves a variety of purposes: as a power dining spot (the service defines discreet), as a place to be seen, and as the site for country French cooking few would expect in a city whose nickname is Cowtown. There are two fixed-price menus at dinner and one at lunch, featuring roasted duck, rack of lamb, and veal dishes. Chef Patrice de Faveri prepares entrées in the open in the comfortable main dining room, and the wine list includes some good values in Bordeaux. *3617 W. 7th St., tel. 817/737–2781. Casual but neat. Reservations required. Closed Sun. and Mon. lunch. AE, MC, V.*

③ **Tours.** The cuisine here is an unlikely combination of
$$$ Southwestern influences and traditional French cooking, but it is more than successful. The menu changes weekly, but it can include dishes such as veal sweetbreads, trout meunière, and fettucine with mushrooms and bacon. The dining room is frilly in a pleasant, un-Texaslike way, with attention to detail; service can be slow, however. If you have time, this is a dignified setting for a discussion without distractions. A more basic menu is on offer at the bar, which stays open until midnight. The weekend brunch, served from 11 AM–2 PM weekends, is recommended. *3500 W. 7th St., tel. 817/870–1672. Casual but neat. Reservations suggested on weekends. Closed for dinner Sun. AE, MC, V.*

③ **Winfield '08's.** One of the best of the new restaurants in
$$ Sundance Square in downtown Fort Worth, Winfield '08's is extremely popular at lunch time. The menu is nothing to get excited about—hamburgers and salads—but the desserts are interesting, and the daily specials are reasonably priced and more than competently prepared. Service

is professional. The newly restored building started life as the 50-room Savoy Hotel in 1908; the Winfield in the restaurant's name refers to Winfield Scott, the Fort Worth tycoon who built the hotel. The dining room's brass and green decor is in keeping with the Victorian style of the original structure. *301 Main St., tel. 817/870–1908. Casual dress. No reservations. AE, MC, V.*

Arlington

❹ **Cacharel.** Located on the ninth floor of an office building
$$$ overlooking the Six Flags Over Texas amusement park, Cacharel is easily the best restaurant in the Mid-Cities, serving simple, country French food in an unintimidating atmosphere. The three-course, fixed-price menu at lunch and dinner includes a choice of fresh seafood, beef, or veal. The duck braised with blackcurrant sauce is worth the 20-minute drive from Dallas or Fort Worth. Cacharel, long a favorite with the local television community, is probably the best spot for a proper business dinner in an area filled with chains and fast-food restaurants. *2221 E. Lamar Blvd., Arlington, tel. 817/640–9981. Jacket and tie suggested. Reservations required. AE, MC, V.*

FREE TIME

Fitness

Hotel Facilities
Most of the area's hotel facilities are open only to guests at the hotel. An exception in Fort Worth is the first-rate health club at the **Worthington** (tel. 817/870–1000); nonguests pay $7 per day.

Health Clubs
The **Downtown Dallas YMCA** (601 N. Akard St., tel. 214/954–0500) is well equipped to provide a variety of workouts, offering a pool, running track, squash and racquetball courts, free-weight and machine rooms, and aerobics classes. The fee for nonmembers is $10 per day.

Jogging
In Dallas, the best place to go jogging is along the 12-mile path around east Dallas's White Rock Lake, site of the annual White Rock Marathon. In Fort Worth, try the 7-mile course west along the Trinity River from downtown to the Cultural District.

Shopping

Dallas
The glitzy **Galleria** (tel. 214/702–7100) and its 185 stores (including Macy's, tel. 214/851–3300; and Marshall Field, tel. 214/851–1461) is the top attraction in North Dallas, while the **Valley View Center** (tel. 214/661–2424) is less than a mile away. The flagship **Neiman Marcus** (1618 Main St., tel. 214/741–6911) has been a downtown landmark for more than 80 years and still attracts many of Dallas's wealthiest shoppers. The **McKinney Avenue** district near downtown includes an Espirit (2425 McKinney Ave., tel. 214/871–8989) superstore for casual women's clothing; the posh Crescent (tel. 214/871–5150) (with Stanley Korshak, a retailer who provides space to designer shops like Ralph Lauren and Donna Karan, as the anchor) across the street; and the Paris-based men's boutique Hippolyte (2800

Routh St., tel. 214/855–5081) a few blocks away in the Quadrangle. **NorthPark Center** (tel. 214/363–7441) on Northwest Highway includes a ritzy Neiman's (No. 400, tel. 214/363–8311) and one of the largest Limited's (women's sportswear) (No. 452, tel. 214/363–7528) in the country among its 150 shops.

It's also possible to save as much as 50% on cowboy boots at outlet stores such as Just Justin (1505 Wycliff Ave., tel. 214/630–2858).

Fort Worth
In downtown Fort Worth, the twin-towered **Tandy Center** (tel. 817/390–3717) features three levels of shops, a privately operated subway, and an ice-skating rink. At the nearby **Sundance Square,** shops and boutiques fill up a two-block area.

The **Stockyards District** in Fort Worth includes about a dozen places to stock up on Western-style souvenirs.

Diversions

Dallas
The **Dallas Museum of Art** (1717 N. Harwood St., tel. 214/922–1200) is best known for its contemporary-style building by architect Edward Larabec Barnes (it's the linchpin of the downtown Arts District), and for its Wendy and Emery Reeves Collection of objets d'art and furniture. The collection is displayed in a room resembling the Reeves's Mediterranean villa.

Fair Park, in south Dallas, is the site of the Cotton Bowl stadium, the Starplex outdoor amphitheater, and a handful of museums, including the Science Place and Museum of Natural History.

The **Sixth Floor** (411 Elm St., tel. 214/653–6666) is on the sixth floor of the old Texas School Book Depository, where Lee Harvey Oswald waited in ambush for President John F. Kennedy. The 9,000-square-foot exhibit on Kennedy and his death is a moving experience.

The **Swiss Avenue Historic District** of houses and mansions stretches for three miles from downtown to Lakewood in east Dallas. The first eight blocks (before Baylor Medical Center) are lined with Victorian gingerbread homes; the last mile (between Munger Ave. and La Vista St.) has dozens of mansions and town houses. Pick up a map of the district at the Dallas Convention & Visitor's Bureau (1201 Elm St., Suite 2000, tel. 214/746–6672.)

Fort Worth
The **Amon Carter Museum** (3501 Camp Bowie Blvd., tel. 817/738–1933) has the world's leading collection of Frederic Remington and Charles Russell paintings and sculptures, and several noteworthy Georgia O'Keeffes.

The **Fort Worth Stockyards** in north Fort Worth, designated a national historic district in 1976, includes the Cowtown Coliseum rodeo arena (tel. 817/625–1025), Billy Bob's Texas honky-tonk (*see* After Hours, below), and a live cattle auction at 10 AM each Monday.

Kimbell Art Museum (3333 Camp Bowie Blvd., tel. 817/332–8451) is one of the best small art museums in the

United States. It is also one of the richest, with the second-largest acquisition budget in the country. Expect to see one or two outstanding examples from each major period from the Renaissance to the early 20th century.

Professional Sports

For football, see the **Dallas Cowboys** at Texas Stadium in Irving (tel. 214/556–2500). Dallas's basketball team, the **Dallas Mavericks,** plays at Reunion Arena (tel. 214/658–7068). Also at Reunion Arena are the **Dallas Sidekicks,** the city's soccer team (tel. 214/361–5425). **Mesquite Championship Rodeo** competitions take place at MCR Arena in Mesquite (tel. 214/285–8777). The region's baseball club, the **Texas Rangers,** plays at Arlington Stadium (tel. 817/273–5100).

The Arts

The Dallas-Fort Worth area offers all of the entertainment options you'd expect in a major regional metropolitian area. The **Fort Worth Ballet** (tel. 817/763–0207) performs at the Tarrant County Convention Center Theater; the home of the **Dallas Opera** (tel. 214/979–0123) is the Music Hall at Fair Park; the **Dallas Symphony Orchestra** (tel. 214/692–0203) plays in the new Morton H. Myerson Center in the Arts District. There's a lively theater scene, led by the **Dallas Theater Center** and the **Majestic Theater,** and Fort Worth's **Casa Manana,** as well as its offbeat **Hip Pocket Theater.** All the major pop groups that visit the area play at the large **Starplex Amphitheater.**

Ticket agencies include Texas Tickets (8840 N. Central Expressway, Dallas, tel. 214/696–8001 or 800/882–9600) and First Row Tickets (11613 N. Central Expressway, Dallas, tel. 214/750–7555). Scalping, incidentally, is legal in Texas.

Casa Manana Playhouse, 3101 W. Lancaster Ave., Fort Worth, tel. 817/332–9319.
Dallas Theater Center, 3636 Turtle Creek Blvd., Dallas, tel. 214/526–8857.
Hip Pocket Theater, 1627 Fairmount Ave., tel. 817/927–2833.
Majestic Theater, 1925 Elm St., Dallas, tel. 214/692–9090.
Morton H. Myerson Center, Pearl and Munger Sts., Dallas, tel. 214/565–9100.
Music Hall at Fair Park, tel. 214/565–1116.
Starplex Amphitheater, 1818 First Ave., Dallas, tel. 214/421–1111.
Tarrant County Convention Center Theater, 1111 Houston St., Fort Worth, tel. 817/332–9222.

After Hours

This area isn't as strong for live music as Austin is, but the club scene is more than healthy. In Dallas, it ranges from the neopunk bars of Deep Ellum, an entertainment district just east of downtown, to the country-and-western spots along Greenville Avenue, to the Yuppie nightclubs in the downtown West End development. In Fort Worth, downtown's Caravan of Dreams offers an eclectic mix of jazz, funk, and new music. In the Stockyards, there are a host of honky-tonks, led by Billy Bob's Texas.

Bars and Lounges

Dallas. The **Library** at the Omni Melrose (3015 Oak Lawn Ave., tel. 214/521–5151) is perfect for a power drink: It's proper, quiet, and sedate. The **Stoneleigh P.** (2926 Maple Ave., tel. 214/871–2346) is more relaxed and informal. The **Scoreboard Sports Bar & Grill** (4872 Belt Line Rd., Addison, tel. 214/788–5444) is one of the few places to get a drink in the dry North Dallas area.

Fort Worth. The **Main Street Bar and Grille** (318 Main St., tel. 817/870–9165) stays open until 2 AM on weekends.

Cabaret

Dallas. Barney Oldfield's (Sheraton Mockingbird, 1893 W. Mockingbird La., tel. 214/634–8850) is a Las Vegas-style showroom with dinner and dancing.

Comedy Clubs

Dallas. The **Improv** (Corner Shopping Center, 8910 N. Central Expressway, tel. 214/750–5858; 4980 Belt Line Rd., Addison, tel. 214/404–8501) features national acts. Dinner reservations are required. In Tarrant County, try the **Comedy Corporation** (Lincoln Square II, Arlington, tel. 817/792–3700) and the **Funny Bone** (Arkansas and Hwy. 360, Arlington, tel. 817/265–2277).

Jazz Clubs

Dallas. The venerable **Poor David's Pub** (1924 Greenville Ave., tel. 214/821–9891) books more Texas blues and rock acts than jazz, but probably is the best live music spot in Dallas—folding chairs and all.

Fort Worth. The **Caravan of Dreams Performing Arts Center** (312 Houston St., tel. 817/877–3000) has a national reputation.

For Singles

Dallas. 8.0 (2800 Routh St., tel. 214/979–0800) tops the McKinney Avenue scene, where the young and the beautiful gather. In the West End, **Dick's Last Resort** (1701 N. Market St., tel. 214/747–0001) is rowdy without being too redneck. **Dallas Alley** (West End Marketplace, tel. 214/988–9378) offers a variety of music, from blues to pop.

Fort Worth. Billy Bob's Texas (2520 Rodeo Plaza, tel. 817/624–7117) must be seen to be believed—a Disneyland of longneck beers and country music. The popular **White Elephant Saloon** in the Stockyards (106 E. Exchange Ave., tel. 817/624–1887), is a country-and-western bar, and trendy **West Side Stories** (3900 Hwy. 377 S., tel. 817/560–7632) is a group of nightclubs offering rock, blues, and pop.

Frankfurt

by Graham Lees

Before World War II, this city on the River Main (pronounced "Mine") boasted one of the best-preserved medieval centers in Europe. Wartime air raids destroyed most of the city's historical monuments. Today, Frankfurt is an abrasive, pushy, hard-headed cosmopolitan city with a downtown forest of glass-and-concrete towers—earning it the nickname "Mainhattan." There's nothing extraordinary about Frankfurt's modern architecture, but no other city center in Europe has so many downtown skyscrapers so closely clustered.

Frankfurt—another nickname is "Bankfurt"—is the financial capital of Germany, although it ranks only sixth in size among the country's cities. It is home to the nation's biggest and most important stock exchange and to offices of some 200 foreign banks and 350 credit institutions. It is also the headquarters of virtually every large German bank, including the nation's central bank, Deutsche Bundesbank.

Frankfurt's commercial prowess is centuries-old (it had a thriving money market as early as the 16th century), but its current leading role in German financial affairs stems from the end of World War II, when Berlin ceased to be the nation's capital.

About half of the city's income today is generated by industry, particularly in the fields of mechanical and electrical engineering, chemicals, and printing and publishing. Continental Europe's biggest international airport, largest hotel, and busiest trade-fair center are here. Frankfurt's important international trade fairs showcase the latest books, furs, and cars. The twice-yearly Frankfurter International Fair displays a wide range of consumer goods.

German reunification and the reestablishment of Berlin as the nation's capital are unlikely to affect Frankfurt's role as financial center for the time being, and it will be years before Leipzig—the other historic German trade-fair center—can provide serious competition for Frankfurt as an exhibition/convention city.

Top Employers

Employer	Type of Enterprise	Parent*/ Headquarters
AEG	Electrical engineering	Frankfurt
Deutsche Bank	Privately owned bank	Frankfurt
Deutsche ICI	Chemicals	ICI (Imperial Chemical Industry)/ London
Dresdner Bank	Privately owned bank	Frankfurt
Frankfurt Airport	Airport	Frankfurt
Hartmann and Braun	Technical instrument manufacturer	Frankfurt
Hoechst	Pharmaceuticals	Frankfurt
Metallgesellschaft	Heavy foundry products manufacturer	Frankfurt
Stadtwerke	All-purpose public utility	Frankfurt
Zurich Vericherungs	Insurance	Zurich

if applicable

ESSENTIAL INFORMATION

We include the Frankfurt telephone area code (069) with all numbers listed below. If you are calling from outside Germany, omit the 0 from the code; if you are calling from within Frankfurt, omit the area code altogether.

The currency of Germany is the mark; abbreviated throughout the chapter as DM.

Government Tourist Offices

German National Tourist Office. In the United States: 747 3rd Ave., New York, NY 10017, tel. 215/308–3300; 444 S. Flower St., Suite 2230, Los Angeles, CA 90071, tel. 213/688–7332.
In Canada: Box 417, 2 Fundy, Place Bonaventure, Montréal H5A 1B8, Quebec, tel. 514/878–9885.
In the United Kingdom: 65 Curzon St., London W1Y 7PE, tel. 071/495–3990.
In Frankfurt: *Hauptbahnof* (main train station), across from platform 23, tel. 069/2128849.

Foreign Trade Information

German Chamber of Commerce. In the United States: 666 5th Ave., New York, NY 10103, tel. 212/974–8830; 104 S. Michigan Ave., Suite 600, Chicago, IL 60603, tel. 312/782–

8557; 3250 Wilshire Blvd., Suite 1612, Los Angeles, CA 90010, tel. 213/381–2236.

In Canada: 1010 rue Sherbrooke Ouest, Suite 1604, Montréal H3A 2R7, Quebec, tel. 514/844–3051; 480 University Ave., Suite 1410, Toronto M5G 1V2, Ontario, tel. 416/596–3355.

In the United Kingdom: 12–13 Suffolk St., St. James, London SW1Y 4HG, tel. 071/236–0294.

Entry Requirements

U.S. and Canadian citizens
Passport only. A visa is required for visitors who remain longer than 90 days.

British citizens
Passport only.

Climate

What follows are the average daily maximum and minimum temperatures for Frankfurt.

Jan.	38F	3C	Feb.	41F	5C	Mar.	52F	11C
	29	– 2		31	– 1		36	2
Apr.	61F	16C	May	68F	20C	June	74F	23C
	43	6		49	9		56	13
July	77F	25C	Aug.	76F	24C	Sept.	70F	21C
	59	15		58	14		52	11
Oct.	58F	14C	Nov.	47F	8C	Dec.	40F	4C
	45	7		38	3		32	0

Airport

Frankfurt Airport is 10 kilometers (6 miles) southwest of downtown and is linked to the city by train and expressway. It is the biggest and busiest airport in Continental Europe, handling about 25 million passengers a year on 70 scheduled airlines. An additional terminal is planned for 1992. The current airport terminal and facilities are constructed in tiers. Below ground are an intercity train station and parking for 6,000 cars; arriving passengers are processed on the ground floor, departing passengers on the second floor. Facilities include a shopping center with a supermarket and 100 shops, three movie theaters, 20 restaurants, a disco, a chapel, and an exhibition gallery.

Airlines

Frankfurt is the home base of the German national airline, Lufthansa, which operates the most flights in and out of the city. Direct flights from North America depart from most major cities, including New York, Boston, Philadelphia, Chicago, Los Angeles, Toronto, and Vancouver. Pan Am has direct flights from New York.

Air France, tel. 069/25660; 800/237–2747.
British Airways, tel. 069/250121; 800/247–9297.
Lufthansa, tel. 069/25701; 800/645/3880.
Pan Am, tel. 069/230591; 800/221–1111.
Swissair, tel. 069/26026; 800/221–4750.

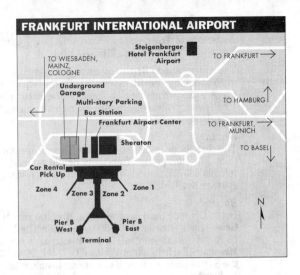

FRANKFURT INTERNATIONAL AIRPORT

Between the Airport and Downtown

The fastest route from the airport to downtown is by city train *(S-Bahn)*.

By Taxi
The drive along A5 (the *Autobahn*), following signs for *Stadtmitte* (downtown), takes about 20 minutes. Allow up to 40 minutes for rush-hour bottlenecks (7 AM–9 AM from the airport, 4 PM–6:30 PM from downtown). The fare is about DM30.

By Bus
There is no express bus between the airport and city center. Local buses that serve the airport area don't go to city center.

By City Train
The S-Bahn's S-15 train runs between the airport terminal and the *Hauptbahnhof* (main train station) in downtown Frankfurt every 10 or 20 minutes from 5:30 AM to 12:30 AM, depending on the time of day. The journey takes 10 minutes and costs DM3.30, or DM4.60 during rush hours.

Car Rentals

The following companies have offices at the airport:

AK Autovermietung, tel. 069/692534.
Avis, tel. 069/6902777; 800/331–1212.
Eurorent, tel. 069/6905250.
Hertz, tel. 069/6905011; 800/654–3131.
InterRent, tel. 069/6905464.
Schuldt/Autohansa, tel. 069/6905575.
Sixt Budget, tel. 069/6905237.

Emergencies

Doctors
For a list of approved physicians and clinics in Frankfurt that belong to the **International Association for Medical**

Assistance to Travelers, contact IAMAT, 417 Center St., Lewiston, NY 14092, tel. 716/754–4883.

The American and British consulates also keep lists of English-speaking health specialists (*see* Important Addresses and Numbers, below). Immediate advice in English on medical emergencies can be obtained by phoning tel. 069/7920200.

Dentists
The consulates issue lists of good English-speaking dentists. For emergency after-hours dental referrals, phone tel. 069/660727; there is often (but not always) an English speaker available.

Hospitals
In the Ostende (east central) area: **Hospital zum Heiligen Geist** (Langestrasse 4–6, 6000, tel. 069/21961); in the Nordend (north central) area: **Rotkreuz Krankenhaus Maingau** (Eschenheimer Anlage 1–5, tel. 069/40330); in the Sachsenhausen (south side) area: **Krankenhaus Sachsenhausen** (Schifferstrasse 10, tel. 069/60591).

Police
Tel. 110.

Ambulance
Tel. 440001.

Important Addresses and Numbers

American Express (Steinweg 5, tel. 069/210548).

Bookstores, English-language. American Book Center (Jahnstr. 36, tel. 069/552816), British Book Shop (Börsenstr. 17, tel. 069/280492).

British Consulate (Bockenheimer Landstr., 51–53, tel. 069/7204060).

Canadian Consulate (Ministry of Industry and Trade, Bockenheimer Landstr. 31, tel. 069/7191990).

Convention and exhibition center. Messe Frankfurt (Friedrich-Ebert-Anlage 57, tel. 069/75751).

Computer rentals. Computer Vermietung Rhein (Feuerbachstr. 26, tel. 069/714020).

Fax service. For round-the-clock service, go to the post office at the main train station (Am Hauptbahnhof, tel. 069/2615120).

Gift shops. Chocolates: Hertie (Zeil 90, ground floor, tel. 069/29861); Florist: Kaufhof (Zeil 116–126, ground floor, tel. 069/21910).

Graphic design studio. Graphische Technic (Mainstr. 143, tel. 069/888677).

Hairstylists. Unisex: Friseur im Westend (Mendelssohnstr. 44, tel. 069/748816), Friseurteam Geog Titze (Landstr. 124, tel. 069/748008).

Health and fitness clubs. *See* Fitness, below.

Limousine service. Limousine Travel (tel. 069/230492).

Liquor stores. Liquor is sold at all department stores and supermarkets.

Mail delivery, overnight. DHL (tel. 069/7752111), Federal Express (tel. 069/230492), TNT Skypack (tel. 069/761066).

Messenger service. Federal Express (tel. 069/77050).

News programs (English-language). Radio: AFN (American Forces Network) 1107 AM, daily on the hour. Some hotels also pick up AFN and CNN (Cable News Network) television.

Pharmacies, late-night. Late-night and 24-hour services are on a rotating basis. If a pharmacy is not open, it will have a sign on the door with the address of one nearby that is. Phone 069/11500 for details.

Secretarial services. Handelskammer (Börsenplatz 8, tel. 069/21970).

Stationery supplies. August Fleischhauer (Zeil 85, tel. 069/280441), Bürocenter Bogen (Goethestr. 20, tel. 069/2990040).

Taxis. Phone the central dispatcher, tel. 069/250001.

Theater tickets. *See* The Arts, below.

Trade Ministry. *Handelskammer* (local chamber of trade and commerce) (Börsenplatz 8, tel. 069/21970).

Train information. English-language information is available at the main train station (Am Hauptbahnhof, tel. 069/23033).

Translation services. Büro Theilhaber (Bischofsweg 1, tel. 069/635566), Dolmetscher Dienst (Uhlandstr. 33, tel. 069/448979).

U.S. Consulate (Seismayerstr. 21, tel. 069/75304).

Telephones

From 8 AM to 6 PM, local calls cost 30 pfennigs for eight minutes; from 6 PM to 8 AM, you get 12 minutes for 30 pfennigs. Public phones take 10-pfennig, DM1, and DM5 coins (there are 100 pfennigs in one Deutschemark). Public telephones with a picture of a bell on front of the booth can receive calls; the phone number is printed on the telephone itself. Most phone booths have calling instructions in English as well as German. To make a call, lift the receiver, deposit the coins, listen for a dial tone, and dial. The amount of unused money is shown on an illuminated dial on the phone. The figures start to blink when your time is about to run out and you need to insert more coins. International calls may be made at phone booths labeled "International," found scattered throughout Frankfurt.

Tipping

It's customary to round out a bill for a bar waiter or a taxi driver: If the tab comes, say, to DM9.80, round out to DM11. Hotel doormen, porters, and room-service waiters get DM2—DM3 at pricier hotels. Use the same range to tip a concierge, depending on the service performed. Service is generally included in a restaurant bill, but if you are pleased with the service, tip 5% extra, up to 10% at fancier establishments. (Give the tip directly to the waiter or waitress rather than leaving cash on the table.)

DOING BUSINESS

Hours

Businesses: weekdays 8 AM–12 PM, 1 PM–4 PM. **Banks:** Mon.–Wed. 8:30 AM–1 PM, 2 PM–4 PM; Thurs. to 4:30 PM, Fri. to 3:30 PM. **Shops:** Mon.–Fri. 8:30 AM–6:30 PM; Sat. 8:30 AM–2 PM, first Sat. of the month, to 6 PM.

National Holidays

New Year's Day; Jan. 6, Drei Könige; Good Friday; Easter Monday; May 1, Labor Day; Ascension Day (40 days after Easter); Whitmonday (the Monday following Whitsunday, which is 50 days after Easter); Corpus Christi (the second Thursday after Whitsunday); Oct. 3, Reunification Day; Nov. 1, All Saints Day; Nov. 20, Repentance Day; Christmas; Dec. 26.

Foreign businesspeople should take note of the holiday many Frankfurt residents take from Christmas to New Year's.

Getting Around

By Car

Excellent perimeter highways and urban freeways keep road traffic moving most of the time, so if you have business in any of the suburban areas, it might be worthwhile to rent a car. If your business is mostly in center city, however, other modes of transportation are preferable. As in most large cities, traffic in Frankfurt is quite congested. In addition, a number of complicated one-way thoroughfares make it difficult to get directly to one's destination if one is unfamiliar with the city, and there are large pedestrian areas closed off to automobile (but not to public transportation) access.

By Taxi

Cabs are not always easy to hail from the sidewalk; some stop, others will pick up only from the city's numerous taxi stands or outside hotels or the train station. Cabs can be ordered by phone (*see* Important Addresses and Numbers, above). Center-city trips cost DM5–DM10. Some areas of the old town, just south of the main square, are pedestrian malls and not accessible by cab. During rush hours, the efficient public transportation system—particularly the subway—is sometimes the fastest way to get around.

Public Transportation

The public transportation system, which operates from 5 AM to 1 AM, is called the FVV. Subway stations are marked by a large, white letter *U* (for *U-bahn*) on a blue background; a large *S* (for *S-bahn*) on a green background denotes the suburban rail network, which is part over-, part underground. Fares are determined by zones, rather than by mode of transportation. Streetcar, bus, and subway tickets are interchangeable; within the time that your ticket is valid (one hour for most inner-city destinations), you can transfer from one part of the system to another. Tickets may be purchased from automatic vending machines accepting coins and notes at all stations and at most street newsstands; on buses and streetcars, they can also be purchased from the driver. You must cancel your own ticket in a time-punching machine on the bus, streetcar, or train station. The simplest, most cost-effective ticket is the *24-Stundenkarte*, providing 24 hours of unlimited travel in the center city for DM7. It's always faster (and at DM3.30–DM4.60 much cheaper) to go by suburban train from the downtown main train station to the airport.

Protocol

Appointments
Germans are punctual people and are invariably early for meetings. They might forgive a foreign businessperson for being slightly late, but not by more than 10 minutes. It's perfectly acceptable to meet in a coffee shop or hotel bar. Even in a beer restaurant, you can order coffee and talk in peace so long as it's not the noon–2 PM lunch period. It's also fine to meet at fancy restaurants, but Germans will not judge you primarily by how much money you spend.

Customs
Shaking hands is a way of life in Germany. People shake hands when they meet, and again when they part. If you visit someone's home, it's polite to shake hands with all the family, including the children. Address adults by their surnames (Frau Schmidt, Herr Mueller), unless specifically invited to use first names. Professional women should be addressed as Frau (Mrs.), even if you know they are single. (Conversely, women service staff, such as waitresses and saleswomen, are addressed as Fräulein (Miss)—even if they are middle-aged and married.) The use of business cards is standard; they are exchanged at the end of a meeting.

Dress
Dress is still relatively formal in Germany. It's better to be overdressed than underdressed. For men, jacket and tie are the safest bets for most occasions. Women certainly can wear nice trousers on social occasions, but suits and dresses are most appropriate for business meetings.

Gifts
The Germans have a special word, *Mitbringsel* (little present), for gifts they give when they visit each other's homes, even if it's just for coffee and cake. A man can present a gift to the hostess of a dinner party, but never to a woman business contact; this might be misconstrued as an advance. Suitable gifts are wine, flowers, or chocolates. Better still would be a small souvenir from your hometown or state.

Toasts and Greetings

To your health!, *Zum Wohl* (zoom VOAL)!
Thank you very much, *Vielen Dank* (FEE-lun DAHNK).
Hello, how are you?, *Guten Tag, wie geht es Ihnen* (GOO-ten TAHK, vee GATE es EE-nen)?
Very well, thank you, *Sehr gut, danke* (zair GOOT, DAHN-kah).
Pleased to meet you, *Sehr erfreut* (ZAIR air-FROIT).
Goodbye, *Auf Wiedersehen* (auf VEE-der-zane).

LODGING

Many hotels of all classes are centered in and near the Westend business district, which encompasses the main train station and the sprawling Messe trade-fair center exhibition halls. However, lack of space has sent some newer and bigger hoteliers to the fringes of the city where they can offer more room and more facilities. Lodgings that are most convenient to business offices and have best access to the airport—being close to the main train station and thus to a quick airport link—are in the Westend area, but these may not always have the best services. The biggest hotel (and one of the best equipped for business purposes) is the Sheraton at the airport. Wherever you plan to stay, you must make room reservations well in advance of arrival. Trade fairs occupy much of the Frankfurt calendar, and rooms are not only harder to find then, but much more expensive. Some hotels will add up to 40% to their rates during major fairs, such as the Book Fair (early October) and the twice-yearly International Fair for Consumer Goods (late February and late August).

Some of the hotels listed below offer weekend or group rates; inquire when making reservations.

Highly recommended lodgings in each price category are indicated by a star ★.

Category	Cost*
$$$$ (Very Expensive)	over DM250
$$$ (Expensive)	DM175–DM250
$$ (Moderate)	under DM175

All prices are for a standard double room, single occupancy, with breakfast, including 14% tax and 10%–15% service charges.

Numbers in the margin correspond to numbered hotel locations on the Frankfurt Lodging and Dining map.

Center City

❸
$$$
Altea. This appealing five-story corner building was constructed in the mid-1980s on a tree-lined street, a five-minute walk from the Messe trade-fair center and a short subway ride from downtown. The lobby offers nothing but a reception area and a few chairs, but rooms are bright and spacious, with functional modern furnishings. The hotel has a "residential" section; apartments designed with the businessperson in mind have separate phone, telex, and fax lines. Apartment guests can cook for themselves or dine in the hotel dining room, which offers good—if not first-rate—nouvelle-style regional specialties. Apartment/car rental packages are available. The bar is a comfortable retreat after a day's work. *A Pullman/Wagons–Lits hotel. Voltastr. 29, 6000, tel. 069/79260, fax 069/79261606. Gen. manager, Peter Bierwirth. 400 doubles, 26 singles, 12 suites, 10 apartments. AE, DC, MC, V.*

❻
$$$
An der Messe. If comfort at a reasonable price (for Frankfurt) is what you want, this small hotel is ideal. All the owner's efforts have gone into giving each guest room its

own charming, Old World decor, using fine, traditional furnishings and fabrics—in happy contrast to the anonymous modern exterior and nondescript modern lobby. Early-to-bed types will appreciate the hotel's location on a quiet, tree-lined street, yet only a five-minute drive from the bustling business quarter. Friendly, personalized service makes up for the lack of facilities. The only food served is a buffet breakfast and snacks (on a shaded terrace in summer). *Westendstr. 104, 6000, tel. 069/747979, fax 069/748349. Gen. manager, Sebastian Schumann. 41 doubles, 6 singles. AE, MC, DC, V.*

③⓪ **Bauer Hotel Scala.** This modest but comfortable small ho-
$$ tel in the heart of the old town is suitable for travelers on tight budgets. All basic facilities are available, but don't expect the lush fittings and services of the larger hotels. The lobby is a small reception area. Rooms have unpretentious modern fittings. The Scala is on a quiet street very close to Ziel, Frankfurt's main pedestrian shopping street, and a short walk to the central business quarter. Public transportation connections are excellent. In all of Frankfurt, you won't find a better-value small conference room (it accommodates up to 20 people). *Schäfergasse 31, 6000, tel. 069/285041, fax 069/284234. Gen. manager, Dieter Kreus. 44 doubles. AE, DC, MC, V.*

★ ⑯ **Continental.** A small lodging with a century-old pedigree,
$$ the renovated Continental offers experienced service, above-average comfort for the price range, and a convenient location opposite the main train station. Subdued lighting and dark-wood paneling are dominant features in public areas and guest rooms. The lobby bar offers a pleasant retreat from the hectic world outside. Though its business services are minimal, the hotel has Frankfurt's most reasonably priced suites. The restaurant is not in the first league, but its friendly service and quiet, relaxing atmosphere are useful for business entertaining. This is one of the best bets for businesspeople traveling at their own expense. *An Inter-Europe hotel. Baselerstr. 56, 6000, tel. 069/230341, fax 069/232914. Gen. manager, Wilhelm Gutöhrle. AE, DC, MC, V. 48 doubles, 21 singles, 5 suites.*

⑬ **Excelsior.** This is the sister hotel to the Monopol next door
$$ (*see* below)—but there the comparison ends. While the Monopol has an Old World feeling, the 10-story Excelsior is a product of the characterless postwar concrete-and-glass style of architecture. However, the interior, though modern, is far from graceless. Clean-lined, Scandinavian-style furnishings fill the public spaces as well as the guest rooms. Business-class rooms are slightly larger than standard rooms, with bigger desks. Only in these rooms are minibar and daily newspaper free—but, then, you pay more for the room. *Mannheimerstr. 7, 6000, tel. 069/256080, fax 069/25608141. Gen. manager, Wolfgang Schleich. 120 doubles, 80 singles. AE, DC, MC, V. Group rates.*

⑪ **Hessischer Hof.** This is a popular business travelers' ho-
$$$$ tel—no tour groups are allowed—located in the middle of the banking/business quarter, a pfennig's throw from the busy trade-fair center. The hotel's motto, "Here I feel like a human being," is borrowed from Goethe, the great literary son of Frankfurt. The writer was not referring to the Hessischer Hof, but the management can lay some claim

FRANKFURT

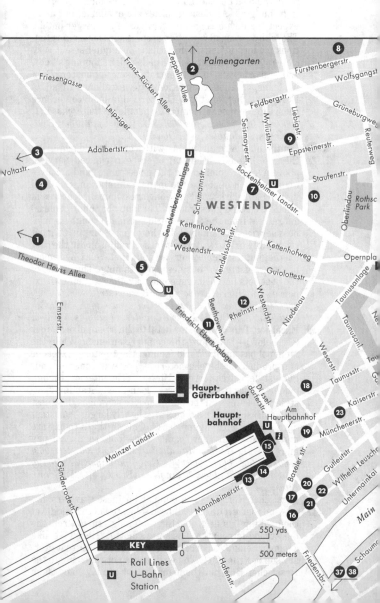

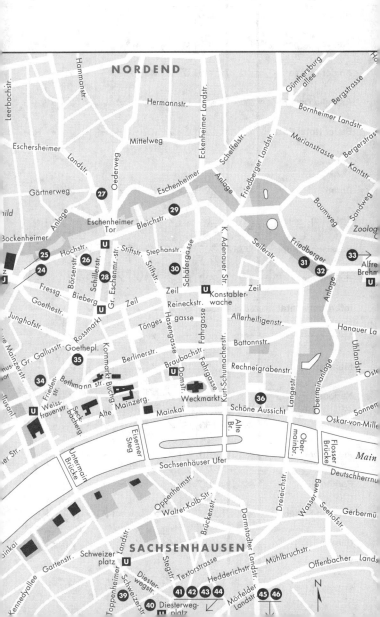

FRANKFURT HOTEL CHART

HOTELS	Price Category	Banquet capacity	No. of meeting rooms	Fax	Telex	Photocopying	Secretarial services	Audiovisual equipment	Translation services	International direct dial	Computer rentals	In-room modem phonejack
Altea	$$$	100	4	✓	✓	-	-	✓	-	✓	-	-
Am Zoo	$$	0	0	-	-	-	-	-	-	✓	-	-
An der Messe	$$$	0	0	✓	✓	-	-	-	-	✓	-	-
Arabella Congress	$$$	500	14	✓	✓	-	✓	✓	✓	-	-	-
Bauer Hotel Scala	$$	20	1	✓	✓	-	-	-	-	✓	-	-
Continental	$$	75	1	✓	✓	-	-	✓	-	✓	-	-
Dorint	$$$	200	3	✓	✓	✓	✓	✓	-	-	-	-
Excelsior	$$	150	3	✓	✓	-	-	✓	-	✓	-	-
Hessischer Hof	$$$$	300	11	✓	✓	✓	-	✓	✓	-	-	-
Holiday Inn	$$$	200	17	✓	✓	✓	✓	✓	-	-	-	-
InterContinental	$$$$	300	9	✓	✓	✓	-	✓	✓	-	✓	-
Marriott	$$$$	600	10	✓	✓	✓	-	✓	-	✓	-	-
Monopol	$$	125	3	✓	✓	✓	-	✓	-	✓	-	-
National	$$$	60	5	✓	✓	✓	-	✓	-	✓	-	-
Novotel	$$	150	13	✓	✓	✓	-	✓	-	✓	-	✓
Palmenhof	$$	50	1	✓	✓	-	-	-	-	✓	-	-
Parkhotel	$$$	200	5	✓	✓	✓	-	-	✓	✓	-	-
Pullman-Savigny	$$$	100	4	✓	✓	✓	-	✓	-	✓	-	-
Queens	$$$	700	5	✓	✓	✓	✓	✓	✓	✓	-	-

$$$$ = over DM250, $$$ = DM175-DM250, $$ = under DM175.
● good, ◑ fair, ○ poor.

| All-news cable channel | Desk | Desk lighting | Bed lighting | In-Room Amenities | | | | | | | Hotel Amenities | | | | | |
				Nonsmoking rooms	In-room checkout	Minibar	Toiletries	Room service	Laundry/Dry cleaning	Pressing	Barber/Hairdresser	Garage	Courtesy airport transport	Sauna	Pool	Exercise room
-	●	◐	●	✓	-	✓	◐	◐	○	◐	-	✓	-	✓	-	◐
-	-	-	●	-	-	-	◐	○	○	◐	-	✓	-	-	-	-
-	●	●	●	-	-	✓	●	○	○	◐	-	✓	-	-	-	-
-	◐	●	●	-	-	✓	◐	◐	◐	◐	-	✓	-	✓	●	-
-	◐	◐	●	-	-	✓	○	○	◐	○	-	-	-	-	-	-
-	●	◐	●	-	-	✓	◐	◐	◐	◐	-	-	-	-	-	-
✓	◐	◐	◐	-	-	-	◐	◐	◐	○	-	✓	-	✓	●	-
✓	●	◐	◐	✓	-	✓	◐	◐	◐	◐	-	✓	-	-	-	-
✓	●	●	●	-	-	✓	●	●	◐	◐	-	✓	✓	-	-	-
✓	◐	●	●	✓	✓	✓	●	●	◐	◐	-	✓	✓	-	○	●
✓	●	●	●	✓	✓	✓	●	●	●	●	✓	✓	-	✓	◐	◐
-	◐	◐	●	✓	✓	✓	◐	◐	◐	◐	-	✓	-	✓	-	-
✓	●	●	◐	✓	-	✓	◐	◐	◐	◐	-	✓	-	-	-	-
-	●	◐	◐	-	-	✓	◐	◐	◐	◐	-	✓	-	-	-	-
✓	●	●	◐	✓	-	✓	●	◐	○	○	-	✓	-	✓	-	●
✓	◐	◐	◐	-	-	✓	●	◐	◐	◐	-	✓	-	-	-	-
✓	●	●	◐	✓	✓	✓	●	◐	○	◐	-	-	-	✓	-	●
✓	●	◐	●	✓	-	✓	◐	◐	◐	◐	-	✓	-	-	-	-
✓	●	◐	●	✓	✓	✓	●	●	◐	◐	✓	✓	-	-	-	-

Room service: ● 24-hour, ◐ 6AM-10PM, ○ other.
Laundry/Dry cleaning: ● same day, ◐ overnight, ○ other.
Pressing: ● immediate, ◐ same day, ○ other.

FRANKFURT HOTEL CHART

HOTELS	Price Category	Banquet capacity	No. of meeting rooms	Fax	Telex	Photocopying	Secretarial services	Audiovisual equipment	Translation services	International direct dial	Computer rentals	In-room modem phone jack
Ramada Caravelle	$$$	400	6	✓	✓	✓	✓	✓	✓	✓	-	-
Scandic Crown	$$$	100	4	✓	✓	-	-	✓	-	✓	-	-
Sheraton	$$$$	500	23	✓	✓	✓	✓	✓	✓	✓	✓	-
Steigenberger Frankfurter Hof	$$$$	450	12	✓	✓	✓	-	✓	-	✓	-	-
Steigenberger Hotel Frankfurt Airport	$$$$	500	33	✓	✓	✓	✓	✓	✓	✓	✓	-
Turm	$$	50	1	✓	-	-	-	-	-	✓	-	-

$$$$ = over DM250, $$$ = DM250-DM175, $$ = under DM175.
● good, ◕ fair, ○ poor.

All-news cable channel	Desk	Desk lighting	Bed lighting	In-Room Amenities	Nonsmoking rooms	In-room checkout	Minibar	Toiletries	Room service	Laundry/Dry cleaning	Pressing	Hotel Amenities	Barber/Hairdresser	Garage	Courtesy airport transport	Sauna	Pool	Exercise room
✓	●	◐	●		✓	-	✓	●	◐	◐	◐		-	✓	✓	-	●	-
✓	●	◐	●		✓	-	✓	●	◐	◐	◐		-	✓	-	✓	●	●
✓	●	●	◐		✓	✓	●	●	●	◐	◐		✓	✓	-	✓	●	●
✓	●	◐	●		✓	✓	●	●	●	●	●		✓	✓	✓	-	-	-
✓	●	◐	◐		✓	✓	✓	●	◐	●	●		-	✓	✓	✓	●	-
-	◐	●	◐		-	-	✓	◐	○	○	○		-	✓	-	-	-	-

Room service: ● 24-hour, ◐ 6AM-10PM, ○ other.
Laundry/Dry cleaning: ● same day, ◐ overnight, ○ other.
Pressing: ● immediate, ◐ same day, ○ other.

to making guests feel wanted. In one of the most exquisite hotel restaurants in Frankfurt, diners are flanked by displays of Napoleonic-era porcelain (the food doesn't quite match the setting, however). The furnishings in both public and guest rooms are French 18th-century reproductions. Most bedrooms are singles, with pale-yellow walls and dark-red leather upholstery. There are a number of salons where private lunches and dinners can be arranged for groups of six or more. Jimmy's piano bar (*see* After Hours, below) attracts an upscale crowd in the evening. *Friedlich-Ebert-Anlage 40, 6000, tel. 069/75400, fax 069/7540924. Gen. manager, Gerhard Köhler. 130 singles, 30 doubles, 7 suites. AE, DC, MC, V.*

★ **㉑**
$$$$
InterContinental. Some of the best equipped and serviced rooms in Frankfurt are to be found inside this 20-story glass-and-concrete block—the biggest of the city hotels—on the banks of the River Main, one mile south of the business district. Rooms are innocuously salmon colored, with deep-pile carpeting. The solid reproduction-antique furnishings, and large working desks, have the businessperson firmly in mind. The 12th floor is reserved for nonsmokers. A conference floor can accommodate up to 800 people. Pan Am and Lufthansa have check-in desks in the shopping arcade. Athletic facilities include a jogging track on the hotel grounds (*see* Fitness, below). One of three hotel restaurants, the Rötisserie (*see* Dining, below), is known for its nouvelle treatment of regional dishes. *An International hotel. Wilhelm-Leuschnerstr. 43, 6000, tel. 069/26050, fax 069/252467. Gen. manager, Andreas Witkowski. 800 rooms, 45 suites. AE, DC, MC, V.*

❺
$$$$
Marriott. No top-hatted concierge will open your car door at the Marriott, where the front entrance is 22 floors up. The hotel occupies 18 floors of Frankfurt's tallest multipurpose skyscraper, in the very heart of the business district. Business facilities, including conference space for 1,200, are top notch. Rooms are Marriott modern, with desks and lighting arranged with the businessperson in mind. A large but cozy lobby offers a cushy retreat for relaxed business discussions. In short, this is a hotel for those seeking efficiency rather than Old World charm. *Hamburger Allee 2, 6000, tel. 069/79550, fax 069/795524312. Gen. manager, Horst Fischer. 591 doubles, 20 suites. AE, DC, MC, V.*

★ **⓮**
$$
Monopol. Sam Spade nursing a bourbon in a chair beside one of the palm trees would go unnoticed in this hotel's lobby. Though newly renovated and refurbished, Monopol retains a 1920s–'30s style in its public spaces. The charm of the decor rubs off on the unobtrusively friendly staff. Guest rooms are spacious and comfortable, although they border on plain; furniture is contemporary Scandinavian, with a salmon-pink color scheme. The contents of the rooms' minibars are free. The prewar stone building sits opposite the main train station—a 10-minute walk to the Messe trade-fair halls and business center, and five minutes by subway to the main shopping district. Even if you're not staying here, the bar (*see* After Hours, below) is a pleasant spot for a pre- or post-prandial business drink. *Mannheimerstr. 11, 6000, tel. 069/256080, fax 069/25608141. Gen. manager, J.M. Shultz. 60 doubles, 20 singles. AE, DC, MC, V.*

⓲ National. This is a surprisingly elegant hotel for a Best
$$$ Western, and the location, opposite the main train station
and a few minutes' cab ride from the trade-fair center, is
convenient. The lobby bar is a popular rendezvous for
business types. The small hotel specializes in services for
business guests, including five ornately decorated confer-
ence rooms. Comfortable bedrooms offer standard facili-
ties, with reproduction antiques in the smaller ones and
authentic antiques in the larger ones. *Baselerstr. 50, 6000,
tel. 069/234841, fax 069/234460. Gen. manager, Dirk
Roggenkämper. 57 doubles, 16 singles. AE, DC, MC, V.*

★ **❹ Novotel.** This nine-story building overlooking the Messe
$$ trade-fair center recalls a factory where something small
and functional, like buttons or safety pins, might be made.
Public spaces are white walled, plain, and angular, with
plastic-veneer furniture. Rooms are anonymous; they're
comfortable but offer few extras. Conference facilities are
excellent, however, reflecting the hotel's chief function as
a businessperson's lodging. The Hemingway Bar is
packed during trade fairs (Ernest would have stayed
away). An Early Bird breakfast buffet service is available
from 4 AM, and the hotel has well-equipped fitness rooms,
which include sauna, solarium, and whirlpool. Overall, the
hotel provides good value in a convenient location.
*Voltastr. 1, 6000, tel. 069/793030, fax 069/79303930. Gen.
manager, Jean-Francois Maljean. 235 doubles. AE, DC,
MC, V.*

★ **❼ Palmenhof.** This small but extremely comfortable gem of-
$$ fers bargain prices in the Westend district, just north of
the main business/trade-fair area. Upscale public rooms
have carved, German-rustic wooden furniture. Guest
rooms are individually styled, some ornately Bavarian,
others sleekly modern. What is lacking in facilities is com-
pensated for in style and coziness. The seafood restau-
rant, Bastei, is ideal for confidential business meals:
Individual alcoves afford privacy, and service is efficient
but unobtrusive. *Bockenheimer Landstr. 89, 6000, tel.
069/75300670, fax 069/75300666. Gen. manager, Paul
Nev. 30 doubles, 20 singles. AE, DC, MC, V.*

⓴ Parkhotel. This red-stone, turn-of-the-century hotel is
$$$ around the corner from the main train station, a few min-
utes' cab ride from the trade-fair center. In 1989–90, it
was thoroughly renovated throughout on elegant modern
lines. The large lobby has marble floors set off by Persian
carpets. Rooms are individually decorated; modern furnishings—including good-quality desks—are elegantly
offset by rich, dark color schemes. Conference rooms have
the latest audiovisual equipment. Though Swiss owned,
the hotel houses one of Frankfurt's best French restaurants, La Truffe (*see* Dining, below). The Casablanca Bar
(*see* After Hours, below) has live piano music. *A
Mövenpick hotel. Wiesenhüttenplatz 28, 6000, tel. 069/
26970, fax 069/26978849. Gen. manager, Elmar Greif. 175
doubles, 50 singles, 4 suites. AE, DC, MC, V.*

⓬ Pullman-Savigny. Completely modernized in late 1986,
$$$ this lodging is only a few minutes' walk from both the main
business district and the city's landmark opera house. The
modern restaurant and bar have curious ceiling drapes
that effect a rather odd, tentlike appearance. The restau-
rant is a bit too cramped for discreet business talks, but
the bar is comfortable for both single drinkers and those

wishing to hold conversations. The large lobby has marble floors and adequate seating for business discussions. Sunny rooms are individually designed, with colorful, Italian-style modern furniture; bathrooms have marble fittings. *A Pullman Wagons–Lits hotel. Savignystr. 14, 6000, tel. 069/75330, fax 069/7533175. Gen. manager, Michael Hartmann. 124 doubles, 7 suites.*

㉒ **Scandic Crown.** This reasonably modish Swedish chain ho-
$$$ tel is close to the main train station and only a mile from the Messe trade-fair center. The level of comfort is appropriate for a hotel midway between first and economy class. The reception area resembles an airline check-in counter, but the staff smiles are genuine. Rooms are comfortable if not homey, with simple modern furnishings and colorful fabrics. Desk space is limited. Business-meeting and conference facilities, however, are top notch, and the Savoy restaurant (*see* Dining, below) is very good. *Wiessenhüttenstr. 42, 6000, tel. 069/273960, fax 069/27396795. Gen. manager, Kurt Mandelsson. 95 doubles, 45 singles, 4 suites. AE, DC, MC, V. Weekend rates.*

★ ㉞ **Steigenberger Frankfurter Hof.** Since the 1880s, when
$$$$ Kaiser Wilhelm's wife stayed in the royal suite, this conspicuously opulent, mid-19th-century, High Renaissance–style structure has catered to Europe's rich and famous. The location, between the old town and the business district, is ideal. There are no public rooms, only salons, decorated in a grand style and served by a cadre of multilingual bellhops. Individually styled rooms are spacious, airy, and furnished with old-fashioned formality; many a well-heeled regular books the same room each visit. The TV channels include American Forces Network—a plus for English-speaking visitors. Even if you don't stay here, or dine in the excellent Français restaurant (*see* Dining, below), stop in at the lobby piano bar (pianist 5 PM–8 PM), a relaxing place for an early-evening drink (*see* After Hours, below). *Am Kaiserplatz, 6000, tel. 069/21502, fax 069/215900. Gen. manager, Bernd Ludwig. 360 rooms, 30 suites. AE, MC, DC, V.*

㉗ **Turm.** This 1970s-era 5-story hotel north of the main
$$ downtown area is a featureless block next to one of the city's architectural landmarks, the early 15th-century Eschenheimer Gate tower. It does, however, offer a level of comfort at reasonable prices in a very expensive town. Rooms are motel modern with wood-veneer furniture and mustard-and-brown carpets; public areas are more cheerful, particularly the steakhouse with its copper-domed bar. The main business quarter is accessible by subway, or a 10-minute cab ride. Rates include a solid buffet breakfast. *Eschersheimer Landstr. 20, 6000, tel. 069/154050, fax 069/553578. Gen. manager, Roger Protz. 60 doubles, 10 singles. AE, DC, MC, V. Closed Dec. 23–Jan. 2.*

South of the River

★ ㊳ **Arabella Congress.** In the suburb of Niederrad, midway
$$$ between the airport and downtown and just 15 minutes by taxi from either, the Arabella is set amid abundant greenery a few steps from Frankfurt's major golf course. The modern 14-story glass-and-concrete building is also adjacent to the city's secondary business district—known as *Bürostadt* (office town). The nondescript exterior hides an almost quaint dark-green and maroon interior, with

heavy, Bavarian-style tapestries and dark, polished wood. The hotel's facilities are oriented toward the business visitor, with 14 fully equipped conference rooms. Many bedrooms are individually decorated in Bavarian-rustic style. Three restaurants and a spacious bar provide plenty of options for after-hours relaxation. Good public transportation links the hotel to both city and airport. *Lyonerstr. 44, 6000, tel. 069/66330, fax 069/6633666. Gen. manager, Stéfan Schörghuber. 200 doubles, 200 singles, 8 suites. AE, DC, MC, V.*

37 **Dorint.** This rectangular block, built in 1988, is south of
$$$ the busy train station/trade-fair district and across the River Main in the suburb of Niederrad. The business district is a 15-minute trip by subway, or 20 minutes by cab; the airport is 10 minutes away by subway. Friendly staff, functional comfort, and smallish guest rooms with Scandinavian-style furniture and pastel color schemes add up to a not-unpleasant atmosphere. Public rooms are plain, bordering on the anonymous. One floor of the seven-story building is set aside for conferences. *Hahnstr. 9, 6000, tel. 069/663060, fax 069/66306600. Gen. manager, Hans Mücke. 150 doubles, 40 singles, 8 suites. AE, DC, MC, V.*

★ 45 **Holiday Inn.** This concrete skyscraper is located among
$$$ the 17th-century half-timbered houses of the Sachsenhausen district, 10 minutes by cab across the River Main to the business quarter and 15 minutes from the airport. Public areas are defined by pale marble and dark leather. Standard rooms have basic Scandinavian-modern fittings; business suites and their reception lounges are more elegant, with glossier furniture and cocktail bars. Two of the 23 floors are reserved for nonsmokers, two more are for business suites. Catering especially to businesspeople, the hotel has 17 meeting rooms accommodating 10–300, and a conference hall seating 400. Facilities include several bars and restaurants, a coffee shop (*see* Business Breakfasts, below), and a fitness floor with workout equipment and a large whirlpool. The location is charming, and this hotel offers the best facilities you can get in this price range. *Mailänderstr. 1, 6000, tel. 069/68020, fax 069/6802333. Gen. manager, Gerhard Grünberg. 404 doubles, 20 suites. AE, DC, MC, V.*

42 **Queens.** The trees of the *Stadtwald* (town forest) surround
$$$ this stylish modern hotel on the southern rim of the city, a 15- to 20-minute drive to center city, and 15 minutes from the airport. Leather chairs in the lobby offer comfortable seating for informal business talks. The modern rooms are glossy and well equipped; some have Jacuzzis, others have added amenities for women travelers. Some accommodations are reserved for nonsmokers. Despite its spacious setting, the hotel has no recreational facilities, but outdoor enthusiasts can jog or stroll through the adjoining woodlands. *A Queens Moat hotel. Isenburger Schneise 40, 6000, tel. 069/67840, fax 069/6702634. Gen. manager, Peter Bertholdt. 148 doubles, 12 singles, 6 suites. AE, DC, MC, V. Weekend rates.*

Ostende/East Central

33 **Am Zoo.** The anonymous white-painted facade of this rea-
$$ sonably priced four-story hotel disguises unexpected comfort inside. Rooms are plain but clean and better than

merely functional, despite the absence of desks. The hotel is in a calm, suburban setting, close to the Frankfurt Zoo, but it's across town from the business district, so expect a 15-minute ride to the trade center, and a 35-minute drive (55 at rush hour) to the airport. The in-house restaurant is cheerful, with unusual stained-glass windows, and the coffee shop has good cakes made on the premises, but neither is appropriate for a business talk; stay downtown for any after-hours meetings. *Alfred-Brehm-Platz 6, 6000, tel. 069/490771, fax 069/439868. Gen. manager, Jean Döll. 60 doubles, 20 singles. AE, DC, MC, V. Closed Dec. 20–Jan. 5.*

Western Suburbs

❶ **Ramada Caravelle.** Four miles west of the downtown dis-
$$$ trict, and close to the freeway, an unattractive 12-story concrete shell disguises competitively priced comfort. Bedrooms (all with balconies) and public areas are fitted with Italian-modern furniture, including soft leather armchairs, and dark-wood paneling; even conference-room seating is cozy. Guests can stroll, jog, or ride rented bicycles (available at the hotel) through adjoining woodlands. There are also tennis and squash courts on the hotel grounds. If your business is downtown, taxi fares in and out could run up a hefty bill, but there's free shuttle-bus service to the airport (8 miles away) from 8 AM to 8 PM. Guests have until 5 PM to check out. *Oeserstr. 180, 6000, tel. 069/39050, fax 069/3808218. Gen. manager, P. M. Herzbach. 200 doubles, 40 singles, 4 suites. AE, DC, MC, V.*

Airport

★ ㊸ **Sheraton.** Staying in the largest hotel in Europe, capable
$$$$ of accommodating 2,100 people, may not sound like heaven on earth, but this one is surprisingly friendly and comfortable. Facilities are complete and top class—from American Forces Network and CNN TV channels in rooms to an automatic translation service in the conference hall. The business-meeting rooms can seat 5–500. Seven eating and drinking venues include Papillon (*see* Dining, below), one of the city's top restaurants. A movie theater and a shopping arcade with hairstylist and beauty salon complete the trappings of this self-contained village. All this, and you're still at the Middle Terminal of Frankfurt's airport. *Flughafen Terminal Mitte, 6000, tel. 069/69770, fax 069/69772209. Gen. manager, Herbert Vollmer. 1,050 doubles, 30 suites. AE, DC, MC, V.*

㊹ **Steigenberger Hotel Frankfurt Airport.** A new business-
$$$$ executive wing, added in 1989 to this 1960s airport hotel, provides 33 conference rooms and a business center with the latest communications services, including translators and couriers. The new wing also includes a VIP lounge and a luxurious DM2,500-a-night suite with its own conference center for up to 12 people. The lobby and other public rooms have elegant traditional fittings. Standard rooms, however, are surprisingly ordinary, with simple modern furniture and pastel color schemes. Desk space is adequate, but lighting is less than ideal. Facilities include a top-floor indoor pool and jogging trails in a huge expanse of adjoining woodland. A weekday airport service counter provides seat reservations and check-in for 24

airlines, as well as a courtesy airport shuttle bus. *Unterschweinstiegestr. 16, 6000, tel. 069/69750, fax 069/ 69752505. Gen. manager, Peter Schuffenhauer. 300 doubles, 150 singles, 46 suites. AE, DC, MC, V.*

DINING

Traditional German cooking tends to be solid, with lots of dark gravies and *Knodel* (dumplings). The most popular meat is pork, which is prepared and served in a multitude of ways—from delicate, melt-in-your-mouth honey-glazed hams to the very filling *Schweinehaxen* (roast pig's knuckle). Unless you are on a restricted diet or are vegetarian, no visit to Germany should exclude sampling the latter. Cuisine tends to be fairly standard throughout Germany—unlike France, there are no strongly distinctive culinary regions. Particular to the Frankfurt area, however, is *Handkäs mit Musik* (slices of cheese covered with raw onions, oil, and vinegar and served with bread and butter), a snack available in the Sachsenhausen cider taverns such as Zum gemalten Haus (*see* review, below). Although traditionally, German cooking tended to have little sympathy for vegetarians, the trend today is toward providing at least one meat-free dish on a menu, and substantial salads are increasingly popular in German restaurants.

Because of its status as a major European air and rail crossroads, Frankfurt has the broadest choice of restaurants in Germany. These range from traditional beer and cider taverns selling regional dishes to gourmet restaurants. Upscale establishments focus on nouvelle fare, light and relatively low in cholesterol; French and Italian restaurants predominate in this category, and the quality is often very high.

Highly recommended restaurants in each price category are indicated by a star ★.

Category	Cost*
$$$$ (Very Expensive)	over DM100
$$$ (Expensive)	DM60–DM100
$$ (Moderate)	under DM60

per person, for a three-course à-la-carte meal, including 14% value added tax (VAT), but excluding drinks and service.

Numbers in the margin correspond to numbered restaurant locations on the Frankfurt Lodging and Dining map.

Wine

The best restaurants tend to offer good, expensive French wines. Elsewhere the emphasis is on German wines, which tend to be sweeter or fruitier, although today's trend in Germany is toward producing drier varieties. The driest German wines, called *Frankenwein*, are from Franconia in northern Bavaria and are best likened to white Burgundy. Both 1985 and 1988 are good years generally for all German wines. Following are the best years for excellent German wines.

Riesling: '71, '76,'79, '82, '83, '87.
Sylvaner: '71, '76, '79, '82, '83, '87.
Ruländer: '71, '76, '79, '82, '83, '87.
Weissburgunder: '71, '76,'79, '82, '83, '87.
Frankenwein: '85, '88.

Beer

Like most German cities, Frankfurt offers a wide variety
of beers. Both local breweries, Binding and Henninger,
produce a range of brews, from the milder Export to the
more bitter Pilsener.

Business Breakfasts

Frankfurt is a town that rolls up its sleeves in the office
first thing in the morning and breaks for an early lunch at
about noon. There are numerous *Stehcafe* (stand-up coffee
shops) that sell hot pretzels, but few places to sit and have
a working breakfast. **Mövenpick** restaurant (Opernplatz
2, tel. 069/20680), on the edge of the business district, has
a noted breakfast room, open from 8 AM, with the day's
newspapers on hand; on Sundays, breakfast becomes an
all-you-can-eat brunch. Businesspeople also meet at the
KaffeeMühle at the Holiday Inn (tel. 069/68020), which
serves a daily buffet breakfast until noon.

Center City

★ ❷ **Börsenkeller.** This dark vault is a favorite lunchtime haunt
$$ of Frankfurt's established male banking and financial
community (the restaurant's name means "stock-ex-
change cellar"). It is next door to Germany's leading ex-
change, and at lunchtime a sober-suited clientele fills the
high-backed booths with animated business talk. Al-
though the atmosphere is more restful in the evening, it is
never a place to dine quietly alone. The cuisine is "new
German"—calorie-conscious regional dishes with fresh
and imaginatively prepared vegetables. Favorite dishes
are venison stew with grapes, bacon, and dumplings; and
leg of veal. There's a good choice of reasonably priced
German wines, including '85 and '88 Rieslings. *Schillerstr.
11, tel. 069/281115. Jacket and tie required. Reservations
required for lunch. AE, DC, MC, V. Closed Sat. evening,
and Sun., except during trade fairs.*

★ ❸ **Brückenkeller.** This highly regarded restaurant near the
$$$ *Dom* (cathedral) in the old town has one of the best chefs,
Hans Haas, and possibly the most complete wine cellar in
Frankfurt. Haas was a student of Munich's Eckart Wit-
zigmann and France's Paul Bocuse before developing his
German nouvelle style. Meals are served in a vaulted 17th-
century cellar with softly lighted nooks and crannies that
are filled with antiques. Dinner is enlivened by a trio of fid-
dlers who ply their gypsy music from table to table. (Feel
free to wave them on.) Haas concentrates on a small menu,
with such specialties as iced cream-of-cucumber soup,
young eel, pigeon cutlets, and veal on tomato vinaigrette.
The wine menu is so vast (85,000 bottles and over 300 varieties) that the wine waiter's advice is usually essential.
*Schützenstr. 6, tel. 069/284238. Casual dress. Reserva-
tions advised. Closed for lunch, and Sun. AE, DC, MC,
V.*

❷ **Eden.** There's no smoking or drinking in this vegetarian
$$ restaurant next door to the stock exchange, where

businesspeople come for a quick, convenient lunch. Furnishings are functional—some would say sterile—but meals are artfully prepared. Try tofu slices with pears and baked cheese, stuffed eggplant, or one of several whole-corn dishes. A broad selection of teas is available. *Rahmhofstr. 4, tel. 069/283189. Casual dress. Reservations advised for lunch. Closed Sat. eve., and Sun. AE, DC.*

★ ⑩ **Erno's Bistro.** Located near Rothschild Park, at the edge
$$$$ of the Westend business area, this top-drawer French restaurant has been catering to discerning diners since the 1970s and is still scoring points with leading German restaurant critics. The decor is clean lined and modern (pale walls, bare tile floor), and on summer days tables are set up on the sidewalk in front. Lunches are busy; business dinners are more relaxed (last orders are taken at about 9 PM). The small menu with Alsace overtones features fish; try turbot with red-and-white grapes, or pike and smoked eel with sauerkraut. A good nonfish entrée is crown roast of lamb served with lightly cooked vegetables. *Liebigstr. 15, tel. 069/721997. Jacket and tie required. Reservations advised. Closed Sat. and Sun., except during trade fairs. AE, DC, MC, V.*

㉞ **Français.** Frankfurt's oldest hotel restaurant offers so-
$$$$ phisticated international fare with a French accent. Today, the dining takes a back seat to the ornate green-and-gold Louis XVI furnishings. Try the seven-course tasting menu (evenings only), or the breast of quail in lentil soup, followed by duck supreme or baked turbot fillets in a mango-and-ginger sauce. This quiet room with well-spaced tables is an excellent setting for an expense-account–financed talk. *In the Steigenberger Frankfurter Hof hotel, Am Kaiserplatz, tel. 069/21502. Jacket and tie required. Reservations advised. Closed Sun., except during trade fairs; closed July. AE, DC, MC; V.*

㉙ **Gildenstuben.** Bohemian cuisine is featured in this bus-
$$ tling tavern with chunky furniture and dark-wood paneled walls. During the summer, up to 500 customers overflow onto a garden terrace that borders a small park where birds' songs rather than car horns pierce the city air. A light meal might include a plate of cold Bohemian hams and cheeses with a Czechoslovakian beer (Pilsener Urquell or Budvar). Among the more substantial dishes are *Svickova* (smoked beef in cream and cranberry sauce with dumplings), and *Schweinelende* (roast sirloin of pork with mushroom sauce and rice). Though service can be slow, the Gildenstuben is conveniently located near the Westend business district and remains open until 4 AM during trade fairs. This is a good spot to come with colleagues and unwind after work. *Bleichstr. 38, tel. 069/283228. Casual dress. Reservations not necessary. No credit cards.*

⑧ **Humperdinck.** The 19th-century composer Engelbert
$$$$ Humperdinck lived in this imposing villa, which today is a first-class French restaurant close to the picturesque Grüneburg Park, just north of the business quarter. A middle-aged expense-account crowd, mostly locals, gathers for a four-course business lunch or a more relaxed dinner, followed by brandy and cigars. This is a place to impress a client, rather than talk serious business. The menu is both nouvelle and classic French, with an empha-

sis on game and fish: goose-liver soup, venison in red-currant sauce, freshwater salmon with mussels in curry sauce. The '85 Burgundy and '86 Chablis are good choices on the extensive French wine list. *Grüneburgweg 95, tel. 069/722122. Jacket and tie required. Reservations required. AE, DC, MC, V. Closed Sat. lunch, and Sun.*

⑮ **Intercity.** Built into the main train station and overlooking
$$ the tracks, this spot is handy for a quick but solid no-frills meal before catching a train, or between appointments. The Intercity is also a useful place for a lunchtime business chat in a district where quiet corners can be hard to find. A varied German-international menu at unbeatable prices is served in a crisp setting with stark, white tablecloths and plain white walls. Try the sizzling steak served on hot oval stones, or *piccata milanaise* (veal cutlets in an egg-and-cheese casserole with spaghetti in tomato sauce). The setting is right for a fruity Rhineland Riesling wine or a locally brewed beer. *Friedrich-Ebert-Anlage, tel. 069/273950. Casual dress. No reservations. No credit cards.*

㉔ **Jacques Offenbach.** For a charming historic setting and
$$$ good nouvelle German and French food, come to this restaurant in the vaulted cellar of the Old Opera House. The restored rooms—not opulent but classy, with subdued lighting and pale walls—are crowded after concerts; for a more relaxed evening, book a table during the performance. Consider beginning with carrot-and-spinach terrine with tuna sauce, or peppered ham with melon. A popular entrée is tender beef fillet with broccoli-filled tomatoes. A good selection of French and German wines is available—try a red Frankenwein of the Müller-Thurgau variety. *Am Opernplatz, tel. 069/1340380. Jacket and tie required. Reservations advised. Closed for lunch. AE, DC, MC, V.*

⑳ **La Truffe.** Recent renovations have introduced a lighter,
$$$$ more modern look, but the substantial oak tables remain (an allusion to the fact that truffles traditionally grow at the foot of oak trees). Though the restaurant is in a Swiss-owned hotel, the cuisine is French nouvelle. Two of the excellent appetizers on the short menu are a unique herb sorbet and a fish strudel. The marinated lamb fillet is a good main-course selection. The young, multilingual staff is friendly and helpful. There's an extensive French wine list. Come to this cheerful place to celebrate a deal or to relax with colleagues. *Parkhotel, Wiesenhüttenplatz 28, tel. 069/26970. Jacket and tie required. Reservations required. Closed Sat. lunch, and Sun. AE, DC, MC, V.*

⑨ **Le Midi.** A soft, yellow-and-white color scheme and nu-
$$$ merous plants and mirrors make this intimate restaurant (only 20 seats) seem larger and airier than it is. Among the worthy appetizers on the classic-French menu are smoked wood-pigeon, and goose livers in pastry with truffle rémoulade. A popular entrée is lamb in rosemary sauce. The cheese cart offers a choice of more than 50. Le Midi sits among the downtown banking offices, and attracts an established business crowd. In summer, tables spill onto the sidewalk in front. *Liebigstr. 47, tel. 069/721428. Jacket and tie required. Reservations required. Closed lunch Sat. and Sun., and first two weeks of Aug. AE, DC, MC, V.*

⑱ **Lunico.** Cool shades of blue dominate this Italian restau-
$$$ rant conveniently located between the main train station

and the old town. Booths are separated by blue-leafed, vine-patterned screens, providing maximum privacy for business dinners. Some chairs are uncomfortably small. Fish and noodle dishes are house specialties; try pan-fried fillets of veal in cream-and-marsala sauce with pasta. The excellent range of Italian wines features a Chianti Classico '85. The kitchen runs nonstop daily noon to midnight—until 4 AM during trade fairs. *Tanusstr. 47, tel. 069/251010. Jacket and tie required. Reservations required. AE, DC, MC, V.*

㉟ Nudelbrett. This basic steak-and-pasta house, part of a
$$ German chain, is situated in the heart of the old town, a short walk from many hotels. It's ideal for a quick, solid lunch in a bright, busy atmosphere festooned with bushy plants. Friendly English-speaking waitresses will help you choose an entrée, but you can't go wrong with a rump or T-bone steak and salad, or one of three main pasta dishes—lasagne, tortellini, or rigatoni—each served with garlic bread and salad. The restaurant also has its own pizza oven. Italian Chianti Classico '86 or '87 is served by the glass or bottle, and there's a good range of beers available. *Kaiserstr. 5, (near Rossmarkt), tel. 069/281214. Casual dress. Reservations not necessary. AE, DC, MC, V.*

⑲ Regent. Although the chief chef was trained at the famous
$$$ Mandarin in Hong Kong, and some of the vegetables are flown in fresh from China, the Regent tends to serve less spicy—one might call them Germanized—Chinese dishes. The food in any case appeals to local businesspeople and to such political leaders as Chancellor Helmut Kohl (a photograph of him towering over the restaurant's manager is prominently displayed). There's an excellent-value lunch menu, though dinner is more pricey. Peking Duck, a popular dish, is not really worth the expense; try the stuffed crab instead, or the five-course seafood special—the fish vary according to season, but are likely to include squid, lobster, halibut, and turbot. No garish gold-and-red decor here, but, rather, dark-wood furniture, plants, and attractive silkscreen paneling. The main train station is nearby. *Kaiserstr. 67, tel. 069/232541. Jacket and tie required. Reservations advised. AE, DC, MC, V.*

★ ㉑ Rôtisserie. The oak-paneled partitions, with their dark-
$$ green velvet curtains and brass rails, simulate the atmosphere of a Victorian London pub and provide a private, comfortable setting for serious business talks. Here, in the flagship dining room of the InterContinental hotel, you can taste German regional specialties cooked with a light nouvelle touch. There's a six-course tasting menu; otherwise, try the turbot schnitzel with salmon mousse, followed by breast of duck with dark cherries, or lobster ragout with basil-flavored noodles. *Wilhelm-Leuschnerstr. 43, tel. 069/26050. Jacket and tie required. Reservations advised. Closed lunch on Sat. and Sun. AE, DC, MC, V.*

㉒ Savoy. This small, warmly decorated restaurant in the
$$$ Swedish-owned Scandic Crown hotel attracts business customers who find the location on the southern edge of the business quarter convenient for a quick, quality lunch. The three-course lunch specials offer good value. The cuisine is international, with such specialties as veal buttons, and fresh lobster in lime sauce, both accompanied by as-

paragus tips on a bed of wild rice. The decor is modern, bright, and cozy: powder-blue upholstered chairs, salmon-pink walls. The staff is friendly and attentive to women dining alone. *Wiesenhüttenstr. 42, tel. 069/273960. Jacket and tie required. Reservations required. AE, DC, MC, V. Closed Sat. and Sun.*

㉓ **Tse Yang.** Close to the main train station and many central
$$$ hotels, this is regarded by many locals as the best Chinese restaurant in town—despite its tendency to Europeanize some of the Cantonese-style dishes. The overzealous staff hovers around diners at close-set tables—not ideal for clinching a business deal. For confidential conversation, try for a corner table near the fish tanks. Though hanging ornaments and lanterns are a Chinese restaurant cliché, the lattice woodwork is a pleasant alternative to the usual red-and-gold flocked wallpaper. Bargain lunchtime specials attract cost-conscious diners. Try chicken breasts in lemon sauce, or veal with broccoli in oyster sauce. Peking duck has to be ordered in advance. French wines are available, as well as Chinese beers. Avoid the overpriced cocktail bar. *Kaiserstr. 67, tel. 069/232541. Jacket and tie required. Reservations advised during trade fairs. AE, DC, MC, V.*

㉕ **Zum Bitburger.** A beer tavern without a long history, this
$$ eye-catching postwar structure near the old town's Alt Oper has mock gas lamps flanking the front door. It's a popular business-lunch spot for middle-management staff at the numerous banking institutions in the neighborhood. Though relatively new, the interior has a warm, traditional feel, with lots of hand-carved polished oak and copper. Regional specialties are served with panache. For a starter, try *Wurstsalat* (sliced cold meats in paprika, oil, and vinegar), followed by Wiener schnitzel with *Spätzle* (light, homemade, finely shredded egg noodles). Bitburger, the bitter brew the restaurant is named after, is one of Germany's favorite pilseners—a perfect complement to this kind of cuisine. *Hochstr. 54, tel. 069/280302. Jacket and tie required. Reservations advised. Closed Sat. and Sun. No credit cards.*

South of the River

㊶ **Bistrot 77.** The cuisine of Alsace is featured in this popular
$$$ business-lunch spot, in the increasingly fashionable suburb of Sachsenhausen, just across the River Main. The stark, modern decor creates a frosty atmosphere that attracts a thirtysomething crowd. Inquire about the moderately priced wines from owner Guy Mosbach's family vineyard. The menu changes frequently; among regular dishes are homemade goose-liver pâté, pike fillets with lentils, and duck in cherry sauce. *Ziegelhüttenweg 1, tel. 069/614040. Casual dress. Reservations advised. Closed Sat. lunch, Sun., and June 15–July 10. AE, DC, MC, V.*

★ ㊵ **Die Gans.** This small bistro in Sachsenhausen is a bit off
$$$ the well-worn gastronomic path, but with its growing reputation for fine Continental cooking with an Italian accent, it is an excellent choice for a business dinner. Some dishes on the limited menu are now among the best in Frankfurt—in particular, the delicatessen plate (goose, venison, lobster, salmon, and caviar on salad greens); tortellini in Gorgonzola sauce; and rabbit with buttered gnocchi. The main room can get cramped at times, but in

summer there's extra room on a garden terrace. The wine
list is small compared with those of restaurants of similar
stature, but it does have some notable Rothschild and
Brion vintages. *Schweizerstr. 70, tel. 069/615076. Casual
dress. Reservations advised. Closed for lunch. AE, DC,
MC, V.*

★ ❸❾ **Zum gemalten Haus.** A colorful alternative to the formal
$$ jacket-and-tie business dining scene, this is one of the best
traditional apple-wine, or cider taverns to be found in
quaint Sachsenhausen: Be prepared to sit with strangers
at communal tables, and to try the local tipple, known as
Ebbelwei (pronounced Abel-veye). There are several
types of cider, from sweet to sour. Among the traditional
dishes are *Rippchen* (juicy smoked pork with sauerkraut),
and Handkäs mit Musik. This is also a good place to
try *Rinderselcher* (smoked beef) and potato salad.
*Schweizerstr. 67, tel. 069/614559. Casual dress. No reser-
vations. Closed Mon. and Tues. No credit cards.*

Ostende/Eastern Suburbs

❸❶ **Casa Toscana.** The light and airy decor and delicate,
$$ white-painted wooden furniture in this comparatively new
Italian restaurant conspire to transport guests to a warm-
er climate. Indeed, in sunny weather the Toscana opens its
doors onto a quiet, flower-filled courtyard. A lunch or ear-
ly-evening business meal in this setting, away from the
bustle of the city, is well worth the 15-minute trek across
town to the *Ostende* (east central) area. Owner Augusto
Marchi offers classic Italian dishes with a regional Tuscan
touch. His *piccata Lombarda* (thin slices of veal in a piquant lemon sauce) is second to none. In season, try the
fresh mussels cooked in white-wine sauce. A dry white
Soave '85 is a perfect accompaniment to the meal, and the
tiramisu an excellent choice for dessert. *Friedberger-
Ebert-Anlage 14, tel. 069/449844. Casual dress. Reservations advised. Closed Sun., except during trade fairs. AE,
DC, MC, V.*

❹❻ **Gourmet.** It's a 12-mile trip southeast of town to this small
$$$$ French restaurant in the Kempinski Hotel, but the
nouvelle cuisine is worth the DM25 cab ride. The atmosphere is subdued—guests tend to speak in whispers—and
the service is attentive but discreet. Popular dishes include veal medallions with wild mushrooms, and lamb fillet in Burgundy sauce. The selection of Burgundies is top
notch; ask for an '85 or '87 vintage. Many guests linger
over coffee or brandy and cigars. *Gravenbruch Kempinski
Hotel, Neu Isenberg 2, 6078, tel. 06102/5050. Jacket and
tie required. Reservations required. Closed lunch Sat.
and Sun., and June. AE, DC, MC, V.*

★ ❸❷ **Kikkoman.** The Japanese soy sauce manufacturer in-
$$$ vested $3 million in Bonsai plants and bamboo, but there's
no need to sit on the floor here; tatami mats hang from the
walls, and meals are served at conventional tables or at a
crescent-shaped bar fitted around a kitchen where diners
watch the chef at work. This is one of the best spots for tra-
ditional Japanese food—from sushi to sukiyaki—in Eu-
rope. Kikkoman is in the new Zoo Passage shopping
arcade next to the city zoo, two miles east of center city.
*Friedberger-Ebert-Anlage 1, tel. 069/4990021. Jacket and
tie required. Reservations advised. AE, DC, MC, V.*

Northern Suburbs

❷ **Windows.** Dine with a view at this revolving restaurant
$$$$ atop the city's 675-foot communications tower. The menu
features international and German dishes. Local business people bring foreign guests here to sample the incomparable eel soup, as well as lobster served on a bed of
pureed lentils, and pork chops in a dark-beer sauce.
Large, healthy salads are also available. Furnishings are
plush and brightly colored—the work of noted German interior designer Philippe Stark. *Wilhelm-Epsteinstr. 20,
tel. 069/533077. Jacket and tie required. Reservations required. AE, DC, MC, V.*

Airport

★ ㊸ **Papillon.** This establishment is lauded by Germany's lead-
$$$$ ing culinary bible, the French Gault Millau guide, as the
world's best airport restaurant. Presided over by a team
of first-class chefs from the Sheraton Hotel, it attracts an
expense-account crowd, who come either to entertain or
to have a serious business meal. The decor of flower-laden
hanging baskets and fancy white drapes is, however, more
appropriate for newlyweds. Attentive young waiters in
crisp livery are eager to advise on the extensive listings—
including daily tasting menus—if you don't feel like working your way through them. Typical dishes include *pot-au-
feu* with wild mushrooms, salmon steak with caviar vinaigrette, and breast of duck in passion-fruit sauce. The
Chablis wines are commendable. *Sheraton Hotel, Airport
Middle Terminal, tel. 069/69770. Jacket and tie required.
Reservations advised. Closed Sat. lunch, and Sun. AE,
DC, MC, V.*

FREE TIME

Fitness

Hotel Facilities
The **InterContinental Hotel** (tel. 069/26050) has the best
facilities, including a large pool and a jogging track, both
open to the public at DM42 per day.

Health Clubs
The **Judokan Fitness Center** (Zeil 109, tel. 069/280565) is
handy to many hotels and offers a wide range of equipment
for an hourly fee of DM21. The **Fitness Center für Frauen**
(Studio 1, Kaiserstr. 10, tel. 069/292916) is close to the
main train station and to numerous downtown hotels; its
DM45-per-day fitness services are tailored specially for
women.

Shopping

Typical souvenirs of Frankfurt are *Struwwelpeter* (pronounced STROO-vell-PA-ter)—puppet dolls named after
the famous childrens' book of the same name by 19th-
century Frankfurt writer Heinrich Hoffmann, and
Bembel, blue-painted stoneware jugs used to dispense apple wine in the city's cider taverns. For porcelain, visit
Willi Lumpp (Kaiserstr. 11, tel. 069/292621), which will
ship overseas. A locally made sweet marzipan-and-almond
delicacy is *Bethmännchen* (pronounced BET-men-chen).
These can be bought at any of the big department stores:

Kaufhof (tel. 069/21910), **Hertie** (tel. 069/29861), or **Karstadt** (tel. 069/29651) on Germany's busiest shopping street, Zeil—a pedestrian mall that stretches through the old town and also houses excellent boutiques.

The streets running off Zeil are home to a series of upscale fashion shops. Top fashions for women are at **Chic** (Kaiserstr. 9, no phone) and **Christian Lacroix Boutique** (Goethestr. 22, tel. 069/288134). For men's clothes, go to **Charly Diehl** (Schneckenhofstr. 17, tel. 069/629555). **Parfümerie Douglas** (Opernplatz 4 and Rossmarkt 15, tel. 069/629482) has one of the largest selections of perfumes.

Try **Dusseldorfer Strasse** for furs, and **Braubachstrasse, Fahrgasse,** and **Weckmarkt** for art and antiques.

Diversions

Börse, Germany's busiest stock exchange, has a visitors' gallery (Börsenplatz Gallery) overlooking the main trading hall, open weekdays 11:30 AM–1:30 PM.

Dom St. Bartholomäus (St. Bartholomew's Cathedral), located on the Domplatz, is a Gothic church where 30 emperors of the Holy Roman Empire were crowned. It is one of the few historic buildings that escaped serious damage during World War II.

Ebbelwei (Cider) Express (Ostbahnhof train station, Danzigerplatz, tel. 069/13682425) is an old, gaily decorated streetcar that takes visitors past many historic buildings every 30 minutes between 1 PM and 6 PM on weekends.

Goethehaus (Grosser Hirschgraben 23, tel. 069/28284), in the old town, was the birthplace and home of one of Germany's most famous literary sons, 18th-century poet Johann Wolfgang von Goethe. Many original family furnishings and memorabilia are on display.

Palmengarten und Botanischer Garten is a complex of lush botanic gardens and tropical greenhouses just a few steps from the main business district.

Römerberg, the historic heart of Frankfurt, is the main square of the old town, which was reconstructed after World War II. One of the buildings flanking the traffic-free square is the **Römer,** the historic town hall where Holy Roman Emperors held lavish coronation banquets.

The medieval town of **Sachsenhausen,** on the south bank of the River Main, still retains an ancient appearance, with winding streets and half-timbered houses, although this suburb of Frankfurt is now also home to chic boutiques and restaurants.

Städelsches Kunstinstitut (Stadel Art Institute) (Schaumainkai 63, tel. 069/617092), located on the Sachsenhausen side of the River Main shore line, houses some of Germany's major art treasures, including paintings by Rembrandt, Rubens, Renoir, and Monet.

The Arts

The **Alt Oper** (Old Opera House, Opernplatz 3, tel. 069/1340400), severely damaged during World War II and lavishly rebuilt as recently as 1981, is the setting for notable concerts and light operettas. The city opera company performs at the **Municipal Opera House** (Theaterplatz, tel. 069/2562434). Other concerts take place at a new cultural venue, the **Künstlerhaus Mouson Turm** (Waldschmidtstr. 4, tel. 069/4058950).

Ticket agencies include **Kartenkiosk Sandrock** (Hauptwache Passage, tel. 069/20115), and the **Römerberg Tourist Office** (Römerberg 27, tel. 069/21238708). The **Frankfurter Wochenschau** is a bimonthly guide to the current arts scene, available from all tourist offices and leading hotels.

After Hours

The annual **German Jazz Festival,** held in September (tel. 069/2128849 or 069/287173 for information), is an event that substantiates Frankfurt's claim to be the leading German jazz city (contested only by Berlin). Bars, bistros, and discos in Sachsenhausen and Bornheim districts increasingly attract a young, smart set. During trade fairs, many places stay open until 4 AM.

Bars and Lounges
A number of the hotels listed in the Lodging section have good bars for a quiet drink with associates; among the toniest is the watering hole at the **Monopol** (tel. 069/256080). A well-heeled '30s-and-'40s business crowd gathers for soothing piano music in the Hotel Hessischer Hof at **Jimmy's** (tel. 069/75400), open until 4 AM; in the early evening (5–8), they come to hear the ivories tinkling in the lounge at the **Steigenberger Frankfurter Hof** (tel. 069/21502). **St. John's Inn** (Grosser Hirschgraben 20, tel. 069/292518) has a cocktail scene that attracts a broader age range; not everyone is admitted, so smart dress is essential. With its British pub–style setting and early closing time (midnight), the **Rob Roy** (corner Neue Mainzerstr. and Opernplatz, tel. 069/20680) draws bankers and business managers who aren't in a hurry to go straight home. It's not an ideal place for women alone.

Jazz Clubs
Der Jazzkeller (Kleine Bockenheimerstr. 18, tel. 069/288537) is a classic smoky cellar that is something of a shrine to German modern jazz lovers of all ages. The tiny **Jazzkneipe** (Berlinerstr. 70, tel. 069/287173) starts late—after 10 PM—with its swing music; be prepared for standing-room-only crowds. **Jazz Life** (Kleine Rittergasse 22, tel. 069/626346) offers everything from Dixieland to rock or pop.

For Singles
The noisy **Bierhaus Mayer-Gustl** (Munchnerstr. 57, tel. 069/232092) caters to people under 30 who want to make friends quickly; the cavernous hall has phones on the tables so guests can call each other up and ask for a dance. An older, more sophisticated crowd heads for the **Casablanca** bar and its Play-It-Again-Sam atmosphere (Parkhotel, tel. 069/26970).

Geneva

by Mavis Guinard and Mary Krienke

Draped at the foot of the Juras and the Alps on the westward tip of Lac Léman (as the natives know it), Geneva is the most cosmopolitan and graceful of Swiss cities. It is a stone's throw from the French border, and the combination of Swiss efficiency and French savoir faire give it a worldly polish rare for a city of only 160,000.

Geneva became a city-state in the Middle Ages, challenging Lyon in importance as a market town. During the Reformation, it sternly enforced what Calvin preached, turning into a Protestant stronghold to which exiled French Huguenots fled, bringing their talents as merchants, watchmakers, jewelers, and bankers. By the 18th century, their skills, widespread contacts, and refined tastes had made Geneva a prosperous and handsome city. In 1815, shortly after Napoleon's defeat, it gave up its autonomy to join the Swiss Confederation. Byron's praise for Lake Léman's romantic shores helped initiate a golden age of tourism, fostered by grand hotels.

Geneva's vocation as a center for international meetings and organizations began when 16 nations signed the Geneva Convention in 1864. The city hosted the League of Nations until World War II, and after the war became European headquarters of the United Nations, with a whole alphabet of international and nongovernmental organizations orbiting around it. It has also been headquarters for the International Red Cross since 1863.

Today, French-speaking Geneva is a city of international meetings and innovative research firms, as well as a center for international banking and finance. Although manufacturing has taken a back seat in this service-oriented town, chemicals and fragrances are still being produced, superb watches are still being made in top-floor ateliers, and precision engineering skills have been adapted to electronics and small, nonpolluting, high-tech ventures in biotechnology, robotics, and computerware. Major auctions add to the glitter of the gem and jewelry business. Aside from the State of Geneva, the biggest employers are service oriented: Retail distribution accounts for only 2% of jobs, banks 1.5%. The tendency is toward highly computerized companies with few employees.

Top Employers

Employer	Type of Enterprise	Parent*/ Headquarters
Compagnie Suisse des Wagons	Transportation	Geneva
Coop	Supermarket	Basel
Credit Suisse	Bank	Zurich
DuPont	Chemical industry	Wilmington, DE
Firmenich	Chemicals, fragrances, and flavors	Geneva
Givaudan	Chemicals, fragrances, and flavors	Geneva
Grand Passage	Department store	Jelmoli/Zurich
Migros	Supermarket	Zurich
Rolex	Watches	Geneva
Societé de Banque Suisse	Bank	Basel
Swissair	Airline	Zurich
Union de Banques-Suisses	Bank	Zurich
Zchokke	Construction engineering	Geneva

*if applicable

ESSENTIAL INFORMATION

We include the Geneva telephone area code (022) with all numbers listed below; if you are calling from outside Switzerland, omit the 0 from the code; if you are calling from within the city, omit the area code altogether.

The currency of Switzerland is the franc, abbreviated throughout the chapter as SwF.

Government Tourist Offices

Swiss National Tourist Office. In the United States: 608 Fifth Ave., New York, NY 10020, tel. 212/757–5944; 260 Stockton St., San Francisco, CA 94108, tel. 415/362–2260.
In Canada: Commerce Court W, Box 215, Commerce Court Postal Station, Toronto, Ontario M5L 1E8, tel. 416/868–0584.
In the United Kingdom: Swiss Center, 1 New Coventry St., London W1V 8EE, tel. 071/734–1921.
In Geneva: Cornavin Station, tel. 022/45.52.00.

Foreign Trade Information

Consulate General of Switzerland. In the United States: 665 Fifth Ave., New York, NY 10022, tel. 212/758–2560;

Olympia Center, Suite 2301, 737 N. Michigan Ave., Chicago, IL 60611, tel. 312/915–0061; 3440 Wilshire Blvd., Suite 817, Los Angeles, CA 90010, tel. 213/388–4127.
In Canada: 1572 Avenue Dr. Penfield, Montréal 83G 1C4, Quebec, tel. 514/932–7181; 154 University Ave., Suite 601, Toronto M5H 3Y9, Ontario, tel. 416/593–5371.
Swiss Embassy in the United Kingdom: 16–18 Montagu Pl., London W1H 2BQ, tel. 071/723–0701.

Entry Requirements

U.S., Canadian, and U.K. Citizens
Passport only. Visas are required for stays longer than 90 days.

Climate

On a narrow plain between two mountain ranges where the river Rhône emerges from Lake Léman, Geneva has long summers followed by a mild fall that can last until November. Then the city disappears in fog, and residents live for weekends, when they can head for nearby mountains bathed in sunshine above the clouds. Temperatures rarely drop below freezing, and snow is a rare sight in the city, but the Genevois frequently hunch up against a biting wind called the "bise." What follows are the average daily maximum and minimum temperatures for Geneva.

Jan.	40F	4C	Feb.	43F	6C	Mar.	50F	10C
	29	−2		31	−1		36	2
Apr.	59F	15C	May	67F	19C	June	74F	23C
	41	5		49	9		56	13
July	77F	25C	Aug.	76F	24C	Sept.	70F	21C
	59	15		58	14		54	12
Oct.	58F	14C	Nov.	47F	8C	Dec.	40F	4C
	45	7		38	3		32	0

Airport

Cointrin Airport is only 3 kilometers (1.5 miles) north of downtown, and is directly linked by rail to Geneva's Cornavin station and points beyond. It now serves 6 million passengers a year and can get congested during holiday travel. Many passengers walk away from the airport carrying just a tote bag thanks to a unique Swiss fly-rail baggage plan that speeds incoming luggage from planes to trains, and forwards it to some 1,500 points around the country.

Airlines

Swissair has the most frequent service. It is also the only airline that flies directly to Geneva, from New York. Crossair is a commuter airline used by many businesspeople to bypass crowded international hubs.

Air Canada, tel. 022/791.03.20; 800/776–3000.
Air France, tel. 022/731.04.00; 800/237–2747.
Crossair, tel. 022/798.88.31.
Pan Am, tel. 022/732.38.34; 800/221–1111.

Swissair, tel. 022/799.31.11; 800/221–4750.
TWA, tel. 022/798.41.61; 800/221–2000.

Between the Airport and Downtown

By Taxi
A taxi is the most convenient and often fastest way to the downtown business center, a 10-minute ride. Cost: about SwF30; no tip.

By Train
Trains leave for Cornavin station every 20 minutes, from 6:35 AM to 11:36 PM. The six-minute ride costs SwF3.40. From the station, you can take a bus, take a taxi, or walk downtown.

By Bus
Bus No. 10 goes to the railway station and continues to Place Bel-Air, which is close to the banks and shops. Cost: SwF1.50.

By Shuttle
Private minibus service is free for guests of airport hotels and of many city hotels. All leave from gate 4 to the right of the arrivals entryway. There is no special airport bus service to the center of town.

Car Rentals

The following companies have booths at the airport:

Avis, tel. 022/798.23.00; 800/331–1212.
Budget, tel. 022/798.22.53; 800/527–0700.
Europcar, tel. 022/798.11.10; 800/227–7368.
Hertz, tel. 022/798.22.02; 800/654–3131.

Emergencies

For a list of approved physicians and clinics in Geneva that belong to the International Association for Medical Assistance to Travelers, contact IAMAT, 417 Center St., Lewiston, NY 14092, tel. 716/754–4883.

Doctors
Association des Médecins (tel. 022/20.25.11) is a doctor's association that provides around-the-clock emergency medical service as well as same-day doctors' appointments. **SOS Médecins á Domicile** (tel. 022/781.17.77) is a 24-hour emergency service.

Dentists
Association des Médecins-Dentistes (tel. 022/732.80.05).

Hospitals
Hôpital Cantonal et Universitaire (24, rue Micheli-du-Crest, tel. 022/22.61.11) and **Hôpital de la Tour** (3, ave. J-D. Maillard, tel. 022/780.01.11) have fully equipped emergency rooms.

Police
Tel. 117.

Ambulance
Tel. 144.

Important Addresses and Numbers

American Express. (7, rue du Mont-Blanc, tel. 022/ 731.76.00); in case of lost credit cards or travelers' checks (tel. 071/384.61.61).

Audiovisual rentals. Action & Light (9, rue Boissonas, tel. 022/42.54.74), Audio/Visuel 16–36 (4, rue du Beulet, tel. 022/44.45.40).

Bookstores (English-language). Elmedia (5, rue Versonnex, tel. 022/736.02.22), Naville (7, rue Ami-Lévrier, tel. 022/732.24.00).

British Consulate (37–39, rue Vermont, tel. 022/ 734.12.02).

Canadian Consulate (1, ch. du Pré-de-la-Bichette, tel. 022/ 733.90.00).

Computer rentals. Cefti (3, ch. Verseuse, Aïre, tel. 022/ 797.12.97), CMI Cie de Micro-Informatique (13, ch. Riantbosson, Meyrin, tel. 022/782.53.52) for one-week-minimum rentals for brand PCs and some laptops.

Convention and exhibition centers. Centre International de Conférences Genève (15, rue Varembé, tel. 022/ 791.91.11), Palexpo (Grand-Saconnex, tel. 022/798.11.11).

Fax services. Facilities in telecommunications office of railway station, main post office (18, rue du Mont-Blanc, tel. 022/739.21.11), and post office in the financial district (rue du Stand/pl. de la Poste, tel. 022/21.00.36).

Formal-wear rentals. Danièle Signerin (8, ave. Calas, tel. 022/47.15.95), Pepino Balestra (20, ave. du Mail, tel. 022/ 28.41.40; by appointment only).

Gift shops. Chocolates: Chocolaterie du Rhône (3, rue de la Confédération, tel. 022/21.56.14), Moreau (12, rue du Marché, tel. 022/28.75.49), Rohr (3, pl. du Molard, tel. 022/21.63.03); Flowers: Le Breuil Fleurs (10, quai Général Guisan, tel. 022/28.50.05), Fleuriot Fleurs (26, rue de la Corraterie, tel. 022/28.36.55; also at the airport and the train station); Gift baskets: Maison Burkard (57, rte. Florissant, tel. 022/47.22.27), Manuel (6, rue Pierre-Fatio, tel. 022/21.61.10).

Graphic design studios. AM Publicité (18, ave. Vibert, Carouge, tel. 022/42.22.77), Andrew Belaieff (3, rampe de la Treille, tel. 022/21.62.27), Joseph Stojan (5, ch. de la Gravire, tel. 022/42.91.80), Kohler & Tondeux (12, ave. Rosemont, tel. 022/735.51.38).

Hairstylists. Unisex: Coiffure-Beauté (2–4, rue François Bonivard, tel. 022/732.46.04), Le Salon (Hotel Richemond, 8–10, rue Adhémar-Fabri, tel. 022/732.22. 18); Women: Viva (6, rue Pierre-Fatio, tel. 022/21.57.71) is better known by the name of its owner, Ebo, who coifs some of the most glamorous heads in town.

Information hot lines. Tel. 022/738.52.00 for tourist information.

Limousine services. Globe Cie de Tourisme Automobile (tel. 022/731.07.50), Prestige Rent-A-Car (tel. 022/ 791.70.77).

Liquor stores. Bignens Vins (4, ave. de Frontenex, tel. 022/735.08.60), Caves du Palais de Justice (1 pl. Bourg-de-Four, tel. 022/29.77.66).

Mail delivery, overnight. Postal "exprs" mail is efficient; letters sent before noon will arrive the same day in the same city, the following day in most of Switzerland. Overseas and pickup service: DHL (tel. 022/44.44.05), Federal Express (tel. 022/798.44.33), TNT (tel. 022/798.68.69).

Messenger service. Tel. 142 for express postal pickup, weekdays 7 AM–7 PM, Sat. 7–noon, delivery within an hour; IC Intercity (tel. 022/798.85.71), Speedy (tel. 022/781.02.44).

News programs (English-language). Radio 74, 88.8 FM, broadcasts BBC World Service News on the hour daily at 8 AM, 9 AM, 1 PM, 6 PM, and 7 PM; CBS-TV news from the previous night can be viewed on Channel 4 weekday mornings at 8 AM.

Office space rentals. Boss (6, rue Guillaume-Tell, 1201, tel. 022/732.64.74) has multilingual office help, communication services, fully equipped offices, and a conference room. Also Genesis (4, rue du Mont-Blanc, tel. 022/732.51.74).

Pharmacies, late-night. Late-night and weekend openings are on a rotating basis. Look under "Pharmacies de Garde" under emergencies (*urgences*) in local papers, or dial tel. 111 or tel. 144; emergency deliveries are possible.

Secretarial services. ABC Executive Services (20, cours de Rive, tel. 022/786.51.46), Boss (6, rue Guillaume-Tell, tel. 022/732.64.74), Business Advisory Services (7, rue Muzy, tel. 022/736.05.40), Genesis (4, rue du Mont-Blanc, tel. 022/732.51.74).

Stationery supplies. Baumann-Jeanneret (49, rue du Stand, tel. 022/21.52.30) or Papeterie Delachaux (27, rue Croix-d'Or, tel. 022/43.66.70) have a large range of office supplies; Brachard (10, rue de la Corratorie, tel. 022/28.60.55) has the most attractive personalized papers, desk paraphernalia, and greeting cards.

Taxis. ABC Radio Taxi (tel. 022/794.71.11 or 022/735.12.34), Centrale Taxi-phone (tel. 022/21.33.33), Central Taxi Dispatch (tel. 141), Cooperative Taxis (tel. 022/20.22.02).

Thomas Cook (64, rue de Lausanne [station], tel. 022/738.45.55).

Trade Ministry. Département de l'Economie Publique (14 rue Hôtel-de-Ville, tel. 022/27.21.11). The International Trade Advisor, in Bern (tel. 031/43.73.42), helps American businesspeople coming to Switzerland with introductions and appointments.

Trade promotion. OPI Office de Promotion de l'Industrie Genevoise (9, rue Boissonas, Acacias, tel. 022/42.42.44).

Train information. Gare Cornavin (Place Cornavin, tel. 022/731.64.50).

Translation services. Transpose (60, ch. du Vieux-Vésenaz, Vésenaz, tel. 022/752.48.83).

U.S. Consulate (1–3, ave. de la Paix, tel. 022/738.76.13 or 022/738.50.95.)

Telephones

To make a local call from a public phone booth, deposit 40 centimes. This is the initial charge to connect the call; each additional minute costs 20 centimes, which you can insert as needed. Instructions in phone booths are graphic and clear, and frequently in English. Dial 111 for an English-speaking operator, 114 for assistance in making long-distance calls; detailed instructions in English can be found on opening pages of phone books. A beep lets you know when your time is up. Prepaid SwF.20 phonecards can be bought at post offices and many newsstands. All Geneva telephone numbers in the 022 region will begin with a 7 (after the 022 code) starting April 25, 1992.

Tipping

Restaurant bills include a 15% service charge; add up to 10% for good service. Give SwF2–SwF5 to doormen, porters carrying bags, concierges (depending on services performed), and room-service waiters. Taxi drivers get no tip, but it's customary to round up the bill, giving the driver the extra small change.

DOING BUSINESS

Hours

Businesses: The hard-working Swiss used to consider 8–6:30 a normal working day, but those hours have shrunk to 8:30 or 9 to 5 or 6. **Banks:** weekdays 8:30–4:30 with one day, usually Wed. to 5:30. Most banks are closed Sat. The centrally located UBS foreign-exchange windows (7, rue de la Confédération) are open Sat. 8:30–5:30. Foreign-exchange windows at the airport are open 6 AM–11 PM daily, including Sun.; at the railway station, weekdays 7:30 AM–7:30 PM, Sat. 8:30–6. **Shops:** Mon. 2–6:30, Tues.–Fri. 9:30–6:30, Sat. 9:30–5. Small shops take a two-hour midday break 12–2.

National Holidays

New Year's Day; Jan. 2; Good Fri., Easter Sun. and Mon.; Ascension Day (Thurs. 40 days after Easter); Pentecost (Mon. 50 days after Easter); Aug. 1, National Holiday; Jeûne Genevois (Thurs. after first Sun. in Sept.); Christmas.

Getting Around

By Car
Geneva has more cars per person than any other city in the world. Traffic can be a nightmare, and limited parking spaces are coveted. If you must drive, an International Driver's License is not needed.

By Taxi
Hailing taxis is not customary, but taxi stands are conveniently located around town. When ordered by phone (*see* Taxis in Important Addresses and Numbers, above), taxis arrive in a matter of minutes. Traffic is heavy during rush hours (7:30 AM–9 AM, 5:30 PM–7 PM.) on the pont du Mont-Blanc; other bridges are less clogged.

Public Transportation

Transportation by bus or tram (no subway) is also fast and efficient. Single-ride tickets are obtained from orange dispensers located at each bus stop; SwF1.50 entitles you to ride all buses and trams within city limits for one hour. Multipleride- and day-tickets are available at most newsstands.

Protocol

Appointments

Appointments should be made well in advance. Serious business discussions are carried on at the office but may be continued less formally over lunch or dinner. Business breakfasts are beginning to catch on. Whether for an office appointment or an invitation to eat at a restaurant, or, more rarely, to a home, punctuality is essential.

Customs

The exchange of business cards is customary. The standard greeting is "Bonjour, Monsieur" or "Bonjour Madame" during the day, or "Bonsoir" in the evening, accompanied by a handshake. By Swiss Federal writ, women are addressed as Madame from age 18.

Dress

Men wear dark business suits, but blazers are increasingly correct business or restaurant attire. Businesswomen tend to wear the ubiquitous jacket over a skirt and shirtwaist, or a simple dress. Perhaps surprising is the casual attire worn even in finer restaurants. Although suits and ties are advised, it is unlikely that one will be turned away for showing up in a pullover and a sports jacket, or even in jeans topped with a smart blazer.

Gifts

When invited for dinner, bring candy, wine, or flowers.

Toasts and Greetings

Hello, how are you? *Bonjour, comment allez-vous* (bohn-ZHOOR, com-MAHNGT AL-lay VOO).
Well, thank you. *Trés bien, merci* (tray byen MAIR-see).
You're welcome. *De rien* (deh ree-EN).
Excuse me. *Pardon* (pahr-DOAN).
Nice to have met you. *Ravi d'avoir fait votre connaissance* (rah-VEE da-VOUAR fay VO-truh con-nay-SANCE).
Good-bye. *Au revoir* (oh re-VOUAR).
To your health. *A votre santé* (ah VO-truh sahn-TAY).

LODGING

For a city of only 160,000, Geneva boasts a disproportionate number of deluxe hotels. No fewer than 16 hold Switzerland's top five-star rating and are priced accordingly high. Some lower-priced alternatives are included below. Switzerland's high standards make it hard to find a really unacceptable room; courtesy and service are generally good. Airport hotels are only 3 kilometers (1.5 miles) from downtown, close to large multinationals (DuPont, Hewlett-Packard, and Digital), high-tech firms, and the Palexpo exhibition center. Lake Léman funnels into the river Rhône, dividing the city into right-bank and left-bank areas. Shops, banks, and offices congregate in the left-bank downtown area. The United Nations and the nongovernment organizations have colonized part of the right bank, at a considerable distance from town and shops. Though there are some good hotels on the left bank, the majority are on the right bank, and the oldest "palaces" solidly front the lake. Those facing the narrowing lake and the reemerging Rhône connect easily to the downtown district by bridges. The advantage of a right-bank hotel location is convenience to railway and airport. At rush hours, Geneva's only bridge across the lake, the Pont du Mont-Blanc, can be a stressful bottleneck.

The three hotels listed in the airport section are each some 1,500 yards from the airport arrivals hall. Courtesy shuttle service is available. There are no flights after 11 PM, so late-night noise shouldn't be a problem. Rail connections are in the airport, just a few minutes away.

A number of the hotels listed below offer corporate rates and/or weekend discounts; inquire when making reservations.

Highly recommended lodgings in each price category are indicated by a star ★.

Category	Cost*
$$$$ (Very Expensive)	over SwF450
$$$ (Expensive)	SwF200–SwF450
$$ (Moderate)	under SwF200

All prices are for a standard double room, single occupancy, including tax and 15% service charge.

Numbers in the margin correspond to numbered hotel locations on the Geneva Lodging and Dining map.

Left Bank

㉜
$$$
Les Armures. Within nose-thumbing distance of the cathedral where Calvin once railed against luxuries, this tiny, family-run, three-story hotel offers many perks, from soft bathrobes to thoughtful service. Quieter front rooms face a cobblestone square shaded by a linden tree. Stitched piqué coverlets lighten massive beds; exposed stone walls enhance antique marquetry tables and carved armoires. The medieval building, carefully restored in 1980, is in the heart of the cobblestoned Old Town, affording a smart business clientele the unusual distraction of ancient buildings and amusing boutiques on the few blocks between the hotel and the main bank district. *1, rue du Puits-St-Pierre, 1204, tel. 022/28.91.72, fax 022/28.98.46. Gen. manager, Nicole Borgeat-Granges, 24 rooms, 4 junior suites. AE, DC, MC, V.*

㉖
$$
Hostellerie de la Vendée. What looks like a dull, '60s-style motel on the outside is really a modest gem of a hotel with a welcome that keeps those who eschew big, impersonal palaces coming back. Owner-manager Joseph Righetto's simple formula of good service at good prices draws a steady trade from banking headquarters and multinational firms moving into this once-quiet residential neighborhood. Rooms are sparsely furnished in bland colors, but many have separate alcoves for working. One of the addi-

GENEVA

GENEVA HOTEL CHART

HOTELS	Price Category	Banquet capacity	No. of meeting rooms	Fax	Telex	Photocopying	Secretarial services	Audiovisual equipment	Translation services	International direct dial	Computer rentals	In-room modem phone jack
Hôtel d'Allèves	$$	0	0	✓	✓	✓	-	-	-	✓	-	-
Ambassador	$$	40	1	✓	✓	✓	-	-	-	✓	-	-
Les Armures	$$$	40	0	✓	✓	✓	-	-	-	✓	-	-
Beau Rivage	$$$	350	6	✓	✓	✓	✓	✓	-	✓	-	-
Les Bergues	$$$$	290	4	✓	✓	✓	✓	✓	-	✓	✓	-
Bristol	$$$	200	3	✓	✓	✓	✓	-	-	✓	-	-
Hôtel de la Cigogne	$$$	25	1	✓	✓	✓	-	-	-	✓	-	-
Cristal	$$	40	1	✓	✓	-	✓	✓	✓	✓	-	-
Grand Pré	$$	0	1	✓	✓	✓	-	-	-	✓	-	-
Holiday Inn Crowne Plaza	$$$	250	10	✓	✓	✓	✓	✓	✓	✓	✓	✓
InterContinental	$$$	750	11	✓	✓	✓	✓	✓	✓	✓	✓	-
Metropole	$$$	200	6	✓	✓	✓	✓	-	✓	✓	✓	-
Mövenpick-Radisson	$$$	250	14	✓	✓	✓	✓	✓	✓	✓	✓	✓
Noga Hilton	$$$	700	14	✓	✓	✓	✓	✓	✓	✓	-	✓
Hôtel de la Paix	$$$	120	4	✓	✓	✓	✓	✓	✓	✓	-	-
Penta	$$$	600	13	✓	✓	✓	✓	✓	✓	✓	-	✓
President	$$$$	150	5	✓	✓	✓	✓	-	✓	✓	✓	✓
Ramada Renaissance	$$$	120	6	✓	✓	✓	✓	✓	✓	✓	-	-
Rex	$$$	30	11	✓	✓	✓	✓	✓	✓	✓	✓	-

$$$$ = over SwF 450, $$$ = SwF 200-SwF 450, $$ = under SwF 200.
● good, ◐ fair, ○ poor.
All hotels listed here have photocopying and fax facilities.

All-news cable channel	Desk	Desk lighting	Bed lighting	In-Room Amenities Nonsmoking rooms	In-room checkout	Minibar	Toiletries	Room service	Laundry/Dry cleaning	Pressing	Hotel Amenities Barber/Hairdresser	Garage	Courtesy airport transport	Sauna	Pool	Exercise room
✓	◐	◐	●	-	-	✓	○	◐	●	●	-	-	-	-	-	-
-	◐	◐	◐	-	-	✓	○	◐	●	●	-	-	-	-	-	-
✓	-	◐	●	-	-	✓	●	◐	●	●	-	-	-	-	-	-
-	●	●	●	-	-	✓	●	●	●	●	-	✓	-	-	-	-
✓	●	●	●	-	-	✓	◐	●	●	●	-	✓	-	-	-	-
✓	◐	◐	◐	-	-	✓	◐	◐	◐	◐	-	-	-	✓	-	●
-	◐	●	●	-	-	✓	●	●	●	●	-	-	-	-	-	-
✓	◐	●	◐	✓	-	✓	◐	-	◐	◐	-	-	-	-	-	-
-	●	●	●	✓	-	✓	●	◐	●	●	-	✓	✓	-	-	-
-	●	●	●	✓	-	✓	●	●	◐	●	✓	✓	✓	✓	●	●
✓	●	●	●	-	-	✓	●	●	●	◐	✓	✓	-	✓	◐	○
✓	●	●	●	-	-	✓	●	◐	◐	●	-	-	-	-	-	-
✓	●	●	●	✓	✓	✓	●	◐	●	●	✓	✓	✓	✓	-	-
✓	●	●	●	✓	✓	✓	●	●	●	●	✓	✓	-	✓	●	●
✓	◐	◐	●	-	✓	✓	●	●	●	●	-	-	-	-	-	-
✓	●	●	●	✓	✓	✓	●	◐	◐	◐	✓	✓	✓	✓	-	◐
✓	●	●	◐	✓	✓	✓	●	◐	●	●	✓	✓	-	-	-	-
✓	●	●	●	✓	-	✓	●	●	●	◐	✓	✓	-	-	-	-
-	◐	●	●	-	-	✓	●	◐	◐	●	-	✓	-	-	-	-

Room service: ● 24-hour, ◐ 6AM-10PM, ○ other.
Laundry/Dry cleaning: ● same day, ◐ overnight, ○ other.
Pressing: ● immediate, ◐ same day, ○ other.

GENEVA HOTEL CHART

HOTELS	Price Category	Business Services Banquet capacity	No. of meeting rooms	Fax	Telex	Photocopying	Secretarial services	Audiovisual equipment	Translation services	International direct dial	Computer rentals	In-room modem phone jack
Le Richemond	$$$$	250	7	✓	✓	✓	✓	✓	✓	✓	✓	-
Hôtel du Rhône	$$$	220	10	✓	✓	✓	✓	✓	✓	✓	✓	✓
Touring Balance	$$	100	1	✓	✓	✓	-	-	-	✓	-	-
Hostellerie de la Vendée	$$	100	4	✓	✓	✓	-	✓	-	✓	-	-
Le Warwick	$$$	200	5	✓	✓	✓	✓	✓	✓	✓	-	-

$$$$** = over SwF 450, **$$$** = SwF 200-Sw F450, **$$ = under SwF 200.
● good, ◖ fair, ○ poor.
All hotels listed here have photocopying and fax facilities.

All-news cable channel	Desk	Desk lighting	Bed lighting	**In-Room Amenities** Nonsmoking rooms	In-room checkout	Minibar	Toiletries	Room service	Laundry/Dry cleaning	Pressing	**Hotel Amenities** Barber/Hairdresser	Garage	Courtesy airport transport	Sauna	Pool	Exercise room
✓	●	●	●	-	-	✓	●	●	●	●	✓	✓	-	-	-	-
✓	●	●	●	✓	-	✓	●	●	●	●	-	✓	-	-	-	-
-	◐	●	●	-	-	✓	○	◐	●	◐	-	-	-	-	-	-
✓	●	●	●	-	-	✓	◐	●	●	◐	-	-	-	-	-	-
-	●	●	●	-	-	✓	◐	●	●	◐	-	-	-	✓	-	-

Room service: ● 24-hour, ◐ 6AM-10PM, ○ other.
Laundry/Dry cleaning: ● same day, ◐ overnight, ○ other.
Pressing: ● immediate, ◐ same day, ○ other.

tions during the most recent renewal in 1989 is a large terrace and additional greenery, which help to relieve the impersonal exterior. The decent restaurant has a loyal following of nonguests as well as guests. *22, ch. de la Vendée, 1213 Petit-Lancy, tel. 022/792.04.11, fax 022/792.05.46. Owner and gen. manager, Joseph Righetto. 33 rooms, 1 suite. AE, DC, MC, V.*

㉝ **Hotel de la Cigogne.** Unwind after a stressful day in the
$$$ fanciful surroundings of a room out of a Baroque German castle, a Swiss chalet, or a futuristic grotto. No two are alike, and 23 have working fireplaces. Furnishings—antiques and one-of-a-kind oddities—are finds of architect/owner René Favre, who gutted this turn-of-the-century hotel in the heart of Geneva's prime shopping/business area and rebuilt it with great style in 1985. The lobby is grandiose in a comfortable way, while the conference room and restaurant are intimate and subdued. The most original hotel in town, it has a faithful clientele, largely French. *A Relais & Châteaux hotel. 17, pl. Longemalle, 1204, tel. 022/21.42.42, fax 022/21.40.65. Gen. manager, Richard Bischoff. 30 rooms, 20 suites (including junior suites). AE, DC, MC, V.*

★ **㉟** **Metropole.** This aging, city-owned, turn-of-the-century
$$$ palace cost Geneva taxpayers a fortune when it was stripped to its shell and rebuilt in the '80s as a prestigious left-bank hotel. A front door to the lake and a back door to Geneva's jewelry row attract a smart cosmopolitan set. Marble stairs lead to a mezzanine lobby with inviting coral velvet sofas, a bar (*see* After Hours, below) with green leather chesterfields, and two restaurants. The simpler of the two, a split-level café called le Grand Quai (*see* Business Breakfasts, below) is *the* place for breakfast, lunch, tea, or snacks, served in the cobblestone square under yellow parasols at the least ray of sunshine. Rooms are very diverse: Coveted corner suites may be handsomely masculine or splendidly Art Deco. Request intimate fifth-floor rooms for windows that frame a lake view over the park. Cosmopolitan businesspeople like the silky restaurant l'Arlequin for business entertaining, as well as the private dining rooms, the conference facilities, and the location, only a short stroll from the left-bank office and bank district. *A Robert F. Warner Distinguished hotel. 34, quai Général Guisan, 1204, tel. 022/21.13.44 or 800/227–8614, fax 022/21.13.50. Gen. manager, André Hauri. 114 rooms, 13 suites. AE, DC, V.*

★ **㉞** **Touring Balance.** Contemporary art from the private col-
$$ lection of one of the city's most important collectors sets the tone of this resolutely modern hotel within a turn-of-the-century landmark building completely reconstructed in 1986. The paintings dominate the lobby, which is otherwise furnished in a lively contemporary style with a large expanse of window that makes one feel part of the bustling city. Rooms are on the small side, but the clean-cut, contemporary furnishings give a feeling of space. Soothing tones of golden beige and gray emphasize the art. Rooms on the top floor have beam ceilings. Levels of taste, comfort, and service are a notch above the town's usual budget offerings. *A Best Western hotel. 13, pl. Longemalle, 1204, tel. 022/28.71.22, fax 022/28.51.41. Gen. manager, Jacques Tritten. 60 rooms, 2 suites. AE, DC, MC, V.*

Right Bank

⓲ **Hôtel d'Allèves.** A location on a secluded, quiet square
$$ midway between the railway station and Geneva's finan-
cial district accounts for this hotel's popularity among
budget-conscious travelers, both business and tourist.
The lobby is small, but one can take refuge in the Coq
Rouge snack bar or, in summer, at tables on the square.
Rooms vary; some are small and decorated with somber
colors that can be oppressive. Rooms on the sixth floor
have tiny balconies, those on the seventh are terraced du-
plexes. The hotel was built in 1957; the most recent reno-
vation was in 1984. Service is adequate and friendly. *13,
passage Kléberg, 1201, tel. 022/732.15.30, fax 022/
738.32.66. Owner and gen. manager, Bernard d'Allèves.
37 rooms, 4 duplex suites. AE, DC, MC, V.*

★ ⓳ **Ambassador.** An ideal Rhône-side location a short bridge-
$$ crossing away from banking and shopping, plus reasonable prices and a helpful concierge, add up to a real bar-
gain in this expensive city. The hitch? Small, nondescript
rooms—yet decently furnished and redone in 1989. Request one in the "11" series for a spacious corner spot overlooking the Rhône at the Pont de la Machine. The lobby is
sparsely furnished in the style of the '70s when the hotel
was built, but the corner restaurant offers pleasant atmosphere and a view. *21, quai des Bergues-place Chevelu,
1201, tel. 022/31.72.00, fax 022/738.90.80. Gen. manager,
B.G. Zamboni. 86 rooms, no suites. AE, DC, MC, V.*

★ ⓳ **Beau Rivage.** The Mayer family has been welcoming lumi-
$$$ naries of government, finance, business, and the arts for
some 125 years with style and impeccable service. The
Duchess of Windsor was a frequent visitor; it was only ap-
propriate that the 1987 auction sale of her fabulous jewels
was conducted here by Sotheby's, whose Geneva head-
quarters are on the premises. From a stunning colon-
naded reception patio completely refurbished and refur-
nished in 1989, one wanders off into smaller lounges invit-
ing a quiet tête-à-tête. Most evenings there's piano music
in the Atrium bar (*see* After Hours, below). Rooms have a
residential quality. Many have eclectic antiques accumu-
lated by the Mayers; the best overlook the lake. First-rate
Le Chat Botté (*see* Dining, below) and more casual Quai 13
(*see* Business Breakfasts, below) are among the popular
Geneva dining spots. *13, quai du Mont-Blanc, 1201, tel.
022/731.02.21, fax 022/786.78.41. Gen. manager, Snuggi
Mayer. 100 rooms, 6 suites. AE, DC, MC.*

★ ㉓ **Les Bergues.** Since 1834, this six-story mansarded hotel
$$$$ has been a Geneva heirloom renowned for its elegance and
the discretion of its staff. From the marble reception hall
to the rooms, renovation is continuing, as is the upkeep of
priceless antiques of Empire or Directoire periods. In the
past few years, modern and business amenities have been
constantly added (the latest redo was in June '90). Floral
fabrics mixed or matched to wallpapers make each room
attractively different. The choicest have views of the lake,
but the quietest may be on the inside court. Bel Étage
suites connect nicely with meeting rooms. Belle Époque
details, crystal chandeliers, trompe l'oeil paneling, and
parquet floors seem to delight diplomats, watchmakers,
bankers, and great auctioneers—who have replaced
grand dukes as privileged guests. A pedestrian bridge

across the river is a favorite connection to the downtown district—so close that shoppers and businesspeople come here for lunch or for a drink at the smartly old-fashioned Le Pavillon. The soigné Amphitryon restaurant is ideal for an important lunch or dinner. *A Trusthouse Forte hotel. 33, quai des Bergues, 1201, tel. 022/731.50.50 or 800/ 223–5672, fax 022/732.19.89. Gen. manager, Reto Grass. 113 rooms, 10 suites. AE, DC, MC, V.*

22 **Bristol.** All the windows of this conservative hotel—built
$$$ toward the end of the 19th century on the now traffic-ridden street between the station and Mont-Blanc bridge— were soundproofed in a 1984 revamping, but rooms over a grassy, tree-planted square surrounded by residential buildings on four sides remain the best bet for quiet. Some doubles are more spacious than others. Eighteenth-century-English reproduction furniture and engravings complement the sedate beige-and-brown decor. From lobby to boardroomlike meeting rooms, the overall look has the classic restraint you'd expect in a men's club; but the bar (*see* After Hours, below), newly jazzed up by a white piano, gets lively at cocktail time. This is the choice of French and American businesspeople or of small tourist groups who like to be in the midst of things. The personnel is snooty but efficient, and is being trained to smile. *10, rue du Mont-Blanc, 1201, tel. 022/732.38.00 or 800/223– 9868, fax 022/34.90.39. Gen. manager, Paul Bougenaux. 95 rooms. 1 suite. AE, DC, MC, V.*

10 **Cristal.** This cheerful little hotel without pretense was
$$ built in 1983 on a quiet back street just steps from the station. Its efficiently sized rooms are identical, with standard-issue hotel furniture and warm colors, providing minimum essentials for the business traveler or tourist who doesn't expect frills. The gleaming green-and-white lobby offers a comfortable seating area near a serene square. The spacious breakfast room with its self-service buffet is a place where anyone would like to start the day. Transportation, parking, shopping, restaurants, and other amenities are conveniently near, and most business offices are only a short walk or bus ride away. *4, rue Pradier, 1201, tel. 022/731.34.00, fax 022/731.70.78. Gen. manager, Catherine Gerber. 79 rooms. AE, DC, MC, V.*

★ **6** **Grand Pré.** This cozy hotel, set in a residential district be-
$$ tween the airport and the UN, was built in 1964 as an answer to Geneva's lack of moderately priced hotels. Budget-conscious return clients prefer its well-lighted, well-fitted rooms to great views; back rooms are quiet but overlook a nondescript yard. A renovation in 1989 has brought in new light-wood Louis Phillip–style furniture upholstered in several pastel schemes, and has updated the tiled bathrooms. A small bar is tucked in back of the lobby. There is no restaurant, and large breakfasts are buffet style, but room service will bring a steak or an omelet to your room. International officials find nearby bus transportation convenient to the UN. There's free shuttle service to the train station or airport. *35, rue du Grand-Pré, 1202, tel. 022/733.91.50, fax 022/734.76.91. Gen. manager, Françoise Strubler. 71 rooms, 9 suites. AE, DC, MC, V.*

★ **21** **Hotel de la Paix.** The rooftop promenade that proved such
$$$ an attraction when this hotel was built in 1857 is gone. Yet the quiet grandeur that eased the bargaining over many

international disputes—from the American Civil War to the Vietnam conflict—remains. Diplomats still comprise a large percentage of guests, joined by international business executives including a strong contingent of Japanese. The main part of the hotel, which underwent a major renovation in 1987, is built around a worldly, six-story atrium. Rooms, most of them spacious, are traditionally decorated in soothing neutral tones with fine antiques scattered here and there. The choicest face the lake, but the hotel is so situated that almost no room, no matter how modest, lacks a pleasant view; almost half have blue-canopied balconies. *11, quai du Mont-Blanc, 1201, tel. 022/732.61.50, fax 022/ 738.87.94. Gen. manager, Olav Vaage. 86 rooms, 14 suites. AE, DC, V.*

❹ **InterContinental.** In its 25 years, this 18-floor skyscraper
$$$ has hosted 75 heads of state who came not just for the rooftop helipad or the view over the UN, but also for a high security label equally attractive to CEOs. Two top-floor presidential suites double as hush-hush meeting rooms linked or separated at will by a skylighted cocktail lounge. The mezzanine of the two-level lobby has spots for a business chat away from the brouhaha. Remodeling that's been ongoing since 1987 has created sand-color, lookalike, business-compatible rooms and compact minisuites on every floor from the fifth up. An indoor pool and enlarged fitness center are scheduled for '92. The heated outdoor pool and tennis courts beside La Pergola's terrace restaurant are summer gathering places; Les Continents (*see* Dining, below) is a diplomatic lunch or dinner choice. The staff is used to catering to a multinational clientele. *7–9, ch. du Petit Saconnex, 1209, tel. 022/734.60.91 or 800/ 33AGAIN, fax 022/734.28.64. Gen. manager, Herbert A. Schott. 311 rooms, 54 suites. AE, DC, MC, V.*

⓲ **Noga Hilton.** The largest deluxe hotel in Switzerland is a
$$$ cosmopolitan, self-contained community on the quays of Lake Léman. One can get lost in the flashy lobby with infinitely reflecting mirrors and acres of sofas. The determinedly modern rooms have lacquered-wood touches; each floor is a different color. Several categories of suites, some with vast marble bathrooms, many with grand views, lead up to the five of presidential class. Le Cygne (*see* Dining, below) is rated by many as Geneva's best; simpler La Grignotière (*see* Business Breakfasts, below) offers the most spacious dining terrace in town, with a view to Mont-Blanc on clear days. The Hilton Fit Club (*see* Fitness, below) is superbly equipped with large exercise rooms, a pool, and outdoor swimming space. Le Grand Casino (*see* The Arts, below) conference/entertainment complex hosts everything from symphony concerts to world-class symposiums. It's a short walk or ride to the shopping and business center, but crossing by shuttle-boat is more fun. *12, quai du Mont-Blanc, 1201, tel. 022/731.98.11, fax 022/738.64.32. Gen. manager, Eric Kuhne. 376 rooms, 38 suites. AE, DC, MC, V.*

⓰ **President.** This lakefront hotel, built in 1962 on the edge of
$$$$ a lovely park, is favored by UN delegates, oil sheiks, and Japanese group tours, but requires a scenic 15-minute hike along the quays and across the bridge to reach downtown. All side windows are cleverly angled to catch a glimpse of the lake. Front rooms, especially the pale, elegant presidential suite, have spectacular views; west

rooms unfortunately also get a closeup of the charred Palais Wilson. Most of the once-garish double rooms have been redone since 1985 in quieter tones, but the ostentatious lobby and gallery still flaunt Gobelins tapestries, Oriental rugs, and marble in profusion. Staff, trained by the hotel's own school and supervised by eminent École Hôtelière graduates, is unusually attentive and friendly. In addition to business facilities, a rare privilege is direct luggage checkout to Swissair flights. *A Swissôtel. 47, quai Wilson, 1211, tel. 022/731.10.00 or 800/637–9477, fax 022/ 731.22.06. Gen. manager, Jacques Favre. 152 rooms, 28 suites. AE, DC, MC, V.*

⓯ **Ramada Renaissance.** The lobby's fancy, precious pink de-
$$$ cor and deep Oriental rugs are unexpected in this seamy district between the train station and Lake Léman. The hotel was built in 1974 and was entirely upscaled and remodeled 10 years later. Rooms in subdued tones are among the largest in town, and tourist groups seem attracted by roomy twin beds wide enough to accommodate a whole family at no extra charge. Eager-to-please hotel trainees staff the front desk. An international array of businesspeople say they return here for reliability and well-equipped modular meeting rooms. At night, a woman alone might prefer to call a cab rather than walk downtown. *19, rue de Zurich, 1201, tel. 022/731.02.41 or 800/ 228–9898, fax 022/738.75.14. Gen. manager, Myriam Vallélian. 219 rooms, 7 suites. AE, MC, V.*

❺ **Rex.** This small hotel of the '50s—revamped in 1984—of-
$$$ fers the unexpected delight of a garden terrace. Red leather chesterfields and hunting prints set a clubby tone at the pub-style bar. Most rooms are fairly large; the quieter back ones look on tidy city yards, and top-floor suites are air-conditioned. Though the hotel, set in a residential section of town, is somewhat removed from the business center, budget-conscious Swiss businesspeople like the convenient public transportation, abundant meeting rooms, and popular restaurant. *A Manotel. 44, Ave. Wendt, 1203, tel. 022/45.71.50, fax 022/44.04.20. Gen. manager, Bernard Lavanchy. 56 rooms, 18 suites. AE, DC, MC, V.*

⓴ **Le Richemond.** This one-time modest, 19th-century pen-
$$$$ sion has come a long way to the jet-set stop-off it is today. The lobby, with its friendly staff, is a good introduction to rooms where lavish decorator details set off the owners' antique finds. Like writer Colette, who spent summers here, well-heeled clients ask for rooms with tiny balconies over a kitsch little park close to the lake. Renovations were begun in the late '80s to attract top-level businesspeople to a status address chosen by celebrities. Bar Le Jardin (*see* After Hours, below) is for aperitifs before light meals served in the plant-filled restaurant. A theatrical extravagance is the rule; and a sumptuous red theme dominates the Salon Émilie, where tea is served from a silver trolley. This is one of the few places in town for dinner dancing. *A Leading Hotels of the World hotel. Jardin Brunswick, 1211, tel. 022/731.14.00 or 800/223–6800, fax 022/731.67.09. Gen. manager, Victor Armleder. 53 doubles, 15 singles, 31 suites. AE, DC, MC, V.*

★ ⓫ **Hôtel du Rhône.** This quintessential business hotel, built
$$$ in 1950, is undergoing a total renovation (to be completed in 1992) to further upgrade its facilities to state-of-the-

art, including a ground-floor business center equipped with Reuters news service. Although part of the elite Rafael Group—a small, exclusive German chain—it retains family ties that prevent it from sinking into the bland business mold. Many rooms are being enlarged, and all are being redone in an efficient yet sybaritic style to provide a well-appointed working environment without making guests feel like they're spending the night at the office. Rooms on the sixth floor are the most colorful you're likely to find in any hotel, although a bit too "boudoir" for some conservative tastes. Although it is located on the Rhône near a bridge leading right to the banking district, the hotel is set off from the bustle of the city's major traffic routes. Le Neptune restaurant serves as the Swiss headquarters for the International Wine Academy—which helps explain the expansive wine list. Small, private dining facilities are available for sensitive discussions. A summer terrace faces the Rhône. On-site parking is available, a rarity in this part of town. *1, quai Turrettini, 1201, tel. 022/731.98.31 or 800/531–6767, fax 022/732.45.58. Gen. manager, Marco Torriani. 215 rooms, 9 suites. AE, DC, MC, V.*

❾ Le Warwick. This most inviting of several hotels facing
$$$ Geneva's train station was completely renovated in 1985. Everything the business traveler can want in this convenient conference spot is within easy walking distance; there's parking under the station, and major public transportation outside. The potential noise of heavy traffic is shut out by double-glazed windows in the plainly furnished rooms, some of them cramped. There's even a view of the lake and mountains from back rooms on the top floor, a few of which have terraces. The nondescript lobby is occasionally invaded by tour groups who join the regular traffic of international businesspeople, including a sizable representation of Americans and Japanese. Service is up to usual Swiss standards. *14, rue de Lausanne, 1202, tel. 022/731.62.50, fax 022/738.99.35. Gen. manager, François Bryan. 167 rooms, 2 suites. AE, DC, MC, V.*

Airport

❸ Holiday Inn Crowne Plaza. Opened in 1989 right next to
$$$ the Palexpo trade-show site, this seven-story hotel is the most livable of the three airport hotels, all more functional than charming. Both the lobby, with its comfortable Art Deco armchairs, and the large, casual pub with tufted banquettes, are easygoing places to meet friends or clients. A curious combination of marble stairs and Plexiglas ramp in the center of the lobby leads to the first floor or down to an elaborate fitness club (*see* Fitness, below) that is centered around a glassed-in pool. Rooms are spacious and furnished with simple, classical 18th-century-English reproductions and requisite soft colors. Nicest rooms overlook the runway toward the Jura mountains. VIP rooms on the top floor enjoy private terraces. Double-glazed windows have to be kept closed to screen out the continuous traffic noise on the nearby superhighway. For those who don't need much sleep, the disco stays open until 4 AM. Except in the top summer months when group tourists abound, the clientele is mostly American and English business travelers visiting nearby multinational firms, or

Swiss attending major trade fairs. Service is professional and agreeable. *26, voie de Moëns, 1218 Grand-Saconnex, tel. 022/791.00.11 or 800/465–4329, fax 022/798.92.73. Gen manager, Christian Maeder. 287 rooms, 15 junior suites, 2 presidential suites. AE, DC, MC, V.*

❶ **Mövenpick-Radisson.** This 11-story hotel—tall for Gene-
$$$ va—opened in January 1990, within the International Centre Cointrin office complex, and close to the World Trade Center business and conference facilities. The World Trade Center Club operates two high-security, business-equipped floors. Mövenpick attracts mostly Germans and Swiss who come for short business trips rather than leisure stays, and appreciate typical Mövenpick touches, such as subdued colors, wood trim, extra-wide beds, built-in desks, and counter space for paperwork. The young personnel is trained for smiling efficiency. The hotel's disco, Arthur's (*see* After Hours, below) is the largest in Switzerland. *A Swiss International hotel. 20, rte. de Prébois, 1215, tel. 022/798.75.75 or 800/228–9822, fax 022/791.02.84. Gen. manager, Max Meyer. 160 doubles, 154 singles, 6 suites. AE, DC, MC, V.*

❷ **Penta.** First-built of the modern hotels near the airport
$$$ (some 20 years ago), the T-shaped Penta has unremitting-
ly functional public rooms. But past a stark, black-marble lobby and unending corridors are small comfortable rooms recently redone in pastels. Views are a toss-up: North rooms afford views of the Jura range beyond the tarmac and airport buildings; south rooms face Geneva's residential districts, the upper ones getting glimpses of the Alps over the rooftops and TV antennas. The cosmopolitan clientele ranges from American skiers to international businesspeople who come for the well-equipped conference facilities. *75–77, ave. Louis Casaï, 1216 Cointrin, tel. 022/798.47.00, fax 022/798.77.58. Gen. manager, Marc Jacot-Guillarmod. 301 rooms, 6 suites. AE, DC, MC, V.*

DINING

The very expensive, precious, gimmicky cuisine that nouvelle has become is beginning to yield to more simple, affordable fare. Originality is still in, and several early-rising, slim young chefs are distingushing themselves by a light approach to the time-honored classics, but even the grander places are shedding pretense and taking on a casual warmth. And unlike the case in many cities, some of the finest dining is to be had in deluxe hotels where competition levels prices. At lunch, from noon to 2, the plat du jour under SwF20 and the business lunch under SwF50 are almost universal. This is the meal for serious business discussions; the evening meal (7–9:30) is the time for serious dining, and entertainment. Some of the best restaurants are in the outlying suburbs. Though the cuisine in Geneva has a French accent and style, there is a good selection of ethnic restaurants in keeping with the makeup of this international city. Although suits and ties are expected in upscale restaurants, it's unlikely that anyone will be turned away for showing up in pullover and sports jacket—surprising in this otherwise uptight town.

Highly recommended restaurants in each category are indicated by a star ★.

Category	Cost*
$$$$ (Very Expensive)	over SwF80
$$$ (Expensive)	SwF50–SwF80
$$ (Moderate)	under SwF50

per person including appetizer, entrée, and dessert, but excluding drinks and 15% service charge.

Numbers in the margin correspond to numbered restaurant locations on the Geneva Lodging and Dining map.

Wine

Due to limited terrains and the high cost of cultivating vineyards on the steep Alpine slopes, Swiss wines tend to be expensive and are rarely exported. Most of the best come from the French-speaking regions of Vaud and Valais. Watch for dry white **Dézaley** and **St-Saphorin** from Lavaux in Vaud, and richer white **Aigle** and **Yvorne** from Chablais. From Valais, **Fendant** and **Johannisberg** are good, crisp whites. The best reds are the Valais's **Dôle,** a Beaujolais-like blend of Pinot Noir and gamay, and the fruity **merlot** of Ticino, the Italian-Swiss region south of the Alps.

Beer

Hürlimann, Haldengut, and Löwenbräu.

Business Breakfasts

These are a new but growing habit here. Generous, buffet-style meals are served at most hotels—the best are at **Beau Rivage** (tel. 022/731.02.21), **Noga Hilton** (tel. 022/731.98.11), and **Metropole** (tel. 022/21.13.44). Also try **Harry's Bar** and **La Coupole** (*see* Clubs, below).

Left Bank

㉜
$$
Les Armures. Suits of armor and tables crowded with tourists may be rather off-putting, but the building is really ancient, and the scent of cheese that lingers in it comes from fondues and raclettes that earn local praise. This is a gathering place, known for business chitchat; about half the clientele is Swiss, and many, including Geneva's mayor, come from government offices across the street. For relative quiet, ask for table 1. Service is friendly but desultory. Such seasonal Genevois specialties as *cardoons* (a local, thistlelike vegetable eaten like celery, usually au gratin) and wild morels appear on the menu, but it's best to join the majority and dip bread cubes in hot, creamy cheese fondue. Swiss and French wines predominate on a surprisingly long list. *1 rue du Puits-Saint-Pierre, tel. 022/28.34.42. Casual dress. Reservations advised. AE, DC, MC, V. Closed Christmas and New Year's.*

★ **㉕**
$$$
Auberge d'Onex. This former golf clubhouse in a Geneva suburb has a faithful following of local businesspeople who come to talk shop and to entertain. Wood paneling; warm reds; a rustic fireplace; and large, comfortable chairs create a clubby look reinforced by proprietor Valentino Rusconi's warm welcome for repeat customers. The

menu offers a cross section of regional Italian standbys, and a huge wedge of Parmesan with aperitifs. Popular entrées include carpaccio garnished with arugula, or risotto and scampi flavored with saffron and ginger, served with suitable wines from a well-tended cellar. A dessert trolley and tempting selection of fruit precede the excellent Italian espresso. *18, route de Loëx, Onex, tel. 022/792.32.59. Jacket recommended. Reservations advised. No credit cards. Closed Sun. and Mon.*

★ ③⓪ **Brasserie Lipp.** This white-tile clone of one of Paris's fa-
$$ vorite hangouts for politicians and intellectuals is out of place on the third floor of a slick shopping center, but this is a failing more than compensated for in summer by a spectacular terrace at the foot of the Old Town. Any time of the year, from noon until late at night, Lipp mirrors Geneva's cosmopolitan character. The menu is mostly basic brasserie fare, with sauerkraut a specialty and the copious platter of seafood a spectacle. The wine list outdoes its Paris counterpart. The informal atmosphere invites spirited conversation so the din can be deafening, but the decibel level is often lower in the Montparnasse Room. This is a meeting place with no frills and quick service. *Confédération Centre, 8, rue de la Confédération, tel. 022/ 29.31.22. Casual but neat. Reservations advised. AE, DC, MC, V.*

④⓪ **Café de la Réunion.** A business clientele comes to this res-
$$$ taurant—in a picturesque village, 10 minutes from Geneva—for its light country lunches. Tables fill two rooms of an ancient stone farmhouse, or sit beneath umbrellas on a pretty summer terrace. Young Patrick Laporte, a fourth-generation chef from Biarritz, received a proper hotel-school education and then cooked in some celebrated French kitchens before striking out on his own with his wife, Caroline, in early 1990. The menu changes every month and might feature breast of chicken stuffed with tomatoes and mushrooms accompanied by fresh pasta; crabmeat lasagna is another possibility. Both wine list and dessert menu offer a varied selection. For a good value try the plat du jour, the business lunch, or either of the two set menus. *2, ch. Sous-Balme, Veyrier, tel. 022/ 784.07.98. Casual dress. Reservations suggested. No credit cards. Closed weekends.*

②⑧ **La Cassolette.** Original bistro fare, prepared by chef Ren
$$$ Fracheboud and served with flair under the attentive eye of his wife, Genevieve, is drawing a growing list of businesspeople and artists to this picturesque corner of Carouge, an artsy suburb of Geneva, 10 minutes by cab from downtown. It is sufficiently removed from city-center bustle to invite relaxed conversation—business or other. The pink-dominated decor softens hard-edged modern furnishings. There are set menus at four prices, including a business lunch. Among à la carte selections are veal fillet in lasagna seasoned with basil and green peppercorns, napped in the lightest tomato sauce; and beef rolls in a Pinot Noir sauce served with baby vegetables. The cheese selection, wine list, and imaginative desserts are several notches above standard bistro fare, as is the service. *31, rue Jacques-Dalphin, Carouge, tel. 022/ 42.03.18. Casual but neat. Reservations required. V. Closed weekends.*

★ ㉔ **L'Escapade.** This restaurant is well named, as it entails es-
$$$$ cape into Geneva's wine-producing countryside for a gastronomic adventure rather than a simple country meal.
It's a calm, relaxed setting in which to entertain customers or talk shop. Christian Parcineau has tucked his jewel
of a restaurant into a verdant setting in Cartigny, 9 kilometers (4½ miles) from Geneva, where it shares an old farmhouse with a contemporary art gallery. One passes the
kitchen on the way to the intimate dining room where art
again sets the scene. An idyllic sculpture garden beyond is
for summer dining. The short menu, which changes every
two weeks, focuses on artfully prepared meat; duck foie
gras is the ideal starter. Wines tend toward the expensive. *31, rue Trabli, Cartigny, tel. 022/756.12.07. Casual
but neat. Reservations required. AE, DC, MC, V. Closed
Sun. and Mon.*

㉛ **Landolt.** When the Mövenpick chain took over this strong-
$$ hold of intellectual argument, where Lenin once had a reg-
ular table, Geneva was ready to be very critical; it still has
mixed views. Landolt is now a glossy, mirrored version of
more typical brasseries nearby. Young chef Christian Le
Flem turns out time-honored standbys like veal cordon
bleu, or sauerkraut in unstinting portions, while experi-
menting with food of a lighter sort. A Breton, he favors
seafood and has a way with mussels whether served in a
soup with vegetables or *marinière* with white wine, gar-
lic, and parsley. University professors and bankers alike
linger over long luncheons ending with old-fashioned des-
serts, and deliberate over a long list of French, Swiss, and
Italian wines. Museum- and theater-goers come by for
first-class snacks; university students still argue in the
moderately priced cellar beerhall, Le Carnotzet. *2, rue de
Candolle, 022/29.05.36. Casual dress. Reservations ad-
vised. Closed Sun. and holidays.*

★ ㊱ **Lion d'Or.** Henri Large's classically French cuisine can be
$$$$ less than perfect at times, but no one can quibble about the
panoramic views over city and lake, the honey-light decor,
the sparkling crystal and silver, or the flower-filled corner
in which to await a table or a taxi. Among diners are celeb-
rities who live in this hillside suburb only minutes from
town, Cologny. The thrifty go to the simpler café or the
summer terrace, where they can expect a warmer ambi-
ence and a shorter, less expensive selection of traditional
dishes from the same kitchen: a blanquette of veal sur-
rounded by baby vegetables, a lake trout au champagne,
or a classic bouillabaisse. Large, who once produced simi-
lar dishes in St. Tropez, has carefully built up an interest-
ing cave, and pays attention to the array of cheeses and a
few tempting desserts. *5, pl. Gautier, Cologny, tel. 022/
736.44.32. Jacket and tie required. Reservations advised.
AE, DC, MC, V. Closed Sat., Sun., Easter, and Dec. 20–
Jan. 20.*

㉗ **Le Marignac.** Chef Louis Pelletier offers two distinct
$$$ styles of dining within the whitewashed walls of his turn-
of-the-century mansion set among ancient trees on the
edge of town. Downstairs, he serves up lightened classic
French cuisine: scallops of duck liver with apple mousse
flavored with Calvados, or small fillet of veal in a cream
sauce laced with port. The upstairs has been turned over
to less-expensive Creole specialties of Mauritius, which
blend Indian, Chinese, and African influences. Both offer

a good range of set menus as well as à la carte selections. The wine list is extensive; the service is cordial but efficient. *32, ave. Eugne-Lance, Grand-Lancy, tel. 022/ 794.04.24. Jacket recommended. Reservations advised. V. Closed Sun.*

㊳ **Parc des Eaux-Vives.** Dining in an 18th-century mansion in
$$$$ one of Geneva's most glorious parks is impressive in every sense of the word. Crystal chandeliers and silver candelabras create a proper ambience for foie gras and champagne. The menu is expansively French: Try the consommé of langoustines under a flaky crust, followed by a gratin of frog's legs, or lightly smoked sea bass. Prices are high—the seven-course *menu des gourmets* is priced at over SwF130—but it's also possible to enjoy a SwF25 plat du jour during summer months on a terrace overlooking a lawn that sweeps toward the lake. *82, quai Gustave-Ador, tel. 022/735.41.40. Jacket advised in the dining room; more casual on the terrace. Reservations required. AE, DC, MC, V. Closed Sun. evening, Nov. 1–May 1; Mon., Jan. 2–Feb. 16.*

㊱ **Le Patio.** Some lawyers, bankers, and stockbrokers who
$$$ work in the Eaux-Vives neighborhood make this extremely popular luncheon spot a daily habit. Their talk animates the place, but, if it's quiet you're after, you can request a table in the back or in one of the intimate niches. The burgundy-accented color scheme warms a rustic interior where candles flicker against the stone walls in the evening. Most midday diners opt for the set-price business lunch, which can start out with a medley of fish in saffron cream sauce, followed by thinly sliced veal against a colorful palette of vegetables. *19, Helvétique, tel. 022/ 736.66.75. Casual but neat. Reservations required. AE, DC, MC, V. Closed weekends and 3 weeks in summer.*

★ ㊲ **Roberto.** Roberto Carugati, the doyen of Italian—from
$$$ North to South—cuisine in Geneva, still packs them in for lunch or dinner: high-powered lawyers, bankers, and businesspeople for the most part, but also impeccably turned-out women who like to lunch in style. There's a considerable amount of table hopping in the large, well-lighted dining room divided into smaller sections with gilded wrought-iron screens. Consider starting with baby artichokes vinaigrette, or slivers of carpaccio or *bresaola* (dried beef) dressed with olive oil and lemon. Also reliable are the house pastas or risotto, veal piccata, and the best scampi in town. The tiramisu, sinfully rich and custardy here, must be tasted to be believed. *10, rue Pierre-Fatio, tel. 022/21.80.33. Jacket recommended. Reservations required. AE, DC, MC, V. Closed Sat. evening, and Sun.*

Right Bank

★ ㉙ **Le Béarn.** Quietly, unobtrusively, Le Béarn continues to
$$$$ satisfy international gastronomes and celebrities who may reserve weeks ahead to savor a refined French cuisine prepared under the sure hand of Jean-Paul Goddard. The atmosphere is suitably formal (crystal and gleaming silver) for a restaurant located near Geneva's private banks. Service is superb: Waiters are accustomed to guests who know their way around food and wine, but are willing to initiate newcomers. If you're in town during truffle season (November–February), the fresh truffle soufflé is a special treat. Other chef's suggestions include pastry-wrapped

langoustines with herbs; and succulent lamb roasted in salt, perfumed with herbs, and served with a gratin of celery and a hint of hazelnuts. The cave is equal to the cuisine and features some excellent local wines. *4, quai de la Poste, tel. 022/21.00.28. Jacket required. Reservations required. DC, MC, V. Closed Sat. lunch, and Sun.*

⓱ Boeuf Rouge. Behind lacy café curtains, this friendly bis-
$$ tro—in an iffy district between the railway station and the lake—might have been lifted bodily from the heart of France. Frosted-glass partitions separate long-haired intellectuals, well-dressed couples sent by nearby grand hotels, and local foodies who tuck in to owner José Farina's robust dishes. It's perfect for an easygoing lunch or informal entertaining. Over a kir, ponder whether to order onion soup grâtinée, a tossed greens-and-bacon salad, or pistacchioed sausage with lentils (the poor man's caviar). Desserts such as the apple *tarte tatin* are gargantuan. The sommelier, in shirtsleeves and long white apron, offers a medium-priced choice of Beaujolais, Burgundy, Côtes-du-Rhône, and Swiss wines. *17, rue Alfred-Vincent, tel. 022/ 732.75.37. Casual dress. Reservations advised. No credit cards. Closed weekends and holidays.*

★ ⓳ Le Chat Botté. This pillar of Geneva gastronomy was given
$$$$ a boost in 1986 with the arrival of Richard Cressac and his energetic, imaginative ideas about French cuisine. Seafood prepared in his kitchen challenges the best coastal establishments without resorting to stylish gimmicks. Roasted lobster scented with coriander and accompanied by mousseline of artichokes, and scallops with wild mushrooms are just two examples. Fine wines are a long-standing tradition. The wood-paneled setting, sedate without being stuffy, is an ideal setting for serious business discussions or late-evening entertaining. Service is first-rate, and, in summer, the lakefront terrace is steeped in flowers. *Hotel Beau Rivage, 13 Quai du Mont-Blanc, tel. 022/ 731.65.32. Jacket and tie required. Reservations advised. AE, DC, MC, V. Closed weekends.*

❼ Chez Bouby. Total lack of pretension and a giant helping of
$$ conviviality make this typically Parisian bistro a great favorite with a large cross-section of Genevois. At lunch you'll encounter bankers and other financial types for whom the short stroll across the bridge is a daily habit; in the evening the crowd runs from politicians and bureaucrats to actors and artists. The standard menu of simple bistro fare is supplemented by daily specials such as filet of salmon served on a bed of lentils with a tangy horseradish sauce. There is a daily three-course bargain at 26 francs for both lunch and dinner. A good selection of wine is available by carafe or bottle. *1, rue Grenus, tel. 022/ 731.09.27. Dress: informal. Reservations advised. MC, V. Closed Sun.*

❽ Chez Jacky. Although red walls, dark-wood booths, well-
$$ worn banquettes, and kitschy touches make this look like every other casual bistro near the train station, the food is a cut above average. Young chef Jacky Gruber developed his knack for light, inventive cuisine while working in the kitchen of Frédy Girardet, Switzerland's most celebrated chef. The *carte* lists saddle of hare with Chinese cabbage, and duck breast with a tangy grapefruitlike garnish among more standard fare. There are reasonably priced *gastronomique* sampling menus and a relatively inexpen-

sive daily *plat du jour*, all served with standard brusque efficiency. Chatter at nearby tables makes this unfit for serious talk, but it fills the local need for a break at noon and for unassuming entertaining in the evening. *9–11, rue Jacques-Necker, tel. 022/732.86.80. Casual but neat. Reservations advised. V. Closed Sat. and Sun.*

4
$$$
Les Continents. Tommy Byrne, a health-conscious young Irish chef, rose from the ranks to head the Inter-Continental's kitchens. Trained by six master chefs, he has a light hand with fish and sauces, relies on virgin olive oil, herbs and spices, shuns butter and cream: He'll wrap langoustines in thin cannelloni pasta, combine a braised lamb chop with roast garlic and parsley puree. Airy desserts with little sugar and unsweetened chocolate appeal to figure-conscious UN delegates. Hushed service and well-separated tables allow quiet discussion. The long wine list is as good value for money as the lunch and dinner menus. Byrne's interest in health and energy foods also shows up in the menus of the InterContinental's simpler **La Pergola** terrace restaurant. *InterContinental Hotel, 7–9, ch. du Petit Saconnex, tel. 022/734.60.91. Casual but neat. Reservations advised. AE, DC, MC, V. Closed Sat., and Sun. noon.*

18
$$$$
Le Cygne. Everything is in harmony: the lakefront view, the discreet decor, the French-accented food, the wine, the service. Young chef Gilles Dupont has left Le Cygne to his well-trained assistant, but it is still too early to predict how well he can follow in Dupont's culinary footsteps. Specialties include delicately smoked sea bass, langoustines in a sauce perfumed with pepper and vanilla, and gratin of chicken flavored with truffles. Eric Curet, named Switzerland's best wine steward in 1989, has one of the city's finest caves at his disposal. No fewer than six dessert trolleys offer an embarrassment of riches, and there's a fine selection of rare old liqueurs and brandies. *Noga Hilton Hotel, 19, quai du Mont-Blanc, tel. 022/731.98.11. Jacket required. Reservations required. AE, DC, MC, V.*

14
$$
Le Mandarin. One of the city's oldest Chinese restaurants, located midway between the railway station and lake, is an exception to the curious Geneva assumption that Chinese cuisine must be expensive. In a 1989 transformation, the requisite lanterns and dragons gave way to an understated decor of natural brick, polished wood, and graphics by famed Chinese artist Zao Wou-Ki. Proprietress Lo-Ju Chu is on hand to oversee the friendly, multilingual service of Cantonese and Szechuan dishes. For good value try the set menus for lunch or dinner. As a service to international businesspeople and diplomats, who make up a large part of her clientele, Mrs. Chu will subdivide the space for groups of 10–30. *1–3, rue de Chantepoulet, tel. 022/732.27.42. Casual dress. Reservations not necessary. AE, DC, MC, V.*

FREE TIME

Fitness

Hotel Facilities
Noga Hilton Fit Club (tel. 022/731.98.11) has the most complete in-town fitness facilities; nonguests pay SwF45 per day for all the facilities. Near the airport, the new **Hol-**

iday Inn Crowne Plaza fitness club (tel. 022/791.00.11) has a full range of facilities, including pool, for SwF25 per day.

Health Clubs

On the Left Bank, centrally located **Gymforme** (15 rue Pierre-Fatio, tel. 022/735.78.67) has a large, well-equipped workout room, a Turkish bath and sauna, and a huge sun terrace with panoramic views of city and lake. A one-day membership costs SwF40. On the Right Bank, **Fitness-Alpes** (4, rue Thalberg, tel. 022/732.77.40) is a real bargain, offering the use of pool, sauna, Turkish bath, and workout equipment for SwF18 per day.

Jogging

Geneva's parks and lakefront quays offer numerous jogging possibilities. One route could go from **Parc Mon Repos** along the left bank quays, across the busy **Pont du Mont-Blanc,** through the **Jardin Anglais,** and along left bank quays as far as the **Yacht Club.** A map of additional, countryside trails is available from the Penta Hotel.

Shopping

If it's upscale, it's on the few blocks of the rue du Rhône— the most famous jewelers and watchmakers are here, including Pâtek Philippe, Piaget, Rolex (at Bucherer), Gubelin, Adler, Van Cleef and Arpels, Harry Winston, Bulgari, Boucheron, and Cartier. The top fashion boutiques are here, too—Hermès, Chanel, Valentino, Ungaro, Yves Saint-Laurent, Armani, Jean-Louis Scherrer, Ralph Lauren, Nina Ricci. Many international travelers prefer to do their serious shopping—especially for jewelry—in the serenity and safety of Geneva rather than in Paris, London, or New York. If you're looking for something more modest and typically Swiss, lace-trimmed handkerchiefs and other delicately detailed linens can be found at **Langenthal** (13, rue du Rhône, tel. 022/28.65.10), and **Au Chalet Suisse** (18, quai Général-Guisan). Swiss gifts and quality souvenirs are sold on the top floor of **Bucherer** (45, rue du Rhône, tel. 022/21.62.66). Curious as it may seem, there is no reliable source of discount watches in Geneva. The same is true of cameras, although **Interdiscount** (6, rue de la Madeleine, 1204, tel. 022/ 28.05.61) has overall good prices on cameras, and video and stereo equipment. Also worth trying is **Photo Verdaine** (4, rue Verdaine, 1204, tel. 022/28.75.90).

Diversions

Cathedral St-Pierre, crowning the Old Town, is Calvinistically austere but has unusually interesting archaeological digs that can be visited.

Jardin Anglais is not only a quayside park with a unique floral clock, but also a regular stop for the white CGN lake steamers cruising around Europe's largest pond. There are lunch cruises in summer (Compagnie Générale de Navigation, tel. 022/21.25.21).

Lakefront quays have wide, flowered sidewalks, good for a long casual stroll on a fine day or evening to enjoy the lake's fabulous changes of color, and the ballet of steamers, small craft, and windsurfs around the **Jet d'Eau,** a 470-foot column of water.

Maison Tavel (6, rue Puits-St. Pierre, tel. 022/28.29.00), a house dating back to the 12th century, offers an inside look at old Geneva.

Geneva's many **museums** are surprisingly inexpensive; some are free. **Musée de l'Horlogerie et de l'Emaillerie** (15, rte. de Malagnou, tel. 022/736.74.12) displays Geneva's antique clocks, watches, and miniatures in an 18th-century mansion setting. Almost next door (1, rte. de Malagnou, tel. 022/735.91.30), the **Musée d'Histoire Naturelle** is a natural history museum with a top-notch dinosaur exhibit. Small, specialized museums include: Oriental art, **Collections Baur** (8 rue Munier-Romilly, tel. 022/46.17.29); primitive art, **Collection Barbier-Müller** (4, rue Ecole-de-Chimie, tel. 022/20.02.53); musical instruments, **Musée des Instruments Anciens de Musique** (23, rue François-Lefort, tel. 022/46.95.65) near the gold-bulbed Russian church. For information on most (but not all) of the museums, call tel. 022/21.43.88.

Old Town (Vieille Ville) is built above the left bank around a hill topped by the Cathedral. It can be reached by walking up the main street, Grand'Rue, or other narrow streets and stairs from many directions. It is ideal for browsing among antiques shops, art galleries, old bookshops, jewelry stores, and so on. Guided tours on cassette with a map can be rented from the tourist office.

Parks at the end of the left-bank quays stretch discontinuously from **Parc Mon Repos** at the lake edge as far as the Bureau International Travail (BIT) and the UN in a manicured network of lawns and rare trees that includes the **Botanical Garden** and its mammoth glass hothouse of exotic rarities. On the right bank, **Parc de la Grange** and **Parc des Eaux Vives** are famous for roses.

Swiss Boat (Quai du Mont-Blanc, tel. 022/732.47.47), on the right bank near Pont du Mont-Blanc, offers short boat rides to glimpse **stately homes** along the lake. CGN (Compagnie Générale de Navigation sur le lac Léman, tel. 022/21.25.21) has white paddleboat steamers that also leave for scheduled stops around Swiss and French shores of the lake.

The United Nations (8–14, Ave. de la Paix, tel. 022/731.02.11) has hour-long guided tours of **Palais des Nations,** the UN European headquarters.

The Arts

The **Grand Théâtre** (pl. Neuve, tel. 022/21.23.11), a 19th-century jewelbox, is the scene for opera and ballet. The highly regarded Orchestre de la Suisse Romande shares the stage of **Victoria Hall** (rue Joseph-Hornung, tel. 022/28.81.21) with orchestras of international repute. Performances at the **Théâtre de Carouge** (39, rue Ancienne, tel. 022/43.43.43) are mostly in French, but during the summer high-quality amateur companies present plays in English. The **Grand Casino** (Noga Hilton, tel. 022/732.06.00) lists foreign dance troupes, musical comedies, and big-name stars among its attractions. For theater (in French), the **Comédie** (6, blvd. des Philosophes, tel. 022/20.50.01) offers excellent productions of classic and contemporary works, as do several smaller theaters about town.

Ticket agencies can be found on **Grand Passage** department store's top floor (13–15, rue du Marché, tel. 022/ 28.91.93), **Forum 2000** (35, rue de la Terrassiére, tel. 022/ 786.55.45), and **Société de Banque Suisse** (2, rue de la Confédération, tel. 022/790.61.11).

After Hours

Bars and Lounges
The most attractive hotel bars are at Le Richemond (tel. 022/731.14.00), the Metropole (tel. 022/21.13.44), the Beau Rivage (tel. 022/731.02.21), and the Bristol (tel. 022/ 732.38.00). Other choices are **La Coupole** (116, rue du Rhône, tel. 022/735.65.44), which has a piano bar and a computer corner to track international financial markets, and **Harry's Bar** (8, rue de la Confédération, tel. 022/ 29.44.21), weighted heavily toward the bankers and portfolio managers.

Clubs
Geneva nightlife is said to begin and end with **Griffin's Club** (36, blvd. Helvétique, tel. 022/735.12.18), a private club/disco/restaurant frequented by the jet set. Griffin's lets in nonmembers on a selective basis—by dress or if the usually excellent dinner is part of the plan. Have your hotel concierge try to swing an introduction. **Club 58** (15 rue Glacis-de-Rive, tel. 022/735.15.15) is also private but less restrictive about nonmembers, and features a strip show in its Pussy Cat Saloon. The **Velvet Club** (7, rue du Jeu-de-l'Arc, tel. 022/735.00.00) is popular among young professionals who like to dance—mostly disco. Near the airport, **Arthur's** (Mövenpick Radisson, tel. 022/798.75.75) is Switzerland's largest disco, covering 3,000 square meters and accommodating 1,500; fortunately, this is broken down in manageable sections, one of them private.

Cabarets
Le Maxim's (2, rue Thalberg, tel. 022/732.99.00) provides Geneva's answer to a Paris floor show. **Ba-Ta-Clan** (15, rue de la Fontaine, tel. 022/29.64.98) has dancing and two strip shows nightly. **New** (4, quai des Forces-Motrices, tel. 022/ 29.30.32) used to be Geneva's top jazz spot but has broadened its repertoire and now calls itself a cultural cabaret; it attracts a young, casual crowd.

Casinos
Aside from the **Grand Casino** in the Noga Hilton (tel. 022/ 732.06.00) where stakes are limited by Swiss law to a paltry SwF5, those in the mood for gambling head for neighboring France. **Casino de Divonne** (tel. 023/50.20.06.63), only 15 minutes away, has a good restaurant and floor shows. This is where big money changes hands. **Le Casino d'Evian** (Royal Club Evian, 74500, Evian les Bains, France, tel. 023/150.75.14.00) is farther afield and has a disco in addition to French- and American-style gambling and a gourmet restaurant.

Hong Kong

by J.D. Brown and Margaret Backenheimer

Hong Kong is regarded by many as the most beautiful harbor city in the Orient. It is certainly the most single-minded business capital, and few locations on earth can boast so many millionaires and Rolls-Royces. Many of its nearly 6 million citizens live in modern apartment towers, which vie with the flashy skyscrapers for domination of the skyline. In Hong Kong the pace is fast, the sidewalks are crowded, the noise level is full bore, the harbor traffic is fascinating. This is a commercial city-state in the Western image, but with a Chinese soul— and with some of the best Chinese food in the world.

Located on the southeast coast of China, Hong Kong is divided into three parts: the New Territories, a sparsely settled expanse of land running south from the Chinese border; Kowloon, the tip of the mainland peninsula, jammed with hotels, shops, and factories; and Hong Kong Island (officially named Victoria Island), the principal business center to the south.

For the past 150 years, Hong Kong has been part of the British Empire. It is now Britain's last great colony in the Orient. The Union Jack was first hoisted on Hong Kong Island in 1841. In 1898, Britain acquired the New Territories as a buffer with China under terms of a 99-year lease; on June 30, 1997, all of Hong Kong will revert to the People's Republic of China, as stipulated in the Sino-British Agreement of 1984.

Despite its imminent takeover by the largest communist nation on earth, Hong Kong in the 1990s remains one of the premier commercial centers in Asia, a mecca for shopping, and the undisputed heavyweight champion of laissez-faire capitalism and free trade. Yet the 1980s did end on some sour notes. Events in China (the stifling austerity program begun in 1988 and the Tiananmen Square massacre of 1989), growing apprehension about China's takeover, and Hong Kong's own recent economic problems have combined to slow the pace of development. During the mid-1980s, Hong Kong's real GDP (Gross Domestic Product) growth was a vigorous 10% annually, but at the beginning of the 1990s, annual expansion had fallen to under 3%. Problems for the 1990s include rising inflation; a continuing exodus of capital, skilled labor, and management; and an investment market dependent on the unpredictable situation in China.

Nevertheless, the business and trade outlook in Hong Kong is upbeat; a cautious optimism prevails. A majority of Hong Kong executives surveyed in 1990 believed that their companies would perform better in the next two years and that Hong Kong would remain a more popular base for regional offices than Singapore. The British government expressed its confidence by announcing construction of a mammoth new container terminal and airport project (US$14.3 billion), intended to bolster the domestic economy and assure Hong Kong's position as a world trade center into the next century.

Hong Kong currently ranks as the world's third largest financial center, second largest container port, and number-one exporter-manufacturer of textiles, clothing, and toys. As the world's largest free port, Hong Kong offers low income and corporate taxes (15%–17%), virtually no capital-gains levies, and the widest door to China's merchandise and labor. Anyone may invest in Hong Kong. Tax on profits is a flat 16.5%; on rental income, 15%.

At present, about 40% of Hong Kong's manufacturing work force is employed in the textile and clothing industry. Hong Kong holds 10% of the world export market in clothing, second only to Italy; 40% of those exports go to the United States. Much of the actual manufacturing, however, has moved to Hong Kong–owned or –managed factories in southern China. Re-exports from China account for 65% of Hong Kong's total exports, and the prices of these manufactured goods are unaffected by Hong Kong's own rising labor and production costs).

Hong Kong's economy is strongly influenced by U.S. trade policies regarding textiles. Should the United States withdraw the Most Favored Nation (MFN) status extended to China, it would affect 70% of Hong Kong's trade with the mainland.

During the 1990s, American businesses are expected to play a larger role in Hong Kong's development. There are now more American residents (15,000) here than British (14,000), Australian (9,000), or Canadian (9,000). American investment in Hong Kong manufacturing is well over US$1 billion, and nearly 50% of Hong Kong's exports go to the United States. As emigration continues apace, service industries have inevitably slipped a notch here and there, but Hong Kong is still fully open to overseas business, trade, and investment.

Note: The Hong Kong dollar is pegged to the U.S. dollar; variations in the exchange rate are miniscule.

Top Employers

Employer	Type of Enterprise	Parent*/ Headquarters
China Light & Power	Utilities	Hong Kong
First Pacific	Investment, management	Hong Kong
Hong Kong Land	Property investment	Hong Kong

Hong Kong Telecom	Communications, telephones	Hong Kong
Hutchison Whampoa	Shipping, trade	Hong Kong
Jardine Matheson	Investment, management	Hong Kong
New World Development	Property development, hotels	Hong Kong
Sun Hung Kai Properties	Property development	Hong Kong
Swire/Cathay Pacific	Aviation, management	Hong Kong
Wharf	Transport, shipping, property	Hong Kong

if applicable

ESSENTIAL INFORMATION

The currency of Hong Kong is the Hong Kong dollar, abbreviated throughout the chapter as HK$.

Government Tourist Offices

Hong Kong Tourist Association (HKTA). In North America: 548 Fifth Ave., Suite 590, New York, NY 10036, tel. 212/869–5008; 333 N. Michigan Ave., Suite 2400, Chicago, IL 60601, tel. 312/782–3872; 361 Post St., Suite 404, San Francisco, CA 94108, tel. 415/781–4582; 10940 Wilshire Blvd., Suite 1220, Los Angeles, CA 90024, tel. 213/208–4582.

In the United Kingdom: 125 Pall Mall, 5th Floor, London SW1Y 5EA, tel. 071/930–4775.

In Hong Kong: Star Ferry Concourse, Tsim Sha Tsui; Shop 8, Basement, Jardine House, 1 Connaught Pl., Central; Shop G–2, Royal Garden Hotel, 69 Mody Rd., Tsim Sha Tsui East. All inquiries can be directed to tel. 801–7177.

Foreign Trade Information

Hong Kong Economic and Trade Office. In North America: 680 Fifth Ave., 22nd Fl., New York, NY 10019, tel. 212/265–8888; 1233, 20th St. NW, Suite 504, Washington D.C. 20036, tel. 202/331–8947; 180 Sutter St., 4th Floor, San Francisco, CA 94104, tel. 415/397–2215.

In the United Kingdom: Hong Kong Government Office, 6 Grafton St., London W1X 3LB, tel. 071/499–9821.

Entry Requirements

U.S. Citizens
Passport only. A visa is required for visits longer than 30 days.

Canadian Citizens
Passport only. A visa is required for visits longer than 90 days.

U.K. Citizens
Passport only. A visa is required for visits longer than 180 days.

Climate

Autumn months (Oct.–Dec.) are mild and sunny (the peak season for tourism), while winters (Jan.–Mar.) are relatively cold, overcast, and a bit dank. Spring months (Apr.–May) bring mixed weather. Summer (June–Sept.) is the season to avoid if possible: days are hot and sticky, with uncomfortably high humidity and occasional typhoons. What follows are the average daily maximum and minimum temperatures for Hong Kong.

Jan.	65F 18C	Feb.	62F 17C	Mar.	66F 19C
	56 13		56 13		60 16
Apr.	75F 24C	May	82F 28C	June	84F 29C
	66 19		74 23		78 26
July	88F 31C	Aug.	88F 31C	Sept.	84F 29C
	78 26		78 26		77 25
Oct.	80F 27C	Nov.	74F 23C	Dec.	68F 20C
	74 23		65 18		59 15

Airport

Kai Tak International Airport, located on the harbor in a crowded residential section of the Kowloon Peninsula, is 5 miles east of the main Kowloon (Tsim Sha Tsui) business district and 8 miles northeast of Central, Hong Kong Island's business district. Direction and counter signs are in English; taxis, buses, and limousines line up at the main entrance. A Hong Kong Tourist Association (HKTA) information desk is open 8 AM–10:30 PM. Departure tax is HK$100 per adult.

Airlines

Hong Kong is the hub city for Cathay Pacific and Dragonair, and for United Airlines's Asia-Pacific operations. Cathay Pacific flies directly from Los Angeles; United flies directly from Chicago, Los Angeles, San Francisco, and Seattle.

British Airways, tel. 868–0303; 800/247–9297.
Canadian Airlines, tel. 868–3123; 800/426–7000.
Cathay Pacific, tel. 747–1888; 800/233–2742.
China Airlines, tel. 868–2299; 800/227–5118.
Dragonair, tel. 736–0202.
Japan Airlines, tel. 523–0081; 800/525–3663.
Northwest, tel. 810–4288; 800/225–2525.
Qantas, tel. 524–2101; 800/227–4500.
Singapore Airlines, tel. 520–2233; 800/742–3333.
Thai International, tel. 529–5601; 800/426–5204.
United, tel. 810–4888; 800/241–6522.

Between the Airport and Downtown

Taxi stands and the Airbus shuttle are both located outside the main entrance (follow signs). Both take about the same time to navigate Hong Kong traffic snarls. Allow 20 minutes to reach the main Kowloon business district (Nathan Road/Star Ferry/Tsim Sha Tsui) and 40 minutes to

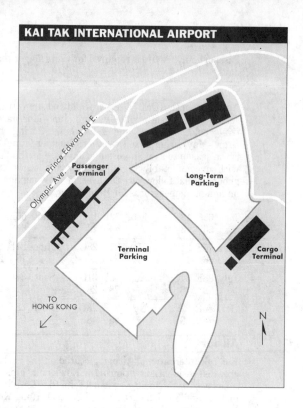

KAI TAK INTERNATIONAL AIRPORT

reach Central District across the harbor on Hong Kong Island (Victoria). Add 20–30 minutes during the always-crowded rush hour (8–9:30 AM, 4–6:30 PM). A few hotels provide courtesy cars or vans; check at the counter inside the main entrance. Some hotels meet guests upon arrival with Rolls Royces, Mercedes-Benz, etc., by prior arrangement at the time of reservations; prices vary for VIP transportation.

By Taxi
Taxis, a bargain, queue up in a continuous line on the closed street outside the main entrance. Cost: HK$20–HK$30 to Kowloon points; HK$60 + HK$20 tunnel fee to the Hong Kong Island side.

By Airbus
Fast, efficient, and comfortable, this is the least expensive form of airport transportation. Line up across from the large route/rate sign just outside the main entrance. Airbus A1 (HK$8) serves 15 hotels in Tsim Sha Tsui, Kowloon; Airbus 2A (HK$10) serves nine Island-side hotels from Central east to Wanchai; Airbus 3A (HK$10) serves three hotels in Causeway Bay; Airbus A4 (HK$6) serves the Mong Kok train station. Departures are every 15–20 minutes from 6:55 AM–midnight, tel. 745-4466.

Car Rentals

There are no car rental offices at the airport. Cars can be rented at hotels and offices in Kowloon and on Hong Kong Island; these rentals often include a professional driver.

Avis (85 Leighton Rd., Causeway Bay, tel. 890–6988) has both self-drive and chauffeur-driven cars that can be reserved in advance from the United States, tel. 800/331–1084.

Hertz (Pacific Star Bldg. 2F, 2 Canton Rd., Tsim Sha Tsui, tel. 367–1021) rents only chauffeur-driven cars that can be reserved in advance from the United States, tel. 800/654–3001.

Emergencies

For a list of approved physicians and clinics in Hong Kong that belong to the International Association for Medical Assistance to Travelers, contact IAMAT, 417 Center St., Lewiston, NY 14092, tel. 716/754–4883. In case of a medical emergency in Hong Kong, dial 999 or contact one of the (24-hour) hospitals listed below.

Doctors and Dentists
Most hotels have a list of accredited doctors and dentists on call.

Hospitals
Hong Kong Adventist Hospital (40 Stubbs Rd., tel. 574–6211), **Queen Mary Hospital** (Pokfulum Rd., tel. 819–2111), **Queen Elizabeth Hospital** (Wylie Rd., tel. 710–2111).

Police
Tel. 527–7177.

Ambulance
Tel. 576–6555.

Important Addresses and Numbers

American Express (Swire House, 8 Connaught Rd., Central, tel. 524–3151; 119 Nathan Rd., Kowloon, tel. 721–0179; emergencies, tel. 843–1775).

Audiovisual rentals. Hiller Pharma Co. HK (Room 2206, Hong Kong Plaza, 186–191 Connaught Rd. W, tel. 549–2647), Multimedia Communications (1/F Kwong Sang Hong Bldg., 6B Heard St., Wanchai, tel. 833–1991).

Bookstores (English-language). Bookazine (Prince's Bldg., 3 Des Voeux Rd., Central, tel. 522–1785), Chung Hwa (450–452 Nathan Rd., Yau Ma Tei, tel. 385–6588), South China Morning Post (Family Bookshop) (313 Ocean Centre, Harbour City, Tsim Sha Tsui, tel. 367–0396; Star Ferry Concourse, Central, tel. 522–1012), Swindon Book Company (13–15 Lock Rd., Tsim Sha Tsui, tel. 311–3732), Wanderlust Books (Travel) (30 Hollywood Rd., Central, tel. 523–2042).

British Consulate. U.K. Commission (Mirror Tower, 61 Mody Rd., Tsim Sha Tsui East, tel. 733–3111).

Canadian Consulate. Canadian Commission (Floors 11–14, Tower 1, Exchange Sq., Connaught Plaza, Central, tel. 810–4321).

Chamber of Commerce. Hong Kong General Chamber of Commerce (United Centre 22F, Queensway, tel. 529–9229).

Computer rentals. Atlantic Computer Systems (Harcourt House, tel. 865–5228).

Convention and exhibition center. Hong Kong Convention and Exhibition Centre (1 Harbour Rd., Wanchai, tel. 864–8888).

Fax services. "Postfax" service at main branch of General Post Office (GPO), Hong Kong side, tel. 522–1071; or at Exchange Square and Hermes House (Middle Rd., Kowloon) offices of Cable & Wireless Company (24-hour service), tel. 732–4336.

Formal-wear rentals. Men: Tuxe Top Co. (18 Hennessy Rd., Wanchai, tel. 529–2179; 16 Peking Rd. 3/F, Tsim Sha Tsui, tel. 366–6311); Women: International Wedding Fashion Centre (Cheng On Bldg., Kowloon, tel. 721–1866).

Gift shops. Chocolates: Peninsula Chocolates (Peninsula Hotel, Salisbury Rd., Tsim Sha Tsui, tel. 366–6251), See's Candies (B66 Landmark Bldg., Central, tel. 523–4977; 404C Taikoo Shing Cityplaza, Quarry Bay, tel. 567–7592; Shop 2119B Ocean Terminal, Harbour City, Tsim Sha Tsui, tel. 735–6488); Flowers: Clover Flower Shop (M36A Prince's Bldg., Central, tel. 522–0638), Greenfield's Flower Shop (2134 Ocean Terminal, Harbour City, Tsim Sha Tsui, tel. 730–4361).

Graphic design studios. Pacific MicroElectronics (2013 Hong Kong Plaza, 186–191 Connaught Rd. W, tel. 559–3978), Peter Chancellor Design Associates (4–10 Thomson Rd., Wanchai, tel. 527–9086).

Hairstylists. Unisex: Ambassador Beauty Salons (Ambassador Hotel Arcade, Tsim Sha Tsui, tel. 366–9093), Ronald Top Stylist (53 Paterson St., 3/F Block A, Causeway Bay, tel. 890–4077).

Health and fitness clubs. *See* Fitness, below.

Information hot lines. Hong Kong Tourist Authority (HKTA) (tel. 801–7177; 8 AM–6 PM daily), shopping advice (tel. 801–7278, weekdays 9 AM–5 PM; Sat. 9 AM–1 PM).

Limousine service. Alex's Tour Service (Mercedes-Benz) (tel. 363–7582).

Liquor store. Remy Nicolas (Swire House, Central, tel. 523–5904; Harbour City, Tsim Sha Tsui, tel. 730–8192).

Mail delivery, overnight. DHL (dozens of branches in subway stations, shopping centers, office buildings, including 13 Mok Cheong St., tel. 765–8111), Federal Express (14/F World Shipping Centre, Canton Rd., Tsim Sha Tsui, tel. 730–3333).

Messenger service. DHL (*see* Mail delivery, above, for addresses; tel. 770–1008).

News programs (English-language). TVB Pearl and ATV Diamond (local television networks), world news morning, evening, and late night; Radio 3 (567 kHz), Radio 4 (91, 100 mHz), hourly news: BBC World Service (96 mHz, 105 mHz), 6 AM–6:45 AM, 5 PM–2 AM.

Office space rentals. American Chamber of Commerce (1030 Swire House, Central, tel. 526–0165), China Traders Centre (Regal Airport Hotel, tel. 718–0333), Far East Executive Services Centre (7 Ice House St. 4F, Central, tel. 521–7461), Harbour International Business Centre (2803 Tower 1, Admiralty Centre, 18 Harcourt Rd., tel. 529–0356).

Pharmacies, late-night. Watson's (28 locations, including Hilton Hotel, Admiralty Centre, Prince's Bldg., New World Centre, Harbour City, and Melbourne Plaza, tel. 523–0666), Manning Dispensary (9 locations including Queensway Plaza, Swire House, Harbour City, and The Landmark, tel. 324–9855).

Secretarial services. Far East Executive Services Centre (7 Ice House St. 4F, Central, tel. 521–7461), Harbour International Business Centre (2803 Tower 1, Admiralty Centre, 18 Harcourt Rd., tel. 529–0356), Margaret Sullivan Secretarial Services (13 Duddell St., Central, tel. 526–5946).

Stationery supplies. Che San (10 Pottinger St., Central, tel. 522–5091), Chun Kee Stationery (11 Lock Rd., Tsim Sha Tsui, tel. 367–4196).

Taxis. Hung Fat Garage (tel. 725–5211, ext. 108), Blue Taxicabs (tel. 711–8719).

Theater tickets. *See* The Arts, below.

Thomas Cook. Mirador Mansion (58A Nathan Rd., Tsim Sha Tsui, tel. 366–9687; Room 141, Duddell St., Central, tel. 526–5701).

Trade Ministry. Hong Kong Trade Development Council (private organization) (1 Harbour Rd. 38F, Wanchai, tel. 833–4333).

Train information. Kowloon-Canton Railway (KCR) (Hung Hom, Kowloon [MTR subway stop: Kowloon Tong], tel. 606–9606).

Translation services. Polyglot Translations (1702 China Bank Bldg., 61 Des Voeux Rd., Central, tel. 521–5689), Translanguage Centre (1604 Tung Wah Mansion, 199 Hennessy Rd., Wanchai, tel. 573–2728).

U.S. Consulate (26 Garden Rd., Central, tel. 523–9011).

Telephones

To use a public phone for a local call, pick up the receiver, deposit HK$1, wait for the tone, and dial the number. Instructions are written in English on the phone. There's no time limit on local calls. Many shops have free phones available for public use as well. For operator assistance, dial 108. Note: Hong Kong was formerly divided into different city codes, but they were eliminated in late 1989. There is now only a country code (852), to be dialed when calling from outside Hong Kong.

Tipping

Most restaurants and hotels include a 10% service charge on the bill. Tip doormen carrying bags to the registration desk HK$5 per item; porters carrying bags to the room get HK$5 per item, minimum of HK$10. Hotel concierges expect HK$10. For room service waiters, tip 5%–10%; for housekeeping, no tip is expected. Give waiters 5%–10% above the included 10% service charge if service was par-

ticularly good. Give taxi drivers spare change or HK$1–
HK$2.

DOING BUSINESS

Hours

Businesses: weekdays 9 to 5 or 6, lunch 1–2; Sat. 9–1.
Banks: weekdays 9–4:30; Sat. 9:30–12:30; varies by bank
and branch. **Shops:** every day 10–6 in Central; 10–9:30 in
Wanchai and Causeway Bay; 10–9 in Tsim Sha Tsui.

National Holidays

New Year's Day; late Jan.–early Feb.,* Chinese New
Year's (3 days); Apr. 5, Ching Ming Festival; late May–
early June,* Dragon Boat Festival; June 11, Queen's
Birthday; late Aug. (last Mon. and preceding Sat. of
month), Liberation Day; mid-Sept.–early Oct,* Mid-Au-
tumn "Moon" Festival (2 days); Christmas Day; Dec. 26,
Boxing Day.

*These holidays are lunar based and change yearly.

Getting Around

By Car
Self-drive car rental is not advised. Traffic is worse than in
Tokyo, parking spots are almost nonexistent, and driving
is on the left side of the road. If you insist on driving yourself, an International Driver's License is required. *See*
Car Rentals, above, for information on renting cars with
or without drivers.

By Taxi
Taxis are numerous, inexpensive, and fairly quick; you
can hail them on the street (they're usually red, and have a
roof sign saying "TAXI" that lights up when the cab is
available) or catch them at queues outside the major hotels. However, they are difficult to find from 4 PM to 7 PM or
when it rains; at those times, it's best to go into a large hotel or restaurant and ask them to phone a cab company for
you.

By Public Transportation
The Mass Transit Railway (MTR) (tel. 750–0710) subway
system is air-conditioned and easy to use, but it is too
crowded to ride during rush hours. Station entrances are
marked with a line symbol representing a man with arms
and legs outstretched. There are clearly marked ticket
machines inside the stations. The system operates from
6 AM to 1 AM; maps are available at the airport, at hotels,
and at bookstores. The cost is HK$2.50–HK$6 for most
destinations. Buses and colorful trams are very inexpensive crosstown alternatives, but are slow and frequently
congested. The Star Ferry (6:30 AM–11:30 PM, tel. 366–
2576) is the quickest, cheapest, and most scenic way to
cross the busy harbor. The cost for the seven-minute ride
is HK$.80 upper deck, HK$.60 lower deck.

Protocol

Appointments
It is important to be prompt. Don't be surprised if a meeting time is assigned by fax or by phone message. Appoint-

ments are frequently changed or canceled. Hong Kong is a business city in a hurry, and often acts that way.

Customs

Hong Kong, long a British colony, is quite at home with Western traditions. Treat business contacts here much as you would in North America or Europe, in a fairly formal, professional manner. Allow your host to play the host's role fully. Shaking hands is the common form of greeting, and "Mr.," "Miss," or "Mrs." are used with the last name. (It's best to wait until asked to use first names.) Business card exchange, at the beginning of a meeting, is now quite common. As a courtesy to Chinese clients, have your card printed in Chinese on the reverse side (this is not expensive to do in Hong Kong; ask at your hotel).

Dress

Hong Kong is as cosmopolitan in fashion as New York or Tokyo. Until familiar with your business contact, dress formally; suits or sports coats with ties are the rule for men; dresses or jackets and skirts for women.

Gifts

Gifts are not normally a part of a business exchange, although fine chocolates and flowers after initial contacts are appreciated. The Chinese frequently do not open gifts on the spot, for fear of embarrassing the giver. Do not give clocks, watches, or hats as gifts; all have negative, superstitious connotations. Thank-you notes are not expected.

Toasts and Greetings

Cantonese rather than Mandarin is the more widely used language in Hong Kong. However, your negotiations and dinners will probably be conducted in English, a language with which Hong Kong businesspeople are quite familiar. The following phrases will be more useful in the street than during business talks.

Hello, how are you? *Neh HO mah?*
Well, thank you. *HO, yow sem.*
Pleased to meet you. *Hun woo.*
Thank you. *Mm-goy.*
You're welcome. *Mm'sai mm-goy.*
Nice to have met you. *HOH goh HING gin dough knee.*
Excuse me. *Doy ing CHOO.*
Goodbye. *WAH-boo-DONG.*
Cheers? *Yum-SING.*

LODGING

Hong Kong has several of the world's finest hotels and many luxury inns of considerable merit. Its high service level is well known in the industry. For the business traveler, this means a large selection of superb hotels, all of which can be booked overseas. The drawback is cost: Hong Kong hotels are priced considerably above comparable offerings elsewhere in Asia. There is a dearth of acceptable budget accommodations in the three-star category as well. Inquire about specials and corporate rates before making a reservation. If your expense account is liberal, consider upgrading to business class; many Hong Kong hotels provide substantially better rooms and services, as well as complimentary food, on their "executive floors," sometimes for as little as HK$100 more a night.

With so many splendid hotels offering roughly comparable business services and accommodations, the leading consideration is often location. The majority of deluxe hotels are on the Kowloon side, either in Tsim Sha Tsui (the central shopping area near the Star Ferry terminal) or in the slightly less convenient Tsim Sha Tsui East area. The Hong Kong side (Victoria Island) contains fewer hotels but more financial institutions and regional headquarters. The Central district is the heart of things; the Western district is under development; the Admiralty and Wanchai districts to the east are rapidly becoming mere extensions of Central; and Causeway Bay and Quarry Bay are far enough east along the waterfront to have their own commercial and industrial attractions.

As we went to press, six major new hotels had opened, all good options for the business traveler: **The Island Shangri-La, Hotel Conrad Hong Kong,** and the **Ritz-Carlton Hong Kong** on the island (Hong Kong) side; and the **Kowloon Panda, Eaton,** and **Prudential** hotels on the Kowloon side.

Highly recommended lodgings in each price category are indicated by a star ★.

Category	Cost*
$$$$ (Very Expensive)	over HK$1,500
$$$ (Expensive)	HK$1,000–HK$1,500
$$ (Moderate)	under HK$1,000

All prices are for a standard double room, single occupancy, excluding 5% tax and 10% service charge.

Numbers in the margin correspond to numbered hotel locations on the Hong Kong Lodging and Dining map.

Kowloon: Tsim Sha Tsui

⑲ **Ambassador.** Nestled in the multiethnic hubbub of lower
$$ Nathan Road, this 1965 hotel is a bright surprise, completely remodeled in 1989 to deliver plenty of luxury for the price. Hallways and elevator lobbies gleam with mirrors and polished wood moldings. The best rooms overlook Nathan Road to the north or Middle Road to the west. All are quiet and well lighted, with horseshoe-shaped desks that afford plenty of room to work. The Ambassador Club executive floors (12 and 13) offer complimentary meeting rooms, in-room fax hook-up, and priority use of the attached business center. Charlotte's (*see* Dining, below) is a nice retreat from the bustle of Nathan Road. *26 Nathan Rd., Tsim Sha Tsui, tel. 366–6321 or 800/448–8355, fax 369–0063. Gen. manager, Patrick San. 262 doubles, 14 suites, 37 business class. AE, CB, DC, MC, V.*

❶ **Grand Tower.** Opened in 1987, this 20-story hotel still feels
$$ brand new. Although catering primarily to tour groups (mainly Japanese), the Grand Tower makes the individual business traveler welcome. The hotel, far up Nathan Road near the bird market, is removed from the clot of tourist shops and hotels, yet right on the subway line (Mongkok Station). It's a favorite of those with business at nearby

factories or offices connected to the import/export trade. Guest rooms are suitably spacious, with tidy bathrooms and coffee/tea setups. The quietest rooms face an uninteresting interior courtyard; upper-floor west-side rooms overlook an industrial portion of the harbor. *627-641 Nathan Rd., Mongkok, tel. 789-0011 or 800/448-8355, fax 789-0945. Gen. manager, Peter Liu. 536 doubles, 13 suites. AE, DC, MC, V.*

★ ⑮ **Holiday Inn Golden Mile.** With 60% of its guests in Hong
$$ Kong on business, this 18-story hotel has become a classic choice among middle-management travelers, especially those connected with the garment industry in Kowloon. Like the hotel service and restaurants, rooms are a notch above the run-of-the-mill Holiday Inn in America, possessing ample space, large, firm beds, built-in desks, and clean marble bathrooms. The Executive Club floors are 8 and 9; nonsmoking rooms are on 10. The lobby is one of the busiest meeting points on lower Nathan Road, where this hotel has maintained a solid reputation since 1975. Delicatessen Corner (*see* Dining, below), tucked away in the hotel's basement shopping arcade, is perfect for a light snack. Subway, ferry, and taxi connections are exceptionally convenient. *50 Nathan Rd., Tsim Sha Tsui, tel. 369-3111 or 800/HOLIDAY, fax 369-8016. Gen. manager, Jean Marc Charpenet. 409 doubles, 59 singles, 9 suites, 120 business class. Rooms for disabled guests. AE, DC, MC, V.*

⑭ **Hyatt Regency Hong Kong.** Centrally situated on Nathan
$$$ Road, but with its entrance at the back, this 17-story tower—Hyatt's first property in Asia (1969)—was renovated and soundproofed in 1988. The lobby combines modern and Oriental motifs in marble and teak; there's plenty of seating, and even a palm reader on duty. There are no views to speak of, but elegant rooms, decorated in earth tones, have separate writing desks and safes. The Regency Club's executive floors (16 and 17) are superb, with additional amenities such as complimentary Continental breakfast and evening cocktails and free use of the conference room. Rooms for nonsmokers are available. There is no pool or fitness center, but service, location, and small decorative touches (fresh flowers, pieces of exquisite lacquerware and porcelain) are outstanding. Hugo's (*see* Dining, below) is an elegant location to wine and dine associates. *67 Nathan Rd., Tsim Sha Tsui, tel. 311-1234 or 800/223-1234, fax 739-8701. Gen. manager, Juergen Wolter. 632 doubles, 17 suites, 74 business class; supersaver rooms by request. Rooms for disabled guests. AE, CB, DC, MC, V.*

★ ⑱ **The Kowloon.** Hong Kong's premier high-tech business
$$ hotel is an 18-story glass-enclosed angular cube sharing expert management with The Peninsula, which blocks part of its harbor view. The Kowloon concentrates more on business services than views. The long lobby is glitzy and overlighted with flight schedules on TV monitors. The small, pastel rooms have clean, tiled bathrooms, triangular bay windows, and TVs with interhotel communications capability. Guests can send telex, telegram, fax, and word-processing texts directly from executive suites and harbor-view rooms (floors 15–18) to the third-floor business center for posting or printing—a first for Hong Kong

HONG KONG

Distance from Kowloon to Hong Kong Island districts has been reduced.

N

Macau Ferry Pier

Victoria Harbour

Connaught Rd. Central

Wing Lok St.

SHEUNG WAN

Des Voeux Rd.

Aberdeen St.

Wellington St.

Queen's Rd.

Stanley St.

Staunton St.

Caine Rd.

Wyndham St.

Central Pedder St.

Chater Rd.

Garden Rd.

Cotton Tree Dr.

Naval Dockyard

Harcourt Rd.

ADMIRALTY

Queen's Way

0   440 yards
0   400 meters

HONG KONG ISLAND

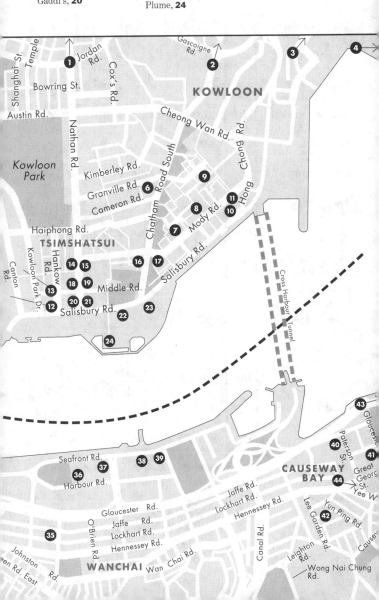

HONG KONG HOTEL CHART

HOTELS	Price Category	Business Services / Banquet capacity	No. of meeting rooms	Fax	Telex	Photocopying	Secretarial services	Audiovisual equipment	Translation services	International direct dial	Computer rentals	In-room modem phone jack
Ambassador	$$	0	2	✓	✓	✓	✓	✓	✓	✓	✓	-
China Merchants	$$	160	7	✓	✓	✓	✓	✓	✓	✓	-	-
Empress	$$	30	1	✓	✓	✓	✓	✓	✓	✓	-	-
Excelsior	$$$	1600	5	✓	✓	✓	✓	✓	✓	✓	✓	-
Furama Kempinski	$$$	576	13	✓	✓	✓	✓	✓	✓	✓	✓	-
Grand Hyatt	$$$$	440	11	✓	✓	✓	✓	✓	✓	✓	✓	-
Grand Plaza	$$	1000	4	✓	✓	✓	✓	✓	✓	✓	-	-
Grand Tower	$$	130	3	✓	✓	✓	✓	✓	✓	✓	-	-
Hilton	$$$$	800	11	✓	✓	✓	✓	✓	✓	✓	✓	-
Holiday Inn Golden Mile	$$	500	5	✓	✓	✓	✓	✓	✓	✓	-	-
Holiday Inn Harbor View	$$$	350	2	✓	✓	✓	✓	✓	✓	✓	✓	✓
Hyatt Regency	$$$	40	1	✓	✓	✓	✓	✓	✓	✓	-	-
Kowloon	$$	0	0	✓	✓	✓	✓	✓	✓	✓	✓	-
Kowloon Shangri-La	$$$$	700	10	✓	✓	✓	✓	✓	✓	✓	✓	✓
Mandarin Oriental	$$$$	700	11	✓	✓	✓	✓	✓	✓	✓	✓	-
Marriott	$$$$	450	12	✓	✓	✓	✓	✓	✓	✓	✓	-
New World	$$$	500	8	✓	✓	✓	✓	✓	✓	✓	-	-
New World Harbor View	$$$	360	3	✓	✓	✓	✓	✓	✓	✓	-	-
Nikko	$$$	300	2	✓	✓	✓	✓	✓	✓	✓	✓	-

$$$$ = over HK$1500, $$$ = HK$ 1000-Hk$1500, $$ = under HK$ 1000.
● good, ◐ fair, ○ poor.

All-news cable channel	Desk	Desk lighting	Bed lighting	**In-Room Amenities** Nonsmoking rooms	In-room checkout	Minibar	Toiletries	Room service	Laundry/Dry cleaning	Pressing	**Hotel Amenities** Barber/Hairdresser	Garage	Courtesy airport transport	Sauna	Pool	Exercise room
-	◐	●	◐	-	-	✓	●	◐	●	●	-	-	✓	-	-	-
-	◐	●	◐	-	-	✓	●	●	●	◐	-	✓	-	✓	-	○
-	◐	◐	○	-	-	✓	○	●	●	●	-	-	-	-	-	-
-	◐	◐	◐	✓	-	✓	◐	●	●	●	✓	-	-	-	-	-
-	●	◐	◐	✓	-	✓	●	◐	●	●	✓	-	-	-	-	-
-	●	●	●	✓	-	✓	●	●	●	●	✓	✓	-	✓	●	●
-	◐	●	◐	-	-	✓	◐	●	●	◐	-	✓	-	✓	●	●
-	●	●	◐	-	-	✓	◐	●	●	●	✓	✓	-	-	-	-
-	●	●	●	✓	-	✓	●	●	●	●	✓	✓	-	✓	●	●
-	◐	◐	◐	✓	-	✓	◐	●	●	●	✓	✓	✓	✓	●	◐
-	●	●	◐	✓	-	●	●	●	●	●	✓	✓	-	✓	●	◐
-	●	◐	●	✓	-	✓	●	●	●	●	✓	-	-	-	-	-
-	◐	◐	◐	✓	-	◐	◐	●	●	●	-	-	-	-	-	-
-	●	●	●	✓	✓	✓	●	●	●	●	✓	✓	✓	✓	◐	●
-	●	●	◐	✓	-	✓	●	●	●	●	✓	✓	-	✓	◐	◐
-	●	●	●	✓	-	✓	●	●	●	●	✓	✓	-	✓	●	●
-	◐	◐	◐	✓	-	✓	◐	◐	●	◐	✓	✓	-	-	●	-
✓	●	◐	●	✓	✓	✓	●	●	●	●	-	✓	-	-	●	-
-	●	◐	●	-	-	✓	●	●	●	●	✓	✓	-	✓	●	◐

Room service: ● 24-hour, ◐ 6AM-10PM, ○ other.
Laundry/Dry cleaning: ● same day, ◐ overnight, ○ other.
Pressing: ● immediate, ◐ same day, ○ other.

HONG KONG HOTEL CHART

HOTELS	Price Category	Banquet capacity	No. of meeting rooms	Fax	Telex	Photocopying	Secretarial services	Audiovisual equipment	Translation services	International direct dial	Computer rentals	In-room modem phone jack
The Omni	$$$	290	5	✓	✓	✓	✓	✓	✓	✓	-	-
Park Lane Radisson	$$$	264	7	✓	✓	✓	✓	✓	✓	✓	✓	-
Peninsula	$$$$	30	1	✓	✓	✓	✓	✓	✓	✓	✓	✓
Ramada Inn Hong Kong	$$	80	3	✓	✓	✓	✓	✓	✓	✓	✓	-
Ramada Inn Kowloon	$$	30	2	✓	✓	✓	✓	✓	✓	✓	✓	-
Ramada Renaissance	$$$	300	4	✓	✓	✓	✓	✓	✓	✓	✓	-
Regal Airport	$$	200	2	✓	✓	✓	✓	✓	✓	✓	✓	-
Regal Meridien	$$$	350	7	✓	✓	✓	✓	✓	✓	✓	✓	-
Regal Riverside	$$	500	14	✓	✓	✓	✓	✓	✓	✓	-	-
Regent	$$$$	650	9	✓	✓	✓	✓	✓	✓	✓	-	-
Royal Garden	$$$	160	2	✓	✓	✓	✓	-	✓	✓	✓	-
Royal Pacific	$$$	150	3	✓	✓	✓	✓	✓	✓	✓	-	-
Sheraton	$$$	480	8	✓	✓	✓	✓	✓	✓	✓	✓	-

$$$$ = over HK$1500, $$$ = HK$ 1000-HK$ 1500, $$ = under HK$ 1000.
● good, ◕ fair, ○ poor.

All-news cable channel	Desk	Desk lighting	Bed lighting	Nonsmoking rooms	In-room checkout	Minibar	Toiletries	Room service	Laundry/Dry cleaning	Pressing	Barber/Hairdresser	Garage	Courtesy airport transport	Sauna	Pool	Exercise room
	In-Room Amenities										**Hotel Amenities**					
-	●	◐	◐	✓	-	✓	◐	●	●	●	✓	✓	-	✓	●	◐
-	◐	◐	◐	-	-	✓	◐	●	◐	●	✓	✓	-	✓	-	◐
-	●	◐	●	✓	-	✓	●	●	●	●	✓	-	-	-	-	-
-	◐	◐	◐	-	-	✓	◐	◐	●	●	-	✓	-	-	-	◐
-	◐	◐	◐	✓	-	✓	●	●	●	●	-	-	-	-	-	-
-	●	●	●	✓	-	✓	●	●	●	●	-	✓	-	-	●	●
-	◐	◐	◐	✓	-	✓	●	●	●	●	✓	✓	-	-	-	-
-	◐	◐	◐	✓	-	✓	◐	●	●	●	✓	✓	✓	✓	-	-
-	◐	◐	◐	-	-	✓	●	●	●	●	✓	✓	-	✓	●	●
-	●	●	●	-	-	✓	●	●	●	●	✓	✓	-	✓	●	◐
-	◐	◐	◐	✓	✓	✓	●	●	●	●	✓	✓	-	✓	-	-
-	●	●	●	-	-	✓	◐	◐	◐	●	✓	✓	-	✓	-	●
-	●	●	◐	✓	-	✓	●	●	●	●	✓	✓	-	✓	●	●

Room service: ● 24-hour, ◐ 6AM-10PM, ○ other.
Laundry/Dry cleaning: ● same day, ◐ overnight, ○ other.
Pressing: ● immediate, ◐ same day, ○ other.

hotels. Rooms are an outstanding bargain; it's no surprise that The Kowloon boasts one of the highest occupancy rates in Hong Kong. *A Peninsula Group hotel. 19–21 Nathan Rd., Tsim Sha Tsui, tel. 369–8698 or 800/262–9467, fax 369–8698. Gen. manager, Anders Poon. 590 doubles, 147 business class. AE, CB, DC, MC, V.*

㉓ **New World.** This 19-story hotel-office-apartment complex
$$$ in the 400-shop New World Centre has catered to business travelers since 1978. It's ready for the 1990s after a recent face-lift. About 160 rooms disappeared during expansion. A large business center has taken the place of the second-floor lobby and disco, and the executive floors (Dynasty Club) now occupy three levels (17–19). Although the inexpensive rooms are gone, the standard rooms are reasonably priced, given this fine location; they are now less cramped and feature safes, better lighting, and separate writing desks. The terraced garden and pool remain a delight. This is no longer a budget hotel, but it's one that has a lot more business facilities to offer. *22 Salisbury Rd., New World Centre, Tsim Sha Tsui, tel. 369–4111 or 800/448–8355, fax 369–9387. Gen. manager, Henry Chan. 339 doubles, 5 singles, 55 suites, 124 business class. AE, CB, DC, MC, V.*

⓬ **The Omni Hong Kong.** This is the most upscale of three sis-
$$$ ter hotels in the mammoth Harbour City–Ocean City shopping center. (The other two are the more modest Omni Prince and Marco Polo hotels.) It's a busy location; in fact, the glittering white-marble lobby with its step-up coffee shop and lounge is a central meeting point for businesspeople. Guest rooms are above-average in size, with pastel color schemes and moderate lighting. Those on the west side of the hotel above the sixth floor have intriguing views of the harbor piers. The 14th floor is reserved exclusively for nonsmokers. The two "Continental" floors at the top (17 and 18) were renovated in 1988; they feature 24-hour butler service and a mini-business center with complimentary boardroom use. The main business center offers a video reference library and PC word processing. The jazz brunch buffet in Gripps (*see* Dining, below) is a wonderful way to spend a Sunday afternoon. There's a rooftop garden pool and fitness center; guests can also use exercise equipment, pool, and tennis and squash courts of the new Pacific Club Kowloon on the pier. *3 Canton Rd., Harbour City, Tsim Sha Tsui, tel. 736–0088 or 800/843–6664, fax 736–0011. Gen. manager, Herbert Sossna. 424 doubles, 84 singles, 95 suites, 117 business class. AE, DC, MC, V.*

★ ⓴ **The Peninsula.** Built on the waterfront in 1928, this Hong
$$$$ Kong landmark has lost none of its legendary luster. Its celebrated high tea (*see* Diversions, below), held in the gold-leaf lobby, is still the best in the East, and its staff (including one member who has been in service here for eight decades) is impeccable. The high-ceiling rooms and suites were tastefully renovated in 1988, and are still the choice of visiting celebrities, world leaders, and business executives. All rooms are fitted with chandeliers, English period furniture, dressing tables, sofas, and writing desks; even the standard bathrooms have Portuguese marble, two washbasins, and separate tubs and showers. There are numerous high-tech touches now: guest messages via television, in-room fax machines, and two-line

telephones. The indefatigible floor attendants and lobby concierges handle every business request. Rolls Royce airport transfers are available for a fee. Even without a formal business center and fitness facilities, this hotel, with its unobtrusive 3-to-1 staff-to-guest ratio, is so upscale it's off the charts. Gaddi's (*see* Dining, below), the hotel's chic French supper club, has been a Hong Kong institution since 1953. The Verandah Lounge (*see* After Hours, below) is a quiet place for an afterwork drink. *A Peninsula Group hotel. Salisbury Rd., Tsim Sha Tsui, tel. 366–6251 or 800/262–9467, fax 722–4170. Gen. manager, Felix Bieger. 190 doubles, 20 suites. AE, CB, DC, MC, V.*

⑬ **Ramada Renaissance.** European elegance is the theme of
$$$ this strategically situated 19-story jewel of Ramada's upscale crown in the Orient; even the elevators and phones play classical music. The lobby is an opulent Louis XVI fantasia with leather furniture and white barrel-vaulted ceilings. Rooms, which have harbor views above the 10th floor, are large, trimmed in mahogany, and contain safes, hands-free speaker phones, spacious work desks, and marble bathrooms with separate tubs and showers. The Renaissance Club executive floors (11 and 12) feature in-room faxes, gold-plated bathroom fixtures, and free limousine airport transfers. The business center, although closed on Sunday, offers plenty for business travelers (70% of the guests) with lap-top PCs for hire, laser printers, and five parlor offices with Murphy beds. The hotel's Italian restaurant, Capriccio's (*see* Dining, below), is a favorite of those out to impress business associates. The rooftop fitness center, pool, and squash courts are state-of-the-art, as is the hotel. *8 Peking Rd., Tsim Sha Tsui, tel. 311–3311 or 800/228–9898, fax 311–6611. Gen. manager, Alain Guernier. 474 doubles, 27 suites, 72 business class. AE, CB, DC, MC, V.*

❺ **Royal Pacific Hotel and Towers.** Part of the new China
$$–$$$ Hong Kong City office complex and Macau Ferry Terminal, this 1989 two-tiered property is 15 minutes (via covered walkway) north of Star Ferry. The compact rooms in the hotel portion are quite moderately priced, with safes, two phones, and surprisingly large bathrooms; the larger, more luxurious rooms and suites in the Tower have better views, but higher price tags. The not-entirely-inviting inner lobby resembles those of swank apartment complexes. The fitness center, with its own coaching staff, has the latest equipment; joggers use a footbridge to cross over to Kowloon Park. Delightful Swiss cuisine and fine views of the harbor are to be had at the Chalet (*see* Dining, below). *33 Canton Rd., China Hong Kong City, Tsim Sha Tsui, tel. 736–1188 or 800/448–8355, fax 736–1212. Gen. manager, John Girard. 383 doubles (hotel), 261 doubles (tower), 22 suites (tower). AE, DC, MC, V.*

㉑ **Sheraton Hong Kong Hotel and Towers.** Long favored by
$$$ business travelers, especially airline crews and executives, the Sheraton has a convenient central location at the south end of Nathan Road. The lobby is a trifle small and noisy, but guest rooms are large and restful, done in pale shades of green and pink, with comfortable seating areas and desks with plenty of lighting. Bathrooms are large, too, with striking green-marble counters and brass fixtures. The newly renovated fifth and sixth floors are best; rooms facing south have full harbor views. The 10th floor

and part of the 12th are for nonsmokers. Sheraton Towers—the executive floors (16 and 17)—has its own private elevator, lounge, and complimentary American breakfast, making it worth the small extra cost. All guests have access to stock reports, flight schedules, a news wire service, personal messages, and hotel bills on their TV screens. *20 Nathan Rd., Tsim Sha Tsui, tel. 369–1111 or 800/325–3535, fax 739–8707. Gen. manager, John Henderson. 741 doubles, 34 singles, 60 suites, 137 business class. AE, CB, DC, MC, V.*

Kowloon: Tsim Sha Tsui East

⑯ **Empress.** This small hotel near the locally famous Wing On
$$ department store/office complex in Tsim Sha Tsui East is a find for the budget business traveler. Most rooms have high ceilings and a spacious feel; those above the standard level include large balconies. Furnishings, carpets, and bathroom tile are worn, but a renovation planned for the 1990s should raise this 1964 hotel to the level of its service. The familylike staff makes up for the lack of a business center by arranging for any requests made by business travelers (40% of its guests). In service, if not yet in facilities, the Empress lives up to its motto: "The Little First Class Hotel." *17–19 Chatham Rd., Tsim Sha Tsui, tel. 366–0211 or 800/448–8355, fax 721–8168. Gen. manager, Johnny Tsang. 186 doubles, 3 suites. AE, DC, MC, V.*

★ ⑩ **Holiday Inn Harbour View.** A top choice of executive busi-
$$$ ness travelers (the majority of the guests), this hotel boasts one of the prime waterfront views in Hong Kong, with rooms and services to match. Rooms are quite spacious; most have a large desk, settee, round table, generous luggage bench, in-room safe, and marble bathroom. Some have sofa beds, creating an office by day. Harborview rooms, and those on the executive floor, cost more, but are superb. The business center (closed Sundays) has an experienced staff and IBM PCs for hire. Rooms for nonsmokers are available. The hotel's fine Continental restaurant, Belvedere (*see* Dining, below), provides an elegant setting for business lunching or dinner entertaining. The rooftop pool is heated and well maintained. There's cross-harbor Hovercraft ferry service to Central (trip time: 5 minutes) within easy walking distance. *70 Mody Rd., Tsim Sha Tsui East, tel. 721–5161 or 800/HOLIDAY, fax 369–5672. Gen. manager, Uwe Boeger. 411 doubles, 27 singles, 9 suites, 93 business class. Rooms for disabled guests. AE, D, MC, V. Expensive.*

⑪ **Nikko Hong Kong.** The lobby, with its massive columns
$$$ and quiet cascading waterfall, sets the tone: a blending of the spectacular with the subtle in this 1988 deluxe Japanese-managed (but Taiwanese-owned) waterside hotel. Although guests are predominantly Japanese (80%), other business travelers will feel at home. Rooms are eclectic in style, with American maple furniture, English country–style bedspreads, and Dutch or antique Japanese framed prints; bathrooms are large, with separate showers and tubs; storage closets and drawers are ample. The executive Nikko floors (14 and 15) are even more elegantly appointed. The business center has complete services and long hours. Rooms on the south side are graced with full, uninterrupted views of Victoria Harbor. Sagano (*see* Dining, below) serves some of the finest Japanese cuisine in

Hong Kong. On request, the Nikko will provide guests with jogging clothes and advice on suitable areas to jog nearby. *72 Mody Rd., Tsim Sha Tsui East, tel. 739–1111 or 800/645–5687, fax 311–3122. Gen. manager, Katsumi Nagasawa. 442 doubles, 19 suites. One room for disabled guests per floor. AE, CB, DC, MC, V.*

★ ⑰ **Kowloon Shangri-La.** Often selected as one of the world's
$$$$ top 10 hotels in surveys of leading business executives, the Shangri-La has one of Hong Kong's best waterfront locations, best Chinese restaurants, best hotel health clubs (complete with water jet–controlled swim-in-place pool), and best business centers (with PCs and fax machines ready for guest-room use). The byword is elegance, from the white marble in the lobby to the white marble in the guest-room baths. The accommodations are spacious, with bay windows, conference-call phones, and bidets. There's a still more deluxe executive floor (Club 21) and a nonsmoking floor (11) where even the room attendants are nonsmokers. The hotel's Coffee Garden (*see* Business Breakfasts, below) is fine for early-morning meetings, and the Shang Palace (*see* Dining, below) is an excellent spot for business entertaining. *64 Mody Rd., Tsim Sha Tsui East, tel. 721–2111 or 800/359–5050, fax 723–8686. Gen. manager, Giovanni Angelini. 678 doubles, 11 singles, 30 suites. AE, CB, DC, MC, V.*

⑥ **Ramada Inn Kowloon.** With 85% of its guests in town on
$$ business, this small three-star inn aims for "business class at economy fare." There's a gas-log fireplace in the cozy lobby; rooms are also cozy—almost too much so—but modern and serviceable. There is a safe in each room, but no dresser or storage drawers, making it difficult to unpack. The best rooms overlook tree-lined Chatham Road from the east side of the upper floors, above the din of traffic. The business center, like the rooms, is small but functional, and its staff is eager to please. Opened in 1988, this Ramada is a sensible, no-frills choice for the business traveler needing a clean, comfortable bed and bath. *73–75 Chatham Rd. S, Tsim Sha Tsui, tel. 311–1100 or 800/228–9898, fax 311–6000. Gen. manager, Loy Chung. 203 doubles, 2 suites. AE, DC, MC, V.*

③ **Regal Airport.** Connected to Kai Tak Airport via an over-
$$ head walkway, this is the hotel of choice for time-conscious business travelers, those in transit, and aerospace executives. Rooms are pleasant creations in pastels; some have Murphy beds and window seats from which there is a spectacular view of planes close overhead. The soundproofing is effective. The business center provides excellent China trade services, including quick visa arrangements, and rental offices. A free shuttle bus runs to Tsim Sha Tsui East every 30 minutes. Rooms and offices are available to transient passengers for partial day use. *A Regal International hotel. Sa Po Rd., Kowloon City, tel. 718–0333 or 800/222–8888, fax 718–4111. Gen. manager, Ike F. M. Perquin. 351 doubles, 49 suites. AE, CB, DC, MC, V.*

⑧ **Regal Meridien.** The busy lobby has a French ambience,
$$$ with chandeliers and reproduction Louis XVI furniture, and many of the business travelers staying here (50% of the guests) are from France, although regulars include Japanese department store executives, too. Rooms are appointed in pastels, light woods, and mirrors; bathrooms in

beige marbles. Corner rooms and suites offer partial harbor views. The business center provides a good reference library, conference room, and private office for hire. There's convenient Hovercraft service to Hong Kong Island's Central district. The classic French cuisine served in Le Restaurant de France (*see* Dining, below) is outstanding; the raspberry napoleon alone is worth the visit. *A Regal International hotel. 71 Mody Rd., Tsim Sha Tsui East, tel. 722–1818 or 800/222–8888, fax 723–6413. Gen. manager, Stefan Pfeiffer. 550 doubles, 40 suites. AE, CB, DC, MC, V.*

★ ㉔ **The Regent Hong Kong.** Since its opening in 1980, The Re-
$$$$ gent has maintained its position at the forefront of the world's great hotels, and its particularly high reputation among American business executives, who make up half the clientele. The red-granite structure is built on the edge of the harbor and features extraordinary uninterrupted views. Everything is superior, including the business center (open every day, with meeting rooms for hire, free typewriters, and a news service update screen), the whirlpools (outside, overlooking Victoria Harbour), the Lobby Lounge (*see* After Hours, below), and the coffee shop (with a two-story glass wall at water level). The spacious guest rooms are beige and orange, with three phones, excellent desk and drawer space, and marble bathrooms with separate showers and sunken tubs. The best rooms have views of the harbor on the south side; some have balconies (third floor). Guest preferences are computerized, an indication of the thorough services here, with a 24-hour butler appointed to every six rooms. There's no need for executive floors; this is the best harborside hotel in Kowloon. There are numerous upscale restaurants on the property, including the Regent Steakhouse and the Plume (*see* Dining, below). *Salisbury Rd., Tsim Sha Tsui, tel. 721–1211 or 800/545–4000, fax 739–4546. Gen. manager, Rudolf Greiner. 521 doubles, 81 suites. AE, CB, DC, MC, V.*

❼ **Royal Garden.** Because of its proximity to a number of ma-
$$$ jor companies, the Royal Garden is a favorite of business travelers in the manufacturing, electronics, and fashion industries. This luxury inn features a spectacular enclosed garden atrium stretching from the third to the fifteenth floor, a haven of greenery with a grand piano standing on an island in a decorative lobby pool. The guest rooms, redecorated in 1988 with Chinese-style furniture and brass trim, are elegant, but some are beginning to show wear. Those on the south side of the building have harbor views, and except for the top floor (16), all rooms encircle the relaxing atrium. The business center has two wood-paneled boardrooms for rent, and plans call for an expansion of business services, including the creation of two executive floors with the latest electronic equipment (such as in-room computer hookups). Lalique, the hotel's restaurant (*see* Dining, below), is a quiet spot for business discussion. The Falcon (*see* After Hours, below) is a great place to unwind. *A Leading Hotels of the World hotel. 69 Mody Rd., Tsim Sha Tsui East, tel. 721–5215 or 800/223–6800, fax 369–9976. Gen. manager, Heinrich L. Kapfenberger. 390 doubles, 43 suites. AE, CB, D, MC, V.*

Hong Kong: Central/Wanchai

㉕ **China Merchants.** Opened in 1987 and standing rather for-
$$ lornly near the waterfront west of Central, this 23-story
hotel is for the budget traveler who wants a taste of China.
Many of the guests are Asian, including Chinese delega-
tions from the mainland, where China Merchants has six
joint-venture properties. Rooms are spartan but clean,
with few amenities; shower curtains appear to have come
from motel stock. "Deluxe" rooms have harbor views. The
business center, despite excellent China information, is
unimpressive. "Hong Kong's first outdoor spa" proves to
be a seldom-used set of Coleman hot tubs; inside are a doz-
en plain exercise machines and a fitness lounge with a
room-size bird cage. For the adventurous business travel-
er on a budget, however, it's suitable, and there is a hotel
shuttle bus to Central. *160–161 Connaught Rd. W, West-
ern District, tel. 559–6888, fax 559–0038. Gen. manager,
Joseph Tung. 276 doubles, 3 suites. AE, DC, MC, V.*

㉛ **Furama Kempinski.** Under new management by the
$$$ German Kempinski group, this 1973, 30-story landmark
with the revolving restaurant on top attracts a high per-
centage of business travelers (over 80% of the guests)
from Japan, Europe, and the United States partly on the
strength of its superb location near the Central financial
and administrative district. Rooms, last renovated in
1988, have earth-tone color schemes and contain safes,
hairdryers, small desks, and spacious marble bathrooms;
those above the 17th floor have views of the harbor or Victoria Peak. Further renovations will enlarge many exist-
ing rooms. The lobby and public areas are bright, with
wonderful carpets in various Oriental motifs. There are
two floors for nonsmokers. The small business center
(closed Sundays) has lap-top PCs and private offices for
hire, and secretaries who can arrange your local appointments. La Ronda (*see* Dining, below), on the top floor of
the hotel, is the most famous revolving restaurant in
Hong Kong. *1 Connaught Rd., Central, tel. 525–5111 or
800/448–8355, fax 529–7405. Gen. manager, Peter Leitgeb.
468 doubles, 55 suites. AE, CB, DC, MC, V.*

★ ㊱ **Grand Hyatt Hong Kong.** This 37-floor skyscraper, opened
$$$$ in 1989 atop the new Hong Kong Convention and Exhibition Centre, quickly became the Island's number-one
place to meet. It is the luxury hotel of choice for many executive travelers (70% of the guests), partly because it is
new and expensive, two values dear to the heart of Hong
Kong. Its lobby, a recreation in Italian black marble and
silvered glass of the romantic 1930s, is the most extravagant in the city; its swimming pool above the Wanchai
harbor is the longest and most stunning; and its health
facilities are the most complete. Harbor-view rooms are
quite large, fitted with custom earth-tone carpets, safes,
full marble bathrooms, even gold-plated faucets. The top
seven floors (Regency Club) are a posh hotel-within-a-hotel, with their own leather-walled lounge, elevators,
boardroom, pool, and concierge service. The home-style
Cantonese cuisine and nostalgic decor of One Harbor Road
(*see* Dining, below) combine to create an impressive dining experience; the Grand Café (*see* Business Breakfasts, below) is a good place for a morning meeting. The business
center is the largest of any Hong Kong hotel. JJ's and the

Champagne Bar (*see* After Hours, below, for both) provide evening entertainment and relaxation. Service continues to improve and should soon equal the exceptional facilities. Shuttle service to Central is provided by a fleet of London-style taxis. *1 Harbour Rd., Wanchai, tel. 861–1234 or 800/233–1234, fax 861–1677. Gen. manager, Ralph Peter Jentes. 573 doubles, 51 suites. AE, DC, MC, V.*

㉚ **Hong Kong Hilton.** Located a short walk uphill from Cen
$$$$ tral offices, near the Peak Tram station, the 25-story Hilton has been frequented by Western business travelers since 1963. The extensive use of marble and teak gives the lobby and public areas a dark but rich appearance. Rooms on the hotel's six highly regarded executive floors have been renovated recently in soft pastels, and equipped with separate writing desks and three phones (local calls are free); among executive-level perks are portable phones. Standard rooms in pastel pinks and greens have many nice touches, including limited-edition prints on the walls, spacious desks, and couches and coffee tables in the comfortable seating areas. Floors 9 and 15 are for nonsmokers. The Hilton maintains a luxury brigantine, the *Wan Fu*, for luncheon and dinner cruises under sail. The hotel's restaurant offers cabaret dinner shows (*see* After Hours, below). *2 Queen's Rd., Central, tel. 523–3111 or 800/445–8667, fax 845–2590. Gen. manager, James Smith. 457 doubles, 87 suites, 200 business class. AE, CB, DC, MC, V.*

㉞ **Hong Kong Marriott.** This 41-story reflective-glass tower,
$$$$ opened in 1989 minutes from Central, attracts many Western business travelers (70% of its guests) with its exceptional rooms, recreational facilities, and direct connection to the new Pacific Place shopping complex. The palatial garden lobby sets the tone, with its three-story atrium filled with greenery, waterfalls, sweeping staircases, skylights, and views of Admiralty harbor. There are three well-run executive floors with a private lounge where complimentary Continental breakfast and evening cocktails and hors d'oeuvres are served. Standard rooms, most with king-size beds, are large, with separate seating areas, well-lighted desks, two phones, spacious bathrooms, and fine views of both water (on the north) and mountain sides (to the south). Guests can view their messages or bills on the room TV. Recreation facilities are impressive, as are services in the business center (open daily) where you can rent a PC or hook up your own to the printers. *88 Queensway, Admiralty, tel. 810–8366 or 800/228–9290, fax 845–0737. Gen. manager, Rene Wurgler. 546 doubles, 41 suites. 48 rooms for nonsmokers, 7 rooms for disabled guests. AE, CB, DC, MC, V.*

★ ㉙ **Mandarin Oriental Hong Kong.** The most venerable hotel
$$$$ on the Island and one of the top hotels in the world, the Mandarin sustains its reputation on the basis of its attentive service, prime location in Central, and elegant accommodations, which attract CEOs and other financial heavyweights. The building, with its signature harborside balconies, dates from 1963, but the rooms were all renovated in the late 1980s. Standard rooms are truly superior: spacious, appointed with chinoiserie lamps and prints, rosewood furniture, teak and burlwood paneling, beige New Zealand carpets, and bathrooms of Portuguese

pink marble—there is even a jogging map on a rope tucked away in guest-room closets. Floors 5 and 12 are non-smoking. The lobby, redesigned by its original creator, is of black marble with white Carrara-marble walkways and gold-painted wood carvings. The Mandarin Grill (*see* Dining, below) is the premier Continental restaurant in Hong Kong. The indoor pool, surrounded by marble columns, resembles a Roman bath. The Mandarin counts on its veteran staff (many with three decades' experience here) to satisfy those who demand excellence. *5 Connaught Rd., Central, tel. 522–0111 or 800/526–6566, fax 810–6190. Gen. manager, Jurg Tuscher. 450 doubles, 35 singles, 56 suites. AE, CB, DC, MC, V.*

⑤ New World Harbour View. This 42-story tower, rising from the eastern wing of the new Hong Kong Convention and Exhibition Centre, is connected by covered walkways to shopping centers, office complexes, and the Wanchai Ferry Pier, with easy cross-harbor connections to the Star Ferry pier in Kowloon. A long, slow escalator leads from the ground-floor entrance to a noisy but comfortable lobby. Hallways in public areas make elaborate use of inset mirrors. Modern-style guest rooms are elegantly appointed, with extensive use of wood trim, limited-edition contemporary prints on the walls, separate writing desks, and large beds. TVs are set up to provide airline information and personal messages. The wood- and gray-marble bathrooms are quite spacious. Rooms on the north side enjoy spectacular harbor views; garden-view rooms on the opposite side overlook the Grand Hyatt's 11th-floor scuptured swimming pool. Two floors are reserved for nonsmokers. About 75% of the guests are business travelers, many of whom choose to stay on the Dynasty Club floors (39–42). The business center has lap-top PCs and mobile phones for hire. There is hotel shuttle service to Central and Causeway Bay. The hotel's disco, the Penthouse (*see* After Hours, below), is a popular night spot. *1 Harbour Rd., Wanchai, tel. 866–2288 or 800/448–8355, fax 866–3388. Gen. manager, Willi Kollmann. 748 doubles, 54 suites, 60 business class. Rooms for disabled guests. AE, DC, MC, V.*

㉟ Ramada Inn Hong Kong. Squeezed into the heart of Wanchai, this Ramada is convenient to nearby commercial development and close to Central by subway or trolley. The lobby is little more than a reception desk, but rooms are modern and comfortable, with two chairs, adequate work space and storage, and a coffee maker. Upper floors are quietest, but there's no view to speak of. A new wing under construction will soon add 50 rooms with their own fax lines, as well as a rooftop pool and health club. The small business center offers complete services, including PC word processing. Extremely well managed, but not showy or long on amenities, this three-star hotel is a smart choice for the budget business traveler needing a handy location. *61–73 Lockhart Rd., Wanchai, tel. 861–1000 or 800/228–9898, fax 865–6023. Gen. manager, Loy Chung. 280 doubles, 4 suites, AE, DC, MC, V.*

Hong Kong: Causeway Bay/Quarry Bay

⑳ Excelsior Hotel. The Island's largest hotel, this 34-story tower next to the World Trade Centre, with a commanding view of the harbor, is frequently the first choice of those with business in Causeway Bay. The two-story lobby of shiny marble and chrome is always bustling. Guest rooms are a bit small, but modern and well appointed after a thorough renovation in 1989; the green-and-gold color scheme and large picture windows seem to lend the room more space, as does the view of the Royal Hong Kong Yacht Club Marina. The expanded business center, open daily, is highly efficient, and has a comfortable lounge with writing desks. Floors 18 and 25 are nonsmoking. The Excelsior Grill (*see* Dining, below) is a popular place for a business meal. Dickens Bar features cool jazz on Sunday afternoons; Talk of the Town is a popular disco (*see* After Hours, below, for both). Although there's no pool or health club, the Excelsior has the Island's only indoor tennis courts, and there is a jogging park nearby. On the whole, service is superb. *A Mandarin Oriental/Leading Hotels of the World hotel. 281 Gloucester Rd., Causeway Bay, tel. 894–8888 or 800/223–6800, fax 895–6459. Gen. manager, Nigel Roberts. 896 doubles, 27 suites. Two rooms for disabled guests (607, 608). AE, CB, DC, MC, V.*

44 **Grand Plaza.** This tower, built in 1988 at the Kornhill
$$ Shopping center, is convenient for travelers with business in Quarry Bay. The lobby is a knockout, the gleaming white marble accented by an elaborately carved Chinese panel and guardian lions. Guest rooms, done in light shades of pink and blue, offer no views of note and are rather sparsely furnished (small, built-in desks, average beds, minimal closet and drawer space). The private-concession health club, open to hotel guests, is one of the best in Hong Kong, with the latest in high-tech computerized equipment, a jogging track, even a miniature golf course; the indoor heated pool with water slide is big enough for laps. The hotel staff has proven exceptionally eager to please its guests. *2 Kornhill Rd., Quarry Bay, tel. 886–0011 or 800/448–8355, fax 886–1738. Gen. manager, Polly Hui. 306 doubles, 42 suites, 150 service apartments. Rooms for disabled guests. AE, DC, MC, V.*

41 **Park Lane Radisson.** Across the street from Victoria Park
$$$ (Hong Kong's largest), near Food Street and other attractions in Causeway Bay, the stately, 27-floor Park Lane caters to travelers on business in the area (40% of the guests). The hotel is affiliated with Japan Airlines; easily half the guests are Japanese. The rooms, renovated in 1989, include marble-top writing desks, two-line telephones, safes, and small marble bathrooms; many have exceptional views of Victoria Peak or the harbor. Premier Club floors (22–24) have all the executive-level extras, such as private concierge service, complimentary breakfast and cocktails served in the executive lounge, free clothes pressing, and upgraded room amenities. The hotel's elegant French restaurant, Parc 27 (*see* Dining, below), is an appropriate spot for entertaining. The business center is well managed, as is the hotel, one of the largest in Hong Kong. *310 Gloucester Rd., Causeway Bay, tel. 890–3355 or 800/333–3333, fax 576–7853. Gen. manager, Kenneth Mullins. 709 doubles, 25 suites, 116 business class. AE, CB, DC, MC, V.*

The New Territories

2 **Regal Riverside.** Located by the Shing Mun River in
$$ Shatin, 45 minutes northeast of Kowloon, this 1986 hotel is

convenient to industries and offices in the New Territories, the zone north of the urban areas of Kowloon and Hong Kong Island; it's also near the enormous New Town Plaza Shopping Centre. Many guests are long-stay business travelers, as well as Asians in tour groups. In this hotel away from the city bustle, with its large grounds and greenery, the ambience is that of a resort; there is an attractive swimming pool, extensive fitness facilities, and a small business center. The large rooms have a resort feel, too, with rattan furniture and broad picture windows. A free shuttle bus runs to Star Ferry. This is a budget-priced but luxurious out-of-town alternative. *A Regal International hotel. Tai Chung Kui Rd., Shatin, New Territories, tel. 649-7878 or 800/222-8888, fax 649-7791. Gen. manager, Douglas A. Barber. 746 doubles, 40 singles, 44 suites. AE, CB, DC, MC, V.*

DINING

Hong Kong is as much a town for gourmets as for shoppers, but most of the Chinese restaurants are not frequented by business travelers; problems with noise, hygiene, and language can be considerable. The upper-echelon Chinese restaurants, however, are quite suitable for visitors doing business and entertaining over a meal. The most common Chinese cuisine is Cantonese, and nowhere is it better prepared than in Hong Kong. The emphasis is on fresh seafood (as close to live as possible), frequently served unadorned or in light, tasty sauces. Other popular regional styles here are Peking (noodle, rather than rice based, heartier than Cantonese), Szechuan (hot, spicy blended dishes), and Chiu Chau (also from the southern China region of Canton, but more robust, with more preserved—pickled, and dried, rather than fresh—dishes, than Cantonese style).

The leading Western cuisine in Hong Kong is Continental, meaning an assortment of French-influenced European and American dishes as served at hotel restaurants and grills. Expect steep prices for dinner, in hotels or not. Dinner is usually an occasion for pleasure, mixed with a bit of business; the idea is to make a suitably grand impression. Set Western lunches, on the other hand, many pitched to "the businessman," are more reasonably priced.

Highly recommended restaurants in each category are indicated by a star ★.

Category	Cost*
$$$$ (Very Expensive)	over HK$500
$$$ (Expensive)	HK$250–HK$500
$$ (Moderate)	under HK$250

per person, including appetizer, entrée, and dessert, but excluding drinks and 10% service charge.

Numbers in the margin correspond to numbered restaurant locations on the Hong Kong Lodging and Dining map.

Wine and Beer

You can easily procure nearly any imported beverage you desire, but those produced on the China mainland are worth sampling. The table wines produced by Dynasty (a joint venture with Remy Martin), and the Tsingtao Chardonnay are surprisingly good. China's premier beer is Tsingtao.

Business Breakfasts

The "power breakfast" is a new concept in Hong Kong, but it is no longer totally alien, and there are a number of good places to meet and talk business in the morning. On the Hong Kong island side, **The Mandarin Grill** (Mandarin Oriental Hotel, tel. 522–0111, ext. 4044) is where CEOs, power brokers, and other high rollers line up for their morning repast and strike big deals. The Grand Hyatt's **Grand Café** (tel. 861–1234) sees a well-turned-out crowd talking seriously over their eggs early in the day. In Kowloon, **The Coffee Garden** (Shangri-La Hotel, tel. 721–1211) has solid fare, fine value, and an extraordinary view. **The Chalet, Gripps,** and **The Regent Steakhouse** are other good venues for business breakfasts in this part of town; *see* Dining reviews, below, for details.

Kowloon: Tsim Sha Tsui

★ ⑬ **Capriccio.** The best Northern Italian food in Hong Kong is
$$$$ found in this neo-Renaissance–style dining room, decorated with Old World frescoes and oil paintings, where CEOs, local dignitaries, and top management from nearby hotels are frequent guests. There is a private room available that seats eight. Chef Silvio Bianchi, a Swiss Italian, has devised a four-course set lunch for businesspeople, using fresh pastas made on the premises. For dinner, the carpaccio with an olive-and-pine-nut vinaigrette is a typical appetizer; and the pastas, carefully presented, receive a Hong Kong touch. The fettucine is served with sautéed prawns under a light cream sauce spiced with fennel and lemon chive; the ravioli are stuffed with lobster and bathed in white-truffle oil. The spumoni desserts are delicate. There's an extensive selection of rare wines and grappas from Italy. Service, attentive but restrained, befits the European decor and gourmet cuisine. This is an excellent location for serious business discussion over a good meal. *Ramada Renaissance Hotel 2F, tel. 311–3311, ext. 2260. Jacket and tie advised. Reservations advised. AE, CB, DC, MC, V.*

⑤ **Chalet.** This sparkling new Swiss restaurant serves some
$$ of the most authentic fondues in the Far East—no surprise, since its manager and chefs are from Switzerland. The decor is polished rustic, with bright wood everywhere: floors, ceilings, tables, chairs. The tables by the chalet windows afford views of the harbor, unlike any in Geneva. The buffet breakfasts and business set lunches are offered at extremely reasonable prices. The best dinner entrée is the fillet of beef Helvetia stuffed with goose liver, served in a light wine sauce. The cheese raclette is superb; the cakes, baked on the premises, are sinful. Waiters and waitresses don traditional Swiss costumes, and, at night, there's even an accordion player. Seating just 80, the Chalet is a reasonably priced choice for business dis-

cussions at lunch, and a leisurely chat at dinner. *Royal Pacific Hotel, tel. 736–1188, ext. 2717. Casual but neat. Reservations accepted, but not needed. AE, DC, MC, V. Closed lunch Sun.*

⑲ Charlotte's. This is the smallest upscale Continental res-
$$$ taurant in town, seating only 40. It overlooks the chaos of lower Nathan Road, but is hushed within, an exquisite haven couched under a coffered ceiling with chandeliers and dark-wood columns. Local businesspeople are attracted in large numbers by the modestly priced four-course set dinners featuring entrées such as salmon fricassee. As in many Hong Kong restaurants, the cuisine focuses strongly on seafood. Manager Anthony So has created the ideal appetizer: an oven-baked lobster bisque with truffles in the shell. The best main course is seafood (garoupa, salmon, shrimp, and scallops) au gratin in a lobster-and-vermouth cream sauce. To celebrate, request a table by the window; for private discussions, there are comfortable booths separated by etched-glass dividers. *Ambassador Hotel 2F, 26 Nathan Rd., Tsim Sha Tsui, tel. 366–6321. Jacket and tie advised in evenings. Reservations required. AE, CB, DC, MC, V.*

⑮ Delicatessen Corner. Hiding out in a dark corner of the
$$ Holiday Inn Golden Mile's shopping arcade basement, this modest café can be a little hard to find, but for a quick meal anytime until midnight it's perfect. Solitary diners, including women alone, won't feel conspicuous here. A gargantuan spread of meats cooked on the premises cools off in lighted cases; the fresh breads to go with the salamis and sausages include all sorts of ryes and a wonderful German black bread. Sandwiches are built to your specifications. The grilled Bavarian meatloaf with fried egg is a good option. Pastries and Swiss chocolate goodies are also baked on the premises, and service is prompt. *Holiday Inn Golden Mile, 50 Nathan Rd., Tsim Sha Tsui, tel. 369–3111, ext. 147 or 250. Casual dress. No reservations. AE, DC, MC, V.*

⑳ Gaddi's. The premier French supper club in Hong Kong
$$$$ since 1953, Gaddi's was remodeled in 1987 and lost none of its renowned elegance. With wall-panel mirrors, corniced ceilings, a royal-blue Tai Ping carpet, and French-crafted chandeliers rescued from a Shanghai hotel, it hardly needed the carved wooden screen created for the Summer Palace in Beijing in 1670—but here it stands, as though in the dining room of a taipan. Swiss chef Peter Hatt now presides over the French cuisine, which is consumed by those who do their business entertaining with little thought to price—or to time. Everything here is savored, nothing rushed. Specialties include lobster tartare with caviar, and king prawns and mussels in a sesame paste (a crispy delight). The set dinner (menu *decouvert*), with a different wine for each course, is a feast. The wine list looks like a novel; for dessert, try the special sampler (four selections). The only thing that won't challenge an expense account here is the set lunch, a relative bargain. *The Peninsula, Salisbury Rd., Tsim Sha Tsui, tel. 366–6251, ext. 3989. Jacket and tie required; black tie not out of place. Reservations required. AE, DC, MC, V.*

㉒ Grand View Noodle Shop. Fast-food outlets long ago in-
$$ vaded and conquered Hong Kong's youth with hamburgers and fries, but the best quick cuisine by a golden mile is

this nothing-but-noodles shop on the lower level of the New World Centre. This is where local businesspeople, shop clerks, and weary shoppers tank up. The service, by young women in aprons and sneakers, is precise; the moment you stick your head in, you're seated with a glass of tea, a saucer of shelled peanuts, and a clean set of chopsticks. The decor is Howard Johnson's East: red lanterns, columns tiled in green bamboo, marble tables, and toadstool green benches. Behind a glass wall, a sweating chef concocts noodle plates in a frenzy. The English-Chinese menu is 100 dishes long. The braised *e-fu* noodles (spaghettilike, made of rice) are delicious, but the mammoth bowl of vermicelli Singapore-style is the best anywhere, a complete meal too good not to finish. For quick lunches, late snacks, or a full meal, you'll never have to resort to McDonald's in Hong Kong. *New World Centre, Salisbury Rd., Tsim Sha Tsui, tel. 369–0470. Casual dress. No reservations. No credit cards.*

⑫ **Gripps.** This Continental grill and lounge in the Harbour
$$$ City shopping complex is easy to reach for a business lunch. A buffet by day, Gripps provides a fine American breakfast spread, an afternoon tea, and, on Sundays, a Jazz Buffet Lunch (noon–3 PM). A supper club by night, Gripps is famous among its regulars for the goose liver on soya sprouts, fillet of pomfret (a Pacific black fish) in champagne, and the salad Mikado (poached oysters with rice). It draws an easygoing late-night crowd who can retire to the attached jazz bar afterwards, where American singers are regular headliners. The setting is luxurious: teak columns, coffered pastel ceiling, floral paintings, and club chairs and sofas encircling an island bar of black granite and brass. There's even a harbor view, making this a cozy spot to unwind and savor one's success. *Omni The Hong Kong Hotel 6F, 3 Canton Rd., Harbour City, Tsim Sha Tsui, tel. 736–1888. Casual but neat. Reservations accepted, but not needed. AE, CB, DC, MC, V.*

⑭ **Hugo's.** Named for an extravagant baron from Bavaria,
$$$$ Hugo's grill is decorated in a duly luxuriant—if rather eclectic—blend of the modern, the rustic, and the Old Germanic (there are tons of European armor on display). It's an elegant venue for a celebratory dinner. Before you arrive, you are assigned a waiter who attends to every detail, including a complimentary rose or cigar following the meal. The cuisine is hearty Continental fare, beautifully presented: steamed mussels in white wine and chives, caviar on blinis, oxtail soup with Kobe beef, flambéed lobster bisque, and prime cuts of Angus beef off the grill. The wine list is one of Hong Kong's best for European vintages. For that very special occasion, reserve a private room on the side, or the 14-seat boardroom. *Hyatt Regency Hotel 2F, 67 Nathan Rd., Tsim Sha Tsui, tel. 311–1234. Jacket and tie required for dinner. Reservations required. AE, CB, DC, MC, V.*

㉔ **Plume.** Executives on generous expense accounts and
$$$$ businesspeople out to impress a client will find this an unrivaled setting. The harbor skyline is perfectly framed at water level; the interior is an exquisite creation in black marble with gold borders, Oriental art works, and handblown glassware. Chef Gerhard Stutz has maintained the highest level in food preparation and presentation, introducing light variations on French country-style cuisine—

the velouté of peas with truffles a notable example. A glass of champagne with a dash of blueberry liqueur starts things off, perfect with the goose-liver and green-pepper-corn pâté served on hot na'an bread freshly baked in the large Indian tandoor oven near the entrance. Equal to the cuisine is the Plume wine cellar, which has 8,000 bottles in a temperature-controlled wood-paneled chamber. Martin Cheng Hing, winner of the first annual Sommelier of the Year award in Hong Kong, stands by to help in your selection. *The Regent Hotel, Salisbury Rd., Tsim Sha Tsui, tel. 721–1211. Jacket and tie required. Reservations required. AE, CB, DC, MC, V. Dinner only.*

㉔ **The Regent Steakhouse.** The mesquite charcoal grill, visi-
$$$ ble from the best tables, is the heart of this American-style restaurant, regarded by many as the finest of its kind in Hong Kong. Certainly the chefs keep it simple and tasty: the large grilled steaks, prawns, and lobster are done to perfection. Idaho potatoes and a salad bar are included with dinner, where the portions are always Texas size, as are the cocktails. The decor—solid wooden chairs and tables, no tablecloths—is not pretentious. Business-people make this a regular lunch stop for salads and steaks, and the health-conscious power breakfast is gaining popularity with its mix-your-own fruit and vegetable plates, natural cereals, yogurts, and German and Swiss breads hot from the restaurant ovens. *The Regent Hotel, Salisbury Rd., Tsim Sha Tsui, tel. 721–1211. Jackets required; no sports shoes. Reservations advised. AE, CB, DC, MC, V.*

Kowloon: Tsim Sha Tsui East

★ ⑩ **Belvedere.** Commanding a fine view of the harbor, the Bel-
$$$ vedere serves Continental cuisine in a country-cottage setting. Attractive partitions enhance privacy. The lunch-time crowd consists of businesspeople partaking of the "Beano" set lunch, a repast of buffet salads and appetizers followed by a choice of six entrées (which usually arrives within 10 minutes). In the evening, the clientele is a mix of expatriates, business travelers, and tourists; the fare is French, with an emphasis on fresh seafood. The crabmeat pancakes with mango dressing are a specialty. Also worth trying are the warm king-prawn salad in caviar dressing, the lobster bisque, and the pan-fried turbot with shallots and burgundy sauce—typical Continental fare in Hong Kong, but consistently well prepared. *Holiday Inn Harbour View, 70 Mody Rd., Tsim Sha Tsui East, tel. 721–5161, ext. 2738. Jacket and tie advised; no jeans or running shoes. Reservations advised. AE, DC, MC, V.*

⑨ **City Chiu Chow Restaurant.** This is a top choice for those
$$ who fancy the specialties of the Swatow region of southern China, particularly the shellfish, and goose dishes cooked in soy. Occupying the entire floor of a shopping and office center, it's a loud, exuberant place—you feel as though you've ridden up an escalator into the middle of an extended family argument. The setting is elegant, with red carpets and crystal chandeliers, but there's no doubt it's a local establishment with hundreds of round tables and a deafening cast of thousands. The choice of shark's fin and bird's nest soups is staggering. You can order abalone by the catty (one-and-a-third pounds) or try sliced whelk with ham, a Chiu Chau specialty, but the sliced soyed

goose with noodles in a rich sauce is difficult to equal. The meal ends with tiny cups of Kwun Yum (Iron Buddha) tea, so named because it is very, very strong. Recommended for a hearty meal and lively conversation. *99 Granville Rd., East Ocean Centre, Tsim Sha Tsui East, tel. 723–6626. Casual dress. Reservations advised for large groups. AE, MC, V.*

7 **Lalique.** Tucked away on the first level of the Royal Gar-
$$$$ den Hotel's splendid atrium, this French restaurant is a tribute to glassmaker René Lalique. The Art Noveau glass doors and screens divide the small dining room into intimate nooks; a number of genuine Lalique figurines and vases are displayed on pedestals. Live music and a tiny dance floor do not detract from quiet discussions over dinner. The two best dinners are the fish potpourri soup flavored with anise and tomato, and the lobster thermidor twice baked with cheese. American steaks and Kobe beef are prepared on a charcoal grill. This is not one of those Continental grills given to heaping your plate high with food; portions tend to be small, in keeping with the restrained and intimate tone set by the glasswork. *Royal Garden Hotel 3F, 69 Mody Rd., Tsim Sha Tsui East, tel. 721–5215, ext. 2000. Jacket and tie required. Reservations advised. AE, DC, MC, V. Dinner only Sun.*

8 **Le Restaurant de France.** Every table bears a pink rose,
$$$$ the emblem of this elegant restaurant, a reliable choice for a business lunch or intimate dinner. The main room, long and narrow, is graced by hand-painted stained-glass ceiling domes and three bronze statues, all imported from France. The French cuisine is classical; many of the top dishes include goose liver. The pan-fried goose liver in a honey-and-vinegar sauce is nearly perfect; follow it with the breast of partridge (accompanied by the ubiquitous goose liver, this time in tandem with truffles and wrapped in a cabbage leaf). For something with less cholesterol, the pan-fried salmon in a red-wine sauce is well prepared. Visiting French chefs often add their own dishes to the menu. Offerings from the wine cellar are extensive. This restaurant is known for its inexpensive gourmet executive lunch and for its pastries; Chef Jean-Yves Gueho's raspberry Napoleon is a must. *Regal Meridien Hotel, 71 Mody Rd., Tsim Sha Tsui East, tel. 722–1818, ext. 201. Jacket and tie required. Reservations required for dinner, advised for lunch. AE, DC, MC, V. Dinner only Sat.; closed Sun.*

11 **Sagano.** Chef Kazuyoshi Yamamoto serves up some of the
$$$$ finest Japanese dishes in Hong Kong, preparing traditional Kyoto recipes with a light touch. The main dining area, spare in keeping with Japanese style, looks out to the harbor. There are also two teppanyaki counters seating eight, a sushi bar accommodating eleven, and four private tatami rooms. Most customers are Japanese, but the set meals make it easy for others to sample a variety of (perhaps unfamiliar) delicacies. The jellyfish marinated in crushed sesame and miso is crisp; the clear soup with duck dumplings is zesty; and the barbecued mackerel with lime is contrastingly sweet. The best dessert is simple, too—the plum ice cream. The wine list has a wide range of European selections, but sake is the appropriate drink here. Sagano is an excellent place to entertain Japanese clients. *Hotel Nikko, 72 Mody Rd., Tsim Sha Tsui East, tel. 739–*

1111, ext. 4215. Jacket and tie advised. Reservations advised. AE, DC, MC, V.

⑰ **Shang Palace.** This celebrated Cantonese dining room in
$$$ the Kowloon Shangri-La basement is a bold and extravagant swirl of reds and golds. Dishes are lavish as well, and served in generous portions. The shark's fin soups are terrific, the small whole suckling pig is a feast in itself, and the fried rice is a specialty of the house. This is a good place to order a wide variety of dim sum; they're light and tasty, made on the premises, and you can be sure that none of your experiments will prove too outlandish. Although Hong Kong Cantonese restaurants are never quiet, massive square columns do break up the floor space here, creating some privacy. A favorite of Chinese, Japanese, and Western businesspeople alike, this is an opulent setting for an unhurried business lunch or a fine, hearty dinner. *Kowloon Shangri-La Hotel, 64 Mody Rd., Tsim Sha Tsui East, tel. 721–2111. Jacket and tie advised. Reservations required. AE, DC, MC, V.*

Kowloon: Lei Yue Mun

④ **Hoi Tin Garden.** The Lei Yue Mun (Carp Fish Gate) area,
$$ about 20 minutes by subway or taxi east of Tsim Sha Tsui East, is a series of small fishing villages tightly packed on a narrow strip in the harbor; it's a popular haunt of local Cantonese in search of the freshest possible seafood. (Take a taxi or the subway to the Lam Tin stop and the No. 14 bus to the end of the line, Sam Ka Tsuen, where a sampan awaits.) Select an entrée from among the live scallops, abalone, lobsters, crabs, shrimp, and other delicacies offered in any of the open stalls here, and take your bagged catch through the village, following the signs to Hoi Tin Garden. There the waiters will help you decide how their chefs should prepare your purchase. You can add side dishes. Steamed shrimp is a good first choice; you shuck the heads and shells with your fingers, cleansing your hands in a tea bowl. If the weather's good, take a table outside on the patio. The staff is expert, attentive, and friendly, speaking minimal English and keeping the plates spotless by rinsing them with a garden hose and drying them on an edge of the tablecloth. This is adventurous dining; going with a local person will smooth the way. *53–59 Praya Rd., Lei Yue Mun, tel. 348–1482. Reservations accepted, but not needed. No credit cards.*

Hong Kong: Central/Wanchai

㉞ **East Ocean Seafood Restaurant.** The best of several new
$$$ restaurants that wed Cantonese cooking with California nouvelle cuisine (there's a branch in California), this is a popular setting for an East/West after-work meeting among the upwardly mobile. Traditional dishes such as braised shark's fin with chicken are prepared with an emphasis on lightness, but the crossover dishes are what's exceptional. Start with the meaty fried spare ribs, the "in" hors d'oeuvre; follow with the drunken prawns, cooked at your table; and finish with Chef Lau Wai Leung's award-winning steamed coconut-custard dumplings and deep-fried macadamia-nut puffs. Service is stylish and upbeat, as is the bright, earth-tone decor, and the presentation of the dishes themselves. *Harbour Centre 3F, 25*

*Harbour Rd., Wanchai, tel. 893–8887. Jacket advised.
Reservations advised. AE, DC, MC, V.*

★ ㉘ **Guangzhou Garden.** Located on the mezzanine level of one
$$$ of Hong Kong's glitziest glass, marble, and chrome harborside office towers, this restaurant offers fine Cantonese dishes to an upscale clientele. Financiers and other businesspeople gather here for fancy set lunches or relaxed dinners with their families or associates. The cuisine is distinguished by its subtle flavors and artful presentation (often employing garnishes of sliced fruits), hallmarks of the Ta Leung style. Few of the selections disappoint. The mock goose (baked slices of tofu with carrots and mushrooms) is smoky in flavor and crunchy on the palate. Both the chicken with walnuts and the shrimp with garlic, while simple, are outstanding. The signature dish is pan-fried milk with crab meat and olive seeds, a trifle exotic for Western tastes. Less strange are the tapioca desserts, especially the sago and honeydew-melon flavors. There's a large selection of Chinese wines. *Two Exchange Square 4F, 8 Connaught Rd., Central, tel. 525–1163. Jacket advised. Reservations required. AE, MC, V.*

★ ㉜ **JK's.** This restaurant just over The Peak with views of
$$$ Lamma Channel serves fine, modern, European dishes with an Oriental touch, mainly to upscale expatriates and local gourmets. In summer, there's a leisurely afternoon tea and set lunch available in the patio garden. Inside, the decor is formal but bright and open, with a skylight in the center, brass chandeliers, oil paintings in gilded frames, and a resident pianist. Executive Chef Walter Gloor uses seasonal local produce with great success in his soups (particularly the lobster bisque) as well as his entrées; mostly from the grill, they are small, light on sauces, and superb. The poached fillet of lemon sole, served in butter sauce on orange-flavored noodles, has a delicate, complex taste. For dessert, don't miss the Grand Marnier crêpes. The wine list is large, strong on vintage ports, and reasonably priced. This is a cheery, first-class spot for business lunch or dinner just over the hill from frantic Central. *100 Peak Rd., The Peak, tel. 849–7788. Jacket and tie required for dinner. Reservations advised. AE, DC, MC, V.*

★ ㉛ **La Ronda.** Hong Kong's most famous revolving restau-
$$$ rant, high atop the Furama, La Ronda was recently redecorated, restoring its claim as a top choice for business lunches in Central. In the evening, it's an easy, comfortable, surprisingly quiet spot to do your business entertaining. The setting is spectacular; as the tables on the outside ring slowly revolve, you can take in the whole of the harbor and The Peak. The service is fast and attentive; the table linen is crisp; the wine list is long and international; and the buffet selections are extensive. In addition to European, Indian, Japanese, and Chinese entrées, there are Thai soups, Italian pastas, and Greek gyros. The dessert soufflés are quite good. The atmosphere perhaps exceeds the cuisine, but as the large number of locals here attest, it is Hong Kong's best buffet for the price and a prime spot for entertaining. *Furama Kempinski Hotel, 1 Connaught Rd., Central, tel. 525–5111, ext. 502. Jacket and tie required for dinner. Reservations required. AE, DC, MC, V. Closed lunch Sun.*

26 **Luk Yu Teahouse.** For Hong Kong's fabled dim sum, this is
$$ the real thing, with crinkled-skin waiters in stained white
shirts, waitresses maneuvering metal cases of steaming
pastries through narrow aisles, gold spittoons underfoot,
and a menu in Chinese only. Convenient and even a bit
classy, it's also the favorite of local businesspeople in Cen-
tral's financial district. The setting is a four-story recon-
structed British teahouse, circa 1925, with ceiling fans,
dark wooden booths, and stained glass. Nothing much else
is English, however. You can order dishes by either cir-
cling the mysterious Chinese characters printed on a
notepad (rather like playing lotto), hailing a trolley and
pointing, or asking a waiter to take you in hand. This is a
place to have fun, to enjoy the atmosphere and din, and to
sample a few new delicacies. The dim sum is not consid-
ered the best in Hong Kong, but it's good enough to draw
in locals by the droves and will probably lure you back sev-
eral times. *24–26 Stanley St., Central, tel. 523–5463. No
reservations. No credit cards.*

★ **29** **Mandarin Grill.** This posh grill is a masterpiece of Hong
$$$$ Kong hotel opulence, with all the elements in a single
split-level creation: etched glass, marble floors, brass
rails, gold trim, teak moldings, crystal lamps, silver
trays, imported linens, carved murals. The quiet tables on
the raised platform in the rear afford a view of the other
diners, of Hong Kong's high society and modern taipans.
The food is almost incidental to the ambience, but it, too,
is celebrated. The grill turns out superb Kobe and Scotch
Angus steaks, Welsh and Tasmanian lamb, and French
poultry. A lobster from the tank is always a good choice;
they know how to prepare it here. Each dish has its own
suggestion of wealth and privilege; eggs Benedict, for ex-
ample, is accompanied by caviar. The wine list reads like a
bid sheet at a Christie's auction. This is Hong Kong's pre-
mier Continental restaurant. *Mandarin Oriental Hotel
1F, 5 Connaught Rd., Central, tel. 522–0111, ext. 4044.
Jacket and tie required. Reservations required. AE, CB,
DC, MC, V.*

★ **36** **One Harbour Road.** A private, glass-walled elevator
$$$$ whisks diners directly to this seventh-floor re-creation of
a taipan's mansion terrace—and to the best home-style
Cantonese cuisine in town. Occupying two levels under a
glass conservatory roof, this is the setting for high-society
dining, but it is not overly formal. The best tables are har-
borside, and the best dishes are the classics: bird's nest
and shark's fin soups, abalone, and a better Peking Duck
than you can find in Peking, displayed, carved, and served
at your table by expert waiters. On Sundays, a dim-sum
brunch is served at 10. The wine list is extensive; try one
of the Chinese vintages for a pleasant change. Restaurant
manager Dino Kwan has succeeded in re-creating 1930s
Hong Kong in cuisine as well as in setting, making this one
of the city's most impressive dining experiences. *Grand
Hyatt Hong Kong Hotel 7F, 1 Harbour Rd., Wanchai, tel.
861–1234. Jacket and tie required. Reservations required.
AE, DC, MC, V.*

33 **Peacock.** This snappy, upbeat East-meets-West restau-
$$$ rant is a favorite of yuppies, chuppies (Chinese yuppies),
businesspeople, and the local smart set. The decor resem-
bles that of a classy art gallery, with glass wall dividers,
forest-green carpeting, a gold-trimmed marble fountain,

raised platforms, and peacock feathers displayed on white pedestals. A business-lunch buffet is spread around the fountain; a few steps up is a curving cocktail lounge and special bars serving fresh juice, sushi, seafood, and tempura. The cuisine is multinational—and sometimes ostentatious: The crabmeat-and-shark's fin soup contains flakes of 24-carat gold. Steaks are stone grilled, the roasted chicken is from a Thai recipe, and Australian specialties include kangaroo-tail soup. Either of two four-course set dinners will keep your budget in tow—one with Japanese and Chinese seafoods, the other with a choice from the grill. Trendy and upscale, this restaurant is pitched to internationally varied groups intent on blending business with gourmet pleasures. *Bond Centre, 89 Queensway, Admiralty, tel. 845–1552. Casual but stylish. Reservations advised. AE, DC, MC, V. Closed Sun.*

39 **$$** **Victoria City Seafood Restaurant.** Though stuffed into a corner on the second floor of an office/shopping complex, this excellent traditional Cantonese restaurant is decorated in high taipan style. Lanterns are big, intricate constructions, dangling like glittering bird cages; chairs are backed with ornate tapestries. Customers are not in awe, however; they arrive in boisterous groups, ready for loud conversation and serious eating. Beyond the showy shark's fin and abalone dishes one expects, there are the simple, attractive seafood dishes such as the pan-fried crab claws, prawns with pepper and chili, and boiled fresh shrimp. The dim sum are lightly seasoned and delicately crusted; the Shanghai minced-pork pie is exceptional. Service is quick, almost brusque, but manager Pang Chung seems to be everywhere, making sure all goes well. *Sun Hung Kai Centre 2F, 30 Harbour Rd., Wanchai, tel. 891–9938. Casual but neat. Reservations advised for dinner and Sun. brunch. AE, DC, MC, V.*

27 **$$$** **Yung Kee.** A short walk from Central, this Cantonese restaurant is highly regarded by locals, although it is too noisy for a serious business discussion. The attraction is its cuisine, the creation of a couple who sold goose dishes from a modest street stall, amassed a fortune, and opened this dining emporium. The most inviting floor is the fourth (use the elevator), but even here the decor is plain—or plain ugly, perhaps, with a low ceiling, bright lights, and no view. The service is quick, but surly and sloppy. The chef, Wong Woon Ming, makes up for it all with his award-winning fillets of frog legs in seafood. (If you're ever going to try frog, this is the place to do it.) Another chef has his own celebrated specialty—poached fillets of lobster with crispy blinis. The leaf mustard with crabmeat is also sumptuous. Whatever you choose, you can count on mild, succulent sauces. This is a fine place to suggest for lunch or dinner if a local Chinese associate asks. *32–40 Wellington St., Central, tel. 523–1562. Casual but neat. Reservations advised. AE, DC, MC, V.*

Hong Kong: Causeway Bay/Quarry Bay

★ **43** **$$** **Casa Mexicana/Texas Rib House.** This Tex-Mex restaurant on a backstreet in Causeway Bay is a favorite of expatriates on weekend outings; on workdays, it's a nice change of pace for lunch or dinner. In the Casa Mexicana dining room the noise level can be high; there's an accomplished band of Filipino mariachis here, and people have been known to dance on the tables. In the rib room down the hall, however, it's always quiet enough for a business discussion. The decor is functional and not too tacky, with woven rugs on the wall and a black-tile floor for south-of-the-border diners, and booths for those on the Texas side. Service is attentive, the fruit margaritas are generous, and the menu is extensive. Combination Mexican dinners include choices of seafood crêpes, chili relleno, quesadillas, and other standbys, as well as skewers of prawns and, oddly, Polish sausage. The Rib Room features ribs, steaks, and Tex-Mex dishes adapted to Cantonese tastes, as well as a decent salad bar. This is the place for hearty portions at fairly low prices, with enough authentic taste to remind you of the real thing. *Victoria Centre, Watson Rd., Causeway Bay East, tel. 566–5560. Casual dress. Reservations required on weekends. AE, DC, MC, V.*

40 **Excelsior Grill.** Newly remodeled in luxurious style (hand-
$$$ painted silk murals, bright wood paneling and latticework) to compete with other hotel grills, this is a favorite haunt of Causeway Bay businesspeople, locals as well as visitors. The inexpensive salad-bar brunch is set up so that you can concoct your own creation or ask your waiter to prepare it (useful if you're in a hurry and engaged in conversation); the hot appetizers are delicious, but more expensive. The showy open grill turns out a special chateaubriand for two. Best dinner choice is the duck-and-walnut mousse, baked in vine leaves and topped with a cream sauce with chives. Dessert crêpes are prepared at your table. An attraction of the grill is its attached Noon Gun Bar, a quiet spot for liqueur coffees and piano music, and the place to be when the historic sixpounder gun is fired on the waterfront below, a custom from earliest taipan days. *The Excelsior 3F, 281 Gloucester Rd., Causeway Bay, tel. 837–6783 or 894–8888. Jacket and tie advised. Reservations advised. AE, CB, DC, MC, V.*

41 **Parc 27.** For a panoramic view of the harbor and Victoria
$$$ Park, this spacious, upscale French restaurant atop the Park Lane Radisson is unsurpassed. It's a comfortable place to talk over business during a three-course set lunch or buffet. The decor—Italian marble floors, a peach-and-gray color scheme, plush carpets, tables spaced widely along the windows—is impressive. For dinner, there are fine appetizers (Russian caviar with sour cream and chives), fragrant entrées (duck in cinnamon-and-pear sauce), and renowned grilled seafood selections (Norwegian salmon, Dover sole, South China king prawns). For dessert, the hot fruit-flavored soufflés are excellent; and the champagne cocktails are a house specialty. The view from the top is enhanced by top cuisine, with unobtrusive service to match. *Park Lane Radisson Hotel 27F, 310 Gloucester Rd., Causeway Bay, tel. 890–3355, ext. 344. Jacket advised. Reservations required. AE, DC, MC, V.*

42 **The Red Pepper.** Though a cut above its Causeway Bay
$$ neighborhood—a fascinating area of rundown shops and alleys—this is still not an elegant restaurant. The thick pillars and garish red-and-gold ceiling, the lanterns and small tables, and especially the rusted beer refrigerator at the rear are typical of Chinese restaurants the world over—except that this one serves some of Hong Kong's most highly regarded Szechuan dishes. Local Chinese and expatriate businesspeople alike favor the mild approach to

Szechuan fare practiced here. The deep-fried crispy rice with shrimp, for example, dressed in a sauce at your table and spooned into a small bowl, is pleasingly mild. So is the popular smoked duck, marinated in oranges. Perhaps the best entrée is the roast spicy duck (simmered in five-spice and peppercorns), but it must be ordered ahead. For 30 years this restaurant has served diners without pretense or a large tab; its veteran waiters are diligent, if a bit curt; and the portions are always large. *7 Lan Fong Rd., Causeway Bay, tel. 577–3811. Casual dress. Reservations advised for dinner. AE, CB, DC, MC, V.*

Other Choices

Food Street

Between Paterson and Cleveland streets, off Causeway Bay, the Food Street open-air mall (tel. 890–3396) has more than two dozen restaurants. Many of them are mediocre, but there's something here for every taste and budget. For fast food, there's the **Dim Sum Kitchen,** with its cramped tables and average pastries. Continental dishes of many sorts are served in a fancier setting at the **Barcelona. Hooraiya Teppanyaki** displays plastic samples of its offerings in the front window; the set-price sukiyaki, sushi, tempura, and *obento* (boxed) lunches are reasonable. Two of the more satisfying spots are the unforgettably named **Boil & Boil Wonderful,** a noisy restaurant favored by locals for its substantial meat-and-vegetable casseroles, and the **Riverside Chinese Restaurant,** sedately appointed with black ladder-back chairs and crisp pink tablecloths, where the specialties are suckling pig, roast goose, Japanese octopus, and "drunken" prawns. This is an inexpensive place to browse for a quick lunch to suit your fancy when you're in the area, a nice change from Western fast food and hotel coffee shops.

Tourist Restaurants

Although mainly catering to tourists, both the **Jumbo Floating Restaurant** in Aberdeen's Shum Wan Harbor (tel. 553–9111), which you reach by sampan, and **The Peak Tower Restaurant** (tel. 849–7381), which you reach by the Peak Tram from upper Central, offer spectacular settings and surprisingly decent food. They're fun the first time around, and are good choices if you are entertaining other business travelers from the West. **Jimmy's Kitchen** (1–3 Wyndham St., Central, tel. 526–5293, or 29 Ashley Rd., Tsim Sha Tsui, tel. 368–4027), a local institution since 1928, is also popular with out-of-towners, as well as with expatriate wheeler-dealers. The rich, heavy, British-German cuisine and the dark-wood and brass decor (suggesting a private club from the Colonial heyday) are the antithesis of everything Cantonese in Hong Kong.

FREE TIME

Fitness

Hotel Facilities

The **Park Lane Radisson** (tel. 890–3355) in Causeway Bay has two floors of the latest fitness and aerobics equipment, and charges HK$100 a day for those not staying at the hotel. The **Sheraton** (tel. 369–1111) and the **Hilton** (tel. 523–3111) make provisions for guests of certain other hotels.

Health Clubs

The **Tom Turk Health Clubs** are located on Hong Kong Island (Bond Centre, West Wing, 13th Floor, 89 Queensway, tel. 521–4541) and in Kowloon (Albion Plaza, 2–6 Granville Rd., Tsim Sha Tsui, tel. 368–0022). All that's required to use the gym, sauna, steam bath, and aerobics facilities is "a membership card to any Fitness Club anywhere in the world." Entrance fees are HK$100 before 5 PM and HK$150 after 5 PM. A monthly fee of HK$200 plus HK$120 per week covers all use from 7 AM to 5 PM; after 5 PM, monthly members pay HK$50 extra.

Jogging

The road around **The Peak,** the harborside promenade from Tsim Sha Tsui east to west, and **Bowen Road** from Stubbs Road to Magazine Gap are the top walking and running spots, especially before work. Visitors are also invited to join the "conversation-speed jogging" groups and "Ladies Walking Groups" organized each week by the Hong Kong Running Clinic (40 Stubbs Rd., tel. 574–6211, ext. 888).

Shopping

Hong Kong is one of the world's great shopping experiences, particularly for clothing and anything Chinese. Nathan Road (Kowloon side) is a **"Golden Mile"** of small shops, featuring some of the least expensive as well as most expensive goods (from cameras to silks) in the world. The vast **Ocean Terminal/Ocean Centre/Harbour City** (Canton Rd., Tsim Sha Tsui, tel. 730–5151) trilevel shopping complex north of Kowloon's Star Ferry Terminal is an endless labyrinth. The **New World Shopping Centre** (18–24 Salisbury Rd., Tsim Sha Tsui, tel. 369–9211) is a third great modern borough of Kowloon shops. On the Island side, the shopping center with the highest gloss is the prestigious **Landmark Building** (Pedder St. and Des Voeux Rd., Central), in the core of Central.

For less-upscale shopping, favorites are the **Stanley Market** in Stanley Village on southern Hong Kong Island (discount designer-label clothing and linens) and **Hollywood Road and Cat Street** in Central (flea markets, bric-a-brac, antiques). **Ladder Street**—or any of the steep alleyways off the main streets west of Central—is filled with stalls worth poking through for crafts, fabrics, flowers, electronics, almost anything on earth.

There are several marvelous Chinese department stores around town, including **Yue Hwa Chinese Products Emporium** (54–64 Nathan Rd., Tsim Sha Tsui, tel. 368–9165), **Chung Kiu Chinese Products Emporium** (17 Hankow Rd., tel. 723–3211; 528–532 Nathan Rd., Tsim Sha Tsui, tel. 780–2351), the **Chinese Arts and Crafts Store** (Silvercord Bldg., 30 Canton Rd., Tsim Sha Tsui, tel. 722–6655), and the **China Products Company** (19–31 Yee Wo St., tel. 890–8321) on Yee Wo Street in Causeway Bay, the location also of several impressive Japanese department stores (Daimaru, Matsuzakaya).

The fashion conscious should try the ultra-chic boutiques in The Landmark and the hotel arcades in the Peninsula, the Regent, and the Mandarin Oriental hotels, as well as the very British department store, **Shui Hing** (23–25 Nathan Rd., Tsim Sha Tsui, tel. 721–1495). Two top men's tailors are **Sam's** (92–94 Nathan Rd., Tsim Sha Tsui, tel. 367–9423) for suits and **Ascot Chang** (Peninsula, tel. 366–2398 and Regent, tel. 367–8319) for shirts. Those inclined toward computers and software should try the **Golden Shopping Centre** (146–152 Fuk Wah St., Sham Shui Po Station, no phone), notorious for bootlegged software, or the more staid-and-true shopping center **Asia Computer Plaza** (Silvercord, 30 Canton Rd., Tsim Sha Tsui, tel. 311–2611).

For those with specific shopping goals, here are some recommended means:

Camera buyers should pay no more in Hong Kong retail stores than they would if ordering by mail from photography-magazine advertisements in the West. Reliable camera dealers include **William's Photo Supply** (Upper Basement, Shop 5, Furama Kempinski Hotel Arcade, 1 Connaught Rd., Central, tel. 522–1268) and **Art Photo Service** (Shop 32, Hilton Hotel Arcade, 2 Queen's Rd., Central, tel. 523–6213).

For watches, avoid buying that US$35 Rolex on the street (it won't last a year and can be confiscated by Customs). Rely instead on official dealers such as the exclusive **Les Must De Cartier (FE) Ltd.** (Shop L1, Peninsula Hotel Arcade, Salisbury Rd., Tsim Sha Tsui, tel. 368–8036) or the ubiquitous and less-pricy **City Chain Co. Ltd.** with 28 locations in Kowloon and 12 on Hong Kong Island (including one at the new One Pacific Place shopping center, 88 Queensway, Central, tel. 845–9403).

Jewelry stores must number in the thousands in Hong Kong. Three of the best are **House of Shen Ltd.** (M20, Peninsula Hotel Arcade, Salisbury Rd., Tsim Sha Tsui, tel. 721–5483), **Larry Jewelry** (G49–50, Edinburgh Tower, The Landmark, Peddar St., Central, tel. 521–1268), and **Kai-Yin and Co. Ltd.** (M1, Mandarin Oriental Hotel Arcade, 5 Connaught Rd., Central, tel. 524–8238) for modern Oriental designs. For pearls (cultured or freshwater), try **The Pearl Gallery** (1/F, New World Tower, 16–18 Queen's Rd., Central, tel. 526–3599); for jade, visit **Jade Creations** (Room 410, Lane Crawford House, 70 Queen's Rd., Central, tel. 522–3598). *See* also Diversions, below.

Oriental rugs are available at some irresistible shops on Wyndham Street and on Hollywood Road as you walk uphill from Central, but the prices are not low. The most highly regarded outlet for locally made Chinese rugs is **Tai Ping Carpets Salon** (Shop 110, Hutchinson House, 10 Harcourt Rd., Central, tel. 522–7138).

In shopping, let the buyer beware. Hong Kong is a free marketplace; its consumer laws are not stringent. Merchants who are members of the Hong Kong Tourist Association (HKTA), however, do subscribe to a set of ethical standards, and consumer complaints against these retailers can be directed to the Membership Department (tel. 801–7177).

Diversions

Aberdeen, on the other side of Hong Kong Island, is home to the largest remaining group of boat dwellers in the Colony, and the Watertours sampans give you a closeup view. Try dim-sum lunch aboard the Jumbo Floating Restaurant. The Watertours sampans all dock under the large Watertour sign on the Aberdeen waterfront. The rate is clearly posted (no haggling necessary). Watertours provides reliable escorted tours (with English-speaking guides) not only for Aberdeen, but for Hong Kong harbor cruises, too. For schedules and bookings, contact your hotel, inquire directly at the Watertours pontoon between the Star Ferry Pier and Ocean Terminal shopping center (Tsim Sha Tsui), or call tel. 525–4808 or 526–3538.

Cheung Chau, the most fascinating of Hong Kong's major outlying islands, offers a taste of old China in miniature. It is easily reached by the hourly ferries from Central Hong Kong.

The Peninsula Hotel's (tel. 366–6251) **high tea** each afternoon (3:30–5:30) is an elegant reminder of Colonial splendor in Hong Kong.

The Jade Market (Kansu St., off Nathan Rd. in Yau Ma Tei) is the place to browse for "penny" jade (very inexpensive, coin-sized pieces), spread out on the sidewalk by traders (10 AM–4 PM).

The Peak provides the best views of the city and harbor. Take the Peak Tram in Central; at the top is a surprisingly fragrant, pollution-free circular walking trail, as relaxing as the ride up on the old tram is nerve-racking.

The Promenade, running from the Kowloon Star Ferry terminal east, possesses the most dazzling views of the Hong Kong skyline and waterfront. It is ideal for a long, relaxing stroll.

The Star Ferry (tel. 366–2576), said to be the most famous harbor crossing on earth, should not be missed, even if you have no business on the other side. It costs just pennies each way, even first class.

Temple Street (Yau Ma Tei district north from the Jordan subway stop in Kowloon) holds a mile-long Night Market extraordinaire every night (8 PM–11 PM), complete with clothing stalls, sidewalk seafood cafés, fortune tellers, dentists, and amateur Chinese opera.

The Arts

The top performing-arts venue is the new **Hong Kong Cultural Centre** (10 Salisbury Rd., Tsim Sha Tsui, tel. 734–2009), which has attracted many international companies and stars since 1989. HKTA puts on free one-hour cultural shows twice weekly in various shopping locations (tel. 801–7177 for current schedule). The **Hong Kong Arts Festival** (Jan./Feb.) and the **Hong Kong International Film Festival** (Apr.) feature innovative works and films (many in spoken or subtitled English). The newest in music and drama (English-language) is staged weekly at **The Fringe Club** (2 Lower Albert Rd., Central, tel. 521–7251). Hong Kong is rightly renowned for Big Business, not High Culture, but it is home to a fine **Philharmonic Orchestra** (tel. 832–7121) and a **Chinese Orchestra** (tel. 334–8465), as well as nearly a dozen semi-professional Cantonese Opera troupes. The best groups often perform at the Hong Kong Cultural Centre or the **Hong Kong Arts Centre** (2 Harbour Rd., Wanchai, tel. 823–0230). For a current listing, check the entertainment sections of either of the two local English-language newspapers, *South China Morning Post* or *Hong Kong Standard*.

Tickets can be purchased through **Ticketmate** outlets at kiosks in the Wanchai, Causeway Bay, Mong Kok, Kwun Tong, and Tsim Sha Tsui subway stations, or at 201 Tower I, Exchange Square, 8 Connaught Pl., Central, tel. 833–9300.

After Hours

Hong Kong's expatriate population is small but active, and business travelers usually feel safe and comfortable in the establishments they have staked out, as listed below.

Entertainment Centers
The newest and most popular night spot is **JJ's** (Grand Hyatt Hotel, tel. 861–1234), a multilevel complex of three dozen video screens, a jazz/blues bar, a disco, and lounges for the sophisticated. The New World Hotel (tel. 369–4111) is creating a similar venue with **The Penthouse**—two top floors of disco, lounges, and private VIP video karaoke (Japanese-style sing-along) rooms.

Bars and Lounges
For sheer luxury and quiet elegance after work, try the **Verandah Lounge** (The Peninsula, tel. 366–6251), the **Lobby Lounge** (The Regent, tel. 721–1211), or the **Champagne Bar** (Grand Hyatt, tel. 861–1234). Local businesspeople usually frequent the **Galley** (Jardine House, Central, tel. 526–3061), the very British **Bull and Bear** (Hutchinson House, Lambeth Walk, tel. 525–7436), or **The Jockey Pub** (Swire House, 2/F, Chater St., Central, tel. 526–1478). **Brown's Winebar** (Tower 2, Exchange Sq., Central, tel. 523–7003) draws a Western stockbroker crowd.

Jazz/Folk Clubs
Dickens Bar in the Excelsior Hotel (tel. 894–8888) regularly showcases the best jazz in town on Sunday afternoons. **Ned Kelly's Last Stand** (11A Ashley Rd., Tsim Sha Tsui, tel. 366–0562) has raucous Dixieland, Aussie style, nightly. **The Wanch** (54 Jaffe Rd., Wanchai, tel. 731–2868) and **Hardy's** (D'Aguilar St., Central, tel. 522–4448) feature live folk music. Groups perform at **The Jazz Club** (34–35 D'Aguilar St., Central, tel. 845–8477) after 8 PM.

Discos
The center of disco hopping is the Lan Kwai Fong area in Central (between Wyndham and D'Aguilar streets), where some top cafés/pubs/discos are concentrated. The best are **Disco Disco** (38 D'Aguilar St., tel. 524–9539), **California** (24–26 Lan Kwai Fong, tel. 521–1345), **Soho** (19–27 Wyndham St., tel. 877–1100), and **1997** (8–11 Lan Kwai Fong, tel. 810–9333). The city's best-known, loudest, and most youthful dancing floor is at **Canton** (World Finance Centre, Harbour City, Tsim Sha Tsui, tel. 735–0209). **Hot Gossip** (tel. 730–6884) next door is quieter and attracts a

slightly older crowd—the chuppies (Chinese yuppies) and expatriate yuppies of Hong Kong. Other popular discos include **The Godown** (Admiralty Centre, tel. 866–2200); **Talk of the Town** (Excelsior Hotel, tel. 837–6786); and, on Saturday and Sunday, the **Falcon** (Royal Garden Hotel, tel. 721–5215, ext. 2021). The truly rich and their admirers dance during and after dinner at the **Casablanca Supper Club** (Marina Tower 8F, 8 Shum Wan Rd., Aberdeen, tel. 555–8321). At most dance clubs, the action starts around 10 PM and often runs until 4 AM; cover charges range from HK$80–HK$120.

Cabarets
The **Hilton Hotel** (dinner shows; tel. 523–3111, ext. 2009) and **Duddell's** (a variety of live performers; 1 Duddell St., Central, tel. 845–2244) occasionally put on good entertainment in this vein.

London

by Kate Sekules

There's no doubt about it, London is sprawling, expensive, and crowded. Yet it remains one of the world's most alluring cities.

A mecca of cultural and economic activity for centuries, London has twice been rebuilt after widespread devastation—the fire of 1666 and the air raids of World War II. It also survived the so-called British disease that followed the war, when one economic crisis followed another.

Although the "Thatcher era" ended in November 1990, with the resignation of the increasingly unpopular prime minister, Margaret Thatcher and the Tories' "enterprise culture" got much of the credit for the recovery from this postwar ailment by curbing the power of the nation's labor leaders, among other steps. The Tories, of course, received considerable help from the North Sea oil and gas revenues and from Britain's entry into the European Economic Community.

The Common Market lure has enticed many American companies the way Buckingham Palace pageantry has enticed tourists. Practically all Fortune 500 companies have a base here, and there's a growing trend for smaller American companies to head over the Atlantic, too. The common language, of course, has a great deal to do with these strong Anglo-American links, making London the obvious springboard to Paris, Frankfurt, and the rest of Europe for companies eager to exploit the open market of 1992 and beyond.

London's layout is as straightforward as a plate of spaghetti, and there's no hint of a grid system to make orientation any easier. Getting around is a pain—high property prices in the late '80s drove companies away from the center, with consequent increases in commuter traffic (and distances between meetings), and the mass-transit system is not the most reliable, though improvements are in progress. On the other hand, the pleasure of London for residents and visitors alike is that its history is tangible. The fact that the city grew over the centuries out of a collection of villages is reflected in the pace and quality of life. To many, London feels like a much smaller place. Expect high-speed super-efficiency, and you may experience delay and frustration. Slow down a little, and you'll see London's charm.

Perhaps more than most great cities, London is constantly evolving. The proliferation of business and retail centers toward the outskirts of the city has been remarkable in recent years. Of these, the Docklands development in the southeast is the most significant—most of the national newspapers have deserted Fleet Street and settled in this former wasteland, as have countless other businesses. Finance and insurance, business and professional services are going, and are currently the fastest growth sectors in London.

Top Employers

Employer	Type of Enterprise	Parent*/ Headquarters
BAT Industries	Tobacco, retail, and paper manufacturers	London
British Aerospace	Aircraft manufacturers	London
British Coal	Coal production	London
British Railways Board	Transportation	London
British Telecom	Telecommunications	London
Electricity Council	Utility	London
General Electric	Industrial and appliance manufacturers	Fairfield, CT
Imperial Chemical Industries	Petrochemicals and pharmaceuticals	London
Post Office		London
Unilever	Food products, detergents	New York

*if applicable

ESSENTIAL INFORMATION

We include the London telephone area codes (071, 081) with all numbers listed below. If you are calling from outside the United Kingdom, omit the 0 from the codes; if you are calling within London, add 71 if you are in an 81 area code, and vice versa.

The currency of England is the pound, abbreviated throughout the chapter as £.

Government Tourist Offices

British Tourist Authority. In the United States: 40 W. 57th St., New York, NY 10019, tel. 212/581–4700; John Hancock Center, Suite 3320, 875 N. Michigan Ave., Chicago, IL 60611, tel. 312/787–0490; World Trade Center, 350 S. Figueroa St., Suite 450, Los Angeles, CA 90071, tel. 213/

628–3525; 2305 Cedar Springs Rd., Suite 210, Dallas, TX
75201, tel. 214/720–4040.
In Canada: 94 Cumberland St., Suite 600, Toronto M5R
3N3, Ontario, tel. 416/925–6326.
In the United Kingdom: Thames Tower, Black's Rd., London W6 9EL, tel. 081/846–9000.

Foreign Trade Information

British Trade Development Office. In the United States: 845
Third Ave., New York, NY 10022, tel. 212/593–2258; 33 N.
Deerborn St., Chicago, IL 60602, tel. 312/346–1810; 3701
Wilshire Blvd., Suite 312, Los Angeles, CA 90010, tel.
213/385–7381.
In Canada: 1155 University St., Suite 901, Montréal H3B
3AF, Quebec, tel. 514/866–5863.
In the United Kingdom: 88–89 Ecclestion Sq., London
SW1V 1PT, tel. 071/215–0574.

Entry Requirements

U.S. and Canadian Citizens
Passport only. A visa is required for visits longer than six
months.

Climate

What follows are the average daily maximum and minimum temperatures for London.

Jan.	45F	7C	Feb.	47F	8C	Mar.	49F	9C
	36	2		36	2		38	3
Apr.	56F	13C	May	63F	17C	June	68F	20C
	40	4		47	8		52	11
July	72F	22C	Aug.	70F	21C	Sept.	65F	18C
	56	13		54	12		50	10
Oct.	58F	14C	Nov.	49F	9C	Dec.	47F	8C
	45	7		40	4		38	3

Airports

Heathrow Airport, the busiest international airport in the
world, is 15 miles west of central London; **Gatwick,** the
world's second busiest international airport, lies 30 miles
to the south of the city.

Airlines

Heathrow Terminal 4 and Gatwick North Terminal serve
British Airways, which flies out of the most U.S. cities
(24), and Montreal, Toronto, and Vancouver; Heathrow
Terminal 3 serves Pan Am, TWA, and Air Canada.
Gatwick South Terminal serves Virgin Atlantic and the
other U.S. airlines, which fly out of major U.S. cities.

Air Canada, tel. 081/759–2331.
American, tel. 0293/502078; 800/433–7300.
British Airways, Gatwick, tel. 0293/518033; 800/247–9297.
British Airways, Heathrow, tel. 081/759–2525; 800/247–
9297.
Continental, tel. 0293/776464; 800/525–0280.
Delta, tel. 0293/502113; 800/221–1212.
Northwest, tel. 0293/502079; 800/225–2525.
Pan Am, tel. 071/409–0688; 800/221–1111.

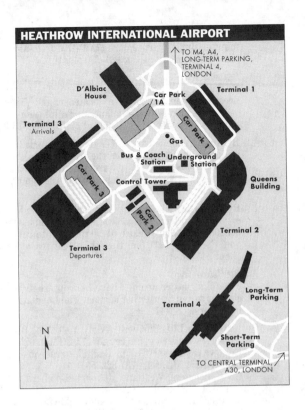

HEATHROW INTERNATIONAL AIRPORT

TO M4, A4, LONG-TERM PARKING, TERMINAL 4, LONDON

D'Albiac House

Car Park 1A

Terminal 1

Terminal 3 Arrivals

Car Park 1

Gas

Bus & Coach Station

Underground Station

Car Park 3

Control Tower

Car Park 2

Queens Building

Terminal 2

Terminal 3 Departures

Terminal 4

Long-Term Parking

N

Short-Term Parking

TO CENTRAL TERMINAL, A30, LONDON

TWA, tel. 081/759–5352; 800/221–2000.
U.S. Air, tel. 071/930–8104; 800/241–6522.
Virgin, tel. 0293/502105; 800/862–8621.

Between the Airports and Downtown

The Underground (also called the Tube) is the most reliable—and least expensive—way to get to downtown from Heathrow. Gatwick has regular rail service into London's Victoria Station, which is much faster and less frustrating than driving or taking a taxi; there is no expressway and traffic is invariably slow.

Heathrow
By Tube. This is the most reliable and direct way to get downtown. The trip takes 50–60 minutes into central London on the Piccadilly Line. Trains run every 3–7 minutes, 5 AM–11:30 PM Mon.–Sat.; 5:50 AM–11:40 PM Sun. Cost: £2.10.

By Bus. The A1 Airbus to Victoria Station departs from Terminal 3 at 15 and 45 minutes past the hour from 6:40 AM to 10:15 PM; and from Terminal 4 at 2 and 32 minutes past the hour until 10:32 PM. The A2 to Euston departs from Terminal 3 every 30 minutes from 6:30 AM to 10 PM; and from Terminal 4 at 17 and 47 minutes past the hour until 10:17 PM. Cost: £4. Night bus N97 goes to Hyde Park Corner and Trafalgar Square. Cost: £1.60.

By Taxi. There are taxi ranks outside the terminals. The drive via the M4 takes 30–40 minutes off-peak, up to 90 minutes during rush hours (7AM–1PM from airport; 9:30 AM, 6 PM from city). Cost: £20–£30 plus tip.

Gatwick

By Rail. This is the most direct route. The Gatwick Express runs nonstop between the airport and Victoria Station, and takes 30–45 minutes. Trains run every 15 minutes during the day, hourly at night. Cost: £6.30.

By Bus. Greenline bus no. 777 goes to Victoria Coach Station, (about 300 yards from the train station) hourly between 5:20 AM and 11 PM from South Terminal Coach Station. The trip takes 45 minutes; up to 90 minutes during peak hours. Cost: £6.

By Taxi. Gatwick Airport Cars can be booked in advance or picked up from the rank in either terminal (tel. 0293/502808). The drive takes 40–90 minutes to central London. Cost: about £20 plus tip. A black cab to Gatwick costs about £45 plus tip.

By Helicopter

The following companies have helicopters available for charter to and from either airport. The London heliport is in Battersea SW11.

Air Hanson Ltd, Business Aviation Centre, Blackbushe Airport, Camberley, Surrey GU17 9LG, tel. 0252/890089.
Bristow Helicopter Group, Redhill Aerodrome, Redhill, Surrey RH1 5JZ, tel. 0737/822353.
CB Helicopters, Westland Heliport, Lombard Rd., London SW11 3RE, tel. 071/228–3232.
McAlpine Helicopters Ltd, Swallowfield Way, Hayes, Middlesex UB3 1SP, tel. 081/848–3522.

Car Rentals

The following companies have booths in or near the airports:

Avis, Gatwick, 0293/29721; Heathrow, 081/897–9321; 800/331–1212.
Budget, Gatwick, 0293/540141; Heathrow, 081/759–2216; 800/527–0700.
Europcar, Gatwick, tel. 0293/31062; Heathrow, 081/897–0811; 800/227–7368.
Hertz, Gatwick, 0293/30555; Heathrow, 081/897–3347; 800/654–3131.

Emergencies

For a list of approved physicians and clinics that belong to the International Association for Medical Assistance to Travelers, contact IAMAT, 417 Center St., Lewiston, NY 14092, tel. 716/754–4883.

American Citizen Services at the American Embassy (24 Grosvenor Sq., W1, tel. 071/499–9000) holds a list of approved doctors and offers assistance in emergencies.
American Medical Incorporation (35 Weymouth St., W1, tel. 071/935–2449 or 071/935–7700) refers patients to the appropriate approved doctor or clinic.

Doctors/Hospitals

The Casualty department of any hospital offers treatment free of charge in cases of genuine emergency. **University College Hospital** (Grafton Way, WC1, tel. 071/387–9300;

Tube: Warren St. or Euston Sq.), **Charing Cross Hospital** (Fulham Palace Rd., W6, tel. 071/846–1234; Tube: Hammersmith).

Dentists
Dental Emergency Service (25 Devonshire Pl., W1, tel. 071/935–4486; 9 AM–5 PM Tues.–Fri.; Tube: Regents Pk.) is a central practice that treats tourists. The **24-hour Private Dental Emergency Service** (tel. 081/677–8383 or 081/546–4444) charges a nonrefundable search fee of up to £6 for referrals.

Police and Ambulance
Tel. 999.

Important Addresses and Numbers

American Express. Central (6 Haymarket, SW1, tel. 071/930–4411), City (52 Cannon St., EC4, tel. 071/248–2671), West (78 Brompton Rd., SW3, tel. 071/584–6182).

Audiovisual rentals. Sightsound (Unit 2, St. Pancras Commercial Centre, 63 Pratt St., NW1, tel. 071/482–5232), Viewplan (Alice Owen Technology Centre, 251–279 Goswell Rd., EC1, tel. 071/734–8833).

Canadian Consulate (Macdonald House, 1 Grosvenor Sq., W1, tel. 071/629–9492).

Computer rentals. Business Systems Group (Business Design Centre, 52 Upper St., Islington Green N1, tel. 071/359–7778).

Convention and exhibition centers. The largest are: Alexandra Palace (Wood Green N22, tel. 081/365–2121), Barbican Centre (Barbican EC2, tel. 071/638–4141), Earls Court (Warwick Rd., SW5, tel. 071/385–1200), Olympia (Kensington W14, tel. 071/385–1200), Olympia Conference Centre (Hammersmith Rd., W14, tel. 071/603–5639), London Arena (Limeharbour E14, tel. 071/538–8880), QEII Conference Centre (Broad Sanctuary, Westminster SW1, tel. 071/222–5000), The London Convention Bureau (26 Grosvenor Gdns., Victoria SW1, tel. 071/730–3450), Wembley Conference Centre (Wembley, tel. 081/902–8833).

Fax services. Central: CCI (15 Whitehall, SW1, tel. 071/930–5322); City: GN Citytel (15–27 Gee St., EC1, tel. 071/588–4567); West: Business Communication Centre (7–11 Kensington High St., W8, tel. 071/938–1721).

Formal-wear rentals. Men: Moss Bros. (88 Regent St., W1, tel. 071/494–0666); Women: One Night Stand (148 Regents Park Rd., NW1, tel. 071/586–2123; 44 Pimlico Rd., SW1, tel. 071/730–8708).

Gift shops. Chocolates: Charbonnel et Walker (28 Old Bond St., W1, tel. 071/491–0939), Godiva (9 Brompton Arc., SW1, tel. 071/589–5557); Flowers: Jane Packer (56 James St., W1, tel. 071/935–2673), Moyses Stevens (6 Bruton St., W1, tel. 071/493–8171); Gift baskets: Telefruit (202 Long La., SE1, tel. 071/403–0555).

Graphic design studios. Design House (Parkway, NW1, tel. 071/482–2815), Lloyd Northover (8 Smart's Pl., WC2, tel. 071/430–1100).

Hairstylists. Unisex: Andrew Lockyer (65 Broadwick St., W1, tel. 071/494–0530); Men's barber: George Trumper (9 Curzon St., W1, tel. 071/499–1850).

Health and fitness clubs. *See* Fitness, below.

Information hot lines. Tourist information (0898/121862), Weather forecast (0898/500401).

Limousine service. London Limousine Company (tel. 071/928–9280).

Liquor stores. Augustus Barnett (36 Wellington St., WC2, tel. 071/836–8767; and branches), Oddbins (7 George St., W1, tel. 071/487–3620; and branches).

Mail Delivery, overnight. Federal Express (tel. 0800/123800), TNT (tel. 081/848–1111).

Messenger service. A to Z (Texryte House, Balmes Rd., N1, tel. 071/254–2000).

News programs. TV: 9 AM, 1, 6, 9 PM, BBC1; 8 AM, 2, 3:50 PM, "Newsnight" (analysis of major stories); weekdays around 10 PM, BBC2; 5 AM, 1, 5:40, 10 PM, ITV; 6 AM, 7 PM, Channel 4. Radio: 6, 7, 8, 9, 11 AM, 12, 1, 4, 5, 6, 7, 10, 12 PM, BBC Radio 4 (720, 756 kHz); on the hour, BBC World Service (648 kHz).

Office space rental. Association of Business Centres (150 Regent St., W1, tel. 071/439–0623).

Pharmacies, late-night. Bliss (5 Marble Arch, W1, tel. 071/723–6116, daily 9 AM–midnight; 50–56 Willesden La., NW6, tel. 071/624–8000, daily 9AM–2 AM), Underwoods (114 Queensway, W2, tel. 071/229–4819, Mon.–Sat. 9 AM–10 PM, Sun. 10 AM–10 PM).

Secretarial services. Angela Pike Associates (9 Curzon St., W1, tel. 071/491–1616).

Stationery supplies. Morgans (22 Goodge St., W1, tel. 071/636–3167).

Taxis. Dial-a-cab (tel. 071/253–5000 [black cabs]), London and City (tel. 071/250–0099 [minicabs]).

Theater tickets. *See* The Arts, below.

Thomas Cook (45 Berkeley St., W1, tel. 071/499–4000; 1 Marble Arch, W1, tel. 071/889–7777; and branches).

Trade Ministry. Department of Trade and Industry (1–19 Victoria St., SW1, tel. 071/215–7877).

Train information. British Rail to South England (tel. 071/928–5100), to West England and South Midlands (tel. 071/262–6767), to Northwest England, East and West Midlands, Scotland, and Ireland (tel. 071/387–7070), to East and Northeast England, and Scotland (tel. 071/278–2477), to Europe (tel. 071/834–2345).

Translation services. Interlingua TTI (Imperial House, Kingsway, WC2, tel. 071/240–5361).

U.S. Embassy (24 Grosvenor Sq., W1, tel. 071/499–9000).

Telephones

Push-Button Pay Phones
Deposit at least 10p before dialing for a two-minute local call. A display shows how much credit is left; a tone warns when you need to deposit more coins; some phones return unused coins.

Dial Pay Phones
These are a dying breed, but a few remain. Dial, then deposit 10p coin(s) at the sound of the beeps.

Card Phones
Phone cards are sold at newsagent's shops, post offices, and some Tube stations. Insert card before dialing; a display shows the available 10p units. The card is returned to you when the receiver is replaced.

Tipping

Tip hotel concierges £1–£5, depending on services performed. Doormen carrying bags to the registration desk get 50p–£1. Porters carrying bags to rooms get 50p–£1 per bag, minimum £1. For room service, tip £1–£3. In restaurants, 10%–15% is usually included in the bill and no extra tip is expected, but £1–£5 or 10% is often left for exceptional service. If in doubt, ask whether service is included. Taxi drivers get 10%, minimum 50p.

DOING BUSINESS

Hours

Businesses: weekdays 9 to 5 or 6. **Banks:** weekdays 9:30–3:30; some have extended hours (e.g., airport and station branches), some open 9:30–12:30 Sat. **Shops:** Mon.–Sat. 9 to 5:30 or 6. West End shops stay open late: Thurs. between 7 and 8 PM; Knightsbridge, Wed. between 7 and 8 PM.

National Holidays

New Year's Day; Easter; May Day, first Mon. after May 1; Spring Bank Holiday, last Mon. in May; Aug. Bank Holiday, last Mon. in Aug., Christmas; Boxing Day, Dec. 26.

Getting Around

Central London traffic is horrendous from 8:30–10 AM, 5–6 PM, and 7–8 PM for "the burst" (cabbie talk for theater hour), so the Tube, despite delays, is usually the most reliable way to get around during these times.

By Car
Traveling by car can be a harrying experience for those not familiar with London's streets; along with the snarls of traffic and strict police enforcement of vehicle "clamping" for illegal parking, you also have to accustom yourself to driving on the "other" side of the road. An International Driver's License is not needed; most rental cars, however, are stick shift.

By Taxi
Licensed, metered black cabs can be hailed in the street when the "for hire" light is on, picked up at a rank, or ordered by phone (*see* Important Addresses and Numbers, above). Drivers have passed an exam and should know ev-

ery tiny mews and the fastest route there. Minicab drivers, who are unlicensed, may not be familiar with some districts of the city, but they offer a cheaper ride and will quote a rate beforehand if asked. Minicabs can't be hailed in the street (you couldn't recognize one anyway, since they are ordinary cars); but must be ordered by phone. There are countless minicab firms in London, most of which are perfectly reliable. Offices tend to have their own account with a local firm.

By Public Transportation
London is divided into six "fare zones" for bus and Tube travel, with rates varying according to length of journey. A daily, weekly, or monthly "Travel card," available from newsagent's shops or Tube stations, is valid for both Tubes and buses and is a good buy if you make more than one round-trip journey a day. Bus routes are often circuitous and best left alone if you're in a hurry.

Protocol

British customs barely differ from those in the United States or Canada. If in doubt, err on the side of formality. It's advisable to use surnames until invited to do otherwise. Business cards are generally exchanged at the end of a meeting.

Appointments
Business lunches are still all the rage, often running well into teatime. Tea has not yet been appropriated as a business meal. Breakfast meetings are possibly a little avant-garde for the stuffier professions, but are increasing in popularity nevertheless. Punctuality is now, and always has been, important to the British.

Dress
Men should wear jackets and ties to meetings—just as they do in North America. Women's power dressing is not quite such a cult here, but the British probably expect it of you, so wear a suit if in doubt.

LODGING

There is no such thing as "the business center" of London. Certainly, most meetings still take place around the West End (midtown), which has the highest concentration of office space, but the City, the square mile that is London's financial and banking center, is surprisingly far to the east, and many businesses are finding Hammersmith, to the west, a convenient site for their new offices. If you're attending a convention or trade show, you may have to spend a lot of time in the Barbican Centre (City), Earls Court (west), or even Alexandra Palace (quite far north) convention centers. The following guide includes hotels in all these areas, with preference given to the West End. But before you make reservations, it's best to study both a city and (if you don't want to be dependent on cabs) an Underground map, so you can determine whether your hotel is easily accessible to the places you'll want most to be near.

Most of the hotels here offer special corporate rates and weekend discounts; inquire when making reservations.

Highly recommended lodgings in all price categories are indicated by a star ★.

Category	Cost*
$$$$ (Very Expensive)	over £125
$$$ (Expensive)	£90–£125
$$ (Moderate)	under £90

All prices are for a standard double room, single occupancy, including 15% value added tax.

Numbers in the margin correspond to numbered hotel locations on the London Lodging and Dining maps.

West End (Mayfair, St. James's, Soho, and Westminster)

③① Athenaeum Hotel. This friendly film-biz favorite attracts *$$$$* many businesspeople (38% of them American). The somewhat dated lobby decor is a peculiar mixture of early-'70s marbleite and polished brass, and traditional leather wing chairs and carriage lamps. Still, it's airy and unfussy, as are the good-size rooms which, with their custom-made yew-wood furniture and pale-yet-butch color schemes, will please those who dislike frills. Suites are simply double the room size; the Carlton type with divider, the Burlington style open plan. Irish linen sheets, Italian-marble bathrooms with power showers, and joggers' suits (ask) and map are standard. The pink English restaurant is popular with adfolk for lunch, and the clubby bar is famous for 56 types of malt whiskey. Rooms 201, 202, and 204, and suites 203 and 205 face Green Park; others look down on Down Street. *A Rank hotel. 116 Piccadilly, W1V 0BJ, tel. 071/499–3464, fax 071/493–1860. Gen. manager, N. Rettie. 90 rooms, 22 suites. AE, CB, DC, MC, V.*

③① Athenaeum Apartments. Adjacent to the Athenaeum Ho- *$$$$* tel, and sharing its facilities and reception, these private, antiques-filled town-house apartments are frequently let for long periods to The Rich and Famous. Units are self-contained right down to ironing boards and coffeemakers. Each apartment has recently undergone a $65,000 face lift. Access to all the hotel's facilities is available and there are two telephone lines in every apartment. *See Atheneum above. 33 apartments. Reduced rates for long-term stays.*

④⓪ Brown's. You slip back a century in the parlorlike lobby *$$$$* with its oak and antiques, frock-coated staff, and the tinkle of teacups from the lounge. Indeed, Queen Victoria used to visit—she probably got lost, too, in the corridors and crannies. Kipling and Agatha Christie wrote at Brown's desks, and Alexander Graham Bell made the first U.K. phone call here. All this history has made Brown's popular with American Anglophiles, including both Roosevelts. Rooms are well maintained, in country-house style with swagged floral curtains and moiré walls. Singles are small, as are the functional tiled bathrooms; rooms at the back of either building are ultra-quiet. The oak-paneled restaurant, L'Aperitif, serves good British grub to chartered surveyors and art dealers, and the George bar lubricates them after work. *A Trusthouse Forte hotel. 34 Albemarle St., W1A 4SW, tel. 071/493–6020 or 800/223–*

5672, fax 071/493–9381. Gen. manager, Bruce Banister. 120 rooms, 13 suites. AE, CB, DC, MC, V.

⑳ **Bryanston Court.** The very central location, reasonable
$$ rates, and well-maintained public rooms of these three connected Georgian town houses are balanced against tiny, rather shabby bedrooms. The lounge and adjoining bar and restaurant are what you would expect in a home of a respectable Edwardian uncle, with a leather chesterfield in the lounge and wing chairs dotted about; all would do fine for a casual meeting—better perhaps than the bleak vinyl-and-formica conference room. Rooms have creaky floors, sinks, and pink walls. Bathrooms are closet sized and mostly bathless. The east-facing rooms at the back are quieter and brighter—111 and 212 are more spacious. The prize for the biggest room goes to 77, on the lower ground floor; it's short on daylight, but it's practically a suite. Roughly half the clientele is American, many of them on business. In short, not a bad place if you're on a budget. *56–60 Great Cumberland Pl., W1H 8DD, tel. 071/ 262–3141 or 800/528–1234, fax 071/262–7248. Gen. manager, M. S. Theodore. 54 rooms. AE, CB, DC, MC, V.*

★ ㉜ **Claridges.** Queen Elizabeth hasn't asked you this time?
$$$$ Never mind, you can stay at Claridges. This discreet, palatial home-from-home for European royalty, bankers, fashion moguls, diplomats, and American presidents quietly secreted behind Bond Street can hardly be faulted. Glide over the marble floors, beneath the chandeliers and grand arches of the Entrance Hall, to order champagne or tea from the liveried footmen in The Foyer lounge (*see* After Hours, below), then sweep up the staircase to a room (or "apartment" as they're known here) decorated by big-name designer David Laws, who does 10 Downing Street, for one. All rooms are different, but reflect one of two styles: authentic Art Deco in the 1932 extension, and traditional English country house elsewhere (the latter includes such follies as Suite 416/7—a Scottish castle). Some singles are smallish, but doubles and suites are enormous. All bathrooms are generous, with windows, 10-inch shower heads, and bells to summon "maid" or "valet," who arrive in a blink because each floor has its own service area. Ask for an outside room if you want a view. Extras include Richard Dalton, Princess Di's hairdresser and two French restaurants—Claridges, highly recommended for important dinners, and the Causerie, intimate and pink and fine for lunch. *A Savoy Group hotel. Brook St., W1A 2JQ, tel. 071/629–8860 or 800/223–6800, fax 071/499–2210. Gen. manager, Ronald Jones, O.B.E. 137 rooms, 53 suites. AE, CB, DC, MC, V.*

㉚ **The Connaught.** Guests here might include several gene-
$$$$ rations of Old English families and the very top banana of one or two multinational corporations—the kind of guest who wouldn't dream of staying anywhere else. Emphatically not a business hotel, the Connaught can nevertheless provide anything at any hour—as any five-star joint should. The desk's too small? Ask for another. The 1897 town house is unsullied by anything modern—except for power showers and hairdryers—and is grand and faded, with quantities of oils and antiques, in a way designers envy but can't duplicate. The staff consists of old retainers who frown upon meetings of any sort but social—this is where you relax after the sordid business is done. Stun-

WEST CENTRAL LONDON

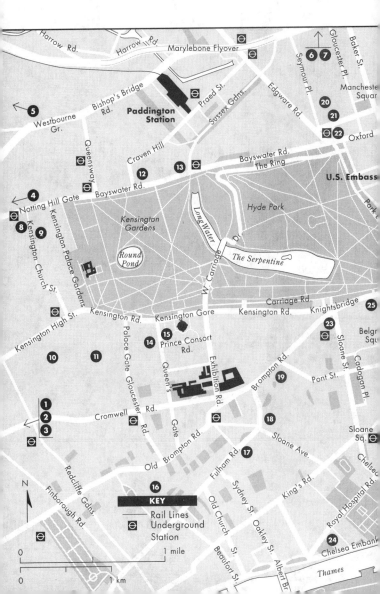

WEST END AND EAST CENTRAL LONDON

LONDON HOTEL CHART

HOTELS	Price Category	Banquet capacity	No. of meeting rooms	Fax	Telex	Photocopying	Secretarial services	Audiovisual equipment	Translation services	International direct dial	Computer rentals	In-room modem phone jack
Athenaeum Apartments & Hotel	$$$$	110	3	✓	✓	✓	✓	✓	-	✓	-	✓
Basil Street	$$	160	3	✓	✓	✓	✓	✓	✓	✓	-	-
The Berkeley	$$$$	280	4	✓	✓	✓	✓	✓	✓	✓	-	✓
Blakes	$$$$	0	0	✓	✓	✓	✓	-	-	✓	-	-
Browns	$$$$	120	7	✓	✓	✓	✓	✓	✓	✓	-	-
Bryanston Court	$$	0	1	✓	✓	✓	-	-	-	✓	-	-
Claridges	$$$$	216	4	✓	✓	✓	✓	✓	✓	✓	-	-
The Connaught	$$$$	22	0	✓	-	✓	-	-	-	✓	-	✓
Cumberland	$$$	1000	7	✓	✓	✓	✓	✓	✓	✓	✓	-
Dolphin Square Apartments	$$	0	3	✓	✓	✓	✓	✓	✓	✓	-	-
The Dorchester	$$$$	550	5	✓	✓	✓	✓	✓	✓	✓	✓	✓
Edward Lear	$$	0	0	✓	-	-	-	-	-	✓	-	-
The Edwardian International	$$$$	600	11	✓	✓	✓	✓	✓	✓	✓	-	-
Flemings	$$$	25	3	✓	✓	✓	-	✓	-	✓	-	-
Gatwick Hilton International	$$$	500	21	✓	✓	✓	✓	✓	✓	✓	✓	-
Gatwick Penta	$$$	180	12	✓	✓	✓	-	✓	-	✓	-	✓
The Gore	$$	0	0	✓	✓	✓	✓	-	-	✓	-	-
The Grafton	$$$	100	9	✓	✓	✓	✓	✓	✓	✓	-	-
Grosvenor House	$$$$	1500	26	✓	✓	✓	✓	✓	✓	✓	✓	✓

$$$$** = over £125, **$$$** =£90 -£125, **$$ = under £90.
● good, ◑ fair, ○ poor.
All hotels listed here have photocopying and fax facilities.

All-news cable channel	Desk	Desk lighting	Bed lighting	Nonsmoking rooms	In-room checkout	Minibar	Toiletries	Room service	Laundry/Dry cleaning	Pressing	Barber/Hairdresser	Garage	Courtesy airport transport	Sauna	Pool	Exercise room
✓	●	●	●	✓	✓	✓	●	●	◑	●	✓	-	-	-	-	-
-	●	●	●	-	-	-	◑	●	◑	○	-	-	-	-	-	-
✓	●	●	●	-	✓	-	●	●	●	●	✓	✓	-	✓	●	◑
✓	-	-	●	-	-	✓	○	●	●	●	-	-	-	-	-	-
✓	◑	◑	●	-	-	✓	●	●	●	◑	✓	-	-	-	-	-
✓	-	-	●	-	-	-	○	◑	◑	○	-	-	-	-	-	-
✓	●	●	●	-	-	-	●	●	●	●	✓	-	-	-	-	-
✓	●	●	●	-	-	-	◑	●	●	●	-	✓	-	-	-	-
✓	●	●	●	✓	✓	✓	○	●	●	◑	-	-	-	-	-	○
-	-	-	●	-	-	-	-	◑	-	-	✓	✓	✓	✓	●	-
✓	●	-	●	✓	-	✓	●	●	●	●	✓	✓	-	-	-	◑
-	-	-	●	-	-	-	●	●	●	●	-	-	-	-	-	-
✓	◑	◑	●	✓	✓	✓	●	●	●	●	✓	✓	✓	✓	◑	◑
-	◑	●	●	-	-	-	●	●	◑	○	-	-	-	-	-	-
✓	◑	●	●	✓	✓	✓	●	●	◑	●	✓	-	-	✓	●	●
✓	◑	●	●	✓	✓	-	◑	●	◑	○	-	-	✓	✓	◑	◑
✓	-	-	●	-	-	✓	-	●	◑	●	-	-	-	-	-	-
-	◑	◑	●	✓	-	-	●	◑	●	●	-	-	✓	-	-	-
✓	●	●	●	✓	✓	✓	●	●	●	●	✓	✓	-	✓	●	●

Room service: ● 24-hour, ◑ 6AM–10PM, ○ other.
Laundry/Dry cleaning: ● same day, ◑ overnight, ○ other.
Pressing: ● immediate, ◑ same day, ○ other.

LONDON HOTEL CHART

HOTELS	Price Category	Business Services										
		Banquet capacity	No. of meeting rooms	Fax	Telex	Photocopying	Secretarial services	Audiovisual equipment	Translation services	International direct dial	Computer rentals	In-room modem phonejack
Hazlitts	$$	0	0	✓	-	✓	-	-	-	✓	-	-
Hilton International Kensington	$$$	200	8	✓	✓	✓	✓	✓	✓	✓	-	-
Kensington Close	$$$	220	8	✓	✓	✓	-	✓	-	✓	-	-
London Hilton on Park Lane	$$$$	1000	15	✓	✓	✓	-	-	-	-	-	-
Le Meridien	$$$$	200	5	✓	✓	✓	✓	✓	✓	✓	-	-
New Barbican	$$	200	11	✓	✓	✓	✓	✓	-	✓	-	-
Plaza on Hyde Park	$$	0	11	✓	✓	✓	✓	✓	✓	✓	-	-
Post House, Heathrow	$$$	200	30	✓	✓	✓	✓	✓	✓	✓	-	-
The Ritz	$$$$	60	3	✓	✓	✓	✓	-	-	✓	-	-
St. James Court	$$$$	150	14	✓	✓	✓	✓	✓	✓	-	-	-
Savoy	$$$$	500	11	✓	✓	✓	✓	✓	✓	✓	-	-
Sheraton Skyline, Heathrow	$$$$	500	6	✓	✓	✓	-	✓	✓	✓	-	-
The Washington	$$$$	80	2	✓	✓	✓	-	✓	-	✓	-	-
White's	$$$$	20	2	✓	✓	✓	✓	✓	-	✓	-	✓

$$$$** = over £125, **$$$** = £90 -£125, **$$ = under £90.
● good, ◐ fair, ○ poor.

All-news cable channel	Desk	Desk lighting	Bed lighting	**In-Room Amenities** Nonsmoking rooms	In-room checkout	Minibar	Toiletries	Room service	Laundry/Dry cleaning	Pressing	**Hotel Amenities** Barber/Hairdresser	Garage	Courtesy airport transport	Sauna	Pool	Exercise room
–	–	–	●	–	–	–	–	○	◐	◐	–	–	–	–	–	–
✓	●	●	●	✓	✓	✓	○	●	◐	◐	✓	✓	–	–	–	–
✓	◐	●	◐	✓	✓	–	○	○	◐	○	–	✓	–	✓	●	◐
✓	●	●	●	✓	✓	✓	●	●	◐	◐	✓	–	✓	✓	–	●
–	◐	◐	◐	✓	–	–	○	–	◐	◐	–	–	–	–	–	–
–	–	–	◐	✓	✓	–	○	●	◐	◐	–	–	–	–	–	–
✓	◐	●	◐	✓	–	–	◐	●	◐	◐	–	✓	✓	✓	–	○
✓	●	●	●	–	✓	✓	●	●	◐	◐	✓	–	–	–	–	–
✓	◐	●	●	✓	–	✓	◐	●	◐	◐	–	–	–	–	–	◐
✓	●	●	●	✓	✓	–	●	●	◐	◐	✓	–	–	–	–	–
✓	◐	–	–	✓	–	–	●	○	◐	◐	✓	✓	✓	✓	●	–
✓	●	●	●	✓	–	✓	●	◐	◐ overnight	◐	–	–	–	–	–	–
✓	●	◐	●	✓	–	✓	●	●	◐	●	✓	✓	–	–	–	–

Room service: ● 24-hour, ◐ 6AM-10PM, ○ other.
Laundry/Dry cleaning: ● same day, ◐ overnight, ○ other.
Pressing: ● immediate, ◐ same day, ○ other.

ning Private Rooms therefore are for banqueting only. Even guests book ahead for the power lunch venue, The Connaught Grill Room and Restaurant (*see* Dining, below). This is the most understated of any of London's grand hotels. *A Savoy Group hotel. Carlos Pl., W1Y 6AL, tel. 071/499–7070 or 800/223–6800, fax 071/495–3262. Gen. manager, Paolo Zago. 90 rooms, 24 suites. MC.*

㉗ Cumberland. This is corporate thinking incarnate, and no
$$$ bad thing if you're after facilities. Some hate piped foyer music, bartenders trained to "react with clients," and restaurants that scream "catering facility." Others need the big bustling lobby, with black leather seats, red-lacquer pillars, and marble-and-chrome detailing; the Business Centre; and the proximity to the City via Marble Arch Tube (literally underfoot). Built in 1933, the hotel has bedrooms of a uniformly medium size and try for the gentleman's-club image in maroon and cream with dark-wood furniture. A recent $16-million face lift means no worries about deterioration, but only front rooms boast views of Park Lane. Executive rooms come with usual extras: trouser press, newspapers. Downstairs are shops, bars, restaurants, and a full range of conference and function facilities. *A Trusthouse Forte hotel. Marble Arch, W1A 4RF, tel. 071/262–1234 or 800/223–5672, fax 071/724–4621. Gen. manager, Mark Elawadi. 886 rooms, 4 suites. AE, CB, DC, MC, V.*

㊷ Dolphin Square Apartments. A unique 1930s-vintage
$$ building houses MPs and titled people on three sides, and guests on the fourth. Gardens, a large pool, squash and tennis courts, a health club, shops, conference rooms, bars, and restaurants make this great for independent types. Okay, so Pimlico isn't central London, but it's accessible—five minutes in a cab to Westminster; the same on foot to the Tube. The apartments are not an interior designer's dream, but they're comfortable. Sixth- (top) floor rooms are "masculine"—done in pin stripes and spartan maroon furnishings. The fifth floor is all pink-and-gray Laura Ashley. Fourth-floor rooms have the best and newest decor, with blue-and-cream Regency stripes and chintz. Until they're refurbished, avoid rooms on floors 1–3 unless you like 1960s-kitsch gold velour and brown vinyl. The dining table, or coffee table in studios, will have to suffice for a desk. There's daily maid and room service, but laundry must be delivered and picked up. Public areas are chic—especially the brasserie and restaurant, where the eccentric jazz singer, George Melly, always seems to be playing. An excellent value. *Dolphin Sq., SW1V 3LX, tel. 071/834–9134 or 617/350–7500 (Boston), fax 071/798–8735. Gen. manager, Jan Devon. 152 apartments. AE, CB, DC, MC, V.*

㉘ The Dorchester. Reopened in 1990 after a refurbishment,
$$$$ the grand old lady of Park Lane has played host to just about everyone famous—from Hollywood stars to royalty. Its profile is higher than that of other five-stars like Claridges or The Connaught, largely due to its magnificent banquet rooms and ballroom, which are perceptibly glitzier than those of its neighbor, Grosvenor House. Decor throughout is in opulent English country house–style, with more than a hint of Art Deco, in keeping with the original 1930s building. Improvements include computerized climate control, double glazing, and remodeled mar-

ble bathrooms. Altogether, the Dorchester has updated itself, with a business center, a health club (no pool), a night club, and an Oriental restaurant added to the facilities you take for granted in a hotel of this caliber. The very British Dorchester Grill has long been a favorite for business entertaining. *Park La., W1A 2HJ, tel. 071/629–8888 or 800/448–8355, fax 071/409–0144. Gen. manager, Ricci Obertelli. 197 rooms, 55 suites. AE, CB, DC, MC, V.*

㉑ **Edward Lear.** Named after the ex-resident author of *The*
$$ *Owl and the Pussycat*, this town-house hotel puts friendliness way ahead of luxury. The owner himself is likely to give you your key—along with a cup of tea and tips about London. Sadly, it's downhill from there, as rooms have a boarding-house atmosphere and few have private bathrooms. Still, accommodations are clean, with flower-sprigged wallpaper and new rust-colored carpets, tea- and coffee-making facilities, and adequate closet space. Triple and family rooms are worth getting for their size; back rooms have quaint views over rooftops; No. 14 is to be avoided—it's a closet. There's no room service and no lounge. Most guests are Americans, Canadians, and Australians, all of whom appreciate the low rates, central location, and huge English breakfasts. *28/30 Seymour St., W1H 5WD, tel. 071/402–5401, fax 071/706–3766. Gen. manager, Duncan McGlashan. 31 rooms. MC, V.*

㊳ **Flemings.** Five Georgian houses just behind Piccadilly are
$$$ done out in generic country-house style, with lots of gilded ebony, palms, and lacy curtains in the pink-marble foyer and lounge. Ubiquitous gilt-framed fake oils are wearing, but dark-veneer furniture and pink-sprigged everything else in bedrooms range from acceptable to very comfortable, depending on the room's size. The tiled, closet-sized bathrooms are undergoing transformation to something nicer in marble this year. A dark-wood paneled, air-conditioned restaurant and bar share the basement with three pastel-colored boardrooms. Ten apartments in two additional houses offer more space and extra amenities; these are a bargain alternative to the Athenaeum Apartments around the corner. *7–12 Half Moon St., W1Y 8BQ, tel. 071/499–2964 or 800/448–8355, fax 071/629–4063. Gen. manager, Neale Monks. 133 rooms, 10 apartments. AE, CB, DC, MC, V.*

㉗ **Grosvenor House.** The Grosvenor is famous for its function
$$$$ rooms (the largest hotel ballroom in Europe, once a skating rink, is here), and its suites and apartments—one of which is home to the Duchess of Argyll. It would like to be famous for its new state-of-the-art business center, next door at 86 Park Lane—18 rooms in American cherry, with knee-high carpets—but its best facility is the health club with a pool large enough for proper laps, and lots of Nautilus equipment in the large gym. Restraint is the word for the decor; bedrooms are taupe, cream, and mulberry, or the colors of Wedgwood china, serious as a dowager aunt. West-facing ones look panoramically over Hyde Park. Lower floors were most recently refurbished. Floor Five is the executive floor, with private lounge and boardroom. Sizes throughout are generous and there are good, tiled bathrooms, most with windows. Lounges are getting a complete makeover. There are three restaurants: Ninety Park Lane (*see* Dining, below), Pasta Vino e Fantasia and the Pavillion, which features a grand Sunday brunch—

fine for an informal meeting. *A Trusthouse Forte hotel. Park La., W1A 3AA, tel. 071/499–6363 or 800/223–5672, fax 071/499–3901. Gen. manager, Pier Vacher. 360 rooms, 70 suites, 160 apartments. AE, CB, DC, MC, V.*

★ ⓭ **Hazlitts.** This is the only hotel in Soho, and it genuinely
$$ feels like a home. The four directors have spent half their lives in country-house auctions collecting prints and etchings, Victorian planters and church pews, Afghan rugs and enough Victorian claw-foot baths for every bathroom. One of their fathers-in-law was a sculptor, and his figurative stone work appears spotlighted in corners and courtyards and bathrooms. Rooms in the three Georgian houses are named after former residents and visitors, and vary enormously. "Jonathan Swift" (yes, he stayed) and "Prussian Resident" are the biggest, and the one suite has a four-poster. Needless to say, all Hazlitts devotees (they're often media types) have their favorite rooms. This hotel is not luxurious, and there are no elevators, no business facilities, limited room service, and a tiny lounge; but Soho is very central, and the best restaurants are here. *6 Frith St., W1V 5TZ, tel. 071/434–1771, fax 071/439–1524. Gen. manager, Alison Jaggar. 23 rooms, 1 suite. AE, DC, MC, V.*

⓭ **London Hilton on Park Lane.** The main foyer is dominated
$$$$ by a vast rectangular bank of chandeliers above a stone balustrade. Around the corner it's '70s teak, smoky glass, and lumpy textile wallhangings, even though most of this flagship Hilton has been redone—from the 26th-floor Executive Lounge to the fourth-floor business center. The meeting rooms are next in line. Bedrooms now come in pink or green pastel with textured vinyl walls, dark-wood furniture, floral fabrics, and black-marble bathrooms. They also have distinctly nonuser-friendly "Roboserve" minibars and that great view (which nonguests can have too, from the top-floor Windows on the World restaurant/ bar [*see* After Hours, below]). Two theme eateries, the French-style Patisserie and *faux* tropical island Trader Vic's, are on the ground floor at the other end from the suites, which are homey—if home is the set of Dallas. The staff is not necessarily helpful or friendly. *22 Park La., W1A 2HH, tel. 071/493–8000 or 800/445–8697, fax 071/ 493–4957. Gen. manager, Jean Robert Loyer. 394 rooms, 54 suites. AE, CB, DC, MC, V.*

⓭ **Le Meridien.** Located above the plushest health club, and
$$$$ boasting one of the prettiest lunch venues (The Terrace Garden) and one of the few *Michelin* starred restaurants in London (The Oak Room), this young addition to Air France's hotel subsidiary has facilities-and-a-half. Although there's nothing wrong with the bedrooms, they are simply standard-issue half country house, half boardroom with pastel walls and reproduction-antique furniture of an upmarket hotel chain—not quite the luxury you might expect. Honey-marble bathrooms with power showers, generous *Lanvin* goodies, and heated towel rails are quite up to scratch though, and suites are more luxurious, especially the Piccadilly Suite with its four-poster bed. There are fine views toward Big Ben from the top front rooms. Champneys Health Club usually commands a membership fee just short of $2,000, but you get to use its Elysian pool, squash courts, Nautilus gym, simulated golf course, snooker tables, Turkish bath, etc., gratis. A busy

business center and 16-channel TV with Reuters keep you in touch. Apart from the Oak Room and Terrace Garden (*see* Business Breakfasts and Dining, below), there's the green-baize Burlington Bar (*see* After Hours, below), which would be fine for a quiet business tête-à-tête. Choose this one for the facilities and location rather than the bedrooms. *A Societé des Hôtels Meridien hotel. 21 Piccadilly, W1V OBH, tel. 071/734–8000 or 800/543–4300, fax 071/437–3574. Gen. manager, Raymond Andre. 254 rooms, 30 suites. AE, CB, DC, MC, V.*

㊹ **The Ritz.** Two surprises: This one is not now related to the
$$$$ Ritz in Paris or Madrid, and, despite its long frontage and its ritzy (no other word for it) grandeur, the Ritz is a fairly small hotel. It seems everything here is gilded, like its role model, Versailles; in fact, it out-palaces most palaces, which is why Queen Joan Collins of Soap will stay nowhere else. She chooses pink from the four room colors; whichever you pick, there'll be many Belle Epoque furbelows, nymphs-and-shepherds frescoes, and the like, and plenty of space. The bathrooms that were redone in brown tiles when Cunard bought the hotel in '76 and smashed the marble baths, are horrendous; redone ones are fine. Public rooms are Louis XVI pink and yellow and gilt, and there's a perfect little Italian Garden off the fabulous Ritz restaurant (*see* Dining, below). The Reuters printout in the lobby and efficient staff help business travelers; function rooms are more for high-profile Events than meetings. Palm Court tea is for tourists. *A Trafalgar House Group hotel. Piccadilly, W1V 9DG, tel. 071/493–8181 or 800/222–0939, fax 071/493–2687. Gen. manager, Terry Holmes. 116 rooms, 14 suites. AE, CB, DC, MC, V.*

㊸ **St. James Court.** Carriages used to pass through the great
$$$$ wrought-iron gates to this hotel's *pièce de résistance*—a restored Edwardian courtyard with fountain and ceramic frieze. Of more interest to the business guest, though, is one of the largest hotel business centers in the city. The health club has good equipment, but limited space and no pool. Throughout the hotel, decor is somewhat bland (the kinder word is masculine) in pale and muddy shades of salmon, buff, and blue. Furniture tends to be sparse and functional, relieved only by the odd painting (and some are very odd indeed). This appeals to tennis stars, apparently; it's the official Wimbledon hotel (actually, the Big Stars rent houses). Some standard rooms are wonderfully large—try asking for a "family room" and you might be lucky. Others are boxy, but overlook the courtyard. There are apartments available, too. The only Eastern influence in this Indian-owned hotel is the food at the Inn of Happiness Szechuan restaurant and the dim sum brunch in the bar, both popular with business lunchers. *A Taj International hotel. Buckingham Ga., SW1E 6AF, tel. 071/834–6655 or 800/458–8825, fax 071/630–7587. Gen. manager, Sam Bhadha. 371 rooms, 19 suites. AE, CB, DC, MC, V.*

㊲ **The Washington.** Built in 1989, this polished hotel is going
$$$$ down very well with businesspeople, although service has yet to be perfected. Gleaming marble and posh, tasseled armchairs in the small lobby lead to a big lounge featuring handwoven carpets and bird's-eye maple paneling. Large, stylish bedrooms in glamorously wide corridors have striking, Deco-ish burred oak furniture and smooth-as-glass carpets. Touch-sensitive light controls, individual

air-conditioning controls, and smart mottled marble-and-chrome bathrooms with power showers and heated towel racks and floors are evidence of attention to detail. In the basement, two connecting meeting rooms are lighted by "daylight" halogen panels. The Madison restaurant has the latest thing for jaded palates—a New Zealand chef. There's free access to the well-equipped Aquilla Health Club; the catch is that it's miles away in South Kensington. *A Sarova hotel. Curzon St., W1Y 8DT, tel. 071/499–7000 or 800/424–2862, fax 071/495–6172. Gen. manager, Virginia Barlow. 173 rooms, 22 suites. AE, CB, DC, MC, V.*

East Central (Bloomsbury, Covent Garden, and The City)

㉟ The Grafton. The lobby doesn't quite achieve the Edwardian ambience it's attempting (the oils are fake), but dark wood, rich blue-and-red carpet, chandelier, and piped Mozart suffice. A major refurbishment, completed in spring 1991, upgraded (not up-priced) 170 rooms and put a new, postmodern Executive Wing in place. Red, from rose to magenta, is the theme color, darker in deluxe bedrooms where chintz is richer and wood is mahogany, paler in standards where you make do with pine and pastel. More red in the Windsor Bar and Lounge is set off by dragged peach pillars, healthy palms, and lots of air freshener. It's relaxing here (for lone women, too) and in total contrast to the basement wine bar, which has bare-wood floors, low prices, and loud music. Piano accompanies Franglais cuisine in the smart, traditional Cliveden. A word to country & western fans: Performers at the London C & W festival (around Easter) stay here. There's a Tube next door (City in 15 minutes) for a quick escape from one of the ugliest streets in central London. *An Edwardian hotel. 130 Tottenham Court Rd., W1P 9HP, tel. 071/387–2555 or 800/447–7011, fax 071/387–7059. Gen. manager, David Tilly. 236 rooms, 5 suites. AE, CB, DC, MC, V.*
$$$

㊾ New Barbican. Just about the only hotel in the City (except for the Great Eastern, tel. 071/283–4363), this functional pit stop is two buildings—a converted warehouse and a 1973 low rise. Open public areas are reminiscent of an airport lounge, with faded ivy-trellis carpet, pink unit seating, melamine tables, and softboard tiles on low ceilings. Boxy bedrooms—in depressing shades of beige, brown, and taupe with lots of pine pretending to be elm—are curiously small, given the generous width of the brightly lighted corridors. The lack of room service could be a problem in this desolate area, and the plasticky restaurant is closed from 10:30 AM to midday, then again at midnight. The nearest bus or Tube is 10 minutes' walk—the same distance as the Barbican Centre. A courtesy bus takes business travelers to the Tube. A trouser press in every room and a parquet-floored, publike bar are new additions. *A Mount Charlotte hotel. Central St., EC1V 8DS, tel. 071/251–1565 or 800/448–8355, fax 071/253–1005. Gen. manager, Ronald Kingston. 468 rooms, 2 suites. AE, CB, DC, MC, V.*
$$

★ ㊽ Savoy. The well-loved, high-profile Savoy plays host to stars and maestri, the titled, the rich, and the powerful. It is grand, but it's comfortably so, with Victorian and Deco public rooms leading down to the Savoy Restaurant and its
$$$$

river views. Rooms are spacious, gracious, and pale, with lots of white plaster moldings and deep carpets. Expect the famous hand-built Savoy beds, linen sheets, huge mirrors, giant shower heads in the bathrooms, and—if you've booked well ahead and are willing to pay extra—the best river views in London. Regulars chat with staff like old friends (fifth-floor valets are known for their sure-fire racing tips). Hold casual meetings in the (always fashionable) American bar, formal ones in the supremely elegant function and boardrooms. The City is 10 minutes away by cab. Though it isn't really business oriented, the Savoy recently was voted one of the world's top 10 business hotels by U.S. travelers. The hotel's colorful and theatrical history is legendary. This is the place where things happen—from top-level deals (Savoy Restaurant, Grill Room, American Bar, and Thames Foyer—*see* Business Breakfasts, Dining, and After Hours, below) to top peoples' parties. Booking now for New Year's 1999. *The Strand, WC2R 0EU, tel. 071/836–4343 or 800/223–6800, fax 071/240–6040. Gen. manager, Herbert Striessnig. 152 rooms, 48 suites. AE, CB, DC, MC, V.*

West Central (Kensington, Knightsbridge)

★ ❷ **Basil Street Hotel.** Owned since 1919 by the same family,
$$ the Basil is dependable and homey and rather eccentric. Welcoming lounges and acres of corridor are full of Oriental carpets, mahogany desks, plump armchairs, and the buzz of conversation. Bedrooms are all completely different; designer chic they're not, but they're as cozy as grandma's country cottage, all antiques and counterpanes. Some lower-priced rooms lack bathrooms. In keeping with the spirit of the place, meeting rooms are informal, looking like somebody's living room crossed with a schoolroom. Guests return again and again, about 65% of them American. Women traveling alone feel particularly comfortable; they have use of the daytime Parrot Club to meet and relax. *Knightsbridge, SW3 1AH, tel. 071/581–3311, fax 071/581–3693. Gen. manager, Steven Korany. 100 rooms, 2 suites. AE, CB, DC, MC, V.*

❷ **The Berkeley.** Rooms are like the apartments of rich and
$$$$ serious British friends. A marble hall with paneled ceiling, an elegant lounge, and abundant antiques belie the building's youth (1972), as do individually decorated bedrooms, featuring mahogany furniture, swathes of curtain, and small armchairs. Many fixtures and fittings—and an entire Lutyens room—were moved wholesale from the original Berkeley, which accounts for the period feel. A unique and spectacular rooftop swimming pool and health club make the Berkeley stand out from the other grand hotels. Three of the suites have conservatories and roof gardens—and in one case, a private sauna. The glittery ballroom has 20 chandeliers and a mirrored ceiling. The triple-tiered Perroquet Bar (*see* After Hours, below) is quiet in the day—fine for a meeting—and has an after-hours liquor license, while the formal French restaurant is impressive enough for lunching or dining clients. *A Savoy Group hotel. Wilton Pl., SW1X 7RL, tel. 071/235–6000 or 800/223–6800, fax 071/235–4330. Gen. manager, Stefano Sebastiani. 133 rooms, 27 suites. AE, CB, DC, MC, V.*

❶ **Blakes.** Utterly unlike anywhere else because owner, cou-
$$$$ turiere, and glitterata Anouska Hempel (aka Lady

Weinberg) hasn't designed anywhere else, this place attracts people who can afford to do what they like while wearing what they like (*haute couture* or shorts) in the most glamorous setting. All is lighted like a Hollywood film and crammed with Murano glass, Biedermeier pieces, chinoiserie, and handmade inlaid wood, extravagant oils and sepia prints, brocades and silks and velvets. Colors are dramatic dark gray, black, and parchment, or lacquered vermillion. For fantasy fiends, a few rooms really take the biscuit: 109 is like a 19-century seraglio; 007 (yes 007) is a pink-moiré apartment, rented by film actors of godlike fame. Other guests are rock stars, big in fashion, or the more unconventional breed of tycoon. They all take taxis because Blakes is rather secluded. Fittingly for this international set, the foyer is like Phileas Fogg's parlor, with antique luggage, a huge tropical parasol, and a noisy budgie. There's an amazingly stylish restaurant, too (*see* Business Breakfasts, below). Many of the rooms are small, but who cares? *33 Roland Gdns., SW7 3PF, tel. 071/370–6701, fax 071/373–0442. Gen. manager, Robert Wauters. 44 rooms, 8 suites. AE, DC, MC, V.*

★ ⑮ **The Gore.** As antiques-bedecked and friendly as its Soho
$$ sister, this beautiful brace of town houses has been in the capable hands of the Hazlitts's crew since 1990. First thing they did was hang 2,600 prints on the buttermilk-and rose-colored walls, and install a brasserie restaurant—useful in this grand, residential area. If you need a desk, say so, as rooms vary greatly. All have hairdryers, antiques, prints, and big South Kensington windows; many have funny little corridors, alcoves, and niches. Some are sheer fantasy—101 is mock Tudor with beams, fireplace, minstrel gallery, stained glass, and Jacobean four-poster (which is often taken out to turn this into a boardroom); 211 has lots of brocades and carved and gilded things, starring the bed Judy Garland brought with her from a film set and left here. An elegant, racing-green lounge with comfy Liberty-print sofas is the only public room, okay for meetings. Like Hazlitts, the Gore looks far more expensive than it is. Pure joy—but as far from a corporate hotel as you can get. *189 Queen's Ga., SW7 5EX, tel. 071/584–6601 or 800/528–1234, fax 071/589–8127. Gen. manager, Jeannie Duncan. 54 rooms. AE, DC, MC, V.*

④ **Hilton International Kensington.** This '70s relic is amaz-
$$$ ingly popular with convention groups (about 55% American), being convenient to Olympia and Earls Court convention centers, and to the growth districts of Hammersmith and White City. By now, the lobby has received an overdue face lift, but the Musak, pink leatherette seats, peculiar blue art, and multilingual babble in the 24-hour bar survive intact. Other improvements are a business center; an executive floor, whose rooms feature small, glassed-in terraces; and a new card lock system. A good-value Japanese restaurant, Hiroko, caters to the high volume of guests from you-know-where. Bedrooms—doubles are acceptable size—have mulberry carpets, burlap-effect walls, small bathrooms, and, frequently, views of other bedrooms, owing to the building's "E" shape. Hilton is spending $8 million to bring the place up half a grade. Newly decorated rooms are marginally preferable due to the improved facilities, but nothing here is exactly

luxurious. *179–199 Holland Park Ave., W11 4UL, tel. 071/ 603–3355 or 800/445–8697, fax 071/602–9397. Gen. manager, Alfred Schoenemann. 592 rooms, 14 suites. AE, CB, DC, MC, V.*

⑩ Kensington Close. Nearer than the Hilton to the exhibition halls and convention centers mentioned above, this three-star has a few features you wouldn't expect from its utilitarian appearance. Best are the health club with pool and squash courts, and a peaceful and secluded terrace called the Water Garden. Perhaps this explains why some very high-ups choose this hotel over the more swanky places. Green-carpeted bedrooms are only just big enough for fitted dark-stained furniture. Superior rooms have trouser presses, hairdryers, better chairs and desks, and some are bigger; Executive Rooms are two knocked into one. Conference rooms are functional boxes, which is better than cheap Edwardian England—style as in so many middle-range hotels. The big blue bar has a nice garden view, but little character. *A Trusthouse Forte hotel. Wrights La., W8 5SP, tel. 071/937–8170 or 800/225–5843, fax 071/937–8289. Gen. manager, Patrick Dempsey. 532 rooms. AE, CB, DC, MC, V.*

$$$

⑬ Plaza on Hyde Park. The Plaza is that rare thing—a modestly priced, central hotel that doesn't feel like a bargain basement. The young, cheery staff and marble-floored lobby are a bright start, though you have to go through a pink neon portico to the bar to find somewhere to sit down. Bedrooms, of the typical pastel colors and marbled wallpaper mold, are too petite for desks (the small coffee table might suffice), but they're cozy enough, and corner ones boast three windows apiece. Bathtubs barely fit into the clinical, tiled bathrooms. Down in Café on the Park, there are rattan chairs, a conservatory, and a pianist not averse to guest participation. For more formal business, there are brand-new meeting rooms. Middle management is keen on the Plaza; accompanying top brass might stay in one of the new executive rooms or mini suites (all the usual trimmings), or a few steps away at White's (*see* below). *A Hilton National hotel. Lancaster Ga., W2 3NA, tel. 071/ 262–5022 or 800/HILTONS, fax 071/724–8666. Gen. manager, Kazim Gurses. 393 rooms, 9 suites. AE, DC, MC, V.*

$$

⑫ White's. Deep carpets, gilt-framed oils and mirrors, feather-cushioned armchairs, and sunny colors make White's hushed, comfortable, and opulent. Spacious bedrooms are like Marie Antoinette's "rustic" cottages with limed-oak furniture, blue-crystal wall lights, and Louis XV–style sofa and chairs. Marble bathrooms have gold-plated fittings and toiletries in little glass *flacons*. Downstairs there's a Victorian gentlemen's bar, and an oak-paneled reading room with cool-mint walls (ideal for a quiet meeting). First-and second-floor front rooms, with lofty ceilings and private balconies facing Hyde Park, are bigger than the two suites. The hotel's restaurant (*see* Business Breakfasts, below) is a quiet spot for a meeting over breakfast. This is the secret refuge of British company directors, who like the slightly off-central location (five minutes' walk to Marble Arch), the solicitous service, and the attention to detail. *A Mount Charlotte Luxury hotel. Lancaster Ga., W2 3NR, tel. 071/262–2711 or 800/448–8355, fax 071/262–2147. Gen. manager, Michael Wills. 52 rooms, 2 suites. AE, CB, DC, MC, V.*

$$$$

Near Heathrow

❶ **The Edwardian International, Heathrow.** A $32-million
$$$$ face lift for this 1959 building means there is every facility
on hand, including a health club with pool, a business center with "video conferencing" (meetings relayed to bedroom TVs), and a ballroom for 500. Bedrooms, as the name
suggests, are Edwardian-style country-house chintz,
with triple glazing, climate control, and—probably
unique in Britain—a personal telephone answering machine. Bathrooms are marble, carpets are handmade,
some beds are four-poster. There's a courtesy coach to all
terminals. The newest and smartest of the airport hotels.
*Bath Rd., Hayes, Middlesex UB3 5AW, tel. 081/759–6311
or 800/447–7011, fax 081/759–4559. Gen. manager, Roman Tobisch. 450 rooms, 17 suites. AE, CB, DC, MC, V.*

❷ **Post House, Heathrow.** Thanks to its location alongside the
$$$ M4 just before the airport, this ugly T-shaped block is
quite a landmark—the first English building many visi-
tors see. Facilities are standard airport-hotel issue, with
soundproofing and climate control in the rather boxy and
drab rooms, conference suites for up to 200, and courtesy
coach to the terminals, but little effort has been made to
elevate the hotel from just an overnight pitstop. Floors
two and three contain executive rooms, with clubby, beige
furnishings; separate check-in; and a small, ill-equipped
gymnasium. *Sipson Rd., West Drayton, Middlesex UB7
0JU, tel. 081/759–2323 or 800/225–5843, fax 081/897–
8659. Gen. manager, Martin Grey. 600 rooms. AE,
MC, V.*

❸ **Sheraton Skyline, Heathrow.** This one tries to make you
$$$$ believe you haven't left the States. Arranged around an
indoor "tropical garden," with bar, pool, palm trees, and
bamboo sunshades, are various shops, sauna, and solari-
um, and a "wild West–style" restaurant with evening cab-
aret. Expect the usual courtesy bus to the terminals,
soundproofed, air-conditioned bedrooms, and conference
facilities for up to 600. Less-standard facilities are a free
bus into central London and 24-hour room service. *Bath
Rd., Hayes, Middlesex UB3 5BP, tel. 081/759–2535 or
800/325–3535, fax 081/750–9150. Gen. manager, Thomas
Hegarty. 355 rooms, 5 suites. AE, CB, DC, MC, V.*

Gatwick

❻❶ **Gatwick Hilton International.** This hotel is actually inside
$$$ the airport, with a covered walkway to the South Termi-
nal and airport transit to the North. The four-star Hilton's
facilities are excellent: There's a pool, hot tub, sauna,
steam room and supervised gym, conference suites for up
to 450, 24-hour room service, as well as the essential climate control and soundproofing. All airport hotels seem to
have beige bedrooms, and this is no exception. They're adequate, if small (the 15 executive rooms are more spacious)
but boast flight information on the TV, meaning you can
leave it till the last minute to check in for your flight at the
desk in the hotel's four-story atrium lobby. *Gatwick Airport, West Sussex RH6 0LL, tel. 0293/518080 or 800/445–
8697, fax 0293/28980. Gen. manager, Richard Thomason.
547 rooms, 5 suites. AE, DC, MC, V.*

❻❷ **Gatwick Penta.** Another four-star with more beige,
$$$ soundproofed, air-conditioned bedrooms, but these are

recently refurbished. Again, there's a courtesy coach to
the airport and conference facilities for up to 150. Leisure
facilities here are as good as the Hilton's, with sauna, solarium, hot tub, pool, supervised gym, and four squash
courts, too. So what differentiates it from other airport
hotels? Nothing, really. *Povey Cross Rd., Horley, Surrey
RH6 0BE, tel. 0293/820169 or 800/225–3456 (New York);
800/238–9877 (Los Angeles); fax 0293/820259. Gen. manager, Norbert Hummel, 260 rooms. AE, CB, DC, MC, V.*

DINING

Now that the days of meat and two soggy vegetables are
long gone, British cuisine is not necessarily a contradic-
tion in terms. Indeed, many of the national dishes—
bangers (sausage) and mash, bubble and squeak (potato and cabbage) have been enthusiastically reappropriat-
ed by the smartest chefs. Thailand has replaced Japan
as trendiest food nation, though Indian restaurants still
outnumber any other ethnic kind. Tapas—the Spanish
appetizers—are ubiquitous barroom accessories and the
latest fad in smart, new restaurants is regional Italian
food (invariably featuring roasted red peppers). The star
chefs now are mainly in Soho and in parts of Kensington
nobody used to know.

Highly recommended restaurants in each price category
are indicated by a star ★.

Category	Cost*
$$$$ (Very Expensive)	over £40
$$$ (Expensive)	£25–£40
$$ (Moderate)	under £25

**per person, including appetizer, entrée, dessert, and 15%
value added tax, but excluding drinks and service.*

*Numbers in the margin correspond to numbered restau-
rant locations on the London Lodging and Dining maps.*

Wine

In Britain, wine is not drunk with every meal as it is on the
Continent. However, it has become increasingly popular
over the past decade. Most wine is imported from France,
Italy, Germany, Australia, and California; exotic imports
are also becoming more accessible.

Beer and Ale

Young's and Fuller's are the only true London beers. Traditional British bitter—a flat, amber-colored, brew—is
being superceded by lager (standard beer) in popularity.
To order bitter in a pub, ask for a pint of "Best."

Business Breakfasts

Chariots of Fire was conceived over breakfast among the
Thai warrior costumes in the stunning and theatrical
black-and-white basement of **Blakes Hotel** (tel. 071/370–
6701)—a not untypical scenario in this best of the media
moguls' breakfast hangouts. **The Dolphin Brasserie** (Dolphin Sq., SW1, tel. 071/834–9134) hasn't yet caught on for

power breakfasts, though a certain group of City financiers has recognized its potential, and meets here regularly in the Deco room with a view over the Dolphin Square
pool. Close to Westminster. **The Savoy Restaurant** (tel.
071/836–4343) was the first and is the best power-breakfast venue. It's important to get one of the tables by the
window, not only because they're the most prestigious,
but because the river view lifts the early morning spirits.
The small Upstairs bar, with a view of the forecourt, has a
more low-key buffet breakfast. **The Terrace Garden** at Le
Meridien (tel. 071/734–8000), with its big glass-conser-
vatory roof and profusion of palms, is also very popular
with all breeds of businesspeople. A lovely setting for
lunch, too. **White's** (tel. 071/262–2711) offers another conservatory terrace for quiet business breakfasts, this one
more accessible for those staying in the west of London or
near Marble Arch.

West End

★ **㉝** **Chez Nico.** If you've heard of two restaurants in London,
$$$$ this is the one that isn't Gavroche. Nico Ladenis used to be
reputed to emerge from the kitchen and chastise the odd
philistine diner, but seems to be growing out of this habit
now that he's happily settled in this opulent West End haven. Even so, do not ask for salt; smoke at your peril. He
can, however, feel justified in occasional displays of ego-
tism; His ability to send hardened restaurant critics and
blasé diners into paroxysms of delight with his perfectly
executed inventions is unparalleled. Even if your restaurant French is up to translating the menu, you can't pre-
dict what will accompany your choice: two sorts of potato
and a creamy cêpe sauce with the duck cônfit; perfect vegetables cooked in sealed containers to retain maximum flavor. For a less-complex taste of the Ladenis style at more
modest prices, there's **Very Simply Nico** (48a Rochester
Row, SW1, tel. 071/630–8061), where former Nico sous-
chef Tony Tobin produces enhanced versions of brasserie
dishes. *35 Great Portland St., W1, tel. 071/436–8846.
Jacket and tie required. Reservations required. MC, V.
Closed weekends, public holidays, 3 weeks in Aug.*

㉚ **The Connaught Grill Room and Restaurant.** Issuing an in-
$$$$ vitation to either of these terribly exclusive hotel dining
rooms is bound to enhance your popularity. The Grill
Room is smaller, discreet, and dignified, paneled and
painted in dark green and gold; the Restaurant is less intimate, more bustling, and elegantly wood paneled. Of the
two, marginally more lunchtime power broking takes
place at the Grill. Both restaurants share the faultless
kitchen of Michel Bourdin, who cooks rather grand
French and traditional English dishes. Thus, you might
have seasonal game roasted with the proper trimmings; or
steak, kidney, and mushroom pie following an asparagus
feuilleté. Melba toast sits on every table, as it does in all
the Savoy Group restaurants in homage to Escoffier, its in-
ventor (it was for Dame Nellie Melba's dieting days) and
the Savoy's first chef. Service is impeccably discreet,
swift, and unobtrusively friendly. The check will be
steep, but it will be worth it. *Carlos Pl., W1, tel. 071/499–
7070. Jacket and tie required. Reservations required. MC.
Closed weekends.*

★ **❷⑥** **Le Gavroche.** The restaurant you've heard of if you've only
$$$$ heard of one, this is the place where Michel Roux's equally
famous brother, Albert, cooks for expense accounters and
very rich people. The haute cuisine is capital-C-Classical;
the menu is freely punctuated with foie gras, lobster,
champagne, etc.; the service is of the sort where two waiters refill your water glass whenever you take a sip and hov-
er to remove silver domes with a synchronized flourish
when the entrée arrives. The food simply cannot be
faulted, except by grouses who feel the high media profile
of the brothers Roux has somehow sullied the purity of the
food god. Albert's famous brother, Michel, earned his
stars at the equally famous **Waterside Inn** (Ferry Rd.,
Bray, Berkshire—around 40 minutes' drive from London,
tel. 0628/20691), probably the most expensive restaurant
in Britain and in one of the prettiest settings. An invitation to that, if you have time, or here, if you don't, should
impress. *43 Upper Brook St., W1, tel. 071/408–0881. Jacket and tie required. Reservations required. AE, DC, MC,
V. Closed weekends, public holidays.*

❸⑨ **Langan's Brasserie.** Perhaps not so packed with celebs as
$$$ when professional bon viveur and insult artist Peter
Langan was around, this art-lined, glamorous restaurant,
part owned by Michael Caine, is still reliable. It used to be
the place you had to book further in advance to visit than
any other, and then you weren't guaranteed anything like
a "good" table, and you might even have been ignomini-
ously banished to the upstairs Venetian Room. Upstairs is
okay now, but some people probably still find it Siberia—
watch whom you invite. The huge—more than 100 dish-
es—French menu veers from rustic to classic. Spinach
soufflé with anchovy sauce seems to be most peoples' fa-
vorite appetizer; *salade frisée* is authentically good
here—and that's hard to find in London. *Cuisine bour-
geoise* staples like boeuf bourguignon are good, too.
There's a compact and perfectly adequate wine list
printed on one side of the menu. *Stratton St., W1, tel. 071/
491–8822. Jacket and tie suggested. Reservations re-
quired. AE, DC, MC, V. Closed Sat. lunch, Sun., public
holidays.*

❷⑦ **Ninety Park Lane.** Pink and plush, festooned with flowers
$$$$ and with part of Lord Forte's private art collection on the
walls, this is a bit like some 19th-century Parisian bou-
doir. The cuisine is French classic in the grand style, and if
truffled foie gras in brioche, quail consommé with sherry,
lobster gratin with mustard seeds steamed with Thai
spices, or duckling breast roasted with balsamic vinegar is
what you desire, you will hardly be disappointed. The
kitchen, under the aegis of three-*Michelin*-star Louis
Outhier, is reliable—the Queen and her mother ate here
on the Queen Mother's birthday, which is probably some
kind of recommendation. The seven-course *Menu Louis
Outhier* is available for gourmands at dinner; also the
light, vegetarian *Menu Potager*. They promise to serve
you lunch within the hour if necessary. There's a separate
paneled alcove (where the Queen Mom dined), but all ta-
bles are quite private, many with banquette seats that put
one in mind of illicit affairs in Hollywood movies. *Grosve-
nor House Hotel, Park La., W1, tel. 071/499–6363, ext.
4205. Jacket and tie required. Reservations required. AE,
DC, MC, V. Closed Sat. lunch, Sun.*

㊺ **Oak Room.** Recently restored *fin de siècle* splendor with
$$$$ limed-oak paneling, gilt, mirrors and chandeliers, and a
Michelin star for inventive cockney chef David Chambers
and French consultant Michel Lorain. They cook in two
separate genres—there's *Cuisine Traditionelle* (spinach
with oysters glazed in a champagne-and-caviar sauce,
roast lobster with mousseline of peppers), and more eclectic, nouvelle-influenced *Cuisine Créative* (gazpacho with
warm langoustines and quenelles of zucchini; scallops and
foie gras with herbs and truffle juice *en papillote)*. This is
where to indulge a taste for all the most expensive ingredients—lobster, oysters, foie gras, frogs' legs, truffles, and
champagne—in exactly the setting you'd prefer them to
be served. It's one of the better hotel dining rooms, frequented by just about every profession, and, occasionally,
royalty. Good for celebrations. *Le Meridien Hotel, 21 Piccadilly, W1, tel. 071/734–8000. Jacket and tie required.
Reservations required. AE, DC, MC, V.*

㊱ **Pizzeria Condotti.** London is, apparently, famous among
$$ American expats for being bad at pizza. Not so. This
place, in deepest Mayfair, is the most stylish of the hand-
ful here—the others being the **Pizza Express** chain and
Pizzeria Castello in darkest Walworth. This belongs to
Enzo Apicella, the cartoonist, and is practically a gallery
of modern art. Pizzas are thin crusted and topped with the
usual good stuff. There are also salads (crab with papaya,
mozzarella, and tomato) for appetizers or for weight
watchers. In the heart of Mayfair, this is a useful place—
especially in the evenings when it's serenely quiet. Lunch-
times are frenetic. *4 Mill St., W1, tel. 071/499–1308. Ca-
sual, smart dress. No reservations. AE, DC, MC, V.
Closed Sun., Christmas.*

㊼ **Poons.** This is a reliable representative of London's tiny
$$ Chinatown, which is centered on Gerrard Street in Soho.
The cooking is Cantonese-style Szechuan—it's hard to
find anything else except in the magnificent Zens (*see* below)—and the specialty is wind-dried meats, which taste
exactly as they sound—not unlike beef jerky. There are
two other Poons. This one, you might say, is the all-pur-
pose version; then there's a posh one in Covent Garden (41
King St., tel. 071/240–1743), smart enough for business
entertaining, with a window into the kitchen and a more
expensive menu than the tiny original (27 Lisle St., tel.
071/437–4549). *4 Leicester St., W1, tel. 071/437–1528. Casual dress. Reservations suggested. No credit cards.
Closed Sun., Christmas.*

㊶ **The Ritz.** With its *trompe l'oeil* sky on the ceiling, swag
$$$$ curtains of gilded vegetation, complicated gold chandeliers, mirrors, marbling, pillars, and pinks, everyone
agrees this is quite the prettiest dining room in London.
Outside is the Ritz's secret little terrace garden with
Green Park beyond—it couldn't be nicer for lunch. Cooking is either traditional (smoked salmon, lobster thermidor, roasts and grills) or modern, featuring interesting
combinations (parfait of smoked salmon and asparagus
with a beetroot dressing; veal filet with lobster on seafood
sauce with vegetable noodles). The post-prandial bouquet
of business-lunch cigars fills Piccadilly. *Piccadilly, W1,
tel. 071/493–8181. Jacket and tie required. Reservations
required. AE, DC, MC, V.*

④ The Veeraswamy. London's oldest Indian restaurant is
$$$ just fine for a business meal. There's plenty of space, a
comfortable pink-and-gray plush decor, big windows over
Regent Street, a separate cocktail bar, and very polite,
uniformed waiters who will help with the menu if help is
needed. Lunch time features a good-value buffet with at
least five meat and fish curries, some vegetable combina-
tions, rice and trimmings, and a fresh fruit salad. Along
with the usual roll call of Indian restaurants, Veeraswa-
my's does things you couldn't get anywhere else: Brain
Masala, for instance, or *Alu Tikki* (spicy lentils and potato
with date, tamarind, and mint chutneys). *99–101 Regent
St., W1, tel. 071/734–1401. Jacket and tie suggested. Res-
ervations advised. AE, DC, MC, V. Closed Christmas.*

Covent Garden

㊹ Bertorelli's. This long-established Italian restaurant, op-
$$ posite the Royal Opera House stage door, attracts its
share of singers and theater-goers, as well as business-
people at lunchtime. Its tiled floor, spruce-white walls,
and cobalt-blue lamps make it smart enough for entertaining; motherly Italian waitresses ensure a warm atmosphere. All the standard Italian dishes are here—*osso
bucco; saltimbocca alla Romana;* mozzarella, tomato, and
basil salad—and there's always a fresh daily fish, pan
fried and served with buttery juices, or roasted with fennel. This cheaper and less trendy alternative to Orso,
around the corner, seems nothing special, at first glance;
but this kind of fresh and reliable cooking, devoid of pre-
tension (together with the cheerful friendliness, reasonable prices, and clean, modern decor) is hard to find,
especially in central London and most especially in Covent
Garden. The wine list is not spectacular, but the olive
bread's great. *44a Floral St., WC2, tel. 071/836–3969.
Jacket and tie suggested. Reservations advised. AE, DC,
MC, V. Closed Christmas.*

★ **㊺ Le Boulestin.** This place has been an oasis in the mayhem
$$$$ of Covent Garden for over 60 years. It's all very comfortable, with rust-washed walls, lots of oils and prints and
chandeliers, and reassuring classic-French cuisine with
the occasional modern twist. From the seasonal menu, ex-
emplary *tournedos* in a Madeira-enriched reduction with
foie gras and truffle might follow a crab sausage with
langoustine coulis, or a warm salad of calves' liver with
raspberry vinegar. Applause for chef and manager Kevin
Kennedy, who will still use raspberry vinegar if he wants,
while all around have gone onto the next snob ingredient.
A thoroughly good time can be had here, devoid of preten-
sion and with no extraneous fuss. Charming French waiters will probably convince you to eat more courses than
you ought to. Good for pampering difficult clients. *1a
Henrietta St., WC2, tel. 071/836–7061. Jacket and tie required. Reservations required. AE, DC, MC, V. Closed
Sat. lunch, Sun., 3 weeks in Aug., Christmas.*

㊻ Joe Allen. One of London's first American-style restau-
$$ rants, Joe Allen is now as ever overpopulated with theater
folk, including a sprinkling of West End stars, who flood in
after final curtain. It's always pretty busy, but if you want
to spot faces, late is the time to arrive. The faces like the
huge salads; the chili and burgers; the fresh, modern

American cooking; the late hours; the profusion of theatrical memorabilia on brick walls—but mainly the presence of other faces. Reviews complain about the decline in service and cooking in recent years, and it's true you can get hustled out in too much of a hurry by the young, long-aproned waiters. It's also true the food can be lackluster, famously large salads included, but it's an institution. Which is the attitude that caused the problem. Not remotely useful for doing business unless you're A&R for a record company. *13 Exeter St., WC2, tel. 071/836–0651. Casual dress. Reservations advised. No credit cards. Closed Christmas.*

★ ⑰ **Orso.** The second in the Joe Allen stable of two, this hang-
$$$ out of actors, singers, and journalists serves modern Italian food in a snazzy basement dining room. Wooden rails on one side overlook what might be the wine cellar but looks more like the dungeon of some Medici palazzo. The menu's always changing, but you get to order in Italian from one side, English from the other. *Crostini* (toasted bread with strong black olives, fresh tomato, and basil) makes a simple first course, as does a salad of arugula and lamb's lettuce with shaved Parmesan, olive oil, and lemon. There are a lot of olives about—chicken with olives and tomatoes is a regular, and sea bass or swordfish might involve some of the good virgin oil they use here. There are plenty of other choices, but it's all good, robust food served on good, robust, hand-painted red-and-blue pottery by a terribly attractive staff. It can get noisy, but then nobody will be able to overhear you. *27 Wellington St., WC2, tel. 071/240–5269. Smart, casual dress. Reservations required. No credit cards. Closed Christmas.*

⑮ **Smollensky's Balloon/Smollensky's On The Strand.** These
$$ two cheap and cheerful American restaurants are very popular with office people. The second has the better decor—a recreation of New York Art Deco—and live bands playing standards from Brubeck to Phil Collins. The first (just off Piccadilly) has a pianist and two-level seating. You get suitably huge portions of filling food, especially steak, of which there are eight cuts, including New York Club for the homesick. These arrive with lots of fries and one of seven sauces on the side. Cocktails, vegetarian dishes, rather rich appetizers and mega-rich desserts called things like "Very, Very Chocolate Fudge Cake" complete the menu. The staff is trained in American "is-everything-OK" style, and the whole experience is a lot more pleasant than it sounds on paper. *1 Dover St., W1, tel. 071/491–1199; 105 The Strand, WC2, tel. 071/497–2101. Casual dress. No reservations. AE, DC, MC, V.*

Soho

⑰ **Alistair Little.** Eponymous chef, Little, impresses trendy
$$$ media types with his fresh and eclectic ideas. Influences as incongruous as Danish and Japanese make brilliant sense, especially when fish is involved. Menus change twice daily, but look for grilled, stuffed baby squid and wicked fig-and-mascarpone tart. The size of the modern dining room—metal lights, Venetian blinds, and simple black chairs—makes it hard to avoid overhearing the neighbors. Modestly priced wines might mean you won't care. *49 Frith St., W1, tel. 071/734–5183. Smart casual dress.*

Reservations required. No credit cards. Closed weekends, Christmas, Easter, 3 weeks in Aug.

51 **Bahn Thai.** Off-duty chefs come here for some of the best
$$ Thai food in London. The smallish, ground-floor dining room has comfortable banquette seats and has been Easternized with hundreds of inverted Oriental parasols on the ceiling. There's an upstairs, too, which is not so cheerful, but which serves an amazingly cheap buffet lunch. The menu includes some 125 dishes. One section carries the helpful warning: "All these sauces tend to be hot and pungent and often not to the taste of non-Thais," but you don't need to risk those with alternatives like a "whole poussin marinated in honey and spices and chargrilled, served with small bowls of hot chili and plum sauce." Owner Philip Harris is English, but has spent a lot of time in Thailand, and his wife is Thai; together they ensure that the food is fresh and always interesting. A place for days off or for foodie clients. *21a Frith St., W1, tel. 071/437–8504. Casual dress. Reservations advised. AE, MC, V. Closed Christmas.*

★ 50 **L'Escargot.** This ever-popular Soho haunt of publishers,
$$$ agents, and people who do things to videos was fashionable from day one, when Alistair Little held the reins in the kitchen. The ground floor is a no-reservations brasserie; upstairs is a more expensive and smarter restaurant presided over by Elena, one of those names to know. Upstairs, downstairs, the food is the same, but do your business higher up. The food is well-executed modern Anglo-French, nouvelle influenced, but with decent-size portions, and particularly good vegetables in selections on sideplates—zucchini with sesame seeds, perhaps, and a carrot puree. Fish is the best choice for entrée—turbot with *buerre blanc* or a salmon fillet poached *à point*, accompanied by a good hollandaise. A snail motif on the carpet and snail-shaped chocolates with the coffee ensure that things don't get too serious. One of the best wine lists you're likely to find was compiled by wine writer and media star Jancis Robinson, who has very helpfully annotated it. *48 Greek St., W1, tel. 071/437–2879. Smart, casual dress. Reservations advised upstairs; no reservations downstairs. AE, DC, MC, V. Closed Sun., public holidays.*

49 **The Gay Hussar.** London literati and left-leaning MPs are
$$ still in residence in this Soho Hungarian institution, even after the departure of much-loved owner Victor Sassie. Mock-tudor paneled, and resembling a Victorian train carriage with bull's-blood colored banquettes along the sides, it's comfortable all right, but hardly private. You will, no doubt, find somebody's tweedy elbow in your blinis, especially after downing the strong Hungarian red or sweet Tokay. Food is served in pre–health conscious portions and includes the famous chilled cherry soup and interesting items like "heroic minced goose." And, as you'd expect, they give great goulash. It is hopeless, obviously, for quiet business meetings but, as the menu says, you can eat well, drink well, live well. *2 Greek St., W1, tel. 071/437–0973. Casual dress. Reservations required. No credit cards. Closed Sun., public holidays.*

46 **Melate.** This Indonesian/Malaysian restaurant, popular
$$ with youthful Londoners, is smarter than you'd expect from the reasonable prices, but it isn't really a business

venue. Lemon grass, ginger, chili, and coconut are principal flavorings in a cuisine that sounds better in its own language. Viz, *mee goreng* (egg noodles with beef and shrimp), *gado-gado* (salad with peanut sauce), *tahu telor* (bean curd omelette). Weird desserts containing kidney beans, syrup, and jello are best left untranslated. Round the corner is **Melati** (21 Great Windmill St., tel. 071/437–2745), which used to be an intimate relation of this place, but got a divorce. The food's just as good there, though the decor is rather harsh in yellow pine and glaring light. Frequented by the same crowd of arty youth and architect trainees. *31 Peter St., W1, tel. 071/437–2011. Casual dress. Weekend reservations advised. AE, MC, V. Closed Sun., public holidays.*

West London

17
$$$$
Bibendum. This star chef's kitchen is housed in one of the best examples of Art Deco architecture in London—the ceramic-faced Michelin building, once a garage, now Terence Conran's design mecca. Conran himself designed the elegant dining room around the original stained-glass windows depicting Monsieur Bibendum, the little Michelin-tire man after whom this place was named. Simon Hopkinson, who came to fame in his own restaurant, Hilaire, cooks hearty reinventions of classic French dishes. He doesn't turn up his nose at *steak au poivre*, for instance—rather he'll make it one of the best you've had; or *tête de veau*, or *boeuf en daube*. Start perhaps with a warm spinach mousse with hollandaise and finish with his Christmas-pudding ice cream. This place helped to breathe new life into what was a rather drab part of the world not that many moons ago. It's had its day as the only place to be seen, but is still very much on the map—book ahead to dine among well-heeled trendies. Wear Chanel. *Michelin House, 81 Fulham Rd., SW3, tel. 071/581–5817. Jacket and tie suggested. Reservations required. MC, V. Closed public holidays.*

9
$$$
Clarke's. Love or hate it, Paris- and California-trained Sally Clarke chooses the menu. It will be composed of whatever was best and freshest at market that morning, unfussily put together by the talented Clarke. It's impossible to speculate on what she might choose to serve, but her style—unsurprisingly—is based on classic French with new-American influence; there might be a salad first, or grilled baby vegetables, then perhaps meat, but probably fish, and there will be complementary wines throughout and the best bread basket around, including fruit and herb varieties, all baked on the premises earlier in the day. If it's liver and you don't like liver, there is nearly always an alternative—albeit difficult to extract—hidden in the kitchen. Vegetarians must request special dishes when they book their table. Prosperous, sociable people sit among the Hockney prints and make like it's a dinner party. At lunchtime there's a choice, and local upscale publishers to take advantage of it. *124 Kensington Church St., W8, tel. 071/221–9225. Smart, casual dress. Reservations advised. MC, V. Closed weekends, public holidays, 2 weeks in Aug.*

19
$$
Grill St. Quentin. This big bright basement done out in peacock blue and gold with a slippery tiled floor is the nearest to Paris you'll get in London. Enterprising execu-

tive manager, Didier Garnier, sent his designer to La Coupole before she set to work on this, so the setting isn't surprising. Generously spaced tables make this ideal for meetings, and choosing from the admirably succinct, simple and classic menu shouldn't take too much valuable time. Appetizers include salads, smoked salmon, foie gras; entrées focus on fish, including today's market buy, or meat—from duck breast to steak—all grilled to your liking and served with large quantities of frîtes. A guide to the French terms for ordering your meat isn't as pretentious as it sounds, as the waiters, imported from across the channel, don't necessarily speak English. They are, however, charming as hell. *2 Yeoman's Row, SW3 (behind 205 Brompton Rd.), tel. 071/581–8377. Smart, casual dress. Reservations advised. AE, DC, MC, V. Closed Sun., public holidays.*

⑱ Joe's Café. Oh that witty name that makes you think of
$$$ greasy-spoon specials when what you actually get is carpaccio and cappuccino in a high-tech gray-on-gray Eva Jiricna interior. And Joe is design maven Joseph Ettedgui who practically invented matte black and for whom the opening of his first restaurant represented yet another direction for his Joseph empire. Between meals it becomes rather casual; more like the café you'd think it is than the fully fledged restaurant it is. Come here to sit uncomfortably in expensive clothes and pick at obscure salad vegetables while trying not to stare at the staff who look like models, or to perch at the bar counter and sip a large espresso without eating. Great for its location and for a quiet lunch without sacrificing aesthetic considerations. *126 Draycott Ave., SW3, tel. 071/225–2217. Casual dress, or see above. Weekend reservations advised. AE, DC, MC, V. Closed Sun. dinner, public holidays.*

★ ⑧ Kensington Place. Another one for the style-conscious,
$$ this time designed by architect Julyan Wickham with plate-glass shop windows and more modernist metal. Rowley Leigh, who has won prizes—but then which serious chef worth his *gros sel* hasn't—draws heavily from various European countries' peasant traditions to produce highly seasoned, strongly flavored dishes. Salt cod and polenta are frequent ingredients, or there might be a potato salad with truffles or foie gras with sweet-corn pancake. It's one of those places on the cutting edge of food fashion, so don't come here expecting to talk turkey—unless that's what you're eating. Lots of local well-known people, and lots of unknown ones who know each other, treat this as their local dining room, so there's a fair amount of table hopping and an awful lot of noise. *201 Kensington Church St., tel. 071/727–3184. Smart, casual dress. Reservations advised. MC, V. Closed Aug. bank holiday, Christmas.*

⑤ 192. Alistair Little put it on the map and, though he's long
$$ since departed, his fresh and interesting style of Anglo-French cooking lives on in this designer den of chrome and blue-stained wood. It gets packed with trendy locals feasting on warm goat-cheese salad and pigeon breasts, and working their way through the well-priced wine list. Downstairs is like a different restaurant, with interconnecting rooms gently lighted, and peace and quiet for lunch. 192 was one of the first restaurants in an area that's now on the up and up; it's still probably the best. *192 Ken-*

*sington Park Rd., W11, tel. 071/229–0482. Casual dress.
Weekend reservations advised. AE, MC, V. Closed Sun.
evening, public holidays.*

⓮ One Ninety Queen's Gate. In art-bedecked dining rooms
$$$ with flowers rampaging over the fireplace, Antony Wor-
ral-Thompson creates robust French peasant–inspired
seasonal menus for patrician consumption. An *amuse-
gueule* might precede a complicated salad of marinated
duck, or shellfish and vegetables set in a lobster aspic with
ginger ("A Jellied Rockpool," says the menu). Then comes
stuffed pigs' feet with sweetbreads, or roasted sea bass
with pine kernels and artichoke. Smart gals in designer
black won't let you order ill-matched courses. An encyclo-
pedic wine list leaves no vine unmined. Perfect for food
snobs, who will enjoy recognizing the occasional mistake,
such as a red-wine sauce overreduced and consequently
too salty—not impressive at this level. *190 Queen's Ga.,
SW7, tel. 071/581–5666. Jacket and tie advised. Reserva-
tions required. AE, DC, MC, V. Closed Sat. lunch,
Christmas.*

㉔ La Tante Clare. Another celebrated chef in another cele-
$$$$ brated restaurant, this time in downtown Chelsea. Pierre
Koffman learned from the brothers Roux and, some say,
has surpassed them. His dining room is pale and rather
modern, incorporating chrome in Deco fashion. His cook-
ing, too, is modern, but the culinary opposite of pale—
warm oysters with marinated salmon, a mousseline of
hare with wild-mushroom sauce, salmon trout encrusted
with herbs, pigs' feet stuffed with sweetbreads. Koffman
now belongs to the older guard of chefs who came to fame
in the late '70s/early '80s and who have now been outdone,
as far as column inches go, by the youngsters—Marco
Pierre White, the *enfant terrible* of **Harvey's** (2 Bellevue
Rd., Wandsworth Common SW17, tel. 081/672–0114—a
bit of a trek, so not reviewed here) chief among them. *68
Royal Hospital Rd., SW3, tel. 071/352–6045. Jacket and
tie required. Reservations required. AE, DC, MC, V.
Closed weekends, 3 weeks at Easter, 3 weeks Aug./Sept.,
Christmas.*

★ ⓫ Wódka. Modern Polish was supposed to catch on, but the
$$ floodgates never opened and we were left with only a
handful, of which this is far and away the best. Charming
owner/manager Jan Woroniecki circulates and chats; the
atmosphere is as relaxed as at a dinner party. The menu
balances between Polish staples (*pierogi, barszcz*
[borscht], *bigos,* and *kulebiak*) and modern Anglo French
(carp terrine with dill sauce, roast guinea fowl with forest
mushrooms). Blinis (especially with herring) are, of
course, essential. The adventurous wine list contains the
odd Chilean or New Zealand bottle, but the thing to drink
is vodka straight from the freezer. Charles Saatchi, the
Evening Standard, various media stars, and Vogueites
use this as their local. It gets very lively in the evenings.
The trendy black tables are rather close together, but
there's a bookable private room downstairs. *12 St. Albans
Gro., W8, tel. 071/937–6513. Smart, casual dress. Reservations advised. AE, MC, V. Closed Sun. lunch, public
holidays.*

North London

❸❹ **Le Bistroquet.** This neighborhood place is off the beaten
$$ track, but *vaut le detour* in summer when the Provençal,
tiled dining rooms opening onto a pretty courtyard come
into their own. Cooking is brasserie-style in the casual
front section; super-brasserie in back, where you'll eat
among TV execs having noisy lunch "meetings" at alcove
tables. Toulouse sausage with pureed, nutmeg-scented
potato (aka bangers and mash) is perennially popular
here, as is brochette of lamb marinated in lime and ginger.
There's always a *salade composée*, a French cheeseboard
in good condition, and an authentic *tarte*. A good neigh-
borhood place, fine for low-key business, too. *275 Camden
High St., NW1, tel. 071/485-9607. Smart, casual dress.
Reservations advised weekends and summer. AE, MC, V.*

❼ **Fleet Tandoori.** This is just one of hundreds of neighbor-
$$ hood Indian restaurants, but a particularly good one,
much beloved of the Hampstead intelligentsia and North
London youth. It's decorated like a comfortable sitting
room, with pale-green carpet and plants, and was one of
the first to deviate from the horrendous raised velveteen
wallpaper, gaudy lamps, and piped sitar music that used
to be the norm. Service is offhand, so it might help to take
a friendly Londoner along for menu translation (every
Londoner is a curry expert). Chicken tikka—or any of the
marinated, boned meats, cooked to sizzling in the clay
oven, or *tandoor*—is essential. Also good is *matar paneer*
(creamy peas and cottage cheese simmered in ginger, coriander, and turmeric). *104 Fleet Rd., NW3, tel. 071/485-
6402. Casual dress. Weekend reservations suggested. AE,
DC, MC, V. Closed Christmas.*

★ ❻ **Zen W3.** Chef Michael Leung has done amazing things to
$$$ Chinese food, taking influences from European and other
Eastern cuisines and leaving out the MSG, so neither this,
nor the other three Zens (**Zen Central,** 20 Queen St., W1,
tel. 071/629-8103; **Zen Chelsea,** Chelsea Cloisters, Sloane
Ave., SW3, tel. 071/589-1781; **Now & Zen,** 4A Upper St.
Martin's La., WC2, tel. 071/497-0376.), bear any relation
to the standard London Chinese restaurant. The design is
coolly theatrical; there's a waterfall down the staircase
handrail and plenty of room between round, white-clothed
tables. Famous people are placed by the huge plate-glass
windows; architects and brassy pop stars go upstairs.
Dishes include some familiar faces, remodeled, along with
originals like "Wrapping Paper"—subtle, wafer-thin
lamb- and mint-leaf pancakes assembled by the tireless
waiter before your very eyes—and broiled chicken breast
with coriander. *83 Hampstead High St., NW3, tel. 071/
794-7863. Jacket and tie suggested. Reservations ad-
vised. AE, DC, MC, V. Closed Christmas.*

The City

❻⓿ **Rouxl Britannia.** This has the debatable honor of being the
$$/$$$ only known restaurant without a full kitchen. It's those
Roux brothers again (of Le Gavroche, the Waterside Inn
at Bray, and TV fame), this time pioneering the *sous-vide*
method of cooking, whereby food is prepared somewhere
else, vacuum sealed, and reheated in this chef-free kitch-
en. That means you get to try Roux cuisine at bargain
rates—and in the City, too, where city-slicker wine bars

outnumber good restaurants by a (square) mile. Upstairs is a restaurant, overlooking unpicturesque Finsbury Circus; downstairs there's the same menu, cheaper, in brasserie conditions—either in a U.S.-style atrium with black-and-white tiles and loud fountain, or in a rather charmless dining room with plastic-rattan chairs and marble tables. And, yes, the French cuisine is good—potted tongue with horseradish sauce, meal-size gravad lax with potato salad, grilled lamb, roast skate with parsley sauce. Strangely free of atmosphere, but ever so useful. *Trident Ct., 14 Finsbury Sq., EC2, tel. 071/256–6997. Jacket and tie suggested. Reservations advised for Restaurant; not accepted for Brasserie. AE, DC, MC, V.*

★ ⑤⑧ **Savoy Grill.** The sweet smell of success overpowers the
$$$$ scent of roast meat in this comfortable, wood-paneled, banquetted dining room where you eat at well-separated tables alongside top newspaper editors and captains of industry. The wonderful waiters are sensitive to needs; they'll pamper you, or leave you alone to plot. The food is not really the point here, which is a shame, because it's excellent. David Sharland's cooking is Very British on one side of the menu, modern French on the other. The dish of the day might be steak, kidney, and oyster pie; or roast beef and Yorkshire pudding. On the French side you might find leek terrine with truffles on a walnut sauce, then broiled duck breast with lime. If the chocolate pie is on the pastry cart, grab it—it explodes in the mouth. *The Strand, WC2, tel. 071/836–4343. Jacket and tie required. Reservations required for lunch. AE, DC, MC, V. Closed Sat. lunch, Sun.*

FREE TIME

Fitness

Hotel Facilities
There are no hotels with health-club facilities that offer day memberships to nonguests.

Health Clubs
There are few outstanding health clubs in London, and most don't offer day rates for nonmembers. Among the ones that have both reasonably good facilities and day memberships are **Ravelles** (52 Brunswick Centre, Russell Sq., WC1, tel. 071/278–2754); **Westside** (201–207 Kensington High St., W8, tel. 071/937–5386); and **Bodys** (250 King's Rd., SW3, tel. 071/351–5682). Dance and aerobics classes are available at **Dance Works** (16 Balderton St., W1, tel. 071/629–6183). Those who are members of the U.S. Health and Tennis Corporation have access to the best health club in London, bar none, **The Barbican** (97 Aldersgate St., EC1, tel. 071/374–0091).

Jogging
Green Park and **St. James's Park** are very central and good for shorter runs. **Hyde Park** and **Kensington Gardens** (they're connected) are much larger. **Regents Park,** especially along its perimeter (2½ miles), is popular, but for a real cross-country trek, head north to **Hampstead** and the Heath.

Shopping

Good buys for gifts include cashmere, lambswool, and other knitwear (**N. Peal,** 54 Burlington Arc., W1, tel. 071/ 493–5378; **The Scotch House,** 2 Brompton Rd., SW3, tel. 071/581–2151; **Marks & Spencer,** 458 Oxford St., W1, tel. 071/935–7954 and branches); Wedgwood, Minton, and Royal Doulton china (**Gered,** 158 Regents St., W1, tel. 071/ 734–7262; or **Harrods,** *see* below), and antiques (Kensington Church St. and Chelsea; also *see* markets, below).

The West End, Knightsbridge, and Covent Garden are the best shopping areas, with **Liberty** (27 Great Marlborough St., W1, tel. 071/734–1234), **Harrods** (87 Brompton Rd., and SW3, tel. 071/730–1234), **Harvey Nichols** (corner Knightsbridge and Sloan St., SW3, tel. 071/235–5000) the top department stores.

Oxford Street is a mile of junk and chain stores. Surrounding streets, though, are still good: Old and New Bond Streets for the most exclusive shops; South Molton Street (especially **Browns** No. 23–27, tel. 071/491–7833) and St. Christopher's Place for fashion. Around Piccadilly, **Burlington Arcade,** W1; and **Fortnum & Mason** (181 Piccadilly, W1, tel. 071/734–8040) are worth looking into for old-fashioned British quality goods of all kinds. The King's Road, once the world center of trendiness, is now a sorry parade of chain stores. North of there, around the **Conran Shop** (81 Fulham Rd., SW3, tel. 071/589–7401), is the new hunting ground for high fashion and design. Then head up to Beauchamp (pr. BEE-chum) Place and the Brompton Road for lots of expensive boutiques. Covent Garden has a bit of everything (Neal Street has specialty shops for shells, hats, tea, beads, ethnic musical instruments, kites, etc.).

For antiques, **Camden Passage** in Islington and **Portobello** in Notting Hill are still reasonable hunting grounds on weekends. Even if you're not buying, it's fun.

Diversions

The British Museum (Great Russell St., Bloomsbury WC1, tel. 071/636–1555) is one of the world's greatest, with many fine collections, particularly Egyptian, Roman, and Greek.

Exhibition Road is the boulevard along which the rest of the great museums are situated (with entrances on Cromwell Road). The **Victoria and Albert** (V&A, tel. 071/938–8500) is a vast temple to all levels of design. Also here are the **Natural History** (tel. 071/938–9123), **Geological** (tel. 071/938–8765), and **Science** (tel. 071/938–8000) museums.

Hampstead is the most picturesque of London's "villages." Visit John Keats's house (Wentworth Pl.) or the fine country estate, Kenwood House (Hampstead La., tel. 081/348–1286) with its superb portrait collection (including Reynolds, Van Dyck, and Gainsborough). Or leave the city behind and just walk on surprisingly rural Hampstead Heath.

Harrods (87 Brompton Rd., SW3, tel. 071/730–1234), the institution, is looking good after extensive renovation.

Browse around the "top people's store" and explore surrounding Knightsbridge.

The National Gallery (Trafalgar Sq., tel. 071/839–3321), with its new extension, houses one of the great 14th- to 19th-century art collections; The **Tate** (Millbank, tel. 071/821–1313) is the place for modern art, with the Clore wing containing the magnificient J. M. W. Turner bequest.

River Trips to Greenwich (National Maritime Museum, tel. 081/858–4422, Royal Observatory, tel. 081/858–1167), Tower Bridge, or the Thames Barrier (London's floodgates) last one to four hours. Boats leave from Westminster Pier (tel. 071/730–4812) or from across Charing Cross Bridge (tel. 071/839–3572) from the South Bank Centre (all boats Apr.–Oct.).

St. Paul's Cathedral (St. Paul's Church yard, EC4, tel. 071/248–2705), is Sir Christopher Wren's finest work. From the Golden Gallery, 627 steps up, there's a panoramic view of London; the Whispering Gallery, lower down inside the dome, is famous for its remarkable acoustics.

The Serpentine Gallery (Kensington Gardens, tel. 071/402–6075) has enterprising exhibitions of modern art and can be combined with a walk around Kensington Gardens, Hyde Park, and the Serpentine lake, where there are rowboats for rent.

Westminster Abbey (tel. 071/222–5152) is London's oldest and most important church, where Britain's kings and queens are crowned. It's overrun by tourist groups in summer. Adjacent are the Houses of Parliament and St. Stephen's Tower (Big Ben).

The Zoo (tel. 071/722–3333) in Regents Park, tragically threatened with closure, needs no explanation; you could take a waterbus on Regents Canal (tel. 071/482–0523) to Camden Town or Little Venice afterwards (Apr.–Sept.).

The Arts

London is a culturally rich capital, and there won't be time to see even a fraction of what's available. Check listings and reviews in *Time Out* or the *Evening Standard* for current events. Among the major venues are The South Bank Arts Complex, including the National Theatre, the National Film Theatre, and the Royal Festival Hall; the Royal Opera House (also home of the Royal Ballet); the English National Opera's Coliseum; and the Barbican Centre, home of the Royal Shakespeare Company. At the majority of the theaters listed below, you can expect to find large, popular shows, big-name stars, or national theater companies; these would be the equivalent of first-run Broadway theaters—but with shows at considerably lower prices. Also listed are a few that would be on par with off-Broadway (here called "fringe") theater, with more avant-garde productions: The Almeida, ICA, Riverside, and Young Vic.

Ticket agencies include **Keith Prowse** (tel. 071/741–9999), which has a New York office (234 W. 44th St., Suite 902, NY, NY 10036, tel. 212/398–1430 or 800/669–8687); the **half-price ticket booth** (Leicester Sq., Mon.–Sat. 2:30–6:30), which sells discounted tickets for that evening's per-

formance at some 45 theaters; and the **Fringe Box Office**
(Duke of York's Theatre, St. Martin's La., WC2, tel. 071/
379–6002).

Aldwych, Aldwych WC2, tel. 071/836–6404.
Almeida, Almeida St., N1, tel. 071/359–4404.
Barbican, Barbican, EC2, tel. 071/638–8891.
Coliseum, St. Martin's La., WC2, tel. 071/836–3161.
Drury Lane, Catherine St., WC2, tel. 071/836–8108.
Haymarket, Haymarket, SW1, tel. 071/930–9832.
ICA Theatre, The Mall, SW1, tel. 071/930–3647.
Lyric Hammersmith, King St., W6, tel. 081/741–3211.
Mermaid, Puddle Dock, EC4, tel. 071/236–5568.
National, (Cottesloe, Lyttleton, and Olivier Theaters),
South Bank Arts Complex, SE1, tel. 071/928–2252.
Old Vic, Waterloo Rd., SE1, tel. 071/928–7616.
Piccadilly, Denman St., W1, tel. 071/437–4506.
Riverside, Crisp Rd., W6, tel. 081/748–3354.
Royal Court, Sloane Sq., SW1, tel. 071/730–1745.
Royal Opera House, Covent Garden, WC2, tel. 071/240–
1066.
St Martin's, West St., WC2, tel. 071/836–1443.
Wyndham's, Charing Cross Rd., WC2, tel. 071/836–3028.
Young Vic, The Cut, SE1, tel. 071/928–6363.

After Hours

England's alcohol licensing laws, deeply unpopular relics
of World War I, mean that the city closes early. After pub
closing at 11 PM, only clubs and restaurants with special
licenses are allowed to serve alcohol, and after midnight
even central London can seem virtually deserted.

Despite the large breweries' efforts to turn them all into
Victorian theme parks, pubs remain central to British social life. Hit the right night in the right place and the famous English reserve melts. Most pubs are still not
particularly comfortable for women on their own, though
this is changing; central ones that serve food and coffee
tend to be more welcoming in this respect. Order at the
bar; a tip is not expected.

Broadly, there are three sorts of nightclubs: membership-
only places like the Groucho, the Zanzibar, and the traditional gentleman's clubs; nightclubs open to all, but usually with a door policy; and "one-nighters"—a generally
short-lived array of trendy clubs for young fashion victims
that rent out an establishment one night a week.

Bars and Lounges
The following hotel bars provide a civilized, grown-up atmosphere for entertaining clients. **American Bar** and
Thames Foyer (Savoy, tel. 071/836–4343) are both large
and comfortable, with great dry martinis. **The Burlington
Bar** (Le Meridien, tel. 071/734–8000) is clubby and central
with green-baize walls, leather sofas, and U.S. channels
on satellite TV. **Claridges** (tel. 071/629–8860) is the grandest there is. Not a bar at all, but a lounge known as The
Foyer—Hungarian orchestra-ette, liveried footmen. The
Perroquet (Berkeley, tel. 071/235–6000) has plush Orien-
tal-ish decor and serves 52 cocktails till 2:30 AM. **Windows
on the World** (Hilton on Park Lane, tel. 071/493–8000) is
for The View.

Brasseries

Offering food, coffee, drink, and music, brasseries entertain younger crowds—they're more for relaxation than
business. **Bar Escoba** (102 Old Brompton Rd., SW7, tel.
071/373–2403) is loud and trendy and serves tapas. **La
Brasserie** (272 Brompton Rd., SW3, tel. 071/584–1668) is
popular and très French. **Café Pacifico** (5 Langley St.,
WC2, tel. 071/379–7728) is one of London's rare Mexican
joints—very noisy. The **Soho Brasserie** (23 Old Compton
St., W1, tel. 071/439–3758) has seen better days, but it's a
useful rendezvous.

Pubs

It's best to find your own favorite, or do as the Londoners
do—install yourself in the nearest one to the hotel and call
it your Local. The following are popular, historic, and/or
picturesque: **The Cheshire Cheese** (145 Fleet St., EC4, tel.
071/353–6170) is touristy and popular, with low ceilings
and sawdust on the floor; Dr. Johnson drank here. The
Coach & Horses (29 Greek St., W1, tel. 071/437–5920) is
where writer Jeffrey Bernard lives; Keith Waterhouse's
play, *Jeffrey Bernard Is Unwell*, is set here. **The Dove** (19
Upper Mall, W6, tel. 081/748–5405), near Hammersmith
Bridge, is a historic pub with a river terrace. **The Flask**
(77 Highgate West Hill, N6, tel. 081/340–7260) is just like
a country inn, but it's a bit of a trek. The **French House** (49
Dean St., W1, tel. 071/437–2799) is another Soho institution. **The Lamb** (94 Lamb's Conduit St., WC1, tel. 071/
405–0713) was Dickens's local and a Bloomsbury Group
haunt. **The Lamb and Flag** (33 Rose St., WC2, tel. 071/
836–4108) dates from 1623. It was known as the Bucket of
Blood when it was a prizefighters' hangout; now it's full of
graphic designers. **The Mayflower** (117 Rotherhithe St.,
SE16, tel. 071/237–4088) is the 17th-century inn from
which the Pilgrims sailed for America. Pleasant river terrace.

Comedy Clubs

The relocated **Comedy Store** (28a Leicester Sq., W1, tel.
071/839–6665) was the first and is the best club. For
others, check *Time Out* listings.

Jazz Clubs

The basement **Bass Clef** (85 Coronet St., N1, tel. 071/729–
2476) regularly hosts excellent line-ups. **The Jazz Café** (56
Newington Grn., N16, tel. 071/359–4936) is for die-hard
modern jazz buffs. **Ronnie Scotts** (47 Frith St., W1, tel.
071/439–0747), daddy of them all, gets the big names.

Nightclubs

Annabel's (44 Berkeley Sq., W1, tel. 071/629–3558), mem-
bership-only haunt of glitterati and royalty, is supposed to
be one of the best clubs in the world, if you can get in.
Gaz's, the longest running one-nighter, is on Thursday
nights at Gossips (69 Dean St., W1, tel. 071/434–4480),
where ska, R&B-type music is played for a completely
mixed, friendly crowd. David Bowie and Lucian Freud
have been spotted here. The enormous **Heaven** (Under the
Arches, Villiers St., W1, tel. 071/839–3852) is the best gay
club, mixed some nights. **Legends** (29 Old Burlington St.,
W1, tel. 071/437–9933) looks great (Eva Jiricna design),
and has a stiff door policy, which changes according to
which night you're there. **Limelight** (136 Shaftsbury Ave.,

WC2, tel. 071/434–1761), based on the New York model, is a cavernous converted church for hip youth. **Stringfellows** (16 Upper St. Martin's La., WC2, tel. 071/240–5534), with glass dance floor and mirrored suede walls, is glitz for flashy showbiz types. **Tramp** (40 Jermyn St., W1, tel. 071/734–0565) is for middle-aged swingers—the kind of place Jackie Collins writes books about.

Los Angeles

by Norman Sklarewitz and Deborah Sroloff

While other parts of the country worried about sluggish business conditions in recent years, Angelenos remained typically upbeat. To a large extent, the area's wide range of industries helped insulate it from wide economic swings. However, the country's budget deficit crisis has triggered nervous talk of slashed orders for military aircraft and missiles, which are manufactured in Southern California, and aerospace industry layoffs were reaching an alarming level in 1990. In addition, a recession in real estate, another focus of the Southern California economy, has had a carryover effect on construction-related businesses.

There's hope, however, that Pentagon cutbacks will be offset by a surge of orders for commercial jetliners and commercial communications satellites. Moreover, a lowering in the cost of housing is likely to draw businesses for which relocation costs had previously been prohibitive. And foreign investors, particularly the Japanese, have continued to acquire everything from "trophy" skyscrapers to golf clubs and resorts, reflecting continuing investor confidence in the city's future.

Supermarket tabloids to the contrary, not all Angelenos are narcissistic diet fanatics who make three-picture deals via cellular car phones while they navigate the freeways in convertibles. While admittedly not Hometown U.S.A., Los Angeles is, in the main, a normal (albeit fun-loving) city—or more precisely, a collection of cities and communities. A stockbroker may live in quiet, bucolic Thousand Oaks and commute 90 minutes each way to Downtown L.A. Or a studio executive may live in sunny Manhattan Beach and drive up to Century City to work.

L.A.'s business pace is often more relaxed than most Easterners are accustomed to. But that doesn't mean people don't work hard. Because of the time difference with the East Coast, stockbrokers and others connected with the financial and commodity markets are at their screens by 6:30 AM. Those who deal with Asia, on the other hand, are waiting at 5 PM for fax and phone calls, when the business day starts in Tokyo and Hong Kong. In the aerospace and high-tech industries, engineers and technicians start work at 8 AM, and many first production shifts begin at 7. However, toilers in the less structured industries are convinced that a script draft, marketing proposal, or financial plan can be read just as effectively at poolside as in an office. And an astounding amount of business is done over lunch and dinner, often at much trendier restaurants than businesspeople frequent in other cities.

Top Employers

Employer	Type of Enterprise	Parent*/ Headquarters
Douglas Aircraft Corp.	Aircraft manufacturer	McDonnell Douglas/ St. Louis
General Telephone Co. of Calif.	Telecommunications	Santa Monica, CA
Hughes Aircraft Co.	Satellites manufacturer	General Motors/ Detroit
Lockheed Corp.	Aircraft manufacturer	Calabasas, CA
May Department Stores	Retail	May Co./ St. Louis
Northrop Corp.	Aircraft manufacturer	Los Angeles
Pacific Bell	Telecommunications	Pacific Telesis/ San Francisco
Rockwell International	Aerospace, electronics manufacturer	El Segundo, CA
Southern California Gas Co.	Utility	Pacific Enterprises/Los Angeles
The Vons Companies, Inc.	Supermarkets	El Monte, CA

if applicable

ESSENTIAL INFORMATION

Climate

Los Angeles enjoys pleasant weather most of the year: warm, sometimes hot, days and cool evenings. Rain does fall from time to time in winter, but even in January it's common to have brilliant, sunny days with temperatures into the 60s and 70s. Spring and early summer are marked by gloomy, overcast mornings; the low clouds invariably burn off by early afternoon. Summers are hot and smoggy—L.A. is making progress in cleaning its air, but those suffering from asthma or other respiratory problems will want to take it easy on smoggy days.

By no means is the entire Los Angeles basin subject to uniform temperatures. In summer, temperatures in the inland valleys—San Fernando and San Gabriel—can climb into the 100s while the coastal communities are in the 70s or 80s.

What follows are the average daily maximum and minimum temperatures for Los Angeles.

Jan.	64F	18C	**Feb.**	64F	18C	**Mar.**	66F	19C
	44	7		46	8		48	9
Apr.	66F	19C	**May**	69F	21C	**June**	71F	22C
	51	11		53	12		57	14
July	75F	24C	**Aug.**	75F	24C	**Sept.**	75F	24C
	60	16		62	17		60	16
Oct.	73F	23C	**Nov.**	71F	22C	**Dec.**	66F	19C
	65	13		48	9		46	8

Airports

Los Angeles International Airport, or LAX, as it is called, fronts the ocean in the southwest corner of the city, 20 miles from Downtown and 12 miles from Beverly Hills. Thanks to a $700-million modernization and expansion program carried out for the 1984 Olympics, LAX has solved most of its congestion problems (except on major holidays, when you should allow up to an extra hour to reach your terminal). Some 80 airlines now serve Southern California through LAX. Most foreign airlines use the Bradley International Terminal; the U.S.-based carriers use the seven other main terminals. All are connected by well-marked shuttles. On the edge of LAX is the West Imperial Terminal, which is used for charter and corporate aircraft as well as MGM Grand Air and LA Air flights. LAX has both nearby short-term parking and less expensive long-term parking on lots served by frequent shuttle buses. For parking information, call tel. 213/646–5707. For general airport information, call tel. 213/646–5252.

The **Burbank-Glendale-Pasadena Airport,** known to locals as Burbank Airport, is a small, low-hassle airport that is ideal for travelers headed to the San Fernando Valley, Glendale/Pasadena area, and Downtown L.A., which is just 13 miles away. Eight major airlines, including Alaska, American, Delta, TWA, United, and USAir, fly in and out of Burbank. Call tel. 818/840–8847 for general information.

Ontario International Airport, in neighboring San Bernardino County, is served by 12 airlines, including United, American, Continental, Delta, Alaska, USAir, Northwest, and Southwest. Ontario, which is 35 miles east of downtown L.A., serves communities in eastern L.A. County as well as such cities as San Bernardino and Riverside. Call tel. 714/983–8282 for information.

Airport Business Facilities

Los Angeles International Airport. Mutual of Omaha Business Service Centers (in Terminals 1, 4, and 7, tel. 213/646–7934) all have fax machines, photocopying, notary public, secretarial service, baggage storage, Western Union, travel insurance, cash advance, Federal Express dropoff, portable fax and cellular phone rentals, phone suites, and conference rooms with catering service. **Skytel** (International Terminal, tel. 213/417–0200) is a mini-hotel with rooms rented by the hour.

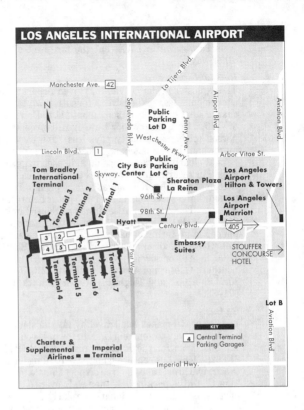

LOS ANGELES INTERNATIONAL AIRPORT

Airlines

Alaska Airlines, tel. 800/426–0333.
American, tel. 213/935–6045 or 800/433–7300.
America West, tel. 800/247–5692.
Continental, tel. 213/271–8733, 213/772–6000, or 800/525–0280.
Delta, tel. 213/386–5510, 818/247–0700, or 800/221–1212.
Hawaiian Air, tel. 800/367–5320.
Midway, tel. 800/621–5700.
Northwest, tel. 213/380–1511 (domestic), 800/447–4747 (international).
Pan Am, tel. 800/221–1111.
Southwest Airlines, tel. 213/485–1221 or 800/531–5601.
TWA, tel. 213/858–8811, 213/484–2244, or 800/221–2000.
United, tel. 213/550–1400, 213/772–2121, or 800/241–6522.
USAir, tel. 213/935–5005 or 800/428–4322.

Between LAX and L.A. Destinations

By Taxi
Cab stands are at the arrival level. Cabs take about 30 minutes in the best of conditions to get Downtown, but during rush hours (6–9 AM and 3–7 PM) and sometimes throughout the day, the trip can take an hour. Cost: about $24 to Downtown and about $22 to the Beverly Hills/Century City area. **LA Taxi** (tel. 213/412–8000) has a flat $24 rate

from Downtown to LAX, but the fare isn't offered the other way.

By Shuttle Van

The explosion in shuttle vans has given airport travelers a convenient, less expensive alternative to taxis. Vans charge a flat rate per person (about $11 to Downtown and $9–$15 to the Century City/Beverly Hills area; the second person in the same party pays less), and they make no more than three stops per vanload. Vans pick up passengers at clearly marked stops outside each baggage-claim area. For return runs to any of the airports, call the shuttle company 24 hours in advance for a pickup. Depending on your hotel's location, allow 1½–3 hours before flight departure. The major shuttle firms are **Super Shuttle** (tel. 213/338–1111), which has the largest fleet and courtesy phones in all terminal baggage-claim areas; **City Shuttle** (tel. 213/419–4000 or 800/262–7433); **Amtrans Shuttle** (tel. 213/532–5999 or 800/356–8671), which travels throughout Southern California; **Airway Shuttle** (tel. 213/769–5555 or 800/446–5766); and **Flightline Airport Shuttle** (tel. 213/971–8265).

By Bus

L.A.'s sprawl makes bus travel by far the slowest, least convenient way to get from LAX to town. If you must take the bus, head for the **Rapid Transit District (RTD)** (tel. 213/626–4455) bus center just outside parking lot C. From the arrival area, take the free airport shuttle bus marked "Lot C" to the parking lot, then walk over to the bus departure islands. Buses depart regularly for Downtown, West Hollywood, Long Beach, the South Bay communities, and Van Nuys. Cost: $1.10; seniors and the disabled, 55¢.

Car Rentals

At LAX, rental cars are kept in surrounding areas, but the major rental companies have reservation desks at arrival levels, outside each baggage claim area. Pickup vans from rental car lots circle the airport regularly.

Alamo, tel. 800/327–9633.
Avis, tel. 800/331–1212.
Budget, tel. 800/527–0700.
Dollar, tel. 800/421–6878.
Hertz, tel. 800/654–3131.
LAX Express, tel. 800/523–9773.
Luxury Line, tel. 213/659–5555 or 800/826–7805 (reserved luxury and sports cars are delivered to customers at LAX; car phones available).
National, tel. 800/227–7368.
Rent-A-Wreck, tel. 213/478–0676 or 800/423–2158.

Emergencies

Doctors

Physicians Referral Service of the L.A. County Medical Association (tel. 213/483–6122), **Psychiatric Referral Service** of the Southern California Psychiatric Society (tel. 213/450–4611).

Dentists
Dentists Referral Service of the L.A. Dental Society (tel. 213/380–7669).

Hospitals
The following hospitals and medical centers have 24-hour emergency rooms and outpatient facilities for nonemergency medical problems: **Cedars-Sinai Medical Center** (8700 Beverly Blvd., L.A., tel. 213/855–5000; emergency room, tel. 213/855–6517); **Hospital of the Good Samaritan** (616 S. Witmer St., Downtown, tel. 213/977–2121; physicians referral, tel. 213/977–2533; 24-hour Ambulatory Care Center, tel. 213/975–1239); **St. Vincent Medical Center** (2131 W. 3rd St., Downtown, tel. 213/484–7111; physicians referral, tel. 213/484–7444); **UCLA Medical Center**, 10822 Le Conte, Westwood, tel. 213/825–0881; emergency room, tel. 213/825–2111).

Important Addresses and Numbers

Audiovisual rentals. AIMM/MFI-Rents (5057 W. Washington Blvd., tel. 213/931–2466 or 800/356–2466), Audio Visual Headquarters (Beverly Hilton Hotel, 9876 Wilshire Blvd., Beverly Hills, tel. 213/205–0054), Visionmaster (1470 W. Hold Ave., Pomona, tel. 714/622–3306 or 800/851–5415).

Chambers of Commerce. Beverly Hills Chamber of Commerce (239 S. Beverly Dr., Beverly Hills, tel. 213/271–8126), Los Angeles Chamber of Commerce (404 S. Bixel St., tel. 213/629–0602), West Hollywood Chamber of Commerce (147 N. Robertson Blvd., West Hollywood, tel. 213/859–8613).

Computer rentals. Computer Rental Center (975 Michillinda Ave., Pasadena, tel. 213/231–6784 or 800/727–3685), Ganton Temporary Computer (1201 S. Flower St., Downtown, tel. 213/785–9319), Micro Computer Rental (1244 Westwood Blvd., Westwood, tel. 213/470–1421), Rent-a-Mac (3944 Wilshire Blvd., tel. 213/651–2011).

Convention & exhibition centers. Los Angeles Convention & Exhibit Center (1201 S. Figueroa St., Downtown, tel. 213/741–1151), Long Beach Convention & Entertainment Center (300 E. Ocean Blvd., Long Beach, tel. 213/436–3636).

Fax services. A Super Facsimile (400 S. Beverly Dr., suite 214, Beverly Hills, tel. 213/553–6161), Copy Mat (24 hours; 6301 Sunset Blvd., Hollywood, tel. 213/461–1222; 5750 Wilshire Blvd., Mid-Wilshire, tel. 213/938–0653; 11988 Wilshire Blvd., West L.A., tel. 213/207–5952), Kinko (731 W. 7th St., Downtown, tel. 213/627–6441), Telex All Services (512 S. San Vincente, West Hollywood, tel. 213/658–6341).

Formal-wear rentals. Gary's Tux Shop (8621 Wilshire Blvd., Beverly Hills, tel. 213/659–7296), Tuxedo Center (7360 Sunset Blvd., Hollywood, tel. 213/874–4200, 4738 Woodman Ave., Sherman Oaks, tel. 818/784–8242, 930 Wilshire Blvd., Santa Monica, tel. 213/393–6707), Wilshire Tuxedo (3822 Wilshire Blvd., Mid-Wilshire, tel. 213/388–2297).

Gift shops. Candy: Ultimate Nut & Candy Co. (Farmer's Market, 3rd and Fairfax, Wilshire district, tel. 213/938–1555); Florists: Broadway Florists (218 W. 5th St., Downtown, tel. 213/626–5511), Crossley's Flowers (7819 Beverly Blvd., Beverly Hills, tel. 213/274–4990); Gift Baskets: Jurgensen's (2 locations: 316 N. Beverly Dr., Beverly Hills, tel. 213/858–7814; 601 S. Lake Ave., Pasadena, tel. 213/681–4861), Lawry's California Center (570 W. Ave. 26, East L.A., tel. 213/224–6800).

Graphic design studios. The Art Director (5512 Wilshire Blvd., Mid-Wilshire, tel. 213/933–9668), Gonz Graphics (3325 Wilshire Blvd., Suite 305, Mid-Wilshire, tel. 213/385–4815).

Hairstylists. Unisex: Alex Roldan Salon (Le Bel Age Hotel, 1020 N. San Vicente Blvd., West Hollywood, tel. 213/855–1113), Juan-Juan Salon (9667 Wilshire Blvd., Beverly Hills, tel. 213/278–5826), José Eber (2 Rodeo Dr., Beverly Hills, tel. 213/278–7646), Style Council (924 Wilshire Blvd., Santa Monica, tel. 213/395–7892), Vidal Sassoon (405 N. Rodeo Dr., Beverly Hills, tel. 213/451–8586).

Information hot lines. Highway conditions (tel. 213/626–7231), L.A. Convention and Visitors Bureau (tel. 213/689–8822), Traveler's Aid (tel. 213/686–0950).

Limousine services. Dav-El Livery, Beverly Hills, 24-hour service (tel. 213/550–0070 or 213/645–8865), Fleetwood Limousine, West L.A. (tel. 213/208–0209), Fox Limousine Service, LAX area, multilingual chauffeurs, 24-hour service (tel. 213/641–9626), V.I.P. Limousine Service, West L.A., also vans and wagons, (tel. 213/273–1505).

Liquor stores. Beverly Hills Liquor Castle (212 S. Beverly Dr., Beverly Hills, tel. 213/273–6000), Liquor Locker (8161 Sunset Blvd., Hollywood, tel. 213/656–1140), Gil Turner's (9101 Sunset Blvd., West Hollywood, tel. 213/271–0030), Gourmet Wine & Spirits (505 S. Flower St., Downtown, tel. 213/489–2666), King's Liquors (3102 Santa Monica Blvd., Santa Monica, tel. 213/828–7100).

Mail delivery, overnight. Airborne Express (tel. 800/826–0144), DHL Worldwide Express (tel. 213/973–7300), Federal Express (tel. 213/687–9767), UPS (tel. 213/626–1551), U.S. Postal Service/Express Mail (24-hour; tel. 213/337–8846).

Messenger services. A & S Messenger & Courier (tel. 213/657–0808), Express Messenger Service (tel. 213/658–6793 in Beverly Hills, 213/629–9159, Downtown), Modern Messenger & Delivery Service (tel. 213/873–4262), Red Arrow Messenger (tel. 213/276–2388 in Beverly Hills/Century City, 213/626–6881, Downtown), Superrush (tel. 213/622–6541).

Office space rentals. Gateway Suites (1801 Ave. of the Stars, Century City, tel. 213/553–6341), Professional Suites at Wilshire (6500 Wilshire Blvd., Suite 500, Wilshire District, tel. 213/651–2333), Raleigh Executive Suites (11444 W. Olympic Blvd., 10th floor, West L.A., tel. 213/312–9500), Roxbury Executive Suites (445 S. Figueroa Blvd., Downtown, tel. 213/612–7700), United Business Center (624 S. Grand Ave., Downtown, tel. 213/689–1454).

Pharmacies, late-night. Horton & Converse Pharmacies (several locations: 7th Street Marketplace, 735 S. Figueroa St., Downtown, tel. 213/623–2838; 11600 Wilshire Blvd., West L.A., tel. 213/478–0801; 9201 Sunset Blvd., West Hollywood, tel. 213/272–0488; 6625 Van Nuys Blvd., Van Nuys, tel. 818/782–6251; 2001 Santa Monica Blvd., Santa Monica, tel. 213/829–3401), Rexall Square Drug (8490 Beverly Blvd., West Hollywood, tel. 213/653–4616).

Radio stations, all-news. KFWB 980 AM, KNX 1070 AM.

Secretarial services. California Transcribing Service (6010 Wilshire Blvd., Suite 400, West L.A., tel. 213/857–5566), Century Secretarial Service (2040 Ave. of the Stars, Century City, tel. 213/277–3329), Helen's Legal Support Services (601 W. 5th St., Suite 500, Downtown, tel. 213/614–1142), McCullough Transcribing Service (527 W. 7th St., Suite 301, Downtown, tel. 213/628–7173), Nancy Ray Secretarial Service (9401 Wilshire Blvd., Suite 650, Beverly Hills, tel. 213/273–7244).

Stationery Supplies. The Green Butterfly (136 Santa Monica Pl., Santa Monica, tel. 213/451–8485), McManus and Morgan (2506 W. 7th St., Downtown, tel. 213/387–4433).

Taxis. There are taxi stands outside major hotels, but otherwise you'll have to call for a cab—and you'll have to call a cab company in your area. Airport: LA Taxi (tel. 213/412–8000); Beverly Hills and West L.A.: Beverly Hills Cab (tel. 213/273–6611) and Rodeo Cab (tel. 213/659–9722); Downtown: LA Taxi (tel. 213/627–7000) and L.A. Checker Cab (tel. 213/393–8905 or 213/201–0775); Hollywood: United Independent Taxi (tel. 213/653–5050); West L.A.: Blue & Yellow Cab (tel. 213/205–0656) and Independent Cab (tel. 213/659–8294).

Train information. Amtrak (Union Station, 800 N. Alameda St., tel. 213/624–0171).

Travel agencies. American Express (several locations: 901 W. 7th St., Downtown, tel. 213/627–4800; 8493 W. 3rd St., West Hollywood, tel. 213/659–1682; 327 N. Beverly Blvd., Beverly Hills, tel. 213/272–9778), Carlson Travel (2040 Ave. of the Stars, Century City, tel. 213/556–2506; 6916 Hollywood Blvd., Hollywood, tel. 213/466–7771; 633 W. 5th St., 25th floor, Downtown, tel. 213/622–3418; 8271 Melrose Ave., West Hollywood, tel. 213/655–4103), Travel Unlimited (9107 Wilshire Blvd., Suite 711, Beverly Hills, tel. 213/274–8826).

Weather (tel. 213/554–1212, 213/209–7211).

LODGING

Visitors to Los Angeles soon find out what the natives have long known: that one spends an inordinate amount of time in automobiles, traveling from one destination to another. Since, as one wag put it, Los Angeles is a series of suburbs in search of a city, everything seems incredibly far away from everything else. With that caveat in mind, choose your hotel carefully. If you have television industry business to conduct, roost yourself near your particular network—the CBS, NBC, and ABC studios are all miles apart. Lockheed Aircraft is over the horizon in Calabasas, while Douglas is down Long Beach way, and Northrup is in Century City. As for film studios, they tend to stay as far apart as snakes and mongooses.

A large number of aerospace and high-tech industries, including Hughes, Rockwell, Ford Aerospace, TRW, and McDonnell Douglas—as well as U.S. Air Force space-related operations and oil refineries—are located near LAX. Consequently, many major hotel chains are in this area, along with upscale motels. Because of their location (and convenience to the San Diego Freeway), these hotels accommodate major conferences and conventions as well as smaller business meetings.

The major airport hotels are located on or just off Century Boulevard, which leads directly into the LAX terminals. Century is not beneath flight paths, so aircraft noise isn't a problem. Unless otherwise indicated, hotel vans cruise the terminals every 10 minutes or so to pick up and drop off guests. Because the hotels at LAX are business-traveler oriented, standard rooms tend to be small.

Fortunately, nearly every urban area and suburban satellite commercial zone features a first-rate hostelry—sometimes, even a world-class one. Many of the older hotels, such as the Regent Beverly Wilshire and the Beverly Hills Hotel, have recently undergone extensive refurbishing. And, considering the rather eclectic local architecture, you're bound to find an inn to suit any aesthetic sensibility, from nouveau mission to postmodern to glitzy.

For organizational purposes, the hotels in this section are grouped into five main areas: Downtown, Hollywood/West Hollywood, Westside (including Beverly Hills, Century City, Bel Air, and Westwood), San Fernando Valley (including Universal City, Burbank, and Warner Center), and Airport/South Bay (LAX and the L.A. Harbor area).

Most hotels listed here offer special corporate rates and weekend packages; inquire when making reservations.

Highly recommended lodgings in each price category are indicated by a ★.

Category	Cost*
$$$$ (Very Expensive)	over $175
$$$ (Expensive)	$125–$175
$$ (Moderate)	under $125

All prices are for a standard double room, single occupancy, excluding tax (12% in L.A., 12.2% in Beverly Hills).

Numbers in the margin correspond to numbered hotel locations on the Los Angeles Lodging and Dining maps.

Downtown

$$$ **Biltmore.** With its Spanish rococo and Italian Renaissance decor, this gorgeous 1920s landmark underwent a painstaking $10-million renovation in 1987. This lush, opulent beauty has soaring, vaulted ceilings, richly colored frescoes, and chandeliers fairly dripping with crystal. The

COASTAL LOS ANGELES

Lodging

Compri Hotel Los Angeles Harbor, **17**

Embassy Suites Hotel, **12**

Hotel Bel-Air, **6**

Los Angeles Airport Hilton and Towers, **14**

Los Angeles Airport Marriott, **13**

Sheraton Plaza La Reina, **11**

Sheraton Universal, **3**

Stouffer Concourse Hotel, **15**

Warner Center Hilton and Towers, **1**

Warner Center Marriott, **2**

Westwood Marquis Hotel and Garden, **7**

Dining

Fino, **16**

Four Oaks, **5**

The Heritage, **10**

Shane, **4**

Trattoria Angeli, **8**

Valentino, **9**

BEVERLY HILLS AND HOLLYWOOD

Lodging

Beverly Hills Hotel and Bungalows, **18**
Century City Inn, **19**
Century Plaza Hotel, **20**
L'Ermitage, **25**
Four Seasons, **26**
Hollywood Roosevelt Hotel, **37**
Regent Beverly Wilshire, **23**
St. James Club, **27**

Dining

Angeli Caffe, **36**
Campanile, **40**
Chapo, **35**
Chaya Brasserie, **29**
Chez Helene, **24**
Citrus, **38**
Ed Debevic's, **31**
Indigo, **34**
Locanda Veneta, **30**

Mandarette, **33**
The Mandarin, **22**
Patina, **39**
Primi, **21**
The Dining Room at the Regent Beverly Wilshire, **23**
Trumps, **28**
Tulipe, **32**

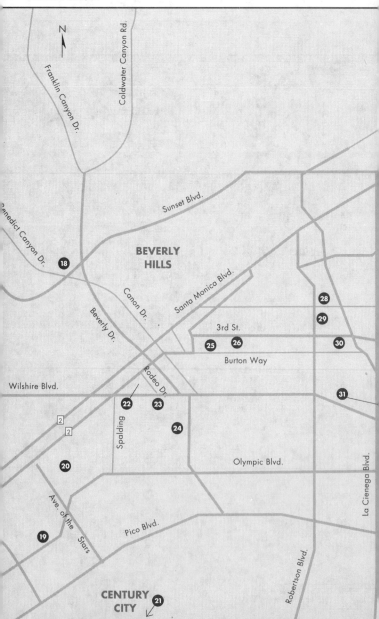

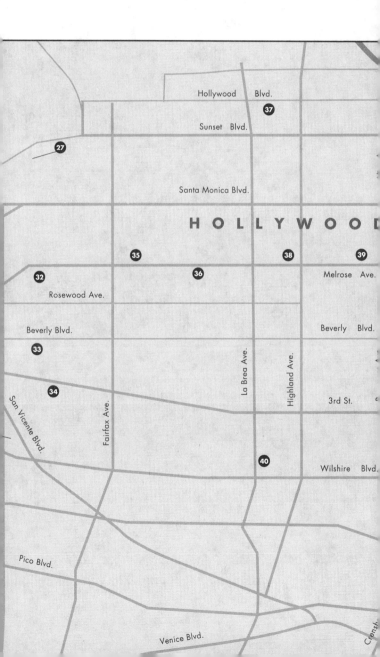

The South East Essex
College of Arts & Technology

DOWNTOWN LOS ANGELES

Lodging

Biltmore, **50**
Bonaventure, **47**
Checkers, **49**
Hyatt Regency, **44**
Los Angeles Hilton and
Towers, **41**
New Otani Hotel and
Gardens, **52**
Sheraton Grande, **46**

Dining

Bernard's, **50**
Checkers, **49**
Crocodile Cafe, **53**
Empress Pavilion, **51**
Engine Co. No. 28, **42**
Parkway Grill, **54**
Rex, Il Ristorante, **48**
Seventh Street
Bistro, **45**
The Tower, **43**

reasonably large, high-ceilinged guest rooms feature most of the modern amenities, although bathrooms still need some upgrading, and the single-line bedside phones don't reach the fold-down work desk. Some rooms have had their original millwork, fine moldings, and other Beaux-Arts details lovingly restored; other rooms are decorated in a more sleek, contemporary fashion. Biltmore is home to the largest hotel health facility (*see* Fitness, below) in the city. Bernard's (*see* Dining, below), the hotel's restaurant, is highly regarded. The Biltmore is well located for Downtown businesspeople—the Grand Avenue and Gallery bars (*see* After Hours, below) are popular afterwork meeting places. However, this is a neighborhood in transition, and Pershing Square, adjacent to the hotel, is a haven for the homeless. *506 S. Grand Ave., 90013, tel. 213/624–1011; in CA, 800/252–0175; in U.S., 800/421–8000; fax 213/612–1628. Managing dir., Randall Villareal. 660 rooms, 40 suites. AE, CB, DC, MC, V.*

⓸⓻ Bonaventure. A staple location for numerous futuristic
$$ Hollywood films, the Blade Runner-esque Bonaventure is a 35-story hotel comprising five slick, cylindrical glass-sheathed towers. Inside, conventioneers and tour groups swarm like drones, milling in confusion around the circular atrium lobby, with its byzantine network of concrete ramps, whooshing glass elevators, and often-long check-in lines. Thirty meeting rooms, including one that holds 3,000, make this the largest convention hotel smack in the center of Downtown. Rooms, many with great views, and all with generic, contemporary corporate decor, are on the cramped side. The 24th floor was recently converted into an executive club floor as part of a major renovation. The Bonaventure is almost a city unto itself—albeit a rather chilly, incoherently planned one: There are 24 shops, a disco, 19 restaurants, and two lounges, including the revolving BonaVista on the 34th floor. *A Westin hotel. 404 S. Figueroa St., 90071, tel. 213/624–1000 or 800/228–3000, fax 213/612–4800. Managing dir., William P. Lucas. 1,408 rooms, 66 suites. AE, D, DC, MC, V.*

★ ⓸⓽ Checkers. Owned by the Ayala Group, which also runs the
$$$$ exquisite Campton Place in San Francisco, Checkers is as intimate and luxurious as a private club, without being the least bit pretentious or stuffy. This elegant, service-oriented smaller hotel is extremely popular with top corporate executives, attorneys, and fast-trackers, and for good reason: Checkers makes you feel important and pampered. This phoenix rose out of the $49-million gutting and renovation of the 1926-vintage Mayflower Hotel in the heart of Downtown. Rooms are on the compact side, but are quietly opulent in muted, soothing shades with expanses of marble, and brass fixtures in the bathrooms. Each room has three two-line phones (with voice mail), and fax machines are available for in-room use at a nominal charge. Among Checkers' many distinctive touches is the cozy mezzanine library, a perfect spot for informal meetings or simply for relaxing. Sports-minded guests are loaned workout garb, and there's a heated lap pool on the rooftop. The eponymous restaurant (*see* Business Breakfasts and Dining, below) is top rate—a destination

LOS ANGELES HOTEL CHART

HOTELS	Price Category	Banquet capacity	No. of meeting rooms	Secretarial services	Audiovisual equipment	Teletype news service	Computer rentals	In-room modem phonejack	All-news cable channel	Desk	Desk lighting	Bed lighting
Airport Hilton and Towers	$$$	2500	40	✓	✓	-	✓	-	✓	◐	●	●
Airport Marriott	$$$	850	37	✓	✓	-	-	-	✓	●	●	●
Beverly Hills Hotel and Bungalows	$$$	550	6	✓	✓	-	✓	✓	✓	●	●	●
The Biltmore	$$$	1000	16	-	✓	-	✓	-	✓	●	●	●
Bonaventure	$$	2000	22	✓	✓	-	-	-	✓	◐	◐	◐
Century City Inn	$$	0	0	✓	-	-	✓	-	-	◐	●	●
Century Plaza	$$$$	2500	23	✓	✓	-	✓	✓	✓	●	●	●
Checkers	$$$$	70	4	✓	✓	-	✓	✓	✓	●	●	●
Compri Hotel Los Angeles Harbor	$$	500	7	-	✓	-	-	-	-	●	●	●
Embassy Suites	$$	180	5	-	-	-	-	✓	✓	●	●	◐
L'Ermitage	$$$	80	2	✓	✓	-	-	-	✓	●	●	●
Four Seasons	$$$$	280	11	✓	✓	-	-	✓	✓	●	●	●
Hilton and Towers	$$$	666	28	✓	✓	-	✓	✓	✓	●	●	●
Hollywood Roosevelt	$$	600	9	-	-	-	-	-	-	●	●	●
Hotel Bel-Air	$$$$	180	2	✓	✓	-	✓	✓	✓	●	●	●
Hyatt Regency	$$	1500	15	-	✓	-	✓	-	✓	-	-	◐
New Otani Hotel and Gardens	$$$	750	8	-	-	-	-	-	-	●	●	●
Regent Beverly Wilshire	$$$$	800	8	✓	✓	-	-	✓	✓	●	●	●
St. James's Club	$$$$	75	3	✓	✓	-	✓	-	✓	●	●	●

$$$$ = over $175, $$$ = $125 -$175, $$ = under $125.
● good, ◐ fair, ○ poor.
All hotels listed here have photocopying and fax facilities.

| In-Room Amenities | | | | | | | | | | Hotel Amenities | | | | | | |
Nonsmoking rooms	In-room checkout	Minibar	Pay movies	VCR/Movie rentals	Hairdryer	Toiletries	Room service	Laundry/Dry cleaning	Pressing	Concierge	Barber/Hairdresser	Garage	Courtesy airport transport	Sauna	Pool	Exercise room
✓	✓	-	✓	✓	✓	●	◐	●	●	✓	✓	✓	✓		●	●
✓	✓	-	✓	-	✓	●	●	◐	◐	✓	✓	✓	✓	✓	●	●
-	-	-	-	✓	✓	●	●	●	●	✓	✓	✓	-	✓	●	●
✓	-	✓	✓	✓	✓	●	●	●	●	✓	✓	✓	-	✓	●	●
✓	✓	✓	✓	✓	✓	◐	●	●	●	✓	✓	✓	-	-	●	○
✓	-	-	-	✓	-	◐	-	●	●	-	-	✓	-	-	-	-
✓	✓	✓	✓	✓	✓	●	●	●	●	✓	✓	✓	-	✓	●	●
✓	-	✓	-	-	✓	●	●	●	●	✓	-	-	-	-	●	●
✓	-	✓	✓	-	-	◐	-	●	●	✓	✓	-	✓	✓	●	●
✓	✓	-	-	✓	-	◐	◐	●	●	-	-	✓	✓	✓	●	●
✓	-	✓	✓	-	-	●	●	●	●	✓	-	-	-	-	●	-
✓	-	✓	✓	✓	-	●	●	●	●	✓	-	✓	-	-	●	●
✓	✓	-	✓	-	-	◐	●	●	◐	✓	✓	✓	-	●	●	●
✓	-	✓	✓	✓	-	◐	●	●	◐	✓	-	✓	-	-	●	●
-	-	✓	-	-	✓	●	●	●	●	✓	-	-	-	-	●	-
✓	✓	-	✓	-	-	◐	●	-	-	✓	-	✓	-	-	-	◐
✓	-	✓	✓	-	-	◐	●	●	●	✓	✓	✓	-	✓	-	-
-	-	-	✓	-	✓	●	●	●	●	✓	-	✓	-	✓	●	●
-	-	✓	-	✓	✓	●	●	●	●	✓	-	✓	-	✓	●	●

Room service: ● 24-hour, ◐ 6AM-10PM, ○ other.
Laundry/Dry cleaning: ● same day, ◐ overnight, ○ other.
Pressing: ● immediate, ◐ same day, ○ other.

LOS ANGELES HOTEL CHART

HOTELS	Price Category	Business Services Banquet capacity	No. of meeting rooms	Secretarial services	Audiovisual equipment	Teletype news service	Computer rentals	In-room modem phone jack	All-news cable channel	Desk	Desk lighting	Bed lighting
Sheraton Grande	$$$	0	0	✓	✓	-	✓	✓	✓	●	●	◗
Sheraton Plaza La Reina	$$	650	99	✓	✓	-	✓	✓	-	●	●	●
Sheraton Universal	$$$	1000	15	✓	✓	-	✓	✓	✓	-	-	●
Stouffer Concourse	$$	1500	42	✓	✓	-	✓	✓	✓	●	●	●
Warner Center Hilton and Towers	$$	0	0	✓	✓	-	-	-	✓	●	●	◗
Warner Center Marriott	$$	800	16	-	✓	-	-	-	✓	●	●	●
Westwood Marquis Hotel and Garden	$$$$	120	6	✓	✓	-	✓	-	✓	●	●	●

$$$$ = over $175, **$$$** = $125 -$175, **$$** = under $125.
● good, ◗ fair, ○ poor.
All hotels listed here have photocopying and fax facilities.

In-Room Amenities	Nonsmoking rooms	In-room checkout	Minibar	Pay movies	VCR/Movie rentals	Hairdryer	Toiletries	Room service	Laundry/Dry cleaning	Pressing	Hotel Amenities	Concierge	Barber/Hairdresser	Garage	Courtesy airport transport	Sauna	Pool	Exercise room
	✓	✓	✓	✓	-	-	◑	●	◐	●		✓	-	✓	-	-	●	-
	✓	✓	✓	✓	-	-	◑	●	●	●		✓	✓	✓	✓	-	●	●
	✓	✓	✓	✓	-	-	◑	●	●	●		✓	-	✓	-	-	●	-
	✓	✓	✓	✓	-	✓	●	●	●	●		✓	-	✓	✓	✓	●	●
	✓	-	✓	✓	-	✓	●	●	●	◑		✓	-	✓	-	✓	●	-
	✓	✓	-	✓	-	-	◑	◑	●	◑		✓	-	✓	-	✓	●	●
	✓	-	✓	-	✓	✓	●	●	●	●		✓	✓	✓	-	✓	●	●

Room service: ● 24-hour, ◑ 6AM-10PM, ○ other.
Laundry/Dry cleaning: ● same day, ◐ overnight, ○ other.
Pressing: ● immediate, ◐ same day, ○ other.

even if you're not staying here. *An Ayala International hotel. 535 S. Grand Ave., 90071, tel. 213/624–0000, 800/ 628–4900, fax 213/626–9906. Gen. manager, Mark McGuffie. 173 rooms, 15 suites. AE, CB, DC, MC, V.*

㊹ **Hyatt Regency.** If location is indeed everything, then the
$$ Hyatt reigns supreme for doing business Downtown. It is situated in a mixed-use office and retail complex that is within walking distance of the Convention Center and most Downtown businesses. Without leaving the premises, guests have access to the 32-story Broadway Plaza office building, the Broadway department store, as well as two floors of shops, restaurants, and various services. A recent, massive renovation and remodeling have essentially made this a new hotel. Standard rooms are more comfortable and roomy than is the norm, each equipped with a desk, good lighting, and a telephone that allows for modem and portable fax transmissions. If you reserve well in advance, for the same rate you can get a larger corner room with city views, but alas, no desk. The top two floors are occupied by the executive-class Regency Club. The Lobby Bar (*see* After Hours, below) offers evening entertainment. *711 S. Hope St., 90017, tel. 213/683–1234, 800/ 233–1234, fax 213/629–3230. Gen. manager, Ralph Suda. 444 rooms, 41 suites. AE, D, DC, MC, V.*

㊶ **Los Angeles Hilton and Towers.** Although it recently un-
$$$ derwent a $70-million renovation and expansion, the Hilton remains a rather cold, impersonal hostelry. Yes, it's been considerably glamorized, and the public areas are picture-perfect, but the ambience is one of rather icy perfection. However, the redo has reversed the Hilton's downward slide, and once again it's a hub for conferences, business meetings, and tour groups. Room decor varies, but generally speaking, the style is soulless corporate contemporary, with inoffensively neutral colors and furnishings. In the Towers—the executive class hotel-within-a-hotel on the top two floors—rooms are exceptionally large and perks include complimentary Continental breakfast and evening hors d'oeuvres. A full-service business center and a variety of shops, services, and restaurants (including Cardini, a swanky, sophisticated Italian eatery, and a 24-hour coffee shop) are among the amenities. Within walking distance are the semichic Seventh Street Marketplace mall, many of Downtown's newer office buildings, and good restaurants such as Engine Co. 28 and Seventh Street Bistro (*see* Dining, below). *930 Wilshire Blvd., 90017, tel. 213/629–4321, 800/445–8667, fax 213/488–9869. Gen. manager, Larry Kirk. 868 rooms, 32 suites. AE, DC, MC, V.*

★ ㊼ **New Otani Hotel and Gardens.** It's no surprise that this re-
$$$ cently refurbished, Japanese-owned hotel, located in the heart of Little Tokyo (on the northeast edge of Downtown), is a favorite of visiting Japanese executives and tour groups. But it's also a peaceful haven for travelers who appreciate a bit of serenity in the middle of the city. Ideally located near city, state, and federal courts and government agencies, it's also close to a gaggle of terrific Japanese restaurants, like Kokekokko (on 2nd St.) and Kappo Kyara (in Little Tokyo Square on Alameda St.). The Japanese Experience package includes a Japanese-style room and some meals (your choice of either Jap-

anese or Western fare). Most rooms, however, have regular beds and faceless, modern decor, with minibars inexplicably located in the bathrooms, and adequate working spaces (though the phones are goofily placed across the room from desks). On the fourth floor is a fine Japanese restaurant, A Thousand Cranes, and a serene half-acre garden complete with ponds and walkways. *120 S. Los Angeles St., 90012, tel. 213/629–1200; in CA, 800/252–0197; in U.S. and Canada, 800/421–8795; fax 213/622–0980. Gen. manager, Kenji Yoshimoto. 434 rooms, 6 suites. AE, DC, MC, V.*

★ ❹❻ **Sheraton Grande.** Though it's Downtown—an easy walk
$$$ from the Stock Exchange and many major office centers— the Grande possesses a rare feeling of seclusion. In the afternoon, a pianist plays in the spacious marble lobby, floor butlers bring pots of coffee with wake-up calls, and a complimentary limo shuttles guests to Beverly Hills. There are no workout facilities on the premises, but guests may use the new YMCA down the street (except during peak late afternoon hours). There's even a blessedly uncrowded movie multiplex next door. The recently renovated rooms, pleasingly decorated, are among the largest Downtown; each has a fine marble bathroom, a desk, and a two-line phone with a modem port and a 10-foot cord. The quiet lobby has many comfortable nooks for informal meetings. *345 S. Figueroa St., 90071, tel. 213/617–1133, 800/325–3535, fax 213/613–0291. Gen. manager, H. Karl Schaefer, 339 rooms, 36 suites. AE, CB, DC, MC, V.*

Hollywood/West Hollywood

❸❼ **Hollywood Roosevelt Hotel.** This once-famous 12-story ho-
$$ tel, closed in 1984, reopened a year later after new owners undertook a complete renovation and sensitive restoration of the original Spanish colonial style (intricate tile work, woodwork, arches, and such, updated with a subtle rose-and-taupe color scheme). Rooms have been modernized, and are very tasteful if not terribly distinctive. A marvelous fillip was added by having artist David Hockney paint the bottom of the hotel's swimming pool— life imitating art imitating life. Guests include lots of starry-eyed tourists (who, unfortunately, won't see too many stars around here), but business travelers wanting to be near major recording studios or other entertainment industries appreciate the hotel's location, as well as its beautiful old meeting rooms, moderate prices, and the Cinegrill (*see* After Hours, below), a terrific, '40s-style jazz supper club. *7000 Hollywood Blvd., Hollywood, 90028, tel. 213/466–7000, fax 213/462–8056. Gen. manager, Bruno Fava. 360 rooms, 20 suites, 80 poolside cabanas. AE, CB, DC, MC, V.*

❷❼ **St. James's Club.** The former Sunset Towers, an imposing
$$$$ apartment building popular with Hollywood stars such as Jean Harlow and Clark Gable, was placed in the National Registry of Historic Places in 1979, and in 1985, a London-based firm spent a bundle turning it into a small hotel with opulent '30s decor and great city views from most of the rooms. Most rooms are suites; there are also some spacious doubles, but practical working space is limited in nonsuite rooms. Although many of the lavish furnishings are costly copies of Art Deco pieces in the Metropolitan Museum in New York, you get a little too much of a good

thing in the suites, which are done in a sort of *uber*-Deco, with overscaled furniture and garish colors. However, the public rooms are as sleek as the sets of *The Gay Divorcée*. The gimmick is that this is a private club—though, in fact, anyone may buy a membership for $8 a day, which will be tacked onto your room rate. In keeping with the club atmosphere, there's a dining room that mimics the great supper clubs of yesteryear in both look and service; a pool; health spa; business center; and secretarial service. *8358 Sunset Blvd., West Hollywood, 90069, tel. 213/654-7100, 800/225-2637, fax 213/654-9287. Gen. manager, Allan Blest. 18 rooms, 44 suites. AE, CB, MC, V.*

Westside/West Los Angeles

★ ⑥ **Hotel Bel-Air.** A night at Hotel Bel-Air is akin to an escape
$$$$ to a parallel universe—a tranquil, luxury-laden Arcadia where swans drift lazily in ponds, towering trees provide a sylvan canopy, and fragrant blooms abound throughout a lush, 12-acre glade, in which the hotel is half hidden. It's a short drive down a canyon road to Sunset Boulevard and Westwood Village, but this isn't the place to stay if you wish to be centrally located; it's really convenient to nowhere. No matter. Guests, many of whom register under assumed names, don't dash in and out to make sales calls—their meetings come to them. The hotel was recently sold to a Japanese company (for a record-setting $110 million—that's $1.2 million per room), but the Bel-Air still bears the imprint of its previous owner, Caroline Hunt Schoellkopf, who had beautifully renovated and expanded it. The hotel's individuality—no two rooms are alike—was greatly due to Schoellkopf's decision to employ five big-name designers, including the late Kalef Aleton, Louis Cataffo, and Betty Garber. Though rooms reflect each designer's style, all share elements like wood-burning fireplaces, and architectural details like window seats, French doors, and hand-stenciled ceiling beams. Rooms and suites are located in six single story California mission-style buildings spread across the grounds; many also have private patios and Jacuzzis. The Hotel Bel-Air Restaurant is one of the classiest, most romantic eateries in town, and the food is imaginative and fabulous, as well. *701 Stone Canyon Road, Bel Air, 90077, tel. 213/472-1211, fax 213/476-5890. Managing dir., Paul Zuest. 59 rooms, 33 suites. AE, CB, DC, MC, V.*

⑱ **Beverly Hills Hotel and Bungalows.** A sprawling, three-
$$$ story pink main building and 21 fabled bungalows (recently outfitted with central air and marble bathrooms) are set amid palm trees and wide lawns on a 12-acre site not far from central Beverly Hills, but not really within walking distance, either. This place is a haven for executives and celebrities who prefer their presence to be known (as opposed to the seclusion and privacy of the Hotel Bel-Air). Amenities include tennis courts, a pool embraced by private cabanas, an exercise room, shops, and restaurants. Rooms in the main building are done in pastels with relatively simple furnishings (although some rooms border on the shabby and reek of cigarette smoke); the standard ones aren't particularly large. A better bet are the "superior" rooms on the main floor, many of which, for the same price, have large private patios. Two-line phones with modem outlets are on all desks, and rooms have VCRs and ac-

cess to a video library. Unless you're a "somebody," service can be awfully sniffy. The legendary Polo Lounge (*see* Business Breakfasts, below) remains a show-business power-meal institution in which the right seat (which is the booth that faces the entrance) is a sure sign of success—the food is decidedly mediocre. The coffee shop, however, is wonderful. *9641 Sunset Blvd., Beverly Hills, 90210, tel. 213/276–2251, fax 213/281–2919. Gen. manager, Kerman Beriker. 247 rooms and 21 bungalows. AE, CB, D, MC, V.*

★ ⑲ **Century City Inn.** It's as difficult to find a well-located,
$$ moderately priced Westside hotel as it is a cruising cab in L.A., which makes this modest businessperson's hotel worth knowing about. Opened in 1988, it's perfectly located for those doing business in Century City or West L.A., and though there are just 46 generic, California-contemporary style rooms, it has a big hotel-style business center complete with copiers, computers, and fax machines. Each room is conveniently equipped with a microwave, refrigerator, and VCR. Service is limited but friendly. *10330 W. Olympic Blvd., Century City, 90064, tel. 213/553–1000, fax 213/277–1633. Gen. manager, Trout Felker. 34 rooms, 12 suites. AE, CB, DC, MC, V.*

⑳ **Century Plaza Hotel.** The Century Plaza rises out of what
$$$$ was once the Twentieth Century-Fox studio backlot, and remains the practical place to stay if you need to be a short walk from Century City's high-rise business and entertainment offices. It's not the city's best or most beautiful hotel—indeed, many think this sweeping, '60s-style, arc-shaped hotel and its adjoining 30-story tower has too many rooms, too much hustle and bustle. All the characterless, blandly contemporary rooms in the massive main building and tower addition have private balconies and views. A thorough renovation marked the hotel's 25th anniversary in 1991. Guests paying corporate rates receive a 50% discount on Super Shuttle van service to LAX, and are entitled to complimentary limo rides to nearby Beverly Hills or Westwood. *A Westin hotel. 2025 Ave. of the Stars, Century City, 90067, tel. 213/277–2000; in U.S., 800/228–3000; in Canada, 800/268–8383; fax 213/551–3355. Managing dir., Bodo Lemke. 683 doubles, 67 suites in main building; 313 rooms, 9 suites in Tower. AE, CB, DC, V.*

★ ㉕ **L'Ermitage.** With baroque music wafting through the inti-
$$$ mate reception area (no grand lobby here), and an impressive collection of original Impressionist paintings on the walls, this all-suite, eight-story hotel, built in 1976, is the closest L.A. comes to a small, luxurious European inn. A recent renovation and added room lighting have brightened the heretofore somber color scheme. Also installed were huge Jacuzzi tubs and showers with steam jets in some of the suites, duvets on beds, and color TVs in the bathrooms. The suites, which resemble plush apartments more than they do hotel rooms, also feature kitchens, dining rooms, and multiple-line phones; and there is free limo service provided to the Beverly Hills-West Hollywood area. Corporate executives and celebrities such as Placido Domingo prefer the large Town House suites. Service throughout the hotel is superb. Le Petit Ermitage next door is a hidden, swanky hospice for stars recovering from plastic surgery. *9291 Burton Way, Beverly Hills, 90210,*

tel. 213/278–3344; in U.S. and Canada, 800/424–4443; fax 213/278–8247. Gen manager, Alexis Eliopulos. AE, MC, V.

★ ㉖ **Four Seasons.** For executives and publishing and enter-
$$$$ tainment industry folk who find the Bel-Air a little too out of the way and the Beverly Hills Hotel a tad too glitzy/tacky, the Four Seasons, opened in 1987, has become the hotel of choice. Its location on the border of Beverly Hills and Los Angeles is convenient to West Hollywood, the Wilshire District, and Beverly Hills. The staff is unfailingly friendly and helpful. Public rooms, which open onto beautifully landscaped terraces and gardens, are appointed with cozy, overstuffed sofas and sink-into chairs. Antiques, spectacular flower displays, and original art, combined with a sense of urban seclusion, make this one of L.A.'s premiere hotels, home to guests ranging from President Bush to the Rolling Stones. Though guest rooms aren't huge, they're flawlessly appointed. Each room offers bathroom TVs, marble vanities, and good desks. Guests who arrive before check-in or whose flights leave after check-out may use an executive suite at no charge. And there's also no tariff for use of in-room fax machines, exercise bikes, shoe shines, and limo rides to Beverly Hills. Windows (*see* After Hours, below) is perfect for tea or a late-evening drink. *300 S. Doheny Dr., L.A., 90048, tel. 213/273–2222; in U.S., 800/332–3442; in Canada, 800/268–6282; fax 213/859–3824. Gen. manager, Kurt Stielhack. 106 rooms, 179 suites. AE, CB, D, MC, V.*

★ ㉓ **Regent Beverly Wilshire.** In 1987, the Hong Kong-based
$$$$ Regent group purchased this tired, landmark hotel, closed it for two years, and spent some $68 million to totally renovate the original (1926) building. Then, in 1990, a health spa was added and the "new" wing, built in 1971, underwent renovation (which is still in progress). This venerable institution, right in the thick of Beverly Hills, once again draws the crème de la crème of the business and entertainment fields. Public rooms are decorated in an elegant Regency/Directoire style; guest rooms follow suit. Accommodations have been enlarged, and are accessorized with antiques. Deluxe-class rooms have sitting areas with sofas and chairs, as well as three TVs and phones. Baths in all rooms have glass shower stalls, separate, spacious bathtubs, and full-length mirrors. Steward service on each floor is impeccable. The business center provides all the customary services, along with space for informal meetings. The Dining Room (*see* Dining, below) is a culinary destination for locals as well as hotel guests. The Cafe (*see* Business Breakfasts, below) is fine for an early meeting, and the Bar (*see* After Hours, below) is a good place to unwind. *9500 Wilshire Blvd., Beverly Hills, 90212, tel. 213/275–5200, 800/421–4354, fax 213/274–2851. Gen. manager, Alain M. Longatte. AE, DC, MC, V.*

❼ **Westwood Marquis Hotel & Garden.** The understated ele-
$$$$ gance of this 15-story, all-suite hotel appeals to the likes of Lee Iacocca and Dustin Hoffman; media and entertainment executives from New York also fill its suites—not bad for a place that used to be a UCLA dorm. Attractive features include efficient yet personable service, a location on a quiet residential street in Westwood Village, and a half-acre garden with two swimming pools. UCLA, Westwood's abundant shops, theaters, restaurants, and

many Wilshire Boulevard office buildings are within walking distance. The one-, two-, and three-bedroom suites are spacious and have comfortable parlors, complete with desks, but are of undistinguished design. The china cabinets housing faux-antique items in the rooms are locked—a rather tacky inference that some guests may be light-fingered. There are several two-line phones in each suite, with voice-mail and modem/fax capabilities. Complimentary limos transport guests to Century City and Beverly Hills. *930 Hilgard Ave., Westwood, 90024, tel. 213/208–8765, 800/421–2317, fax 213/824–0355. Gen. manager, Jacques Camus. 285 suites. AE, CB, DC, MC, V.*

San Fernando Valley

❸ **Sheraton Universal.** On the same property as Universal
$$$ Studios and MCA's monolithic headquarters, this 20-story hotel is also close to The Burbank Studios and the many businesses in Burbank and Studio City. A tram takes guests to the MCA building, specialty restaurants (although what most of them specialize in is lousy food), and the studio tour. Built in 1969, the Sheraton completed an extensive renovation in 1990; now marble floors (in the baths and entries), minibars, and safes are standard in all rooms. Unfortunately, the lobby still looks like the leftover set from a Gothic horror movie. Also added was a sports bar named for Telly Savalas, who has lived in the hotel for 20 years. The contemporary rooms, done in the ubiquitous corporate/Southwestern mode endemic to current hotel redos, are a bit larger than the norm, and most have terrific views of the Valley. Its size and amenities make this hotel popular for meetings and conferences of all sizes. *333 Universal Terrace Pkwy., Universal City, 91608, tel. 818/980–1212, 800/325–3535, fax 818/985–4980. Gen. manager, Creston Woods. 423 rooms, 23 suites. AE, CB, DC, MC, V.*

❶ **Warner Center Hilton and Towers.** Opened in late 1989, this
$$ 15-story business-oriented hotel is located in the western end of the Valley, in the middle of the sprawling, prefab Warner Center business/retail/residential megalopolis. Rooms, decorated in an inoffensive, phony Art Deco fashion, are relatively large; those on the Towers floors have such extras as two-line phones with call-waiting. The Towers has the usual executive-class services, along with complimentary breakfast and hors d'oeuvres. Use of the large athletic club next door is available to guests for $10 a day (no charge for Towers patrons), but use of the pool is free. There's no business center, but the hotel will send and receive faxes, make copies, and provide guests with computers. *6360 Canoga Ave., Woodland Hills, 91367, tel. 818/595–1000, 800/445–8667, fax 818/595–1090. Gen. manager, Uwe Holtorf. 313 rooms, 23 suites. AE, CB, DC, V.*

❷ **Warner Center Marriott.** Opened in 1986 at a cost of $55
$$ million, this humongous hotel was the first property in the then newly developed Warner Center. The focus here is on business; 80% of the clientele consists of folks dealing with the major insurance companies, defense contractors, and high-tech industries that have relocated to the area in recent years. It's also a major center for meetings and conventions, boasting meeting rooms of every size, and two huge kitchens to service them all, including one kosher

kitchen. Rooms, done in the usual soft pastels, have sitting areas and good work space. The top two floors are devoted to an executive-class hotel-within-a-hotel. *21850 Oxnard Ave., Woodland Hills, 91367, tel. 818/887–4800, 818/228–9290, fax 818/340–5893. Gen. manager, Rene Boskoff. 453 rooms, 20 suites. AE, DC, MC, V.*

Airport/South Bay

⑰ **Compri Hotel Los Angeles Harbor.** Opened in 1989 in
$$ L.A.'s port community of San Pedro, this is a business hotel with some resort amenities. The three-story property is located on a multi-acre parcel overlooking a marina, and is well positioned for travelers doing business in the South Bay and the industrial areas around the L.A. Harbor. Rooms are compact yet functional. The Compri Club, a large, informal meeting and working area—sort of a grown-up rumpus room—off the main lobby, is complete with big-screen TV, telephone-equipped desks, and a library. Here a complimentary, cooked-to-order breakfast is served, along with early evening cocktails and late-night snacks. There are also two lighted tennis courts. *2800 Via Cabrilla Marina, San Pedro, 90731, tel. 213/ 514–3344, fax 213/547–9612. Gen. manager, Jeffrey K. Protzman. 212 rooms, 12 suites. AE, CB, DC, MC, V.*

⑫ **Embassy Suites Hotel.** It's difficult to take a hotel corpora-
$$ tion that "hires" Garfield as its spokescat too seriously, but practicality and economy are the strong suits at the second of the Embassy chain's properties at LAX (the other, just off the Imperial Terminal on the south side of LAX, is named Embassy Suites Hotel-LAX/Imperial, so if you hop aboard a courtesy van upon arrival, make sure you're headed for the right one). The spacious rooms, amenities, and color schemes are standard for the chain, yet are a cut above most hotels in this range. A full breakfast is complimentary. Facilities include an indoor pool, 4,100 square feet of banquet or meeting space, seven conference suites, and guest laundry facilities. *9801 Airport Blvd., L.A., 90045 tel. 213/215–1000, 800/634–0066, fax 213/215–1952. Gen. manager, Anthony Lovoy. 215 suites (7 for disabled). AE, CB, DC, MC, V.*

⑭ **Los Angeles Airport Hilton and Towers.** More than 85,000
$$$ square feet of meeting and conference space make this 17-story hotel, with its dramatic smoked-glass and granite exterior, one of the world's largest airport hotels and conference centers. The top two floors are devoted to the executive-class Towers, which offer a complimentary Continental breakfast, evening hors d'oeuvres, and a boardroom for informal meetings. The lounge has the same view of the south runways as the LAX control tower. There are five restaurants and a fully equipped business center, yet the generic, corporate-looking rooms lack good workspace. However, despite its immense size and all the hustle and bustle, this is a good place to stay if you need to be in the area. *5711 W. Century Blvd., L.A., tel. 213/410– 4000, 800/445–8667, fax 213/410–6250. Gen. manager, John Elford. 1,200 rooms, 79 suites. AE, CB, DC, MC, V.*

⑬ **Los Angeles Airport Marriott.** Formerly the flagship of the
$$$ Marriott chain, this 1973-built hotel was one of LAX's first luxury properties. Though large and very busy, the Marriott manages to maintain a friendly, warm atmos-

phere that sets it apart from other airport inns. It recently underwent a major renovation; the top two of the 18 floors are concierge levels, offering a private lounge, complimentary Continental breakfast, evening hors d'oeuvres, and space for small meetings. Standard rooms are reasonably spacious and contemporary in style, with two phones and good desks. A business center provides secretarial services, including word processing. Three restaurants, retail shops, a laundry room (something few hotels have), and a pool complete with swim-up bar are on the grounds. *5855 W. Century Blvd., L.A., 90045, tel. 213/ 641–5700, fax 213/337–5358. Gen. manager, Charlton W. Hines. 993 rooms, 19 suites. AE, DC, MC, V.*

⑪ **Sheraton Plaza La Reina.** With more than 100 meeting
$$ rooms ranging from the intimate to the grand, the Sheraton lives and breathes business—the overall mood is one of cool functionality, not elegance. Though the ambience is somewhat cold, the staff more than makes up for that with its amiability and helpfulness. The modern rooms, in requisite pastels, get larger the higher up they are; you can request one with a sitting area or work desk. As with the other airport hotels, this place has a variety of services, including retail shops, self-service laundry, business center, three lounges, and two restaurants. A free shuttle runs every few hours to Manhattan Beach and a nearby mall. *6101 W. Century Blvd., L.A., 90045, tel. 213/642– 1111, fax 213/410–1267. Gen. manager, Jerry Golenor, 641 rooms, 166 suites. AE, DC, MC, V.*

⑮ **Stouffer Concourse Hotel.** In addition to providing plenty
$$ of work-related facilities, this efficient, 12-story hotel has 18 corner suites with terraces equipped with private spas—a nice, sybaritic touch for the business traveler. The top two stories are the Club Floors, which have standard-size rooms with upgraded amenities and a lounge that serves complimentary Continental breakfast. Guests in the regular rooms (which are comfortable, contemporary, and characterless) are brought coffee and a morning paper with wake-up calls. Meeting facilities include a large, tiered theater and a range of conference rooms. TV monitors in the lobby display flight information from the major airlines. *5400 W. Century Blvd., L.A., 90045, tel. 213/216–5858, 800/468–3571, fax 213/645–8053. Gen. manager, John Reiss. 703 rooms, 47 suites. AE, DC, MC, V.*

DINING

by Merrill Shindler

When it comes to eating in Los Angeles, the first thing you must understand is that this is a city without a center. Even if you're searching for what cynics consider to be L.A.'s best-known contribution to American regional cuisine—surf 'n' turf—you're probably going to have to drive some distance to find it. But the drive is often worth it, for hidden in the midst of this urban and suburban sprawl are culinary treasures that rival the finest in the world. After decades of slavishly following the cooking styles of other cities (as in "New York-style Italian" or "Hong Kong-style Chinese"), L.A.'s chefs, especially its young chefs, have headed for regions not formerly explored—or even imagined. At cocktail parties, the conversation may begin with housing prices, but it inevitably works its way to restaurants. In L.A., eating well keeps the wheels of commerce and entertainment well lubricated.

A note about dress: Ties are not expected in any but a very few formal restaurants (though they're common at the Downtown places, just because the locals have to wear them to work). L.A.'s large entertainment, design, and fashion industries are notoriously casual, and you'll look like an out-of-towner if you wear a businesslike pin-striped suit (unless it's an Armani) to such trendy spots as Trumps or Citrus; men are well advised to pack a hip sportcoat, and women a casual-chic ensemble, for fashionable L.A. dining.

The restaurants that follow are scattered all over the L.A. basin, though most are in the most central areas popular with travelers and residents alike. They are divided into these categories: Downtown, Hollywood/West Hollywood (including the central L.A. area), Westside (including Beverly Hills, West L.A., and Santa Monica), San Gabriel Valley, and South Bay (not far from LAX).

Highly recommended restaurants in each price category are indicated by a ★.

Category	Cost*
$$$$ (Very Expensive)	over $50
$$$ (Expensive)	$26–$50
$$ (Moderate)	$10–$25
$ (Inexpensive)	under $10

per person, excluding drinks, service, and 6½% sales tax.

Numbers in the margin correspond to numbered restaurant locations on the Los Angeles Lodging and Dining maps.

Business Breakfasts

Unlike New York, home of the power breakfast, Los Angeles is not a city where many residents go out for breakfast, even to do business. The morning ritual for most Angelenos consists of a 3-mile jog and a hearty breakfast of Ultra Slim-Fast, followed by an hour stuck in traffic. But for those who must meet for breakfast, certain spots predominate. Downtown, there's a superb breakfast at the elegant **Checkers** (Checkers Hotel, tel. 213/624–0000). Breakfast at the **Polo Lounge** (Beverly Hills Hotel, tel. 213/276–2251) is not a wonderful meal, but the local power brokers (most in show business) feel a sentimental attachment to it. Nearby, in the **Cafe at the Regent Beverly Wilshire** (tel. 213/274–8179), the food is much better, the setting more convenient, and the service great. And both writers and actors love informal **Hugo's** (8401 Santa Monica Blvd., West Hollywood, tel. 213/654–3993), whose Italian dishes include an exceptionally filling spaghetti carbonara mixed with scrambled eggs.

Downtown

⑤⓪ Bernard's. After a multimillion-dollar restoration, the
$$$$ Biltmore has returned from its dowdy decline to the ranks
of one of L.A.'s great hotels. And its tastefully ornate dining room has returned as well, revived after the departure
of its founding father, Bernard Jacoupy (who now runs
West L.A.'s Lunaria). The room is noted for its indirect
lighting, its quiet atmosphere, and the privacy of its few,
widely spaced tables, making it especially appropriate for
discreet business meetings. The menu is a paean to
nouvelle cuisine—modest portions of chartreuse of lobster and sweetbreads with a "butter" of fresh peas, and
steamed red snapper served on a bed of creamed parsley.
A harp player fills the room with soothing sounds.
*Biltmore Hotel, 515 S. Olive St., tel. 213/612–1580. Jacket
and tie required. Reservations essential. AE, CB, DC,
MC, V.*

★ ④⑨ Checkers. Checkers sits ever so elegantly in the rear of the
$$$$ hotel of the same name, the Southern California branch of
San Francisco's fine Campton Place. Open for breakfast,
lunch, and dinner, it's one of downtown's best business
restaurants. Its quiet, soothing space, with peachy-pastel
colors, soft lighting, abundant flowers, and white linens, is
tucked in the midst of the high-rise frenzy that's busily
giving L.A. its long-awaited skyline. The menu is best described as new American: sweet-potato waffles and duck
hash for breakfast, smoked ham shanks with roasted crab
apples for lunch, hickory smoked duck with a chestnut flan
for dinner. It sounds eccentric, but it tastes wonderful.
You'll certainly impress your guests here—and please
yourself as well. *535 S. Grand Ave., tel. 213/624–0000.
Jacket and tie advised. Reservations essential. AE, CB,
DC, MC, V.*

⑤① Empress Pavilion. This is the premier Hong Kong-style
$$ Chinese restaurant in Chinatown, capable of seating some
800 diners in an elegantly appointed room that swarms
with hosts, waiters, and busboys. Come lunchtime, much
of Chinatown shows up for the dim sum, a wide assort-
ment of dumplings served from rolling carts that criss-
cross the dining room, feeding groups of 10 or 12 at a time.
The noise level remains high at dinnertime, as banquet ta-
bles are piled high with steaming bowls of shark's fin soup
and heaping platters of Peking duck emerging at a frantic
rate from the kitchen. Despite the size of the place, and
the huge menu, the service is superb—but the noise
makes it more a place for fun, not work. *Bamboo Plaza,
988 N. Hill St., tel. 213/617–9898. Informal dress. Reser-
vations essential. AE, MC, V.*

★ ④② Engine Co. No. 28. An old firehouse, on the verge of being
$$ demolished, was saved as an historical landmark and
turned into one of downtown's best American restaurants
(and bars, *see* After Hours, below). The high-ceilinged
room is reminiscent of the grills of San Francisco—filled
with gleaming woodwork and booths, serviced by bar-
tenders who know how to make a proper martini and a
kitchen that can cook a steak black and blue. This is Guy
Food—steaks and chops, chili, meatloaf, superb onion
rings, and thin, crisp fries sprinkled with chili pepper.
The comfortable upholstered booths offer a good sense of
privacy for conversation, and the larger tables in back are

comfortable for meetings. *644 S. Figueroa St., tel. 213/ 624–6996. Business casual dress. Reservations essential. AE, MC, V.*

48 **Rex, Il Ristorante.** What is arguably the most expensive
$$$$ restaurant in town is inarguably the most elegant. A virtual museum of Art Deco, it occupies the ground floor of the Art Deco Oviatt Building, a beacon of taste in the midst of L.A.'s transitional Downtown area. Even the doors were made by Lalique. Inside is a superb bar on the upstairs balcony, with a black marble dance floor and a pianist who plays like Bobby Short. Below, in the dining room (a one-time haberdashery), tables sit far apart, offering a maximum of privacy. After years of serving miniature portions of Italian *nuova cucina*, Rex has a skilled new chef whose cooking is a bit heartier in style and larger in portion; dishes include a potato soup with tuna, pappardelle noodles with quail and artichoke hearts, and incomparable veal chops. The large wine list is predictably pricey. In all, expect to be wowed—and to pay a pretty penny. Though this is a fine spot for top-drawer business entertaining, the sheer dazzle of the room makes meetings seem distinctly out of place. *617 S. Olive St., tel. 213/627– 2300. Jacket and tie advised. Reservations essential. AE, CB, DC, MC, V.*

45 **Seventh Street Bistro.** Along with Rex, Checkers, and
$$$$ Bernard's, this place completes the quadrumvirate of downtown's most elegant restaurants. The surprisingly modern space is situated within the exquisitely restored Fine Arts Building (don't miss the adjacent lobby, with its remarkable fountains and murals). Don't let the word "bistro" fool you—this is a formal nouvelle French restaurant, with elegant service, subdued lighting, and one of the best chefs in town. Try the cold cream of watercress soup served with Santa Monica bay shrimp fritters, duck breast with rhubarb purée, or crayfish salad wrapped in sautéed eggplant. In the staid world of Downtown dining, chef Laurent Quenioux's creations would be considered outlandish if they didn't work so well—you'd never believe a celery-root purée could taste so good. *815 W. 7th St., tel. 213/627–1242. Jacket and tie advised. Reservations required. AE, CB, DC, MC, V.*

43 **The Tower.** Though Los Angeles stretches from the moun-
$$$ tains to the sea, there are few restaurants that afford vistas of the basin. The Tower, which sits atop the Transamerica Building, offers the best view of any restaurant in town (you can even helicopter to the roof of the building and walk down the stairs into the restaurant, a decidedly memorable experience). On a very clear evening, you can watch planes land and take off at distant LAX and admire the sunset over Santa Monica. After several years of serving dated Continental cuisine, the Tower has become one of L.A.'s few remaining classic French restaurants, featuring chicken au Grand Marnier, steak au poivre, and duckling with olives. The restaurant is on several levels, so every table offers a view. This is a fine setting for a business meeting. *1150 S. Olive St., 32nd floor, tel. 213/746–1554. Jacket and tie strongly advised. Reservations required. AE, CB, DC, MC, V.*

Hollywood/West Hollywood

★ **36** **Angeli Caffe.** There's hardly a restaurant more definitively
$$ casual—or more constantly crowded—than Angeli, which
sits in the very heart (and indeed may actually *be* the
heart) of the ultratrendy Melrose district. Angeli is noth-
ing more than a pair of busy, minimalist rooms, with floor-
to-ceiling windows facing the street and an open kitchen
balancing the back of each room. Tables are small and
crowded, not the sort of setting for a business deal—but a
great spot for very amusing people-watching. The anti-
pasto plates are like no others: an assortment of smoked
meats, baked ricotta tartlets, fried eggplant, grilled ol-
ives, and small rice and potato croquettes. The pizzas are
among the most authentic this side of Naples. *7274 Mel-
rose Ave., Hollywood, tel. 213/936–9086. (Also:* **Trattoria
Angeli,** *11651 Santa Monica Blvd., West L.A., tel. 213/
478–1191; and* **Angeli Mare,** *Marina Marketplace, 13455
Maxella Ave., Marina del Rey, tel. 213/822–1984.) Casu-
al dress. Reservations essential. AE, MC, V.*

40 **Campanile.** Named for the tower that crowns this 1928,
$$$ Charlie Chaplin-built landmark, Campanile is run by the
married team of Mark Peel and Nancy Silverton, veterans
of Michael's, Spago, and Maxwell's Plum in New York.
Campanile is a wonderful-looking restaurant. You enter
through a fine café, with a bar off to one side, a rustic fountain in the middle of the room, and a skylight overhead
that allows you to look up at the looming campanile. Beyond the café is a long, cloisterlike room, with tables on
one side and the kitchen on the other. In back is a dining
room with an isolated balcony running around its perimeter (some think the balcony is too removed from the action,
but it's much preferred for doing business). The food is, at
once, Californian, French, Italian, Mediterranean, and
many permutations in between, and virtually everything
is cooked with olive oil. The poached mozzarella with pesto
and the grilled prime rib are memorable; every table receives incredible breads from the adjacent bakery and a
steaming plate of grilled vegetables. Silverton made her
name as a pastry chef for very good reason. Service can
sometimes drag. *624 S. La Brea Ave., Wilshire District,
tel. 213/938–1447. Studied casual dress. Reservations required. AE, MC, V.*

35 **Chapo.** The owners are Philipe and Hilde Leiaghat, whose
$$ previous restaurant was the De Pottekyker (The Curi-
osity) in Antwerp. Their latest effort is a moderate-
ly priced California-French-Italian-Belgian restaurant
which serves, among other things, a spectacular tomato-
corn soup. The menu includes baked goat cheese with fat
croutons flavored with olive tapenade, and grilled chicken
with a light goat cheese sauce and a heap of french fries,
something the Belgians make better than anyone else. If
you pretend the rice tart is rice pudding, you'll be in com-
fort-food heaven. Located in the middle of too-hip Mel-
rose, the setting is serenely quiet and candlelighted, a
nice spot for an impromptu business meeting. *7661 Mel-
rose Ave., Hollywood, tel. 213/655–2924. Casual dress.
Reservations helpful. AE, MC, V.*

29 **Chaya Brasserie.** This fashionable celebrity haunt is
$$$ owned by the Tsunodas, a family of restaurateurs in Japan
since the 17th century. Despite the family's venerable tra-

dition, Chaya Brasserie is radically modern. Situated
next door to Cedars-Sinai Medical Center on the edge of
West Hollywood, it serves food that's mostly Franco-Cali-
fornian, with some Japanese touches. You dine under a
high beamed ceiling, in a room awash with mirrors and
potted palms, with a casual brasserie atmosphere. The
menu lists grilled smoked eel on pumpernickel points,
poached red snapper stuffed with artichoke, lamb chops
with a rosemary pesto sauce, and pan-fried oysters in a
puff pastry with a sorrel cream sauce. Portions can be substantial, and it's all delicious. Only meet here with those
who are tolerant of more than a little ambient noise. *8741
Alden Dr., central L.A., tel. 213/859–8833. Casual dress.
Reservations essential. AE, MC, V.*

★ ❸❽ **Citrus.** Citrus is the brainchild of chubby, avuncular
$$$ Michel Richard, who spent many years being L.A.'s favor-
ite French pastry chef before becoming the city's overall
favorite chef. This is perhaps the best restaurant in town,
a perfect combination of superb food and the casual Los
Angeles style that's evident in every aspect of Citrus: the
oversize white patiolike room with its curious indoor um-
brellas; the spotless glass-walled kitchen, where you can
see chefs and assistants bustling about; and chatty, well-
informed waiters who help customers put together the
best meal possible. The Hollywood Power People love Cit-
rus, which has remained (along with Spago) the hottest
ticket in town for several years. The undeniable bottom
line is that the food is remarkable—Richard is always
there, tasting in the kitchen, greeting customers at their
tables, worrying that something's wrong. Business meet-
ings work especially well in the privacy of the small room
to the right of the hostess's desk. *6703 Melrose Ave., Hol-
lywood, tel. 213/857–0034. Casual dress (many in jacket
and tie). Reservations strongly advised. AE, MC, V.*

★ ❸❹ **Indigo.** It's hard to be blue in Indigo, which is basically one
$$ big room, where you can see who's eating what with whom.
Behind a window at the far end is a garden, complete with
a faux waterfall and a little fisherman trolling in it, an offbeat memento from the Thai restaurant that once filled
this space near West Hollywood. With its small, kitschy
touches, Indigo doesn't seem quite real. There's more
than just a creative menu writer at work here—the food
tastes as great as it sounds. It's hard to choose between
such starters as Chinese crisp-fried baby squid in a spicy
chili sauce and chicken and spinach potstickers with a mint
dipping sauce. Main dishes include a Thai shrimp and papaya salad, a super grilled chicken (with rosemary and
garlic), and wonderful charred lamb loin brochettes and
flank steaks—really charred, not faux charred as at too
many places. They make their own bread, too, flavored
with rosemary and garlic. It's a good space for casual
meetings or just a good time. *8222-½ W. 3rd St., central
L.A., tel. 213/653–0140. Casual dress. Reservations advised. AE, MC, V.*

★ ❸⓪ **Locanda Veneta.** This small, incredibly popular trattoria
$$ may be across the street from Cedars-Sinai Medical Cen-
ter and down the block from the Beverly Center, but when
you're at your table you'll swear you're in Venice on a
warm summer's night, with the evening breeze flowing
through the windows. The image of Venice is further rein-
forced by the green olive oil being poured over the carpac-

cio and the sizzle of the roast lamb (served in a mustard and walnut sauce). Close your eyes (or drink enough Pinot grigio) and you'll imagine you hear the songs of the gondoliers. It's hard to choose from the simple menu—perhaps the *frittura di bianchetti* (pan-fried whitebait served with a fine pile of vinegared onions cooked to a mush) or the *trittico di mozzarelle,* a trio of freshly made mozzarellas with tomatoes, basil, and olive oil. Unfortunately, the noise level of this fine but extremely cozy spot makes it inappropriate for meetings; come here for the pleasure of the cuisine, and the company. *8368 W. 3rd St., central L.A., tel. 213/274–1893. Casual dress. Reservations required. AE, MC, V.*

33 **Mandarette.** Like sushi, dim sum is a recent discovery for
$ most Americans. But unlike sushi, it was never intended to be eaten at any old time of the day. Dim sum is meant to be eaten during late morning, or in the early afternoon as a sort of pick-me-up. But at this offspring of the far grander Mandarin, dim sum and then some are served into the small hours of the morning. Located near the Beverly Center and West Hollywood, the room is as spare as can be—a big shoebox with a high ceiling and lots of industrial appointments. The dishes range from dim sum standbys (dumplings, pastries, and so forth) to miniature versions of full-fledged Chinese dishes. Under the *Binh* and *Bao* (Breads and Pancakes) heading are a hot dog Mandarette (actually a Chinese pork sausage), onion pancakes, and a spiced-beef sandwich. The menu continues through garlic catfish, clams in black-bean sauce, and Szechuan noodles—none bigger than a snack, at snack prices. A good restaurant for fun food, but not a great one for meetings. *8386 Beverly Blvd., central L.A., tel. 213/655–6115. Casual dress. Reservations advised. AE, MC, V.*

★ **39** **Patina.** Its exterior is so understated that you can easily
$$$$ drive by without noticing the place at all. Even after you've left your car with a parking valet, it's tricky to find the front door—it looks like the delivery entrance. But that's just a little witticism, for as soon as you walk in, you're in an elegant space filled with muted tones, soft light, and lots of little tables placed so close together that it looks as though they've tried to squeeze a large restaurant into a very small space. Superchef Joachim Splichal has pulled out all the stops in creating a menu that keeps fans coming back again and again. Consider the whimsy (stronger at lunch than dinner) of dishes like a corn blini "sandwich" filled with marinated salmon; a soufflé (how French) of grits (how American) with Herkimer cheddar and an apple-smoked bacon sauce; and a red bell pepper soup served with a tiny bacon, lettuce, and tomato sandwich. Quiet discussions are best held in the smaller room to the right of the entrance. This is an excellent place for entertaining clients who are serious about food. *5955 Melrose Ave., Hollywood, tel. 213/467–1108. Jacket and tie advised. Reservations essential. AE, MC, V.*

★ **28** **Trumps.** In many ways, this is the quintessential Los An-
$$$ geles restaurant. From its ultracool look (white walls hung with Major Art, white ceiling rafters, huge concrete tables) to its power tea (wedged in between the power lunch and power dinner), it is a gathering spot for the Angelenos of the future. Sitting among the designers, agents, and assorted beautiful people, you don't just feel

like you're on the cutting edge, you feel like you're the edge itself. There's food (and service) to match: potato pancakes with goat cheese and sautéed apples; tuna grilled rare with eggplant caviar; superb fried chicken with mashed potatoes and gravy. Chef Michael Roberts shares his recipes in a fine book, *Secret Ingredients*. But every day in this restaurant, he proves it takes more than recipes to make great food. Despite the noise, lots of business (usually in the creative fields) is done here; for meetings, there's an excellent private space right next to the bar, with a fine view of the celebrities coming and going across the street at Morton's. *8764 Melrose Ave., West Hollywood, tel. 213/855–1480. Casual-chic dress. Reservations required. AE, MC, V.*

㉜ **Tulipe.** This large, glass-walled, fairly stark place with a
$$$ sizable open kitchen is warmed by both the people who work here and the people who eat here. It's a pleasure far beyond the sum of its parts, though that sum is a significant one. In the kitchen are owners/chefs Roland Gilbert (ex of Bernard's and Califia) and Maurice Peguet (ex of the California Club). Their food has French roots, though there's plenty of California tossed in for good measure. Duck is grilled with acacia honey and Oriental spices; a most commendable braised veal shank comes with an assortment of vegetables and crunchy cabbage; and Louisiana shrimp are wrapped in savoy cabbage leaves and served in a ginger sauce. There's a Chinese/Japanese edge to the food, adding one more set of ingredients to this particular mélange. They may not recognize this food in Paris, but melting-pot Angelenos have no trouble making it their own. Both the food and the wine list are very fairly priced. This is a good space for quiet talks, though there's no private room. *8360 Melrose Ave., West Hollywood, tel. 213/655–7400. Jacket advised. Reservations strongly advised. AE, MC, V.*

Westside

㉔ **Chez Helene.** This light and airy Beverly Hills cottage is
$$ reminiscent of the small French bistros popular in the late '50s and early '60s, the friendly little places where the service was casual, the food better than decent, and the ambience conducive to lingering. Despite its location in Beverly Hills, it looks like it's in the middle of Provence, with its sweet outdoor patio, polished wood, and farmhouse interior. The menu is quite small and reasonably priced. Try the rich, intensely flavored cream of tomato soup. The onion soup is a straightforward rendition of one of the most beloved clichés of French cuisine, as are the escargots de Bourgogne, the trio of quiches (eaten by the occasional real man), and the house pâté. You can talk comfortably here, but it isn't wholly appropriate for serious business meetings. *267 S. Beverly Dr., Beverly Hills, tel. 213/276–1558. Casual dress. Reservations advised. AE, MC, V.*

★ ㉓ **The Dining Room at the Regent Beverly Wilshire.** The
$$$ many dining rooms at the old Beverly Wilshire hotel have boiled down to just The Dining Room at the new Regent Beverly Wilshire. The room is at once highly classical and stringently modern; trompe l'oeil, gleaming woodwork, and bucolic murals blend with a massive kitchen-under-glass. It's a formal room but a comfortable one, and it's one

of L.A.'s best for an elegant working breakfast, lunch, or dinner, or for fine business entertaining. The daily-changing menu is less formal (and less expensive) than you'd expect, given the dazzling decor and excellent service. The food is basically American, lightly influenced by France, Italy, and Japan. You can have an excellent meal here that's as American as anything you'll find in the Midwest: clam chowder, Cobb salad (infinitely better than the one served at the Brown Derby), veal chops with garlicked mashed potatoes, and cheesecake. It's a winning combination. *9500 Wilshire Blvd., Beverly Hills, tel. 213/275–4282. Jacket advised. Reservations advised. AE, CB, DC, MC, V.*

㉛ Ed Debevic's. After a hard day crunching numbers on your
$ laptop, there's nothing like the old-fashioned fun at Ed's. It doesn't take reservations, but it's not a bad place to wait—and wait you will. This is L.A.'s best re-creation of a '50-style diner, which is no small praise in a town that has been buried beneath a mudslide of born-again meatloaf and gum-cracking waitresses. Signs on the walls proclaim "The more you tip—the nicer we are" and "Eat it—then beat it." The staff hams it up, occasionally bursting into song. The food is pure nostalgia, only better—and for Beverly Hills, it's dirt cheap. The cheeseburger comes topped with a combination of American, Cheddar, Swiss, and Velveeta. The tasty Five-Way Chili is mixed with macaroni, cheese, and onions. The meatloaf is a hash-house classic, and it comes with—says the menu—frozen vegetables. Honesty this rare is worth waiting for. This is a place for after-work zaniness, not meetings. *134 N. La Cienega Blvd., Beverly Hills, tel. 213/659–1952. Very casual dress. No reservations. No credit cards.*

❺ Four Oaks. Nestled in the midst of Beverly Glen, this place
$$$$ spent years being the prettiest restaurant in town with the most mediocre food. And then, after several failed attempts at being revived, it was finally reborn. The new chef, Peter Roelant, is a young graduate of Girardet and L'Orangerie. And though he's clearly learned his classical lessons well, the food has evolved into a tidy sort of California-French, with small touches from Italy and Japan—in other words, an eminently modern menu. Dishes include white-potato soup with smoked morels, a homemade terrine of duck foie gras with a kumquat chutney, and baby chicken in a rock-salt crust with country vegetables. The exceptional beauty and serenity of the setting make this an excellent place for small meetings and refined entertaining. *2181 N. Beverly Glen Blvd., Beverly Glen, tel. 213/470–2265. Jacket advised (many in tie). Reservations required. AE, MC, V.*

❿ The Heritage. One feels obliged to dress properly here
$$$ (though not all do—this is Santa Monica, after all). Nearly a century ago, when this grand old Victorian was designed by one Summer P. Hunt, it was known as the Kyte House. Today, it is a traditionalist's haven, a handsome, old-money-style American setting that would do Ralph Lauren proud. The food is gentrified American—things get no wilder than the wild honey with which the California quail is glazed. There's a fine braised veal shank, terrific steak tartare, and an excellent culotte steak broiled over bay leaves. It's worth noting that the entrée prices,

which are mostly in the mid-teens, include big plates with lots of side dishes, so you probably won't need to order the à la carte vegetables. This is ideal for dignified working meals, and the many rooms upstairs are excellent private meeting spots. *2640 Main St., Santa Monica, tel. 213/ 392–4956. Jacket and tie advised. Reservations advised. AE, MC, V.*

★ ㉒ **The Mandarin.** When the Mandarin was gutted by fire sev-
$$$ eral years ago, everyone thought owner Cecilia Chiang would rebuild it and continue to produce some of the best, most elegant Chinese food in town. But instead she passed on ownership to her son Philip, who had shown his wit in a casual Chinese bistro called Mandarette. The result is a restaurant that's best described as an upscale version of Mandarette know-how. The portentousness of the old place is gone; this is a place for those who wear Armani, and wear him well. It serves what may be the best Chinese food in L.A.—it's certainly the best in Beverly Hills. It's also highly ideal for meetings, especially in the small alcove rooms; be sure to preorder the meal so your guests won't be distracted with menus. *430 N. Camden Dr., Beverly Hills, tel. 213/272–0267. Jacket advised. Reservations advised. AE, CB, DC, MC, V.*

★ ㉑ **Primi.** At the heart of casual dining in L.A. is that '80s
$$ phenomenon called grazing. And L.A.'s prime grazing spot is a casually elegant room, with angels hidden in the decor, called Primi, short for *primi piatti,* Italian for "first plates." Several dozen Italian appetizers are served in both the main room, with its open kitchen, and the garden room. The best way to go is to order the tasting menu of three cold appetizers, three hot appetizers, three pastas, and dessert. Expect such dishes as shreds of grilled pigeon served with soft white cannellini beans and black truffles; gnocchetti, little potato dumplings in the colors of the Italian flag (red, green, and white); and risotto with seafood with porcini or herbs. Each dish is just a nibble, proof that tasty things come in small packages. It's a good meeting space, though the multiplicity of the dishes may be a bit distracting. *10543 W. Pico Blvd., West L.A., tel. 213/475–9235. Casual dress. Reservations advised. AE, MC, V.*

④ **Shane.** Hidden in back of the Beverly Glen Circle shopping
$$ center, this Italian-Southwestern restaurant is unique while being quintessentially L.A. The wild, colorful Southwestern decor is pure love-it-or-hate-it stuff, with tile snakes crawling around the room—it's anything but neutral and beige. Even the dishware makes a statement. Oddly, the food that sits atop these plates is fairly recognizable, despite its eccentric Italian-Southwestern roots. The pizzas are all tasty (lamb sausage, sage, and red chili; or chicken and tomatillo salsa; or pancetta and shiitake mushrooms), and the duck tostada and the beef quesadilla are unusually good. Although this is an informal spot, you can have quiet talks in the upstairs dining area. *2932 Beverly Glen Circle, Beverly Glen, tel. 213/470–6223. Casual dress. Reservations advised. AE, MC, V.*

⑨ **Valentino.** That the food has always been superb at Valen-
$$$$ tino is something few would deny. That the ambience at Valentino was dreary was also something few would argue

against. So master restaurateur Piero Selvaggio shut down his place several years ago and redid everything. Though the exterior still looks like a stucco bunker, the inside has been opened up and stylized, a series of rooms painted in muted, powdery pastels, with a Milanese stylishness in the lighting and decorative touches. Ask Selvaggio to create a meal for you, and out of the kitchen will come such things as bread crusts with beautiful glass pitchers of obscure olive oils; buffalo ricotta with basil leaves; prosciutto with white beans and Parmesan; small pancakes filled with radicchio and cheese—in other words, Italian cooking as it's eaten in Italy. One caveat: Leaving yourself in Selvaggio's hands is not inexpensive. But it certainly is good. Valentino's is also excellent for business meals of all sizes and types. *3115 Pico Blvd., Santa Monica, tel. 213/829-4313. Jacket and tie advised. Reservations required. AE, CB, DC, MC, V.*

San Gabriel Valley

❸ Crocodile Café. This is the creation of the nearby Parkway
$ Grill, which has been described as the "Spago of Pasadena." It's a successful attempt to create a place where people can go for fun and good, cheap California cuisine. The café setting—a pleasant outdoor patio and a bright, minimalist interior designed around the hectic open kitchen—is noisy, cheerful, and easygoing. The food can be strikingly good, in particular the black bean and sirloin chili. Then there are the chubby red Anaheim chilies stuffed with smoked jack cheese; the excellent oakwood-grilled burgers, which come with a small mountain of very crisp fries; and the barbecued-chicken and smoked-gouda pizza. For those in Pasadena or in not-far-away Downtown L.A., this is a great spot for a lively, casual night off. *140 S. Lake St., Pasadena, tel. 818/449-9900. Casual dress. No reservations. MC, V.*

★ ❺ Parkway Grill. This is a warm and wonderfully open place,
$$$ with brick walls, high ceilings, and a small forest of plants and trees. When you enter, you stand on a platform that overlooks an open kitchen in which a bevy of chefs is making pizzas and composing salads. It's a nearly perfect piece of design, blending the traditional with the modern. The design of the menu is equally successful. The dishes are utterly revisionist Americana; for the most part, they never existed in anyone's past. Consider such appetizers as delicate corn cakes with warm oysters, small sausages, and a slightly spicy tomatillo sauce; black-bean soup with smoked pork and a lime cream; and roasted chilies filled with smoked chicken, corn, cilantro, and cheese. Think of marvelous pizzas topped with lamb sausage, grilled eggplant, smoked chicken and cilantro, or even black beans and smoked pork. It sounds odd, but it tastes good. This is an excellent spot for business lunches and dinners, and there's a fine private room for larger meetings. *510 S. Arroyo Pkwy., Pasadena, tel. 818/795-1001. Jacket advised. Reservations advised. AE, MC, V.*

Airport/South Bay

⓰ Fino. This is a child of the South Bay's widely acclaimed
$$ Chez Melange, a three-ring culinary circus that makes you

wonder why more places aren't doing it this way—and this well. Tucked in a mini-mall south of Pacific Coast Highway, Fino is an assortment of smallish rooms on several levels, with rough white walls, a red-tile interior "roof," Mediterranean decorative touches, and a semiopen kitchen raging on the ground floor. Waiters who work the upper floor develop legs of steel; bounding up those steps laden with plates of lamb loin, duck with white beans and sausage, and braised escarole stuffed with prosciutto balanced on their forearms takes a lot of skill. Fino defines itself as, "a bistro featuring the rustic foods of Spain, France, and Italy," though you taste mostly Italy, and its requisite garlic and olive oil. The quieter upstairs dining area is good for informal business meetings; downstairs is the place for a good time. *24530 Hawthorne Blvd., Torrance, tel. 213/373–1952. Casual dress. Reservations strongly advised. AE, MC, V.*

FREE TIME

Fitness

Hotel Facilities
Downtown's **Biltmore Health Club** (tel. 213/612–1567) is the city's largest hotel club. Hotel guests are charged $8 during the week, nonguests pay $10 a day.

Health Clubs
There are many **Holiday Spa Health Clubs** around town (tel. 800/669–3200, for locations and information); most have a decent collection of gym equipment, pools, and fitness classes. Fees vary, and there's usually a one-week minimum membership. The new **Ketchum Downtown YMCA** (401 S. Hope St., tel. 213/624–2348) has outstanding facilities and charges $10 daily ($15 if you arrive prime-time, between 4:30 and 7:30 PM). The **Sports Connection** (8612 Santa Monica Blvd., West Hollywood, tel. 213/652–7440; 2929 31st St., Santa Monica, tel. 213/450–4464; and locations in outlying areas), a good health-club chain with extensive facilities, admits out-of-town guests for $15 a day.

Jogging
Runners and walkers staying Downtown will have to make their course on the wide sidewalks, or drive north to **Griffith Park,** which has many hillside trails. Visitors to the Westside can jog on the grassy median on **Burton Way** between La Cienega Boulevard and Beverly Hills. In Beverly Hills, there are gravel paths along **Sunset Boulevard** and **Santa Monica Boulevard.** Crisscrossing Beverly Hills are many wide, quiet, tree-lined side streets that are excellent for running or walking. The best (and most smog-free) Westside running area is the grassy median on **San Vicente Boulevard** between Brentwood and Santa Monica, ending at Ocean Avenue overlooking the beach. And of course, there are many options for those who like to run on sand; *see* Beaches, in the Diversion section, below.

Shopping

Los Angeles is a great shopping town, but as with everything here, it often involves a trip by car. Most shoppers head for one of the many sprawling malls scattered throughout the city; they may have a rather depressing uniformity and preponderance of chain stores, but for a busy traveler they're perfect for one-stop shopping. There are also some excellent neighborhood shopping areas throughout town, most notably the expensive, tourist-thronged shops of Beverly Hills's **Rodeo** (pronounced "Ro-DAY-o"), **Cañon** (pronounced "Canyon"), and **Beverly** drives, and **Wilshire Boulevard.** Other good streets to walk and shop are yupscale **Montana Avenue** in Santa Monica, arty **Main Street** in Venice, hip **Melrose Avenue** in Holly-wood, small-town **Larchmont Boulevard** in Hancock Park, **Sunset Plaza** in West Hollywood, and conservative **Lake Street** in Pasadena.

Downtown

ARCO Plaza (Fifth & Flower Sts., tel. 213/625–2132), with its 7 acres of shopping and dining on two levels, is one of the largest subterranean shopping centers in the coun-try, and one of the most disappointing. Downtown's **Sev-enth Street Marketplace** (Figueroa St. at 7th St., tel. 213/955–7150) is home to a good Bullock's, a small but choice array of upscale shops, like Ann Taylor and Godiva, and a fast-food court. Bargain-hunters flock to the **Cooper Building** (860 S. Los Angeles St., tel. 213/622–1139), in which some 70 shops sell heavily discounted, major-label men's, women's, and children's clothing and accessories, along with cosmetics and linens.

West Hollywood, Westside, Beverly Hills

The famed **Beverly Center** (8500 Beverly Blvd., tel. 213/854–0070), on the edge of the Wilshire District and West Hollywood, is home to more than 200 shops and restau-rants, including a 13-screen cinema complex. The mix of shops slants toward the young and aggressively chic. On the street level is the legendary (and *always* mobbed) Hard Rock Café. The **Century City Shopping Center & Marketplace** (10250 Santa Monica Blvd., Century City, tel. 213/553–5300) is a large, very pleasant outdoor mall with lots of upscale shops (Charles Jourdan, Ann Taylor, The Pottery Barn), a 14-theater complex, and dozens of places to eat. In West L.A., the **Westside Pavilion** (10800 W. Pico Blvd., tel. 213/474–6255) is a striking three-story atrium-style center with a good mix of shops (The Cash-mere People, Victoria's Secret), restaurants, and movie theaters. The most famous shopping area, **Rodeo Drive,** is often compared to Fifth Avenue in New York or Via Condotti in Rome. Along several blocks of North Rodeo Drive, between Wilshire and Santa Monica boulevards, are such stores as Giorgio (327 Rodeo Dr., tel. 213/274–0200), Battaglia (306 Rodeo Dr., tel. 213/276–7184), Polo/Ralph Lauren (444 Rodeo Dr., tel. 213/281–7200), Theo-dore (453 Rodeo Dr., tel. 213/276–9691), Montana (463 Ro-deo Dr., tel. 213/273–7925), Giorgio Armani (436 Rodeo Dr., tel. 213/271–5555), Krizia (410 Rodeo Dr., tel. 213/276–5411), Alaïa (313 Rodeo Dr., tel. 213/275–7313), and Chanel (301 Rodeo Dr., tel. 213/278–5500).

Diversions

The new **Gene Autry Western Heritage Museum** (4700 Zoo Dr., Griffith Park, tel. 213/667–2000) displays a worth-while collection of art and artifacts from the early West.

Beaches abound in Southern California; the widest, most popular, and most convenient beach is Santa Monica Beach (tel. 213/394–3266); check to be sure its waters are clean enough for safe swimming. Take the Santa Monica Freeway about 20 miles west from Downtown. Swimmers can also head north on Pacific Coast Highway to **Zuma** (tel. 213/457–9891) or the beaches near the Ventura County Line.

The **California Afro-American Museum** (600 State Dr., Exposition Park, tel. 213/744–7432) documents the Afro-American experience in the Americas.

The recently expanded **California Museum of Science & Industry** (700 State Dr., Exposition Park, tel. 213/744–7400) is filled with fascinating exhibits on science, technology, and health.

Card clubs in the communities of Gardena and Bell Gardens (5 miles from Downtown) offer legal table (mostly poker) gaming. **The Bicycle Club** (7301 Eastern Ave., Bell Gardens, tel. 213/806–4646) is the world's largest such casino. Another card room is the **Normandie Casino & Dinner Theater** (1045 W. Rosecrans Ave., Gardena, tel. 213/715–7400).

Downtown walking tours of L.A.'s marvelous old buildings (yes, L.A. has a history) are led on Saturday mornings by the Los Angeles Conservancy (tel. 213/623–CITY or 213/623–TOURS).

Early risers staying Downtown should visit the **Flower Market** (Wall St. between 7th and 8th Sts.) around 5–6 AM. In scenes reminiscent of Holland, local growers and importers deliver truckloads of fragrant blooms to some 100 wholesalers. In the same area is the bustling **Produce Market,** where, in similar scenes of bustling predawn activity, fresh fruits and vegetables are unloaded and transferred to trucks from supermarkets and grocers.

The spectacularly sited **J. Paul Getty Museum** (17985 Pacific Coast Hwy., Malibu, tel. 213/459–7611) is home to an extensive collection of Greek and Roman antiquities, plus pre-20th-century Western art, all housed in a re-creation of a first-century A.D. Roman country villa.

Golf West (tel. 818/340–9202) organizes corporate and organizational golf outings and tournaments for groups only.

Grand Central Market (317 S. Broadway, Downtown) may be in L.A., but it's a scene straight out of a Latin American market town. Local Latino shoppers come to shop for familiar groceries and household goods; terrific Latino fast food is available.

Heli LA (tel. 213/553–4354) offers various dramatic sightseeing dinner helicopter flights over Los Angeles. It's not cheap at $299 per person, but it's an unforgettable experience.

Hollywood On Location (8644 Wilshire Blvd., Beverly Hills, tel. 213/659–9165) sells (for $29) a daily list and precise map of some 35 locations where movies, TV series, and music videos are being shot. It's a great chance to see how Hollywood works—and perhaps even to see a few stars.

The **Los Angeles County Museum of Art** (5905 Wilshire Blvd., Wilshire District, tel. 213/857–6111) attempts with some success to be L.A.'s cultural heart and soul. The five museum buildings around a spacious central court include the new Pavilion for Japanese Art and the Atlantic Richfield Gallery of Modern Art. Classic films are also screened regularly.

The **Los Angeles Zoo** (5333 Zoo Dr., Griffith Park, tel. 213/666–4650) is the sprawling (and intriguing) home to more than 2,000 rare and exotic mammals, birds, and reptiles in naturalistic settings.

The **Museum of Contemporary Art** (250 S. Grand Ave., Downtown, tel. 213/626–6222) is both a spectacular building (designed by Arata Isozaki) and an excellent center for new art, including media and performing arts. The gift shop and café alone are worth a visit.

The **Museum of Flying** (2771 Donald Douglas Loop, Santa Monica, tel. 213/392–8822) at the Santa Monica Airport details L.A.'s rich aviation history, with its restored historical military and commercial aircraft.

The **George C. Page Museum of La Brea Discoveries** (5801 Wilshire Blvd., Wilshire District, tel. 213/857–6311 or 213/936–2230) houses the collection of Ice Age fossils recovered from the asphalt deposits (the famed La Brea Tar Pits) that surround the museum.

Power and sail boats of all sizes are rented by the hour from Rent-a-Sail in Marina del Rey (tel. 213/271–2677).

The **Southwest Museum** (234 Museum Dr., Highland Park, tel. 213/221–2164 or 213/221–2163) is an excellent museum that holds exhibits on Native American cultures from Alaska to South America, with a particular emphasis on local tribes.

The **Wells Fargo History Museum** (333 S. Grand Ave., Downtown, tel. 213/253–7166) uses stagecoaches, photos, and other relics to illustrate California's Gold Rush days.

Professional Sports

Baseball: Los Angeles Dodgers (Dodger Stadium, 1000 Elysian Park Ave., L.A., tel. 213/224–1400), **California Angels** (Anaheim Stadium, Anaheim, tel. 714/634–2100). **Basketball: Los Angeles Lakers** (Great Western Forum, 3900 W. Manchester Blvd., Inglewood, tel. 213/419–3142), **Los Angeles Clippers** (Los Angeles Memorial Sports Arena, 3939 S. Figueroa St., tel. 213/748–0500). **Football: Los Angeles Rams** (Anaheim Stadium, Anaheim, tel. 714/937–6767 or 213/227–4748), **Los Angeles Raiders** (scheduled to play in the Los Angeles Coliseum but still negotiating for a new home; tel. 213/322–5901). **Hockey: Los Angeles Kings** (Great Western Forum, tel. 213/480–3232).

The Arts

Although movies and television dominate the performing arts in Los Angeles, the stage is still quite active; in fact, it's not unusual for major Hollywood performers, nostalgic for the live theater, to appear in one of the area's small houses. For the most complete listing of weekly events, get the current issue of *Los Angeles* or *California* magazine. The Calendar section of the Los Angeles *Times* also offers a wide survey of Los Angeles arts events, as do the more irreverent free publications, the *L.A. Weekly* and the *L.A. Reader.* The largest venue for live theater is downtown's Music Center, which comprises the Ahmanson Theatre (seating 2,071); the Dorothy Chandler Pavilion, the 3,200 seat home to musical extravaganzas; and the Mark Taper Forum, a more intimate and experimental theater. The other major L.A. theaters are the Shubert Theater in Century City, and Hollywood's James A. Doolittle Theatre and Henry Fonda Theater. Smaller, more avant-garde venues include the Canon Theatre, Colony Studio Theatre, Park Plaza, and Taper, Too, a 99-seat space at the John Anson Ford Theater near the Hollywood Bowl.

The Los Angeles Philharmonic makes its summer home at the famous Hollywood Bowl; a concert under the stars here is a memorable experience. From October to May, the Philharmonic performs at the Dorothy Chandler Pavilion, which also showcases major dance troupes.

The following are good venues for tickets: **Al Brooks Tickets** (900 Wilshire Blvd., Downtown, tel. 213/626–5863); **Front Row Center** (404 S. Figueroa, Suite 105, Downtown, tel. 213/488–0020); **Murray's Tickets** (740 W. Martin Luther King Jr. Blvd., Downtown, tel. 213/234–0123); **Ticketmaster** (tel. 213/480–3232); **Ticketron** (6060 W. Manchester, Westchester, tel. 213/642–5708); **Ticket Times** (9925 Venice Blvd., Culver City, tel. 213/202–0053).

Ahmanson Theatre, 135 N. Grand Ave., Downtown, tel. 213/972–7403.

Canon Theatre, 205 N. Canon Dr., Beverly Hills, tel. 213/466–9966.

Colony Studio Theatre, 1944 Riverside Dr., Beverly Hills, tel. 213/665–3011.

Dorothy Chandler Pavilion, 135 N. Grand Ave., Downtown, tel. 213/972–7200.

Henry Fonda Theater, 6126 Hollywood Blvd., Hollywood, tel. 213/410–1062.

Hollywood Bowl, 2301 N. Highland Ave., Hollywood, tel. 213/850–2000.

James A. Doolittle Theatre, 1615 N. Vine St., Hollywood, tel. 213/410–1062.

Mark Taper Forum, 135 N. Grand Ave., Downtown, tel. 213/972–7337.

Park Plaza, 607 S. Park View, Downtown, tel. 213/466–1767.

Shubert Theater, 2020 Ave. of the Stars, Century City, tel. 800/233–3123.

Taper, Too, 2580 Cahuenga Blvd. E, Hollywood, tel. 213/972–7392.

After Hours

Clubs are scattered across the city, but many of the best are in the Hollywood/West Hollywood area; not surprisingly, they tend to attract the young and the restless. Despite the high energy level, this is an early-to-bed city, and its safe to say that by 2 AM most clubs are closed. The accent is on trendy rock clubs, smooth country-western establishments, intimate jazz spots, and comedy clubs. City residents usually don't gravitate to hotels, except for a quiet evening of soft piano music, often accompanied by sentimental vocalists.

Bars and Lounges
Downtown: The small bar at **Engine Co. No. 28** (644 S. Figueroa St., tel. 213/624–6996) is a traditional spot popular with the Brooks Brothers set. The **Lobby Bar** (Hyatt Regency, tel. 213/683–1234) is an unpretentious, comfortable, and convenient gathering spot that offers live entertainment and a happy hour buffet. The **Grand Avenue Bar** (Biltmore Hotel, tel. 213/624–1011) is a cool, sophisticated marble hideaway with good music and hors d'oeuvres.

Westside: The serenely sophisticated **Windows** (Four Seasons Hotel, tel. 213/273–2222) is something of a mecca for Beverly Hills business types. Afternoon tea is poured, and there's a pianist in the evening. Perhaps the best Westside bar for doing business and unwinding is **The Bar, Regent Beverly Wilshire** (tel. 213/275–5200), a very elegant spot with the atmosphere of a gentleman's club in which women feel right at home. There's piano music from 4 PM and complimentary hors d'oeuvres from 5 to 7. **Jimmy's Bar** (201 Moreno Dr., Beverly Hills, tel. 213/879–2394), located just off the restaurant's main dining room, is a gathering spot for local society, celebrities, and show-business dealmakers. Those wanting to people-watch and check out the trendy side of L.A.'s bar scene might consider **DC3** (Santa Monica Airport, 31st St. entrance, Santa Monica, tel. 213/399–2323), the **West Beach Café** (60 N. Venice Blvd., Venice, 213/823–5396), **Eureka** (1845 S. Bundy Dr., West L.A., tel. 213/447–8000), and **Maple Drive** (345 N. Maple Dr., Beverly Hills, tel. 213/274–9800).

Nightclubs/Dancing
Bar One (9229 Sunset Blvd., West Hollywood, tel. 213/271–8355) is an intimate combination of restaurant and disco; a DJ plays rap, hip hop, and rock. Don't expect to get in unless you're with someone the door host recognizes. The trendy **China Club** (1600 Argyle St., Hollywood, tel. 213/469–1600) serves California cuisine for late dinners and showcases live music during the week and DJs on weekends. The clientele is casually well dressed and well heeled. **Club Lingerie** (6507 W. Sunset Blvd., Hollywood, tel. 213/466–8557) is a fashionable spot to hear live rock and check out hip Angelenos. For a classic disco (with live music and an adjoining restaurant), head for **Spice** (7070 Hollywood Blvd., Hollywood, tel. 213/856–9638). **The Troubadour** (9081 Santa Monica Blvd., Hollywood, tel. 213/276–6168), once L.A.'s folk/rock center, is now a haven for heavy metal. You have to like it loud if you come here. Young execs, entertainment industry folk, and offbeat trendsetters frequent **Vertigo** (333 S. Boylston St., Downtown, behind the Pacific Stock Exchange, tel. 213/

747–4849), a huge, stylish nightclub that features live music and dancing. Also check out **Roxbury** (8225 W. Sunset Blvd., W. Hollywood, tel. 213/656–1750) and **Highland Grounds** (742 N. Highland Ave., Hollywood, tel. 213/466–1507).

Comedy Clubs

The most famous are the **Comedy Store** (8433 W. Sunset Blvd., West Hollywood, tel. 213/656–6225) and **The Improvisation** (8162 Melrose Ave., West Hollywood, tel. 213/651–2583). Also good are the **Laugh Factory** (8001 W. Sunset Blvd., West Hollywood, tel. 213/656–1336) and **Igby's** (11637 W. Pico Blvd., West L.A., tel. 213/477–3553). For a change of pace and lots of laughs, don't miss the show at the **Groundlings Theatre** (7303 Melrose Ave., Hollywood, tel. 213/934–9700), a very funny mix of improvisation and ensemble sketch comedy.

Cabarets

Café Largo (432 N. Fairfax, Hollywood, tel. 213/852–1073) has taken the cabaret to new heights, with its cutting-edge live entertainment, jazz, performance art, readings, and good dinners. Traditionalists will adore **The Cinegrill** (Hollywood Roosevelt Hotel, 7000 Hollywood Blvd., Hollywood, tel. 213/466–7000), a beautiful, sophisticated '40s-style supper club featuring great torch singers and jazz music. **Oscar's** (8210 Sunset Blvd., West Hollywood, tel. 213/654–3457) serves up jazz and the blues in an English pub atmosphere. **Verdi** (1519 Wilshire Blvd., Santa Monica, tel. 213/393–0706) combines Northern Italian food and a chic decor with fairly serious performances of opera and light opera.

Jazz Clubs

The gorgeous former lobby area of the Biltmore Hotel, the **Gallery** bar (tel. 213/624–1011), is a popular gathering spot for businesspeople after work and on into the evening. The live jazz is mellow and pleasant. **Café Mondrian** (Le Mondrian Hotel, 8440 Sunset Blvd., West Hollywood, tel. 213/650–8999) showcases jazz and pop artists in an intimate lounge setting. Big-name jazz acts perform in the large room at the **Catalina Bar & Grill** (1640 N. Cahuenga Blvd., Hollywood, tel. 213/466–2210). **Nucleus Nuance** (7267 Melrose Ave., Hollywood, tel. 213/939–8666) is a small, lovely spot in which to dine (Continental cuisine), dance, and listen to traditional jazz and jazz-tinged pop. The comfortable **Vine Street Bar & Grill** (1610 N. Vine St., Hollywood, tel. 213/463–4375) attracts such fine performers as Etta James and George Shearing.

Milan

by Laura Colby and Barbara Walsh Angelillo

There is very little that is Latin about Italy's business center. The clatter of streetcars on cobbled streets, the stately 19th-century homes, and the chilly, foggy winters remind one more of London or Vienna than of an Italian city. Indeed, Milan has few Roman ruins. Only the marble columns at the Porta Romana remind visitors that this city was a center of transalpine commerce long before the Lombards arrived more than 1,500 years ago.

That Milan is still a center of commerce and industry is abundantly clear. Working days begin early, before the sun is up. Lunches are gulped at stand-up counters in bars, not lingered over for hours. People walk—and drive—as though they are in a hurry, and indeed they are, moving at an often furious pace.

Milan is Italy's headquarters for fashion, design, and furniture—which are among Italy's biggest exports to the United States. It is also the country's financial headquarters, location of the stock market and investment companies, and headquarters to almost all of Italy's leading banks. Other big industries include auto-making (Alfa Romeo has its headquarters here), chemicals, and rubber. In addition, the city has thousands of small and midsize manufacturers making and exporting everything from window shades to shoelaces.

In fact, most Milanese will tell you, in their clipped local accent, that Milan is not only Italy's business center, it is the country's unofficial capital. The 1.5 million hard-working Milanese (3 million in the Milan metropolitan area) regard Rome, seat of political power, with a mixture of resignation and disdain. Rome, they feel, is a place that lives off the sweat of Northerners' brows; Milan is the country's economic engine. But whether the Milanese like it or not, business travelers aren't about to confuse this city with Frankfurt. Milan is still very much a part of Italy, sharing some of its foibles and much of its charm.

Top Employers

Employer	Type of Enterprise	Parent*/ Headquarters
Alfa Romeo	Automobile manufacturers	Fiat/Turin

Banca Commerciale Italiana	Commercial bank	IRI/Rome
Cassa di Risparmio delle Provincie Lombarde, or Cariplo	Savings bank	Milan
CIR (Cie. Industriali Riunite)	Financial and industrial cos. throughout Europe, including C. Olivetti & Co.	Milan
Credito Italiano	Commercial bank	IRI/Rome
Esso Italiana SpA	Oil	Exxon/Florham Park, NJ
The Ferruzzi Group	Agro-industrial, industrial, and financial cos.	Milan
Fininvest SpA	Media, real estate, advertising, publishing, retail (Standa chain)	Milan
Italtel SpA	Telecommunications equipment	AT&T/New York City
Montedison SpA	Chemicals	Milan
Pirelli SpA	Tire and cable manufacturers	Milan

*if applicable

ESSENTIAL INFORMATION

We include the Milan telephone area code (02) with all numbers listed below. If you are calling from outside Italy, omit the zero from the code. If you are calling within the city, drop the code altogether.

The currency of Italy is the lire.

Government Tourist Offices

Italian Government Travel Office (ENIT). In the United States: 630 5th Ave., Suite 1565, New York, NY 10111, tel. 212/245–4822; 500 N. Michigan Ave., Suite 1046, Chicago, IL 60611, tel. 312/644–0990; 360 Post St., Suite 801, San Francisco, CA 94108, tel. 415/392–6206.
In Canada: 1 Place Ville Marie, Suite 1914, Montréal H3B 3M9, Quebec, tel. 514/866–7667.
In the United Kingdom: 1 Princes St., London W1R 8AY, tel. 071/408–1254.
In Milan: Via Marconi 1, tel. 02/809662; Central Station, tel. 02/669–0432.

Foreign Trade Information

Italian Chamber of Commerce. In the United States: 350 5th Ave., Suite 3015, New York, NY 10118, tel. 212/279–5520; 126 Grand Ave., Chicago, IL 60610, tel. 312/661–1336; 11520 San Vincente Blvd., Suite 101, Los Angeles, CA 90049, tel. 213/826–9898.
In Canada: 550 rue Sherbrooke Ouest, Bureau 680, Montréal H3A 1BA, Quebec, tel. 514/844–4249; 901 Lawrence Ave. W, Suite 306, Toronto M6A 1C3, Ontario, tel. 416/789–7169.
In the United Kingdom: 418-427 Walmar House, 296 Regent St., London W1R 6AE, tel. 071/637–3153.

Entry Requirements

U.S. and Canadian Citizens
Passport only. Visa required for visits of longer than 90 days.

British Citizens
Passport only.

Climate

Milan, located in the Lombardy region, on the Po plain, is rimmed on the north by the Alps. Thus sheltered from chilly northern winds, Milan has much milder winters than you might expect. But Milan pays a price: the lack of wind leads to the city's dreaded fog, which can close airports without warning any time during April through October. The sheltered location, combined with Milan's considerable industrial production, has a serious climatic effect: smog. A World Health Organization report in 1989 listed Milan as one of the 10 worst cities in the world for certain types of air pollution. Visitors with asthma or other respiratory problems may want to schedule their trips for the spring and autumn months, when pollution is less severe. During any season, people with such illnesses or allergies would be well advised to bring a store of medications.

What follows are the average maximum and minimum daily temperatures for Milan.

Jan.	41F	5C	Feb.	46F	8C	Mar.	55F	13C
	32	0		36	2		43	6
Apr.	64F	18C	May	73F	23C	June	81F	27C
	50	10		57	14		63	17
July	84F	29C	Aug.	82F	28C	Sept.	75F	24C
	68	20		66	19		61	16
Oct.	63F	17C	Nov.	50F	10C	Dec.	43F	6C
	52	11		43	6		36	2

Airports

Milan has two airports, **Linate,** which is mainly for domestic and European flights, and **Malpensa,** for intercontinental and some continental flights. Linate, only 10 kilometers (6 miles) east of center city, is by far the preferable airport. However, it is Europe's most notorious for fog and so should be avoided if possible in the winter during the early morning and late evening; if you must fly here

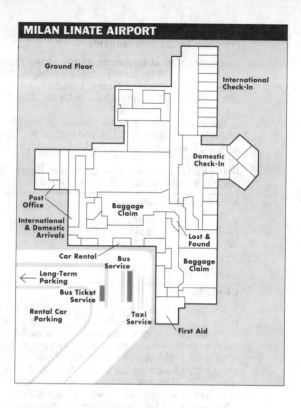

MILAN LINATE AIRPORT

in winter, try to take off or land from about 11 AM to 5 PM, when fog is least likely to be a problem.

At 50 kilometers (31 miles) northwest of the city, Malpensa is less convenient than Linate, but it tends to be far less crowded and more efficient in terms of processing passengers and managing the overall flow of air traffic. By virtue of its distance from the city's air pollution, Malpensa often stays open when Linate is fogged in. Don't be surprised if your winter flight to Linate is diverted here.

A word about strikes: Italy's airlines and airports have been plagued by them, but they are usually announced several weeks in advance. If you are planning a trip to Milan, check with either your travel agent or, better still, your local contact in Italy, to determine whether any labor actions are expected for times during which you will be traveling.

Airlines

Alitalia, the national airline, has the most flights to Milan, as well as an agreement that funnels passengers to United Airlines in the United States. Milan is also served by Pan Am. Most domestic flights are handled by Alitalia or its sister airline, ATI. Some local routes, such as Milan to Sardinia, are handled by private airlines such as Alisarda. At Linate's private air terminal, Cessna jets for six to nine passengers can be chartered from Ciga Aviation.

Alisarda, tel. 02/809658.
Alitalia, tel. 02/2831 (information); tel. 02/2830 (reservations); 800/223–5730.
Ciga Aviation, tel. 02/733–316 or 02/718–104.
Pan Am, tel. 02/877241; 800/221–1111.
TWA, tel. 02/77961; 800/221–2000.

Between the Airports and Downtown

By Taxi
A yellow taxi from Linate to Milan center city costs from 15,000 to 20,000 lire, depending on the traffic and time of day. During nonpeak hours the trip should take about 20 minutes, during peak hours (8–10 AM from Linate, 6–7 PM from Milan), about 40 minutes. A taxi from Malpensa, which will run double the fare shown on the meter because the airport is outside city limits, costs about 100,000 lire. The trip takes about 40 minutes during nonpeak hours, 70–80 minutes during peak hours.

By Bus
Buses connect both airports with Milan, stopping at the central train station. The fare from Linate is 2,500 lire on the special **SEAV** airport bus, or 800 lire on the municipal bus (ATM No. 73), which also stops at Piazza San Babila in the business district. The SEAV buses run until flights stop, and municipal buses run from about 6 AM–midnight. Both leave from the airport about every 20 minutes. Buses from Malpensa take one hour and cost 8,000 lire. They leave when filled, not before.

Car Rentals

The following companies have offices at both Linate and Malpensa airports:

Automobile Club d'Italia, tel. 02/77451.
Avis, tel. 1678–63063 (toll-free); 800/331–1212.
Budget, tel. 02/6709228; 800/527–0700.
Hertz, tel. 02/20483; 800/654–3131.

Emergencies

For a list of approved physicians and clinics in Milan that belong to the International Association for Medical Assistance to Travelers, contact IAMAT, 417 Center St., Lewiston, NY 14092, tel. 716/754–4883.

Doctors
The **American Consulate** (tel. 02/652–841) maintains a list of specialized practitioners who speak English. Emergency medical assistance can be obtained by dialing the Red Cross Emergency Service (tel. 3883).

Dentists
Istituto Stomatologico (via Pace 12, tel. 02/5462751), a privately owned clinic, can handle dental emergencies.

Hospitals
The **Fatebenefratelli Hospital** (Corso di Porto Nuova 23, tel. 02/63631) is the best centrally located hospital; there is usually English-speaking staff at the emergency room *(pronto soccorso)*.

Police and Ambulance
Tel. 113.

Important Addresses and Numbers

American Express (via Brera 3, lost cards tel. 02/85571, travel office tel. 02/85571, card information tel. 02/72282).

Audiovisual rentals. Universal Video Corporation (via E. Reguzzoni 15, tel. 02/6473612).

Bookstores (English-language). American Bookstore (via Camperio 16, tel. 02/870944), English Bookshop (via Mascheroni 12, tel. 02/4694468), Feltrinelli Bookstore (via Manzoni 12, tel. 02/700386).

Canadian Consulate (via Vittor Pisani 19, tel. 02/6697451).

Computer rentals. Lomani (Srl. Corso Lodi 59, tel. 02/5693335).

Convention Center. Fiera di Milano (Largo Domodossola 1, tel. 02/49971).

Fax services. There are no independent fax services; almost every small business has its own machine. All major hotels have fax services.

Formal-wear rentals. Abbigliamento Bianchi (via Salvio Giuliano 5/3, tel. 02/435725).

Gift shops. Chocolates: Cova (via Montenapoleone 8, tel. 02/793187), Galli (Corso Porta Romana 2, tel. 02/871629), Marchesi (via Santa Maria alla Porta 13, tel. 02/876730); Gourmet gift baskets: Peck (via Spadari 9, tel. 02/860842); Florist: Radaelli (via Manzoni 16, tel. 02/76002876).

Graphic design studio. Grafiche Diodoro (Srl. via Diodoro Siculo 20, tel. 02/6425274).

Hairstylists. Men: Antica Barberia Cola (via Morone 3, tel. 02/874312), Benito (via Rovello 1, tel. 02/879238); Women: Jean Louis David (via Marcona 70, tel. 02/743558), Wally Prandi (via Solari 43, tel. 02/48950692).

Health and fitness clubs. *See* Fitness, below.

Limousine service. VIP Limousine (tel. 02/6592158).

Liquor stores. Enoteca Ronchi (via S. Maurilio 7, tel. 02/808988) for wine; liquor is sold in every supermarket or food store.

Mail delivery, overnight. DHL International (tel. 02/57571), Federal Express (tel. 02/5064151), TNT Skypak (tel. 02/31081), UPS (tel. 02/5079166).

Messenger services. City Cross (tel. 02/234048241), Milano Express (tel. 02/8386).

News programs (English-language). TeleMontecarlo broadcasts the previous night's CBS Evening News every morning at 7:30 and 8. CNN is available at some hotels.

Office space rentals. S.B.C. (via Sansovino 8, tel. 02/29405518), International Business Center (Corso Europa 12, tel. 02/5456211).

Pharmacies, late-night. The pharmacy on the upper level of Milan Central Station is open 24 hours. Others take turns staying open late and on weekends; addresses of open pharmacies are posted on each pharmacy, or call tel. 02/192.

Secretarial services. Business Office (corso Plebisciti 9, tel. 02/744645), Organizzazione Segreterie (corso Concordia, 11, tel. 02/793553).

Stationery supplies. Cartoleria de Magistris (via Meravigli 12/14, tel. 02/873295), Carta e Penna (via Torino 60, tel. 02/873703).

Taxis. Radio-Taxi (tel. 02/6767, 02/5251, 02/5353, 02/8388, or 02/8585).

Theater tickets. *See* The Arts, below.

Thomas Cook (via Dante 4, tel. 02/863620).

Trade Ministry. Milan Chamber of Commerce and Industry (via Meravigli 9B, tel. 02/85151, fax 02/85154245), Camera di Commercio Americana in Italia (via Cantu 1, tel. 02/8690661).

Train information. Station Centrale (Piazza Duca d'Aosta, tel. 02/67500).

Translation services. Jones Meyer (via Settembrini 24, tel. 02/29402828), Studio Traduzioni Sandona (via A. Ristori 6, tel. 02/20612).

U.S. Consulate (Largo Donegani 1, tel. 02/652841).

Telephones

Local calls cost 200 lire. Pay phones take either a 200-lire coin, two 100-lire coins, or a *gettone*, a ridged copper token worth 200 lire, available at post offices or cigarette counters. If you happen upon an older phone that takes only the tokens, insert the *gettone* (which doesn't drop right away), dial your number, wait for an answer, then complete the connection by pushing the knob at the token slot. You can talk for nine minutes before having to insert more coins or another *gettone*. For long-distance direct-dialing, insert at least five coins and have more handy; unused coins will be returned when you pull the knob. New *scheda* telephones take phone cards sold at Telefoni offices in denominations of 3,000, 6,000, or 9,000 lire. The number of units available to you are shown on an automatic display at the beginning of and throughout the call. It's not currently possible to charge calls to a credit card in Italy. There is one exception—holders of an AT&T credit card can call USA Direct at 172–0011 to reach the U.S. For general information in English on calling in Europe and the Mediterranean area, dial 176.

Tipping

Tipping in Italy is appreciated, but not obligatory. In hotels, a porter carrying bags to your room should get about 1,000 lire per bag. A hotel doorman who has hailed cabs for you and helped you into or out of taxis should get 1,000 lire–2,000 lire at the end of your stay. Room service gets 2,000–5,000 lire (the high end of the range only in deluxe hotels), depending on the time of day and what you ordered.

For short taxi rides (10,000 lire or less), a tip of 500 lire–1,000 lire is standard. Most people just round off the fare to the nearest 1,000 lire and let the driver keep the change. On longer trips, such as to the airport, a tip of around 10% is common.

Most restaurants include a service charge of 10%–18% in the bill. The menu will usually say *servizio compreso* to indicate this, or your bill will include a line labeled *servizio* near the bottom. In this case, add a tip of about 5% only if the service is especially good. (In a family-run restaurant, it's not common practice to tip the owner if he waits on you; only regular waiters should be tipped.) When having coffee or drinks in a bar or café, you should leave a small tip (100 lire–500 lire) for the barman or waiter.

DOING BUSINESS

Hours

Hours of different types of businesses vary widely in Milan, and business travelers can find themselves easily putting in 12 hour days to deal with them all. Here are some guidelines: **Banks:** weekdays 8:30–1:30 and 3–4. (Don't arrive less than 15 minutes from closing time; the cashier may refuse to serve you.) **Public offices:** weekdays 8–1:30. **Businesses:** weekdays 8:30–6:30, lunch break from 1 to 2:30 or 3:00. Secretaries and other support staff members usually leave for the day by about 6 PM, but you can often find managers, even in some public offices, at their desks until 8 PM or later. **Shops:** Mon.–Sat. 9–7. Some close for lunch from 1 to 3 or 4, but most clothing stores in the center of town are open all day. **Grocery stores:** Usually open Mon.–Sat. 8:30–12:30 and 3–7:30, closed one afternoon during the week, usually Mon.

National Holidays

New Year's Day; Easter; Apr. 25, Liberation Day; May 1, Labor Day (May Day); June 2, Republic Day; Aug. 15, Ferragosto; Nov. 1, All Saint's Day; Dec. 7, the feast of St. Ambrose, Milan's patron saint; Dec. 25 and 26, Christmas; New Year's Eve.

Ferragosto, originally a religious holiday (the Assumption), now serves as an unofficial deadline for departure on summer vacation. Most businesses, shops, restaurants, bars and newsstands are shut up tight for 15 days or more around this time of year. Italians like to use their many holidays to *fare il ponte*—literally, "to make a bridge" between a midweek holiday and the weekend. Certain times of year, such as Christmas and the mid-summer holiday, are to be avoided for business trips because many people are taking long weekends and it may be hard to get anything done.

Getting Around

The fastest way to get around is by subway. Taxis are the most comfortable means, and are fast too, now that traffic in center city has been restricted.

By Car
It is not only inadvisable but illegal for visitors to drive in Milan city center; because of serious pollution, there is a ban on all unnecessary traffic in the area. Only cars with special resident permits are allowed; others will be stopped and ticketed, and parked cars may be towed.

By Taxi

Use yellow cabs only, and don't expect to hail a cab unless you are waiting at a cab stand (marked "Taxi"), found throughout the city. Taxis can also be telephoned in advance (*see* Important Addresses and Numbers, above); they are dispatched by operator according to their proximity to the caller. Some but not all taxis accept credit cards; request this service in advance.

By Subway

Milan's subway network, the Metropolitana, is modern, fast, and easy to use. "MM" signs mark Metropolitana stations. There are three lines. The ATM, or city transport authority, has an information office on the mezzanine of the Duomo Metro station (tel. 02/875494). Tickets are sold at newsstands at every stop, and in ticket machines for exact change only. The fare is 1,000 lire, and the subway runs from 6:20 AM to midnight.

By Bus and Streetcar

There is an extensive network, which is very crowded during rush hours, but otherwise pleasant to use. Tickets are sold at newsstands, tobacco shops, and bars. One ticket (1,000 lire) is valid for 75 minutes on all buses and streetcars and for one subway ride. Daily tickets, offering unrestricted travel for 24 hours on all public transportation lines, are on sale at the Duomo Metro station ATM Information Office, and at Stazione Centrale Metro station. Cost: 8,000 lire. Tickets must be validated in machines at the MM entrance, and on buses and streetcars.

Protocol

Appointments

Punctuality is appreciated for business meetings, and you should call your host if you will be more than 15 minutes late for an appointment. Nonetheless, lateness is common in Italy and you should not be offended if you are kept waiting by your host for up to a quarter of an hour. Both men and women should shake hands on being introduced, and smile without false enthusiasm. Business cards should be exchanged at the beginning of a prearranged meeting. However, if you meet someone casually, at a convention or cocktail party, you should offer to exchange cards when you part company.

Customs

Although Italians generally are friendly, they do not expect to be called by their first names when they meet you. Honorific titles are very important here. Anyone who has graduated from university is a *dottore*. Men are almost always called Dottore, but if they are engineering graduates, they are called *Ingegnere* (in-gen-NYEA-reh). Male lawyers are addressed as *Avvocato*, -*a* for women (ah-vo-CAH-toh, -tah). A company president or chairman is addressed as *Presidente*.

A note about women in business: With the exception of fields such as fashion and advertising, they are rare in high positions. An Italian woman, other than a clerical or secretarial worker, should usually be addressed as *Dottoressa*. But take your cue from how the woman introduces herself or how she is introduced to you—some women prefer to be called *Signora*. Secretaries usually are called *Signora* or

Signorina, depending on age and whether they are married. A clue for telling the difference: A secretary might be called *Signora Barbara* (using her first name), while an executive would be *Signora Rossi* (her last name). Men here still open doors for women, help them on with their coats, and are loathe to let women pick up the check in restaurants (flashing a company credit card is a face-saving technique). Men of the old school may greet a woman visitor with a *baciamano*—kiss on the hand. Generally, this is just the way Italian men have been brought up to treat women. Men and women can expect to be questioned about their personal lives: Are you married? Do you have children? What does your spouse do? Women traveling alone aren't frowned upon at all, they are just a bit of a rarity and so are treated with curiosity.

Dress

Corporate executives and professionals dress with conservative elegance, wearing meticulously tailored two- or three-piece suits and beautiful Italian silk ties. Those in the fashion and design world tend to show more imaginative flair; many prefer Missoni-type knit jackets to suit jackets. Women in business dress with great style, but stay on the conservative edge of high fashion trends.

Gifts

It's more likely that you will be invited to dinner out with an associate, who may bring a spouse, then be asked to his or her home. If you are invited to dinner at someone's home, however, it's best to send flowers, to be delivered before you arrive. Bringing along fancy chocolates or cakes is also appropriate, but it's unwise to bring wine unless you are absolutely certain of your host's tastes.

Toasts and Greetings

Hello, how are you? *Buon giorno, come sta?* (Bwon JOR-no, co-meh sta).
Well, thank you. *Bene, grazie* (BEH-nay, GRAHTZ-ee-ay).
Pleased to meet you. *Piacere* (Pee-a-CHAYR-ay).
Thank you. *Grazie* (GRAHTZ-ee-ay).
You're welcome. *Prego* (PRAY-go).
Excuse me. *Miscusi* (mee SKOO-zee).
Nice to have met you. *E stato un piacere conoscerla* (Ay STAH-to oon pee-a-CHAYR-ay con-O-shayr-lah).
Goodbye. *ArriverderLa* (ah-ree-vay-DAYR-lah).
Cheers. *Salute* (sah-Loo-tay).
Ciao (chow). This greeting, which means both hello and good-bye, is used strictly between friends. Your business colleague will not be amused if you use this word.

LODGING

Unlike most Italian cities, Milan has few tourists, and its lodging industry generally caters to business travelers of all types. In Italy, that translates into high prices geared to expense-account travelers—especially in hotel restaurants. Phone charges, too, tend to be outrageous; if you can, make U.S. calls with an AT&T credit card and use one of the public SIP telephone centers for long distance calls. (There's an excellent one, which will also place collect international phone calls for you, in the Galleria Vittorio Emanuele.)

Milan is a city of trade fairs, and its hotels tend to be completely booked during the months of March, April (when the major international trade fair is held), September, and October, and on many days in December and January. Reserve far in advance to avoid disappointments. In August, many hotels are closed.

Despite the business focus and the apparent emphasis on physical luxury, Italian hotels often lack the most basic services that Americans take for granted. Phone connections can be dreadful—be prepared and be patient. Health facilities are rare. In-room modems are virtually nonexistent. And room service may operate only the same hours as the hotel's restaurant, if at all.

Milan is spread out, and it will not always be possible for you to stay near the place where you are going to be working. The very top international hotels tend to be grouped near the huge, Fascist-era Stazione Centrale (Central Train Station). Many businesses have headquarters in this area. However, traffic is heavy and drug users tend to congregate around here. Although the hotels themselves are well policed and quite safe, travelers who like to explore the city on foot on free evenings might be better advised to stick with hotels around the Duomo, the heart of the city, near shopping, sightseeing, and traditional cafés and restaurants. Another option is to stay in the Fiera, the trade fair area at the western edge of the city, a rather drab, but not unsafe, neighborhood that's convenient if you plan to be spending most of your time at a nearby show.

A number of hotels listed here offer corporate rates and/or weekend discounts; inquire when making reservations.

Highly recommended lodgings in each price category are indicated by a star ★.

Category	Cost*
$$$$ (Very Expensive)	over 350,000 lire
$$$ (Expensive)	250,001 lire–350,000 lire
$$ (Moderate)	150,000 lire–250,000 lire
$ (Inexpensive)	under 150,000 lire

All prices are for a standard double room, single occupancy, including 19% value added tax (VAT).

Numbers in the margin correspond to numbered hotel locations on the Milan Lodging and Dining map.

Duomo

❿ **Antica Locanda Solferino.** This hotel is a favorite of visit-
$$ ing correspondents at the nearby *Corriere Della Sera*, Italy's best known newspaper; accommodations should be reserved far in advance. The rooms are in demand because this family-style hotel in Milan's Brera district provides excellent value. The building is 19th century, but the rooms were all recently redecorated with peasant-print bedspreads, low bedside lamps draped with lace-edged

cloths, and 19th-century prints on the walls. There's very little in the way of public space, just a small lounge/reception area. *via Castelfidardo 2, 20100, tel. 02/657–0129, fax 02/656460. Gen. manager, Curzio Castelli. 11 doubles. V. Closed Aug. 7–17, Dec. 24–Jan. 4.*

★ **㉓** **Hotel Brunelleschi.** A drab, slate-gray exterior hides one
$$$ of Milan's real lodging gems. Rooms were redone in 1988–89, and are decorated in the efficient, ultramodern blond wood, pale flowered prints, and black paneling that characterizes up-to-the-minute Milanese interior design. Rooms, though on the small side, feature spacious, well-lighted desks and are equipped with computer-card door locks. Service is discreet but friendly—also a rarity in Milan. Ask for a room facing the interior courtyard; there is no view, but you will avoid the traffic noise on busy via Larga, below. So far, few Americans have discovered this hotel, which is frequented mainly by low-profile Japanese and German business travelers. It also serves a copious breakfast buffet—everything from bacon and eggs to meusli—included in the price of the room. *via Baracchini 12, 20123, tel. 02/8843, fax 02/870144. Gen. manager, Sebastiano Colacicco. 80 singles, 40 doubles, 5 suites. AE, DC, MC, V.*

㉔ **Hotel Canada.** This is a friendly and functional small hotel
$ only a few steps from Piazza del Duomo, and at the edge of the lively Corso di Porta Romana, a residential quarter lined with shops and restaurants. Frequented by business travelers on a budget, mostly Italians, it's run by a husband-and-wife team. Rooms, recently renovated, are spacious, with good lighting and desks; the modern furnishings are nondescript. Recommended for those who want a good location at a good price, but aren't too exigent about amenities or prestige. *via Santa Sofia 16, 20122, tel. 02/8052527, fax 02/58300282. Gen. manager, Alberto San Gregorio. 23 doubles, 12 singles. AE, DC, MC, V.*

㉒ **Grand Hotel Duomo.** Just a few steps from the Piazza del
$$$ Duomo, this hotel is frequented by a chic international clientele, including many on business. The hotel was designed by Giuseppe Mengoni, a late-19th-century architect who liked to use unexpected juxtapositions of forms from various periods, and his most famous work is attached to the hotel: The Galleria Vittorio Emanuele. The two-story cathedral-ceiling lobby was redone in classic mid-20th century fashion, with lots of marble and Oriental rugs. These also appear in most of the rooms, similarly traditional, and decorated in golds and browns. All duplex suites, the second-floor breakfast room, and rooms on the first, second, and third floors have views of the Gothic statues and spires of the city's cathedral. Service is aloof but functional. *via San Raffaele 1, 20121, tel. 02/8833, fax 02/877552. Gen. manager, Cesare Ghirardi. 76 singles, 66 doubles, 18 suites. MC, V. Closed Aug.*

㉗ **Jolly Hotel President.** This is the hotel of choice for travel-
$$$ ers who want to be assured of what they are getting in advance. All rooms have equal amenities in this gray steel-and-stone modern nine-story high rise: firm double beds with attractive polka-dot print spreads, bright modern lighting, functional desks, and an alarm clock hooked up into the telephone system that you can program for a wake-up call. It's best to ask for a room facing the Largo

MILAN

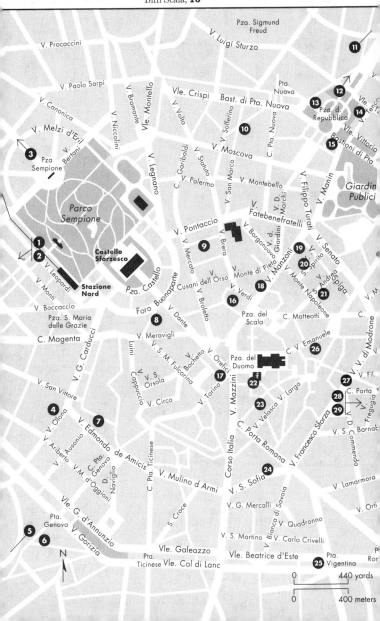

MILAN HOTEL CHART

HOTELS	Price Category	Business Services / Banquet capacity	No. of meeting rooms	Fax	Telex	Photocopying	Secretarial services	Audiovisual equipment	Translation services	International direct dial	Computer rentals	In-room modem phone jack
Air Hotel	$$	100	7	✓	✓	✓	-	✓	-	✓	-	-
Antica Locanda Soiferino	$$	0	0	✓	-	✓	-	-	-	✓	-	-
Brunelleschi	$$$	60	2	✓	✓	✓	-	✓	-	✓	-	-
Canada	$	0	1	✓	✓	✓	-	-	-	✓	-	-
Duca di Milan	$$$$	100	3	✓	✓	✓	✓	-	✓	✓	-	-
Hotel d'Este	$$	60	2	✓	✓	✓	✓	✓	✓	✓	-	-
Excelsior Gallia	$$$$	700	9	✓	✓	✓	✓	✓	✓	✓	-	-
Grand Hotel Brun	$$$	700	7	✓	✓	✓	✓	✓	✓	✓	-	-
Grand Hotel Duomo	$$$	50	1	✓	✓	✓	-	-	-	✓	-	-
Jolly Hotel President	$$$	100	4	✓	✓	✓	-	✓	-	✓	-	-
Jolly Touring	$$$	120	5	✓	✓	✓	-	-	-	✓	-	-
Manzoni	$	0	0	✓	-	✓	-	-	-	✓	-	-
Palace	$$$$	400	2	✓	✓	✓	-	-	-	✓	-	-
Pierre	$$$$	40	1	✓	✓	✓	✓	✓	✓	✓	-	-
Principe di Savoia	$$$$	400	11	✓	✓	✓	✓	-	✓	✓	-	-

$$$$ = over 350,000 lire, $$$ = 250,000 lire-350,000 lire, $$ = under 250,000 lire
● good, ◑ fair, ○ poor.

All-news cable channel	Desk	Desk lighting	Bed lighting	In-Room Amenities	Nonsmoking rooms	In-room checkout	Minibar	Toiletries	Room service	Laundry/Dry cleaning	Pressing	Hotel Amenities	Barber/Hairdresser	Garage	Courtesy airport transport	Sauna	Pool	Exercise room	
✓	◐	◐	◐		-	-	✓	◐	○	●	●		-	✓	✓	-	-	-	
-	-	-	◐		-	-	-	○	-	-	-		-	-	-	-	-	-	
✓	◐	◐	◐		-	-	✓	◐	◐	●	●		-	✓	-	-	-	-	
-	◐	◐	●		-	-	✓	◐	◐	◐	●		-	✓	-	-	-	-	
✓	●	◐	●		-	✓	✓	◐	◐	●	●		-	✓	-	-	-	-	
-	●	●	●		-	-	✓	◐	◐	●	●		-	✓	-	-	-	-	
✓	◐	◐	◐		✓	-	✓	●	◐	●	●		-	-	-	✓	○	●	
✓	◐	◐	●		-	-	✓	◐	◐	●	●		✓	✓	-	-	-	-	
-	◐	◐	◐		-	-	✓	◐	◐	●	●		-	✓	-	-	-	-	
✓	◐	◐	●		✓	-	✓	◐	◐	◐	◐		-	✓	✓	-	-	-	
✓	◐	◐	◐		-	-	✓	◐	◐	●	●		-	✓	✓	-	-	-	
-	○	○	○		-	-	-	○	○	-	-		-	✓	-	-	-	-	
✓	○	◐	●		-	-	✓	◐	◐	●	●		✓	✓	-	✓	-	●	
✓	●	●	●		-	-	✓	●	●	●	●		-	-	-	-	-	-	
✓	◐	◐	●		-	-	✓	●	●	●	●		✓	✓	-	✓	●	●	

Room service: ● 24-hour, ◐ 6AM–10PM, ○ other.
Laundry/Dry cleaning: ● same day, ◐ overnight, ○ other.
Pressing: ● immediate, ◐ same day, ○ other.

Augusto, and on a high floor. These afford views of the nearby spires of the Duomo, and some have small balconies. The restaurant is overpriced, but comfortable and friendly to guests dining alone. Frequented by department-store fashion buyers and executives, many of them American, the hotel also has a spacious bar and lounge area off the lobby. *Largo Augusto 10, 20122, tel. 02/7746, fax 02/783449. Gen. manager, Mario Mortula. 35 singles, 171 doubles, 14 minisuites, 1 suite. AE, DC, MC, V.*

★ ❷⓿ **Hotel Manzoni.** This charming small hotel in a 19th-centu-
$ ry palazzo just off Milan's most-traveled fashion street, the via Montenapoleone, draws models and people in the antiques business. But none of the snobbiness associated with those professions spills over into the hotel. Service is friendly and attentive. Rooms are modern, with print bedspreads and curtains, writing tables with lamps, and firm mattresses. Those facing the street have views of the quaint, well-restored 19th-century houses lining the via Santo Spirito, and are quiet in the evening after shops close. Other rooms look out onto a small courtyard. *via Santo Spirito 20, tel. 02/76005697, fax 02/784212. Gen. manager Renato Gigli. 28 doubles, 24 singles. No credit cards.*

Train Station Area

❶❸ **Duca di Milano.** One of the city's first hotels to be designed
$$$$ mainly for business travelers, this hotel has all its rooms arranged as suites, so that guests can have a separate room or alcove with a very spacious desk. Furnishings are modern, but rooms manage to avoid being too stark and officelike with such luxurious details as wood-trimmed furniture, brass lamps, and antique prints. Rooms facing the street have a view of the public gardens. The hallways and public rooms add elegance with potted palms, oil paintings, and antique furniture. *A Ciga hotel. Piazza della Repubblica 13, 20124, tel. 02/6284, fax 02/6555966. Gen. manager, Leone Jannuzzi. 50 double suites, 10 single suites. AE, DC, MC, V.*

❶❶ **Excelsior Gallia.** This is a favorite for top business execu-
$$$$ tives, many of whom hold press conferences or conventions in the hotel's spacious 1930s-era salons or in its luminous rooftop meeting hall, with views of the marble Mussolini-era train station across the street. Rooms are decorated in a variety of styles, all with vast bathrooms, gilt-edged mirrors, and chenille bedspreads. The hotel lobby is opulent, with plush Oriental carpets, and uniformed footmen provide attentive service. Gallia's Restaurant is renowned for both traditional Italian and more modern, creative cuisine; it is an excellent spot for a business lunch. The bar (*see After Hours, below*) is the place to meet with clients for a drink. *A Trusthouse Forte hotel. Piazza Duca D'Aosta 9, 20124, tel. 02/6785, fax 02/656306. Gen. manager, Valentino Bertolini. 44 singles, 198 doubles, 10 suites. AE, DC, MC, V.*

❶❺ **Jolly Touring.** Part of the Jolly chain, this eight-story ho-
$$$ tel, built in the 1930s, offers the same modern comforts as the Jolly President, but at a slightly lower price, reflecting the less prestigious—yet still convenient—location near the railroad station. Rooms have the standard functional decor found throughout the chain—dark brown and beige fabrics, built-in furniture well equipped with read-

ing lights, radio, call bells, etc., and desks and armchairs. A mixed bag of business travelers stays here, from Japanese salesmen to Roman senators. The wood-paneled lobby, with a cappuccino bar, is a bit cramped, especially around check-out time. *via Ugo Tarchetti 2, 20121, tel. 02/ 6335, fax 02/6592209, Gen. manager, Carlo De Poli. 240 doubles, 30 singles. AE, DC, MC, V.*

★ **⑭** **Hotel Palace.** Milan's most luxurious business hotel, built
$$$$ in the 1960s in the large-windowed block style of the era, the Palace is located halfway between the Duomo and the train station, facing Piazza della Repubblica and looking across to its splashier sister hotel, the Principe di Savoia. Where the Principe di Savoia draws a glitzier crowd of celebrities, the Palace is geared to serve a top-level business clientele. Over the past few years, this hotel has been completely renovated. Bedrooms are spacious and decorated in early-19th-century Empire style, with highly polished mahogany furniture, fine fabrics in soft pastels or deep reds or blues, and lovely old prints. Public areas have an air of understated luxury with deep carpets, comfortable armchairs, and elegant flower arrangements. The Casanova Grill, with well-spaced tables and light, and fresh-from-the-market specialties, is a good spot for a lunch meeting. *Piazza della Repubblica 20, 20124, tel. 02/6336, fax 02/65448, Gen. manager, Sandro Matassini. 42 singles, 166 doubles, 8 suites. AE, DC, MC, V.*

⑫ **Hotel Principe di Savoia.** This quiet, luxurious hotel is the
$$$$ top of the line for Milan. Although it has a Piazza della Repubblica address, it's set away from the bustle of that busy square. The hotel, renovated during 1990, is furnished in turn-of-the-century Lombard style: dark-wood period furniture, polished brass light fixtures, and frescoes in the public areas. Rooms are vast, and furnished with antique desks, wallpaper, 19th-century prints, and hand-blown Venetian glass chandeliers. The bar (*see* After Hours, below) is a rendezvous for Milan's top executives throughout the day. The drawback is that this hotel is not in a neighborhood where guests can stroll about and discover the city; after dark, near the railway station, it can become dangerous. But no matter: Most guests here— from Elton John to Margaret Thatcher—don't travel by foot. *A Ciga hotel. Piazza della Repubblica 17, 20124, tel. 02/6230, fax 02/6595838. Gen. manager, Giorgio Daina. 193 doubles, 52 suites. AE, DC, MC, V.*

Near Sant'Ambrogio

★ **❼** **Pierre.** Located on the inner beltway, near the medieval
$$$$ church of Sant'Ambrogio, this renovated 19th-century building is one of Milan's newest luxury hotels, opened in late 1987. Each room is furnished in a different style, with elegant color-coordinated fabrics, objets d'art, a variety of modern and antique furnishings, and pure linen bed sheets. Everything is electronic: You can open the curtains, turn off the lights, have personal messages from the front desk appear on your TV screen—all by pressing the buttons on your remote control. The restaurant serves fine classic Italian cuisine in a quiet, plush room with a verandah looking out onto a minuscule garden courtyard. The bar (*see* After Hours, below) is a good spot for meeting clients. This hotel, with a 50% American clientele, draws top-level business travelers as well as elite tourists. *Via de*

Amicis 32, tel. 02/8056220, fax 02/8052157. Gen. manager, Carlo Standilini. 12 singles, 29 doubles, 6 junior suites. AE, DC, MC, V.

Near Porta Romana

㉕ **Hotel d'Este.** This comfortable, clean hotel with efficient
$$ service is a 20-minute walk south from center city, near
the Bocconi University, a leading business school. Rooms
are large, well lighted, and functional—indeed, rather
spartan. The hotel has no frills, but it does have all the
basics. Clientele includes many business travelers from
other parts of Italy, and a fair number of women business
travelers. The hotel is in a safe, residential neighborhood
dotted with inexpensive restaurants and shops. *viale
Bligny 23, 20136, tel. 02/5454330, fax 02/5454330. Gen.
manager, Luca Brancaleoni. 46 doubles, 32 singles, 1
suite. No credit cards.*

Fiera District

❶ **Grand Hotel Brun.** This modern seven-story building with
$$$ two wings is in a rather desolate suburb of Milan, but its
elegance, excellent service, easy access to center city, and
proximity to the Fiera—the site of the fashion collections
and countless other trade shows—make up for the drab
surroundings. In addition to the fashion trade, members
of Milan's champion soccer team and their entourages also
frequent this hotel. Inside, there is nothing drab about the
Brun. Rooms are spacious, with tasteful designer bedspreads and curtains, plush carpeting, and enormous twin
beds. All rooms also have two telephones, one of them in
the bath. Some travelers stay here just for the Ascot restaurant, whose modern, creative cuisine and smoked
salmon and foie gras are among the best in Milan. *via Cal-
dera 21, 20153, tel. 02/45271, fax 02/4526055. Gen. manager, Giovanni Battista Modestini. 306 doubles, 24 suites.
AE, DC, MC, V.*

Airport

㉙ **Air Hotel.** Located ¼ mile from Linate airport, this mod-
$$ ern four-star hotel built in 1988 is convenient for both
travelers with early morning flights and those doing busi-
ness at the many firms nearby. Rooms are sound-proofed
and well equipped. Furnishings are comfortable and con-
temporary. *via Idroscalo 4, 20090, Novegro Segrate, tel.
02/7560256, fax 02/7561294. Gen. manager, Roberto Di
Barletta. 60 double rooms. AE, DC, MC, V.*

DINING

Milanese businesspeople tend to frequent classic trat-
torias, many of them specializing in Tuscan cooking and
seafood; here the term trattoria is not necessarily synony-
mous with moderate prices, as it generally is elsewhere in
Italy. Paradoxically, you can get fresher seafood in this in-
land city than on the coast: The choice of the catch is
whisked to Milan by truck from Italy's main fishing ports.
As a result, however, seafood is often even more expensive
than other items on the menu; it's often priced by weight.

Unlike most Italian regions, Lombardy exhibits a north-
ern European preference for butter rather than oil as its

cooking medium, which imparts a rich and distinctive flavor to the cuisine. Among the most popular specialties is *ossobucco alla Milanese*, veal knuckle served with rissoto. *Risotto Milanese* uses chicken broth and adds saffron, which gives the dish a rich yellow color. The lakes in the region are a good source of freshwater fish, particularly trout and pike. Gorgonzola, the rich veined cheese, and *panettone*, a raised fluffy fruitcake, both come from Milan.

The Milanese love to eat, and if they can do business at the same time, they are perfectly happy. Restaurants in Milan are like theaters—places where the dramas of love and money are played out. It is here, too, that the real social life of the city takes place, a fact that gives extra importance to a restaurant's class and decor. Being part of the crowd that frequents a certain restaurant is extremely important to businesspeople in this city; it allows them to keep an eye on what is going on.

This explains why getting a table in many Milan restaurants can be a complex affair. Night after night, the best restaurants are filled with marketing executives, models, fashion designers—all those who belong, and many of those who would like to belong. When going to a first-rate Milan restaurant, it is always best to bring along your Italian business colleagues. Not only will they be able to obtain a reservation, but they will also be able to tell you who the people are at the next table, and whether you should know about them or not. As is often the case in a city where most people are dining on expense accounts, prices at Milan restaurants can be outrageous.

Highly recommended restaurants in each price category are indicated by a star ★.

Category	Cost*
$$$$ (Very Expensive)	over 180,000 lire
$$$ (Expensive)	100,000 lire–180,000 lire
$$ (Moderate)	under 100,000 lire

Prices are per person, including appetizer, entrée, and dessert, but excluding drinks and service (there is no tax).

Numbers in the margin correspond to numbered restaurant locations on the Milan Lodging and Dining map.

Wine

The Lombardy region, of which Milan is the capital, produces good wine, but Milanese prefer the wines of neighboring Piedmont, about 30 miles away. It is here that most of the famous Italian reds are made—those deep, gravelly wines with complex noses. Milan's best restaurants all have cellars full of these heady Piedmont wines, and they go very well with the roast meat dishes that are often found on the menus.

Barolo, from Piedmont, is the uncontested king of Italian vineyards. Made from the black, nebbiolo grape, it is kept in barrels for at least two or three years, and sometimes as many as five, before being bottled. The long aging process in the wood gives the wine an astringency and weight that some find hard to appreciate. Barolo is a bit much for a business meal, especially since it requires a relatively long time to breathe before it can be fully appreciated. The best restaurants serve it in glasses that look like huge brandy snifters. If your guest is a wine lover, though, he may be impressed by your choice.

Barbaresco is probably the best expensive Piedmont red to choose for a business lunch. It is also made from nebbiolo, but spends rather less time in the wood. This gives it a certain astringency, but leaves a fruity zest that is reminiscent of a good burgundy.

Another Piedmont red, the light and fruity Dolcetto, is good on a warm day when you don't want anything too heavy. It should never be more than two or three years old. Gavi, or Cortese di Gavi is the most distinguished Piedmontese white. It has a complex nose that recalls white burgundy. It is made from the Cortese grape, grown in the same areas of the Piedmont as Barolo and Barbaresco.

Lombardy does boast two good local reds. The first, Oltrepo Pavese, is made from a blending of local grapes. It often is sold under a fantasy name, like "Buttafuoco" (firebreather) or "Babbacarlo" (grandfather Carlo). Avoid the one called "Sangue di Giuda" (Judas's blood) which tends to be sickly-sweet. Best vintages vary from brand to brand; ask the waiter to recommend a good one.

Lombardy's second good local wine is a red from the Valtellina, the Alpine region next to Switzerland. The wine is made from a mixture of nebbiolo and local grapes, and is sold under a variety of names. "Inferno" or "Sassella" tend to be excellent wine buys, since the two years they are aged in barrels give them a hearty astringency.

Following are the best years for these excellent Italian wines:

Barolo: 64, 78, 80.
Barbaresco: 79, 82, 85.
Dolcetto: 85, 86, 87.
Gavi: 86, 87.
Oltrepo Pavese: 83.

Beer and Ale

Italian beer is of no special interest to beer lovers. It is light and frothy, and relatively expensive; a mug costs about twice what you would pay in the United States. Birra Peroni is the principal brand. A wide selection of imported beer is available.

Business Breakfasts

Business breakfasts are not common among Italians, but those used to working with Americans will not be averse to having an early morning meeting over cappuccino. Outside of the hotels, however, there are no places that would accommodate a quiet meeting; the cafés are mostly bustling and cramped. The two best hotels in which to meet are the **Jolly President** (tel. 02/7746) and the **Principe di Savoia** (tel. 02/6230), both with spacious dining rooms suitable for discussions.

Center City

⑲ **Bice.** The unimposing front of this busy restaurant belies
$$$ its understated elegance, with white linen tablecloths, antique sideboards, and plush rugs. Bice is packed every day at lunchtime with photographers, fashion designers, and buyers. Tables are close together, and the place is noisy, but food and service are excellent. Try the selection of risottos, especially the *risotto agli asparagi* (rice cooked in an asparagus sauce), or the *risotto alla trevigiana* (creamy rice with radicchio salad, a specialty of the Veneto region). There are excellent fish and steaks as second courses, and the wine list is ample. *via Borgospesso 12, tel. 02/76002572. Reservations required. Casual chic dress. AE, DC, MC, V. Closed Mon., Tues. lunch, and Aug.*

⑯ **Biffi Scala.** Next to Milan's famous opera house, this res-
$$$$ taurant is a haunt of the rich and powerful. Milan banker Enrico Cuccia—who orchestrated most of the important Italian business deals in the last half-century and whose office is just around the corner—is a regular here. A place to meet with the financial elite, Biffi Scala offers calm, modern elegance and luxury foods like caviar and foie gras. A specialty is carpaccio: thin slices of raw beef topped with Parmesan cheese, bitter herbs, and olive oil. The wine cellar is interesting, though not wide-ranging. *via Filodrammatici 2, tel. 866651. Jacket advised. Reservations essential. AE, DC, MC, V. Closed Sun., Aug. 10–20, Dec. 24–Jan. 6.*

★ ㉑ **Boeucc** (pronounced "butch"). Across from the home of
$$$ the great 19th century Milanese writer Alessandro Manzoni is the best Milanese restaurant in the city. The decor is that of a 19th-century palazzo, with satin curtains and antique furniture; the building was designed by the architect Piermarini, who built La Scala Opera House. There is an awning-covered courtyard garden for warm-weather dining. The traditional atmosphere has always attracted the great and famous of the city, like former Italian prime minister Bettino Craxi, a Milan native; indeed, such is the importance of Boeucc that foreigners will find it very difficult to get a table. With luck, your business colleagues will take you here (and they might appreciate your asking them to come). It's the ideal place for what Italians call *rappresentanza*—making an impression on a client or showing a colleague a good time. Boeucc is the place to try the famous *risotto alla Milanese*, Lombardy rice flavored with saffron, or to sample a huge chateaubriand, made with the great beef of the region. It also specializes in *fettuccine agli scampi* (homemade egg noodles with crayfish in a basil and tomato sauce). Boeucc probably has the best cellar in Milan for traditional red wines. Accompany beef or veal dishes with a Piedmontese Barbaresco or Barolo. *Piazza Belgioioso 2, tel. 02/790224. Reservations essential. Jacket advised. Closed Sat., Sun. lunch, Good Fri.–Easter, Aug., Dec. 24–Jan. 2.*

⑱ **Don Lisander.** Smack in the center of Milan's business dis-
$$$ trict, this former chapel overlooking a garden offers superb fresh local meats and vegetables. Inside, designer lighting, abstract prints, and a modern terra-cotta tile floor create a chic, contemporary setting in which to try the famous Italian mushrooms, *funghi porcini*, grilled

over a wood fire, or really fresh fish and pasta. In the summer, have an elegant outdoor lunch in the garden courtyard, which is covered by an awning and lined with marble statues. The wine list is good. *via Manzoni 12a, tel. 02/790130. Jacket required. Reservations required. AE, DC, MC, V. Closed Sat. eve., Sun., Aug. 7–21, Dec. 20–Jan. 6.*

❹ Orti di Leonardo. This is one of Milan's newer eateries, lo-
$$$ cated in a converted convent with vaulted brick ceilings. Service is attentive but unobtrusive at this elegant restaurant. Gray and creamy-white walls are hung with paintings, most of them by well-known contemporary artists. Three separate dining areas—the main longish hall and two smaller rooms to either side—offer a choice to diners. The cuisine is international, but includes some interesting Italian specialties. Try the *ravioli di anatra*, duck-filled ravioli with a simple butter sauce; *branzino*, grilled sea bass; or *pesce spada*, grilled swordfish. This restaurant attracts a business crowd, especially at lunch. *via Aristide de'Togni 6, tel. 02/4983476. Jacket advised. Reservations advised. AE, DC, MC, V. Closed Sun., Aug.*

❽ Quattro Mori. Right next to the Milan business district,
$$$ this restaurant is always filled with stockbrokers and financial analysts; it sometimes appears to be the executive dining room of the nearby companies, such as tire-maker Pirelli. Just a few steps from the reconstructed 15th-century Sforza castle, and a lovely garden, this is an excellent place to have a business lunch. The seafood, of superior quality, is absolutely fresh and suits top management's low-cholestorol requirements. The antipasto selection, both of marinated cooked vegetables or mixtures of marinated seafood—shrimp, octopus, and *moscardini* (tiny squid)—are exceptional. *via San Giovanni sul Muro 2, tel. 870617. Jacket advised. Reservations required. AE, DC, MC, V. Closed Sat. lunch, Sun., Aug.*

★ ⑰ Ristorante Peck. In the heart of the business district, this
$$$ is one of the world's great Italian restaurants. Established by Francesco Peck at the end of the 19th century as a kind of delicatessen, Peck now takes up almost a whole street with its fine food stores. But the best that Peck offers is decidedly in the discreetly decorated blond-wood paneled dining room, where the important businesspeople of the city meet. Peck has succeeded in offering the best of traditional Northern Italian (especially Milanese) fare, cooked to perfection, as well as maintaining one of the most creative kitchens on the peninsula. Red mullet in dill and coriander-flavored gelatine, and *ravioli di branzino* (stuffed with sea bass) are examples of the high creative level this restaurant maintains. Snails stewed in tomato sauce with polenta (*lumache con polenta*) provide a sample of traditional flair. The cellar has great wines from all over Italy, with special focus on the complex, heavy whites of the Friuli region. This is also one of the few restaurants in Milan where the service is impeccable. It is the ideal place for clinching a business deal or for discreet negotiations. *via Victor Hugo 4, tel. 876774. Jacket advised. Reservations essential. AE, DC, MC, V. Closed Sun. and July.*

㉖ Savini. This is known as the restaurant for the power bro-
$$$$ kers of the city. The decor is similar to that of the nearby 19th-century opera house, La Scala; the wood-paneled rooms, with their luxurious curtains, often remind the

visitor more of an opera stage set than of a restaurant. However, business acquaintances may want to take you to lunch or dinner here. Some of the food is interesting, although many of the recipes have not changed for a long time. This is the right restaurant to sample the famous *costoletta alla Milanese*—the breaded veal cutlet that is a specialty of the city. The cellar is adequate, and prices are sky-high. *Galleria Vittorio Emanuele, tel. 02/805–8343. Reservations advised for evening. Jacket advised. AE, DC, MC, V. Closed Sun., Aug. 1–21, Dec. 24–Jan. 3.*

❾ **Trattoria dell'Angolo.** This two-story restaurant in Milan's
$$ central Brera district is a favorite with bankers and brokers at lunchtime, and with a trendier crowd at dinner. Ask for a table in the quieter upstairs room at noontime—both rooms are quiet in the evening. The pasta is excellent—try fresh spinach and ricotta cheese ravioli in a light tomato sauce, or gnocchi served with tomato sauce and cheese. Beamed ceilings, exposed brick, and yellow and brown tablecloths set the mood here for a friendly, not-too-formal meal. *via Fior Chiari, tel. 02/8058495. Jacket advised. Reservations advised. AE, DC, MC, V. Closed Sat. lunch, Sun., Jan. 1–7, Aug. 5–25.*

Porta Vittoria

★ ㉘ **Gualtiero Marchesi.** Gualtiero Marchesi is the only Italian
$$$$ chef ever to have won a three-star Michelin rating. He created "nouvelle cuisine," Italian-style, championing the new French school in a country where traditions die hard and convincing his countrymen that small portions in complex combinations represented the new culinary ideal. Although the decor of his small restaurant is functional, even cold, a meal here is a once-in-a-lifetime experience. It's well worth the 15-minute cab ride to this residential neighborhood. Obviously, getting a table is not an easy matter, and it would be wise to reserve at least a few days in advance. The ravioli with herbs and shrimp, or the eggplant with sweet and sour sauce and shrimp (*caponatina di melanzane in agrodolce con gamberi saltati*) are among the stellar selections. *via Bonvesin de la Riva 9, tel. 02/ 741246. Reservations required. Jacket and tie required. AE, DC, MC, V. Closed Sun. and Mon. lunch, Good Fri.– Easter Mon., all Aug., Dec. 24–Jan. 8.*

Near Piazzale Giovanni delle Bande Nere

❷ **Aimo e Nadia.** This somewhat out-of-the-way restaurant,
$$$$ about 20–25 minutes by taxi from the center city, boasts the most inventive versions of classic Italian cuisine in the city. Ultrafresh vegetables and the highest grades of meat are combined with unusual spices and herbs. As a result of her inventive larder, chef Nadia has attracted the ultra chic crowd in this snobbish city. Fashion and marketing are bywords here, and getting a table is not an easy matter. If you succeed, don't miss the anchovies with fresh mozzarella, or the beef with ginger. The cellar is of the highest level, and service is, too. *via Montecuccoli 6, tel. 416886. Jacket advised. Reservations essential. AE, DC, V. Closed Sat. lunch, Sun., Aug.*

Corso Sempione Area

★ ❸ **Montecristo.** It's located a bit out of the way for busi-
$$$ nesspeople—in the residential Corso Sempione area,

about a half hour walk, 15 minutes by taxi from the Duomo—but its fish specialties attract a loyal following of influential lawyers. The rather stark blue and white decor, with tanks of multicolored fish providing a contrast, makes for a pleasant change for a business lunch or dinner. All the grilled fish here are superb, and the pasta and fish dishes, like spaghetti with lobster, are made with the light, unobtrusive sauces usually found only in Naples. Not very formal, this is a good place to bring a business associate that you know fairly well. There's a good selection of white wines in addition to reds. *via Prina 17, tel. 02/312760. Jacket advised. Reservations advised. AE, DC, MC, V. Closed Tues., Sat. lunch, Aug., Dec. 24–Jan. 2.*

I Navigli

★ ❻ **La Scaletta.** This restaurant is located in the picturesque
$$$$ quarter known as "I Navigli," or the canals, but its outward appearance isn't impressive. La Scaletta is next to a minor train station, in a dirty square, and the little stairway that leads up to the dining room makes you think it's an annex to the station. But once inside, you get a different impression. Linen, crystal, books, and paintings all create a warm, welcoming ambience in this intimate and most unusual restaurant. Chef "Mamma" Pina Bellini, whose reputation was already established throughout Europe before she became the chef here, maintains the highest level in her kitchen. Try the salt-cod salad, or fish gnocchi (dumplings), *tagliolini* noodles with clams and broccoli, or, for the adventurous, rice with snails. There's a superb cellar with great wines from small producers that don't always make their way into the best restaurants. *Piazza Stazione Genova 3, tel. 8350290. Jacket advised. Reservations essential. Closed Sun., Mon., Easter, Aug., Dec. 24–Jan. 6. No credit cards.*

★ ❺ **Osteria dei Binari.** A long time ago, this first-class restau-
$$$ rant was a working man's dive near the railroad. Although the railroad still runs past it, the restaurant is now in the center of the gentrified Navigli section of Milan, and, on most nights, it is filled with journalists, local politicians, and businesspeople. The elegant mirrored dining room looks out on one of the most charming gardens in the city. It is the ideal place to go in the spring or summer, when one can sit outside, but even in winter the romance of the city makes itself felt here. Cuisine is a mixture of classic Milanese and Piedmontese cooking. Try the local antipasti; the *creîspelle*, or crêpes stuffed with spinach and cheese; or *manzo in crosta*, tender beef in a pastry crust. The cellar has a number of interesting wines, all served with great care. First-rate service makes this an excellent choice. It's one of the great local finds that few foreigners ever get to see. *via Tortona 1, tel. 02/8399428. Casual dress. Reservations advised. Dinner only. Closed Sun. and Aug. 10–17.*

FREE TIME

Fitness

Hotel Facilities
There are few hotels that have health clubs. The Brunelleschi and the Excelsior Gallia have facilities, but they are not open to nonguests.

Health Clubs
Health clubs in Milan do not generally admit guests, unless they are accompanied by a member. The following clubs have monthly memberships available (and may be persuaded to accept guests on a day-rate basis). Milan's ultra-chic set, from models to marketing executives, belongs to the **Club Francesco Conti** (via Cerva 4, tel. 02/7600014), which has a roof-top garden and swimming pool, open in summer. The **Skorpion Health Club** (Corso Vittorio Emanuele 24, tel. 02/781424) and **American Contourella** (via Montenapoleone 10, tel. 02/76005290) offer gymnastics, massage, and warm-up facilities.

Jogging
Jogging in the streets of Milan may be more harmful to your health than beneficial, given the hair-raising traffic and its attendent fumes. The best places to jog are around the zoo at the **Giardini Pubblici,** along **via Palestro,** or on the grounds of the **Castello Sforzesco,** a moated reconstruction of the imposing 15th-century fortress built by the Sforza family. Milan has a large population of heroin addicts who throng the parks after dark, so jogging at night is to be avoided.

Shopping

As Italy's and perhaps Europe's wealthiest city—and as the capital of the country's booming fashion and interior design industries—Milan has boutiques to enthrall even the most jaded shoppers. Better still for business travelers, these are located right in the business district, wedged between discreet bank offices and stock brokerage houses on via Manzoni, via Montenapoleone, via della Spiga, via Sant'Andrea, and the Corso Vittorio Emanuele. Some of the most renowned women's fashion boutiques within this small area are **Armani** (via Sant'Andrea 9, tel. 02/792757), **Ferre** (via Sant'Andrea 10a, tel. 02/794864), **Valentino** (via Santo Spirito 3, tel. 02/790285), **Coveri** (via San Pietro all'Orto, tel. 02/76001624), **Pupi Solari** (via Mascheroni 12, tel. 02/463325), which also has a children's boutique; and **Lange** (via Sant'Andrea 11, tel. 02/794133). The best of the men's clothing stores in this part of town include **Valentino** (via Montenapoleone 20, tel. 02/790285), **Tincati** (via Verri 11, tel. 02/76009928, with branches at Piazzale Oberdan 2 and Viale Piave 41), **Ermenegildo Zegna** (via Verri 3, tel. 02/795521), and **Barba's** (via Sant'Andrea 21, tel. 02/76005505). Both sexes will find something to covet at **Missoni** (via Montenapoleone 1, tel. 02/76000906) and **Gucci** (via Montenapoleone 5, tel. 02/5456621).

For leather goods, **Prada** (Galleria Vittorio Emanuele 63, tel. 02/876979) is a classic. The Prada shop at via Spiga 5 (tel. 02/76008636) has more trendy fashions in handbags, travel bags, and umbrellas. **Valextra** (Piazza San Babila 3, tel. 02/76002989) specializes in attaché cases and leather accessories for businesspeople. The inimitable Italian style in footwear for men and women is well represented at **Ferragamo** (via Montenapoleone 3, tel. 02/76000054) and **Beltrami** (via Montenapoleone 16, tel. 02/76002975).

If the latest suits by Giorgio Armani, dresses by Valentino, textiles from Missoni, or hand-blown glass by Vennini of Venice aren't within your budget, try **Fimpar** (Corso Vittorio Emanuele 1, no tel.). Its attentive multilingual staff will show you attractive tweed suits or gabardine trousers that are sold under the store's own brand name at very reasonable prices. And at **Michela Mercantini** (Corso Venezia 8, tel. 02/709745), you can find cut-rate designer outfits that were worn by models at fashion shows. Another outlet for discounted designer fashions is **Vestistock** (viale Romagna 19, tel. 02/7490502).

Right across from Il Duomo, the cathedral, is **La Rinascente** (tel. 02/23961), an efficient department store with English-speaking clerks and special services for tourists, such as help with the paperwork needed to get a refund of Italy's hefty value-added tax (VAT). The only other upscale department store is **Coin** (Corso Vercelli, tel. 02/48005160 and Piazzale Loreto, tel. 02/2826179). The **UPIM** chain, with branches all over Italy, carries a wide variety of low-priced goods—from stationery to toothbrushes to clothing—of medium quality.

Gastronomes should try the **Peck** stores (via Victor Hugo 4, tel. 02/861040 and via Cantu 3, tel. 02/693017), a group of boutiques selling the finest Italian food, to take out or to eat on the premises. You can take home handmade pasta, olive oil, fresh cheese, or dried porcini mushrooms. Peck also has tasty cooked dishes that are ideal for the traveler tired of dining out. Ask for *una forchetta* (oo-na for-KEHT-ta), which means a fork, with your risotto or lasagna.

Diversions

If museums aren't for you, take a stroll around the **Brera** district surrounding Milan's most famous art museum, the Pinacoteca Brera (*see* below). With small, well-kept palazzi housing chic shops, restaurants, and cafés on the ground floor, this is Milan's equivalent of Greenwich Village.

The massive brick fortress, **Castello Sforzesco** (Piazza Castello), that sprawls across the northern artery of the city at Piazza Castello houses collections of Lombard sculptures, paintings, antiques, armor, and ceramics, including Michelangelo's *Rondanini Pieta*, his last work. It's nice to take a stroll through the castle's courtyard and into the Parco Sempione beyond for a rare respite from Milan's snarled traffic.

Milan's center and symbol, the massive **Duomo** (cathedral) was begun in 1396 by the Visconti family, who wanted to outdo rival Florentine lords by building a grander church. Worked on for centuries, and still unfinished, the Duomo has become a Milanese epithet for something that never gets done. Its vast, shadowy interior has startlingly beautiful Gothic stained-glass windows. The exterior is a riot of statues, spires, and gargoyles, capped by the golden statue of the Madonnina (little Madonna), a symbol of Milan. An elevator to the roof affords a stunning view of Milan and the Alps when the weather is fine.

The two-tiered, cross-shaped **Galleria Vittorio Emanuele**—one of the world's earliest and most elegant shopping malls—was built by the architect Mengoni in 1867. Sandwiched between Piazza della Scala and the Duomo, it is still the center of Milan city life. It's a perfect place to stop for a cappuccino or coffee and people-watch, especially around 5 PM.

In a free hour, you can get a feel for the way the bourgeois of Milan once lived by strolling through the **Museo Poldi Pezzoli** (via Manzoni 12, tel. 02/794889), a 19th-century villa whose art-loving owner bequeathed it to the city as a museum. Particularly noteworthy among the collections are paintings from the Botticelli school, and the swords and armor.

The little-visited **Navigli** quarter of Milan was, until a few years ago, a working-class neighborhood, and is now slowly becoming a gentrified quarter of charming shops and cafés. The Navigli are the only remaining canals of the dozens that used to reach into central Milan from the nearby Ticino River, and they are still the site of a regatta and canoe race every spring.

One of Italy's most stunning painting collections, in the **Pinacoteca Brera** (via Brera 28, tel. 02/80837), includes works by Raphael, Tintoretto, Caravaggio, and Mantegna (his *Dead Christ* is housed here). The large collection, which encompasses the 20th century, will probably require several hours.

If you like Romanesque art, **Sant'Ambrogio** (Piazza Sant'-Ambrogio) church, named after Milan's patron saint, is not to be missed. Begun in the fourth century by Saint Ambrose on the site of a cemetery of Christian martyrs, it was renovated several times, most recently in the 12th century. Noteworthy are its carved capitals, apse mosaic, marble choir, and gold and silver altar.

Santa Maria Della Grazie (Corso Magenta) is the site of Milan's most famous work of art, Leonardo Da Vinci's *Last Supper*. The painting, which has been badly damaged by age and pollution, is currently restored, and though it still can be viewed by visitors, it is faded and hardly visible in a vast, dark room with several sets of railings separating it from the crowds.

If you can't get tickets to a performance at **La Scala** (Piazza della Scala), the most famous opera house in the world, you can still see the gilt and red-velvet wedding cake of a theater and learn about its history at the museum next-door (tel. 02/8053418).

The Arts

The most famous spectacle in Milan is **La Scala Opera,** which presents some of the world's most impressive operatic productions. The house is invariably sold out in advance in opera season; sometimes your local host can help you find tickets if he or she is well connected. Otherwise, check at your hotel or try to book tickets at the CIT travel agencies elsewhere in Italy and in foreign countries, but no more than 10 days before the performance. The opera season begins early in December and ends in May. The concert season runs from May to the end of June and from September through November. There is a brief ballet season in September. Programs are available at principal travel agencies and tourist information offices in Italy and abroad. (Box Office, Teatro alla Scala, Piazza della Scala, tel. 02/809126. Open Tues.–Sun., 10–1 and 3:30–5:30. Tickets for the same evening's performance are on sale from 5:30.)

In addition to La Scala's opera and ballet seasons, the official orchestra of the **RAI** (Italian state radio and television) has a full season of concerts (Corso Sempione 27, tel. 02/38881). **Angelicum** (Piazza Sant'Angelo 2, tel. 02/6592748) and **Pomeriggi Musicali** (via Kramer 5, tel. 02/799974) also offer musical programs. Chamber music concerts are organized by the **Società del Quartetto** (Corso Mattcotti 9, tel. 02/706850).

Although Milan also has an active theater life, there are unlikely to be any productions in English; however, there are some good cinemas that show films in the original language. For information on opera, ballet, and concerts, consult the city's Municipal Information Office (*see* below).

The **Municipal Information Office** (Galleria Vittorio Emanuele, Piazza della Scala side, tel. 02/87054) will book tickets for you. **La Biglietteria** (Corso Garibaldi 81, tel. 02/6590188) also books and sells tickets for performances of all kinds.

After Hours

Milan's bustling streets become almost completely deserted after business hours, with the exception of the central areas, such as Piazza del Duomo, and the Brera section.

Bars and Lounges
For drinks, try the Art Deco **Bar Magenta** (Corso Magenta 13, at the corner of via Carducci, tel. 02/8053808), the in place for youthful managers, trendy marketing executives, and foreign fashion models to sip aperitifs. It's in a busy but chic section of town. In the Brera section, the **Bar Jamaica** (via Brera 26, no tel.), once known as an artists' and writers' hangout, is a favorite place for everyone from the literary crowd to business managers. **Café Pacifico** (via Cornalia 2, tel. 02/6690078) offers an American-style wood-paneled bar populated by a boisterous but friendly crowd. There's good Mexican food here, too, and this is probably the only place in Italy where you can order a pitcher of Margaritas. For more sedate imbibing, **Gershwin's** (via Corrado il Salico 10, tel. 02/8497722) is a relaxed piano bar where Cole Porter and Noel Coward, along with the bar's namesake, figure in the repertoire. The best hotel bars for elegant after-hours business discussions are those of the **Hotel Pierre** (tel. 02/8056220), the **Principe di Savoia** (tel. 02/6230), and the **Excelsior Gallia** (tel. 02/6277).

Jazz

Le Scimmie (via Ascanio Sforza 49, tel. 02/8391874) is a good spot for cool jazz in a relaxed atmosphere. **Capolinea** (via Lodovico il Moro 119, tel. 02/470524) offers jazz concerts, with occasional visiting stars.

Nightclubs

Charly Max (via Marconi 2, tel. 02/871416) and **Nepentha** (Piazza Diaz 1, tel. 02/804837) are good bets for an evening of dinner and dancing—but don't expect the entertainment to come cheap.

Discos

Disco lovers with egos of steel can head to **Plastic** (viale Umbria 120, tel. 02/743674), where the doorman selects the clientele for its chic look. Also recently opened is a lower-key snack bar/café next door. The city's best known rock club/disco, **Rolling Stone** (Corso XXII Marzo 32, tel. 02/733172), usually features big-name bands, often from the United States or Britain.

Montréal

by Patricia Lowe

Montréal has made good business sense since 1611, when entrepreneur and explorer Samuel de Champlain first set up a fur-trading post on a strategic 32-mile-long island in the St. Lawrence River. Settlement by the French followed in 1642, a milestone that will be marked by 350th-anniversary celebrations in Montréal in 1992.

The city's history as first a French then a British possession has led to endless language and power feuds between its French- and English-speaking populations. Officially, Montréal is French-speaking, but unofficially, it's English as well, as evidenced in the names of its early tycoons—Allan, Drummond, McGill, McTavish, Shaughnessy, and Van Horne—which live on in museums (the Shaughnessy House of the Canadian Centre for Architecture, for example), the leading university (McGill), and many street signs.

Today, with the approach of celebrations that will mark Montréal's founding, major multinationals, like Lavalin, the homegrown engineering firm, and Teleglobe Canada, are erecting the city's tallest (51-story) office tower, at 1000 rue la Gauchetière. IBM is building an enormous complex at 1250 blvd. René-Lévesque. Other consortiums and private foundations are renovating museums (including the McCord Museum) and restoring monuments.

The municipality is also rebuilding sidewalks and major arteries. The downside of all this activity is that city streets are a tangle of muddied walkways, workmen, cement trucks, and cranes. What should be a five-minute cab ride may stretch to almost half an hour. It's fortunate for the business traveler that most office towers and shopping complexes are clustered in a downtown core. Cabs are abundant, and the subway system is linked with "the city below," Montréal's unique response to its harsh climate. In winter, Montréalers can travel below ground on more than eight miles of walkways leading to métro, train, and bus stations, major hotels, businesses, boutiques, restaurants, banks, movie theaters, and the two main convention centers, the Palais des Congrès and Place Bonaventure.

Translation and simultaneous interpretation services abound, international firms and banks from Shanghai, Paris, Italy, and the United States do business here; and the Federal Business Development Bank operates from Place Victoria. Montréal is the headquarters of the International Air Transport Association and the United Nations International Civil Aviation Organization. Long a center for high-level international meetings, the city is well equipped with support services, which make this a good place to do business, whatever your language.

Top Employers

Employer	Type of Enterprise	Parent*/ Headquarters
Alcan Aluminum	Aluminum manufacturing	Montréal
BCE	Investment and holding company	Montréal
Canadian National	Freight services	CPI Rail/ Montréal
Canadian Pacific	Transportation	Montréal
Canada Post Corp.	Postal service	Montréal
Hydro-Quebec	Electric company	Montréal
Power Corporation	Investment and holding company	Montréal
Provigo	Food and convenience distribution	Montréal
Steinberg	Supermarket chain	Montréal

if applicable

ESSENTIAL INFORMATION

Climate

What follows are the average daily maximum and minimum temperatures for Montréal.

Jan.	23F	−5C	**Feb.**	25F	−4C	**Mar.**	36F	2C
	9	−13		12	−11		23	−5
Apr.	52F	11C	**May**	65F	18C	**June**	74F	23C
	36	2		48	9		58	14
July	79F	26C	**Aug.**	76F	24C	**Sept.**	68F	20C
	63	17		61	16		53	12
Oct.	57F	14C	**Nov.**	42F	6C	**Dec.**	27F	−3C
	43	6		32	0		16	−9

Airports

Montréal International Airport is divided into two terminals. The first is in Dorval, a suburb 14 miles west of the city; the second is called Mirabel, and is about 30 miles north. The Dorval terminal is used for all domestic and U.S. flights and Mirabel serves all other destinations.

Airport Business Facilities

Mirabel Terminal. Le Château de l'Aeroport Mirabel (connected by walkway to the Main Terminal, tel. 514/476–1611) has fax machines, photocopying, conference rooms with catering service, a fitness center, and day rates for rooms. **Dorval Terminal** has no business facilities.

Airlines

Montréal is a hub city for Air Canada.

Air Canada, tel. 514/393–3333 (U.S. and Canadian destinations), 514/393–1111 (other destinations), or 800/776–3000.
Air France, tel. 514/284–2825 or 800/237–2747.
Air Ontario, tel. 514/393–3333 or 514/393–3888.
American, tel. 800/433–7300.
British Airways, tel. 514/287–9133 or 800/247–9297.
Canadian Airlines International, tel. 514/286–1212 or 800/387–2737.
City Express, tel. 514/485–2489 or 800/387–3060.
Delta, tel. 514/337–5520 or 800/221–1212.
United, tel. 514/875–4333 or 800/241–6522.

Between the Airports and Downtown

By Taxi
From Dorval, taxis take 30–60 minutes during rush hour (8:30–10 AM and 4:30–5:30 PM) and 20–30 minutes at nonpeak times. From Mirabel, a cab ride generally takes 45 minutes to one hour. Dispatchers (who do not accept tips) at both airports hail the taxis, and fares are legally set: Unmetered rates are Can$19 from Dorval and Can$45 from Mirabel.

By Limousine
Limousines, also reserved through airport dispatchers at the arrivals exit, are on a set-fare system as well. The cost is Can$27.50 from Dorval and Can$55 from Mirabel.

By Bus
Aerocar (tel. 514/397–9999) is the cheapest way to get downtown, and, if a bus is standing ready to depart, it's often quicker than taking a cab. The buses stop at various hotels in the downtown area. Buses begin running at about 5 AM to both terminals; the Dorval bus runs until 11:10 PM, the Mirabel bus runs until 2 AM. They leave every 20 minutes from Dorval and every ½ hour from Mirabel (every 30 minutes and every hour, respectively, on weekends). The cost is Can$7 from Dorval and Can$9 from Mirabel.

Car Rentals

Avis, tel. 514/636–1902 (Dorval), 514/476–3481 (Mirabel) or 800/331–1212.
Budget, tel. 514/636–0052 (Dorval), 514/476–2687 (Mirabel) or 800/527–0700.
Hertz, tel. 514/636–9530 (Dorval), 514/476–3385 (Mirabel) or 800/654–3131.
Thrifty/Viabec, tel. 514/631–5567 (Dorval), 514/476–0496 (Mirabel) or 800/367–2277.

Tilden, tel. 514/636–9030 (Dorval), 514/476–3460 (Mirabel) or 800/227–7368.

Emergencies

Doctors
Jewish General Hospital (3755 rue Côte-Ste-Catherine, tel. 514/340–8222), **Montréal General Hospital** (1650 av. Cedar, tel. 514/937–6011), **Royal Victoria Hospital** (687 av. Pine ouest, tel. 514/842–1231).

Dentists
Côte-des-Neiges Dental Centre (5845 rue Côte-des-Neiges, Suite 100, tel. 514/731–7721), **Dental Centre** (1414 rue Drummond, Suite 412, tel. 514/281–1023), **Emergency Dental Services** (800 blvd. René-Lévesque ouest, tel. 514/875–7971).

Important Addresses and Numbers

Audiovisual rentals. Audio-Visual and Video (pl. Bonaventure and 475 av. President Kennedy, tel. 514/844–9865), NDG Photo (1197 Sq. Phillips, tel. 514/866–2965), Photo Service (222 rue Notre-Dame ouest, tel. 514/849–2291), Visual Planning (6805 blvd. Décarie, tel. 514/739–3116).

Chamber of Commerce. Montréal Board of Trade (1080 Côte Beaver Hall, tel. 514/878–4651).

Computer rentals. Centre Micro-Informatique CIAP (1690 rue Gilford, tel. 514/522–2427), Co-Rent (500 rue Sherbrooke ouest, tel. 514/843–8888), Ordiloc (4425 rue Ste-Catherine ouest, tel. 514/934–1348).

Convention and exhibition centers. Palais des Congrès (201 rue Viger ouest, tel. 514/871–8226), Place Bonaventure (pl. Bonaventure, tel. 514/397–2355).

Fax services. Canadac (7520 rue Côte-de-Liesse, tel. 514/735–1411), Officium (475 av. du Président Kennedy, tel. 514/284–2246), Ricoh Facsimile (1150 rue Golf, Verdun, tel. 514/769–2552).

Formal-wear rentals. Classy Formal Wear (486 rue Ste-Catherine ouest, tel. 514/861–5416 and 1227 carré Phillips, tel. 514/875–9938).

Gift shops. Flowers: Cupidon (2288 rue Fleury est, tel. 514/382–6111), McKenna (4509 rue Côtes-des-Neiges, tel. 514/731–4992), Pinkerton Flower (5127 rue Sherbrooke ouest, tel. 514/487–7330); Gift Baskets and Candy: Eaton Department Store Gourmet Shop (677 rue Ste-Catherine ouest, tel. 514/284–8361), Laura Secord (1 pl. Ville-Marie, tel. 514/861–7867 and 1007 rue Ste-Catherine ouest, tel. 514/843–5708).

Graphic design studios. Graf 18 (1130 rue Sherbrooke ouest, tel. 514/849–1784), Graphème Communication Design (1558 av. Dr. Penfield, tel. 514/932–2615), Montréal Creative Centre (407 rue Dowd, Vieux-Montréal, tel. 514/861–6323).

Hairstylists. Unisex: La Coupe (1115 rue Sherbrooke ouest, tel. 514/288–6131), Gibson's (Le Reine Elizabeth, 900 blvd. René-Lévesque, tel. 514/866–6639), Vag (pl. Bonaventure, Centrale Station tunnel, tel. 514/866–9279 and 2015 rue Crescent, tel. 514/844–9656).

Health and fitness clubs. *See* Fitness, below.

Information hot lines. Bus and métro (tel. 514/288–6287), Canadian Automobile Association (tel. 514/861–1313 for emergencies, or 514/861–7111 for information), Entertainment (CHOM-FM, tel. 514/790–0718 and Montréal Today, tel. 514/352–2500), Road conditions (tel. 514/861–1313 or 514/873–4121).

Limousine services. Contact (tel. 514/875–8746), G. T. V. (tel. 514/871–8888), Murray Hill (tel. 514/937–5466).

Liquor stores. Maison des Vins (505 av. President Kennedy, tel. 514/873–2274), Société des Alcools du Québec (1 pl. Ville-Marie, tel. 514/861–6616; 1067 pl. Bonaventure, tel. 514/861–7037; 800 pl. Victoria, tel. 514/875–6180; and 426 Complexe Desjardins, tel. 514/844–8721).

Mail delivery, overnight. DHL International Express (tel. 514/636–8703), Federal Express (tel. 514/345–0130), TNT Skypak (tel. 514/636–6983).

Messenger services. Blitz 24 (tel. 514/321–0646), Express Service Courier (tel. 514/526–4434), Purolator Courier (tel. 514/731–1000).

Office space rental. Travelex Business Centre (1253 av. McGill College, tel. 514/871–8616).

Pharmacies, late-night. Cumberland Drug (1004 rue Ste-Catherine ouest, tel. 514/866–7791), Jean Coutu (1836 rue Ste-Catherine ouest, tel. 514/933–4221).

Secretarial services. A&A (1117 rue Ste-Catherine ouest, tel. 514/288–3795), ExecuCentre (1200 av. McGill College, tel. 514/393–1100), Travelex Business Centre (1253 av. McGill College, tel. 514/871–8616).

Stationery supplies. Pilon (1 pl. Ville-Marie, tel. 514/861–9497; 280 rue St-Jacques, tel. 514/842–4171; and Windsor building, 1170 rue Peel, tel. 514/861–4640), Wilson Stationers (Place Montréal Trust, tel. 514/499–9851 and Alexis Nihon Plaza, tel. 514/937–3579).

Taxis. Diamond (tel. 514/273–6331), LaSalle (tel. 514/277–2552), Veteran's (tel. 514/273–6351).

Theater tickets. *See* The Arts, below.

Train information. Amtrak (Central Station, 935 rue la Gauchetière ouest, tel. 800/426–8725), Via Rail (Central Station, 935 rue la Gauchetière ouest, tel. 514/871–1331).

Travel agents. American Express Travel Services (in all La Baie department stores and at 1141 blvd. de Maisonneuve ouest, tel. 514/284–3300), Thomas Cook (2020 rue University, tel. 514/398–0555 or 514/842–2541).

Weather (tel. 514/636–3026 or 514/636–3282).

LODGING

Travelers do well in most Montréal hotels, even in those that are moderately priced. Most of the major hotels are downtown, between rue Guy and rue Berri, a generally safe area even after dark. Some motels on the outskirts of town and tiny "bargain hotels" in the city can be a disappointment.

Most of the hotels listed below offer corporate rates and weekend discounts; inquire when making reservations.

Highly recommended lodgings in each price category are indicated by a star ★.

Category	Cost*
$$$$ (Very Expensive)	over Can$150
$$$ (Expensive)	Can$121–Can$150
$$ (Moderate)	under Can$120

All prices are for a standard double room, single occupancy, excluding the 10% provincial accommodation tax, 7% federal goods and service tax, and 15% service charge.

Numbers in the margin correspond to numbered hotel locations on the Montréal Lodging and Dining map.

Downtown

6
$$
Auberge Ramada Centre-Ville. The exterior of this seven-story building in a dreary section of rue Guy is unexceptional, but inside you'll find a friendly staff and a welcoming lobby. Corridors on unrenovated floors are a bit dingy and the worse for wear. However, the renovated plum-and-mauve rooms are neat, clean, and well furnished, each with bedside tables, a coffee table, and two armchairs. Rooms with queen-size beds are reserved for single guests and are spacious and fully equipped, but their white-tile bathrooms are small and toiletries are skimpy. The sixth and seventh floors are reserved for business clientele who place a premium on peace and quiet. The neighborhood, just below bustling boulevard René-Lévesque, can be a bit threatening at night. La Buisonnière restaurant is a good choice if you're dining alone. *1005 rue Guy, H3H 2K4, tel. 514/866–4611 or 800/268–8930, fax 514/866–8718. Gen. manager, Michel Garnier. 199 doubles, 6 suites. AE, CB, D, MC, V.*

★ 17
$$$$
Bonaventure Hilton International. This hotel is perched atop the Place Bonaventure Center, with its busy mall and exhibition space, and overlooks 2½ acres of gardens and streams. It is also connected to Central Station and Place Ville-Marie's underground shopping complex. Contemporary comfort characterizes the spacious doubles and suites, which were redecorated in 1989. All have brightly lighted desks, work/dining tables, love seats, and easy chairs framed by large windows. Inside garden units are recommended; those facing west may have their view cut off by the rapidly rising building next door. Lobby restaurants include the imposing Castillon (*see* Dining, below) and Le Portage (*see* After Hours, below); the Belvedere Bar (*see* After Hours, below) is a classy piano lounge. *A*

MONTRÉAL

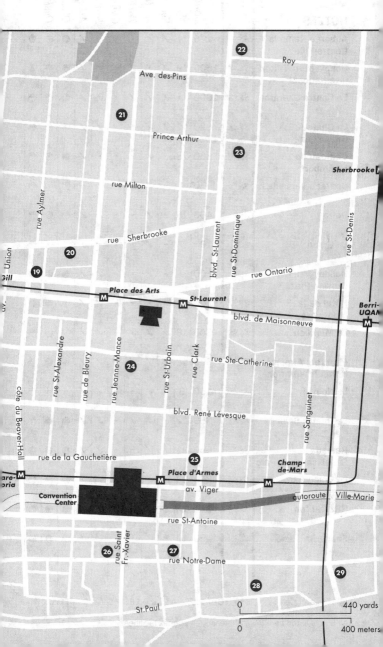

MONTRÉAL HOTEL CHART

HOTELS	Price Category	Business Services / Banquet capacity	No. of meeting rooms	Secretarial services	Audiovisual equipment	Translation Service	Computer rentals	In-room modem phonejack	All-news cable channel	Desk	Desk lighting	Bed lighting
Auberge Ramada Centre-Ville	$$	175	11	✓	-	-	-	-	✓	●	◐	●
Bonaventure Hilton International	$$$$	1600	19	✓	✓	✓	-	✓	✓	●	●	●
Le Centre Sheraton	$$$$	1000	11	✓	✓	✓	-	✓	✓	●	◐	◐
Le Château Champlain	$$$$	620	11	✓	✓	-	✓	✓	✓	◐	◐	◐
Château de L'aéroport	$$$	360	28	-	✓	-	-	-	✓	●	◐	◐
Château Versailles	$$	0	4	-	✓	-	-	✓	-	○	○	◐
Delta	$$$	400	15	-	✓	-	✓	✓	✓	◐	●	◐
Le Grand	$$$	1100	13	-	✓	-	-	-	✓	○	◐	◐
Holiday Inn Crowne Plaza	$$$	600	9	-	✓	-	-	✓	✓	●	●	●
Hôtel de la Montagne	$$$	100	2	-	-	-	-	✓	✓	●	●	●
Le Méridien	$$$$	800	18	-	✓	✓	-	✓	✓	○	○	◐
Montreal Airport Hilton International	$$$	500	18	✓	✓	-	-	✓	✓	●	●	◐
Le Nouvel	$$	150	6	-	✓	-	-	✓	✓	-	-	◐
Le Quatre Saisons	$$$$	650	12	✓	✓	✓	-	✓	✓	●	●	◐
Ramada Renaissance du Parc	$$$	550	21	✓	✓	-	-	✓	✓	●	●	●
Le Reine Elizabeth	$$$$	2800	23	✓	✓	-	✓	✓	✓	●	◐	◐
Ritz-Carlton	$$$$	350	12	-	✓	-	-	✓	✓	●	●	◐
Shangrila	$$$	450	10	-	✓	-	-	✓	✓	◐	◐	●

$$$$ = over Can $150, **$$$** = Can $120-Can $150, **$$** = under Can $120.
● good, ◐ fair, ○ poor.
All hotels listed here have photocopying and fax facilities.

| In-Room Amenities | | | | | | | | | | Hotel Amenities | | | | | | |
Nonsmoking rooms	In-room checkout	Minibar	Pay movies	VCR/Movie rentals	Hairdryer	Toiletries	Room service	Laundry/Dry cleaning	Pressing	Concierge	Barber/Hairdresser	Garage	Courtesy airport transport	Sauna	Pool	Exercise room
✓	✓	-	✓	-	-	○	○	◐	○	✓	-	✓	-	✓	◐	◐
✓	✓	✓	✓	-	-	●	●	●	◐	✓	-	✓	-	✓	●	○
✓	✓	✓	✓	✓	-	◐	◐	◐	◐	✓	✓	✓	-	✓	●	◐
✓	-	✓	✓	-	-	●	◐	◐	○	✓	✓	◐	-	✓	◐	◐
-	-	-	✓	✓	◐	◐	○	○	○	✓	✓	-	-	✓	◐	-
✓	-	✓	-	-	✓	○	-	-	-	-	-	-	-	-	-	-
✓	-	✓	✓	-	✓	◐	●	◐	○	-	✓	✓	-	✓	●	●
✓	-	✓	✓	-	-	◐	●	●	○	✓	-	✓	-	✓	◐	◐
✓	-	✓	✓	-	-	○	◐	◐	○	✓	✓	✓	-	✓	◐	◐
-	-	✓	-	✓	✓	●	◐	●	◐	✓	-	✓	-	-	◐	-
✓	-	✓	✓	-	✓	◐	●	◐	◐	✓	-	✓	-	✓	●	-
✓	✓	✓	✓	✓	-	◐	●	◐	●	✓	-	✓	✓	✓	●	◐
-	-	✓	-	-	✓	-	-	◐	-	✓	-	✓	-	-	◐	-
✓	✓	✓	✓	-	✓	●	●	●	●	✓	-	✓	-	✓	◐	●
✓	-	-	✓	-	-	◐	◐	●	◐	✓	✓	✓	✓	✓	●	●
✓	-	✓	✓	-	-	◐	◐	●	◐	✓	✓	✓	-	-	-	-
✓	-	-	✓	-	✓	●	◐	●	◐	✓	✓	✓	-	-	-	-
✓	-	✓	✓	-	✓	●	◐	●	◐	✓	✓	-	-	-	-	-

Room service: ● 24-hour, ◐ 6AM-10PM, ○ other.
Laundry/Dry cleaning: ● same day, ◐ overnight, ○ other.
Pressing: ● immediate, ◐ same day, ○ other.

*Hilton International hotel. 1 pl. Bonaventure, H5A 1E4,
tel. 514/878–2332 or 800/445–8667; in Canada, 800/268–
9275; fax 514/878–3881. Gen. manager, Robert Frigère.
374 doubles, 13 suites, 7 executive suites. AE, CB, D,
MC, V.*

⑫ **Le Centre Sheraton.** This utilitarian, 37-story concrete
$$$$ tower is near the financial high rises on boulevard René-
Lévesque and has been a prime location for business travelers since 1982. The staff is welcoming, and the concierge
is particularly helpful. Smallish double rooms are outfitted with creamy pastel tones and pale-wood furnishings.
Guests staying in executive-class rooms, on levels 30 and
31, can take tea at the lounge on 32. The lounge also serves
the more luxurious Towers floors (32–36) that, for higher
rates, offer better accommodations, private check-in/
check-out, and a boardroom. A health club, the relaxing
L'Impromptu bar (*see* After Hours, below), and the rooftop restaurant, Le Point de Vue, are three more pluses.
*1201 blvd. René-Lévesque ouest, H3B 2L7, tel. 514/878–
2000 or 800/325–3535, fax 514/878–3958. Gen. manager,
Alfred Heim. 800 doubles, 18 suites, 60 business-class.
AE, CB, D, MC, V.*

⑮ **Le Château Champlain.** Facing Windsor Station and Do-
$$$$ minion Square, the 36-story skyscraper with distinctive
half-moon-shape windows is favored by British guests,
such as Prince Phillip, who stayed in the 35th-floor Royal
Suite. A cage of tiny tropical birds is a grace note in the
gold-ceilinged, marble-floored lobby, which gives way to
wide, quiet halls. The rooms are clustered in groups of
three in small alcoves off the corridors, adding a feeling of
privacy. Brocade-pattern wallpaper and upholstery appear worn in some rooms, but reproductions of Louis XVI,
Second Empire, and Queen Anne furnishings lend touches
of luxury. Every unit has a dressing room. Guests staying
on the three business floors get express check-in/check-
out and a lounge. The Château is home to Le Caf' Conc'
(*see* After Hours, below) and the Escapade, on the 36th
floor, which offers a good buffet dinner nightly. *A Canadian Pacific hotel. 1 pl. du Canada, H3B 2L7, tel. 514/878–
9000 or 800/268–9411; in Canada, 800/828–7447; in Ontario or Quebec, 800/268–9420; fax 514/878–6761. Gen.
manager, Paolo de Pol. 516 doubles, 40 suites, 60 business-class. AE, CB, D, MC, V.*

❹ **Château Versailles.** Four Edwardian, semidetached, lime-
$$ stone townhouses in a quiet downtown residential section
are a find if you like Old World charm at bargain prices.
Guests must put up with a few inconveniences such as the
lack of cable TV. In 1989 the Villeneuve family, which
owns the complex, added a 12-story, 1960s-style wing
across rue Sherbrooke. Called La Tour Versailles, it pro-
vides modern though spartan accommodations. Visiting
journalists usually opt for the old-fashioned rooms, with
decorative fireplaces and chaise longues; however, some
rooms lack desks, and back rooms may face a brick wall. In
comparison to the townhouse complex, the annex feels
brand-new and empty, although some rooms on the upper
floors have fine views southward to the St. Lawrence. The
Scandinavian-style furnishings are appropriate in the
airy rooms, many of which are equipped with kitchen-
ettes. *1659 rue Sherbrooke ouest, H3H 1I3, tel. 514/933–*

3611 or 800/361–3664; in Canada, 800/361–7199; fax 514/ 933–7102. Gen. manager, Germain Villeneuve. 70 deluxe doubles in Château, 105 doubles and 2 penthouse suites in La Tour. AE, MC, V.

★ ⑲ **Delta Hotel.** Built as a 24-story condominium, this is one of
$$$ the better choices visitors can make for convenience, comfort, and cost. It's in the commercial core, near the McGill métro station, and caters to a business, convention, and group clientele. Staff is polite and friendly. Accommodations are comfortably traditional, and the rose or pale blue color scheme blends well with the Velveteen armchairs with ottomans, and the stained-wood cabinets concealing minibars and televisions. Bathrooms, however, are on the small size and towels are skimpy. Most units, with the exception of those on the corners, have concrete balconies. Signature Service, designed for business travelers, offers better rooms with more amenities; however, all units are roughly the same size. The hotel is at its best in summer, when the garden courtyard off rue Sherbrooke is in bloom and the outdoor pool is open. Cellular phone rentals are a handy plus. *A Delta hotel. 475 av. President Kennedy, H3A 2T4, tel. 514/286–1986 or 800/877–1133; in Canada, 800/268–1133; fax 514/284–4342. Gen. manager, Carel Forlkesma. 400 doubles, 8 suites, 50 business-class. AE, CB, D, MC, V.*

⑱ **Le Grand Hôtel.** Opened in 1977, this 30-story property at-
$$$ tracts business people with its proximity to the convention center and underground access to Place Victoria's stock exchange and métro station. However, the hotel does have drawbacks. Public areas are sparsely furnished with worn modular-style chairs and chipped marble tables and some rooms reflect this general neglect. Panoramic-view glass elevators and the vine-bedecked atrium lobby are holdovers from the hotel's early days as a Hyatt. Standard rooms are '60s contemporary; all, including twin-bedded accommodations for single travelers, are the same size. Ongoing refurbishment will add desks to every room; now only 100 rooms have them. From the sixth story up, sweeping views from floor-to-ceiling windows give rooms a feeling of spaciousness. A concierge oversees the 24-floor Le Privé, which offers extra amenities. The hotel hosts Montréal's only revolving restaurant, Le Tour de Ville. *A Hôtel des Gouverneurs hotel. 777 rue University, H3C 3Z7, tel. 514/879–1370 or 800/361–8155, fax 514/879–1761. Gen. manager, Anthony Tuor. 673 doubles, 47 singles, 10 suites, and 1 business-class suite. AE, CB, DC, MC, V.*

⑳ **Holiday Inn Crowne Plaza.** Near McGill métro station and
$$$ the university, this 20-story hotel is invaded by college students every fall weekend and by business travelers year-round on weekdays. Despite the hotel's heavy traffic, the overworked staff is efficient and relatively friendly. Entirely renovated between 1987 and 1988, the '60s-era building was given a glittering marquee above the entrance. In contrast, rooms are decorated in peaceful gray-blues and pastels. Although the bathrooms are tiny, alcoves provide separate sinks and vanities. Some suites have lovely views of Mont Royal, and all resemble model-home rooms, down to the parquet floors. Two executive floors offer express check-in/check-out, priority reservations, and a lounge. Cellular phones can be rented at the front desk. Of the two restaurants, Les Verrières is the

better. *420 rue Sherbrooke ouest, H3A 1B4, tel. 514/842–6111 or 800/465–4329, fax 514/842–9381. Gen. manager, Guy Lemieux. 425 doubles, 6 suites, 58 business-class. AE, CB, D, MC, V.*

⑨ **Hôtel de la Montagne.** A rather ordinary apartment build-
$$$ ing when it was built in 1982, this property has been ele-
gantly transformed and now contains the city's most
inviting lobby, graced by an eclectic collection of Edward-
ian, Neo-Classic, and Biedermeier furnishings. A gilded
nymph adorns the central fountain, and around her cavort
elephants and sphinxes. The upstairs corridors are nar-
row, dim, and occasionally stuffy, but the plush rooms are
spacious and feature golden-oak or dark wood French-Co-
lonial furnishings. In the suites, handsome four-poster
beds are hung with fabric that matches the spreads and
drapes. There's no health club, but suites are equipped
with their own rowing machines; guests in any type of
room will be provided with a machine at no charge upon
request. Luxurious bathrooms in the suites include
Jacuzzis. The hotel's owner is also the proprietor of
Thursday's/Les Beaux Jeudis, a restaurant and night spot
on rue Crescent that is connected by a tunnel with the lob-
by. The two lobby bars are popular with locals and thirty-
forty-something visitors; the restaurant, Le Lutetia (*see*
Dining, below) is highly esteemed. *1430 rue de la
Montagne, H3G 1Z5, tel. 514/288–5656 or 800/361–6262;
in Canada, 800/361–6262; fax 514/288–9658. Gen. manag-
er, Alain J. M. Pauquet. 122 doubles, 14 suites. AE, CB,
D, MC, V.*

★ ㉑ **Hôtel Ramada Renaissance du Parc.** This 14-story brick
$$$ tower targets a business clientele by means of incentives
and packages. The hotel is often, and undeservedly, over-
looked, partially due to its location in a quieter part of
downtown, 2½ blocks north of rue Sherbrooke. Much of
the darkish lobby is occupied by the Puzzles bar (*see* After
Hours, below); otherwise, there's not much public space.
The building resembles a modern apartment complex and
is part of the La Cité housing-and-commercial project; elevators from the lobby give direct access to a newly rede-
veloped underground mall. All rooms are pleasantly
decorated; those with northwest exposures offer unique
views of the Mont Royal cross. The top-floor Club Renaissance is for executives who want private check-in/check-
out, buffet, and bar service, and a boardroom for private
meetings. Cellular phones can be rented. This is the only
hotel in the city with an outdoor tennis court. *3624 av. du
Parc, H2X 3P8, tel. 514/288–6666 or 800/228–9898; for the
hearing impaired, 800/228–3232; in Canada, 800/268–
8930; fax 514/588–2469. Gen. manager, Marc Hamel. 416
doubles, 10 suites, 28 kings, 2 business-class suites. AE,
CB, D, MC, V.*

㉔ **Le Méridien.** Built for the 1976 Summer Olympics (Mick
$$$$ and Bianca Jagger were the first guests to stay in the
Presidential Suite that August), this 12-story appendage
to the Complexe Desjardins is the only hotel directly
linked to the convention center. The Place des Arts cultural complex is just across the street. Although the chain is
known for its elegance, the Montréal Méridien may be a
disappointment to guests expecting more-posh surroundings; the lobby, for instance, opens onto the bustling mall.
The rooms, decorated in soft tones, are on the small side

for a luxury hotel. Tiny vanities, beneath make-up mirrors, must double as desks; perhaps the hotel's business center is meant to compensate. Business travelers have a separate floor called Le Club President with additional perks: a lounge, express check-in/check-out, and a private boardroom. Le Club Restaurant is recommended for quiet, candlelit business dinners. *4 Complexe Desjardins, H5B 1E5, tel. 514/285–1450 or 800/543–4300; in Canada, 800/361–8234; fax 514/285–1243. Gen. manager, Jean-Claude Andrieux. 574 doubles, 22 suites, 5 executive suites. AE, CB, D, MC, V.*

★ ❸   **Le Nouvel Hotel.** A complex of three high-rises built be-
$$ tween 1985 and 1987, this convenient, moderately priced hotel in western downtown is known for its young, eager staff. The hotel itself may not have much personality, but its expansive studio and apartment suites are cheerful and spotless and boast wide balconies. All apartment-style units have kitchenettes and dining areas. Furnishings are contemporary boxy, in salmon, pink, and aqua tones; and every living room and studio has an added sofa bed. Although dining tables are wide enough to substitute for desks, their overhead lighting is more suited to romantic dinners. The quietest units are on the 10th–12th floors, where rooms with a northwest exposure have the best views. Bathrooms are basic. There are minibars in suites, but no room service; breakfast, lunch, and dinner are available in the Entr'acte restaurant. *A Nouvel Hôtel. 1740 blvd. René-Lévesque, H3H 1R3, tel. 514/931–8841 or 800/363–6063. Gen. manager, Jean Baervoets. 124 studios, 124 2½-room units. AE, MC, V.*

★ ⓮   **Le Quatre Saisons.** The most luxurious of Montréal's ho-
$$$$ tels, this 31-story tower has commanded the prime Peel-Sherbrooke intersection since 1976. Travelers who want every amenity will prefer this hotel to the Ritz-Carlton, its rival down the street; however, the Quatre Saisons does not have the reputation for old-European charm or fine dining that its neighbor has cultivated. Contemporary elegance prevails, from the stunning flower arrangements in the Oriental lobby to the dark wood cabinets that enclose the guest room television sets. Cheerful, satiny chintz brightens many standard doubles, and mahogany desks with brass lamps look ready for business. Suites are expansive and offer exhilirating views. French doors divide living rooms and bedrooms. Le Restaurant (*see* Business Breakfasts, below) is the home of the power breakfast or lunch, and the L'Apero Bar (*see* After Hours, below) is the place to go after work or after hours. *A Four Seasons hotel. 1050 rue Sherbrooke ouest, H3A 2R6, tel. 514/284–1110 or 800/332–3442; in Canada, 800/268–6282; fax 514/845–3025. Gen. manager, Kuno Fasel. 272 doubles, 28 suites. AE, CB, D, MC, V.*

⓰   **Le Reine Elizabeth.** Built in 1957 and still the biggest hotel
$$$$ in town, this downtown establishment near the train station caters to business travelers and tour groups. It has also hosted Queen Elizabeth, Neil Armstrong, and Charles de Gaulle and is still celebrated as the site of John and Yoko's bed-in for peace. The hotel's ground floor, frequently likened to a train station, could put off first-time visitors, who will find the lobby cavernous and loud; ongoing renovations should change its glitzy '50s decor. Standard rooms are cozy and restful and are furnished

with love seats and pine desks and cabinets. The dark-green-marble bathrooms are cramped. Business-class guests stay on floors 16 and 17 and enjoy extra amenities, including Continental breakfast, fresh plants, minibars, and a separate check-in/check-out. A glass elevator leads from these floors to Montréal's most intimate business lounge, with a woodburning fireplace in winter and a buffet. The Beaver Club (*see* Dining, below) is well known and one of the best restaurants in the city. Les Voyageurs (*see* After Hours, below) is good for quiet business talks over drinks. *A Canadian Pacific hotel. 900 rue René-Lévesque ouest, H3B 4A5, tel. 514/861-3511 or 800/828-7447; in Canada, 800/268-9420; fax 514/861-3536. Gen. manager, George Villedary. 276 singles, 495 doubles, 158 regular suites, 35 studios, 60 mini-suites, 19 executive suites. AE, CB, D, MC, V.*

★ ⑪ **Hôtel Ritz-Carlton.** Within two blocks of McGill Universi-
$$$$ ty and the Montréal Museum, the Ritz has drawn executive travelers since 1912, when Canadian-born publishing tycoon Lord Beaverbrook made the nine-story, neoclassical limestone building his preferred hotel. The Ritz is still a favorite with those who like to travel in style and don't care about in-house fitness facilities. The spacious black-and-gold lobby is set off by a curving staircase. Elegant doubles and suites feature crystal chandeliers and some antique furnishings as well as desks with inlaid leather and brass lamps. Each smart white-and-slate marble bathroom has built-in shelves for mounds of fluffy towels and robes. Better suites are fitted with working fireplaces. French doors separate the bedrooms from sitting rooms, which segue into compact dining areas with buffet and bar. Uninspiring views of surrounding offices don't seem to faze repeat visitors. The hotel's Café du Paris (*see* Dining, below) is excellent for business breakfasts and dinners; the Ritz Garden (*see* Diversions, below) offers lovely afternoon teas; and Le Grand Prix (*see* After Hours, below) provides a refined setting for a drink with associates. *Member of the Leading Hotels of the World. 1228 rue Sherbrooke ouest, H3G 1H6, tel. 514/842-4212 or 800/223-6800; in Canada, 800/363-0366; fax 514/842-3383. Gen. manager, René Gounel. 205 doubles, 35 suites. AE, CB, D, MC, V.*

⑬ **Shangrila Hotel.** Although it shares the Peel-Sherbrooke
$$$ locale with Le Quatre Saisons, this 20-story concrete tower is on a more modest scale. The lobby is small and serene, with an Oriental motif. The Eastern theme continues in the rooms, which are spacious and bright, except for the queen-bedded units (for single guests), which are small and overwhelmed with furniture. Suites feel airy, thanks to their cityscape panoramas, some from glass doors leading to private terraces. Bathrooms are unremarkable. Fitness addicts can stay in rooms that have private mini gyms. Corporate Class offers upgraded rooms, express check-in/check-out, and a lounge. The hotel's restaurants, the Dynastic de Ming (try the peanut-butter-flavor Chinese ravioli; it tastes better than it sounds) and Cafe Park Expresse (offering counter service) are both good. *A Best Western Hotel. 3407 rue Peel, H3A 1W7, tel. 514/288-4141 or 800/648-7200; in Canada, 800/361-7791; fax 514/288-3021. Gen. manager, Pierre Quintal. 153 doubles, 15 suites. AE, CB, D, MC, V.*

Airport

Dorval

★ ❷ **Montréal Airport Hilton International.** Considering its lo-
$$$ cation in a dreary expanse alongside the Dorval terminal,
the Hilton is an unexpectedly pleasant stopover. A 1989
renovation spruced up the hotel, adding a marble lobby
and a solarium between the restaurant and garden-pool
area. A proficient staff has perfected the airport/hotel
transfer routine, carefully settling half-dazed early-morn-
ing travelers into shuttles for the two-minute trip to
Dorval, next door. Guest rooms are small but capture the
ambience of a private club, with dark wood and sturdy
wingback chairs. All rooms are soundproof, but units in
the Tower annex are the quietest. There are studio suites,
meeting facilities, and an executive floor with added
amenities. *A Hilton International hotel. 12505 chemin
Côte-de-Liesse, Dorval, H9P 1B7, tel. 514/631-2411 or
800/445-8667, fax 514/631-0192. Gen. manager, Gaston
Viallet. 483 doubles, 20 suites. AE, CB, D, MC, V.*

Mirabel

❶ **Château de l'Aéroport.** Conveniently connected to the air-
$$$ port at Mirabel, this location is ideal for passengers arriv-
ing or leaving on late-night flights. The hotel is built
around an atrium and spacious indoor pool, a setting that
attracts Montréalers on weekend escape packages.
*Aéroport International de Montréal, C.P. 60, Mirabel,
J7N 1A2, tel. 514/476-1611; in Quebec, 800/361-0924.
Gen. manager, Regis Nadeau. 362 rooms. AE, CB,
MC, V.*

DINING

There are more than 3,500 restaurants in Montréal, over
10,000 if the surrounding suburbs are included. Nouvelle
cuisine, once a staple in French restaurants, is no longer
new; and menus seem to be returning to heartier fare. Recently, a few Mexican restaurants have opened along with
places that look to other parts of North America, especially California, for inspiration. However, traditional French
restaurants are still most popular with both residents and
visitors, and restaurants serving regional favorites like
meat pies, Gaspé salmon, *moules* (mussels), maple-syrup
dishes, and sugar pie continue to hold their own.

Highly recommended restaurants in each category are indicated by a star ★.

Category	Cost*
$$$$ (Very Expensive)	over $30
$$$ (Expensive)	$20–$30
$$ (Moderate)	under $20

*All prices are per person, including appetizer, entrée,
and dessert, but excluding drinks, service, and 10% meal
tax.*

*Numbers in the margin correspond to numbered restau-
rant locations on the Montréal Lodging and Dining map.*

Business Breakfasts

A. L. Van Houtte. Fresh-ground coffee, café au lait, and muffins are a successful formula for the more than 50 outlets of this café, most of them downtown and in major complexes like place Bonaventure and place Ville-Marie. *1083 Beaver Hall Hill, tel. 514/861–4604, and 1001 blvd. de Maisonneuve ouest, tel. 514/845–5922.*

Café de Paris. The Ritz-Carlton's highly esteemed restaurant (*see* Downtown, below) serves a wide choice of breakfasts in formal surroundings characterized by crisp white napery and careful, hushed service. Newspapers are available at the entrance, and there is a generous buffet for business people on the run. *Hôtel Ritz-Carlton, tel. 514/842–4212.*

Lux. This trendy restaurant-bar-cum-newsstand serves breakfast 24 hours a day in an off-the-beaten-track neighborhood that locals like to compare to New York's Soho. Vestiges of the building's former life—as a factory—are retained in the metal stairways around the bar. *5220 blvd. St-Laurent (Laurier métro, bus no. 55), tel. 514/271–9272.*

Picnic. Downstairs from the William Tell Restaurant, this cheerful Swiss chalet offers sit-down and takeout breakfasts beginning at 8 AM. Waitresses in dirndls preside while the regulars from surrounding office towers pick up fresh-baked blueberry muffins. Those with more time can relax over one of the most reasonable breakfasts in town. In summer a tiny outdoor terrace serves the same morning menu. *2055 rue Stanley, tel. 514/288–0139.*

Le Restaurant. The dining room of Le Quatre Saisons is best known as the originator of the Montréal power breakfast. You can get a welcoming cup of coffee and complimentary paper in the downstairs room, and the Captain's Table at the back can seat up to 12, for power get-togethers. Chrome-and-black leatherette chairs look like office furnishings, but fresh tulips and baby orchids brighten each table. A low-calorie, -sodium, and -fat menu is available. *Le Quatre Saison, tel. 514/284–1110.*

La Tulipe Noire. For most of the day, this café is jammed. However, breakfast is a quiet time, and employees of Alcan Aluminium upstairs make this an early morning rendezvous, as do guests from the nearby Ritz-Carlton and Quatre Saisons. It's a pretty spot, with frosted-glass sconces, and an open courtyard in summer. The youthful staff is friendly, even on gray November mornings. Some people prefer to sit at the coffee bar in back for a quick chocolate-chip muffin and cappuccino. *2100 rue Stanley, tel. 514/285–1255.* •

Chinatown

 Tai Kim Lung. This small restaurant in the heart of Chinatown draws a loyal lunchtime crowd from neighboring federal offices at Complex Guy-Favreau, as well as delegates escaping the convention center down the street. Wedged between two larger establishments, the restaurant, with its beige, nondescript facade, is easy to miss. The decor is also simple; the leatherette-quilted bar dates back some 30 years. Reasonably priced business lunches include four or five selections of Szechuan or Cantonese dishes, such as beef with Chinese vegetables, or fillet of doré (walleye pike) in garlic sauce. At dinner, when business is slower, more extensive menus are featured, along with tropical drinks. *74 rue Lagauchetière ouest, tel. 514/861–7556. Casual dress. AE, MC, V. Closed Sun. lunch.*

Downtown

★ **⑯** **Beaver Club.** Maitre d' Charles Ploem oversees Montréal's
$$$$ most famous dining room, a favorite of former mayor Jean Dapeau and just about every Québec politician, including Canadian prime minister Brian Mulroney. Named for a private club started by fur-trading voyageurs in the 18th century, it's been a part of Le Reine Elizabeth hotel since 1958. Executives like to be seen here, and there are still some members whose copper plates engraved with their names share the back brick wall with an aging buffalo hide. Best for quiet business meetings in the evening, the restaurant can be cheerfully noisy at noon. Regulars like the special, a thick slice of roast beef au jus accompanied by a baked potato. Lighter meals might start with consommé of feathered game and morels beneath a crust, and include an entrée of roasted, lightly smoked salmon with a champagne-vinegar sauce. The dessert cart displays tiers of pastries, Black Forest cakes, and cheesecakes. The wine list ranges from a rare Sauternes to an enjoyable Entre-Deux Mers. *Le Reine Elizabeth, 900 blvd. René-Lévesque ouest, tel. 514/861–3511. Jacket and tie required. Reservations required. AE, CB, D, MC, V.*

㉓ **La Cabane Grecque.** A good selection of reasonably priced
$$ Greek dishes; sunny, plant-filled dining rooms; and friendly service make this an inviting place to relax after work. Glassed-in on two sides, it's a fine vantage point for watching rue Prince Arthur, the city's first and most-popular pedestrian mall and a mecca for McGill University students as well as an older, trendy crowd. The generous shish kebab platter is a good bet, as is the moussaka, made with eggplant, squash, potatoes, and ground beef. *102 rue Prince Arthur est, tel. 514/849–0122. Casual dress. AE, MC, V.*

★ **⑪** **Café de Paris.** Don't be misled by the informal name—this
$$$$ café in the Ritz-Carlton is an elegant establishment with ornate gilt mirrors and lovely floral arrangements framing clusters of fawn-colored banquettes. Its walls are covered in golden watered silk, and a row of French doors at the back opens onto a private garden. Present and former prime ministers Mulroney and Trudeau drop by, and retired Canadian governor general Jeanne Sauvé enjoys summertime dining on the terrace around the duck pond. Most diners opt for one of the room's classic dishes, which includes light Dover sole with wild rice. The chef also prepares a six-course menu de degustation, with venison or veal as the entrée. There are low-calorie, salt-free dishes. Strawberries with whipped cream go well with the little cookies and bonbons served at the end of every meal. *Hôtel Ritz-Carlton, 1228 rue Sherbrooke ouest, tel. 514/842–4212. Jacket and tie required. Reservations required. AE, CB, D, MC, V.*

★ **⑰** **Le Castillon.** The Bonaventure Hilton's dining room is a
$$$$ modern-day replica of a baronial castle. In winter a roaring fire greets guests as they enter the lobby and in summer glass sliding doors open onto a terrace shaded by firs and birches. Wherever diners sit they have a view of trees

and sky. The stone walls are hung with tapestries, and the beamed ceiling supports huge, carved-wood chandeliers. Maroon banquettes offer the most comfortable and private areas. Waiters in knee breeches serve food that is surprisingly light and nouvelle. A favorite dish is scallops braised with butter and dill, surrounded by baby carrots and new potatoes. Roast pheasant is the house specialty; other recommended selections are the medallions of lamb with braised peppers, and the roast of the day, always good and reasonably priced. At lunchtime the front dining area by the fireplace features a 55-minute business menu. *Bonaventure Hilton International. 1 pl. Bonaventure, tel. 514/878–2332. Jacket and tie required. Reservations advised. AE, CB, D, MC, V.*

18
$$$
Chez Antoine. Stockbrokers gravitate to this popular bistro and grill in the tunnel that links Le Grand Hôtel with the Place Victoria exchange. Even during the busy lunch hour you can find privacy in a tranquil corner. Tiffany-style lamps, frosted glass, and Art Deco tilework depicting romantic Edwardian figures create a cheery ambience. Chez Antoine excels at grilled selections, prepared over mesquite, Canadian maple, or hickory woods. Grilled quail is a specialty, as is grilled scampi with curry. Luncheon fare also includes salads and sandwiches. Abstainers will appreciate the nonalcoholic "wine list." *Le Grand Hôtel, 777 rue University, tel. 514/879–1370. Casual dress. Reservations advised for dinner. AE, CB, D, MC, V.*

5
$$$
Chez Pauzé. Established in 1862, this is one of the few remaining fine restaurants that once clustered on rue Ste-Catherine. The somewhat outdated maritime decor sets the stage for seafood specialties. Sconces and chandeliers are replicas of ships's wheels, and a swordfish trophy guards the bar entrance. Lone diners are fussed over by attentive waitresses. Reasonably priced business lunches are featured Tuesday through Friday 11:30–2:30. The à la carte menu may feature creamy lobster stew or a thick lobster sandwich on brown bread. Clam chowder makes an economical, filling meal. Dinner is more extensive and expensive and is especially good when lobster is in season. *1657 rue Ste-Catherine ouest, tel. 514/932–6118. Casual dress. Reservations advised for dinner. AE, CB, D, MC, V. Closed Mon.*

★ 8
$$$$
Les Halles. An evening here will take you back to the era of Paris's old market district. It's the most talked-about restaurant in Montréal, and all four dining rooms are usually full. On the first floor a charcuterie serves a high-spirited crowd. For a quiet meeting sit upstairs, where the atmosphere is more restrained. The menu offers a selection of classic French and nouvelle cuisine, and appetizers include a hare pâté with apples and juniper berries. Among the main dishes are *magret de canard de Barbarie* (breast of duck with Cumberland sauce), and filet of beef with mushrooms and foie gras. For dessert try the homemade sorbet or the pastries. A reasonably priced business lunch is offered Tuesday through Friday 11:45–2:30. *1450 rue Crescent, tel. 514/844–2328. Jacket advised in the evening. Reservations required. AE, CB, D, MC, V. Closed Mon. and some holidays.*

⑩ Katsura. Located near the Hôtel Ritz-Carlton, this Japanese restaurant, the most elegant in the city, is always jammed with local and international clientele. Business groups meet in private tatami rooms or in the relatively quiet alcove off the sushi bar. Service in the alcove is not always efficient, and the area can become hot and stuffy. Tastefully decorated with Japanese screens and prints, the restaurant manages to be both contemporary and cozy, and knowledgeable waitresses are exceptionally helpful. Although there is a good wine list, most diners start off with hot saki. The generous sushi-and-sashimi combination platter is a comprehensive selection. Shabu-shabu is prepared here for two with slices of beef and vegetables thinly cut and boiled in broth at the table. Fixed-price, eight- to 12-course dinners provide a good sampling of the house specialties. *2170 rue de la Montagne, tel. 514/849–1172. Casual dress. Reservations required, except at the sushi bar. AE, CB, D, MC, V.*

$$$

⑨ Le Lutetia. This valentine of a dining room in the Hôtel de la Montagne is a frothy confection of needlepoint chairs, cabbage-rose rugs, lacey tablecloths, and candy-box murals of clouds and cherubs. Popular for power breakfasts and lunches, as well as for Sunday brunch, Lutetia's kitchen is highly regarded for its nouvelle cuisine. All-inclusive lunches range from mushroom quiche to roast beef. The fresh fettuccine with shredded vegetables and shrimp is light, yet as satisfying as the steak tartare, and the lamb medallions "perfumed" with fresh mint. Oenophiles praise the wine cellar, which, in 1987, won a gold medal as the best in Québec. *Hôtel de la Montagne, 1430 rue de la Montagne, tel. 514/288–5656. Jacket advised. Reservations advised. AE, D, MC, V.*

$$$

★ ⑦ Le Mas des Oliviers. This restaurant's name ("The Olive Grove") and its white stucco walls and black wrought-iron grillwork conjure images of Provence. Although the food is not quite so lyrical as the images suggest, the restaurant has come into its own since it was taken over by Jacques Muller a decade ago. You'll like the look of the place: the fresh green napery, the imposing refectory table displaying wine and cheese, and the dark wood bar. The soup of the day, simmering in an old black cauldron, is a good way to start. Some entrées are exceptional. A wise choice is the grilled, lightly seasoned lamb chops, or the steak *sauvage*, marinated in white wine, thyme, sage, rosemary, laurel, and garlic. Frogs' legs, and the tender double entrecôte in a red-wine sauce flavored with shallots, are also excellent. Crêpes suzette and rich chocolate profiteroles are popular desserts. *1216 rue Bishop, tel. 514/861–6733. Casual dress. Reservations advised. AE, D, MC, V. Closed weekend lunch.*

$$$

★ ㉒ Moishe's Steak House. Those who have business with the clothing concerns around boulevard St-Laurent, Montréal's "Main," which divides the city into east and west, and visitors in the area will enjoy this institution, famous among beef-lovers since 1938. The down-at-the-heels storefront—and the restaurant's dirty white siding and green plastic awnings—shouldn't put off first-time visitors. The pace is hectic, and the expert waiters busy and often brusque, but the atmosphere is clubby and comfortable and the steaks are prime quality, particularly the tender Red Brand filet mignon broiled over charcoal.

$$$

Other offerings include marinated shish kebab, mixed
grill, lamb chops, and boiled beef. Deli mainstays uch as
pickled herring, chopped liver, and fresh pickled salmon
are also available as appetizers. *3961 blvd. St-Laurent,
tel. 514/845–3509. Casual dress. AE, D, MC, V.*

Vieux-Montréal

★ **26**   **Chez Delmo.** This Vieux-Montréal restaurant, near the
$$$$ Notre-Dame Basilica, has been an institution for fresh
seafood since 1910. Delmo's offers communal lunch in the
front room at two long, polished, wood bars for a crowd of
individual diners and couples, and more private tables in
the back dining room. A lunchtime favorite with the regular clientele of judges, lawyers, journalists, and actors is
the seafood plate, offering crab, lobster, shrimp, and scallops on a bed of Boston lettuce. Curried-shrimp casserole
with rice; and Dover sole belle meunière are also house
specialties. Thanks to two experienced chefs, Luigi Bordi
and Enja Bertoli, almost any selection is a good choice.
The white house wine, a Muscadet, is available by the
glass at the bar and is reasonably priced. However, the
wine list includes a good selection of labels and can be expensive. For dessert, the crème caramel is exceptional.
*211 rue Notre-Dame, tel. 514/849–4061. Casual dress.
Reservations advised for dinner. AE, CB, D, MC, V.
Closed Sun., two weeks in mid-summer, Christmas week.*

★ **29**   **Les Filles du Roy.** Although it's been called corny, this res-
$$$ taurant seems to please everyone from summertime tour-
ists to busy executives. Named in honor of the women sent
by Louis XIV to marry colonists in New France, the res-
taurant has cream-color wainscoting, casement windows,
and fluffy curtains that frame a view of the Historic Quar-
ter's cobblestoned rue Bonsecours. Today's "filles" wear
18th-century garb and are happy to describe typical
Québécois fare featured at the luncheon buffet and dinner.
The hearty platters are not for everyone, but the menu is
balanced with such lighter dishes as salmon, fillet of sole,
and chicken and veal dishes. The enormous Québec plat-
ter holds *tourtière* (meat pie), meatballs, sausage, and
mashed potatoes in gravy. Other regional dishes include
cipaille St-Jean (three-meat pie), and ham in maple syr-
up. Sweet sugar pie is another local favorite. There is an
extensive wine list and a good house wine, Cuvée des
Filles du Roy. *415 rue Bonsecours, tel. 514/849–3535.
Jacket advised in evening. Reservations advised; re-
quired for opera evening. AE, CB, D, MC, V.*

27   **La Sorosa.** Always busy with diners from nearby office
$$ towers and the courthouse, this Italian restaurant in
Vieux-Montréal is a barn of a place with exposed beams
and brick walls adorned with collectibles that include an
old-fashioned baby's sleigh and faded wedding photos.
Sterno candles light the room and keep the pizzas hot, too.
The quietest area is the mezzanine balcony overlooking
rue Notre-Dame; by noon there is usually a line and most
of these tables are taken. Salads, pastas, and *croques-
monsieurs* are popular. The wine list favors Italian labels;
red house wine, in half liters and smaller carafes, can be
harsh but goes down well with the pizza. Service is often
brusque. *56 rue Notre-Dame ouest, tel. 514/844–8595. Casual dress. AE, MC, V. Closed Sun.*

㉘ **Le St-Amable.** Cozily ensconced in an 18th-century field-
$$$$ stone building off place Jacques Cartier, this is a splurge
even for visitors on an expense account. But everything
about the restaurant bolsters Montréal's reputation for
fine dining in artful surroundings. Thick exposed brick
walls give a sense of history to the upstairs dining room.
The intimate bar is lit by candles. Usually quiet, except
during the holiday season, the setting is an excellent background for a business lunch or dinner. Waiters are solicitous but never intrusive. Evening meals feature classics
for which the restaurant is known—breast of duckling in
cream sauce with red peppercorns and apples; and medallions of veal in sherry. The thick and flavorful chateaubri-
and—filet mignon with truffles for two—is just the dish
with which to seal a business agreement. The fare is
hearty and filling, but try to leave room for the desserts,
which range from millefeuilles to cherries jubilee. *188 rue
St-Amable, tel. 514/866–3471. Jacket advised. Reservations advised. AE, CB, D, MC, V. Closed weekend lunch.*

FREE TIME

Fitness

Hotel Facilities
The **Centre Sheraton** (tel. 514/878–2000) is the only hotel
health club open to nonguests; a Can$8 daily fee or special
weekly rates are available.

Health Clubs
The **YMCA** (1450 rue Stanley, across from Peel métro, tel.
514/849–8393), downtown, is open to visitors for a Can$8
fee. The **YWCA** (1355 blvd. René-Lévesque ouest, tel. 514/
866–9941), downtown, is open to visitors for Can$6 week-
days, Can$4 weekends and holidays.

Jogging
Mont Royal is a favorite jogging route and offers challenging trails. Stairs at the top of rue Peel, rue Drummond,
and avenue du Musée lead to avenue Pine, across which
you jog to reach the main mountain path. Le Quatre
Saisons provides guests with maps of various park routes.
Another joggers' rendezvous is the **Vieux-Port** bicycle
path along the harbor.

Shopping

Le Rouet Métiers d'Art craft stores (136 rue St-Paul,
Vieux-Montréal, tel. 514/875–2333, and 700 rue Ste-Catherine ouest, tel. 514/861–8401) are good bets for tasteful and reasonably priced Québec-made items such as
ceramics, hand-embroidered clothing, copper and enamel
jewelry, and wooden toys. Fine carvings, prints, and tapestries are available at the **Eskimo Art Gallery** (1434 rue
Sherbrooke ouest). **Henry Birks and Sons** (1240 Carré
Phillips, tel. 514/397–2510), a longtime Montréal firm at
square Phillips, is the place for jewelry, china, and silver.

The central shopping area extends from **Baie** department
store (585 rue Ste-Catherine ouest, tel. 514/281–4422), at
square Phillips, westward to **Ogilvy** department store
(1307 rue Ste-Catherine ouest, tel. 514/842–7711). Rue
Ste-Catherine cuts through this roughly 20-square-block
zone and is lined with boutiques and major stores. With

the exception of **Holt Renfrew** (1300 rue Sherbrooke ouest, tel. 514/842–5111), all department stores have Ste-Catherine addresses, as do a number of major complexes, like the **Eaton Centre** (677 rue Ste-Catherine ouest). If you don't have much time, the **Eaton** department store at the Centre is your best bet. Here you can find anything from Canadian souvenirs to Canadian furs. Other leading shopping complexes include the underground mall at **Place Ville-Marie, Place Bonaventure, Place Victoria, Complexe Guy-Favreau** (connected to the convention center), and **Complexe Desjardins.** Rue St-Denis eastward, and rue Crescent westward of blvd. St-Laurent are the two streets for trendy fashions. Rue Sherbrooke ouest, with which they both intersect, is lined with expensive designer salons, antiques shops, and art galleries. High-fashion shops for men include **Brisson & Brisson** (1472 rue Sherbrooke ouest, tel. 514/937–7456), **Giorgio de Montréal** (1176 rue Sherbrooke ouest, tel. 514/287–1928), and **Uomo Moda** (1452 rue Peel, tel. 514/844–1008). Among dozens of women's haute couture salons are **Bruestle** (1490 rue Sherbrook ouest), **Raffinati,** and **Valentino,** at Ogilvy; **Ralph Lauren** (1300 rue Sherbrooke ouest, tel. 514/284–3988, for men and children, too) next door to Holt Renfrew on rue Sherbrooke ouest, and **Ungaro** (1430 rue Sherbrooke ouest, tel. 514/844–8970).

Diversions

Montréal Harbour Cruises (Victoria Pier at the Vieux-Port, tel. 514/842–3871) let you drift down the St-Lawrence on any one of six daily trips, including an evening cocktail-and-dinner cruise. Tickets are available at Info-Touriste on square Dorchester. Cruises run from May to October.

The Montréal Museum of Fine Arts (1379 rue Sherbrooke ouest, tel. 514/285–1600), the oldest in Canada (1861), holds a large collection of European and North American fine and decorative art. A massive expansion is underway across rue Sherbrooke.

Mont Royal offers a quick escape, particularly in fall, when Montréal maples burst into scarlet and orange. Jogging, biking, a restful lake, acres of rolling lawns, and wooded trails are all easily accessible via steps at the top of rues Drummond, Peel, and du Musée downtown.

Murray Hill Tours (1380 rue Barré, tel. 514/937–5311) gives a general overview of the city on a four-hour bus tour leaving from square Dorchester's InfoTouriste center and major hotels. Tickets are on sale at the hotels and the main departure point (1001 sq. Dorchester).

In summer drop by the **Ritz Garden** (Hôtel Ritz-Carlton, tel. 514/842–4212) for tea near the fluffy Brome ducklings, and relax amid the flowers and sculptures in Canada's most famous backyard.

A walk along **rue Sherbrooke** eastward to rue University, and west as far as rue Guy, introduces visitors to Montréal's "Square Mile," where wealthy families lived a century ago. The turreted limestone mansions look much as they did before the street became a center for museums, sculpture cafés, outdoor terraces, and intriguing art and antiques galleries.

Take a **sleigh ride** over Mont Royal and view the cityscape from the wooded mountaintop lookout. Bring your skates, or rent them at the chalet (tel. 514/653–0751) for a quick spin around Beaver Lake, to the accompaniment of the "Skater's Waltz."

Vieux-Montréal (Champ-de-Mars métro) is for browsers who want to stroll among historic greystone houses and stop off at a bistro or sidewalk café for a pick-me-up.

Professional Sports

Hockey fans can see the **Canadiens** at the Forum (2313 rue Ste-Catherine ouest, tel. 514/932–2582). The baseball team, the **Expos,** plays in the Olympic Stadium (4545 av. Pierre-de-Coubertin, tel. 514/253–3434 for information; 514/253–0700 or 800/361–0658, in Québec and Ottawa, for tickets). **Supra de Montréal** play soccer in Centre Claude-Robillard (1000 rue Emile-Journault, tel. 514/739–6266).

The Arts

The **Place des Arts** (PdA) complex (1501 rue Jeanne-Mance, tel. 514/842–2112) is the main center for the performing arts and home to the Montréal Symphony Orchestra, Les Grands Ballets Canadiens, and the Opéra de Montréal. The renovated **Théâtre Saint-Denis** (1594 rue St-Denis, tel. 514/849–4211) and the **Spectrum** (318 rue Ste-Catherine ouest, tel. 514/861–5851) are venues for musicals and jazz. Most drama is aimed at French-speaking audiences, but the **Centaur Théâtre** (453 rue St-Francoís-Xavier, tel. 514/288–3161) concentrates on English productions. The **Saidye Bronfman Centre** (5170 rue Côte-Ste-Catherine, tel. 514/739–2301) has had uneven success with English-language plays but highlights first-rate Yiddish (simultaneous-translation) drama twice a year.

Ticket agencies include **Ticketron** (sq. Phillips, tel. 514/ 277–2552, and Sears Store branches) and **Teletron** (tel. 514/288–2525).

After Hours

Bars and Lounges
Le Grand Prix, in the Hôtel Ritz-Carlton (tel. 514/842–4212), is a sophisticated rendezvous for a drink with clients. **Moby Dick** (1188 rue Sherbrooke ouest, tel. 514/285–1637) is flush with young professionals at happy hour. In the lobby of the Hôtel Ramada Renaissance du Parc, **Puzzles** (tel. 514/288–6666) features jazz during the week and dancing cheek-to-cheek on Saturday. Hotel piano bars are usually good for a quiet business tête à tête. Try, among others, the Bonaventure Hilton's **Belvedere Bar** (tel. 514/ 878–2332); **L'Impromptu,** the lobby bar at Le Centre Sheraton (tel. 514/878–2000); Le Quatre Saisons' **L'Apero** (tel. 514/284–1110); the Manoir LeMoyne's **Bar Frédéric** (2100 De-Maisonneuve, tel. 514/931–8861); and Le Reine Elizabeth's **Les Voyageurs** (tel. 514/861–3511).

Cabarets

Le Portage (Bonaventure Hilton International, 1 pl. Bonaventure, tel. 514/878–2332) spotlights singers, jazz musicians, small combos, and occasionally a comedy act. **Le
Caf' Conc'** (Le Château Champlain, pl. du Canada, tel.
514/878–9000) offers a can-can show and variety acts.

Comedy Clubs

Try the **Comedy Nest** (1459 rue Crescent, tel. 514/849–
6378), one of the sites for the "Just for Laughs" festival.
This annual summer festival (tel. 514/845–3155) is an international, multilingual celebration of comedy at various
theaters around Montréal.

Jazz Clubs

Owner and bassist Charlie Biddle and a host of guest musicians play at **Biddle's** (2060 rue Aylmer, tel. 514/842–
8656). Other possibilities include: **L'Air du Temps** (191 rue
St-Paul ouest, tel. 514/842–2003) and **Le Grill Café** (183
rue St-Paul ouest, tel. 514/397–1044).

For Singles

Thursday's/Les Beaux Jeudis (Hôtel de la Montagne, 1430
de la Montagne, tel. 514/288–5656) stands out as the most
popular singles meeting place in town. A couple of disco
choices: **Metropolis** (59 rue Ste-Catherine est, tel. 514/288–
5559), the biggest disco in town, is awash in high-tech la-
sers, throbbing music, and multiple dance floors. **L'Esprit**
(1234 rue de la Montagne, tel. 514/397–1711) is another favorite of young singles.

New York

by Roger Lowenstein

The 1980s were, in general, a prosperous time for New York—a welcome rebound from its 1970s brush with bankruptcy. With the notable exception of the 1987 crash, Wall Street and other white-collar industries boomed; employment soared; new hotels and skyscrapers changed the skyline; and whole neighborhoods on the West Side, Lower East Side, and Brooklyn were reclaimed from blight. New York's retail establishments—from groceries to boutiques—never looked brighter.

Tourists and natives benefited from a new convention center, a renovated zoo, a new waterfront district at Battery Park City, and, more important, an overhauling of the subway system. New graffiti-free cars were installed and stations began to get long-overdue facelifts. As real estate prices soared, some of New York's most famous buildings, including parts of Rockefeller Center and Citicorp Center, were sold to cash-rich foreigners.

But the real estate boom that fed the city's coffers and seemed at times to be the inescapable conversation topic at any gathering of New Yorkers also brought problems. The city's residents were joined by some of its corporations in being unable to afford the rents. Exxon, Mobil, and J.C. Penney left town. NBC and Chase Manhattan threatened to leave, but were given generous inducements by City Hall to stay. And as the 1990s got under way, the prosperous times were clearly coming to an end. Wall Street, still under the shadow of the 1987 stock market crash, continued to cut back on its employees and its bonuses. Advertising, another major New York industry, slumped, and development stalled. And the City Government was again badly strapped for funds.

Violent and drug-related crime, as in other cities, has been on the rise, but tourists, with a few notable exceptions, have usually been unaffected by it. What average citizens have been unable to avoid is the striking juxtaposition between rich and poor. A seemingly endless stream of homeless people often disconcert and disturb visitors and New York residents alike.

That said, New York still has twice the verve of almost any other town. To get the most out of it, remember to allow for a little delay, even confusion, in getting from one place to another, and try to indulge in, rather than just tolerate,

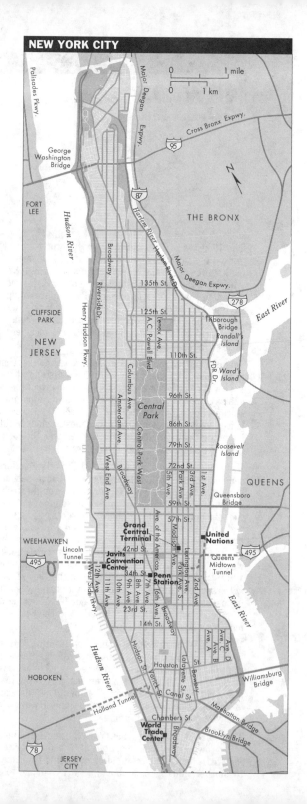

the city's diversity. As always, the best way to mine the city's riches is to walk its streets (with reasonable care).

Top Employers

Employer	Type of Enterprise	Parent*/ Headquarters
American Express/ Shearson Lehman Hutton	Travel, credit card, broker-age firm	New York
Chase Manhattan Bank	Bank	New York
Citicorp	Bank	New York
Consolidated Edison	Utilities	New York
R.H. Macy	Department store	New York
Manufacturers Hanover Trust Co.	Bank	New York
Merrill Lynch & Co.	Financial services	New York
New York Telephone	Telephone company	NYNEX/ New York
New York University	University	New York
Pan American	Airline	New York

*if applicable

ESSENTIAL INFORMATION

Climate

What follows are the average daily maximum and minimum temperatures for New York.

Jan.	41F 29	5C −2	Feb.	43F 29	6C −2	Mar.	47F 34	8C 1
Apr.	61F 45	16C 7	May	70F 54	21C 12	June	81F 63	27C 17
July	85F 70	29C 21	Aug.	83F 68	28C 20	Sept.	76F 61	24C 16
Oct.	69F 52	19C 11	Nov.	56F 43	13C 6	Dec.	43F 31	6C −1

Airports

John F. Kennedy International Airport is 15 miles east of midtown Manhattan. Though few will be unimpressed by its vital statistics (31 million passengers a year, 16,000 parking spaces, and a total surface area equal to one third of Manhattan Island), the airport is unwieldy and is the least convenient of the three that serve New York. Half the traffic is from overseas.

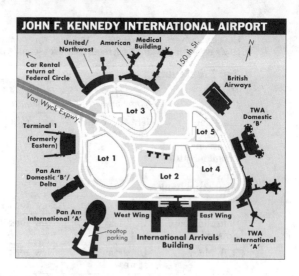

JOHN F. KENNEDY INTERNATIONAL AIRPORT

LaGuardia Airport, eight miles east of Manhattan, primarily handles short-haul domestic flights. Though much smaller than JFK, it accommodates 24 million people a year and is growing—perhaps too quickly. In recent years, its on-time record has been among the worst in the U.S.

Newark International Airport, 16 miles southwest of midtown, handles 22 million passengers a year, making it one of the country's biggest. Unlike the other metropolitan-area airports, however, Newark is not operating beyond its designed capacity. That, plus a user-friendly and accessible roadway system, make this a good choice, especially for those staying in downtown Manhattan. About 10% of the traffic is international.

Airport Business Facilities

John F. Kennedy International Airport. There are no business service centers or hotels in the terminals.

LaGuardia Airport. Mutual of Omaha Business Service Center (Second fl., Main Terminal, near USAir and United, tel. 718/478–1414) has fax machines, photocopying, baggage storage, Western Union, travel insurance, cash advance, and phone suites. Another branch at the Delta terminal (tel. 718/651–6725) has baggage storage and travel insurance.

Newark International Airport. There are no business services here except the airline clubs and insurance machines.

Airlines

In general, the major domestic carriers serve all three airports. The Trump and Pan American shuttles connecting New York with Washington and Boston operate out of LaGuardia. Continental is the primary carrier out of Newark.

Air Canada, tel. 212/869–1900 or 800/776–3000.
American, tel. 800/433–7300.
Continental, tel. 212/319–9494 or 800/525–0280.
Delta, tel. 212/239–0700 or 800/221–1212.
Midway, tel. 800/621–5700 or 800/621–5700.
Northwest, tel. 212/736–1220 or 800/225–2525.
Pan Am, tel. 212/687–2600 or 800/221–1111.
TWA, tel. 212/290–2121 or 800/221–2000.
Trump Shuttle, tel. 800/247–8786.
United, tel. 800/241–6522.
USAir, tel. 800/428–4322.

Between the Airports and Downtown

By Helicopter
This is the fastest way to get into town. **New York Helicopter** (tel. 800/645–3494) flies from JFK (TWA Terminal A) to midtown, at 34th Street on the East River, in 10 minutes; flights leave every half hour from 1:45 PM until 7:15 PM. Cost: $65.88, though the ride is free for first-class passengers on some airlines. **Trump Air Helicopter Service** (tel. 800/448–4000 or 800/247–8786) flies between LaGuardia (Trump Shuttle terminal) and its Pier 6 Wall Street terminal (at South St. and Water St.) in six minutes, from 8 AM until 6:15 PM. Cost: $60.

By Taxi
The trip to midtown is about 30 minutes from LaGuardia, 30–45 minutes from Newark, and an hour from JFK, but travelers should allow for considerable traffic delays, especially (but not exclusively) during rush hours. From LaGuardia the most direct route into midtown is via the Queens-Midtown Tunnel, but during rush hours the Triboro Bridge route is often quicker. From JFK, take the Belt Parkway and Brooklyn Battery Tunnel into lower Manhattan and the 34th Street Tunnel into midtown. The Holland Tunnel is the best route from Newark. Cost: about $17 from LaGuardia, $30–$35 from JFK, and $30–$35 from Newark, plus tolls and tip. At Newark, "Share-and-Save" group rates are available for up to four passengers between 8 AM and midnight; make arrangements with the airport's taxi dispatcher.

By Ferry
Pan Am operates a water shuttle (tel. 800/543–3779) from LaGuardia's Marine Air Terminal, which serves the Pan Am Shuttle. It runs from 7:45 AM–6:45 PM, and stops at Pier 11, at Wall Street and South Street, and at 35th Street on the East River. The trip takes 45 minutes to downtown and 30 minutes to midtown. Cost: $20.

By Minibus or Van
Gray Line Air Shuttle (tel. 212/757–6840) will take you from the three area airports directly to your midtown hotel for $11 per person from LaGuardia, $14 from Kennedy, and $16 from Newark; prices are slightly higher for locations from 30th to 14th streets and from 64th to 95th streets. Buses leave every 15 minutes from JFK and LaGuardia, every 20 minutes from Newark; they run from 7 AM to midnight at JFK, 8 AM to midnight at LaGuardia and Newark. Make arrangements at the ground transportation counter.

By Bus
Carey Airport Express (tel. 718/632–0500, 718/632–0506, and 800/284–0909) runs buses from both New York airports to six hotels and terminals in midtown Manhattan. Buses from LaGuardia run every 20 minutes from 7 AM to midnight; travel time is 25–45 minutes, depending on traffic. Cost: $8.50. Buses from JFK run every half hour from 6 AM to midnight. Travel time is 45–75 minutes. Cost: $11. **Olympia Trails** (tel. 212/964–6233) runs buses every 15 minutes from 6 AM to midnight between Newark and Manhattan. The trip is 25 minutes to the World Trade Center and 35–45 minutes to Grand Central Station. Cost: $7.

For information on bus service between the three metropolitan airports call 800/AIR–RIDE.

Car Rentals

The following companies have booths at all three metropolitan airports:

Avis, tel. 800/331–1212.
Budget, tel. 800/527–0700.
Hertz, tel. 800/654–3131.
National, tel. 800/328–4567.
Thrifty, tel. 800/367–2277.

Emergencies

Doctors
Affiliated Physicians of St. Vincent's (5 World Trade Center, tel. 212/775–1218), **Central Park West Medical** (2 W. 86th St., tel. 212/769–1700, doctors always on call), **Lincoln Medical Practice** (1995 Broadway, tel. 212/787–8770, doctors always on call).

Dentists
Concerned Dental Care (30 E. 40th St., tel. 212/696–4979), **Preventative Dental Associates** (200 Madison Ave., tel. 212/213–2004 and 210 E. 86th St., tel. 212/685–7169).

Hospitals
Beth Israel Medical Center (First Ave. & 16th St., tel. 212/420–2000), **Mount Sinai Hospital** (100th St. & Fifth Ave., tel. 212/241–6500), **New York Eye & Ear Infirmary** (310 E. 14th St. & Second Ave., tel. 212/598–1313), **New York Hospital-Cornell Medical Center** (525 E. 68th St., tel. 212/472–5454), **New York University Medical Center** (560 First Ave., between 32nd & 33rd Sts., tel. 212/340–7300), **St. Vincent's Hospital & Medical Center** (153 W. 11th St. at Seventh Ave., tel. 212/790–7000).

Important Addresses and Numbers

Audiovisual rentals. Olden Camera & Lens (1265 Broadway bet. 33rd St. and 32nd St., tel. 212/725–1234), VRI Scharff (599 11th Ave., tel. 212/582–4400).

Chamber of Commerce (200 Madison Ave., tel. 212/561–2020).

Computer rentals. The Computer Factory (219 E. 44th St., tel. 212/953–2233; 11 W. 52nd St., tel. 212/664–0170), Microrent (14 Leonard St., tel. 212/925–6455).

Convention and exhibition centers. Jacob J. Javits Convention Center (36th St. and 11th Ave., tel. 212/216–2000).

There is also convention space at Pier 88 (tel. 212/466–7985), and at Pier 90 (tel. 212/466–7974). For more information, call the New York Convention & Visitors Bureau (tel. 212/397–8222).

Fax services. AAA Service Resource Industries (67 Wall St., tel. 212/943–1111), Abco Typing & Mail Service (60 E. 42nd St., tel. 212/697–1360), Electronic Systems Plus (120 W. 44th St., tel. 212/302–5477), Mailboxes Etc. USA (217 E. 86th St., tel. 212/996–7900).

Formal-wear rentals. A.T. Harris (47 E. 44th St., tel. 212/682–6325), Jack & Co. Formal Wear (128 E. 86th St., tel. 212/722–4455).

Gift shops. Chocolates: Godiva Chocolatier (560 Lexington Ave., tel. 212/980–9810; 33 Maiden Lane, tel. 212/809–8990; and 701 Fifth Ave., tel. 212/593–2845), Jo-Ann's Nut House (25 W. 33rd St. [lobby of the Empire State Building], tel. 212/279–1809); Flowers: Christatos & Koster (201 E. 64th St., tel. 212/838–0022, New York's most famous florist), Christie's Flowers (71 Broadway, tel. 212/425–2644).

Graphic design studios. Bloch, Graulich, Whelan (333 Park Ave., tel. 212/473–7033), Commercial Arts (122 W. 27th St., tel. 212/243–1905).

Hairstylists. Unisex: Jean-Louis David (Roosevelt Hotel, 45 E. 45th St., tel. 212/661–9600, where no appointment is necessary), Vidal Sassoon (767 Fifth Ave., tel. 212/535–9200); Women: Elizabeth Arden (691 Fifth Ave., tel. 212/832–3225).

Health and fitness clubs. *See* Fitness, below.

Information hot lines. Movies (tel. 212/777–3456), Sports (tel. 212/976–1313).

Limousine services. Battery City Car & Limousine Service (tel. 212/947–9696), Concord Luxury Limousine (tel. 212/230–1600), Limousine and Chauffeur Service (tel. 212/222–8247), Limousine by Ari (tel. 212/472–2226), London Town Cars (tel. 212/988–9700).

Liquor stores. Famous Wines & Liquors (27 William St., tel. 212/422–4743), Morrell & Co. (535 Madison Ave., tel. 212/688–9370), Sherry Lehmann (679 Madison Ave., tel. 212/838–7500).

Mail delivery, overnight. DHL Worldwide Courier Express (tel. 718/917–8000), Federal Express (tel. 212/777–6500), TNT Skypak (tel. 800/558–5555), UPS (tel. 212/695–7500), U.S. Postal Service Express Mail (212/330–5250).

Messenger services. Able Motorized Delivery Service (tel. 212/687–5515), Allboro Messenger Service (tel. 212/532–5959), Bullit Courier (tel. 212/952–4343, downtown; and tel. 212/983–7400, midtown).

Office space rental. World-Wide Business Centres (575 Madison Ave., tel. 212/605–0200).

Pharmacies, late-night. Jaros Drug (25 Central Park West, tel. 212/247–8080), Kaufman Pharmacy (557 Lexington Ave., tel. 212/755–2266), Star Pharmacy (1540 First Ave., tel. 212/737–4324).

Radio stations, all-news. WCBS, 880 AM; WINS, 1010 AM.

Secretarial services. Dial-A-Secretary (521 Fifth Ave. and 149 E. 81st St., tel. 212/348–9575), HQ Services & Offices (730 Fifth Ave., tel. 212/333–8700; 237 Park Ave., tel. 212/949–0722; 666 Fifth Ave., tel. 212/541–3800), Wordflow (162 Madison Ave., tel. 212/725–5111).

Stationery supplies. Airline Stationers (284 Madison Ave., tel. 212/532–6525), Grolan Stationers (1800 Broadway, tel. 212/247–2676), Ropal Stationery (1283 Third Ave., tel. 212/988–3548), Times Circle East (61 E. 45th St., tel. 212/682–0820).

Taxis. Minute Men Taxi (tel. 718/899–5600), Taxi Town (tel. 212/315–1490), Uptown Taxi (tel. 212/304–3989).

Theater tickets. *See* The Arts, below.

Train information. Amtrak (tel. 212/582–6875 or 800/872–7245) and the Long Island Railroad (tel. 718/454–5477) depart from Pennsylvania Station at Seventh Ave. and 33rd St; Metro North (tel. 212/532–4900) departs from Grand Central Station, at Lexington Ave. and 42nd St.

Travel agents. American Express (150 E. 42nd St., tel. 212/687–3700; American Express Tower C, World Financial Center, 200 Vesey St., tel. 212/640–5130; and 374 Park Ave., tel. 212/421–8240), Liberty Travel (1430 Third Ave., tel. 212/772–3808; 298 Madison Avenue, tel. 212/689–5600; 50 Broad St., tel. 212/363–2320), Thomas Cook Travel (2 Penn Plaza, tel. 212/967–4390; 160 E. 53rd St., tel. 212/755–9780).

Weather (tel. 212/976–1212).

LODGING

New York's hotels are concentrated in midtown (usually defined as the area between 42nd and 59th streets and between the East River and Avenue of the Americas). This is home base for the lion's share of New York's major law firms and large corporations. However, the boundary lines of midtown have blurred as development has pushed west into the theater district. Hotels there are a bit farther from the heart of the business zone, but not much. The big difference is one of style. Midtown is consistently fast-paced, corporate, and somewhat sterile; the theater area, a blend of small businesses—including those that make the garment and diamond trade, as well as show business—is serious by day and colorful (some would say raffish) by night. Female travelers especially should note: this neighborhood has been coming back for a long time but still has a way to go.

Travelers who want a break from the monotony of skyscrapers when the work day is over should consider hotels on the Upper East Side, just a short taxi ride or a longish walk from midtown. Enticing restaurants cater to the area's well-to-do locals, and the streetscape is dotted with museums, galleries, and boutiques. Hotels in the residential streets south of midtown (grouped here with midtown hotels) offer convenience and quiet, though the area is somewhat short on pizzazz.

The downtown financial district has only one hotel, and it's easily the most convenient for those doing business on Wall Street. The airport hotels may suffice for people on one-night stopovers, but are not advisable for those planning repeated trips to midtown.

Most hotels listed here offer special corporate rates and weekend discounts; inquire when making reservations.

Highly recommended lodgings in each price category are indicated by a star ★.

Category	Cost*
$$$$ (Very Expensive)	over $210
$$$ (Expensive)	$150–$210
$$ (Moderate)	under $150

All prices are for a standard double room, single occupancy, excluding 13.25% and $2 a day taxes.

Numbers in the margin correspond to numbered hotel locations on the New York Lodging and Dining maps.

Wall Street

★ **52** $$$ **Vista International.** The style is plain-vanilla functional, but rooms are comfortable, and the location makes the hotel a must for those who need to be near Wall Street. Among its other standard amenities, the Vista offers computers for hire and a 22nd-floor fitness center with a 50-foot pool, jogging track, and weight room overlooking the Hudson River. Guests on two executive floors have the run of a lounge and open bar. The best rooms are those overlooking the World Trade Center plaza, stunning when lit up at night. Book in advance; though other developments are in the works, at press time this remained the Wall Street area's only hotel. *A Hilton International hotel, 3 World Trade Center, 10048, tel. 212/938–9100 or 800/445–8667, fax 212/372–2231. Gen. manager, Roman Rickenbacher. 769 rooms, 25 suites. AE, CB, D, DC, V.*

Midtown/Theater District/Gramercy

★ **36** $$ **Algonquin.** Famous writers put the hotel on the map by holding court in the Blue Bar, today a hangout of the theater set as well as literary types. The Oak Room is still a good bet to view cabaret acts and to enjoy pretheater dinner, and the oak-paneled lobby, a cozy place for reading and subdued conversation, doesn't seem to have changed since 1902. It's a good place to have a drink with a highbrow client, but you'll go upstairs to a cramped bedroom and smallish bath. Rooms on all 12 floors have recently been refurbished, so they no longer have a boarding house feel; most of them now have desks. Still, it's best to come for the scene and the location, convenient to midtown—but not if you need to spend a lot of time working in your room. *An Aoki hotel. 59 W. 44th St., 10036, tel. 212/840–6800 or 800/548–0345, fax 212/944–1419. Gen. manager, Edward Pitt. 139 rooms, 24 suites. AE, CB, DC, MC, V.*

MIDTOWN NEW YORK CITY

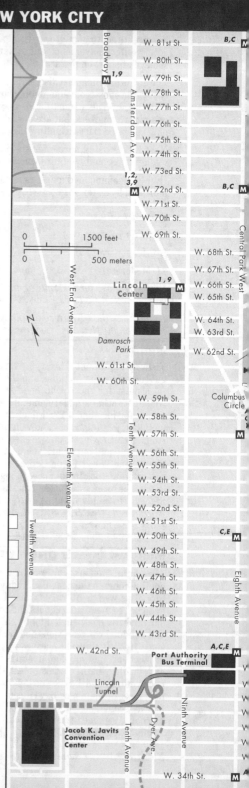

Lodging

Algonquin, **36**
Beekman Tower, **32**
Carlyle, **1**
Grand Hyatt, **38**
Hotel Elysée, **22**
Kitano, **39**
Lowell, **5**
Marriott Marquis, **35**
Mayfair Regent, **4**
Mayflower, **6**
New York Hilton &
Towers, **23**
Parc 51, **26**
Park Lane Hotel, **10**
Le Parker Meridien, **12**
Peninsula New York, **18**
Plaza, **11**
Regency, **7**
Royalton, **37**
San Carlos, **30**
Sheraton Park Ave., **40**
Sheraton Squire, **25**
Sherry Netherland, **8**
Waldorf-Astoria, **31**
Westbury, **2**

Dining

Adrienne, **18**
Aquavit, **20**
Aurora, **34**
Le Bernardin, **27**
La Caravelle, **14**
Le Cirque, **4**
La Côte Basque, **15**
Le Cygne, **21**
The Four Seasons, **24**
Lafayette, **13**
Lutèce, **28**
Michael's, **17**
The Quilted Giraffe, **16**
The Rainbow Room, **29**
La Reserve, **33**
Restaurant Raphael, **19**
San Domenico, **9**
Sign of the Dove, **3**

DOWNTOWN NEW YORK CITY

1,2,3,9 Ⓜ **41**

Ⓜ B,D,F,
N,Q,R

Penn
on Station
n

Ⓜ **1,9**

Broadway

**Empire State
Building**

Ⓜ **6**

Ⓜ N,R

Lexington Avenue

Third Avenue

Second Avenue

First Avenue

FDR Drive

Avenue C

East River

42 Ⓜ **6**

Seventh
Avenue

Ⓜ **1,9**

Ⓜ F,Q N,R

*Madison
Square
Park*

Ⓜ **6**

Ⓜ **6**

43

*Gramercy
Park*

*Cooper
Village*

Z

Ⓜ **1**

44

*Union
Square*

4,5,6
Ⓜ B,L,
N,Q,R

E. 16th St.
E. 15th St.

2 Ⓜ
,9

Ⓜ F,L,Q

Fourth Ave.

Broadway

Ⓜ L

Ⓜ L E. 14th St.

nwich Ave.

Christopher
St.

*Tompkins
Square Park*

FDR Drive

averly Place

Ⓜ **1,9**

N,R Ⓜ Ⓜ **6**

Lafayette
St.

*Washington
Square Park*

Ⓜ A,C,E,F,B,
D,Q,JFK

Seventh Avenue S.

Ⓜ **1,9**

Ⓜ C,E

Ⓜ **6**

The Bowery

Ⓜ F

Avenue A

Avenue B

Avenue C

Avenue D

B,D,F,Q
Houston St. Ⓜ

W. Broadway

**B,D,
F,Q
4,6**
Ⓜ

N, R Ⓜ
Broadway

Ⓜ **6**

J,M Ⓜ

Orchard St.

J,M,Z
Ⓜ

Williamsb
Bridge

Broome St.

45

Ⓜ A,C,E
¹Ⓜ

tts St.

Greenwich St.

West Side Highway

Canal St.

B,D,Q Ⓜ

Eldridge St.

Canal St. Ⓜ F

N,R Ⓜ **4,5,6**
Ⓜ
Ⓜ J,M,Z

Ⓜ **1,9**

46 **47**

Church St.

Centre St.

*Chatham
Square*

Manhattan Bridge

48

49 **50** **51**

Chambers St. Ⓜ
1,2,3,9

N,R Ⓜ **2,3**

A, E Ⓜ

N,R Ⓜ

*City
Hall*

4,5,6
Ⓜ
J,M,Z

**World
Trade
Center**

A,C
Ⓜ J,M,R

2,3

Brooklyn Bridge

orld
ential
nter

52 **53**

4,5
N,R Ⓜ 1,9 St.

Ⓜ **2,3**

Trinity Pl.

Broadway

Nassau St.

Ⓜ **2,3** Wall St.
J,M,R

Park

West St.

Ⓜ
1,N,R **4,5**

4,5
Ⓜ

*Battery
Park*

N,R Ⓜ

BROOK
HEIGH

NEW YORK CITY HOTEL CHART

HOTELS	Price Category	Business Services Banquet capacity	No. of meeting rooms	Secretarial services	Audiovisual equipment	Teletype news service	Computer rentals	In-room modem phonejack	All-news cable channel	Desk	Desk lighting	Bed lighting
Algonquin	$$	100	3	-	-	-	-	-	✓	-	-	◐
Beekman Towers	$$$	125	1	-	-	-	-	-	-	◐	◐	●
The Carlyle	$$$$	120	2	-	✓	-	-	✓	✓	●	●	●
Gramercy Park	$$$$	200	5	-	-	-	-	-	✓	◐	◐	○
Grand Hyatt	$$$$	150	20	✓	✓	-	-	✓	✓	-	-	◐
Hilton and Towers	$$$	2800	47	✓	✓	✓	✓	-	✓	●	●	◐
Hotel Elysée	$$$	50	0	-	-	-	-	-	✓	◐	●	●
JFK Plaza	$$	250	12	-	✓	-	-	✓	✓	●	●	◐
Kitano	$$	0	0	-	-	-	-	-	-	◐	◐	○
LaGuardia Marriott Airport Hotel	$$$	400	13	-	-	-	-	-	-	◐	◐	◐
Lowell	$$$$	50	1	-	✓	-	-	✓	✓	●	●	●
Marriott Marquis	$$$$	200	47	-	-	-	-	✓	✓	●	●	●
Mayfair Regent	$$$$	40	2	✓	✓	-	-	✓	✓	●	●	●
Mayflower	$$	100	3	-	-	-	-	-	✓	◐	◐	◐
Parc 51	$$$$	70	2	✓	✓	-	-	✓	✓	●	●	◐
Le Parker Meridien	$$$$	300	7	✓	✓	✓	-	✓	✓	◐	●	●
Park Lane	$$$	20	1	-	-	-	-	✓	✓	◐	◐	◐
Peninsula	$$$$	180	6	-	✓	-	-	✓	✓	●	●	○
Penta	$$	1500	34	-	✓	-	-	✓	✓	◐	◐	◐

$$$$ = over $210, **$$$** = $150 -$210, **$$** = under $150.
● good, ◐ fair, ○ poor.
All hotels listed here have photocopying and fax facilities.

| In-Room Amenities | | | | | | | | | | Hotel Amenities | | | | | | |
Nonsmoking rooms	In-room checkout	Minibar	Pay movies	VCR/Movie rentals	Hairdryer	Toiletries	Room service	Laundry/Dry cleaning	Pressing	Concierge	Barber/Hairdresser	Garage	Courtesy airport transport	Sauna	Pool	Exercise room
-	-	-	-	-	-	○	◐	●	●	✓	-	-	-	-	-	-
-	-	-	✓	-	-	●	◐	●	●	-	-	-	-	-	-	-
-	-	✓	-	✓	✓	●	●	●	●	✓	✓	✓	-	✓	-	●
-	-	-	✓	-	-	-	◐	◐	●	✓	✓	-	-	-	-	-
✓	✓	-	✓	✓	-	●	●	●	●	✓	-	✓	-	-	-	-
✓	✓	✓	✓	-	-	●	●	◐	◐	✓	✓	✓	-	✓	-	●
-	-	-	-	-	✓	●	○	●	◐	-	-	✓	-	-	-	-
✓	-	-	-	-	✓	●	◐	●	○	✓	-	✓	✓	✓	◐	◐
-	-	-	✓	-	-	○	-	○	◐	✓	-	-	-	-	-	-
✓	-	-	✓	-	-	○	◐	●	◐	-	-	✓	✓	✓	●	◐
-	-	✓	-	✓	-	●	●	●	●	✓	-	✓	-	-	-	-
✓	✓	-	✓	-	-	●	●	●	○	✓	-	-	-	-	-	●
-	-	-	-	-	✓	●	●	●	●	✓	-	-	-	-	-	-
-	✓	-	-	-	-	○	◐	●	◐	-	-	-	-	-	-	-
✓	-	-	-	✓	-	●	●	●	●	✓	-	✓	-	✓	-	-
✓	✓	✓	✓	✓	✓	●	●	●	◐	✓	-	✓	-	✓	●	●
✓	-	-	✓	✓	✓	●	●	●	●	✓	✓	✓	-	-	-	-
✓	-	✓	-	-	✓	●	●	●	●	✓	-	✓	-	✓	●	●
✓	-	-	✓	-	-	-	◐	●	◐	-	✓	✓	✓	✓	-	-

Room service: ● 24-hour, ◐ 6AM-10PM, ○ other.
Laundry/Dry cleaning: ● same day, ◐ overnight, ○ other.
Pressing: ● immediate, ◐ same day, ○ other.

NEW YORK CITY HOTEL CHART

HOTELS	Price Category	Business Services Banquet capacity	No. of meeting rooms	Secretarial services	Audiovisual equipment	Teletype news service	Computer rentals	In-room modem phonejack	All-news cable channel	Desk	Desk lighting	Bed lighting
The Plaza	$$$$	700	18	-	✓	-	-	✓	✓	●	●	●
Regency	$$$$	150	3	-	-	-	-	-	✓	●	●	●
The Royalton	$$$	0	0	-	-	-	-	✓	✓	●	●	●
San Carlos	$$	0	0	-	-	-	-	✓	✓	●	●	●
Sheraton Park Avenue	$$$	100	3	-	✓	-	-	✓	✓	●	●	●
Sheraton Squire	$$$	400	7	-	✓	-	-	-	✓	◐	●	◐
Sherry Netherland	$$$	400	0	-	-	-	-	✓	✓	◐	◐	◐
Waldorf-Astoria	$$$$	1600	25	✓	✓	-	-	-	✓	●	●	●
Vista International Newark Airport	$$	600	6	✓	✓	-	✓	-	✓	◐	◐	◐
Vista International Wall Street	$$$	1000	16	✓	✓	-	✓	✓	✓	◐	◐	◐
Westbury	$$$$	250	5	-	✓	-	-	✓	✓	●	●	◐

$$$$ = over $210, $$$ = $150 -$210, $$ = under $150.
● good, ◐ fair, ○ poor.
All hotels listed here have photocopying and fax facilities.

| In-Room Amenities | | | | | | | | | | Hotel Amenities | | | | | | |
Nonsmoking rooms	In-room checkout	Minibar	Pay movies	VCR/Movie rentals	Hairdryer	Toiletries	Room service	Laundry/Dry cleaning	Pressing	Concierge	Barber/Hairdresser	Garage	Courtesy airport transport	Sauna	Pool	Exercise room
✓	-	✓	✓	-	-	●	●	●	●	✓	✓	✓	-	✓	-	-
-	-	-	✓	✓	✓	●	●	●	●	✓	✓	✓	-	✓	-	●
✓	✓	-	-	✓	-	●	●	●	●	✓	-	✓	-	✓	●	●
-	✓	-	-	-	-	○	◐	●	○	-	-	-	-	-	-	-
✓	✓	-	✓	-	✓	●	●	●	◐	✓	-	✓	-	✓	-	-
✓	-	-	✓	-	-	●	●	●	●	✓	✓	✓	-	-	●	-
-	-	-	-	✓	-	●	◐	●	●	✓	✓	-	-	-	-	-
✓	✓	✓	✓	-	-	●	●	◐	●	✓	✓	✓	-	-	-	-
✓	✓	-	✓	-	-	●	●	◐	◐	✓	-	✓	✓	✓	◐	●
✓	✓	✓	✓	-	✓	○	●	●	◐	✓	✓	✓	-	✓	●	●
✓	-	✓	✓	-	✓	●	●	●	●	✓	-	✓	-	-	-	-

Room service: ● 24-hour, ◐ 6AM-10PM, ○ other.
Laundry/Dry cleaning: ● same day, ◐ overnight, ○ other.
Pressing: ● immediate, ◐ same day, ○ other.

㉜ **Beekman Tower.** This good-value, all-suite hotel is recom-
$$$ mended for travelers seeking an extended stay in a quiet,
homelike environment. Favored by business people and
by diplomats serving the nearby United Nations, the 1929
Art Deco establishment sports Top of the Tower, a cock-
tail lounge and famed nightspot. The homey rooms have
traditional mahogany furnishings as well as kitchens with
enough counter space to be the envy of many New
Yorkers; the upper floors afford East River views. Avoid
the studio suites, however, if you need a desk. As part of
an ongoing room-by-room restoration, the Beekman re-
cently added a health club and restaurant. *Manhattan
East Suite Hotels. 3 Mitchell Pl., 10017, tel. 212/355–7300
or 800/637–8483, fax 212/753–9366. Gen. manager, Bob
Hansen. 172 suites. AE, CB, DC, MC, V.*

㊸ **Gramercy Park.** A nice change from the many soulless
$$$$ brass-and-chrome midtown hotels, this 18-story estab-
lishment offers its guests the key to one of Manhattan's
only private parks. Set in a quiet residential neighbor-
hood, a couple of subway stops closer to Wall Street, the
Gramercy Park offers a personal touch, catering to even
unusual requests with efficiency and grace. But the warm,
wood-paneled lobby and alluring bar have a disappointing
follow-through. Rooms are poorly lighted, bathroom tiles
are chipped, and the cheerless mood pervades even those
rooms that have been recently renovated. The lower
floors, on occasion, are noisy—attributable in part to the
rock bands that stay here (along with clothing manufac-
turers and gift and toy industry people). *2 Lexington
Ave., 10010, tel. 212/475–4320 or 800/221–4083, fax 212/
505–0535. Gen. manager, Thomas O'Brien. 220 rooms,
140 suites. AE, DC, MC, V.*

㊳ **Grand Hyatt.** People move about the brassy, floodlit lobby
$$$$ of this 34-story hotel, revamped in 1981, at an almost fre-
netic pace. You may not admire such flourishes as the
lobby's marble waterfall (subtlety was never the strong
suit of Donald Trump, the developer and part-owner), but
the hotel has an energy that captures the spirit of the city.
One apt touch: Diners in the glass-walled Crystal Foun-
tain can watch the 42nd Street traffic reflected in mirrored
ceilings. The mostly business clientele enjoy the proximi-
ty to the transportation hub of Grand Central Station, as
well as the spacious, quiet rooms, but the absence of desks
is a shortcoming. Sports fans, note: You could run into
Magic Johnson in the elevator—the hotel is a favorite with
out-of-town athletic teams. *Park Ave. at Grand Central,
10017, tel. 212/883–1234 or 800/233–1234, fax 212/697–
3772. Gen. manager, Gale Garvin. 1,293 rooms, 54 suites.
AE, CB, D, DC, MC, V.*

㉒ **Hotel Elysée.** Via word of mouth, this small hotel has
$$$ developed a loyal clientele who prize its intimate, French
country-inn ambience. Close to a wealth of fine restau-
rants, the Elysée is valued by business travelers—especially Europeans and Japanese—who want character and
charm along with the convenience of midtown. The rooms
are spacious, comfortable, and warmly furnished, if not
plush; all have terraces, some overlooking 54th Street.
Other pluses are the seafood restaurant and the Monkey
Bar, which has comedy and cabaret acts. *60 E. 54th St.,
10022, tel. 212/753–1066, fax 212/980–9278. Gen. manager, Sy Pinto. 95 rooms, 15 suites. AE, CB, DC, MC, V.*

㊴ Kitano. Tokyo newspapers are delivered daily to this Japa-
$$ nese-owned and -staffed hotel, whose clientele is about
70% Japanese. The Kitano is also popular with fashion
buyers doing business in the nearby garment district. It
offers good value and a helpful staff; the location, in a quiet
area, just south of midtown, is also a plus. But the ambi-
ence—from the piped-in lobby music to the flourescent
lighting—owes more to a suburban shopping mall than it
does to the Orient, and room desks are the sort seen at ga-
rage sales. *66 Park Ave., 10016, tel. 212/685-0022, fax
212/532-5615. Gen. manager, Yoshiomi F. Nakajima. 86
rooms, 12 suites. AE, CB, DC, MC, V.*

㉟ Marriott Marquis. This huge, 48-floor hotel, part of the up-
$$$$ grade of the still sleazy theater district, opened in 1985
and largely caters to groups attending the city's Jacob
Javits Convention Center. Every detail of the design—
rooms wrapping around an atrium, glass elevators, re-
volving rooftop restaurant—is familiar, but the patented
look, cloned from sunbelt establishments, seems out of
place on Times Square. Though the lower seven floors of
stores, restaurants, and meeting places are reminiscent of
a shopping mall, the rooms and baths are unusually spa-
cious and comfortable; those on the front side, though a
trifle noisy, offer spectacular views of Broadway. *1535
Broadway, 10036, tel. 212/398-1900 or 800/228-9290.
Gen. manager, Thomas Reese. 1,733 rooms, 141 suites.
AE, CB, D, DC, MC, V.*

★ ㉓ New York Hilton & Towers. This no-nonsense hotel is prob-
$$$ ably the best in midtown for purely business needs, as is
evidenced by a largely business clientele. Guests can give
dictation 24 hours a day and get prompt, printed tran-
scripts. A business center has private work stations with
personal computers as well as a Dow Jones news ticker and
information services. Those staying in the hotel's executive tower get complimentary breakfasts and drinks with
free hors d'oeuvres on a 39th-floor lounge. The rooms have
slick, black-top furniture and a clean, corporate look. A
new, Manhattan-style steakhouse has a lot of old-fashioned character, but unless you favor pulsating music and
flashing lights, you can skip the nightclub, which is oddly
out of place. *1335 Ave. of the Americas, 10019, tel. 212/
586-7000 or 800/445-8667, fax 212/315-1374. Gen. manager, John Power. 1,922 rooms, 112 suites. AE, CB, D,
DC, MC, V.*

㉖ Parc 51. Opened in 1986 as the Grand Bay, this is perhaps
$$$$ the most luxurious of the new hotels springing up in the
theater district. Catering to law firms, accounting firms,
and other businesses pioneering on the west side, the hotel has only seven floors; guests who want to avoid the
noise of Seventh Avenue should ask for an interior room.
Compensations are a pampering staff and 24-hour-a-day
concierge service, along with plush, French provincial
rooms with ample sitting areas, and luxurious baths with
60-gallon tubs as well as bidets, TVs, and telephones. The
lobby, with its classical paintings and quiet fern bar, has
an understated elegance, and the mezzanine breakfasts
are perfect for morning business meetings. *Park Lane Hotels International. 152 W. 51st St., 10019, tel. 212/765-
1900, fax 212/541-6604. Gen. manager, Guenter Richter.
126 rooms, 52 suites. AE, CB, DC, MC, V.*

⑫ **Parker Meridien.** This distinctly French hotel boasts a
$$$$ warm and lively lobby animated by a jazz piano bar. Visitors from nearby Carnegie Hall and the theater district come for the ground-floor buffets. In addition to a full health club, Le Parker Meridien has a skylit penthouse swimming pool. The only disappointment is the rooms, furnished in spare, contemporary style; they seem a bit too modest for a hotel in this price category. The higher floors are quietest. The mostly business clientele draws heavily from West Coast entertainment industry people visiting the nearby networks. *A Meridien hotel. 118 W. 57th St., 10019, tel. 212/245–5000 or 800/543–4300, fax 212/307–1776. Gen. manager, Serge Denis. 494 rooms, 207 suites. AE, CB, DC, MC, V.*

⑩ **Park Lane Hotel.** If you're not from Miami Beach you may
$$$ find this 1972, 46-floor hotel a bit overstated. The lobby is done up in light marble, wood paneling, mirrors, and the inevitable crystal chandeliers, but the effect is of glitz rather than grandeur. Still, the Central Park views are second to none, and the location is within walking distance of most of midtown. The rooms are spacious and come with fridges, scales, shoe-shine facilities, and phones by beds and desks; their old-fashioned furnishings are surprisingly plain, however. Guests are lavished with attention by the staff, and the hotel seems undisturbed by the myriad legal problems of its most famous long-time resident—who also happens to be its owner—Leona Helmsley. *Helmsley Hotels. 36 Central Park S., 10019, tel. 212/371–4000 or 800/221–4982, fax 212/319–9065. Gen. manager, Anton Gotsche. 601 rooms, 25 suites. AE, CB, DC, MC, V.*

⑱ **Peninsula New York.** The hotel was known as Maxim's un-
$$$$ til 1988, when it reopened under its present name. The new management has made mostly superficial changes; the accent is still French, and still luxurious, the tone somewhat formal. The Fifth Avenue location appeals mainly to Fortune 500 executives, but celebs stay here, too. Practically every room has a photograph of Sara Bernhardt, one of the many Art Nouveau touches in the establishment. Everything about the rooms is plush—note the large bathtubs and gold fixtures. The three-floor health spa is one of the city's best. *A Peninsula Group hotel. 700 Fifth Ave., 10019, tel. 212/247–2200 or 800/262–9467, fax 212/903–3949. Gen. manager, Manfred Timmel. 220 rooms, 30 suites. AE, DC, MC, V.*

㊶ **Penta.** A hangout of Glenn Miller in the Big Band era, this
$$ 1919 Beaux Arts classic (designed by McKim Mead & White) has lost some of its shine with the decline of the neighborhood, which suffers from an overabundance of panhandlers and a general social malaise. Still, the hotel is popular with convention-goers and business groups. The rooms are adequate, although the decor leans to tacky still-life prints. The upper floors are a bit worn; the lower floors, refurbished in 1985, are the best bet. Guests staying on the sixth floor can go from the conference center to their quarters without stepping in an elevator. Another plus: young, energetic staff members. Many have been hired recently and most are bubbling over with an eagerness to help. The Penta is convenient to the subway and to shopping (Macy's is a block away). *401 Seventh Ave., 10001, tel. 212/736–5000 or 800/447–3682, fax 212/502–*

8712. Gen. manager, Kenneth Walles. 1,680 rooms, 25 suites. AE, CB, DC, MC, V.

★ ⓫ **The Plaza.** Owner Donald Trump has too many copies of
$$$$ his autobiography on display in the hotel store, but the Plaza is arguably still the grandest of New York's hotels, attracting show biz guests as well as business and sports VIPs. The original 1907 moldings and crystal chandeliers lend an elegance to the guest quarters, but save for the suites, they are otherwise surprisingly ordinary and the rates quite steep. The Plaza's appeal is in its location, on the high-rent border of Central Park, and in its Baroque public spaces. The dark panelled Oak Room, with painted murals and leather armchairs, is ideal for business meals. Most notable is the gold-trimmed Palm Court, serving light fare and desserts—perfect for listening to piano and violin duets and for just passing time. *Fifth Avenue at Central Park S., 10019, tel. 212/759–3000 or 800/228–3000, fax 212/759–3167. Gen. manager, Richard Wilhelm. 705 rooms, 109 suites. AE, CB, D, DC, MC, V.*

㊲ **The Royalton.** This super-chic hotel, whipped up in 1988
$$$ by the duo that created Studio 54, has the same flair as that disco for capturing a sense of scene. The museum gallery-like interior, the creation of avant garde designer Philippe Starck, includes a hypermodern lobby with horn-shaped lights, harpoon-legged stools, and employees in severe black Mao jackets. The comfortable rooms have a seductive charm—the beds are tucked between pairs of portholes, and the bathrooms are done in green slate; many of them have five-foot round tubs. An in-house tape library holds 500 films. Not surprisingly, movie, record, design, and entertainment types figure prominently on this midtown hotel's guest list. Indeed, everything and everyone here is beautiful, but some will find the self-conscious and unrelenting attention to design tiresome. *44 W. 44th St., 10036, tel. 212/869–4400 or 800/635–9013, fax 212/869–8965. Gen. manager, Alex de Toth. 154 rooms, 16 suites. AE, CB, DC, MC, V.*

★ ㉚ **San Carlos.** This small, owner-operated hotel offers priva-
$$ cy, reasonable rates, and a residential feeling in the heart of midtown. U.N. diplomats and Japanese and Brazilian businessmen who stay here lend an international accent, and all are well attended by the efficient staff. The rooms are equipped with sleek, modern furnishings and small kitchens, and the decor is bright, spare, and uncluttered. Rooms in the back, off the street, are recommended. *150 E. 50th St., 10022, tel. 212/755–1800 or 800/722–2012, fax 212/688–9778. Gen. manager, Robert Kaminsky. 140 rooms, 60 suites. AE, CB, DC, MC, V.*

㊵ **Sheraton Park Avenue.** This hotel has about as much per-
$$$ sonality and charm as one might expect from a chain, but its location, just south of midtown, is perfect for no-nonsense business travelers. The rooms, recently renovated, are comfortable, and have telephones in the bath. The lower floors on the 37th Street side can be noisy; the rooms overlooking Park Avenue have the best views. Garment industry people, executives with business on Wall Street, and Europeans of various interests are among the guests. Try out the jazz (four nights a week) in the Judge's Chamber. *45 Park Ave., 10016, tel. 212/685–7676 or 800/325–3535, fax 212/889–3193. Gen. manager, James Bennett. 133 rooms, 18 suites. AE, CB, D, DC, MC, V.*

㉕ **Sheraton Squire.** This hotel is generally packed with busi-
$$$ ness travelers, but it's hard to tell why. The ground-floor
coffee shop is neon depressing, the lobby has all the ambi-
ence of an airport lounge, and the room decor is tacky. The
last room renovation was in 1983 and the next is overdue:
paint is peeling on some walls, and some bedboards are
spotted. Rooms overlooking Seventh Avenue are noisy,
and the smallish lobby is jammed with patrons and a bit
confused. One plus is the staff, many of whom have been
here for years and do their best to overlook the chaos and
keep the guests content. The west side location is close to
midtown, Broadway, and the Jacob Javitz Convention
Center. *790 Seventh Ave., 10019, tel. 212/581–3300 or 800/
325–3535, fax 212/541–9219. Gen. manager, Andrew
Katz. 713 rooms, 7 suites. AE, CB, D, DC, MC, V.*

★ ㉛ **Waldorf-Astoria.** The Waldorf, built in 1931 and restored
$$$$ in 1986, evokes an era when great public places were re-
vered as monuments and meeting grounds. The Art Deco
lobby is a sort of idealized, bustling city, where no one
seems to be at cross purposes, and elegance transcends all
the hubbub—see especially the Cocktail Terrace, where a
harpist sets the tone. Rooms are plush and luxurious,
from the gold bath fixtures to the separate dressing areas
and solid mahogany furnishings. The hotel has a well-
equipped business center, and a staff capable of translat-
ing 60 languages. Although the salad to which the hotel
gave its name is still served here, a Japanese restaurant,
Inagiku, is becoming the most admired of the Waldorf's
various dining spots. *A Hilton hotel. 301 Park Ave.,
10022, tel. 212/355–3000 or 800/445–8667, fax 212/872–
4799. Gen. manager, Per Hellman. 1,410 rooms, 300
suites. AE, CB, DC, MC, V.*

Upper East Side and Lincoln Center

★ ❶ **The Carlyle.** A favorite of celebrities—Jack Nicholson is a
$$$$ regular—who are wont to wave at each other in the hotel
tea room, the Carlyle is also a haven for corporate big-
wigs, who sail in and out in limousines to offices down-
town. The decor may be English country, but modern
amenities abound: most of the large, ultra-plush rooms in-
clude Jacuzzi, bidet, pantry with fridge, compact disk
player, stereo, bathroom phone, and fax machine. The up-
per floors facing south offer stunning views of the midtown
skyline. The Carlyle has twice as many staff members as
rooms, yet its muraled bar, restaurant, and nightclub are
what make this hotel a New York institution. Jazz pianist
Bobby Short—also an institution—is in his third decade
at the Café Carlyle (*see* Bars and Lounges, below). *35 E.
76th St., 10021, tel. 212/744–1600 or 800/227–5737, fax
212/717–4682. Gen. manager, Dan Camp. 100 rooms, 90
suites. AE, CB, DC, MC, V.*

★ ❺ **The Lowell.** This small, mostly suite hotel is the ultimate
$$$$ for those looking for a European flavor and elegant, spa-
cious quarters. The rooms, with their eclectic mix of En-
glish and French furnishings, wood-burning fireplaces,
and 18th- and 19th-century prints, are very homey, and in-
clude desks both practical *and* stylish; all also feature full
kitchens, and bathroom telephones. The Pembroke Room,
serving Continental cuisine and afternoon tea, is a good
hideaway for business meals. Few hotels are pricier than
the Lowell, but few have better service (the staff outnum-

bers the guests). On a quiet, east-side street, close to galleries and bookstores as well as to midtown, the hotel is a favorite of executives traveling with spouses. *28 E. 63rd St., 10021, tel. 212/838–1400, fax 212/319–4230. Gen. manager, Lynne Hunter Gray. 13 rooms, 48 suites. AE, CB, DC, MC, V.*

❹ Mayfair Regent. A fine location—in an upscale residential
$$$$ district, but close to midtown—and Continental-style attention to detail help this gracious hotel draw a large number of European business travelers and dignitaries. The rich terra cotta color of the walls in the elegant lobby is accented by the upholstery of the dark-wood furniture; the arches, palm fronds, and Oriental vases of an adjoining lounge make it a lovely setting for a light lunch or afternoon tea. The complete refurbishing in 1988–89 of the original 1925 structure left the spacious, light rooms and suites with charm intact while adding such modern business amenities as 4-line telephones (at least two in each accommodation). There are no on-premises exercise facilities, but stationary bikes are available on request. Umbrellas, unlimited free local calls, and humidifiers in each room are among the other special touches. The superlative Le Cirque restaurant (*see* Dining, below) has an entrance off the hotel lobby. *A Regent International hotel; member of Leading Hotels of the World. 610 Park Ave., 10021, tel. 212/288–0800 or 800/223–0542, fax 212/737–0538. Gen. manager, Dario Mariotti. 27 singles, 69 doubles, 105 suites. AE, CB, DC, MC, V.*

❻ Mayflower. If you're seeking a crisp, corporate look, you
$$ won't find it here. The lobby is dreary and a bit run-down. The spacious rooms and suites, recently redone, have pantries, fridges, and oversized closets (one reason the hotel is a favorite of actors and Bolshoi Ballet members), but the nondescript modern decor is nothing to write home about. What the Mayflower does offer is a friendly and informal ambience and a Central Park West location, appreciated by conventioneers, Lincoln Center- and theater-goers, and all who prefer Manhattan's more relaxed and heterogeneous West Side. Park-front rooms have views as good as any, but be prepared for street noise. Music in the hotel's Conservatory Bar and Restaurant is a neighborhood favorite. *15 Central Park W., 10023, tel. 212/265–0060 or 800/223–4164, fax 212/265–5098. Gen. manager, Michael Fenn. 190 rooms, 410 suites. AE, CB, D, DC, MC, V.*

❼ Regency. The exclusive and residential Park Avenue ad-
$$$$ dress may explain why Dustin Hoffman and Frank Sinatra—as well as many wealthy South Americans—are frequent guests. All the amenities, and most of the luxuries, are here (an executive favorite: telephones are placed on desks as well as on nightstands). The restaurant, "540 Park," is famed for power breakfasts, and the rooms, recently restored, combine modern baths with reproductions of 18th-century furniture. But the Regency doesn't have the grandeur to justify its price, and it's a bit too stuffy to qualify as intimate. Though it bills itself as "residential," music from weddings in the hotel ballroom is audible in the lobby. *Loews Hotels. 540 Park Ave., 10021, tel. 212/759–4100 or 800/243–1166, fax 212/826–5674. Gen. manager, John Beier. 320 rooms, 70 suites. AE, DC, MC, V.*

★ **❽** **Sherry Netherland.** Considering its Old New York reputa-
$$$ tion, its Fifth Avenue location, and its air of elegance, this
vintage 1927 hotel offers surprising value. Its chief attri-
butes are the spacious, traditional rooms—try for one
with a Central Park view—the quiet, subdued tone, and a
staff that prides itself on knowing its guests. (The bell
captain has been on the job for more than 30 years.) CEOs,
Hollywood celebrities, and fashion moguls are among the
clientele, and many come for long stays. A room renova-
tion is on-going, but some guests say it isn't necessary.
The wooden, hand-painted elevator is a gem. *781 Fifth
Ave., 10022, tel. 212/355–2800 or 800/223–0522, fax 212/
319–4306. Gen. manager, Louis Ventresca. 98 rooms, 25
suites. AE.*

❷ **Westbury.** With a restaurant called The Polo, this hotel in
$$$$ the heart of New York's gallery district is perfect for the
prep school set. And with socialites, diplomats, foreign
dignitaries, and camera-shy celebrities heading the guest
list, is it any wonder the lobby is a tad stiff? Thanks to the
staff's policy of catering to guests' whims, the hotel has a
high ratio of regular customers. The understated elegance
of the rooms, recently renovated in English manor house
style, should appeal to business travelers, as should their
noiselessness. The Westbury's rates are as exclusive as its
ambience. *Trusthouse Forte Hotels. 15 E. 69th St., 10021,
tel. 212/535–2000 or 800/225–5843, fax 212/535–5058.
Gen. manager, Stefan Simkovics. 180 rooms, 55 suites.
AE, CB, DC, MC, V.*

Airport

$$ **JFK Plaza Hotel.** This contemporary-style, 12-story hotel, a 5- to 10-minute drive from the terminals at John F.
Kennedy International airport, is out of the flight path of
most of the airport's traffic. Guests on the concierge level
get free Continental breakfasts and hors d'oeuvres; general amenities include a weight room. *Heller-White Hotels. 135–30 140th St., 11436, tel. 718/659–6000 or 800/
445–7177, fax 718/659–4755. Gen. manager, Bill McGlad-
dery. 349 rooms, 21 suites. AE, CB, D, DC, MC, V.*

$$$ **LaGuardia Marriott Airport Hotel.** A quarter-mile from
the airport and—barring traffic—within 20 minutes of
Manhattan, this 1981 hotel is out of the direct line of most
of the flights. A concierge floor with a bar and free Conti-
nental breakfasts recently opened. *102–05 Ditmars
Blvd., East Elmhurst, 11369, tel. 718/565–8900 or 800/
228–9290, fax 718/899–0764. Gen. manager, William
Archard. 432 rooms, 5 suites. AE, CB, D, DC, MC, V.*

$$ **Vista International.** Opened in 1988, the Vista is five minutes from Newark airport and 20 minutes, in light traffic,
from Manhattan. Triple-glazed glass doors keep airport
noise to a minimum. The hotel caters to businesspeople,
but guests who need to go into Manhattan should bear in
mind that traffic in the Jersey–New York tunnels can be
especially slow (in both directions) at rush hours and at
various other unpredictable times. *A Hilton International hotel. 1170 Spring St., Elizabeth, NJ, 07201, tel. 201/
351–3900 or 800/678–4782, fax 201/355–8059. Gen. manager, Cindy Estis. 370 rooms, 6 suites. AE, CB, D, DC,
MC, V.*

DINING

by Elaine Hamilton

The restaurant scene in New York, like the city itself, is constantly changing as new places open and close, new cuisines come and go, and chefs hop around from one kitchen to another. Along with "spa" cuisine and Northern Italian food, bistro cooking has become the current craze. Even if no one knows what next year will bring, one thing is certain: there are few places in the world where one can eat as well as in New York City. In the past decade, many top French and Italian chefs have moved here, and their influence has spread throughout the city's better restaurants. Many of the top hotels have upgraded their eateries—some of the best food in town is now to be found in hotel dining rooms. At the same time, the quality of the produce available has improved dramatically. There has never been such a variety of fresh ingredients for the chef to choose from.

The following guide lists restaurants that are congenial either to business discussion or entertaining. It includes well-known and less-discovered places. In addition, after the reviews is a listing of some of the best or most unusual ethnic restaurants the city has to offer. Although most are not appropriate for business meals, they help represent what makes dining in New York a unique experience.

Highly recommended restaurants in each of these categories are indicated by a star ★.

Category	Cost*
$$$$ (Very Expensive)	over $55
$$$ (Expensive)	$38–$55
$$ (Moderate)	under $38

per person, including appetizer, entrée, and dessert, but excluding drinks, service, and 8¼% sales tax.

Numbers in the margin correspond to numbered restaurant locations on the New York Lodging and Dining maps.

Business Breakfasts

Many of the city's top hotels also serve the now legendary "power breakfast." **Café Pierre** in the Hotel Pierre (2 E. 61st St., tel. 212/940–8185) has a dining room in the grand style of the '30s and '40s and serves a business breakfast that includes chipped beef and (for the health conscious) Egg Beaters. **The Carlyle Restaurant** (Carlyle Hotel, tel. 212/744–1600) presents a top-notch breakfast buffet in an elegant, classic Georgian-style setting. **The Regency** (Regency Hotel, tel. 212/749–4200) is the place where the power breakfast originated. On any weekday morning you can find the city's business leaders wheeling and dealing here over kippers and eggs.

Midtown

⓲ **Adrienne.** International business travelers, many from
$$$$ the Far East, congregate in this second-floor dining room of the Hotel Peninsula. Comfortable chairs, thick carpets,

and a low noise level make this a good place for serious business talk, although the Art Nouveau decor is uninspired and the atmosphere just slightly stuffy. The food, however, is first-rate. The chef, Gray Kunz, a young Swiss protégé of master chef Fredy Girardet, is unquestionably a rising star; his cooking is a fascinating blend of East and West (he worked for a while in Hong Kong). Some of his dishes are dazzling, especially those featuring fish, such as snapper with curry and cardamom, or steamed sole. The cheese tray is exceptional and the wine list excellent. *Peninsula Hotel, 700 Fifth Ave. at 55th St., tel. 212/903-3918. Jacket and tie required. Reservations advised. AE, CB, DC, MC, V. Closed Sun. dinner.*

②⓪ **Aquavit.** Aquavit offers the best and most sophisticated
$$$ Scandinavian food New York City has seen for years. Christer Larsson, a Swedish-born chef who trained in restaurants and hotels in Europe, does wonders with such exotic specialties as juniper-smoked salmon, moose, Arctic venison, snow grouse, and cloudberries. You walk into a sleek café that serves inexpensive light meals and Danish open-face sandwiches; in the handsome formal dining room beneath it, a seven-story atrium between two townhouses, the leaves of silver birch trees rustle as endless sheets of water pour down a gray tiled wall. In addition to the extensive wine list, there is a choice of seven kinds of beer and eight kinds of aquavit. *13 W. 54th St., tel. 212/307-7311. Jackets required downstairs, no dress code upstairs. Reservations suggested downstairs, not accepted upstairs. AE, MC, V. Closed Sun.*

③④ **Aurora.** At lunchtime Joseph Baum's restaurant resem-
$$$$ bles a corporate dining room, so packed is it with business-people. Sometimes it can be hard to get reservations, as this has become one of the city's major business lunch places. Comfortable leather chairs, tables placed far apart, wood paneling, and a soothing pink glow make this a relaxed spot for a serious discussion. A special grill menu is served at the long horseshoe-shaped bar. Chef Andrew Wilkinson produces classic but innovative French food. Try ravioli with sea scallops, oysters on the half shell with spicy veal sausage, roast pigeon with garlic sauce, salmon in a horseradish crust, and, for dessert, saffron ice cream and warm chocolate mousse cake. Service is professional and unobtrusive. *60 E. 49th St., tel. 212/692-9292. Jacket and tie required. Reservations advised. AE, CB, DC, MC, V. Closed Sun.*

②④ **The Four Seasons.** No other restaurant in New York serves
$$$$ up quite such a big-league lunch as the Four Seasons in the Seagram's Building. Every working day in the Grill Room, a no-nonsense masculine setting of leather and wood, with enormous hanging brass rod sculptures by Richard Lippold, the big guns in publishing, finance, and politics make deals over small bottles of Seagram's soda water and spa cuisine. At night, the Pool Room with its gurgling waters and tubs of ficus trees caters to out-of-town businesspeople. Chef Christian Albin is skilled and inventive (especially with game, polenta, and terrines) but not all the dishes are a success. Try frog's legs in flaky pastry, fettucine primavera, roast pigeon, and any of the desserts. Service can be offhand and if you are unknown you may be seated in "Siberia"—upstairs in the back. Private rooms accommodate 10–22 people. *99 E.*

52nd St., tel. 212/754–9494. Jacket and tie required. Reservations advised. AE, DC, MC, V. Closed Sun. and major holidays.

⑭
$$$$
La Caravelle. With its lipstick-red banquettes and postwar murals of Paris, this restaurant is a throwback to the 1950s; you could picture the Duke and Duchess of Windsor walking in at any minute. Bright and elegant, this is a good setting for business or post-business pleasure at lunch as well as dinner. Chef Frank Chanpli produces exciting variations on classic French themes. Try the fresh foie gras, roast duck with cranberries, crab ravioli, and such exceptional desserts as chocolate Charlotte or apple tart from the trolley. The impeccable service is of the old school, with dishes prepared at tableside. *33 W. 55th St., tel. 212/586–4252. Jacket and tie required. Reservations advised. AE, CB, DC, MC, V. Closed Sun. and major holidays.*

⑮
$$$$
La Côte Basque. The noise and table hopping can be distracting for serious business, but this restaurant also turns out superb classic French cooking. Pretty murals of the French coast, red banquettes, and a chic clientele lend a touch of glamour. You can feel a bit out of things, though, if you are seated in the newer dining room to the left—and indeed, customers not known to the management are often placed here. Tables in front of the bar, as you walk in, are quieter than those in the main dining room. Jean-Jacques Rachoux now looks after the customers and staff, while Michel Fitoussi oversees the kitchen. The food is elaborate, intensely flavored, and highly decorated with two-tone sauces painted with fanciful designs. Particularly recommended are the charcuterie, pâtés and terrines, roast duck, rack of lamb, and cassoulet Toulousain. Fresh berries and hot soufflés are the best desserts. *5 E. 55th St., tel. 212/688–6525. Jacket and tie required. Reservations advised. AE, CB, D, MC, V. Closed Sun. and major holidays.*

⑬
$$$$
Lafayette. The Swiss-owned Drake Hotel's plush, quiet dining room is a little bland and dowdy, but the food—French with Mediterranean and Southeast Asian influences—is not. The menu is overseen by Louis Outhier, who had a three-star restaurant in the French Riviera, and his protégé, Jean-Georges Vongerichten, who trained at L'Auberge de L'Ill in Alsace. Among the stellar choices are sweetbreads with foie gras, whole sea bass in pastry crust, baby goat with chick peas, and chocolate soufflé gratin. Lafayette now serves a special three-course lunch for hurried businesspeople and guarantees to get you out within half an hour. *Drake Hotel, 65 E. 56th St., tel. 212/ 832–1565. Jacket and tie required. Reservations advised. AE, CB, D, MC, V. Closed Aug.*

★ ㉝
$$$$
La Reserve. Without fanfare, La Reserve has taken its place among the city's best French restaurants. The cooking is classically based but with a light touch. The restaurant's two dining rooms are large, quiet, and comfortable, with enormous chandeliers, beige-and-peach banquettes, and chairs generously proportioned to accommodate those accustomed to a steady diet of rich French food. Owner Jean-Louis Missud is a conservationist, and named his restaurant after the wetlands reserve on the New Jersey shore overlooking Manhattan, pictured in huge murals in the first room. Some good choices are a jellied crayfish

consommé, bavarois of smoked salmon topped with red caviar, grilled quail in hazelnut vinaigrette, and lamb noisettes with green peppercorns. Save room for dessert. *4 W. 49th St., tel. 212/247-2993. Jacket and tie required. Reservations advised. AE, CB, DC, MC, V. Closed Sun.*

㉗ **Le Bernardin.** This French fish restaurant on the ground
$$$$ floor of the Equitable building is both luxurious and clubby, with high teak ceilings and dark blue walls decorated with large oil paintings of fishermen. Tables are well spaced, making this an ideal spot for private conversations—and indeed, virtually all the clientele look to be here on business. The fish is as fresh as you'll get anywhere, and chef Gilbert LeCoze's food can be dazzling, even if inconsistent. Among the more arresting preparations are a carpaccio of tuna, oysters cooked with truffles and served on seaweed, and salmon dishes such as gravlax potato salad or roulade of salmon, stuffed with spinach. Finish off with a caramel sampler, which includes caramel ice cream, crème caramel, oeuf à la neige, and caramel mousse. *155 W. 51st St., tel. 212/489-1515. Jacket and tie required. Reservations advised well in advance. AE, CB, V. Closed Sun.*

★ ❹ **Le Cirque.** This is less a restaurant in which to do business
$$$$ than a place to celebrate after a deal has been made. It's boisterous, noisy, amusing, and filled with celebrities and society types blowing kisses across the crowded dining room. Owner Sirio Maccioni is a New York legend and a master at making it all work. The classic French food prepared by the young Burgundian chef, Daniel Boulud, is nothing short of great—and the menu is vast. Try the scallops with black truffles (listed as "sea scallops fantasy in black tie"), sautéed fresh foie gras, pot au feu, or roast chicken with lemon garlic and herbs. The crème brûlée is justifiably renowned. The wine list is one of the city's best, with many good choices at reasonable prices. *58 E. 65th St., in the Mayfair-Regent Hotel, tel. 212/794-9292. Jacket and tie required. Reservations advised well in advance. AE, CB, DC. Closed Sun., major holidays, and first 3 weeks of July.*

㉑ **Le Cygne.** Despite handsome new quarters, this restau-
$$$$ rant went into decline for a few years until the arrival of chef Jean Michel Bergougnoux, who formerly worked at Lutèce. Now the pretty pastel dining rooms (on two floors of a townhouse) are a fitting backdrop to the fine French cuisine being produced here. A dual winding staircase leads to the upper level, which has arched ceilings and opaque glass panels; the downstairs is decorated with bright murals of wildflowers. Parties of more than four should request upstairs seating—tables are larger and more widely spaced. On both floors the noise level is low and the service first-rate. Among the many excellent entrées are bouillabaisse, breast of chicken with leeks and truffles, and fettuccine with wild mushrooms; top the evening off with a cassis delight. *55 E. 54th St., tel. 212/759-5941. Jacket and tie required. Reservations advised. AE, DC, MC, V. Closed Sun., major holidays, and 3 weeks in Aug.*

★ ㉘ **Lutèce.** Also on two floors of a townhouse, with a garden
$$$$ room in back, Lutèce is one of New York's best French restaurants, but you may have to wait a month for a reservation. André Soltner is a dedicated chef whose classic

French and Alsatian dishes make the wait worthwhile.
(He also consistently tours the dining room to make suggestions and check on the meal; if he makes a recommendation, follow it.) People are often surprised at the
informality of Lutèce—it doesn't have the stiffness of
many haute cuisine establishments. In some ways it sees
itself as a high-class bistro—and the customers who come
here tend to be passionate about food. Try the Alsatian onion tart, choucroute garni, roast pheasant or venison,
chicken sauté au Riesling, or tarte tatin. The prix fixe
lunch is a very good value. *249 E. 50th St., tel. 212/752–
2225. Jacket and tie required. Reservations advised well
in advance. AE, DC, CB. Closed Sun., Mon. lunch, Sat.
in June and July, all major holidays, and Aug.–Labor
Day weekend.*

⑰ **Michael's.** Chef Michael McCarty recently brought his
$$$ brand of California cuisine from Santa Monica to New
York. The large dining rooms are hung with lithographs
by Jasper Johns, Frank Stella, and David Hockney, and
bas-reliefs by Robert Graham. During the day, the res-
taurant is bright and cheerful, with a view onto the street,
and, in the back, a skylight and courtyard gardens. De-
spite a menu that spells out the life-history of each ingre-
dient, much of the food at Michael's is superior. Try the
Malpèque oysters, gravlax with mustard dill sauce and
brioche toast, lobster salad, grilled rabbit in mustard
cream sauce, or grilled saddle of lamb with red wine,
blackcurrants, and thyme. Michael's has a particularly im-
pressive wine list with many unusual choices from small
California vineyards at reasonable prices. *24 W. 55th St.,
tel. 212/753–7295. Casual dress. Reservations advised.
AE, DC, CB, MC, V.*

㊷ **Park Bistro.** If you are doing business near or around low-
$$ er Park Avenue, this is a good place for a casual lunch.
Publishers and magazine editors congregate here for su-
perior Provençal cooking at reasonable prices. The restaurant feels like an authentic old-style bistro, complete
with French film posters, lace curtains, leather banquettes, and a bustling, glassed-in kitchen at the back.
Jean-Michel Diot's dishes are redolent of the Mediterranean, infused with garlic, olive oil, and fresh herbs, plus
out-of-the-ordinary seasonings, such as whole baby onions, fennel, and salsify. Try cold shellfish soup, codfish
(cabillaud) with fried leeks and mashed potatoes, leg of
lamb with flageolets, and roasted rabbit. The short wine
list (on the back of the menu) is reasonably priced and interesting, with some good selections from Provence. *414
Park Ave., tel. 212/689–1360. Casual dress. Reservations
advised. AE, DC. Closed Sun. and Sat. lunch.*

★ ⑯ **The Quilted Giraffe.** The most expensive restaurant in
$$$$ New York—usually filled with rich foreign businessmen—The Quilted Giraffe is also one of the most impressive both in decor and cuisine. The dramatic new quarters
in the AT&T building on Madison Avenue at 55th Street
feature stainless steel walls, gray leather banquettes, and
speckled granite floors; lavish flower arrangements add
color and warmth. Chef Barry Wine turns out food that is
out of the ordinary and unforgettable. Among the delights
are beggar's purses (tiny crêpes filled with caviar and
crème fraiche), home-smoked salmon, confit of duck, and
rack of lamb with Chinese mustard. Some desserts worth

the calories are pecan squares and chocolate soufflé with espresso ice cream. *550 Madison Ave., tel. 212/593–1221. Jacket and tie required. Reservations advised well in advance. AE, MC, V. Closed Sun., lunch.*

㉙ **The Rainbow Room.** The famous 1930s supper club has un-
$$$$ dergone extensive renovations under the supervision of restaurateur Joseph Baum and designer Milton Glaser. Now, complete with revolving dance floor, seating on three levels, silk walls, and giant bandstand, it brings back a more glamorous era. It's an experience not to be missed—a great place to celebrate a business deal. The room itself, with one of the most magnificent views in Manhattan, is a stunning example of Art Moderne. In addition to contemporary French fare, much of the menu is deliberately retro—some of the dishes, such as lobster thermidor, tournedos Rossini, and oysters Rockefeller, date back to the 1930s and '40s. For a finishing touch you can order a baked Alaska flambé. *30 Rockefeller Plaza, tel. 212/632–5100. Jacket and tie required. Reservations advised several weeks in advance. AE. Dinner only; closed Mon.*

⑲ **Restaurant Raphael.** A quiet spot in bustling midtown,
$$$$ this intimate, demure townhouse is understandably popular with French business visitors. With its fireplace and outdoor garden (where you can dine in the summer), it fits everyone's image of the quintessential Parisian dining room. A new chef, Kurt Beverly, has taken over the kitchen, but to date, this restaurant, supervised by owners Mira and Raphael Edery, has consistently produced classic French cooking at its best. Among the commendable choices on the current menu are wild mushroom flan, grilled jumbo shrimp, roast loin of lamb with ratatouille purée, Gascogny-style duck breast with celery root and apple, and, to finish, chocolate soufflé with crème anglaise or apple tart in a thin pastry shell. Service is impeccable but the wine list, while offering many French vintages to go with the food, is predictable. *33 W. 54th St., tel. 212/ 582–8993. Jacket and tie required. Reservations advised. AE, CB, DC, MC, V. Closed Sun., Sat. from Memorial to Labor Day.*

⑨ **San Domenico.** New York's most expensive Italian restau-
$$$$ rant caters to lawyers, businesspeople, wealthy Europeans, and followers of fashion. The large, comfortable dining rooms have terra cotta floors, ocher-tinted walls, and lots of marble and leather. Chefs Paul Bartolotta and Valentino Marcatulii produce refined Northern Italian cuisine—plus "spa" dishes at lunchtime for those watching their waistlines. Pasta dishes are superior (especially seafood ravioli); also recommended are the sautéed goose liver with fried onions, rabbit in a casserole with grilled polenta, and roast squab with borlotti beans. The wine list is extensive and offers many unusual and interesting Italian vintages—but also complements the food in price. *240 Central Park S., tel. 212/265–5959. Jacket and tie required. Reservations advised. AE, CB, DC, MC, V. Closed Sun., Sat. lunch.*

③ **Sign of the Dove.** After years of serving appalling food at
$$$ outrageous prices to an audience largely from out of town, this restaurant, with the help of consultant Clark Wolf and chef Andrew D'Amico, has finally become one of the city's most exciting spots. The rooms are elegant and romantic,

separated by brick arches and decorated with beautiful flower arrangements; the lighting is soft and flattering, and an attractive piano bar near the entrance is a nice spot for cocktails. Tables are well spaced for conversation but service can be slow; be prepared to linger over your meal. The food is French/American with oriental influences. Try, according to season, ravioli stuffed with duck confit and mushrooms, homemade pastas, or venison with polenta. Desserts, especially crème brûlée, are also excellent, and the wine list superior, with reasonable prices. *1110 Third Ave., tel. 212/861–8080. Jacket required. Reservations advised. AE, CB, DC, MC, V. Closed Mon. lunch.*

Lower Manhattan

45 **Alison on Dominick Street.** Alison Price took a chance
$$ when she opened this discreet, attractive restaurant in a landmark townhouse tucked away on a downtown side street, but it quickly became a hit, especially among downtown artists and Wall Street executives. Now it is hard to get a table here at peak hours without a week's notice. Dark-blue velvet curtains, cream colored walls, and framed photographs create a pleasant, understated ambience. Customers whose local hangout is Lutèce find no cause to complain about the food here: Chef Thomas Valenti's cooking, with its Provençal overtones, is creative, boldly seasoned, and flavorful. Try roast guinea hen with wild mushroom risotto, pan-seared breast of Muscovy duck, lamb shank with fava and white beans, bread pudding, or pear and walnut tart. *38 Dominick St., between Hudson and Varick, tel. 212/727–1188. Casual dress. Reservations advised. AE, CB, DC, MC, V. Closed Sun. and major holidays.*

47 **Arqua.** Light Italian cooking is served here in a soaring
$$ dining room with mottled amber-ocher walls that could be in a palazzo in Venice. The contrast between the huge space and the stark decor of this restaurant has been much imitated all over the city. Some of the customers come straight from their Wall Street offices, briefcases in hand, after work. Come for lunch if a quiet discussion is what's on the agenda. The small menu (in Italian only) focuses on Venetian dishes: fresh pasta, risotto, polenta, seafood. The food can be superb, but it's uneven; first courses and pastas are the best. The carpaccio, radicchio with melted cheese, homemade pastas (especially papardelle with sausage and radicchio), and the cheesecake with lemon and raspberry sauces are all highly recommended. *281 Church St. at White St., tel. 212/334–1888. Casual dress. Reservations advised. AE. Closed Sun.*

49 **Bouley.** The beautiful formal dining room here is reminis-
$$$$ cent of that in a top French country hotel, with high arched ceilings, flattering lighting, and Impressionist landscapes. Even though the tables are well spaced, the room can get noisy at night, and service can be distracted—all of which does not deter the Wall Street crowd that frequents the place. David Bouley, a young American chef, serves New American cuisine that is often brilliant but at times erratic. His best dishes are game and fish. Among the top choices are guinea hen in port wine sauce, pigeon with savoy cabbage and grilled foie gras, roasted halibut with rosemary oil, monkfish with garlic, bacon, and cabbage, and for dessert, bitter chocolate sorbet. The

wine list is excellent, with many unusual choices. *165 Duane St. between Hudson and Greenwich Sts., tel. 212/ 608–3852. Jacket and tie required. Reservations advised. AE, CB, DC, MC, V. Closed Sun.*

48
$$$$
Chanterelle. This austere French restaurant in a soaring post-modern dining room is a perfect spot for business—and given the location, it predictably attracts a Wall Street clientele (as well as many Japanese business travelers). The effect here is grandeur mixed with functionalism. The starkness of the decor is alleviated by magnificent, immense flower arrangements. Chef David Waltuck turns out some inspired creations of New American cuisine, although there are some misfires. Among the recommended choices are the grilled seafood sausage, seared foie gras, or rack of lamb with thyme and mustard; for finishers, there's a superior cheeseboard, lemon tart with blackberry coulis, or chocolate mille feuille with coffee sauce. The wine is interesting but exorbitant, and the sommelier is extremely helpful. *2 Harrison St. at Hudson St., tel. 212/966–6960. Jacket and tie required. Reservations advised. AE, CB, D, DC, MC, V. Dinner only; closed Sun., Mon., major holidays, first week of Jan., and July.*

50
$$
Duane Park Café. Two Japanese chefs with backgrounds in Cajun, Italian, and American food have opened a restaurant that serves another new style of cooking: Northern Italian and American regional with a dash of Japanese and French. Dishes are grounded in the classics but are at the same time esoteric and subtle; the oriental touch comes in the seasonings. The modern brown-and-black dining room is comfortable, quiet, and attractive in an understated way. A well-heeled art crowd, plus business people from Wall Street, are the usual customers. The wine list is short but reasonably priced (wine tastings are held here in the early evening during the week). For entrées, the crisp-skinned roast mackerel, risotto with shrimp, mussels and scallops, skate wings with ponzu sauce (a Japanese vinegar), and duck with balsamic vinegar are all commendable; pear hazelnut tart with raspberry coulis is a good dessert choice. *157 Duane St., tel. 212/ 732–5555. Casual dress. Reservations advised. AE, CB, DC, MC, V. Closed Sat. lunch, Sun.*

★ 46
$$$
Montrachet. Among the New Wave of downtown restaurants with spare interiors and a reverential focus on the food, Montrachet is the least stiff, and attracts a following both from midtown and downtown business communities. Prices are lower than at comparable restaurants, and the prix-fixe menus are a real bargain. The setting is vaguely post-modern—a softly-lit converted industrial space with light-green walls, rust-colored banquettes, and a small, attractive bar. Chef Debra Ponzek's style has evolved from a modern French tradition. Her cooking is exceptional: bold and innovative, with clever combinations that work, such as salmon with lentils and red wine, or baby pheasant with orzo and olives. The distinguished wine list has interesting selections at all prices. *239 W. Brdwy. at White St., tel. 212/219–2777. Casual dress. Reservations advised. AE. Dinner only except Fri. when lunch is served. Closed Sun.*

51
$$
The Odeon. After nearly a decade, the Odeon has evolved into a genuine bistro, and it is extremely popular both

with Wall Street executives and local artists. The occasional limousine purrs outside the door, but prices are reasonable and the restaurant has become the sort of place people can drop in casually without a reservation on slow nights and expect to get a table before they've finished their second drink at the bar. The decor is simple, comfortable and attractive, a former 1930s working man's cafeteria updated to serve the new breed of workers in the area. Chef Stephen Lyle turns out good, straightforward but updated bistro specialties, among them squid in cornmeal with red-pepper garlic mayonnaise, grilled salmon, and steak frites; some light finishers are a pucker-inducing lemon tart or fruit sorbets. *145 West Broadway at Thomas St., tel. 212/233-0507. Casual dress. Reservations advised. AE, CB, DC, MC, V.*

★ ❹❹ **Union Square Café.** Book publishers have made this their
$$ downtown club at lunchtime, perhaps because the eclectic menu, with a Northern Italian flair, is good and reasonably priced. Of the three informal dining rooms, decorated with splashy paintings or murals, the most comfortable is the main one a few steps down in front of the bar. The signature of the cooking here is freshness. Try risotto made with fried sage leaves, spinach, and prosciutto; green gnocchi in a yellow tomato sauce topped with melted cheese; palliard of lamb; or fried calamari with anchovy mayonnaise. Also recommended are the oysters—different kinds are on the menu, fresh daily—and the generous hamburgers. The wine list is distinguished. *21 E. 16th St., tel. 212/243-4020. Casual dress. Reservations advised. AE, MC, V. Closed Sun.*

❺❸ **Windows on the World.** Don't come here for the food; the
$$$$ view makes better eating. Stick to plain dishes such as oysters on the half shell, marinated salmon with cucumber and yogurt sauce, rack of lamb, and lemon tart. The view and the wine list, however, are unbeatable, and if the former doesn't distract too much from the conversation, this is an impressive spot for a business dinner (for lunch during the workday week the restaurant is a private club; there is a surcharge for nonmembers). The large rose, cream, and beige dining room is reminiscent of that in an ocean liner—it's built on tiers with brass railings so all the tables get a view. In keeping with the nautical motif, members of the staff wear white uniforms with gold epaulettes; in addition, they're extremely helpful, especially when you are trying to make your way through the remarkable wine list. (For oenophiles, there is another restaurant here, Cellar in the Sky, which lacks a view but specializes in matching wines with a special four- or five-course menu.) *One World Trade Center, 107th floor, tel. 212/938-1111. Jacket and tie required. Reservations required. AE, CB, DC, MC, V.*

Ethnic

Chinese
There are Chinese restaurants on almost every block of the city, some better than others, but almost all offer a great variety of dishes. Chinatown is, of course, a prime source for an authentic meal. Three recommended Chinatown restaurants are **The Oriental Pearl Restaurant** (103 Mott St., tel. 212/219-8388); the **Nice Restaurant** (35 E. Broadway, tel. 212/406-9510) for dim sum; and the **Silver**

Palace (50 Bowery, tel. 212/964–1204). Uptown, near Lincoln Center, **Shun Lee West** (43 W. 65th St., tel. 212/595–8895) provides an elegant preconcert meal, with the **Shun Lee Café** right next door for a more casual, dim sum experience.

Japanese

Some good Japanese restaurants are **The Tatany Restaurant** (388 Third Ave., tel. 212/686–1871) and **Tatany Village** (62 Greenwich Ave., tel. 212/675–6195); **Japonica** (90 University Pl., tel. 212/243–7752) has some of the freshest sushi in the city.

Delicatessans

Carnegie Restaurant & Delicatessan (854 Seventh Ave., between 54th and 55th Sts., tel. 212/757–2245) is a classic place to indulge in New York deli "cuisine"; for the scene and the hot dogs, try **Katz's** (205 E. Houston St., tel. 212/254–2246); also for the experience, **Sammy's Famous Roumanian** (157 Chrystie St., tel. 212/673–5526); and for kosher rather than kosher-style there's the **Second Avenue Delicatessan** (156 Second Ave., tel. 212/677–0606).

Indian

Good, inexpensive Indian restaurants abound on Sixth Street between First and Second avenues. If you don't mind roughing it (in most places you bring your own alcohol), it's well worth the trip. On that block **Passage to India** (308 E. Sixth St., tel. 212/529–5770), one of the few places with a liquor license, is good; uptown, the chef at **Dawat** (210 E. 58th St., tel. 212/355–7555) was advised by the cookbook author and chef Madhur Jaffrey; and **Akbar** (475 Park Ave., tel. 212/838–1717) has a staff that is particularly friendly.

Others

Periyali (35 W. 20th St., tel. 212/463–7890) serves good Greek food and attracts a publishing crowd. **Teresa Coffee Shop and Restaurant** (103 First Ave., tel. 212/228–0604), casual and inexpensive, offers hearty authentic Polish fare. **Sun Lee Oak** (77 W. 46th St., tel. 212/869–9958) lets you barbecue Korean-style at the table. For spicy Thai cuisine, **Tommy Tang's** (323 Greenwich Ave., tel. 212/334–9190) is a good pick. **Zarela's** (953 Second Ave., tel. 212/644–6740) serves out-of-the-ordinary Mexican food in a relaxed atmosphere. For a Brazilian meal in a lively, fun setting, try **Cabana Carioca** (123 W. 45th St., tel. 212/581–8008; and 133 W. 45th St., tel. 212/730–8375).

FREE TIME

Fitness

Hotel Facilities

Hotel health clubs in New York generally are open only to hotel guests and regular members, but several independent health clubs accept guests on a walk-in, one-day basis.

Health Clubs

Battery Park Fitness (375 South End Ave., tel. 212/321–1117) has a 50-foot pool, aerobics, free weights, Nautilus, Jacuzzi, rowing machines, treadmills, and stationary cycles. A one-day pass is $26. **ABC Health Spa** (500 E. 83rd

St., tel. 212/772–8760) has a 44-foot pool, sauna, steam, Jacuzzi, weights, and stationary cycles. Daily cost: $12.50. The **Vanderbilt YMCA** (224 E. 47th St., tel. 212/ 755–2410) and the **West Side YMCA** (5 W. 63rd St., tel. 212/ 787–4400) have 75-foot pools. The Vanderbilt branch has aerobics, Nautilus, free weights, and an indoor track and gym. Daily cost: $10. The West Side branch has weights, Nautilus, rowing machines, an indoor track, stationary cycles, racquetball, and squash. Daily cost: $12.

Jogging
The best, by far, is the 1½-mile reservoir track and 6-mile roadway in **Central Park,** a pastoral setting enlivened by views of the skyline. During the day the park fairly swarms with runners and cyclists; still, side roads or paths should be avoided. If you must run after dark, don't go alone, and stay south of 96th Street (women especially should never run alone at night). On the west side, **Riverside Park,** from 72nd to 96th streets is also popular and offers Hudson River views. On the east side, joggers can run through **Carl Schurz Park** from 90th to 84th streets and then follow the East River walkway to the United Nations, but the ambience is marred by the East River Drive expressway.

Shopping

In New York, unlike in most American cities, shopping has yet to become dependent on the automobile. New Yorkers shop wherever they walk, and they walk just about anywhere. One of the most quintessentially New York stores is **Zabar's** (2245 Broadway, tel. 212/787–2000), a temple of hanging sausages and coffee beans from around the world where the act of buying gourmet foods and housewares is transformed into an almost religious experience. A toy store that is similarly connected to the Manhattan zeitgeist—and where the looking is almost as much fun as the buying—is **F.A.O. Schwarz** (767 Fifth Ave., tel. 212/644–9400). **Mythology Unlimited** (370 Columbus Ave.) has a funky array of antique toys, alligator rafts, Mexican art, cookie jars, etc. The **Metropolitan Museum gift shop** (82nd St. and Fifth Ave., tel. 212/570–3726) has prints, date books, jewelry, neckties, scarves, and other gifts based on reproductions from the museum collection. **47th St. Photo** (67 W. 47th St.; 115 W. 45th St., both at tel. 212/398–1410; or downtown on 116 Nassau St., tel. 212/732–3370) has the last word in watches, electronics, computers, radios and yes, even camera equipment and supplies, at low prices.

Macy's, the world's biggest store (Sixth Ave. and 34th St., tel. 212/695–4400), is one of New York's best for clothing, housewares, and linens. **Bloomingdale's** is its uptown rival (59th St. and Lexington Ave., tel. 212/725–2000). **Barney's New York** (106 Seventh Ave. at 17th St., tel. 212/ 929–9000) is one of the city's most popular stores for its wide and well-chosen selection of men's suits and women's wear. **Paul Stuart** (45th St. and Madison Ave., tel. 212/ 682–0320) is very exclusive and has a superb array of men's wear and a smaller, though equally smart, selection of women's clothes. **Henri Bendel** (10 W. 57th St., tel. 212/ 247–1100) is an upscale favorite of women executives.

The toniest **jewelry stores** are on **Fifth Avenue** between 42nd and 59th streets. Cheaper prices can be found in the diamond district, on **West 47th Street** between Fifth and Sixth avenues, but be prepared to haggle with the local merchants.

Diversions

For a wonderful walk, just slightly off the beaten path, cross the **Brooklyn Bridge.** Supported by a spider web of cables, the bridge, completed in 1883, has a drama and beauty matched by few; the same may be said for its views of the lower Manhattan skyline.

Central Park, designed by Frederick Law Olmstead and Calvert Vaux, keeps 843 acres of New York out of the mitts of real estate developers. Its woodlands and open knolls look much as they might have before the arrival of Dutch settlers. Contemporary natives use it as a giant backyard for cycling, jogging, walking, softball, concerts, and people-watching. The renovated zoo is beautifully landscaped.

Circle Line (42nd St. & 12th Ave., tel. 212/563–3200) **cruises around Manhattan Island** in three hours. Those pressed for time might prefer the lesser known Seaport Line (Pier 16, at Fulton and South Sts., tel. 212/669–9400), which tours the southern end of the island and returns in only 90 minutes. Both are open March–Nov.

Fifth Avenue is the main drag for elegant and pricey window shopping. Good destinations are **Rockefeller Center** (48th to 52nd Sts.), with its statue of Atlas, shopping, and wintertime skating, and **St. Patrick's Cathedral** (50th to 51st Sts.), an arched, granite, French Gothic structure dating to 1879.

If you don't mind heights, **New York's best views** are from the Observation Deck of Two World Trade Center (tel. 212/466–7377), and from the Observatory of the Empire State building (350 Fifth Ave., between 33rd and 34th Sts., tel. 212/736–3100).

Madison Avenue from 50th to 86th streets is lined with galleries, shops, boutiques, and coffee shops.

Metropolitan Museum of Art (82nd St. and Fifth Ave., tel. 212/535–7710) runs the gamut from the ancient Near East, Egypt, and the Orient to contemporary European and American styles. But it's the daunting collection of European Old Masters, à la Rembrandt and Raphael, that makes this one of the world's great museums.

Museum of Modern Art (11 W. 53rd St., tel. 212/708–9480) is notable for Picasso's *Desmoiselles d'Avignon*, perhaps the landmark work of cubism, and Monet's soothing *Water Lilies.* Picasso's *Pregnant Goat*, a hauntingly realistic sculpture, is itself worth the price of admission.

Neighborhoods in New York are too numerous to name. One good one is SoHo, a collection of small streets between Houston and Canal where browsers will find a wealth of art galleries, as well as fashions, merchandise, and cafés with an artsy tone. Another one worth visiting, just a bit to the east and teeming with restaurants, is Chinatown. For an endless choice of cafés and small artsy shops, visit Greenwich Village between 10th and Houston streets and from Broadway to the Hudson River.

Short stops—perfect for chance run-ins and stolen hours—abound. The **International Center of Photography** has a branch at 1133 Avenue of the Americas and 43rd St. (tel. 212/768–4680). The **Frick Collection,** housed in the splendid old home of a steel baron (1 E. 70th St. and Fifth Ave., tel. 212/288–0700), houses such gems as Rembrandt's Polish Rider and Holbein's portrait of Sir Thomas More. AT&T's **InfoQuest** (550 Madison Ave. between 55th and 56th Sts., tel. 212/605–5140) features interactive science exhibits on robotics, electronic voice recognition, and other high-tech topics. The **IBM Gallery of Science of Art** (590 Madison Ave., between 56th and 57th Sts., tel. 212/745–6100) has a permanent computer exhibit, visiting art collections, and an atrium café. In addition to its main, 75th Street and Madison locus, The **Whitney Museum of American Art** (tel. 212/570–3676) has bite-sized, rotating samples of American artists—including, at times, such figures as Warhol and Hopper—at three downtown and midtown branches (33 Maiden Lane; Equitable Center, Seventh Ave. between 51st and 52nd Sts.; Philip Morris, 120 Park Ave., between 41st and 42nd Sts.). A good place to kill time in midtown is the lobby of **Citicorp Center** (Lexington Ave. between 53rd and 54th Sts.), with its restaurants, shops, and concerts. Downtown, try the magnificent, palm-shaded, glass-enclosed atrium at the **Winter Garden** in the World Financial Center, also offering shops, restaurants, and concerts (West St. between Liberty and Vesey Sts., tel. 212/945–0505).

South Street Seaport (Fulton St., tel. 212/732–7678) is New York's answer to the national craze for waterfront marketplaces. Open-air entertainment, a maritime museum, and tall sailing ships round out the usual collection of restaurants and trendy stores facing the East River. The wholesale Fulton Fish Market, still in business during the early morning hours and still pungent, is a New York original.

Wall Street, the country's financial center, was the first part of Manhattan settled by the Dutch. Any walking tour of its narrow, crooked streets should include the New York Stock Exchange (Wall & Broad Sts., tel. 212/656–5167), and Fraunces Tavern (Broad & Pearl Sts., tel. 212/269–0144), the site of General Washington's emotional farewell dinner for his officers, and one of the few remaining restored Colonial buildings (1719) in New York.

For more: the New York Convention & Visitors Bureau, tel. 212/397–8222, has a complete and yet wonderfully concise calendar of events.

Professional Sports

Baseball. Mets, Shea Stadium, Flushing, Queens, tel. 718/507–8499; **Yankees,** Yankee Stadium, the Bronx, tel. 212/293–6000. **Football. Giants,** Giant Stadium, East Rutherford, NJ, tel. 201/935–8222; **Jets,** Giant Stadium, tel. 212/421–6600. **Basketball. Knicks,** Madison Square Garden, Manhattan, tel. 212/563–8000; **Nets,** Brendan Byrne Arena, East Rutherford, NJ, tel. 201/935–3900. **Hockey. Rangers,** Madison Square Garden, tel. 212/563–8000; **Dev-**

ils, Brendan Byrne Arena, East Rutherford, NJ, tel. 201/
935–3900; **Islanders,** Nassau Veteran's Memorial Coliseum, Uniondale, Long Island, tel. 516/794–4100.

The Arts

Anyone who doubts that New York is the country's arts
capital should talk to a waiter or waitress. Nearly everyone, it seems, is an aspiring (or moonlighting) actor, ac-
tress, dancer, or musician. Besides its 30 or so Broadway
theaters, New York has dozens of Off Broadway houses
and scores of neighborhood Off Off Broadway theaters.
The city's diverse selection of music and dance argues
against singling out any one stage, but Carnegie Hall must
be mentioned as the best place to hear concerts. Lincoln
Center is home to the Metropolitan Opera, the American
Ballet Theatre, the New York Philharmonic, the New
York City Ballet, the New York City Opera, and a first-
rate (and moderately priced) Broadway stage, the Vivian
Beaumont. Two modern dance groups appear at City Cen-
ter Theater: Alvin Ailey American Dance Theater and
Martha Graham Dance Company. At Christmastime and
other times, the Rockettes kick up their legs at Radio City
Music Hall.

New York is also replete with smaller stages and music
halls where the setting is more intimate and the talent is
first-rate. One that is close to East Side hotels and features classical and other concerts is the 92nd Street
YMHA. Travelers should consult the listings in local
newspapers or magazines. (The New York Convention &
Visitors Bureau calendar of events is also a good guide; *see*
Diversions, above.)

Ticket agencies include **Miller Ticket Service** (2 E. 61st
St., lobby of the Pierre Hotel, tel. 212/757–5210), **Nite on
New York Town Inc.** (430 W. 34th St., tel. 212/947–0819),
and **Downtown Theater Ticket Agency** (71 Broadway., tel.
212/425–6410). **TKTS (Times Square Theater Center)** has
half-price tickets to same-day performances (if you're
willing to wait in line and to take your chances on what's
available) of Broadway and Off Broadway shows. Two locations: Broadway & 47th St. at Times Square and in the
mezzanine of Two World Trade Center (which is less
crowded). For information on hours call tel. 212/354–5800.
The **Theater Development Fund NYC/ON STAGE** hot line
for information on theater, dance, and music is 212/587–
1111 or, outside of New York State, 800/782–4369.

Alice Tully Hall, Lincoln Center, 65th St. and Broadway,
tel. 212/362–1911.
Avery Fisher Hall, Lincoln Center, tel. 212/874–2424.
Brooklyn Academy of Music, 30 Lafayette Ave., Brooklyn,
tel. 718/636–4100.
Carnegie Hall, 57th St. and Seventh Ave., tel. 212/247–
7800.
City Center Theater, 131 West 55th St., tel. 212/581–7907.
Joyce Theater, 175 Eighth Ave., tel. 212/242–0800.
Metropolitan Opera, Lincoln Center, tel. 212/362–6000.
New York State Theater, Lincoln Center, tel. 212/870–
5570.
92nd St. YMHA, 92nd St. & Lexington Ave., tel. 212/996–
1100.

Radio City Music Hall, 1260 Ave. of the Americas, tel. 212/247–4777.

Town Hall, 123 W. 43rd St., tel. 212/840–2824.

After Hours

There is life after dark all over town, but night crawling can be classified into four geographic turfs: Greenwich Village and SoHo, midtown, the upper east side, and the upper west side. The Village and SoHo, in lower Manhattan, are trendiest; midtown is favored by establishment types. Uptown night spots, both east and west, draw hordes of young professionals, many of them singles, but the west-side crowd is ethnically diverse and informal. On the east side, the accent is glitzier and the bills are larger.

Bars and Lounges
For a quiet drink with clients, hotel bars are usually best. Try, among others, the **Plaza,** the **Carlyle,** the **Algonquin,** and the **Westbury** (*see* Lodging, above). The **Palio** (151 W. 51st St. at Seventh Ave., tel. 212/245–4850) is flush with executives. The open bar overlooking the main terminal area at **Grand Central Station** (enter at Vanderbilt and 42nd Sts., tel. 212/883–0009) is jammed with people-watchers. If you want to wow clients—or yourself—with views and elegance, try the **Rainbow Room** (RCA Building, 30 Rockefeller Plaza, tel. 212/632–5100); **Windows on the World** (1 World Trade Center, tel. 212/938–1100); and **River Café** (1 Water St., Brooklyn, tel. 718/522–5200). Sports nuts will enjoy the big screens and, if they're lucky, catch a glimpse of the restaurant's namesake, at **Mickey Mantle's Restaurant Sports Bar** (42 Central Park S., tel. 212/688–7777).

Cabarets
For the likes of the Gershwins, Rodgers and Hart, Cole Porter, et al sung in lively, intimate settings, the **Algonquin** and the **Carlyle** hotels are the best bets (*see* Lodging, above). **Rainbow & Stars** (RCA Building, 30 Rockefeller Plaza, tel. 212/632–5000) sports spectacular views in a glitzier, 65th-floor setting. Dinner and music are offered at **Jan Wallman's** (49 W. 44th St., tel. 212/764–8930). Hotels with pianists and/or singers include the **Drake** (440 Park Ave. at 56th St., 212/421–0900), **Parc 51,** the **Marriott Marquis,** the **Parker Meridien,** the **InterContinental** (111 E. 48th St., tel. 212/755–5900), and the **Westbury** (*see* Lodging, above, for addresses and telephone numbers).

Clubs
The club scene in New York is constantly changing, practically from week to week. What's in today can, literally, be gone tomorrow. There are no guarantees that the following will still be open by the time you visit, but they've proved to have some staying power.

Heartbreak (179 Varick St., tel. 212/691–2388) pays homage to the '50s with a bust of the King on the bar, a linoleum dance floor, a luncheonette, and kitschy touches everywhere. **Mars** (10th Ave. at 13th St., tel. 212/691–6262) is still hot after over a year as *the* place to go. Take your pick among five levels. The door staff is *very* particular. **M.K.** (204 5th Ave., tel. 212/779–1340) has a SoHo-chic design that attracts a celebrity crowd to this supper club noted for its number of film premiere parties. **Nell's** (246

W. 14th St., tel. 212/675–1567) reintroduced sophistication to nightlife. The tone in the upstairs jazz salon is Victorian; downstairs is for tête-à-têtes and dancing. **Regine's** (502 Park Ave., tel. 212/806–0990) attracts the international set for dancing and listening to a variety of contemporary sounds. **Stringfellows** (35 E. 21st St., tel. 212/254–2444), a British import, is for the jet-and-blank-check set. At 11, mirrored panels unveil a dance floor, where commodities traders, TV commentators, and famous fashion designers invade each other's personal space.

Comedy Clubs

The talent varies but is often quite good. The best-known clubs are on the upper east side, including **Catch A Rising Star** (1487 First Ave., tel. 212/794–1906), **Comic Strip** (1568 Second Ave., tel. 212/861–9386), and **Dangerfield's**—owned by Rodney, who on rare occasions performs here (1118 First Ave., tel. 212/593–1650). In midtown try **Monkey Bar,** in the Elysée Hotel (*see* Lodging, above). **Stand-Up New York** (236 W. 78th St., tel. 212/595–0850), a bit off the beaten track, draws a local Upper West Side crowd.

Jazz Clubs

The Village is the place for jazz. The list (by no means complete) includes **Village Gate** (160 Bleecker St., tel. 212/475–5120), **Village Vanguard** (178 Seventh Ave. S., tel. 212/255–4037), **Sweet Basil** (88 Seventh Ave. S., tel. 212/242–1785), and **Blue Note** (131 W. 3rd St., tel. 212/475–8592). **Sounds of Brazil (S-O-B's)** (204 Varick St. at W. Houston St., tel. 212/243–4940) has music from exactly where you'd expect, and also from the Caribbean and elsewhere. In midtown, in addition to the many hotels with jazz bars, there is **Michael's Pub** (211 E. 55th St., tel. 212/758–2272) and **Red Blazer Too** (349 W. 46th St., tel. 212/262–3112). For egg rolls with rhythm, **Fortune Garden Pavilion** (209 E. 49th St., tel. 212/753–0101) combines a greenhouse ambience with jazz and Chinese food.

For Singles

With the exception of grand, formal settings, singles feel comfortable just about anywhere in New York. The hotel lounges and low-key bars on the east side are generally more relaxed than the pick-up joints. You can meet people or enjoy the scene, no questions asked. A few choices: **Ravelled Sleave** (1387 Third Ave., tel. 212/628–8814), **Brighton Grill** (1313 Third Ave., tel. 212/988–6663), **Island** (1305 Madison Ave., tel. 212/996–1200), **Elio's** (1621 Second Ave., tel. 212/772–2242), **Sam's Cafe** (1406 Third Ave., tel. 212/988–5300), which is owned by Mariel Hemingway, and the celebrity/literary salon, **Elaine's** (1703 Second Ave., tel. 212/534–8103).

Paris

by Phil Revzin

The City of Light won that title not only because of its enduring intellectual preeminence but also because of its shimmering beauty. To have visited Paris is to have acquired a new standard for judging the beauty of cities. Small wonder that it has so thoroughly fascinated writers, poets, and artists for centuries.

Straddling the Seine River, the city has 20 arrondissements, or boroughs, each with an appointed mayor. Alongside the Seine on the Champs-de-Mars is the Eiffel Tower, the city's chief landmark.

On the Right Bank of the Seine is the commercial and business center, with fashionable streets and shops. Here, along tree-lined boulevards, are the Arc de Triomphe, Elysée Palace, the Opéra, Comedie Française, and the Louvre. The floodlit monuments along the major boulevards are as strikingly handsome at night as during the day.

Paris spread to the river's Left Bank after the city was conquered by Julius Caesar in 52 BC. The catacombs under Montparnasse and the baths in the Cluny Museum remain from the Roman period. The Left Bank, which contains the Sorbonne, the French Academy, the Pantheon, and the Luxembourg Palace and Gardens, is the city's governmental and intellectual center. The old Latin Quarter here is the preserve of university life, as it has been for a thousand years.

At the city's center, in the Seine, is the Ile de la Cité. The island is dominated by the Cathedral of Notre Dame de Paris and the Palais de Justice.

The way French business is conducted has probably changed more over the past five years than during the past 45. Plans are proceeding to abolish most internal trade barriers within the European Community, and French businesses are determined to play a central role in this wider market. As a result, they have shucked a lot of past stereotypes: They are learning languages; hiring bright young staff from across Europe; and opening offices in Britain, Germany, and Spain. They are also reorganizing marketing structures along regional, not national, lines. The upheavals in Eastern Europe are also attracting attention, and the still-promised land of North America has seen a dizzying number of acquisitions by large French companies.

Paris has always been the headquarters for companies whose factories stretch across the country and into the rest of Europe. (On the other hand, France's biggest industry—government—is decentralizing, moving staff out of Paris and closer to the people it governs.) Service industries continue to flourish in Paris, which is in a close race with Frankfurt and Milan for the title of Europe's second biggest financial center, after London. Most of the world's major banks are represented here, and the Paris Bourse (Stock Exchange) has finally thrown off rules and customs dating to Napoléon, and begun to trade shares via computer.

The scope and swiftness of these changes has meant a huge adjustment for French businesses. The people at the best French firms have learned to be less haughty; they work as long and as hard as it takes to close a deal, and are even willing to speak English and German. Having to be accountable to shareholders—often Americans and/or Germans—has taken its toll. The French still enjoy a long lunch washed down with plenty of good wine, but these days they are as likely to do business over a 7:30 AM breakfast of croissants and coffee.

The city has adapted, too. More hotels offer services geared to the business traveler. The once notoriously slow French post office now offers express mail services to compete with DHL and Federal Express. The phones work, and buying a France Telecom phone card at a tobacconist or post office provides access to thousands of well-maintained phone booths, without the need for coins. Businesses and travelers alike are relying increasingly on the Minitel database system, which provide information and permits users to reserve airplane, train, and theater tickets without going through a travel agent.

Through it all, however, Paris's legendary beauty and *joie de vivre* haven't changed a bit. If anything, the extensive renovations made for the 1989 bicentennial of the French Revolution, and President François Mitterrand's *Grands Travaux* (Great Works), including the Arch at La Défense and the new Bastille Opéra, have made the City of Light more seductive than ever.

Top Employers

Employer	Type of Enterprise	Parent*/ Headquarters
Bouygues	Construction	Paris
CGE	Utility	Paris
Elf-Aquitaine	Oil	Paris
Pechiney	Aluminum	Paris
PSA	Automobiles	Paris
Renault	Automobiles	Paris
Rhône-Poulenc	Chemicals	Paris
Saint-Gobain	Glass	Paris

Thomson	Electronics	Paris
Total	Oil	Paris

if applicable

ESSENTIAL INFORMATION

All French phone numbers now have eight digits, and all Paris numbers start with the number 4. When dialing Paris from the provinces, add 161 before the eight digits. The area code is built in to the telephone numbers listed below. Dial all the numbers in the series.

The currency of France is the franc, abbreviated throughout the chapter as F.

Government Tourist Offices

French Government Tourist Office. In the United States: 610 Fifth Ave., New York, NY 10020, tel. 212/315–0888; 645 N. Michigan Ave., Chicago, IL 60611, tel. 312/337–6301; 2305 Cedar Springs Rd., Dallas, TX 75201, tel. 214/720–4010; 9454 Wilshire Blvd., Beverly Hills, CA 90212, tel. 213/271–6665; 1 Hallidie Plaza, Suite 250, San Francisco, CA 94102, tel. 415/986–4174.
In Canada: 1981 McGill College, Suite 490, Montréal H3A 2W9, Quebec, tel. 514/288–4264; 1 Dundas St. W, Suite 2405, Box 8, Toronto M5G 173, Ontario, tel. 416/593–4723.
In the United Kingdom: 178 Piccadilly, London WIV OAL, tel. 071/491–7622 or 071/499–6911.
In Paris: 127 av. des Champs-Elysées, tel. 47.23.61.72.

Foreign Trade Information

Embassy of France Trade Offices. In the United States: 810 Seventh Ave., 38th Floor, New York, NY 10019, tel. 212/307–8800; One East Wacker Drive, Suite 3730, Chicago, Il 60601, tel. 312/661–1880; Gateway West Building, Suite 921, 1801 Ave. of the Stars, Los Angeles, CA 90067, tel. 213/879–1847.
In Canada: Case postale 177, Place Bonaventure, Montréal P.Q. H5A 1A7, Quebec, tel. 514/878–9851; 210 Dundas St. Suite 800, Toronto M5G 2E8, Ontario, tel. 416/977–9671.
In the United Kingdom: 21–24 Grosvenor Pl,. London SWIX 7HU, tel. 071/235–7080

Entry Requirements

U.S. and Canadian Citizens
Passport only. A visa is required for visits longer than 90 days.

U.K. Citizens
Passport only. No work permit is required.

Climate

What follows are the average daily maximum and minimum temperatures for Paris.

Jan.	43F	6C	**Feb.**	45F	7C	**Mar.**	54F	12C
	34	1		34	1		39	4

Apr.	61F	16C	May	68F	20C	June	73F	23C
	43	6		50	10		55	13
July	77F	25C	Aug.	75F	24C	Sept.	70F	21C
	59	15		57	14		54	12
Oct.	61F	16C	Nov.	50F	10C	Dec.	45F	7C
	46	8		41	5		36	2

Airports

Charles de Gaulle Airport is 15 miles northeast of the city center; **Le Bourget Airport,** for private planes, is nearby. **Orly Airport** is 10 miles south of the city center. Most transatlantic and European flights go to de Gaulle, but many use Orly, as do almost all charter flights and nearly all domestic flights. The airport used depends on the carrier rather than the destination. Taxis or buses are the fastest way to get from Orly to Paris; train or métro are best from de Gaulle.

Airlines

Air France has the most flights in and out of de Gaulle from its own convenient new terminal. Air Inter, the domestic carrier, flies out of Orly.

Air France, tel. 45.35.61.61; 800/237–2747.
Air Inter, tel. 42.89.38.88.
American, tel. 42.89.05.22; 800/433–7300.
British Airways, tel. 47.78.14.14; 800/247–9297.
Continental, tel. 42.25.31.81; 800/231–0856.
Lufthansa, tel. 42.65.37.35; 800/645–3880
Pan Am, tel. 42.66.45.45; 800/221–1111.
SAS, tel. 47.42.06.14; 800/221–2350.
TWA, tel. 47.20.62.11; 800/241–6522.

Between Charles de Gaulle Airport and Downtown

By Taxi
Taxis take about 30 minutes at nonpeak hours and can take more than an hour during rush hours (7 AM–9 AM from the airport, 4:30 PM–8 PM from the city). The most direct route to the center is the A1, exit Porte de la Chapelle. Cost: 150–200F.

By Train
The superfast **RER express subway line B** runs every 15 minutes from 5 AM to midnight between the airport and Gare du Nord and other stations. It takes 30 minutes and is the quickest way into town during rush hours. A shuttle bus links airport terminals to the train station. Two drawbacks: There isn't much space for luggage, and train cars tend to get overcrowded with commuters. Cost: 27.50F.

By Bus
Cheaper than taxis but prone to the same traffic snarls, **Air France buses** run every 12 minutes from 6 AM to 11:30 PM; they depart from just outside the terminal doors to Porte Maillot, two métro stops from the Champs-Elysées. The trip takes between 30 minutes and one hour. There is plenty of luggage space. Cost: 36F.

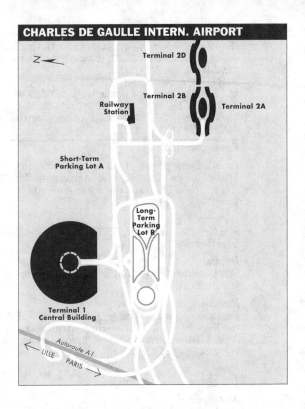

CHARLES DE GAULLE INTERN. AIRPORT

Terminal 2D

Terminal 2B

Railway Station

Terminal 2A

Short-Term Parking Lot A

Long-Term Parking Lot R

Terminal 1 Central Building

Autoroute A1

LILLE

PARIS

Between Orly Airport and Downtown

By Taxi
Taxis take 20 to 30 minutes in off-peak hours and 30 to 40 minutes during rush hours. The most direct route is straight north past Gare Montparnasse. Cost: 100–150F. If you're going to a suburb, you must take a more expensive suburban taxi marked "Banlieue."

By Train
RER line C serves Orly, which is linked to the terminals by shuttle bus. It leaves every 15 minutes from 5 AM to 11:35 PM and takes about 35 minutes. Cost: 22F.

By Bus
Air France buses link Orly and a terminal at Invalides. They leave every 12 minutes from 5:45 AM to 11 PM and take from 25 to 40 minutes. If requested, the bus will stop at Porte d'Orléans, Gare Montparnasse, and the Duroc métro station. Cost: 29F. The Orlybus also links Orly and the Denfert-Rochereau métro station; it leaves every 15 minutes from 6:30 AM to 11:30 PM and takes 25 minutes. Cost: 18.50F.

Car Rentals

These companies have booths in both de Gaulle and Orly airports, as well as offices across town:

Avis, Orly South, tel. 49.75.44.97, Orly West, tel. 49.75.44.91; Charles de Gaulle 1, tel. 48.62.34.34, Charles de Gaulle 2, tel. 48.62.59.59; 800/331–1212.

Europcar (National), Orly, tel. 49.75.47.47; Charles de Gaulle 1, tel. 48.62.33.33, Charles de Gaulle 2, tel. 48.62.56.47; 800/227–7368.

Hertz, Orly South, tel. 49.75.37.52, Orly West, tel. 46.87.10.44; Charles de Gaulle 1, tel. 48.62.29.00, Charles de Gaulle 2, tel. 48.62.58.58; 800/654–3131.

Thrifty, Orly, tel. 05.16.02.75; Charles de Gaulle, tel. 34.29.90.50; 800/367–2277.

Emergencies

For a list of approved physicians and clinics in Paris that belong to the International Association for Medical Assistance to Travelers, contact IAMAT, 417 Center St., Lewiston, NY 14092, tel. 716/754–4883.

Doctors
SOS Medecins (tel. 47.07.77.77) is an English-speaking referral service.

Dentists
SOS Dentistes (tel. 43.37.51.00) is an English-speaking referral service.

Hospitals
English-speaking medical services are provided at **American Hospital** (63, bd. Victor-Hugo, Neuilly, tel. 47.47.53. 00) and **Hetford British Hospital** (3, rue Barbes, Levallois-Perret, tel. 47.58.13.13).

Police
Tel. 17.

Ambulance
Tel. 18 or 45.67.50.50.

Important Addresses and Numbers

American Express (11, rue Scribe, 9e, tel. 42.66.09.99).

Audiovisual rentals. Inter Congres (16, rue Armand-Carrel, 19e, tel. 42.00.70.01), Reels on Wheels (7, rue Decrés, 14e, tel. 45.42.58.66).

Bookstores (English language). Brentanos (37, av. de l'Opéra, 2e, tel. 42.61.52.50), Galignani (224, rue de Rivoli, 1er, tel. 42.60.76.07), Shakespeare & Co. (37, rue de la Bucherie, 5e, no tel.), W. H. Smith (248, rue de Rivoli, 1er, tel. 42.60.37.97).

British Embassy and Consulate (35, rue du Faubourg St-Honoré, 8e, tel. 42.66.91.42).

Canadian Embassy and Consulate (35, av. Montaigne, 8e, tel. 47.23.01.01).

Computer rentals. Computerloc (43, rue du Schemin-Vert, Boulougne, tel. 46.09.15.50), Locamicro (3, rue St-Felicité, 15e, tel. 45.32.80.01).

Convention and exhibition centers. CNIT-World Trade Center (4, pl. Défense, Puteaux, tel. 47.73.66.44), Palais des Congrès 2, pl. Porte-Maillot, 17e, tel. 40.68.22.22), Parc des Expositions (Porte de Versailles, 15e, tel. 48.42.87.00), Paris Nord-Villepente (near Charles de Gaulle Airport, tel. 48.63.30.59).

Fax services. Bossburo (91, rue du Faubourg St-Honoré, 8e, tel. 42.66.90.75), Post Office (tel. 40.28.20.00).

Formal-wear rentals. Au Cor de Chasse (40, rue de Buci, 6e, tel. 43.62.51.89), Autour de Minuit (5, av. de l'Opéra, 1er, tel. 42.60.68.13).

Gift shops. Chocolates: Leonidas (9, rue Auber, 9e, tel. 47.42.61.78), Salon du Chocolat (11 blvd. Courcelles, 8e, tel. 45.22.07.27); Flowers: Lachaume (10, rue Royale, 8e, tel. 42.60.57.26), Massot (5, rue du Cherche-Midi, 6e, tel. 45.48.70.31).

Hairstylists. Unisex: Jean-Louis David (47, rue Pierre-Charron, 8e, tel. 43.59.82.08), Michele & Heinz (4, rue de la Tremouille, 8e, tel. 47.23.75.55), Men: Defosse (19, av. Matignon, 8e, tel. 43.59.95.13).

Health and fitness clubs *See* Fitness, below.

Information hot lines Goings-on and tourist information in English (tel. 47.20.88.98); SOS Help (tel. 47.23.80.80; English-language crisis hot line; 3 PM– 11 PM).

Limousine services. Carey (tel. 42.65.54.20), International Limousine (tel. 45.74.89.72).

Liquor stores. Gargantua (284, rue St-Honoré, 1er, tel. 42.60.52.54), Georges Duboeuf (wines) (9, rue Marbeuf, 8e, tel. 47.20.71.23), Nicolas (pl. de la Madeleine, 8e, and throughout town).

Mail delivery, overnight. Chronopost (at all French post offices), DHL (tel. 48.63.70.00), Federal Express (tel. 47.99.39.00).

Messenger services. Courses Service (tel. 43.44.67.35), Vecteur (tel. 42.23.60.69).

News programs (English-language). CBS Evening News (daily, 7 AM) on Canal Plus (TV channel 4).

Office space rental. Le Satellite (8, rue Copernic, 16e, tel. 47.27.15.59).

Pharmacies, late-night. Centre Opéra (6, bd. des Capucines, 9e, tel. 42.65.88.29), Derby (84, av. des Champs-Elysées, 8e, tel. 45.62.02.41).

Secretarial services. Dernis (23, av. de Wagram, 17e, tel. 46.22.98.98), Erom (84, rue de Richelieu, 2e, tel. 42.96.50.63), Interim Nation (63, bd. Haussmann, 8e, tel. 42.65.61.26).

Stationery supplies. Cassegrain (422, rue St-Honoré, 8e, tel. 42.60.20.08), Copix (5, rue Pasquier, 8e, tel. 42.65.06.93), Montaigne (48, rue Pierre-Charron, 8e, tel. 47.20.00.25).

Taxis. Artaxi (tel. 42.41.50.50), Bleu (tel. 42.02.42.02), Taxi Etoile (tel. 42.70.41.41).

Theater tickets. *See* The Arts, below.

Thomas Cook (Gare de l'Est, 10e, tel. 42.09.51.97).

Trade Ministry (41, quai Branly, 7e, tel. 45.50.71.11).

Train information (tel. 45.82.50.50). Main stations include Gare d'Austerlitz, Gare de L'est, Gare de Lyon, Gare Montparnasse, Gare du Nord, and Gare St-Lazare.

Translation service. Cabinet de la Hanse (44, rue de la Boetie, 8e, tel. 45.63.81.18).

U.S. Consulate (2, rue St-Florentin, 1er, tel. 42.96.14.88).

U.S. Embassy (2, av. Gabriel, 8e, tel. 42.96.12.02).

Telephones

The French phone system is now a joy. Pay phones are available on street corners and in métro and train stations, post offices, and most corner bars and tobacconists. Coin phones take 50 centimes and one-, two-, and five-franc coins. Local calls cost 1F for three minutes. Lift the receiver, put in coins, and dial. Unused coins are returned at the end of the call, or if there is no answer. Emergency calls are free.

Card phones, which do not take coins, are increasingly common. The *telecartes* that enable you to make calls can be purchased at many train stations, post offices, and shops. Lift the receiver, put the card in the slot (arrow first), close the door over the card, and dial. Remaining units on your card are shown on an LED display. Telecartes are essential if you use pay phones frequently.

Tipping

The customary tip at the better hotels is 5F for doormen and 10F for hotel porters carrying bags. Tip concierges in the same range, depending on the service they provide for you. Room service and waiters' tips of 15% will be included in your bill. Tip more only for extra service. Taxi drivers expect a few francs in addition to the 15% already built into the fare.

DOING BUSINESS

Hours

Businesses: weekdays 9–1 and 3–7. **Banks:** weekdays 9–4:30. **Shops:** Mon.–Sat., 9–6 or 6:30; smaller shops may take a lunch hour or open on Sun. mornings.

National Holidays

New Year's Day; Good Fri.; Easter Sun.; May 1, Labor Day; May 8, Armistice Day; Ascension (40 days after Easter); Whit Mon. (50 days after Easter); July 14, Bastille Day; mid-Aug., Assumption; Nov. 1, All Saints' Day; Dec. 24; Christmas.

Getting Around

By Car

Paris weekday traffic is a mess. It is far easier to take the métro or walk. If you must have a car, a valid U.S. license is all that is needed to rent one. Check individual rental companies to see if insurance is included in the rental price. Parking garages are strategically located throughout the city—look for blue-and-white signs marked "P."

By Taxi

To hail a taxi on the street, look for cabs with their roof lights lit, or look for a taxi stand (marked with a blue-and-white "Taxi" sign) on the major streets. (To call a taxi, *see* Important Addresses and Numbers, above.)

By Public Transportation

The ubiquitous métro is easy to master, and costs 5F. Buses cost 5F, and their major destinations are displayed on side panels. Routes also are displayed on complicated route maps at each bus stop.

Protocol

Appointments

Although business meetings rarely start on time, it is best to be punctual—just be prepared to wait. If you're running more than 15 minutes late, call ahead. It is appropriate to hold meetings in private offices, conference rooms at hotels, or restaurants. It is inappropriate to hold them in hotel bedrooms, except for suites, or in bars.

Customs

Always call business acquaintances by honorifics and last names (e.g., Monsieur Dupond), unless you are asked to call them by their first names. If an executive's subordinates call him Monsieur le Président, then follow suit. If you're speaking French, never use the familiar *tu* form unless you are invited to. Shake hands at the start and end of meetings, meals, and visits, no matter how many times you've met the person before. Women should offer their hand, not wait for it to be grabbed. Cheek-pecking occurs only between good friends of opposite sexes, not business acquaintances; it's done twice on each side. Exchange business cards at the start of a first meeting. (French business cards are often huge.) Business conversation is much more formal than in the United States; don't be the first to introduce such subjects as spouses, hobbies, children, pets, or professional sports. Meetings and business meals may seem to last forever, with nothing happening. It's not your fault, and you shouldn't try to speed things up. Everything takes longer here; appointments are often hard to get, but quiet persistence pays.

Dress

For men, a suit or sport coat and tie is needed for almost every business situation. A sports shirt is acceptable for more informal gatherings, such as country houses or country clubs. Women should stress elegance over power dressing. And leave sneakers at home—French women don't wear them on the métro or anywhere in public, except to exercise.

Gifts

Gifts are usually not exchanged in business situations, unless the gift is a sample of a salesperson's wares. If invited to a private home for dinner, bring a bouquet of flowers, a potted plant, or a box of fancy chocolates.

Toasts and Greetings

Hello, how are you? *Bonjour, comment allez-vous?* (Bohn-ZHOOR, come-AHNT ah-lay voo).
Very well, thank you. *Trés bien, merci* (TRAY bee-en, mer-see).

Nice to have met you. *Ravi d'avoir fait votre connaissance* (Rah-VEE da-VOUAR fay VO-truh con-nay-SAHNS).

Thank you very much. *Merci beaucoup* (Mer-see boh-COO).

You're welcome. *Il n'y a pas de quoi* (Eel nyah PAH deh kwah).

Excuse me. *Pardon* (Pahr-DOHN).

Cheers! *A votre santé!* (Ah voh-truh sahn-TAY).

LODGING

Unquestionably one of the world's great hotel cities, Paris is a joy for the business traveler tired of dreary, cookie-cutter hotel rooms. From small Left Bank charmers to stately Right Bank mansions to contemporary, service-oriented places, there's a Paris hotel for every type of businessperson. The larger Right Bank hotels, particularly those located between the Opéra and the Louvre and those near the Arc de Triomphe, cater more to the business traveler than do the smaller, homier places on the Left Bank, though these are nonetheless recommended for those seeking atmosphere more than modern amenities. The venerable palaces remain as grand as ever; in fact, most have been recently renovated. Of late, more chain hotels have sprung up; they try to compete with the grand hotels by offering more modern amenities and business services.

Unlike many cities, Paris doesn't have a "downtown" or a financial district. Instead, its businesses—and its hotels—are spread across the city's 20 arrondissements. Fortunately, the excellent métro makes location a lesser concern in Paris than elsewhere, since you can usually get from one point to another with ease and speed. In general, the better Right Bank hotels are clustered in the 1st and 8th arrondissements, not far from the Seine; the better Left Bank places are found in the 6th arrondissement. One tip: If you'll be doing business at La Défense, don't stay in that area, which is isolated and unattractive. Instead, choose one of the Right Bank hotels, particularly in the 17th arrondissement. The contemporary hotels of the 17th arrondissement are also ideal for those visiting the convention center. The airport hotels are strictly functional.

Most of the large Paris hotels listed below offer weekend discounts and corporate rates; inquire when making reservations.

Highly recommended lodgings in each price category are indicated by a star ★.

Category	Cost*
$$$$ (Very Expensive)	over 1,500F
$$$ (Expensive)	1,000F–1,500F
$$ (Moderate)	under 1,000F

All prices are for a standard double room, single occupancy, including 28% value added tax and 15% service charge.

Numbers in the margin correspond to numbered hotel locations on the Paris Lodging and Dining map.

Right Bank

㉑
$$$$
Bristol. Although it's almost across the street from the Elysée Palace (the French White House), the 66-year-old Bristol houses more traveling bankers and financiers than politicians; in fact, the hotel actively discourages statesmen, especially if they bring a lot of gun-toting bodyguards (the staff talks up the "cult of discretion" that permeates the atmosphere). The lobby, which stretches over most of the ground floor, is replete with 19th-century tapestries and 23 Baccarat crystal chandeliers. All of the traditional, antique-filled rooms have been recently redecorated, most in quiet whites and off-whites. The stunning white-marble bathrooms come complete with separate shower stalls (rare in an old Paris hotel). The fine main restaurant is a good place for an early-morning meeting (*see* Business Breakfasts, below); it also has one of the best wine cellars in Paris. *Leading Hotels of the World. 112, rue du Faubourg St-Honoré, 8e, tel. 42.66.91.45, fax 42.66.68.68. Gen. manager, Raymond Marcelin. 195 rooms, 43 suites. AE, DC, MC, V.*

㉘
$$
Cambon. In contrast to the grand hotels along the nearby rue du Rivoli (like the Crillon and the Meurice), the Cambon is a small, well-kept haven of calm that is being discovered by more and more business travelers. Madame Simeon mother-hens everyone who stays in her 44 contemporary rooms, all of which have marble-walled bathrooms with all the latest gadgets. A concerted renovation campaign has brought spacious modern armoires, cable TV, and direct-dial phones into all the rooms; this, alas, has resulted in a commensurate rise in prices. Insist on being shown your room before settling in, since some are uncomfortably small. There is no restaurant, but breakfast and afternoon tea are served in the newly redecorated lobby, and English-language newspapers and books are available next door at W. H. Smith. *3, rue Cambon, 1er, tel. 42.60.38.09, fax 42.60.30.59. Gen. manager, Jacqueline Simeon. 44 rooms. No air conditioning. AE, DC, MC, V.*

❶
$$$
Concorde–La Fayette. This huge skyscraper hotel between the Arc de Triomphe and La Défense perches atop the Palais des Congrès convention center, which also houses movie theaters, an Air France bus terminal that serves de Gaulle Airport, and boutiques. The new Top Club, an executive-class hotel-within-a-hotel that is unique in Paris, offers stunning views of central Paris (ask for a southern exposure). Top Club guests have an express checkout line in the lobby, along with access to a top-floor lounge offering free drinks, coffee, newspapers, and a secretarial staff. Guests in standard rooms can use the scenic rooftop bar and the rooftop golf practice rooms. The midsize bedrooms all have electric trouser presses, but otherwise they have the generic contemporary look—soothing pastels, neutral furnishings—found at most skyscraper hotels. The hotel organizes group jogging and offers courtesy bus service to nearby tennis courts and golf courses. *3, pl. de Général-Koenig, Porte Maillot, 17e, tel. 40.68.50.68, fax 40.68.50.43. Gen. manager, Michel Blazy. 1,000 rooms. AE, DC, MC, V.*

PARIS

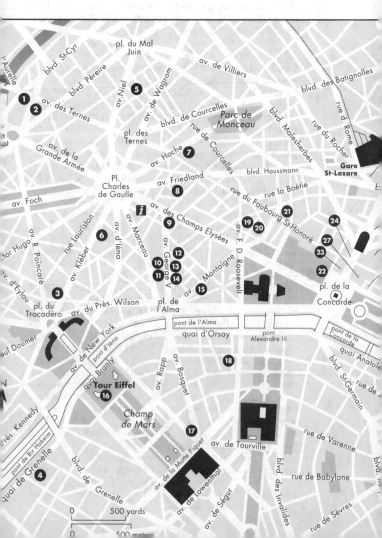

PARIS HOTEL CHART

| HOTELS | Price Category | Business Services | | | | | | | | | | |
---	---	Banquet capacity	No. of meeting rooms	Fax	Telex	Photocopying	Secretarial services	Audiovisual equipment	Translation services	International direct dial	Computer rentals	In-room modem phone jack
L'Abbaye St.-Germain	$$	0	0	-	-	-	-	-	-	✓	-	✓
Arcade	$$	100	3	✓	✓	✓	-	✓	-	✓	-	-
Bristol	$$$$	150	7	✓	✓	✓	-	-	-	✓	-	-
Cambon	$$	0	0	✓	✓	✓	-	-	-	✓	-	✓
Concorde La Fayette	$$$	2000	15	✓	✓	✓	✓	✓	✓	✓	-	✓
George V	$$$$	400	21	✓	✓	✓	-	✓	-	✓	-	✓
Grand	$$$$	500	20	✓	✓	✓	✓	✓	-	✓	-	✓
Hilton Orly	$$	400	19	✓	✓	✓	✓	✓	-	✓	-	✓
Holiday Inn	$$	120	10	✓	✓	✓	-	✓	-	✓	-	✓
L'Hôtel	$$$	0	1	✓	✓	✓	-	-	-	✓	-	-
Hôtel de Crillon	$$$$	100	7	✓	✓	✓	-	✓	-	✓	-	-
Hôtel Lotti	$$$	24	2	✓	✓	✓	-	-	-	✓	-	✓
InterContinental	$$$$	910	11	✓	✓	✓	-	✓	-	✓	✓	-
Lutétia	$$$	600	12	✓	✓	✓	-	✓	-	✓	-	✓
Marriott Prince de Galles	$$$$	200	5	✓	✓	✓	✓	✓	-	✓	-	✓
Méridien Etoile	$$$	1000	7	✓	✓	✓	✓	✓	✓	✓	-	✓
Meurice	$$$	150	6	✓	✓	✓	✓	✓	✓	✓	-	✓
Nikko	$$$	600	12	✓	✓	✓	✓	✓	-	✓	-	-
Novotel	$$$	40	8	✓	✓	✓	-	-	-	✓	-	✓

$$$$ = over 1,500 F, $$$ = 1,000 F-1,500 F, $$ = under 1,000 F.
● good, ◑ fair, ○ poor.

All-news cable channel	Desk	Desk lighting	Bed lighting	In-Room Amenities	Nonsmoking rooms	In-room checkout	Minibar	Toiletries	Room service	Laundry/Dry cleaning	Pressing	Hotel Amenities	Barber/Hairdresser	Garage	Courtesy airport transport	Sauna	Pool	Exercise room
✓	○	○	◐		-	-	-	○	-	◐	◐		-	-	-	-	-	-
✓	◐	◐	◐		-	-	-	-	-	-	-		-	✓	✓	-	-	-
✓	●	●	●		-	-	✓	◐	●	●	●		✓	✓	-	✓	●	-
✓	●	◐	●		-	-	✓	●	-	●	●		-	-	-	-	-	-
✓	●	●	●		✓	-	✓	●	●	●	●		✓	✓	✓	-	-	-
✓	●	●	●		-	-	✓	●	●	●	●		✓	-	-	-	-	-
✓	●	●	●		✓	✓	✓	●	●	●	●		-	-	-	✓	-	●
✓	●	●	●		✓	✓	✓	◐	●	◐	◐		-	✓	✓	-	-	-
✓	●	●	●		✓	-	✓	●	●	●	●		-	✓	✓	✓	-	●
✓	○	○	◐		-	-	✓	○	●	●	●		-	-	-	-	-	-
✓	●	●	●		-	-	✓	●	●	●	●		-	-	-	-	-	-
✓	●	●	●		✓	-	✓	●	●	●	●		-	-	-	-	-	-
-	◐	○	◐		-	-	✓	●	●	●	●		-	-	-	-	-	-
✓	●	●	●		✓	✓	✓	●	●	●	●		✓	-	-	-	-	-
✓	●	●	●		-	-	✓	●	●	●	●		-	-	-	-	-	-
✓	●	●	●		-	-	✓	●	●	●	●		-	-	-	-	-	-
-	●	●	◐		✓	-	✓	●	●	◐	◐		✓	✓	✓	✓	●	●
-	●	●	◐		-	✓	✓	-	◐	●	●		-	✓	✓	-	-	-

Room service: ● 24-hour, ◐ 6AM-10PM, ○ other.
Laundry/Dry cleaning: ● same day, ◐ overnight, ○ other.
Pressing: ● immediate, ◐ same day, ○ other.

PARIS HOTEL CHART

HOTELS	Price Category	Business Services Banquet capacity	No. of meeting rooms	Fax	Telex	Photocopying	Secretarial services	Audiovisual equipment	Translation services	International direct dial	Computer rentals	In-room modem phone jack
Plaza-Athénée	$$$$	100	4	✓	✓	✓	-	✓	-	✓	✓	✓
Raphaël	$$$	50	4	✓	✓	✓	-	✓	-	✓	-	✓
Relais Christine	$$$	0	1	✓	✓	✓	-	✓	-	✓	-	✓
Ritz	$$$$	100	4	✓	✓	✓	-	✓	-	✓	-	✓
Royal Monceau	$$$$	300	7	✓	✓	✓	✓	-	-	✓	-	-
Sofitel	$$	500	12	✓	✓	✓	✓	✓	✓	✓	-	✓

$$$$** = over 1,500 F, **$$$** = 1,000 F-1,500 F, **$$ = under 1,000 F.
● good, ◐ fair, ○ poor.

All-news cable channel	Desk	Desk lighting	Bed lighting	In-Room Amenities	Nonsmoking rooms	In-room checkout	Minibar	Toiletries	Room service	Laundry/Dry cleaning	Pressing	Hotel Amenities	Barber/Hairdresser	Garage	Courtesy airport transport	Sauna	Pool	Exercise room
✓	●	●	●		-	-	✓	●	●	●	●		✓	-	-	-	-	-
-	●	●	●		-	-	✓	◐	●	●	●		✓	-	-	-	-	-
-	●	●	●		-	-	✓	●	○	●	●		-	✓	-	-	-	-
✓	●	●	●		-	-	✓	●	●	●	●		✓	✓	-	✓	●	●
✓	●	●	●		-	-	✓	●	●	●	●		✓	✓	-	✓	●	●
✓	●	●	●		✓	✓	✓	●	●	●	●		-	✓	✓	✓	●	●

Room service: ● 24-hour, ◐ 6AM-10PM, ○ other.
Laundry/Dry cleaning: ● same day, ◐ overnight, ○ other.
Pressing: ● immediate, ◐ same day, ○ other.

⑩ **George V.** Long one of Paris's grandest hotels, the George
$$$$ V has recently been repolished and refurbished to emerge
once again as a star in Europe's hotel firmament. A grill
was opened to complement Les Princes, the haute-cuisine
eatery (*see* Business Breakfasts, below). The vast, col-
umned lobby, a gathering spot for an attractive international crowd, now affords more seating space. Bathrooms
are marble lined and modern. Bedrooms are unusually
big, even for an old Paris hotel, and lavishly furnished
with large, comfortable beds and antique side tables and
desks. Soundproofed windows block out traffic noise;
rooms on the inner courtyard are particularly quiet. Since
terrorist scares and dollar fluctuations have led to a drop
in American business visitors, the George V has been
making a concerted marketing effort to attract more Europeans and Japanese. *A Trust House Forte hotel; Leading Hotels of the World. 31, av. George-V, 8e, tel.
47.23.54.00, fax 47.23.54.00. Gen. manager, Michel
Bonnetot. 292 rooms, 59 suites. AE, DC, MC, V.*

㊱ **Grand.** Popular with business travelers of all types, the
$$$$ Grand has an efficient modernity (even an impersonality)
that belies its 130 years. A $20-million renovation pro-
gram has rebuilt the Court of Honor, where drinks and
meals are now served under a greenhouse-style roof, and
installed a well-equipped (but poolless) workout club on
the top floor and a 24-hour business communications center on the first floor. The Café de la Paix (*see* Dining, below) has been returned to its former opulence. Still to be
completed is the transformation of the main lobby, flanked
by green marble columns, into a more open-plan greeting
area. Despite double windows in all the large rooms, most
guests still prefer those overlooking the inner courtyards;
streets are busy around the Opéra, which is right across
the boulevard. The "business rooms," with beds that fold
up into the wall, can be transformed into meeting rooms.
*An InterContinental hotel. 2, rue Scribe, 9e, tel.
42.68.12.13, fax 42.66.12.51. Gen. manager, Frank
Mielert. 515 rooms, 30 suites. AE, DC, MC, V.*

㉓ **Hôtel de Crillon.** To stay here is to live a little French his-
$$$$ tory. The 18th-century palace on the place de la Concorde
became a hotel in 1909, and not long thereafter was the
site of the signing of the League of Nations charter by
Woodrow Wilson. Since then it has played host to generations of diplomats, politicians, sports stars, and, above all,
businesspeople. The latest renovation has reached most of
the large rooms—whose fabric walls, silk drapes, and elegant woodwork are the work of Paris haute-couturier
Sonia Rykiel—and most of the corridors, which are being
recarpeted and repainted. The main restaurant, Les Ambassadeurs (*see* Business Breakfasts, below), serves some
of Paris's finest and most innovative cooking. From bell-
boy to general manager, the staff is professional and discreet. Bathrooms are now marble lined, rooms have been
ultrasoundproofed, and all feature elegant Louis XIV-
style furnishings. Beds are large and firm. The wood-paneled bar is a gathering place for U.S. Embassy types and a
quietly glittering sampling of Crillon customers. Money
and power don't shout at the Crillon; they whisper. *Leading Hotels of the World; Relais & Châteaux. 10, pl. de la
Concorde, 8e, tel. 42.65.24.24, fax 47.42.72.10. Gen. manager, Hervé Houdré. 163 rooms. AE, DC, MC, V.*

③ Hôtel Lotti. A faithful international business clientele,
$$$ supplemented by an increasing number of Italian tourists
lured by the parent Italian chain's promotions, stays at
this comfortable, midsize hotel snuggled among bigger,
better known, and much more expensive neighbors, such
as the Meurice and the InterContinental. (Mr. Lotti, a for-
mer headwaiter at what was to become the InterConti-
nental, opened this hotel in 1910 on the advice of the Duke
of Westminster, who sought a more intimate place to
stay.) Double rooms are surprisingly spacious, but single
rooms are tiny. Although the staff is attentive, don't ex-
pect all the business and personal conveniences of a mas-
sive Ramada; charm has its disadvantages. *A Jolly hotel.
7, rue de Castiglione, 1er, tel. 42.60.37.34, fax 40.15.93.
56. Gen. manager, Massimo Amato. 133 rooms, 5 suites.
AE, DC, MC, V.*

③ InterContinental. Because this hotel began life in 1878 as
$$$$ the Continental and didn't become a member of the Inter-
Continental chain until 1968, it's a far cry from the plain-
vanilla skyscrapers common to the group. Thanks in part
to the hotel's excellent location near the Tuileries and the
Opéra, the lobby and the terrace restaurant are cross-
roads for international businesspeople, politicians, and
opera stars (Jessye Norman lives here when in town). The
recently remodeled, quite large rooms on the third,
fourth, and fifth floors are done in soothing pastels, with
glistening marble bathrooms and a rich, modern look; ren-
ovation is continuing on the two lower guest floors. The
best rooms are the spacious (and more costly) fourth-floor
"executive rooms," which have couches and coffee tables.
If you want the view of the Tuileries and the Left Bank,
ask for a street room; if you crave quiet, request a room on
the Court of Honor. The ground floor was recently rear-
ranged, leaving the magnificent baroque Napoléon and
Imperial rooms but adding smaller conference rooms. *3,
rue Castiglione, 1er, tel. 42.60.37.80, fax 42.61.14.03.
Gen. manager, Frederick de Roode. 452 rooms, 62 suites.
AE, DC, MC, V.*

⑪ Marriott Prince de Galles. This smallish hotel is the rela-
$$$$ tively happy marriage of Marriott efficiency and Parisian
charm. The rooms have more antiques than most
Marriotts, though the overall decor isn't as elegant as at
the George V next door. But what it lacks in genuine ele-
gance it makes up in service, which makes it popular with
American businesspeople. This is virtually the only hotel
in Paris that provides phone jacks for personal computers.
It also offers in-room checkout and has all the features
you'd expect from a modern 1,000-room behemoth, except
for a pool or health club. Most of the Art Deco mosaic-tiled
bathrooms are giving way to marble as redecoration con-
tinues. The 60-year-old wooden doors are being replaced
by thicker ones, and all rooms have smoke detectors, a rel-
ative rarity in Paris. *33, av. George-V, 8e, tel. 47.23.55.11,
fax 47.20.96.92. Gen. manager, Douwe Cramer. 140
rooms, 31 suites. AE, DC, MC, V.*

② Méridien Etoile. This purely functional business hotel, lo-
$$$ cated between La Défense and the Arc de Triomphe, of-
fers standard comforts in standard rooms—and a good
dose of the Méridien chain's attentive service. Conveniences include a lobby secretarial service and (because of
the chain's affiliation with Air France) a desk to check

bags directly onto Air France flights. Air France buses leave from across the street. The Méridien is home to a well-regarded restaurant, Le Clos Longchamp, and the main bar becomes the lively Lionel Hampton Jazz Club (*see* After Hours, below) after 10 PM. *81, bd. Gouvion St-Cyr, 17e, tel. 40.68.34.34, fax 40.68.31.31. Gen. manager, Maurice Tapie. 1,012 rooms, 15 suites. AE, DC, MC, V.*

㉝ **Meurice.** This home-away-from-home for heiresses, CEOs,
$$$ and a cross-section of the world's super rich dates from 1815. It was getting rave reviews from English visitors in the 1820s, was reborn in 1907 to the delight of the crowned heads of Europe, and has just been given yet another veneer of elegance by its new owner, CIGA, the group controlled by the Aga Khan. All is marble and mirrors, tapestries and Persian rugs, antiques and Ormolu clocks. Rooms and beds are large, suites are sumptuous, and the flawless service puts an emphasis on discretion. The renovation opened up and lightened the exquisite Salon Pompadour and other public rooms, and even the bedrooms, many redone in blue-and-white checked walls hung with prints of prancing nymphs, are much less gloomy than they once were. Business services—and virtually anything imaginable—are available from the omni-competent concierges. But—perish the thought!—you won't find anything so crass and workaday as a business center or health club. *A CIGA hotel. 228, rue de Rivoli, 1er, tel. 42.60.38.60, fax 40.15.92.31, telex 230673. Gen. manager, Philippe Roche. 152 rooms, 35 suites. AE, DC, MC, V.*

★ ⑮ **Plaza-Athénée.** This 80-year-old, recently renovated hotel
$$$$ is the glittering heart of the Right Bank's fashion and entertainment industries. Public rooms and bedrooms (rich with antiques and thick drapes) glow with a quiet elegance. Breakfast (*see* Business Breakfasts, below) and lunch crowds reflect the hotel's location amid many of Paris's most elegant fashion houses and nearby television and radio stations; the Art Deco grill room attracts a high-society, mainly Parisian lunch set, and each afternoon an astonishing collection of elegant people take tea in the drape-lined ground-floor gallery. The English Bar (*see* After Hours, below) is a popular spot for a drink with associates. But there's more than glamour to the Plaza-Athénée—it's also an excellent business hotel, combining a good location with meeting rooms and business services. Amenities include whirlpool tubs in most of the bathrooms; some rooms feature TVs that hydraulically withdraw into fabric-covered side tables. The hotel boasts that it employs two staff members for every room and spends more on fresh flowers than it does on electricity. The best views are from rooms that overlook the inner courtyard, a veritable sea of climbing ivy during the spring and summer. *A Trust House Forte hotel; Leading Hotels of the World. 25, av. Montaigne, 8e, tel. 47.23.78.33, fax 47.20.20.70. Gen. manager, Franco Cozzo. 200 rooms. AE, DC, MC, V.*

❻ **Raphaël.** The Raphaël is a throwback to a gentler era,
$$$ when dark wood and tapestries did the work of central heating. It is the place for the business traveler who wants Paris headquarters just off the Champs-Elysées, who wants to stay in a gigantic, wood-paneled, antique-furnished bedroom, perhaps with a sitting room, and who doesn't mind if the bathroom fixtures date to 1925. The

tone is set by the softly lit entrance hall, lined with oil paintings of nymphs and pink-cheeked maidens in bowers, leading to a comfortable bar and small, elegant restaurant. Service is discreetly efficient, and the staff is aware that most of the clientele—heavily American—are businesspeople, leavened with a refreshing mix of artists and musicians. Each room is slightly different than the next; most habitués have learned to ask for their favorites. *17, av. Kléber, 16e, tel. 45.02.16.00, fax 45.01.21.50. Gen. manager, Alain Astier. 77 rooms, 12 suites. AE, DC, MC, V.*

③⓪ $$$$ **Ritz.** Founded as a temple of luxury by Cesar Ritz, this legendary haven of the flamboyantly wealthy has been regilded at a cost of $150 million by owner Mohammed al-Fayed (who also owns Harrods department store in London). From the Imperial Suite (40,000F a night) to the well-hidden discothèque, the decor is as ornate as the clientele. Rooms are spacious, comfortable, and discreetly endowed with all the latest gimmickry, including a control panel hidden in the nightstand. The staff is ubiquitous, helpful, and multilingual. Some of Paris's best food is served in Espadon, around an attractive courtyard garden. The health club (*see* Fitness, below), a sort of neo-Romanesque temple of sweat, is worth a visit if only for a look at the trompe l'oeil murals surrounding the pool. Although there is no comfortable gathering place in the lobbies, the three wood-paneled bars (one boasting a bust of ex-patron Ernest Hemingway) are inviting and usually quiet (*see* After Hours, below). *Leading Hotels of the World. 15, pl. Vendome, 1er, tel. 42.60.38.30, fax 42.86.00.91. Gen. manager, Frank Klein. 143 rooms, 47 suites. AE, DC, MC, V.*

❼ $$$$ **Royal Monceau.** This well-located hotel is aimed straight at the business traveler, from the exceptionally helpful staff to the small VIP room (open to all free of charge) equipped with a Reuters foreign-exchange terminal and a fax machine. Two other features set this place apart from Paris's other grand old hotels: a round, glassed-in terrace restaurant serving French cuisine (the hotel's other dining room is one of Paris's best Italian restaurants) and a ground-floor health club—free for guests—with a small pool and the best-equipped weight rooms and gymnasium in Paris (*see* Fitness, below). The clientele is nearly 100% businesspeople, with the heavily American preponderance increasingly giving way to Japanese. *37, av. Hoche, 8e, tel. 45.61.98.00, fax 45.63.28.93. Gen. manager, Michel-André Pottier. 180 rooms, 40 suites. AE, DC, MC, V.*

Left Bank

★ ㊷ $$ **L'Abbaye St-Germain.** This small Left Bank hotel, a former mansion, is more a charming place to sleep than an efficient place to conduct business. Rooms are smallish, although the suites, with sitting room downstairs and bedroom upstairs, are comfortable without being lavish. The welcoming public lounges and flower-filled courtyard garden are better than those at most small hotels. There's no restaurant, but breakfast is served. Its main trump card is location, near the Latin Quarter—no particular business advantage, but loads of atmosphere. *10, rue Cassette, 6e, tel. 45.44.38.11. Gen. manager, Pierre*

Lafortune. 44 rooms, 4 suites. No air conditioning. No credit cards.

40 **L'Hôtel.** This small Latin Quarter hotel is popular with
$$$ artists, musicians, and a few loyal bankers and financiers, who love its atmosphere of a bygone Paris. The rooms open off a circular stairwell decorated with plaster-cast medallions of Greek gods. There are two spectacular rooms: number 16, where Oscar Wilde died, and number 36, where French music-hall queen Mistinguette once lived. The former is lined with bookshelves, has a non-working fireplace, and is full of pictures and memorabilia of Wilde. The latter is startling Art Deco, from the furry white bedspread to the mirrored dressing table. Apart from these two, the rooms are fairly ordinary, with tiny bathrooms and even tinier bathtubs. The staff is helpful but overworked. Stay here for charm, to eat at the restaurant (Belier), and to drink in the air of the Left Bank. *13, rue des Beaux-Arts, 6e, tel. 43.25.27.22, fax 43.25.64.81. Gen. manager, Alain-Philippe Feutré. 27 rooms, 2 suites. AE, DC, MC, V.*

41 **Lutétia.** The first step into the Left Bank's largest hotel
$$$ takes you straight back to the 1910s and '20s. Scurrying about the Art Nouveau-style lobby are bellboys in red uniforms and red pillbox hats, looking like they just stepped out of an old Philip Morris ad. The rooms maintain the theme, with reproductions of Art Deco and Art Nouveau furnishings and prints. Everything was recently renovated, with particular care given to the meeting and seminar rooms. Many of the guests—upscale tourists and business travelers—prefer the interior rooms, although thick window glass has been installed in rooms overlooking busy boulevard Raspail and rue de Sèvres. All rooms are large; suites are huge. *A Concorde Group hotel. 45, bd. Raspail, 6e, tel. 45.44.38.10, fax 45.44.50.50. Gen. manager, Jean-Marc de Margerie. 300 rooms, 17 suites. AE, CB, DC, MC, V.*

4 **Nikko.** The only hotel in a small but growing 15th-arron-
$$$ dissement business district near the Eiffel Tower, this large international-modern place is popular with Japanese and international business travelers and airline crews. Convenience and service make up for the lack of charm. The contemporary, rather spare rooms are small-ish, though well furnished, and most have a small entry-way with table and chair that makes them seem bigger. Most standard rooms were recently redecorated, and some of these are nicer than the unredecorated luxury rooms. Best rooms are on the upper floors, which afford views over the Seine toward La Défense. In addition to the three restaurants, business meals may be enjoyed in several private dining rooms; also available are glassed-in reading and smoking rooms in the lobby. The hotel's health-club facilities (*see* Fitness, below) include a pool with retractable roof. *61, quai de Grenelle, 15e, tel. 45.75.62.62, fax 45.75.42.35. Gen. manager, Jean-Louis Ory. 777 rooms, 2 suites. AE, DC, MC, V.*

43 **Relais Christine.** This hotel is the essence of the Left
$$$ Bank, a converted 17th-century abbey tucked between busy boulevard St-Germain and the Seine, just across from Notre Dame. All rooms are large, with restored wooden beams; the best overlook the flower-filled garden.

Bathrooms have just been redone in marble. The clientele is 80% North American, and nearly all are here on business. There is no restaurant, but dozens are nearby. The vaulted lobby provides plenty of nooks for private chats. The staff is attentive to the needs of business travelers, even though the hotel isn't set up for big meetings. Its strong points are charm, location, and comfort. The suites are duplex-style: sitting room downstairs, bedroom upstairs. *3, rue Christine, 6e, tel. 43.26.71.80, fax 43.26.89.38. Gen. manager, Jean-Jacques Regnault. 51 rooms, 13 suites. AE, DC, MC, V.*

Airport

$$ **Arcade.** This is the low-budget choice for those trapped at Charles de Gaulle. Its great advantage is convenience; it's located right at the train station that links Paris to de Gaulle. Otherwise, you get what you pay for: Rooms are small and ordinary; there are no bathtubs, only shower stalls. The hotel clearly meets a demand, however—the new addition has just tacked on 170 more rooms. Shuttle buses run every five minutes to the terminals. There's a restaurant, but you're better off walking over to the Novotel, on the other side of the train station. *A Pullman International hotel. Gare SNCF-RER, Aeroport Charles-de-Gaulle, tel. 48.62.49.49, fax 48.62.54.22. Gen. manager, Wilfried Keestra. 530 rooms, 15 suites. MC, V.*

$$ **Holiday Inn.** Frequent shuttle buses link this generic-looking contemporary hotel on the edge of the Charles de Gaulle Airport to the terminals and the train station. For a few more francs you can have a slightly larger room (including a free-standing desk, trouser press, and bathrobe) on the fourth-story "executive" floor. Meeting rooms are well organized and plentiful, the lobby is pleasant for waiting or drinks, and the health club is small but well equipped. There is a convenient shuttle-bus waiting area just inside the main door. *1, allee du Verger, Roissy-en-France, tel. 34.29.30.00, fax 34.29.90.52. Gen. manager, Wolfgang Dittis. 250 rooms. AE, DC, MC, V.*

$$ **Hilton Orly.** This concrete-block hotel overlooking the Orly runways was built in 1965 and is in the midst of major renovation. Work has been completed on the first and third floors of the main building, which are refurnished in polished pine and offer much more desk space. Rooms are standard international-hotel in all respects. Double-thick windows keep out most of the airport noise. The many meeting and seminar rooms are well furnished, and the staff is skilled in setting up meetings. On site are travel and insurance agencies. Frequent shuttle buses will take you to the terminals, but you can walk to the south terminal in a pinch. *Aeroport Orly, tel. 46.87.33.88, fax 48.78.06.75. Gen. manager, Joseph Albrand. 366 rooms. AE, DC, MC, V.*

★ **Novotel.** In 1988, this large, fast-growing French chain
$$$ opened this airport hotel at the train station that links Paris to de Gaulle. Its eight meeting rooms are small, but they're equipped with moveable walls that allow the creation of large rooms. Bedrooms are standard for this type of contemporary hotel, and the amenities are equally standard: satellite TV, minibars, and the like. The staff is well attuned to the needs of the business traveler, and there's even a TV screen in the lobby displaying airline depar-

tures and arrivals. This is both a pleasant and efficient place for a quick meeting. *Gare SNCF-RER, Aeroport Charles-de-Gaulle, tel. 48.62.00.53, fax 48.62.00.11. Gen. manager, Remy Rein. 201 rooms, 2 suites. AE, DC, MC, V.*

$$ **Sofitel.** This chain hotel within de Gaulle Airport is linked by shuttle buses to the terminals and the train station. The modern, pastel-hued rooms are smallish and otherwise like those in any other middle-of-the-road chain hotel. There is a rooftop restaurant from which to watch the planes, and a pool and health club. Meeting rooms are large, and the staff works well with conference organizers. An efficient spot for a meeting. *Aeroport Charles-de-Gaulle, tel. 48.62.23.23, fax 48.62.78.49. Gen. manager, Gérard Toupet. 352 rooms, 8 suites. AE, DC, MC, V.*

DINING

In Paris, food is not just something to fill you up. It's an obsession, an art, a subject of endless debate. Wines, and wine lists, are of equal—perhaps even greater—fascination to the French. So if you're doing business with Parisians, you'll find yourself spending a lot of time at the lunch and dinner table. In general, lunch is the time to talk shop and get some work done; dinner is customarily a time to focus on the food and the socializing. Neither meal will be rushed; at the finest restaurants, a three-hour, multicourse lunch, with wine, is the norm.

Although the days of puny portions are over, the creative spirit of nouvelle cuisine remains. Most of today's French cooking is made with less butter and cream, and Parisian chefs are working wonders with fresh seafood. French chefs also have rediscovered their roots, leaving behind some of the frillier excesses of haute cuisine in favor of the deeply satisfying tastes from France's many regions.

Reservations are almost always accepted, and they're almost always required in the best restaurants (in fact, at the very top places, you'll need to reserve weeks or even months in advance). Be aware that reservations are carefully honored, so either show up on time or call. And plan on dressing well at the better restaurants: suits for men and dresses or ensembles for women.

Dining well in Paris makes for a considerable investment, but even the most expensive restaurants offer *prix-fixe* (fixed-price) tasting menus at dinner and, often, bargain menus at lunch, which can help keep bills down. These menus are not only good value, but also often permit you to taste many of the chef's specialties.

Highly recommended restaurants in each price category are indicated by a star ★.

Category	Cost*
$$$$ (Very Expensive)	over 500F
$$$ (Expensive)	300F–500F
$$ (Moderate)	under 300F

per person, including appetizer, entrée, dessert, 28% value added tax, and 15% service charge, but excluding drinks.

Numbers in the margin correspond to numbered locations on the Paris Lodging and Dining map.

Wine

Following are the best years for the great French wines.

Red Bordeaux: '88, '86, '85, '83, '82, '78, '70.
White Bordeaux: '86, '85, '83, '81, '71, '70.
Red Burgundy: '85, '78, '76.
White Burgundy: '86, '85, '83, '79.

Business Breakfasts

Increasingly, French movers and shakers are sharing their morning croissants and café au lait with clients, usually at the large Right Bank hotels. Reservations are needed at all of the following. The **Plaza Athénée** (tel. 47.23.78.33) draws a fashion and finance crowd. The **George V** (tel. 47.23.54.00) usually boasts a sprinkling of politicians, as does the **Bristol** (tel. 42.66.91.45), which is almost directly across the street from the Elysée Palace, where the president lives. The **Crillon** (tel. 42.65.24.24) glitters with diplomats and dignitaries.

Note: The French follow strict rules when drinking their coffee. In the morning, it's served in a gigantic cup with a separate pitcher of warm milk, and called *café au lait.* At lunch and in the afternoon, they drink a small cup of strong coffee with sugar but no milk. If you want milk, ask for a *café crème,* which is a café au lait with the milk already added. In the evening, everyone drinks coffee strong and black; you can ask for a café crème, but you might not get it. More and more restaurants are offering decaffeinated coffee.

Right Bank

③④ **Angelina.** The most famous tea room in Paris, this was
$$ once a bastion of prim society ladies but is now also home to a unique mix of footsore tourists from the Louvre, white-gloved matrons from the provinces, and chic Paris teenagers out for a spree. As ever, black-clad waitresses serve Paris's best hot chocolate (along with a glass of water) in white porcelain china, carried on a silver tray. The decor is faded elegant, with painted plaster columns and heavy velvet drapes. Tea cakes include extravagant chocolate and meringue creations; there are also several main courses, though they tend to be overpriced. The tasty salads, particularly *Les Années Folles* (foie gras on radicchio), are a better value. Angelina is hardly a place for a business meeting, but it's a Parisian experience that's not to be missed—and it's a good Right Bank location for a quick lunch. *226, rue de Rivoli, 1er, tel. 42.60.82.00. Casual dress. No reservations. AE, DC, V.*

④⑤ **Au Cochon d'Or des Halles.** Not to be confused with Au
$$$ Pied du Cochon, around the corner, this is a smaller, much quieter, lesser-known place to have grilled kidneys, roast pork, or a juicy steak with marvelous *frites* (french fries)—the sort of simple fare that recalls the days when Les Halles was Paris's meat and fruit market and a home

to good rustic restaurants. Tables are closer together upstairs than down, and the prices are a bit high, but the coziness and good food more than compensate. If you're planning a working meal, request one of the banquettes. The wine list is heavy on Beaujolais. *31, rue du Jour, 1er, tel. 42.36.38.31. Jacket and tie advised. Reservations advised. AE, DC, V. Closed Sun.*

44 **Beauvilliers.** This is the best-known restaurant in Mont-
$$$ martre, and one of the prettiest in Paris. Politicians, actors, and well-heeled businesspeople flock to the intimate, flower-strewn rooms that Edouard Carlier has decorated with 19th-century engravings and paintings, most celebrating food. First-rate service and a serene atmosphere make this a fine place for a sophisticated working lunch. The cuisine is rich and elegant, with hearty plates of game in season and stews of rabbit and pigeon year-round. The prix-fixe lunch menu is a particularly good value, and most of the wines on the long list are reasonably priced. It's a long trek—30 minutes or so by métro—from the center of town, but it's well worth the trip. And despite its popularity, a table can usually be found, particularly at lunch. *52, rue Lamarck, 18e, tel. 42.54.54.42. Jacket and tie advised. Reservations advised. MC, V. Closed Mon. lunch, Sun., and first two weeks of Sept.*

19 **Le Boeuf Sur Le Toit.** This two-story bistro is in the same
$$ family as Julien (*see* below), but it has a completely different atmosphere. "The Cow on the Roof" is all '20s-style Art Deco, always full of life and noise. The clientele of middle managers and show-biz types—more of the latter later in the evening—comes for the oyster and shellfish platters, served on giant mounds of ice, or honest plates of steak with frites. The staff is attentive, if harried. The extensive menu also offers well-prepared fresh fish, *cassoulet* (bean-and-sausage casserole), and chops. The wine list is long and pricey, but the "Flo" label champagne is reasonable. This is not a place for a quiet business meeting to clinch the deal, but for the celebration afterwards. The downstairs restaurant houses a piano bar. *34, rue du Colisée, 8e, tel. 43.59.83.80. Casual dress. Reservations advised. AE, DC, V. Moderate.*

36 **Café de la Paix.** Also called the Opéra, this huge, beautiful
$$$ restaurant in the Grand hotel is a gathering place for Paris's financial community. Tables are sufficiently private, and the conversations held at them are almost exclusively business-oriented. The decor has recently been restored to its 19th-century glory, all gilding and silver serving pieces, and the food remains the same: traditional hearty French, including roast beef carved on the trolley, served with nicely arranged green beans and potatoes, and fresh seafood platters and oysters in season. The formal service and genteel elegance make this a popular place to host an important business gathering—a lunch or dinner invitation here is much coveted by Parisians. The wine list is long and expensive, though there are usually a few moderately priced (though young) Bordeaux. *3, pl. de l'Opéra, 9e, tel. 47.42.97.02. Jacket and tie required. Reservations advised. AE, DC, MC, V. Closed Aug.*

14 **Chez Edgard.** At lunch or dinner this traditional-looking
$$ brasserie (etched glass, tile, burnished woodwork) is filled with journalists, politicians of all parties, and a sprinkling of businesspeople. Host Paul Benmussa flits from table to

table, greeting ministers and ex-ministers and instigating and exchanging gossip. The food is simple—fresh oysters and seasonal seafood platters, steak with frites, roast pork, duck breast—and similar to that of one hundred other brasseries in Paris. The reasons to come here are the personal attention and the politician-watching; bring along someone who can recognize the diners, or ask Benmussa. *4, rue Marbeuf, 8e, tel. 47.20.51.15. Jacket and tie advised. Reservations advised. AE, DC, MC, V. Closed Sun.*

㊲ Drouant. Best known to Parisians as the place where the
$$$ judges eat before awarding the prestigious Prix Goncourt literary prize, this sprawling restaurant was relaunched a few years ago by the people who run Jules Verne in the Eiffel Tower. The plush, red-toned main dining room has once again become a chandelier-lit palace of haute cuisine, and the former Grill has been renamed Le Café and given a nautical decor and seafood menu. Several ornate private rooms are available for lunch or dinner. The most famous dish is the fricassée of lobster, but there are many other worthy fresh seafood dishes (try the warm oysters), as well as steaks and roasts. The clientele comes primarily from the worlds of publishing and finance. Hosting a meal here is sure to impress. *18, rue Gaillon, 2e, tel. 42.65. 15.16. Jacket and tie required in main dining room, advised in Le Café. Reservations advised. AE, DC, MC, V.*

㉕ L'Ecluse. At this chain, you can taste some of France's
$$ best and most expensive Bordeaux wines by the glass, accompanied by light, well-prepared dishes: fresh noodles with foie gras or bone marrow, a plate of assorted smoked fish, chicken breast in white wine sauce, and one of the best chocolate cakes in Paris. But the wine is the star. Médocs, Haut Médocs, Margaux . . . for a few dollars a glass you can see what all the fuss is about over the great French wines. Some of the locations have terraces for outdoor summer dining, or tables in the wine cellar. Regardless of the setting, each is a good place to have a fun lunch or to relax with a glass of wine after work, joining the crowd of office workers and middle-management types. *15, pl. de la Madeleine, 8e, tel. 42.65.34.69; rue Mondetour, 1er, tel. 47.03.30.73. 64; rue François-1er, 8e, tel. 47.20.77.09; 4, rue Halevy, 9e, tel. 47.42.62.33. Left Bank: 15, quai des Grands-Augustins, 6e, tel. 46.33.58.74. Casual dress. Reservations advised. CB.*

㉒ Espace Cardin. In a small pavilion in the gardens just off
$$ the place de la Concorde, across the street from the U.S. Embassy, a youngish clientele drawn from nearby banks and show-business establishments crowds this spare, modern, art-lined room and the summer terrace for the massive prix-fixe buffets. There are usually 30 to 40 hors d'oeuvres, including herring, smoked salmon, salads, and slices of ham and beef; 2 or 3 hot main dishes; and 20 to 30 desserts, including chocolate cakes, mousses, and fruit tarts. You can have an appetizer, main course, and dessert, or just an appetizer and dessert. Particularly in the summer, this place makes for a relatively quick and pleasant change from the three-hour lunch. Tables are well spaced, but the place is noisy anyway, so don't plan on conducting serious business meetings. *1, av. Gabriel, 8e, tel. 42.66.11.70. Casual dress. Lunchtime reservations advised. AE, DC, MC, V.*

⑬ **La Fermette Marbeuf 1900.** Art Deco thrives here—the
$$$ real thing in one room, an undetectable copy in the other.
This huge, busy restaurant serves standard brasserie fare
(oysters, sauerkraut with sausages, steak with frites) at a
reasonable price. But because of its size, service can be
slow, and the menu is annoyingly inflexible; you can have,
for example, the prepared salmon dish on the menu, but
you may not be able to get a plain piece of grilled salmon.
The saddle of lamb is quite good. There are many wines for
less than 100F a bottle, a rarity in Paris. The combination
of stained-glass nymphs, good steaks and seafood, and a
location not far from the Champs-Elysées draws big
crowds of middle-management businesspeople and tour-
ists. It's usually pretty noisy, even in the back rooms; this
is a place for fun, not business. *5, rue Marbeuf, 8e, tel.*
47.20.63.53. Casual dress. Reservations advised. AE,
DC, MC, V.

❾ **Fouquets.** The most famous restaurant on the Champs-
$$$ Elysées was recently declared a historic monument, sav-
ing it from real estate developers after an outpouring of
protest from its faithful clientele of actors, dress designers, and other chic Parisians. The fun isn't so much in the
brasserie cuisine (tasty but unexceptional steaks, seafood, and such daily specials as crusty roast pork served
from a silver trolley) as in the atmosphere. You can eat in
the sumptuously furnished upstairs dining room, where
quiet conversation is possible, or downstairs on the
crowded, glassed-in terrace, where the object is to see and
be seen. Either way, your French guests will be delighted
with an invitation here. *99, av. des Champs-Elysées, 8e,*
tel. 47.23.70.60. Jacket and tie advised. Reservations ad-
vised. AE, DC, MC, V.

㉟ **Garnier.** This two-story, glass-fronted seafood restaurant
$$$ overlooking the not very scenic Gare St-Lazare offers ex-
ceptionally fresh and well-prepared platters of oysters
and assorted shellfish, along with lightly grilled fillets of
salmon, sole, and other fresh-daily fish. The wines are pri-
marily white, and many are reasonably priced. It's a little
quieter up the circular staircase on the second floor, but
not worth waiting for if there's a table available down-
stairs. Although it's across from a train station in a not
particularly pretty neighborhood, this is a safe area, and
the contemporary decor—gray fabric walls, fish swim-
ming in large tanks, modern art on the walls—is stylish.
The clientele is button-down business. *111, rue St-Lazare,*
8e, tel. 43.87.50.40. Casual dress. Reservations advised.
DC, V. Closed Aug.

㉖ **Goumard.** Fresh fish reigns at this small restaurant just
$$$ behind La Madeleine church. The blue-and-white walls,
the nautical touches, and the leather-aproned shellfish
sheller, who carries his wares through the dining room,
create an appropriately salty setting. The conservative
business clientele chooses from the pick of that morning's
market. The menu usually includes several appetizers
made with shrimp, scallops, and mussels, often served on
a bed of cabbage or other vegetables; and main courses can
include a plate of shellfish, an assortment of fresh fish from
the Mediterranean, or a meaty chunk of sea bass. The
large selection of white wines includes many expensive
Burgundies and a reasonable Sancerre. A good place for a
working lunch. *17, rue Duphot, 1er, tel. 42.60.36.07. Jack-*

*et and tie advised. Reservations advised, especially at
lunch. AE, DC, MC, V. Closed Sun.*

★ ❸❾ **Le Grand Véfour.** Business entertaining doesn't get any
$$$$ better than this: The combination of the 18th-century decor and some of the finest cuisine in Paris makes a meal
here an unforgettable experience. Located in a corner of
the Palais Royale (which it shares with the Supreme Court
and the Culture Ministry), it is lined with plush red banquettes studded with plaques commemorating notables
from the reigns of Napoléons I and III. Elegance doesn't
stop at the mirrors or painted ceilings; even the table settings are works of crystal-and-china art. Dishes range
from lobster casseroles to divinely tender lamb chops.
Portions are generous; this is not the pretty but undersize
nouvelle cuisine you might expect in such a setting. Desserts, including various fruit concoctions, are extrava-
gantly good, and the wine list is extensive and expensive.
*17, rue de Beaujolais, 1er, tel. 42.96.56.27. Jacket and tie
required. Reservations required. AE, DC, MC, V. Closed
Sat. lunch, Sun., and Aug.*

❸ **Jamin.** Joël Robuchon's intimate restaurant is perhaps the
$$$$ most revered in the world among devoted foodies and the
rich and powerful. Unfortunately, this makes getting one
of the 45 seats in the delicate dining room (green walls,
glass dividers, floral fabrics, white ceramics) about as
easy as getting a seat on the space shuttle. But if you've
got connections, a great concierge, or several months in
advance to plan, you can experience cooking of unsurpassed skill and creativity—and you can make a powerful
impression on your Parisian clients or colleagues.
Robuchon changes his dishes regularly; examples include
spiced duck with foie gras and turnips, rack of lamb with a
crust of crumbled truffles, and a potato purée that takes
the humble tuber to unprecendented heights. All the details, from the gracious service to the world-class wine list
to the refined desserts, combine to create a gastronomic
heaven on earth. *32, rue de Longchamp, 16e, tel.
47.27.12.27. Jacket and tie required. Reservations required. V. Closed Sat., Sun., and July.*

❹❾ **Julien.** This carefully maintained member of the Flo chain
$$ is a boisterous piece of Belle Epoque dining history, offer-
ing an all-too-rare chance to experience an old-style Pari-
sian bistro. Although it is located in a down-at-the-heels
neighborhood that can be scary (though not really danger-
ous) after dark, taxis discharge passengers into the hands
of a uniformed doorman and the warmth of the entrance
foyer. A cavernous dining room, with a restored Belle
Epoque decor and a riotous collection of fancy old hats and
fox stoles, welcomes diners ranging from Scandinavian
models to American businesspeople to French wedding
parties. The menu is bistro classic: cold or hot oysters and
other shellfish, a *salade riche* of foie gras, cassoulet rich in
beans and goose fat, solid steaks and chops, and nonde-
script desserts. The wine selection is limited, but prices
are reasonable. Julien is quite popular for business enter-
taining. *16, rue du Faubourg St-Denis, 10e, tel. 47.70.
12.06. Casual dress. Reservations strongly advised. AE,
DC, V.*

★ ❷❼ **Lescure.** Well located between the U.S. Consulate and the
$$ InterContinental hotel (and near many other Right Bank
hotels), this place is a real find for a relaxed, inexpensive,

nonworking meal. In summer, a few tables are placed on the quiet street; inside the tiny restaurant are long wooden tables, which you may be asked to share with others. Strings of garlic and old wine bottles hang from the walls and ceiling. Like the staff, the dishes hail from Limousin, in west-central France: stewed chicken, a wonderful and generous portion of warm pâté in a flaky crust, and *confit de canard* (rich, moist duck that has been preserved in its own fat). There are always inexpensive and good house wines. Most waiters speak English; members of the U.S. diplomatic corps visit frequently. *7, rue de Mondovi, 1er, tel. 42.60.18.91. Casual dress. Reservations advised. V. Closed Sat. dinner, Sun., and July.*

★ **⑤** **Michel Rostang.** Chef Rostang is one of the great young
$$$$ masters of French cuisine, spreading his fame through new bistros in Paris, New York, and the Caribbean. But when in Paris he is here at his stove, with his wife graciously tending the elegantly draped, softly lit dining rooms, with well-spaced tables and walls adorned with food-related oil paintings. Ravioli stuffed with cheese or seafood is the best-known first course; main courses include roast Breton crayfish, delicately cooked roast beef, and hearty roast guinea fowl. Any dessert made from chocolate or apples is sensational. Both the cheese tray and the wine list are extensive. Rostang's creations are best savored over a relaxed dinner or a very long lunch; it would be a shame to rush through such extraordinary food. Consequently, most businesspeople save this place for celebrations rather than deal making, the better to concentrate on the meal. *20, rue Rennequin, 17e, tel. 47.63.40.77. Jacket and tie advised. Reservations required. MC, V. Closed Sat. lunch, Sun., and first two weeks of Aug.*

㉔ **Le Moulin du Village.** This restaurant attached to the pop-
$$$ ular Blue Fox Bar recently moved from the stable of British wine expert Steven Spurrier to that of fellow British wine expert Michael Williamson. Both men continue to select the excellent wines, and the food is better than ever. Fresh fish dishes are particularly well prepared, especially the sea bass and salmon. The marinated salmon appetizer is exceptional, as is the rich, dark slice of chocolate terrine. The staff knows its wines, and wine prices are reasonable—though the food carries a rather stiff tab. The copious *plat de jour* (daily special) comes with a glass of wine. A relaxed business-embassy crowd comes for lunch. The atmosphere is intimate downstairs, with the tables too close together for really private business discussions. The upstairs room is usually less crowded. *Cité Berryer, 25, rue Royale, 8e, tel. 42.65.08.47. Casual dress. Lunch reservations advised. V. Closed Sat. and Sun.*

⑫ **Oh! Poivrier.** For a light, pleasant meal near the Champs-
$$ Elysées and elsewhere around town, try this chain of fastish-food restaurants. The simple menu offers assorted sandwiches, grilled with chicken or ham and cheese, and salad platters with foie gras, ham, or sliced duck breast, served with toasted bread. Desserts include light and dark chocolate mousses in geometrical shapes. Several types of fruit juices are available, in addition to wine, beer, and mineral water. The price is right, which is why lunchtime sees a considerable crowd of office workers. The

decor is sort of jungle modern, built around a pyramid symbol. *60, rue Pierre-Charron, 8e, tel. 42.25.28.65. 121, bd. Malesherbes, 8e, tel. 42.25.24.94. 2, bd. Haussmann, 9e, tel. 42.46.22.24. 2, av. du Maine, 15e, tel. 45.48.98.94. 1, av. Versailles, 16e, tel. 42.88.20.22. Left Bank: 25, quai des Grands-Augustins, 6e, tel. 43.29.41.77. 143, bd. Raspail, 6e, tel. 43.26.98.27. Suburbs: 168, av. Charles-de-Gaulle, Neuilly, tel. 47.47.59.17. Casual dress. V.*

㉔ Le Petit Montmorency. This elegant restaurant just off the
$$$ Champs-Elysées is relatively unknown, except to the faithful legion of financiers from nearby merchant banks who have made it their outside company canteen. Giant floral centerpieces separate the tables from each other, affording privacy and encouraging business talk. The traditional food is beautifully presented in generous portions. Outstanding dishes include warm *pâté en croûte* (goose liver pâté in a light crust), foie gras, and delicious fresh salmon cooked on one side—the warm plate cooks the other side while you eat it. The wine list is long and expensive. *5, rue Rabelais, 8e, tel. 42.25.11.19. Jacket and tie advised. Reservations required. MC, V. Closed Sat., Sun., and Aug.*

★ ㊻ Pharamond. One of the most authentic turn-of-the-centu-
$$$ ry restaurants still going in Les Halles, Pharamond serves substantial specialties from Normandy to a substantial clientele. Most of the Parisian diners will be eating tripe, served in a warming dish on a brass tripod; grilled pig's feet; or *andouillette*, a sausage made from the pig's insides. Other features are a robust selection of ocean fish and usually a pork or beef roast served from a silver trolley. Service can be slow when the place is full, as it usually is, though the noise level is moderate. A spiral staircase leads to an ordinary-looking upstairs room; opt instead for the mirrored, ceramic-tiled, red-plush ground-floor room. This is a fine place for a working lunch. *24, rue de la Grande-Truanderie, 1er, tel. 42.33.06.72. Jacket and tie advised. Reservations advised. AE, DC, MC, V. Closed Mon. lunch, Sun., and mid-July to mid-August.*

㊳ Pierre Traiteur. Long an institution among Parisian finan-
$$$ ciers, this old restaurant near the Bourse (stock exchange) has lost none of its charm. Amid an old-fashioned, darkly glittering interior, groups of men in dark suits quietly talk business while eating such bourgeois dishes as stuffed saddle of lamb served with potatoes au gratin, as generations have done. The food is hardly nouvelle, and it's not particularly imaginative, but it pleases the conservative clientele. Hidden behind the Palais Royale, this restaurant isn't as well known to non-Parisians as some of its more visible competitors. The wine list includes lesser-known bottles from places other than Bordeaux or Burgundy, at manageable prices. *10, rue de Richelieu, 1er, tel. 42.96.09.17. Jacket and tie advised. Reservations advised. AE, DC, V. Closed Sat., Sun., and Aug.*

㉙ Le Soufflé. As the name suggests, soufflés are the stars of
$$ this venerable restaurant near the place de la Concorde and many Right Bank hotels. There are main-course soufflés of cheese or smoked salmon and avocado, among others, and for dessert—surprise!—there are more soufflés: chocolate or hazelnut, for example. It's not for everyone, but if you like soufflés you'll be in heaven. Those who don't like them will be satisifed with the regular fish-and-

meat main courses. Both back and front rooms (each with a pleasant but unremarkable decor) afford plenty of privacy for business meals. The crowd is a mix of local business-people and tourists. *36, rue Mont-Thabor, 1er, tel. 42.60.27.19. Casual dress. Reservations advised. AE, DC, MC, V. Closed Sun.*

★ **❽** **Taillevent.** Jean-Claude Vrinat continues to draw a clien-
$$$$ tele studded with stars of politics, business, and the arts to one of the world's most famous restaurants. The fame is deserved: Taillevent's cuisine is brilliantly nouvelle without being precious or silly. Famous starters include lobster and turtle ravioli; main dishes include superbly cooked duck and lamb. The cheese tray is huge, but not as huge as the astounding wine list, with prices ranging from the affordable to the stratospheric. The waiters seem to have extrasensory powers—if you wish for something, it appears as if by magic. Taillevent occupies a dignified old two-story townhouse not far from the Arc de Triomphe, with a formal, stately interior done in light colors. If you invite a client here, they'll know you're serious; if they invite you, go. Private rooms are available. *15, rue Lamennais, 8e, tel. 45.63.39.94. Jacket and tie required. Reservations required. MC, V. Closed Sat., Sun., last week of July, and first three weeks of Aug.*

Left Bank

★ **⓰** **Bellecour.** Tucked away behind Napoléon's tomb at
$$$ Invalides, this Lyon-style bistro is always packed with neighborhood locals, politicians, and businesspeople from all over town—but few tourists find their way here. The regulars come not so much for the attractive but ordinary decor (oil paintings, draperies) as for the large portions of delicious Lyonnais food, such as fresh turbot or red mullet, lightly fried and served on a bed of shredded vegetables, or cod smothered in a gratin of breadcrumbs. As a starter, the crayfish ravioli is exceptional. Ask the waiter to recommend a plat de jour. The wine list tilts heavily to white Burgundies, which are as expensive here as they are everywhere else in Paris. Desserts, such as the café mousse, are rich but exquisite. *22, rue Surcouf, 7e, tel. 45.51.46.93. Jacket and tie advised. Reservations required. AE, DC, MC, V. Closed Sat., Sun., and last two weeks of Aug.*

⓱ **Le Bourdonnais.** Not far from the Eiffel Tower, this res-
$$$ taurant is relatively unknown but highly recommended for a quiet business lunch or dinner, thanks to its serenity, attentive service, and excellent food. The culinary style is basic nouvelle: tasty terrines of chicken or duck, simple but perfectly prepared medallions of lamb, rosy-pink slices of duck breast, and one or two types of fresh fish served with a light sauce. For dessert, try the chocolate-hazelnut cake. Though not particularly innovative, the decor is appealing, with flowers, soothing colors, and large, well-spaced tables. *113, av. de la Bourdonnais, 7e, tel. 47.05.47.96. Jacket and tie required. Reservations advised. AE, V.*

⓸ **Brasserie de l'Ile St-Louis.** This raucous, rowdy Alsatian
$$ beer hall serves arguably the best *choucroute* (sauerkraut and sausages) and cassoulet in Paris. The long, bare wooden tables are impossibly close together, and you'll almost certainly be asked to sit with people you don't know, so

this is no place to conduct business. But you'll be able to overhear highly entertaining conversations from an eclectic crowd—students, senior citizens, tourists, businesspeople—and it's a great place for some after-work fun. The waiters weave through the narrow aisles with the grace of Olympic ice skaters, and they all speak several languages, sometimes all at once. The herring in cream sauce, served with warm potatoes, is a favorite appetizer. *55, quai de Bourbon, 4e, tel. 43.54.02.59. Casual dress. No reservations. No credit cards. Closed Thurs. lunch, Wed., and Aug.*

L'Ecluse. *See* Right Bank Restaurants, above.

★ **⑯ Jules Verne.** In many parts of the world, rooftop view restaurants are home to the dreariest food. So naturally you'd expect the restaurant high up in the Eiffel Tower to be a tourist-filled temple of overpriced pseudo-gourmet cooking. But leave it to the French to perfect the view restaurant; for once, the food is as spectacular as the vista. A terribly chic international crowd (including a surprising number of Parisians, many of them working businesspeople) tear their eyes away from the panorama to pay attention to the sophisticated contemporary French cuisine. The veal with lemon and vanilla is superb, as is just about everything else. Not everybody likes the dramatically lit black erector-set interior, but you're here to gaze at Paris, not the decor. Window seats may be reserved, and they're the hardest to get, but the view from everywhere is good. Wines are pricey. *Eiffel Tower, 7e, tel. 45.55.61.44. Reservations required. Jacket and tie required. AE, DC, MC, V.*
$$$$

Oh! Poivrier. *See* Right Bank Restaurants, above.

★ **㊼ Tour d'Argent.** This is what foreigners think of as the quintessential French restaurant: impeccable food and service, an endless wine list, and an unbeatable view of Notre Dame from a few select tables, all followed by a staggering bill. Longtime owner Claude Terrail has fixed some past problems with the consistency of the food, and he continues his legal battle against a sound-alike, downmarket Tour d'Argent over by the new Bastille Opéra. Nouvelle cuisine will never darken Tour d'Argent's doors—this is rich, pretty, haute-French cooking in the grand style. Have the duck, served with a flourish in two portions, after which you'll be given a souvenir postcard with your fowl's special serial number. Other time-honored specialties are fresh foie gras and a truffle ragoût. Tables are well spaced, conversation is serious and quiet, and diners tend to be French, American, and Japanese executives dressed in dark suits. It's essential to make reservations at least a week in advance, though occasionally there's a last-minute cancellation. The Tour is one of the few super-elegant restaurants open Saturday and Sunday nights. *15, quai de la Tournelle, 5e, tel. 43.54.23.31. Jacket and tie required. Reservations required. AE, DC, MC, V. Closed Mon.*
$$$$

FREE TIME

Fitness

Hotel Facilities

The extraordinary Roman-style health club at the **Ritz** (tel. 42.60.38.30) and the well-equipped weight rooms at the **Royal Monceau** (tel. 45.61.98.00) reflect major efforts by the big hotels to improve their health-club facilities. Also, the **Nikko** (tel. 45.75.67.62) has weight rooms and a pool with retractable roof to allow sunbathing. All three hotels allow nonguests to use their health clubs, for fees that vary depending on the facilities used.

Health Clubs
Gyms and health clubs are mushrooming (and often closing as fast as they open) all over Paris. Recommended ar **City Forum** (85, av. François-Arago, Nanterre, te. 47.29.91.91, fee: 140F per day), **Forest Hills** (4, rue Louis Armand, 15e, tel. 40.60.10.00, fee: 140F per day), an **Garden Gym** (65, av. Champs-Elysée, 8e, tel. 42.25.87.2(fee: 100F per day). Forest Hills and Garden Gym have se\ eral other branches.

Jogging
It's not just Americans—the French do it, too. The be: jogging routes are around and through the **Tuileries** ga: dens in front of the Louvre, in the **Champs de Mars** in fror of the Eiffel Tower, in the **Luxembourg Gardens** on th Left Bank, and in either of the two large parks on Paris periphery: the **Bois de Boulogne** to the west and the **Bo de Vincennes** to the east.

Shopping

Paris's top department stores are the Right Bank A **Printemps** (64, bd. Haussmann, 9e, Right Bank, te 42.82.50.00) and **Galeries Lafayette** down the block (40, b Haussmann, tel. 42.82.34.56). Both have large selection of clothing, perfume, and housewares, as does the Le Bank's **Bon Marché** (22, rue de Sèvres, 7e, tel. 45.4\ 21.22). Also on the Left Bank the **Bazaar de l'Hôtel de Vill** (52, rue de Rivoli, 4e, tel. 42.74.90.00) has the best har ware department in Paris, in the basement, and clothin and housewares on other floors.

Many of the world's most elegant clothiers and perfumer have shops on one or all of Paris's main shopping streets o the Right Bank. Two of these are the elegant avenue Mor taigne and rue Faubourg St-Honoré (both home to suc designers as **Karl Lagerfeld, Christian Dior, Hermès, an Lanvin**), continuing on to rue St-Honoré across rue Ro yale. For perfume and cosmetics, try **Annick Goutal** (14 rue de Castiglione, ler, tel. 42.60.52.82) or **Sephora** (66 ru Chausée d'Antin, 9e, tel. 42.82.06.22)

Rue des Sts-Pères on the Left Bank is the place to go fo top-quality footwear. **Carel** (No. 78, tel. 42.22.71.65) an **Maud Frizon** (No. 79, tel. 42.60.30.01) are two goo choices. Paris's FAO Schwartz, called **Au Nain Bleu** (The Blue Dwarf; 408, rue St-Honoré, 8e tel. 42.60.39.01) is a fabulous three-story toy shop. Loyal customers include Michael Jackson. Rue Royale itself, between La Mad eleine church and place de la Concorde, houses designers **(Pierre Cardin, L'Oréal)** and jewelers **(Chaumet, Van Cleef et Arpels)**. The arcaded rue de Rivoli, from place de la Concorde past the Louvre, has small boutiques of every description.

Most Paris shops, including the swankiest clothes design ers, have major sales twice a year, in January and July.

Otherwise, shops specializing in clothes with the labels cut out—known as *degriffé*—offer bargains for the careful shopper. Degriffé shops open and close with alarming frequency; ask your concierge to recommend the best ones of the moment.

The place de la Madeleine (8e) features two of Paris's best fancy food shops: **Hediard,** at number 21, and **Fauchon,** at number 26. Both have English-speaking salespeople.

Diversions

Paris is one of the great walking towns in the world. Go to the museums, of course, but if the weather allows, walk to and between them. From the tree-lined *grand boulevards* of the Right Bank to the narrow maze of the Left Bank, Paris always surprises. Boulevard Haussmann and, of course, the Champs-Elysées on the Right Bank and Boulevard St-Germain and Boulevard St-Michel on the Left Bank are good places to start a stroll.

The Bâteaux Mouches (literally, housefly boats), which leave from Pont d'Alma (8e, tel. 42.25.96.10) every half hour during good weather, are the best way to see Paris from the Seine. Meals on board are expensive and disappointing.

The Bois de Boulogne is Paris's Central Park, though located west of the center of town. Amid acres of footpaths and forests, it houses two racetracks, several restaurants, and, at night, an array of prostitutes of all descriptions.

The Eiffel Tower (Champs de Mars, 7e, tel. 45.55.91.11) is worth both gazing up at by night, particularly with the new lighting that gives it a shimmering, spider-web look, and gazing down from by day, from any of the three observation platforms.

Invalides (Hôtel des Invalides, 7e, tel. 45.51.92.84) houses Napoléon's grand tomb under a newly regilded golden dome, along with a mammoth museum of military artifacts.

The Louvre (rue de Rivoli, 1er, tel. 40.20.51.51) should be seen in small chunks on many visits, but at least go through I.M. Pei's controversial new glass pyramid entrance hall and see as much as you can. Closed Tues.

The Marais, essentially the 3rd and 4th arrondissement, is the best neighborhood in Paris for an aimless walk, seeing and smelling the streets crowded with garment workers, falafel stands, and small art galleries, all overseen by graceful old mansions. Rue du Temple and Rue du Rosiers, or street of the rosebushes, are good starting places.

Musée d'Orsay (1, rue de Bellechasse, 7e, tel. 45.49.11.11), the spectacular converted train station that now houses virtually all of Paris's mammoth collection of paintings and sculpture dating from 1848 to 1914, also demands several visits. If you have time for only one, go straight up to the third floor to see the Impressionists. Closed Mon.

Notre Dame Cathedral on the Ile de la Cité in the middle of the Seine is Paris's spiritual heart, though it's often overrun with tourists. The best time to visit is just after Sunday morning Mass. Be sure to walk over to the nearby church of St-Michel, in the courtyard of the Conciergerie police station. It features beautifully restored frescoes downstairs and stunning stained-glass windows upstairs. Both churches offer frequent concerts; a Baroque recital or a quartet playing Vivaldi upstairs at St-Michel is an extraordinary treat.

The Palais Royal, built by the all-powerful Cardinal Richelieu in the 17th century, is probably the most stunning example extant of Paris's past glory, with a mammoth courtyard sheltering peaceful gardens and Daniel Buren's controversial zebra-striped columns. Take the time to walk through the gardens and under the arcades.

While strolling the Marais district (*see* above), stop into the **Picasso Museum** (rue de Thorigny, tel. 42.71.25.21), home to a fascinating collection of the great modernist's work.

Place Vendôme features Napoléon triumphant on his column in the center, surrounded by some of the most expensive jewelry shops on earth.

The Arts

The new **Opéra de la Bastille** has taken lyric opera away from the **Palais Garnier** at the place de l'Opéra, which now houses ballet. The **Salle Pleyel** is the major symphony hall, the **Comedie Française** the major drama center. The **Théâtre Musical de Paris** offers a wide selection of opera, ballet, and classical music. The **Palais de Congrès** often hosts plays or visiting dance troupes. Rock stars usually play the huge **Palais Omnisports** at Bercy, or the **Zenith,** on the east side of town.

Paris is probably the best movie city in the world. Hundreds of cinemas show old and new films from all over the world. Most of them are dubbed into French—the initials VF on posters or at the box office indicate that this is the case. The initials VO mean the film is shown with its original soundtrack, with French subtitles. Most VO theaters tend to be along the Champs-Elysées or in the Latin Quarter. Several weekly guides, such as *Pariscope* (which appears each Wed.), list everything going on in the arts.

Tickets to most theaters and musical performances can be bought through hotel concierges, ticket bureaus, or at any of the several locations of the **FNAC** bookstore chain, such as the one in the Forum des Halles shopping center or at 26, av. de Wagram, near the Arc de Triomphe. The **discount ticket** booth in the middle of place de la Madeleine (8e, no tel.) sells half-price seats for that evening's performances.

Comedie Française, Palais Royale, 1er, tel. 40.15.00.15.
Opéra de la Bastille, pl. de la Bastille, 12e, tel. 43.42.92.92.
Palais des Congrès, Porte Maillot, 17e, tel. 46.40.22.22.
Palais Garnier, rue Scribe, 9e, tel. 47.42.53.71.
Palais Omnisports de Paris Bercy, 8, bd. Bercy, 12e, tel. 43.42.01.23.
Salle Pleyel, 252, rue du Faubourg St-Honoré, 8e, tel. 45.63.88.73.
Théâtre Musical de Paris, pl. du Chatelet, 1er, tel. 42.21.00.86.

Zenith, Parc de la Villette, 211, av. Jean-Jaurès, 19e, tel.
42.40.60.00.

After Hours

Bars and Lounges
Hemingway's ghost still haunts both **Harry's Bar** (5, rue
Daunou, 2e, tel. 42.61.71.14) and the mahogany-paneled
bar graced by his bust in the **Ritz** (tel. 42.60.38.30) hotel.
Both naturally attract Americans and journalists. The
major hotels all have popular bars, the most comfortable
being the **English Bar** (tel. 47.23.78.33) at the Plaza
Athénée, the grandest being at the **Crillon** (tel.
42.65.24.24). For a younger, more relaxed crowd of Parisian yuppies, try **Kitty O'Shea's** (10, rue des Capucines,
2e, tel. 40.15.00.30).

Cabaret
Paris's famous nightclubs attract mainly tourists. **Crazy
Horse** (12, av. George-V, 8e, tel. 47.23.32.32) and **Lido**
(116 bis, av. des Champs-Elysées, 8e, tel. 45.63.11.61) are
located near the Arc de Triomphe. **Moulin Rouge** (pl.
Blanche, 18e, tel. 46.06.00.19) and **Folies-Bergère** (32, rue
Richer, 9e, tel. 42.46.77.11) harken back to the days when
it was safe to walk after dark in the raunchier areas of
Pigalle. All feature scantily clad girls, bad multilingual comedians, and dinner and a show for 200 to 600F per person.

Cafés
Although it's getting pretty difficult to find poets and phi-
losophers spending all their time at sidewalk cafés, the institution is alive and thriving. Paris's cafés are still the
best refuge for weary tourists or for pressure-free unwinding after a long day. The best cafés for people-watching tend to be along the great boulevards of the Left Bank:
bd. St-Germain and bd. St-Michel. Among the best and
most famous is **Les Deux Magots** (6, pl. St-Germain-des-
Prés, 6e, tel. 45.48.55.25), across from the old St-
Germain-des-Prés church and just down the street from
the Ecole des Beaux-Arts, from which many of its artistic
customers come. Others include **Le Select** (99, bd. du
Montparnasse, 6e, tel. 42.22.65.27), across the street
from the equally famous and recently remodeled **La
Coupole** (122, bd. du Montparnasse, 6e, tel. 47.20.14.20).
A tiny cup of strong coffee at any of these cafés can top the
$2 mark, but just one cup gives you the right to sit, read
the paper, and argue for as long as you like. Coffee and
drinks are cheaper if you have them standing up at the
bar.

Jazz Clubs
France's love affair with jazz, both American and home
grown, continues. Clubs include **New Morning** (7–9, rue
des Petites-Ecuries, 10e, tel. 45.23.51.41) on the Right
Bank and, on the Left Bank, **Caveau de la Huchette** (5, rue
de la Huchette, 5e, tel. 43.26.65.05), one of the great old
smoke- and music-filled basement clubs in Europe. The
Méridien hotel (Porte Maillot, 17e, tel. 47.58.12.30) is
home to the **Lionel Hampton Jazz Club,** which features occasional appearances by the great man himself.

For Singles

Rock clubs include **Le Palace** (8, rue du Faubourg Montmartre, 9e, tel. 42.46.10.87) and **Le Rex** (5, bd. Poissonnière, 2e, tel. 42.36.83.98). For a New York–style glitzy disco, go to **Regine's** (49, rue de Ponthieu, 8e, tel. 43.59.21.60).

San Francisco

by Barbara Koeth

In 1848, gold was discovered in the sleepy settlement of San Francisco, which had been founded by the Spaniards in 1776. Periods of frantic building have marked the city's progress ever since. Developers now fight bitterly against residents who seek to preserve the city's architectural past and unusual natural beauty.

The city is one of the most scenic in the world: In clear weather its precipitously steep hillsides bring to mind a Mediterranean seaport with a compact city center and outlying residential areas glittering in the sun. On foggy days (and there are many) San Francisco takes on a surreal aspect as skyscrapers and apartment towers disappear into mist-shrouded hills.

Tourism is the number one industry, but San Francisco also attracts a wide range of businesses. The headquarters of many of the nation's leading corporations, including BankAmerica, Chevron, Pacific Telesis, Shaklee, Transamerica, and Wells Fargo, are located here. The financial district—dominated by the dark, looming Bank of America and the pyramid-shaped, glass-and-concrete Transamerica Building—centers on Montgomery Street, between Market Street and the Embarcadero. More than 200,000 people are employed in the area, which is home to the Pacific Stock Exchange. The city's vital foreign trade sector is served by more than 80 foreign banks, which maintain representative offices or agencies in the city.

The population of San Francisco is about 732,000, but the city draws heavily on the Bay Area for its work force. The Chamber of Commerce estimates that there are 285,000 intracity commuters, and as many as 225,000 commuters from outside the city limits. Salaries in the Bay Area run 15%–20% higher than the national average, with San Francisco in the lead.

Top Employers

Employer	Type of Enterprise	Parent*/ Headquarters
American Building Maintenance	Building services	San Francisco

AMFAC Inc.	Distribution and retail	San Francisco
BankAmerica Corp.	Banking	San Francisco
Chevron Corp.	Oil and gas	San Francisco
McKesson Corp.	Wholesale services	San Francisco
Pacific Gas & Electric	Utility	San Francisco
Pacific Telesis Group	Telecommunications	San Francisco
Potlatch Corp.	Paper and forest products	San Francisco
TransAmerica Corp.	Financial services	San Francisco
Wells Fargo & Co.	Banking	San Francisco

*if applicable

ESSENTIAL INFORMATION

Climate

What follows are the average daily maximum and minimum temperatures for San Francisco.

Jan. 55F 13C 41 5	**Feb.** 59F 15C 42 6	**Mar.** 60F 16C 44 7
Apr. 62F 17C 46 8	**May** 66F 19C 48 9	**June** 69F 21C 51 11
July 69F 21C 51 11	**Aug.** 69F 21C 53 12	**Sept.** 73F 23C 51 11
Oct. 69F 21C 50 10	**Nov.** 64F 18C 44 7	**Dec.** 57F 14C 42 6

Airports

San Francisco International Airport (tel. 415/761–0800) is about 16 miles south of the city, off U.S. 101. **Oakland International Airport** (tel. 415/577–4000) is about the same distance east of the city, across San Francisco Bay via I–80 east and I–580 south. There is still a lot of construction going on in the freeway area due to the earthquake in 1989. Roads from the airport to the city should be clearly marked for detours. If you're doing business in the city, use SFIA. If you have business in the East Bay area, consider booking a flight into OIA.

Airport Business Facilities

Mutual of Omaha Business Service Center (upper level of SFIA the South Terminal, between Eastern and Southwest airlines ticket counters, tel. 415/877–0369) has fax machines, photocopying, a notary public, ticket pickup, Western Union, travel insurance, cash advance, Federal Express, phone suites, and a conference room. **AT&T** (SFIA International Terminal, by Phillipine Airlines, tel. 415/877–0269) has fax machines, a small meeting room, and phone suites. **Great Haircuts Barber Shop** (North Terminal, tel. 415/877–8440) has showers.

Airlines

Alaska Air, tel. 800/426–0333.
American, tel. 415/398–4434 or 800/433–7300.
Continental, tel. 415/397–8818 or 800/525–0280.
Delta, tel. 415/552–5700 or 800/221–1212.
Piedmont, tel. 415/956–8636 or 800/251–5720.
Southwest, tel. 415/885–1221 or 800/531–5601.
TWA, tel. 415/864–5731 or 800/221–2000.
United, tel. 415/397–2100 or 800/241–6522.
USAir, tel. 415/956–8636 or 800/428–4322.

Between the Airports and Downtown

By Taxi
Taxis from San Francisco International Airport (SFIA) to downtown take 20–30 minutes and cost about $30. The trip from Oakland International Airport (OIA) takes 30–45 minutes, 60 minutes during rush hour, when traffic snarls on the San Francisco-Oakland Bay Bridge. Morning rush hour is 6:30–8:30 AM; afternoon rush hour, 4–6 PM. Cost: about $35.

By Bus
The **Airporter** (tel. 415/673–2433) provides bus service between SFIA and several convenient locations downtown, including major hotels. Call for the stop nearest your destination. Buses run every 15–30 minutes, 5:30–12:45 AM. Cost: $4.

By Van
Supershuttle will take you from SFIA to anywhere within the city limits of San Francisco, 24 hours a day. At the airport, after picking up your luggage, call 415/871–7800 and a van will usually pick you up within five minutes. Cost: $10. **Yellow Airport Shuttle** (tel. 415/282–7433) also offers service 24 hours a day, leaving every 15 minutes from the upper level of SFIA. Cost: $9. The trip takes 20–30 minutes.

By Rail
Rail service is available from OIA during daytime and early evening hours via shuttle bus to the Oakland Coliseum Arena **BART** (Bay Area Rapid Transit, tel. 415/788–BART) station. However, this is the least convenient way to get downtown. The shuttle to the BART station costs $1. The BART fare to Montgomery Street in downtown San Francisco is $1.90.

Car Rentals

Avis, Budget, Dollar, and Hertz have booths at both airports. National has one at Oakland International.

Avis, tel. 415/562–9000 or 800/331–1212.
Budget, tel. 415/568–4770 or 800/527–0700.
Dollar, tel. 415/638–2750 or 800/421–6868.
Hertz, tel. 415/568–6777 or 800/654–3131.
National, tel. 415/632–2225 or 800/328–4567.

Emergencies

Doctors

Access Health Care provides drop-in medical care at three San Francisco locations daily, 8–8: 1604 Union St. at Franklin St., tel. 415/775–7766; 26 California St. at Drumm St., tel. 415/397–2881; 5748 Geary Blvd. at 22nd Ave., tel. 415/221–9233.

Dentists

The **San Francisco Dental Office,** 132 Embarcadero, between Mission and Howard Sts., tel. 415/777–5115, provides 24-hour emergency service. It also offers dental care by appointment.

Hospitals

Two hospitals have 24-hour emergency rooms: **San Francisco General Hospital,** 1001 Potrero Hill, tel. 415/821–8200, and the **Medical Center** at the University of California, San Francisco, 500 Parnassus Ave. at 3rd Ave., near Golden Gate Park, tel. 415/476–1000.

Important Addresses and Numbers

Audiovisual rentals. McCune Audio/Visual/Video (tel. 415/777–2700), Photo & Sound (tel. 415/882–7600). Both have many locations; call for the one nearest you.

Chamber of Commerce (465 California St., tel. 415/392–4511).

Computer rentals. *See* Audiovisual rentals, above.

Convention and exhibition centers. Moscone Center (747 Howard St., tel. 415/947–4000), Brooks Hall/Civic Auditorium Complex (99 Grove St., Civic Center, tel. 415/974–4000), The San Francisco Fashion Center at Showplace Square (650 Seventh St., tel. 415/864–1561).

Fax services. Copymat (several locations: 705 Market St., downtown, tel. 415/882–7377; 1 Maritime Plaza, Embarcadero, tel. 415/392–1757; 505 Sansome St., financial district, tel. 415/421–2327; 1898 Union St., Marina district, tel. 415/567–8933; 120 Howard St., SoMa district, tel. 415/957–1700), Red Carpet Service (821 Market St., tel. 415/495–1910).

Formal-wear rentals. Black and White Formal Wear, for men and women (1211 Sutter St., tel. 415/673–0625).

Gift shops. Flowers and Gift Baskets: Podesta Baldocchi (2525 California St., tel. 415/346–1300), San Francisco Florists and Gifts (220 Montgomery St., tel. 415/781–5900); Gourmet foods: Williams-Sonoma (576 Sutter St., tel. 415/982–0295); Chocolates: Godiva (The Galleria, 50 Post St., tel. 415/982–6798).

Graphic design studios. One Stop Graphics (27 Sutter St., tel. 415/781–8600).

Hairstylists. Unisex: Mayer's for Hair, no appointment necessary (245 Powell St., tel. 415/981–1310), Transitions (166 Grant Ave., tel. 415/433–7174).

Health and fitness clubs. *See* Fitness, below.

Information hot line (tel. 415/391–2001 for a recorded message listing daily events and activities).

Limousine services. A Classic Ride, Vintage Limousines (tel. 415/626–0433), Carey of San Francisco/Nob Hill Limousine (tel. 415/468–7550), Opera Plaza Limousines (tel. 415/826–9636).

Liquor stores. Fred O. Foster (51 2nd St., tel. 415/362–4775), John Walker & Co. (175 Sutter St., tel. 415/986–2707), The Wine Shop (2175 Chestnut St., tel. 415/567–4725).

Mail delivery, overnight. DHL Worldwide Express (tel. 415/345–9400), Federal Express (tel. 415/877–9000), TNT Skypak (tel. 415/692–9600), UPS (tel. 415/952–5200), U.S. Postal Service Express Mail (tel. 415/621–6792).

Messenger service. Quicksilver Messenger Service (tel. 415/495–4360), Silver Bullet Courier (tel. 415/777–5100), Western Messenger Service (tel. 415/864–4100).

Office space rental. Roxbury Executive Offices (1 Sansome St., tel. 415/951–4600 and 388 Market St., tel. 415/296–2500).

Pharmacies, late-night. Walgreen Drugstore (135 Powell St., near Union Sq., tel. 415/391–4433) open to midnight. Also, Mandarin (895 Washington St., tel. 415/989–9292), though not open late, offers free delivery.

Radio stations, all-news. KGO 810 AM, KCBS 740 AM, KQED 88.5 FM.

Secretarial service. Support Office Services (tel. 415/391–4578).

Stationery supplies. Minden's Stationers (1 Market Plaza, tel. 415/777–2550), Russ Building Stationers (235 Montgomery St., tel. 415/392–7169).

Taxis. Luxor Cab (tel. 415/282–4141), Veteran's Taxicab Company (tel. 415/552–1300), Yellow Cab (tel. 415/626–2345).

Theater tickets. *See* The Arts, below.

Train information. Bay Area Rapid Transit (BART, tel. 415/788–BART), CalTrain Peninsula Commute Service (CALTRAIN, tel. 415/557–8661), San Francisco Municipal Railway System (MUNI, tel. 415/673–MUNI), Amtrak (First and Mission Sts., tel. 415/982–8512).

Travel agents. American Express (several locations: 237 Post St., downtown, tel. 415/981–5533; 295 California St., financial district, tel. 415/788–4367; 2500 Mason St., Sheraton Hotel, Fisherman's Wharf, tel. 415/788–3025), Tyree & Associates, Personalized Tours & Travel (tel. 415/333–3250).

Weather (tel. 415/936–0100).

LODGING

Despite an unusually large number of hotel rooms for a city its size, San Francisco's hotel prices are high. The competitive situation provides good value, though, and just might spoil the hotel experience for you in other cities. Upgraded services and amenities are becoming standard: this is a city of complimentary papers, overnight shoe-shines, and terry-cloth robes. It's not unusual to be greeted by name by the hotel concierge and the doorman. Many of the ultra-deluxe modern hotels provide attentive, Asian-style hospitality. They offer personal service and European-style ambience at only slightly lower prices.

"The City," as it's called by northern Californians, is very compact. All of the Downtown/City Center hotels are within easy walking distance of the business and financial district.

Most of the hotels listed here offer special corporate rates and weekend discounts; inquire when making reservations.

Highly recommended lodgings in each price category are indicated by a star. ★

Category	Cost*
$$$$ (Very Expensive)	over $225
$$$ (Expensive)	$150–$225
$$ (Moderate)	under $150

All prices are for a standard double room, single occupancy, excluding 11% San Francisco hotel tax.

Numbers in the margin correspond to numbered hotels on the San Francisco Lodging and Dining map.

Downtown/City Center

❻
$$$$
Fairmont Hotel and Tower. Built atop fashionable Nob Hill in 1907, this landmark hotel has a magnificent carriage entrance leading to an opulent lobby with more red velvet than one could imagine. Guest rooms in the Tower, which was added in 1961, have the best views, but have a modern, almost anonymous look. Those in the original building provide a more elegant ambience, with period architectural details restored. Although it caters to large convention groups, the hotel is quite luxurious; standard amenities include hair dryers, terry robes, and shoe-shine machines. Extensive renovations in 1989 included state-of-the-art phone services in each room, complete with voice-mail features and jacks for modems and computers; the concierge handles arrangements for other business support services. The exclusive Nob Hill Club, a spa and fitness center on the hotel's Terrace level, is available to guests. The Crown Room (*see* After Hours, below) is a good spot for a scenic drink. *950 Mason St., 94106, tel. 415/772–5000 or 800/527–4727, fax 415/772–5086. Gen. manager, Herman Wiener. 600 rooms, 62 suites. AE, CB, DC, MC, V.*

★ ㉕
$$$
Four Seasons Clift Hotel. This was the exclusive spot for the exclusive set in the 1920s and '30s. Today, it's the only 5-star and 5-diamond hotel in San Francisco (the ultimate ratings by the Mobil Travel Guide and AAA, respectively), and it sets local standards for luxury accommodations, concierge services, and congenial atmosphere. Since 1981, more than $1 million dollars has been spent each year so that the 75-year-old landmark could give its more modern high-rise competition a run for the money. And it does—with aplomb. Almost all doubles are spacious enough for a comfortable seating area; deluxe rooms, created from two

smaller rooms have a larger seating area. Rooms have fine fabrics, original artwork, period reproduction furnishings, and tasteful appointments that create an elegant, residential atmosphere. Each room has two phone lines. Baths are small but have every amenity. The 16th and 17th floors house the Business Center, 11 deluxe penthouse rooms, and two large boardrooms for private meetings. The French Room is the place for power breakfasts and dinners; the Sunday brunch is outstanding (*see* Dining, below). High tea in the lobby is a San Francisco institution (*see* Diversions, below), and the Redwood Room (*see* After Hours, below) draws an upscale crowd at the end of the working day. *495 Geary St., 94102, tel. 415/775–4700 or 800/332–3442, fax 415/776–9238. Gen. manager, Paul V. Pusateri. 329 rooms, 18 suites. AE, CB, DC, MC, V.*

㉒ **Galleria Park Hotel.** This European-style "boutique" ho-
$$ tel in the heart of the financial district opened in 1984, and was refurbished and redecorated in 1988. It features Art Nouveau decor in the lobby, including a marble entry with striking etched glass, a sculpted wood-burning fireplace, and a glazed crystal skylight. Guest rooms are decorated in light-hued floral patterns and pale wood furniture. Rooms on the lower floors are quite small, as are all the bathrooms, but the soundproofing throughout is excellent, an important factor given the hotel's busy location. Business amenities are minimal, but each room has a well-lighted desk with direct-dial telephone. Three small meeting rooms accommodate groups of 12–60. Room service is limited; Bentley's, a commendable seafood restaurant, offers gourmet room service in the early morning and evening hours only. There is a rooftop park and jogging track. *A Kimco hotel. 191 Sutter St., 94104, tel. 415/781–3060 or 800/792–9855, fax 415/433–4409. Gen. manager, John Brocklehurst. 177 rooms, 8 suites. AE, CB, DC, MC, V.*

★ ㉑ **Grand Hyatt San Francisco.** After a top-to-bottom $20 mil-
$$$ lion renovation, completed in 1990, this 36-story hotel is indeed grand. Its large, open-air plaza area is a wonderfully extravagant use of space. The hotel is just steps from Union Square. Guest rooms are elegantly decorated in dark walnut and rich burgundy, and include two phones and television sets as standard amenities. The Executive Business Center is the most complete in San Francisco, providing a long list of business and on-line information services including stock market quotes and averages and the Dow Jones QuickSearch, which accesses corporate reports, as well as facilities for issuing airline tickets and boarding passes. *345 Stockton St., 94108, tel. 415/398–1234 or 800/233–1234, fax 415/392–2536. Gen. manager, Marc Ellin. 693 rooms, including 92 concierge level, 25 suites, and 6 penthouse suites. AE, CB, DC, MC, V.*

⓯ **Hyatt Regency San Francisco.** This luxury convention ho-
$$$ tel is part of the eight-block Embarcadero Center business and shopping complex, just minutes from Moscone Convention Center, Union Square shopping, Fisherman's Wharf, and other visitor attractions. The 20-story building has a 300-foot-long sky-lighted lobby with full-size trees, a running stream, and enough greenery to landscape a small park. When it opened in 1973, the Hyatt's high-tech futuristic design was on the cutting edge. Times have changed, though, and in 1990 all rooms and most of the public spaces were redecorated to provide a warmer

SAN FRANCISCO

SAN FRANCISCO HOTEL CHART

HOTELS	Price Category	Business Services / Banquet capacity	No. of meeting rooms	Secretarial services	Audiovisual equipment	Teletype news service	Computer rentals	In-room modem phone jack	All-news cable channel	Desk	Desk lighting	Bed lighting
Airport Hilton	*$$*	700	27	✓	✓	✓	✓	✓	✓	●	●	●
Airport Marriott	*$$*	1200	7	✓	✓	-	✓	✓	✓	◐	◐	◐
The Claremont Resort	*$$$$*	400	15	✓	✓	-	✓	-	✓	●	●	●
Fairmont Hotel and Tower	*$$$$*	1900	19	✓	✓	-	✓	✓	✓	●	●	●
Four Seasons Cliff	*$$$*	180	9	✓	✓	-	✓	✓	✓	●	●	●
Galleria Park	*$$*	50	3	✓	✓	-	✓	✓	✓	●	●	●
Grand Hyatt	*$$$*	700	18	✓	✓	✓	✓	✓	✓	●	●	●
Hilton and Towers	*$$$*	3000	61	✓	✓	-	✓	✓	✓	●	●	●
Hyatt Regency	*$$$*	1500	35	✓	✓	✓	✓	✓	✓	◐	◐	◐
The Inn at Union Square	*$$*	0	0	✓	-	-	-	-	✓	◐	◐	◐
Mandarin Oriental	*$$$$*	100	3	✓	✓	-	✓	✓	✓	●	●	●
Marriott	*$$$*	3350	21	✓	✓	-	✓	-	✓	◐	◐	◐
Meridian	*$$$$*	100	4	✓	✓	-	✓	✓	✓	●	●	●
Nikko	*$$$*	500	9	✓	✓	✓	✓	✓	✓	●	●	●
Nob Hill Lambourne	*$$$$*	0	0	✓	✓	-	✓	✓	✓	●	●	●
The Pan Pacific	*$$$*	500	13	✓	✓	-	✓	✓	✓	◐	◐	◐
Prescott	*$$*	0	0	✓	-	-	✓	✓	✓	●	●	●
The Stanford Court	*$$$*	400	2	✓	✓	-	✓	✓	✓	◐	●	●
The Westin St. Francis	*$$$*	1100	27	✓	✓	-	-	✓	✓	◐	◐	◐

$$$$ = over $225, $$$ = $150-$225, $$= under $150.
● good, ◐ fair, ○ poor.
All hotels listed here have photocopying and fax facilities.

| In-Room Amenities | | | | | | | | | | Hotel Amenities | | | | | | |
Nonsmoking rooms	In-room checkout	Minibar	Pay movies	VCR/Movie rentals	Hairdryer	Toiletries	Room service	Laundry/Dry cleaning	Pressing	Concierge	Barber/Hairdresser	Garage	Courtesy airport transport	Sauna	Pool	Exercise room
✓	✓	✓	✓	✓	✓	●	◐	●	●	–	–	✓	✓	–	●	●
✓	✓	–	✓	–	✓	◐	●	●	●	✓	–	✓	✓	✓	●	●
✓	✓	✓	✓	✓	–	◐	◐	●	●	✓	✓	✓	–	✓	●	●
✓	✓	✓	–	–	✓	●	●	●	●	✓	✓	✓	–	✓	–	●
✓	✓	✓	✓	✓	–	●	●	●	●	✓	–	✓	–	–	–	–
✓	–	✓	✓	✓	–	◐	○	●	●	✓	–	✓	–	–	–	–
✓	✓	✓	✓	–	–	●	●	●	●	✓	✓	✓	–	–	–	●
✓	✓	✓	–	–	✓	●	●	●	●	✓	✓	✓	–	✓	●	●
✓	✓	✓	–	–	–	◐	●	●	●	✓	–	✓	–	–	–	–
✓	–	✓	✓	–	–	◐	○	●	●	✓	–	✓	–	–	–	–
✓	✓	✓	–	–	✓	●	●	●	●	✓	✓	✓	–	–	–	–
✓	✓	✓	–	–	✓	◐	●	●	●	✓	–	✓	–	✓	●	●
✓	✓	✓	✓	–	–	●	●	●	●	✓	–	✓	–	–	–	–
✓	✓	✓	✓	–	–	●	●	●	●	✓	✓	✓	–	✓	●	●
✓	✓	✓	✓	✓	✓	●	–	●	●	✓	–	✓	–	–	–	–
✓	–	✓	✓	✓	✓	●	●	●	●	✓	–	✓	–	–	–	–
✓	✓	✓	✓	–	✓	●	○	●	●	✓	–	✓	–	–	–	–
✓	✓	✓	✓	–	✓	●	●	●	●	✓	–	✓	–	–	–	–
✓	✓	✓	✓	–	–	◐	●	●	●	✓	✓	✓	–	–	–	–

Room service: ● 24-hour, ◐ 6AM–10PM, ○ other.
Laundry/Dry cleaning: ● same day, ◐ overnight, ○ other.
Pressing: ● immediate, ◐ same day, ○ other.

atmosphere, though rooms are still standard Hyatt issue. The phone system was also upgraded to provide two lines in each room and voice mail features. Each room contains a work area with a well-lighted desk; a full range of business services including teleconference calling is available at the business center. Equinox, San Francisco's only revolving rooftop restaurant and cocktail lounge, is a good place for a drink with a view (*see* After Hours, below). *5 Embarcadero Center, 94111, tel. 415/788–1234 or 800/ 233–1234, fax 415/989–7448. Gen. manager, Charles McElroy 803 rooms, 110 concierge level, including 44 suites. AE, CB, DC, MC, V.*

㉚ $$ The Inn at Union Square. This small, elegant hotel in the heart of downtown San Francisco offers service and comfort in the European tradition. Security-conscious travelers will appreciate the locked front door (with doorbell) and keyed access elevator. Built in 1924, the Inn was completely renovated in 1981. Each room is decorated differently, with Georgian-style furniture and designer fabrics; many have king-size canopied beds with goosedown pillows. Each of the four guest-room floors has its own intimate lobby where guests are served a complimentary Continental breakfast, afternoon tea, and wine and hors d'oeuvres in the evening. The sixth-floor penthouse boasts a wood-burning fireplace and private whirlpool bath and sauna. All business services are provided by the front desk staff; the penthouse will accommodate up to eight people for meetings. *440 Post St., 94102, tel. 415/397– 3510 or 800/288–4346, fax 415/989–0529. Gen. manager, Brooks Bayly. 31 rooms, 7 suites, 1 penthouse suite. AE, CB, MC, DC, V.*

★ ⓭ $$$$ Mandarin Oriental, San Francisco. In the middle of the historic "Dollar Block," in the heart of the city's financial district, this hotel occupies the top 11 floors of the 48-story First Interstate Center. The unique positioning of the double towers ensures each of the guest rooms an unobstructed view of the city and the Bay. Because there are only 14 rooms on each floor, guests are ensured a high degree of quiet, privacy, and security. The luxuriously appointed rooms have a distinctly residential feeling, complete with a pleasantly chiming doorbell. The 22 Mandarin rooms have screened living areas and huge polished-marble bathrooms with floor-to-ceiling windows next to the extra-deep soaking tubs. All rooms have three phones with two phone lines, extra large desk, and remote control television and radio with speakers in the bathroom. Personal amenities are outstanding, including lightweight and terry-cloth robes, and Thai silk slippers to take home with you. The lobby level Business Center provides all professional services and includes a private conference room. The restaurant here, Silks (*see* Dining, below), is first-rate. *222 Sansome St., 94104–2792, tel. 415/885– 0999 or 800/622–0404, fax 415/433–0289. Gen. manager, Wolfgang K. Hultner. 154 rooms, 6 suites. AE, CB, DC, MC, V.*

★ ㉙ $$$$ Hotel Meridien San Francisco. When it opened in 1983, this 36-story sky-rise hotel was at the cutting edge of the newly respectable SoMa (South of Market) area. Today, the opulent hotel, with expansive rooms, elegant furnishings, and fabulous floor-to-ceiling windows, is at the heart of the new downtown area, just a block from Moscone Center. A $20 million redecoration, which began early in 1990, gilded the lily. Personal and business amenities are top notch; all rooms have desks and well-lighted work areas. The distinctively French atmosphere that pervades the hotel is best showcased in the Pierre restaurant (*see* Dining, below), which serves contemporary California-French cuisine. There's a fully staffed Business Center and a currency exchange in the lobby. *50 3rd St., 94103, tel. 415/974–6400 or 800/543–4300, fax 415/543–8268. Gen. manager, Cyril Isnard. 675 rooms, 26 suites. AE, CB, DC, MC, V.*

★ ❷ **Hotel Nikko San Francisco.** Oriental-style tranquility
$$$ marks this sleekly modern hotel, just minutes from the downtown financial district. From the soothing sound of falling water in the white marble lobby, to the mauve and pearl-gray room decor, the mood throughout the 25-story hotel is serene. Guest rooms feature expansive windows, furniture with simple lines, and recessed lighting. Well-designed, contemporary desks and swivel reading lamps are standard, as are radio and television speakers in the bathrooms. The fifth-floor fitness center features two dry saunas, two traditional *ofuros* (Japanese soaking tubs), a *kamaburo* (Japanese sauna), and the city's only glass-enclosed swimming pool and whirlpool. Exercise clothing, towels, lockers, and full amenities are provided for guests at no extra charge. The Executive Assistance Center is staffed 12 hours every weekday, and offers complete business service support, including personal computers in small partitioned offices, a television monitor, VCR and video-editing equipment, and a paper shredder. *222 Mason St., 94102, tel. 415/394–1111 or 800/645–5687, fax 415/421–0455. Gen. manager, Andrews Kirmse. 522 rooms, 27 suites, 2 Japanese tatami suites. AE, CB, DC, MC, V.*

❽ **Nob Hill Lambourne.** At this high-tech hotel, a full range
$$$$ of business services is provided in the privacy of your own room; there's a fax machine with dedicated phone line, and a personal computer with preloaded software, including Lotus 1-2-3 and Wordperfect 5.0. On-line computer services include both Lexis and Nexis data bases. Opened late in 1989, the three-story hotel attracts many travelers in the legal and financial-services industry. And no wonder. Full secretarial support, personalized voice mail and answering services, desktop publishing, and boardroom facilities make the Nob Hill Lambourne seem like a San Francisco branch office. The accommodations are decorated with custom-designed furnishings that mix contemporary and period styles. Each room is oversized, with a queen-size bed, a separate work area, and a fully outfitted kitchen area. Although complimentary Continental breakfast is served, there is no other food service. Room rates include airport pickup in a London-style taxi. *725 Pine St., 94108, tel. 415/433–2287 or 800/274–8466, fax 415/433–0975. Gen. manager, Cyndi Weber. 20 rooms, 6 suites. AE, CB, DC, MC, V.*

❶❽ **The Pan Pacific Hotel San Francisco.** Known as the
$$$ Portman until it was acquired by the Pan Pacific Hotel and Resort chain in 1990, this 21-story hotel in the heart of downtown is noteworthy for its high degree of personal service and impeccable standards of privacy. There is round-the-clock concierge and valet service, a private club for off-hours meetings or relaxing, and no set check-

out time. The third-floor lobby is a riot of marble, glass, and chrome, complete with architect John Portman's signature glass capsule elevators. A sculpture of four dancing nudes, inspired by Matisse's *The Dance*, and a fountain are positioned directly under the 17-story atrium skylight. The rooms are spacious, and the rose-color marble baths are immense, with separate soaking tubs and shower stalls. The dressing areas have miniscreen TV sets. There are two-line phones at the desk, bedside, and in the bathroom, with call waiting and voice mail features. The Executive Conference Center has its own dining facility and a separate concierge staff. *500 Post St., 94102, tel. 415/771–8600 or 800/533–6465, fax 415/398–0267. Gen. manager, Patrick J. Mene. 330 rooms, 19 suites. AE, CB, DC, MC, V.*

★ ⑰ **Prescott Hotel.** This is one of San Francisco's newest "bou-
$$ tique" hotels, opened in 1989. Small and elegant, with a gracious lobby with blazing hearth-style fireplace and richly upholstered custom furniture, it offers a good location a block from Union Square. The accommodations conjure up a Ralph Lauren bedroom with deep green, rich burgundy, and dark wood decor. Terry robes, hair dryers, makeup mirrors, and limousine transportation to the financial district are standard amenities, and all rooms have desks and phone jacks for data transmission. The Mendocino penthouse takes up the entire seventh floor, and includes a secluded rooftop deck with hot tub and garden. Guests are guaranteed preferred seating at Postrio, Wolfgang Puck's restaurant sensation (*see* Dining, below), which also supplies room service during limited hours. *A Kimco hotel. 545 Post St., 94102, tel. 415/563–0303 or 800/ 283–7322, fax 415/563–6831. Gen. manager, Patrick Sampson. 109 rooms, 7 suites, 1 penthouse suite. AE, CB, DC, MC, V.*

㉖ **San Francisco Hilton and Towers.** A $210 million renova-
$$$ tion and expansion in 1988 made this the biggest hotel in San Francisco. Originally built in 1964, with a 1972 addition, it takes up an entire city block in the center of downtown with three towers of 19, 23, and 46 floors. The sleekly modern lobby bustles with activity, and each building serves a different market: business, convention, and leisure. The concierge-level rooms in the newest tower are the best bet for business travelers, with upscale furnishings, lots of greenery, and upgraded amenities; desks and two-line phones are standard. It's worth having a drink at Cityscape, the restaurant at the top of the highest tower; it commands a 360-degree view of the city and the Bay, and has a unique retractable skylight (*see* After Hours, below). There's a complete business center, and a health club with a heated outdoor pool on a sheltered deck— quite unexpected in the middle of the city. *1 Hilton Sq., 94102, tel. 415/771–1400 or 800/445–8667, fax 415/771– 6807. Gen. manager, Holger Gantz. 1,891 rooms (107 concierge level, 190 suites). AE, CB, DC, MC, V.*

㉘ **San Francisco Marriott.** Part of the San Francisco redevel-
$$$ opment project known as "Yerba Buena Gardens," this huge 40-story hotel has changed the San Francisco skyline with its distinctive design—modern Art Deco with large fanlike windows across the top. This major meeting and convention facility, which opened in 1989, is one block from Moscone Center. It is a factory of sorts: Rooms are

small but functional, with standard California-pastel decor. The concierge level rooms on the 18th and 19th floors afford less anonymity. They feature upgraded amenities and a private lounge. Recreational facilities include a full-service health club, with the city's largest indoor swimming pool; weight, exercise, and massage rooms; whirlpool; and sauna. In addition to the largest ballroom west of Las Vegas, the hotel has 21 self-contained conference suites suitable for groups from 5 to 150. The Business Communications Center provides all business services, including paging devices and beepers. *777 Market St., 94103, tel. 415/896–1600 or 800/228–9290, fax 415/777–2799. Gen. manager, Alain Piallat. 1,500 rooms (98 concierge level, 134 suites). AE, CB, DC, MC, V.*

★ **❼** **The Stanford Court.** Acquisition by Stouffer Hotels and
$$$ Resorts in 1989 brought a number of immediate changes to this prestigious Nob Hill luxury hotel, including 24-hour room service. More important was the elimination of the 75¢ surcharge previously billed to guests to place phone calls, and the elimination of charges for incoming fax messages. The lobby area, which was refurbished in 1989, showcases Baccarat chandeliers, Carrara marble, and French Provincial furniture; it's a lovely setting for afternoon tea (*see* Diversions, below). All guest rooms were completely refurbished in 1990, and decorated with deep-tone floral print fabrics and dark wood furnishings; minibars and safes were added. But all this was icing on the cake: standard amenities at this nine-story hotel already included television sets in each bathroom, two telephones with call-waiting features in each bedroom, and all-day, complimentary car service anywhere in the city. Built in 1919 as a luxury apartment building, the hotel has spacious rooms, with high ceilings and detailed moldings. A fully staffed business center opened in 1990. *905 California St., 94108, tel. 415/989–3500 or 800/468–3571, fax 415/986–8195. Gen. manager, Creighton Casper. 402 rooms, 34 suites. AE, CB, DC, MC, V.*

㉔ **The Westin St. Francis.** In 1972, the addition of a 32-story
$$$ tower doubled the number of rooms in this historic (1904) hotel, which dominates one side of famed Union Square and overlooks the financial district. A $53 million renovation, completed in 1987, preserved and enhanced historical details in the original lobby and guest rooms, but provided contemporary furnishings throughout. The Tower rooms are the best bet, featuring upgraded amenities and well-lighted work areas. Five bronze-tinted glass external elevators provide access to the Tower guest rooms, the much touted nightclub, Oz (*see* After Hours, below), the highly rated Victor's restaurant, and a breathtaking panorama of San Francisco and environs. The lobby's Compass Rose restaurant (*see* Diversions, below) offers high tea in style. *335 Powell St., 94102, tel. 415/397–7000 or 800/228–3000, fax 415/774–0124. Gen. manager, Hans Bruland. 1,202 rooms, 84 suites. AE, CB, DC, MC, V.*

Airport

㉟ **San Francisco Airport Hilton.** Unlike most airport hotels,
$$ this property has a resort look and feel to it. The hotel opened in 1960, but was renovated in 1989. Most rooms are oversized, with small bathrooms, and all have complete business amenities including two-line phones and well-

lighted desks and work areas. Many overlook the heated
Olympic-size pool or the garden courtyard, and some have
patios opening onto the pool area. The fully staffed business center has a PC work station and the latest office
equipment. There's also a well-equipped fitness center.
Though ideal for large meetings, the hotel also caters to
smaller groups with well-designed and comfortable executive conference facilities. *San Francisco International
Airport, 94128, tel. 415/589-0770 or 800/445-8667, fax
415/589-0770. Gen. manager, Richard Groves. 540 rooms,
9 suites. AE, CB, DC, MC, V.*

36 **San Francisco Airport Marriott.** This 11-story hotel has a
$$ bright and attractive public lobby, with picture windows
that have panoramic views of the bay and the airport run-
ways. The hallways, though, are narrow and dark. Stan-
dard rooms are small but functional, with adequate desks
and lighting; concierge level rooms and suites are the best
bets. There's a fully equipped health club complete with
saunas, whirlpool, and indoor pool. *1800 Old Bayshore
Hwy., Burlingame, 94010, tel. 415/692-9100 or 800/228-
9290, fax 415/692-9861. Gen. manager, Steve Sharple.
684 rooms (55 concierge level, 21 suites). AE, CB, DC,
MC, V.*

Oakland

★ 33 **The Claremont Resort.** This legendary Victorian-style ho-
$$$$ tel, surrounded by 22 acres of landscaped gardens in the
Oakland/Berkeley hills, celebrated its 75th anniversary in
1990. Less than 30 minutes from downtown San Francis-
co, it offers all the advantages of a self-contained resort in
an urban setting, as well as a $6 million, 25,000-square-
foot, European-style spa facility, opened in 1989. The
high-ceilinged lobby showcases contemporary artwork—
the largest collection by Pacific Northwest artists assem-
bled outside of a museum. Guest rooms are unusually spa-
cious, and many feature seating areas; all have upgraded
bathrooms. The cuisine served in the Pavilion Restaurant
is top notch, and the views across the bay to San Francisco
and the peninsula and north to Mt. Tamalpais are excep-
tional. The Gallery is noted for premium wines by the
glass; the Terrace Bar provides music and dancing. More
than $28 million has been invested in the property over the
past 10 years, much of it in the conference center, which
draws major corporate clients. A staffed business center
provides professional services. *41 Tunnel Rd., Box 23363,
Oakland, 94623, tel. 415/843-3000, fax 415/843-6239.
Gen. manager, Lenny Fisher. 239 rooms, 30 suites. AE,
CB, DC, MC, V.*

DINING

by Colleen Dunn Bates

For more than a century, San Francisco has reigned as the
undisputed restaurant capital of the West. In the last two
decades, excellent restaurants have opened in Los Ange-
les and San Diego and in towns from Seattle to Santa Fe.
But San Francisco remains an eating town nonpareil. Its
hotel restaurants are unsurpassed. Its Asian food—Cam-
bodian, Vietnamese, Korean, Japanese, Chinese—is won-
derful. Its classic "old San Francisco" eateries remain

infused with charm and civility. And its California cuisine is inventive and flavorful.

Because of its compactness, San Francisco is ideal for the hungry business traveler. Within downtown's financial district/Union Square/Civic Center hub are some of the West's very best restaurants (Masa's, Fleur de Lys, Stars, and Postrio, to name just a few). Chinatown and North Beach (San Francisco's Little Italy) are just a short walk or cab ride north; trendy South of Market (SoMa) is an equally short hop south. The city's restaurants usually reflect the immediate neighborhood—more tourists in Union Square, more government employees and arts lovers in the Civic Center/Opera area, more bankers and business people in the financial district, more high-style yuppies in SoMa. But you'll usually find a refreshing mix of patrons almost everywhere.

San Francisco may be in California, but when it comes to wardrobe, don't expect the anything-goes attitude of Los Angeles. Thanks to a colder climate and more conservative populace, people dress up a bit at the city's best restaurants. Jackets and ties are the norm at practically all higher-end downtown establishments, even if they're not required. Things are a bit more casual in SoMa and, of course, at most of the ethnic restaurants.

Highly recommended restaurants in each price range are indicated by a star ★.

Category	Cost*
$$$$ (Very Expensive)	over $50
$$$ (Expensive)	$31–$50
$$ (Moderate)	$20–$30
$ (Inexpensive)	under $20

*per person, including an appetizer, entrée, and dessert, but excluding drinks, service, and 6.75% sales tax.

Numbers in the margin correspond to numbered restaurants on the San Francisco Lodging and Dining map.

Business Breakfasts

Hands down, the best business breakfast spot in the city is **Campton Place** (340 Stockton St., tel. 415/781–5155). It offers a dignified setting, exceptional contemporary American food (old-fashioned waffles topped with all sorts of tasty things, superb corned-beef hash, first-rate breads), and a convenient Union Square location. For another take on the all-American breakfast, this time in a chic farmhouse-kitchen setting, make the trek to the Marina district to **Doidge's** (2217 Union St., tel. 415/921–2149). Make a reservation, too, since the dreamy pancakes, nitrite-free bacon, and perfectly poached eggs keep the tables full. Despite the name, Union Square's **French Room,** at the Four Seasons Clift Hotel (tel. 415/775–4700), serves such tasty American standards as oatmeal and scrambled eggs; the setting is quiet and conservatively opulent—perfect for an important business breakfast. For something a bit different—and for a lively atmosphere and stunning decor of gleaming marble, polished wood, high ceilings, and an open kitchen—try **Il Fornaio** in the Embarcadero area (1265 Battery St., tel. 415/986–0100): Even bacon 'n' eggs are exceptional, particularly when ordered with Italian smoked bacon and toasted, triple-thick slices of Il Fornaio's famous breads. To make the trendiest breakfast scene in town, reserve a table at **Postrio,** at the Prescott Hotel in Union Square (tel. 415/776–7825). This glamorous multilevel restaurant is the latest project of California-cuisine King Wolfgang Puck, and serves such innovative dishes as soft scrambled eggs with lobster, mascarpone, and chives.

Downtown

★ ❹ **Amelio's.** Like Ernie's (*see* below), Amelio's has been one
$$$$ of San Francisco's best known restaurants for decades. And like Ernie's, this once-tired North Beach warhorse was given a new lease on life by gifted chef Jacky Robert, who made Ernie's kitchen hum again before coming here. In an elegant, warmly decorated (rich woods, floral fabrics), quiet dining room, a smooth staff serves Robert's creative yet not too fussy contemporary French dishes, either à la carte or via one of two fine fixed-price menus. Dishes change regularly; you can expect such creations as woven bicolor pasta with Hawaiian prawns and scallops, a green salad with a brie "pancake," rack of lamb with an Oriental-style soy marinade, and exquisite chocolate desserts. The wine list is expensive but full of good choices. Amelio's is a short cab ride from downtown and an excellent spot for business entertaining. *1630 Powell St., tel. 415/397–4339. Jacket and tie advised. Reservations advised. AE, DC, MC, V. Dinner only. Closed Mon. and Tues. (closings vary).*

⓫ **The Blue Fox.** Redone from head to foot by a new owner,
$$$ the new Blue Fox combines an opulent decor (mirrored and draped walls, light colors, chandeliers) with equally opulent Northern Italian food, flawless service, and a well-dressed financial district clientele—making it an ideal spot for serious business entertaining. The food is almost too pretty to eat—almost. Try the venison carpaccio with essence of white truffle, any of the rich, perfect risotti, the first-rate veal dishes, and the fresh seafood, such as the simple, grilled red mullet with bitter greens. And take advantage of the excellent Italian wine list. The small, terribly refined bar serves as a predinner rendezvous. A short walk from downtown's office towers, The Blue Fox is probably the most elegant Italian restaurant in the city. *659 Merchant St., tel. 415/981–1177. Jacket and tie advised. Reservations advised. AE, CB, DC, MC, V. Dinner only. Closed Sun.*

㉓ **Campton Place.** Despite the departure of famed chef
$$$ Bradley Ogden, this hotel restaurant remains very good, turning out delicious contemporary American food. And it's as handsome as ever, in that luxury-hotel style that's currently popular: white linens on large tables, peach-color fabric walls, tall windows, upholstered chairs, and dramatic floral displays. It's a great place for both business meals and business entertaining; the well-spaced freestanding tables in the center of the room afford more privacy than the banquettes against the wall. The food combines American ingredients and inspirations with the creativity and technique normally associated with French

cooking. Breakfast is inspired (*see* Business Breakfasts, above), the lunchtime salads are marvels, and dinner is always intriguing, with such offerings as grilled asparagus with morels and a pancetta vinaigrette, spring lamb chops with a Gorgonzola crust, and guinea-hen with crisp potatoes and spinach. For sweets, try chocolate mousse torte with apricot brandy sauce, or butterscotch pie. *340 Stockton St., tel. 415/781–5155. Jacket and tie advised. Reservations advised. AE, CB, DC, MC, V.*

⑤ Cypress Club. Located in the historic Jackson Square area
$$$ of downtown, this wild new restaurant looks like a speakeasy designed for Ali Baba and Dick Tracy. You enter through a curtain into a room aswirl with curving, oversized shapes and exotic materials: fat, rounded dividers made of pounded copper, overstuffed mohair seats, a cartoonlike mural, and more. Even those who don't like the look admit that it's loads of fun. The contemporary American food isn't quite as weird as the decor, but it's definitely inventive. Seared scallops with fennel seed and a saffron vinaigrette, and charred pork loin with honey dates and ginger are among the tasty choices. The pastry chef is already legendary; people come here just for her caramel crème brûlée, and nut brioche pudding on warm poached fruit. The setting is a bit outlandish for serious business talks (though there's an excellent private room in back for meetings), but its a perfect spot for entertaining adventurous clients. *500 Jackson St., Financial District, tel. 415/296–8555. Jacket advised. Reservations strongly advised. AE, CB, DC, MC, V.*

★ ⑲ Donatello. Haute Italian cuisine is the order of the day in
$$$$ these adjoining dining rooms in the Donatello hotel. Both are ultraswank, almost stuffy visions of Old World splendor; mirrors and Italian marble dominate one, richly patterned Fortuny fabrics set a cozier tone in the other. Don't expect hearty fare—presentations are refined, almost a bit precious, and not exactly served with a generous hand. But there's no doubting that the kitchen is skilled and the flavors are outstanding. Popular dishes include sautéed fresh shiitake mushrooms with garlic, spinach, and pancetta; tasty eggplant and zucchini with tomato sauce, Fontina cheese, and oregano; and tender rack of lamb with rosemary, pancetta, and garlic. The service and wine list live up to the setting and the very high prices. The well-spaced tables and discreet atmosphere facilitate business conversation. *501 Post St., Union Square, tel. 415/441–7100. Jacket and tie advised. Reservations advised. Dinner only. AE, CB, D, DC, MC, V.*

⑩ Ernie's. You may not believe it upon entering, but this
$$$$ legendary spot began in 1934 as a humble Italian joint. Today, it is perhaps San Francisco's most elegant restaurant—popular with a moneyed, middle-aged crowd of locals and tourists, who appreciate the well-spaced tables, gleaming woodwork, silk-covered walls, fine silver, and unequaled service. And the wine list has done nothing but improve over the last half century. Many famous old restaurants stick with the tried and true, which then becomes tired and dull, but not Ernie's. The food has had its downs over the decades, but for the last several years it has been worthy of the decor and reputation. The dishes are updated French, neither too stodgy nor too strange; try the game pâté en croûte with seasonal mushrooms,

grilled tuna with a tropical-fruit coulis, rack of lamb in puff pastry with garlic sauce, and special-occasion desserts. If you need to impress someone, holding a dinner here will do the trick. On the border of the financial district and North Beach, Ernie's is a five-minute cab ride from most downtown hotels. *847 Montgomery St., tel. 415/ 397–5969. Jacket and tie required. Reservations advised. AE, CB, DC, MC, V. Dinner only.*

★ ⑯ **Fleur de Lys.** Rivaling Masa's (*see* below) as one of the best
$$$$ French restaurants in Northern California, Fleur de Lys deserves every bit of its national reputation. Chef/co-owner Hubert Keller turns out contemporary French masterpieces that taste as wonderful as they look. A hollowed baked potato hiding an herbed breast of squab, sautéed foie gras served on lettuce leaves with slices of duck breast, roasted lamb chops wrapped in an airy vegetable mousseline, a chocolate-mousse-and-meringue swan swimming on a raspberry pond—few restaurants outside of France serve such marvels. Hearty meat-and-potatoes types may find Fleur de Lys's food a bit precious, but gourmets will be in heaven—as will wine lovers. The dining room's dramatic use of hand-painted, rich red fabric draping the ceiling and walls, gives a feeling rather like that of a Sultan's banquet tent. The clientele is made up of soberly dressed executives and food lovers of all sorts; it's a good place for serious business entertaining and discussions, though it's more a place to pay attention to your meal, not your paperwork. Dinners are fixed-price only. *777 Sutter St., tel. 415/673–7779. Jacket and tie required. Reservations strongly advised. AE, DC, MC, V. Dinner only. Closed Sun.*

★ ❷ **Fog City Diner.** A rip-roaring hit from the day it opened,
$$ the Fog City Diner is a winning blend of old San Francisco charm and contemporary California-cuisine zing. San Francisco's mythical hard-boiled private eye Sam Spade would have felt at home in this waterfront hangout on the border of the financial district and North Beach, hunching over a steak and a scotch in one of the booths; also at home is a pride of wine-drinking Yuppies and well-dressed stockbroker types looking more for fun than shop talk. Fog City really does look like a diner, albeit a snazzy one, with polished wood, tile floors, upholstered booths, and '40s-style lighting. The food of chef/owner Cindy Pawlcyn is down-home American with a twist: crab cakes with a sherry-cayenne mayonnaise, skirt steak with a tomato aioli, sesame chicken with shiitake mushrooms, even a chili dog. Desserts—fruit pies, crème brûlée, chocolate cake—are richly satisfying. Service is helpful and efficient. Wines are rather pricey, and at peak times the noise level is considerable. *1300 Battery St., tel. 415/982–2000. Jacket advised, but anything goes. Reservations strongly advised. MC, V.*

❸ **Il Fornaio.** A chain of bakeries in Italy spawned an equally
$$ successful minichain of bakeries and cafés in America, which in turn spawned the crown jewels of the Il Fornaio empire: three full-fledged restaurants, this one on the edge of the financial district and North Beach, one north in Marin County, and one south in Del Mar. The stunning decor (gleaming white marble, polished dark wood, high ceilings, open kitchen, outdoor terrace) and appealing, well-prepared contemporary Northern Italian fare have

made this one of San Francisco's hot spots, particularly popular at lunch with a well-dressed business crowd. The noise level at lunch and dinner makes it a better place for entertaining than conducting serious business, but it's a superb spot for a breakfast meeting (*see* Business Breakfasts, above). The lengthy lunch and dinner menu includes a crisp, puffy *bomba* (pizzalike bread) topped with smoked prosciutto; intensely flavorful foccacia with Gorgonzola and Parmesan; lots of pastas and pizzas; and simple grilled fish and veal chops. And this is one place where you don't want to pass up the bread basket. *1265 Battery St., tel. 415/986-0100. Casual dress, but during the week most are in business attire. Reservations advised. AE, DC, MC, V.*

㉕ **French Room.** A grand old dining room in a grand old hotel, the French Room is a fine place for a business breakfast, lunch, or dinner. The Four Seasons management has skillfully kept the best of the old without neglecting contemporary comforts, amenities, and cuisine, which is why this place is so popular with executives from the worlds of fashion, retail, and real estate. Under a dazzling panoply of crystal chandeliers, a polished staff tends to the quietly wealthy clientele seated on richly upholstered chairs amid huge potted palms. If you're in the mood for familiar Continental fare, go for the excellent Caesar salad and the flawless prime rib with English popovers. If you're feeling a bit more adventurous, try some of chef Kelly Mills's fine Asian-influenced dishes, such as scallops and Chinese broccoli in a black-bean-and-ginger sauce, and crab cakes with a papaya and coriander relish. Even the firmest resolves weaken at the sight of the gleaming silver dessert cart. California's best are well represented on the wine list. The central Union Square location makes this a short walk from most downtown sites. *Four Seasons Clift Hotel, 495 Geary St., tel. 415/775-4700. Jacket and tie required. Reservations advised. AE, CB, DC, MC, V.*

$$$

★ ❶ **Greens.** This vegetarian restaurant deserves all the acclaim it gets. Greens takes meatless eating to unprecedented levels—and it throws in such perks as a sweeping bay/Golden Gate Bridge view and a remarkable California wine list. Salads are exemplary, made with tasty organic greens and all sorts of good things—oranges, *frisée* (curly endive), and olives; assorted lettuces, mangoes, pecans. The menu also features rich, earthy breads, savory pizzas and pastas, herbed-cheese sandwiches on thick grilled bread, creative entrées, juicy cobblers, and a decidedly unhealthful chocolate hazelnut cake. Service can be a bit distracted. Located in one of Fort Mason's warehouse buildings (near Fisherman's Wharf), Greens has an homey, '70s-style decor, with polished wood floors, lots of plants, and huge windows. It's a great place to entertain vegetarian clients, and its meditative atmosphere allows for private talk. Friday and Saturday dinners are fixed-price only. *Building A, Fort Mason, tel. 415/771-6222. Casual dress. Reservations required. MC, V. Closed Sun. for dinner, and Mon.*

$$

★ ❾ **Masa's.** Quite likely the best restaurant in San Francisco — perhaps in all of California—Masa's remains the hottest culinary ticket in town; you'll probably need to make reservations three weeks in advance. It attained widespread notoriety in 1984 when chef Masa Kobayashi was mysteriously murdered (the case is still unsolved), but its real

$$$$

claim to fame is its inspired contemporary French cuisine, now prepared by Julian Serrano. Although it's not exceptionally attractive, the small room is quiet and richly comfortable, with gray fabric walls, framed mirrors, vaguely contemporary black chairs, white linens, and elegantly simple appointments (oversize white china, clean-line crystal stemware). For maximum privacy, request a table along the wall. The wine list is full of treasures, the service is correct, if a tad haughty at times, and the food is unforgettable. Try the lobster-and-endive salad, incomparable foie gras, simple but perfect duck breast served with a poached winter pear, cheeses almost as good as those in France's best restaurants, and dreamy desserts, from the crème brûlée to the richly flavorful sorbets. The Union Square location is easily accessible, and the atmosphere and food make Masa's ideal for business entertaining of the first order. *648 Bush St., tel. 415/989–7154. Jacket and tie required. Reservations required. AE, DC, MC, V. Dinner only. Closed Mon.*

★ ㉙ **Pierre.** California cuisine is all well and good, but some-
$$$ times the occasion demands nothing but the finest classic French: decadent foie gras, sublime sauces, rich Bordeaux wines, petit fours with your coffee, and service by impeccably trained waiters who don't chat you up. That's exactly what you'll get at Pierre, the excellent dining room in the sleek Hotel Meridien, just south of Market Street and a quarter's throw from the financial district. You'll find all the components of a fine French meal here, plus a soothing, elegant dining room done in gray and cream, with candles on the tables and a baby grand in the corner. Game dishes such as roast pheasant with an orange and green-peppercorn sauce are specialties; also popular are roast lotte (monkfish) with sweet garlic, and an eggplant flan. The wine list, once exclusively French, is home to an increasing number of good Californian bottles. The frequent Master Chef's special dinners, prepared by some of the world's best chefs, are always worthwhile. Popular with well-dressed professionals, Pierre is good for both a working dinner and entertaining. *Hotel Meridien, 50 3rd St., tel. 415/974–6400. Jacket and tie required. Reservations advised. AE, CB, D, DC, MC, V. Dinner only. Closed Mon.*

★ ⑰ **Postrio.** L.A.-bashing is a favorite sport of San Francis-
$$$ cans, particularly when it comes to restaurants. So it came as quite a surprise to see how quickly and fervently the City by the Bay embraced this Union Square venture of L.A. wunderchef Wolfgang Puck. You'll need to make reservations at least a week in advance to get a table here, but the effort is well worth it. The most fashionable crowd in town, ranging from financial district whiz kids to society matrons, decorate a whimsical yet lovely three-level space that allows for great people-watching. Try to get a table on the lower level. It's the heart of the place, dominated by a sweeping staircase, large open kitchen, tall windows, and wacky space-age light fixtures. The second level is the next best thing. You'll eat excellent contemporary American food, even better than that served at Puck's legendary Spago in L.A. Try the crab cakes, the Chinese sausage on a bed of warm cabbage, the roast chicken with mashed potatoes, and the homey American desserts—actually, try anything, for it's all delicious. De-

spite the scene, the noise level isn't too daunting, though this is more a place for entertaining than working. Postrio is also a superb place for a breakfast meeting (*see* Business Breakfasts above). *Prescott Hotel, 545 Post St., tel. 415/ 776-7825. Jacket and tie advised. Reservations strongly advised. AE, CB, DC, MC, V.*

⑬ **Silks.** Although hotel dining rooms are too often dreary
$$$ places serving mediocre food, San Francisco has more than its share of first-rate hotel restaurants. One of the best is also one of the newest: Silks, in the dramatic Mandarin Oriental Hotel atop an office tower. (Unfortunately, the restaurant is on the second floor of the tower, so it doesn't have the same incredible views as the guest rooms.) Restaurants don't get much more attractive and serenely comfortable than this: extremely well-spaced tables set with white china and fine crystal; cream-color paneled walls inset with mirrors; thick gray carpeting; plush, fully upholstered armchairs; and a centerpiece laden with flowers, foodstuffs, and liqueurs. Despite the hotel's Asian roots, the intriguing, skillfully prepared cuisine is French-Californian: shrimp and corn chowder, grilled chicken wings in a red-sesame mole sauce, roast squab with chèvre tucked under its skin, gorgeous desserts. Service lives up to the food and decor. The financial district location means a big turnout by the business set. *Mandarin Oriental Hotel, 222 Sansome St., tel. 415/885-0999. Jacket and tie required. Reservations advised. AE, DC, MC, V.*

⑭ **Tadich Grill.** You haven't been to San Francisco if you
$$ haven't been to Tadich's, which has been around since the Gold Rush. The high-back wooden booths, starched white linens, crowded mahogany bar-counter, wonderfully brusque (some say surly) white-jacketed waiters, and heaps of tangy sourdough bread are all as San Franciscan as it gets. You'll have a long wait if you want a lunchtime booth, but the people-watching—middle-aged men in Brooks Brothers suits, younger financial district hotshots, tourists, old-timers, you name it—will keep you amused. No baby greens or Santa Barbara shrimp here; this is real food for unpretentious eaters, with an emphasis on fresh seafood: cioppino as good as it gets, grilled swordfish and salmon, wonderful sand dabs, textbook rice pudding, and simple wines served in small tumblers. A short walk from most downtown offices, Tadich's is a fun spot for business entertaining or a not-too-serious working meal, and its counter is perfect for the solo diner. *240 California St., tel. 415/391-2373. Jacket suggested (most diners are in business attire). No reservations. No credit cards. Closed weekends.*

⑫ **Yank Sing.** For a delicious change of pace at lunch, head for
$ this sophisticated dim sum restaurant. Most dim sum places are frenzied and noisy, with huge tables of Chinese families and swarms of women wheeling around carts laden with Chinese dumplings, pastries, and various small dishes. But Yank Sing, in the financial district, has successfully sought out a primarily non-Asian business-lunch crowd, which returns for the outstanding food, good service, relative quiet, and handsome, contemporary setting (flowers, white linens, parquet floors, etched-glass room dividers). The dim sum still comes by on carts, but the servers are more gracious than is the norm in such

eateries. Every offering is beautifully fresh and tasty; try the potstickers, spring rolls, sui mai, rice noodles, silver-wrapped chicken, and all sorts of dumplings filled with shrimp, chicken, pork, and vegetables. And by business-lunch standards, the prices are a bargain. *427 Battery St., tel. 415/362–1640. Informal dress. Reservations suggested. AE, DC, MC, V. Lunch only.*

Civic Center

★ ③ Hayes Street Grill. Curiously, the port town of San Fran-
$$ cisco isn't exactly thick with really good seafood restaurants. But it does have the Hayes Street Grill. The place doesn't look like much—an attractive but very simple two-room café, with bentwood chairs, hardwood floors, blackboard menus, and a good bit of noise—but the seafood is impeccably fresh and the service really hustles. Try any of the salads (especially smoked chicken and mango), then move on to one of the mesquite-grilled or sautéed fish dishes such as swordfish, snapper, salmon, or soft-shell crabs. Pasta fans will usually find a delicious shellfish pasta or two. A word of caution: The desserts, from the acclaimed crème brûlée to the retro fruit cobblers, will take away any virtuous feeling you had from eating fish. This is a good spot for a sociable Civic Center-area lunch or a casual business dinner before attending the nearby symphony or opera. *320 Hayes St., tel. 415/863–5545. Informal dress (jacket suggested). Reservations advised. MC, V. Closed Sun.*

★ ③ Stars. Stars owner/chef Jeremiah Tower is perhaps best
$$$ known for being profiled in a Dewar's Scotch ad. Fortunately, his celebrity status is matched with tremendous talent—despite the hype, Stars really does serve celestial food. Tower's kitchen crew turns out contemporary American dishes that almost always work, whether they be humble (the perfect hot dog served at the bar), homey (black-bean soup with sour cream and salsa), or inventive (Hawaiian tuna tartare with cilantro-chili vinaigrette, sesame cucumbers, and ginger cream). And the desserts—French silk pie, fresh berry pies, and cobblers—are incomparable. Several years after opening, Stars is still as vibrant as ever, always packed with the town's movers and shakers, along with curious tourists, devout foodies, and those attending the nearby opera or symphony. If you can't get a reservation, or are watching your pennies, drop in for a light meal and/or dessert at the bar or counter, which has a great view of the bustle in the open kitchen. At night, the noise level in this huge, handsome, bistro-style place (all gleaming wood and brass, with French posters, white linens, and old-fashioned glass light fixtures) is considerable. Stars is great for a working lunch—as long as you request a table in the quieter room to the right of the entrance—and for festive business entertaining at night. *150 Redwood Alley, tel. 415/861–7827. Jacket suggested. Reservations strongly advised. AE, CB, DC, MC, V.*

South of Market

③ Eddie Jacks. If you want to eat well *and* make the trendy
$$ SoMa scene (just south of downtown), head for Eddie Jacks, an industrial looking modern place that offers terrific California fare and a wine list full of good values, in-

cluding excellent wines by the glass. And, unlike most SoMa eateries, the noise level isn't mind-numbing (though it isn't hushed, either). Dishes of note include addictive fried polenta sticks with a Gorgonzola dipping sauce, a delicious lamb sandwich with goat cheese and red onions, unusual pastas, and good seafood (savory seafood stew, rare tuna in a soy marinade). The atmosphere is vibrant yet not too chaotic, the decor is reminiscent of New York's SoHo (with a warehouse feel, high-tech black chairs, ceiling fans, and stage props decorating the walls), and the prices are quite fair. Though not appropriate for a serious business meal, this is a perfect place for hip business entertaining. *1151 Folsom St., tel. 415/626–2388. Casual dress. Reservations strongly advised. AE, MC, V. Closed Sun.*

Berkeley

★ ❸ Chez Panisse and Café at Chez Panisse. The years go by, $$$$/$$ and Alice Water's Chez Panisse remains a shrine to California cuisine—you still need to call a month in advance for reservations. In a homey, almost plain setting of dark, clean-line woodwork, wooden banquettes, low-slung armchairs, and white linens, an eclectic mix of diners is served a single five-course fixed-price dinner, which changes nightly. Chef Paul Bertolli is an Italophile, so you may be treated to an excellent pasta or risotto, but in general his dishes are resolutely American/Californian. Preparations are usually extremely simple, and the quality of ingredients and cooking is exceptional. One recent dinner included delicious white-corn soup, a classic Chez Panisse baby-greens salad, and flavorful beef simply roasted with a rock-salt crust. Upstairs at the Café at Chez Panisse, where reservations aren't taken and the mood and food are more casual, you can lunch or dine on the famous pizzas and calzones topped with roasted garlic and goat cheese; hearty grilled radicchio with aioli; and satisfying roast chicken. Service can be snooty both upstairs and down. The wine selection in both places is superb. The Berkeley location doesn't make the two Chez Panisses convenient for most business-meal occasions, but they're worth the trek if you're a devout food-lover—or if you're entertaining one. *1517 Shattuck Ave. Chez Panisse: tel. 415/548–5525. Jacket advised. Reservations required. AE, DC, MC, V. Dinner only. Closed Sun. and Mon. Café: tel. 415/548–5049. Casual dress. AE, DC, MC, V. Closed Sun.*

Ethnic

San Francisco is blessed with outstanding ethnic restaurants, particularly those representing the countries of the Pacific Rim. Following are some of the best ethnic places in the more accessible parts of the city.

Angkor Palace (1769 Lombard St., Marina District, tel. 415/931–2830) offers sophisticated Cambodian cuisine, lovely Cambodian-palace decor, and a good wine list. **Celadon** (881 Clay St., Chinatown, tel. 415/982–1168) is an elegant Hong Kong-style Chinese restaurant with first-rate food. **China Moon Café** (639 Post St., Union Square, tel. 415/775–4789), run by acclaimed chef Barbara Tropp, serves intriguing, creative Chinese/Californian dishes in a simple café setting. **Fuku-Sushi** (Japan Center West, 1581

Webster St., Japantown, tel. 415/346–3030) has excellent sushi, comfortable decor, and doting service. **Golden Turtle** (2211 Van Ness Ave., Van Ness, tel. 415/441–4419) serves up fabulous Vietnamese food in an opulent setting. **Kinokawa** (347 Grant Ave., Union Square, tel. 415/398–8226) is a good bet for fine sushi and good grilled dishes in a prime downtown location. **Peacock** (2800 Van Ness Ave., Van Ness, tel. 415/928–7001), set in a serene Victorian mansion, offers admirable Indian food. **Phnom Penh** (631 Larkin St., Polk Gulch, tel. 415/775–5979) is one of the city's finest Cambodian restaurants, with a friendly atmosphere, delicious food, and good French wines. **Royal Thai** (951 Clement St., Richmond district, tel. 415/386–1795) may be a bit out of the way, but it's worth the trek for wonderful Thai food, lovely decor, and an intimate, romantic atmosphere. **Wu Kong** (1 Rincon Center, 101 Spear St., financial district, tel. 415/957–9300) is the hottest Chinese restaurant in town, featuring Shanghai-style cuisine, a stylish decor, and a very good wine list.

FREE TIME

Fitness

Hotel Facilities
The following are the top fitness centers in San Francisco hotels; all are open to nonguests for a day rate. **Nikko Fitness Center,** Hotel Nikko San Francisco (tel. 415/394–1111), $20; **Nob Hill Club,** Fairmont Hotel, (tel. 415/772–5393), $15; **San Francisco Hilton Health Club,** (tel. 415/771–1400, ext. 6333), $10.

Health Clubs
The following health clubs have excellent facilities and day rates for guests: **24 Hour Nautilus Fitness Center** (1355 Sutter St., tel. 415/776–2200), **Northpoint Health Club** (2310 Powell St., tel. 415/989–1449), and **Physis** (1 Post St., tel. 415/989–7310).

Shopping

Union Square recalls old San Francisco. It's a landmark park in the heart of downtown bounded by Powell, Stockton, Geary, and Post streets and is lined with traditional department stores, including Gump's, Macy's, I. Magnin, Neiman-Marcus, and Saks Fifth Avenue. The three-level **Crocker Galleria** (tel. 415/392–0100) at 50 Post Street has more than 50 shops and restaurants under a great glass vault. The newest and most elegant shopping mall is **San Francisco Centre** (tel. 415/495–5656), at Fifth and Market streets. Its spiral escalator leads to more than 100 stores, topped by Nordstrom's, which occupies five floors of the nine-story vertical mall. Its central location makes it perfect for one-stop quick shopping. There are more than 175 retail shops, boutiques, restaurants, cafés, and galleries in the **Embarcadero Center** (tel. 415/772–0500), a five-block complex at the foot of Market Street that looks out over San Francisco Bay.

Ghirardelli Square is a renovated 19th century chocolate-spice-coffee-woolen works complex overlooking Aquatic Park that attracts tourists to its more than 70 shops, galleries, outdoor cafés, and restaurants. Nearby, the **Can-**

nery (tel. 415/771–3112)—a refurbished produce cannery at Fisherman's Wharf—has 50 additional shops, galleries, restaurants, and cafés.

Not to be confused with Union Square is **Union Street,** a trendy upscale stretch of shops and restaurants five blocks south of the Golden Gate National Recreation Area, where you'll find expensive boutiques and gift shops. Even **Haight Street** shops have become sophisticated; you'll still find tie-dyed and vintage '40s and '50s clothing, as well as Art Deco jewelry, but prices are inflated.

Diversions

Riding San Francisco's **cable cars** is a memorable experience: the views are spectacular, and clanging up the city's steepest hills is exhilarating. The Powell-Mason line (No. 59) and the Powell-Hyde line (No. 60) terminate at Fisherman's Wharf.

Chinatown is a 24-block city within a city, with the largest Chinese community outside of Asia. The area stretches from Bay Street south to California Street, and from downtown Sansome Street to Van Ness Avenue. Nighttime, the area is as busy as it is during the day.

Cruise San Francisco Bay day and night with Red & White Fleet (Pier 41 & 43½, Fisherman's Wharf, tel. 415/546–2896) or Blue & Gold Fleet (Pier 39, West Marina, tel. 415/781–7877).

Embarcadero Center (*see* Shopping, above) is a three-tiered pedestrian mall extending five blocks west from the landmark Ferry Building at the foot of Market Street. The complex has major outlet stores, like Ann Taylor and the Gap, as well as restaurants, but what's interesting here is the contemporary art, especially the immense Louise Nevelson sculpture.

Ghirardelli Square, the **Cannery, Fisherman's Wharf,** and **Pier 39** hug the promenade along the waterfront, with lots of shops and restaurants, and crowds of tourists—many of whom come to see the group of sea lions who have settled in at the end of Pier 39 (left-hand side).

Wear warm clothing and be prepared for wind and mist if you walk across the almost 2-mile-long **Golden Gate Bridge.** Mini Bus No. 28 takes you to the toll plaza on the city side; the view from the vista point on the Marin side is outstanding.

The eastern section of the 1,000-acre **Golden Gate Park** has three museums: the **M.H. de Young Memorial Museum** (tel. 415/221–4811), which has 44 galleries showing the development of Western cultures from the time of ancient Egypt to the 20th century; the **Asian Art Museum of San Francisco** (tel. 415/668–8921), which houses the world-famous Avery Brundage collection of more than 10,000 sculptures, paintings, and ceramics illustrating major periods of Asian art; and the **California Academy of Sciences** (tel. 415/750–7145), one of the top five natural-history museums in the country, featuring an aquarium and a planetarium.

High tea is served 3–4 in the Four Season Clift Hotel Lobby (tel. 415/775–4700), where you'll be treated as graciously as any guest. Tea is also served at the Stanford Court Hotel Lobby (tel. 415/989–3500); the Compass Rose in the Westin St. Francis Hotel (tel. 415/397–7000); and at the Rotunda, in the Neiman-Marcus store (150 Stockton St., tel. 415/362–3900).

The Museum of Modern Art (McAllister St. and Van Ness Ave., in the Civic Center, tel. 415/863–8800) includes works by contemporary masters Paul Klee, Jackson Pollock, Robert Motherwell, Alexander Calder, Henri Matisse, and Clyfford Still.

The National Maritime Museum (Aquatic Park, at the foot of Polk St., tel. 415/556–8177) showcases ship models, photographs, maps and other artifacts, and includes the **Hyde Street Pier** (two blocks east, tel. 415/556–6435), where the *Eureka*, a sidewheel ferry, and the *C.A. Thayer*, a three-masted schooner, can be boarded.

Professional Sports

San Francisco's baseball club, the **San Francisco Giants**, plays at Candlestick Park (tel. 415/467–8000). The Oakland team, the **Oakland Athletics,** plays at Oakland Coliseum Stadium (tel. 415/638–0500). The city's **basketball** team, the **Golden State Warriors,** appears at Oakland Coliseum Arena (tel. 415/638–6000). And the **San Francisco 49ers,** the city's football team, keeps Candlestick Park (tel. 415/468–2249) packed in the autumn.

The Arts

A single block of Geary Street makes up San Francisco's "theater row," but there are commercial theaters throughout the downtown area.

The city's major theater group, the **American Conservatory Theater,** sets the standard by which other Northern California resident theater companies are judged; performances are held at the **Herbst Theatre** (Van Ness Ave. at McAllister St., tel. 415/552–3656). Across the Bay, the **Berkeley Repertory Theatre** (2025 Addison St., Berkeley, tel. 415/845–4700) offers a more contemporary mix that includes classics and new plays, and is the major rival for leadership in the region.

Commercial, Broadway-style shows are the mainstay at the **Curran Theater** (445 Geary St., tel. 415/673–4400), the **Golden Gate Theatre** (Golden Gate Ave. at Taylor St., tel. 415/474–3800), and the **Orpheum Theater** (1192 Market St., tel. 415/474–3800).

The **San Francisco Symphony, San Francisco Opera,** and the **San Francisco Ballet**—the city's three major performing-arts organizations—perform in the downtown Civic Center complex, the first at **Louise M. Davies Symphony Hall** (Van Ness Ave. at Grove St., tel. 415/431–5400), the latter two at the **War Memorial Opera House** (Van Ness at Grove St., tel. 415/864–3300).

Ticket agencies include **City Box Office** (141 Kearny St., tel. 415/392–4400), **St. Francis Theatre and Sports Tickets,** Westin St. Francis Hotel (tel. 415/362–3500), **BASS** (tel. 415/762–2277), and **Ticketron** (tel. 415/392–SHOW). Try **STBS** (Stockton St. side of Union Square, Thurs.–Sat., noon–7:30; tel. 415/433–STBS for recorded information) for day-of-performance tickets for selected music, dance, and theater events at half-price, as well as advance, full-price tickets. Cash sales only; no reservations or telephone orders.

After Hours

The greatest concentration of nightlife outside of the hotels is found in the North Beach/Broadway and South of Market (SoMa) areas, but there are bars and discos scattered throughout the waterfront and outer neighborhoods, too.

Skyline Bars
Not to be missed in scenic San Francisco, the city's skyline bars—many of them in the major hotels—are a good option for a drink with colleagues or business contacts. The best is **The Carnelian Room** (555 California St., tel. 415/433–7500) at the top of the 52-story Bank of America Building. It has a clubby feeling and a forever view. At the top of the 46-story San Francisco Hilton, **Cityscape** (tel. 415/771–1400) offers a spectacular 360-degree view under a unique retractable skylight. The view begins in the glass-enclosed elevator that takes you 24 stories to the **Crown Room** in the Fairmont Hotel (tel. 415/772–5131). At the top of the Hyatt Regency, the **Equinox** (tel. 415/788–1234) completes a 360-degree revolution every 45 minutes. The fabulous vistas are just part of the ambience at the elegant, landmark setting at the **Top of the Mark** in the Mark Hopkins Hotel (1 Nob Hill, tel. 415/392–3434).

Bars
The Redwood Room in the Four Seasons Clift Hotel (tel. 415/775–4700) is an Art Deco landmark where an upscale group in their 30s and 40s come to relax. The **House of Shields** (39 New Montgomery St., tel. 415/392–7732), just across from the Sheraton Palace Hotel, has the feel of an old-time San Francisco saloon. In the heart of downtown, **John's Grill** (63 Ellis St., tel. 415/986–0069) was featured in *The Maltese Falcon,* and mystery fans will revel in its Hammett memorabilia. Scores of office workers in the financial district enjoy friendly libations at **The Holding Company** (2 Embarcadero Center, tel. 415/986–0797), one of the area's most popular weeknight watering holes.

Cabarets
The wacky musical revue at **Club Fugazi** (678 Green St., tel. 415/421–4222) has been running for more than a decade; reservations are a must. Female impersonators have been the draw at **Finocchio's** (506 Broadway, tel. 415/982–9388) for 50 years. The **Plush Room** in the Hotel York (940 Sutter St., tel. 415/885–6800) provides big-name entertainment in an elegant atmosphere.

Comedy Clubs
Super stand-up comics perform at the crowded **Cobb's Comedy Club** (2801 Leavenworth St., in the Cannery, tel. 415/928–4329). There's a more local crowd at **Lipp's Bar and Grill** (201 9th St., tel. 415/552–3466), an all-improv club that showcases outstanding troupes; Robin Williams has been known to drop in. Jay Leno and Whoopie Goldberg launched their careers at the **Punch Line** (444 Battery St., tel. 415/397–7573), which continues to feature top talent.

Jazz Clubs

Jazz greats, including Stan Getz, have performed at **Kimball's** (300 Grove St., tel. 415/861–5555). Johnny Coals and Clifford Jordan appear fairly regularly at **Milestones** (376 5th St., tel. 415/777–9997). **Roland's** (2313 Van Ness Ave. at Union St., tel. 415/567–1063) is a comfortable place that draws a local crowd.

Rock Clubs

City Nights (715 Harrison St., tel. 415/546–7774) offers dancing to disks in sumptuous surroundings. In the SoMa area, the **DNA Lounge** (375 11th St., near Harrison St., tel. 415/626–2532) has live bands on Fridays and Saturdays. The **Great American Music Hall** (859 O'Farrell St., between Polk and Larkin Sts., tel. 415/885–0750) offers an eclectic schedule of live bands; call ahead to see who's appearing. Panoramic views are part of the decor at **Oz** (tel. 415/397–7000), an upscale disco at the top of the Westin St. Francis, reached via a glass elevator. You'll find crowds of young professionals, sometimes 2,000 strong, rocking at **Southside** (1190 Folsom St., tel. 415/431–3332).

For Singles

Channel's (No. 1 Embarcadero Center, tel. 415/956–8768) is a financial district watering hole that's popular on weeknights. **Harry's Bar and American Grill** (500 Van Ness Ave., tel. 415/864–2779) attracts an upscale crowd. **Perry's** (1944 Union St. at Buchanan St., tel. 415/922–9022) is one of the city's best singles bars; it's usually jam-packed. All of these clubs serve a 20s–40s crowd.

Seoul

by Sharon Spence

The Republic of Korea (South Korea) represents one of the great economic miracles of modern times. In 1953, after 35 years as a Japanese colony, and after the devastating effects of World War II and a three-year civil war, South Korea was poorer than most African countries. Today, South Korea has risen from the ashes. Its GNP has gone from $2 billion in 1962 to $210 billion in 1990. One element of South Korea's success has been its commitment to improve facilities for both business travelers and tourists. In preparation for Seoul's 1988 Summer Olympics, for example, state-of-the-art convention hotels and exhibition centers were built, the subway was modernized, and the World Trade Center was created.

South Korea has opened its doors to international business relationships. South Korean–American bilateral trade has flourished, growing from $150 billion in 1961 to $360 billion in 1990. But eager to lessen its dependence on the United States for trade, South Korea has begun sending its manufactured goods to Europe—Britain, Germany, and other members of the European Community.

Consumer electronic products top the list of South Korea's export-based economy. Well-known conglomerates such as Daewoo, Hyundai, Lucky-Goldstar, and Samsung dominate the industry. The clothing and footwear industries also continue to thrive, but "made in Korea" no longer suggests cheap goods. As other countries, including China and Indonesia, undercut South Korea's labor costs, clothing and footwear manufacturers are beginning to stress quality and fashion, sometimes selling goods under their own brand names. South Korean consumers themselves are more able to buy quality products and services as their per capita income continues to grow—from $1,500 in 1981 to $5,000 in 1990.

Seoul, founded 100 years before Christopher Columbus discovered the Americas, has been a mercantile center for centuries. But compared to Korea's 5,000-year history, the capital city is relatively new. Surrounded by craggy mountains, Seoul is a city of contrasts. Its modern buildings (all of them built within the past 25 years) tower over 14th-century palaces. Gray-suited executives hurry down a street bedecked with Buddhist lanterns. A farmer herds his goats through an underpass of computer stores and ginseng showrooms. And a sidewalk vendor sells imported bananas next to Gucci bags.

In recent years, Westerners have become accustomed to news of antigovernment demonstrations, led by students (there are more than 40 universities in Seoul) and young factory workers calling for a more democratic government and free elections.

But political unrest hasn't devastated this emerging metropolis, by any means. Considering that almost one quarter of South Korea's population lives in Seoul's crowded urban area, the city is relatively clean and friendly and its crime rate is low—virtues owed as much to the city's hardworking, educated population as to the rigid class structure and Confucian philosophy that has shaped this nation.

Top Employers

Employer	Type of Enterprise	Parent*/ Headquarters
Daewoo Corp.	Steel, chemicals, textiles, machinery	Seoul
Hanjin Electronics	Transmitters, audio/video equipment	Seoul
Hyosung Corp.	Steel, metals, chemicals, construction, textiles	Seoul
Hyundai Corp.	Automobiles, steel, metals, chemicals, fabrics	Seoul
Korea Explosive	Explosives, chemicals, lathes, gas meters	Seoul
Lucky-Goldstar International	Chemicals, electronics, tele-communications	Seoul
Samsung Co. Ltd.	Chemicals, iron, steel, electronics	Seoul
Ssangyong Corp.	Cement, paper, diesel engines, medical products, petrochemicals	Seoul
Sunkyong Ltd.	Electronics, plywood, footwear, textiles	Seoul

| **Yukong, Ltd.** | Gasoline, solvents, asphalt, lube oil | Seoul |

*if applicable

ESSENTIAL INFORMATION

We include the Seoul telephone area code (02) with all numbers listed below. If you are calling from outside South Korea, omit the 0 from the code. If you are calling from within Seoul, omit the area code altogether.

The currency of Korea is the chon, abbreviated throughout the chapter as W.

Government Tourist Offices

Korea National Tourism Corporation (KNTC). In the United States: 460 Park Ave., Suite 400, New York, NY 10022, tel. 212/688–7543; 230 N. Michigan Ave., Suite 1500, Chicago, IL 60601, tel. 312/346–6660; 501 W. 6th St., Suite 323, Los Angeles, CA 90014, tel. 213/623–1226; c/o Ehrig and Associates, 4th Vine Bldg., Seattle, WA 98121, tel. 206/623–6666; 1188 Bishop St., Century Sq., Honolulu, HI 96813, tel. 808/521–8066.
In Canada: 480 University Ave., Suite 406, Toronto, M5G 1V2, Ontario, tel. 416/348–9056.
In the United Kingdom: Vogue House, 2nd floor, 1 Hanover Sq., London W1R 9RD, tel. 071/409–2100.
KNTC Tourist Information Center. In Seoul: 10a Ta-dong, Chung-Ku, tel. 02/757–0086; Kimpo Airport, tel. 02/665–0086; Seoul City Tourist Information Center, behind City Hall, tel. 02/731–6337; Seoul Express Bus Terminal, tel. 02/598–3246.

Foreign Trade Information

Korean Trade Center. In the United States: 460 Park Ave., Suite 402, New York, NY 10022, 212/826–0900; 111 E. Wacker Dr., Suite 519, Chicago, IL 60601, tel. 312/644–4323; 700 S. Flower St., Suite 3220, Los Angeles, CA 90017, tel. 213/627–9426.
In Canada: 65 Queen St. W, The Thompson Bldg., Suite 600, Toronto M5H 2M5, Ontario, tel. 416/368–3399.
In the United Kingdom: Vincent House, ground floor, Vincent Sq., London SW1P 2NB, tel. 071/834–5082.

Entry Requirements

U.S. and Canadian Citizens
Passport only. A visa is required for stays longer than 15 days.

U.K. Citizens
Passport only. A visa is required for stays longer than 60 days.

Climate

Seoul's monsoon season runs from mid-June to mid-July, and a mild typhoon season arrives in August. Spring in Seoul is cool and breezy, summer is hot and humid, fall has warmer days and cooler nights, and winter is crisp and chilly with occasional snowfall. What follows are the average daily maximum and minimum temperatures for Seoul.

Jan.	32F	0C	Feb.	37F	3C	Mar.	46F	8C
	16	– 9		20	– 7		29	– 2
Apr.	62F	17C	May	72F	22C	June	80F	27C
	41	5		51	11		60	16
July	84F	29C	Aug.	88F	31C	Sept.	78F	26C
	70	21		72	22		59	15
Oct.	66F	19C	Nov.	51F	11C	Dec.	37F	3C
	44	7		32	0		20	– 7

Airport

Kimp'o International Airport is 11 miles west of downtown. The new **City Air Terminal** (159-1 Samsung-dong, Kangman-gu, tel. 02/551–0777), open since April 1990, is in Seoul's World Trade Center complex and has facilities for airline reservations and baggage check-in.

Airlines

Although many international airlines offer service to Seoul, Korean Air (KAL), the national carrier, provides the most frequent domestic and international service. Korean, Delta, and United offer direct service from New York City. Korean and Northwest offer direct flights from Los Angeles.

American, tel. 02/766–3314; 800/433–7300.
British Airways, tel. 02/774–5511; 800/247–9297.
Cathay Pacific Airways, tel. 02/778–0326; 800/233–2742.
Delta, tel. 02/754–1921; 800/241–4141.
Japan Airlines, tel. 02/757–1711; 800/525–3663.
Korean Air, tel. 02/755–2221; 800/223–1155.
Northwest, tel. 02/733–4191; 800/447–4747.
Thai Airways, tel. 02/754–9950; 800/426–5204.
United, tel. 02/757–1691; 800/241–6522.

Between the Airport and Downtown

Many hotels offer free shuttle service every 30 minutes. Check for hotel signs along the curb outside the baggage area.

By Taxi
The best transportation is by taxi; the trip into town takes about 30 minutes; during rush hours (7:30–9:30 AM and 5:30–7:30 PM) add another 45 minutes to the trip. Although Seoul is spread out, no destination in the city area should take longer than 45 minutes in nonpeak hours. Cost: W2,700–W3,000, excluding tip. Taxis wait just outside the baggage-claim area; follow the taxi icon signs.

By Bus
Airport express buses, which run from 5:20 AM to 10 PM, are convenient for getting to many downtown hotels. Bus No. 600 departs every seven minutes and stops at the Palace Hotel in Chamshil. Bus No. 601 runs every 10 minutes to the Sheraton Walker Hill Hotel, with hotel stops at the Koreana, Lotte, Plaza, President, and Westin Chosun. Travel time to the city is 45 minutes, and the one-way fare is W500. During rush hours the trip may take another 45

minutes; schedule any business appointments accordingly.

Car Rentals

The following companies have booths at the airport:

Arirang, tel. 02/695–0340.
Avis, tel. 02/737–7878; 800/331–1212.
Changwon, tel. 02/556–2008.
Hertz, tel. 02/585–0801; 800/654–3131.
New Korea, tel. 02/676–0031.
Sambo, tel. 02/797–5711.
Sungsan, tel. 02/552–1566.
The Korea Express, tel. 02/719–7295.
VIP, tel. 02/557–8081.

Emergencies

For a list of approved physicians and clinics in Seoul that belong to the International Association for Medical Assistance to Travelers, contact IAMAT, 417 Center St., Lewiston, NY 14092, tel. 716/754–4883.

Doctors
Seoul Diagnostic Medical Clinic (Hanaro Bldg. 3F, 194-4 Insa-dong, Chongro-gu, tel. 02/732–0303).

Dentists
Kain Dentists (Lotte World Clinic 6F, 40-1 Chamshil-dong, Songpa-gu, tel. 02/419–2811).

Hospitals
Ewha Women's University Hospital (70 Chongo 6-ga, Chongo-gu, tel. 02/762–5061), **Severance Hospital** (134 Shinch'on-dong, Sodaemun-gu, tel. 02/392–0161).

Police
Tel. 112.

Ambulance
Tel. 119.

Important Addresses and Numbers

American Express (Chongro 1-1, Chongro-gu, tel. 02/720–6250).

Audiovisual rentals. Most major hotels. Also, the Unico Business Center (Hotel Lotte 3F, 1 Sogong-dong, Chung-gu, tel. 02/771–10, ext. 5067).

Bookstores (English-language). Kyobo Book Center (147 Sejongno, Chongno-gu, tel. 02/730–7891).

British Embassy (4 Chong-dong, Chung-gu, tel. 02/735–7341).

Canadian Embassy (Kolon Bldg. 10F, 45 Mugyo-dong, Chung-gu, tel. 02/776–4062).

Chamber of Commerce (45 T'aep'yongno 2-ga, Chung-gu, tel. 02/757–0757).

Computer rentals. Unico Business Center (Hotel Lotte 3F, 1 Sogong-dong, Chung-gu, tel. 02/771–10, ext. 5067), World Trade Center (159 Samsong-dong, Kangnam-gu, tel. 02/551–2700). Also available in most major hotels.

Convention and exhibition centers. Korean Exhibition Center (KOEX), World Trade Center Complex (159 Samsong-dong, Kangnam-gu, tel. 02/551–0114), DLI 63 Convention Center (DLI Bldg., 60 Yoido-dong, Yongdungpo-gu, tel. 02/789–5700).

Fax service. Available in all major hotels and at the Central Post Office (21 Ch'ungmuro 1-ga, Chung-gu, tel. 02/775–0014).

Formal-wear rentals. Sunshine Formal Wear House (11-1 Chung Moo, 2-ga, Choog-gu, tel. 02/776–5130).

Gift shops. Lotte Department Store (1 Sogong-dong, Chung-gu, tel. 02/771–25), Tiffany (2-176 It'aewŏn-dong, Yongsan-gu, tel. 02/797–9507). Chocolates, flowers, and other gift items can also be purchased in the shopping arcades of most major hotels.

Graphic design studios. Ms. Kim's Printing (119 It'aewŏn-dong, Youngsan-gu, tel. 02/798–3691).

Hairstylists. Unisex: Nicky Beauty Shop (300-24 Dongbu, Inchon-dong, Younsan-gu, tel. 02/794–1740). There are also beauty and barber shops in most major hotels.

Health and fitness clubs. *See* Fitness, below.

Information hot lines. Korea Tourist Information (tel. 02/757–0086).

Limousine service. Korean Rent-A-Car (tel. 02/585–0801).

Liquor stores. Lotte Duty Free Shop (Lotte Department Store, 1 Sogong-dong, Chung-gu, tel. 02/771–25).

Mail delivery, overnight. DHL (tel. 02/716–0001), Federal Express (tel. 02/793–6991), TNT Skypak (tel. 02/694–6666), UPS (tel. 02/690–2488).

Messenger services. Available at all major hotels.

News programs (English-language). English-language broadcasting is limited to the Armed Forces Korea Network on AM and FM radio and Channel 2 on television. Check with your hotel for frequencies; see the English daily newspapers (the *Korea Herald* or the *Korea Times*) for programming schedules.

Office space rental. U.S. Trade Center (82 Sejong-ro, Chongro-ku, tel. 02/732–2601). Several major hotels, including the Lotte, InterContinental, and Westin Chosun, rent temporary space (guests only).

Pharmacies, late-night. Chung 11 Drugstore (34-77 It'aewŏn-dong, Youngsan-gu, tel. 02/797–7163).

Secretarial services. Unico Business Center (Hotel Lotte, tel. 02/774–2617), World Trade Center (159 Samsong-dong, Kangnam-gu, tel. 02/551–2700); also available through business centers of major hotels.

Stationery supplies. Kyobo Book Center (147 Sejongno, Chongno-gu, tel. 02/730–7891), Lotte Department Store (1 Sogong-dong, Chung-gu, tel. 02/771–25).

Taxis. City taxis (tel. 02/414–0150).

Theater tickets. *See* The Arts, below.

Trade Ministry. Korea Trade Promotion (159 Samsun-dong, Kangnam-ku, tel. 02/551–4181), U.S. Trade Center (82 Sejong-ro, Chongro-ku, tel. 02/732–2601).

Train information. Korean RR Station (2-122 Bongrae-dong, Chang-ku, tel. 02/392–0078).

Translation services. Unico Business Center (Hotel Lotte, tel. 02/774–2617), World Trade Center (159 Samsong-dong, Kangnam-gu, tel. 02/551–2700); also available through business centers of major hotels.

U.S. Embassy (82 Sejongno, Chongro-ku, tel. 02/732–2601).

Telephones

Local calls can be made from orange or gray pay phones in most public places. Insert two W10 coins for three minutes of local service. A warning beep will sound and the line will automatically cut off after three minutes; inserting more money will not extend the call.

Ideally, long distance calls should be made from any major hotel because their international operators speak English. Alternately, they can be made on the gray phones found in most large buildings and along the major streets. Listen for a dial tone, drop in a W100 coin, and wait for the operator who will let you know how many other coins are necessary. Have W100 and W10 coins ready, and insert as needed. If you hear beeps before your call is finished, insert additional coins. Some gray phones take telephone cards, which are on sale in shops close to the telephone boxes. Cards come in W3,000, W5,000, and W10,000 units. For operator-assisted calls, dial 007.

Tipping

Tips have not traditionally been a part of Korean custom. A 10% service charge is already added to bills in hotels and restaurants. You may leave an extra 10% for outstanding service, but it is not expected. It is not necessary to tip a taxi driver unless he assists you with luggage, in which case W700 is customary.

DOING BUSINESS

Hours

Businesses: weekdays 9–6, Sat. 9–1. **Banks:** weekdays 9:30–4:30, Sat. 9:30–1:30. **Shops:** hours vary, but those in major markets are generally open 8–9 every day. **Department stores:** daily 10:30–7:30.

National Holidays

New Year's Day; Feb. 6, Folklore Day; Mar. 1, Independence Movement Day; Apr. 5, Arbor Day; May 5, Children's Day; May 12, Buddha's Birthday; June 6, Memorial Day; July 17, Constitution Day; Aug. 15, Liberation Day; Sept. 14/15, Chusok (Korean Thanksgiving); Oct. 1, Armed Forces Day; Oct. 3, National Foundation Day; Oct. 9, Hangul Day (celebrates the anniversary of the Korean written language, created by King Sejong in 1443); Christmas Day.

Getting Around

If you're staying in center city, walking is the easiest and fastest way to get to business appointments. Seoul's low crime rate makes it quite safe for walking any time of day or night. However, as drivers do not give the right of way to pedestrians, extreme caution is advised when stepping off curbs and crossing streets. Fortunately, most street crossings are underground.

By Car
Rental cars are plentiful in Korea; drivers must have an International Driver's License, be over 21 years of age, and possess a valid passport. However, due to traffic congestion and lack of available parking and street signs in English, self-driving is not recommended. Visitors are encouraged to obtain the services of a driver from one of the car-rental firms. The cost is the equivalent of $30 for a 10-hour day, plus the driver's meals and any additional expenses.

By Taxi
There are three classes of taxi service in Seoul; regular, "88," and hotel taxis (also called "tourist" taxis). Regular taxis, usually painted green or yellow, are available at taxi stands along the major streets. The fare is W600 for the first 1.24 miles, and W50 for each additional ¼ mile; expect a 20% surcharge from midnight to 4 AM. Taxis referred to as "88" are slightly roomier than regular cabs and are also available at street taxi stands. The fare is W800 for the first 1.24 miles and W100 for each additional ¼ mile. It is possible to hail regular or "88" cabs from the street. Hotel or "tourist" taxis are always queued in front of major hotels. Fares start at W3,000.

By Public Transportation
Subway stations and trains have been modernized, allowing travelers to get anywhere in the city easily and cheaply. Signs are written in the Roman alphabet and subway-stop maps are posted. Four lines to various city points have greatly eased the rush-hour crush. Tickets can be purchased at automatic vending machines or station ticket windows. Your ticket is your entrance and exit pass, so hold on to it. Basic subway fare is W200.

There are two types of city buses—local and express. Local buses are frequent, reliable, and cheap; they're fine if hanging on to an overhead strap surrounded by local shoppers isn't a problem for you. Bus tokens are available from small booths located near most bus stops. Tokens are W140, regardless of distance; cash fare aboard the bus is W150. Local buses are marked with numbers and signs in blue and red on the front, side, and rear. City express buses, called *chwasok* (seat) buses, pick up only the number of passengers for which they have seats. They stop less frequently than local buses and cost W400. Maps of the bus system are available at most hotels.

Protocol

Appointments
Being on time for appointments is very important. Because of the constant, slow-moving traffic, allow extra time for getting to meetings. Prior to setting up initial ap-

pointments, firms should obtain formal introductions through an intermediary. Most Koreans prefer to conduct business in their offices, but some may choose to meet for lunch in your hotel restaurant.

Customs
It is proper to use Mr., Mrs., or Miss in addressing a new business aquaintance. If you are meeting a woman, it is a good idea to ask her secretary if she goes by Mrs. or Miss. The term Ms. is not yet commonly used. It is standard to shake hands with both men and women.

Always carry a business card. Korean businesspeople will not be comfortable until they know the company and position of the person they are meeting. Offer your card with both hands—a sign of respect—and accept cards in the same manner. Take the time to read the other person's card, rather than hastily putting it away.

In business meetings, do not assume that everything you say in English is completely understood. Emphasize and repeat your key points. Use audiovisual aids and brochures (preferably in Korean) to make yourself clear. Hire an interpreter, when necessary, to facilitate communication in meetings and negotiations. Don't push your position too hard. Koreans do not appreciate arguments, and may appear to acquiesce simply to permit discussion to continue harmoniously. Allow sufficient time for your Korean counterparts to come to a decision.

The popular local saying, "make a friend first, a client second," illustrates the importance Koreans place on strong personal ties in business relationships. The details of a contract matter, but so does the character of the person who signs it. Therefore, it is important to develop and actively foster mutual trust. Social interaction is an integral part of business in Korea, so accept offers for entertainment and be sure to reciprocate.

Dress
Classic suits in subdued colors are proper business attire for both men and women. Avoid bright, flashy clothing and accessories, as well as heavy cologne or perfume. Slacks are not worn by women in business settings, but are perfectly acceptable in informal situations.

Gifts
Suitable gifts for executives include everything from quality leather goods, pens, and silk ties and scarves, to simple souvenirs from your hometown. Korean businesspeople will also be pleased if you simply treat them to a nice meal and drinks. Once you have established a solid business relationship, you may be invited to your Korean associate's home. If so, an expensive liquor, good cognac, or champagne would make an appropriate gift.

Toasts and Greetings

Hello, how are you? *AHN-yung hah-seem-YEE-kah.*
Well, thank you. *Yeh, KAHM-sah HAHM-nee-dah.*
Pleased to meet you. *Mahn-nah-SOH pan-gap-sum-NAY-dah.*
Thank you. *KAHM-sah HAHM-nee-dah.*
You're welcome. *Chun-MAHN-ay-YOH.*
Excuse me. *Mee-AHN HAHM-nee-dah.*

Goodbye, nice to have met you. *AHN-yung-hee kah-SEEP-see-yoh*.

Cheers. *Goon BYE*.

LODGING

An amazing range of accommodations is available in Seoul, from first-class luxury hotels with dozens of restaurants and fully equipped health clubs, to no-frills hotels suitable only for sleeping. Quality of service and amenities is generally reflected in the price, though prices in Seoul tend to be high.

Traffic congestion makes it a wise idea to stay in a hotel within walking distance of your business activities. Hotels in the City Plaza area are in the commercial center of the city, near the major banks, newspapers, and government offices; those in the Namsam area are in the quieter park region just south of downtown. Hotels south of the Han River are closest to the World Trade Center, the Korean Exhibition Center (KOEX), and the new up-and-coming industrial/commercial district on Yoido Island (home of Lucky Goldstar, the Korea Broadcasting System, and the Korea Stock Exchange). There are also a few deluxe properties nestled in the quieter outskirts of Seoul, a short commute to downtown businesses.

Corporate rates and weekend or seasonal discounts are available at a number of the hotels; inquire when making reservations.

Highly recommended lodgings in each price category are indicated by a star ★.

Category	*Cost**
$$$$ (Very Expensive)	over W112,000
$$$ (Expensive)	W98,000–W112,000
$$ (Moderate)	under W98,000

*All prices are for a standard double room, single occupancy, excluding 10% service charge. Foreigners are not charged a hotel tax.

Numbers in the margin correspond to numbered hotel locations on the Seoul Lodging and Dining maps.

Downtown/City Hall Plaza Area

㉓
$$$$

Hotel Lotte. In the heart of Seoul's main business and shopping district, this very large, sleek hotel, built in 1979, is particularly popular with Japanese and European executives. The lobby is the size of several football fields, with huge crystal chandeliers and gleaming marble floors. Rooms in the original wing are small, and furnished with pink bedspreads and drapes and dark-wood Oriental furnishings. Rooms in the new wing, added in 1988, are more spacious and brighter, and decorated in modern pastel fabrics and gold-trimmed French-style wooden furniture with delicately carved feet. Guests staying in rooms in the Executive Salon have access to private meeting rooms, secretarial service, and separate check-in and checkout. Several restaurants and bars in the hotel are suitable for entertaining, notably Benkay, Café Gardenia, and La Cantina (*see* Dining, below), and the Lobby Lounge and Disco Bistro (*see* After Hours, below). This bustling hotel offers plenty of convenience, but little in the way of warm personal service. *The Lotte Group. 1 Sokong-dong, Chung-gu, tel. 02/771–10 or 800/225–6883, fax 02/752–3758. Gen. manager, Kiichiro Ohba. 1,207 rooms, 113 suites. Free airport shuttle bus. AE, DC, MC, V.*

★ ㉘ **King Sejong Hotel.** Built in 1966, this 15-story hotel near
$$ the city's import offices and department stores is one of Seoul's last bargains. The lobby exudes elegance and style, with its long marble floors and walls, soft recessed lighting, and live plants. Renovated in 1989, guest rooms are bright and spacious, but decorated in low-budget, motel-style green-and-blue floral prints, with small wooden dressers and unusually small TV sets. Fresh flowers are placed daily in the average-size bathrooms. South-side rooms have views of Seoul Tower and Namsan Mountain. A drawback for female guests: The hotel health club and sauna are for men only. Otherwise, the convenient downtown location, reasonable prices, and comfortable guest rooms make this the best selection for business travelers on a tight budget. *61-3, 2-ga Ch'ungmu-ro, Chung-gu, tel. 02/776–1811 or 800/223–9868, fax 02/ 755–4906. Gen. manager, Sung Kwang Kim. 236 rooms, 14 suites. AE, DC, MC, V.*

㉘ **Koreana.** This moderately priced, 24-story hotel is conve-
$$$ niently located next to the city's major newspaper and government offices. The black-marble floor and low ceiling give the lobby a claustrophobic feel. Standard rooms are cramped, with worn pink couches and bedspreads, sturdy oak dressers, and small desks with inadequate lighting from lamps mounted high on the wall. Recently redecorated rooms on the 17th and 18th floors—with views of either Toksu Palace or the bustling streets below—are the better choices. Business services are limited to copying, faxing, and typing. There is a tailor, barber, gift shop, and travel agency in the lower lobby, and the hotel provides free airport shuttle service. *61, 1-ka Taepyung-ro, Chung-gu, tel. 02/730–9911 or 800/251–4848, fax 02/ 734–0665. Gen. manager, Key Nam Kim. 278 rooms, 2 suites. AE, DC, MC, V.*

㉙ **New Seoul Hotel.** Within walking distance of City Hall, the
$$ Korean Press Center, and Toksu Palace, this 17-floor hotel offers good value for simple accommodations in the primary business district. Most guests are Japanese and European business travelers. The lobby's black-and-white-tile floor, gray leather couches, and lush trees are welcoming. Sparsely decorated guest rooms are small but clean, with tiny single beds, small dressers and desks, and cramped bathrooms offering only the bare necessities. *Wanja* (Korean sliding doors) cover the windows, permitting only partial outdoor views. Rooms with larger built-in desks and computer tables for adequate work space are available on request. Corner suites above the 10th floor look out over downtown Seoul, and are roomier and more comfortably furnished. *29-1, 1-ka Taepyung-ro, Chung-gu, tel. 02/735–9071, fax 02/735–6212. Gen. manager. C.Y. Lee. 129 rooms, 16 suites. AE, MC.*

㉑ **President.** Built in 1971 and renovated in 1984, this 33-
$$ story high rise offers no-frills accommodations within

GREATER SEOUL

Lodging
Hotel Inter-
Continental, **14**
Hotel Lotte World, **16**
Hotel Manhattan, **5**
Hyatt Regency
Seoul, **10**
Ramada Olympia
Hotel, **2**

Ramada Renaissance
Hotel Seoul, **13**
Seoul Garden, **4**
Seoul Palace Hotel, **11**
Sheraton Walker
Hill, **15**
Swiss Grand Hotel, **1**

Dining
Baron's Restaurant, **14**
Dae Won Gak, **3**
Firenze, **14**
Ka Ya Rang, **9**
London Pub, **6**
Moghul, **8**

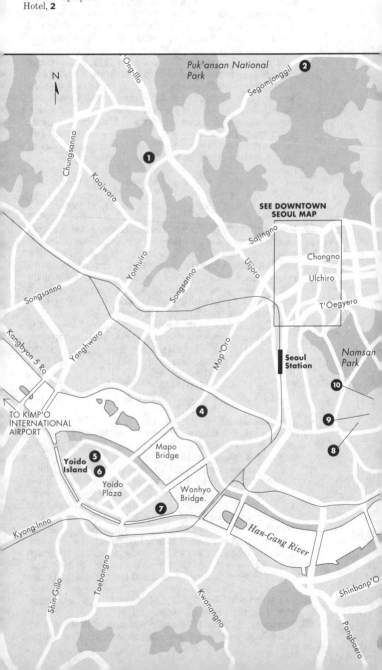

SEE DOWNTOWN
SEOUL MAP

Chongno

Ulchiro

T'Oegyero

Namsan
Park

Seoul
Station

Puk'ansan National
Park

Saitingno

Uljiro

Songsanno

Map'Oro

Yonhuiro

Yanghwaro

Kaajwaro

Chungsanno

I'Ong-Illo

Segomjonggil

Songsanno

Kangbyon 5 Ro

TO KIMP'O
INTERNATIONAL
AIRPORT

Mapo
Bridge

Yoido
Island

Yoido
Plaza

Wonhyo
Bridge.

Han-Gang River

Kyong-Inno

Shin-Gillo

Taebangno

Kwanangno

Shinbanp'O

Pangbaero

DOWNTOWN SEOUL

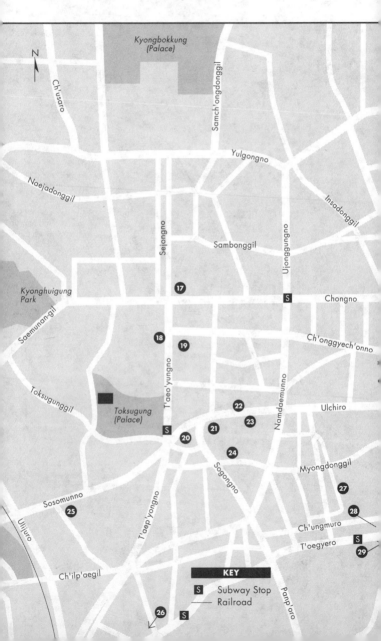

N

Kyongbokkung
(Palace)

Ch'usaro

Samch'ongdonggil

Yulgongno

Naejadonggil

Insadonggil

Sejongno

Sambonggil

Uljongunno

Kyonghuigung
Park

Chongno

Saemunan-gil

🅢

Ch'onggyech'onno

18

19

T'aeo'yungno

Namdaemunno

Ulchiro

Toksugunggil

Toksugung
(Palace)

🅢

22

23

Sogongno

20

21

Myongdonggil

24

27

Sosomunno

25

T'aep'yongno

28

Ch'ungmuro

🅢

Uljiro

T'oegyero

29

Ch'ilp'aegil

KEY

🅢 Subway Stop
— Railroad

26 🅢

Panp'oro

walking distance of downtown businesses and shops. The lobby is stark, with dark-wood walls and threadbare burgundy chairs. Rooms look out over City Hall through tiny, dismal windows. The vinyl wall coverings and worn fabrics and furnishings have a second-hand-store feel. Bathrooms are cramped, with a minimum of amenities. One bright note is the business center, which offers free consulting on networking with Korean corporations. For those who aren't particular about amenities and luxury, this hotel offers a good location at economical rates. *188-3, 1-ka, Ulchiro, Chung-gu, tel. 02/753–3131 or 800/448–8355, fax 02/752–7417. Gen. manager, Young Sup Park. 261 rooms, 16 suites. AE, DC, MC, V.*

❹ **Seoul Garden.** Just 10 minutes from downtown, near the
$$ Yoido Island business zone, this cozy 16-story hotel, built in 1979, was renovated in 1989. Although the hotel is Korean-owned and -operated, it is devoid of Oriental decor; once inside the hotel, it's hard to tell whether you're in Asia or middle America. The well-lighted, simply decorated lobby is bustling—there's a gift shop, convenient airline ticket office, and sparkling lobby lounge complete with white baby grand. The spacious rooms are attractively decorated in sophisticated green and peach fabrics, with modern dressers, desks, and tables of blond wood. Room windows—unlike those in many hotels—can be opened for a view of Seoul's busy city streets. The "Ladies Gold Card Club" entitles returning female guests to discounts in the hotel's restaurants and health club. *169-1, Dowha-dong, Mapo-gu, tel. 02/717–9441 or 800/251–4848, fax 02/715–9441. Gen. manager, K.J. Whang. 394 rooms, 6 suites. AE, DC, MC, V.*

⑳ **Seoul Plaza.** Located across the street from City Hall, this
$$$ 22-story hotel, built in 1976 and renovated in 1989, is sophisticated but casual. The very friendly service, modern business facilities, and ideal location for downtown business appointments and shopping make this an excellent location for travelers. It's also a favorite of the Bolshoi Ballet and Belgium's Prince Albert. The lobby's cornflower-blue carpet, blond wood, and marble furnishings exude elegance and charm. The spacious front rooms, decorated in a chic beige-and-apricot color scheme, overlook the National Museum and Toksu Palace; those in back have views of Namsan Mountain. For an unusual experience, try one of the two *Ondol* suites, furnished in typical Korean style, with low tables and thick futons for sleeping on the floor. Other suites are elegantly appointed in Western-style, with grand antique desks and wardrobes. The lower level of the hotel offers a number of convenient services such as an English newsstand and bookstore, flower shop, bakery, barber/beauty shop, and business center offering secretarial and translation services. *23, 2-ka, Taipyung-ro, Chung-gu, tel. 02/771–22 or 800/447–2311, fax 02/755–8897. Gen. manager, In Soo Park. 427 rooms, 94 suites. AE, DC, MC.*

★ ㉔ **Westin Chosun.** This sleek, modern hotel, visited by Presidents Nixon, Ford, and Reagan, is best known for its superb personal service and warm, cozy atmosphere. The well-trained staff is gracious and attentive to every detail. Within walking distance of Seoul's business, financial, and embassy district, this 20-floor high rise features an intimate marbled lobby with beautiful Oriental murals on the

SEOUL HOTEL CHART

HOTELS	Price Category	Business Services		Fax	Telex	Photocopying	Secretarial services	Audiovisual equipment	Translation services	International direct dial	Computer rentals	In-room modem phone jack
		Banquet capacity	No. of meeting rooms									
Garden	$$	600	6	✓	✓	✓	✓	✓	✓	✓	✓	-
Hilton	$$$$	3500	12	✓	✓	✓	✓	✓	✓	✓	✓	✓
Hyatt Regency	$$$$	2000	8	✓	✓	✓	✓	✓	✓	✓	✓	✓
InterContinental	$$$$	800	18	✓	✓	✓	✓	✓	✓	✓	-	✓
King Sejong	$$	200	7	✓	✓	✓	✓	✓	✓	✓	✓	✓
Koreana	$$$	200	4	✓	✓	✓	✓	✓	✓	✓	-	✓
Lotte	$$$$	1800	12	✓	✓	✓	✓	✓	✓	✓	✓	✓
Lotte World	$$$$	1800	6	✓	✓	✓	✓	✓	✓	✓	✓	✓
Manhattan	$$	70	1	✓	✓	-	-	✓	-	-	✓	-
New Seoul	$$	250	2	✓	✓	✓	✓	✓	✓	✓	-	✓
President	$$	250	3	✓	✓	✓	✓	✓	✓	✓	-	✓
Ramada Olympia	$$$	350	10	✓	✓	✓	✓	✓	✓	✓	✓	-
Ramada Renaissance	$$$	700	7	✓	✓	✓	✓	✓	✓	✓	✓	-
Palace	$$	600	6	✓	✓	✓	✓	✓	✓	✓	-	✓
Plaza	$$$	600	7	✓	✓	✓	✓	✓	✓	✓	✓	✓
Sheraton Walker Hill	$$$$	1000	17	✓	✓	✓	✓	✓	✓	✓	✓	✓
Shilla	$$$$	1400	16	✓	✓	✓	✓	✓	✓	✓	✓	-
Swiss Grand	$$$	600	8	✓	✓	✓	✓	✓	✓	✓	✓	✓
Westin Chosun	$$$$	800	5	✓	✓	✓	✓	✓	✓	✓	✓	✓

$$$$** = over W 112,000, **$$$** = W 98,000-W 112,000, **$$ = under W 98,000.
● good, ◗ fair, ○ poor.

All-news cable channel	Desk	Desk lighting	Bed lighting	**In-Room Amenities** Nonsmoking rooms	In-room checkout	Minibar	Toiletries	Room service	Laundry/Dry cleaning	Pressing	**Hotel Amenities** Barber/Hairdresser	Garage	Courtesy airport transport	Sauna	Pool	Exercise room
✓	●	●	●	✓	✓	✓	●	●	●	●	✓	✓	✓	✓	–	–
✓	●	●	●	✓	✓	✓	●	●	●	●	✓	✓	✓	✓	●	●
✓	●	●	●	–	✓	✓	●	●	●	●	✓	✓	–	✓	●	●
–	●	●	◐	✓	–	●	●	●	●	●	✓	✓	–	✓	●	●
✓	●	●	◐	✓	✓	●	●	●	●	●	✓	✓	✓	✓	–	●
✓	●	◐	◐	–	–	●	●	●	●	●	✓	✓	✓	–	–	–
✓	●	●	●	✓	–	●	●	●	●	●	✓	✓	✓	●	●	●
–	○	○	◐	✓	–	✓	◐	●	●	●	✓	✓	–	✓	–	◐
✓	◐	○	◐	–	–	✓	●	●	●	◐	✓	✓	✓	–	–	–
✓	●	●	●	–	✓	✓	●	●	●	●	✓	✓	✓	–	–	–
–	●	●	●	✓	✓	✓	●	●	●	●	✓	–	●	●	●	●
✓	●	●	●	✓	–	✓	●	●	●	●	✓	✓	✓	✓	●	●
✓	●	●	●	–	–	✓	◐	●	●	●	✓	✓	✓	✓	–	●
✓	●	●	●	✓	✓	✓	◐	●	●	●	✓	✓	✓	–	–	–
✓	●	●	●	✓	–	●	●	●	●	●	✓	✓	✓	✓	●	●
–	●	●	●	✓	✓	✓	●	●	●	●	✓	–	✓	✓	●	●
✓	●	●	●	✓	✓	✓	●	●	●	●	✓	✓	✓	✓	●	●
–	●	●	●	✓	–	✓	●	●	●	●	✓	✓	–	✓	●	●

Room service: ● 24-hour, ◐ 6AM-10PM, ○ other.
Laundry/Dry cleaning: ● same day, ◐ overnight, ○ other.
Pressing: ● immediate, ◐ same day, ○ other.

walls and elevator doors. Built in 1970, the Westin Chosun was totally renovated in 1990; upgraded guest rooms now feature luxurious furnishings in soothing, elegant pastel fabrics. Early risers in rooms on the east side are treated to the spectacular sight of sunrise behind the majestic Temple of Heaven. Guests on executive-class floors (16–18) enjoy such added amenities and services as complimentary breakfast, free admission to the fitness center/ outdoor pool, express checkout, and multilingual secretarial assistance. The complimentary "Women Executives' Package" features smaller terry-cloth robes and slippers, padded hangers, and makeup mirrors. The hotel has numerous restaurants suitable for entertaining associates, including Café Royal (*see* Business Breakfasts, below), Ninth Gate, the Orchid Room, and Yesterdays (*see* Dining, below, for all three); there are also several outstanding bars and lounges, such as the Ninth Gate Bar and Xanadu Nightclub (*see* After Hours, below, for both). *87 Sokong-dong, Chung-gu, tel. 02/771–05 or 800/228–3000, fax 02/752–1443. Gen. manager, David Shackleton. 452 rooms, 24 suites. AE, CB, DC, MC, V.*

Namsam Area

① Hyatt Regency Seoul. Set amid 18 acres of waterfalls and
$$$$ landscaped gardens, this luxurious hotel, built in 1978 and renovated in 1988, is only 10 minutes from downtown and within walking distance of the famous It'aewŏn shopping district. The massive lobby overflows with trees, Oriental paintings, and inviting couches. Guest rooms are spacious and sunny, and decorated in sophisticated green velvet fabrics; furnishings include firm queen-size beds, large free-standing desks, light-oak dressers, and cozy seating areas. Bathrooms are ample, with marble countertops and all the amenities guests might need. There is even a handy pants press in each room. Single women travelers are automatically upgraded to rooms on the executive-class Regency Club floors. J.J. Mahoney's (*see* After Hours, below), located in the basement, is one of the most popular night spots in town. *747-7 Hannam-dong, Yongsan-gu, tel. 02/797–1234 or 800/228–9000, fax 02/798–6953. Gen. manager, Michael Jauslin. 574 rooms, 33 suites. AE, DC, MC, V.*

★ ② **Seoul Hilton.** This elegant 22-story high rise, within
$$$$ walking distance of Seoul's main banking district, is often the first choice of American executives. The lobby features a dramatic, three-story atrium with huge bronze pillars, an Italian marble fountain, and Henry Moore's famous sculpture, *Large Reclining Woman.* Room decor also sets the Hilton apart from more mundanely decorated hotels. Polished Korean chests, sliding *changmun* (latticed wood and paper) window screens, and local art tastefully accent the elegant pale-green fabrics and gleaming Western-style fittings in the spacious guest rooms. Other amenities include a glass-enclosed indoor pool, a convenient outdoor jogging track, sunbathing terrace, and a well-run business center. The Rainforest bar and the Oak Room lounge (*see* After Hours, below) are suitable spots for serious discussions over drinks or for evening entertaining. *395, 5-ka, Namdaemun-no, Chung-gu, tel. 02/ 753–7788 or 800/932–3322, fax 02/754–2510. Gen. manag-*

er, Andreas Bossard. 824 rooms, 66 suites. AE, CB, DC, MC, V.

★ **㉙** **Shilla Hotel.** Set on 23 acres of gardens and waterfalls, the
$$$$ stately Shilla is one of Seoul's top hotels—the home away
from home for visiting royalty and top business leaders
from around the globe. Its lobby is hushed and opulent,
with bamboo walls, stone carvings, thick cinnamon carpeting, and an unusual cascading-glass chandelier. Rooms
are spacious and elegant, with large, well-lighted writing
desks, king- or queen-size beds with pale-green brocade
spreads, immaculate bathrooms with black marble countertops, separate vanity tables with makeup/shaving mirrors, and fresh air vents (a treat for those who don't like
air-conditioning); rooms above the fifth floor have delightful views of Namsan Mountain. Guests staying in Executive Class rooms on the seventh floor enjoy upgraded room
amenities, complimentary airport limo service, access to
conference rooms, and other helpful business services.
Plans are underway for a new fitness center. *Member,
Leading Hotels of the World group. 202, 2-ga Janchung-
dong, Chung-gu, tel. 02/ 233–3131 or 800/448–8355, fax
02/233–5073. Gen. manager, Bong-Shik Kang. 504 rooms,
116 suites. AE, DC, MC, V.*

South of Han River

★ **⓱** **Hotel InterContinental.** Built in 1988 for the Seoul Olym-
$$$$ pics, this luxury hotel is the closest to the Korea Exhibition Center and the newly opened City Air Terminal in the
World Trade Center. The lobby atrium is palatial, with inviting couches, 40-foot trees, brightly colored carpets,
and magnificent wooden balconies. The well-appointed
guest rooms are enormous, with built-in wet bars, limited-edition prints on the walls, free-standing marble-
topped desks, and plush couches with marble end tables in
spacious seating areas. Sumptuous bathrooms have granite tubs and countertops and separate glass-enclosed
shower stalls. There is a small but well-equipped health
club with a 25-meter indoor lap pool, and several outstanding restaurants, including Baron's, Firenze (*see* Dining,
below), and the Sarang-Bang Coffee Shop (*see* Business
Breakfasts, below). Shopping options are plentiful, with
an extensive basement shopping arcade connected to a
major department store next door. *159-1 Samsung-dong,
Kangnam-gu, tel. 02/555–5656 or 800/332–4246, fax 02/
552–6422. Gen manager, Benrouz Tamdyidi. 400 rooms,
200 suites. AE, CB, DC, MC, V.*

⓰ **Hotel Lotte World.** Ten minutes from the World Trade
$$$$ Center and the Korea Exhibition Center (KOEX), this
massive 33-story property, built in 1988, is Korea's largest hotel/shopping/amusement complex. The mad dash of
bodies passing through the huge marble lobby brings to
mind New York's Grand Central Station. Guest rooms are
modern, fairly spacious, and furnished in a pink-and-white
French Provincial decor; fresh flowers sit atop the white
marble countertop in the bathrooms. With two large Dis-
ney-like theme parks (one of them indoors), this hotel is a
favorite among Japanese tour groups and other leisure
travelers. Adjoining the hotel is a duty-free shopping
mall, a folklore exhibition center, and a sports center with
two pools, exercise and sauna facilities, bowling lanes,
squash courts, and a golf driving range. There is free

shuttle service to KOEX, the Itaewon shopping district, and the downtown area. Although popular among convention-goers and families, this is not the location for business travelers seeking a quiet, serious atmosphere conducive to work. *The Lotte Group. 40-1 Chamshil-dong, Kangdong-gu, tel. 02/419–7000 or 800/225–6883, fax 02/417–3655. Gen. manager, Yoshiro Takahashi. 458 rooms, 45 suites, AD, DC, MC, V.*

❺ **Hotel Manhattan.** Located on Yoido Island, close to the
$$ National Assembly Building, the Japanese Trade office, and major corporations like IBM and the Munwha Broadcasting Corporation, this 15-story hotel, built in 1978 and renovated in 1990, is very low on ambience, but offers clean, budget-priced accommodations. Standard rooms have tiny single beds with rattan headboards and nubby white cotton bedspreads, small dressers jammed in the closets, portable TV sets, and no desks. On the positive side, some rooms have pleasant views of the the Han River and others have views of the city streets of this rapidly developing new business district. A small business center in the lobby offers minimal services. *13-3 Yoido-dong, Yongdungpo-gu, tel. 02/780–8001, fax 02/784–2332. Gen. manager, Park Hyung Bum. 180 rooms, 2 suites. AE, DC, V.*

⑬ **Ramada Renaissance Hotel Seoul.** This 25-floor high rise,
$$$ built in 1988, is in the heart of Seoul's fastest-growing new business district just west of KOEX and the World Trade Center. It is much more elegant than its counterpart across town and is more fully equipped for business conventions and meetings. Towering wooden columns, trees, antique Korean chests, and plush couches in intimate groupings decorate the sprawling lobby. Guest rooms, done in light shades of green and plum, are spacious and contemporary, with large, firm beds, shiny brass lamps on marble-topped writing desks, and handsome Korean-style wardrobes with carved walnut doors and brass hinges. A basketful of amenities is perched atop black marble countertops in the roomy bathrooms. The Regency Club on floors 20-22 offers larger, executive-class rooms with upgraded amenities and personalized business services. *676 Yoksam-dong, Kangnam-gu, tel. 02/555–0501 or 800/272–6263, fax 02/553–8118. Gen. manager, Johannes G. Jahns. 551 rooms, 21 suites. AE, CB, DC, MC, V.*

⑪ **Seoul Palace Hotel.** The plastic plants and artificial cherry
$$ trees in the lobby are tacky, but the hotel's proximity to Seoul's Express Bus Terminal makes it convenient for those traveling by bus to points beyond Seoul. The Seoul Palace is also one of the few moderately priced hotels in the vicinity of the World Trade Center. Visitors who have business with Korea's Government Supply Center make up a large part of the guest list. Hallways are gloomy, with faded carpeting, but the midsize rooms are clean, with basic motel-style furniture and worn pink carpets, drapes, and bedspreads. Fitness facilities are for men only. *631 Banpo-dong, Socho-gu, tel. 02/532–0101 or 800/ 251–4848, fax 02/532–0399. Gen. manager, Yim Seung Soon. 194 rooms, 6 suites. AE, DC, MC, V.*

Outskirts

❷ **Ramada Olympia Hotel.** Located just 15 minutes from
$$$ downtown Seoul, this 12-story hotel, built in 1964 and ren-
ovated in 1989, is a pleasant escape from the city's conges-
tion. The beige marble lobby with wood accents creates a
serene atmosphere for weary business travelers. Guest
rooms are sunny and spacious, with simple rather than
luxurious maple-wood furnishings and pink and mint-
green candy-striped fabrics. Sturdy maple desks with
ample lighting sit next to large picture windows overlook-
ing the Bukak Mountains just behind the hotel. Health
facilities are extensive: five floors of exercise equipment,
an aerobics room, saunas, a golf driving range, and indoor
and outdoor pools with dining terraces. Free shuttle serv-
ice is provided to downtown offices, cultural spots, and
shopping. *108-2 Pyung Chang-dong, Chongno-gu, tel. 02/
323-5121 or 800/272-6232, fax 02/353-8688. Gen. manag-
er, Wang S. Kim. 298 rooms, 12 suites. AE, DC, MC, V.*

❺ **Sheraton Walker Hill.** Built in 1963 on 139 landscaped
$$$$ acres overlooking Seoul, this newly renovated resort ho-
tel has its own major convention and cultural center, 30
minutes away from downtown's congestion. The lobby,
created by American designer Harold Thompson, fea-
tures carved teak sunflower columns that tower over
plants, waterfalls, and pale-green upholstered couches.
Bright and airy guest rooms in subtle green color schemes
overlook the Hans River and have such elegant touches as
polished cherry wood and brass-trimmed Korean chests
and spacious marble-topped desks. The cramped plastic
unit bathrooms are a drawback. The hotel offers plenty of
nightlife, with Kayagum Theater, an entertaining dinner
theater showcasing Korean music, folkdancing, and a Las
Vegas–style revue on ice; Reflections Disco; and Casino
Walker Hill (*see* After Hours, below), the only gambling
spot in Seoul. *21 Kwangjang-dong, Sungdong-gu, tel. 02/
453-0121 or 800/325-3535, fax 02/452-6867. Gen. manag-
er, Jay Hahn. 570 rooms, 67 suites. AE, CB, DC, MC, V.*

★ ❶ **Swiss Grand Hotel.** This intimate, 12-story property, lo-
$$$ cated in a secluded mountainside park 15 minutes north of
downtown, is one of Seoul's most elegant hotels. The atri-
um lobby showcases antiques and colorful modern art
scattered among marble staircases and flowing waterfalls.
The opulently decorated mauve and green guest rooms
have brocade spreads on comfortable double beds, large
chestnut desks with bright lamps, and intimate balconies
where guests can sit and enjoy the fresh mountain air and
relaxing scenery. This resortlike hotel has a fully
equipped fitness club with indoor pool and a nicely landscaped jogging path that winds around the hotel and into
the surrounding hills. The hotel staff is very friendly and
accommodating; they will even meet your associates at
the airport or babysit if needed. Free shuttle bus service
provides convenient connections to downtown and the
It'aewŏn shopping and entertainment district. *A Swissotel. 210 Hongeun-dong, Sodaemun-gu, tel. 02/356-5656
or 800/637-9477, fax 02/356-7799. Gen. manager, Pierre
Urs Stacher. 374 rooms, 26 suites. AE, CB, DC, MC, V.*

DINING

Westerners are usually delighted to find that many Korean dishes are ideally suited to their meat-and-vegetable tastes. Koreans tend to favor beef dishes like *pulgogi* (thin slices of beef marinated in soy or sesame sauce and cooked over a hot charcoal grill), *kujolp'an* (cooked meat and vegetables arranged on a large platter with a stack of Korean pancakes in the center), and *shinsollo* (meat, fish, vegetables, and bean curd in a beef broth).

Of course, the amount of spice in some Korean fare takes a bit of getting used to. Some examples to try with caution include *pibimbap* (cooked rice mixed with bits of meat, seasoned vegetables, and red pepper), *naengmyon* (thin buckwheat noodles in cold beef broth with chopped scallions and hot mustard), and of course *kimchi*, the spicy pickled cabbage served at virtually all meals.

Eating out is a pleasure in Korea, with its abundance of good restaurants. Beyond the many establishments specializing in local fare, a multitude of restaurants offer a wide variety of international cuisine.

Highly recommended restaurants in each price category are indicated by a star ★.

Category	Cost*
$$$$ (Very Expensive)	over W28,000
$$$ (Expensive)	W21,000–W28,000
$$ (Moderate)	under W21,000

per person, including appetizer, entrée, and dessert, but excluding drinks, service, and 10% sales tax.

Numbers in the margin correspond to numbered restaurant locations on the Seoul Lodging and Dining maps.

Wine and Beer

Korean vintages are *majuang* (white wine) and *papjoo* (deceivingly mild, milky-white rice wine). They are somewhat acidic, but worth a try. Your best bet is to stick with the imported wines served in better restaurants. The local brews, OB Beer and Crown Beer, are both refreshing and delicious.

Business Breakfasts

Because Koreans enjoy meeting over any meal, not so much to discuss business as to socialize and strengthen business ties, the "power breakfast" is very popular here. The best breakfast buffets and Sunday brunches are offered at the **Café Royale** (tel. 02/771–05) in the lobby of the Westin Chosun, the **Sarang-Bang Coffee Shop** (tel. 02/555–5656) in the Hotel InterContinental, and the **Business Hall Coffee Shop** (1-Bun Ji, 1-Ka Chongro, Chongro-gu, tel. 02/739–8830) in the lobby of the Kyobo Building.

Downtown/City Hall Plaza Area

㉓ **Benkay.** With its peaceful pebble gardens, serene ikebana
$$$$ flower arrangements, and gleaming black lacquer tables in private tatami-mat rooms, Benkay is an elegant venue for

business entertaining. Open for lunch and dinner, it is a favorite among Japanese and Korean executives and politicians. Chef Musha is a master of presentation; his carefully orchestrated meals are almost too beautiful to eat. Try the fresh broiled mackerel or steamed sweet fish with teriyaki sauce. The tempura, sukiyaki, and other well-known Japanese dishes are also excellent choices. Both the quiet sushi bar and the main dining room are comfortable for those who are dining alone. *Hotel Lotte, 1 Sokong-dong, Chung-gu, tel. 02/771–10, ext. 5211. Jacket suggested. Reservations required. AE, DC, MC, V.*

㉓ **Café Gardenia.** Blue stained-glass panels, pink velvet
$$ chairs, and full-grown trees make this a cheerful restaurant for a quick business lunch or dinner after work. With a buffet of over 80 dishes, Café Gardenia is a great way to sample an amazing variety of Korean dishes. The grilled spare ribs are excellent, as are the succulent, fragrant Korean vegetables. Try the ginseng cocktail. Tables are spaced rather closely, providing little privacy for the primarily Korean and European clientele. *Hotel Lotte, 1 Sokong-dong, Chung-gu, tel. 02/771–10, ext. 5222. Casual dress. No reservations. AE, DC, MC, V.*

⑰ **L'abri.** For an elegant, classic French meal, dine in one of
$$$$ Seoul's few downtown French restaurants, on the second floor of the Kyobo Building, overlooking a beautiful indoor tree garden. The atmosphere here is more formal than in most of Seoul's restaurants, with pink and green brocade banquettes, white linen tablecloths, and silver service. Chef/general manager Alan Boudet Fenouillet creates specialties like fresh *irba* (a local fish) poached in wine, served with cheese and mushrooms, and tender lamb cutlets in tomato sauce. Also reliable are the smoked scallops, lobster sautéed in brandy, and orange kiwi mousse. The service is attentive, and tables are well spaced for privacy. Ambassadors and top corporate executives are among the regular patrons who entertain important associates here. *1-Bun Ji, 1-ka Chongro, Chongro-gu, tel. 02/739–8830. Jacket and tie required. Reservations required. AE, CB, DC, MC, V. Closed Sun., holidays.*

㉒ **La Cantina.** A welcome haven for pasta and steak lovers,
$$ this intimate Italian restaurant is in the lobby of the Samsung building in the heart of downtown. Surrounded by Italian ink drawings, posters, and sculptures, an international crowd dines on Chef Chung Kwung Tak's Northern Italian cuisine. Specialties include homemade lasagna, tagliatelle with Alfredo sauce, thick imported American steaks, and rich zabaglione for dessert. The extensive wine list includes chianti and Korean Majuang. Canned music and closely spaced tables make this spot more appropriate for relaxation than for doing business. *50 1-Ka Ulji-ro, Chung-gu, tel. 02/777–2579. Casual dress. Reservations advised. AE, DC, MC, V. Closed holidays.*

㉗ **Myong-dong Kyo-ja.** Located in the middle of the business
$$ and shopping district along Myong-dong, this is where the locals come for quick, nourishing bowls of noodles and dumplings. It is a noisy place, with bargain-basement tables and chairs, but it's worth a try if you're in the neighborhood and ready to taste some simple local fare. There are only four items on the menu, all priced under US$4; refills on soup and rice are free. Take a taxi or walk, as

there is no parking in the area. *25-2, 2-ga, Myong-dong, Chung-gu, tel. 02/776–5348. Casual dress. No reservations. V. Closed holidays.*

★ ❷ **Ninth Gate.** Ninth Gate, one of the most elegant restau-
$$$$ rants in Korea, caters to the city's top business leaders, politicians, and journalists. The beige velvet chairs, soft lighting, fresh flower arrangements, and stunning views of the historic Temple of Heaven create a serene atmosphere for enjoying the superb cuisine. The European chef uses fresh imported ingredients, such as California asparagus, to create his nouvelle French entrées like tender roast lamb loin with tarragon port-wine sauce and asparagus pancakes. Also delicious is the steamed fresh sea bream with lobster butter sauce and angel-hair pasta. Under the direction of Kim Kyung Ran, the only female sommelier in Korea, the extensive wine cellar contains 350 international selections. If you are looking for an impressive spot to entertain important associates, Ninth Gate will certainly fit the bill. *The Westin Chosun Hotel, 87 SoKong-dong, Chung-gu, tel. 02/771–05. Jacket advised. Reservations required. AE, CB, DC, MC, V.*

★ ❷ **Orchid Room.** Only a very confident and experienced res-
$$ taurant could arrange a buffet that includes Chinese, Korean, Japanese, and Western foods, and do so successfully. This is a favorite lunch spot of locals as well as Americans and Japanese in town on business. The sunny rooftop room has a terrific bird's eye view of the city. Recommended from the vast buffet are sushi, sashimi, ravioli in tomato sauce, cold roast beef with tartar sauce, abalone soup, and cherry cheesecake. You won't need to eat dinner after lunching in this delightful restaurant. Its central downtown location and something-for-every-taste buffet make it ideal for almost any business lunch. *Westin Chosun Hotel, 87 SoKong-dong, Chung-gu, tel. 02/771–05. Jacket advised. No reservations required. AE, CB, DC, MC, V. Closed holidays.*

❷⑤ **Press Club.** As the name implies, this restaurant on the
$$ 19th floor of the Daily News Building is the haunt of many Korean and foreign press members working at the *Seoul Daily News*. Journalists deep in conversation and smoke relax in the brown leather chairs that line the floor-to-ceiling windows that look out over the city. Owned and operated by the highly respected Shilla Hotel (*see* above), the boisterous Press Club serves simple but delicious sandwiches, hamburgers, and salads. It is a fun local spot to pick up a quick lunch and the latest news. *25 1-ga Taepyongro, Chung-gu, tel. 02/731–7545. Jacket required. Reservations advised. AE, DC, MC, V. Closed holidays.*

❷ **Yesterdays.** This friendly, casual restaurant is located in
$$ the bustling shopping arcade of the Westin Chosun Hotel. The eclectic menu offers Hungarian goulash soup, crispy cheese and mushroom pizza, spaghetti Bolognese, grilled veal bratwurst, panfried seabream meunière, and fresh chef's salads. The red-and-white checkered tablecloths, period photos, and wine racks lining the walls create a comfortable atmosphere suitable for an informal business lunch with associates or a quick meal alone after work. *Westin Chosun Hotel, 87 SoKong-dong, Chung-gu, tel. 02/771–05. Casual dress. No reservations. AE, CB, DC, MC, V. Closed holidays.*

Namsam Area

★ ❾ **Ka Ya Rang.** For a fun place to entertain clients, consider
$$$$ Ka Ya Rang, one of Seoul's most famous Korean restaurants. The large dining room and smaller private rooms are simple but elegant, with salmon-hued floors, Oriental wallpaper, and sliding *wanja* doors. Ten highly trained chefs serve expertly prepared "palace" dishes—traditional specialties once reserved for Korean royalty, but now widely popular. Especially delightful are *kujal pan*, soft pancakes wrapped around nine different vegetables and dipped in hot mustard sauce. Also good is the fish-and-vegetable casserole in the charcoal-heated *shinseon-ro* pot. Have the sweet chewy lotus root for dessert. *239-4 It'aewŏn-dong, Yongsan-gu. tel. 02/797-4000. Casual dress. Reservations required. AE, DC, MC, V. Closed holidays.*

❽ **Moghul.** In the heart of the It'aewŏn shopping district,
$$ this is one of the few Pakistani restaurants. It offers a welcome change from the vegetable-oriented Korean cuisine. Especially good is the fish tandoori, which is barbecued on charcoal and served with spiced butter-and-lemon sauce. Also delicious is the chicken *galfrazy*, sautéed in butter with onions, tomatoes, green chilies, and fresh ginger. A cool OB beer will help counteract the spices. This is a good place to relax with colleagues, not to impress your business associates. *116-2 It'aewŏn-dong, Yongsan-gu, tel. 02/ 796-5501. Casual dress. Reservations suggested. AE, DC, V.*

South of Han River

★ ⓮ **Baron's Restaurant.** One of Seoul's top nouvelle French
$$$$ restaurants, Baron's offers spectacular city views from its 34th-floor vantage point atop the Hotel InterContinental. This is a very quiet place for serious business or client entertainment. Diners relax in private alcoves with window views, in plush leather chairs surrounded by black marble and Korean pottery. Chef Alan Duval presents his entrées with flair, particularly the fresh broiled sea scallops with herb sauce and wild rice and the rare roast lamb chops in mustard sauce with artichoke hearts. Fresh strawberry tarts complete a very satisfying meal. A variety of French, Australian, and Korean wines are available. The attentive but unobtrusive service and the quiet atmosphere make this spot conducive for business discussions. *Hotel InterContinental, 159-1 Samsong-dong, Kangnam-gu, tel. 02/553-8181, ext. 7631. Jacket and tie required. Reservations required. AE, DC, CB, MC, V. Closed Sun.*

★ ⓯ **Firenze.** Dine under a sapphire-blue mural sky in this ele-
$$$ gant Italian restaurant in the lobby of the InterContinental hotel. Popular among tourists and business travelers for both lunch and dinner, Firenze is a chic bistro featuring outstanding Northern Italian cuisine and soft classical guitar music. Diners select from an array of delicacies on the antipasto cart wheeled to their table. Favorite entrées include marinated salmon in pink pepper and olive oil, homemade fettucine in *quattro formaggi* (four cheese) sauce, and grilled sirloin topped with herbed mixed vegetables. A second cart reveals a mouth-watering selection of desserts; the chocolate mousse is irresistible. Firenze is elegant enough for entertaining. *Hotel InterContinen-*

tal, 159-1 Samsong-dong, Kangnam-gu, tel. 02/559-7607. Jacket and tie required. Reservations required. AE, DC, MC, V.

⑥ **London Pub.** With Scottish kilt–type red-and-green plaid
$$ carpet, plush leather chairs, and framed ship models, this Old World pub is a cozy place for an informal business lunch or relaxed meal after work. Although blaring music videos make it difficult for the crowd of local business-people to converse near the bar, there are plenty of quiet tables in the dining room. The pepper steak, shrimp fried rice, and garden salads are excellent. Pizza, hamburgers, pork chops, and spaghetti are also on the menu. French and Korean wines are available, as are cocktails and beer. *Korea Federation Small Business Bldg. B1, 16-2 Yoido-dong, Yongdungpo-gu, tel. 02/783–7701. Casual dress. Reservations required. AE, CB, DC, MC, V. Closed Sun., holidays.*

⑦ **Paengni Hyang Chinese Restaurant.** This restaurant is a
$$$$ favorite among executives of IBM, Litton, Samsung, and other nearby offices for a working lunch or dinner. Elegant Oriental murals and beveled glass dragons accent the six private meeting rooms; the small dining room affords spectacular views of Yoido and the outskirts of Seoul. Top choices among the many beautifully presented Cantonese and Mandarin dishes are braised prawns in chili sauce, abalone and pine mushrooms, fresh asparagus with scallops, and bird's nest soup with crab eggs. There is also a fine selection of French, German, Chinese, and Korean wines. *DLI Building 57F, Yoido-dong, Yongdungpo-gu, tel. 02/ 789-5741. Jacket and tie required. Reservations required. AE, DC, MC, V.*

⑫ **Rose Garden.** On a bustling city street of boutiques and
$$ bistros near the Palace Hotel, this charming Northern Italian restaurant is filled with floral murals, plants, and fresh roses. A noisy crowd of tourists, shoppers, and business executives dine on the homemade pizza and spaghetti, fresh chef's salads, and imported American steaks. Among the 10 different steak dishes served, the tender T-bone with mushrooms is best. The lobster and salmon courses are not as fresh as they could be, having been "fresh frozen" rather than flown in daily. Cocktails, local and imported beer, and wine are served. The Rose Garden is a relaxing place for dining after work or shopping. *11 Bangbae Jungang-ro, Bangbae-dong, tel. 02/537–1101. Casual but neat. Reservations accepted. AE, MC, V.*

⑦ **Sky View Lounge.** On the 59th floor of the Daehan Life
$$$ Building, this luxurious Continental restaurant, with upholstered wooden chairs, crystal chandeliers, and lush greenery, offers one of the city's most spectacular views. It is a popular choice with a Korean and European clientele for serious business lunches and after-hours entertaining. Menu selections include beef, lamb, chicken, and seafood. The broiled prawns in herbed butter sauce, grilled lobster, and crêpes suzette are top sellers. A good selection of Austrian, French, German, American, and Korean wines are served. Ask for a table next to the large picture windows. *60 Yoido-dong, Yongdungpo-gu, tel. 02/ 789-5904. Jacket and tie advised. Reservations advised. AE, DC, MC, V.*

Outskirts

★ ❸
$$$$

Dae Won Gak. Nestled among the woods high above Seoul is a complex of 60 wooden huts where guests are treated to sumptuous Korean feasts and traditional entertainment. Climbing up the rock stairway to the private huts, visitors are met by the sounds of rushing waterfalls, soft classical music, and the murmered greetings of the staff. Charming hostesses in Korean *hanbok* dresses help diners select from the many entrées. Specialties include beef sirloin and ribs, boiled vegetables, steamed jumbo shrimp, and buckwheat noodle soup. Following the meal, dancers and musicians in traditional costume perform Korean folksongs. Dae Won Gak is sophisticated rather than touristy; many local and foreign business executives do their entertaining here. *323 Songbuk, Songbuk-gu, tel. 02/762–0034. Jacket advised. Reservations required. AE, DC, MC, V.*

FREE TIME

Fitness

Hotel Facilities
Most of the major hotels have excellent health clubs, but they are reserved for guest use only; however, facilities at the Hilton and Ramada Olympic are open to nonguests. The **Seoul Hilton** (tel. 02/753–7788) has the most extensive facilities, with an indoor swimming pool, gymnasium, jogging track, sauna, and sun terrace. The **Ramada Olympia** (tel. 02/323–5121) has five floors in its Fitness Center, including indoor/outdoor pools, a beauty salon, aerobics room, weight room, golf driving range, and Turkish bath. Both facilities cost W9,800 per day.

Health Clubs
Besides those at the major hotels, there are no health clubs open to temporary members.

Jogging
The best jogging areas are found on the historic, picturesque palace grounds of **Ch'angdŏkkung, Kyŏngbokkung,** and **Toksukung.** There are also manicured jogging paths on the grounds of the **Swiss Grand** and **Shilla** hotels. The **Westin Chosun** can provide a map of suitable jogging routes in its neighborhood.

Shopping

Korea has a wide variety of quality items including fur (mink, fox, beaver, etc.), custom and ready-made clothing and shoes, eel-skin and leather goods, ceramics, lacquerware, silk, dolls, antiques, semiprecious stones, ginseng, and brassware.

The major shopping districts are **Myong-dong** (fashion), **It'aewŏn** (bargains on consumer goods), **Insa-dong** (Korean arts and crafts), **Changan-dong** and **Tapshimni-dong** (antiques), **Tongdaemun** (large open-air market for silks, household goods), and **Namdemun** (another open-air market for produce, clothing, and jewelry). Take along a calculator and a translator, if possible.

The top department stores near the primary business districts are **Korea Diamond Duty Free Department Store** (77 Mugyo-dong, Chung-gu, tel. 02/757–7101), **Shinsegae De-**

partment Store (52-5 Ch'ungmuro 1-ga, Chung-gu, tel. 02/
754–1234), and the **Lotte Shopping Center** (1 Sogong-
dong, Chung-gu, tel. 02/771–25). Of the three, Lotte offers the largest variety of both Korean and international
goods. Department store prices are much higher than
those in the markets and shopping districts; however, English is more likely to be spoken by department store
clerks.

There are numerous boutiques around town for chic fashions. **Elle Boutique** (260-184 It'aewŏn-dong, Yongsan-
gu, tel. 02/792–2364) carries a fine selection of elegant
women's dresses and suits. **Lee Kwanghee** (260-199 It'aewŏn-dong, Yongsan-gu, tel. 02/797–3739) has the best
sportswear. For fashionable men's clothing, recommended shops are **Bando** (63-1 Ch'ungmuro, 2-ga, Chung-
ku, tel. 02/756–1343) and **SS Fashion** (50-5, Myong-dong 2,
Chung-ku, tel. 02/777–5004).

For antiques, head to **Hanbo Antiques** (188 Insa-dong,
Chongro-ku, tel. 02/739–3531). For silks, try **Shinwa Silks**
(87 Sogong-dong, Chung-ku, tel. 02/757–6888); for ceramics, go to **Koryo-sa** (28-1 Insa-dong, Chongro-ku, tel. 02/
732–2820); and for semiprecious stones, try **Jeil Amethyst**
(87 Sogong-dong, Chung-ku, tel. 02/778–2212).

Diversions

Seoul is a fascinating combination of new and old: Mirrored high-rise hotels reflect the edifices of centuries-old
palaces and modern department stores compete with bustling open-air markets. A stroll around Seoul will reveal
an enthralling diversity of architecture, shops, and people. The following sights can be appreciated even by travelers with limited time.

Ch'angdŏkkung Palace (2 Waryong-dong, Chongno-gu) is
the best preserved of the five palaces of the Yi Dynasty
(the royal family that ruled Korea from 1392 to 1910). Of
interest on the palace grounds are Piwon (the Secret Garden)—80 acres of blossoms, ponds, and pavilions— and
Naksonjae, the home of Princess Pang-ja (Masàko), the
surviving widow of the dynasty's last crown prince.

Chongmyo (1 Hunjong-dong, Chongno-gu), once a sacred
shrine containing the carved stone ancestral tablets of all
the Yi kings and queens, is now a beautiful public park. It
still serves its ceremonial function the first Sunday in
May, when an elaborate Confucian ritual is held.

The **Daehan Life Insurance Building** (50 Youido-dong,
Yongdungpo-ku, tel. 02/784–0063) is the tallest skyscraper in Asia, with 60 floors above ground and three below.
This "Golden Tower" contains an Imax cinema, a Sea
World Aquarium, a convention hall, a shopping center,
several restaurants, and an observation deck with a bird's
eye view of Seoul and surrounding neighborhoods.

Tucked away in Seoul Grand Park in Kwach'on, a suburb
of Seoul, is the **National Museum of Contemporary Art**
(7058-1 Makkye-dong, Kong-gido, tel. 02/503–7744). Designed to resemble an ancient Korean fortress, this ul-
tramodern building houses 3,000 works of modern art
including sculpture, three-dimensional art, and Korean
paintings, handicrafts, and engravings. Don't miss inter-

nationally renowned Nam June Paik's video art installation, "The more, the better." The museum also features works by Andy Warhol, Joseph Beuys, and Claude Viallet.

The **Korea Folk Village** (107 Borari Kiheung-myon, Yongin-gun, tel. 02/776–6869), 30 minutes south of Seoul in Kyonggi-do Province near Suwon, is an open-air living museum that presents rural Korean life of a century ago. This is not a tourist theme park, but truly educational, with exhibits such as a typical farmhouse, an operating blacksmith's shop, and a brass forge, all run by locals—a fortune teller, calligrapher, embroiderers, basketweavers, and paper makers. It's worth seeing if you have a free day.

Kyongbokkung Palace (1 Sejongno, Chongno-gu, tel. 02/732–1931) is the largest and most important of the royal palaces. This "Palace of Shining Happiness" was the home of Yi T'Aejo, the founder of the Yi Dynasty, who ordered it built in 1395. On the palace grounds are numerous historic stone pagodas, two well-preserved lotus ponds (one of which has lotuses that bloom each July), and the **National Folklore Museum** (tel. 02/720–3138), well worth a stop if you enjoy native crafts.

If you fancy a pleasant short hike, head up the mountain in Namsam Park to **Seoul Tower.** From the platform atop the tower, you can appreciate a more intimate view of downtown Seoul than the view from the DLI Building in Yoido. A high-speed elevator whisks you to the circular observation deck and dining room. The tower also houses a grill, snack bar, coffeehouse, souvenir shops, and a tropical aquarium.

Surrounded by modern city high rises, **Toksukung Palace** (5-1 Chong-dong, Chung-gu), or the "Palace of Virtuous Longevity," has a number of buildings constructed of stone rather than wood, reflecting 19th-century Western architecture rather than traditional Korean styles. The main gate and throne rooms are surrounded by fragrant flower gardens in spring, providing a refreshing break from the din of the city outside.

The Arts

Seoul hosts a wide variety of cultural entertainment, from classical Korean dramas to modern ballet and Broadway shows. You can hear classical Korean court music at the **Korea House Art Theater** (80-20 P'il-dong, 2-ga, Chung-gu, tel. 02/266–9101), or enjoy traditional Korean-style theater outdoors at the **National Theater** complex (San 14-16 Changdu'ung-dong 2-ga, Chung-gu, tel. 02/274–1153), which also houses the **National Classical Music Institute.** Opera and ballet are often performed at the **Sejong Cultural Center** (81-3 Sejong-no, Chongno-gu, tel. 02/736–2721), or at the National Theater.

For a schedule of current events, check the *Korea Herald* or *Korea Times.* Tickets are available at box offices and at the **Kyobo Book Store** (1-1 Chongro, Chongro-ku, tel. 02/730–7891).

After Hours

Singles will probably feel the most comfortable in the up-scale lounges and lively nightclubs of the major hotels. Most Westerners appreciate the quiet, sophisticated atmosphere of the hotel bars for after-hours entertaining as well.

Bars and Lounges
You will find an elite mix of locals and business travelers at the **Ninth Gate Bar** (Westin Chosun, tel. 02/771–05), an elegant, comfortable spot with live entertainment provided by a Filipino band. Two of the best lounges in town for quiet conversation over drinks are the elegant **Oak Room** (Seoul Hilton, tel. 02/753–3788) and the informal but pleasant **Gallery** (The Plaza, tel. 02/756–1112). If you're searching for an elegant spot for evening entertaining, try **Reflections** (Sheraton Walker Hill, tel. 02/444–8211), where a sophisticated crowd gathers to drink and mingle. Suitable clubs outside the major hotels include **Casanova** (83-5 Myong-dong 2-ga, Chung-gu, tel. 02/776–2473), **Myhouse** (52-13 Myong-dong 2-ga, Chung-gu, tel. 02/777–6861), and **Giant Night Club** (45-10 Sansung-dong, Kangnam-gu, tel. 02/549–1161).

Jazz Clubs
J.J. Mahoney's (Hyatt Regency, tel. 02/798–0066), one of the only places in town to catch good live jazz, is a fun spot for a light meal, drinks, and dancing amid a boisterous American, Korean, and European crowd. This large entertainment complex houses a disco, a deli, several green-house bars, an outdoor terrace, and a pub with music videos, darts, and billiards. Another popular haunt for jazz lovers is **All That Jazz** (tel. 02/795–5701) in the heart of the It'aewŏn shopping district.

Cabaret
The Sheraton Walker Hill (tel. 02/444–8211) offers a Las Vegas–style revue and another floorshow featuring Korean folkdance and music in the **Kayagum Theater Restaurant.** The hotel also has the city's only casino.

Discos
Disco Bistro (Hotel Lotte, tel. 02/771–10, ext. 5281) offers cocktails and dancing under a neon "sky" from 7 PM to 3 AM. The **Rain Forest** (Seoul Hilton, tel. 02/753–7788) is a favorite among businesspeople and journalists for drinks and people-watching. **Xanadu** (Westin Chosun, tel. 02/771–05), popular with the young Europeans living and working in Seoul, is a lively spot for dancing.

Singapore

by Marc Rouen

Singapore, a city-state of some 3 million people, is at the forefront of the rapidly expanding and developing economies of Southeast Asia. As the most industrialized of the region's cities, it has excellent air links and telecommunications, and a solid, well-oiled infrastructure.

Singapore was founded as a British trading post in 1819. In 1971, when the last of the British military forces left the island, Singapore raced to modernize. Since the 1950s, under the leadership of Lee Kuan Yew—former prime minister and still the guiding force behind Goh Chok Tong's present government—Singapore has had relatively little overt corruption or crime.

Strict laws and education programs keep drugs from eating away at the fabric of society. The streets are well lit and litter-free, with clearly marked crosswalks, and there is an excellent and inexpensive public transport system. Education is free and compulsory. Every schoolchild must study English and either Mandarin, Malay, or Tamil (the four official languages).

All these benefits have been bought at a price. Critics accuse the People's Action Party of social programming, promoting a bland uniformity, and infringement of individual rights.

Singaporeans don't necessarily like the fact that the party will decide their future, but most accept the sacrifices they must make, recognizing that Singapore is safe, clean, and prosperous, largely as a result of the party's firm control and acumen.

Skyscrapers line the Shenton Way financial district, and air-conditioned shopping malls and glitzy hotels line the Orchard Road tourist strip. Most of the population now live in apartment blocks on estates that have replaced the old *kampongs* (villages). In recent years, the government has realized the value of retaining the city's architectural heritage, and tucked among the modern buildings are areas of restored old shophouses and imposing British colonial buildings. Unlike many former colonies, Singapore has retained the old British names for its streets.

The government has put great effort into creating a unified nation out of this multiracial island, where the population is 76% Chinese, 15% Malay, 6% Indian, and the balance, Eurasian. Each race retains its unique cultural identity, but all manage to live together with an unusual degree of harmony.

Trading has always been Singapore's life-blood. In line with its image as a modern, efficient business city, it is encouraging high-technology industries and phasing out labor-intensive ones, and training workers to upgrade their skills to suit the new trades. Electronics and computer-component manufacturing have grown in importance, while ship repairing and support services for the oil industry in nearby Indonesia have begun to play a smaller role in the nation's economy.

Foreign investment is actively sought by the government's Economic Development Board, and tax breaks are given to companies that set up operational headquarters here. Singapore is also growing as a financial center, both in the region and as part of a worldwide financial network. Its real estate is attracting increasing attention from Hong Kong investors nervous about the British colony's return to Chinese rule in 1997.

In a city-state like Singapore, the government is the largest employer. In the private sector, the list is as follows:

Top Employers

Employer	Type of Enterprise	Parent*/ Headquarters
AT&T Consumer Products	Electrical products	New York, NY
Hewlett-Packard	Computers	Palo Alto, CA
Int'l Airport Services	Transportation	Changi, Singapore
Matsushita Electrical	Electrical equipment	Osaka, Japan
McDonald's	Fast-food chain	Oakbrook, IL
Miniscribe Peripheral	Computer peripherals	Longmont, CO
Philips Singapore	Electrical equipment	Eindhoven, Netherlands
Seagate Technologies	Computer disk drives	Scotts Valley, CA
Singapore Airlines	Transportation	Singapore
Singapore Bus Services	Transportation	Singapore

*if applicable

ESSENTIAL INFORMATION

The currency of Singapore is the dollar, abbreviated throughout the chapter as S$.

Government Tourist Offices

Singapore Tourist Promotion Board. In the United States: 590 Fifth Ave., 12th Floor, New York, NY 10036, tel. 212/302–4861; 333 N. Michigan Ave., Suite 818, Chicago, IL 60601, tel. 312/704–4200; 8484 Wilshire Blvd., Suite 510, Beverly Hills, CA 90211, tel. 213/852–1901.

In Canada: 175 Bloor St. E, Suite 1112, North Tower, Toronto N4W 3R8, Ontario, tel. 416/323–9139.

In the United Kingdom: Carrington House, 126–130 Regent St., London W1R 5FE, tel. 071/437–0033.

In Singapore: Raffles City Tower, 250 North Bridge Rd., tel. 330–0431 or 339–6622.

Foreign Trade Information

Singapore Trade Development Board (STDB). In the United States: 745 5th Ave., Suite 1601, New York, NY 10151, tel. 212/421–2207; Los Angeles World Trade Center, 350 S. Figueroa St., Suite 272, Los Angeles, CA 90071, tel. 213/617–7358 or 213/617–7359.

In Canada: STDB c/o Overseas Union Bank of Singapore, The Standard Life Centre, 10th Floor, 121 King St. W, Toronto M5H 3T9, Ontario tel. 416/363–8227; c/o United Overseas Bank Canada, Park Place Suite 880, 666 Burrard St., Vancouver BC V6C 2X8, tel. 604/662–7055.

In the United Kingdom: 5 Chesam St., London SW1 X8D, tel. 071/245–9709.

In Singapore: 1 Maritime Sq., #03–01 World Trade Centre, Telok Blangah Rd., Singapore 0409, tel. 271–9388.

Entry Requirements

U.S. Citizens
Passport only. A visa is required for stays longer than 90 days.

Canadian and U.K. Citizens
Passport only. A visa is required for stays longer than 14 days.

Climate

Located less than one degree north of the equator, Singapore is hot and humid all year, and has a short, heavy tropical downpour every day or two. During the rainy season, from late-November to mid-January, rain is very heavy and the temperature usually falls slightly. Otherwise, the heat is constant year-round. What follows are the average daily maximum and minimum temperatures for Singapore.

Jan.	82F	28C	**Feb.**	88F	31C	**Mar.**	88F	31C
	75	25		81	27		81	27
Apr.	88F	31C	**May**	88F	31C	**June**	88F	31C
	81	27		81	27		81	27
July	88F	31C	**Aug.**	88F	31C	**Sept.**	88F	31C
	81	27		81	27		81	27
Oct.	88F	31C	**Nov.**	88F	31C	**Dec.**	82F	28C
	81	27		81	27		75	25

Airport

Changi International Airport, easily Asia's best, is located on the eastern end of the island, 11 miles north of downtown. Scheduled international flights go exclusively to Changi.

Airlines

Singapore is home base for the national carrier, Singapore Airlines, which has the most frequent flights. Both Singapore and United fly direct from Los Angeles (with a stop in Tokyo) and from San Francisco (with a stop in Hong Kong). Flying from the east North American coast cuts the flight by five hours. Finnair, in particular, promotes this route from New York, with a change of planes in Helsinki.

Cathay Pacific, tel. 533–1333; 800/663–8868.
Finnair, tel. 733–3377; 800/950–5000.
Japan Airlines (JAL), tel. 221–0522; 800/525–3663.
Malaysian, tel. 336–6777.
Northwest, tel. 235–7166; 800/225–2525.
Singapore Airlines, tel. 223/8888; 800/742–3333.
TWA, tel. 298–9911; 800/221–2000.
United, tel. 220–0711; 800/538–2929.

Between the Airport and Downtown

Many hotels provide transportation by limousine or minibus; inquire when making reservations. Note that there is no helicopter service into town. The Mass Rapid Transit railway does not operate to the airport.

By Taxi
Taxis are the best way to get downtown. They are plentiful and follow the most direct routes—there are no "scenic tours." The trip along either the Pan-Island Expressway or East Coast Parkway takes 20–25 minutes, even in rush hours (8:30–9:30 AM and 5–6:30 PM), and costs about S$14 plus a S$3 airport departure surcharge. The Singaporean government actively discourages tipping; taxi drivers are not tipped by Singaporeans, who become upset when they see tourists tip.

By Bus
There is no express service. Singapore Bus Services's No. 390 bus goes downtown but is not recommended because it is slow, uncomfortable, and there is no air-conditioning or storage space for luggage. However, the price is right—only S$.90 one way.

Car Rentals

Avis and Thrifty have booths at the airport; Hertz, Ken Air, and Toyota have offices in town. Hertz and Toyota charge additional fees for airport dropoffs. Ken Air's cars cannot be returned at the airport.

AA Toyota Rental, tel. 475–3855.
Avis, tel. 542–8855; 800/331–1212.
Hertz, tel. 447–3388; 800/654–3131.
Ken Air, tel. 737–82892.
Thrifty, tel. 542–7288; 800/367–2277.

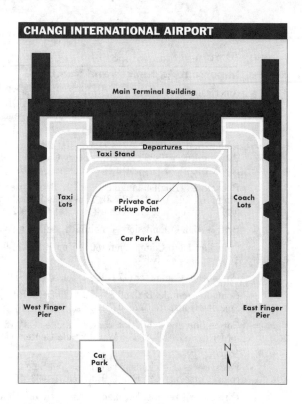

CHANGI INTERNATIONAL AIRPORT

Main Terminal Building

Departures

Taxi Stand

Taxi Lots

Private Car Pickup Point

Coach Lots

Car Park A

West Finger Pier

East Finger Pier

N

Car Park B

Emergencies

For a list of approved physicians and clinics in Singapore that belong to the International Association for Medical Assistance to Travelers, contact IAMAT, 417 Center St., Lewiston, NY 14092, tel. 716/754–4883.

Doctors
The Ming Clinic (19 Tanglin Rd., #12-02 Tanglin Shopping Center, tel. 235–8166; after business hours, tel. 535–8833.

Dentists
International Plaza Dental Surgeons (10 Anson Rd., #02-39 International Plaza, tel. 220–6230 or 535–8833) and **Claymore Dental Surgeons** (#05-11B Orchard Towers, 400 Orchard Rd., tel. 732–5226 or 533–0088) both have 24-hour emergency service.

Hospitals
Private Mount Elizabeth Hospital (3 Mount Elizabeth, tel. 737–2666), **Gleneagles Hospital** (4/6 Napier Rd., tel. 473–7222), and **The American Hospital of Singapore** (321 Joo Chiat Pl., tel. 344–7588) have 24-hour accident and emergency departments. **Singapore General Hospital** (Outram Rd., tel. 222–3322) also has 24-hour emergency services and is accustomed to treating foreigners.

Police
Tel. 999.

Fire/Ambulance
Tel. 995.

Important Addresses and Numbers

American Express (#14-00 UOL Bldg., Somerset Rd., tel. 235–8133) for travel-related services; #16-00 UOL Bldg., Somerset Rd., tel. 737–8188) open for emergencies, 24 hours.

Audiovisual rentals. AV-Science Marketing (22 Pasir Panjang Rd., #10-28 PSA Multi-Story Complex, tel. 278–8283).

Bookstores (English-language). MPH Bookstores (71-75 Stamford Rd., tel. 336–3633), Times The Bookshop (#04-08/15 Centrepoint, 176 Orchard Rd., tel. 734–9022).

British High Commission (Tanglin Rd., tel. 473–9333).

Canadian High Commission (80 Anson Rd., #14-00 IMB Towers, tel. 235–6363).

Chamber of Commerce (47 Hill St., tel. 337–8381).

Computer rentals. Bizland Systems (25 Delta Rd., #10-01 Seiclene House, tel. 278–1771).

Convention and exhibition centers. Raffles City (2 Stamford Rd., tel. 338–8585), World Trade Center (tel. 274–7111).

Fax services. Hotel business centers and Singapore Telecoms (Comcentre, 31 Exeter Rd., tel. 734–3344).

Formal-wear rentals. For men: Fashion Tailors Menswear (#02-01/42, and 43 Orchard Plaza, tel. 734–7206), National Tailor (582 Balastier Rd., tel. 251–4463); there are no formal-wear rentals for women.

Gift shops. Chocolates: Teuscher (C.K. Tang Department Store, 320 Orchard Rd., tel. 737–5500); Flowers: Fun's Florist & Nursery (#B1-26 Hong Leong Bldg., 16 Raffles Quay, tel. 220–8575), Nouvelle Florist (1 Raffles Pl., #03-05 OUB Centre, tel. 532–3733); Gift baskets: Dial-A-Gift Services (42 Emerald Hill Rd., tel. 737–7909), Noel Hampers & Gifts (15 Moonstone La., tel. 285–1133).

Graphic design studios. Addison Design Consultants Asia Pacific (1589 Cecil St., #08-03 Dapenso Bldg., tel. 225–3766), Cato Design (2 Stamford Rd., #12-02 Raffles City Tower, tel. 339–1313).

Hairstylists. Unisex: Brown's Salon (14 Scotts Rd., #05-24 Far East Plaza, tel. 737–9277), Rever Hair Design (#02-40/41 The Paragon, 300 Orchard Rd., tel. 235–0678).

Health and fitness clubs. *See* Fitness, below.

Limousine services. Avis Limousine Service (Avis Rent-A-Car, tel. 737–1668), Friendly Transport Service (tel. 235–6928).

Liquor stores. Cold Storage Supermarket (#B1-05 Centrepoint, 176 Orchard Rd., tel. 737–4835), Jason's Supermarket (#01-01 Orchard Towers, 400 Orchard Rd., tel. 235–4355).

Mail delivery, overnight. DHL Worldwide Express (tel. 334–8911), Federal Express (tel. 743–2626), TNT Skypak (tel. 742–9000), UPS (tel. 542–5151).

Messenger services. On-Call Couriers (tel. 532–5088), Steiner Courier (tel. 337–4214).

News programs, English-language. Radio: SBC Radio 1, "News in Brief," every hour on the hour, bulletins at 7 AM, 8 AM, 1 PM, 7 PM, and 10 PM; BBC World Service relay has bulletins, headlines, or news programs every hour on the hour. TV: Singapore Broadcasting Corporation, Channel 5, 9 PM.

Office-space rentals. Jones Lang Wootton (#45-00 Shell Tower, 50 Raffles Pl., tel. 220–3888), Richard Ellis (#12-01 Hong Kong Bank Bldg., 21 Collyer Quay, tel. 224–8181), Servcop Serviced Offices (#36-00 Hong Leong Bldg., 16 Raffles Quay, tel. 225–5535).

Pharmacies, late-night. Guardian Pharmacy (#B1-05 Centrepoint, 176 Orchard Rd., tel. 732–0893), open until 9 PM.

Secretarial services. Bez Secretarial Services (#03-26 Furama Hotel and Shopping Center, 60 Eu Tong Seng St., tel. 535–3988), Drake Training and Personnel (#16-02 Hong Leong Bldg., 16 Raffles Quay, tel. 224–3488).

Stationery supplies. Alcol Stationery (1 Raffles Pl., #03-07/08 OUB Center, tel. 533–2345), Allmarks Stationery Company (1 Maritime Sq., #01-04 World Trade Center, tel. 270–1520).

Taxis. NTUC Comfort (tel. 452–5555), SABS Taxi Service (tel. 250–0700), Singapore Commuter (tel. 474–7707).

Theater tickets. *See* The Arts, below.

Thomas Cook (04–15 The Amara, 165 Tanjung Pagara Rd., tel. 221–0222).

Trade Ministry (48th Floor, Treasury Bldg., 8 Shenton Way, tel. 225–9911).

Train information. Malaysian Railway Administration (Singapore Station, Keppel Rd., tel. 222–5165; booking and fare inquiries, tel. 221–6994).

Translation services. Interlingua Language Services (141 Cecil St., #06-01 Tung Ann Association Bldg., tel. 222–3755), Worldwide Translation Services (64 Lloyd Rd., tel. 737–7672).

U.S. Embassy (30 Hill St., tel. 338–0251).

Telephones

To make a call on a coin-operated phone, pick up the receiver, listen for the dial tone, insert a 10-cent coin, then dial the seven-digit number. After three minutes, a buzzer will sound when it's time to insert another coin. The Telecoms phone card can be useful if you'll be making several long-distance calls during your stay. The cards can be purchased in denominations of S$10, S$20, and S$50. The price of each call is deducted from the card total, and your balance is roughly indicated by the punched hole in the card. Phone cards are available from post offices and

Telecoms Customer Services outlets. Telephones that accept the phone card are most frequently found in shopping centers, post offices, subway stations, and at the airport. For cardphones, pick up the receiver, listen for the dial tone, then insert the card and dial the number.

Tipping

Tipping is officially discouraged. Nevertheless, it is common to tip doormen, porters, and room service, but not waiters or taxi drivers. Doorman carrying bags to the registration desk get S$1–S$2. Tip porters carrying bags to your room S$2–S$3. For room service, tip S$1–S$2. The concierge gets S$2.

DOING BUSINESS

Hours

Businesses: weekdays 9–1, 2–5:30; Sat. 9–1. **Banks:** weekdays 10–3; Sat. 10–11:30 AM. **Shops:** daily 10:30 AM–10 PM.

National Holidays

New Year's Day; Jan./Feb.,* Chinese New Year; Good Fri.; May 1, Labor Day; April/May,* Hari Raya Puasa; May,* Vesak Day; July,* Hari Raya Haji; Aug. 9, National Day; Oct./Nov.,* Deepavali; Christmas Day.

*These holidays are lunar based and change yearly.

Getting Around

Singapore is very compact and easy to negotiate. The best ways to travel are by taxi and public transportation.

By Car
Traffic jams are few, but the one-way systems can be confusing for visitors. In addition, a Restricted Zone—covering the Shenton Way business district and most of the Orchard Road shopping and hotels district—requires one to buy a S$3 license to enter the zone from Monday through Saturday 7:30–10:15 AM and Monday through Friday 4:30–6:30 PM. Licenses may be purchased from one of the kiosks located on the approach roads to the Zone, but the kiosks are difficult to identify, and drivers must be on the lookout for signs for them.

By Taxi
Taxis are inexpensive and plentiful. In center city, go to a cab stand; in other areas, hail a taxi in the street. When traffic in the business district is restricted (*see* By Car, above) passengers taking a taxi into the Restricted Zone must pay for the S$3 license, unless the taxi already displays one. A S$1 surcharge is imposed for all trips leaving the Zone weekdays between 4 and 7 PM, and Saturdays between noon and 3 PM.

By Public Transportation
The Mass Rapid Transit (MRT) subway is fast, clean, safe, efficient, and inexpensive. It provides a good link between the Orchard Road shopping/hotel belt and the Shenton Way financial district, and most other parts of the island. Fares range from S$.50 to S$1.60. Tickets can be purchased in the stations from vending machines (which give change) or at a booth. Insert the magnetic ticket in the

turnstyle to get on and off the platform. Easy-to-follow route maps are prominently displayed in all the stations.

Buses are comfortable and fairly easy to use, although crowded at peak times; some are air-conditioned. Signs are in English. Fares start at S$.30 and no trip will cost more than S$.90. Exact change is necessary and should be deposited in the box as you enter the bus. Buses run from 5:30 or 6 AM to around 11:30 PM.

Protocol

Appointments

Singaporeans tend to be late for appointments; nevertheless, it is courteous to arrive on time. Meet at your contact's office or in your hotel lobby. In general, business meals take place at lunch rather than dinner. If your business contact entertains you after hours, it will be at a restaurant—never at his or her home.

Customs

Singaporeans are conservative, so do not use first names unless you are invited to do so. Remember that the first word in a Chinese name is the surname. Use Mr. or Mrs. as titles; Ms. is rarely used here. A firm handshake and warm "hello" will serve as greeting; Muslim Malaysians bring their hand back to touch their chest after shaking hands, and you should follow suit. Business cards are exchanged at the beginning of a meeting, and must be given and received using *both* hands—never the left one only. It's polite to study the card and hold on to it as you speak.

Dress

In Singapore's hot weather, it's perfectly appropriate for men to forego their suit jackets—a good shirt and tie are fine. During evenings and casual occasions, a short-sleeved shirt and slacks are appropriate almost anywhere except upscale restaurants, where a long-sleeved shirt and tie are acceptable; a jacket may be needed for cocktail parties and for glacially air-conditioned hotel and restaurant dining rooms. For women, a jacket and skirt are best for day-time appointments; slacks are generally reserved for casual wear.

Gifts

Gift-giving is not customary in a business context, but if you want to give something, a pen or similar item with your company name or logo is safest. Never give clocks or watches (signifying approaching death), white flowers (associated with death), or knives (signifying the severing of a friendship).

Toasts and Greetings

Multiracial Singapore has four official languages—English, Chinese (increasingly Mandarin, rather than other dialects), Malay (which has a Roman alphabet), and Tamil. English is widely spoken, Tamil is seldom used.

Cantonese

Hello, how are you? *Neh HO mah?*
Well, thank you. *HO, yow sem.*
Pleased to meet you. *Hun woo.*
Thank you. *Mm-goy.*
You're welcome. *Mm'sai mm-goy.*

Excuse me. *Doy ing CHOO.*
Nice to have met you. *HOH goh HING gin doh nee.*
Goodbye. *WAH-boo-DONG.*
Cheers! *Yum-SING.*

Malay
Hello, how are you? *AH-pah kah-BAR?*
Well, thank you. *Kah-BAR bike.*
Pleased to meet you. *SAY-yah seh-NANG* BET-teh-MOO
DEN-gah-MOO.
Thank you. *Teh*-REE-mah kah-SAY.
You're welcome. *SAH-mah Sah-mah.*
Excuse me. *Mah-AHF.*
Nice to have met you. *SAH-lah-maht.*
Goodbye. If leaving: *SAH-lah-maht ting-GAH.* If some-
one else is leaving: *SAH-lah-maht jah-LAHN.*
Cheers! No equivalent.*
*Malays, being Muslim, do not drink alcohol.

LODGING

Hotels in Singapore are generally of a very high standard,
and half a dozen—the Shangri-La, Oriental, Goodwood
Park, Mandarin, Hyatt, and Sheraton Towers—will satisfy the most discerning and well-heeled of travelers. (The
most famous hotel, Raffles, is closed until 1992 for restoration and redevelopment.) Most are located around Orchard Road, a shopping and entertainment area that
draws tourists and evening revelers. However, it's less
than 10 minutes by cab or subway from here to the busi-
ness/financial district. Some of the newest hotels, including the Marina Mandarin and the Oriental, are located in
Marina Square, a minicity created by a vast reclamation
project that pushed back the seafront. There are more
than 200 shops and restaurants in the area. Hotel rates
here reflect the high prices of the real estate on which they
stand. Raffles City is home to two megahotels, the Westin
Plaza and Westin Stamford. And several properties are located right in Shenton Way, the primary business district, but this area is deserted after dark.

If you're planning to mix business with the pleasure of
shopping and nightlife, the Orchard Street area will serve
you best. If you're going to be spending most of your time
at a convention, you'll most likely want to stay in either
Marina Square or Raffles City. However, location should
not be overemphasized. Singapore is a relatively compact
city, and taxis and public transportation allow you to travel between one area and another in a matter of minutes.

Room rates have jumped about 55% in the past year, but
Singapore's hotels still offer good value, high standards,
and such business-oriented facilities as business centers
with secretarial services and reference libraries. All
those listed below have swimming pools, and most have in-
house fitness centers. A tourism boom has pushed up hotel
occupancies; rooms are becoming increasingly difficult to
book in August and around Christmas, so plan well in advance if you plan to visit during these times.

Most hotels listed below offer corporate rates; inquire
when making reservations.

Highly recommended lodgings in each price category are indicated by a star ★.

Category	Cost*
$$$$ (Very Expensive)	over S$300
$$$ (Expensive)	S$200–S$300
$$ (Moderate)	under S$200

All prices are for a standard double room, single occupancy, excluding 4% tax and 10% service charge.

Numbers in the margin correspond to numbered hotel locations on the Singapore Lodging and Dining map.

Orchard Road Area

❷ **ANA Hotel.** On an exclusive residential hill, a 10-minute
$$ walk from the shopping/entertainment area, the 14-story ANA Hotel has a modern facade but turn-of-the-century ambience, with wood paneling and columns throughout the public areas. Built in 1978, it was renovated in 1990. Guest rooms follow a trend toward classic European design, with soft peach and light-blue color schemes and floral prints. Curtains are tucked behind arched pelmets, and furniture is of stained teak. All rooms have separate writing desks, personal safes, tea/coffee-making facilities, mist-free shaving mirrors, and remote controls for both the television set and radio. Beige marble bathrooms have speckled granite vanity tops. Among the best rooms are the third-floor cabanas, which have private terraces with direct access to the swimming pool. The hotel is popular with business travelers. *An All Nippon Airways property. 16 Nassim Hill, 1025, tel. 732–1222 or 800/858–4849, fax 235–1516. Gen. manager, Guido Jonas. 437 twins/doubles, 19 suites. AE, DC, MC, V.*

❼ **Boulevard.** The Boulevard, a three-minute walk from the
$$$ Orchard Road/Scotts Road intersection (the hub of the shopping/entertainment area), is under the same management as the grand Goodwood Park hotel (*see* below) but lacks a strong identity of its own. It has been a good-value alternative to pricier places in the past, but current room-rate increases have eroded this advantage. Rooms in the older (1974), 10-story Cuscaden wing of this family-oriented property have more space than others in the hotel, and overlook quiet Cuscaden Road. Those in the 15-story Orchard wing overlook busy Orchard Boulevard. Rooms are done in peach-colored pastels with varnished dark-wood trim. The Orchard wing was refurbished in 1984, the Cuscaden wing in early 1991. All rooms have wall unit desks of reasonable size and tea/coffee-making facilities. Public areas are bland, in spite of an atrium lobby dominated by a 15-story aluminium sculpture. All told, the Boulevard offers unexciting but acceptable accommodations. *A Goodwood Park property. 200 Orchard Blvd., 1024, tel. 737–2911 or 800/421–0536, fax 737–8449. Gen. manager, Elizabeth Khoo Lim. 208 twins, 298 doubles, 19 suites. AE, DC, MC, V.*

⓰ **Crown Prince.** Corporate travelers, especially Japanese,
$$$ as well as Japanese tour groups, are attracted to this Japanese-run property in the heart of the shopping and entertainment area. Members of the Brunei royal family,

SINGAPORE

Lodging
ANA Hotel, **2**
Avant, **21**
Boulevard, **7**
Carlton, **35**
Crown Prince, **16**
Dynasty, **11**
Goodwood Park, **13**
Hilton, **9**
Holiday Inn Park View, **26**
Hyatt Regency, **12**
Marina Mandarin, **40**
Mandarin, **18**
Meridien, **27**
New Otani, **29**
Omni Marco Polo, **4**
Orchard, **6**
Oriental, **41**
Pan Pacific, **42**
Regent, **5**
Royal Holiday Inn Crowne Plaza, **10**
Shangri-La, **3**
Sheraton Towers, **14**
Tai-Pan Ramada, **34**
Westin Plaza, **36**
Westin Stamford, **37**

Key

North-South MRT line
East-West MRT line
Railroad lines
Subway stop
Ferry

SINGAPORE HOTEL CHART

HOTELS	Price Category	Business Services — Banquet capacity	No. of meeting rooms	Fax	Telex	Photocopying	Secretarial services	Audiovisual equipment	Translation services	International direct dial	Computer rentals	In-room modem phone jack
ANA Hotel	$$	250	1	✓	✓	✓	✓	✓	✓	✓	-	-
Avant	$$	625	6	✓	✓	✓	✓	✓	✓	✓	✓	-
Boulevard	$$$	230	5	✓	✓	✓	✓	✓	✓	✓	✓	-
Carlton	$$	350	8	✓	✓	✓	✓	✓	-	✓	✓	-
Crown Prince	$$$	130	4	✓	✓	✓	✓	✓	✓	✓	✓	✓
Dynasty	$$$	550	6	✓	✓	✓	✓	✓	✓	✓	✓	-
Goodwood Park	$$$	300	4	✓	✓	✓	✓	✓	✓	✓	✓	-
Hilton	$$$	600	9	✓	✓	✓	✓	✓	✓	✓	-	-
Holiday Inn Park View	$$$	200	4	✓	✓	✓	✓	✓	✓	✓	✓	-
Hyatt Regency	$$$$	520	18	✓	✓	✓	✓	✓	✓	✓	✓	-
Mandarin	$$$$	1060	8	✓	✓	✓	✓	✓	✓	✓	✓	-
Marina Mandarin	$$$$	700	13	✓	✓	✓	✓	✓	✓	✓	✓	✓
Meridien	$$	600	5	✓	✓	✓	✓	✓	✓	✓	✓	-
New Otani	$$$	600	4	✓	✓	✓	✓	✓	✓	✓	✓	-
Omni Marco Polo	$$$	160	5	✓	✓	✓	✓	✓	✓	✓	✓	-
Orchard	$$	70	2	✓	✓	✓	✓	✓	✓	✓	✓	-
Oriental	$$$$	450	6	✓	✓	✓	✓	✓	✓	✓	✓	-
Pan Pacific	$$$	300	15	✓	✓	✓	✓	✓	✓	✓	✓	✓
Regent	$$$	1000	7	✓	✓	✓	✓	✓	-	✓	-	-

$$$$ = over S$300, $$$ = S$200 - S$300, $$ = under S$200.
● good, ◕ fair, ○ poor.

All-news cable channel	Desk	Desk lighting	Bed lighting	**In-Room Amenities** Nonsmoking rooms	In-room checkout	Minibar	Toiletries	Room service	Laundry/Dry cleaning	Pressing	**Hotel Amenities** Barber/Hairdresser	Garage	Courtesy airport transport	Sauna	Pool	Exercise room
–	●	●	●	✓	✓	✓	●	●	●	●	✓	✓	–	✓	●	◐
–	●	●	●	–	–	✓	●	●	●	●	✓	✓	–	✓	●	●
–	●	●	●	–	–	✓	●	●	●	●	✓	–	–	–	●	◐
✓	●	●	●	✓	–	✓	◐	●	●	●	✓	✓	–	✓	●	◐
✓	●	●	●	✓	–	✓	●	●	●	●	–	✓	–	–	●	–
–	●	●	●	✓	–	✓	●	●	●	●	✓	✓	–	✓	●	●
–	●	●	●	✓	–	●	●	●	●	●	✓	✓	–	–	●	–
✓	●	●	●	✓	–	✓	●	●	●	●	✓	✓	–	✓	●	●
✓	●	●	●	✓	–	✓	●	●	●	●	–	✓	–	✓	●	◐
✓	●	●	●	✓	✓	✓	●	●	●	●	✓	✓	–	✓	●	●
✓	●	●	●	✓	–	✓	●	●	●	●	✓	✓	–	✓	●	●
✓	●	●	●	✓	–	✓	●	●	●	●	✓	✓	–	✓	●	●
✓	●	◐	◐	✓	–	✓	●	●	●	●	✓	✓	–	✓	●	–
–	●	●	●	✓	–	✓	●	●	●	●	✓	✓	–	✓	●	●
✓	◐	●	●	–	–	✓	◐	●	●	●	✓	✓	–	–	◐	–
✓	●	●	●	✓	–	✓	●	●	●	●	–	✓	–	✓	●	●
✓	●	●	●	✓	✓	✓	●	●	●	●	✓	✓	✓	✓	●	●
–	●	●	●	✓	✓	✓	●	●	●	●	✓	–	–	✓	●	●

Room service: ● 24-hour, ◐ 6AM–10PM, ○ other.
Laundry/Dry cleaning: ● same day, ◐ overnight, ○ other.
Pressing: ● immediate, ◐ same day, ○ other.

SINGAPORE HOTEL CHART

HOTELS	Price Category	Business Services / Banquet capacity	No. of meeting rooms	Fax	Telex	Photocopying	Secretarial services	Audiovisual equipment	Translation services	International direct dial	Computer rentals	In-room modem phone jack
Royal Holiday Inn Crowne Plaza	$$	300	5	✓	✓	✓	✓	✓	✓	✓	✓	
Shangri-La	$$$	1400	13	✓	✓	✓	✓	✓	✓	✓	✓	✓
Sheraton Towers	$$$$	500	4	✓	✓	✓	✓	✓	-	✓	✓	-
Tai-Pan Ramada	$$	600	3	✓	✓	✓	✓	✓	✓	✓	-	-
Westin Plaza	$$$	4420	30	✓	✓	✓	✓	✓	✓	✓	✓	✓
Westin Stamford	$$$	4420	30	✓	✓	✓	✓	✓	✓	✓	✓	✓

$$$$ = over S$300, **$$$** = S$200 - S$300, **$$** = under S$200.
● good, ◗ fair, ○ poor.

All-news cable channel	Desk	Desk lighting	Bed lighting	In-Room Amenities Nonsmoking rooms	In-room checkout	Minibar	Toiletries	Room service	Laundry/Dry cleaning	Pressing	Hotel Amenities Barber/Hairdresser	Garage	Courtesy airport transport	Sauna	Pool	Exercise room
✓	●	●	●	✓	–	✓	●	●	●	●	✓	✓	–	✓	●	–
–	●	●	●	✓	–	✓	●	●	●	●	✓	–	–	✓	●	●
–	●	●	●	✓	✓	✓	●	●	●	●	–	✓	–	✓	●	●
–	●	●	●	✓	–	✓	●	●	●	●	✓	✓	–	✓	●	◐
✓	●	●	●	✓	–	✓	●	●	●	●	✓	✓	–	✓	●	●
✓	●	●	●	✓	–	✓	●	●	●	●	✓	✓	–	✓	●	●

Room service: ● 24-hour, ◐ 6AM–10PM, ○ other.
Laundry/Dry cleaning: ● same day, ◐ overnight, ○ other.
Pressing: ● immediate, ◐ same day, ○ other.

Malaysian government ministers, and Hong Kong film stars frequently book suites here. The lobby's cream marble and red carpeting are softly lighted by Austrian crystal chandeliers. Rooms are pleasant but unremarkable. The oak furniture is trimmed with brass, and all rooms have writing desks and dressing tables. Bathrooms have ceramic-tiled floors and Italian marble vanity tops. Guest rooms facing Bideford Road are quieter than ones fronting busy Orchard Road. The general ambience is one of efficiency rather than warmth. *A Prince Hotels property. 270 Orchard Rd., 0923, tel. 732–1111 or 800/448–8355, fax 732–7018. Gen. manager, Tomoki Haruno. 287 twins/doubles, 16 suites. AE, DC, MC, V.*

🔟 **Dynasty.** This distinctive skyscraper—a 33-story, yellow
$$$ pagoda, topped by a roof that looks like a green sun hat with a red bobble—is a modern (1982) landmark that's been featured in many a tourist's snapshot. It's located at the heart of the hotel/shopping area, opposite a subway station and adjacent to C.K. Tang, Singapore's best department store, owned by the same family. Despite the almost overpowering Chinese character of the design and decor—the lobby is dominated by 24 massive teak panels carved with events from China's history—the Dynasty's Western-style comforts and efficient management make it a central base for business travelers and a good value. Chinoiserie also extends to the well-appointed guest rooms, which are being renovated and upgraded. (New superior rooms are planned with off-white walls, satin curtains, marble-topped coffee tables, and furniture in mahogany and black-painted wood.) Deluxe rooms are decorated in traditional grays and blues, with brass lamps and brass-legged tables. The new Junior Suites have bolder colors. All rooms have separate seating areas, free-standing writing desks, spacious marble bathrooms, and tea/coffee-making facilities. The best rooms face Orchard and Scotts roads, above the 11th floor; below that, traffic may be noisy. Fax machines and hand-held phones are available for rent. There is no seating in the lobby for those not ordering drinks. *320 Orchard Rd., 0923, tel. 734–9900 or 800/448–8355, fax 733–5251. Gen. manager, Richard Oon. 351 twins/doubles, 14 suites. AE, CB, DC, MC, V.*

★ 🔢 **Goodwood Park.** Those who want class and clout head for
$$$ this truly grand hotel. The ornate, wedding cake–like structure was built in 1900 as the Teutonia Club, and served as an entertainment center, guest house, Japanese officers' quarters, and site of the war crimes court before becoming a hotel after World War II. The hotel has been tastefully extended and restored and sits in lush gardens close to Orchard Road. Service is gracious and efficient; guests are remembered by name. Refurbished in 1990, the spacious, elegant guest rooms blend the old and new, with Queen Anne–style furniture and marble bathrooms. Suites in the original Tower building have the most cachet; those suites in the Parklane wing are reserved for long-term guests. Suites by the poolside are the most popular—they have louvred windows and doors that open onto the gardens. High tea is accompanied by a string quartet. There are two swimming pools, but no fitness center. *A Goodwood Group hotel. 22 Scotts Rd., 0922, tel. 734–7766 or 800/421–0536, fax 732–8558. Gen. manager, Mavis Oei. 123 twins/doubles, 108 suites. AE, CB, DC, MC, V.*

⑨ **Hilton.** Western design with local touches set the tone of
$$$ this well-established property in the Orchard Road shopping and entertainment area. Although one of Singapore's first international-standard hotels (built in 1968), it has been well maintained, and service is efficient, making it popular with corporate guests as well as upscale tourists. The functional lobby has a russet marble floor, embroidered wall hangings, abstract paintings, and a comfortable seating area. In the guest rooms, textiles in bold red and blue contrast with earth-tone carpets and walls; work of local artists adds an Oriental flavor. All rooms have spacious writing desks with table lamps and telephone extensions. The 12 top-floor Givenchy Suites have private check-in, butler service, a concierge, and such luxuries as steambaths and whirlpool baths. All guests have access to excellent health club facilities (*see* Fitness, below). For a quiet drink, try the Lounge (*see* After Hours, below). The elegant Harbour Grill (*see* Dining, below) is one of the best dining rooms in Singapore for business entertaining. *581 Orchard Rd., 0923, tel. 737–2233 or 800/445–8667, fax 732–2917. Gen. manager, Oskar von Kretschmann. 386 doubles, 20 singles, 29 suites. AE, DC, MC, V.*

㉖ **Holiday Inn Park View.** Holiday Inns tend to offer better
$$$ quality accommodations in Asia than in other parts of the world, and the Park View is no exception. Centrally located just off busy Orchard Road and facing the president's official home (rooms overlooking the grounds have the most pleasant views), it is the smaller of the chain's two Singapore properties. Until about two years ago, this was the executive's choice Holiday Inn. Though still popular with traveling businesspeople, the Royal Holiday Inn (*see* below) now attracts the upper end of the corporate market. A polished brown marble and black granite lobby sets the tone, and tasteful, modern clean lines are carried through in the pastel guest rooms with matte-black furniture, three telephones, room safes and remote-control television. Service is friendly and efficient. *11 Cavenagh Rd., 0922, tel. 733–8333 or 800/465–4329, fax 734–4593. Gen. manager, Andreas Obrist. 130 doubles, 168 singles, 19 suites. AE, CB, DC, MC, V.*

⑫ **Hyatt Regency.** At the center of the entertainment/shopping area, the Hyatt recently underwent a restructuring
$$$$ and refurbishment that converted half its accommodations to suites. The previously large, open lobby, which used to serve as a meeting place for Singaporeans and travelers alike, has been divided into a lounge and seating areas, with dark-brown marble floors, wood paneling, sofas, and Chinese lamps, artifacts, and paintings. A tropical garden with 16 mini waterfalls and the Canopy Bar (*see* After Hours, below) have been added. The 20-story main tower (1971) now includes six Regency Terrace executive floors; rooms here are attractive and comfortable, with excellent facilities, including dual-line telephones, two television sets, king-size beds, and spacious writing desks. The modern Asian theme is reflected in pale-wood furniture and lacquered Chinese cabinets. Rooms in the adjoining Regency Terrace (1985) catch the light from the attractive triangular bay windows. All bathrooms are marble, with separate shower stalls. The Hyatt is the home of Nutmeg's (*see* Dining, below), a delightfully laid-back restaurant, and Brannigan's (*see* After Hours, be-

low), a popular basement-level bar. There are also dinner-theater performances in the hotel (*see* The Arts, below). The hotel's young and enthusiastic staff is encouraged to show initiative, and an efficient concierge team is available to help with special requests. Other pluses are the 24-hour business center and two swimming pools. This is a fine choice for business travelers who are looking for something one step up from the Holiday Inns. *10-12 Scotts Rd., 0922, tel. 733–1188 or 800/228–9000, fax 732–1676. Gen. manager, Arthur Holliger. 448 doubles, 300 suites. AE, DC, MC, V.*

⑱ Mandarin. From the outside, this hotel at the heart of the
$$$$ shopping/entertainment area seems to be nothing but two plain tower blocks. Inside, however, are touches of Oriental splendor, with gold-leaf ceilings, Chinese murals, and antique vases in the lobby. The South Wing guest rooms, last renovated in 1980, have a more subdued Chinese decor, with lacquered cabinets, carved door handles, and Chinese lamps. Newly renovated rooms in the main building, decorated in Western modern-hotel style, seem bland in comparison, but serve corporate travelers well with such amenities as personal safes, VCRs, and separate seating areas. Marble bathrooms have bidets and separate shower stalls. The hotel's Pine Court restaurant (*see* Dining, below) is suitable for business meals. For a taste of local culture, attend one of the hotel's dinner-theater shows (*see* The Arts, below). *A Mandarin Singapore International property. 333 Orchard Rd., 0923, tel. 737–4411 or 800/228–6800, fax 732–2361. Gen. manager, Jean Fernand Wasser. 771 twins, 304 doubles, 59 suites. AE, DC, MC, V.*

㉗ Meridien. A strong French flavor (including greetings of
$$ "bonjour" on the telephone) permeates this 1983, French government–owned low rise on the shopping/hotel strip. The white marble-floored atrium lobby, with graceful, slow-rising elevators, is not easy to locate because its entrance is on a side street off Orchard Road. Rooms blend East and West with silk-screened Chinese murals, king-size beds, separate seating areas, and spacious writing desks. Rooms on the concierge level—the seventh-floor Le Club Président—have extra features, such as butler service, use of meeting rooms at no charge, and discounts on business-center services, as well as upgraded toiletries in baths. *100 Orchard Rd., 0923, tel. 733–8855 or 800/543–4300, fax 732–7886. Gen. manager, Helmut Gaisberger. 299 doubles, 58 singles, 39 executive rooms, 17 suites, 2 rooms for disabled guests. AE, CB, DC, V.*

㉙ New Otani. The Japanese-run New Otani is a high rise,
$$$ five minutes by cab from both the Orchard Road shopping/entertainment belt and the main financial area. It is located above a shopping complex amid a wilderness of semi-abandoned warehouses earmarked for rejuvenation as a tourist attraction within the next few years. Guests escape the depressing surroundings by heading for the cheerful and comfortable seventh-floor lobby. Like the Crown Prince, the New Otani has a loyal Japanese clientele. Recently refurbished guest rooms have been lightened with pastel shades; furnishings include large, firm beds and free-standing desks. Most of the marble bathrooms have separate shower compartments. Ask for a harbor view, and try to avoid rooms overlooking the

warehouses. The staff goes out of its way to be helpful and friendly, which partly makes up for the location. *177A River Valley Rd., 0617, tel. 338–3333 or 800/421–8795, fax 339–2854. Gen. manager, Chester Ikei. 368 twins/ doubles, 22 suites. AE, DC, MC, V.*

★ ❹ **Omni Marco Polo.** Though located in a residential and em-
$$$ bassy district, a 15-minute walk from the shopping/enter-tainment area and a 10-minute cab ride from the main business area, the Marco Polo, opened in 1968, one of the best business hotels in Singapore. The lobby is elegant, with marble and dark varnished wood, and plenty of seat-ing. The original Continental wing has been renovated to return it to the high standard from which it had slipped in the early 1980s. Rooms here are comfortable, with Euro-pean hotel–style decor (thick curtains are pulled back and tied by sashes). The 10 Terrace rooms facing the swim-ming pool are the most popular. The Tanglin Wing (1980) rooms have a dated look, with orange upholstery and tan-colored varnished furniture; however, some of these have extra-large desks. The fitness center is probably the best in town (*see* Fitness, below), and the jogging circuit at the Botanic Gardens is nearby. The long-serving staff is well trained. *An Omni Hotels Asia-Pacific property. Tanglin Rd., 1024, tel. 474–7141 or 800/223–5652, fax 471–0521. Gen. manager, Dieter Loewe. 545 doubles, 58 suites. AE, DC, MC, V.*

❻ **Orchard.** This 19-story property at the top end of bustling
$$ Orchard Road (farthest from Shenton Way) opened in 1980 and will soon add a second wing. Its location provides a central base, but accommodations are functional rather than luxurious. The dull-looking lobby throngs with mill-ing tour-group guests. However, the two upper floors—transformed into the Harvesters' Club—offer separate check-in, complimentary breakfast, and cocktails. Rooms have light-green walls and carpets, and floral bedspreads; those in the new wing have separate shower stalls in the bathrooms. Upper-floor and rear-wing rooms are quiet-est. Only 136 rooms have desks, and not all have hair dry-ers, which is unusual for a Singapore hotel. The swimming pool is rather small. *A CDL Hotels International proper-ty. 442 Orchard Rd., 0923, tel. 734–7766 or 800/448–8355, fax 733–0482. Gen. manager, Ali Alavi. 167 twins, 112 doubles, 56 business class, 6 suites, 1 room for disabled guests. AE, CB, DC, MC, V.*

★ ❺ **Regent.** The Regent, with its atrium lobby, was refur-
$$$ bished in early 1991 to bring it up to the standard of other properties in this highly rated chain that attracts the top end of the business travel market. Though only a five-minute walk from the Orchard Road shopping and enter-tainment area, it has a residential feeling, created by an eclectic blend of contemporary and traditional styles and materials. The lobby is furnished with rich fabrics, warm woods, rugs, and white marble; lush greenery surrounds the glass elevators. The well-appointed guest rooms, dec-orated in the requisite pastels, combine Asian elegance with understated luxury. Furnishings include firm king-size beds, free-standing writing desks, and comfortable seating areas. Baths have a good range of toiletries, from plush towels to cotton balls. If you want a large balcony, ask for a room on the east or west terrace. Service is up to high Regent standards. *A Regent International hotel. 1*

*Cuscaden Rd., 1024, tel. 733–8888 or 800/545–4000, fax
732–8838. Gen. manager, Bruno Brunner. 441 twins/
doubles, 42 suites. AE, CB, DC, MC, V.*

★ ⑩   **Royal Holiday Inn Crowne Plaza.** The first of Singapore's
$$ two Holiday Inns, opened in 1974, was upgraded in 1990 to
the chain's top Crowne Plaza category. The Sultan of Bru-
nei owns the 15-story property, and the busy lobby is now
decorated in rather heavy, classical European style, with
dark-wood paneling and molding. Standard guest rooms,
with large beds, separate seating areas, and wall-unit
desks, incorporate the latest technology, including digital
safes and computerized remote television and radio con-
trol units. In contrast to the public spaces, rooms are done
in soft pastels, with upholstered bleached-ash furniture,
marble coffee tables, and marble baths. King Leisure
rooms have large free-standing desks for more work
space. The 15th-floor Executive Club has butler service.
Squash and badminton courts and a fitness center are in
the works. Located in the heart of the entertainment and
shopping area, this hotel provides good value for the mon-
ey. *25 Scotts Rd., 0922, tel. 737–7966 or 800/465–4329, fax
737–6646. Gen. manager, Jean Ricoux. 329 doubles, 88
singles, 30 suites, 49 business class. AE, CB, DC, MC, V.*

★ ❸   **Shangri-La.** This elegant and unique business/resort ho-
$$$ tel, considered the crème de la crème of Singapore hotels,
sits among lush tropical gardens in center city, five min-
utes' walk from the Orchard Road entertainment and
shopping area. Rooms in the 24-story tower, built in 1971,
are small, but have such extras as safes, and three telephones. The rattan, maple, and cherry-wood furniture
blend East and West. Rooms in the tropical Garden Wing
(1978) are more spacious and have cane and batik decor.
The exclusive Valley Wing has a private entrance and is
linked to the other buildings by a skybridge; rooms here
are much larger and more luxurious, and include comfortable sofas and chaise lounges, as well as spacious writing
desks. Xanadu's (*see* After Hours, below) is where the
younger set heads for dancing. The Latour (Continental)
and Nadaman (Japanese) restaurants (*see* Dining, below,
for both) are among the city's best. A loyal staff ensures
smooth service. Indoor and outdoor pools, squash courts,
and a 24-hour business center are extra perks. *Orange
Grove Rd., 0923, tel. 737–3644 or 800/457–5050, fax 733–
7220. Gen. manager, Andrew Quinlan. 750 rooms, 60
suites. AE, DC, MC, V.*

★ ⑭   **Sheraton Towers.** The Sheraton, opened in 1985, pampers
$$$$ its guests with service and attention to detail. Executive
floor–type services are offered throughout the hotel.
Rates include a packing and unpacking service, a pressing
service, breakfast, daily cocktail hour, evening room
snacks, and full toiletry kits. The same quality is reflected
in the furnishings—crystal and polished marble and
brass. The lobby features a magnificent staircase with a
brass-bound teak handrail. The atrium coffee shop's floor-
to-ceiling window overlooks a garden and a waterfall. The
staff is warm and unfailingly attentive. Not surprisingly,
the Sheraton Towers attracts a very high percentage of
business travelers and repeat guests. Li Bai, the hotel's
Chinese restaurant (*see* Dining, below), is an impressive
spot for evening business entertaining. Domus (*see* Business Breakfasts, below) is fine for brunch. *39 Scotts Rd.,*

0922, tel. 737–6888 or 800/334–8484, fax 737–1072. Gen. manager, Carl Kono. 354 twins/doubles, 30 cabanas, 22 suites. AE, CB, DC, MC, V.

Marina Square/Raffles City Area

★ ㉟ **Carlton.** At the south end of the Orchard Road hotel/shop-
$$ ping strip and close to the financial area and convention fa-
cilities is a modern (1988), 26-floor property that has the
ambience of a smaller, cozier hotel, and relatively reason-
able room rates. It is a good place to stay if you want to
hold down costs without appearing cheap. The spacious
marble lobby has plenty of seating. Reasonably sized
rooms, adorned with paintings of old Singapore, have
light-wood furnishings, firm beds, comfortable seating
areas, and sturdy writing desks. Suites overlooking the
bay offer the best views. Telephone jacks for modems can
be arranged. Hair dryers are standard on the executive
floors. The exercise room has limited equipment. *76 Bras
Basah Rd., 0718, tel. 338–8333 or 800/448–8355, fax 339–
4866. Gen. manager, Evan Pavlakis. 350 twins/doubles,
20 suites, 20 business class. AE, DC, MC, V.*

㊵ **Marina Mandarin.** As at the other hotels on Marina
$$$$ Square, the John Portman–designed atrium is the Marina
Mandarin's focal point. It narrows as it ascends 21 floors to
a tinted skylight that filters light into the lobby and onto
the 36-meter-long mobile suspended from the ceiling. The
entrance to the hotel is at street level, and the meeting
rooms are on the second and third floors, so the lobby area
on the fourth floor is relatively peaceful. Opened in 1986,
the hotel has an elegant Chinese theme carried through-
out the rooms, with such touches as Chinese brush paint-
ings and gold colored carpets. All baths are spacious,
marble-finished, with separate showers, bidets, and full-
length mirrors. Rooms overlooking the harbor have the
best views. Rooms on the concierge floor—the Marina
Club—have additional amenities, such as terry-cloth
bathrobes, butler service, and complimentary breakfast
and cocktails. The Captain's Bar (*see* After Hours, below)
is a relaxing spot for drinks after work. Fitness facilities
are good, and the swimming pool has underwater stereo
music. Newer, more attractive, and better designed than
its sister property on Orchard Road, the Marina Mandarin
is an efficiently run hotel and the next best choice (after
the Oriental, *see* below) for corporate travelers who want
to stay in the Marina Square area. *6 Raffles Blvd., #01-100
Marina Square, 0103, tel. 338–3388 or 800/223–6800, fax
339–4977. Gen. manager, Achim Ihlenfeld. 340 twins, 205
suites, 30 business class. AE, DC, MC, V.*

★ ㊶ **Oriental.** It's difficult to choose between the Shangri-La
$$$$ and the Oriental—both vie for top position in the Singa-
pore hotel market. The triangular-shaped Oriental—sis-
ter of Bangkok's famed Oriental and Hong Kong's
Mandarin Oriental—is geared toward business travelers
who appreciate understated elegance, efficiency, and un-
obtrusive, intelligent service. This Marina Square hotel
has an elegant 19-story atrium lobby. Guest rooms' peach
and soft-green color scheme and natural-wood furniture
lend a feeling of tranquility. All rooms have safes and mar-
ble bathrooms with separate showers. Because of the ho-
tel's pyramidal shape, rooms have one of three views—
over the city, harbor, or surrounding park. The Cafe Palm

(*see* Business Breakfasts, below) serves one of the best breakfast buffets in Singapore. Fourchettes, the hotel's French restaurant (*see* Dining, below), is an excellent spot for business entertaining. Service is one of the Oriental's strongest points; smaller than many of the modern Singaporean hotels in its class, it has a well-trained staff that is able to cater to guests' individual needs. *A Mandarin Oriental property. 5 Raffles Ave., Marina Square, 0103, tel. 338–0066 or 800/526–6566, fax 339–9537. Gen. manager, Wolfgang Pachler. 454 twins/doubles, 61 suites. AE, DC, MC, V.*

42 **Pan Pacific.** This link in a growing Japanese chain attracts
$$$ a mix of tour groups (especially Japanese) and business travelers. Of the three Marina Square hotels, this one is the largest and least expensive. Its 35-floor atrium lobby, with second-floor reception area, is rather soulless and functional, except for a huge pink fabric mobile hanging from the ceiling. Rooms are furnished in earth tones and have free-standing writing desks and marble bathrooms with separate showers. Upper floors offer the best harbor and city views. Past guests range from Prince Bolkiah of Brunei, to Commonwealth heads of government, to singer Gloria Estefan. There's a wide range of restaurants, including The Seafood Place—good for a casual business lunch or a relaxing dinner (*see* Dining, below). The swimming pool features underwater stereo. *7 Raffles Blvd., Marina Square, 0103, tel. 336–8111 or 800/448–8355, fax 339–1861. Gen. manager, John Roozemond. 434 twins, 355 doubles, 37 suites. AE, DC, MC, V.*

34 **Tai-Pan Ramada.** Nearing the end of its second decade as
$$ the main Ramada hotel in Singapore, the Tai-Pan has no particularly outstanding features, except that it offers basic comforts at comparatively reasonable rates. The second-floor lobby is bright and cheerful, although the connected bar—popular during happy hours—can be noisy. Rooms are finished in rosewood and have oversize beds, desks, and tea/coffee-making facilities. The exercise room is small. It's a short walk to the Raffles City convention center, and a five-minute cab ride to either the shopping or financial districts. The hotel provides a complimentary air-conditioned shuttle bus to both areas, as well as to Chinatown, four times a day on weekdays. This is a good alternative, but the Carlton (*see* above) provides more creative comforts for the same price. *101 Victoria St., tel. 336–0811 or 800/228–9898, fax 339–7019. Gen. manager, William Wong. 308 twins, 104 doubles, 15 suites. AE, DC, MC, V.*

36 37 **Westin Plaza** and **Westin Stamford.** Of these twin hotels in
$$$ the mammoth Raffles City complex, the Plaza is the smaller and higher-priced and caters to the business executive, while the Stamford attracts package-tour travelers and convention delegates. Combined, the hotels offer more than 2,000 guest rooms and uniformity. They are certainly not intimate, custom-service hotels—the trademark of many Singapore establishments—but instead, bustling convention city properties. Located next to the Raffles Hotel between Marina Square and the bottom of Orchard Road (they are a 10-minute taxi ride from the Orchard and Scotts roads intersection), these hotels have formed a hub of their own, with 100 or more shops (including a department store), convention facilities, and 17 restaurants, of

which the best-known is the Compass Rose (*see* Dining, below), with Continental fare. Also within the complex is a relaxing jazz club, Somerset's (*see* After Hours, below), a disco, a fitness center, two outdoor pools, six tennis courts, and four squash courts. For business meetings and banquets, there are convention rooms, including the largest column-free meeting room in the world. Function rooms have comprehensive support facilities and services, such as sophisticated audiovisual capabilities, simultaneous translation, boardroom suites, a closed-circuit TV system linking all meeting rooms, and a 24-hour business center. *2 Stamford Rd., 0617, tel. 338–8585 or 800/228–3000, fax 336–5117. Gen. manager, Michel Geday. Stamford, 1,257 rooms; Plaza, 796 rooms. AE, DC, MC, V.*

Shenton Way Business District

㉑ **Avant.** The striking, futuristic exterior of this black-glass
$$ cylinder, with bubble elevators dominating its 27-story atrium, contrasts with the more traditional feel of its smallish guest rooms. Previously called the Glass Hotel, it is located between the shopping and business districts, and attracts more tour groups than corporate travelers, but is worth considering if you want to hold down travel costs. A refurbishment program is under way; ask for a refinished standard or an upgraded deluxe room. Furnishings combine rosewood and teak. There are free-standing desks and separate seating areas suitable for work. The hotel is surrounded by blocks of public housing, which are quiet after dark, so for nightlife, you'll have to take a 10-minute cab ride to the entertainment district. *317 Outram Rd., 0316, tel. 733–0188, fax 733–0989. Gen. manager, Frank Kuhn. 266 twins, 217 doubles, 22 suites. AE, DC, MC, V.*

DINING

Singapore vies with Hong Kong for the role of top restaurant city in the East, if not the world. Here, you'll find excellent restaurants specializing in home-grown fare (known as Nonya, or Peranakan, cuisine—*see* Nonya and Baba review, below) and in foods from Malaysia, Indonesia, Thailand, Vietnam, Korea, Japan, all parts of China, and North India, as well as from Europe and the United States. And, as befits an island, Singapore has numerous seafood restaurants, many offering dishes representing a variety of national cuisines.

Chinese make up about 76% of Singapore's population, so Chinese cuisines naturally predominate. Cantonese and Teochew (Chiu Chau—from the Swatow area of China) cuisines are the best represented in the city. Teochew cuisine is fairly bland, as Cantonese is, but dishes tend to be steamed rather than fried. That generalization not withstanding, recommended Teochew dishes include fried *kuay teow* (rice noodles fried with cockles, beansprouts, and pieces of Chinese sausage), and a dessert of sweet yam paste with ginko nuts and coconut milk. Of the cuisine from China's Hainan Island, off the north coast of North Vietnam, worth trying is "chicken rice": rice cooked in the broth of and served with a chicken lightly poached in ginger and spring onions, with a hot-and-sour chili dipping sauce. Also popular is Fukienese cuisine, which emphasizes soups and stews with rich, meaty stocks. Dishes to order are braised pork belly served with buns, fried oysters, and turtle soup. Hunanese cooking, another favorite, is dominated by sugar and spices; it tends to be more rustic. One of the most famous dishes is beggar's chicken, wrapped in lotus leaves and baked in a sealed covering of clay. Other tasty options are pigeon soup in bamboo cups, fried layers of bean curd skin, and honey ham served with bread.

Hotel restaurants are among the best, most popular, and most convenient spots for business entertaining in Singapore. They also serve the best Western food in town. More adventurous diners, however, have a wealth of options from open-air stalls, where a meal costs just a few dollars and business tycoons share tables with laborers, to gourmet restaurants that can cost several hundred dollars a head. Outdoor establishments usually have more ambience than hotel restaurants—and are popular with smokers, who are not permitted, by law, to light up in enclosed air-conditioned dining rooms.

Highly recommended restaurants in each price category are indicated by a star ★.

Category	Cost*
$$$$ (Very Expensive)	over S$90
$$$ (Expensive)	S$45–S$90
$$ (Moderate)	under S$45

per person, including appetizer, entrée, and dessert, but excluding drinks, service, and 4% tax.

Numbers in the margin correspond to numbered restaurant locations on the Singapore Lodging and Dining map.

Wine and Beer

Singapore does not produce wines. However, a reasonable selection of French, German, Australian, and some Californian wines are generally available in the better restaurants, where they tend to be expensive, starting at about S$36 a bottle. The top-selling, locally produced beers are Anchor and Tiger.

Business Breakfasts

Business breakfasts are not common in Singapore, although urgent meetings can be scheduled in your hotel coffee shop. Nor is business a usually conducted at weekend brunches, which, as a rule, do not start until noon. **Cafe Palm** (Oriental Hotel, tel. 338–0066) and **Domus** (Sheraton Towers, tel. 737–6888) serve the best breakfast buffets.

Orchard Road Area

★ **㉔** **Aziza's.** This quaint, prewar terrace house off the Orchard
$$ Road hotel belt, with its soft lighting, warm, earthy colors and batik paintings, is one of the few upscale Malay restaurants. It attracts mainly Malays—a good sign—plus a sprinkling of Chinese, and Western expatriates. The menu is extensive, with some creative dishes such as *sayor*

damai (vegetables with shredded chicken and prawns in beef stock) and charcoal-grilled chicken with herbs; however, the best dishes are sometimes unavailable by 9:30 PM. The wine selection is limited, but beer or fresh-squeezed lime juice go better with Malay food anyway. Waitresses in traditional dress are helpful, friendly, and informal. This is a good place for entertaining Malay business contacts; tables are fairly close, but the noise level is low. *36 Emerald Hill, tel. 235–1130. Casual dress. Reservations advised. AE, CB, DC, MC, V. Closed Sun. lunch.*

㉓ **Casablanca.** As in the film, lots of expatriates hang around
$$ in this charming terrace house in Singapore's first architectural conservation area, just off busy Orchard Road. Its whitewashed interior, decorated with Bogart and Bergman photos, attracts relaxed management types and look-at-me advertising people. Food is Continental (both classic and nouvelle cuisine). The menu is simple and changes regularly; daily specials are listed on blackboards. Ingredients are fresh and meals have a home-cooked quality. The roast lamb loin with seasonal vegetables in a pastry basket is recommended. For dessert, the lemon soufflé pancake is excellent. The reasonable selection of mainly French wines is somewhat steeply priced. Service is friendly yet polished. This is a good place for entertaining, although tables are too close and the room too noisy for serious business discussions. The front section away from the bar is quieter. *7 Emerald Hill, tel. 235–9328. Casual but neat dress. Reservations advised. AE, DC, MC, V. Closed Sun.*

⑰ **China Palace.** This large, reasonably priced restaurant is
$$ conveniently located a short walk off Orchard Road on the second floor of an office building. One of the older Szechuan restaurants, it is decorated in traditional style, with wooden screens, dragon moldings, and red carpets. It is busy at both lunchtime and in the evening and is good for business entertaining, but do not expect to discuss deals here; instead, concentrate on such authentic fare as Monk Jumps Over The Wall (casserole of shark's fin, abalone, chicken, scallops, sea cucumber, fish maw, and vegetables) and deer and duck meat steamed in a basket. The big draw is the Chinese imperial banquet for 10 people, eaten with cloisonné and enamel chopsticks. *20 Bideford Rd., #02-00 Wellington Bldg., tel. 235–1378. Casual dress. Reservations suggested. AE, DC, V. Closed Chinese New Year.*

㊲ **Compass Rose.** The Compass Rose is not for vertigo suffer-
$$$$ ers, sitting as it does on the 70th floor of the world's tallest hotel, with mostly unobstructed panoramic views across Singapore, Indonesia, and Malaysia through the floor-to-ceiling windows. It is a place suited more for celebrating a deal than for serious business entertaining. Singapore's prime minister brought Britain's Queen Elizabeth here for lunch. Greenery breaks up the room, and lighting is low to highlight the city scapes below that some would say are more memorable than the cuisine. The barbecued pigeon, marinated with honey and palm wine, is a flavorsome example of the innovative menu that combines Continental and Chinese dishes and ingredients. Dutch veal medallions in creamy morel sauce with seasonal vegetables is another good choice. Ask the waiter about the daily specials. Service is courteous and attentive. French,

Swiss, and Australian wines are featured on the wide
wine list. *Westin Stamford Hotel, 2 Stamford Rd., tel.
338–8585. Casual but neat dress. Reservations required.
AE, DC, MC, V.*

⑮ ㉛ **Fook Yuen Seafood Restaurant.** The two branches of this
$$ Cantonese restaurant (one in the hotel/shopping area, the
other on the fringe of the financial area) serve similar fare
and are both better suited for a relaxed meal with col-
leagues than for business entertaining. Both have basic
traditional Chinese decor. Tables are too close and the din-
ing rooms are noisy, but the seafood is among the best in
the city and ingredients are fresh. Favorites include large
steamed prawns, and fried mixed vegetables with scallops
and oyster sauce. However, the specialty is the *din xin*
lunch of snacks and tidbits, which draws full houses, even
though all the dishes tend to be plunked on the table at the
same time. Even if you have a reservation, your table may
be given away unless you arrive early. Write off the curt-
and-hurried service as a cultural experience and enjoy the
food. The wine selection is very limited. *290 Orchard Rd.,
#03-05/08 The Paragon, tel. 235–2211; 95 South Bridge
Rd., #01-01 South Bridge Center, tel. 532–7778. Casual
dress. Reservations required, but not always honored.
AE, DC, MC, V. Closed Chinese New Year.*

★ ⑨ **Harbour Grill.** For serious business negotiations, the un-
$$$$ derstated elegance of this restaurant, with its large, well-
spaced tables and the subdued hum of deals in progress, is
ideal. Popular with executives for both lunch and dinner, it
has an unhurried air, and serves classic Continental fare
such as prime roast rib of U.S. beef with salad and baked
potato, as well as more innovative fare such as blanquette
of salmon with mushrooms and baby onions. The wine list
is smallish and expensive—mostly French, with a few
German, Californian, and Australian bottles. Service is
excellent, courteous, and unobtrusive. Its excellent food
and atmosphere make the Harbour Grill a favorite for en-
tertaining. *Hilton Hotel, 581 Orchard Rd., tel. 737–2233.
Jacket and tie advised. Reservations recommended. AE,
DC, MC, V. Closed for lunch weekends and holidays.*

⑳ **Han Do.** This small Korean restaurant is a haven of tran-
$$$ quility in the heart of Orchard Road. Bamboo and rice-
paper screens divide it into several semiprivate sections,
keeping down noise levels and allowing business talks over
a meal. South Korean embassy officials, who appreciate
the authentic Korean fare, often entertain here. The Korean *bulgogi* barbecue of sliced, marinated beef and the
kalbi (beef short ribs grilled over charcoal) are deservedly
popular. Avoid the *kimchi*, that hot, pickled cabbage
found on every Korean table, if you plan to meet business
contacts after lunch or to go anywhere after dinner—it
tends to linger on the breath. A small selection of wines,
some Korean, is available. Service is efficient. *321 Orchard Rd., #05-01/07 Orchard Shopping Center, tel. 235–
8451. Casual but neat dress. Reservations suggested. AE,
DC, MC, V. Closed Chinese New Year.*

㉒ **Kirin Court.** Kirin Court is conveniently located on a side
$$ street off the Orchard Road hotel and shopping area. With
chandeliers and green carpets, it is a cheerful, brightly
lighted, fairly noisy place popular with both business-
people (it has five private function rooms) and families. It
specializes in Cantonese seafood and shark's fin dishes,

but the comprehensive menu offers plenty of alternatives. Pork ribs simmered in a sauce of five Chinese spices and rice wine are tasty. The barbecued Peking duck is justifiably popular; the remaining meat clinging to the bones is taken back to the kitchen and served later in the meal, fried with beansprouts so that diners can enjoy every bite—the mark of a quality restaurant. Brandy with ice is the popular drink, but some Chinese wines are available. Service is generally polite and efficient, but becomes a bit ragged at peak times. *20 Devonshire Rd., tel. 732–1188. Smart, casual dress. Reservations recommended. AE, DC, MC, V. Closed Chinese New Year.*

❸ **Latour.** Silver candlesticks, glass chandeliers, starched
$$$ white tablecloths, and warm shades of peach set the tone for quality dining in this prestigious location. With the dinner music kept low, this centrally located place is a good bet for business discussions. The large menu is mainly classic Continental, but mixes Eastern and Western dishes to create a memorable meal. Among the best are lobster ragout, fillet of pomfret, and blueberry soufflé. A separate menu, which changes every three months, features seasonal specialties. The comprehensive wine list includes a 1943 Château Rothschild priced at around US$550. Service is smooth and courteous. *Shangri-La Hotel, Orange Grove Rd., tel. 737–3644. Jacket and tie recommended. Reservations required. AE, DC, MC, V.*

★ ⓮ **Li Bai.** If you want to impress a Chinese business associ-
$$$ ate, head for Li Bai, a restaurant that combines contemporary red-and-black Oriental richness with Western minimalism. Ivory chopsticks and jade tableware are set on the well-spaced tables, each decorated with a single flower. The well-trained staff provides highly attentive, knowledgeable service. Two private rooms, each seating 12, are available for private meetings. The menu, changed quarterly, features innovative Cantonese fare with highlighted specialties such as barbecued, boned, and sliced duckling with fresh mangoes and lemon sauce, and whelks with fresh asparagus in oyster-and-shrimp sauce. The wine list is comprehensive and includes eight Chinese wines as well as Japanese sake. Many customers will be in smart, casual clothes, but you will probably feel more comfortable in a suit. *Sheraton Towers Hotel, 39 Scotts Rd., tel. 737–6888. Casual but neat attire. Reservations required. AE, DC, MC, V.*

❸ **Nadaman.** The country inn–style Nadaman occupies the
$$$ top floor of the Shangri-La's tower in an exclusive residential area, and is particularly popular with Japanese executives. Tables look right into the backyards of some of Singapore's smartest homes. However, the main attraction is the wide range of Japanese dishes. Although local flavors have crept into some dishes, most are authentic and the raw fish is as fresh as can be. There are four private tatami rooms, as well as a Western-style private dining room. Set lunches offer a wide variety of dishes and keep down costs; the elegant, 10-course *kaiseki* dinners (formal Japanese banquets) range up to S$150 a head for certain seasonal specialties. Sake or cold beer is the best accompaniment, but the wine list is comprehensive. Service is attentive and friendly. This is an elegant location to entertain. *Shangri-La Hotel, Orange Grove Rd., tel. 737–*

3644. Jacket and tie advised. Reservations required. AE, DC, MC, V.

㉘ **Nonya and Baba.** To get close to a client's heart, take him
$$ or her for local, Peranakan-style cooking—an exotic blend
of Chinese and Malay influences with Thai overtones. Cre-
ated by immigrants from China's Fujian province who
married local Malays, dishes are either spicy and rich in
coconut milk, or spicy and sour. It's a five-minute cab ride
from Orchard Road to this simple, cozy terraced shop rich
in nostalgia: marbletopped tables, old-fashioned chairs
and lamps, ceiling fans, and walls decorated with
Peranakan artifacts. The whole deep-fried fish is particu-
larly tasty with its dip of soy sauce, chili, and red onion.
Desserts are limited to a few dishes, such as *gula malacca*
(cold sago with brown cane syrup). There is no wine list.
Service is warm and friendly. This is the real Singapore,
but do not expect to discuss business here. *262 River Val-
ley Rd., tel. 734–1382. Casual dress. Reservations ad-
vised. MC, V. Closed Chinese New Year.*

⑫ **Nutmegs.** The new California cuisine, with unusual food
$$$ combinations and light textures, is featured in this stylish
black-and-white Art Deco room. It's popular for business
lunches, especially with younger executives. Comfortable
booths along the walls offer privacy to discuss deals, but in
the evenings a jazz band in the adjoining lounge sets the
tone for relaxed dining. There is also music during the
Sunday brunch. Designer breads, crispy rôtisserie duckling with four sauces, and exotic marriages of ingredients
in other dishes complement traditional favorites such as
charcoal-grilled steaks and seafood. Californian wines
dominate; Robert Mondavi's Chardonnay and Pinot Noir
are two safe choices. The staff takes pride in its work;
service is friendly and efficient. *Hyatt Hotel, 10-12 Scotts
Rd., tel. 733–1188, ext. 2462. Casual but neat dress. Reservations advised. AE, CB, DC, MC, V.*

㉕ **Parkway Thai.** The downtown sister of an east Singapore
$$ eatery, the Parkway Thai makes the best of its shopping
center location, but high rents force the tables close to-
gether. The Thai menu is comprehensive. Try the fleshy,
barbequed cotton fish, dipped into a spicy seafood sauce,
and the chili-hot *tom yum* prawn soup served over a warm-
er. Pineapple rice (fried rice with chunks of pork and pine-
apple in curry) is not really a Thai dish, but is worth
ordering anyway. For a Thai restaurant, there's an unusu-
ally wide choice of desserts. There is no wine list, but beer
or soft drinks go well with this hot cuisine. Service by
waitresses in Thai costumes is usually gracious and atten-
tive, but can slip a little when the restaurant is full. This is
a place to visit for the high standard of its food, rather
than for a business meal. *176 Orchard Rd., #01-59/62
Centrepoint, tel. 737–8080. Casual dress. No reserva-
tions. MC, V. Closed Chinese New Year.*

⑱ **Pine Court.** If you want Peking duck, this is the place. It is
$$$ carefully prepared, with fragrant, crispy skin, and is one
of the specialties of this high-ceilinged restaurant, taste-
fully decorated in earthy browns and reds, highlighted
with discreet touches of gold—a pleasant change from the
usual gaudy red-and-green Chinese restaurant decor. In
addition to the duck, the extensive menu also includes
large and tasty crispy fried prawns in a light batter. The
wine list is long, and the service is polished and efficient.

The Pine Court is suitable for business lunches or dinners, and is conveniently located in the Orchard Road hotel area. *Mandarin Singapore, 333 Orchard Rd., tel. 737–4411. Smart, casual dress. Reservations essential. AE, CB, DC, MC, V.*

⑲ **Saigon.** Cane chairs, ceiling fans, and soft lighting conjure
$$ up colonial Vietnam—a good setting for either adventurous business entertaining or a meal with associates. Tables are well-spaced, and banquettes are comfortable. Reasonably priced Vietnamese dishes are authentic, tasty, light, and not too oily. The menu is surprisingly large, although it has only four or five dessert selections. The prawn tamarind soup has an intriguing sour-sweet flavor, and the deep-fried spring rolls have a classic sauce of vinegar, fish, chili, and garlic. The Saigon tea is flavored with jasmine and pandan (a plant used mainly for its brilliant green color). The wine list is limited; try instead the Saigon Special with brandy added. Service is efficient and friendly. Saigon is off the Orchard Road hotel/shopping strip, tucked away on the fourth floor of a quiet building. *15 Cairnhill Rd., #04-03 Cairnhill Place, tel. 235–0626. Casual dress. Reservations advised. AE, DC, MC, V.*

㉙ **Sanur.** Located in the sterile surroundings of a shopping
$$ center is a small, unpretentious restaurant serving authentic, standard Indonesian dishes. Lighting is subdued and the small rattan tables and chairs are close together, but this place is always crowded (long lines sometimes form) and is more for a quick meal after work than for entertaining. Try *ayam panggang* (deep-fried spicy chicken), beef *rendang* (cubed beef simmered in coconut milk and spices), or *sambal udang* (prawns in a very hot sauce). Beer or lime juice is a better accompaniment than anything from the limited wine list. Waitresses are very friendly and helpful, and considerate of those dining alone. *176 Orchard Rd., #04-17/18 Centrepoint, tel. 734–2192. Casual dress. Reservations essential. AE, DC, MC, V.*

⑧ **Suntory.** Exquisite Japanese atmosphere and service
$$$$ draw dark-suited Japanese businesspeople with large expense accounts to the centrally located Suntory, which has a Japanese garden with carp swimming in a pond, and four eating areas: sushi and tempura bars and the teppanyaki and shabu-shabu rooms. Traditional-style Japanese service is practiced in four private tatami rooms. Elsewhere, the kimono-clad waitresses are unobtrusive but friendly and helpful. All portions are small, so expect to order numerous dishes. For a main course, try the well-prepared classic sukiyaki. Suntory brewery's beer-fed and massaged beef is an extravagance worth trying. Leave room for a scoop of delicately flavored green-tea ice cream. *402 Orchard Rd., #06-01/02 Delfi Orchard, tel. 732–5111. Casual but neat dress. Reservations advised. AE, DC, MC, V. Closed Chinese New Year.*

㉕ **Swatow Teochew.** This is one of the new breed of Chinese
$$ restaurants that breaks away from the traditional decor of red, gold, and green and large tables crammed together, and instead, offers diners a small but tastefully decorated dining area, with Chinese art, in which to conduct private conversations. Tucked away on the fifth floor of an Orchard Road shopping center, Swatow Teochew is not easy to find but is worth the hunt, for it is far more attractive

than its faded elder sister in the financial district, and its robust Teochew fare is just as good. Among the better dishes are braised goose, braised shark's fin, and typical Teochew yam pudding with ginko nuts. The wine selection is very small. Service is friendly and efficient; ask the helpful senior staff to recommend dishes. *176 Orchard Rd., #05-16 Centrepoint, tel. 235-4719. Casual but neat dress. Reservations required for lunch, recommended for dinner. AE, DC, MC, V. Closed Chinese New Year.*

Shenton Way Business District

★ ❸⓪ **Moti Mahal.** Moti Mahal means "pearl palace"—an appro-
$$$ priate name for delightful North Indian cuisine served in an ugly shell of a restaurant. The decor is so unfortunate it's almost kitsch: dim lighting, dark wallpaper, uncomfortable booths along the walls, a strong smell of incense, old tablecloths, and chipped crockery. But all this becomes insignificant once you try the tasty fare. Customers are mainly local regulars content to eat rather than talk. Staff will make recommendations if the huge menu confuses you—the chicken tikka (boneless tandoori chicken) and mutton kurma (mildly spicy mutton in a creamy sauce) are particularly good. A small wine list is available. Moti Mahal is pricy for North Indian fare, but it's close to the financial district and worthwhile. *18 Murray Terrace, tel. 221-4338. Casual dress. AE, DC, MC, V.*

❸⓽ **Oscar's.** This basement restaurant in the financial district
$$$ is crowded at lunchtime but almost deserted in the evenings. It is popular for business lunches, although the fairly high noise level probably precludes serious negotiations. A spiral staircase leads to this bright, cheery, brasserie-type place with a split-level black-and-white checkered marble floor, gleaming brass rails, and mirrors. Avoid the banquette seats, which are too low for the tables; the bar has stools for single diners. The classic Continental food is of consistent, rather than startling, quality, and the 30-minute lunch includes snacks and some British fare. Among the better dishes are the seafood combo (salmon, prawns, scallops, and kurau fish on a bed of young leeks, lightly glazed in ginger sauce) and veal Oscar's (pan-fried veal loin with ham, mushrooms, and Gruyere cheese, served with noodles and seasoned vegetables). The wine list is short and mainly French, with some Californian and Australian offerings. Service is attentive and swift. *30 Robinson Rd., #B1-00 Tuan Sing Tower, tel. 223-4033. Casual but neat dress. Weekday lunch reservations required. AE, DC, V. Closed Sun. and holidays.*

★ ❸⓼ **The Pinnacle.** On the 60th floor of Overseas Union Bank
$$$$ Center in the heart of the financial district, this triangular restaurant has spectacular views of Singapore from two sides—specify a window seat when making a reservation. Oriental artifacts from the bank chairman's private collection are on display. This is a good choice for a business dinner, and private function rooms are available. The Pinnacle marries East and West by offering both Cantonese and Continental cuisine. Choices are limited, but almost everything is good. The Monk Jumps Over The Wall (a potpourri of shark's fin, abalone, chicken, scallops, sea cucumber, and fish maw) and the broiled salmon steak with caramel vinegar are excellent choices. The wine list is fair

and includes 13 champagnes. Service is efficient and polite, as one would expect from the price. The Pinnacle is highly recommended for its prime location and innovative food. *1 Raffles Pl., #60-00 OUB Center, tel. 532–5631. Jacket and tie advised. Reservations required. AE, DC, V. Closed Sun. and holidays, except for private functions.*

Marina Square/Raffles City Area

❸❸ Annalakshmi. The carved chairs and tables and the Hindu
$$ artifacts make this warm, incense-scented restaurant appear expensive, but in fact it serves very moderately priced Indian vegetarian fare, with great emphasis on authenticity, quality, and nutritional value. The à la carte menu is fairly extensive, but the uninitiated may prefer one of the good-value set lunches and dinners from the mild Northern and spicy Southern Indian cuisines. *Dosais* (pizza-sized thin vegetable-filled pancakes served with three spicy dipping sauces) and *idlis* (steamed rice flour and lentil patties) are recommended. Annalakshmi's staff belongs to a religious association, so the sari-clad waitresses tend to be grave and serene, rather than polished and efficient. No alcohol is served. Good for a business dinner with an Indian contact, especially if you want to get away early: the restaurant closes at 9:30 PM. *5 Coleman St., #02-10 Excelsior Hotel Shopping Center, tel. 339–3007. Casual dress. Reservations advised. AE, DC, MC, V. Closed Thurs. dinners, and Deepavali day and the day after.*

★ ❹❶ Fourchettes. Glass and brass partitions between some of
$$$ the well-spaced, candle-lighted tables lend extra privacy to diners in this gracious, brass-and-oak room, making it an excellent choice for business entertaining or high-powered negotiations against a background of soft harp or violin-and-guitar music. Close to the financial district, it has a fairly small French/English menu that concentrates on quality and attractive presentation. The snails in puff pastry with morel mushroom sauce are a good appetizer; for a main course, try the turbot baked in a pastry case with champagne sauce and mushrooms. The cheese trolley offers a good selection, and the wine list has a wide range of quality French and other wines. Service is attentive yet unobtrusive. *Oriental Singapore Hotel, 5 Raffles Ave., tel. 338–0066. Casual but neat attire. Reservations advised. AE, DC, MC, V. Closed lunchtime Sat.*

❹❷ The Seafood Place. Ingenious decor—rustic beach huts
$$ amid sea-blue marine aquariums and large murals of a fishing village—disguises The Seafood Place's hotel location and sets the mood for casual entertaining. Eating here with a business contact might even break the ice and enable you to set a deal in motion. The crab-shaped menu offers plenty of fresh local favorites such as fried crab with sambal chili sauce, and steamed live prawns with egg white. Among the recommended desserts is fried jackfruit with coconut ice cream. Staff are well-informed and do not try to hurry diners. The wine list is comprehensive. *Pan Pacific Hotel, 7 Raffles Blvd., tel. 336–8111, ext. 4234. Casual. Reservations advised. AE, DC, MC, V. Closed Sun. lunch.*

Suburbs

㉜ Banana Leaf Apolo. This noisy, tacky, basic restaurant,
$$ decorated with track lights, Formica tables, and hard
chairs is famed for its fiery South Indian fare eaten off a
strip of banana leaf. You can ask for a spoon and fork; oth-
erwise, custom dictates that you eat with your right hand.
The restaurant is located on the edge of "Little India," a
10-minute cab ride from center city, and its clientele in-
cludes families and local businesspeople. There is no
menu; just point to the spicy items on display or speak to
one of the staff who hovers behind you and remembers
everything. The fish-head curry—the eyes are prized—is
a top seller here; other good choices are the fried chicken
and prawns, and chicken masala in spicy coconut milk.
Plain or saffron rice and stewed vegetables come with all
orders. Beer is served, but will only make you hotter; best
stick to fresh lime juice. *56 Race Course Rd., tel. 293–
8682. Casual dress. AE, DC, MC, V. Closed Deepavali
day and the day after.*

★ ㊸ Choon Hoon Seng. It's worth the 25-minute cab ride from
$$ downtown to the northern shore where you'll find excellent seafood and plenty of local color in an unspoiled, rus-
tic corner of fast-disappearing old Singapore. Here
customers sit at rickety open-air tables overlooking the
Straits of Johore to neighboring Malaysia. It is one of
three breezy restaurants at the end of the road, and is always crowded with local people and expatriates who come
for a hearty feast at moderate prices. The precracked chili
crabs are a highlight of almost every meal. The deep-fried
baby squid, with a sweetish brown sauce, and freshly
steamed prawns are also good bets. Service is unpolished
but efficient. Chilled beer is the drink that goes best with a
casual meal like this, so do not expect a wine list. *892
Punggol Rd., tel. 288–3472. Casual attire. No reservations. No credit cards. Closed Chinese New Year.*

❶ El Felipe's Cantina. If you develop a craving for Tex-Mex,
$$ take a 10-minute cab ride from center city to the original
branch of El Felipe's Cantina in Holland Village, which
has more charm than the others. American co-owner Phil-
ip Gibson is often on hand to chat in this cozy, casual place
where margaritas are served in jam jars and the staff is
young and friendly. It's popular with expatriates and
young locals, and its wooden bar counter and small tables
are always crowded and noisy. The warm, cheerful atmos-
phere makes this a good choice for a relaxed meal. The en-
chiladas are fine, as is the grilled marinated chicken with
onions and green peppers served in a taco shell with re-
fried beans, guacamole, and sour cream. One of the more
unusual desserts is the Tequila Sunset—orange sherbet
topped with sliced peaches, raspberry sauce, and tequila.
*34 Lorong Mambong, tel. 468–1530. Casual dress. Week-
end reservations required. AE, DC, MC, V.*

㊹ Long Beach. It's a 15-minute cab ride from center city
$$ along the east coast to this old-fashioned, noisy, and casual seafood restaurant with more charm than any of the ten
restaurants in the nearby new Seafood Centre. Tanks of
live fish line the walls of the air-conditioned interior, but
opt for a table outside under the trees. Portions are large,
prices are reasonable, and your clients will appreciate
your choice for relaxed business entertaining. Try the

black-pepper crabs, crabs in chili sauce, deep-fried baby squid, live "drunken" prawns, or steamed prawns. Beer and soft drinks are served. The harried staff assumes diners know what is on the menu, so ask for help. *610 Bedok Rd., tel. 445–8833. Casual dress. Reservations advised. AE, DC, MC, V. Dinner only. Closed Chinese New Year.*

FREE TIME

Fitness

Hotel Facilities

The **Omni Marco Polo's Clark Hatch Physical Fitness Center** (tel. 474–7141) is the best-equipped and -managed hotel club, with free weights, sauna, and steam baths, Olympic-size pool, and aerobic classes. Nonguests are charged S$20 a session. The **Hilton Fitness Center** (tel. 737–2233) is also good; nonguests can take advantage of the sauna and pool, free weights and fitness machines, and aerobics classes for S$15 a session.

Health Clubs

The **Fiscal Fitness Center** (1 Raffles Pl., #06-00 OUB Center, tel. 535–5678), conveniently located in the financial district, has all the latest equipment and facilities and charges nonmembers S$10 per visit. Nonmembers can also use the free weights and equipment at **Gold's Gym Singapore** (1 Selegie Rd., #B1-13/32 Paradiz Center, tel. 339–0822), a branch of the well-known chain; fees are S$20 for the first visit and S$15 for subsequent visits.

Jogging

A very attractive running path traverses the lush grounds of the **Botanical Gardens** on Cluny Road. The waterfront at **Marina Bay** near Marina Square/Raffles City is less attractive, but still popular among joggers.

Shopping

The bargain prices for which Singapore was once famous no longer exist. The intense competition among shops prevents them from buying and selling in volume. Also, with a growing economy and a standard of living second in Asia only to Japan's, Singapore has a strong dollar and high overheads for importing agents and retail outlets.

There are still bargains, but the saving may not be great. Good values are found in fashion goods (Singapore has become a fashion contracting center, since it does not have the quota restrictions Hong Kong and other Asian cities do), handcrafted rosewood furniture, Chinese objets d'art, and Oriental carpets.

When shopping, look for the Singapore Tourist Promotion Board logo—a gold Merlion (a lion's head with a fish tail) on a red background. This signifies that the retailer is recommended by the STPB and the Singapore Retail Merchants Association. Members are required to sell at "reasonable prices," give receipts, and display price tags indicating the discount as well as what is included in the price. If the object is a camera, for example, the price tag must say whether the camera bag, lenses, etc., are included in the displayed price.

Street stalls or bargain shops have designer-label merchandise for ridiculously low prices; they are all fakes. Sport shirts with famous-name labels and logos—Lacoste, Pierre Cardin, Giordano—filter in from Thailand and Hong Kong and are often of the same quality as the original product but at a third the price. Deeply discounted leather goods with such labels as Cartier, Etienne Aigner, and Gucci at these shops are most certainly frauds, and the quality may be inferior.

Street peddlers sell quartz watches, mainly from Taiwan, bearing the names of great Swiss or French watchmakers or European design houses for about S$30; they are fakes, but the timing mechanisms are just as good as those in watches that cost a hundred times more. Many Singaporeans consider the imitations the smarter buy. The greatest of the fakes is the "solid gold Rolex," which comes complete with serial number for S$100. You might buy it as a lark, but it looks so good, you could have a problem at Customs.

The main shopping area is Orchard Road, which is lined with hotel shopping arcades and massive malls with up to 800 shops in each. Of these, **Lucky Plaza** (no phone) and **Far East Plaza** (tel. 732–7038) are a bit downmarket, with pokey, crowded shops; **Centrepoint** (tel. 235–6629), **Marina Square** (no phone), the **Promenade** (no phone), and the **Paragon** (no phone), are all well run, with reliable shops and good varieties of merchandise. Oriental handicrafts and knick-knacks make attractive gifts and can be found everywhere. For something a little more classy—say, Oriental antiques or jewelry—try the **Tanglin Shopping Center** (no phone).

The top department store in Singapore for variety of items and quality of goods is **C.K. Tang** (320 Orchard Rd., tel. 737–5500). Others, also reliable, are **Metro** (several branches; try the one at The Paragon, 290 Orchard Rd., tel. 235–2811), **Sogo** (Raffles City complex, tel. 339–1100), **Robinson's** (Levels 1-5, Centrepoint, 176 Orchard Rd., tel. 733–0888), and **Isetan** (Wisma Atria, 435 Orchard Rd., tel. 733–7777). Excellent boutiques for women include **Glamourette** (300 Orchard Rd., #02-02/03 The Promenade, tel. 734–3137) and **Joy's** (6 Scotts Rd., #02-09/10 Scotts Shopping Center, tel. 235–3540). For off-the-rack menswear, stick to the department stores. A reliable tailor is **Lloyd's Kimberly Tailor** (583 Orchard Rd., #01-31 Forum Galleria, tel. 737–5254).

For electronics, **Cost Plus** (6 Scotts Rd., #04-09/09 Scotts Shopping Center, tel. 235–1557) is hassle-free, but be sure to get the maker's warranty.

Diversions

Those who appreciate period architecture will enjoy a cab ride through **Alexandra Park,** an enclave of beautiful old black-and-white colonial homes left behind by the British. **Emerald Hill Road,** off Orchard Road, is another good area; it is Singapore's first conservation area, where highly ornate, turn-of-the-century terrace houses provide a refreshing contrast to modern tower blocks.

The **Botanical Gardens,** off Cluny Road, provide an ideal escape from the bustle of downtown Singapore. Begun in Victorian times as a collection of tropical trees and plants, the gardens have now spread to 74 acres, with a large lake and masses of shrubs, flowers, and trees (including 98-foot fan palms). The orchid beds are breathtaking, with specimens of some 250 varieties, many of them very rare.

Chinatown, near the Singapore River and financial center, is best appreciated on foot rather than by tour bus. Here you will see ornately decorated shophouses (two-story buildings with shops or small factories on the ground floor and living quarters upstairs), temples, mosques, and traditional medicine shops; you can sample fresh spring rolls, have something written in calligraphy, purchase a lion-dance costume, or just wander through the bustling markets. Start your stroll along the Singapore River and wind your way through the side streets off South Bridge Road until you reach the IBM Towers on Anson Road.

Little India, in the Serangoon Road area, has all the sights, sounds, and spicy smells of India. Go by cab, and then wander on foot to get the most out of your visit to this unique district. There are several temples of interest, as well as numerous shops selling Indian spices, textiles, brass goods, porcelain, and antiques.

Housed in a grand colonial building topped by a silver dome, the **National Museum** (Stamford Rd., tel. 337–7355) has numerous well-designed displays that convey this young country's history. The renowned Haw Par Jade Collection is showcased here as well.

Newton Circus Hawker Center is a brash, colorful collection of outdoor dining stalls selling fresh fruit juices, beer, seafood, and Chinese, Malaysian, and Indian dishes. Have at least one meal here to savor the color, but check prices first—if you think you are being taken advantage of, ask a local person to query the prices. Conditions are hygienic.

Sultan Mosque and the surrounding area of two-story storefronts and terrace houses give visitors a good feel for the history of Singapore's Malay community. This is a place to meander, taking time to browse through shops selling batik, rich silks and velvets, perfumes, and various handicrafts, and sample Malaysian food at simple outdoor cafés.

The Arts

Now that Singapore has established itself as a commercial center, the arts are being officially encouraged, but options are fairly limited in view of the size of the population, some 3 million. The Singapore Symphony Orchestra performs regularly on Friday and Saturday nights at the **Victoria Theater and Concert Hall** (9 Empress Pl., tel. 337–7490); Sunday night performances usually feature visiting orchestras or musical groups. Chinese opera, traditional dance, and other cultural activities are occasionally staged here, too. The **Drama Center** (Canning Rise, tel. 336–0005) and **Kallang Theatre** (Stadium Walk, tel. 345–8488) are the main locations for touring companies. **Kallang Stadium** (Stadium Walk, tel. 345–8488) is reserved for large-scale productions and touring companies, but the acoustics are rather poor. Colorful cultural song and dance reviews are featured in dinner-theater performances at the **Mandarin Hotel** (tel. 737–4411) and the **Hyatt Regency** (tel. 733–1188).

Tickets are available at the information counters at **Centrepoint Shopping Center** (176 Orchard Rd., tel. 235–6629) and the **C.K. Tang Department Store** (320 Orchard Rd., tel. 737–5500).

After Hours

Singapore's nightlife is staid compared to that of nearby cities such as Bangkok, Manila, and even Kuala Lumpur. Orchard Road—"the street that never sleeps," as the local newspaper describes it—is often barely awake after 10 PM, but most of the action is in this area. Choose carefully and you can probably find something to suit, but don't expect to have any stories to relate when you get back home.

Bars and Lounges
For a relaxing drink after work, **Bibi's** (180 Orchard Rd., Peranakan Pl., tel. 732–6966) is tropically casual, with antiques, ceiling fans, rattan furniture, and greenery. For a quiet drink with clients, the **Captain's Bar** (Oriental Hotel, tel. 338–0066) is appropriately plush, and has a pianist. Also try the **Canopy Bar** (Hyatt Regency, tel. 733–1188), Singapore's first champagne and wine bar. **The Lounge,** on the lobby level of the Hilton (tel. 737–2233) is also a good spot for a quiet drink.

Cabarets
Although not what Westerners usually regard as a cabaret, the **Golden Million** (Peninsula Hotel, tel. 336–6993) is a vast Chinese nightclub with floor shows featuring local and foreign bands and singers. Because this is a hostess bar, drink prices are very high: S$250 for a bottle of Scotch whiskey. **Top Ten** (400 Orchard Rd., #05-18A Orchard Towers, tel. 732–3077) is a theater lounge where top local and touring foreign bands perform. The walls of this converted cinema are painted like the Manhattan skyline. It is always crowded with local people and resident foreigners.

Discos
A slightly older crowd will feel comfortable at **Xanadu** (Shangri-La Hotel, tel. 737–3644), but the younger group heads for **Ridley's Has The Rubber** (Century Park Sheraton, 16 Nassim Hill, tel. 732–1222) and **The Warehouse** (River View Hotel, 382 Havelock Rd., tel. 732–9922), a converted warehouse with the latest sound and video systems.

Jazz Clubs
It is loud at **Saxophone** (23 Cuppage Terr., tel. 235–8385), a casual, ties-off place with a Continental restaurant over the tiny bar; opt for an outside table. **Somerset's** (Westin Stamford and Plaza, tel. 338–8585) is roomier, smarter, and less noisy; the focus here is on New Orleans–style jazz.

For Singles
Popular **Brannigan's** (Hyatt Hotel, tel. 733–1188) attracts a mixture of locals and expatriates. Singles of both sexes

will feel comfortable here, and may even meet someone. The bar counter at **Somerset's** (*see* above) is also a good spot to mingle with unattached people, as is **Bibi's** (*see* above).

Sydney

by Chris Pritchard

Canberra is Australia's federal capital, and Melbourne, second only to Sydney in size, is home to the headquarters of some leading companies and banks. But Sydney is Australia's lively, cosmopolitan heart, its leading commercial center. The downtown area, known locally as the central business district (or CBD), is relatively compact. But the city also has a vast suburban sprawl stretching about 50 miles from north to south, and the greater Sydney area is home to about 3.5 million people (one of every five Australians lives here).

Although Britain ruled from 1788 until the Commonwealth of Australia (as the nation is officially called) was established in 1901, Sydney has little of the Old World flavor of a European city. The downtown area and the large shopping malls in suburbia are distinctly North American in appearance, and the harborside location and temperate climate have promoted an informal, outdoor-oriented, California-type lifestyle. Indeed, Sydney is often compared with San Francisco, despite a less hilly topography. For the feel of "old" Sydney, stroll among the sandstone buildings in the compact, historic Rocks area adjoining downtown, where many fine restaurants are located. Most Sydneysiders (as residents are known) prize the leisure component of life, and a memorable part of your trip may well be a harbor cruise on the pleasure boat of a local contact or indulging in local wines and seafood with the gleamingly white-roofed Opera House and "coat hanger" Harbor Bridge in the background.

There is significant foreign investment in Sydney's tourism, banking, insurance, manufacturing (such as pharmaceuticals and machinery), and service industries. Overseas investors, particularly from Japan and Southeast Asia, have been major buyers and developers of hotels, office towers, and residential properties.

Opponents of immigration contend that the high number of new residents being granted entry should be cut back until the economy improves. Proponents counter that only by continuing to take in a big flow of newcomers (many now from Southeast Asia rather than from Europe) can national development be spurred. Certainly, for many business travelers, the increasingly multicultural face of Australia means this is a more interesting place to visit than it was, say, a decade ago.

Top Employers

Employer	Type of Enterprise	Parent*/ Headquarters
Alcan Australia Ltd.	Aluminum production and product manufacture	Alcan/Montréal, Canada
Amatil Ltd.	Beverage bottler and franchise; manufacturer of cigarettes, foods, and packaging	Sydney
ANI Corp. Ltd.	Manufacturer of railroad cars, heavy machinery, and electrical goods; auto dealerships chain	Sydney
Boral Ltd.	Construction materials	Sydney
Brambles Industries Ltd.	Heavy machinery and crane rental; container rental; transportation; security equipment manufacture	Sydney
Burns Philp & Co. Ltd.	Wholesale merchant; travel agencies; manufacturer of photographic equipment	Sydney
General Property Trust	Property investment and development	Sydney
Lend Lease Corp. Ltd.	Property development and construction	Sydney
Pioneer Concrete Service Ltd.	Cement and concrete production; gas and oil exploration	Sydney
Westpac Banking Corp.	Financial services; travel agency	Sydney

* *if applicable*

ESSENTIAL INFORMATION

We include the Sydney telephone area code (02) with all numbers listed below. If you are calling from outside Australia, omit the 0 from the code; if you are calling from within Sydney, omit the area code altogether.

The currency of Australia is the dollar, abbreviated throughout the chapter as A$.

Government Tourist Offices

Australian Tourist Commission (ATC). In the United States: 489 Fifth Ave., New York, NY 10017, tel. 212/687–6300; 150 N. Michigan Ave., Chicago, IL 60601, tel. 312/781–5150; 2121 Ave. of the Stars, Suite 1200, Los Angeles, CA 90067, tel. 213/552–1988.

In Canada: 2 Bloor St. W, Suite 1730, Toronto, M4W 3E2, Ontario, tel. 416/925–9575.

In the United Kingdom: Gemini House, 10–18 Putney Hill, London SW15, tel. 081/780–2027.

In Sydney: Travel Center of New South Wales, Pitt and Spring Sts., tel. 02/231–4444.

Foreign Trade Information

Australian Trade Commission. In the United States: 630 Fifth Ave., New York, NY 10111, tel. 212/245–4000; 321 N. Clark St., Quaker Tower Suite 2930, Chicago, IL 60610, tel. 312/644–5556; 611 North Larchmont Blvd., Los Angeles, CA 90004, tel. 213/469–4300.

In Canada: 175 Bloor St. E, Suite 314/316, Toronto, M4W 3R8, Ontario, tel. 416/323–1155.

In the United Kingdom: The Strand, London WC2B 4LA, tel. 071/438–8326.

Entry Requirements

U.S., Canadian, and U.K. Citizens
Passport and visa required. Visas are issued free of charge by any Australian embassy or consulate.

Consulates
In the United States: Australian Consulate General, 636 Fifth Ave., 4th Floor, New York, NY 10111, tel. 212/582–0640.

In Canada: Australian High Commission, Suite 710, 50 O'Connor St., Ottawa, K1P 6L2, Ontario, tel. 613/236–0841.

In the United Kingdom: Australian High Commission, Australia House, The Strand, London WC2B 4LA, tel. 071/379–4334.

Climate

Sydney is a temperate city—warmest summer months are January and February. Spring and fall are crisp but sunny. July is the coldest month. In summer, despite numerous hot and sunny days, several days in a row of rain are not unusual. What follows are the average daily minimum and maximum temperatures for Sydney.

Jan.	79F	26C	Feb.	79F	26C	Mar.	76F	24C
	65	18		65	18		63	17
Apr.	72F	22C	May	67F	19C	June	61F	16C
	58	14		52	11		49	9
July	61F	16C	Aug.	63F	17C	Sept.	67F	17C
	49	9		49	9		52	11
Oct.	72F	22C	Nov.	74F	23C	Dec.	77F	25C
	56	13		61	16		63	17

Airport

Kingford Smith International Airport is about 6 miles south of downtown Sydney. The two domestic airline terminals, although separate from the international terminal building, use the same runways and are linked to it by shuttle buses. Most international flights arrive in the early morning, after a 5 AM airport curfew is lifted, contributing to congestion in the overused international terminal. International departure tax is A$10. The domestic airlines (Ansett, Australian) have good club lounges in their terminals, some with reciprocal deals with major airlines—so check if your membership card will get you into their lounge. Airline arrivals/departures information: Domestic (tel. 02/0055–14626); International (tel. 02/0055–14627).

Airlines

Qantas Airways has the most flights to Sydney; its North American gateways are Los Angeles and San Francisco. It is exclusively an international carrier; the two first-class domestic carriers are Australian and Ansett Airlines. East-West Airlines also has jet service to many domestic destinations. American, Continental, United, and Qantas all have direct flights from North America, with connections in Honolulu.

Air New Zealand, 02/965–4111.
American, tel. 02/251–3288; 800/433–7300.
Ansett Airlines, tel. 02/268–1555.
Ansett New Zealand, tel. 02/268–1010.
Australian Airlines, tel. 02/693–3333; 800/922–5122.
British Airways, tel. 02/258–3300; 800/247–9297.
Canadian Airlines International, tel. 02/297–843; 800/426–7000.
Continental, tel. 02/232–8222; 800/525–0280.
East-West Airlines, tel. 02/268–1166.
Eastern Australian Airlines, tel. 02/693–1000.
Japan Airlines, tel. 02/233–4500; 800/525–3663.
Qantas, 02/957–0111; 800/227–4500.
Singapore Airlines, tel. 02/236–0111; 800/742–3333.
United, tel. 02/237–8888; 800/241–6522.

Between the Airport and Downtown

Taxis are the most convenient way to get downtown. Travel time is about 20 minutes by cab, or 30–40 minutes during rush hours (7:30–9 AM; 4:30–6PM). Some hotels have courtesy transportation; check when making hotel reservations.

By Taxi
There is a cab stand immediately outside the arrivals level. Metered cabs will cost A$13–A$20, with a maximum of 50 cents surcharge for luggage (charged by weight) and a A$1.50 toll for crossing the Sydney Harbor Bridge.

By Bus
The bright yellow **Airport Express** leaves from outside the international arrivals hall at 20-minute intervals, stopping to pick up passengers at domestic terminals. The trip to downtown Sydney costs A$5. Travel time to the city is about 30 minutes (40–50 minutes during rush hours), with stops at the Sydney Terminal railroad station and along

downtown's George Street (you can walk to several major hotels from here, or easily catch a cab).

Car Rentals

The following companies have booths at the airport:

Avis, tel. 02/561–2877; 800/331–1212.
Budget, tel. 02/339–8811; 800/527–0700.
Hertz, tel. 02/360–6621; 800/654–3131.
Thrifty, tel. 02/357–5399; 800/367–2277.

Dollar (tel. 02/332–1032; 800/421–6968) and **National** (tel. 02/332–1233; 800/328–4657) don't have airport booths, but they will meet flights. Local firms are less expensive; they don't meet flights but will usually deliver cars to hotels. Among the most reliable are **King's Cross Rent-A-Car** (tel. 02/361–0637) and **ABC Rent-A-Car** (tel. 02/357–7700).

Emergencies

For a list of approved physicians and clinics in Sydney that belong to the International Association for Medical Assistance to Travelers, contact IAMAT, 417 Center St., Lewiston, NY 14092, tel. 716/754–4883.

Doctors
Executive Health Medicenter (47 Phillip St., tel. 02/276–963), **Women's Medical Center** (10 Martin Pl., tel. 02/231–2366).

Dentists
Dental Emergency Services and Central Dental Laboratory (793 George St., tel. 02/211–1011).

Hospitals
St. Vincent's Hospital (corner of Victoria and Burton Sts., Darlinghurst, tel. 02/339–1111), **Sydney Hospital** (Macquarie St., tel. 02/228–2111).

Ambulance, Fire, Police
Tel. 000.

Important Addresses and Numbers

American Express (388 George St., tel. 02/886–1111).

Audiovisual rentals. Haycom Staging Propriety Ltd. (Unit 20, 17-21 Bowden St., Alexandria, tel. 02/319–0466).

British Consulate (Gold Fields House, Alfred St., Circular Quay, tel. 02/277–521).

Canadian Consulate (50 Bridge St., tel. 02/231–6522).

Computer rentals. Tech Rental (18 Hilly St., Mortlake, tel. 02/736–2066).

Convention and exhibition center. Sydney Convention and Exhibition Center (Darling Harbor, tel. 02/282–5000).

Fax services. Abbot Secretarial Services (14 Martin Pl., tel. 02/244–8988), Queens Court Business Center (118-122 Queen St., Woollahra, tel. 02/327–8296), Fax Bureau (119 Willoughby Rd., Crows Nest, tel. 02/436–0422).

Formal-wear rentals. American and Telford Formal Hire (Watson House, 2nd floor, 300 George St., tel. 02/232–1602).

Gift shops. Chocolates: Sweet Art (96 Oxford St., dington, tel. 02/361–6617); Flowers: Pearson's Florist (Queen Victoria Bldg., George St., tel. 02/389–0111); Gift baskets: A Basket For You (81 Military Rd., Neutral Bay, tel. 02/953–1033).

Graphic design studio. Imagecorp (50 Miller St., North Sydney, tel. 02/954–4066).

Hairstylists. Wentworth Men's Hairdressers (Lower Level, Sheraton-Wentworth Hotel, 61-101 Philip St., 02/233–2525); Trumps Hairdressing, unisex but mainly women (Qantas International Center, 243 George St., tel. 02/272–316).

Health and fitness clubs. *See* Fitness, below.

Information hot lines. Sydney Tourist Attractions (tel. 02/0055–20554), Sydney Nightlife (tel. 02/0055–20551), Ticketek Inpho for concerts, theaters (tel. 02/0055–50551).

Limousine services. Astra Limousines (tel. 02/699–2233), Legion Limousines (tel. 02/699–9722).

Liquor stores. Oddbins (46 York St., tel. 02/295–075), Paddington Fine Wines (306 South Dowling St., Paddington, tel. 02/332–1811).

Mail delivery, overnight. DHL International (tel. 02/317–8333), Federal Express (tel. 02/693–1544), TNT Skypak (tel. 02/319–2333), UPS (02/663–0774).

News programs. Radio: Australian Broadcasting Corporation (ABC) Radio National (AM 576) at 6 PM. TV: for international coverage, Special Broadcasting Service, SBS channel 0 (VHF), at 6:30 PM; best national coverage is on ABC, channel 2 at 7 PM.

Office space rentals. The Plaza (14 Marin Pl., tel. 02/233–7476), Servcorp (MLC Center, Corner Castlereagh and King Sts., tel. 02/238–2100), Sydney Commercial Center (99 York St., tel. 02/220–6700).

Pharmacies, late-night. Fountain Pharmacy (137 Maclay St., Potts Point, tel. 02/358–6463), Kings Cross Pharmacy (190 Victoria St., Kings Cross, tel. 02/358–5848).

Secretarial services. Cullen's Secretarial (34 Hunter St., tel. 02/235–0411), Intercity Business Center (203–233 New South Head Rd., Edgecliff, tel. 02/327–8333), Sydney Executive Centers (133 Alexander St., Crows Nest, tel. 02/439–5488).

Stationery supplies. Hemsworth Stationery Propriety Ltd. (44 Pitt St., tel. 02/272–949), W.C. Penfold & Co. Propriety Ltd., 88 Pitt St., tel. 02/233–5777).

Taxis. Combined (tel. 02/332–8888), Legion (tel. 02/20–918), Manly Warringah (tel. 02/977–9111), Premier (tel. 02/897–4000), St. George (tel. 02/533–1166).

Theater tickets. *See* The Arts, below.

Thomas Cook (175 Pitt St., tel. 02/229–6611).

Trade Ministry. Dept. of Foreign Affairs and Trade (100 William St., tel. 02/358–0222), International Trade Devel-

....nter (203 New South Head Rd., Edgecliff, tel. ....57).

.... information. Central Railway Station (Eddy Ave., 02/219–1067).

Translation services. European and Asian Language Center (Dymocks Bldg., 428 George St., tel. 02/233–1749), Associated Translators and Linguists (72 Pitt St., tel. 02/ 231–3288).

U.S. Consulate (corner Park and Elizabeth Sts., tel. 02/ 261–9200).

Weather (tel. 02/0055–29800).

Telephones

To make a local call, lift the receiver, drop in one 20-cent and one 10-cent coin, and dial. You get unlimited time for this 30 cents on a local call. For long distance calls, you can initially put in up to A$1 in any mix of 10-, 20-, 50-cent, and A$1 coins; deposit more coins when the red light near the dial starts flashing. If the call is unsuccessful, replace the receiver and the coins will be returned. Red pay phones are for local calls only. Dial "0" for collect calls; no money is needed. Phones accepting stored-value phone cards (sold at newsstands and other outlets) are being installed throughout the city.

Tipping

Concierge: A$2–A$5; doormen carrying bags to registration desk: A$1–A$2; porters carrying bags to room: A$1– A$2; room service: 10%; waiters: 10% (15% at a first-class restaurant when service is good); taxi drivers: round off to the nearest dollar, but for longer rides such as airport trips give about A$1–A$1.50.

DOING BUSINESS

Hours

Businesses: weekdays 9–5:30. **Banks:** weekdays 9:30–4, Fri. until 5. **Shops:** weekdays 9–5:30; many stores open to 8 PM Thurs., some stores open to 1 PM or as late as 4 PM on Sat., some stores open 10–4 Sun., particularly in tourist areas.

National Holidays

New Year's Day; Jan. 26, Australia Day; Good Fri.; Easter; Easter Mon.; April 16, Anzac Day; second Mon. in June, Queen's Birthday; first Mon. in Aug., Bank Holiday; first Mon. in Oct., Labor Day; Christmas; Dec. 26, Boxing Day.

Getting Around

By Car
Although Sydney drivers can be aggressive, the city is relatively easy to negotiate by car. Remember to drive on the left. Police road blocks (with alcohol Breathalyser tests) are commonplace, especially at night.

By Taxi
Taxis can be hailed on the street, hired at cab stands, ordered by your hotel, or summoned by phone (*see* Impor-

tant Addresses and Numbers, above). Expect
2:30–3:30 PM, when many drivers are involved in sh.
changeovers; during rush hours; and when it rains.

By Public Transportation
The downtown bus network is extensive. Ask at your hotel
for a map; fares begin at A$1.20. There's no need to have
exact change, but drivers will not accept 1-cent or 2-cent
coins, and may refuse bills larger than A$5. The elevated
monorail loop is convenient for those going to Darling
Harbor's convention, entertainment, and shopping facilities. Fare is A$2; a handy downtown station is City Cen-
ter, next to the Pitt Street entrance of the Hilton.

Protocol

Appointments
Australians have a reputation for informality, but you
should still be on time for appointments, or call to say
you're running late. Lunch meetings are common. If your
appointment is in the late afternoon, you'll probably end
up downing Australian beers at a nearby watering hole.

Customs
Australian customs are similar to North American ones,
but less formal than those in Great Britain. Australians
are quick to switch to first names as soon as a rapport is
established, often even at the first handshake. It's not
over-familiarity, it's simply the local norm. Nevertheless,
business cards are invariably exchanged—but without
ceremony.

Dress
Wear suits for business meetings (lightweight in summer),
smart casual clothes for dinner at a local associate's house,
and casual attire (even walking shorts and sandals) for a
Sunday barbecue in a suburban backyard. It's fine to take
off your jacket during a meeting. Women executives
should dress as they would at home, bearing in mind that,
in summer, bright colors and light fabrics are popular.

Gifts
If you are invited to someone's home, flowers or candy are
appropriate. Gifts aren't otherwise expected. However,
on return visits, after friendships are established, it's appropriate to bring something—a present evocative of your
home state, for instance.

LODGING

For most business travelers, an address in the heart of
downtown Sydney will be most convenient. However, the
city is compact enough that you can stay in other neighborhoods and still be able to walk or take a short cab ride
to downtown appointments. Excellent accommodations
also are available in The Rocks, a historic harborside area
that was the site of Sydney's original British settlement;
Chinatown, an increasingly upscale retail and restaurant
area adjoining the south end of downtown, and close to the
Darling Harbor convention facilities; and Kings Cross, the
city's lively nightlife area, a five-minute cab ride from center city. You can even stay at one of Sydney's best beaches,
and make an easy daily commute—13 minutes via hydro-

etings. Most Sydney hotels offer corporate ... or weekend discounts; inquire when making reservations.

...ly recommended lodgings in each price category are indicated by a star ★.

Category	Cost*
$$$$ (Very Expensive)	over A$241
$$$ (Expensive)	A$178–A$241
$$ (Moderate)	under A$178

All prices are for a standard double room, single occupancy. No taxes or service charges are added to Australian hotel bills.

Numbers in the margin correspond to numbered hotel locations on the Sydney Lodging and Dining map.

Downtown, Chinatown, and The Rocks

㉑
$$$ **Golden Gate Park Plaza.** This modern 18-floor high rise, opened in 1989, is located in a quiet corner of Chinatown, an easy walk to Darling Harbor, and a brisk 10-minute stroll to the heart of downtown. The busy black-marble lobby is furnished with comfortable couches and chairs; business guests can also stop for drinks in the mezzanine lounge. The rooms, some with balconies, are among the city's largest, and are furnished in pastels and light woods. Granite dominates the bathrooms. The hotel, which has played host to several major conventions, houses the Taiping (*see* Dining, below), one of Sydney's more sophisticated Chinese restaurants. There is a putting green on the premises. *A Park Inns International hotel. 169-179 Thomas St., 2000, tel. 02/281–6888, 800/ 437–7275, fax 02/281–6688. Gen. manager, Colin Southcoombe. 235 rooms, 15 suites. AE, DC, MC, V.*

⑲
$$$ **Hilton.** Formerly Sydney's top hotel, the Hilton is still among the city's best-run properties. A well-located downtown high-rise, it was built in 1973 and is currently being refurbished. Rooms, though smallish, are cheerfully decorated with light wood, brass light fittings, pastel hues, and prints of Australian landscapes. Rooms begin on the 20th floor of a 43-story building—above office space— and all have city views, some with the harbor as a backdrop. One drawback: the Hilton has busy restaurants, a cabaret (*see* After Hours, below), and bars that attract young, rowdy crowds from the local market. The San Francisco Grill (*see* Dining, below), the exception, attracts a sedate business crowd at lunch. The hotel's Henry the Ninth Bar is a pleasant spot to relax after work and listen to live Irish music. *259 Pitt St., 2000, tel. 02/266– 0610, 800/445–8667, fax 02/265–6065. Gen. manager, Oded Lifschitz. 556 rooms, 29 suites. AE, CB, DC, MC, V.*

⑩
$$$ **Holiday Inn Menzies.** The Menzies, as it's known, is a big, busy, mid-downtown property. The 14-story building was built in 1963, and completely refurbished in 1990. Rooms are done in earth tones, with fabric wall coverings and Victorian-style furniture. Ask for a room in the north wing; they're larger, and some overlook leafy Wynyard Park. Though the mirrored lobby area is small for a hotel of this size, there are numerous restaurants and bars. The

intimate Piano Bar, above the lobby, is a good p[...]
quiet, private conversation in cedar-paneled surroun[...]
ings. *14 Carrington St., 2000, tel. 02/20232, 800/465–4329,
fax 02/290–3819. Gen. manager, Norbert Uhlig. 401
rooms, 41 suites. AE, DC, MC, V.*

★ ⑰ **InterContinental.** One of Sydney's most distinctive hotels
$$$$ combines the New South Wales Treasury building—a colonial landmark built in 1849—with a modern 31-story
tower. The Treasury building's domed Italianate indoor
courtyard serves as the lobby area, and from there graceful sandstone arcades lead to restaurants and shops. Cocktails and afternoon tea are served in the Cortille lobby
bar. Accommodations are large and modern, with cream-
colored fabrics, capacious armchairs, fresh Australian
wildflowers, and pen-and-ink drawings of Australian
scenes; unusually large desks are positioned along
ultralarge windows. The best rooms have harbor views.
The InterContinental's dining room, Treasury (*see* Dining, below), is one of the best hotel restaurants in Sydney.
Executive floors offer extra amenities such as butler service, and video and CD libraries. *An InterContinental hotel. 117 Macquarie St., 2000, tel. 02/230–0200, 800/327–
0200, fax 251–2342. Gen. manager, Wolfgang Grimm. 424
rooms, 42 suites. AE, CB, DC, MC, V.*

★ ⑥ **Old Sydney Parkroyal.** This hybrid in the historic Rocks
$$$ quarter, only a few minutes on foot from downtown, is
part modern building and part 1926 warehouse: The eight-
story, officially protected 1926 walls form two sides of the
atrium, but everything else in the hotel complex dates
from 1984. Renovations were completed in September,
1990. The sweeping lobby, which looks as though it be-
longs to a far larger place, and greenery-and-flag-be-
decked atrium provide access to Argyle Lane, a shopping
mall fringed by old buildings, restaurants, and handi-
craft stores. The best of the hotel's spacious, modern
rooms—now done in pinks and grays—have views of Syd-
ney Opera House (as does the rooftop pool). Popular with
North American tourists, this property nevertheless has
a core of business regulars—many of whom stay here to
enjoy the Rocks ambience but go up the street to the Club
Bar at the Regent of Sydney to meet business guests they
want to impress. *A Southern Pacific Hotel, 55 George St.,
2000, tel. 02/252–0524, 800/421–0536, fax 02/251–2092.
Gen. manager, Peter A. Hobbs. 170 rooms, 4 suites. AE,
DC, MC, V.*

⑤ **Park Hyatt.** This new (1990) hotel isn't yet fully into its
$$$$ stride, but aspires to be Sydney's top property. It's al-
ready on a par with the InterContinental, Regent, and
Ritz Carlton—and already commands the city's top price.
The Park Hyatt's location can't be beat: The pink low rise,
with its harborside rooms, is in the heart of The Rocks,
on a tranquil waterfront cove overlooking the busy harbor
and with postcard views of the Opera House. The staff has
been culled from other leading Sydney hotels, and service
standards are very high. Despite the property's laid-back
harborside feel, its business services are excellent too.
Rooms, in light hues, are spacious, with large desks facing
the water. Some have balconies. Bathrooms have TV sets
mounted above the tubs. The bright, stylish public areas
have floor-to-ceiling windows. For business entertaining,
the hotel's main restaurant, Number 7, is quickly making

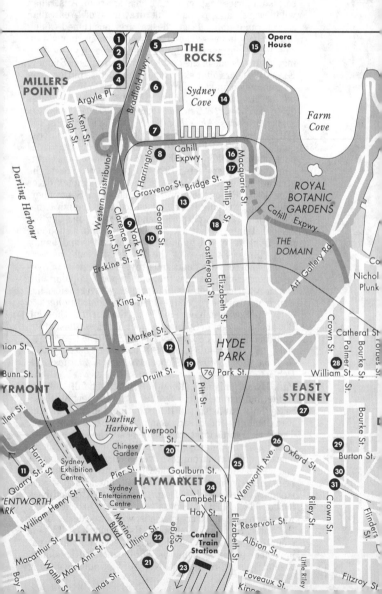

KEY

— Rail Lines
- - - Monorail

SYDNEY HOTEL CHART

HOTELS	Price Category	Business Services Banquet capacity	No. of meeting rooms	Fax	Telex	Photocopying	Secretarial services	Audiovisual equipment	Translation services	International direct dial	Computer rentals	In-room modem phonejack
Airport Hilton	$$$	500	7	✓	✓	✓	✓	✓	✓	✓	✓	✓
Boulevard Parkroyal	$$$	480	7	✓	✓	✓	✓	✓	✓	✓	✓	✓
Centra North Sydney	$$$	0	0	✓	✓	✓	✓	✓	–	✓	–	–
Gazebo	$$	380	6	✓	✓	✓	–	✓	–	✓	–	✓
Golden Gate Park Plaza	$$$	270	8	✓	✓	✓	✓	✓	✓	✓	✓	✓
Hilton	$$$	640	8	✓	✓	✓	✓	✓	✓	✓	✓	✓
Holiday Inn Menzies	$$$	350	7	✓	✓	✓	✓	✓	✓	✓	✓	✓
Hyatt Kingsgate	$$$	600	14	✓	✓	✓	✓	✓	✓	✓	✓	–
InterContinental	$$$$	300	10	✓	✓	✓	✓	✓	✓	✓	✓	✓
Manly Pacific Parkroyal	$$$	600	7	✓	✓	✓	✓	✓	✓	✓	✓	–
Nikko	$$$	500	7	✓	✓	✓	✓	✓	✓	✓	✓	–
Old Sydney Parkroyal	$$$	40	1	✓	✓	✓	✓	✓	✓	✓	✓	–
Park Hyatt	$$$$	55	4	✓	✓	✓	✓	✓	✓	✓	–	✓
Ramada Renaissance	$$$	250	4	✓	✓	✓	✓	✓	✓	✓	✓	✓
Regent of Sydney	$$$$	600	7	✓	✓	✓	✓	✓	✓	✓	✓	✓
Resort Hotel Macquarie	$$$	200	10	✓	✓	✓	✓	✓	✓	✓	–	–
Ritz-Carlton	$$$$	100	2	✓	✓	✓	✓	✓	✓	✓	✓	✓
Royal Garden	$$	0	0	✓	✓	✓	✓	–	✓	✓	–	–
Russell	$$	0	0	✓	✓	✓	–	–	–	✓	–	–

$$$$ = over A$241, **$$$** = A$178 - A$241, **$$** = under A$178.
● good, ◕ fair, ○ poor.

All-news cable channel	Desk	Desk lighting	Bed lighting	In-Room Amenities Nonsmoking rooms	In-room checkout	Minibar	Toiletries	Room service	Laundry/Dry cleaning	Pressing	Hotel Amenities Barber/Hairdresser	Garage	Courtesy airport transport	Sauna	Pool	Exercise room
✓	●	●	●	✓	✓	✓	●	●	●	●	-	✓	✓	-	●	-
✓	●	●	●	✓	✓	✓	●	●	●	●	✓	✓	-	✓	-	-
-	●	●	●	✓	✓	✓	◐	●	◐	●	-	✓	-	-	◐	-
✓	◐	◐	●	-	-	✓	◐	●	●	●	-	✓	✓	✓	●	-
✓	●	●	●	✓	✓	✓	●	●	●	●	-	✓	✓	-	●	-
✓	●	●	●	✓	✓	✓	●	●	●	●	✓	✓	-	✓	●	●
✓	●	●	●	✓	-	✓	◐	●	●	●	-	-	✓	✓	●	◐
-	●	●	●	✓	✓	✓	●	●	●	●	✓	✓	✓	✓	◐	◐
✓	●	●	●	✓	✓	✓	●	●	●	●	✓	✓	-	✓	●	●
✓	●	●	●	✓	✓	✓	●	●	●	●	-	✓	-	●	●	●
-	●	●	●	✓	✓	✓	●	●	●	●	-	✓	-	-	●	-
-	●	●	●	✓	-	✓	●	●	●	●	-	✓	-	✓	○	-
-	●	●	●	✓	✓	✓	●	●	●	●	✓	✓	-	✓	●	●
-	●	●	●	✓	-	✓	●	●	●	◐	-	✓	-	✓	●	◐
✓	●	●	●	-	✓	✓	●	●	●	●	✓	✓	-	-	●	-
-	●	●	●	✓	✓	✓	◐	●	●	-	-	✓	-	✓	●	●
✓	●	●	●	✓	✓	✓	●	●	●	●	-	✓	✓	✓	●	●
✓	●	●	●	✓	-	✓	●	◐	●	◐	-	✓	✓	✓	●	-
-	●	●	●	-	-	-	-	●	●	●	-	✓	✓	-	-	-

Room service: ● 24-hour, ◐ 6AM-10PM, ○ other.
Laundry/Dry cleaning: ● same day, ◐ overnight, ○ other.
Pressing: ● immediate, ◐ same day, ○ other.

SYDNEY HOTEL CHART

HOTELS	Price Category	Banquet capacity	No. of meeting rooms	Fax	Telex	Photocopying	Secretarial services	Audiovisual equipment	Translation services	International direct dial	Computer rentals	In-room modem phone jack
Sebel Town House	$$$	400	6	✓	✓	✓	✓	✓	✓	✓	–	✓
Sheraton Wentworth	$$$	630	6	✓	✓	✓	✓	✓	✓	✓	✓	✓
Southern Cross	$$$	220	4	✓	✓	✓	✓	✓	✓	✓	✓	✓
Wynyard Travelodge	$$$	300	4	✓	✓	✓	✓	✓	–	✓	✓	–

$$$$ = over A$241, $$$ = A$178 - A$241, $$ = under A$178.
● good, ◑ fair, ○ poor.

All-news cable channel	Desk	Desk lighting	Bed lighting	In-Room Amenities	Nonsmoking rooms	In-room checkout	Minibar	Toiletries	Room service	Laundry/Dry cleaning	Pressing	Hotel Amenities	Barber/Hairdresser	Garage	Courtesy airport transport	Sauna	Pool	Exercise room
✓	●	●	●		✓	-	✓	●	●	●	●		✓	✓	-	✓	●	●
✓	●	●	●		✓	-	✓	●	●	◐	●		✓	✓	-	-	-	◐
-	●	●	●		-	-	✓	●	●	●	●		-	-	✓	✓	●	◐
✓	●	●	●		✓	-	✓	●	●	●	●		-	✓	-	-	-	-

Room service: ● 24-hour, ◐ 6AM–10PM, ○ other.
Laundry/Dry cleaning: ● same day, ◐ overnight, ○ other.
Pressing: ● immediate, ◐ same day, ○ other.

its mark as a chic spot for Australian and Continental cuisine. *7 Hickson Rd., 2000, tel. 02/241–1234, 800/233–1234, fax 02/256–1555. Gen. manager, Willi Martin. 147 rooms, 12 suites. AE, CB, DC, MC, V.*

⑬ **Ramada Renaissance.** This 32-floor high rise (with four
$$$ Renaissance Club Executive Floors) opened in 1989 in an excellent location for central-city business. Generally bland and modern public areas are made attractive by original Australian art and colonial antiques. A famous old two-story Aussie pub, incorporated in the design, now serves as the hotel's busy banker-and-broker bar, and, on the upper level, as its fine-dining restaurant, Raphaels (*see* Dining, below). Guest rooms are decorated in varying light hues, some with cheery floral fabrics; suites have Colonial-era antiques, including four-poster beds in some. Ask for a room with a harbor view. The Oyster Bar has become a place to be seen for business lunchers; many well-known faces in the financial district zip in for a fast order of famous Sydney oysters and a glass of Australian wine. *30 Pitt St., 2000, tel. 02/259–7000, 800/228–9898, fax 02/252–1999. Gen manager, Ulrich Renner. 494 rooms, 68 suites. AE, CB, DC, MC, V.*

★ ⑧ **Regent of Sydney.** This 34-floor high rise, built in 1982 at
$$$$ the border of downtown and The Rocks, and a short walk from the Sydney Opera House, draws a loyal following of well-heeled guests. The three-story lobby, with its potted trees and polished pink marble, hums softly with discreet activity. A room renovation program was recently completed. Most accommodations are done in pastels, with light Tasmanian oak tables and writing desks; in many rooms, there are harbor views encompassing both the Harbor Bridge and Sydney Opera House through floor-to-ceiling windows. Sydney's best hotel restaurant, Kables (*see* Dining, below), is here, and the Club bar (*see* After Hours, below) is a popular after-work gathering place for businesspeople. *A Regent International hotel, 199 George St., 2000, tel. 02/238–0000, 800/545–4000, fax 02/251–2851. Gen. manager, Ted Wright. 578 rooms, 42 suites. AE, CB, DC, MC, V.*

⑯ **Ritz-Carlton.** It's still too soon to judge this small, clublike
$$$$ property near the New South Wales State Parliament building. Opened in August 1990, it promises to provide all the attention to personal service that has distinguished the Ritz-Carlton hotel chain. Elegant guest rooms, with classical French influence, are among the city's largest; most have balconies. A European ambience is achieved in the formal, marble-floored public areas with 18th- and 19th-century oil paintings, fireplaces, and well-chosen antiques. The Café, a spacious brasserie, attracts many corporate lunchers with its high standards and location in the business district. *A Ritz-Carlton hotel. 93 Macquarie St., 2000, tel. 02/252–4600, 800/241–3333, fax 02/252–4286. Gen. manager, Thomas A. Klein. 93 rooms, 13 suites. AE, CB, DC, MC, V.*

㉔ **Royal Garden.** This modern 13-floor building, opened in
$$ 1989 at the edge of Chinatown, is one of those free-from-personality places: small, functional, with clean rooms and an efficient, eager-to-please staff. It's in a good location for downtown meetings, but the best reason for staying here would be to cut costs. A bonus is the Royal Court, the hotel's highly regarded Cantonese restaurant. Most of

the hotel's guests are package tourists. *431-439 Pitt St., 2000, tel. 02/281-6999, fax 02/281-6988. Gen. manager, Robert Craig. 120 rooms, 40 suites. AE, DC, MC, V.*

★ **7** **Russell.** Like an exclusive European *pension*, the 102-
$$ year-old, creamy pink, three-story Russell—a few doors down from the Regent of Sydney—is the local leader among increasingly popular boutique hotels. A discovery that's highly regarded by its regulars, the Russell is not the most convenient for business travelers who don't have an office base in the city—or aren't prepared to zip next door to use the Regent's five-star facilities. This doesn't stop theatrical agents (and movie actors such as Bryan Brown and his wife, Rachel Ward), as well as advertising executives, from checking in. Rooms—some with fireplaces—are all individually decorated: For example, an Australian colonial room is done in rose and green, a blue-and-white country-style room features white wicker chairs, and another is decorated in Laura Ashley–type florals. Of the 18 rooms, only 5 have their own bathrooms. (All rooms are supplied with designer bathrobes, however—useful if you have to go padding down the hall.) *143A George St., 2000, tel. 02/241-3543, fax 02/252-1652. Gen manager, Carl Malmberg. 18 rooms. AE, DC, MC, V.*

18 **Sheraton Wentworth.** At the heart of Sydney's financial
$$$ area, this 35-year-old hotel has high occupancy rates built on a core of business and professional repeat visitors. The red-carpeted, crystal-chandeliered lobby has a Lobby Bar (*see* After Hours, below) that's been the scene of many a hushed business meeting. In recent years the bar's heavily masculine accent has softened—they even serve sushi—and women, alone or in groups, are no longer an oddity here. The recently refurbished rooms, where heavy, dark woods have given way to salmon-pink and similar pastels, are well appointed. The hotel has a complimentary hospitality suite for early arrivals (especially helpful for travelers arriving from the United States) and late departures. *61-101 Philip St., 2000, tel. 02/230-0700, 800/325-3532, fax 02/227-9133. Gen manager, Art Nigro. 401 rooms, 32 suites. AE, DC, MC, V.*

25 **Southern Cross.** In 1983, a former warren of garment fac-
$$$ tories was gutted and re-emerged as the five-star Southern Cross hotel. The nine-floor building was refurbished in 1988. Guests, a mix of businesspeople and tourists, have included Whitney Houston and Stevie Wonder. The property isn't the city's most opulent, but it's modern and comfortable. The lobby is small, with cushy armchairs and couches, and the rooms are spacious and furnished in browns and beiges. This address is convenient for downtown business and is also handy for Chinatown and the Darling Harbor area. For a taste of local political and social controversies, examine the original drawings by leading political cartoonists in the off-the-lobby Cartoon Bar. *Corner of Elizabeth and Goulburn Sts., 2000, tel. 02/20987, 800/448-8355, fax 02/211-1806. Gen. manager, George Bedwani. 168 rooms, 13 suites. AE, DC, MC, V.*

9 **Wynyard Travelodge.** This well-staffed, 21-story high rise
$$$ was built in 1976 and last renovated in 1986. The guests are mostly business travelers who appreciate the hotel's no-nonsense style. Aside from their excellent city views, large desks, and comfy chairs, rooms are forgettable.

During busy times, the small lobby, done in gray marble and bleached wood, can get very crowded. Kache (*see* Dining, below), a rooftop restaurant and bar, is a pleasant place for evening cocktails. *A Southern Pacific Hotel. 7-9 York St., 2000, tel. 02/20254, 800/421–0536, fax 02/ 262–2416. Gen. manager, Herbert Nussbaumer. 119 rooms, 1 suite. AE, DC, MC, V.*

Kings Cross

❷⓼
$$$
Boulevard Parkroyal. Though most business visitors prefer to stay downtown, others like to be close to the Kings Cross entertainment quarter. For those who can't decide, the Boulevard Parkroyal is appropriate—it's a five-minute walk uphill to Kings Cross and an eight-minute walk, mostly downhill, to the downtown area. The hotel was built in 1973 and refurbished in 1987. Some of the larger-than-average rooms have bright floral bedspreads and drapes. Others are decorated in a stark Japanese style, with slim black-framed chairs and shiny black-topped wooden desks. The lobby, furnished with deep armchairs and Persian rugs, has a small lounge area where drinks are served from a cart. The rooftop bar/restaurant offers lovely views of the harbor and the Botanic Gardens. *A Southern Pacific Hotel. 90 William St., 2011, tel.`02/357– 2277, 800/421–0536, fax 02/356–3786. Gen. manager, Ko Buisman. 274 rooms, 12 suites. AE, DC, MC, V.*

★ ❸⓺
$$
Gazebo. This hotel next to the El Alamein Fountain in Kings Cross, at the boundary of the Elizabeth Bay area, has been a circular landmark since 1967. The 18-floor, 400-room Gazebo had a new rectangular wing built in 1985, but wise guests will insist on an upper-level, harbor-view room in the old wing (despite the property's sluggish elevators; avoid noisy rooms near the elevators). Accommodations aren't great, but the telephones have wires long enough to allow one to work on the curved balcony while enjoying a vista of Sydney's harbor, Harbor Bridge, and Opera House. At sunset, the rooftop Panorama Room Bar is well worth a visit. The busy lobby is often cluttered with the baggage of Japanese package tourists, and there are quite a few business travelers attracted by upscale amenities at moderate prices (even though business facilities are very basic). *2 Elizabeth Bay Rd., Elizabeth Bay, 2011, tel. 02/358–1999, fax 02/356–2951. Gen. manager, Peter Wise. 390 rooms, 10 suites. AE, DC, MC, V.*

❸⓷
$$$
Kingsgate. This landmark behind the big Kings Cross Coca-Cola sign is a rather standard Hyatt—and definitely No. 2 now that the Park Hyatt has opened. The hotel's public areas are blandly unimpressive (except for the justly celebrated Craigend restaurant, which draws a loyal lunchtime business crowd). Service, however, is good and the business center is first-class. The hotel depends heavily on package-tour groups, conventions, and air crews, but there is a body of loyal business travelers attracted by its location in the heart of the Kings Cross nightlife area and its easy accessibility (a 5-minute cab ride) to downtown. Guest rooms—upgraded in 1987—are modern, with good desk space (plus gray leather sofas and armchairs in suites). Rooms on the upper floors of this 33-story tower have superb city-and-harbor views. There are three Regency club floors, which provide executive perks. *Top of William St., 2011, tel. 02/356–1234, 800/228–9000, fax 02/*

356–4150. Gen. manager, Mustafa Issa. 267 rooms, 15 suites. AE, DC, MC, V.

㉟ **Nikko.** Part of the Japan Airlines–owned accommodation
$$$ chain, the Nikko, opened in September 1990, is unapologetically ultramodern in decor. Business services are good, because the hotel is geared to Japan's globe-trotting businessfolk. It's too soon to judge either service or clientele, but the hotel is likely to attract many North American and European business travelers; public areas are already filled with gray suits. A two-minute walk from the nightlife of Kings Cross, in a neighborhood called Potts Point, the 17-story hotel is seven minutes by cab, in average traffic, from downtown. (This is a handy area for taxis.) The chic, modern rooms, done in pastel shades, all have harbor views. Try the Tavern Bar for its informal "Aussie pub" atmosphere. *81 Macleay St., Potts Point, 2011, tel. 02/357–3300, 800/645–5687, fax 02/358–6631. Gen. manager, Jean-Marie Leclercq. 457 rooms, 13 suites. AE, CB, DC, MC, V.*

㊲ **Sebel Town House.** In the residential Elizabeth Bay area,
$$$ only a two-minute walk from Kings Cross, this 11-story property (built in 1963 but refurbished in 1988) is less than 10 minutes from downtown. Business guests are often in the music, film, or advertising industries, and movie stars such as Tom Selleck and Shirley Maclaine also favor "the Sebel." The rooftop pool and the hotel's small bar—lined with framed photos of celebrity guests—are the places to rub shoulders with whomever the groupies camped out across the street are waiting for. Wood-paneled rooms, many with city and harbor views, are spacious and comfortable, with large desks and deep armchairs in pastel shades. Drawbacks: The switchboard is sometimes slow to answer incoming calls, and the staff tends to make much more fuss over those it recognizes. *25 Elizabeth Bay Rd., 2011, tel. 02/358–3244, 800/223–6800, fax 02/357–1926. Gen. manager, Michael J. Hall. 142 rooms, 26 suites. AE, DC, MC, V.*

Suburbs

② **Centra North Sydney.** Just across the Sydney Harbor
$$$ Bridge from downtown is North Sydney, home to much of the advertising, insurance, and computer industries. A time-saving option, if you have business in North Sydney and you want to avoid a daily bridge commute of 5–15 minutes, is this 1970-vintage, 14-floor property, which was smartly spruced up in 1990. The hotel is within walking distance of most North Sydney businesses. All the rooms are motel modern, done in pastel shades with Aussie prints on the walls; the ones on the higher floors have the best harbor views. The business services are efficient, and the lobby is small but functional. Although the hotel's restaurant and bar are just acceptable, the area is awash with good dining and drinking choices. *A Southern Pacific Hotel. 17 Blue St., North Sydney, 2060, tel. 02/955–0499, 800/421–0536, fax 02/922–3689. Gen. manager, Ross Smith. 215 rooms. AE, DC, MC, V.*

★ ① **Manly Pacific Parkroyal.** For travelers with time to com-
$$$ bine business with pleasure, the Manly Pacific Parkroyal, located just across the street from one of Sydney's best beaches, is the place to stay. This modern seven-floor hotel, renovated in 1989, has large rooms with balconies (ask

for a room with a water view) and relaxing sky-blue, pink, or beige furnishings. The downtown area is easily accessible by hydrofoil or fast catamaran (13 minutes to Circular Quay), and Manly has many good restaurants as well as shops. Joggers will enjoy running along the beachfront promenade. *A Southern Pacific Hotel. 55 N. Steyne, Manly, 2095, tel. 02/977–7666, 800/421–0536, fax 02/977–7822. Gen. manager, Karl Kranzie. 180 rooms, 10 suites. AE, DC, MC, V.*

⑪ **Resort Hotel Macquarie.** This all-suite hotel is 10 miles
$$$ from downtown, amid computer companies and other light industry. The property makes the most of its almost rural location; its rooms are built around a vast swimming pool, and facilities include a jogging track and tennis courts. Golf is nearby. The all-suite configuration is appealing to businesspeople who use the extra room (with desk) as either a sitting room or as a daytime office. The atmosphere in the rooms and public areas is warm and clublike, with dark woods and deep red coloring. In the evenings, the bar is thick with corporate talk. *Corner of Epping and Herring Rds., North Ryde, 2113, tel. 02/805–1888, 800/448–8355, fax 02/805–0538. Gen. manager, Robyn Stevenson. 228 suites. AE, DC, MC, V.*

Airport

㉓ **Sydney Airport Hilton.** This compact, 11-floor property
$$$ was recently refurbished with Australian country-style furnishings. Rooms are smallish, well soundproofed, and have good-size desks. The cocktail bar hums with aviation industry gossip at night, and Amy's is the airport area's lively nightspot. *20 Levey St., Arncliffe, 2205, tel. 02/597–0122, 800/445–8667, fax 02/597–6381. Gen. manager, Ruth Harrison. 170 rooms, 10 suites. AE, DC, MC, V.*

DINING

An increasingly cosmopolitan city, Sydney offers diners a wide choice of cuisines. As you might expect, there are restaurants with standard European and Continental menus, but you'll also find a few small eateries serving African or South American food, or Maori food from neighboring New Zealand. Many Asian cuisines are available here too, even Burmese and Laotian.

"Modern Australian"—nouvelle-influenced French-style cuisine using fresh Australian meats, seafood, and vegetables—is becoming increasingly popular. But it's also possible to find places serving traditional country-style "Aussie roasts"—English-influenced beef and lamb dishes served in generous portions. In addition, "bush tucker"—the food of aborigines and early settlers—is becoming available at some upscale establishments. The adventurous might try crocodile or buffalo from the Northern Territory, or witchety grubs, small insects that are an aboriginal delicacy.

Sydney's restaurants range from tiny oyster bars to flashy, faddish eateries and luxurious hotel dining rooms. The latest trend is toward informal brasserie-style establishments. Since the city is so compact, most restaurants, even those in the inner suburbs, are easily accessible by cab.

Highly recommended restaurants in each category are indicated by a star ★.

Category	Cost*
$$$$ (Very Expensive)	over A$85
$$$ (Expensive)	A$35–A$85
$$ (Moderate)	under A$35

per person, including appetizer, entrée, and dessert but excluding drinks and tips. There are no service charges or taxes.

Numbers in the margin correspond to numbered restaurant locations on the Sydney Lodging and Dining map.

Wine

Following are the best years for these excellent Australian wines:

Whites
Hunter Valley Semillion: 79, 84
Yarra Valley Chardonnay: 83, 68

Reds
Margaret River Cabernet-Sauvignon: 82, 84

Beer and Ale

In bottles try Hahn or Toohey's Dry. On tap try Fosters.

Business Breakfasts

Power breakfasts are becoming increasingly popular, although they are still not a common custom. However, it's perfectly acceptable to ask an associate to meet you for breakfast. Numerous downtown coffee shops serve reasonable breakfasts; typical and above average is **La Cité** (Queen Victoria Building, opposite the Hilton, George St., tel. 02/267–9171). But hotel coffee shops or restaurants are your best bets: The **InterContinental** (tel. 02/230–0200), **Regent** (tel. 02/238–0000), and **Sebel Town House** (tel. 02/358–3244) are top choices in this department.

Brunches have a growing following on Sundays: join a smart-casual set for seafood and champagne at **Jordan's** (197 Harborside Festival Marketplace, Darling Harbor, tel. 02/281–3711), and then stroll through Darling Harbor's exhibitions, boutiques, and bars (some with live jazz). However, the most popular brunch custom in Sydney is to head for Chinatown for *dim sum*. Recommended among several Hong Kong-style places are the large **Marigold** (299 Sussex St., tel. 02/264–6744) and the small **May Flower** (160 Thomas St., tel. 02/211–1602).

Downtown and Nearby

★ ㉜   **Afrilanka.** Amel and Mohamed Digne wanted to open a
$$$ restaurant but couldn't agree on whether to go for his homeland cuisine (Senegalese) or hers (Sri Lankan). The result: They serve both. Decorated with African masks on one wall, Sri Lankan artifacts on the other, Afrilanka is a

small, friendly place, perfect for dining alone after work. The tables are laid with black cloths, and the waiters wear floor-length West African robes. Asian dishes are confined to those of Sri Lanka, but the African section takes in dishes from all over that continent. From Sri Lanka, try a spicy beef curry; from Africa, there's couscous, or *theibo diene* (a spicy fish dish from the Ivory Coast). *237 Oxford St., tel. 02/360–4946. Smart, casual dress. Reservations advised. MC, V. Dinner only; closed Sun.*

★ ❷⓻ **Beppi's.** A Sydney institution, this 35-year-old establish-
$$$ ment—doyen of the city's Italian eateries—is a favorite of business leaders and show-biz celebrities, many of whom are known to owner Beppi Polese. First-class Italian food and highly professional, noncondescending service have helped build a big clientele over the years. The restaurant, decorated in deep reds and lots of mirrors, is an excellent venue for business conversation: though not overly spacious, the dining room affords a more-than-adequate degree of privacy. Poached Atlantic salmon with chive mayonnaise is a good choice here, as are the mussels *all'agro* (marinated in olive oil and lemon dressing). There's a well-chosen and extensive wine list. *Corner of Yurong and Stanley Sts., East Sydney, tel. 02/360–4558. Jacket and tie preferred. Reservations advised. AE, DC, MC, V. Closed Sun.*

❷⓺ **Burdekin Dining Room.** This old-style "Aussie pub" has a
$$$ busy street-level bar, but that's not the attraction here. In the back of the building is the basement Dug Out Bar, serving Sydney's best martini, made by much-praised bartender Justin Brash. Upstairs (take the creaking steel-cage elevator) is the Burdekin's dining room, a small (45-seater) but uncramped Art Deco oasis. Regulars here include businesspeople, media types, and fashion designers from nearby clothing companies. Recommended on the small menu, which has a seafood emphasis, are grilled barramundi (a highly regarded fish from Australian waters) and poached Tasmanian salmon. *2-4 Oxford St., tel. 02/331–1046. Smart, casual dress. Reservations essential. AE, DC, MC, V. Closed Sun.*

❷⓪ **Capitan Torres.** On Sydney's small "Spanish strip" at the
$$ edge of Chinatown, Capitan Torres is decorated with lots of wrought iron, heavy wooden beams, tiled floors, and white-plastered walls hung with wood-carved pictures. The high-back chairs provide a feeling of privacy—and noise levels at night allow conversation but make eavesdropping difficult. To enjoy Sydney seafood Spanish-style, try the *combinado de mariscos* (mussels, squid, prawns, and several types of fish in a moderately spicy sauce) or *parrillada de pescado* (mixed grilled seafood). This is also a good Sunday brunch spot. *73 Liverpool St., tel. 02/264–5574. Smart, casual dress. Reservations not necessary. AE, DC, MC, V.*

★ ❸⓷ **Chitose.** This is one of Sydney's most outstanding Japa-
$$$ nese restaurants. Located off the lobby of the Hyatt Kingsgate, this starkly modern spot is done in black lacquer and gray with marble floors. The dining area has well-spaced tables for business conversation, and private tatami rooms are down a flight of stairs. However, if the occasion doesn't demand privacy, it's far better to opt for the well-stocked sushi bar. Aside from sushi and sashimi, rewarding choices here would be grilled *unajyu* (freshwa-

ter eel) or *hitokuchi hirekatsu* (breaded deep-fried pork fillet). *412 Kingsgate Shopping Center, Top of William St. (enter from Hyatt Kingsgate lobby), tel. 02/358–6932. Smart, casual dress. Reservations advised. AE, DC, MC, V. Closed Monday; dinner only weekends.*

⑮ **Harbor Restaurant.** Go around the back of Sydney Opera
$$$ House; there, at the water's edge, beneath the unique, sail-like roof, is the Harbor Restaurant. Within easy walking distance of the downtown business area, this nautical blue-and-white restaurant is rather bare of decor, but then you're here for a priceless harbor vista. It's a good choice for an informal head-to-head business discussion while wrestling with fresh crab and lobster. Less messy options: King prawn salad or poached Tasmanian ocean trout. Most tables are outdoors. Though somewhat touristy, this place nonetheless attracts a large number of locals with its well-presented, superbly fresh Sydney seafood. High prices keep out the tour-bus hordes. *Sydney Opera House, Northern Broadwalk, tel. 02/250–7581. Smart, casual dress. Reservations not necessary. AE, DC, MC, V. Closed Sun.*

★ ⑫ **Jin Jiang.** In an upstairs corner of the Queen Victoria
$$$ Building—an expensive downtown shopping mall—is one of Sydney's two most sophisticated Chinese restaurants (the other is Cleveland—*see* below). Chairs and tables are made of Chinese rosewoods; turquoise tablecloths complement the furnishings. The chefs and some of the waiters are here from China on arrangement with the Chinese government. This is one of the downtown area's best spots for business discussions, with ample space between tables, and an attentive and knowledgeable staff. Sesame chicken or deep-fried squid dipped in rock salt and pepper are notable dishes. *2nd floor, Queen Victoria Building, George St., (opposite the Hilton), tel. 02/261–3388. Smart, casual dress. Reservations advised. AE, DC, MC, V.*

★ ⑧ **Kables.** For business entertaining, the Regent of Sydney's
$$$$ flagship restaurant is the safe place to go on those occasions when you can't afford to have anything go wrong. Large tables are set far apart in the elegant, spacious room, where diners enjoy a standard of service equaled only by the InterContinental's Treasury (*see* below). Expect to spend at least 90 minutes at lunch and several hours at dinner. The menu is modern Australian, with French and other European influences. For quality and originality, the food here is among the best available in Sydney—with prices to match. Appetizers include lasagna of white Queensland scallops with asparagus, tomato, and tarragon coulis. Among French Canadian chef Serge Dansereau's main courses is roast rack of Australian lamb with sweetcorn cakes, chili, and mint chutney. The extensive international wine list features prized Australian vintages. Service is impeccable. *Regent of Sydney, 179 George St., tel. 02/238–0000. Jacket and tie required. Reservations required. AE, CB, DC, MC, V.*

⑨ **Kache.** Located at top of the Wynyard Travelodge, Kache
$$$ has great Sydney skyline views. It's one of those often-full business lunch places that no one seems to have heard of (except, presumably, the many regulars); you may impress your colleagues by bringing them to this "secret" spot. Although the menu is modern-Australian-cum-European, the decor has Japanese touches—clean lines, an

outdoor Japanese garden with a decorative pool—and a good deal more style than the hotel beneath it. Recommendations include Snowy Mountain rainbow trout, poached with a lime sabayon; and Australian beef fillet medallions with Burgundy and blackcurrant sauce. The fare is well above the standard one might expect from a rooftop dining room. *Wynyard Travelodge, 7-9 York St., tel. 02/20254. Jacket and tie preferred; smart, casual dress acceptable. Reservations advised. AE, DC, MC, V. Closed weekends.*

㉙ **La Fine Bouche.** Tony Bilson, one of Sydney's most influ-
$$$ ential chefs, worked at several prime locations around town before he opened his own French-influenced modern Australian restaurant on one floor of a three-story former warehouse/office building close to downtown. Long, padded benches run along the rather spare, brightly lighted room, providing seating for tables well spaced for private talks. Plain pastel-blue walls are hung with large contemporary Australian paintings. The fixed-price menu offers a choice of two or three courses; there's no à la carte option. Bilson changes the menu radically with regularity. Try exotica such as duck's neck in pastry—or staples such as roasted rack of lamb with herbs. *191 Palmer St., East Sydney, tel. 02/331-4821. Smart, casual dress. Reservations advised. AE, DC, MC, V. Closed Sun., Tues., lunch.*

★ ❸ ㉒ **Malaya.** Long a scruffy hangout for students, professors,
$$ and journalists, the Malaya was reborn in 1987 a few doors from its old location. Now, excellent Malaysian fare is served amid elegant, modern, gray-and-black Italian decor. Prices have remained low, so students from the nearby University of Sydney are still here, as are editorial types from the *Sydney Morning Herald* and *Australian Financial Review*, but there's been an infusion of businesspeople, too. Bowls of noodle-based *laksa* (chicken or seafood are best) and spicy beef *rendang* (a curry dish) are popular. Also popular are satays (beef or seafood on skewers, with peanut sauce). There's a similarly appointed branch, with identical menu, in the North Sydney business area. *761 George St., tel. 02/211-0946. (Also: 86 Walker St., North Sydney, tel. 02/955-4306). Casual dress. Reservations not necessary. AE, DC, MC, V. Closed Sun.; for lunch, Sat.*

㉞ **Natalino's.** Although not Sydney's top Italian restaurant,
$$$ this is arguably the most pleasant for a long, leisurely chat. Service is by career waiters (rare in Australia, where waiting is often a student's meal ticket) who know their jobs well. Tiled floors, whitewashed walls, and Italianate bric-a-brac create a generic Italian look, but it's attractive nevertheless. On a fine day you can dine on the grapevine-covered outdoor terrace—the best choice in summer. A table indoors near the roaring fire is a cheerful winter option. The house specialty is *pollo alla Natalino* (chicken cooked in white wine and rosemary). Among the pastas, the tagliatelle marinara (with seafood) is always fresh. *1 Kellet St., tel. 02/358-4752. Smart, casual dress. Reservations not necessary. AE, DC, MC, V.*

★ ㉚ **Old Saigon.** Vietnamese-Australian Kim Robinson does
$$ the cooking; her American-Australian husband, ex-*Newsweek* correspondent Carl Robinson, plays host at the finest Vietnamese restaurant in town. Venison and boar

are used in a variety of dishes; more mainstream are *mi xao don chay* (fried yellow egg noodles with mixed vegetables), *bo xa ot* (braised beef with lemongrass and chili), and *heo nuong* (marinated pork grilled on skewers). The decor here is plain—travel posters from pre-Communist Vietnam, maps of Indochina. Regulars include a large contingent of foreign correspondents who enjoy the informal atmosphere and authentic dishes. *107 Oxford St., Darlinghurst, tel. 02/332–4434. Casual dress. Reservations not necessary. No credit cards.*

㉛ **P & P.** This is not the fanciest Thai restaurant, nor the one
$$ with the longest menu. But it does offer some of the city's tastiest Thai food at very low prices. The simple, small storefront is jammed with tables; decor is limited to a few dog-eared Thai travel posters. Regulars are a broad cross section of Sydney society: businesspeople in suits, theater and media people in blue jeans, post-punk art students in obligatory black outfits. Best dishes: *pla choo chee* (deep-fried whole fish with chili paste and coriander) and *gang keow warn gai* (chicken with green curry and coconut milk). *4 Flinders St., Taylor Sq., tel. 02/332–3135. Casual dress. Reservations not necessary. V.*

⑬ **Rafael's.** In this hotel dining room, with its pale-blue walls
$$$$ and alcoves (the most private tables are behind columns), the mood is one of subdued elegance. Located in part of a historic Sydney building incorporated in the modern, high-rise Ramada Renaissance, Rafael's appeals to corporate clients who value it as a quiet and classy place to do business—and to have an excellent meal. Chef Dieter Grun allows Asian influences to complement his mixed European cuisine: loin of lamb with Japanese noodles, for instance, or pork tenderloin with *wasabi* (Japanese horseradish). Service can't be faulted. Small private rooms are available for parties of two to as many as 12. *Ramada Renaissance, 30 Pitt St., Jacket and tie required. Reservations required. AE, DC, MC, V.*

⑲ **San Francisco Grill.** For culinary conservatives who shun
$$$$ the adventurous cuisine served in some Sydney hotel dining rooms these days, the Hilton's San Francisco Grill is made to order. The dim, clubbish, wood-paneled room and its adjoining Champagne Bar have escaped the refurbishments that have modernized the rest of the Hilton. It's still very much a staid dining room for serious business lunches; men in navy blue suits are huddled deep in conversation. Service is attentive but not obtrusive. The atmosphere is appropriate for generous portions of prime Australian roast beef, roast lamb, or sirloin, panfried with bone marrow, an herb crust, and a shallot sauce. *Hilton, 259 Pitt St., tel. 02/266–0610. Jacket and tie required. Reservations advised. AE, DC, MC, V. Lunch only, closed Sun.*

★ ⑭ **Sydney Cove Oyster Bar.** Take your choice—Sydney rock
$$ oysters or local prawns served with beer or wine at a tiny restaurant on the walkway between Circular Quay and the Sydney Opera House. They can be savored with any of a limited selection of Australian beers, wines, and champagnes. Decor is nonexistent; there are a few stools at the counter, and outdoor tables under umbrellas where you can enjoy a short lunch break or a longer after-work session, and take in the vista of the Sydney Opera House, Harbor Bridge, and passing water traffic. Somehow, on

Fridays and Saturdays, they squeeze in a jazz band. *1 Circular Quay E, tel. 02/272–937. Casual dress. No reservations. AE, DC, MC, V.*

★ ⑰ **Treasury.** Located in the historic New South Wales Treas-
$$$$ ury building (now incorporated into the modern InterContinental Hotel), the Treasury is one of Sydney's top hotel
restaurants. A tone of British colonial-style luxury is set
by the crystal chandeliers, turn-of-the-century artwork,
canopied drapes, and comfortable period armchairs at im-
maculately set tables. Lighting is subdued, and tables are
among Sydney's best spaced. The clientele is a combination of businesspeople (the financial district is down the
street), politicians from nearby South Wales State Parliament, and well-heeled independent tourists. Chef Gerard
Madani's choice dishes on the nouvelle-influenced modern
Australian menu include an appetizer of warm, pink-eye
potato salad with fresh chive cream dressing and Beluga
caviar; and a main course of roasted rack of lamb with
couscous and fresh date sauce. The list of Australian and
foreign wines and ports in the large cellar is exceptional.
*InterContinental Hotel, 117 Macquarie St., tel. 02/230–
0200. Jacket and tie required. Reservations required. AE,
CB, DC, MC, V.*

Suburbs

★ ㊶ **Cleveland.** In the inner suburbs of Double Bay, a short cab
$$$ ride from most hotels, is an elegant outpost of a 23-branch
Hong Kong chain featuring Chinese dining at its most
stylish. The decor is modern, with a sleek, expensive look:
plenty of marble, a giant crystal chandelier, and crisp
white table linens. And the Chinese menu, which empha-
sizes Szechuan and vegetarian dishes, is among the best in
town. Consider starting with a platter of vegetarian appe-
tizers, including bean curd made to resemble barbecued
pork; or shark's-fin soup. In warm weather, cold steamed
chicken with jellyfish (served with strong English mus-
tard) is a tasty option. Diners here include many of the lo-
cal Chinese business community's movers and shakers. *63
Bay St., Double Bay, tel. 02/327–6877. Smart, casual
dress. Reservations not necessary. AE, DC, MC, V.*

④ **Doyles on the Beach.** There are other branches- but Doyles
$$$ on the Beach in Watsons Bay is probably Australia's most
famous restaurant. Food critics dismiss it as an upmarket
fish-and-chip shop, others denigrate it as a tourist trap.
There's truth in both assertions. Nevertheless, it's also
true that locals almost always outnumber out-of-towners.
All come for silver dory fillets and French fries; char-
grilled gem fish cutlets with lemon butter; or tuna and
kingfish sashimi. The staff is helpful but hassled. The decor is forgettable—what people come for are the views of
the Opera House and the sailboat-filled harbor. Doyle's
has a fun water-taxi service from downtown (Circular
Quay)—call the restaurant for a schedule. *11 Marine Parade, Watsons Bay, tel. 02/337–2007. Casual dress. Reservations not necessary. AE, DC, MC, V.*

★ ㊴ **Oasis Seros.** This small (60-seat) restaurant in the trendy
$$$$ inner suburb of Paddington is the winner of several key culinary awards. The stylishly stark, modern gray room is
made only slightly less austere by a few Australian paintings. The food, prepared by renowned Sydney chef Phillip
Searle, is modern Australian, with French influences. Lo-

cal celebrities and upscale businesspeople are among the
clientele in this current "in" spot. Popular dishes include
seared hare stuffed with beet, horseradish, and chili; and
guinea fowl baked in clay and stuffed with wild and black
rice. For dessert, try the "checkerboard" of anise ice
cream, pineapple sorbet, and licorice. *495 Oxford St.,
Paddington, tel. 02/361-3377. Smart, casual dress. Reservations essential. AE, DC, MC, V. Closed Sun., Mon.*

★ ❸ **Paddington Inn Bistro.** Surprisingly for a dining room in a
$$ pub, this one in trendy Paddington has a locally celebrated
chef, and serves French bistro-style fare, with some Ital-
ian and Aussie dishes as well. The decor is simple: bright
pink kitchen-style chairs, farmhouse-style tables, and
walls dominated by blackboards on which are chalked a
large menu and a huge wine list. Diners at lunch include
well-heeled shoppers, fashion retailers from a nearby bou-
tique row, and a business crowd that's in-the-know about
food. Evenings are busy and noisier, with a large gay com-
ponent. Appetizers include a warm tomato salad. A good
choice among the seafood-dominated main courses is suc-
culent cod fillets with a hint of saffron. Private rooms are
available for small parties. *338 Oxford St., Paddington,
tel. 02/361-4402. Smart, casual dress. MC, V. Closed for
dinner Mon.*

❹ **Pappadum's.** This elegant, sophisticated spot serves some
$$$ of the best Indian food in Sydney. Northern Indian cuisine
is dominant, but popular dishes from elsewhere in the
country—including a few Madras-style—are also featured. The dining room is a brightly lighted expanse of
white tablecloths, plain white walls, and spotless gray
carpeting. Guests can also sit on a glassed-in balcony.
There is sufficient space between tables for business talk,
and, if conversation lags, a view through glass of chefs at
work at their *tandoor* (clay oven). Waiters are competent,
but have been primed to overexplain—an irritating habit.
Tandoori chicken is deservedly popular; other worthwhile
suggestions include beef *vindaloo* (specify whether you
want this normally spicy curry mild or extra-spicy) and
lamb *Madras* (a brown sauce even spicier than the
vindaloo). *55 Bay St., Double Bay, tel. 02/325-510.
Smart, casual dress. Reservations advised. AE, DC, MC,
V.*

FREE TIME

Fitness

Hotel Facilities
The well-equipped **Clark Hatch Fitness Center** (117 Macquarie St., tel. 02/251-3486), part of an international
chain, is located in the InterContinental Hotel. A day's access to gym equipment, sauna, and pool is A$20.

Health Clubs
Many health clubs offer short-term memberships, but the
best value (and best equipped) is **City Gym** (107 Crown
St., Darlinghurst, tel. 02/360-6247), open 24 hours. Daily
fee is A$10.

Jogging
The most accessible route, because it's at the edge of
downtown, is from Circular Quay, past Sydney Opera

House, through the Botanic Gardens, and back into the downtown area at Macquarie Street; it's less than 2 miles round trip. Or take a cab and join the joggers in **Centennial Park** (like New York's Central Park, only safer).

Shopping

Australia is famous for opals. For jewelry made from these semiprecious stones, check **Gemtech** (50 Park St., tel. 02/267–7939) or **Opal Fields** (155 George St., The Rocks, tel. 02/247–6800). **Ausfurs** (Clocktower Sq., corner of Harrington and Argyle Sts., The Rocks, tel. 02/247–3160) sells sheepskins and sheepskin products. Leather goods, including luggage, are sold at **Hunt Leather** (141 George St., tel. 02/272–208). The largest souvenir and handicraft selection is in the small shops in the **Argyle Center** (Argyle and Playfair Sts., The Rocks). The top shopping mall is the **Queen Victoria Building** (George St., opposite Hilton Hotel). When you show your outbound ticket and passport, you can get good duty-free bargains at **Downtown Duty Free** (Victoria Walk, Queen Victoria Building, opposite Hilton Hotel, George St., tel. 02/267–7944). Australian aboriginal arts and crafts make unusual and thoughtful gifts; try **Aboriginal Artists' Gallery** (477 Kent St., tel. 02/261–29290).

The two main department stores in town are **David Jones** (133 Elizabeth St., tel. 02/226–5544) and **Grace Bros.** (436 George St., tel. 02/238–9111). The former is a bit more opulent, but both are relatively upscale and have a good cross section of goods in all departments, including sections selling quality Australian souvenirs.

Diversions

The **Art Gallery of New South Wales** (Art Gallery Rd., tel. 02/225–1700) has exhibitions of Colonial-era and modern Australian art, as well as a good selection of aboriginal art.

At the **Australian Museum** (6 College St., tel. 02/339–8225), there are aboriginal and Papua New Guinean lifestyle displays and extensive exhibits of Australian wildlife, geology, and social history.

Take a cab or bus (get details from your concierge) to **Bondi Beach,** Australia's most famous stretch of sand. The south end is mostly topless. There are many restaurants—from good to indifferent—opposite the beach.

Darling Harbor convention-and-entertainment complex is conveniently reached by a three-minute, A$2, elevated-monorail ride from downtown. Here, boutiques offer a wide choice of souvenirs and fashions; restaurants serve Aussie seafood; and bars feature jazz, rock, and traditional Irish-influenced Australian-colonial folk music.

The oceanside resort suburb of **Manly** is less than 15 minutes from downtown by hydrofoil or fast catamaran (35 minutes by slow ferry). Crammed with shops and restaurants, it's also home to a great surfing beach. The trip to Manly is a practical way to see the harbor if time is limited. An alternative is to take a quick harbor cruise (lunch hour is pleasant). The biggest operator, leaving from No. 6

Jetty, Circular Quay, is **Captain Cook Cruises** (tel. 02/251–5007).

A pleasant diversion for an hour or two is to amble down George Street, past the Regent of Sydney Hotel on your left and Circular Quay on your right, into the historic **Rocks** district—a quarter filled with restaurants and bars, handicraft and souvenir stores, and fine old sandstone buildings, dating from the days of British rule.

The Arts

The Metro section in the Friday *Sydney Morning Herald* contains a comprehensive guide to weekly happenings. Check events at the **Sydney Opera House** (Bennelong Pt., tel. 02/250–7111) for drama, opera, and orchestral concerts. **Sydney Entertainment Center** (Chinatown, tel. 02/211–2222) features pop and rock concerts. **Belvoir Street Theater** (925 Belvoir St., Surry Hills, tel. 02/699–325) puts on avant garde productions. The Australian Film Institute's **Chauvel Cinema** (Oxford St., Paddington, tel. 02/361–5398) shows homegrown Australian films and documentaries.

For credit-card bookings, call **Ticketek** (tel. 02/266–4800). Discount tickets are sold from **Halftix,** a booth at Martin Place and Castlereagh streets (tel. 02/357–1364).

After Hours

Sydney's main nightlife area is Kings Cross, an anything-goes combat zone that includes numerous restaurants, stylish bars and nightclubs, sleazy bars and nightclubs, strip clubs, sex shows, streetwalkers, massage parlors, and good jazz spots. An alternative nightlife area is the nearby **Oxford Street** strip—mostly gay but increasingly also attracting a straight clientele.

Bars and Lounges
The Regent of Sydney's **Club Bar** (tel. 02/238–0000) is ideal for an after-work drink, if a quiet environment is needed for serious business conversation. The best bar for unwinding at the end of the day in banker-and-broker territory is **Syd's** (Westpac Plaza, corner of George and Margaret Sts., tel. 02/247–8203). In the heart of Kings Cross, and a favorite of North American visitors, is the smoky, 24-hour **Bourbon and Beefsteak** (24 Darlinghurst Rd., Kings Cross, tel. 02/358–1144). Dress ranges from torn jeans to designer suits. Unaccompanied women probably will feel uneasy here; this is lounge-lizard territory.

Cabaret
In dreadfully short supply, cabaret barely warrants a mention in Sydney. One exception is the **Hilton** (tel. 02/266–0610), which continues to present expensive foreign acts and showcase top local talent.

Comedy Clubs
Several clubs offer live stand-up comedy, but the funniest lineup is usually at the **Comedy Store** (278 Cleveland St., Surry Hills, tel. 02/699–5371).

Jazz Clubs
The **Real Ale Cafe** (66 King St., tel. 02/262–32277) and **Round Midnight** (2 Roslyns St., Kings Cross, tel. 02/356–4045) are top jazz clubs, featuring leading local names and

foreign performers. Unaccompanied women should feel more comfortable at the former, in the heart of the downtown area. **Soup Plus** (358 George St., tel. 02/297–728) is ideal for women alone, since many female tourists, mostly from Europe, choose it for a night out.

For Singles

The **Cauldron** (206 Darlinghurst Rd., tel. 02/331–1523), a dark spot on the edge of Kings Cross, and **Rogues** (Oxford Sq., 16 Oxford St., tel. 02/332–1718) are popular discos. **Williams** (Boulevard Hotel, 90 William St., tel. 02/357–2277) is pleasant on Sunday nights, when a piano bar format replaces the disco, but even here women should be prepared to be hassled. A nice, safe nightspot is **Nonki's** (Kingsgate Shopping center, corner of Darlinghurst and Bayswater Rds., Kings Cross, tel. 02/357–7100), a Japanese tavern with many private alcoves, attracting a mixed crowd of visitors, backpackers, and businesspeople. In The Rocks historic quarter, head for **Phillip's Foote** (101 George St., tel. 02/241–1485), a laid-back wine bar and restaurant (open late) with a casual mix of businesspeople and tourists. It's one of the most pleasant, unpressured, and nonthreatening singles haunts; unfortunately, it closes at midnight.

Tokyo

by Jared Lubarsky

Of all the major cities in the world, Tokyo is perhaps the hardest for Westerners to understand, to feel comfortable in, to put in perspective. To begin with, there is the sheer, outrageous size of it. Tokyo incorporates 23 wards, 26 smaller cities, seven towns, and eight villages, together sprawling 55 miles east to west and 15 miles north to south. The wards alone enclose an area of 227 square miles—home to some 8.5 million people. Over two million of them pass through Shinjuku Station, one of the major hubs in the transportation network, every day.

Tokyo is a state-of-the-art financial marketplace, where billions of dollars are whisked electronically around the globe every day, and where the automatic cash dispensers shut down at 6 PM. It's a city of exquisite politeness, where taxi drivers open the door for you when you get in and out—and where the man in the subway will push an old woman out of the way to get a seat. A city of astonishing beauty in its small details, it also has some of the ugliest buildings on the planet—and generates 20,000 tons of garbage a day. It installed its first electric light in 1833—and still has hundreds of thousands of households without a bathtub.

Probably the one overwhelming fact of life for Tokyo as a business city is that it is also the seat of government. Laws and regulations in Japan, especially those that relate to any aspect of doing business, are written not by legislators but by bureaucrats; the letter of the law itself is extremely loose and ambiguous. Part of the enormous power the bureaucrats wield is the freedom they have to interpret the rules they draft. If you are a Japanese businessperson with a new undertaking, you simply have to know what the bureaucrats are thinking; you need the kinds of personal contacts in agencies like the Ministry of International Trade and Industry, the Ministry of Finance, or the Ministry of Posts and Telecommunications, that enable you to pick up the phone and find out where you stand. Like it or not, then, you need to have headquarters in Tokyo.

In 1987, the Tokyo Stock Exchange surpassed New York's to become, in terms of the dollar value of transactions, the largest in the world. It has become imperative for organizations, public and private, seeking a share of Japan's mushrooming investments abroad to have a presence in Tokyo.

This has driven the cost of commercial real estate in the city to astronomical levels. Space in one new office building on the block next to Tokyo Station, for example, was offered when it opened in 1990 for about $2,600 per square foot—a jump of 300% over market prices in that area the year before. While this is an extreme case, rents of $1,000 per square foot in the central wards of Chuo, Chiyoda, and Minato are the rule rather than the exception. Location in Tokyo is so crucial that most prospective tenants just bite the bullet, but an increasing number of major corporations are looking elsewhere. Over the past two years, many of them have been lured to large-scale real estate developments that opened or are about to open in neighboring Chiba Prefecture (at Makuhari), in Yokohama (at Minato Mirai), and along the Tokyo waterfront; these projects combine more attractive rents with infrastructure advantages like satellite communications and nearby convention facilities. Foreign business travelers already familiar with the city center will find calls and conferences taking them farther and farther afield from now on.

Top Employers

Employer	Type of Enterprise	Parent*/ Headquarters
Fujitsu	Communications equipment	Tokyo
Hitachi	Electric machinery	Tokyo
Honda Motors	Automobiles	Tokyo
Mitsubishi Electric	Electric machinery	Tokyo
Mitsubishi Heavy Industries	Heavy electric machinery	Tokyo
NEC	Communications equipment	Tokyo
Nippon Telegraph & Telephone	Communications	Tokyo
Nissan	Automobiles	Tokyo
Toshiba	Electric machinery	Tokyo

*if applicable

ESSENTIAL INFORMATION

We show the Tokyo telephone area code (03) with all listed numbers; if you are calling from outside Japan, omit the 0; if you are calling from within Tokyo, drop the area code altogether.

The currency of Japan is the yen, abbreviated throughout the chapter as ¥.

Government Tourist Offices

Japan National Tourist Organization (JNTO). In the United States: 630 Fifth Ave., Suite 2101, New York, NY 10111, tel. 212/757–5640; 402 N. Michigan Ave., Chicago, IL 60601, tel. 312/222–0874; 2121 San Jacinto St., Suite 980, Dallas, TX 75201, tel. 214/754–1820; 360 Post St., Suite 401, San Francisco, CA 94108, tel. 415/989–7140; 624 S. Grand Ave., Suite 2640, Los Angeles, CA 90017, tel. 213/623–1952.

In Canada: 165 University Ave., Toronto M5H 3B8, Ontario, tel. 416/366–7140.

In the United Kingdom: 167 Regent St., London W1R 7FD, tel. 071/734–9638.

In Tokyo: The Tourist Information Center (TIC), Kotani Bldg., 1–6–6 Yurakucho, Chiyoda-ku, tel. 03/503–1461.

Foreign Trade Information

Japan External Trade Offices (JETRO). In the United States: McGraw-Hill Bldg., 44th floor, 1221 Avenue of the Americas, New York, NY 10020, tel. 212/997–0400; 401 N. Michigan Ave., Suite 660, Chicago, IL 60611, tel. 312/527–9000.

In Canada: Britannica House, 151 Bloor St. West, Suite 700, Toronto M5S 1T7, Ontario, tel. 416/962–5050; Place Montreal Trust Tower, 1800 McGill College Ave., Suite 2902, Montreal H3A 3J6, Quebec, tel. 514/849–5911.

In the United Kingdom: Leconfield House, Curzon St., London WIY 7FB, tel. 071/493–7226.

Entry Requirements

U.S. and Canadian Citizens
Passport only. Visa required for visits longer than 90 days.

U.K. Citizens
Passport only. Visa required for visits longer than 180 days.

Climate

Tokyo has mild winters and snowfalls are rare, but summers are hot and extremely humid. The annual rainfall averages about 55 inches; there are especially wet periods June through July, and again in late September (the typhoon season). The weather is best in early May and mid-October. What follows are the average daily maximum and minimum temperatures for Tokyo.

Jan.	46F	8C	**Feb.**	48F	9C	**Mar.**	53F	12C
	29	– 2		30	– 1		35	2
Apr.	62F	17C	**May**	72F	22C	**June**	75F	24C
	46	8		53	12		62	17
July	82F	28C	**Aug.**	86F	30C	**Sept.**	78F	26C
	70	21		72	22		66	19
Oct.	70F	21C	**Nov.**	60F	16C	**Dec.**	51F	11C
	56	13		42	6		33	1

Airports

Tokyo is served by two airports. **Haneda,** the domestic airport, is 10 miles to the southwest, on Tokyo Bay; the **New Tokyo International Airport** (more commonly known as Narita) is Tokyo's primary international airport, and is 50 miles northeast of the city. City Air Link (tel. 03/212–3747) runs helicopter flights between Narita and Haneda airports (¥16,850 one way). Narita, with its enormous volume of traffic (nearly 10 million Japanese went abroad in 1990), is notorious for its long lines at passport and baggage inspection counters; the arrivals lobby is often jammed with people and luggage carts. Haneda, on the other hand, has ample terminal space, though waiting areas are uncomfortable. Narita is the only airport in Japan that imposes a departure, or "facilities-use" tax (¥2,000 per person).

Airlines

All Nippon Airways, Japan Airlines, and Japan Air System provide the most frequent domestic service in and out of Haneda. There is also one international carrier authorized to land at Haneda: Taiwan's China Airlines, which flies to Japan from New York, Los Angeles, and San Francisco. Over 40 carriers have regular international flights to Narita; 13 of these have departures from North American cities. Airlines that offer the most frequent service are listed below.

All Nippon Airways, tel. 03/272–1212; 800/235–9262.
American, tel. 03/214–2111; 800/433–7300.
Canadian Airlines International, tel. 03/281–7426; 800/426–7000.
China Airlines, tel. 03/436–1661; 800/227–5118.
Continental, tel. 03/592–1631; 800/525–0280.
Delta, tel. 03/275–7000; 800/327–2850.
Japan Airlines, tel. 03/457–1121; 800/525–3663.
Japan Air System, tel. 03/747–8111.
Korean Air, tel. 03/211–3311; 800/223–1155.
Northwest, tel. 03/432–6000; 800/447–4747.
United, tel. 03/817–4411; 800/241–6522.

Between the Airports and Downtown

By Taxi
Cabs are the most convenient way to get directly to your destination—and the most expensive: The metered fare to one of the downtown Tokyo hotels from Haneda will be about ¥7,500, and from Narita it will be more than ¥20,000. Three or four people with baggage might want to share one of the larger "wagon taxis;" the meter rate is the same. At nonpeak hours, the ride from Haneda takes about 30 minutes and the ride from Narita takes about 90 minutes; when traffic builds up on the one and only highway connection, the latter can take as long as three hours.

By Bus
From Haneda, the Airport Limousine Bus provides service to major hotels in the Shinjuku section of Tokyo: Cost is ¥1,000 and hours of operation are 9 AM–10 PM. From Narita, two services, the Airport Limousine Bus and the Airport Express Bus, run to major hotels in each section of the city: Ginza, Akasaka, Shinagawa, Shinjuku, Shiba.

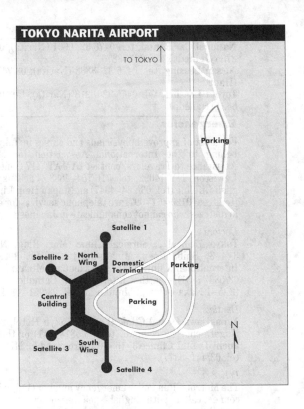

TOKYO NARITA AIRPORT

TO TOKYO ↑

Parking

Satellite 1

Satellite 2   North Wing   Domestic Terminal   Parking

Central Building   Parking

Satellite 3   South Wing

Satellite 4

N

The fare is ¥2,700; tickets are sold at the counter directly across the arrivals lobby from the customs area exit. Buses leave from just outside the terminal exit; tickets have the departure time stamped on them and are valid only for that bus. Even if you are not staying at one of the destination hotels, these buses are fairly convenient; take one to the nearest drop-off, and use a taxi for the remaining distance. The major drawback is that there are only one or two buses an hour, at best, to any given section of the city, and there are no buses at all to most destinations after 10 PM.

By Train
Haneda has a quick (17-minute) and inexpensive (¥270) monorail connection to the city center. There are no rail connections directly to or from Narita Airport. There are, however, shuttle buses from the terminal to the private Keisei Line Airport Station (6 minutes) and Japan Railway Station in Narita City (25 minutes). Keisei Line trains run every 30–40 minutes to the terminal in Ueno; depending on which train you take, the ride takes either 66 or 81 minutes. Cost: ¥1,750 for the Skyliner; ¥1,030 for the Limited Express. JR trains also go to Ueno, with connections there on the Yamanote loop line to other parts of the city. Cost: ¥2,520 for the Limited Express (85 minutes); ¥1,090 for the rapid service (105 minutes).

Car Rentals

The following companies have desks at the airports:

National Car Rental, tel. 0476/32–0601 (Narita); 03/747–
8785 (Haneda); 800/227–3876.
Nissan Leasing, tel. 0476/32–8888 (Narita); 03/747–8782
(Haneda).
Toyota Leasing, tel. 0476/32–8218 (Narita); tel. 03/742–
6681 (Haneda).

Emergencies

For a list of approved physicians and clinics in Tokyo that
belong to the International Association for Medical
Assistance to Travelers, contact IAMAT, 417 Center St.,
Lewiston, NY 14092, tel. 716/754–4883. The Tokyo English Lifeline (tel. 03/264–4347) and Japan Help Line (tel.
[toll free] 0120/461–997) are telephone services for anyone
in distress who cannot communicate in Japanese.

Doctors
Tokyo Medical & Surgical Clinic (Mori Bldg. No. 32,
3–4–30 Shiba Koen, Minato-ku, tel. 03/436–3028); the
International Clinic (1–5–9 Azabudai, Minato-ku, tel.
03/583–7831); or the **International Catholic Hospital**
(2–5–1 Naka-Ochiai, Shinjuku-ku, tel. 03/951–1111).

Dentists
Yanagisawa Dental Clinic (Capitol Tokyu Hotel, 2–10–3
Nagata-cho, Chiyoda-ku, tel. 03/581–4511) or the **Yam-
auchi Dental Clinic** (3–16–10 Shiroganedai, Minato-ku,
tel. 03/441–8377).

Police
The Metropolitan Police emergency number (110) will also
connect callers with English-speaking interpreters on 24-
hour duty.

Ambulance
Tel. 119.

Important Addresses and Numbers

American Express (Toranomon-Mitsui Bldg., 3–8–1
Kasumigaseki, Chiyoda-ku, tel. 03/508–2400 [travel ser-
vices] or 03/595–4571 [banking]; Ginza Four Stars Bldg.,
4–4–1 Ginza, Chuo-ku, tel. 03/564–4381).

Audiovisual rentals. Rental Shop ACOM (1–34–11 Shinjuku, Shinjuku-ku, tel. 03/350–5081).

Bookstores (English-language). Jena (5–6–1 Ginza, Chuo-
ku, tel. 03/571–2960), Kinokuniya (3–17–7 Shinjuku,
Shinjuku-ku, tel. 03/354–0131), Maruzen (2–3–10 Nihon-
bashi, Chuo-ku, tel. 03/272–7211). *Note:* These are
Japanese-language bookstores with special sections of
material in English.

British Embassy and Consulate (1 Ichiban-cho, Chiyoda-
ku, tel. 03/265–5511).

Canadian Embassy (7–3–38 Akasaka, Minato-ku, tel. 03/
408–2101).

Chamber of Commerce. Japan Junior Chamber (2–14–3
Irakawa-cho, Chiyoda-ku, tel. 03/234–5601).

Computer rentals. Hard to find. The best bet is the Business Service Center at your hotel.

Convention and exhibition centers. Nippon Convention Center (3–16 Chuo 2-chome, Chiba Prefecture, tel. 0472/ 25–1700), Sunshine City Convention Center (3–1–1 Higashi Ikebukuo, Toshima-ku, tel. 03/989–3486), Tokyo International Fair Grounds (5–3–53 Harumi, Chuo-ku, tel. 03/533–5311), Tokyo Ryutsu Center (6–1–1 Heiwajima, Ohta-ku, tel. 03/767–2162), Tokyo Trade Center Taito Hall (2–6–5 Hanakawado, Taito-ku, tel. 03/844– 6151), World Trade Center of Japan (2–4–1 Hamamatsu-cho, Minato-ku, tel. 03/435–5650).

Fax service. These machines have become so widespread that there is no real market for independent service outlets. Your hotel will send and receive facsimiles for you (if you've managed to find a hotel without a fax machine, it's not likely to have running water either); otherwise, most larger stations on the Japan Railway loop line around the city have service corners, where you can send facsimiles locally at standard telephone time rates.

Formal-wear rentals. Ricky Sarani (3–3–12 Azabu-dai, Minato-ku, tel. 03/587–0648).

Gift shops. Chocolates/Sweets: Mitsukoshi Department Store (4–6–16 Ginza, Chuo-ku, tel. 03/562–1111); Florists: Goto Hanaten (5–1–3 Roppongi, Minato-ku, tel. 03/ 4–8–8211), Kokusai Florist Tokyo (3–1–1 Marunouchi, Chiyoda-ku, tel. 03/212–8741).

Graphic design studios. Concept International (Time & Life Bldg., 2–3–6 Otemachi, Chiyoda-ku, tel. 03/242– 3421), Destination West (Hoshi Bldg. No. 304, 27–3 Sakuragaoka-cho, Shibuya-ku, tel. 03/463–8565), Early Birds (1–40–14 Komagome, Toshima-ku, tel. 03/944– 6559), Jude Brand (5–14–14 Sendagaya, Shibuya-ku, tel. 03/352–1960), P & B International (Heights Akaska No. 406, 7–6–52 Akasaka, Minato-ku, tel. 03/589–3299).

Hairstylists. Unisex: André Bernard (Horaya Bldg., 4th floor, 5–2–1 Roppongi, Minato-ku, tel. 03/404–0616), From New York (Hanatsubaki Bldg., 3rd floor, 3–15–23 Roppongi, Minato-ku, tel. 03/401–6555).

Health and fitness clubs. *See* Fitness, below.

Information hot lines. Teletourist Information (recorded information on current cultural events, in English, tel. 03/ 503–2911).

Limousine services. Hinomaru Transportation (tel. 03/ 505–0707), Hotel Okura Limousine Service (Carry Japan) (tel. 03/583–2424).

Liquor stores. All downtown department stores (*see* Shopping, below) have sections devoted to wines and spirits on the lower level; one of the best is the Liquor Cellar (Yuraku-cho Seibu Department Store, Mullion Bldg. B1, 2–5–1 Yuraku-cho, Minato-ku, tel. 03/286–5583).

Mail delivery, overnight. DHL (tel. 03/865–2580), Federal Express (tel. [toll free] 0120/003–200), UPS-Yamato Transport (tel. 03/541–3411).

Messenger services. Bike Kyubin (tel. [toll free] 0120/37– 8199), Business Kyubin (tel. 03/370–1111), Quick Motorcycle Express (tel. 03/317–9911), The Sugu (tel. 03/306–

0055). *Note:* Dispatchers are unlikely to speak or understand English.

News programs (English-language). Radio: The U.S. military's Far East Network (FEN) has the only English-language news programming available on the standard broadcast bands (810 FM); call tel. 0425/52–2511 for information. TV: KTYO (tel. 03/359–5100) is a local 24-hour English-language station, but available only on cable; major hotels that have the CNN all-news channel on their cable TV system will also have KTYO.

Office space rentals. International Executive Office–Tokyo (4–6–10 Yotsuya, Shinjuku-ku, tel. 03/379–1331), Jardine Business Centre–Tokyo (ABS Bldg., 2–4–16 Kudan Minami, Chiyoda-ku, tel. 03/239–2811), Sanko Estate (Shuwa Bldg. No. 4, 8–10–5 Ginza, Chuo-ku, tel. 03/574–6862).

Pharmacies. American Pharmacy (Hibiya Park Bldg., 1–8–1 Yuraku-cho, Chiyoda-ku, tel. 03/271–4034), Hill Pharmacy (4–1–6 Roppongi, Minato-ku, tel. 03/583–5044). These close at 7 PM; there are no late-night pharmacies.

Secretarial services. Girl Friday (Shin Aoyama Bldg., 1–1–1 Minami Aoyama, Minato-ku, tel. 03/404–0789), Interlanguage Service System (Capitol Tokyu Hotel, 2–10–3 Nagata-cho, Chiyoda-ku, tel. 03/508–9020), Japan Convention Services (Nippon Press Center Bldg., 4th floor, 2–2–1 Uchisaiwai-cho, Chiyoda-ku, tel. 03/508–1211), Manpower Japan (Toshiba EMI Nagata-cho Bldg., 2–4–8 Nagata-cho, Chiyoda-ku, tel. 03/506–8888), Temporary Center Corporation (Nippon Press Center Bldg., 2–2–1 Uchisaiwai-cho, Chiyoda-ku, tel. 03/508–1431).

Stationery supplies. Itoya (2–7–15 Ginza, Chuo-ku, tel. 03/561–8311). Supplies are also available in major department stores (*see* Shopping, below) and bookstores (*see* above).

Taxis. Checker Cab (tel. 03/563–5151), Green Cab (tel. 03/203–8181), Hinomaru Cab (tel. 03/814–1111), Kokusai Taxi (tel. 03/491–6001), Tokyo Musen Taxi (tel. 03/330–2111). *Note:* Dispatchers are unlikely to understand or speak English.

Theater tickets. *See* The Arts, below.

Thomas Cook (Ascend Kanda Bldg., 6th floor, 10 Kanda Toyama-cho, Chuo-ku, tel. 03/254–4041).

Trade Ministry. Ministry of International Trade and Industry (1–3–1 Kasumigaseki, Chiyoda-ku, tel. 03/501–1551).

Train information. Tokyo Station (1–9–1 Marunoeuchi, Chiyoda-ku), JR East InfoLine (tel. 03/423–0111, Mon.–Fri. 9 AM–6 PM only).

Translation services. Diplomatt (5–3–20 Toranomon, Minato-ku, tel. 03/472–6090), Interlanguage Service System (Capitol Tokyu Hotel, 2–10–3 Nagata-cho, Chiyoda-ku, tel. 03/580–9020), Japan Convention Services (Nippon Press Center Bldg., 4th floor, 2–2–1 Uchisaiwai-cho, Chiyoda-ku, tel. 03/508–1215), Japan Translation Center

(1–21 Kanda Nishiki-cho, Chiyoda-ku, tel. 03/291–0655), Linguapower (Shibuya Kyowa Bldg., 2–20–11 Shibuya, Shibuya-ku, tel. 03/498–5181), Simul International (Kowa Bldg. No. 9, 1–8–10 Akasaka, Minato-ku, tel. 03/586–5641), Temporary Center Corporation (Nippon Press Center Bldg., 2–2–1 Uchisaiwai-cho, Chiyoda-ku, tel. 03/508–1431).

U.S. Embassy (1–10–5 Akasaka, Minato-ku, tel. 03/224–5000).

Telephones

Calls from public phones are charged at the rate of ¥10 for three minutes; deposit coins after you pick up the receiver, and wait for a dial tone. Red and pink phones accept only ¥10 coins; yellow phones take both ¥10 and ¥100 coins. Neither one gives you more than a split second of warning before it buzzes and disconnects your call; carry plenty of change to feed the machine. Better yet, use the green phones, which accept magnetically coded "telephone cards," available at any kiosk, convenience store, department store, or hotel lobby in denominations of ¥500, ¥1,000, ¥3,000, and ¥5,000: A digital display on the phone tells you how much time you have left on your card.

Tipping

Generally speaking, there is no tipping in Japan. International hotels and restaurants normally add a 10% or 15% service charge to your bill; you may wish to tip the driver of a car you have hired by the day about ¥1,000, but otherwise this is a custom you can safely forget.

DOING BUSINESS

Hours

Businesses: Mon.–Fri. 8:30 or 9 to 5:30 or 6; to noon on Sat. (An increasing number of firms are closing on Sat.) **Banks:** weekdays 9–3; closed on national holidays. **Shops:** daily, 10–8. **Department stores:** 10 to 6 or 7, including weekends and national holidays. Closed one day midweek (this varies from store to store).

National Holidays

New Year's Day; Jan. 15, Adult's Day; Feb. 11, National Foundation Day; Mar. 20 or 21, Spring Equinox; Apr. 29, Greenery Day; May 3, Constitution Memorial Day; May 5, Children's Day; Sept. 15, Respect for the Aged Day; Sept. 23 or 24, Autumnal Equinox; Oct. 10, Health and Sports Day; Nov. 3, Culture Day; Nov. 23, Labor Thanksgiving Day; Dec. 23, The Emperor's Birthday.

Getting Around

By Car
It's not advisable to drive in Tokyo. Highways are poorly marked in English; local streets—most without names—are often narrow, congested, and confusing. Driving, as in the United Kingdom, is on the left side. Compact cars rent for about ¥6,000 a day (an International Driver's License is required); gasoline, tolls, and parking fees are extremely high. Cars must be returned to the same office where

they were rented—usually before 8 PM to avoid additional charges.

By Train

Daunting in its sheer size, Tokyo is in fact an extremely easy city to negotiate by public transportation—a system obliged to cope with 4 or 5 million commuters a day simply *has* to be efficient, extensive, and reasonably easy to understand. Most places you're likely to go are within five minutes' walk of a train or subway station, and station stops are always marked in English. On the **National Railway (JR)**, trains are color coded, making it easy to identify the different lines. The **Yamanote Line** (green or silver with green stripes) makes a 35-kilometer loop around the central wards of the city; the 29 stops include the major "hub" stations of Tokyo, Yuraku-cho, Shimbashi, Shinagawa, Shibuya, Shinjuku, and Ueno. The **Chuo Line** (orange) and **Sobu Line** (yellow) run east and west through the loop. JR fares start at ¥120; most stations have a chart in English somewhere above the row of ticket vending machines, so you can check the fare to your destination; if not, you can simply buy the cheapest ticket and pay the difference at the other end. In any case, hold on to your ticket—you'll have to turn it in at the exit. Tickets are valid only on the day you buy them, but if you plan to use the JR a lot, you can save time and trouble with an **Orange Card,** available at any station office. The cards are electronically coded for ¥1,000–¥5,600 worth of fares. At vending machines with orange panels, you insert the card and punch the cost of the ticket; that amount is automatically deducted. Bear in mind that from 7–9:30 AM and 5–7 PM the trains are packed to bursting with commuters; avoid them if possible. During these hours, there is no smoking in JR stations or on platforms.

By Subway

Tokyo has 10 subway lines: maps, bilingual signs at entrances, and even the trains themselves are color coded for easy identification. Trains run about every five minutes 5 AM–midnight. Fares start at ¥120. The network of interconnections (subway-to-subway and train-to-subway) is particularly good; one transfer—two at most—will get you to any part of the city you're likely to visit in less than an hour. At some stations—like Otemachi, Ginza, and Iidabashi—long underground passageways connect the various lines, and it does take time to get from one to another. Directions, however, are clearly marked. Less helpful is the system of signs that tells you which of the 15 or 20 exits from a large station will bring you above ground closest to your destination: Only a few stations have such signs in English.

By Taxi

Taxi fares in Tokyo are among the highest in the world; the meter starts running at ¥540 and ticks away at the rate of ¥80 every 370 meters (about one-fifth of a mile). There are also smaller cabs, called *kogata*, which start at ¥520. Between 11 PM and 5 AM, a 30% surcharge is added to the fare. Hailing a taxi during the day is seldom a problem. In the Ginza, drivers are allowed to stop for passengers only in designated areas; elsewhere, you need only step off the curb and raise your arm. If the cab already has a fare, there will be a green light on the dashboard; if not, the light will be red. Night changes the rules a bit: A cab with a red light may not stop for you because the driver has a radio call or is heading for an area where he can pick up a long profitable fare to the suburbs. Between 11 PM and 2 AM on Friday and Saturday nights, you have to be very lucky to get a cab in any of the major entertainment districts; in Ginza, it is virtually impossible.

Protocol

Appointments
Perfecters of the "just-on-time" inventory system, the Japanese take promptness seriously, for both business and social engagements. Addresses can be complicated, and traffic is usually heavy, so allow for plenty of extra time to get where you're going.

Customs
When addressing Japanese colleagues, it's best to stick with family names with the honorary suffix *san;* even long-time colleagues in Japan rarely use each other's first names. Hearty informality is not likely to make a good impression, especially at first meetings; nor is an overly aggressive approach to negotiations. Losing your temper, or betraying impatience when things are not moving at the pace you'd like, will instantly—and permanently—sour your deal.

A special note to women traveling on business: Bear in mind that there are still very few women in executive positions in the Japanese business world, and many Japanese businessmen do not yet know how to interact with you. They may be uncomfortable, aloof, or patronizing. Be patient, and, if the need arises, make the point firmly that you expect to be treated professionally as an equal.

Bowing is an elaborate ritual among the Japanese themselves; their perceptions of each other's age, status, and connections determine how deeply they incline, and for how long. Although you're likely to manage only an awkward imitation of the proper form, the attempt will be appreciated as an earnest expression of your good will. The Japanese have become so accustomed to dealing with Westerners that they no longer expect a bow, and will often thrust out a hand to shake. When shaking hands, be sure to keep your grip light; the Japanese do not share the notion that strength of grip is a reflection of character.

Business cards are mandatory in Japan. On a few days' notice, most major airlines can have them printed up in both English and Japanese for business travelers, and ready when you arrive in Tokyo; if not, the Executive Service centers at the better hotels can prepare them for you overnight. The Japanese are sensitive to titles and ranks, so make sure that your card indicates your position in the company. They make a point of reading the business cards they receive studiously, and put the cards in front of them on a table or desk as they begin a meeting; do likewise, rather than simply shoving them in your pocket.

Dress
A dark suit, white shirt, and subdued tie are virtually the uniform of the Japanese businessman, even in the warmest weather. Dressing in similar style is expected of you.

Businesswomen should stick to suits in subdued colors; avoid wearing high heels if you will, as a result, tower over the Japanese, and try to keep makeup, perfume, and accessories to a minimum; avoid anything that might accentuate your femininity or intimidate Japanese colleagues.

Gifts

Gifts play an important role in doing business in Japan; they are exchanged when starting a new venture, at the close of successful negotiations, when bidding farewell to visiting VIPs, and in a variety of other situations. When the Japanese visit someone, they always take a gift—an example you'd do well to follow. Suitable gifts for executives include wine and liquor, leather goods, silk ties and scarves, famous-label accessories, and fresh fruits, beef, or salmon (though these must be certified by the U.S. Department of Agriculture before entering Japan).

One special caveat: If you are invited to play golf—an occasion the Japanese use for a lot of confidential business discussions—you may want to ask about "hole-in-one insurance." In Japan, the golfer who makes a hole-in-one does not simply tip the caddy extra and buy his foursome a round of drinks; he is expected to buy presents and host an extravagant celebration that can run into thousands of dollars. Yes, there really *is* an insurance policy that covers the cost.

Toasts and Greetings

How are you? *Oh-GEHN-key dess kah.*
Well, thank you. *GEHN-key-dess ah-lee-GAH-toh.*
Pleased to meet you. *Hah-gee-may-MAHSH-teh.*
Thank you. *Ah-lee-GAH-toh.*
You're welcome. *Doh ee-tah-shee-MAHSH-teh.*
Nice to have met you. *Oh-AYE DEHK-teh YOH kah-tah.*
Excuse me. Soo-mee-mah-SEN.
Goodbye. Sah-yoh-NAH-lah.
Cheers! KAHN-pie.

LODGING

Tokyo has an incredible array of accommodations, but those that meet the basic needs of business travelers—proximity to major business destinations, space to spread out and work in the hotel room, suitable facilities for meetings and appointments—are surprisingly few and costly. There are, of course, any number of moderately priced accommodations in Tokyo. The so-called business hotels, however, tend to be poorly located; they have tiny rooms (in many you can literally touch the walls on both sides); services are minimal, and the staff rarely speaks anything but Japanese. If you are traveling on a very limited budget, one of the choices listed as "moderate" will put a comfortable roof over your head, but don't expect much more.

Hotels listed below are divided geographically into three sections: one roughly to the west of the Imperial Palace, one to the east, and the third to the south. The area to the west includes Shinjuku—slated, with the completion of the new City Hall, to become the administrative "heart" of the city—as well as Roppongi, Akasaka, and Aoyama. These centers of fashion and glitzy night life are also home to many of the companies involved in high technology, real estate, and international finance. The area east of the Palace embraces Kasumigaseki, Marunouchi, and Ginza. Located here are the ministries of the national government and many of the headquarters of major institutions in banking, manufacture, commerce, and international trade. South is less convenient to most businesses, but those who need to be near the Tokyo Trade Center might want to stay here.

Highly recommended lodgings in each price category are indicated by a star ★.

Category	Cost*
$$$$ (Very Expensive)	over ¥21,000
$$$ (Expensive)	¥16,000–¥21,000
$$ (Moderate)	under ¥16,000

All prices are for a standard double room, single occupancy, excluding 10% tax and 10%–15% service charge.

Numbers in the margin correspond to numbered hotel locations on the Tokyo Lodging and Dining maps.

West

㉗
$$$$
Akasaka Prince. Designed by renowned architect Kenzo Tange, this hotel looks something like a 40-story piece of aluminum window track, standing on end. The lobby is uninviting at best, all slabs of white marble, hard edged and cold. The rooms, decorated in white and pale gray, have wide windows that run the length of the outside wall to create an impression of space, but the impression doesn't really hold up. Bathrooms, even in the better accommodations, are especially small; most are step-up plastic modular units with only 6′3″ of headroom. The service here is professional and correct, but for a hotel that draws almost half its clientele from foreign business travelers, the staff is a bit inclined to freeze when confronted with the unexpected request. Built in 1983, the Akasaka Prince is convenient to Japanese national government buildings and the offices of major corporations in the Kasumigaseki and Toranomon areas; the only access, however, is across a bridge to a five-way intersection: If you elect to stay here, beware of bottlenecks and allow extra time to make your appointments. Rooms high on the north side, facing the Imperial Palace, afford fine panoramic views of the city. Tokyo's power brokers often entertain in La Trianon (*see* Dining, below). *Prince Hotels. 1–2–Kioi-cho, Chiyoda-ku, 102, tel. 03/234–1111 or 800/542–8686, fax 03/262–5163. Gen. manager, Akinami Nakai. 530 doubles, 103 singles, 68 suites. AE, DC, MC, V.*

㉘
$$$
Akasaka Tokyu. Like the nearby New Otani and Akasaka Prince, the Tokyu, built in 1969, is conveniently located for anyone with appointments in Toranomon or Kasumigaseki; in those two areas, and in Aoyama, are a considerable number of the city's major international law firms. Compared to the neighboring hotels, however, the Akasaka Tokyu gets far fewer bookings—around 15%—from foreign business travelers. The Executive Center is just a counter in the third-floor lobby that farms out requests for translation or secretarial services. Rooms and

GREATER TOKYO

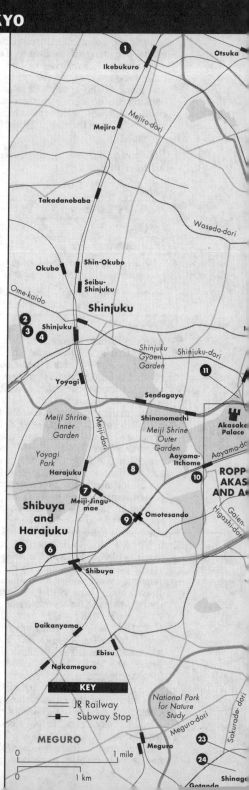

public areas are undistinguished in style and amenities are minimal: no pool, no health club, no rooms set aside for nonsmokers. Long and low (14 stories), with rooms all opening onto a single corridor, it affords no particular view. What recommends it most is the fact that its single rooms—renovated in 1990—are somewhat larger and more comfortable than those in most other hotels of this class. *2–14–3 Nagata-cho, Chiyoda-ku, 100, tel. 03/580–2311; in New York, 800/822–0016; in Los Angeles, 800/624–5068; fax 03/580–6066. Gen. manager, Seiji Ohta. 242 doubles, 293 singles. AE, DC, MC, V.*

㊲ **ANA Hotel Tokyo.** Owned and operated by All Nippon Air-
$$$$ ways, this 37-story hotel was built in 1986 in the neo-zig-gurat style: glitzy, high-tech, complete with fountain in the split-level atrium lobby. ANA hired Howard Hirsch Associates of Los Angeles to design the rooms and public spaces; soft pastels and good lighting take some of the edge off its otherwise impersonal "where-are-we-this-time?" international effect. The hotel is just a two-minute walk from the American Embassy; next door is Ark Hills, the newest and largest office building and residential complex in central Tokyo, where a number of the leading American investment banks and securities traders are located. The building faces the Expressway, which can be noisy; ask for one of the rooms on the west side opposite the highway, with views of Tokyo Tower and the Bay—especially on the 34th floor, which has its own concierge and breakfast room. The main banquet room is equipped for conferences with simultaneous interpretation; the Business Center can arrange a limousine pickup at the airport. *1–12–33 Akasaka, Minato-ku, 107, tel. 03/505–1111, fax 03/505–1155. Gen. manager, Yu Murakawa. 783 doubles, 65 singles, 31 suites. AE, DC, MC, V.*

★ ㉚ **Capitol Tokyu Hotel.** Built in 1964, the flagship of the
$$$$ Tokyu chain has an old-fashioned, sturdy air of comfort about it, with a decor that might have been designed by a disciple of Frank Lloyd Wright. The dark-wood furnishings in the guest rooms are offset by traditional Japanese sliding paper screens on the windows, softening the light. Small by the standards of Tokyo's first-class hotels, it boasts nearly two permanent staff members to every guest, and the service is excellent. Convenient to the American Embassy and the offices of major offshore banks and trading companies, the Capitol Tokyu draws about half its clientele from foreign business travelers, many of them repeat. Quiet and discreet, the hotel maintains some permanent suites as unofficial offices for "advisors" to major corporations—men who are nominally retired but enormously influential in business and political circles. Best room in the house is no. 827, overlooking the nearby Hiei Shrine; other good choices are on the Executive floors (9th and 10th), with views of the hotel garden. *2–10–3 Nagata-cho, Chiyoda-ku, 100, tel. 03/581–4511; in New York, 800/822–0016; in Los Angeles, 800/624–5068; fax 03/581–5822. Gen. manager, Yoshihide Hirase. 383 doubles, 50 singles, 19 suites. AE, CB, DC, MC, V.*

❸ **Century Hyatt Tokyo.** The decor in the lobby here is the
$$$$ usual Century Hyatt overkill: three huge bulbous chandeliers, echo-chamber marble floors and glass walls, elevator gondolas ringed with lights, interior windows with stained-glass trim. The furnishings in the guest rooms are

ROPPONGI, AKASAKA, AND AOYAMA

KASUMIGASEKI, MARUNOUCHI, AND GINZA

Lodging
Annex Dai-Ichi Hotel, **42**
Ginza Tokyu Hotel, **50**
Hotel Atamiso, **49**
Imperial Hotel, **41**
Marunouchi Hotel, **39**
Palace Hotel, **38**
Ramada Renaissance Ginza Tobu, **47**
Seiyo Ginza, **48**

Dining
Ashoka, **45**
Attore, **48**
Balalaika, **46**
Edo-Gin, **51**
Heichinrou, **40**
Ketel's, **44**
Sabatini di Firenze, **43**

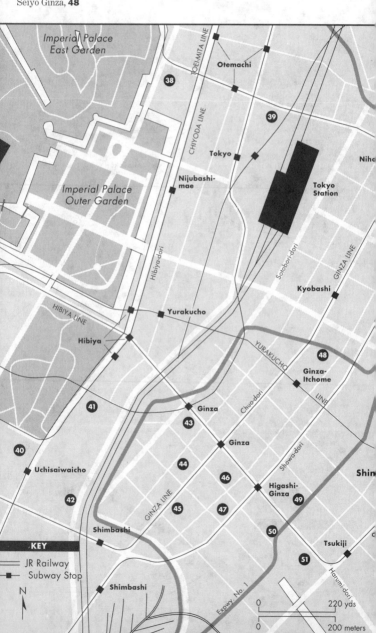

assembly-line modern; why the standard twin has only one armchair remains a mystery. Standard rooms in general are small; you have to move up a notch to "Superior" for a desk with decent working space. Built in 1980, this 28-story hotel is next door to the new Tokyo City Hall and within easy walking distance to the cluster of skyscraper buildings in Shinjuku that house many of the city's high-tech companies. The Century Hyatt gets about 30% of its bookings from foreign business travelers but has not yet geared up to provide basic business services. Rooms on the east side, from the 15th floor up, overlook Shinjuku Central Park; on rare days when the air is perfectly clear, you can even see Mt. Fuji. *2–7–2 Nishi-Shinjuku, Shinjuku-ku, 160, tel. 03/349–0111 or 800/233–1234, fax 03/344–5575. Gen. manager, Yoshihiko Sakurada. 722 doubles, 17 singles, 22 suites. AE, CB, DC, MC, V.*

★ ⑱ **Fairmount Hotel.** Nostalgia buffs will love the Fairmount,
$$$ a place that did a major renovation in 1988 and still has the water pipes exposed—neatly wrapped and painted, of course, but exposed just the same. In relentlessly high-tech Tokyo, you'd have to look long for a hotel with pull-chain ventilators and real tile in the bathrooms; the Fairmount has all that, and furniture (a little chipped) that Sears Roebuck must have phased out of its catalogue in 1955. The hotel isn't seedy, mind you: just old (it was built in 1951) and a bit set in its ways. Some of the staff members have been here over 20 years. The guests are over 50% foreign, some of them booked in by the nearby British Embassy, and many of them repeat visitors who have come to like its faded, friendly atmosphere. The best thing about the seven-story Fairmount is its frontage on the park that runs along the east side of the Imperial Palace grounds; rooms facing the park have a wonderful view of the moat and Chidori-ga-fuchi pond, where Tokyo couples take rented rowboats out on summer Sunday afternoons. *2–1–17 Kudan-Minami, Chiyoda-ku, 102, tel. 03/262–1151, fax 03/262–2476. Gen. manager, Sadao Sumiya. 112 doubles, 93 singles, 3 suites. AE, DC, MC, V.*

★ ⑰ **Hotel Okura.** The *Institutional Investor* magazine poll
$$$$ consistently rates the Okura among the three best hotels in the world; this is the kind of place you can return to two years later and the duty manager will still remember your name. The lobby, inspired by the traditional Japanese sense of space and scale, has the serenity of an old-fashioned private club. Determined to rank No. 1 in the poll, the hotel recently completed a two-year renovation, increasing the number of business suites and commissioning English designer David Hicks to do the new pastel interiors. It has also started 24-hour room service. The Okura is across the street from the American Embassy, up the hill from the Japan External Trade Organization, and in easy reach of major corporate headquarters like IBM Japan and all Japanese government ministries. The main building dates to 1962; the 13-story South Wing, built 10 years later and separated from the main building by an underground shopping arcade, is the quieter part of the hotel. From the fifth floor up, rooms on the street side have spectacular views of Tokyo Tower at night. The Toh-ka-lin Restaurant on the second floor serves some of the best Chinese cuisine in town (*see* Dining, below). The Highlander Bar, on the first floor of the main building, stocks

TOKYO HOTEL CHART

HOTELS	Price Category	Banquet capacity	No. of meeting rooms	Fax	Telex	Photocopying	Secretarial services	Audiovisual equipment	Translation services	International direct dial	Computer rentals	In-room modem phone jack
Akasaka Prince	$$$$	1600	30	✓	✓	✓	✓	✓	✓	✓	✓	✓
Akasaka Tokyu	$$$	200	6	✓	✓	✓	✓	✓	✓	✓	✓	-
ANA Hotel Tokyo	$$$$	2200	13	✓	✓	✓	✓	✓	✓	✓	-	-
Annex Dai-Ichi	$$$	30	4	✓	✓	✓	-	✓	-	✓	-	-
Atamiso	$$	120	4	✓	✓	✓	-	✓	-	-	-	-
Capitol Tokyu	$$$$	1000	10	✓	✓	✓	✓	✓	✓	✓	-	-
Century Hyatt	$$$$	1400	23	✓	✓	✓	✓	✓	✓	✓	✓	✓
Fairmount	$$$	150	2	✓	✓	✓	-	✓	-	✓	-	-
Ginza Tokyu	$$$	350	11	✓	✓	✓	✓	✓	✓	✓	-	-
Hilltop	$$$	100	11	✓	✓	✓	-	✓	-	✓	-	-
Imperial	$$$$	2000	27	✓	✓	✓	✓	✓	✓	✓	✓	✓
Keio Plaza	$$$$	1500	32	✓	✓	✓	✓	✓	✓	✓	✓	✓
Marunouchi	$$	250	8	✓	✓	✓	-	-	-	-	-	-
Miyako	$$$	400	0	✓	✓	✓	-	-	-	✓	-	-
New Otani	$$$$	3000	48	✓	✓	✓	✓	✓	✓	✓	✓	-
New Takanawa Prince	$$$	5000	13	✓	✓	✓	✓	✓	✓	✓	✓	-
Okura	$$$$	2000	35	✓	✓	✓	✓	✓	✓	✓	✓	✓
Pacific Meridien	$$$	2500	19	✓	✓	✓	✓	✓	✓	✓	✓	✓
Palace	$$$$	1000	19	✓	✓	✓	✓	✓	✓	✓	-	-

$$$$ = over ¥21,000, $$$ = ¥16,000 - ¥21,000, $$ = under ¥16,000.
● good, ◐ fair, ○ poor.

All-news cable channel	Desk	Desk lighting	Bed lighting	In-Room Amenities / Nonsmoking rooms	In-room checkout	Minibar	Toiletries	Room service	Laundry/Dry cleaning	Pressing	Hotel Amenities / Barber/Hairdresser	Garage	Courtesy airport transport	Sauna	Pool	Exercise room
✓	●	◐	●	✓	✓	✓	●	●	●	●	–	✓	–	–	–	–
✓	●	◐	◐	–	–	✓	○	◐	●	●	✓	✓	✓	✓	–	–
✓	●	●	●	✓	–	✓	●	◐	◐	◐	✓	✓	–	✓	◐	–
✓	●	●	●	✓	–	✓	●	◐	●	●	–	✓	–	–	–	–
–	○	◐	○	–	–	✓	○	◐	●	●	✓	✓	–	–	–	–
✓	●	●	◐	–	–	✓	●	●	●	●	✓	✓	–	–	◐	–
✓	◐	◐	◐	✓	–	✓	●	◐	●	●	✓	✓	–	✓	●	◐
✓	○	◐	◐	–	–	✓	○	◐	●	●	✓	–	–	✓	–	–
✓	◐	●	●	✓	–	✓	●	◐	●	●	✓	✓	–	✓	–	–
✓	●	○	◐	–	–	✓	○	◐	●	●	✓	✓	–	–	◐	–
✓	●	◐	○	✓	–	✓	●	◐	●	●	✓	✓	✓	–	–	–
–	◐	◐	●	–	–	✓	○	○	●	●	✓	–	–	–	–	–
✓	◐	◐	◐	–	✓	✓	●	◐	●	●	✓	–	–	✓	◐	◐
✓	●	●	●	✓	–	✓	●	◐	●	●	✓	✓	–	✓	●	●
✓	–	–	◐	✓	–	✓	◐	●	●	●	✓	✓	–	–	●	–
✓	●	●	●	✓	–	✓	●	●	●	●	✓	✓	✓	✓	●	●
✓	●	●	●	✓	–	✓	●	◐	●	●	✓	✓	–	✓	●	–
✓	●	◐	◐	✓	–	✓	●	◐	●	●	✓	✓	–	–	–	–

Room service: ● 24-hour, ◐ 6AM-10PM, ○ other.
Laundry/Dry cleaning: ● same day, ◐ overnight, ○ other.
Pressing: ● immediate, ◐ same day, ○ other.

TOKYO HOTEL CHART

HOTELS	Price Category	Banquet capacity	No. of meeting rooms	Fax	Telex	Photocopying	Secretarial services	Audiovisual equipment	Translation services	International direct dial	Computer rentals	In-room modem phone jack
President	$$	100	3	✓	✓	✓	✓	✓	-	✓	✓	-
Ramada Renaissance Ginza	$$$$	400	6	✓	✓	✓	✓	✓	✓	✓	-	-
Roppongi Prince	$$$	80	8	✓	✓	✓	-	-	-	✓	-	-
Royal Park	$$$	1300	12	✓	✓	✓	✓	✓	✓	✓	✓	✓
Seiyo Ginza	$$$$	150	3	✓	✓	✓	✓	✓	✓	✓	-	✓
Takanawa Prince	$$$	750	25	✓	✓	✓	-	✓	-	✓	-	-
Tokyo Hilton	$$$$	1300	17	✓	✓	✓	✓	✓	✓	✓	-	-
Tokyo Prince	$$$$	2400	25	✓	✓	✓	✓	✓	✓	✓	✓	-

$$$$** = over ¥21,000, **$$$** = ¥16,000 - ¥21,000, **$$ = under ¥16,000.
● good, ◔ fair, ○ poor.

All-news cable channel	Desk	Desk lighting	Bed lighting	**In-Room Amenities** Nonsmoking rooms	In-room checkout	Minibar	Toiletries	Room service	Laundry/Dry cleaning	Pressing	**Hotel Amenities** Barber/Hairdresser	Garage	Courtesy airport transport	Sauna	Pool	Exercise room
✓	◐	◐	◐	-	✓	✓	○	○	●	●	-	✓	-	-	-	-
✓	●	●	◐	-	-	✓	●	●	●	●	✓	✓	-	-	-	-
✓	◐	◐	○	-	-	✓	○	●	●	●	-	✓	-	-	●	-
✓	●	●	●	✓	-	✓	●	◐	●	●	✓	●	-	✓	◐	●
✓	●	●	●	-	-	✓	●	●	●	●	-	✓	-	-	-	●
✓	◐	◐	◐	✓	-	✓	○	●	●	●	✓	●	-	-	●	-
✓	●	●	●	✓	✓	✓	●	●	●	●	✓	✓	-	✓	◐	●
✓	◐	◐	◐	✓	-	✓	○	●	●	●	✓	✓	-	-	●	-

Room service: ● 24-hour, ◐ 6AM-10PM, ○ other.
Laundry/Dry cleaning: ● same day, ◐ overnight, ○ other.
Pressing: ● immediate, ◐ same day, ○ other.

224 different brands of Scotch—48 of them single malt (*see* After Hours, below). *Member, Leading Hotels of the World. 2-10-4 Toranomon, Minato-ku, 105, tel. 03/582-0111, fax 03/582-3707. Gen. manager, Tatsuro Goto. 626 doubles, 180 singles, 53 suites. AE, CB, DC, MC, V.*

❹ Keio Plaza. This is the largest of the hotels in the new city
$$$$ "center" on the west side of Shinjuku. Built in 1971, it is the oldest of the area's skyscraper hotels and—at 47 floors—still the city's tallest. A second tower was added in 1979, and a major renovation completed in 1990; neither gave the Keio Plaza much in the way of intimacy. The lobby and arcades are like a badly planned airport—laid out without character or definition, with pillars everywhere and comfortable seating nowhere. The hotel was built more with banquet revenue and Japanese bookings in mind, and only in recent years has been getting a fairly high percentage of foreign business travelers. Even so, business facilities are unexpectedly good here. The Executive Service Center is one of the few in Tokyo that can do color photocopying, or have dual-language business cards printed in 24 hours. There are also several meeting rooms and banquet halls with international teleconference capability. Guest rooms have good desk space and big picture windows; those on the west side, overlooking Shinjuku Central Park, are the best. *An InterContinental hotel. 2-2-1 Nishi-Shinjuku, Shinjuku-ku, 160, tel. 03/344-0111 or 800/222-5346, fax 03/344-0247. Gen. manager, Katsuhiro Todoroki. 1,328 doubles, 134 singles, 20 suites. AE, CB, DC, MC, V.*

★ ㉖ New Otani. The Otani is not so much a hotel as an urban
$$$$ sprawl. The 17-story main building opened in 1964, on a rise of land once embraced by the defenses of Edo Castle (a section of the moat still survives); the hotel has been growing ever since, buying the rest of the hill piece by piece for a tower annex (completed in 1974), mammoth banquet facilities, arcades and restaurants, and private clubs. The latest addition, scheduled for completion this year, is the Garden Court, an office building to be 30% occupied by foreign firms—primarily banks and securities companies—and connected with the hotel for catering and other support services. The Otani still derives some 15% of its bookings from tour groups, and the main lobby can feel like Grand Central Station at times, but since it was chosen to host the Tokyo Summit Meeting of the Industrialized Nations in 1979 it has been consciously upgrading itself as an international facility for negotiators, diplomats, and business travelers. A major renovation project begun in 1989 leaves the main building with fewer but larger rooms, all equipped with fax machines. The deluxe twins have walk-in closets and glass shower stalls. For work space and facilities, the Executive Service Center is probably the best in town. Showcase restaurants include La Tour d'Argent, the world's only clone of the Tour d'Argent in Paris (*see* Dining, below). Trader Vic's is a good place for a quiet drink (*see* After Hours, below). Ask for a room facing the spectacular 10-acre Japanese garden in the center of the complex, which dates back to the 15th century. *4-1 Kioi-cho, Chiyoda-ku, 102, tel. 03/265-1111; in New York, 800/421-8795; in Los Angeles, 800/252-0197; fax 03/221-2619. Gen. manager, Kazuhiko Otani.*

1,490 doubles, 180 singles, 125 suites. AE, CB, DC, MC, V.

★ ❿ **President Hotel.** This hotel recommends itself more for its
$$ location than for its amenities; if you have dealings with the Honda Company headquarters next door or with one of the law firms or advertising agencies in the Twin Tower Building across the street, the President is ideal. Built in 1980, it's among the best of the local "business hotels." Most rooms are small singles, with tiny bathrooms and no closets at all, but the decor—blond-wood furniture, flowered print drapes and bedspreads—makes them intimate and comfortable. Ask for a room on the top (13th) floor, overlooking the grounds of the Crown Prince's residence and the State Guesthouse. The staff members are friendly and eager to please; with a foreign business clientele approaching 35%, their English is well above the level of most hotels in this category. The harp and piano in the lobby are not merely decorative; there's chamber music here every evening from 7:30 to 11:30. You can unwind over a drink while you listen—if you manage to catch one of the half-dozen small tables. *2–2–3 Minami-Aoyama, Minato-ku, 107, tel. 03/497–0111, fax 03/401–4816. Gen. manager, Naohiko Motohashi. 57 doubles, 155 singles, 2 suites. AE, DC, MC, V.*

❸❻ **Roppongi Prince Hotel.** The memorable feature of this ho-
$$$ tel is a Plexiglas-walled swimming pool in its open central courtyard. In the summer, the pool is filled by day with Tokyo's epicene Gilded Youth (the females are the ones with tops to their bathing suits); if you have no interest in watching them cavort in their fishbowl, there's no compelling reason to stay at the Roppongi Prince—unless you have business at the headquarters of IBM Japan, only a minute's walk away. At nine stories, the hotel (built in 1984) enjoys no particular views. The hotel lobby is very small, decorated mostly in frosted glass and black marble; guest rooms have clean, functional lines, with space-age silver-gray couches, black tables and desks. Beds are very low off the floor, evoking the feeling of traditional futons. Bathrooms are tiny. *3–2–7 Roppongi, Minato-ku, 106, tel. 03/587–1111, fax 03/587–0770. Gen. manager, Hirokazu Wakita. 174 doubles, 30 singles, 12 suites. AE, DC, MC, V.*

★ ❷ **Tokyo Hilton Hotel.** Built in 1984, the Hilton is the newest
$$$$ of the three upscale hotels on the west side of Shinjuku, and—at 38 stories—the largest Hilton in Asia. Well over half the bookings here are by foreign business travelers. Renovations in 1990 added two executive floors, bringing the total to five; the Executive Lounge on the 17th has several small meeting rooms, good work spaces, and its own check-in/check-out concierge service. The lounge in the main lobby, with its two-story, thick marble columns and its spiral staircase sheathed in copper, seems a bit overdone, but the chairs are deep and comfortable, and despite the surrounding traffic, it's a surprisingly quiet place to talk business over a drink. Twin rooms on the executive floors have deep blue carpeting, brass-bound walnut furniture, and sliding *shoji* screens instead of drapes; the feeling is one of muted luxury. On a clear day, west-facing rooms afford views of Mt. Fuji. A special feature for the fitness-minded guest is two rooftop tennis courts, with a full-time resident coach, open 7 AM to 9 PM. *6–6–2 Nishi-*

Shinjuku, Shinjuku-ku, 160, tel. 03/344–5111 or 800/223–1146, fax 03/342–6094. Gen. manager, Hiroshi Nakamura. 723 doubles (business class: 134), 45 suites. AE, CB, DC, MC, V.

East

㊷ **Annex Dai-Ichi Hotel.** Words that mean one thing in English can often mean something quite different to the Japanese. The Annex is not, in fact, an annex at all; right next door to the Shimbashi Dai-Ichi Hotel and owned by the same organization, it is operated as an entirely separate hotel. The old Dai-Ichi is slated for demolition; the Annex, built in 1989, is the first of three new hotels planned for this strategic location. The lobby of the Annex is in the geometric black and white of current fashion; it is architecturally interesting and tastefully done. Rooms are designed in coordinated pastels—understated, but with a sense of luxury provided by touches like marble washstands, full-length double wardrobe mirrors, and (on the Hibiya side of the building) extra-ample desks of walnut and brass, running the length of the window. The Annex is relatively small; the building goes up 20 stories, but the 13th through 20th floors are occupied by the head offices of the Tokyo Seimei insurance company. Conference rooms are on the third floor, which also has a well-appointed lounge exclusively for guests of the hotel. Business services are minimal, but the staff is friendly and eager to help. Shimbashi is a short cab ride to the office towers and government buildings of Hibiya and Kasumigaseki, or to the International Trade Center in Hamamatsu-cho. *1–5–2 Uchisaiwai-cho, Chiyoda-ku, 100, tel. 03/503–5611, fax 03/503–5777. Gen. manager, Masato Aota. 160 doubles, 10 suites. AE, DC, MC, V.*

㊿ **Ginza Tokyu Hotel.** Built in 1960, the 10-story Tokyu manages to avoid anything a foreign visitor would find architecturally distinctive; it is a basic gray slab of a building, with a large open lobby, carpeted and softly lighted. Rooms have beige-patterned wallpaper and assembly-line furniture; all singles are on the inner side, overlooking an empty courtyard. Bathtubs are square, and impossibly small. Foreign business travelers (about 30% of the bookings) are likely to choose the Tokyu for its location; the headquarters of Nissan Motors are across the street; and the advertising and publishing houses of Higashi-Ginza are only a few minutes' walk. Staff people are professionally correct, but you get the impression they're a bit overworked. *5–15–9 Ginza, Chuo-ku, 104, tel. 03/541–2411; in New York, 800/822–0016; in Los Angeles, 800/624–5068; fax 3541–6622. Gen. manager, Shinya Ishida. 249 doubles, 194 singles, 3 suites. AE, DC, MC, V.*

★ ⑲ **Hilltop Hotel.** There aren't many hotels in Tokyo that let you use the word "charming" with a straight face; the Hilltop is one of them. It was designed in 1937 by an American architect who enjoyed a local vogue at the time, and put up buildings in this same mini–Empire State style all over town. The seven-story Hilltop has two sitting rooms in the lobby, one of them with a grandfather clock; guest rooms have real wood windowsills and lampshades with fringes. Somebody's grandmother must have picked the furniture; the only thing you really wish she hadn't done was pick that particular bilious shade of green for the carpets. Best rooms are the double-bed singles on the third and fourth floor, on the southwest side, overlooking a small park; an annex was added in 1970, but the rooms are about the same size and have no character at all. About 70% of the guests are Japanese business travelers and academics (Meiji University is next door); for the foreign business traveler, the location is a bit remote, unless you're dealing in electronics with nearby Hitachi—but the Japan Railway crosstown line that takes you quickly into the city center is only a five-minute walk. *1–1 Surugadai, Kanda, Chiyoda-ku, 101, tel. 03/293–2311, fax 03/233–4567. Gen. manager, Yusuke Akiyama. 41 doubles, 30 singles, 2 suites. AE, CB, DC, MC, V.*

49
$$
Hotel Atamiso. Originally a traditional-style Japanese inn, the Atamiso was rebuilt in 1980 as a 10-story Western-style hotel. The owner has tried to keep the best of both worlds with "combination" rooms—one section with a bed and odd bits of Western furniture, another (about 8' × 10') with a traditional low table and tatami-mat floors. The Nissan Motor Co. headquarters is within easy walking distance; this part of East Ginza is also home ground for Dentsu, Japan's mammoth advertising agency, and to a number of major publishing houses. Not far from the Tsukiji Central Market, the area teems with good sushi restaurants, and the Kabuki Theater is just around the corner. The hotel itself has relatively little to offer. Most of the lobby space is taken up by a big stainless steel–clad column in the center; rooms are small, and unit baths—with barely six feet of clearance—are truly tiny. The Atamiso badly needs a renovation. But the friendly staff tries hard, and bookings by foreigner travelers have slowly climbed to about 20% as the word gets around. *4–14–3 Ginza, Chuo-ku 104, tel. 03/541–3621, fax 03/541–3263. Gen. manager, Sachiko Yamamoto. 40 doubles, 33 singles, 3 suites. AE, DC, MC, V.*

★ 41
$$$$
Imperial Hotel. Japan's very first attempt at a Western-style grand hotel, the Imperial was built in 1891; the second incarnation, designed by Frank Lloyd Wright, opened just in time to greet the Great Kanto Earthquake of 1923—and was the only major building in Tokyo to survive intact. The present 17-story main building dates to 1975; a 31-story tower annex, with somewhat smaller rooms but wonderful panoramic views of the city, was added in 1983. The hotel draws about 80% business travelers (60% of them foreign); its location, between the Imperial Palace and the Ginza, is ideal for anyone with business in the Marunouchi financial district, Hibiya, or the government centers in Kasumigaseki. The Imperial is proud of its place and history—perhaps a little more than it should be as growth has somewhat dulled the edge on its tradition of personal service. The Executive Service Lounge, for example, could have more to offer: There's a small conference room—and a piano—but no individual work spaces. The pillared main lobby is spacious and elegantly appointed, but the overall impression is one of too much traffic. Power breakfasts at Les Saisons (*see* Dining, below), on the mezzanine, are especially popular with visiting businesspeople. The Old Imperial Bar (*see* After Hours, below) is furnished in part with frescoes and stone latticework preserved when Frank Lloyd Wright's brilliant work was torn down. *Member, Leading Hotels of the*

*World. 1–1–1 Uchisaiwai-cho, Chiyoda-ku, 100, tel. 03/
504–; in New York, 800/223–6800; in Los Angeles, 800/
323–7500; fax 03/504–1258. Gen. manager, Ichiro
Inumaru. 1,062 doubles, 76 suites. AE, CB, DC, MC, V.*

㉟ Marunouchi Hotel. Built in 1924, and renovated in 1964,
$$ before foreigners started coming to Japan in any apprecia-
ble numbers, the Marunouchi reflects the unspoken ex-
pectations of the Japanese business traveler, namely, if
you can just get close enough to the action, comfort is a bo-
nus you don't even *think* of demanding. And the nine-story
Marunouchi is indeed close to the action—within easy
walking distance of the corporate headquarters of the
Mitsui and Mitsubishi banking/trading conglomerates,
Fujitsu, Nomura Securities, the Federation of Economic
Organizations, and the Bank of Japan, to name only a few.
The hotel itself could use another major remodeling; the
price is certainly right for the location, but amenities are
few. The lobby is small, the adjacent lounge and coffee
shop are noisy and crowded, and early morning checkout
can be a hassle. The furniture is worn, and foreigners will
find it undersized; the red plush settees and mauve car-
pets must have been picked out before anyone in Japan
ever heard the word "design." Best rooms are the deluxe
twins on the second and third floors, on the inner side of
the building (avoid the avenue side: it gets noisy). Dating
back to the 1964 renovation, these rooms are appreciably
larger than the rooms in more modern business hotels;
they have real tile baths, and room dividers and lacquered
cabinets evoke something of the traditional Japanese
sense of decor. *1–6–3 Marunouchi, Chiyoda-ku, 100, tel.
03/215–2151, fax 03/215–8036. Gen. manager, Kiyoshi Ko-
bayashi. 132 doubles, 61 singles, 1 suite. AE, DC, MC, V.*

★ ㊳ Palace Hotel. Of the first-class hotels in Tokyo, the 10-sto-
$$$$ ry Palace is closest to the Otemachi and Marunouchi finan-
cial districts. It's within walking distance of the local
offices of major American corporate law firms, foreign and
domestic banks, and insurance and securities companies.
It caters, in fact, almost 100% to business travelers, and
the service is excellent. For the guest with a little time to
spare, the hotel is also just across the street from the East
Garden of the Imperial Palace—the only part of the
grounds open to the public. Built in 1934, the hotel retains
a deliberately low-key and old-fashioned (some would say
dowdy) ambience, quiet and dignified, with low ceilings
and dark-wood furniture in the lobby and guest rooms.
Best rooms in the house, for the Imperial Palace view, are
nos. 837 and 937. The lounge and Swan Terrace restaurant
both have full-length windows that look out on the impos-
ing stone walls of the Palace moat. The hotel maintains its
own fleet of chauffeur-driven limousines for hire. *Associ-
ate Member, CIGA Hotels. 1–1–1 Marunouchi, Chiyoda-
ku, 100, tel. 03/211–5211 or 800/223–0888, fax 03/211–
6987. Gen. manager, Masao Yoshihara. 274 doubles, 124
singles, 6 suites. AE, CB, DC, MC, V.*

㊼ Ramada Renaissance Ginza Tobu. The upscale Ramada ho-
$$$$ tels have a certain predictable glitter wherever you find
them; the Tokyo version is no exception. The lobby is a
large open square; twin spiral staircases in the center,
with brass railings and glass-rod chandeliers overhead,
lead down to the restaurants on the floor below. Guest
rooms are of a decent size, with blond-wood furniture, flo-

ral print drapes and bedspreads, in the kind of good taste
that gives you no clue at all to what country you might be
in. Opened in 1987, the hotel prides itself on the Renaissance (10th) and Executive Suite (11th) floors at the top of
the building, but there's less here than meets the eye: You
need your room key to access these two levels on the elevator, but apart from a small lounge and a concierge service,
the amenities do not differ very much from those in rooms
on the floors below. If your business is with the nearby
Honda Motor Company, or one of the publishers or ad
agencies in this area, the location couldn't be better;
you're also within walking distance of the Kabuki Theater
and the upscale shops and department stores of the Ginza.
The Marunouchi financial district is only five minutes by
cab. Night owls take note: The Ramada Renaissance has
one of the only 24-hour hotel coffee shops in town. *6–14–10
Ginza, Chuo-ku, 104, tel. 03/546–0111 or 800/228–9898,
fax 03/546–8990. Gen. manager, Eiichi Kasai. 163 doubles, 34 singles, 9 suites. AE, DC, MC, V.*

★ ❷⓿ **Royal Park Hotel.** This hotel would recommend itself if
$$$ only for the connecting passageway to the Tokyo City Air
Terminal, where you can complete all your check-in proce-
dures before you climb on the bus for Narita Airport.
There's no luxury—especially at the end of an intensive
business trip—like being able to pack, ring for the bell-
hop, and not have to touch your baggage again until it
comes off the conveyor belt back home. In terms of loca-
tion, however, the Royal Park has even more going for it:
It's a short walk to the IBM Hakozaki Building, the Tokyo
Stock Exchange, and the offices of most major Japanese
securities companies; it's five minutes by cab to the
Marunouchi and Otemachi financial districts; and a sub-
way station (Hanzomon Line) in the basement puts you
within 20 minutes of anywhere else in town. Built in 1989,
the 20-story Royal Park is well designed in the bargain.
The large, open lobby has perhaps a bit more marble than
it needs, and the inevitable space-age chandelier, but this
is offset by wood-paneled columns, brass trim, and lots of
comfortable lounge space. Guest rooms, done in coordi-
nated neutral grays and browns, have good proportions;
deluxe twins have handsome escritoires instead of built-in
desktops. Ask for a room on one of the Executive Floors
(16th–18th) with a northeast view of the Sumida River;
another good option is a room lower down (6th–8th floors)
on the opposite side, overlooking the hotel's delightful
fifth-floor Japanese garden. The Royal Park gets about
45% of its bookings from foreign business travelers, main-
ly American and European; the staff is on its toes, eager to
please, and proud of the hotel. *A Nikko International ho-
tel. 2–1–1 Nihonbashi-Kakigaracho, Chuo-ku, 103, tel.
03/667–1111 or 800/645–5687, fax 03/665–7212. Gen. man-
ager, Yutaka Nakamura. 430 doubles, 11 singles, 9
suites. AE, CB, DC, MC, V.*

★ ❹⓼ **Seiyo Ginza.** This is it: the classiest act in town. Nothing so
$$$$ crass as a check-in lobby here: You walk up the pink-mar-
ble staircase to the salon and take a seat at the inlaid ma-
hogany desk, while your "personal secretary" deals with
these tiresome formalities. Built in 1987, the Seiyo mark-
ed the entry of the Saison Group merchandising conglom-
erate into the hotel business; Saison went on to acquire a

majority share in the InterContinental chain, and the Seiyo was used to develop expertise in running a world-class luxury bivouac. The Seiyo is small (80 rooms on 12 floors), and a staff of 240 caters to your every need. The lounge areas were designed by Toronto-based William Noel Lee (and the Presidential Suite by Rena Dumas/Hermes); the soft coordinated neutral tones in the guest rooms are a kind of trademark of the Saison fashion statement. All rooms have glass-enclosed stall showers, bathtubs that would accommodate a string quartet, separate boudoirs with seven-foot mirrors on the closet doors, and VCRs that access a 200-tape video library. The Seiyo is not especially well situated (a section of the Tokyo Expressway runs right past it), but its location—a few minutes from the heart of the Ginza and the Marunouchi financial district—is otherwise excellent. On the lower level, the hotel connects directly with the 774-seat Saison Theatre; on this floor, too, is the Attore (*see* Dining, below), Tokyo's best Italian restaurant, and Pastorale (*see* Dining, below), an elegant venue for important breakfast meetings. *Member, Relais & Chateaux, Preferred Hotels of the World. A Seiyo Continental hotel. 1–11–2 Ginza, Chuo-ku, 104, tel. 03/535–1111 or 800/447–3496, fax 03/ 535–1110. Gen. manager, Eiji Shigeta. 52 doubles, 28 suites. AE, DC, MC, V.*

South

★ ㉕
$$$
Hotel Pacific Meridien. Built in 1971 on the grounds of a former imperial family estate, the Pacific Meridien enjoys an unusual amount of ambient space—and makes the best of it. It has, for example, one of the three largest hotel gardens in Tokyo; it also has the city's largest hotel pool. The location is not exactly central (Sony is one of the few major corporations with headquarters in this area), but from the Japan Railway station across the street you can be in the Marunouchi business district—or down the bay in Yokohama—in 20 minutes. The hotel itself is basically a 30-story slab; lobby and lounge areas rely heavily on fancy lighting fixtures to disguise the uninspired architecture. Guest rooms were renovated in 1990, however, and done rather well, with pale-green drapes, beige and blond-wood furniture, and full-length mirrors on closet doors. Though the hotel gets about 25% of its bookings from foreign business travelers, it hasn't put much effort into an Executive Center, and farms out most of the services you are likely to need. The senior staff, on the other hand, is very pleasant and eager to please. Contact the hotel branch office in Los Angeles (tel. 213/413–5109) about membership in the Pacific Club International, which entitles you to a 10% discount on room rates, and late checkout privileges. *3–13–3 Takanawa, Minato-ku, 108, tel. 03/ 445–6711 or 800/543–4300, fax 03/445–5733. Gen. manager, Hiroshi Sato. 614 doubles, 299 singles, 41 suites. AE, CB, DC, MC, V.*

㉒
$$$
Miyako Hotel Tokyo. Somewhat inconvenient for the foreign business traveler, the Miyako is nevertheless a comfortable fallback choice when better-situated hotels are full. Built in 1980, it is part of a chain with headquarters in Kyoto; the flagship Miyako there is the city's oldest and finest Western-style hotel. Guests in the 12-story Tokyo

Miyako are predominantly Japanese, relatively few of
them traveling on business. The hotel gets much of its revenue from the new banquet section, completed in 1986.
The large L-shaped lobby is a lounge with big picture windows that look out on a garden. Guest rooms are fairly spacious; furnishings are assembly-line basic. The hotel runs
its own courtesy minibus to the nearest station on the Japan Railway loop line, at Meguro, but if you're staying
here plan instead on getting around by cab, and allow for a
little extra time. *1–1–50 Shiroganedai, Minato-ku, 108,
tel. 03/447–3111, fax 03/447–3133. Gen. manager, Mr.
Komaki. 500 doubles, 19 singles, 12 suites. AE, DC, MC,
V.*

㉔ **New Takanawa Prince Hotel.** Built in 1982 on the theory
$$$ that bigger is better, the 15-story New Takanawa is a
long, white rectangle, scalloped with little, round balco-
nies that nobody ever seems to use, rising the whole
length of the hill from Shinagawa Station. At the far end is
a banquet hall that can accommodate 5,000 people; be-
tween the hotel and the original Takanawa Prince (*see* be-
low) is yet another banquet complex, completed last year,
bringing the combined capacity to 7,990. Acres of marble
lobby, labyrinthine corridors, and an arcade connect
these various facilities; the overall effect is a bit daunting.
While receptions and weddings account for a particularly
high percentage of the hotel's cash flow, the business trav-
eler is not neglected. One unique feature of the well-ap-
pointed Business Communication Space on the first floor is
a meeting room that can be rented in three-hour blocks of
time, available 24 hours a day. Guest rooms, on the other
hand, tend to be frilly, with patterned wallpaper, chande-
liers, Empire vanity tables—but no work space. The New
Takanawa is a reasonable choice if you have business at
the nearby Sony headquarters; few other major corpora-
tions have offices in this part of town. *3–13–1 Takanawa,
Minato-ku, 108, tel. 03/442–1111 or 800/542–8686, fax 03/
444–1234. Gen. manager, Takeo Miyazawa. 894 doubles,
74 singles, 32 suites. AE, DC, MC, V.*

㉓ **Takanawa Prince Hotel.** This is the older (1971) and small-
$$$ er (14 floors) of the two hotels on the same property, sepa-
rated from the mammoth New Takanawa Prince by a fine
Japanese garden with a fish pond. It caters more to the individual business traveler, and ought to be a quieter, more
peaceful place to stay; certainly the lobby, with its low
ceilings and comfortable proportions, is more promising.
With less traffic to manage, however, the staff seems to
scurry more; at worst, their sense of urgency can be conta-
gious. Renovated in 1988, guest rooms have pale-red carpets, pink bedspreads, and light-wood furniture; the
effect is light and airy, but there's nothing of special character about them. Rooms on the east side overlook the
garden and an inviting outdoor pool. The hotel has no
business center of its own but shares the ample facilities of
the New Takanawa Prince next door. Perhaps the best
thing about the Prince is the Kihinkan Guest House, a
lovely old stone structure in the style of a French manor
house, built in the late 19th century, that can be used for
formal luncheons, dinner parties, and meetings. *3–13–1
Takanawa, Minato-ku, 108, tel. 03/447–1111 or 800/542–
8686, fax 03/446–0849. Gen. manager, Takeo Miyazawa.
307 doubles, 77 singles, 14 suites. AE, DC, MC, V.*

㉑ **Tokyo Prince Hotel.** Except for its proximity to the World
$$$$ Trade Center Building and the Tokyo Trade Center, the
11-story Tokyo Prince offers little in the way of location
except the charm of wide-open spaces. Built in the pro-
jecting-roof style favored by the architects who were making Tokyo over for the 1964 Olympics, it is the flagship of
the Prince hotel chain. The approach is a long, tree-lined
avenue with parking lots on both sides. Rooms on the
south side overlook the gardens of Shiba Park and the
landmark Zozoji Temple. The lobby has low, paneled ceilings and marble floors, and a lounge with red plush
couches. Though rooms were renovated in 1989, the general impression is still a bit threadbare. As in most Prince
hotels, the staff is snap-to competent at the things it
knows best (tour groups and routine requests), but tends
to freeze when you ask for something out of the ordinary.
*3–3–1 Shiba Koen, Minato-ku, 105, tel. 03/432–1111 or
800/542–8686, fax 03/434–5551. Gen. manager, Toshijimi
Motoi. 380 doubles, 87 singles, 17 suites. AE, DC, MC,
V.*

DINING

At last count, there were over 187,000 bars and restaurants in Tokyo. Japanese companies nationwide spend
about $65 million a day (that, at least, is what they report
to the tax authorities) on business entertainment, and a
high percentage of that is spent in this city. Wining and
dining, then, is a very major component in the local way of
life.

Tokyo is not really an "international" city yet; in many
ways, it is still stubbornly provincial. Whatever the rest of
the world has pronounced good, however, eventually
makes its way here—sometimes in astonishing variety.
French, Italian, Chinese, Indian, Middle Eastern, Latin,
East European—it's hard to think of a national cuisine
that goes unrepresented, as Japanese chefs by the thousands go abroad, learn their craft at great restaurants,
and come home to make their mark in Tokyo.

A noteworthy feature of entertaining in Tokyo is that the
city's finest hotels also have some of its best restaurants.
Another is the generally high quality of French food. A
number of France's best-known restaurants have established branches and joint ventures in Tokyo, and regularly
send their chefs over to supervise; some of them stay, find
backers, and open restaurants of their own. The style almost everywhere is nouvelle, but more and more restaurants are making their reputations on the interesting
fusion of French and Japanese culinary traditions, with
poetically beautiful presentations, in bowls and dishes of
different shapes and patterns; and fresh Japanese ingredients, like *shimeji* mushrooms and local wild vegetables.

A few pointers are in order on the geography of food and
drink. There is superb Japanese food all over the city, but
lovers of sushi swear (with excellent reason) by Tsukiji;
the sushi bars in this area, around the central fish market,
tend to have the best ingredients, to serve the biggest
portions, and to charge the most reasonable prices. Tempura is reliable almost everywhere, especially at branches

of the well-established, citywide chains, but Tokyoites will usually confess that the best tempura restaurants are "downtown," in the older working-class neighborhoods around the Asakusa Kannon Temple.

The quintessential Japanese restaurant is the *ryotei:* a large, villalike establishment, usually walled off from the bustle of the outside world, with a number of small, private dining rooms. The rooms are all in traditional style, with tatami-mat floors and low tables, and a hanging scroll or a flower arrangement in the alcove. Members of the staff are assigned to each room, to serve the many different dishes that constitute the meal, pour your sake, and provide light conversation. ("Waitress" is the wrong word; "attendant" is closer, but there really isn't a suitable term in English.) A visit to a ryotei is an adventure—an encounter with foods you've never seen before, with a graceful, almost ritualized style of service, unique to Japan and centuries old. The ryotei is also the kind of restaurant preferred by the older generation of political and business leaders for serious, private negotiations. Many parts of the city are proverbial for their ryotei; the top houses tend to be in Akasaka, Tsukiji, Asakusa and nearby Yanagibashi, and Shimbashi.

Highly recommended restaurants in each price category are indicated by a star ★.

Category	Cost*
$$$$ (Very Expensive)	over ¥7,000
$$$ (Expensive)	¥5,000–¥7,000
$$ (Moderate)	under ¥5,000

per person, including appetizer, entrée, and dessert, but excluding drinks, service, 10% sales tax, and 3% consumption tax.

Numbers in the margin correspond to numbered restaurant locations on the Tokyo Lodging and Dining maps.

Wine and Beer

The Japanese are not known for wine production, primarily because the drink of choice is sake. On a typical night on the town, the Japanese businessman will start off drinking beer (usually Asahi, Kirin, Sapporo, or Suntory), move on to sake, then graduate to *mizuwari* (scotch and water) as the evening wears on. If you prefer wine with your meal, rest assured that most restaurants in Tokyo stock an assortment of imported vintages.

Business Breakfasts

This is not exactly a deep-rooted custom here, but an increasing number of your Japanese counterparts—especially those in law, consulting, advertising, and market research—will feel comfortable enough with this sort of meeting to make it productive. Venue is the problem; apart from the hotels, there are virtually no restaurants in Tokyo open for breakfast that can offer the privacy and comfort you'd want. If your hotel has an Executive Floor, it's likely to serve a Continental breakfast in the lounge; for more elegant surroundings, two of the most popular restaurants are **Les Saisons** at the Imperial Hotel (tel. 03/504–111) and **Pastorale** at the Hotel Seiyo Ginza (tel. 03/535–1111). Reserve well in advance if you're not a guest.

East

⑮ $$ Ashoka. The owners of this Indian restaurant set out to provide a decor commensurate with its fashionable address. The room is hushed and spacious; incense perfumes the air, the lighting is recessed, carpets are thick, and floor-to-ceiling windows overlook Chuo-dori, the main street of the Ginza. The waiters have spiffy uniforms; the *thali* (a selection of curries and other specialties of the house) is served on a figured brass tray. All in all, a good show for the Raj. The *Khandari nan* (a flat bread with nuts and raisins) is excellent; so is the chicken tikka, boneless chunks marinated and cooked in the tandoor clay oven. *Pearl Bldg. 2nd floor, 7–9–18 Ginza, Chuo-ku, tel. 03/572–2377. Casual dress. Reservations advised. AE, DC, MC, V.*

★ ⑱ $$$$ Attore. The Italian restaurant of the ever-so-elegant Seiyo Hotel is divided into two sections. The "casual" side, with seating for 60, has a bar counter, banquettes, and a see-through glass wall to the kitchen; the comfortable room has track lighting and potted plants, marble floors, and ethnic-print tablecloths. The "formal" side, with seating for 40, is the better choice for a quiet business dinner; the mauve wall panels and carpets, armchairs, and soft recessed light are likely to put your client in a relaxed and expansive frame of mind. On either side of the room, at any rate, you get what is hands-down the best Italian cuisine in Tokyo; chef Katsuyuki Muroi trained for six years in Tuscany and Northern Italy, and acquired a wonderful repertoire. Try the pâté of pheasant and porcini mushrooms with white-truffle cheese sauce, or the walnut-smoked lamb chops with sun-dried tomatoes. *Hotel Seiyo Ginza, 1–11–2 Ginza, Chuo-ku, tel. 03/535–1111. Jacket and tie required. Reservations advised. AE, DC, MC, V.*

⑯ $$$ Balalaika. In this age of perestroika, someone may come up with a nouvelle version of Russian cooking; until then, this is the place to go when you are seriously hungry. The Balalaika is by no means cheap, but it serves an excellent sort of ballast, if you have the room to stow it away. Try chicken Kiev, *blinchiki* (small, sweet pancakes with garnishes of red and black caviar), or *solyanka* (a savory broth with sausage and vegetables)—just the thing to sop up with the excellent black bread. A Balalakia Trio entertains every evening from 6; off the main dining room, simply furnished and softly lighted, are three small banquet rooms for private parties, just right for business discussions. *5–9–9 Ginza, Chuo-ku, tel. 03/572–8387. Casual dress. Weekend reservations advised. AE, DC, MC, V.*

㉑ $$$ Edo-Gin. In an area that teems with sushi bars, Edo-Gin maintains its reputation as one of the best. Portions have shrunk a bit lately, but you'd have to visit once every few years, like a time-lapse photograph, to notice. Edo-Gin still serves up generous slabs of fish that drape over the vinegared rice, rather than perch demurely on top. The centerpiece of the main room is a huge tank in which the day's ingredients swim about until they are required; you can't get any fresher than that. A good place to unwind with a client when the day is done. *4–5–1 Tsukiji,*

Chuo-ku, tel. 03/543–4405. Casual dress. No reservations. AE, DC, MC, V.

★ ⑳ **Heichinrou.** This branch of one of the oldest and best res-
$$$ taurants in Yokohama's Chinatown occupies the top floor
of a prestigious office building about five minutes' walk
from the Imperial Hotel, and commands a spectacular
view of Hibiya Park and the Imperial Palace grounds.
Much of the clientele comes from the law offices, securities
firms, and foreign banks on the floors below. The decor is
rich but subdued, the lighting is soft, the linen is impecca-
ble. The banquet room seats 100, and the "VIP Room" has
separate telephone service for power lunches. The cuisine
is Cantonese, and first-rate; specialties of the house in-
clude stir-fried beef with mango, and Peking duck with
shrimp balls. *Fukoku Seimei Bldg., 28th floor, 2–2–2 Uchi-
saiwai-cho, Chiyoda-ku, tel. 03/508–0555. Jacket and tie
required. Reservations advised, especially for tables by
the window. AE, DC, MC, V. Closed Sun. and holidays.*

⑭ **Ketel's.** Helmut Ketel came to Tokyo and went into the
$$$$ food business just after World War I; the same family—by
now in the third generation—has been running the busi-
ness ever since. The first floor of present-day Ketel's
(which opened in 1930) is a restaurant-pub, with seating
for about 40; the main dining room, one flight down, seats
70 in quiet comfort. Ketel's does not go overboard on at-
mospheric effects; the emphasis instead is on good, solid
German food, and plenty of it. Try the sausage salad, and
the sauerbraten with potato dumplings. Not the best
place for a business meeting—especially when the other
customers start singing along with the piano and clarinet;
come here instead to unwind. *5–5–15 Ginza, Chuo-ku, tel.
03/571–5056. Casual dress. Weekend reservations ad-
vised. AE, DC, MC.*

⑬ **Sabatini di Firenze.** The owner and chef at the original
$$$$ Ristorante Sabatini in Florence spend half the year in Tok-
yo, looking after their joint venture, on the seventh floor
of the Sony Building, at the Sukiya-bashi intersection in
the heart of the Ginza. The setting, naturally, is *très* Flor-
entine, with marble floors and sculpted paneling, beams
and pilasters, sconces and chandeliers. Phalanxes of ma-
hogany service carts glide hither and yon. The antipasto of
chicken livers *alla Fiorentina* (sautéed and served over
croutons with diced ham) is very good, as is the *pennette* (a
thick, round, hollow pasta) in cream sauce. A good place to
take that important client, to warm up the relationship.
*5–3–1 Ginza, Chuo-ku, tel. 03/573–0013. Jacket and tie
required. Reservations advised. AE, DC, MC, V.*

West and South

★ ⑯ **La Belle Époque.** The flagship restaurant of the Hotel
$$$$ Okura, across the street from the American Embassy, La
Belle Époque is a monument to the Japanese passion for
Art Nouveau, with the curvilinear, graceful touches of an
Aubrey Beardsley or Gustav Klimt, including panels of
stained glass separating the tables into flowered alcoves.
A chanson singer holds forth every evening to the strains
of a harp and piano. From the north dining room, there's a
fine view of the city, with the Eiffel-inspired Tokyo Tower
in the foreground. The cuisine is French *classique*; chef
Philippe Mouchel has three-star credentials, having
trained at both the Restaurant Paul Bocuse and the Mou-

lin de Mougins. Favorites here include *dorado Amadai* (sea bream in balsamic vinaigrette with garnish of candied tomatoes) and mushroom-stuffed chicken breast with asparagus. *2–10–4 Toranomon, Minato-ku, tel. 03/505–6073. Jacket and tie required. Reservations required. AE, DC, MC, V. Dinner only.*

★ ㉛ **Bengawan Solo.** The Japanese, whose own aesthetic tradition demands a separate dish for every item in a meal, have
$$$ to overcome a certain resistance to the Indonesian custom of *rijsttafel* (a smorgasbord tray full of curries, skewered items, and sauces), but in fact, they've been overcoming it at Bengawan Solo for about 30 years; this is one of the oldest foreign restaurants in Tokyo. A back room was added about 10 years ago without appreciably reducing the amiable clutter of batik pictures, shadow puppets, carvings, and pennants that make up the decor. The eight-course rijsttafel is spicy-hot, and ample; if it doesn't quite stretch for two, order an extra *Gado-Gado* salad (a mixture of bean sprouts, fried rice crackers, and vegetables in peanut sauce). Start unwinding here after the business day; the bars and discos of Roppongi are just a short walk away. *7–18–13 Roppongi, Minato-ku, tel. 03/408–5969. Casual dress. Reservations advised. AE, DC, MC, V.*

⑫ **Borsalino.** The accent at Borsalino, a five-minute walk
$$$ from the Roppongi intersection, is Milanese; the decor is all right angles and designer concepts, in black and white, but softened with a few tall plants. The buffet puts an admirable selection of antipasti on display, such as scallops and green beans in Marsala sauce (made with cream and Marsala wine); ratatouille of diced eggplant, tomatoes, and zucchini; and omelet *aux fines herbes*. The *fritto misto*, or fried assortment of, in this case shrimp and squid, is another must. Comfortable banquettes make this a good place to talk over the finer points of your deal. *6–8–21 Roppongi, Minato-ku, tel. 03/401–7751. Casual dress. Reservations advised. AE, DC, MC, V. Closed Mon.*

㉘ **Budo-tei.** The word *budo-tei* in Japanese means "grape ar-
$$$ bor," and this is a restaurant that prides itself on its thoughtfully chosen selection of wines. It's also the kind of quiet, friendly place where they remember your name, and put aside a piece of your favorite dessert when you call in your reservation. The French nouvelle menu changes frequently, but you can always count on a good entrecôte of beef or filet Mignon. The decor is modest: hardwood floors, ceiling beams, a few good pieces of sculpture and pottery highlighted in niches along the bare white walls. The three-course lunch—at ¥1,700—is probably the best bargain in town. A good place for a working meal. *Akasaka Tokyu Plaza 1st floor, 2–14–3 Nagata-cho, Chiyoda-ku, tel. 03/593–0123. Jacket and tie required for dinner. Reservations advised. AE, DC, MC, V. Closed Sun. and holidays.*

㉜ **Castle Praha.** Czechoslovakian cooking is an interesting
$$$ style that tends, like German cooking, to emphasize veal and pork, various kinds of sausages, potatoes, and dumplings. The Castle Praha is spacious and comfortable by Tokyo standards, with seating for perhaps 160 in the main section, and two rooms for private parties. The high ceilings are set off by fixtures of Czechoslovakian crystal; at night, the view of Roppongi—from 17 stories up—is superb. A violinist and accordion player stroll from table to

table every evening, with a repertoire of romantic Bohemian melodies. Try the pork cutlet Bratislava Castle, stuffed with mild sausage, grilled, and served with a paprika-and-sour cream sauce. *Tonichi Bldg., 17th floor, 6–2–31 Roppongi, Minato-ku, tel. 03/405-2831. Casual dress. Reservations advised for a table by the window. AE, DC, MC.*

⑤ **Chez Matsuo.** Shoto is the kind of neighborhood you don't
$$$$ expect in the inner city—a sort of sedate Beverly Hills, with its stately homes (the governor of Tokyo's among them) hidden discreetly behind walls half a block long. Chez Matsuo occupies the first floor of a lovely, old, two-story house in Western style. The two dining rooms look out on the garden, where you can dine by candlelight on summer evenings. Owner-chef Matsuo studied his craft in Paris, and in London as a sommelier. His food is nouvelle; the specialty is supreme of duck. Other recommended dishes are foie gras with *daikon* (Japanese white radish) and roast duck with garnish of candied apples. A good place to wine and dine that important client. *1–23–15 Shoto, Shibuya-ku, tel. 03/465-0610. Jacket and tie required. Reservations advised. AE, DC, MC, V. Closed Mon.*

★ ⑪ **Fukudaya.** This is not a restaurant you decide to just "try"
$$$$ on your own, even if you could; ryotei of this caliber are reluctant to take a reservation from somebody they don't already know. Fukudaya is the kind of place the Japanese themselves pick to host people they most want to impress. And Fukudaya *is* impressive, with graceful attendants in exquisite kimonos; silk cushions and lacquered armrests; private gardens with flagstone walks, manicured to perfection; and a seemingly endless series of courses—small portions of fish and seafood and vegetables, arranged like works of art. The sake comes in Imari porcelain cups—yours to take home, as a parting gift. Not a place for a working dinner, but where, with the right word and the right moment, you can nail down the deal. *6 Kioi-cho, Chiyodu-ku, tel. 03/261-8577. Jacket and tie required. Reservations required. No credit cards. Closed Sun. and holidays.*

⑬ **Ganchan.** The Japanese expect their sushi bars to be im-
$$ maculately clean and light; they expect *yakitori* joints, which specialize in bits of chicken and vegetables charcoal-broiled on skewers, to be smoky, noisy and cluttered—like Ganchan. There's counter seating only, for about 15; you have to squeeze to get to the chairs in back by the kitchen. Walls are festooned with festival masks, paper kites and lanterns, handwritten menus, and greeting cards from celebrity patrons. Behind the counter, the cooks yell at each other, fan the grill, and serve up enormous schooners of beer. Try the *tsukune* (balls of minced chicken), and the fresh asparagus wrapped in bacon. No business to be done here: just good fun. *6–8–23 Roppongi, Minato-ku, tel. 03/478-0092. Casual dress. No reservations. V. Dinner only.*

㉝ **Go-nin Hyakusho (Five Farmers).** The specialty here is
$$ Tohoku cooking, from the northeastern part of Japan—hearty food, strong on boiled vegetables and grilled fish, served in an interesting variety of folk-craft dishes, bowls, and baskets. The floor under the tables and counter spaces is on two levels, so you can stretch your legs. Five Farmers has an especially fine collection of lacquer chests

and other antiques from Tohoku farmhouses. Try the *oden* (a bubbling assortment of fish cakes and vegetables served on a hibachi), or the fried stuffed crab. *Roppongi Square Bldg., 4th floor, 3–10–3 Roppongi, Minato-ku, tel. 03/470–1675. Casual dress. No reservations. AE, DC, MC, V. Closed Sun.*

★ ❸❹ **Inakaya.** The style is *robata-yaki* (charcoal-grilled cook-
$$$ ery); the ambience is pure theater. In the center of this restaurant is a large U-shaped counter; behind it, on a platform, two cooks in traditional garb sit on cushions at the grill, with a wonderful cornucopia of food spread out below them—fresh vegetables, fish and seafood, skewers of beef and chicken. Point to what you want, or tell your waiter (they all speak a little English), and the cook fetches your choice out of the display on an eight-foot wooden paddle, prepares it, and passes it back across the counter. A place very popular with the foreign business community. *Reine Bldg., 1st floor, 5–3–4 Roppongi, Minato-ku, tel. 03/408–5040. Casual dress. No reserva-tions; expect a half-hour wait any evening after 7. AE, DC, MC, V. Dinner only.*

❾ **L'Orangerie.** Fashion is the key word here at this nouvelle
$$$$ restaurant on the fifth floor of the Hanae Mori Building, just a minute's walk from the intersection of Aoyama-dori and Omote-sando, where you can't throw a stone in any di-rection without breaking the window of a designer boutique. The restaurant itself is a joint venture of L'Orangerie in Paris and Mme. Mori's own formidable em-pire in couture. A muted elegance marks the decor: Cream walls and deep brown carpets, accented with a few good French landscapes, create an atmosphere of muted ele-gance. Mirrors add depth to a room that seats only 40. The menu—an ambitious one to begin with—changes ev-ery two weeks; the salad of sautéed sweetbreads, when they have it, is excellent. Lunch and dinner menus are very pricey; the buffet brunch is a particularly good bet on a warm Sunday between 11 AM and 2:30 PM, when for ¥3,000 you can sit out in the courtyard, amid the grape ar-bors and orange trees, and count the Armani jackets. *Hanae Mori Bldg., 5th floor, Minato-ku, 3–6–1 Kita-Aoyama, tel. 03/407–7461. Jacket and tie required at din-ner. Reservations required. AE, DC, MC, V.*

❽ **La Patata.** One feels that La Patata arrived in Tokyo by
$$$ way of the Berkeley Gourmet Ghetto: it's in the most yuppified part of town, and makes every effort to belong there. There's a blackboard out front, propped on a wood-en chair, with the chef's suggestions of the day chalked in Italian and Japanese; there are brass fixtures and ceiling beams, huge potted plants, old travel posters, an espresso machine on the bar, and a see-through kitchen with a hanging array of copper pans. "Trendy restaurant! Trendy restaurant!" it screams—but La Patata is as seri-ous about its food as it is about its image, and serves up a very fine Italian meal. They make their own prosciutto here, and their own rich tortes and cakes; for a main course try the *boleto misto* (mixed fried seafood). A bit cramped for a business meal. *2–9–11 Jingumae, Shibuya-ku, tel. 03/403–9664. Casual but neat. Reservations ad-vised. AE, DC, MC, V. Closed Mon.*

❶❺ **Sankoen.** With the Embassy of the Republic of Korea a
$$ few blocks away, Sankoen is in a neighborhood thick with

Korean barbecue joints; not much seems to distinguish one from another. A few years back, however, Sankoen suddenly caught on, and people started coming in droves—not just the neighborhood families, but music production and PR people from the nearby studios. Folks in shiny shoes would pull up and let their ladies out to stand in line, while they parked the Mercedes. The Sankoen opened a branch, then moved its main operation across the street to new two-story quarters; late into the night, people are still waiting in line to get in. Korean barbecue is a smoky affair; you cook your own dinner—thin slices of meat and vegetables—on a gas grill at your table. The whole process is a bit too busy for business discussions; this is the kind of place where you and your Japanese client can get to know each other. Sankoen makes a great salad to go with its *kalbi* (brisket). *1–8–7 Azabu Juban, Minato-ku, tel. 03/585–6306. Casual dress. No reservations. AE, MC.*

★ ❶ **Sasashu.** Strictly speaking, Sasashu is not a restaurant
$$$ but an *izakaya* (a sake bar with food). It's included here for two reasons: first, because it stocks only the finest and rarest, the Latours and Mouton-Rothschilds, of sake; and second—the Japanese wouldn't dream of drinking well without eating well—because it serves the best food of any izakaya in town. Sasashu is a rambling two-story building in traditional style, with thick beams and step-up tatami floors. The specialty is salmon steak, brushed with sake and soy sauce and broiled over a charcoal hibachi. Bring your Japanese business contacts here; they're bound to enjoy themselves—and come away deeply impressed that you even know about places like this. *2–2 Ikebukuro, Toshima-ku, tel. 03/971–6796. Casual dress. Reservations advised, especially Jan.–Feb. AE, DC, MC. Closed Sun. Dinner only.*

❼ **South China.** This is a Chinese restaurant for every-
$$ body—or at least for everybody you know, and most of their friends. South China occupies the three basement floors of a building near the main entrance to the Meiji Shrine; it can hold a reception for a thousand people, or a banquet for a hundred, and boasts 13 smaller rooms for private parties. How many tons of red lacquer have gone into the decor is anybody's guess. The menu is on a commensurate scale—with over 200 entries, about half of them Cantonese. The 35 cooks can also handle the fiery Szechuan cuisine, as well as Peking and Shanghai styles. Specialties include shark's fin with crab meat, and Peking duck. *Co-op Olympia Bldg. B1-3, 6–35 Jingu-mae, Shibuya-ku, tel. 03/400–0031. Casual dress. Reservations accepted but not required. AE, DC, MC, V.*

❸❺ **Spago.** This is, so far, the only venture overseas by
$$$$ trendsetting Spago of Los Angeles. Owner-chef-celebrity Wolfgang Puck comes here periodically to oversee the authenticity of his "California cuisine." Will duck-sausage pizza with boursin cheese and pearl onions ever be as American as apple pie? Maybe. In the meanwhile, Spago is a comfortable, well-lighted place with ample spaces, painted pink and white and adorned with potted palms. Service is smooth, and the tables on the glassed-in veranda attract a fair sample of Tokyo's Gilded Youth. *5–7–8 Roppongi, Minato-ku, tel. 03/423–4025. Casual dress. Reservations advised. AE, DC, MC, V.*

⓮ Stockholm. The claim to fame here is the smorgasbord—
$$$$ which, being unpronounceable in Japanese, is usually called a "Viking." At Stockholm, the groaning board is very good indeed—take your choice of deviled eggs with caviar, herring in sour cream, shrimp, salmon, smoked hams, and pâtés, roast chicken, steak tartare, salads of every description, cheeses and fruits, and pastries. You can also order from an extensive dinner and à la carte menu; the specialty is loin of reindeer steak. Elegance is the keynote, with deep leather chairs in the bar, brick archways, and royal-blue carpeting and tapestries on the walls. A quiet, convivial place for business discussions. *Sweden Center Bldg. B1, 6–11–9 Roppongi, Minato-ku, tel. 03/ 403–9046. Jacket and tie required. Reservations advised. AE, DC, MC, V.*

➏ Tenmatsu. You don't really have to spend a lot of money to
$$$ enjoy a first-rate tempura restaurant, and Tenmatsu proves the point. The best seats in the house, as in any *tempura-ya* (tempura restaurant), are at the immaculate wooden counter, where your tidbits of choice are taken straight from the hot oil and served up immediately. You also get to watch the chef in action; Tenmatsu's brand of good-natured professional hospitality adds to your enjoyment of the meal. You can rely on a set menu, or order à la carte from delicacies like lotus root, shrimp, *unagi* (eel), and *kisu* (a small, white freshwater fish). Fine for a relaxed evening with colleagues or clients, but a bit cramped for a serious working dinner. *1–6–1 Dogenzaka, Shibuya-ku, tel. 03/462–2815. Casual dress. Reservations advised for counter seating. DC, V.*

★ ⓱ Toh-Ka-Lin. On the second floor of the Hotel Okura, the
$$$$ Toh-Ka-Lin rates as one of the best Chinese restaurants in the city. Downstairs, decorum reigns; up here, the mood is one of cheerful clatter. The Toh-Ka-Lin is a favorite with Tokyo's film and media personalities as well as with business guests of the hotel. The cuisine is eclectic; two stellar examples are the Peking duck and the sautéed quail wrapped in lettuce leaf. Those who don't find it a little bizarre to drink fine French wines with Chinese food can choose from one of the most extensive wine lists in town—including 11 different champagnes. *Hotel Okura, 2–10–4 Toranomon, tel. 03/505–6068. Casual but neat. Reservations accepted but not required. AE, CB, DC, MC, V.*

㉙ Tokyo Joe's. The very first foreign branch of famed Miami
$$$$ Joe's was in Osaka, a city where volume-for-value really counts in the reputation of a restaurant. The Tokyo branch opened about four years ago and upholds its reputation the same way—by serving enormous quantities of stone crabs, with melted butter and mustard mayonnaise. The turnover is fierce; waiters in long red aprons scurry to keep up with it, but the service is remarkably smooth. This is a noisy place, with no room to speak of between tables, so abandon thoughts of business and devote your attention to the crabs—flown in fresh from the Florida Keys, their one and only habitat. Top off (if you have room) with Key Lime pie. *Akasaka Eight-One Bldg. B1, Nagata-cho 2–13–5, Chiyoda-ku, tel. 03/508–0325. Casual but neat. Reservations advised. AE, DC, MC, V.*

㉖ La Tour d'Argent. The pride of the New Otani Hotel since
$$$$ 1984, La Tour d'Argent is a worthy scion of its ritzy Parisian parent. In the foyer, in a glass case, is the table set-

ting at the Café Anglais—forerunner to the original Tour d'Argent—where Bismarck held a dinner in 1867 for Tsar Alexander II of Russia and Emperor William I of Prussia. Dominating the main dining room is the enormous drapery-sculpted marble carving table, with its silver duck press; the specialty of the house, naturally, is *caneton* (breast of duck). Just as in Paris, you receive a card recording the number of the duck you were served. The roast duckling in green-pepper sauce and the pan-fried red snapper in lemon-flavored herb sauce are good alternatives. *New Otani Hotel, 4–1 Kioi-cho, Chiyoda-ku, tel. 03/239–3111. Jacket and tie required. Reservations required. AE, DC, MC, V. Dinner only.*

27 **Le Trianon.** In 1976 chef Sadao Hotta came over from the
$$$$ Tokyo branch of Maxim's to open Le Trianon in the old guest house of the Akasaka Prince Hotel. The house was built for the king of Korea, in the style of a French country estate, with parquet floors, lofty wooden beams, and stained-glass windows. The restaurant, which takes up the whole second floor, has seven private dining rooms; the largest will hold a party of 12. Many of the regular clientele work in the nearby centers of power: the National Diet, the Liberal-Democratic Party headquarters, and the Supreme Court. Veal in goose liver and truffle sauce, and mousseline of sea bass with creamed sea-urchin sauce are specialties here. *Akasaka Prince Hotel, 1–2 Kioi-cho, Chiyoda-ku, tel. 03/234–1111. Jacket and tie required. Reservations required. AE, DC, MC, V.*

FREE TIME

Fitness

Hotel Facilities
None of the hotel health facilities are open to persons not registered at the hotel.

Health Clubs
Sports and fitness clubs in Tokyo operate for the most part on life-membership systems; only the **Clark Hatch Fitness Center** (Azabu Towers, 2–1–3 Azabudai, Minato-ku, tel. 03/584–4092) offers a one-week temporary membership, at ¥5,000 (no daily memberships available). Facilities include Nautilus equipment and a sauna.

Jogging
The course of choice for joggers who work in the city center is the scenic 5-kilometer run around the **Imperial Palace.** Even better, for broad avenues and open spaces, are **Yoyogi Park** and the playing fields of the **Meiji Jingu Outer Gardens.**

Shopping

Unless you're a determined shopper with lots of time for exploring, Tokyo is not a place where you can expect to find bargains. And while the shelves abound with brand-name luxury goods from all over the world, it's also a strangely difficult place to find things traditionally Japanese that aren't just as available—and maybe even cheaper—back home.

Two factors, however, ease the busy traveler's burden. One is the tendency for certain districts to specialize in a particular kind of merchandise. The famous case in point, and a tourist attraction in its own right, is **Akihabara**— block after block of stores that deal in discount electronic and electrical consumer goods, with a combined annual turnover well in excess of ¥30 trillion. **Shinjuku** is the place to go for discount camera equipment. **Kanda** is known for its booksellers. **Aoyama** and **Omote-sando** have perhaps the highest concentration of designer boutiques for men's and women's fashions. **Asakusa**—especially the narrow streets around the Asakusa Kannon Temple—is known for traditional craft products like fans, kimono fabrics, handmade boxwood combs, tools, and hair ornaments.

The other useful factor is the prevalence of arcades and "theme" buildings (vertical malls, you might call them) and the abundance of department stores that make shopping a one-stop affair. For example, at the **International Arcade,** a few steps from the Imperial Hotel, you'll find a selection of shops offering everything from woodblock prints to pearls, from kimonos to sub-miniature tape recorders—all at quite reasonable prices. Most of the vertical malls, like **Parco** (14 Udagawa-cho, Shibuya-ku) or the **From 1st Building** (3–6–1 Kita-Aoyama, Minato-ku) tend to rent their space to quality clothing boutiques. **Isetan** (3–14–1 Shinjuku, Shinjuku-ku, tel. 03/352–1111; closed Wed.), **Mitsukoshi** (4–6–16 Ginza, Chuo-ku, tel. 03/562–1111; closed Mon.), and **Seibu** (2–1 Udagawa-cho, Shibuya-ku, tel. 03/462–0111; closed Wed.) offer the best selection of goods and are the most upscale of the many department stores around Tokyo.

Still looking for something uniquely Japanese? Try the **Crafts Center** (Plaza 246, 3–1–1 Minami-Aoyama, tel. 03/403–2460) or the **Oriental Bazaar** (5–9–13 Jingumae, Shibuya-ku, tel. 03/400–3933) for a general range of merchandise. For folkcrafts, try **Ishizuka** (1–5–20 Yaesu, Chuo-ku, tel. 03/275–2991); for handmade paper products, **Washikobo** (1–8–10 Nishi-Azabu, Minato-ku, tel. 03/405–1841); for lacquerware, **Inachu Japan** (1–5–2 Akasaka, Minato-ku, tel. 03/582–4451); for woodblock prints, **Matsushita Associates** (6–3–12 Minami-Aoyama, Shibuya-ku, tel. 03/407–4966); and for antiques, the **Tokyo Old Folk Craft and Antique Center** (1–23–1 Jimbo-cho, Kanda, Chiyoda-ku, tel. 03/295–7112), which has over 50 dealers in one building.

Diversions

A free weekend afternoon? Take in a **baseball** game at the new Tokyo Dome (also known as Korakuen Stadium, 1–3–61 Koraku, Bunkyo-ku, tel. 03/811–2111). You can't get a better sociology lesson in the way the Japanese can take something from another culture and make it their own.

Explore one or two of the smaller **museums** in Tokyo with unique special collections. These are comfortable, well-designed spaces that you won't have to share with hordes of other visitors. Among these are the **Japanese Sword Museum** (4–25–10 Yoyogi, Shibuya-ku, tel. 03/379–1386), with over 6,000 swords, of which 30 are designated National Treasures; the **Ota Memorial Museum of Art** (1–10–10 Jingumae, Shibuya-ku, tel. 03/403–0880), with some

12,000 *ukiyoe* woodblock prints; the **Nezu Institute of Fine Arts** (6–5–36 Minami-Aoyama, Minato-ku, tel. 03/400–2536), with an outstanding collection of Chinese bronzes, Korean celedons, and Japanese scroll paintings; and the **Idemitsu Museum of Arts** (3–1–1 Marunouchi, Chiyoda-ku, tel. 03/213–9402), especially strong in Chinese porcelains and Japanese ceramics.

Sensoji, or the Asakusa Kannon Temple, is more than a tourist attraction; it's the spiritual heart of Tokyo's hustling, jostling, gossiping "downtown"—the older, working-class part of the city. Take a free hour or two to walk around the narrow side streets and arcades of this section, and see how eighth-generation-and-proud-of-it Tokyoites spend their day.

Don't miss **sumo wrestling,** if there's a tournament scheduled at the Kokugikan Stadium (1–3 Yokoami, Sumida-ku, tel. 03/623–5111) while you're in town. If not, you might want to take an early-morning stroll through Ryogoku, the district on the north side of the Sumida River; most of the *heya* (stables, where the wrestlers live and train) are located in this area, and you can sometimes get to watch a practice session.

At 5 AM the **Tsukiji Central Market** starts auctioning off some 90% of the fish to be consumed that day by the 11 million inhabitants of Tokyo. By 8 it's all over—and the action in between is really worth watching. About 15,000 people work here, in almost as many tiny shops and auction spaces, sprawling over 54 acres. Men in rubber boots and aprons wheel long wooden pushcarts, stacked with every imaginable variety of seafood, through impossibly narrow passages at impossibly frantic speeds—and somehow never get in each other's way.

Ueno Koen, once the site of a great temple complex, has been a public park for more than a century; it's the basket in which the government put most of its first cultural eggs—including the **Zoological Garden** (9–93 Ueno Koen, Taito-ku, tel. 03/828–5171), the **National Science Museum** (7–20 Ueno Koen, Taito-ku, tel. 03/828–5131), and the **Tokyo National Museum** (13–9 Ueno Koen, Taito-ku, tel. 03/828–1111). The latter consists of four buildings, grouped around a courtyard; of these, the **Horyuji Treasure Hall,** open only on Thursdays, houses 319 breathtaking works from the 7th-century Horyuji Temple in Nara. Also in Ueno Park is the **Toshogu Shrine** (9–8 Ueno Koen, Taito-ku, tel. 03/822–3455), a companion work to the Toshogu Shrine in Nikko, mausoleum and memorial to the first Tokugawa shogun 2, Ieyasu—worshipped after his death as "The Great Incarnation Who Illuminates the East." The shrine dates to 1627 and has survived intact through countless disasters, making it perhaps the oldest collection of buildings in Tokyo.

The Arts

Few cities have as much to offer as Tokyo in the performing arts. It has Japan's own great stage traditions: Kabuki, Noh, Bunraku puppet drama, music, and dance. **Kabuki-za** is the best place to see Kabuki, built especially for that purpose in 1925. The **National Theater of Japan** hosts Kabuki companies from outside Tokyo. The city also has a wide variety of music. Pop music and rock concerts are staged at **Budokan.** And Western classical music, including opera, can be heard at **Suntory Hall** and **Tokyo Bunka Kaikan.** For chamber music, a new venue, designed by architect Arata Isozaki, is **Casals Hall.** Modern theater also exists here—in somewhat limited choices, to be sure, unless you can follow dialogue in Japanese—but Western repertory companies can always find receptive audiences here for plays in English. In recent years musicals have become enormously popular with Japanese audiences; it doesn't take long for a show that hits in New York or London to open at the **Imperial Theater.** Japan has yet to develop any serious strength of its own in opera or ballet, but for that reason touring companies like the Metropolitan and the Bolshoi, Sadler's Wells and the Bayerische Staatsoper find Tokyo a very compelling place—as well they might, when ¥20,000 seats are sold out even before the box office opens. Traditional Japanese dance can be seen at the National Theater.

Ticket agencies with numbers to call in English include **Ticket Pia** (tel. 03/769–4134 or 03/237–9990 for classical music) and **Saison Ticket** (tel. 03/286–5482 or 03/980–6060 for classical music). A third option is the **Playguide** agency, which has outlets in most department stores and in other locations all over the city; you can stop in or call the main office (Playguide Bldg., 2–6–4 Ginza, Chuo-ku, tel. 03/561–8821) and ask for the nearest counter. Note that agencies normally do not have tickets for same-day performances, only for advanced booking.

Budokan, 2–3 Kita-no-maru, Chiyoda-ku, tel. 03/216–0781.
Casals Hall, 1–6 Kanda Surugadai, Chiyoda-ku, tel. 03/294–1229.
Imperial Theater, 3–1–1 Marunouchi, Chiyoda-ku, tel. 03/213–7221.
Kabuki-za, 4–12–15 Ginza, Chuo-ku, tel. 03/541–3131.
National Theater of Japan, 4–1 Hayabusa-cho, Chiyoda-ku, tel. 03/265–7411.
Suntory Hall, 1–13–1 Akasaka, Minato-ku, tel. 03/505–1001.
Tokyo Bunka Kaikan, 5–45 Ueno Koen, Taito-ku, tel. 03/828–2111.

After Hours

One warning holds equally true for the elegance of the Ginza and the seediness of Shinjuku's Kabuki-cho: Don't wander into places you don't already know. Ginza is Expense Account Heaven for the Japanese businessman; many of the bars and clubs in this area just keep running tabs and present them to the company at the end of the month. They maintain the cozy simplicity of this arrangement by discouraging strangers—especially strangers who might go into cardiac arrest when they see the size of the bill. Ginza watering holes also tend to close before midnight. Kabuki-cho, on the other hand, welcomes the unwary stranger with open arms. There are joints in this area that don't close until morning; they specialize in luring the customer and charging astronomical prices for a few recycled beers. If you're exploring on your own, stick to Akasaka and Roppongi, two areas popular with foreign residents of Tokyo that afford more than enough reliable and interesting options.

Bars and Lounges

For a quiet drink with clients, **Trader Vic's** (New Otani Hotel, tel. 03/265–1111) is an Establishment standby, as is the **Old Imperial Bar** (Imperial Hotel, tel. 03/504–1111). **Temps** (Dai-ni Lene Bldg., 4th floor, 5-3-1 Roppongi, Minato-ku, tel. 03/404–0661) draws a crowd of soul-music fans to its encyclopedic record collection. The younger, well-heeled party animal heads for **The Hard Rock Café** (5-4-20 Roppongi, Minato-ku, tel. 03/408–7018); if you get hungry late at night, this place could well have the best hamburger in town. **Le Club** (Plaza Kay B1, 5-1-1 Minami-Azabu, Minato-ku, tel. 03/402–5730), with its quiet Japanese-modern interior, is a low-key venue for a business conversation. The **Highlander Bar** (Hotel Okura, tel. 03/582–0111) is another good spot for a business discussion over drinks.

Cabarets

There aren't many choices in this category, for a city of Tokyo's size. The **New Latin Quarter** (2-13-8 Nagata-cho, Chiyoda-ku, tel. 03/581–1326) has the kind of velvet-curtain decor that conjures up scenes in gangster movies; the **Cordon Blue** (6-6-4 Akasaka, Minato-ku, tel. 03/582–7800) is a restaurant theater with topless dancers.

Jazz Clubs

Body and Soul (7-14-12 Roppongi, Minato-ku, tel. 03/408–2094) is a small, dedicated club where local musicians often show up after hours when their own gigs are finished, and sit in with the featured performers. **Satin Doll** (Haiyuza Bldg., 3rd floor, 4-9-2 Roppongi, Minato-ku, tel. 03/401–3080) is larger and more elegantly appointed; the crowds are mixed, both in age and in degree of seriousness about jazz. Newcomer on the block is **The Blue Note** (5-13-3 Aoyama, Minato-ku, tel. 03/407–5781), which books international headliners, charges top dollar, and draws a lot of people who come more for the cachet than for the music.

For Singles

The tone can go downhill fast after 2 AM at **Charleston** (3-8-11 Roppongi, Minato-ku, tel. 03/402–0372), a perennial favorite with Tokyo's expat community. Low-keyed and friendlier is **Maggie's Revenge** (3-8-12 Roppongi, Minato-ku, tel. 03/479–1096), a successfully transplanted Australian pub.

Toronto

by Allan Gould and Suzanne McGee

Local Indians gave the name "Toronto," believed to mean "a place of meetings," to the spot where the Humber and Don rivers come together and join with Lake Ontario. The site first hosted a busy Indian village, then a French trading post, and, in the late 1700s, a British town named York, before it was incorporated in 1834 as a Canadian city.

Toronto is still a place of meetings, the prime place to do business in English-speaking Canada. In response to growing separatist sentiment during the 1970s in Montréal, many national companies relocated here, and those companies have been joined by others. Hong Kong money is starting to flow into the city, along with that country's new entrepreneurs, who are fleeing the prospect of living the strictures of the People's Republic of China. At the same time, cost of living in Toronto has increased dramatically in recent years, and high rental fees have lead several major corporations to shift headquarters to the suburbs or away from the area altogether.

But although subject to typical big-city annoyances such as congested rush hours, Toronto is still a good place to live—if one can afford it. It is clean and relatively crime free. It is also the country's cultural capital. Once homogenous to the point of tedium, Toronto is now ethnically diverse; recent immigrant groups include Greeks, Portuguese, Italians, Vietnamese, Chinese, and Hungarians. With the conclusion of the free trade agreement between Canada and the United States, business travel has stepped up considerably, and services offered to business travelers have kept pace. Toronto is one of the few cities in North America where it is still possible to attend business meetings, dine in style, and attend an excellent concert or play before retiring for the night without having walked more than six blocks from your hotel.

Top Employers

Employer	Type of Enterprise	Parent*/ Headquarters
A&P Food Stores	Groceries	Toronto
Canada Life Assurance	Insurance	Toronto

Ellis Don Construction Limited	Construction	London, Ontario
F. W. Woolworth Co. Limited	Retail	Toronto
Honeywell Limited	Computers	Toronto
Indal Limited	Manufacturing	Toronto
Kodak Canada Inc.	Photographic equipment	Toronto
Maclean-Huntre Ltd.	Communications	Toronto
Royal Trust Company	Real estate	Toronto
Sun Life Assurance	Insurance	Toronto
Toronto Star Newspapers Ltd.	Newspapers	Toronto

if applicable

ESSENTIAL INFORMATION

Climate

What follows are the average daily maximum and minimum temperatures for Toronto.

Jan.	30F 16	−1C −9	Feb.	30F 15	−1C −9	Mar.	37F 23	3C −5
Apr.	50F 34	10C 1	May	63F 44	17C 7	June	73F 54	23C 12
July	79F 59	26C 15	Aug.	77F 58	25C 14	Sept.	69F 51	21C 11
Oct.	56F 40	13C 4	Nov.	43F 31	6C −1	Dec.	33F 21	1C −6

Airports

Pearson International (simply called "the Toronto airport"), 18 miles from the city center, serves Toronto and most of southwestern Ontario. Try to avoid arrivals at Terminal 1, which is overcrowded and has inadequate baggage handling facilities. (Although most flights use Pearson, **Toronto Island Airport,** about 25 minutes from downtown, also offers commuter service to nearby cities, notably Ottawa, Montreal, and Newark, NJ. Shuttle service from the Royal York Hotel to the Toronto Island Airport—by bus and then by ferry—is provided free by the airport's major carrier, City Express, but this airline's planes are small and propeller-driven, flights are less frequent, delays are not uncommon, and there are few alternative flights if delays are extensive.

Airport Business Facilities

A **Swiss Hotel** with business facilities is planned to open in the summer of 1991 at Pearson International, within the new Terminal 3 currently under construction.

Airlines

Toronto is a hub city for both Air Canada and Canadian Airlines International. Air Canada, USAir, and American Airlines fly between here and the northeastern U.S. most often; Northwest has frequent flights to and from Chicago.

Air Canada, tel. 416/925–2311 or 800/422–6232.
American, tel. 800/433–7300.
Canadian Airlines International, tel. 416/675–2211 or 800/387–2737.
City Express, tel. 416/360–4444 or 800/387–3060 (Island).
Delta, tel. 416/868–1717 or 800/843–9378.
Midway, tel. 800/621–5760.
Northwest, tel. 800/225–2525.
United, tel. 416/362–5000 or 800/241–6522.
USAir, tel. 416/361–1560 or 800/428–4322.

Between Toronto Airport and Downtown

By Taxi
A cab downtown can take more than an hour during rush hour, 25–30 minutes if traffic is light. To avoid delays, travelers are advised to arrive or depart between 9 AM and 3 PM or after 7 PM. Fares from the airport are flat rates that depend on the destination. Taxis and limos to a hotel or business by the lake usually run more than Can$35. It is slightly more expensive to head uptown or to Yorkville, and about Can$40–Can$45 to go to the city's northeast corner (the area of Don Mills or Scarborough). Most limousine services have a minimum charge of Can$15, which gets you to an airport hotel. To Mississauga, charges run about Can$25.

By Bus
Grey Coach (tel. 416/393–7911) runs buses to most major downtown hotels at 20-minute intervals, from 6 AM to midnight daily. The fare is about Can$11. This is often a good bet when the airport is busy, as even at the best of times there is a dearth of taxis and limos. Grey Coach also transports travelers to three subway stops: two in the north (Yorkdale and York Mills) and one in the west (Islington).

By Subway
Subway travel is less expensive (Can$5–$8) but not recommended unless you're on a stringent budget and don't mind carrying your own luggage. Allow 1½–2 hours to reach center city. Buses run every 20 minutes from both terminals to Islington and Kipling stations (in the west end, on the Bloor line) and to Yorkdale (in the north of the city, on the Yonge line). The subway runs between 6 AM–12:30 AM.

Car Rentals

The following companies have booths in the terminals.

Avis, tel. 416/964–2051 or 800/331–1212.
Budget Rent-a-Car, tel. 416/673–3322 or 800/527–0700.

Hertz, tel. 416/961–3320 or 800/223–6472; in NY, 800/522–5568.
National, tel. 416/488–2400 or 800/227–7368.

Emergencies

Doctors
Dial-a-Doctor (tel. 416/492–4713).

Dentists
Yonge Finch Dental Centre (5650 Yonge St., tel. 416/222–6122), **Toronto Eaton Centre** (Dundas and Yonge Sts., tel. 416/585–9133), **Metro Central** (24-hour service, tel. 416/787–1275), **Metro West** (including airport, tel. 416/622–5235).

Hospitals
Mount Sinai (600 University Ave. near Dundas, tel. 416/596–4200), **Toronto General** (University Ave. and Dundas St., tel. 416/595–3111), **Toronto Western** (399 Bathurst St., at Dundas St., tel. 416/368–2581), **North York General** (4001 Leslie St., near the 401, tel. 416/756–6000), **Etobicoke General** (101 Humber College, near airport, tel. 416/747–3528).

Important Addresses and Numbers

Audiovisual rentals. Metrocom (21 Goodridge St., tel. 416/259–1772).

Chamber of Commerce. The Board of Trade of Metropolitan Toronto (1 First Canadian Place, tel. 416/366–6811).

Computer Rentals. CO/RENT Computer Stores (2 Berkeley St., Suite 305, tel. 416/366–7368), Drexis Computer Rentals (100 Richmond St. E, Suite 320, tel. 416/366–9199), Vernon Computer Rentals (81st St. Clair Ave. E, tel. 416/963–9340).

Convention and Exhibition Centers. Canadian Exposition and Conference Centre (272 Attwell Drive, Etobicoke, tel. 416/675–6500), Exhibition Place (tel. 416/393–6076), International Centre (6900 Airport Rd., Mississauga, tel. 416/677–6131), Metro Toronto Convention Centre (255 Front St. W, tel. 416/585–8000).

Fax services. Businex Business Centres (801 York Mills; 3800 Steeles Ave. W; 833 The Queensway; 3100 Steeles Ave. W, 24-hour services; tel. 416/739–5000 for all stores).

Formal-wear rentals. Freeman Formalwear (556 Yonge St., tel. 416/920–2727), Syd Silver Formals (500 Yonge St., tel. 416/923–4611).

Gift shops. Chocolates: Chocolate Messenger (1574 Bayview, South of Eglinton, tel. 416/488–1414). Flowers: King Edward Florist (37 King St. E, tel. 416/366–6501), Queen's Quay Florist (at Harbourfront, tel. 416/865–1388, open daily). Fruit baskets: Gift O'Fruit (964 Eglinton St. W, tel. 416/787–4505).

Graphic design studios. GJW Graphics Services (1120 Tapscott Rd., Unit #3, Scarborough, tel. 416/298–7050), The Printing House (Citibank Pl., 123 Front St. W, tel. 416/865–1660), Syrograph International (517 Wellington St. W, Suite 301, tel. 416/599–8094).

Hairstylists. Unisex: De Berardini Salon (Eaton Centre, tel. 416/979–9292). Men: Roula's Exclusive Men's (Inn on the Park, Leslie and Englinton Ave. E, tel. 416/447–9780).

Health and fitness clubs. *See* Fitness, below.

Information hot lines. Metropolitan Toronto Convention and Visitors Association (tel. 416/368–9821), Canadian Auto Association Road Report (tel. 416/966–3000).

Limousine services. Airline Limousine (tel. 416/675–7181), Carey Limousine (tel. 416/466–8776 or 800/336–4747), Rosedale Livery (tel. 416/677–9444 or 800/268–4967).

Liquor stores. Pearson International Airport (Terminal 1, tel. 416/676–3945, Terminal 2, tel. 416/676–3695), Toronto Eaton Centre (Dundas and Yonge Sts., tel. 416/979–9978), Union Station (Front and Bay Sts., tel. 416/368–9644).

Mail delivery, overnight. DHL International (tel. 416/244–3278), Federal Express (tel. 416/897–9322), TNT Skypak (tel. 416/678–2770), UPS (tel. 416/736–3800).

Messenger services. Canada Post (tel. 416/973–5757), Win-Jam (tel. 416/431–5232).

Office space rental. Global Office (Drake International, 55 Bloor St. W, tel. 416/928–1300).

Pharmacies, late-night. Lucliff Place (700 Bay and Gerrard Sts., tel. 416/979–2424), Pharma Plus Drugmart (Wellesley and Church Sts., tel. 416/924–7760).

Radio stations, all-news. Canada's only all-news station closed in 1989 but CBC 740 AM and CBC 94.1 FM both have world news at the top of every hour.

Secretarial service. Support Office Systems (80 Richmond St. W, tel. 416/362–0859, open daily).

Stationery supplies. Grand & Toy (several locations, including: 120 Adelaide St. W, tel. 416/363–0022; 347 Bay St., tel. 416/366–0753; 777 Bay St., tel. 416/977–5100; 144 Bloor St. W, tel. 416/928–0213; Toronto Eaton Centre, Yonge and Dundas Sts., tel. 416/598–0144; 60 Yonge St., tel. 416/364–6481).

Taxis. Beck (tel. 416/449–6911), Co-op (tel. 416/364–8161), Diamond (tel. 416/366–6868), Metro (tel. 416/363–5611).

Theater tickets. *See* The Arts, below.

Train information. Union Station, Front St. W between Yonge and York Sts.: Amtrak (tel. 800/872–7245), Via Rail (tel. 416/366–8411).

Travel agents. Goliger's Travel (214 King St. W and other locations, tel. 416/593–6168), Marlin Travel (Commerce Ct., tel. 416/363–4911), P. Lawson Travel (131 Bloor St. W, tel. 416/926–6380; 33 Yonge St., tel. 416/365–7360; First Canadian Pl., tel. 416/862–0607).

Weather (tel. 416/676–3066).

LODGING

As Canada's largest city and financial center, Toronto offers a wide variety of business-oriented hotels, many of which were built in the past 20 years. Business travelers who want to be within a few minutes' walk of their morning meetings often opt for hotels that belong to the Sheraton, Hilton, or Canadian Pacific chains. All are located in the downtown core, have similar rates, and cater primarily to business travelers or conventioneers. The downtown tends to be deserted early, except for theater- and concert-goers, but is within easy access of good restaurants and evening shopping. Many of the best Toronto hotels are located in the Yorkville area, a 5- to 10-minute cab ride from downtown, which has many excellent restaurants and upscale stores that stay open late on Thursday nights. It's not advisable to stay at airport hotels or in the northeast section of the city unless you're doing business in those areas. You'll have to fight rush-hour traffic if you want to get downtown—a fate many commuters feel no amount of luxury justifies. All but the airport and northeastern hotels are within easy access of Toronto's main attractions.

Most of the hotels listed offer corporate rates and weekend discounts; inquire when making reservations.

Highly recommended properties in each category are indicated with a star ★.

Category	Cost*
$$$$ (Very Expensive)	over Can$175
$$$ (Expensive)	Can$125–Can$175
$$ (Moderate)	under Can$125

All prices are for a standard double room, single occupancy, excluding 8% city tax, 7% value-added tax, and 5% service charge.

Numbers in the margin correspond to numbers on the Toronto Dining and Lodging map.

Downtown/Center City

㉓ **Chestnut Park Hotel.** This 26-story hotel, which opened in
$$$ 1989, stands just behind the futuristic New City Hall and only steps from the financial district—an exceedingly convenient location for business travelers. The glass-enclosed lobby is handsomely turned out with Asian art, Chinese screens and vases, and handcarved rosewood chairs. The hotel's owner is a serious collector of exotic art, especially textiles, and the hotel is connected at the mezzanine level with a Museum of Textiles. Cozy guest rooms are furnished with bleached-pine furniture; bathrooms are standard. Executive suites have whirlpool tubs. *108 Chestnut St., M5G 1R3, tel. 416/977–5000 or 800/668–6600, fax 416/977–9513. Gen. manager, John Pye. 520 rooms, 8 suites. AE, CB, DC, MC, V.*

㉓ **Delta Chelsea Inn.** One of the largest hotels in the British
$$ Commonwealth, the Chelsea recently finished several renovations and an $80-million expansion, including the addi-

TORONTO

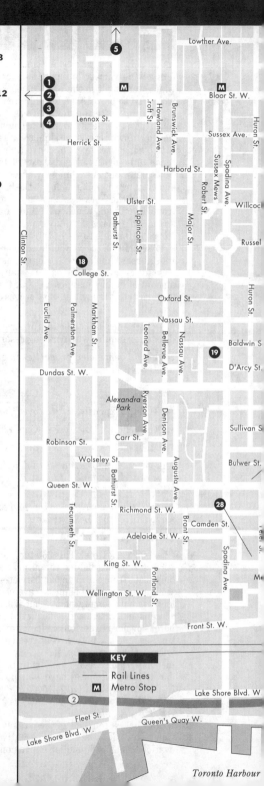

Toronto Harbour

TORONTO HOTEL CHART

HOTELS	Price Category	Banquet capacity	No. of meeting rooms	Secretarial services	Audiovisual equipment	Teletype news service	Computer rentals	In-room modem phone jack	All-news cable channel	Desk	Desk lighting	Bed lighting
Bristol Place	$$$$	400	16	✓	✓	✓	✓	✓	-	●	◐	●
Chestnut Park	$$$	400	19	✓	✓	-	-	✓	✓	◐	◐	●
Delta Chelea Inn	$$	1870	26	✓	✓	-	-	✓	✓	●	●	●
Four Seasons	$$$$	675	20	✓	✓	-	✓	-	✓	◐	●	●
Harbour Castle Westin	$$$$	2500	25	✓	✓	-	-	-	✓	◐	◐	◐
Hilton International	$$$	1000	18	✓	✓	✓	✓	✓	-	●	●	●
L'Hôtel	$$$	500	15	✓	✓	-	-	-	✓	●	◐	●
Ibis	$$	120	6	-	✓	-	-	-	-	●	◐	●
Inn on the Park	$$$$	1400	26	✓	✓	-	✓	-	✓	✓	✓	✓
Journey's End Hotel	$$	0	0	-	-	-	-	✓	✓	◐	◐	◐
Journey's End Suites	$$	0	0	✓	-	-	-	✓	✓	◐	●	◐
King Edward	$$$$	350	12	✓	✓	-	-	✓	✓	●	●	●
Novotel Toronto Centre	$$	150	6	✓	✓	-	✓	-	✓	◐	◐	◐
Park Plaza	$$$	400	12	✓	✓	-	✓	✓	✓	-	-	●
Regal Constellation	$$	2800	72	✓	✓	-	-	-	✓	◐	◐	◐
Royal York	$$$	1380	34	✓	✓	✓	✓	✓	✓	◐	◐	●
Sheraton Centre	$$$	1800	36	✓	✓	✓	✓	✓	✓	●	●	●
Skydome	$$$	250	4	✓	✓	-	✓	✓	✓	●	●	●
Sutton Place	$$$$	350	17	✓	✓	-	✓	✓	✓	◐	◐	◐

$$$$ = over Can$175, **$$$** = Can$125-Can$175, **$$** = under Can$125.
● good, ◐ fair, ○ poor.
All hotels listed here have photocopying and fax facilities.

In-Room Amenities Nonsmoking rooms	In-room checkout	Minibar	Pay movies	VCR/Movie rentals	Hairdryer	Toiletries	Room service	Laundry/Dry cleaning	Pressing	**Hotel Amenities** Concierge	Barber/Hairdresser	Garage	Courtesy airport transport	Sauna	Pool	Exercise room
✓	✓	✓	✓	✓	✓	◐	●	●	●	✓	✓	-	-	✓	◐	◐
✓	-	✓	✓	-	●	●	●	●	●	✓	-	✓	-	✓	◐	◐
✓	✓	✓	✓	-	-	●	●	●	●	✓	✓	✓	-	✓	●	●
✓	-	✓	-	✓	●	●	●	●	●	✓	✓	✓	-	✓	●	●
✓	-	✓	✓	✓	-	◐	●	●	●	✓	✓	✓	-	✓	◐	●
✓	-	✓	✓	-	-	◐	●	●	●	✓	✓	✓	-	✓	◐	◐
✓	-	✓	✓	-	-	◐	●	●	●	✓	-	✓	-	✓	●	◐
✓	-	-	✓	-	-	◐	-	●	●	-	-	✓	-	-	-	-
✓	-	✓	✓	✓	✓	●	●	●	●	✓	✓	-	-	✓	●	●
-	-	✓	✓	-	-	-	-	●	◐	-	-	✓	-	✓	-	-
-	-	✓	✓	✓	-	◐	○	●	●	-	-	✓	-	-	-	-
✓	-	✓	✓	✓	●	●	●	●	●	✓	✓	✓	-	✓	-	◐
✓	-	✓	✓	✓	✓	◐	◐	◐	●	✓	-	✓	-	✓	●	◐
✓	✓	✓	✓	✓	✓	◐	●	◐	●	✓	✓	✓	-	-	-	◐
✓	-	-	✓	-	✓	◐	●	●	●	✓	✓	✓	-	✓	●	◐
✓	✓	✓	✓	-	✓	●	◐	●	●	✓	✓	-	-	✓	◐	●
✓	✓	✓	✓	-	✓	●	●	●	●	✓	✓	✓	-	✓	●	●
✓	-	✓	✓	-	-	●	●	●	◐	-	✓	✓	-	✓	◐	◐
✓	-	✓	✓	✓	✓	◐	●	●	●	✓	✓	✓	-	✓	◐	●

Room service: ● 24-hour, ◐ 6AM–10PM, ○ other.
Laundry/Dry cleaning: ● same day, ◐ overnight, ○ other.
Pressing: ● immediate, ◐ same day, ○ other.

tion of a business center, a glass-enclosed spa, an exercise room, and a pool. Rooms are bright and modern, with dark wood furniture; some are more spacious than others. Ask for the east- and west-facing rooms in the south wing, overlooking downtown and the lake. Signature Service Rooms include such extras as Continental breakfast. Because this is still one of the lowest-priced major hotels in the city and just a short walk from downtown, it draws many families and tour groups; tours alone represent 50% of the business. *33 Gerrard St. at Yonge St., M5G 1Z5, tel. 416/595–1975 or 800/877–1133, fax 416/585–4393. Gen. manager, Rekha Khote. 1,600 rooms. AE, CB, DC, MC, V.*

★ ⑫ **Four Seasons Toronto.** Built in 1972, this is the No. 1 choice
$$$$ for Toronto executives who need to lodge an important visitor. On the edge of Toronto's fashionable Yorkville district, it is a 5- to 10-minute cab ride from the financial center, and only a 5-minute walk to some of Toronto's best restaurants and shops. The elegant rooms are decorated in earth tones and feature tasteful artwork. Suites are filled with antiques and fresh flowers; those on the 31st floor come equipped with stereos and VCRs. The hotel's staff is renowned for its service. A business center on the fourth floor is staffed 9–5 weekdays, but never closes. A masseuse and a car rental office are on the premises. The Café (*see* Business Breakfasts, below) is a good place for a morning meeting, and the highly rated French restaurant has an intimate air and a substantial degree of privacy for lunch or dinner entertaining. *21 Avenue Rd., M5R 2G1, tel. 416/964–0411 or 800/332–3442, fax 416/964–2301. Gen. manager, Raymond Jacobi. 379 rooms, 47 twins, 70 queens, 95 kings, 30 suites, 7 penthouse suites. AE, CB, DC, MC, V.*

㊱ **Harbour Castle Westin.** A favorite with conventioneers,
$$$$ the hotel's two 30-story towers on the lakefront are just steps from the Harbourfront complex and the ferry to the Toronto Islands. The uptown business core is some distance away, but the hotel offers guests a shuttle service. All rooms have lake views; corner rooms also look north to the glittering towers of the city. This former Hilton was built in 1975; the North Tower was renovated in 1990. The swimming pool, squash courts, and health club are among the best in town. Guest rooms are all in pastel colors, with marble-top desks and night stands, and bathroom phones. The Executive Club floors (21–23) offer concierge service, a lounge with an honor bar, Continental breakfast, and access to the health club. *1 Harbour Sq., M5J 1A6, tel. 416/869–1600 or 800/228–3000, fax 416/869–0573. Gen. manager, Rick Layton. 950 rooms. AE, CB, DC, MC, V.*

㉜ **Hilton International Toronto.** The advantages here can be
$$$ summed up in one word: convenience. It's only a few minutes' walk to most major downtown office towers, restaurants, and shops. Built in 1979, this 32-story tower used to be a Westin hotel, and travel agents frequently confuse it with the Harbour Castle Westin; it's wise to double check (the Hilton is the better bet). The spacious rooms are standard fare with comfortable furnishings and requisite pastel decor. Business-class rooms are somewhat larger but have furniture disappointingly similar to that of standard rooms. Furnishings in the suites are Sears modern; guests may prefer to relax in the business-class lounge, with its

large television set and billiards table. Other business-class perks include free local calls and in-house cable movies. *145 Richmond St. W, M5H 2L2, tel. 416/869–3456, fax 416/869–1478. Gen. manager, Horst Angelkotter. 601 rooms, 46 suites, 179 kings, 376 queens or doubles. AE, CB, DC, MC, V.*

★ ③ **L'Hôtel.** Open since 1984 and connected directly to
$$$ Toronto's convention center, this hotel is not only a favorite for conventioneers but also houses Canada's prime minister on his Toronto visits. The hotel is a few minutes' walk west from Union Station. Views are dismal—railway tracks, construction sites, office buildings, and only glimpses of the lake—but rooms are comfortable and in excellent repair (those on upper floors get less train noise). Nice touches include telephones with two lines and a hold button. Business-class rooms are larger and offer such features as stereos and full dining suites. Gold Class guests have private check-in service, free use of a boardroom, and a Victorian-style lounge where private breakfasts are served. The decor takes a turn toward the garish in some hospitality suites. Throughout, comfortable modern sofas and beds mix with the occasional reproduction antique sidetable or wingchair. The competent though not outstanding staff will provide most business services. *225 Front St. W, M5V 2X3, tel. 416/597–1400 or 800/828–7447, fax 416/597–8128. Gen. manager, Claude Sauve. 463 rooms, 36 suites, 427 doubles. AE, CB, D, DC, MC, V.*

㉒ **Hotel Ibis.** This reasonably priced 11-story hotel is a mem-
$$ ber of the same French chain as the Novotel (*see* below). Opened in 1988, it is only a few blocks from the Eaton Centre and not much further from the business district. Although rates are attractive, the somewhat seedy neighborhood does not make women on their own feel at ease taking an evening stroll. The comfortable, standard-size rooms have the necessities, but few frills. Passes to a nearby health club are available. Staff members are cordial but not particularly knowledgeable. *Accor chain. 240 Jarvis St., M5B 2B8, tel. 416/593–9400 or 800/221–4542, fax 416/593–8426. Gen. manager, Patrice Basile. 294 rooms, 164 singles, 122 doubles, 10 for the disabled. AE, CB, DC, MC, V.*

㊵ **Journey's End Hotel.** Rooms in this brick 14-story hotel,
$$ which opened in 1989, are spartan but spacious and well-lighted, with large work tables. Furniture and bathrooms are about what you would expect for the moderate price. On bright days, the modest lobby is flooded with sunlight. Amenities are few (free local phone calls are a plus), but the hotel is just a 10-minute walk from downtown. *111 Lombard St., near Jarvis, M5B 2B8, tel. 416/367–5555 or 800/668–4200; 416/624–8200, in Toronto, fax 416/367–3470. Gen. manager, Deidre Sloan. 196 rooms. AE, CB, DC, MC, V.*

★ ㊳ **King Edward Hotel.** After many years of neglect, this Ed-
$$$$ wardian classic has been thoroughly renovated. Some of the restoration was less than sensitive; the kitschy arbor in the dining room desecrates one of the city's great interiors. Still, the building is a splendid structure. Now restored to its pink marble grandeur, it attracts a well-heeled clientele (including royalty); one of the Shamrock Summits between Canada's prime minister, Brian Mulroney, and President Reagan took place here. Guest

rooms—all renovated by mid-1991—have an English country motif, and the floral wallpaper pattern is echoed in the curtains and bedspreads. The location, two blocks from King and Bay streets (the latter is Canada's Wall Street) is a plus, as is the hotel's Café Victoria, with its excellent business breakfasts (*see* Business Breakfasts, below). The Lobby Lounge (*see* After Hours, below) is a good spot for a quiet drink. *A Trusthouse Forte Exclusive Hotel. 37 King St. E, M5C 1E9, tel. 416/863-9700 or 800/ 225-5843, fax 416/863-5232; guest fax, 416/367-5515. Gen. manager, James Batt. 315 rooms. AE, CB, DC, MC, V.*

★ ⑨ **Novotel Toronto Centre.** This moderately priced hotel
$$ opened in late 1987. South of the main business district, it is within walking distance of downtown and caters to budget-conscious travelers who insist on service and quality. The stunning neoclassical gray building, fronted with columns and arches, promises—and delivers—a little more than the typical budget hotel. Rooms are basic but pleasant, with modern decor. The neighborhood is good, too; the O'Keefe Centre is just steps away, as is shopping along Front Street East. Among the cookie-cutter steak-and-seafood restaurants that dominate the area are a handful of attractive bistros. Unless you request a room facing north with a view of the city, you risk overlooking the city's railroad system. *Accor chain. 45 The Esplanade (one block below Front Street E, near Yonge St.), M5E 1W2, tel. 416/367-8900 or 800/221-3185, fax 416/360-8285. Gen. manager, Ricardo Perran. 226 rooms, 7 suites, 219 doubles. AE, CB, DC, MC, V.*

⑪ **Park Plaza.** If there were desks in the 64 small rooms and
$$$ suites in the recently renovated South Tower, this half-century-old hostelry would give the nearby Four Seasons serious competition. Desks are planned for the larger rooms in the North Tower, being renovated, along with the lobby. Scheduled for completion in late 1992, these 200 rooms will do well to match the decor of those in the South Tower, where the atmosphere of a private home is created by individually decorated accommodations in pale earth tones, and the occasional antique vanity mixed among the Bauhaus-style furniture. Some suites feature added luxuries such as quilted comforters and TV sets in the marble bathrooms, which have separate vanity areas. A business center and fitness facilities are in the works. The elegant rooftop restaurant-and-bar (*see* Business Breakfasts, below) is a power breakfast spot in the morning and a favorite haunt for literati in the evening. The staff is generally gracious, but waiters can be supercilious. *Preferred Hotels Worldwide. 4 Avenue Rd., corner of Bloor St. W, M5R 2E8, tel. 416/924-5471 or 800/268-4928, fax 416/924-4933. Gen. manager, David L. Dennis. 64 rooms (264 by mid-1992), 20 suites. AE, CB, DC, MC, V.*

㉟ **Royal York.** Until recently, the Royal York, built in 1929,
$$$ was the standard against which other Toronto hotels were measured. Most rooms, however, are on the small side, and although refurbished, they retain the somewhat dark, heavy air of Victoriana. Business-class rooms are a few square feet larger than standard rooms. Ask for accommodations on the upper floors with a southwest view, as far as possible from the noisy elevators. Some guests report problems with the aging heating system, which can over-

heat rooms. Bathrooms are dark marble and have new fixtures. The hotel's underground link to Toronto's railway station as well as to many of its major office towers helps explain why some 70% of the guests are business travelers. *A Canadian Pacific Hotel. 100 Front St. W, M5J 1E3, tel. 416/368–2511; 800/828–7447; in Canada, 800/368–9411, fax 416/368–2884. Gen. manager, Pietter Bougain. 1,438 rooms. AE, CB, DC, MC, V.*

★ ③③   **Sheraton Centre.** Those who prize convenience over all
$$$ else will appreciate this central location and its labyrinthine underground connection to most major office buildings. The majority of guests are conventioneers, and the lobby resembles an airport lounge in size, decor, and volume of people rushing through it. The newly renovated rooms (floors 5–25) are standard Sheraton fare, with a pleasant decor in floral patterns. Desks are small, but rooms also have tables. Unrenovated rooms are rather dilapidated. Business-class travelers get a well-furnished lounge with free breakfast and hors d'oeuvres; however, their rooms are disappointingly small and some are in bad repair. The best bet for avoiding lobby noise are the "Cabana rooms," which open onto either the pool or a terrace garden. For a fee, male business-class travelers have access to a private health club within the hotel complex. The staff is cheerful but sometimes seems overburdened. *123 Queen St. W, M5H 2M9, tel. 416/361–1000; 800/325–3535; hearing impaired, 800/325–1717, fax 416/947–4874. Gen. manager, Marcel P. van Aelst. 1,430 rooms, 78 suites. AE, CB, DC, MC, V.*

③⓪   **Skydome Hotel.** Not only is this one of the best values
$$$ downtown, but guests in many of the rooms can watch baseball or football games at Toronto's new stadium from their bedroom windows. Other rooms have views of the downtown skyline. The decor throughout the hotel is slick and futuristic, but comfort hasn't been sacrificed to style. Some rooms are small, but rates for them are proportionately lower. Business-class accommodations are spacious, and occupants have access to a private lounge for breakfast or drinks. The friendly staff tends to get flustered when hordes try to check in as a ball game is starting. The surrounding area is safe, if a trifle bleak. The financial district is a 10-minute walk; cabs can take longer if there's a game on. *A Canadian Pacific Hotel. 45 Peter St. S, M5V 3B4, tel. 416/361–1400 or 800/828–7447. Gen. manager, Ray P. Thompson. 348 rooms, 71 suites. AE, CB, DC, MC, V.*

★ ⑰   **Sutton Place Hotel.** This European-owned luxury hotel,
$$$$ one of the city's most impressive, occupies 16 stories of a 33-floor tower close to provincial government offices and thus is a favorite with lobbyists and lawyers. Afternoon tea is served off the lobby in an antique-filled lounge. Built in 1967, the hotel underwent renovations in 1988, including construction of a business center. Standard rooms are spacious and stylish, done in light, airy pastels; some adjoin parlors. Each suite has a different decor, though most include Oriental rugs and antiques. Butler service is available on the 18th floor, and also by special arrangement for all other guests. The neighborhood is a bit cut off from most business, shopping, and entertainment. To compensate, the hotel offers complimentary limousine service to the financial district. The staff is polite and efficient, but

warmth is reserved for favorite return guests. *A Kempinski Hotel. 955 Bay St., M5S 2A2, tel. 416/924–9221 or 800/268–3790, fax 416/924–1778. Gen. manager, Hans Gerhardt. 108 rooms, 72 suites. AE, CB, DC, MC, V.*

Northeast of Toronto

❾ Inn on the Park. This resort hotel, part of the Four Sea-
$$$$ sons chain, is a 20-minute drive north of downtown. The advantages of the tranquil setting are offset by the distance from both the airport and downtown offices. The 600 acres have miles of trails for cross-country skiing, hiking, and jogging, as well as facilities for tennis, racquetball, squash, and horseback riding. The newly renovated lobby has marble floors, a rock garden, and a large fireplace. All rooms have dark wood armoires with matching headboards, side tables, and desks. The main building has 14 floors, the tower, 22. All deluxe accommodations are in the tower; these rooms are large, with spacious bathrooms, walk-in closets, and park or city views. Inner-courtyard rooms and the main building have balconies. Meeting facilities are superb, as is the service. *1100 Eglinton Ave. E, M3C 1H8. tel. 416/444–2561 or 800/332–3442. fax 416/446–3308. Gen. manager, Klaus Tenter. 568 rooms, 22 suites.*

Airport

★ ❶ Bristol Place. This 15-floor airport hotel has always been
$$$$ elegant, and after a major renovation in 1987, it is more attractive than ever. The three-story atrium/lobby has a traditional, European air, with soft colors, classical columns, Oriental carpets, and tasteful flower arrangements. Guest rooms have mahogany armoires, tables, desks, and minibars. Indoor and outdoor pools, a sauna, and a small exercise room add to the appeal. The hotel runs an airport bus from the arrival level; it's a two-minute ride. Airport noise should not be a problem for most, but rooms facing east are quietest. *950 Dixon Rd., M9W 5N4; tel. 416/675–9444, fax 416/675–4426. Gen. manager, Nick Vesely. 287 rooms, including 160 singles. AE, DC, MC, V.*

★ ❸ Journey's End Suites. Like its downtown cousin (*see*
$$ *above*), this all-suite property is a reasonably priced option. Each suite is spacious, with a good-size table and four chairs in the living room, and French doors closing off the bedroom. The business center has all the basic facilities, and a courtesy bus runs to and from the airport every half-hour. Free local calls and a special day rate make this an excellent deal for budget travelers. *262 Carlingview Dr., Etobicoke, M9W 5G1, tel. 416/674–8442 or 800/668–4200. Gen. manager, Dykran Zabunyan. 258 suites. AE, D, MC, V.*

❷ Regal Constellation. This airport hotel has the facilities
$$ and sophistication of many downtown properties. It was built in 1960, and a new wing was added in 1984; all rooms were renovated between 1989 and 1991. The ballroom holds 3,000, and there are 75 individual meeting rooms. The executive floors offer minisuites with handsome desks, sitting areas, and attractive oak furniture—all in bright, contemporary colors that vary from room to room. An airport bus runs every 30 minutes between 4:30 AM and 1 AM. Airplanes do not fly over the hotel, so noise is not a

major problem. *A Regal Hotel. 900 Dixon Rd., M9W 1J7, tel. 416/675–1500 or 800/268–4838, fax 416/675–1738. Gen. manager, Michael Kalmar. 900 rooms. AE, D, MC, V.*

DINING

Toronto's dining scene has gone far beyond the city's bland British meat-and-potatoes beginnings and now includes an encouraging selection of ethnic restaurants. Recent years have seen what the *Toronto Globe and Mail* restaurant critic has dubbed "the bistroization of Toronto," thanks to a new exciting generation of chefs. There are no real regional specialties as in, say, New Orleans, but the choices are wide and varied—the same as in any cosmopolitan U.S. city. Businesspeople frequent all the fine restaurants below, both for lunch and dinner. After-hours dining is available at most of them.

Highly recommended restaurants in each price category are indicated by a star ★.

Category	Cost*
$$$$ (Very Expensive)	over Can$35
$$$ (Expensive)	Can$27–Can$35
$$ (Moderate)	Can$15–Can$26
$ (Inexpensive)	under Can$15

per person, including appetizer, entrée, and dessert, but excluding drinks, service, and 8% sales tax.

Numbers in the margin correspond to numbered restaurants on the Toronto Lodging and Dining map.

Business Breakfasts

Café Victoria (tel. 416/863–9700), on the main level of the King Edward Hotel, is popular for power breakfasts near the financial area; it's noted for poached eggs in phyllo dough with sautéed mushrooms and Canadian bacon, and broiled kippers with scrambled eggs on toast. **Le Café,** in the Four Seasons Hotel (tel. 416/964–0411), serves the old favorites—corned beef hash, bacon and eggs—as well as lighter fare. Service is attentive, and accommodates time restraints. Booths or secluded alcoves (seating 6–8) afford privacy. The **Prince Arthur Room** of the Park Plaza (tel. 416/924–5471) is Canada's primary business breakfast spot. Hearty repasts and a lighter Jogger's Breakfast come with a spectacular view.

Downtown

★ ㉕ **The Avocado Club.** Until mid-1990, the Avocado Club was
$$ known as Beaujolais and was considered one of the city's best and most expensive restaurants. Then the same inspired owners and chef gave the place an entirely new, less expensive menu and look. In this converted warehouse, a few blocks east of the financial district, along the chic Queen Street West strip, Impressionist prints have given way to a riot of hot mustard, pink, and turquoise colors to match the menu's new spicy flavors. Appetizers include curried mussel salad with apples and new potatoes, and

soba noodle salad with sushi ginger. Main dishes include tandoori spiced pork loins with curried onions, and lamb chili. Publishers and ad execs continue to dine here at lunch, and a noisier sports and entertainment crowd pours in for dinner. The upstairs dining area is the best option for a quiet meeting. *165 John St., tel. 416/598–4656. Casual dress. Reservations required. AE, MC, V. Closed Sat. lunch, Sun. Moderate.*

★ ㉔ **Bamboo** An offbeat setting—a converted industrial laun-
$$ dry—and unusual Caribbean/Thai specialties have proved to be a draw for a young and chic TV, movie, and rock-music crowd. Because the dining area is always noisy, this is not a place for business meetings, but for relaxing after work. The decor is eclectic, with yellow walls, light green ceilings, and African and Indonesian art. Gado gado nut salad, Thai noodles, pan-fried sea bass, and red snapper are among the flavorful offerings. After 10 PM, there's live reggae and Caribbean music. *312 Queen St. W, tel. 416/593–5771. Casual dress, no reservations. AE, MC, V. Closed Sun.*

㉑ **Bangkok Garden.** The scent of teak and a faint odor of in-
$$$$ cense set the stage for some of Toronto's best Thai cuisine. Watch out for the fake crab, but don't miss the noodle dishes, which are the house specialties. The restaurant is elegant and quiet with teak paneling, Thai artifacts, and a small stream that runs through the dining area. Downstairs is The Brass Flamingo, a bar whose menu is more limited, though it still includes noodle dishes and the unique Boxing Stadium chicken. It's a good place to grab lunch, or even an early dinner. Menu items in both sections are thoughtfully coded according to spice level. *18 Elm St., near Eaton Centre, tel. 416/977–6748. Jacket and tie suggested, reservations recommended. AE, DC, MC, V. Closed Sat. lunch, Sun.*

★ ㉗ **Le Bistingo.** Claude Bouillet, one of Toronto's finest
$$$$ French chefs—part classic, part nouvelle—has his domain here among the Queen Street West shops, just a few blocks west of City Hall. This charming, low-key bistro has French windows with lace curtains, and large, round tables, well spaced for privacy. The prime minister is a regular, and lawyers, media stars, and business executives often lunch here, requesting the less noisy tables in the back when business is on the agenda. Reliable choices include the medallions of duck and any of the fresh fish dishes. The wine list is strong on French and California selections. *349 Queen St. W, tel. 416/598–3490. Casual dress. Reservations required. AE, MC, V. Closed Sat. lunch, Sun.*

★ ⑯ **Bistro 990.** This French Provençal-style bistro, complete
$$$ with open kitchen and mock-Chagall murals, is just across from the Sutton Place Hotel. Service tends to be quick at lunch and more leisurely at night. The place is packed for both meals, and low ceilings add to the noise level, but tables in the corners or at the back can be reserved for quiet talk. Roasted breast of duck, sea scallops, and salmon with peppercorns and olive oil all draw rave reviews. The wine list includes French, Australian, Californian, German, and Spanish labels. *990 Bay St., tel. 416/921–9990. Casual dress. Reservations advised. AE, MC, V. Closed Sat. afternoon and holidays.*

41 **Bombay Palace.** Part of a chain that stretches from New
$$ Delhi to New York, this offers the best tandoori chicken in
town, along with the usual North Indian fare. Another
tasty specialty is the vegetarian Navrattan curry. Al-
though the exterior and neighborhood are unprepossess-
ing, the red plush interior is upscale and the service is
nearly impeccable. The clientele is diverse and includes
the pretheater crowd. This is one of a handful of good
downtown restaurants open on Sunday. *71 Jarvi St., tel.
416/368–8048. Casual dress. Reservations suggested. AE,
DC, MC, V.*

7 19 28 **Eating Counter.** This excellent Cantonese minichain has
$ three locations: one near the Art Gallery of Ontario; a sec-
ond one near SkyDome; and a third uptown, on Yonge St.
near St. Clair Avenue West. Businesspeople and lawyers
flock to all three; meetings at the tables near the front
window and in the corners are quietest. The decor at these
eateries is nonexistent, but the food is top rate, particu-
larly the Szechuan shrimp, lobster, and chicken dishes, all
in garlic sauce. There are a few French wines available. *23
Baldwin St., near Dundas St., tel. 416/977–7028; 56 Peter
St. near SkyDome, tel. 416/977–2828; 1560 Yonge St., just
above St. Clair Ave. W, tel. 416/323–0171. Casual dress.
Reservations advised. AE, DC, MC, V.*

★ 29 **La Fenice.** Convenient to both the Royal Alexandra thea-
$$$$ ter and Roy Thomson Hall, this is a popular spot for
preperformance Northern Italian meals as well as for
business lunches. Though usually full and often noisy, it's
worth the hassle. The antipasto is a feast for the senses,
with treats such as mint-flavored grilled eggplant. Grilled
fish is the real specialty, but veal dishes also come highly
recommended. The extra virgin olive oil is pressed espe-
cially for the restaurant, and the chef's own watercolors
decorate the terra-cotta walls. *319 King St. W, tel. 416/
585–2377. Reservations recommended. Jacket and tie
suggested. Closed lunch, Sat.; Sun. AE, DC, MC, V.*

39 **Nami.** This is where Japanese businesspeople like to wine
$$$$ and dine their business contacts. Especially recom-
mended is the robata-yaki, or barbecue grill. Otherwise,
sample the seafood, the light and crispy tempura, or the
fresh sushi and sashimi. Some half-Western dishes have
crept on to the menu. The service ranges from mediocre to
attentive, depending on the day and the individual waiter.
The location is convenient to the business district. *55 Ade-
laide St. E, tel. 416/362–7373. Jacket and tie, reservations
recommended. AE, DC, MC, V. Closed lunch, Sat.; Sun.*

26 **The Parrot.** For many years, this bistro near the financial
$$$ district was Toronto's only high quality vegetarian res-
taurant; today carnivores have the most choices, but there
are still some good meatless dishes on offer. Track lighting, marble-top tables, black metal chairs, and changing
exhibits of oil paintings and photos offer a pleasant setting
for a blend of Continental and international specialties,
prepared by a French-Canadian chef. The menu changes
frequently, but the *gnocchi di spinaci* appetizer (dumplings of riccota and spinach in a rich gorgonzola cheese
sauce), sweetbreads, chicken breasts in amaretto cream
sauce garnished with cashews and almonds, and pastas
are all highly recommended. Quiet conversation is best at
tables 9 and 11 along the brick wall; elsewhere, it can be
noisy. The wine list is strong on American reds and

whites. *325 Queen St. W, near University Ave., tel. 416/ 593–0899. Casual dress. Reservations accepted. AE, MC, V. Closed Sun. and Mon. lunch, 2 weeks around Christmas, first 2 weeks of summer.*

⑬ Le Trou Normand. As the name suggests, this restaurant
$$$ specializes in French dishes from Normandy. Calvados, an apple brandy, appears frequently in sauces; the omelets are renowned and make a good light lunch or dinner. Other Norman dishes include treats like duck livers sautéed with apple jelly, and grilled pork tenderloin with goat cheese sauce. Desserts, notably *clafouti*, a fruit tart with a custard base, are worth forgetting a diet for. The atmosphere is quiet and relaxed, and the restaurant, which contains three homelike rooms, resembles an unpretentious country inn. Generous portions and attentive service make this a pleasant alternative to fighting for tables and service at better known French restaurants. *90 Yorkville Ave., tel. 416/967–5956. Casual dress. Reservations recommended. AE, DC, MC, V. Closed Sun. lunch.*

㉞ Winston's. Some of the city's top lawyers, politicians, and
$$$$ lawyers-turned-politicians lunch here daily at their personal tables, giving this resolutely nontrendy restaurant the feel of a private club rather than a public dining room. The vichyssoise is a highlight of the menu, much of which consists of good but predictable prenouvelle cuisine. Dependable entrées include beef Wellington and a range of soufflés. People come here because of the restaurant's reputation as a power meeting place; they don't expect an adventure in dining. *104 Adelaide St. W, tel. 416/363–1627. Tie and jacket required, reservations required. AE, DC, MC, V. Closed lunch Sat.; Sun.*

⑭ Zero. True aficionados of Japanese cuisine are not de-
$$ terred by Zero's basement location or its unprepossessing appearance; in fact, the 30-seat room is consistently jammed with homesick Japanese businesspeople and students. The best bets are the set dinners, particularly tempura or *unagi* (broiled, marinated sea eel). Also offered are many dishes rarely found outside Japanese homes, such as *kimpira-gobo*, a mountain root chopped up and marinated with a tangy sesame-based sauce. The cuisine is simpler than that of Nami, but portions are bigger. *69 Yorkville Ave. (enter off street, down a flight of stairs), tel. 416/961–8349. Casual dress. Reservations suggested. AE, MC, V.*

North Toronto

⑧ Centro. One of the best of the trendy Italian restaurants in
$$$$ the city, Centro sets a proper mood with soaring columns, photos of street scenes of the chef's hometown (Asolo, Italy), and warm, Mediterranean pinks and yellows. Large business groups request the quiet upstairs mezzanine; a private room in the wine cellar is often booked for parties. The menu is Northern Italian, with strong California overtones. Specialties include tuna carpaccio, grilled veal chop and roast American lamb, and polenta with gorgonzola mascarpone sauce. Desserts are made on the premises. Italian wines are very well represented, but there are California, French, and Australian labels as well. *2472 Yonge St., tel. 416/483–2211. Casual dress. Reservations required. AE, CB, DC, MC, V. Closed lunch; Sun., Christmastime.*

⑱ Palmerston. Despite an out-of-the-way location, 1½ miles
$$$$ from the financial district, lawyers, business executives, and entertainers come here regularly to sample the nouvelle American creations of chef Jamie Kennedy. Among the light, tasty, and unfussy dishes are fresh lamb and fish, cooked to near perfection, and trout fillets in champagne sauce. Wonderful ice creams and fresh breads and pastries are all made in-house. Menus change according to the availability of ingredients. The former storefront has pale pink walls hung with rotating exhibits of paintings and photographs. The wood bar at the entrance and the long, narrow dining area create a cozy and unpretentious atmosphere. The wine list includes Australian, Californian, and Canadian varieties. *488 College St., at Palmerston Ave., tel. 416/922–9277. Casual dress. Reservations advised. AE, CB, DC, MC, V. Closed lunch.*

★ ⑩ Pronto. This striking, bistro-style restaurant has an open
$$$$ kitchen and a chic contemporary look to match its cuisine, which can be described as Northern Italian with North American twists. Mirrors and large abstract paintings add to the flamboyant, stylish ambience; recessed lighting adds an air of intimacy to an otherwise crowded, busy setting. Among dependable dishes on the seasonable menu are barbequed shrimp with sweet potato fettuccine, and peppered tuna steak—all with sauces that enhance rather than disguise natural flavors. One sees world-class entertainers and the CEOs of Canada's Top 500 here, although the usual noise level is not conducive to serious business discussion; if you want to try to talk, request a table away from the loud kitchen and front door. The private stock of Italian, French, and California wines is impressive. *692 Mount Pleasant Rd., south of Eglinton Ave.; tel. 416/486–1111. Jacket optional. Reservations required. Call weeks ahead for weekends. AE, CB, D, MC, V.*

❻ Scaramouche. This elegant French restaurant, with fine
$$$$ views of downtown Toronto, is located in a small apartment building on the peak of the Avenue Road hill, just south of St. Clair and about 3 miles north of the financial center. Tables are well spaced, but some are quieter than others, and only six are directly in front of windows; call early to request a table for serious conversation or good views. The Continental cuisine is usually satisfying, if rarely daring. Seasonal specialties include Atlantic salmon house-smoked and grilled with horse radish cream sauce, organic filet Mignon with caramelized shallot sauce, and a salmon tartare starter with caviar and cucumber. The affiliated Pasta Bar next door is much less expensive; both have well-rounded wine lists. There is complimentary valet parking. *1 Benevenuto Pl. (entrance off Edmund Ave., on west side of Avenue Rd.; tel. 416/961–8011. Jacket optional. Reservations recommended starting Sept. Closed lunch Sat.; Sun. AE, CB, DC, MC, V.*

★ ❺ United Bakers. This superior dairy restaurant, about 15–
$ 20 minutes by cab from downtown, is now overseen by a third generation of the original owners, the Ladovsky family. The soups are superlative, from the daily green pea to twice-weekly barley, bean, vegetable, and potato, to the Friday-only cabbage. Dishes such as gefilte fish, carp, whitefish, cheese blintzes, vegetarian lasagna, and Greek and Caesar salads match those found at downtown

establishments for three times the price. This place is worth the journey. *In Lawrence Plaza, corner of Bathurst and Lawrence Sts., tel. 416/789-0519. Casual dress. No reservations. MC, V.*

Airport

❹ **Café Creole.** For many years this restaurant off the main
$$$ lobby of the Skyline Hotel was known for its Cajun specialties. The accent has shifted to such standard Continental fare as steamed salmon fillets and sautéed scallops in broth, but some old standards remain, such as the delicious potato pecan pie and bread pudding for dessert. Everything is prepared to order, so don't come here if you're in a hurry. Table 99, the "chef's table," is the quietest place in this large, 165-seat room. *655 Dixon Rd. at Martingrove, near the airport, tel. 416/244-5200. Jacket advised. Reservations advised. Closed Sat. lunch. AE, CB, DC, MC, V.*

FREE TIME

Fitness

Hotel Facilities
Some of the best fitness clubs can be found at the hotels, but the only one with daily fees (Can$5) for nonguests is the **Harbour Castle Westin** (tel. 416/869-1600).

Health Clubs
Bloor Park Club, inside Hudson's Bay Centre (at Bloor and Yonge Sts., tel. 416/922-1262), has a Can$10 guest pass. Facilities include a pool, squash courts, weights, an outdoor track, a sauna, and whirlpool. For facilities that include racquetball, squash, tennis, Nautilus, pool, and weights, **Parkview Club** (behind the Inn on the Park, tel. 416/441-6163) charges Can$15 a day.

Jogging
The **Martin Goodman Trail,** a 12-mile path along the waterfront from the Balmy Beach Club in the east end to the western beaches southwest of High Park, offers a scenic run; phone the *Toronto Star* (tel. 416/367-2000) for a map. **The Toronto Islands,** a 10-minute ferry ride from the foot of Bay Street, just beneath the Harbour Castle Westin, offer good paths and a spectacular view of downtown.

Shopping

Eaton's and **Simpson's,** both large, moderately priced department stores, anchor the **Eaton Centre** (290 Yonge St., tel. 416/598-2322), downtown Toronto's major shopping area. With more than 300 stores convenient to the business district and enclosed from bad weather, this is the place to find virtually anything you need. It's also one of the city's major tourist attractions. Less expensive stores tend to be on the first floor, more expensive ones above.

The **Yorkville Avenue/Bloor Street area** is where you'll find the big fashion names. Yorkville Avenue, once Canada's equivalent of San Francisco's Haight Street, has become a mecca for those who would rather spend money than make love or war. Streets to explore include Cumberland and Scollard—both running parallel to Bloor Street—and Hazelton Avenue, running north from Yorkville Avenue near Avenue Road. The area is filled with famous designer boutiques, expensive jewelry shops, chichi cafés, and art galleries. Look for **Creed's** (45 Bloor St. W, tel. 416/923–1000) and **Holt Renfrew**, across the street (50 Bloor St. W, tel. 416/922–2333), for women's clothing (Holt's also has men's and children's departments); **Georg Jensen** (95 Bloor St. W, tel. 416/924–7707) for crystal; and **Boutique Quinto** (110 Bloor St. W, tel. 416/928–0954) or **David's** (89 Bloor St. W, tel. 416/928–9199) for shoes. On Yorkville Avenue, you'll find many antiques dealers. Bargain-hunters should check out **William Ashley** (50 Bloor St. W, tel. 416/964–2900) for discounted china and silverware.

If Bloor Street is Toronto's Rodeo Drive, the area around **Queen Street West** is its SoHo. Boutiques for young designers, new and used bookstores, vintage clothing shops, two shops devoted exclusively to comic books, and some of the city's most avant-garde galleries are to be found beginning at University Avenue and going westward past Bathurst Street, and along side streets. **Art Metropole** (788 King St. W, tel. 416/367–2304) specializes in limited edition art books. **Prime Canadian Crafts** (299 Queen St. W, tel. 416/593–5750) sells Canadian-made artifacts. **Atomic Age** (350 Queen St. W, tel. 416/977–1296) sells clothes by the trendiest young designers (no pinstripes allowed).

Mirvish Village (Markham St., a block south of Bloor St. W) is a one-block assortment of bookstores, antique shops, and boutiques. On Sunday, the Harbourfront features Canada's biggest antiques market (professional dealers are here Tues.–Fri.). Also at Harbourfront is the **Queen's Quay Terminal** (tel. 416/363–4411), a renovated warehouse that houses boutiques, crafts stalls, patisseries, and gift shops. There's a free shuttle bus from Union Station (parking is expensive).

Diversions

The Art Gallery of Ontario (317 Dundas St. W, tel. 416/977–0414) offers an eclectic collection that ranges from medieval European to contemporary Canadian, as well as the world's largest collection of Henry Moore sculptures.

The Beaches area, in Toronto's east end from Coxwell Avenue eastward along Queen Street, has evolved from a village on the city's outskirts into a trendy Sunday and summer haunt for young professionals. It boasts a 4-mile boardwalk along the lakefront as well as a beach, but swimming isn't advised because of Lake Ontario's pollution.

Casa Loma (1 Austin Terr., tel. 416/923–1171), a European-style castle built in 1913 by an entrepreneur for $3 million, has 98 rooms, two towers, secret panels, and fine views of downtown Toronto. It's about a 10-minute cab ride from downtown.

Toronto's **Chinatown,** where more than 100,000 Chinese live, is a colorful setting for an afternoon stroll, particularly on Sunday. The area runs along Spadina Avenue, from Queen Street up to College Street, and along Dundas Street from Bay Street west almost to Bathurst Street. Visitors can eye cryptic medical labels at an herbalist, sniff the tantalizing aroma of roast duck hanging in shop windows, or buy pork buns to eat while strolling around.

CN Tower (301 Front St. W, tel. 416/360–8500) is Toronto's second most popular attraction (the Eaton Centre is the first; *see* Shopping, above). The tallest freestanding structure in the world (1,815 feet, or 147 stories tall), it offers spectacular views of the city—even extending to the spray of Niagara Falls, 80 miles to the south. Go on clear days only.

Toronto's nod to the waterfront "theme park" development trend is **Harbourfront** (at the foot of Bay Street by Lake Ontario, tel. 416/364–5665), which features galleries, boutiques, poetry readings, concerts, and boat tours of the harbor.

Metropolitan Toronto Public Library (789 Yonge St., tel. 416/393–7000), with its magnificent atrium, is one of the most inviting libraries in the world—open stacks, glass-enclosed elevators, audio carrels with headphones, and more than 10,000 albums to listen to. There's even an Arthur Canon Doyle Room for Sherlock Holmes fans.

It's a 30-minute ride from downtown to the **Metropolitan Toronto Zoo** (Meadowvale Rd., just north of Hwy. 401; tel. 416/392–5900), which was built to exhibit animals in natural habitats.

Ontario Place (South of Lakeshore Blvd., across from the Canadian National Exhibition grounds, tel. 416/965–7711) is a family-oriented waterfront complex, including a six-story movie theater, outdoor arena for concerts, a Children's Village, and a World War II destroyer. Open May–Sept.

The Ontario Science Centre (7700 Don Mills Rd., about 7 miles northeast of downtown, tel. 416/429–4100) has live demonstrations of lasers, glassblowing, papermaking, electricity, and a gift shop filled with science books and experiments.

Royal Ontario Museum (southwest corner of Bloor St. W and University Ave., tel. 416/586–5549) has a good dinosaur collection, an Evolution Gallery, a Roman Gallery, and a noted collection of Chinese art. Tickets include admission to **The Gardiner Museum** across the street, whose exhibits include a collection of Meissen porcelain.

Behind the Harbour Castle Westin Hotel, ferries debark regularly for the small group of **Toronto Islands** (tel. 416/363–1112), less than 10 minutes offshore. Here you can jog, ride a rented bike, fish, or just relax and enjoy the views.

Professional Sports

The **Toronto Blue Jays** (tel. 416/595–0011, baseball) and the **Toronto Argonauts** (tel. 416/595–1131, football) appear at the Skydome. The city's hockey team, the **Toronto Maple Leafs** (tel. 416/977–1641), plays at Maple Leaf Gardens.

The Arts

Roy Thomson Hall (60 Simcoe St., tel. 416/593–4828), home of the Toronto Symphony Orchestra, also hosts visiting orchestras as well as pop performers. **St. Lawrence Centre for the Arts** (Front St. at Scott St., tel. 416/366–7723) presents everything from live theater by the Canadian Stage Company to debates on political issues to chamber music. **The O'Keefe Centre** (1 Front St. E, tel. 416/872–2262), the largest of the city's halls, is home to the Canadian Opera Company and the National Ballet of Canada, as well as to those rock groups and other performers with the drawing power to fill it. **Royal Alexandra Theater** (260 King St. W, tel. 416/593–4211), a restored 1907 theater, offers everything from classic drama to Broadway musicals and new Canadian plays. The lavishly restored 1920-vintage vaudeville theater, **Pantages** (63 Yonge Street, tel. 416/362–3216), puts on Broadway road shows.

The best sources for information are the weekly "What's On" section of the *Toronto Star*, which appears on Fridays, the Saturday *Globe and Mail*, or the free weekly publications *Now* and *Metropolitan*.

Half-price tickets are available on the day of performance from **Five Star Tickets,** in the lobby of the Royal Ontario Museum (in winter), or at Yonge and Dundas streets outside the Eaton Centre the rest of the year. All sales are final and cash only, and a small service charge is added to the ticket price. Tickets are also sold through **Ticketmaster** (tel. 416/872–2233).

After Hours

Bars and Lounges

Club Twenty-Two (22 St. Thomas St., tel. 416/979–2341), in the Windsor Arms Hotel, is a glamorous spot for an after-work drink. Local stockbrokers visit **The Amsterdam** (133 John St., tel. 416/595–8201) after work for excellent home-brewed beer (the food, unfortunately, isn't so good). Don't come if you want peace and quiet, however—especially on Fridays, when it turns into a singles bar. Reservations are a must. **The Bellari Café** (100 Cumberland St., near Bay and Bloor Sts., tel. 416/964–2222), in the upscale Yorkville area, has dancing to Top 40 music played by a DJ, and tables outside in summer for those who want to escape the noise. **The Madison Restaurant** (14 Madison Ave., tel. 416/927–1722) is a British-style pub on three floors with two outdoor terraces and wall-to-wall people, all playing darts and singing along with the pianist. For drinks or snacks, **Remy's** (115 Yorkville Ave., near Avenue Rd., tel. 416/968–9429) has brass, class, two outdoor patios, and a European atmosphere. **Movenpick** (165 York St., tel. 416/366–5234) has a wine bar that draws a business clientele from about 6 PM. **Quotes** (220 King St., tel. 416/979–7697) serves drinks and light snacks in a relaxing atmosphere. This is a favorite after-performance haunt for actors at the Royal Alexandra Theater next door. **Denison's** (75 Victoria St., tel. 416/360–5877) is another brew-pub, like the Amsterdam, but with a more relaxed atmosphere.

The Barrister's Bar at the Hilton (tel. 416/869–3456) offers a subdued, quiet setting for after-hours business discussions. **The Rooftop Bar** at the Park Plaza (tel. 416/924–5471), a favorite among Toronto's literary set, has a fireplace, which makes it a cozy spot for a drink on a winter evening. **The Lobby Bar** at The Four Seasons (tel. 416/964–0411) has window tables, which offer a fair amount of privacy for business discussions when the bar is full. Businesspeople from nearby offices gather at the quiet **Lobby Lounge** of the King Edward Hotel (tel. 416/863–9700).

Cabaret and Comedy Clubs
Second City (110 Lombard St., tel. 416/863–1111) usually offers great comedy fare, though much of the humor may be lost on those unfamiliar with Canadian politics and culture. **Yuk-Yuk's Komedy Kabaret** (1280 Bay St., just above Bloor St., and 2355 Yonge St., just above Eglington, tel. 416/967–6425) has a dopey name, but Howie Mandel and many other top comics got their start here.

Jazz Clubs
Café des Copains (48 Wellington St. E, near Yonge St., tel. 416/869–0148) has a romantic yet casual atmosphere and a clientele of serious jazz lovers who come to hear a different solo jazz pianist every two weeks. **George's Spaghetti House** (290 Dundas St. E, tel. 416/923–9887) is in a fairly scruffy neighborhood but is the oldest continuously running jazz club in the city. **Meyer's Deli,** at two locations (185 King St. W, near University Ave., and 69 Yorkville Ave., near Bay and Bloor Sts., both tel. 416/593–4189), has solid deli food and good jazz, including late-night sets on Friday and Saturday.

Rhythm and Blues
Club Bluenote (128 Pears Ave., tel. 416/921–1109) is the champion of R&B in Toronto and attracts visiting musicians and singers; when Whitney Houston is in town, this is where she goes.

For Singles
An upscale 25-to-35-year-old crowd puts on its smartest outfits for a night at **Berlin** (2335 Yonge St., tel. 416/489–7777), a multilevel club with a Continental dinner menu and a seven-piece band for jazz, pop, and R&B. **P.W.D. Dinkel's** (88 Yorkville Ave., tel. 416/923–9689) is frequented by a thirtysomething crowd that comes to hear live bands play Top 40-style music. **StiLife** (217 Richmond St. W, tel. 416/593–6116) is a restaurant/bar/dancing club with metallic and modular decor, and a DJ. **Studebaker's** (150 Pearl St., tel. 416/591–7960) is the 1950s revisited, with colorful memorabilia, a jukebox, and a DJ. During the week, the business crowd comes here, more male than female. Celebrities frequently drop in, too.

Washington, DC

by Sharon Geltner
Introduction with Deborah Papier

To a surprising degree, Washington is a city much like any other. True, it doesn't have a baseball team, but, in most other respects, life in the nation's capital is not that different from life elsewhere in the nation. People are born here, grow up, get jobs, and have children. Very often, they live out their lives without ever testifying before Congress, being indicted for influence peddling, or attending a state dinner at the White House.

Which is not to say that the government does not cast a long shadow over the city. "Washington means Business" is the city's slogan, but the biggest business of all is the Federal government, which employs about half a million local workers (out of a population of 630,000). Second is tourism, which brings in annual revenue of some $2 billion. Washington's downtown rents are the second highest in the nation, partly because developers can't build higher than the Capitol. This flat terrain has caused the business district to be called "K Street Canyon."

There's concern now over whether government spending cuts will level the city's economy. Local forecasters say not, because the economy is diversifying into high tech, financial, and information services. By the year 2000, professional workers should number 750,000—about 27% of all workers—clerical 26%, service 15%. Statistics aside, politics is still *the* business of this workaholic town, where people pride themselves on how early they get up.

It is often said that Washington does not have any real neighborhoods the way nearby Baltimore does. Although it's true that Washingtonians are not given to huddling together on their front stoops, each area of the city does have a clearly defined personality. Georgetown, one of the city's most inbred, exclusive communities—its residents successfully fought to keep out the subway—is a magnet for the young and the restless for miles around. Dupont Circle is Washington's bohemian neighborhood, where the artists and activists used to live before the rents got too high; now it's home to the most visible segment of the city's gay community. And adjacent Adams Morgan, the city's most intensely ethnic neighborhood, has begun to lose some of its Hispanic flavor, but you're still likely to hear more Spanish than English on the streets here.

Wealth and poverty have always coexisted here, but until recently poverty kept its distance. It's now omnipresent, wearing a very human face. Still, there's no denying that Washington, the world's first planned capital city, is also one of its most beautiful. And though the Federal government dominates the city psychologically, there are parts of the capital where you can leave politics behind. World-class museums and art galleries (nearly all of them free), tree-shaded and flower-filled parks and gardens, bars and restaurants that benefit from a large and creative immigrant community, and nightlife that seems to get better with every passing year are as much a part of Washington as floor debates or filibusters.

Top Employers

Employer	Type of Enterprise	Parent*/ Headquarters
Federal Government		Washington, DC
Gannett Company, Inc.	Newspaper chain	Arlington, VA
Giant	Groceries	Landover, MD
GEICO	Insurance	Bethesda, MD
Martin Marietta Corp.	Defense, weapons manufacture	Bethesda, MD
Marriott Corp.	Hotels	Bethesda, MD
MCI Communications	Telecommunications	Washington, DC
NVR L. P.	Housing, construction	McLean, VA
Potomac Electric Power Co. (PEPCO)	Utility	Washington, DC
USAir	Airline	Arlington, VA
Washington Post	Newspaper	Washington, DC

*if applicable

ESSENTIAL INFORMATION

Climate

What follows are the average daily maximum and minimum temperatures for Washington, DC.

Jan.	47F	8C	**Feb.**	47F	8C	**Mar.**	56F	13C
	34	−1		31	−1		38	3
Apr.	67F	19C	**May**	76F	24C	**June**	85F	29C
	47	8		58	14		65	18
July	88F	31C	**Aug.**	86F	30C	**Sept.**	79F	26C
	70	21		68	20		61	16
Oct.	70F	21C	**Nov.**	56F	13C	**Dec.**	47F	8C
	52	11		41	5		32	0

Airports

National Airport is just 3 miles south of downtown. **Dulles Airport** is 26 miles northwest, and principally handles international flights. **Baltimore Washington International** (BWI), in Maryland, is 28 miles from Washington and less convenient than the other two.

Airport Business Facilities

National Airport. Mutual of Omaha Business Service Center (Main Terminal, close to the Trump Shuttle, tel. 703/685–2453) has fax machines, photocopying, secretarial service, ticket pickup, baggage storage, Western Union, travel insurance, cash advance, and conference rooms.

Airlines

Dulles is the hub airport for United Airlines.

America West, tel. 800/247–5692.
American, tel. 202/393–2345 or 800/433–7300.
Continental, tel. 202/478–9700 or 800/525–0280.
Delta, tel. 202/468–2282 or 800/221–1212.
Midway, tel. 800/621–5700.
Northwest, tel. 202/737–7333 or 800/225–2525.
Pan Am, tel. 202/845–8000 or 800/221–1111.
Trump Shuttle, tel. 800/247–8786.
TWA, tel. 202/737–7400 or 800/221–2000.
United, tel. 202/742–4600 or 800/428–4322.
USAir, tel. 202/783–4500 or 800/428–4322.

Between the Airports and Downtown

By Taxi
This is the fastest way to get downtown from National (less than 30 minutes, even during rush hours). Ask the dispatcher for a DC cab, which is on the zone system: it costs about $11 to get downtown. Virginia and Maryland cabs are not zoned by district but metered and therefore more expensive. The trip from Dulles costs about $36; from BWI, about $42.

By Subway
From National, walk about 15 minutes to the National Airport Metro station (you'll see it when you leave the terminal) or take a free shuttle bus that departs across from the North terminal. The ride downtown takes about 20 minutes and costs $1.25–$2.25. There is no metro connection to Dulles or BWI.

By Train
At BWI, free shuttle buses take passengers to and from the train station. Amtrak (tel. 800/872–7245) and MARC (Maryland Rail Commuter Service, tel. 800/325–7245) trains run between the station and Washington's Union Station from about 6 AM to 11 PM. The cost for the 40-minute ride is $11 on Amtrak ($21 on the Metroliner) and $4.25 on a MARC Train.

By Bus
Dulles and BWI are served by the buses of **Washington Flyer** (tel. 703/685–1400). The ride downtown costs $12 and takes 45–60 minutes. Buses go to the downtown terminal at 1517 K St. NW, and connect with vans that go to

major hotels. The **Metro Bus Service** runs from National, but it's much less complicated to take the subway.

By Limousine
Reserve ahead or call from all three airports for a **Diplomat** limousine or sedan (tel. 202/589–7620). The cost from National is $33 ($23 for a sedan); from Dulles, $60 (sedan, $42); from BWI, $90 (sedan, $75).

Car Rentals

The following car rental companies have booths in or near National Airport:

Alamo, tel. 703/478–9597 or 800/327–9633.
Avis, tel. 202/467–6588 or 800/331–1212.
Budget, tel. 202/628–2752 or 800/527–0700.
Enterprise, tel. 202/393–0900 or 800/325–0700.
Hertz, tel. 703/979–6300 or 800/654–3131.
National, tel. 202/842–7454 or 800/328–4567.
Thrifty, tel. 202/783–0400 or 800/367–2277.

Emergencies

Doctors
Prologue Medical Referral (tel. 202/362–8677), **Physicians Home Service** (2440 M St. NW, Suite 620, tel. 202/331–3888).

Dentists
D.C. Dental Society (tel. 202/547–7613), **Dental Referral Bureau** (tel. 202/723–5323).

Hospitals
Capitol Hill Hospital (700 Constitution Ave., NE, tel. 202/269–8750), **George Washington University Hospital** (2150 Pennsylvania Ave. NW, tel. 202/994–3211), **Georgetown University Hospital** (3800 Reservoir Rd. NW, tel. 202/784–2118).

Important Addresses and Numbers

Audiovisual rentals. AVCOM (1006 6th St. NW, tel. 202/408–0444), Crews Control (1025 Thomas Jefferson St. NW, Suite 312, tel. 202/625–1900 or 800/545–2739).

Chamber of Commerce (1411 K St. NW, No. 500, tel. 202/347–7201).

Computer rentals. The Standard (1528 K St. NW, tel. 202/628–4940), ComputeRental (666 11th St. NW, Suite 1050, tel. 202/347–1582).

Convention center (9th & H Sts. NW, tel. 202/789–7000).

Fax services. AVCOM (1006 6th St. NW, tel. 202/408–0444), Lancaster Business Centers (16th & K Sts. NW, tel. 202/628–3614), Mail Boxes, Etc. (3220 N St. NW, tel. 202/342–0707; 2000 Pennsylvania Ave. NW, tel. 202/457–8166; 1718 M St. NW, tel. 202/785–3604), Presentation Group (2121 Wisconsin Ave. NW, Suite 55, tel. 202/337–5500).

Formal-wear rental. Royal Formal & Bridal (1328 G St. NW, tel. 202/737–7144).

Gift shops. Chocolates: Schoffs Belgian Chocolatier (2000 Pennsylvania Ave. NW, tel. 202/452–0924); Flowers: Blackistone's (1427 H St. NW, tel. 202/726–2700).

Graphic design studios. AlphaGraphics Printshops of the Future (1436 New York Ave. NW, tel. 202/638–1767), Balmar Printing, Graphics and 24-hour Copy Centers (1225 Eye St. NW, tel. 202/659–3610).

Hairstylists. Milton Pitts (Sheraton Carlton, 16th & K Sts. NW, tel. 202/638–2626, ext. 6733) has been barber to the presidents since 1969; at Rendezvouz in the Park (Park Hyatt, 24th & M Sts. NW, tel. 202/789–1234), Yves Graux cuts Barbara Bush's hair. When Nancy Reagan was in town she had hers done by Robin Weir (2134 P St. NW, tel. 202/861–0444).

Health and fitness clubs. *See* Fitness, below.

Information hot lines. Emergency (other than police/fire/ambulance, tel. 202/8DC–HELP), International Visitors Information Service (tel. 202/783–6540).

Limousine services. Bush-Martin Limousine Service (tel. 202/829–9719), Capital City Limousine (tel. 202/387–6217 or 800/441–6676), Carey Limousine (4345 42nd St. NW, Suite 300, tel. 202/537–5370).

Liquor stores. Capitol Hill Liquor (323 Pennsylvania Ave. SE, tel. 202/543–2900), Central Liquor Store (726 9th St. NW, tel. 202/737–2800), Connecticut Avenue Liquors (1529 Connecticut Ave. NW, tel. 202/332–0240), Dixie Liquor (3429 M St. NW, tel. 202/337–4412).

Mail delivery, overnight. DHL Worldwide Express (tel. 800/225–5345), Federal Express (tel. 800/238–5355), TNT Skypak (tel. 703/550–1000), UPS (tel. 301/595–9090), U.S. Postal Service Express Mail (tel. 202/636–1404).

Messenger services. Apple Courier (tel. 202/293–0930), Metro Delivery (tel. 202/387–8200), Quick Messenger Service, daily, 24 hours (tel. 202/783–3600), Washington Express Services (tel. 202/265–9200).

Office-space rentals. U.S. Office (1825 Eye St. NW, Suite 400, tel. 202/429–2000).

Pharmacies, late-night. Peoples at Dupont Circle (18th & Connecticut Ave. NW, tel. 202/785–1466), Peoples at Thomas Circle (14th St. & Massachusetts Ave. NW, tel. 202/628–0720).

Radio stations, all-news. WNTR 1050 AM, WTOP 1500 AM, WRC 980 AM.

Secretarial services. Advantage (1750 K St. NW, Suite 490, tel. 202/293–0232), Talent Tree Personnel (1101 17th St. NW, tel. 202/833–4880).

Stationery supplies. Ginns Office Products (7 locations, including: 1208 18th St. NW, tel. 202/833–6112), Jacobs Gardner Supply (10 locations, including: 1101 17th St. NW, tel. 202/293–3880 and 1353 Connecticut Ave. NW, tel. 202/872–9000).

Taxis. Capitol Cab (tel. 202/546–2400), Diamond Cab (tel. 202/387–6200), Yellow Cab (tel. 202/544–1212).

Theater Tickets. *See* The Arts, below.

Train information. Amtrak at Union Station (1st St. & Massachusetts Ave. NE, 800/872–7245 or 202/484–7540).

Travel agents. American Express Travel Service (3 locations: 1150 Connecticut Ave. NW, tel. 202/457–1300; 1776 Pennsylvania Ave. NW, tel. 202/289–8800; 1001 G St. NW, tel. 202/393–0095), Ask Mr. Foster Travel Service (4 locations: 1230 Connecticut Ave. NW, tel. 202/783–4255; 1120 Connecticut Ave. NW, tel. 202/466–8510; 1700 K St. NW, tel. 202/861–7700; 1800 G St. NW, tel. 202/682–9114).

Weather (tel. 202/936–1212).

LODGING

Washington's new hotels are lavish and, to keep up, most of the older ones have been extensively—and expensively—refurbished. This competition makes amenities that might be noteworthy in other cities almost standard here—desks, minibars, two-line phones, modem hookups, cable TV sets hidden in armoires, robes, double beds, express checkout, hair dryers, and so on.

But this doesn't mean you always have to pay top dollar. Summertime rates at many top hotels are reasonable, even when Congress is in session. Note, however, that some of the less expensive downtown hotels, particularly those east of the business district, are no bargain because they're in borderline neighborhoods. Although all the hotels listed below are in safe areas, visitors going out alone at night would be wise, as a rule, to travel by cab.

Your business appointments needn't determine where you'll stay. The Convention Center area is a bit dreary. For a livelier stay near shopping and entertainment, Georgetown is probably a better bet. Capitol Hill is quiet after working hours, but more entertaining than the Convention Center area.

Almost all the hotels listed below offer corporate rates and weekend discounts; inquire when making reservations.

Highly recommended lodgings in each price category are indicated by a star ★.

Category	Cost*
$$$$ (Very Expensive)	over $195
$$$ (Expensive)	$150–$195
$$ (Moderate)	under $150

*All prices are for a standard double room, single occupancy, excluding 11% room tax and $1.50 occupancy charge.

Numbers in the margin correspond to numbered hotel locations on the Washington, DC, Lodging and Dining map.

Downtown

㉓
$$$$

Hay-Adams. With the White House as its near neighbor, this hotel on Lafayette Park has serious snob appeal—mostly for corporate executives and lawyers during the week, and couples on weekends. Built in 1927, it boasts a medieval-style lobby with a 17th-century Medici tapestry, arches, and shelves of leather-bound books. Women guests are usually booked in rooms decorated in pink and cream; men, in rooms with a blue-and-cream color scheme. All accommodations are decorated in English country house styles and are equally tasteful, even the smaller ones. Bathrooms tend to be small and worn; doors have original knobs and have to be slammed shut. Rooms on the south side have views of the White House. The best junior suite is 744. The Adams Room is a popular spot for power breakfasts (*see* Business Breakfasts, below). *Murdock Hotels. 1 Lafayette Sq. NW, 20006, tel. 202/638–6600 or 800/424–5054, fax 202/638–2716. Gen. manager, William Trimble. 144 rooms, 20 suites. AE, CB, DC, MC, V.*

★ ㉕ **Hotel Washington.** This oldest continuously operating ho-
$$ tel in town, and now a national monument, is neither big, flashy, well known—nor overly expensive. It boasts the best views and suites at prices one-third less than those of other luxury hotels. This elegant period piece was restored in 1988 for its 70th anniversary at a cost of $12 million. The hotel has retained its Edwardian character, and a Gibson girl would not feel out of place in the opulent lobby. The hotel's central location near the Treasury is a plus. All rooms, some of which overlook White House grounds, are furnished with mahogany reproductions of 18th-century antiques; in keeping with the American Colonial tone, the dominant color is Williamsburg blue. Bathrooms are heavy with Italian marble. There are reasonably priced suites with Pennsylvania Avenue views. Washingtonians bring visitors to the rooftop bar for views of the White House grounds and the Washington Monument. The Two Continents restaurant (*see* Business Breakfasts, below) is a good venue for a morning meeting. *Gal-Tex. 15th & Pennsylvania Ave. NW, 20004, tel. 202/638–5900 or 800/424–9540, fax 202/638–5900, ext. 3999. Gen. manager, Muneer Deen. 350 rooms, 17 suites. AE, CB, DC, MC, V.*

★ ⑳ **Jefferson.** Built in 1923 and restored in 1989, the Jefferson
$$$ is just four blocks from the White House. The hotel has long been a favorite of Washington's elite; Cabinet members have stayed here, and George Bush's family settled in during the '89 inauguration. The staff remembers guests' names; laundry is hand-ironed and delivered in wicker baskets. The design touches are unusual and creative: Red-tipped white roses and oranges poked with cloves scent the lobby; black wallpaper with white sprigs gives character to one guest room, while a bright green Federal secretary desk brightens another. Striped divans, Japanese screens, grandfather clocks, antique lingerie chests, and Venetian glass reproductions are among the furnishings in the individually decorated rooms. Suites have phones with conference-call capability and speed dialing, as well as stereos and CD players; all rooms have VCRs and large desks. The Jefferson (*see* Business Breakfasts, below) dining room is a sunny spot for an early morning meeting. *Prudential-Bache. 16th & M Sts. NW, 20006, tel. 202/347–2200 or 800/223–6800, fax 202/331–7982. Gen. manager, Elmer Coppoolse. 100 rooms, 32 suites. AE, CB, DC, MC, V.*

㉗ **J. W. Marriott.** There's an even mix of tourists and
$$$$ businesspeople in this 15-story hotel, built in 1980, and attached to the National Press Building, National Theatre, and National Place shopping mall. Metro Center subway

WASHINGTON DC

WASHINGTON, DC HOTEL CHART

HOTELS	Price Category	Business Services — Banquet capacity	No. of meeting rooms	Secretarial services	Audiovisual equipment	Teletype news service	Computer rentals	In-room modem phone jack	All-news cable channel	Desk	Desk lighting	Bed lighting
Four Seasons	$$$$	500	4	✓	✓	-	✓	✓	✓	●	●	◐
The Grand	$$$	220	5	✓	✓	-	-	✓	✓	●	◐	◐
Hay Adams	$$$$	200	3	✓	✓	-	✓	✓	✓	●	●	●
Hotel Washington	$$	600	8	✓	✓	-	-	-	-	●	●	●
Hyatt Dulles	$$$	350	7	✓	✓	-	-	✓	✓	●	●	●
Hyatt Regency Capitol Hill	$$$	1500	12	✓	✓	-	✓	-	✓	●	●	●
Jefferson	$$$	65	5	✓	✓	-	✓	✓	✓	●	●	●
J.W. Marriott	$$$$	1300	10	✓	✓	-	✓	✓	✓	●	◐	◐
Mayflower	$$	700	20	✓	✓	-	✓	✓	✓	◐	○	○
Morrison Clark Inn	$$$	125	2	✓	✓	-	✓	✓	-	●	◐	◐
Park Hyatt	$$$$	500	2	✓	✓	-	✓	✓	✓	●	◐	●
Phoenix Park	$$	100	1	✓	✓	-	✓	✓	✓	◐	●	◐
Ramada Renaissance	$$	2000	20	✓	✓	-	✓	✓	✓	◐	◐	◐
Ritz-Carlton Pentagon City	$$$	600	9	✓	✓	-	✓	✓	✓	●	●	●
Sheraton-Carlton	$$$$	650	7	✓	✓	-	✓	✓	✓	○	○	◐
Washington Court	$$$	350	10	✓	✓	-	✓	✓	✓	◐	◐	◐
Watergate	$$$$	500	9	✓	✓	-	✓	✓	✓	●	●	●
Westin	$$$	500	8	✓	✓	-	✓	✓	✓	◐	◐	◐
Willard InterContinental	$$$$	400	13	✓	✓	✓	-	-	✓	●	◐	●

$$$$ = over $195, $$$ = $150-$195, $$ = under $150.
● good, ◐ fair, ○ poor.
All hotels listed here have photocopying and fax facilities.

| In-Room Amenities | | | | | | | | | | Hotel Amenities | | | | | | |
Nonsmoking rooms	In-room checkout	Minibar	Pay movies	VCR/Movie rentals	Hairdryer	Toiletries	Room service	Laundry/Dry cleaning	Pressing	Concierge	Barber/Hairdresser	Garage	Courtesy airport transport	Sauna	Pool	Exercise room
✓	✓	✓	✓	-	✓	●	●	●	●	✓	✓	✓	-	✓	●	●
✓	-	✓	✓	-	✓	●	●	●	●	✓	-	✓	-	-	◐	◐
✓	-	✓	✓	✓	✓	●	●	●	●	✓	-	✓	-	-	-	-
✓	-	-	✓	-	✓	●	◐	●	●	-	-	✓	-	-	-	◐
✓	-	-	✓	-	✓	◐	◐	●	●	-	-	-	✓	✓	◐	◐
✓	✓	✓	✓	✓	✓	◐	●	●	●	✓	✓	✓	-	✓	●	◐
✓	-	✓	✓	-	✓	●	●	●	●	✓	-	✓	-	-	-	-
✓	✓	✓	✓	-	✓	○	●	●	●	✓	✓	✓	-	✓	●	●
✓	✓	✓	✓	✓	✓	◐	●	●	●	✓	✓	-	-	-	-	-
✓	-	-	✓	✓	✓	●	◐	●	●	✓	-	✓	-	-	-	-
✓	-	✓	✓	✓	✓	●	●	●	●	✓	✓	✓	-	✓	◐	●
✓	-	✓	✓	✓	✓	◐	●	●	●	✓	-	✓	-	-	-	-
✓	-	✓	✓	✓	-	◐	●	●	●	✓	✓	✓	-	✓	●	●
✓	✓	✓	✓	-	✓	●	●	●	●	✓	-	✓	✓	✓	●	◐
✓	✓	✓	✓	✓	✓	●	●	●	●	✓	✓	✓	-	-	-	◐
✓	-	✓	✓	✓	✓	●	●	●	●	✓	-	✓	-	✓	-	◐
✓	-	✓	✓	✓	✓	●	●	●	●	✓	✓	✓	-	✓	●	●
✓	-	✓	✓	✓	✓	●	●	●	●	✓	✓	✓	-	✓	●	●
✓	✓	✓	✓	✓	✓	●	●	●	●	✓	-	✓	-	-	-	-

Room service: ● 24-hour, ◐ 6AM-10PM, ○ other.
Laundry/Dry cleaning: ● same day, ◐ overnight, ○ other.
Pressing: ● immediate, ◐ same day, ○ other.

is two blocks east, and Smithsonian museums and monuments are a few blocks south. Industrial-strength chandeliers hang above pink metal columns and white marble floors in the well-trafficked lobby of this massive hotel. (A nearby video arcade adds to the general hubbub.) Perks for Marriott guests include hair dryers on request and video check-out and breakfast order. VIPs stay on the 14th floor, with attractive parquet floors but some glass/brass bloopers; spectacular balcony views compensate for any decor deficiencies. Best views are on the Pennsylvania Avenue side. The executive lounge offers a free, light breakfast, snacks, an honor bar, and views of the Treasury park. There's also a health club with a lap pool, spacious sundeck, large Jacuzzi, and sauna. *1331 Pennsylvania Ave. NW, 20004, tel. 202/393–2000 or 800/228–9290, fax 202/626–6965. Gen. manager, John Dixon. 773 rooms, 51 suites. AE, CB, DC, MC, V.*

⑲ **Mayflower.** It seems that anyone who's anyone ends up at
$$ the Mayflower. Harry Truman and JFK lived here, and J. Edgar Hoover came for lunch daily for 25 years. Built in 1925, in what is now the heart of downtown, the 10-story hotel, now part of the Stouffer chain, was restored in 1984, although the west wing rooms are still to be done. The smallest rooms in the west wing have no desks, no bathroom amenities, and unsightly exposed pipes. Renovated rooms have Federal-period reproduction furnishings; bathrooms have been redone in marble. None of the rooms in either section of the hotel is huge, not even the suites. Lighting is a bit dim, but guests can borrow lamps from the front desk. Rooms facing bustling Connecticut Avenue have the best views, but those looking out on DeSales Street are quieter. The lobby, with its historical photos and large model of the *Mayflower*, is an ornate promenade stretching under a skylight for an entire block from Connecticut Avenue to 17th Street; it's *the* place to people-watch. Head to the mezzanine for quiet talks. Nicholas restaurant is well regarded for business meetings. The hotel offers Stouffer's systemwide "Meetings Express" service: with eight hours' notice, a guest can arrange a conference down to every detail—including catering, secretarial services, and audiovisual equipment (tel. 800/872–6338). *A Stouffer hotel. 1127 Connecticut Ave. NW, 20036, tel. 202/347–3000 or 800/468–3571, fax 202/466–9082. Gen. manager, Barry Swenson. 721 rooms, 85 suites. AE, CB, DC, MC, V.*

㉒ **Sheraton-Carlton.** This eight-story property was built in
$$$$ 1926 and underwent a major renovation in 1988 that enlarged many rooms and restored the hotel's grandeur. The hotel is in a bustling business sector, but the lobby is an opulent blend of Baroque and Rococo styles, with stucco arches, chandeliers, and a Florentine carpet of gold, green, and lavender. Even the elevators are decorated—with carved wooden griffins. Though rooms are furnished with antique reproductions, they don't quite live up to the promise of the lobby. The hotel provides 24-hour butler service, and exercise equipment will be delivered to rooms on request. Other in-room perks are three phones with call waiting, and a bathroom TV speaker. Desks, however, are the smallest of any major hotel in town. *A Sheraton hotel. 16th & K Sts. NW, 20006, tel. 202/638–2626 or 800/*

325–3535, fax 202/638–4231. Gen. manager, Michel Ducamp. 200 rooms, 36 suites. AE, CB, DC, MC, V.

★ ❷❻ **Willard InterContinental.** The Willard, two blocks from
$$$$ the White House, was meticulously restored to its 1901 appearance in a renovation completed in 1986. Since then, 20 heads of state have stayed on the Secret Service-approved sixth floor. The hotel's rich history includes visits by Mark Twain and Nathaniel Hawthorne (who was covering the Civil War). The term "lobbyist" was inspired by those attempting to curry favor with prominent guests in the hotel's richly decorated lobby during the Grant administration. Martin Luther King, Jr., wrote his "I have a dream" speech here. The new Willard presents an opulent, Beaux-Arts feast for the eye. Book well in advance for the 45 rooms facing Pennsylvania Avenue and the Washington Monument; if they're not available, choose G Street over noisy 14th Street. Rooms are furnished with mahogany Queen Anne reproductions. Two restaurants, the Occidental and the Willard, have won national acclaim. Upon request, rooms can be outfitted with fax machines. *1401 Pennsylvania Ave. NW, 20004, tel. 202/628–9100 or 800/327–0200, fax 202/637–7326. Gen. manager, K.L. Jeffrey. 365 rooms, 37 suites. AE, CB, DC, MC, V.*

West End

❾ **Grand.** The eight-story Grand, completed in 1984, has a
$$$ simple, understated lobby without gilt, chrome, or ornate flourishes. Good-size rooms are unfussy, too, with muted tones and clean lines. Windows open, phones have hold buttons, and tables are stocked with plenty of local magazines. Some rooms have French doors (no balconies) overlooking a European-style courtyard. Bathrooms are exceptionally opulent, with dark green marble sinks and tubs with whirlpool jets. Fax machines are installed in rooms upon request. The Grand Promenade, with its brass columns, murals, plush chairs, and courtyard views, is a good place for private talks. The Rose 'n' Crown pub is clubby, with plenty of privacy in an alcove hidden behind dark paneled walls. The hotel is a short walk from Georgetown and the Foggy Bottom Metro. *Kaempfer Company. 2350 M St. NW, 20037, tel. 202/429–0100 or 800/848–0016, fax 202/429–9759. Gen. manager, Samir Darwich. 236 rooms, 16 suites. AE, CB, D, MC, V.*

❽ **Park Hyatt.** Like its neighbors, the Grand and the Westin,
$$$$ this 10-story 1986 building on "hotel corner" is within walking distance of Georgetown, the State Department, "the K Street Corridor" of office buildings, and the shops and restaurants of Dupont Circle. Though it's a chain hotel, it's less bustling and more intimate than the representative of the Westin chain across the street. The lobby is decorated with flowers, ornate furniture, and a patterned marble floor. Rooms are less opulent, but spacious, with muted colors, good bed lamps, two-line telephones, and TVs in the bathrooms. The business center is open 24 hours. The health club is more for relaxing than working out; the pool is not big enough for lap swimming. *24th & M Sts. NW, 20037, tel. 202/789–1234 or 800/922–7275, fax 202/457–8823. Gen. manager, Paul Limbert. 224 rooms, including 130 suites. AE, CB, DC, MC, V.*

❻ **Watergate.** Though considered the top address in town,
$$$$ this famous 14-story hotel has some drawbacks. It has to

contend with a homeless shelter in the neighborhood, and it's part of the Watergate Complex, a serpentine configuration of curved black-and-white high rises faced with sawtooth balconies (ubiquitous maps guide guests through the labyrinth). Although the hotel, renovated by the designer who did the Westin and Willard, is fresh, with lots of pink and green and a sleek black-and-white marble lobby, there remains an odd underground feeling in many of the public areas, which are windowless. However, no other hotel offers views of the Potomac, Kennedy Center, and Key Bridge (less expensive rooms have a pleasant view of the pool and greenery). And though rooms are a bit prim, in a Ralph-Lauren-British-country-manor kind of way, they have such modern amenities as double-line phones. The health club is a chic outpost (*see* Fitness, below). There are many stores on site, including a bike rental shop. A complimentary limousine is available for rides to and from business appointments. *Pan American Properties. 2650 Virginia Ave. NW, 20037, tel. 202/965–2300 or 800/424–2736, fax 202/337–7915. Gen. manager, Alan Fitzgerald. 238 rooms, 119 suites. AE, CB, DC, MC, V.*

❼ Westin. Scenes in the movie *Broadcast News* were filmed
$$$ in the high-tech auditorium, and Jesse Jackson exercises here in Washington's best hotel health club (*see* Fitness, below). Guests can walk to offices on K Street and environs, or to the shops and restaurants of Georgetown. The sand-color 10-story building is perfectly nondescript, but indoors the white marble lobby is elegantly spare and sunny, with a two-story glass enclosure overlooking a brick courtyard. Rooms are average size, if a bit narrow, in a restful blue. The Executive Club floor has upgraded rooms, a staff of 19, and complimentary breakfast and snacks. The velvet banquettes in the elegant Colonnade restaurant are ideal for private talks. *All Nippon Airways. 24th & M Sts. NW, 20037, tel. 202/429–2400 or 800/228–3000, fax 202/457–5010. Gen. manager, Michael Sansbury. 417 rooms, 4 suites. AE, CB, DC, MC, V.*

Capitol Hill

㉚ Hyatt Regency. When the Hyatt opened in 1976, it was an
$$$ urban pioneer in shabby north Capitol Hill. Now, with the renovation of Union Station and the opening of other hotels, this 11-story convention hotel is trying to keep up. The lobby is an awkward triangle with a brown-tile floor that the skylight and chrome accents don't brighten much. Elsewhere in the hotel, browns are being replaced by more cheerful pastels. Still, the most light in the hotel is over the swimming pool and lounge area in the new health club. Rooms are a good size; upgraded rooms have bathroom phones, robes, and access to the 11th floor executive lounge. Ask for accommodations on the top floors, which still have views of, but are farther from, the rusty atrium roof. At night, from Hugo's Steakhouse, you can see the Capitol's lighted dome. The luncheon buffet in the lobby is a good value; the seafood stew in Jonah's Oyster Kitchen is excellent (Jonah's also has an upscale lunch counter for single travelers). Sunday brunch at the Park Promenade (*see* Business Breakfasts, below) is among the best in town. Video rentals are available in the lounge. *400 New Jersey Ave. NW, 20001, tel. 202/737–1234 or 800/223–*

1234, fax 202/393–7927. Gen. manager, Charly Assaly. 834 rooms, 31 suites. AE, CB, DC, MC, V.

③② Phoenix Park. This eight-story hotel, built in 1921 and re-
$$ furbished in 1986, is named after a park in Dublin, and the Irish theme is carried throughout. "Yards of beer" in glasses three feet tall are served in the bars around the hotel. The Dubliner bar is one of the most popular in town, and by day it serves as a casual meeting spot for businesspeople who hold informal talks at the small tables. The hotel lobby is fairly serene, with Oriental rugs on a marble floor and a handsome curving staircase. Rooms are furnished in tones of aqua or mauve. Desks are small. Draperies and spreads are in heavy floral patterns; furniture is boxy, except for the carved headboards. Corner rooms are preferable, but not on the floor over the bar. The Phoenix's greatest advantage for business travelers is its location—one block from the trains, shops, and restaurants at Union Station, and three blocks from the Capitol. *Irish Hospitality. 520 North Capitol St. NW, 20001, tel. 202/638–6900 or 800/824–5419, fax 202/393–3236. Gen. manager, Joseph Zarza. 87 rooms, 9 suites. AE, CB, MC, V.*

③① Washington Court. Three blocks north of the Capitol,
$$$ Washington's tallest hotel (15 stories) has a showpiece of a lobby, outfitted with salmon-color marble, glass elevators, and a one-story-high waterfall. Guest rooms are done in soothing pastels and include ornate armoires. Closets have such thoughtful touches as tie racks and padded hangers. All bathrooms have television sets. Some rooms have great views of the Capitol, others overlook the Washington Monument. All have comfortable couches. Exercise equipment is delivered to rooms on request. *Harbaugh Hotels. 525 New Jersey Ave. NW, 20001, tel. 202/628–2100 or 800/321–3010, fax 202/737–2641. Gen. manager, Marty Kaufman. 266 rooms, 14 suites. AE, CB, DC, MC, V.*

Convention Center

②⑧ Morrison Clark Inn. Mamie Eisenhower held teas in these
$$$ two Victorian townhouses that were built in 1865 and restored in 1987. Twelve guest rooms are decorated in turn-of-the-century style, with rich, dark colors and heavy fabrics. Some rooms have marble desks at bay windows, but you may need to request extra light for working. Rooms in the modern wing have a lighter, country feel, with pastel colors and wicker furniture. All baths are modern, with phones. Guest perks include complimentary limousine service, Continental breakfast, and newspapers. Try the restaurant, where, it's rumored, Barbara Bush favors the boneless chicken breast. *DEC Development. Massachussetts Ave. & 11th St. NW, 20001, tel. 202/898–1200 or 800/332–7898, fax 202/289–8576. Gen. manager, Michael Such. 54 rooms, 24 suites. AE, CB, DC, MC, V.*

②⑨ Ramada Renaissance-Techworld. Behind a bleak, black 15-
$$ story facade is a skylighted lobby festooned with Christmas lights and a bar, hidden under a pagoda—a garish entrance to a good-value hotel built in 1989. This is a lobby that screams "Look at me," but you won't want to. In the guest rooms, cherrywood dressers and tables sit on teal-blue carpets. Bedspreads and curtains share a cinnamon-

and-teal floral pattern reflected in the requisite landscape paintings on the cream-color walls. There's a well-outfitted health club (*see* Fitness, below), executive lounge, decently priced restaurants with private alcoves, pay-fax machine, and shops—all just across from the convention center. The Techworld business complex is an easy walk through an Oriental-style garden. *999 9th St. NW, 20001, tel. 202/898–9000 or 800/228–2828, fax 202/789–4213. Gen. manager, Josef Ebner, 800 rooms, 61 suites.*

Georgetown

❺ **Four Seasons.** A polished staff is at your service the mo-
$$$$ ment you approach the doors of this contemporary hotel between Georgetown and Foggy Bottom. The attractive lobby is lined with more than 2,000 plants set along brick paths, hanging from balconies, and encircling fountains. In the upstairs corridors, linens are stored in armoires, so chambermaids' carts never block the halls (instead, you'll find jars of Peruvian lilies in the hallways). Rooms were redecorated in 1990 with overstuffed goosedown armchairs, leather-top desks, and silk moiré wall coverings. Baths, heavy with beige Carrara marble, have fresh orchids or roses. Best accommodations face the C&O canal (and freeway), the quietest face the courtyard. Suites with locking desks and folding doors between bedrooms and parlors are suitable for meetings. The Aux Beaux Champs restaurant is well regarded locally. Free limo service is provided. *2800 Pennsylvania Ave. NW, 20007, tel. 202/342–0444 or 800/332–3442, fax 202/944–2076. Gen. manager, Stan Bromley. 197 rooms, 30 suites. AE, CB, D, MC, V.*

Airport

❶ **Hyatt Dulles.** This 14-story hotel, built in 1989, is 3 miles
$$$ from Dulles International, and is linked to the airport by a free, half-hourly shuttle. Downtown is about 40 minutes away by taxi. Soundproof guest rooms are suite-sized. A parlor area, with seating for four, is set off from the bed by a credenza. All rooms have two-line telephones, and the women's rooms—closer to the elevators—have hair dryers in the bathrooms. A pianist performs near the fountain in the two-story atrium. This is a warmer and more elegant place to stay than the standard airport hotel. *2300 Dulles Corner Blvd., Herndon, VA, 22070, tel. 703/834–1234 or 800/223–1234, fax 703/742–3410. 300 rooms. AE, CB, DC, MC, V.*

❸❻ **Ritz-Carlton, Pentagon City.** This luxurious establish-
$$$ ment, in a vast and pricy shopping mall five minutes from National Airport, opened in the spring of 1990. It is a 15-minute taxi ride, and less than a half-hour subway ride, from downtown. Rooms have Federal reproduction furnishings, silk drapes, and framed botanical prints. Beds are covered with heavy quilted spreads. Two-line phones are standard. The building is insulated against jet noise. The lavish appointments and meticulous upkeep make this a splendid oddity among airport hotels. *1250 S. Hayes St., Arlington, VA 22202 tel. 703/415–5000 or 800/241–3333, fax 703/415–5061. 345 rooms, 41 suites. AE, CB, DC, MC, V.*

DINING

In the last few years, Italian restaurants have come to rival French restaurants, which for a long time set the standards in fine dining in the city. There has also been an explosion of the kind of cooking usually called New American. You can find almost any kind of food in Washington, from Nepalese to Salvadoran to Ethiopian; in only one category is the city falling short these days, and that's Chinese. Many of the deluxe restaurants are in a 12-block area radiating northwest from 16th and K streets NW—also the location of many of the city's blue-chip law firms. These are the restaurants that feed expense-account diners and provide the most elegant atmosphere. The other area of town for dining, though more for pleasure than business, is Georgetown, whose central intersection is Wisconsin Avenue and M Street. Georgetown contains some of the city's trendiest dining spots, with elegant eateries right next door to hole-in-the-wall carryouts.

For an inexpensive meal when you're on your own, try one of the subsidized government cafeterias—at the Library of Congress, Federal Reserve Board, Supreme Court, or Congressional office buildings.

Highly recommended restaurants in each price category are indicated by a star ★.

Category	Cost*
$$$$ (Very Expensive)	over $40
$$$ (Expensive)	$20–$40
$$ (Moderate)	under $20

per person, including appetizer, entrée, and dessert, but excluding drinks, service, and 9% sales tax.

Numbers in the margin correspond to numbered restaurant locations on the Washington, DC, Lodging and Dining map.

Business Breakfasts

If the purpose of your meeting is to impress people, eat at **The Adams Room** in the Hay-Adams (tel. 202/638–6600), with its colorful, colonial-style decor and its views of Lafayette Park and the White House. Breakfasts are served up traditionally with meats; lighter fare is also available. **The Jefferson** (tel. 202/347–2200) is a bright, quiet spot with old-fashion wooden chairs and large tables—perfect for opening manila folders and getting down to business. **Two Continents**, at the Hotel Washington (tel. 202/638–5900), offers the best breakfast value with a large, varied buffet and a formal atmosphere suitable for quiet talks. The recently restored restaurant is still (unfairly) burdened with a ho-hum reputation, so privacy won't be a problem.

Best brunches (in order): **Key Bridge Marriott** (1401 Lee Hwy., Arlington, VA, tel. 703/524–6400), **Hyatt Regency** (tel. 202/737–1234), **Sheraton Washington** (2660 Woodley Rd. NW, tel. 202/328–2000), **Clyde's Georgetown** (3236

M St. NW, tel. 202/333–0294), **Vista International** (1400 M St. NW, tel. 202/429–1700).

Downtown

㉑ **Bombay Club.** Many embassy and business types confer in
$$$$ this Indian restaurant. A block-and-a-half from both the White House and the K Street business district, the restaurant smacks of Empire, with lots of rattan, spacious banquettes, well-spaced side tables with lamps, and copper and brass antiques. Try lamb rogan josh, cooked with saffron and yogurt, chicken tikka morsels with mint sauce, tandoori chicken or shrimp, or Chesapeake crabmeat masala with tomatoes, onions, and curry. The combination (silver) platter gives you a choice of six dishes. The service is more professional than warm. *815 Connecticut Ave. NW, tel. 202/659–3727. Jacket and tie. Reservations advised. AE, CB, DC, MC, V. Closed lunch Sat.*

⓭ **C. F. Folks.** Located amid pricy power-lunch eateries is
$$ this popular white-collar lunch counter with a small outdoor patio for additional seating in warmer months. A tiny spot for solo dining, it numbers among its specialties thick, delicious soups, such as black bean. The clientele is largely young office workers. Every day brings its own cuisine, from Cajun on Mondays to Middle Eastern on Fridays. *1225 19th St. NW, tel. 202/293–0162. Casual dress. No credit cards. Lunch only; closed weekends.*

⓱ **Duke Zeibert's.** Washington's power elite—and more than
$$$ 400 others—lunch on designer deli dishes by the soaring glass walls overlooking the bustle of Connecticut Avenue. The staff is less than alert, except when serving celebrities, who get the prestigious center tables and slaps on the back from Duke himself. Matzo ball soup is the signature item; rich chopped chicken liver and beef hash are also dependable. The heavy cheesecake has a glutinous strawberry topping, omitted on request. The interior is more subtle than the atmosphere. *1050 Connecticut Ave. NW, tel. 202/466–3730. Jacket and tie. Reservations advised. AE, DC, MC, V. Closed lunch Sun.*

㉔ **Old Ebbitt Grill.** This Washington institution has settled
$$ into elegant, Victorian saloon digs. Lots of locals dine here, notably "Schedule-C types" (political appointees) from the Treasury Department and the White House next door. Businesspeople come for friendly chats, not to conclude deals. Stick to simple dishes, such as grilled fish and some of the best burgers in town. Service by young, aproned staff members is briskly courteous. Open to 3 AM. *675 15th St. NW, tel. 202/347–4801. Casual dress. Reservations suggested. AE, CB, DC, MC, V.*

⓬ **I Ricci.** Three weeks after his inauguration, George Bush
$$$$ ate at this restaurant, which features the earthy cuisine of Tuscany. Immediately the most sought-after people began arriving in droves. Located on a major tributary of K Street, this is a convenient and discreet-yet-glamorous site for private-sector summits. The burnt orange walls are painted with vines and flowers, with matching terracotta and Ginori china from Italy. The open kitchen has a huge wood-burning oven. Unusual meats, such as baby goat, leg of rabbit, and quail, are featured. Appetizers include *la fettunta*, grilled garlic bread with white beans

and tomato; *topini*, potato dumplings with tomato sauce; and ricotta and spinach tortelloni. *1220 19th St. NW, tel. 202/835–0459. Jacket and tie. AE, CB, MC, V. Closed for lunch Sat.; Sun.*

⓲ **Tabard Inn.** With its artfully artless decor, absentminded
$$$ waiters, and quasihealth food menu, the Tabard is an idiosyncratic restaurant with a devoted clientele of baby boomers. The dark-panel club room is slightly shabby, but the courtyard is delightful. The Inn is suitable for relaxed lunch discussions, with just enough noise to foil eavesdroppers. At night, the atmosphere turns romantic with low lights and candles. The health-conscious chef is always inventing new treatments for the staple ingredients on her California/French nouvelle-style menu. Softshell crabs, for instance, have appeared sautéed with a cornmeal coating, and the chicken salad features walnut-bread croutons and a blue-cheese-and-buttermilk dressing. The wine list is laden with California labels, but also includes some organically grown Italian wines. The staff is friendly and knowledgeable. *1739 N. St. NW, tel. 202/785–1277. Casual dress. Reservations advised for dinner; accepted for lunch before 12:15; required anytime for parties of 5 or more. MC, V.*

⓯ **La Taberna del Alabardero.** The owner, who opened his
$$$$ first restaurant in Madrid, has achieved a formal Old World ambience in this upscale Spanish restaurant. Bilevel dining offers a chance to spot plenty of guests, but lawyers come here for a quiet place to talk. The restaurant is one block from 18th and K Streets, one of the busiest business-district intersections. The kitchen turns out creditable Basque shrimp with mushrooms, fried squid, filet Mignon with Rioja wine sauce, and paella and peppers stuffed with crab in a saffron sauce. The kitchen is visible in the main dining room. The staff comports itself with classic Spanish *cortesia*. *18th & Eye Sts. NW, tel. 202/429–2200. Jacket and tie. Closed for lunch Sat.; Sun. AE, DC, MC, V.*

⓰ **21 Federal.** Washington investors discovered the original
$$$$ in Nantucket and brought a branch to DC in 1988. A private dining room is separated from the main room by glass walls so that, as one critic said, "everyone can be aware of the exclusive gathering they weren't invited to." This trendy eatery is also staging ground for the Hollywood practice of taking phone calls at the table. The food is new American; among the specialties are mushroom streudel, lobster and corn chowder, scallops and shrimp fettuccine, roast goose, herb-crusted sole with chive butter, and lobster/crab cakes with corn okra relish. The place is noisy, so serious negotiations are out of the question. The bar and surrounding tables are of black granite—striking, against the black-and-white marble floor. The staff is helpful and only a trifle too familiar. Generally, the clientele is lower-middle-age, upper-middle-class, and highly fashion conscious. The wine list is French and Californian, with more than half a dozen available by the glass. *1736 L St. NW, 202/331–9771. Jacket and tie. Reservations advised. AE, CB, MC, V. Closed lunch Sat; Sun.*

⓫ **Vincenzo.** This Italian seafood restaurant is a popular
$$$ business spot, in part because of the pleasant Mediterranean-style decor, with red tile floors and white stucco

walls. Located in the trendy Dupont Circle neighborhood, near sidewalk cafés and art galleries, Vincenzo is within 10 blocks of most major law firms and corporate offices. Tables are decently spaced, making them suitable for negotiations. The main dining room downstairs is quieter and better lighted, but smoking is not permitted there. Try a whole grilled fish, such as grouper, red snapper, or pompano. Fish stews in spicy tomato broth, and grilled scallops are also delicious. Pasta is prepared with spicy sauces, but tends to be a bit chewy. Wines are exclusively Italian, and only two are available by the glass. *1606 20th St. NW, tel. 202/667-0047. Jacket and tie. AE, CB, MC, V. Closed for lunch weekends.*

West End

★ ⑭ **Dominique's.** The front room is rustic, complete with
$$$ stuffed animal heads mounted on the wall; the back rooms have ornate tapestries, white columns, and stained glass—more fitting for a restaurant serving some of the best classic French food in town (few people actually order the rattlesnake and kangaroo appetizers Dominique's is so famous for). Local restaurant-goers voted Dominique's decor the city's prettiest. Specialties include shrimp in garlic sauce, fillet of beef, and duck pie. Near the World Bank complex, two blocks from the K Street lawyer-lobbyist promenade, and three blocks from the White House, this restaurant serves both private and public sectors. Tables are close together, inhibiting highly confidential talks; the noise level is acceptable. *1900 Pennsylvania Ave. NW, tel. 202/452-1126. Jacket and tie. Reservations advised. AE, MC, V. Closed for lunch weekends.*

★ ⑩ **Jockey Club.** Nancy Reagan ate here regularly, if you can
$$$$ call "just a salad" eating. People come in smug and curious, proud to be here and wondering who else is around. Order a Coke and the stiff and punctilious waiters insist upon adding "lay-mone." Still, the place isn't as intimidating as it may sound—and the food is excellent. The decor in three adjoining rooms is countrified, with heavy wooden beams, white stucco walls, red-and-white plaid tablecloths, and lots of paintings of dogs, horses, and ships. Commerce Secretary Robert Mosbacher and Lee Iaccoca are regulars. Most diners want to sit in the first, most visible room, lining up against the back wall so they don't miss anyone. Tables in the back two rooms are farther apart and offer more privacy. On the whole, the menu is classic Continental. Crab cakes are distinguished by their meatiness rather than by unusual spicing; breast of duck is prepared with morels and port sauce; the double-grilled lamb chop is accompanied by rosemary and tomato sauce. The Grand Marnier chocolate tart is excellent. The wine list is evenly divided between France and California; a small selection is available by the glass. *Ritz-Carlton, 2100 Massachusetts Ave. NW, tel. 202/659-8000. Jacket and tie. Reservations advised. AE, MC, DC, V.*

Capitol Hill

㉞ **Adirondacks.** Inside Union Station is this restored 1907
$$$ Beaux Arts masterpiece, complete with soaring barrel-vault ceilings, gilded moldings, chandeliers, artwork by De Kooning, Hockney, and Motherwell on the walls, and Michael Graves china on the tables. The staff is friendly,

and the food is prepared in an unusual and appealing California style. Pork tenderloin is prepared with garlic and sun-dried tomatoes, and the roasted duck breast has a distinctive green peppercorn sauce. California labels dominate the pricy wine list, but France comes close; there are Australian and Spanish selections, too. Tables near the entrance are quietest. This is a perfect place to fête your Congressional representative, as the Capitol is practically next door. It's convenient, too, for those fresh off the Metroliner, or just about to board. *Union Station, 50 Massachusetts Ave. NE, tel. 202/682–1840. Jacket and tie. Reservations advised. AE, CB, DC, MC, V.*

35 **La Brasserie.** Conveniently near the Capitol, La Brasserie
$$$ is noted as the place for Congressional working dinners over breast of duck or seafood prepared with a French flair. The salmon, smoked on the premises, is served as an appetizer with capers, chopped onions, and toast, or in a salad of mixed greens. The seafood is fresh and distinctively prepared; for instance, the unbreaded crab cakes are made with red peppers and shallots, and baked—not deep-fried. Lobster is baked in layers of pastry. The restaurant, which occupies two townhouses, has several small rooms (one holds only five tables) and a main dining room. Collectors' plates and scenes of France decorate the walls. Dim lighting, artwork in heavy gilt frames, and plenty of fresh flowers on the tables create a cozy ambience. In summer, diners prefer to sit outside on the patio. Private rooms seating 4–40 can be reserved. Service is efficient and polite, not fawning. Wines are mostly French, with a few Virginian labels among the Americans, which are otherwise from California; a dozen are available by the glass. *239 Massachusetts Ave. NE, tel. 202/546–9154. Jacket and tie. Reservations advised. AE, MC, V.*

33 **La Colline.** Lunchtime meetings are the rule here among a
$$$ rogue's gallery of political photos (Ted Kennedy's is signed, "Let the Good Times Roll"). A bistro with lots of light and hanging plants, La Colline's best buy is the three-course fixed-price dinner. The menu, which changes daily, is reliable; most popular dishes are the bouillabaisse and cassoulet. The fricassée of shellfish includes scallops, shrimp, and lobster, and shiitake mushrooms in a dry vermouth-and-cream sauce. The breast of duck is served in an Oriental marinade. The wine list is two-thirds French, with the remainder Californian. Eight wines, plus one Champagne, are available by the glass. The service, efficient at midday, is very slow at night. Either time, you may spy a famous senator, but too many gladhanders will be stopping by his table for you to see him for long. The back-slapping and elbow-rubbing can be distracting, but otherwise your discussions will not be disturbed. Best tables for talks are near the captain's post. *400 North Capitol St. NW, tel. 202/737–0400. Jacket and tie. Reservations advised. AE, CB, MC, V.*

30 **Mel Krupin's.** Krupin, Duke Ziebert's former head waiter
$$$ (*see above*), is usually on hand to greet diners at this bilevel Capitol Hill restaurant. Upstairs is Mel's Deli, fine for sandwiches or a solo breakfast or lunch. Downstairs, you're part of the macho Washington scene that includes athletes, reporters, and old-fashion politicos. The setting is subdued, with plenty of the expected dark wood, and surprisingly delicate upholstery on the Queen Anne

chairs in the section facing the lobby. Many booths are in the center of the room. Waiters are frank, even sassy, and—like the prime rib and crab cakes they serve—dependable. The sirloin is the outstanding item but, like the rest of the conventional menu, distinguished only by its consistency. *Washington Court, 525 New Jersey Ave. NW, tel. 202/628–2100. Jacket and tie. Reservations advised. AE, CB, MC, V.*

Georgetown

② **Bamiyan.** Afghani food is largely unknown in the West.
$$ That's a pity, because the country's cuisine is quite appealing, unusual enough to be interesting but not so strange as to be intimidating. Bamiyan is the oldest and arguably the best Afghani restaurant in the area, even though it does look like a motel that has seen better days. Kebabs—of chicken, beef, or lamb—are succulent. More adventurous souls should try the *quabili palow* (lamb with saffron rice, carrots, and raisins) or the *aushak* (dumplings with scallions, meat sauce, and yogurt). For a side vegetable, order the sautéed pumpkin; it will make you forget every other winter squash dish you've ever had. *3320 M St. NW, tel. 202/338–1896. Reservations accepted. Casual dress. AE, MC, V. Closed lunch.*

③ **Germaine's.** This elegant Pan-Asian restaurant, over a
$$$ video store in northern Georgetown, has a romantic story behind it. The eponymous Vietnamese owner met her husband, an American news photographer (whose work now hangs on the walls), in Saigon during the war. He returned to Vietnam to rescue his wife's family as Saigon fell, and many of Germaine's relatives now work in the restaurant. David Brinkley, Sam Donaldson, and the ambassadors from Japan, Singapore, and Germany eat here often. The tasty Korean-style beef is hot and spicy and has the chewy texture of beef jerky. The Southeast Asian menu includes a commendable "pine cone fish" that is both a specialty and a spectacle: Filleted and scored before it is deep-fried in a light tempura batter, it comes out looking like a pine cone split open. The lower-ceilinged front room, facing Wisconsin Avenue, is quieter than the atrium. In addition to an ample selection of international wines, the restaurant offers nearly 20 imported beers, including the rare Maui Lager. *2400 Wisconsin Ave. NW, tel. 202/ 965–1185. Jacket and tie. Reservations advised. AE, DC, MC, V.*

④ **1789.** Named not for the year of the French Revolution but
$$$$ for the adoption of the U.S. Constitution and the founding of Georgetown University next door, this is an appropriately serene place to eat. Most diners are couples; for business purposes, the tone is right for toasting the conclusion of an agreement rather than for hammering out its details. Currier & Ives prints, wooden Venetian blinds, and an intricately carved antique mahogany sideboard lend to the main dining room the air of a sumptuous country inn. The livelier Pub Room has a five-stool bar. Waiters, in black tie, are reserved and attentive. The seasonal Continental menu is usually strong on fish dishes such as sautéed striped bass. Also popular are medallions of duck. Wines are from France and California and are reasonably priced. *1226 36th St. NW, tel. 202/965–1789. Jacket required. Reservations advised. AE, CB, DC, MC, V.*

FREE TIME

Fitness

Hotel Facilities

Westin Fitness Center at the Westin Hotel (tel. 202/457–5000) has the best facilities, including a two-lane pool, pounds of exercise equipment, and aerobics classes. **Hyatt Regency,** near Capitol Hill (tel. 202/737–1234), has similar facilities. **Ramada Renaissance Techworld** (tel. 202/898–9000) and the **Watergate** (tel. 202/965–2300) also have good clubs with lap pools. Nonguests pay $10–$15 a day.

Health Clubs

Most downtown facilities do not allow one-day members. Some hotels give passes to the modern, seven-story **YMCA** (1711 Rhode Island Ave. NW, tel. 202/862–9688), the largest downtown fitness center.

Jogging

The **Mall,** between the Capitol and Washington Monument, has a 3-mile gravel path. Some people continue west on the grass from the Monument to the Lincoln Memorial. The **Hains Point Loop** takes joggers along a scenic 3-mile waterfront path. Take a cab there, and don't go after dark.

Shopping

Though **Georgetown** is not on a subway line and parking is next to impossible (take a cab), people still flock here for the antiques and craft shops and high-style clothing boutiques. From the intersection of Wisconsin Avenue and M Street, walk west on M Street and north on Wisconsin.

The city's department stores can be found in the "new" downtown, which is still being built. Its fulcrum is **Metro Center** (tel. 202/637–7000), which spans 11th and 12th streets NW along G Street. Here you'll find two of the best department stores, **Hechts** (12th & G Sts., tel. 202/628–6661) and **Woodward & Lothrop** (11th & F Sts., tel. 202/347–5300).

An even newer project is the renovation of **Union Station** (tel. 202/371–9441) at Massachusetts Avenue NE. Resplendent with marble floors and gilded, vaulted ceilings, this is now both a working train station and a mall with three levels of stores selling everything from designer jellybeans to trendy clothes.

For high quality country crafts, try **Appalachian Spring** (Union Station and 1415 Wisconsin Ave. NW, tel. 202/682–0505 or 202/337–5780). You can buy quality Americana at **Celebrate America!** (National Press Building, 14th & F Sts., tel. 202/638–4681) and the **Decatur House Museum Shop** (Lafayette Sq., tel. 202/842–1856). For American art, pottery, and antiques, try **Chenonceau** (2314 18th St. NW, tel. 202/667–1651). For unique, upscale gifts, visit the gift shops at the **Smithsonian** (tel. 202/357–2700).

Diversions

First-time visitors to Washington will want to see the icons of American government: **Jefferson Memorial** (15th St. SW on the south shore of the Tidal Basin, tel. 202/426–6841); **Lincoln Memorial** (west end of the Mall at 23rd St.

NW, between Constitution & Independence Aves. NW, tel. 202/426–6841), with the **Vietnam Veterans Memorial** close by; **Washington Monument** (center of Mall, Constitution Ave. and 15th St. NW, tel. 202/426–6839); **White House** (1600 Pennsylvania Ave. NW, tel. 202/456–7041, tape, or 202/456–2000; the line forms at the Ellipse before noon, often around 9 AM); and the **U.S. Capitol** (east end of the Mall, tel. 202/225–6827).

The following are a selection of other options for those with extra time on their hands.

Walk up to 13 miles along the scenic **C&O Canal towpath,** starting in Georgetown.

Georgetown, with its trendy shops, restaurants, and galleries, is fun to explore (*see* Shopping, above).

The **National Museum of Women in the Arts** (1250 New York Ave. NW, tel. 202/783–5000) is the first museum in the world dedicated to women artists. The permanent collection of more than 500 works ranges from the Renaissance to the present and includes paintings, drawings, sculpture, prints, and photographs.

Cruise to **Mt. Vernon** (tel. 703/780–2000), George Washington's beautiful estate in Virginia, on the *Spirit of Washington* (Pier 4, 6th & Water Sts., tel. 202/554–1542). Before the cruise, stroll among seafood restaurants and fish stands along the waterfront.

The **National Archives** (Constitution Ave. between 7th & 9th Sts. NW, tel. 202/323–3000) house the Declaration of Independence and the U.S. Constitution.

The **National Gallery of Art** (Constitution Ave. at 4th St. NW, tel. 202/737–4215) has one of the world's foremost collections of paintings, sculptures, and graphics, including the only DaVinci outside of Europe. The domed west building has works from the 13th to the 20th century; I.M. Pei's angular east building displays modern art exclusively.

Not far from the Convention Center is the **National Portrait Gallery** (8th & F Sts. NW, tel. 202/357–1300). Its collection includes photographs from the Civil War era, and life casts of Abraham Lincoln's face and hands.

Stroll around the **Tidal Basin,** the small walled lake in front of the Jefferson Memorial, particularly in spring when the cherry blossoms are in bloom. Or rent a pedal boat at the Tidal Basin Boat House (15th St. & Maine Ave. NW, tel. 202/484–0206).

The **U.S. Botanic Garden** (Maryland Ave. & 1st St. SW, tel. 202/226–4082 or 202/225–7099) is especially delightful in the winter, with its conservatory offering sanctuary to cactii, ferns, and orchids.

Tour the **U. S. Supreme Court** (1st & East Capitol Sts. NE, tel. 202/479–3499) and the **Capitol** (tel. 202/225–6827) across the street.

Professional Sports

DC's basketball team, the **Bullets** (tel. 301/350–3400), and the hockey team, the **Capitals** (tel. 301/350–3400), appear at Capital Centre. The town's football team, the **Redskins** (tel. 202/546–2222), plays at RFK Stadium.

The Arts

In the past 20 years, this cultural backwater has been transformed into a cultural capital. **The Kennedy Center** is home to the National Symphony Orchestra and host to Broadway shows, ballet, modern dance, and opera. The Center is actually four stages under one roof: the Concert Hall, the Opera House, the Eisenhower Theater (usually for drama), and the Terrace Theater (for experimental works and chamber groups).

The Arena Stage is the city's most respected resident company—the first theater outside New York to win a Tony Award. There are three theaters: the theater-in-the-round Arena, the proscenium Kreeger, and the cabaret-style old Vat Room.

Ford's Theatre, looking much the way it did when President Lincoln was shot, is host mainly to musicals, many with family appeal. **National Theatre** presents pre- and post-Broadway shows. **Shakespeare Theatre** at the Folger presents works by the bard and his contemporaries in an Elizabethan-type setting. Several art galleries present highly regarded chamber concert series, including the **National Gallery** (which also offers free concerts Sun., 7 PM, in the Garden Court), **Corcoran Gallery of Art,** the **Folger Shakespeare Library,** and the **Phillips Collection** (free concerts Sun., 5 PM, Labor Day–Memorial Day).

The "Weekend" section in Friday's *Washington Post* is the best guide to coming events. The Post's daily "Guide to the Lively Arts" also lists cultural events. The *Washington Times's* "Weekend" section comes out on Thursday. Also consult the "City Lights" section in the monthly *Washingtonian* magazine.

Instant-Charge (tel. 202/857–0900) sells tickets to Kennedy Center only; **Metro Center TICKETplace** (F Street Plaza between 12th & 13th Sts. NW, tel. 202/842–5387) has day-of-performance tickets at half price; **TicketCenter** (tel. 202/432–0200 or 800/448–9009) sells tickets to Capital Centre, Wolf Trap, and Ford's Theatre. Tickets to most events are available through **Ticketron** (1101 17th St. NW, tel. 202/659–2601). **Premier Theatre Seats** (tel. 202/963–6161), **Top Centre Tickets** (tel. 202/452–9040), and **Ticket Connections** (tel. 202/587–6850) sell tickets on short notice, sometimes to otherwise sold-out productions, for a $15–$25 surcharge.

Arena Stage (6th St. & Maine Ave. SW, tel. 202/488–3300).
Corcoran Gallery Concert Series (17th St. & New York Ave. NW, tel. 202/638–3211).
Folger Shakespeare Library Concerts (201 E. Capitol St. SE, tel. 202/544–4600).
Ford's Theatre (511 10th St. NW, tel. 202/347–4833).
John F. Kennedy Center for the Performing Arts (one block

south of Virginia and New Hampshire Ave. NW, tel. 202/
254–3600 or 800/424–8504).

National Gallery Concerts (6th St. & Constitution Ave.
NW, West Building, tel. 202/737–4215).

National Theatre (1321 Pennsylvania Ave. NW, tel. 202/
783–3372 or 800/233–3123).

Phillips Collection Concerts (1600 21st St. NW, tel. 202/
387–2151).

Shakespeare Theatre at the Folger (201 E. Capitol St. SE,
tel. 202/546–4000).

After Hours

Bars and Lounges

For a quiet talk with clients, **Madeo** (1113 23rd St. NW,
tel. 202/457–0057), with its indoor garden, is the most elegant. It is sophisticated but not stuffy, and offbeat types
come from the artsy cinema next door. **The Guards** (2915 M
St. NW, tel. 202/965–2350) has a hushed atmosphere, and
is favored by "cave dwellers" (old-money native Washingtonians). **The Dupont Plaza Hotel** (Dupont Circle NW, tel.
202/483–6000) has a piano lounge and a separate, quieter
room with views of Dupont Circle and its picturesque
fountain. **The Front Page** (19th & New Hampshire Sts.
NW, tel. 202/296–6500) is loud and jam-packed, especially
at Thursday Happy Hours, when under-30 office workers
come to let off steam.

Cabarets

Capitol Steps, a satirical group made up of Congressional
staffers, performs at **Chelsea's Georgetown** (1055 Thomas
Jefferson St. NW, tel. 202/683–8330). **Mrs. Foggybottom
& Friends/Marquee Cabaret** (Omni Shoreham Hotel, 2500
Calvert St. NW, tel. 202/745–1023) performs musical po-
litical satire.

Comedy Clubs

Comedy Café (1520 K St. NW, tel. 202/638–5653) brings in
comics from all over the east coast. Don't expect sophisticated political humor—not unless there's a crude and/or
silly angle. But the audience loves it. **Garvin's Comedy
Club** (1335 Greens Ct.; L St. between 13th & 14th Sts.
NW, tel. 202/726–1334) features top acts.

Jazz Clubs

Blues Alley (rear of 1073 Wisconsin Ave. NW, tel. 202/
337–4141) serves up jazz in an intimate, casual setting.
Anton's 1201 Club (1201 Pennsylvania Ave. NW, tel. 202/
783–1201), an Art Deco supper club, is one of the most sophisticated spots in town and a good place to take clients;
former Speaker of the House Jim Wright used to take refuge here when his fortunes were at their worst.

For Singles

The Bayou (3135 K St. NW, under Whitehurst Fwy., tel.
202/333–2897) features rowdy rock bands, rough wooden
tables, and an easy-going, beer-swigging crowd. **Bull-
feathers** (410 1st St. SE, tel. 202/543–5005) is for yuppies
and preppies, many of whom are from the nearby Congressional offices. **The Fifth Column** (915 F St. NW, tel.
202/393–3632) is a converted downtown bank where a
youngish crowd poses in black ensembles and punk hair-
dos amid neon sculpture and foreign videos.

Zurich

by Nancy Coons

As the financial capital of Switzerland and safekeeper to the world, Zurich is setting its heavy gold Rolex to 1992. Sleek, sharp, and cosmopolitan, this humming commercial center draped along the Limmat River leads a relatively provincial nation (women still don't vote in the Appenzell region), whose primary resources are banks and Alpine slopes. Switzerland has come to depend increasingly on the ever-broadening Euromarket, and this fiercely capitalist society no doubt will be supping with more socialist-oriented neighbors and learning the humble art of compromise.

This won't be an easy transition. Native Zurichers are a proud lot, one moment in a righteous rage over microscopic details, the next radiating urbane grace and the hospitality that has made tourism Switzerland's greatest natural resource. The most combative and diligent among their softer-spoken neighbors in Switzerland's provinces, Zurichers make themselves heard—which may be why their stock exchange is fourth in the world, after New York's, London's, and Tokyo's: 636 billion Swiss francs change hands at the Bourse every year; no other place on the planet trades more gold.

Zurich has been a center of commerce since the Middle Ages, when merchants and tradesmen organized into powerful progressive guilds. But it took Alfred Escher, a political and financial genius, to bring the banking industry to Zurich at the end of the 19th century; now Rolls-Royces roar past Escher's statue in the Bahnhofplatz. Although the city is dominated by its famous banks, the chief landmark is the two-tower Grossmunster Cathedral on Oberdorfstgrasse, a 12th-century edifice that harbored 16th-century religious reformer Huldreich Zwingli and the prosecuted Protestants. Einstein, Lenin, and James Joyce lived in Zurich, and Joyce is buried here.

Zurichers do business in four or five languages, responding not only to the cultural mix within their own country, where different regions may speak French, Italian, or any variety of Swiss-German dialects, but to the influx of foreigners as well. About 360,000—nearly a quarter of Zurich's population—come from abroad, including bankers dressed in Savile Row suits as well as blue-overalled workers who polish the brass on corporate doors. English is spoken widely and well, and more and more documents are being translated into Japanese.

When you combine this linguistic facility with the country's legendary efficiency, graceful architecture, and exceptional discretion, you get the most comfortable, effective, and pleasant place to do business in Europe.

Top Employers

Employer	Type of Enterprise	Parent*/ Headquarters
Alusuisse	Aluminum	Zurich
Asea, Brown Boveri	Electronics	Zurich
Careal	Diversified	Zurich
Cosa Liebermann	International trade	UHAG/Zurich
Diethelm	International trade, pharmaceuticals, retail	Zurich
Elektrowatt	Utility (electricity)	Zurich
Jacobs Suchard	Coffee, chocolate	Zurich
Kuoni Travel	Travel	Zurich
Migros	Retail	Zurich
Oerlikon-Buhrle	Machine tools, weapons	Zurich

if applicable

ESSENTIAL INFORMATION

We include the Zurich telephone area code (01) with all listed numbers. If you are calling from outside Switzerland, omit the zero from the code. If you are calling within the city, drop the code all together.

The currency of Switzerland is the franc, abbreviated throughout the chapter as SwF.

Government Tourist Offices

Swiss National Tourist Office. In the United States: 608 5th Ave., New York, NY 10020, tel. 212/757–5944; 260 Stockton St., San Francisco, CA 94108, tel. 415/362–2260.
In Canada: Commerce Court W, Box 215, Commerce Court Postal Station, Toronto M5L 1E8, Ontario, tel. 416/868–0584.
In the United Kingdom: Swiss Center, 1 New Coventry St., London W1V 8EE, tel. 071/734–1921.
In Zurich: Bahnhofplatz 15 (Main Station), tel. 01/211.40.00.

Foreign Trade Information

Consulate General of Switzerland. In the United States: 665 5th Ave., New York, NY 10022, tel. 212/758–2560; Olympia Center, Suite 2301, 737 N. Michigan Ave., Chicago, IL

60611, tel. 312/915–0061; 3440 Wilshire Blvd., Suite 817, Los Angeles, CA 90010, tel. 213/388–4127.

In Canada: 1572 Avenue Dr., Penifield, Montréal 83G 1C4, Quebec, tel. 514/932–7181; 154 University Ave., Suite 601, Toronto M5H 3Y9, Ontario, tel. 071/593–5371.

Swiss Embassy in the United Kingdom: 16–18 Montagu Pl., London W1H 2BQ, tel. 071/723–0701.

Entry Requirements

U.S., British, and Canadian Citizens
Passport only. Visa required for visits of more than 90 days.

Climate

What follows are the average daily maximum and minimum temperatures for Zurich.

Jan.	36F	2C	Feb.	41F	5C	Mar.	50F	10C
	27	−3		29	−2		34	1
Apr.	59F	15C	May	67F	19C	June	74F	23C
	40	4		47	8		54	12
July	77F	25C	Aug.	76F	24C	Sept.	68F	20C
	58	14		56	13		52	11
Oct.	58F	14C	Nov.	45F	7C	Dec.	38F	3C
	43	6		36	2		29	−2

Airport

Zurich International Airport is at Kloten, 7 miles north of center city. One of the 10 busiest airports in the world, it is served by about 60 airlines.

Airlines

Swissair has the most frequent flights. **Crossair** is Switzerland's domestic airline. American, Pan Am, and TWA have nonstop service to Zurich from New York. In addition, American flies nonstop from Chicago and Pan Am flies nonstop from Los Angeles.

Air France, tel. 01/813.74.22; 800/237–2747.
American, tel. 01/221.31.10; 800/443–7300.
British Airways, tel. 01/816.24.04; 800/247–9297.
Crossair, tel. 01/816.27.00.
Lufthansa, tel. 01/816.28.00; 800/645–3880.
Pan Am, tel. 01/816.35.51; 800/221–1111.
Swissair, tel. 01/251.34.34; 800/221–4750.
TWA, tel. 01/816.41.11; 800/221–2000.

Between the Airport and Downtown

By Train
The quickest—and least expensive—way to get into the center of town if you're traveling light is to take the **Swiss Federal Railway** feeder train at the sleek railroad station across the terminal. The trip to the main station (tel. 01/245.31.11) in downtown Zurich takes 10 minutes; the price is 4.60 SwF one way. Trains run every 20–30 minutes from 5 AM–midnight, about five times an hour.

By Taxi
Cabs are the most direct way to get to your hotel, but they cost 40–45 SwF. They take about 20 minutes at nonpeak

hours and up to 40 minutes at rush hour (7–8:30 AM from the airport, 5–6:30 PM from the center).

By Shuttle
A reputable private minivan shuttle, **Fretz Limousine Service** (Gasometerstrasse 9, tel. 01/272.24.44), runs every 30 minutes in the morning from 6:30 AM and hourly in the afternoon until 8:15 PM, from the airport to the center, where it stops at most hotels (hotel names are listed on the side of the minivans). Cost: 16 SwF. After hours take a taxi—renting an off-hours private shuttle through Fretz costs 108 SwF or more.

By Limousine
Fretz Limousine Service (*see* above) also rents chauffeured limousines (Rolls, Mercedes, BMW, stretch or not) by the hour, half day, or full day. Full-day rates run from 540 to 1,200 SwF, depending on the type of limo. If you reserve an airport pickup and your flight is delayed (which happens often in this very busy airport), you'll pay, of course, for the chauffeur's wait. The international **Carey** limousine line (Pfingstweiderstrasse 31A, tel. 01/271.33.82) is competitive.

Car Rentals

The following car rental firms have offices in or near the Kloten airport:

Avis, tel. 01/813.00.84; 800/331–1212.
Budget, tel. 01/813.31.31; 800/527–0700.
Europcar, tel. 01/813.20.44; 800/227–7368.
Hertz, tel. 01/814.05.11; 800/654–3131.

Emergencies

For a listing of approved physicians and clinics in Zurich that belong to the International Association for Medical Assistance to Travelers, contact IAMAT, 417 Center St., Lewiston, NY 14092, tel. 716/754–4883.

Doctors and Dentists
The city of Zurich sponsors an excellent—and free—24-hour medical and dental emergency referral service called **Notfälldienst,** tel. 01/261.61.00, staffed by English-speaking operators who will refer you to a doctor or dentist, send a doctor to your hotel, or, if necessary, summon an ambulance. An alternative 24-hour service can be reached at 01/361.61.61.

Hospitals
Contact the accident department of **Zurich Universitätsspital** (Schmelzbergstrasse 8, tram 6 to ETH Zentrum/University, tel. 01/255.11.11).

Important Addresses and Numbers

American Express (Bahnhofstrasse 20, tel. 01/211.83.70).

Audiovisual rentals. Hausmann (Bahnhofstrasse B91, tel. 01/211.37.83).

Bookstores (English-language). Daeniker (In Gassen 11, tel. 01/211.27.04), Payot (Bahnhofstrasse 9, tel. 01/211.54.52).

British Embassy (Dufourstrasse 56, tel. 01/47.15.20).

Computer rentals. Computerzentrum Fisch (Stampfenbachplatz 4, tel. 01/363.67.67), Executive Business Services (Usteristrasse 23, Lowenplatz, tel. 01/219.81.11).

Convention and exhibition centers. Hallenstadion (Wallisellenstrasse 45, tel. 01/312.77.77), Kongresshaus (Gotthardstrasse 5, tel. 01/201.61.88), Zuspa (Thurgauerstrasse 7, Zurich-Oerlikon, tel. 01/311.50.55).

Fax services. Fax and telex machines are located at public phone cabins in the PTT office (Fusslistrasse 6), and at the main rail station (Hauptbahnhof).

Gift shops. Chocolates: Teuscher (Storchengasse 9, in the Globus department store, tel. 01/221.33.11 and Café Schober, Napfgasse 4, tel. 01/251.80.60, Sprungli (Paradeplatz and Lowenplatz, tel. 01/221.17.22) Florists: Blumen Fitze (Augustinergasse 20, tel. 01/221.21.61), Blumen-Kramer (Bahnhofstrasse 38, tel. 01/211.46.35).

Graphic design studio. Orell Füssli Graphisches Betriebe (Dietzingerstrasse 3, tel. 01/466.77.11).

Hairstylists. Unisex: The salons at the Baur au Lac hotel (tel. 01/221–1650) and the Savoy Baur en Ville (tel. 01/211.53.60).

Health and fitness clubs. *See* Fitness, below.

Limousine services. Fretz (tel. 01/272.24.44), Carey (tel. 01/271.33.82)

Liquor store. Statskellerei Des Kantons Zurich (Hirschengraben 13, tel. 01/251.23.47).

Mail delivery, overnight. DHL (tel. 01/301.16.00), Federal Express (tel. 01/311.33.66),TNT Skypak (tel. 01/272.22.70), UPS (tel. 01/57–2755).

Messenger services. City Link (tel. 01/301.13.13), Kurier (tel. 01/383.66.66).

News programs, English-language. America's all-news TV channel, CNN, is available in most of the better hotels.

Office space rental. Executive Business Services (Usteristrasse 23, Lowenplatz, tel. 01/219.81.11).

Pharmacy, 24-hour. Bellevue Apotheke (Theaterstrasse 14, tel. 01/252.44.11).

Secretarial services. Friedel Interim Skript (Rislingstrasse 4, tel. 01/221.15.15), International Office Services (Rennweg 32, tel. 01/214.61.11).

Stationery supplies. Büro-Fürrer (2 locations: Munsterhof 13, tel. 01/211.15.55; Shopville, tel. 01/211.80.71), Rüegg-Naeheli (Börsenstrasse 12, tel. 01/221.15.15).

Taxis. Taxiphon (tel. 01/271.11.11), Zentrale (tel. 01/44–4441).

Theater tickets. *See* The Arts, below.

Thomas Cook (Talacker 42, tel. 01/211.87.10).

Trade Ministry. Internationale Handelskammer (Börsenstrasse 26, tel. 01/221.27.07).

Train information. Swiss Federal Railways (Bahnhofplatz, tel. 01/245.31.11).

Translation services. Berlitz (Limmatquai 72, tel. 01/251.03.63), Inlingua (Limmatstrasse 23, tel. 01/271.55.66).

U.S. Embassy (Zollikerstrasse 141, tel. 01/55–2566).

Telephones

Public telephones in Switzerland are straightforward: Pick up the receiver, put in a minimum of 40 rappen or centimes—the German and French names, respectively, for the same coin—for a three-minute local call (five minutes on Sundays or holidays). A digital readout tells you how much money you've put in and warns you when it's time to add more. You also can buy a 10 SwF card from the post office, insert it in most public phones, and watch the minutes tick off, 10 rappen at a time.

Tipping

For doormen carrying bags to the registration desk, tip 1–2 SwF; for porters bringing bags to your room, 1–2 SwF; for room service, 1 SwF. Because 15% service is included in every restaurant and liquor bill, you are not expected to add an American-style tip. However, it is customary to add 2–5 SwF for good service and 10 SwF for exceptional service; no matter what, you should round up to the nearest franc. Because bills are often settled in person at tableside (except at the most formal spots), hand the tip directly to the server, rather than leave it on the table behind you. Taxi drivers get about 10% of the bill.

DOING BUSINESS

Hours

Businesses: weekdays 8–noon, 1–5:30. **Banks:** Mon.–Wed. and Fri. 8:15–4:30, Thurs. 8:15–6 (Union Bank of Switzerland, Swiss Bank Corporation, and Credit Suisse keep Sat. hours as well). **Shops:** weekdays 8–6:30, Sat. 8–4 (some downtown stores stay open to 9 PM on Thurs., and many are closed Mon. morning).

National Holidays

New Year's Day and Jan. 2; Good Friday; Easter Sunday; Easter Monday; May 1, Labor Day; Ascension, 40 days after Easter; Pentecost, 50 days after Easter; Aug. 1, National Holiday; Christmas; Dec. 26, Boxing Day.

Getting Around

By Car
Cars are more of a nuisance than a convenience—Zurich's concentrated downtown and efficient tram system make walking and/or trams the easiest and quickest means of getting around.

By Public Transportation
The tram service in downtown Zurich is excellent—fast, frequent, and, of course, punctual to a fault. All-day passes (5 SwF), which can be purchased at booths in the larger tram stops (such as Paradeplatz), are a good deal for visitors. Single-trip tickets are sold in vending machines at every tram stop.

By Taxi
If you can find one, cabs can be hailed on the street (they're available if the light on top is lit) or telephoned (*see* Important Addresses and Numbers, above). They're also usually lined up outside the train station and major hotels.

Protocol

Appointments
Promptness is next to godliness for the Swiss, and arriving early or late is simply unacceptable—you may find yourself in the unusual professional position of being snubbed or scolded like a child (scolding, however, is common here, by colleagues and strangers alike; you may, if you like, scold back). Restaurants and hotel lobbies are acceptable meeting places, but most popular with the Swiss are the comfortable private meeting areas that the better hotels reserve for their guests.

Customs
As in most of Europe, address people by their last names unless invited to use the first. Zurich is a predominantly German city; use the "Frau" or "Herr" before the name. Handshakes and business cards are standard form.

Dress
Zurichers are a formal, well-groomed people who seem to live in suits round the clock. Sober business suits are the norm for businesswomen as well. Find out before you arrive if any events will be black tie; renting a tux is quite difficult (the fastidious Swiss are appalled at the idea of renting clothing that has been worn by strangers).

Gifts
If you're invited to a Zuricher's home, bring more than flowers or wine. A small, wrapped gift—a vase, some scented soaps, a picture frame—will put you in good stead with your hosts.

Toasts and Greetings

Zurichers speak their own lilting German dialect, called *Schwyzerdutsch* (shvit-zer-dootch). You may substitute any form of German gracefully, though English is widely understood. But before you plunge into English with a stranger or shopkeeper, many Zurichers prefer that you ask if they speak English first; they almost always do, but if they don't they lose face and may snub you. Give them the chance to say *"Moment bitte"* (Just a minute) so they can rush for the aid of an associate.

Cheers! *Prost!* (proast).
Hello, *Gruezi* (GROOT-see).
Nice to meet you, *S'hat mich g'freut sie z'traffa* (zat mish gah-FROIT zee Z'TREH-feh).
Thank you, *Merci vielmal* (MEHR-see FEEL-mall).
Good-bye (formal), *Uf wiederluege* (oof VEE-der-LOOEH-ga).
Good-bye (informal), *Tschau* (ciao, chow).

LODGING

Zurich is an excellent destination for the business traveler for many reasons, not the least of which is its superb hotels: Most of them adhere to the highest standards in architecture, comfort, amenities, and service. The city is so compact and easy to negotiate that almost every hotel is well located for business and pleasure. In general, many of the grand hotels are found on the Bahnhofstrasse side of the Limmat River, the commercial hub of Zurich that's home to banks, embassies, government offices, and many shops. Across one of the many bridges on the Limmatquai side, the mood is younger and livelier, thanks to the many night spots and good restaurants; many Zurich landmarks are also found here. Whichever side you settle on, you'll be just a few minutes by foot or tram from wherever you need to be.

Even in a country famous for extraordinarily high standards in hotel services, you can still go wrong from time to time, landing in that rare, poorly managed spot with an ill-trained staff and fixtures gone to seed. The hotels listed below, however, are among the best for business travelers.

Except in the more modern international chains, Swiss singles often have single beds, and double rooms have twinned mattresses with sheets tucked firmly down the middle. However, most hotels now provide some standard double beds, known as French beds, and more and more hotels are offering these to single travelers.

Highly recommended lodgings in each price category are indicated by a star ★.

Category	Cost*
$$$$ (Very Expensive)	over 250 SwF
$$$ (Expensive)	150 SwF–250 SwF
$$ (Moderate)	under 150 SwF

All prices are for a standard single room, and include tax and 15% service charges.

Numbers in the margin correspond to numbered hotel locations on the Zurich Lodging and Dining map.

Bahnhofstrasse Side

 Ascot. This 1950s structure in the heart of the business/
$$$ banking district was renovated in 1987, and it now presents a fresh, gleaming face to its mostly business guests. The style and source are Milanese, from the checkerboard marble, brass, and dark wood, to the paintings of sad-eyed waifs that crowd the walls. Singles have full French beds; corner doubles are slightly larger. The front rooms over Tessinerplatz (the site of the city's second train station, with convenient tram connections) have balconies overlooking the traffic; some have air-conditioning, so you needn't open windows at night. It's a 15-minute walk (or a quick tram ride) from the Bahnhofstrasse. *Tessinerplatz 9, CH–8002, tel. 01/201.18.00, fax 01/202.72.10. Gen.*

manager, Herbert Reichel. 70 rooms, 4 suites. AE, DC, MC, V.

★ ❷ **Baur au Lac.** This hoary, highbrow patrician of Swiss ho-
$$$$ tels—every wingback seeming to shelter a financial newspaper and a Davidoff cigar—was born in 1844. Though it's
silvered at the temples, it is by no means over the hill. Its
back is turned to the hum of Bahnhofstrasse commerce,
and its front rooms overlook the lake, canal, and manicured lawns of a private park. The lobby and halls are
hushed, and the understated decor is firmly fixed in the
age of reason. Luxurious corner suites are vast and light;
the lakeside corner junior suites (priced as deluxe doubles) are an excellent value. The masculine *zunfthaus* (la-
borer's guild-hall) decor of the well-known Grill Room (*see*
Dining, below) draws loyal Zurich businesspeople. Breakfast at the Pavillon (*see* Business Breakfasts, below) will
impress your colleagues. Extras include a Rolls-Royce
airport shuttle, a private men's club, a nightclub open to
club members and hotel guests, and an exceptional wine
cellar. *Talstrasse 1, CH–8022, tel. 01/221.16.50, fax 01/
221.81.39. Gen. manager, Michel Rey. 140 rooms, 16
suites. AE, CB, DC, MC, V.*

❼ **City.** In a convenient setting close to the Bahnhofstrasse,
$$$ the main train station, and the Lowenstrasse shopping
district, this quirky little hostelry for businesspeople has
just been given a chic, understated polish, with that neu-
tral pastel look common to Swiss hotels. Singles are the
norm here, with oddly shaped rooms and baths, some on a
dollhouse scale (tiny bed, tiny desk, tiny shower). Of the 73
rooms, 56 are singles; most doubles are in back and have a
bathtub only. Service is friendly but limited. *Lowen-
strasse 34, CH–8021, tel. 01/211.20.55, fax 01/212.00.36.
Gen. manager, Stephan Knubel. 73 rooms. AE, DC,
MC, V.*

❷ **Glärnischhof.** This anonymous 1955 banking district stan-
$$$ dard—its '60s scarlet-and-harvest-gold decor preserved
with a curator's respect—is finally changing personality,
and what a change it is. All junior suites and rooms on the
two top floors have been transformed to glamorous,
postmodern Eurostyle, all halogen lighting, woven wall
coverings, and faux malachite, with full desks. Once small
bathrooms have been expanded. Suites are no bargain,
but the Jacuzzi, three phones, and revolving marble television tower may suit the taste of latter-day playboys. The
windows in the standard doubles lack double glazing,
which is all the more reason to ask for an upper-floor room.
*A Best Western hotel. Claridenstrasse 30, CH–8022, tel.
01/202.47.47, fax 01/201.01.64. Gen. manager, Urs
Mathys. 67 rooms, 3 suites. AE, DC, MC, V.*

❿ **Glockenhof.** Sometimes hotels with the best locations
$$ don't concern themselves with upkeep; their convenience
alone brings them enough business. Thus, only 10% of the
rooms in this modest old central hotel have been renovated
since, apparently, the invention of walnut-grain Formica.
The newer rooms boast fresh, pretty pastels, but chances
are good you'll land in a Scandi-bland setting of red and
gold. Back rooms overlook a quiet garden court. Located
two blocks from the Bahnhofstrasse, this is a handy crash
pad for traveling salespeople. There are no conference fa-
cilities. *A Best Western hotel. Sihlstrasse 31, CH–8023,*

ZURICH

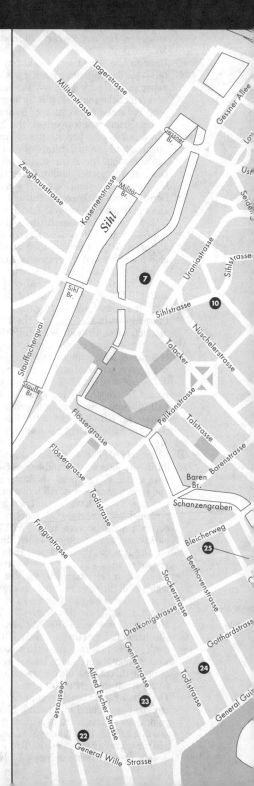

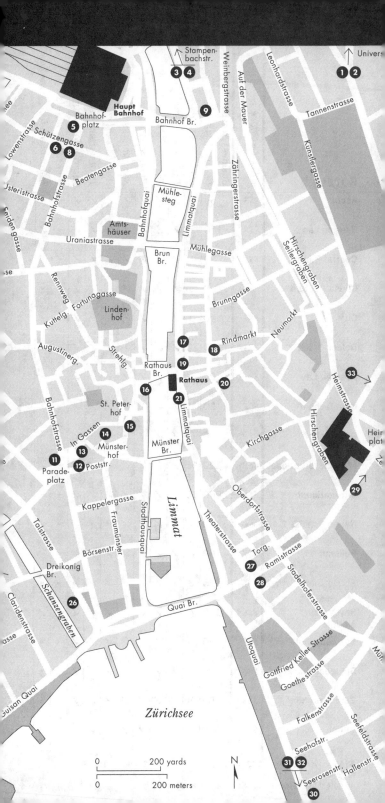

ZURICH HOTEL CHART

HOTELS	Price Category	Banquet capacity	No. of meeting rooms	Fax	Telex	Photocopying	Secretarial services	Audiovisual equipment	Translation services	International direct dial	Computer rentals	In-room modem phone jack
Ascot	$$$	50	1	✓	✓	✓	✓	✓	✓	✓	-	-
Baur au Lac	$$$$	150	2	✓	✓	✓	✓	✓	✓	✓	-	✓
Central Plaza	$$$	30	1	✓	✓	✓	✓	✓	✓	✓	-	✓
Chesa Rustica	$$	0	0	✓	✓	✓	✓	-	✓	✓	-	-
City	$$$	0	0	✓	✓	✓	-	-	-	✓	-	-
Dolder Grand	$$$$	250	10	✓	✓	✓	✓	-	✓	✓	-	-
Eden au Lac	$$$$	20	1	✓	✓	✓	✓	-	✓	✓	-	-
Glärnischhof	$$$	50	2	✓	✓	✓	✓	✓	✓	✓	-	✓
Glockenhof	$$	0	0	✓	✓	✓	-	-	-	✓	-	-
Hilton International	$$$$	320	15	✓	✓	✓	✓	✓	✓	✓	-	✓
International	$$$	600	10	✓	✓	✓	✓	✓	✓	✓	-	-
Neues Schloss	$$$	25	1	✓	✓	✓	✓	-	✓	✓	-	-
Pullman	$$$	100	6	✓	✓	✓	✓	✓	✓	✓	-	-
St. Gotthard	$$$	65	3	✓	✓	✓	✓	✓	✓	✓	-	-
Savoy Baur en Ville	$$$$	130	4	✓	✓	✓	✓	✓	✓	✓	-	✓
Schweizerhof	$$$	40	3	✓	✓	✓	✓	✓	✓	✓	-	-
Splugenschloss	$$$	30	1	✓	✓	✓	✓	✓	✓	✓	-	-
Zum Storchen	$$$	50	3	✓	✓	✓	✓	✓	✓	✓	-	-
Zurich	$$$	300	8	✓	✓	✓	✓	✓	✓	✓	-	✓

$$$$ = over 250 SWF, $$$ = 150 SWF-250 SWF, $$ = under 150 SWF.
● good, ◕ fair, ○ poor.
All hotels listed here have photocopying and fax facilities.

All-news cable channel	Desk	Desk lighting	Bed lighting	In-Room Amenities	Nonsmoking rooms	In-room checkout	Minibar	Toiletries	Room service	Laundry/Dry cleaning	Pressing	Hotel Amenities	Barber/Hairdresser	Garage	Courtesy airport transport	Sauna	Pool	Exercise room
✓	●	●	●		-		✓	●	○	●	●		-	✓	-	-	-	-
✓	●	●	●		-	-	✓	●	◐	●	●		✓	✓	-	-	-	-
✓	●	●	●		✓	-	✓	●	◐	●	●		✓	✓	-	-	-	-
✓	●	●	●		-	-	✓	●	◐	●	●		-	✓	-	-	-	-
-	○	◐	●		-	-	✓	◐	◐	●	●		-	✓	-	-	-	-
✓	●	●	●		-	-	✓	●	●	●	●		✓	✓	-	-	-	-
✓	◐	●	●		-	-	✓	●	◐	●	●		-	-	-	✓	-	-
✓	●	●	●		-	-	✓	●	◐	●	●		-	✓	-	-	-	-
✓	◐	◐	●		-	-	✓	◐	○	◐	◐		-	✓	-	-	-	-
✓	●	●	●		✓	✓	✓	●	◐	●	●		-	-	✓	✓	-	-
✓	●	●	●		✓	-	✓	●	●	●	●		✓	✓	-	✓	●	◐
✓	●	●	●		-	-	✓	●	◐	●	●		-	-	-	-	-	-
✓	◐	●	◐		-	-	✓	●	◐	●	●		-	✓	-	-	-	-
✓	●	●	●		-	-	✓	●	◐	●	●		-	-	-	✓	-	-
✓	●	●	●		-	-	✓	●	◐	●	●		✓	-	-	-	-	-
✓	◐	◐	●		-	-	✓	●	○	●	●		-	-	-	-	-	-
✓	◐	●	●		✓	-	✓	●	◐	●	●		-	-	-	-	-	-
✓	●	●	●		-	-	✓	●	◐	●	●		-	-	-	-	-	-
✓	●	●	●		-	-	✓	●	◐	●	●		✓	✓	-	✓	●	●

Room service: ● 24-hour, ◐ 6AM–10PM, ○ other.
Laundry/Dry cleaning: ● same day, ◐ overnight, ○ other.
Pressing: ● immediate, ◐ same day, ○ other.

tel. 01/211.56.50, fax 01/211.56.60. Gen. manager, Walter Hediger. 106 rooms. AE, DC, MC, V.

㉔ **Neues Schloss.** Headed by Bernard Seiler, an heir to the
$$$ Zermatt hotel dynasty, this small, discreet hotel in the business district shows its bloodlines. Behind a cold quasifascist modern facade, the entrance parlor radiates a warm welcome, and the traditional decor throughout is as meticulous and comfortable as a private home. Rooms are pristine, done in jewel tones and unfussy florals; comforts include filtered fresh air and personal safes. Renovations are adding a junior suite and enlarging bathrooms in 15 rooms. Some singles are small, but singles with French beds are available for less than the cost of a double room. A breakfast buffet is served in Le Jardin, a popular adjoining French restaurant that bustles with dealmakers at lunch. *Stockerstrasse 17, CH–8022, tel. 01/201.65.50, fax 01/201.64.18. Gen. manager, Bernard Seiler. 60 rooms, 1 suite. AE, DC, MC, V.*

★ ❽ **St. Gotthard.** It's a man's world here—the dull roar of
$$$ male voices and the thick smoke of good cigars fill the burnished-brass-and-leather public spaces, and a deal is cooking in every corner. At lunchtime, La Bouillabaisse looks like a private men's club, and Hummer- und Austernbar (Lobster and Oyster Bar) is extremely popular with Zurichers of both sexes (*see* Dining, below). Over the last 100 years, guests have included the famous and infamous, from Maria Callas to Henry Kissinger, Mussolini to the Shah of Iran. Concierges seem to double as secretaries—they'll make photocopies, mail packages, even arrange for translations. Rooms have a solid, homey feel, with heavy fabrics, strong colors, and glossy metallic accents; the junior suites, with Bahnhofstrasse views, are a good value. Most singles are on the noisier side in the back, though all their windows are soundproofed. The train station is only steps away. *Bahnhofstrasse 87, CH–8023, tel. 01/211.55.00, fax 01/211.24.19. Gen. manager, Stefan Serafin. 135 rooms, 7 suites. AE, DC, MC, V.*

★ ⓬ **Savoy Baur en Ville.** The oldest hotel in Zurich (1838), re-
$$$$ built in 1975 as an airtight urban gem, is also the most expensive—and it's worth it. Located right on the city's chic central square, Paradeplatz, and thus at the hub of the banking, shopping, and sightseeing districts, this landmark offers international powerbrokers the works: soundproof conference rooms (roaring fireplace optional), a "cone-of-silence" ultrasoundproof phone booth outside the meeting spaces, and a birch-paneled guild room that's home to a men's club dating from 1492. Service is labor intensive (the flower budget alone is 100,000 SwF per year) and the staff is well trained. The current decor (renovations are continual; all is renewed every 10 years) is warm and eclectically postmodern, with pearwood cabinetry, brass, and chintz fabrics. You don't get glitzy extras here (no pool, gym, bathrobes, or lavish breakfast buffet), but location is everything—once you're at the Savoy, you've arrived. *Am Paradeplatz, CH–8022, tel. 01/211.53.60, fax 01/211.14. 67. Gen. managers, Manfred and Christina Hörger. 112 rooms, 15 suites. AE, CB, DC, MC, V.*

❺ **Schweizerhof.** An island of triple-glazed silence in the
$$$ midst of the roar of the Bahnhofplatz, this centrally located landmark balances an air of hushed discretion with

the warmth of a welcoming staff. Renovations are maintaining the timeless decor (subdued yet sleek, with warm pastel colors) of the comfortable rooms. Standard singles may be small; French-bed double rooms have more space. Deluxe doubles have bay windows and chandeliers. The hotel is steps from the train station, and thus an easy airport connection, which pleases the mostly business clientele. Located at the busy, less luxurious end of the Bahnhofstrasse, near the Langstrasse and Lowenstrasse shopping areas, Schweizerhof is also just one tram stop from the entertainment district. *Bahnhofplatz, Box 6375, CH–8023, tel. 01/211.86.40, fax 01/211.35.05. Gen. manager, H.U. Stässle. 115 rooms, 1 suite. AE, DC, MC, V.*

㉓ **Splugenschloss.** Located southeast of the Bahnhofstrasse
$$$ in a modern quarter packed with American firms (including Manufacturers Hanover and Chase Manhattan), these converted turn-of-the-century luxury apartments have become a Relais & Châteaux property, with all the implications of history and architectural grandeur that designation confers. Despite the rather feminine, nonutilitarian accommodations—somewhat fussy pastel rooms with ornate moldings, impressive antiques, and exquisite (if virtually useless) writing desks—nearly half the clientele is American businesspeople. The public areas are an appealing hodgepodge of Old World pomp and airport-modern convenience, with good central conversation areas. Welcome touches include a breakfast buffet, nonsmoking rooms, some automatic beds, and—the latest Swiss hotel fad—a combination bidet/toilet. *A Relais & Châteaux hotel. Splugenstrasse 2, CH–8002, tel. 01/201.08.00, fax 01/201.42.86. Gen. manager, Benno Welschen. 55 rooms, 13 suites. AE, DC, MC, V.*

★ ⑯ **Zum Storchen.** The setting is the picture-prettiest in cen-
$$$ tral Zurich (overlooking the swans and bridges of the Limmat River, with views of Old Town and Grossmünster towers), as well as the most convenient to business, shopping, and sightseeing. It's icing on the cake, therefore, to find sleek, contemporary rooms (done in the neutral Swiss fashion, with the usual pastels), commendable restaurants, unusually attractive conference facilities, and a helpful, cheerful staff. Built in 1939 on the site of a building traced back to 1357, it was renovated in 1990 to its current impeccable state; the public areas are stylishly contemporary, with black leather and glass à la Mies Van der Rohe. Riverfront doubles and corner luxury doubles include in-room breakfast and unbeatable views. Banquet rooms have various combinations of murals, antiques, parquet, ceiling moldings, and, of course, those views. The Rotisserie (*see* Business Breakfasts, below) is a pretty spot for a morning meeting. The energetic can jog along Lake Zurich with the general manager mornings at 6:15. *Weinplatz 2, CH–8001, tel. 01/211.55.10, fax 01/211.64.51. Gen. manager, Jean-Philippe Jaussi. 77 rooms. AE, DC, MC, V.*

Limmatquai Side

⑨ **Central Plaza.** This old hotel (built in 1883) is eager to
$$$ please a young, often American, crowd; while the exterior says landmark, the interior, gutted and rebuilt in 1984,

says chain-hotel glitz. The lavish old atrium fountain and palm court have been compressed into a modest entrance space, and piano bars, champagne bars, American bars, and theme restaurants follow claustrophobic suit. Most of the bedrooms are more graciously arranged, including comfortable singles (eight out of 10 have showers only) and lavish junior suites complete with round beds. Only the full corner suites seem a bit cramped. Although the Meyer-Elwert family has owned the hotel for generations, its support staff is young and occasionally less than polished. The location, directly across the river from the Bahnhofstrasse, is ideal for the young or energetic, who can walk to the entertainment quarter (Niederdorf) or hop a tram directly outside the entrance. *Central 1, CH–8001, tel. 01/251.55.55, fax 01/251.85.35. Gen. managers, Robert and Alex Meyer. 98 rooms, 10 suites. AE, DC, MC, V.*

⑰ **Chesa Rustica.** This location combines convenience with
$$ history, and the river views across to Zurich's oldest quarter are some of the best in town. Buildings on this site have been traced as far back as 1280; the most recent structure was transformed into a hotel in 1970. Rooms are spare, with rustic touches—dark woods lend a chunky, almost Spanish look—but the tile bathrooms are new and roomy. A generous breakfast buffet is served in the medieval *zunfthaus*-style restaurant. Smaller back rooms, away from the traffic along the river, lack views but are quieter. The Old Town/entertainment district is behind the hotel, and the Bahnhofstrasse and its chic shopping are just across a scenic bridge. There are no conference or business facilities, and service is limited, but all the standard conveniences (TV sets, phones) are here. Champagnertreff (*see* After Hours, below) offers piano music in an Art Deco setting. *Limmatquai 70, CH–8001, tel. 01/251.92.91, fax 01/261.01.79. 23 rooms. AE, DC, MC, V.*

★ ㉝ **Dolder Grand.** A cross between Camp David and Queen
$$$$ Maria Theresa's summer palace, this sprawling Victorian estate is a luxurious, self-sufficient retreat from the city center. With 10 cushy conference rooms, extensive banquet space, a spectacularly situated French restaurant, a pool with a wave machine, a golf course, tennis courts, ice skating, and quarters for your entourage, you needn't venture into the city jungle at all—though it's just 10 minutes to the center by hotel bus. Opened in 1899 as a summer resort, this fin-de-siècle mélange of turrets, cupolas, and half timbers wasn't expanded until 1964, when a jarring modern wing added 60 rooms and suites. Inside, however, no contrast is evident—all the good-size rooms are inviting, done in feminine florals—and the garden/forest views from the back rooms are nearly as pleasant as the magnificent front-room views of the golf course, park, and city. More florid than the Baur, more grandiose than the Savoy, it's an opera set for a summit of world powers. The dining room (*see* Business Breakfasts, below) makes an elegant, if somewhat remote, setting for a morning meeting. Other luxuries include 2 PM check-out and chartered limos if you want to pop over to St. Moritz. *Kurhausstrasse 65, CH–8032, tel. 01/251.62.31, fax 01/251.88.29. Gen.*

manager, Henry J. Hunold. 180 rooms, 12 suites. AE, CB, DC, MC, V.

30 **Eden au Lac.** A jet-lagged traveler might blink at the view
$$$$ and think he disembarked in Geneva, waking in this lakefront grande dame that overlooks bobbing yachts and a tree-lined promenade. On a considerably humbler scale than its fellow five-stars, and tucked at the edge of the city center (the neighborhood, past the Opernhaus, is now slightly down at the heels), the Eden has maintained traditions founded in 1909 with a costly 1970s renovation and a new 1989 decor. Rooms are done in prim pastels, with delicate (if semifunctional) writing desks, and the public spaces beyond the sweep of the grand entrance have a cozy, musty feel. Business travelers from all over the world make the Eden their Zurich home. *Utoquai 45, CH–8023, tel. 01/261.94.04, fax 01/261.94.09. Gen. manager, Ruedi Bartschi. 49 rooms, 3 suites. AE, DC, MC, V.*

4 **Pullman.** Though its prices are competitive with the St.
$$$ Gotthard and Zum Storchen, this international hotel clone offers considerably less for the money: small, low-ceiling rooms (some singles feel smaller than those in a trailer), limited lighting and desk space (some have no desk at all), and a location slightly apart from both the city center and transportation. But such extras as a fresh new decor (albeit in the generic American chain-motel style), large beds, air-conditioning, trouser presses, and a movie channel help compensate, and the conference facilities—this spot's raison d'être—are ample. *Stampfenbachstrasse 60, CH–8035, tel. 01/363.33.63, fax 01/363.33.18. Gen. manager, Philip C. Brunner. 134 rooms, suite options. AE, DC, MC, V.*

3 **Zurich.** A lone concession to the new world in a city that
$$$ hosts some of the world's great old hotels, this 19-floor cookie-cutter-modern glass tower (opened 1972) could have sprouted along any freeway in America. The public areas are on an airport scale, with strictly '70s-style furnishings and Scandinavian accents; the decor in the rooms is mixed, depending on the room's most recent renovation—old ones are an anonymous white, with limited workspace, but the newest are warm and colorful, with good, big desks (in all cases, happily, the windows open). A newly opened wing boasts air conditioning and outlets for faxes and computers. Conference facilities are vast and forgettable. Views, of course, are stunning, but the location is less than ideal: It's a 10-minute walk to the nearest tram and a 20-minute walk to the city center, and you don't want to cut through the park across the river that looks so pastoral from the 19th floor—it's the local drug and crime center. Those who don't like walking past porno movie houses on the way to the tram should stick to cabs. The vast health club and pool costs guests 25 SwF a day. *Neumuhlequai 42, CH–8001, tel. 01/363.63.63, fax 01/363.60.15. Gen. manager, Marc Bloch. 290 rooms, 10 suites. AE, DC, MC, V.*

Airport

1 **Hilton International.** Dine at Sutter's Grill, drink at the
$$$$ Bonanza Bar—or concede you're in Switzerland and let dirndled waitresses serve you fondue under the cowbells of the Swiss Chalet. You needn't see more of the country than you wish: everything is here. In a nation devoted to

coddling the first-class traveler with Old World service and tradition, a no-surprises, impersonal chain hotel—even a top-drawer one—seems anachronistic. That said, as a Hilton it can't be faulted, and some of its American-style extras may come as a relief: smoke detectors, air-conditioning, computer modem jacks, bathroom scales, nonsmoking areas, and—so lanky Yankees can stretch out—no single beds. Nestled like a suburban country club in freeway-side meadowlands, it's low-slung and spacious, with banquet facilities for 320, 15 conference rooms, and suites with exponential flexibility. *Hohenbühlstrasse 10, CH–8058, tel. 01/810.31.31, fax 01/810.93.66. Gen. manager, Frederick Leuenberger. 286 rooms, 18 suites. AE, DC, MC, V.*

❷ **International.** Another all-business hotel, rising 32 glossy
$$$ stories above a village train station smack between downtown and the airport, this 1972 Swissôtel venture focuses more on its facilities than on its functional, plain-vanilla rooms. Guest rooms were not part of the renovation program on the upper-floors, which took place after a 1988 fire caused a code crackdown throughout Zurich. These remodeled floors are now stunning and distinctly unusual for a Swiss hotel: At the 31st-floor health club you can swim with a view of the distant city lights, and there's a high-style panoramic restaurant and lighted-floor disco. Ten slick conference rooms (also renovated after the fire) hold up to 700. At ground level are shops and a connector to the sizable local mall. Extras include air conditioning, double beds, bathroom scales, and full 24-hour room service. *A Swissôtel hotel. Am Marktplatz Oerlikon, CH–8050, tel. 01/311.43.41, fax 01/312.44.68. Gen. manager, Hans Hauri. 350 rooms, 11 suites. AE, DC, MC, V.*

DINING

A solid city with traditional tastes, Zurich remains aloof for the most part from the foodie fast track. Even though most of its prestige restaurants tend toward no-longer-nouvelle contemporary cuisine, some favorite places feature Germanic meats, potatoes, hearty sauces, and plenty of salt. No matter what the cuisine, quality, service, and presentation are usually impeccable, and portions (except, ironically, in the prestige spots) are astonishingly generous—at the traditional restaurants, even the elegant ones, meals invariably include seconds. If your arteries allow, squeeze in a few café pastries, and don't leave without sampling the local chocolate truffles—many restaurants make their own to compete with the big-name chocolatiers.

Zurichers normally eat lunch at noon, and it's their largest meal of the day. It's also the meal of choice for conducting business—in fact, most restaurants appeal to business-people with bargain fixed-price lunch menus. About 8 PM is the fashionable time to sit down to dinner; the evening meal is customarily a time for socializing, not talking shop.

Highly recommended restaurants in each price category are indicated by a star ★.

Category	Cost*
$$$$ (Very Expensive)	over 100 SwF
$$$ (Expensive)	50 SwF–100 SwF
$$ (Moderate)	under 50 SwF

*per person, including appetizer, entrée, dessert, tax, and 15% service (automatically included), but excluding drinks.

Numbers in the margin correspond with numbered restaurant locations on the Zurich Lodging and Dining map.

Wine

Due to limited terrains and the high cost of cultivating vineyards on steep Alpine slopes, Swiss wines tend to be expensive and are rarely exported. Most of the best come from the French-speaking regions of Vaud and Valais. Watch for dry white **Dézaley** and **St-Saphorin** from Lavaux in Vaud, and richer white **Aigle** and **Yvorne** from Chablais. From Valais, **Fendant** and **Johannisberg** are good, crisp whites. The best reds are the Valais's **Dôle**, a Beaujolais-like blend of pinot noir and gamay, and the fruity merlot of **Ticino**, the Italian-Swiss region south of the Alps.

Beer

Hürlimann, Haldengut, Löwenbräu.

Business Breakfasts

Switzerland's first-class hotels inevitably include breakfast in the price of the room, so business travelers tend to play host to local clients, meeting them at their home away from home. There's no need to tussle over the check—good waiters simply glance at your room key, and the charges for the extra breakfasts will appear on the bill when you check out. If impressive breakfast venues figure prominently in your meeting strategy, consider staying at the Baur au Lac in spring and summer to breakfast at the **Pavillon** (tel. 01/221.16.50), which overlooks manicured private lawns. Breakfast at Zum Storchen is served in the **Rotisserie** (tel. 01/211.55.10), which overlooks the swans on the Limmat River. A **Dolder Grand** (tel. 01/251.62.31) breakfast on the hill over the city is spectacular, but it's out of the way for many clients.

Bahnhofstrasse Side

★ ⑭ **Bierhalle Kropf.** This 100-year-old beer hall, complete
$$ with elaborate murals and a stuffed boar's head, is considerably smaller than the neighboring Zeughauskeller, but the bustle, clatter, wisecracking, and often crotchety waitresses more than make up for it—and the food is top-notch for the genre. Try *leberknodli* (liver dumplings), sausages with *rösti* (hash brown potatoes), and *apfelköchli* (fried apple slices)—and don't pass up the wonderful chewy *boerli* bread or the fresh house beer. Tables are shared, so you'll get to know your neighbors, most of whom are locals. This is a great spot for casual, after-work fun. *In Gassen 16, tel. 01/221.18.05. Casual dress. Reservations advised. AE, DC, MC, V.*

㉖ **Grill Room.** Though this local institution shares the re-
$$$$ fined menu of the Baur au Lac's more formal Restaurant

Français (where Max Kehl apprenticed), Zurich business-people prefer its wood-and-leather ambience and treat it like the traditional men's club it resembles, with its stone fireplace, Gothic woodwork, and American high-stool bar. Despite the handful of token plain grilled meats, "grill" is mostly a figure of speech—the cuisine is a lofty, dependable blend of elaborately prepared seafood, fowl, and desserts. Go elsewhere for radical innovations; this chef of long standing follows the straight and narrow. Specialties include fillet of turbot with leeks, breast of duck with glazed pearl onions, and homemade chocolate truffles. The wine list is international and extensive. This is a solid, reliable business-lunch spot. *Hotel Baur au Lac, tel. 01/ 221.16.50. Jacket and tie required. Reservations required. AE, DC, MC, V.*

6
$$$
Hummer- und Austernbar. Zurichers love this hotel restaurant: The oyster bar setting is intimate in the extreme, both for romance and for rubbing elbows (almost literally) with fashionable neighbors, who may think your whispers were meant for them. (The main dining room, separate from the oyster bar, is roomier, but this is still more a place for fun than private business talks.) The decor suggests a fin-de-siècle café, all polished wood, candlelight, and soft pastels. *Hummer- und austern* means lobster and oysters, which are the menu's main thrusts, and prices are accordingly high, sometimes determined by weight. Popular variations on the seafood theme include Brittany lobster poached in champagne sauce and St-Pierre (John Dory) flambeed with fennel. The champagne flows as freely as the Limmat. *St. Gotthard, tel. 01/211.55.00. Jacket and tie advised. Reservations advised. AE, DC, MC, V.*

11
$$
Sprungli. There are locations all over Zurich, but it's the Paradeplatz flagship, with its high ceilings and brasserie decor, that draws the Louis Vuitton set for meticulous and abundant sweets—and a business crowd for good, light lunch plates like homemade gnocchi and tasty salads. Don't leave without buying some incomparable *truffes du jour* from the sweet shop below. A Zurich landmark since 1836, Sprungli is ideal for a quick, nonworking lunch. *Paradeplatz, tel. 01/211.07.95. Casual dress (though many in jacket and tie). No reservations. AE, DC, MC, V. Lunch only.*

★ 15
$$$
Veltliner Keller. Built in 1325, it's been a restaurant since 1551. Decorated in the intricate carved-wood style of the Grison Alps (the wood is a rare mountain pine), this rustic yet sophisticated eatery manages to bring Alpine coziness to the Limmat without the slightest touch of the tourist trap. It was named for its traditional cellar storage of Italo-Swiss wines (*valtellina* in Italian), which were carried over the Alps and imported to Zurich. Despite the emphasis on heavy meat standards, the kitchen is flexible and equally deft with seafood. Specialties include a good Grison barley soup (in dialect, *schoppa da giuotta*), veal steak with Gorgonzola sauce, and outstanding winter-nut mousses. Of the two pretty dining rooms, the upstairs one has tables too close for private talks; background noise on the downstairs level allows conversations not to be overheard, but at tables by the cash register you might have trouble hearing the person across the table. Veltliner wines are still offered, but, alas, the old wine cellar is

gone. Nonetheless, Zurichers come here to impress out-of-town clients. *Schlüsselgasse 8, tel. 01/221.32.28. Jacket and tie advised. Reservations advised. AE, DC, MC, V. Closed 3 weeks midsummer and Christmas holidays.*

⑬ **Zeughauskeller.** This enormous, stone-walled, beamed-
$$ ceilinged, 15th-century armory has been converted to a popular beer hall where families, shoppers, tourists, and businesspeople share long tables and gobble up hearty meat dishes (pot roasts and loads of sausages) and good draft Hürlimann beer. Unlike the shabbier beer halls in Niederdorf, this one is clean and bourgeois, reflecting its upscale Paradeplatz location; you can, however, roll up your sleeves. Waiters work at a dead run and may have to shout over the roaring crowd and kitchen clatter. Evenings are sometimes quieter (hot food is served until 10:30), but this is still more a place for fun than work. *Bahnhofstrasse 28 (at Paradeplatz), tel. 01/211.26.90. Casual dress. Reservations advised at lunch. No credit cards.*

Limmatquai Side

★ ㉙ **Agnes Amberg.** The best restaurant in central Zurich
$$$$ showcases the creations of a former home economics teacher, an inspired and ambitious chef whose tiny, painterly nouvelle-cuisine creations may be dated but are nonetheless exquisite. Despite the feminine decor, all pistachio, ruffles, and silver detail, the clientele is divided evenly between ladies-who-lunch and French-cuffed businesspeople in serious summit. Three *menus dégustations* (tasting menus) are priced according to the number of courses (portions are minuscule, so opt for more if you're hungry); low-calorie tasting menus will be prepared if two or more request them. If you're looking for a bargain, you shouldn't come here, but the daily lunch special carries a relatively reasonable price. The ambience is hushed and formal, and there's enough privacy for an impressive business tête-à-tête. Specialties include sautéed foie gras in cabbage with rock salt and Szechuan pepper, and guinea-fowl on a leek fondue with a honey-vinegar sauce. The desserts are as pretty as they are puny. *Hottingerstrasse 5, CH–8032, tel. 01/251.26.26. Jacket and tie advised. Reservations required. AE, DC, MC, V. Dinner only Mon. and Sat.; closed Sun.*

㉑ **Haus zum Ruden.** The tradition of *zunfthaus* (laborers'
$$$ guild-house) restaurants runs strong in Zurich, and a visit to at least one is a must if you want to experience the ancient culture that molded contemporary Zurich tastes. As medieval guilds grew more affluent and influential, they built sumptuous meeting halls. Converted to restaurants today, they still function as clubhouses for modern guild members and display ancient—some still extant—family seals. This 1295 zunfthaus is the most culinarily ambitious of the lot and also the most spectacular, with river views, pastel linens, and a barrel-vaulted ceiling with 30-foot beams. Slick modern improvements—including a glassed-in elevator—manage to blend with the ancient decor to give the place a cutting-edge air. The pricey market cuisine includes paupiettes of sole and salmon with saffron, and veal with a foie gras cream. Service is jovial, if cavalier. Particularly impressive at night, this zunfthaus is

more a place for entertaining than working. *Limmatquai 42, tel. 01/261.95.66. Jacket advised. Reservations advised, required at dinner. AE, DC, MC, V.*

★ ㉘ **Kronenhalle.** Once a haven to Strauss, Stravinsky,
$$$ Brecht, and Joyce, and now a favorite of Rudolf Nureyev, Catherine Deneuve, and Yves St. Laurent, this beloved landmark near the opera house and theater is as much a gallery as a fine restaurant. Every panel of gleaming wood wainscoting frames original works of post-impressionist art, many donated by such once-regular customers as Picasso, Braque, and Miró; some of them are portraits of Hulda Zumsteg, who owned the restaurant from 1921 until her death in 1985. Her son Gustav carries on the tradition, serving hearty regional daily specials as well as more polished French classics. You can indulge in sautéed tournedos with truffle sauce or breast of guinea-fowl with nuts and grapes in a wine sauce—but nobody will object if you have a simple sausage. Of three lovely dining rooms, the main-floor brasserie (decked with emblems of all the local guilds) is the liveliest and most popular for working lunches; reserve as soon as you get into town. Two smaller rooms are more hushed and intimate. The cozy adjoining bar serves prize-winning cocktails to well-heeled crowds. *Rämistrasse 4, tel. 01/251.02.56. Jacket and tie advised. Reservations advised. AE, MC, DC, V.*

㉗ **Odeon.** As Parisian as the name implies, this historic
$$ hangout once sheltered a pre-Revolutionary Lenin, who nursed a coffee and read the house's daily papers. Today the black-attired crowd is just as intense, exuding a tonic air of counterculture chic mixed with pungent no-filter cigarette smoke. Under high ceilings in a Belle Epoque setting, the hipsters nosh on generic pastas, sandwiches, and desserts—the scene's the thing, not the food. *Am Bellevue, tel. 01/251.16.50. Casual dress. No reservations. AE, DC, MC, V.*

㉙ **Schober.** Like stepping into a Victorian wedding cake,
$$ with woodwork as ornate as the molded plaster ceilings and counters piled high with elaborate sweets, this is the coziest of Zurich's cafés, as well as the oldest (founded 1834). Serving only beverages and sweets, Schober is an ideal Old Town stop for homemade hot chocolate and splendid cakes. It's particularly popular with Zurich's working women, who stop in for a pick-me-up after work. *Napfgasse 4, tel. 01/251.80.60. Casual dress. No reservations. No credit cards. Open until 6:30 PM; closed weekends.*

⑲ **Zunfthaus zur Saffran.** Cavernous, spare (even a bit
$$$ bleak), and dating in various forms from 1389, this dark-wood *zunfthaus* has lovely views toward the Limmat River and the ancient Rathaus (town hall). As a result of recent changes, the staff is young and friendly. There's plenty of room for lunch discussions, and businesspeople take full advantage of that fact. Besides the usual *zunfthaus* fare (like *geschnetzeltes kalbfleisch*—veal in cream sauce—with rösti potatoes), try the excellent goulash *nach chorherrenart* (choirmen's style). Pluses include homemade ice creams and good guild wine. *Limmatquai 54, tel. 01/261.65.65. Casual but neat. Reservations advised. AE, DC, MC, V. Dinner only weekends.*

⑱ **Zunfthaus zur Schmiden.** *Schmiden* were blacksmiths and
$$$ barbers, and their guild house (acquired in 1412) is a mag-

nificent mix of Gothic wood, leaded glass, and tile stoves. The lively public restaurant encourages business conversation, and tableside service is formal but never stuffy. This is classic Zurich chow: austere clear soups, enormous portions of veal or calves' liver in rich cream sauces, and enough rösti potatoes per portion to feed four. The good house wine bears the guild label. Like all guild houses, this place offers attractive banquet spaces, some more exquisite than the restaurant itself. *Marktgasse 20, tel. 01/ 251.52.87. Informal dress, though business wear is standard. Reservations advised. AE, DC, MC, V.*

Suburbs

★ ③ **Chez Max.** Some rate him with Bocuse and Girardet for cu-
$$$$ linary expertise, but chef Max Kehl draws as many kudos for the beauty of his preparations. While the menu shows less and less Japanese influence (Kehl made his name with Franco-Japonaise blends), the emphasis remains on the precise, the exquisite, and the oddly juxtaposed. Specialties include salmon and langoustine in an urchin-coral sauce, and lamb in a rosemary-hazelnut butter. The restaurant's decor blends serene traditional English woods with splashes of modern art, and the ambience—despite the management's flair for the creative and bohemian—is as formal as the impeccable service. Chez Max serves only evening meals these days (except for Saturday lunch), so business gatherings tend to be relaxed, candlelighted rewards for a good day's work. By Zurich standards, this place is out of the way, but the 10-minute cab ride will take you along Lake Zurich's shore. *Seestrasse 53, Zollikon, tel. 01/391.88.77. Jacket and tie advised. Reservations required. AE, DC, MC, V. Dinner only (except Sat.); closed Sun., Mon.*

★ ③ **Petermann's Kunststuben.** Neck and neck with Agnes
$$$$ Amberg (*see* above) for culinary achievement and high prices, but harder to reach for lunch (take the train to Kusnacht or a 15-minute cab ride along Lake Zurich's northeast shore), this culinary mecca showcases the *cuisine du marché* (market cuisine) of Horst Petermann, a German from Hamburg with an innovative French flair. Specialties change with season and whim, but may include tempura of lobster tail in vanilla butter, turbot roasted in veal juice with a confit of shallots, or sweetbreads with a caper sabayon. The rather ordinary decor is pristine and masculine, warmed with baskets of flowers; the taste is focused on the kitchen, where it counts. Hushed conversation suggests the typical Swiss reverence for great cuisine, though the business-lunch crowds are a bit livelier. Excellent service and a good wine list complete the picture. *Seestrasse 160, Kusnacht, tel. 01/910.07.15. Jacket and tie advised. Reservations required. AE, DC, MC, V. Closed Sun., Mon.*

FREE TIME

Fitness

Hotel Facilities

The **Zurich** hotel's Atmos club (tel. 01/363.63.63) charges guests and nonguests alike 25 SwF per day for unlimited access to its sizable pool, Turkish bath, whirlpool, and sundeck.

Health Clubs

A banking-district locale and American ownership makes the **Luxor** (Glärnishstrasse 35, tel. 01/202.38.38) the most popular club for downtown visitors; it has four squash courts, Stairmasters, saunas, a steambath, and a whirlpool, but no pool. Cost: 25 SwF per day; the adjoining Glärnischhof hotel offers discounts to its guests. Members of U.S. Town Sports International or New York Sports Clubs are admitted free of charge.

Jogging

Of Zurich's seven Vita-Parcours jogging tracks, the closest to the center is at **Allmend Sportplatz** (tram 13 to the last stop), conveniently placed between two cemeteries.

Shopping

Though folk crafts from all over Switzerland can be bought here (from **Heimatwerk** tel. 01/211.57.80, Rennweg 14 or Bahnhofstrasse 2), Zurich is Switzerland's sophisticated capital of luxury shopping, with a heavy emphasis on leather goods, watches, high fashion, and, of course, chocolate. The famous **Bahnhofstrasse** is the Fifth Avenue of Switzerland; the lovely old area around **Storchengasse** is full of elite boutiques; and young, casual shops are in the **Niederdorf** neighborhood. Zurich's top department stores are **Globus** (Bahnhofstrasse at Lowenplatz, tel. 01/221.33.11), **Jelmoli** (Bahnhofstrasse at Seidengasse, tel. 01/220.44.11), and **Vilan** (Bahnhofstrasse 75, tel. 01/229.51.11).

Bally of Switzerland's leather goods are widely available, especially at **Bally Capitol** (66 Bahnhofstrasse, tel. 01/211.35.15). You'll also find excellent leather goods at **Madler** (26 Bahnhofstrasse, tel. 01/211.75.70), **Leder Locher** (Bahnhofstrasse 92, tel. 01/211.70.82 and Munsterhof 18, tel. 01/211.18.64), and **Fendi** (Paradeplatz, tel. 01/221.16.11). Watches made in the French-Swiss region are sold at **Beyer** (31 Bahnhofstrasse tel. 01/221.10.80), **Bucherer** (Bahnhofstrasse 50, tel. 01/211.26.35), and **Les Ambassadeurs** (Bahnhofstrasse 64, tel. 01/211.18.10). For high fashion for women, **Weinberg** (Bahnhofstrasse 10, tel. 01/211.29.54) and **Grieder** (Bahnhofstrasse 30, tel. 01/211.33.60) offer a lofty mix, and the **Trois Pommes** boutiques (Storchengasse 6/7, tel. 01/211.02.39) carry Jil Sander, Alaïa, and Comme des Garçons; **Giorgio Armani** men's and women's shops are at Zinnengasse 6 and 4, respectively, tel. 01/211.23.48; **Gianni Versace** is displayed at Storchengasse 23, tel. 01/211.06.21; and **Beatrice Dreher Presents** (In Gassen 14, tel. 01/211.13.48) offers Chloé and Krizia. For chocolate, **Teuscher** (Storchengasse 9, in the Globus department store, tel. 01/221.33.11, and at Café Schober, Napfgasse 4, tel. 01/221.33.11), and **Sprungli** (Paradeplatz and Lowen-platz) are neck and neck for the title of Zurich's best, with Sprungli surpassing on truffes du jour and Teuscher leading in champagne truffles.

Diversions

The **Bahnhofstrasse** between Rennweg and the lake, particularly around Paradeplatz, is one of the most luxurious window-shopping stretches in Europe.

Fraumünster, parallel to the Munsterhof, is a Gothic church with a slender Baroque spire and stained-glass windows by Marc Chagall and Augusto Giacometti (the sculptor's father).

The **Kunsthaus** museum (Heimplatz 1, tel. 01/251.67.55) features a first-class collection of Swiss and Zuricher paintings in addition to old and modern masters.

Lindenhof, the site of Zurich's first Roman settlements (there are visible remains), is a pleasant elevated city park, with larger-than-life outdoor chess and excellent views of the Limmat River. A stroll up Augustinergasse to the medieval square by St. Peterskirche gives a good sense of **Old Town** (the one on the Bahnhofstrasse side; there's another across the river in Niederdorf). Continue down Schlusselgasse to spot the excavated Roman baths exposed under a narrow alley stair (Thermengasse). You'll emerge on Storchengasse, an elite shopping neighborhood.

The **Schweizerisches Landesmuseum** (Swiss National Museum, Museumstrasse 2, tel. 01/221.10.10), located behind the rail station, is an excellent cultural museum, exhibiting objects from the span of Swiss history, from prehistoric weapons and farm implements to stained glass, costumes, and watches.

The Arts

The **Tonhalle Orchestra** (Claridenstrasse 7, tel. 01/201.15.80), named for the fine concert hall inaugurated by Brahms in 1895, has been gaining stature recently under the baton of Hiroshi Wakasugi. Under music director Christopf Groszer and conductor Ralph Weikert, the company of the opulent **Opernhaus** (Falkenstrasse 1, tel. 01/251.69.22) is widely recognized. The **Schauspielhaus** (Ramistrasse 34, tel. 01/251.11.11) features top-drawer theater in German, with several affiliated smaller theaters and cabarets covering experimental grounds. Films are almost always shown in their original language; for American movies, check listings for the initials "v.o." (version originale) or "E/d/f" (English with Deutsch/Franzosisch subtitles).

Ticket sources include **BiZZ** (Billettzentrale Kulturpavillon, Werdmuhleplatz, tel. 01/221.22.83), **Jecklin** (Ramistrasse 30, tel. 01/251.59.00), and **Musik Hug** (Limmatquai 26, tel. 01/47.16.00).

After Hours

Bars and Lounges

If you're suffering withdrawal from your cellular phone, join fellow workaholics at the **Investor's Club** (Nuschelerstrasse 9, tel. 01/211.26.60), where you can lunch, drink, snack, and watch overhead monitors track the New York and Zurich stock exchange and worldwide financial news. Chic, lively crowds pack hip-to-hip at the **Kronenhalle** bar (Ramistrasse 4, tel. 01/251.66.69), whose bartender has won international awards for unusual mixed drinks. **Champagnertreff** (Central 1, tel. 01/251.55.55) at the Central Plaza hotel is a popular piano bar in an updated Art Deco setting. A younger, artier set gathers into the wee hours at **Odeon** (Am Bellevue, tel. 01/251.16.50). Casual beer halls like **Bierhalle Kropf** (In Gassen 16, tel. 01/221.18.05) and **Zeughauskeller** (Bahnhofstrasse 28, tel. 01/211.26.90) are good for letting your hair down.

Dancing

Birdwatcher's Club (Schutzengasse 16, tel. 01/211.50.58) is an upscale, jackets-only bar with a disco dance floor, but you must have a membership card or go as a member's guest. **Le Petit Prince** (Bleicherweg 21, tel. 01/202.17.39) draws an elite, well-heeled crowd, including business travelers. **Nautic Club** opens onto the lakefront on summer nights (Wythenquai 61, tel. 01/202.66.76). **Mascot** (Theaterstrasse 10, tel. 01/252.44.81) is currently popular with an eclectic group (including businesspeople) on weekdays; young people flock here on weekends.

Jazz Club

Jazz is the exclusive domain of **Casa Bar,** (Munstergasse 30, tel. 01/47.20.02), where international artists pass through daily.

ADDRESSES

Name

Address

Telephone

Fax

Name

Address

Telephone

Fax

Name

Address

Telephone

Fax

Name

Address

Telephone

Fax

Name

Address

Telephone

Fax

ADDRESSES

Name

Address

Telephone

Fax

Name

Address

Telephone

Fax

Name

Address

Telephone

Fax

Name

Address

Telephone

Fax

Name

Address

Telephone

Fax

NOTES

FODOR'S TRAVEL GUIDES

U.S. Guides

Alaska
Arizona
Boston
California
Cape Cod
The Carolinas & the
  Georgia Coast
The Chesapeake
  Region
Chicago
Colorado
Disney World & the
  Orlando Area
Florida
Hawaii
Las Vegas
Los Angeles

Maui
Miami & the
  Keys
New England
New Mexico
New Orleans
New York City
New York City
  (Pocket Guide)
Pacific North Coast
Philadelphia & the
  Pennsylvania
  Dutch Country
Puerto Rico
  (Pocket Guide)
The Rockies
San Diego

San Francisco
San Francisco
  (Pocket Guide)
The South
Texas
USA
The Upper Great
  Lakes Region
Vacations in
  New York State
Vacations on the
  Jersey Shore
Virgin Islands
Virginia & Maryland
Waikiki
Washington, D.C.

Foreign Guides

Acapulco
Amsterdam
Australia
Austria
The Bahamas
The Bahamas
  (Pocket Guide)
Baja & the Pacific
  Coast Resorts
Barbados
Belgium &
  Luxembourg
Bermuda
Brazil
Budget Europe
Canada
Canada's Atlantic
  Provinces
Cancun, Cozumel,
  Yucatan Peninsula
Caribbean
Central America
China
Eastern Europe
Egypt
Europe
Europe's Great
  Cities
France

Germany
Great Britain
Greece
The Himalayan
  Countries
Holland
Hong Kong
India
Ireland
Israel
Italy
Italy 's Great Cities
Jamaica
Japan
Kenya, Tanzania,
  Seychelles
Korea
Lisbon
London
London Companion
London
  (Pocket Guide)
Madrid & Barcelona
Mexico
Mexico City
Montreal &
  Quebec City
Morocco
Munich

New Zealand
Paris
Paris
  (Pocket Guide)
Portugal
Rio de Janeiro
Rome
Saint Martin/
  Sint Maarten
Scandinavia
Scandinavian
  Cities
Scotland
Singapore
South America
South Pacific
Southeast Asia
Soviet Union
Spain
Sweden
Switzerland
Sydney
Thailand
Tokyo
Toronto
Turkey
Vienna & the
  Danube Valley
Yugoslavia

Wall Street Journal Guides to Business Travel

Europe
International Cities

The Pacific Rim
USA & Canada

Special-Interest Guides

Cruises and Ports
  of Call
Healthy Escapes
Fodor's Flashmaps
  New York

Fodor's Flashmaps
  Washington, D.C.
Shopping in Europe
Skiing in North
  America

Smart Shopper's
  Guide to London
Sunday in
  New York
Touring Europe